Advance Praise for
Literature: A Pocket Anthology

W9-BGK-280

"Gwynn's prose features the vitality of the casual, various, and friendly, while remaining always to the point, immediately informative, yet without any taint of academic fustiness."

> Barry Spacks
> *University of California, Santa Barbara*

"I find the Introduction clear and concise and I think that it makes the book versatile enough for courses of many levels."

> Margaret Noel Sipple
> *Northern Virginia Community College*

"I applaud your inclusion of a wide range of living poets."

> James Hirsh
> *Georgia State University*

"The material on quoting and documentation is fabulous."

> Terry Rasmussen
> *Casper College*

"Gwynn has managed to make many (if not all) of the points larger, more unwieldy anthologies make in a very short space, and his tone is methodical and sympathetic."

> Carol Ann Davis
> *College of Charleston*

"The strengths of Gwynn's anthologies are the price, the selection of contemporary works, and the introductory/background material."

> Kathleen Dale
> *University of Wisconsin, Milwaukee*

"What the Pocket Anthology can promise is that the teacher can have a 'spine' for the course—a sequence of base texts at a cut-rate price—so that students won't feel the pinch if they have to pay . . . for some of the single plays on the syllabus."

> Kevin Kerrane
> *University of Delaware*

R. S. Gwynn has edited several other books, including *Poetry: A Pocket Anthology, Drama: A Pocket Anthology, Fiction: A Pocket Anthology, The Longman Anthology of Short Fiction* (with Dana Gioia), and two volumes of *The Dictionary of Literary Biography.* He has also authored five collections of poetry, including *No Word of Farewell: Selected Poems: 1970–2000.*

Professor Gwynn teaches at Lamar University in Beaumont, Texas.

Literature

A Pocket Anthology

Edited by

R. S. Gwynn
Lamar University

PENGUIN ACADEMICS

Longman

New York   San Francisco   Boston
London   Toronto   Sydney   Tokyo   Singapore   Madrid
Mexico City   Munich   Paris   Cape Town   Hong Kong   Montreal

Editor-in-Chief: Joseph Terry
Acquisitions Editor: Erika Berg
Marketing Manager: Melanie Craig
Production Manager: Donna DeBenedictis
Project Coordination and Electronic Page Makeup: The Clarinda Company
Senior Cover Designer/Manager: Nancy Danahy
Cover Illustration/Photo: © Tony Stone Images
Senior Manufacturing Buyer: Dennis J. Para
Printer and Binder: R.R. Donnelley & Sons Company/Crawfordsville
Cover Printer: Phoenix Color Corp.

For permission to use copyrighted material, grateful acknowledgment is made
to the copyright holders on pp. 1423–1430, which are hereby made part of this
copyright page.

Copyright © 2002 by Addison-Wesley Educational Publishers Inc.

All rights reserved. No part of this publication may be reproduced, stored in a
retrieval system, or transmitted, in any form or by any means, electronic,
mechanical, photocopying, recording, or otherwise, without the prior written
permission of the publisher. Printed in the United States.

Please visit our website at http://www.ablongman.com/gwynn

For more information about the Penguin Academics series, please contact us by
mail at Longman Publishers, attn. Marketing Department, 1185 Avenue of the
Americas, 25th Floor, New York, NY 10036, or by e-mail at www.ablongman.com

ISBN 0-321-01114-7

1 2 3 4 5 6 7 8 9 10—DOC—04 03 02 01

Contents

Introduction to Drama   70

Writing About Literature   98

Fiction   129

Poetry   531

Drama   901

Preface

When the *Pocket Anthology* series first appeared almost a decade ago, our chief aim was to offer a clear alternative to the anthologies of fiction, poetry, and drama that were available at the time. *Literature: A Penguin Pocket Anthology* incorporates the contents of *Fiction: A Pocket Anthology* (3rd ed.), *Poetry: A Pocket Anthology* (3rd ed.), and *Drama: A Pocket Anthology* (2nd ed.). Additionally, *Literature* can be bundled with one or more of the rich selection of the most popular Penguin titles, which Longman offers at significantly reduced prices. Your Longman representative can supply full details about these books and available Penguin titles.

Literature addresses the four wishes and concerns most commonly expressed by both instructors and students. First, of course, is the variety of selections it contains. Admittedly, a pocket anthology has to be very selective in its contents, so we are especially proud that the thirty-seven stories, over three hundred poems, and nine plays in this book include both established canonical writers from ancient Greece to the present as well as many newer voices who reflect the diversity of gender, ethnic background, and national origin that is essential to any study of contemporary literature. We are also pleased that approximately one-third of the selections in *Literature* are by women, and that international and minority writers comprise roughly one-quarter of its contents. More important, the contents of *Literature* have been shaped by the advice of experienced instructors who have cited stories, poems, and plays which are most often taught and which possess proven appeal to students. The editor has also made a strong effort to include a number of works that reflect contemporary social questions and thus will easily stimulate classroom discussion and writing assignments. We strongly believe that the stories in *Literature* will provide a reading

experience that is not only educational but thought-provoking and en-
joyable as well.

Our second aim was flexibility. We wanted a book that could be used
as a primary text in a variety of courses, ranging from introduction to
literature courses to classes in research methods and application of literary theory to mixed-genre courses in creative writing. *Literature* contains, in addition to its generous selection of stories, poems, and plays,
biographical headnotes for authors, an introduction that covers the
techniques and terminology of each of the three major literary genres,
and a concise section on writing about literature and on research procedures. As an aid to student writing assignments, *Literature* also contains
an appendix which groups works from all three genres thematically and
provides suggestions for the application of a range of critical approaches. As a futher aid to instructors and students, our website at
http://www.ablongman.com/gwynn provides discussion questions,
suggestions for writing topics, links to other useful websites, and commentary on the authors and selections; much of this material has been
provided by instructors and students themselves. In addition, our website contains online versions of the medieval morality play *Everyman*
and Oscar Wilde's comedy of manners *The Importance of Being Ernest*,
as well as links to some classic plays, including works by Aphra Behn,
Oliver Goldsmith, and George Bernard Shaw.

Third, we wanted an affordable book. Full-sized introductory literature books now cost upwards of $60, and even the compact editions of
these books represent a significant expense for students. Longman is
committed to keeping the price of the *Literature* reasonable without
compromising on design or typeface. We believe that readers will find
the attractive layout of *Literature* preferable to the cramped margins
and minuscule fonts found in many other literature textbooks. Because
of its low cost, *Literature* may be easily supplemented in individual
courses with handbooks of grammar and usage, with manuals of style,
with introductions to critical theory, with textbooks on research methods, or with instructional texts in creative writing. The low price of
Literature reflects the original claims of the *Pocket Anthology* series,
that these books represent "a new standard of value."

Finally, we stressed portability. Many instructors expressed concern
for students who must carry large literature books, many of which now
approach 2000 pages, across large campuses in backpacks already

laden with books and materials for other courses. A semester is a short time, and few courses can cover more than a fraction of the material that many full-sized collections contain. Because of the focus of *Literature* is on primary texts, we are able to offer roughly the same number of poems, stories, and plays as much larger books. While *Literature* still may be a snug fit in most pockets, we trust that sympathetic instructors and their students will be grateful for a book that does not add a physical burden to the already heavy intellectual one required by college courses.

In closing, we would like to express our gratitude to the instructors who reviewed all or part of *Literature: A Pocket Anthology* series and offered invaluable recommendations for improvements: Melanie Abrams, California State University, San Bernadino; Herman Asarnow, University of Portland; Edward Bodie, University of South Carolina, Columbia; Francis Burch, St. Joseph's University; Jeff Cofer, Bellevue Community College; Kathleen Dale, University of Wisconsin–Milwaukee; Carol Ann Davis, College of Charleston; Michael de Benedictis, Miami-Dade Community College; Verna Foster, Loyola University, Chicago; Janet Gardner, University of Massachusetts, Dartmouth; Christine Gilmore, University of Toledo; James Hirsh, Georgia State University; Edward H. Hoeppner, Oakland University; Dennis G. Jerz, University of Wisconsin–Eau Claire; Kevin Kerrane, University of Delaware; Daniel Kline, University of Alaska, Anchorage; Jennifer Maier, Seattle Pacific University; Janet McCann, Texas A & M University, College Station; Susan Morehouse, Alfred University; Terry Rasmussen, Casper College; R. Clay Reynolds, University of Texas, Dallas; Daniel Sheridan, University of North Dakota; Porter Shreve, University of Michigan, Milwaukee; Barry Spacks, University of California, Santa Barbara; Margaret Sipple, Northern Virginia Community College; James Stick, Des Moines Area Community College; and Karin Westman, Kansas State University; and Robin Woods, Ripon College.

R. S. Gwynn
Lamar University

Introduction to Literature

Explore, Experiment, Expand: Three Reasons to Study Literature

It is a good day in Belton Hall 105. The instructor has assigned a short story by a well-known contemporary American writer, and even though spring is making its presence felt among the campus trees and shrubs, no one is gazing wistfully out the open windows. Some interest is stirring in even the back rows of the classroom, hands go up quickly and, instead of lecturing, all the instructor has to do is field one question and raise another. The days when his teaching technique consisted of a recitation of details for note-taking—the parts of a plot, the structure of a sonnet, the origins of tragedy—seem like memories of gray winter afternoons, and the students' eyes, some of them flashing with anger, focus on one another instead of on the pages of their notebooks. One student complains that the story places women in a subordinate role and turns them into objects of the narrator's lustful eye; another counters that such behavior is exactly what one should expect from the story's protagonist, a teenaged boy working at a dull job in a supermarket. The instructor is clearly enjoying himself, feeling lucky to be playing the role of referee in the debate, which has grown animated as the members of the class add their opinions and take sides. On occasions like this, discussing and arguing about literature seems as natural as talking about sports, campus gossip, or the movies. It is a good day in Belton Hall 105.

But on the other days—the days of lectures, inscrutable diagrams on the chalkboard, eyes that would rather look at anything other than a piece of lined paper—instructors and students alike ponder the toughest questions of all: What's the point of this? Why do we have to study literature? What value is this study to me? As a way of introducing *Literature: A Pocket Anthology*, I have chosen three words—explore, experiment, expand—to suggest some good reasons why the study of literature is invaluable to any educational experience.

Explore

"We are such stuff/As dreams are made on; and our little life/Is rounded with a sleep," says Shakespeare's great magician Prospero. Our experience of the world is limited by time and place, and even the most resolute traveler can only superficially come to know the complex blends of cultures that make up our world. The act of reading literature allows us a means of imaginatively entering minds and civilizations that may seem distant to us but actually are only as remote as a turn of the page. To read *Oedipus the King* is to recapture something of the awe with which the Athenians of Sophocles' day witnessed the dramatic reenactments of their ancient religious mysteries. In reading such a play we may also realize that the questions the ancient Greeks asked about human destiny are the same ones we still ponder today. True, we may never travel to Africa, but by reading a story by Chinua Achebe we can learn something about customs that in some ways resemble our own but in others seem foreign and strange. A poem by a contemporary American poet like Ellen Bryant Voight may bring with it the shock of recognition we reserve for those experiences that touch us most deeply. In literature we are allowed the possibility of inhabiting, for a brief time, lives and minds that are not our own. Men can learn from Adrienne Rich what it feels to be a rape victim; women can learn how the protagonist of Dagoberto Gilb's "Look on the Bright Side," a husband and father, deals with an act of economic injustice. We can see the world through the eyes of people of genders, races, historical eras, and social classes that may resemble or vastly differ from our own. The perspectives and subjects we explore in literature are as varied and sometimes as troubling as life itself, but in investigating them we can broaden our understanding of life in ways that other fields of academic study cannot equal. We might eventually agree that the insight which we gain from a literary experience is equal or even superior to the experience itself. "How frugal is the Chariot/That bears the Human soul," said Emily Dickinson, speaking of the readily available pleasures of reading.

Experiment

Literature does not write itself, and even the most vivid experience does not automatically translate into a memorable poem, story, or play. To the writer, every event that he or she considers as a likely subject presents a problem in literary form. Which of the genres—drama, fiction, or poetry—can best depict an experience, and which of each genre's innumerable sub-types—comedy or tragedy, short story or novel, open-form poem or sonnet—will work best? To study literature is to learn that every play, story, or poem that has ever been written involves some kind of experiment in literary technique, and much of the study of literature must be given over to questioning why artists make the choices that they do. Edgar Allan Poe once wrote an essay, "The Philosophy of Composition," about how he came to write his famous poem "The Raven," in which he explained in detail the decisions that he made about rhythm, language, setting, and even the sounds of individual words. But many readers have found that "The Raven," or for that matter any successful piece of literature, adds up to more than the sum of its parts; not even the creator has the last word on what the experiment has uncovered. As serious readers, our job is often to go beneath the surface to reveal the underlying structures and meanings. We may never write a short story, poem, or play ourselves, but in being entertained and perhaps instructed by a writer's skill with words, we gain some insight into one of the greatest human mysteries—the motives and methods of those who make art literally out of nothing. To read literature with the goal of learning how it is made is to understand literature not as life itself but as an artful imitation of it. As Richard Wilbur, observing his own daughter's attempts to write a short story, says to her, "It is always a matter, my darling,/Of life or death . . . ." And then he adds, ". . . as I had forgotten."

Expand

We expand our understanding by reading, by discussing what we have read, and by writing about it. When talking about a poem in a classroom group, students are often surprised to find that the way one reads a certain passage is not quite the same as a classmate's interpretation and that both differ from the instructor's. Literature is not a science and many of the meanings we attach to individual works remain largely matters of speculation. This is not to claim that all interpretations, no matter how far-fetched, are equally valid; it is only to observe that complex works of literature offer different channels of interpretation for readers, as any survey of available criticism of a given text will quickly demonstrate. The student's chance to speak his or her piece most often takes the form of the essay answer on an examination, in the theme or thesis paper, or in the research project. The job of making assertions, backing them up with references to the text, and locating support from outside sources may not be the most exciting aspect of literary study, but it remains the primary way through which students may demonstrate that their initial attempts to understand a story, poem, or play have grown and deepened. In analyzing, researching, and writing about literature, we expand our minds as we realize that none of us has the final word. As in life, the qualifications and adjustments we make as we respond to literary works teach us something about the necessity of not taking things at face value; there is always one more question to ask, one more possibility to weigh and test.

It is no coincidence that the three words that I have chosen all begin with the prefix *ex*-, which means "out of." One of the most common questions from students that I have heard over the years is "What are we supposed to get *out of* this (story, poem, play)?" I may be turning the phrase slightly, but if you have really savored the full experience that good literature offers, then the first thing you should get "out of" will be your own skin—when you do that you will answer your own question. For a few moments you may lose your own identity and see through the eyes of an ancient Greek, a modern Nigerian, or a contemporary American woman, and you may just find that in some significant way your own manner of looking at the world will never be quite the same again.

In beginning our study of literature, we must first look at the different literary genres—fiction, poetry, and drama—and discuss their different methods and techniques. Each genre, or type, of literature has its own history and terminology, some of which may be shared with other genres. In the introductory discussions of fiction, poetry, and drama that follow, certain important terms appear in boldface type. An index of critical terms is found at the end of this book.

Introduction to Fiction

The Telling of the Tale

The memory begins with a scene like this: the circle contains about thirty boys and girls, all in their preteen years and dressed identically in khaki shorts and t-shirts, who sit on upended sections of logs around a leaping fire. The sun has just dropped beneath the rim of a nearby mountain, and a hint of damp chill steals into the August woods. It is the last night of camp, and they have gathered to sing songs and receive awards. Now one of the counselors, a college student who could pass for an older brother of any of the campers, puts away his guitar and nods to his colleague, a young woman who steps into the ring of firelight and begins to speak. "Many, many years ago," she begins, her solemn voice describing three characters—a brave warrior, a maiden with a beautiful, silvery laugh, a wolf cub raised as a pet—"on a night not too different from this . . . ." The surrounding woods seem to grow darker as the campers lean forward towards the rise and fall of her voice and the blaze of the flames. Caught in the spell of her words, they have momentarily left television and MP3 players behind, enacting one of the human race's oldest rituals as they respond to the simple magic of the storyteller's art.

Before we can begin to examine the elements of literary fiction we must bear in mind that literature in its written form is historically a recent innovation; indeed, its two most common modern forms, the short story and the novel, have been in existence for little more than two centuries. Yet long before the invention of writing, for thousands of years ancient peoples developed complex **oral traditions** of literature; these primitive stories, dealing with the creation of the cosmos and the origins of gods and goddesses, formed a body of **myths,** supernatural narratives widely believed to be true by the people of a given culture, and **legends,** popular stories about characters and events that may contain trace elements of historical truth. Even in modern societies elements of this primitive folklore survive in regional or ethnic tales passed on through the generations, most often taking the written form of **folk tales** collected by literary scholars; **fairy tales,** like Charles Perrault's "Beauty and the Beast" or Hans Christian Andersen's "The Little Mermaid"; **beast fables,** stories with animal characters such as those of Aesop (c. 550 BC) or Joel Chandler Harris (1848–1908); or **parables,** short realistic tales like those found in the Gospels. Many of these, especially the fables and parables, are to some degree **didactic,** with the narrative events illustrating a **moral** that is either stated or implied.

Even in modern societies other ancient forms of oral literature still enjoy a good state of health. These include **anecdotes,** accounts of single incidents usually involving a well-known person, and **riddles** and **jokes** of all types, which often seem to spring into circulation overnight and often unwittingly mirror the basic situations and coarse humor of venerable **fabliaux**—short, realistic tales from the Middle Ages which often turn on a bawdy situation. Recently, much attention has been given to **urban legends,** so named by folklorist Jan Brunvand, which are short narratives involving grotesque incidents that are widely accepted as true. The title of one of Dr. Brunvand's collections, *The Vanishing Hitchhiker,* refers to a ghost tale that many Americans have heard in one of its many versions.

When myths and legends are assembled around the exploits of a great hero, the result is the **folk epic,** a long narrative in elevated style that is generally considered a starting point for any culture's literary history. Like most types of oral folk literature, epics were originally composed in verse for the sake of memorization, but they otherwise contain the same elements as modern literary forms like the short story and novel. For example, the individual **episodes** of Homer's *Odyssey*—such as Odysseus outwitting the Cyclops or his adventures with the sorceress Circe—can stand alone as exciting tales and also can fit into the larger structure of the epic, like chapters in a novel. Later authors, living in societies which had invented writing, consciously imitated the style of folk epics in composing **literary epics;** the *Aeneid* by Virgil (70–19 BC) and *The Divine Comedy* by Dante (1265–1321) are two famous examples. In the Middle Ages **romances,** written in both verse and prose, gained great popularity among all social classes. These tales of chivalry involving a knightly hero and a series of exciting, if improbable, adventures were ridiculed by Cervantes (1547–1616) in *Don Quixote*, a realistic account of an impoverished Spanish gentleman driven mad by reading too many romances. The eventual form that Cervantes gave Don Quixote's adventures was perhaps influenced by **picaresque novels** like the anonymous *Lazarillo of Tormes* (c. 1450), which involved a young orphan (or *pícaro*, Spanish for "rascal") in a series of loosely connected adventures. These picaresque tales are rightly considered the ancestors of modern realistic fiction. Many novels, from Henry Fielding's *Tom Jones* to Mark Twain's *The Adventures of Huckleberry Finn* to J. D. Salinger's *The Catcher in the Rye* and Jack Kerouac's *On the Road*, borrow their structure from the picaresque novel, and the modern short story is indebted to its often stark level of realism.

The Short Story

There is no agreement on the precise origins of the modern short story. One important influence in its development was the Italian **novella** of the late Middle Ages and Renaissance. The most famous collection of these realistic prose narratives is *The Decameron* by Boccaccio (1313–1375). *The Decameron*, in which the individual stories are narrated by young men and women who have taken to the country to escape a plague, is an example of a **frame tale,** in which the stories are "framed" by a larger narrative. The famous Arabian collection *A Thousand and One Nights* is one of the earliest examples of this genre (brilliantly resurrected here by Tim Gautreaux in "Died and Gone to Vegas" and likewise the structure of recent films like *Pulp Fiction* and *Magnolia*). In translation these tales were popular in other countries and widely imitated. In writing his plays, Shakespeare frequently borrowed from Italian writers; his tragedy *Othello* takes its plot from a sensational novella by Giraldi Cinthio. We still use the term **novella** for short stories that are long enough (usually over 15,000 words) to be published separately in book form. Count Leo Tolstoy's *The Death of Ivan Ilyich* is a classic Russian example, and Ernest Hemingway's *The Old Man and the Sea* is one of the best known novellas in American literature.

The first half of the nineteenth century is the great period of the growth of the short story as a distinct **literary genre,** or type, and its rise takes place in many countries at roughly the same time. Many reasons for this rapid development could be put forth, but perhaps the most important was the literary market established by newspapers and magazines aimed at middle-class audiences. The United States, with its increasingly high rate of literacy and expanding middle class, led the way in this period; Washington Irving's tales like "Rip Van Winkle" and "The Legend of Sleepy Hollow" were among the first American writings to attain international popularity. Edgar Allan Poe, the first great theorist of the short story and one of its notable practitioners in this period, supported himself primarily (although not very prosperously) as a magazine editor and contributor, and thus had a large personal stake in promoting short fiction. Poe's influential review of Nathaniel Hawthorne's *Twice-Told Tales* in 1842 first stated the theory that a short story ought to be a unified artistic creation, as carefully shaped as a sonnet.

> *A skillful literary artist has constructed a tale. If wise, he has not fashioned his thoughts to accommodate his incidents; but having conceived, with deliberate care, a certain unique or single effect to be wrought out, he then invents such incidents—he then combines such events as may best aid him in establishing this preconceived effect. If his very initial sequence tend not to the outbringing of this effect, then he has failed in his first step. In the whole composition there should be no word written, of which the tendency, direct or indirect, is not to the one pre-established design. And by such means, with such care and skill, a picture is at length painted which leaves in the mind of him who contemplates it with a kindred art, a sense of the fullest satisfaction.*

This idea of the *single effect* is perhaps Poe's most important contribution to the development of the short story as a serious literary genre.

Most of Hawthorne's and Poe's stories are perhaps more properly termed **tales,** if by that term we mean narratives that contain elements which are exotic or supernatural and which depart from the level of ordinary experience. Poe himself established many of the conventions of the horror, science fiction, and detective tales still being written and read today. **Formula fiction,** which rigidly follow the clichés and conventions of a particular genre, is sometimes half-affectionately called **pulp fiction** (the source of title for Quentin Tarantino's film), a reminder of the low-grade paper once used in inexpensive magazines. Still, the tale remains a lively tradition among serious artists as well. Among the contemporary stories collected in this volume, selections by Borges, Jackson, Faulkner, Oates, and others show their debt to the tradition of the tale.

The short story continued to develop in the nineteenth century, and its evolution was part of the larger literary movement of **realism,** which profoundly influenced the arts in the middle years of the nineteenth century with its "slice of life" approach to subject matter that, in early centuries, would have been deemed inappropriate for serious treatment. It has been rightly noted that realism simply represents the effect of democracy on literary history. Celebrating its appearance as early as 1837, Ralph Waldo Emerson noted, "The literature of the poor, the feelings of the child, the philosophy of the street, the meaning of household life, are the topics of the time." **Naturalism,** an outgrowth of realism that emerged in the second half of the nineteenth century, also proved influential because it joined realistic treatments of everyday life with understandings of human behavior drawn from the new sciences of psychology and sociology. A story from this collection, such as Willa Cather's "Paul's Case," reveals in its title (with its overtones of "case study") the almost clinical approach to fictional characters. Both realism and naturalism remain vital currents in contemporary short fiction, as stories here by Raymond Carver, Alice Walker, and Bobbie Ann Mason will attest.

The twentieth century saw the short story rise to its highest level of popularity and just as rapidly decline in its influence as a literary form. During the first half of the century, when many magazines like *Collier's* and the *Saturday Evening Post* paid large sums for short stories by important authors, the genre flourished. F. Scott Fitzgerald, a frequent contributor to these magazines, kept a meticulous ledger in which he noted that, in one six-month period in 1922–1923, he earned over $15,000 from magazine sales alone. A decade later, in the depths of the depression, Fitzgerald complained that stories that earlier would have sold for prices in excess of $4000 now commanded only $2500. If these amounts do not seem exorbitant, remember that we are talking about times when a new automobile sold for under $1000 and a gallon of gasoline cost a dime! Today, when virtually every college in the country employs one or more writers-in-residence whose primary income comes not from publishing but from teaching, we tend perhaps to underestimate the impact that economic realities have had on the history of literature.

In the second half of the century, many of the established magazines that regularly ran serious fiction ceased publication. Search a typical magazine rack and you will find only one weekly magazine, *The New*

Yorker, and a handful of monthlies containing short stories. Reading tastes have changed, and increased competition from television and other forms of entertainment have made the writing of short stories an expensive pastime. Still, the pages of so-called little magazines and literary quarterlies continue to provide outlets for publication, and new writers seem undeterred by the prospect of being paid with little more than what one disgruntled writer has called "two free copies of what I've already got." Almost every writer of short fiction prominent today first appeared in small-circulation periodicals of this type, and many have continued to publish in magazines that can offer, instead of money, prestige and a discriminating readership numbering in the hundreds. Indeed, the little magazines traditionally have been hospitable to many kinds of **experimental fiction** that editors of commercial magazines would never have considered. If the quantity of contemporary short fiction being published has shrunk from what it was in prior decades, the quality, one might argue, has remained the same or even improved. When we look at lists of recent winners of the Pulitzer or Nobel prizes, we discover many writers who have counted the short story as their first home.

Reading and Analyzing Short Fiction

We read for many reasons. In our daily lives most of our reading is strictly utilitarian—it is part of our jobs or education—or informational, as we scan the headlines of a daily newspaper for current events, business trends, or sports scores. We read short stories and other types of fiction for differing reasons. Sometimes our motive is simply to be entertained and to pass the time. Reading matter of this type is usually termed **escapist literature** and includes such popular categories as romance and detective novels, science fiction tales, westerns, and gothic novels. Or we might consciously choose to read "inspirational" fiction that is obviously didactic and contains messages or moral lessons that apply to our own lives. Literary reading, however, occupies a position between the two extremes. Serious literature should certainly entertain us, but on a deeper level than, say, a half-hour episode of a television comedy show does. Similarly, it may also contain an ethical theme with which we can identify, even if it does not try to "preach" its moral message to the reader. A short story that we can treat as a serious work of art will not yield all of its subtlety at first glance; in order to understand

and appreciate its author's achievement fully we may have to examine its components—its plot, characterization, point of view, theme, setting, and style and symbolism—noting how each part contributes to the story's overall effect. With that purpose in mind, let us read a very brief example by a modern American master of the genre, John Cheever's "Reunion" (p. 312).

Plot

In his discussion of tragedy in the *Poetics*, Aristotle (384–322 BC) gives first importance to **plot** as an element of a play, and most readers would agree that it holds a similar position in a work of fiction. Indeed, if we tell a friend about a short story we have enjoyed we will probably give a **synopsis** or brief summary of its incidents. In the case of a very brief story like "Reunion," this synopsis is only a few sentences long:

> *In "Reunion" the narrator, a teenaged boy traveling by train, meets his estranged father during a stop for lunch in New York City. Over the course of an hour and a half, the father's alcoholism and potentially abusive personality are revealed. The story ends with the narrator boarding his train, indicating that this was the last time he saw his father, possibly by choice.*

Plot may be defined as a story's sequence of incidents, arranged in dramatic order. One is tempted to insert the word "chronological," but doing so would exclude many stories that depart from this strict ordering of events. Although its use is more characteristic in longer works like novels, many stories employ the **flashback** to narrate incidents in the past. William Faulkner's "A Rose for Emily" begins with the funeral of the title character and then goes back in time to relate events that occurred as many as fifty years earlier. Margaret Atwood's "Happy Endings" dispenses with a single plot line entirely, offering numerous possibilities for the fates of her characters. Conversely, writers sometimes use **foreshadowing** to provide hints of future actions in the story; an effective use of foreshadowing prevents a story's outcome from seeming haphazard or contrived. Of course, the manner in which stories handle time is largely illusory. During scenes with dialogue and action, time is slowed down by descriptive and explanatory phrases. At other times, stories cover gaps in chronology or leap over uneventful periods with transitional phrases and passages; the opening sentence of the second paragraph of "Reunion" ("We went out of the station and up a side street to a restaurant.") compresses into a second or two an action that in reality would have taken at least several minutes. Even though "Reunion" does not take serious liberties with chronological time as we experience it, the ninety minutes of action in the story is compressed into about ten minutes of the reader's time. A plot like this, in which the action is more or less continuous within a single day, is called a **unified plot;** one which stretches over weeks or even longer periods and thus consists of isolated scenes connected by a thin tissue of transitional devices is called an **episodic plot.**

When we speak of the **dramatic structure** of a story, we refer to the exact way in which our emotional involvement in its plot is increased and relaxed. As Janet Burroway observes of the short story in *Writing Fiction, "Only* trouble is interesting." If we are not quickly engaged by the situation of a story and caught up in its plot, then we pronounce the cruellest of all critical verdicts on it by closing the book. The first part of this dramatic structure is the **exposition,** which provides the reader with essential information—who, what, when, where—he or she needs to know before continuing. Although writers of sophisticated fiction may try to disguise the fact, they often begin their stories with a version of the "Once upon a time" opening common to fairy tales. A variation on this type of beginning, called the **in medias res** ("in the middle of things") opening after the conventions of the old epic poems, may actually open with a "blind" bit of action before supplying its context. The exposition of "Reunion" is fairly straightforward; in the first paragraph we learn who (Charlie and his father), what (a lunchtime meeting between trains), when (noon to 1:30 PM), and where (in and near Grand Central Station in Manhattan). Cheever might have begun the story with a slightly more "dramatic" sentence ("At twelve o'clock sharp I saw him coming through the crowd.") but he would have to have provided the essential contextual information in short order to avoid unnecessarily confusing the reader.

Exposition in a story usually describes a stable situation, even if it is not an entirely happy one. Charlie tells us that his parents' divorce is three years old and that he has not seen his father in that time. If he had not taken the step of writing the letter arranging the "reunion," that state of affairs might have gone on indefinitely. The appearance of "trouble" constitutes the second part of a plot, the **complication,** which is the appearance of some circumstance or event that shakes up the stable situation and begins the **rising action** of the story. Complication in a story may be either external and internal, or a combination of the two. A stroke of fortune such as illness or accident which affects a character is a typical example of an external complication, a problem that the character cannot ignore. An internal complication, in contrast, may not be immediately apparent, for it may result from a character's deep-seated uncertainties, dissatisfactions, and fears. The external complication in "Reunion" is the father's series of confrontations with waiters; the internal complication is Charlie's growing sense of pity and revulsion. Typically, the complication of a plot is heightened by **conflict** between two characters who have different personalities and goals. Charlie is overjoyed to see his father at the beginning of the story but, despite his knowledge that he will grow up to "be something like him," he is more than eager to escape his company at the end, even if he is unconsciously trying to run away from his own "future and . . . doom."

The body of a story is called the rising action and usually contains a number of scenes, containing action and dialogue, which build to **moments of crisis,** points in the story where a resolution of the complication momentarily seems at hand but quickly disappears. Aristotle used the term **peripety** for these moments of reversal, as the hopes of the characters rise and fall. Thus, in "Reunion" all that needs to be resolved, at least on the surface, is for the characters to order lunch, eat, and return in time for the departing train. The father's increasingly obnoxious behavior, however, keeps postponing this resolution until the reunion has turned from a happy occasion to something very different. Unlike most stories, "Reunion" has a rising action as rigidly structured as a joke, with its four similar restaurant scenes that gradually escalate in absurdity as the father's senseless rage increases.

The central moment of crisis in a plot is the **climax,** or moment of greatest tension, which inaugurates the **falling action** of the story, in which the built-up tension is finally released. Some stories, particularly those involving a heavy use of suspense, have a steep "dramatic curve" and the writer uses all of his or her skills to impel the reader toward the final confrontation. Among writers included in this anthology, Edgar Allan Poe is the master of this kind of plot construction, as thousands of readers who have observed the struggles of the protagonist of "The Pit and the Pendulum" to escape the steadily descending blade will attest. Often one encounters the **trick ending** (also called the **O. Henry end-**

ing after the pen name of William Sidney Porter, a popular writer of the late nineteenth century). A climax such as this depends on a quick reversal of the situation from an unexpected source; its success is always relative to the degree to which the reader is surprised when it occurs. The ending of Kate Chopin's "The Story of an Hour" hits both its protagonist and its reader with the same surprise. More typically, modern short stories instead rely on climactic devices that are somewhat subtler than unexpected plot twists. Many modern writers have followed James Joyce's lead in building not to a climactic event but to a moment of spiritual insight or revelation, what Joyce termed an **epiphany.** Epiphanies can take many forms, from an overheard chance remark that seems significant in the context of the story to a character's unpitying gaze at himself in a mirror. In the hands of a melodramatic writer insistent on sentimental happy endings "Reunion" might have concluded with Charlie delivering a "tough love" sermon to his father, who would then fall to his knees and beg his son's forgiveness, having seen the error of his ways. Cheever's more realistic method of climax is, in this case, to avoid the confrontation altogether as Charlie escapes to his train.

The final part of a plot is the **dénouement,** or **resolution.** The French term literally refers to the untying of a knot, and we might compare the emotional release of a story's ending to a piece of cloth that has been twisted tighter and tighter and is then untwisted as the action winds down. The dénouement returns the characters to another stable situation. Just as fairy tales traditionally end with "And they lived happily ever after," many stories conclude with an indication of what the future holds for the characters. In the case of "Reunion," we return to the estrangement between Charlie and his father that existed at the beginning of the story, although this time all indications are that it will be a permanent one. A story's dénouement may be termed either closed or open. A **closed dénouement** ties up everything neatly and explains all unanswered questions the reader might have; a typical example is the "Elementary, my dear Watson" explanation of any remaining loose ends that is provided by the sleuth Sherlock Holmes in the final paragraphs of Arthur Conan Doyle's famous tales. An **open dénouement** leaves us with a few tantalizing questions; the last phrase of "Reunion," which consciously mirrors the story's opening sentence, does not explicitly state *why* Charlie never sees his father again. Was it strictly his own choice? Did the father die soon after their meeting? Were other factors involved? We do not know, of course, and such an ending invites us to speculate.

One final word about plots: The fledgling writer attempting to invent a totally original plot is doomed to failure, and it is no exaggeration to say that there is nothing (or at least not much) new under the sun where plots of short stories are concerned. Plots may be refurbished with new characters and settings, but they still draw on what psychologist Carl Jung called **archetypes,** universal types of characters and situations that all human beings carry in their unconscious mind. Plots deriving from these archetypes may be found in ancient mythologies, fairy tales, and even in contemporary fiction. Among a few of the most familiar are the triangle plot, a love story involving three people; the quest plot, which is unified around a group of characters on a journey; and the transformation plot, in which a weak or physically unattractive character changes radically in the course of the story. "Reunion" is an example of one of the most widely used of all archetypal plots, the **initiation story.** In a plot of this type, the main character, usually a child or adolescent, undergoes an experience (or **rite of passage**) that prepares him or her for adulthood. In this book such stories as John Updike's "A & P" and Joyce Carol Oates's "Where Are You Going, Where Have You Been?" share the same archetype, although they differ in almost every other respect.

Characterization

Every story hinges on the actions undertaken by its main character, or **protagonist,** a term drawn from ancient Greek tragedy (literally "first debater") that is more useful in discussions of fiction than such misleading terms as hero or heroine. Additionally, stories may contain an opposing character, or **antagonist,** with whom the protagonist is drawn into conflict. In many modern stories there is little, in any traditional sense, that is heroic about the protagonists; it may be more accurate to use a negative term, **anti-hero,** to designate one who occupies center stage but otherwise seems incapable of fitting the traditional heroic mold. For example, the title character of Willa Cather's "Paul's Case" is a social misfit, a thief, and finally suicidal. Indeed, writers of the last century have often been so reluctant to seem didactic in presenting characters that are "moral beacons" that they go to the opposite extreme in presenting protagonists whom we regard with pity or even disgust, rather than with admiration.

A character in a short story may be termed either a **flat character** or a **round character,** depending on the depth of detail the writer supplies. In "Reunion," the father is essentially a flat character, rendered with a few quick strokes of the pen and reduced to a single personality trait, his alcoholic rudeness. Flat minor characters in stories are often **stock characters,** stereotypes who may be necessary to advance the plot but otherwise are not deserving of more than the barest outlines of description. Round characters are given more than one trait, some of which may even seem contradictory, and are explored in depth as the author delves into the character's past and even into his or her unconscious mind. Characters of this type, usually a story's protagonist, begin to approach the level of complexity that we associate with real human beings.

Development and **motivation** are also important in any consideration of a story's characters. Characters can be either **static** or **dynamic** depending on the degree to which they change in the course of the story. In "Reunion," the father is a static character. His personality was fixed long before the story opens, and there seems no likelihood that he will ever alter his course. But Charlie does attain some understanding in the course of the story, even if it is at the cost of his own disillusionment with what he wants his father to be. If development in a character is usually clear in a story, then motivation—the reasons the reader is given for a character's actions—may not be so obvious. In many cases, an author will simply tell us what is going on in a character's mind, but in others we are denied access to this level of understanding. Although we can speculate, playing the amateur psychiatrist, about Charlie's father's strange behavior, we are not given any direct insight into his own view of his actions. In some stories, writers may try to plug directly into a character's thoughts by using **interior monologue,** a direct presentation of thought that is somewhat like a soliloquy in drama, or **stream-of-consciousness,** an attempt to duplicate raw sensory data in the same disordered state that the mind receives it. As useful as these last two devices can be in explaining motivation, they sometimes place excessive demands on readers' patience, for they require sifting through a jumble of thoughts and impressions whose significance is unclear.

Description of characters also helps us to understand the author's intent. In real life we are told from an early age not to judge people by external appearance, but in fiction the opposite is more often the case: Physical description is invariably a sign of what lurks beneath the surface. Given the brevity of most short stories, these physical details may be minimal but revealing in the author's choice of particulars. Cheever has Charlie describe his father at first as only "a big, good-looking man."

Remarkably, the author then uses his protagonist's sense of smell to make the character vivid: Charlie breathes in "a rich compound of whiskey, aftershave lotion, shoe polish, woolens, and the rankness of a mature male." In that burst of imagery we may momentarily overlook the most important item in the list, the evidence that Charlie's father has been drinking in the morning. Other elements may add to our understanding of its characters. Many writers take particular care in naming their characters in such a way as to draw attention to aspects of their personalities. This device (often termed **characternym**) is sometimes obvious—as with Hawthorne's Young Goodman Brown and his wife Faith—and sometimes not; in one of her stories Flannery O'Connor calls an unscrupulous seducer Manley Pointer, a name that a moment's thought reveals as an outrageous pun. Similarly, actions in the story such as speech patterns and mannerisms may also disclose personality traits. A character's misuse of grammar or stilted vocabulary can *show* us a great deal more about his or her background and self-image than a whole page of background information or analysis. Charlie's father's gestures and loud attempts at ordering in various foreign languages grow more embarrassing until his tongue-tied request for two "Bibson Geefeaters" (a "Beefeater Gibson" is a potent martini made from a well-known brand of gin) comes as the punch line to a grotesque joke on himself.

Point of View

When we speak of a politician's **point of view** on an issue we mean his or her attitude toward it, pro or con. In fiction, however, the term point of view is employed in a specialized sense, referring to the question of *authority* in the story. Every story has a **narrator,** a voice that provides the reader with information about and insight into characters and incidents; but in some cases the identity of this voice of authority is not immediately apparent. The narrative voice may be that of a character in the story, or it may come from outside the story. Being too literal-minded about the matter of point of view usually is a mistake, and we usually have to accept certain **narrative conventions** without questioning them too seriously if we are to enjoy reading stories. Thus, when we finish reading a detective story narrated by the sleuth himself, we do not worry ourselves speculating about when such a busy character found time to jot down the events of the story. Similarly, we accept as a convention the fact that a narrator may suddenly jump from simply recording a conversation to telling us what one of its participants is thinking. Very early in our lives we learn how stories are told, just as we have been conditioned to make a mental transition while watching a movie, when our perspective shifts in the blink of an eye from one character's frightened stare, to the flashing barrel of a gun, to a hand clutching a chest, to another character's sneer of triumph.

Almost all narrative points of view can be classified as either first-person or third-person. In **first-person narration,** the narrator is a **participant** in the action. He or she may be either a major character (which is the case with Charlie in "Reunion") or a minor character, who may be close to the event in time or distant from it. Although it is never directly stated, it seems likely that the adult Charlie is narrating an account of something that happened years before; thus, his repeated phrase about the last time he saw his father has a finality about it that goes far beyond a simple statement like "The last time I saw my father was a week ago in Grand Central Station." In general, first-person stories may seem more immediate than third-person stories, but they are limited by the simple fact that the narrator must be present at all times and must also have some knowledge of what is going on. If, for example, an attempt had been made to tell "Reunion" from the point of view of one of the restaurant waiters, the narrator might have had to resort to eavesdropping on Charlie and his father in order to report their circumstances. The ability of the narrator to tell the story accurately is also important. An **unreliable narrator,** either through naïvete, ignorance, or impaired mental processes, relates events in such a distorted manner that the reader, who has come to recognize the narrator's unreliability, literally has to turn the character's reporting on its head to make sense. Imagine how we would read "Reunion" if it had been told from the boozy, self-deluding point of view of Charlie's father.

Third-person narration, by definition, employs a **nonparticipant** narrator, a voice of authority which never reveals its source and is capable of moving from place to place to describe action and report dialogue. In third-person stories the question of reliability is rarely an issue, but the matter of **omniscience,** the degree to which the "all-knowing" narrator can reveal the thoughts of characters, is. **Total omniscience** means that the narrator knows everything about the characters' lives—their pasts, presents, and futures—and may reveal the thoughts of anyone in the story. An **editorial point of view** goes even farther, allowing the god-like author to comment directly on the action (also called **authorial intrusion**).

Most contemporary authors avoid total omniscience in short fiction, perhaps sensing that a story's strength is dissipated if more than one perspective is used. Instead, they employ **limited omniscience,** also called **selective omniscience** or the **method of central intelligence,** thereby limiting themselves to the thoughts and perceptions of a single character. This point of view is perhaps the most flexible of all because it allows the writer to compromise between the immediacy of first-person narration and the mobility of third-person narration. A further departure from omniscience is the **dramatic point of view** (also called the **objective point of view**). Here the narrator simply reports dialogue and action with minimal interpretation and does not delve into characters' minds. As the name implies, the dramatic point of view approximates the experience of reading a play; readers are provided only with set descriptions, stage directions, and dialogue, and thus must supply motivations that are based solely on this external evidence.

Technically, other points of view are possible, although they are rarely used. Stories have been told in the second person (note the use of the imperative verbs and an implied "you" in Lorrie Moore's "How to Talk to Your Mother (Notes)." A plural point of view also may be employed (William Faulkner's "A Rose for Emily" is one example), but such points of view are difficult to sustain and may quickly prove distracting to readers. Also, there is an unwritten rule that point of view should be consistent throughout a story, although occasionally a writer may utilize multiple perspectives to illustrate how the "truth" of any incident is always relative to the way in which it is witnessed.

Theme

We have already discussed the manner in which fables and other types of didactic literature make their purpose clear by explicitly stating a moral or interpretation at the end of the story. Literary fiction, however, is usually much more subtle in revealing its **theme,** the overall meaning the reader derives from the story. Most of the early reading we did as children probably fell into two distinct categories—sheer entertainment or overt didacticism—with very little middle ground. Thus, many readers, coming to serious fiction for the first time, want either to avoid the tedious search for a "message" or to complain, "If the author was trying to say that then why didn't she just come right out and *say* it!" To further complicate matters, the theoretical manner in which we analyze stories and the preconceptions we bring to bear on them may result in multiple interpretations of meaning. No single statement of theme is likely to be the "correct" one, although it is fair to say that some seem more likely than others.

What, then, is the theme of "Reunion"? A reader insistent on a moral might denounce Charlie's father, inveighing against "demon rum" and its destructive effect on "family values." Another reader, slightly more charitable, might recognize alcoholism as a disease and feel some amount of sympathy for the father. Yet another, perhaps entirely too self-righteous, might fault Charlie for running away from his father, interpreting the older man's actions as a subconscious cry for help. If we investigate Cheever's own troubled biography and note his own serious problems with both parenthood and alcoholism, we may read the story as a psychological confession, with Cheever himself simultaneously playing the roles of father and son. With so many possibilities before us, it is perhaps best to summarize a story's theme broadly:

> *'Reunion,' like most initiation stories, is about growth through loss of innocence. Children have to learn, often through painful experience, that they are not responsible for their parents' well-being, and sometimes they must distance themselves from their parents in order to survive.*

Such a statement does not encompass every possible nuance of the story's theme, but it does at least provide us with a starting point for arguing about the finer points of Cheever's meanings.

Still, many modern authors are not always reticent about revealing their themes. A moralist like Flannery O'Connor perceives her characters' shortcomings and judges them according to her own Roman Catholic moral standards. Alice Walker has tackled social themes like female genital mutilation in her fiction. Margaret Atwood's feminism is rarely hidden in her stories and poems. Many modern stories are in fact **allegorical tales,** in which the literal events point to a parallel sequence of symbolic ideas. In many stories the literal setting of the story, a doctor's waiting room, for example, or a crowded city bus, is a **microcosm,** a "small world" that reflects the tensions of the larger world outside. Thus, despite their outward sophistication, many of the stories included here reveal their debt to the ancient ethical functions of fables and parables.

Setting

Novelists can lavish pages of prose on details of setting, just as they can describe characters down to such minutiae as the contents of their pockets. But short story writers, hemmed in by limitations of space, rarely have such luxury and must ordinarily limit themselves to very selective descriptions of time and place. When a writer like Edgar Allan Poe goes into great detail in his descriptions (for example, in the opening sentences of "The Fall of the House of Usher") it is likely that **atmosphere,** the emotional aura surrounding a certain setting, is more important to him than the actual physical locale.

Setting is simply the time and place of a story, and in most cases the details of description are given to the reader directly by the narrator. A story may employ multiple locations in its different scenes, and its time frame may encompass a few hours or many years. "Reunion" is a story with relatively few details of setting. Because Cheever wrote his stories almost exclusively for *The New Yorker*, it is not necessary for him to describe the interior of Grand Central Station to an audience doubtless familiar with it; excessive details here would probably be irrelevant. Similarly, he spends no more than a sentence or two describing each of the restaurants: One has "a lot of horse tack on the walls," one is "Italian," and the other two are not described at all. The time setting is also relatively unimportant here. We know that the action is taking place during the lunch hour on a weekday, probably in the summer, but as far as a more specific time is concerned, we know little or nothing. "Reunion" could be taking place today or fifty years ago or, for that matter, twenty years from now.

Some stories, however, depend on their **locale** or time setting much more heavily and thus demand fuller exposition of setting. **Historical fiction** usually pays great attention to the altered landscapes and customs of bygone eras. A writer who carelessly lets an alarm clock go off in a story set in the early 1800s has committed an anachronism which may be only slightly more obvious than another writer's use of contemporary slang in the same setting. **Local color fiction** depends heavily on the unique characteristics of a particular area, usually a rural one that is off the beaten path. Such places have become increasingly rare in contemporary America, but the deep South and Alaska still provide locales that possess intrinsic interest. Some southern writers, like William Faulkner or Flannery O'Connor, first established their reputations as practitioners of **regionalism,** setting most of their work in a particular area or country. A recent American writer like Bobbie Ann Mason reveals in virtually every one of the stories in her first collection, *Shiloh and Other Stories,* her deep roots in her native Kentucky. A South American writer like Gabriel García Márquez continually draws us into the strange world of Colombian villages cut off from the contemporary world, places where past and present, history and folklore, natural and supernatural, seamlessly join in what has been labeled **magic realism.**

Stories contain both specific and general settings. The specific setting is the precise time(s) and place(s) where the action takes place. The general setting of a story, what is called its **enveloping action,** is its sense of the "times" and how its characters interact with events and social currents in the larger world. We have already mentioned how the specific setting of a story often is a microcosm that reflects the doings of society at large. It is impossible to read stories by Flannery O'Connor or Alice Walker and not be made aware of the social changes that have transformed the rural South in the last thirty years. Stories sometimes depend on readers' ability to bring their knowledge of history and culture to bear on the events taking place. In reading a story like Ralph Ellison's "A Party Down at the Square," younger readers may be unaware of the widespread horrors of lynchings in an America that older readers can painfully recall.

Style and Symbol

Style in fiction refers equally to the characteristics of language in a particular story and to the same characteristics in a writer's complete works. The more individual a writer's style is, the easier it is to write a **parody,** or satirical imitation, of it, as the well-publicized annual "Faux Faulkner" and "International Imitation Hemingway" contests attest. A detailed analysis of the style in an individual story might include attention to such matters as diction, sentence structure, punctuation (or the lack thereof), and use of figurative language. In English we usually make a distinction between the differing qualities of words—standard versus slang usage,

Latinate versus Germanic vocabulary, abstract versus concrete diction, and so on. While such matters are most meaningful only in the context of an individual story or an author's work in general, we can clearly see the difference between one character who says, "I have profited to a great degree from the educational benefits of the realm of experience," and another who says, "I graduated from the school of hard knocks." However, in analyzing style we must be sensitive to the literary fashions of periods other than our own; it is senseless to fault Poe for "flowery diction" when we compare his use of language to that of his contemporaries. The prevailing fashion in fiction today is for the unadorned starkness of writers like Bobbie Ann Mason and Raymond Carver, a type of literature that has been disparagingly called "K-Mart realism" by one critic. Still, one should not be surprised if, as we move forward in a new century, fashions shift and writers compete to outdo Faulkner at his most ornate.

The style of "Reunion" is for the most part straightforward, with few flourishes of vocabulary (if we except the foreign phrases) or sentence structure. About the only significant departure from this plain style is in the opening paragraph, where Charlie momentarily rises to a slightly elevated rhetorical plateau: ". . . as soon as I saw him I felt that he was my father, my flesh and blood, my future and my doom." The **tone** of the story, or what we can indirectly determine about the author's own feelings about its events from his choice of words, is also carefully controlled. Cheever avoids the twin pitfalls of sentimentality on the one hand and cynicism on the other by deftly walking an emotional tightrope. After the opening paragraph, at no point does Charlie tell us how he feels, instead letting his father's actions speak for themselves. There are points in "Reunion" where we may laugh, but it is an uncomfortable laugh at which we probably feel a little guilty. The possible tones available for use in any given story may run through the whole range of human emotions, from outright comedy or satirical contempt to pathos of the most wrenching sort. It is possible for an unwary reader to fail to appreciate the keen edge of Flannery O'Connor's irony or the profound skepticism of Jorge Luis Borges, but this failure should not be laid at the feet of the writers. Appreciation of a writer's tone of voice can often be difficult to master, coming only after the experience of reading a wide range of stories and comparing how irony may or may not be present in them.

Like tone of voice, symbolism in stories is often a troublesome affair for beginning readers, as is indicated by the oft-heard phrase "hidden meanings." Are authors doing their best to conceal, rather than reveal, the significance of actions and things in their works? Usually they are not, but superficial reading of a story may barely scratch the surface of its full complexity. Symbolism may occur in any of the elements discussed above: A plot or character or setting may have some symbolic value. There is little heavy symbolism in "Reunion," but if we think about the title, with its suggestions of emotional warmth, and the setting, a busy train station, we can see that Cheever has chosen his title carefully, and it has both ironic and symbolic overtones.

If the details of a plot seem consistently symbolic, with each detail clearly pointing the way to some obvious larger meaning, then we are reading **allegory.** An allegorical reading of Hawthorne's "Young Goodman Brown," the first story in this collection, might focus on how the protagonist's and his wife's names represent untested virtue and religious fidelity, respectively, and how the dark forest mirrors the confusion of Brown's soul. Many stories do not use symbolism is so obvious a way, however. In a given story, an author may employ a **traditional symbol,** a thing that most members of a culture instantly recognize as possessing a shared symbolic meaning. We may recognize a white gown or a red rose symbolizing, on the one hand, innocence and, on the other, romantic love without having to think very deeply about either. Familiarity with an individual author's works may also help us to recognize a **private symbol,** a symbol that the author has made his or her own by repeated usage. To cite one example, Flannery O'Connor's use of bursts of bright light generally herald some kind of dawning spiritual revelation in the mind of one of her characters. Another writer may use certain colors, situations, and actions repeatedly; it is hard to read much of Poe's fiction without becoming aware of the personal horror that small, confined spaces represent for the author. Finally, we may identify an **incidental symbol** in a story. This may be a thing or action that ordinarily would have not deeper meaning but acquires one in a particular story. Paying close attention to the way an author repeats certain details or otherwise points to their significance is the key. Understanding what a symbol *means* is often less important than merely realizing that it *exists.* The exact meaning of an incidental symbol is usually open to interpretation and multiple interpretations of its implications do not necessarily contradict one another.

Introduction to Poetry

An Anecdote: Where Poetry Starts

The room is not particularly grand, a large lecture hall in one of the old buildings on the college campus, and the small group of first-year students whose literature class has been dismissed so that they can attend the poetry reading have taken seats near the back of the room. They have been encouraged to come for several weeks by their instructor, and when she enters she looks around the room and nods in their direction, smiling.

The seats gradually fill. The crowd is a mixed one—several men and women known by sight as senior faculty members; a scattering of other older visitors, many of them apparently from the community; a large contingent of instructors and graduate students from the English Department sitting in the front rows; and small clusters of undergraduates scattered throughout the room.

One of the students scans the crowd, wondering aloud which is the poet. On the walk to the reading, several fellow class members decided that the poet, a cadaverous grey-haired man wrapped in a black cloak, would recite his poems in a resonant monotone, preferably with a strong breeze tossing his hair. Speculating on how the wind effect might be managed inside a lecture hall made them laugh.

Now the crowd grows quiet as the students' instructor steps to the podium and adjusts the microphone. She makes a few complimentary remarks about the strong turnout and thanks several benefactors for their financial support of poetry at the university. Then she introduces the guest. Her students know most of this information, for they have studied several of his poems in class that week, but they are still slightly surprised when he rises to polite applause and takes the lectern. The balding middle-aged man wearing a chambray shirt and loosely knotted tie could be taken for a professor in any campus department, and when he adjusts his glasses and clears his throat, blinking at the audience, there is little about poet.

Surprisingly, he does not begin with a poem. Instead, in a relaxed voice he tells an anecdote about his younger daughter and an overdue science project. When he moves from the background story into reading the poem itself, there is little change in his volume level, and his tone remains conversational. The students find that the poem, which they had discussed in class only a couple of days before, takes on new meaning when its origins are explained by the poet himself. They find themselves listening attentively to his words, even laughing out loud several times. The hour goes by quickly, and at its end their applause, like that of the rest of the audience, is long and sincere.

At the next class meeting, the instructor asks for reactions to the reading. Although some of the class members are slightly critical, faulting the speaker for his informal manner and his failure to maintain eye contact with the room, most of the remarks are positive. The comments that surface most often have to do with how much more meaningful the poems in the textbook become when the poet explains how he came to write them. They now know that one poem is actually spoken in the voice of the poet's dead father and that another is addressed to a friend who was paralyzed in an automobile accident. Although these things could perhaps be inferred from the poems alone, the students are unanimous in their opinion that knowing the details beforehand adds a great deal to the first impression a poem makes. As one student puts it, "It's just that a poem makes a lot more sense when you know who's talking and when and where it's supposed to be taking place."

"It always helps to know where poetry starts," adds one of her classmates.

Speaker, Listener, and Context

The situation described above is hardly unique. Instructors have long been encouraging, even begging, their students to attend events like one described and the college poetry reading has become, for many Americans, the closest encounter students will have with this complex and often perplexing art form. But what students often find at such readings, sometimes to their amazement, is that poetry need not be intimidating or obscure. Poems that are *performed* provide a gentle reminder that the roots of poetry, like those of all literature, were originally part of the **oral tradition.** In ancient societies, stories and poems were passed down from generation to generation and recited for all members of the tribe, from the wizened elders to the youngest children. For most of its long history, poetry has been a popular art form aimed at audiences (remember that the word audience means "hearers"). It is only recently, in the last three or four decades, that its most visible signs of life are to be found on college campuses. Still, it is perhaps worth noting that we are exposed daily to a great deal of poetry in oral form, primarily through the medium of recorded song lyrics. The unique qualities of poetry throughout the ages, that is, its ability to tell stories or summarize complicated emotions in a few well-chosen words, are demonstrated whenever we memorize the lines of a popular song and sing them to ourselves.

Of course, poetry written primarily for the page is usually more demanding than song lyrics. Writers of popular songs aim at a wide commercial audience, and this simple fact of economics, added to the fact that the lyrics are not intended primarily for publication but for being recorded with all the resources of studio technology, tends to make many song lyrics relatively uninteresting when they appear in print. But a poem will exist primarily as a printed text, although its effect may be enhanced greatly through a skillful oral performance in which the poet can also explain the background of the poem, its setting and speaker, and the circumstances under which it was written. In general, these details, so crucial to understanding a poem yet so often only implied when the poem appears in print, are called the **dramatic situation** of a poem. Situation can be summed up in a question: *Who is speaking to whom under what circumstances?* If the poet fails to provide us with clues or if we are careless in picking up the information that is provided, then we may begin reading with no sense of reference and, thus, may go far astray. Even such words as "on," "upon," or "to" in titles can be crucial to our understanding of dramatic situation, telling us something about an event or object that provided the stimulus for the poem or about the identity of the "you" addressed in the poem.

An illustration may be helpful. Suppose we look at what is unquestionably the most widely known poem ever written by an American. It
is a poem which virtually all Americans can recite in part and, in fact,
do so by the millions every week. Yet if we were told that this poem is
unusual because its best-known section is a long, unanswered question,
addressed by the speaker to a nearby companion, about whether or not
the object named in the title even exists, then it is likely that most of
us would be confused. Before going further, let us look at the poem.

The Star-Spangled Banner

O say, can you see, by the dawn's early light,
    What so proudly we hailed at the twilight's last gleaming?
Whose broad stripes and bright stars thro' the perilous fight,
    O'er the ramparts we watched, were so gallantly streaming!
And the rockets' red glare, the bombs bursting in air,
    Gave proof through the night that our flag was still there:
O say, does that star-spangled banner yet wave
    O'er the land of the free and the home of the brave?

On the shore, dimly seen thro' the mists of the deep,
    Where the foe's haughty host in dread silence reposes,
What is that which the breeze, o'er the towering steep,
    As it fitfully blows, now conceals, now discloses?
Now it catches the gleam of the morning's first beam,
    In full glory reflected now shines on the stream:
'Tis the star-spangled banner! O long may it wave
    O'er the land of the free and the home of the brave!

And where is that band who so vauntingly swore
    That the havoc of war and the battle's confusion
A home and a country should leave us no more?
    Their blood has washed out their foul footsteps' pollution.
No refuge could save the hireling and slave
    From the terror of flight, or the gloom of the grave:
And the star-spangled banner in triumph doth wave
    O'er the land of the free and the home of the brave!

Oh! thus be it ever, when freemen shall stand
    Between their loved homes and the war's desolation!

Blest with victory and peace, may the heav'n-rescued land
Praise the Pow'r that hath made and preserved us a nation.
Then conquer we must, when our cause it is just,
And this be our motto: "In God is our trust."
And the star-spangled banner in triumph shall wave
O'er the land of the free and the home of the brave!

"Now wait a minute!" you may be complaining. "The Star-Spangled Banner' is a *song*, not a poem. And what's this question business? Don't we always sing it while facing the flag? Besides, it's just a patriotic song. Nobody really worries about what it *means*."

In answer to the first comment, "The Star-Spangled Banner" *was* in fact written as a poem and was set to music only after its composition. Most of us will probably agree that the words are not particularly well-suited to the melody (which was taken, curiously, from a popular British barroom ballad) and the song remains notoriously difficult to sing, even for professional performers. Garth Brooks, the popular country singer, once remarked before attempting it at a Super Bowl that it "is one of the hardest songs to sing," implying that the audience at such an event always seems ready to witness a failure. In its original form, "The Star-Spangled Banner" (or "The Defense of Fort McHenry," the title under which it was first published) is an example of **occasional verse,** a poem that is written about or for an important event (or occasion), sometimes private but usually of some public significance. Although poems of this type are not often printed on the front pages of newspapers as they once were, they are still being written. Enough poems appeared after the assassination of President John F. Kennedy in 1963 to fill a book, *Of Poetry and Power,* and the Challenger disaster of 1985 stimulated a similar outpouring of occasional poems, one of them by Howard Nemerov, who served as poet laureate of the United States. More recently, Maya Angelou recited "On the Pulse of Morning" at the first inauguration of President Clinton, and Miller Williams read "Of History and Hope" at the second. The author of "The Star-Spangled Banner," Francis Scott Key (1779–1843), wrote poetry as an avocation. Yet like many men and women who are not professional writers, Key was so deeply moved by an event that he witnessed that occasional poetry was the only medium through which he could express his feelings.

Now let's go back to our question about dramatic situation, taking it one part at a time: Who is speaking? A technical word that is often used to designate the speaker of a poem is **persona** (plural: **personae**), a word that meant "mask" in ancient Greek. Even though the persona of "The Star-Spangled Banner" never uses the word "I" in the poem, the speaker seems to be Key himself, a fact that can be verified by biographical research. Still, it is probably safer to look at poems carefully to see if they give any evidence that the speaker is someone other than the poet. Poems like "Ulysses" by Alfred, Lord Tennyson or "Porphyria's Lover" by Robert Browning have titles that identify personae who are, respectively, a character from ancient epic poetry and an unnamed man who is confessing the murder of his lover, Porphyria. In neither case is the persona to be identified with the poet himself. Other poems may be somewhat more problematical. Edgar Allan Poe's "The Raven," like many of Poe's short stories, is spoken by a persona who is not to be identified with the author, even though he shares many of the same morbid preoccupations of Poe's other characters. Even Sylvia Plath, a poet usually associated with an extremely candid form of autobiographical poetry known as **confessional poetry,** on a BBC broadcast identified the persona of her masterpiece "Daddy" as an invented character, "a girl with an Electra complex." Although it now is clear that Plath used many autobiographical details in her poem, readers who try to identify her as a victim of child abuse on its evidence should instead turn to Plath's journals and the many biographies that have been written about her. Sometimes poems have more than one persona, which is the case with Thomas Hardy's "The Ruined Maid" and Robert Frost's "Home Burial," two poems which consist almost entirely of dialogue. In other poems, for instance in many ballads, the voice may simply be a third-person **narrator** such as we might find in a short story or novel. Thus, although it is perhaps true that many poems (including the majority of those included here) are in fact spoken by the poet out of his or her most private feelings, it is not a good idea to leap too quickly to the assumption that the persona of a poem is identical to the poet and shares his or her views. Conclusions about the degree to which a poem is autobiographical can be verified only by research and familiarity with a poet's other works.

To return to our question: Who is speaking to whom? Another useful term is **auditor,** the person or persons spoken to in a poem. Some poems identify no auditor; others clearly do specify an auditor or auditors, in most cases identified by name or by the second-person pronoun "you" (or "thee/thou" in older poetry). Again, the title may give clues:

Poe's "To Helen" is addressed to the famous beauty of Homeric legend; Robert Herrick's "To the Virgins, to Make Much of Time" is addressed to a group of young women; William Cullen Bryant's "To the Fringed Gentian" is addressed to a common New England wildflower. (The figure of speech **apostrophe**—discussed later in this introduction—is used when a nonhuman, inanimate, or abstract thing is directly addressed.) Relatively few poems are addressed directly to the reader, so when we read the opening of William Shakespeare's Sonnet 18 ("Shall I compare thee to a summer's day?") we should keep in mind that he is not addressing us but another individual, in this case a young male friend who is referred to in many of the sonnets. A powerful poem like Claude McKay's "If We Must Die" begins in this manner:

> If we must die, let it not be like hogs
> Hunted and penned in an inglorious spot,
> While round us bark the mad and hungry dogs,
> Making their mock at our accursed lot.

Later in the poem McKay identifies his auditors as "Kinsmen." Without outside help, about all we can say with certainty at first glance is that the poet seems to be addressing a group of companions who share his desperate situation; when we learn, possibly through research, that McKay was an African-American poet writing in reaction to race riots during the 1920s, the symbolic nature of his exhortation becomes clearer.

Now the final part of the question: Who is speaking to whom *under what circumstances?* First, we might ask if there is a relationship, either implied or stated, between persona and auditor. Obviously many love poems take the form of verbal transactions between two parties and, because relationships have their ups and downs, these shifts of mood are reflected in the poetry. One famous example is Michael Drayton's sonnet "Since There's No Help," which begins with the persona threatening to end the relationship with the auditor but which ends with an apparent reconciliation. Such "courtship ritual" poems as John Donne's "The Flea" and Andrew Marvell's "To His Coy Mistress" are witty arguments in favor of the couple's engaging in sexual relations—no more, no less. An example from poetry about marital love is Matthew Arnold's "Dover Beach," with ends with the plea "Ah, love, let us be true/To one another" as the only hope for stability the persona can find in a world filled with uncertainty and fear. Even an age disparity between persona and auditor can lend meaning to a poem, which is the case with the Herrick poem mentioned earlier and a dialogue poem like John Crowe Ransom's "Piazza Piece," a classic example of the debate between innocence and experience.

Other questions relating to circumstances of the dramatic situation might concern the poem's physical setting (if any), time (of day, year, historical era), even such matters as weather. Thomas Hardy's "Neutral Tones" provides a good example of a poem in which the setting, a gray winter day in a barren outdoor location, symbolically reinforces the persona's memory of the bitter end of a love affair. The shift in setting from the springtime idyll to the "cold hillside" in John Keats's "La Belle Dame sans Merci" cannot be overlooked in discussing the persona's disillusionment. Of course, many poems are explicitly occasional and may even contain an **epigraph** (see Gwendolyn Brooks's "We Real Cool"), a brief explanatory statement or quotation, or a **dedication,** which explains the setting. Sometimes footnotes or even outside research may be necessary. John Milton's "On the Late Massacre in Piedmont" will make little sense to readers if they do not know that the poet is reacting to the massacre of a group of Waldensian Protestants by Roman Catholic soldiers on Easter Sunday, 1655. Milton, an English Puritan, uses the occasion to attack the papacy as a "triple tyrant" and the "Babylonian woe."

To return, then, one final time to "The Star-Spangled Banner," let us apply our question to the poem. We have already determined that Key is the persona. Who is the "you" mentioned four words into the poem? It seems clear that Key is addressing an auditor standing close to him, either a single individual or a group, as he asks the auditor if he can see the flag that they both observed for the last time the previous day at sundown. Key tells us that it is now the first moment of dawn, and that even though the flag could be glimpsed periodically in the "rockets' red glare" of the bombardment throughout the night, it cannot be clearly seen now. It is a crucial question, for if the flag is no longer flying "o'er the ramparts," it will mean that the fort has fallen to the enemy. The tension mounts and moves into the second stanza, where at last, "thro' the mists of the deep," the flag can be discerned, "dimly seen" at first, then clearly as it "catches the gleam" of the full sunlight.

The full story of how Key came to write the poem is fairly well-known and supports this reading. The events which the poem describes took place on September 13–14, 1814, during the War of 1812. Key, a lawyer, came aboard a British warship anchored off Baltimore to argue for the release of a client and friend who had been taken hostage by the

British. Key won his friend's release, but the British captain, fearing that he might reveal information he had learned on board, kept Key overnight, releasing him and his client in the morning. It was during that night that Key witnessed the bombardment and with it, the failure of the British to take Baltimore. The final half of the poem celebrates the victory and offers a hopeful prayer that God will continue to smile on America "when our cause . . . is just." One might well argue that Key's phrase "conquer we must" contradicts the spirit of the earlier parts of the poem, but few people have argued that "The Star-Spangled Banner" is a consistently great poem. Still, it is an effective piece of patriotic verse that has a few moments of real drama, expressed in a vivid manner that lets its readers become eyewitnesses to an incident from American history.

Lyric, Narrative, Dramatic

The starting point for all literary criticism in Western civilization is Aristotle's *Poetics*, a work dating from the fourth century BC. Although Aristotle's remarks on drama, tragedy in particular, are more complete than his analysis of other types of literature, he does mention three main types of poetry: lyric, epic, and dithyrambic. In doing so, Aristotle outlines for the first time a theory of literature based on **genres,** or separate categories delineated by distinct style, form, and content. This threefold division remains useful today, although in two cases different terminology is employed. The first genre, **lyric poetry,** originally comprised brief poems that were meant to be sung or chanted to the accompaniment of a lyre. Today we still use the word "lyrics" in a specialized sense when referring to the words of a song, but lyric poetry has become such a large category that it includes virtually all poems that are primarily *about* a subject and contain little narrative content. The subject of a lyric poem may be the poet's emotions, an abstract idea, a satirical insight, or a description of a person or place. The persona in a lyric is usually closely identified with the poet himself or herself, because we tend to identify the essence of poetry with personal, subjective expression of feelings or ideas, lyric poetry remains the largest genre, with a number of subtypes. Among them are the **epigram,** a short, satirical lyric usually aimed at a specific person; the **elegy,** a lyric on the occasion of a death; and the **ode,** a long lyric in elevated language on a serious theme.

Aristotle's second genre, the epic, has been expanded to include all types of **narrative poetry,** that is, poetry whose main function is to tell a story. Like prose fiction, narrative poems have plots, characters, setting, and point-of-view, and may be discussed in the same terms as, say, a short story. The **epic** is a long narrative poem about the exploits of a hero. **Folk epics** like *The Iliad* or *Beowulf* were originally intended for public recitation and existed in oral form for a long period of time before they were transcribed. Little or nothing is known about the authors of folk epics; even Homer, the purported author of the *Iliad* and the *Odyssey,* is primarily a legendary character. **Literary epics,** like Dante's *Inferno* or Henry Wadsworth Longfellow's *The Song of Hiawatha,* differ in that they are the products of known authors who *wrote* their poems for publication. **Ballads** generally are shorter narratives with song-like qualities which often include rhyme and repeated refrains. **Folk ballads,** like folk epics, come from the oral tradition and are usually published anonymously; "Bonny Barbara Allan" and "Sir Patrick Spens" are typical examples. **Art** or **literary ballads** are conscious imitations of the ballad style by later poets and are generally somewhat more sophisticated than folk ballads in their techniques. Examples of this popular genre include Keats's "La Belle Dame sans Merci," Coleridge's famous long art ballad, "The Rime of the Ancient Mariner," and a recent example like Marilyn Nelson's "Ballad of Aunt Geneva." There are also other types of narrative poetry that have been popular through the centuries. **Metrical romances,** verse tales of the exploits of knights, were a popular genre during the Middle Ages and the Renaissance; Edmund Spenser's *The Faerie Queene* is one of the most ambitious examples of the type. At the opposite extreme are **mock-heroic narratives** like John Dryden's *MacFlecknoe* or Lord Byron's *Don Juan,* which spoof the conventions of epic poetry for comic or satirical effect. **Realistic narratives** of medium length (under 1000 lines) like Robert Frost's "Home Burial" or, more recently, Leon Stokesbury's "Evening End," have been popular since the early nineteenth century and are sometimes discussed as "poetic novels" or "short stories in verse."

There is no exact contemporary analogue for Aristotle's third category, **dithyrambic** poetry. This type of poem, composed to be chanted at religious rituals by a chorus, was the forerunner of tragedy. Today this third type is usually called **dramatic poetry,** because it has perhaps as much in common with the separate genre of drama as with lyric and narrative poetry. In general, the persona in a dramatic poem is an invented character not to be identified with the poet. The poem is presented as a speech or dialogue that might be acted out like a soliloquy or scene from a play. The **dramatic monologue** is a speech for a single character, usually delivered to a silent auditor. Notable examples are Tennyson's "Ulysses" and Browning's "My Last Duchess." A dramatic monologue sometimes implies, in the words of its persona, a distinct setting and interplay between persona and auditor. At the close of "Ulysses" the aged hero urges his "mariners" to listen closely and to observe the ship in the harbor waiting to take them off on a final voyage. Dramatic poetry can also take the form of **dialogue poetry,** in which two personae speak alternately. Examples are Christina Rossetti's "Up-Hill" and Hardy's "The Ruined Maid." A popular type of dialogue poem that originated in the Middle Ages was the **débat,** or mock-debate, in which two characters, usually personified abstractions like the Soul and the Body, argued their respective merits.

Although it is easy enough to find examples of "pure" lyrics, narratives, and dramatic monologues, sometimes the distinction between the three major types may become blurred, even in the same poem. "The Star-Spangled Banner," for example, contains elements of all three genres. The opening stanza, with its vivid re-creation of a question asked at dawn, is closest to dramatic poetry. The second and third stanzas, which tell of the outcome of the battle, are primarily narrative. The final stanza, with its patriotic effusion and religious sentiment, is lyrical. Still, the three-fold division is useful in discussing a single author's various ways of dealing with subjects or in comparing examples of one type by separate authors. To cite three poems by the same poet in this collection, we might look at William Blake's "The Tyger," "A Poison Tree," and "The Chimney Sweeper." The first of these is a descriptive lyric, dwelling primarily on the symbolic meaning of the tiger's appearance; the second is a narrative that relates, in the allegorical manner of a parable, the events leading up to a murder; and the third is a short dramatic monologue spoken by the persona identified in the title.

The Language of Poetry

One of the most persistent myths about poetry is that its language is artificial, "flowery," and essentially different from the language that people speak every day. Although these beliefs may be true of some poetry, one can easily find numerous examples that demonstrate poetic diction of an entirely different sort. It is impossible to characterize poetic language narrowly, for poetry, which is after all the art of language, covers the widest possible range of linguistic possibilities. For example, here are several passages from different poets, all describing birds:

> Hail to thee, blithe Spirit!
>   Bird thou never wert—
> That from Heaven, or near it,
>   Pourest thy full heart
> In profuse strains of unpremeditated art.
>
> Higher still and higher
>   From the earth thou springest
> Like a cloud of fire;
>   The blue deep thou wingest,
> And singing still dost soar, and soaring ever singest.
>
> Percy Bysshe Shelley, "To a Skylark"

> I caught this morning morning's minion, king-
> dom of daylight's dauphin, dapple-dawn-drawn Falcon, in his riding
> Of the rolling level underneath him steady air, and striding
> High there, how he rung upon the rein of a wimpling wing
> In his ecstacy!
>
> Gerard Manley Hopkins, "The Windhover"

> When the lilac-scent was in the air and Fifth-month grass was
>   growing,
> Up this seashore in some briers,
> Two feather'd guests from Alabama, two together,
> And their nest, and four light-green eggs spotted with brown,
> And every day the he-bird to and fro near at hand,
> And every day the she-bird crouch'd on her nest, silent, with
>   bright eyes,
> And every day I, a curious boy, never too close, never disturbing
>   them,
> Cautiously peering, absorbing, translating.
>
> Walt Whitman, "Out of the Cradle Endlessly Rocking"

At once a voice arose among
  The bleak twigs overhead
In a full-hearted evensong
  Of joy illimited;
An aged thrush, frail, gaunt, and small,
  In blast-beruffled plume,
Had chosen thus to fling his soul
  Upon the growing gloom.

Thomas Hardy, "The Darkling Thrush"

There is a singer everyone has heard,
Loud, a mid-summer and a mid-wood bird,
Who makes the solid tree trunks sound again.
He says that leaves are old and that for flowers
Mid-summer is to spring as one to ten.

Robert Frost, "The Oven Bird"

The blue booby lives
on the bare rocks
of Galápagos
and fears nothing.
It is a simple life:
they live on fish,
and there are few predators.

James Tate, "The Blue Booby"

Of these quotes, only Shelley's from the early nineteenth century possesses the stereotypical characteristics of what we mean when we use the term "poetic" in a negative sense. Poetry, like any other art form, follows fashions that change over the years; by Shelley's day, the use of "thee" and "thou" and their related verb forms ("wert" and "wingest") had come full circle from their original use as a familiar form of the second person employed to address intimates and servants to an artificially heightened grammatical form reserved for prayers and poetry. Hopkins's language, from a poem of the 1870s, is artificial in an entirely different way; here the poet's **idiom,** the personal use of words that marks his poetry, is highly idiosyncratic; indeed, it would be hard to mistake a poem by Hopkins, with its muscular monosyllables and rich texture of sound patterns, with one by any other poet. Whitman's diction should present few difficulties; the only oddity here is the use of "Fifth-month" instead of "May," a linguistic inheritance, perhaps, from the poet's Quaker mother. Of course, one might argue that Whitman's "naturalness" results from his use of his free verse, but both Hardy and Frost, who write rhymed, metrical verse, are hardly less natural. When we move to the contemporary period, we can find little difference between the language of many poems and conversational speech, as Tate's lines indicate.

Still, in reading a poem, particularly one from the past, we should be aware of certain problems that may impede our understanding. **Diction** refers to the individual words in a poem and may be classified in several ways. A poem's **level of diction** can range from slang at one extreme to formal usage at the other, although in an age in which most poems use a level of diction that stays in the middle of the scale, ranging from conversational and standard levels, these distinctions are useful only when a poet is being self-consciously formal (perhaps for ironic effect) or going to the opposite extreme to imitate the language of the streets. In past eras the term **poetic diction** was used to indicate a level of speech somehow refined above ordinary usage and, thus, somehow superior to it. Today the same term would most likely be used as a way of criticizing a poet's language. We should keep in mind that the slang of one era may become the standard usage of another, as is the case with "O.K." which has become a universal expression.

A good dictionary is useful in many ways, particularly in dealing with **archaisms** (words that are no longer in common use) and other words that may not be familiar to the reader. Take, for example, the opening lines of Edgar Allan Poe's "To Helen":

> Helen, thy beauty is to me
>   Like those Nicean barks of yore,
> That gently, o'er a perfumed sea,
>   The weary, way-worn wanderer bore
>   To his own native shore.

Several words here may give trouble to the average contemporary reader. First, "o'er," like "ne'er" or similar words like "falt'ring" and "glimm'ring," is simply a contraction; this dropping of a letter, called **syncope,** is done for the sake of maintaining the poem's meter; in the third stanza of "The Star-Spangled Banner," the words "Pow'r" and "heav'n" are contracted for the same reason. "Barks of yore" will probably send most of us to the dictionary, for our sense of "bark" as either the outer surface of a tree or the noise that a dog makes does not fit here; likewise, "yore" is unfamiliar, possibly archaic. Looking up the literal sense of a word in a dictionary discloses its **denotation,** or literal meaning. Thus, we find that "barks" are small sailing ships and that "yore" refers to the distant past. Of course, Poe could have said "ships of the past" or a similar phrase, but his word choice was perhaps dictated by **connotation,** the implied meaning or feel that some words have acquired; it may be that even in Poe's day "barks of yore" had a remote quality that somehow evoked ancient Greece in a way that, say, "ancient ships" would not. But what are we to make of "Nicean," a proper adjective that sounds geographical but does not appear in either the dictionary or gazetteer? In this case we have encountered an example of a **coinage,** or **neologism,** a word made up by the poet. Speculation on the source of "Nicean" has ranged from Nice, in the south of France, to Phoenician, but it is likely that Poe simply coined the word for its exotic sound. Similarly, we might note that the phrase "weary, way-worn wanderer" contains words that seem to have been chosen primarily for their alliterated sounds.

When we put a poem into our own words, we **paraphrase** it, a practice that is often useful when passages are had to understand. Other than diction, **syntax,** the order of words in a sentence, may also give readers problems. Syntax in poetry, particularly in poems that use rhyme, is likely to be different from that of both speech and prose; if a poet decides to rhyme in a certain pattern, then word order must be modified to fit the formal design, and this may present difficulties to readers in understanding the grammar of a passage. Here is the opening of a familiar piece of American patriotic verse: "My country, 'tis of thee,/Sweet land of liberty,/Of thee I sing." What is the subject of this sentence? Would you be surprised to learn that the subject is "it" (contained in the contraction "'tis"—"It is of thee, my country, sweet land of liberty, of thee [that] I sing")? The passage from Poe's poem presents few difficulties of this order but does contain one example of **inversion,** words that fall out of their expected order (a related syntactical problem lies in **ellipsis,** words that are consciously omitted by the poet). If we do not allow for this, we are likely to be confused by "the weary, way-worn wanderer bore/To his own native shore." The wanderer bore *what?* A quick mental sentence diagram shows that "wanderer" is the direct object of "bore," not its subject. A good paraphrase should simplify both diction and syntax: "Helen, to me your beauty is like those Nicean (?) ships of the ancient past that carried the weary, travel-worn wanderer gently over a perfumed sea to his own native land." In paraphrasing, only the potentially troublesome words and phrases should be substituted, leaving the original language as intact as possible. Paraphrasing is a useful first step toward unfolding a poem's literal sense, but it obviously takes few of a poet's specific nuances of language into account; words like "cool," "cold," "chilly," and "frigid" may denote the same thing, but each has its own connotation. "Poetry," Robert Frost famously remarked, "is what is lost in translation." He might have extended the complaint to include paraphrase as well.

Several other matters relevant to poetic language are worth mentioning. **Etymology,** the study of the sources of words, is a particularly rewarding topic in English because our language has such an unusually rich history—just compare an unabridged French dictionary to its English counterpart. Old English (or Anglo-Saxon), the ancient language of the British Isles, was part of the Germanic family of languages. When the Norman French successfully invaded Britain in 1066 they brought with them their own language, part of the Romance language family (all originally derived from Latin). By the time of Chaucer's death in 1400 these two linguistic traditions had merged into a single language, Middle English, that can be read today, despite its differences in spelling, pronunciation, and vocabulary. We can still, however, distinguish the words that show their Germanic heritage from those of Latinate origin, and despite the fact that English is rich in synonyms, the Germanic and Latinate words often have different connotations. "Smart" (from the Old English *smeart*) is not quite the same as "intelligent" (from the Latin *intellegent*). A "mapmaker" is subtly different from a "cartographer"—ask yourself which would have ink on his fingers. Although a poet's preference for words of a certain origin is not always immediately clear, we can readily distinguish the wide gulf that separates a statement like "I live in a house with my folks" from "I abide in a residence with my parents."

A final tension exists in poems between their use of **concrete diction** and **abstract diction.** Concrete words denote that which can be perceived by the senses, and the vividness of a poem's language resides primarily in the way it uses **imagery,** sensory details denoting specific physical experiences. Because sight is the most important of the five senses, **visual imagery** ("a dim light"; "a dirty rag"; "a golden daffodil") predominates in poems, but we should also be alert for striking examples of the other types of imagery: **auditory** ("a pounding surf"), **tactile** ("a scratchy beard"),

olfactory ("the scent of apple blossoms"), and **gustatory** ("the bitter tang of gin"). The use of specific imagery has always been crucial for poetry. Consider, for example, of the way Chaucer uses brilliantly chosen concrete details—a nun's coral jewelry, a monk's hood lined with fur, a festering sore on a cook's shin—to bring his pilgrims to life in the prologue to *The Canterbury Tales.* In the early twentieth century, a group of poets led by Americans Ezra Pound and H. D. (Hilda Doolittle) pioneered a poetic movement called **imagism,** in which concrete details predominate in short descriptive poems (see H. D.'s "Sea Rose"). "Go in fear of abstractions," commanded Pound, and his friend William Carlos Williams modified the remark to become a poetic credo: "No ideas but in things."

Still, for most poets abstract words remain important because they carry the burden of a poem's overall meaning or theme. William Butler Yeats's "Leda and the Swan" provides a good example of how concrete and abstract diction coexists in a poem. In reading this account of the myth in which Zeus, in the form of a swan, rapes and impregnates a human woman and thus sets in action the chain of events that leads to the Trojan War (Leda was the mother of Helen of Troy), we will probably be struck at first by the way that tactile imagery ("a sudden blow," fingers attempting to "push/The feathered glory" away, "A shudder in the loins") is used to describe an act of sexual violation. Even though some abstract words ("terrified," "vague," "glory," "strange") appear in the first eight lines of the poem they are all linked closely to concrete words like "fingers," "feathered," and "heart." In the last two lines of the poem, Yeats uses three large abstractions—"knowledge," "power," and "indifferent"—to state his theme (or at least ask the crucial rhetorical question about the meaning of the myth). More often than not, one can expect to encounter the largest number of abstract words near the conclusion of poems. Probably the most famous abstract statement in English poetry John Keats's "'Beauty is truth, truth beauty,' that is all/Ye know on earth, and all ye need to know" appears in the last two lines of a fifty-line poem that is filled with lush, sensory details of description.

Two other devices sometimes govern a poet's choice of words. **Onomatopoeia** refers to individual words like "splash" or "thud" whose meanings are closely related to their sounds. Auditory imagery in a poem can often be enhanced by the use of onomatopoeic words. In some cases, however, a whole line can be called onomatopoeic, even if it contains no single word that illustrates the device. Thomas Hardy uses this line to describe the pounding of distant surf: "Where hill-hid tides throb, throe on throe." Here the repetition of similar sounds helps to imitate the sound of the ocean. A second device is the **pun,** the use of one word to imply the additional meaning of a similar-sounding word (the formal term is **paranomasia**). Thus, when Anne Bradstreet compares her first book to an illegitimate child, she addresses the book in this manner: "If for thy Father asked, say thou had'st none;/And for thy Mother, she alas is poor./Which caused her thus to send thee out of door." The closeness of the interjection "alas" to the article and noun "a lass" is hardly coincidental. Poets in Bradstreet's day considered the pun a staple of their repertoire, even in serious poetry, but contemporary poets are more likely to use it primarily for comic effect:

> They have a dozen children; it's their diet,
> For they have bread too often. Please don't try it (Anonymous)

More often than not, puns like these will elicit a groan from the audience, a response that may be exactly what the poet desires.

Figurative Language

We use figurative language in everyday speech without thinking of the poetic functions of the same devices. We can always relate experience in a purely literal fashion: "His table manners were deplorable. Mother scolded him severely, and Dad said some angry words to him. He left the table embarrassed and with his feelings hurt." But a more vivid way of saying the same thing might employ language used not in the literal but in the figurative sense. Thus, another version might run, "He made an absolute pig of himself. Mother jumped on his back about it, and Dad scorched his ears. You should have seen him slink off like a scolded puppy." At least four comparisons are made here in an attempt to describe one character's table manners, his mother's scolding, his father's words, and the manner in which the character retreated from the table. In every case, the thing being described, what is called the **tenor** of the figure of speech, is linked with a concrete image or **vehicle.** All of the types of figurative language, what are called **figures of speech,** or **tropes,** involve some kind of comparison, either explicit or implied. Thus, two of the figures in the above example specifically compare aspects of the character's behavior to animal behavior. The other two imply parental words that were delivered with strong physical force or extreme anger. Some of the most common figures of speech are:

Metaphor: a direct comparison between two unlike things. Metaphors may take several forms.

> His words were sharp knives.
> The sharp knife of his words cut through the silence.
> He spoke sharp, cutting words with his knife-edged voice.
> His words knifed through the still air.
> *I will speak daggers to her but use none.* (Shakespeare, *Hamlet*)

Implied metaphor: a metaphor in which either the tenor or vehicle is implied, not stated.

> The running back gathered steam and chugged toward the endzone.

Here the player is compared to a steam locomotive without naming it explicitly.

> *While smoke on its chin, that slithering gun*
> *Coiled back from its windowsill* (X. J. Kennedy)

In this passage from a poem about the assassination of President John F. Kennedy, Lee Harvey Oswald's rifle is indirectly compared ("coiled back" and "slithering") with a snake that has struck its victim.

Simile: a comparison using "like," "as," or "than" as a connective device.

> *My love is like a red, red rose* (Robert Burns)
> My love smells as sweet as a rose.
> My love looks fresher than a newly budded rose.

Conceit: an extended or far-fetched metaphor, in most cases comparing things that apparently have almost nothing in common.

> *Make me, O Lord, thy spinning wheel complete.* . . . (Edward Taylor)

The poem, "Huswifery," draws an analogy between the process of salvation and the manufacture of cloth, ending with the persona attired in "holy robes for glory."

Petrarchan conceit: named after the first great master of the sonnet, is a clichéd comparison usually relating to a woman's beauty (see Thomas Campion's "There Is a Garden in Her Face"; Shakespeare's Sonnet 130 parodies this type of trope). The **metaphysical conceit** refers to the extended comparisons favored by such so-called metaphysical poets as John Donne, George Herbert, and Edward Taylor. The conceit in the final three stanzas of Donne's "A Valediction: Forbidding Mourning" compares the poet and his wife with a pair of drafting compasses, hardly an image that most people would choose to celebrate marital fidelity.

Hyperbole: an overstatement, a comparison using conscious exaggeration.

He threw the ball so fast it caught the catcher's mitt on fire.

And I will love thee still, my dear,
Till a' the seas gang dry. (Robert Burns)

Understatement: the opposite of hyperbole.

"I don't think we're in Kansas anymore, Toto." (says Dorothy in
  The Wizard of Oz)

The space between is but an hour,
The frail duration of a flower. (Philip Freneau)

Freneau is understating the wild honeysuckle's lifespan by saying it is "but an hour." Because, by implication, he is also talking about human life, the understatement is even more pronounced.

I watched him; and the sight was not so fair
As one or two that I have seen elsewhere. (Edwin Arlington
  Robinson)

In "How Annandale Went Out," the persona is a physician who is about to perform euthanasia on a friend dying in agony. Understatement is often used in conjunction with verbal irony (see below).

Allusion: a metaphor making a direct comparison to a historical or literary event or character, a myth, a biblical reference, and so forth.

He is a Samson of strength but a Judas of duplicity.

He dreamed of Thebes and Camelot,
And Priam's neighbors. (Edwin Arlington Robinson)

Metonymy: use of a related object to stand for the thing actually being talked about.

It's the only white-collar street in this blue-collar town.

And O ye high-flown quills that soar the skies,
And ever with your prey still catch your praise. (Anne Bradstreet)

Here, Bradstreet speaks of critics who may be hostile to her work. She identifies them as "quill," referring to their quill pens.

He stood among a crowed a Drumahair;
His heart hung all upon a silken dress. (William Butler Yeats)

The title character of "The Man Who Dreamed of Faeryland" was interested in the woman *in* the dress, not the dress itself.

Synecdoche: use of a part for the whole, or vice versa.

The crowned heads of Europe were in attendance.
Before the indifferent beak could let her drop. (William Butler
    Yeats)

Personification: giving human characteristics to nonhuman things or to abstractions.

Justice weighs the evidence in her golden scales.
The ocean cursed and spat at us.

Of all her train, the hands of Spring
First plant thee in the watery mould. (William Cullen Bryant)

Bryant personifies spring by giving it hands with which to plant the yellow violet, which is one of the first wildflowers to appear in the season.

Apostrophe: a variety of personification in which a nonhuman thing, abstraction, or person not physically present is directly addressed as if it could respond.

> *Milton! Thou shouldst be living at this hour.* (William Wordsworth)

> *Is it, O man, with such discordant noises,*
>   *With such accursed instruments as these,*
> *Thou drownest Nature's sweet and kindly voices,*
>   *And jarrest the celestial harmonies?* (Henry Wadsworth
> Longfellow)

Longfellow is addressing the human race in general.

Paradox: and apparent contradiction or illogical statement.

> I'll never forget old what's-his-name.

> *His hand hath made this noble work which Stands,*
> *His Glorious Handiwork not made by hands.* (Edward Taylor)

Taylor is describing God's creation of the universe, which He willed into being.

Oxymoron: a short paradox, usually consisting of an adjective and noun with conflicting meanings.

> The touch of her lips was sweet agony.

> *Progress is a comfortable disease* (e. e. cummings)
> *A terrible beauty is born.* (William Butler Yeats)

Synesthesia: a conscious mixing of two different types of sensory experience.

> A raw, red wind rushed from the north.

> *Leaves cast in casual potpourris*
> *Whisper their scents from pits and cellar-holes* (Richard Wilbur)

Transferred epithet: not, strictly speaking, a trope, it occurs when an adjective is "transferred" from the word it actually modifies to a nearby word.

The plowman homeward plods his weary way. (Thomas Gray)

In this example, the plowman is weary, not the path ("way") he walks upon.

Allegory and Symbol

Related to the figurative devices are the various types of symbolism that may occur in poems. We have already discussed how symbolism works in fiction, but its use in poetry is perhaps even more complex. In many cases, a poem may seem so simple on the surface that we feel impelled to read deeper meanings into it. Robert Frost's "Stopping by Woods on a Snowy Evening" is a classic case in point. There is nothing wrong with searching for larger significance in a poem, but the reader should perhaps be wary of leaping to conclusions about symbolic meanings before fully exhausting the literal sense of a poem. Whatever the case, both allegory and symbolism share the demand that the reader supply abstract or general meanings to the specific concrete details of the poem.

The simplest form that this substitution takes occurs in **allegory.** An allegory is usually a narrative that exists on at least two levels simultaneously, a concrete literal level and a second level of abstract meaning; throughout an allegory a consistent sequence of parallels exists between the literal and the abstract. Sometimes allegories may imply third or fourth levels of meaning as well, especially in long allegorical poems like Dante's *The Divine Comedy*, which has been interpreted on personal, political, ethical, and Christian levels. The characters and actions in an allegory explicitly signify the abstract level of meaning, and generally this second level of meaning is what the poet primarily intends to convey. For example, Robert Southwell's "The Burning Babe" is filled with fantastic incidents and paradoxical speech that are made clear in the poem's last line: "And straight I called unto mind that it was Christmas day." The literal burning babe of the title is the Christ child, who predicts his own future to the amazed watcher. Thus, in interpreting the poem, the reader must substitute theological terms like "redemption" or "original sin" for the literal details it contains.

Two types of prose allegories, the fable and parable, have been universally popular. A fable is a short, nonrealistic narrative that is told to illustrate a universal moral concept. A parable is similar but generally contains realistic characters and events. Thus, Aesop's fable of the tortoise and the hare, instead of telling us something about animal behavior, illustrates the virtue of persistence against seemingly unbeatable competition. Jesus' parable of the Good Samaritan tells the story of a man who is robbed and beaten and eventually rescued by a stranger of another race in order to define the concept of "neighbor" for a questioning lawyer. Poetic allegories like George Herbert's "Redemption" or Christina Rossetti's "Up-Hill" can be read in Christian terms as symbolic accounts of the process of salvation. Robert Burns's witty ballad "John Barleycorn" tells on the literal surface the story of a violent murder, but the astute reader quickly discovers that the underlying meaning involves the poet's native Scotland's legendary taste for strong drink.

Many poems contain symbolic elements that are somewhat more elusive in meaning than the simple one-for-one equivalences presented by allegory. A **symbol,** then, is any concrete thing or any action in a poem that implies a meaning beyond its literal sense. Many of these things or actions are called **traditional symbols,** that is, symbols that hold roughly the same meanings for members of a given society. Certain flowers, colors, natural objects, and religious emblems possess meanings that we can generally agree on. A white lily and a red rose suggest, respectively, mourning and passion. Few western cultures would associate a black dress with a festive occasion or a red one with purity and innocence. Dawn and rainbows are traditional natural symbols of hope and new beginnings. It would be unlikely for a poet to mention a cross without expecting readers think of its Christian symbolism. Other types of symbols can be identified in poems that are otherwise not allegorical. A **private symbol** is one that has acquired certain meanings from a single poet's repeated use of it. William Butler Yeats's use of "gyres" is explained in some of his prose writings as a symbol for the turning of historical cycles, and his use of the word in his poems obviously goes beyond the literal level. Some visionary poets like Yeats and William Blake devised complicated private symbolic systems, a sort of alternative mythology, and understanding the full import of these symbols becomes primarily the task of critics who have specialized in these poets. Other poets may employ **incidental symbols,** things that are not usually considered symbolic but may be in a particular poem, or symbolic acts, a situation or response that seems of greater than literal import. As noted earlier, one of the most famous poems using these two devices is Robert

Frost's "Stopping by Woods on a Snowy Evening." In this poem some readers see the "lovely, dark and deep" woods as both inviting and threatening, and want to view the persona's rejection of their allure ("But I have promises to keep/And miles to go before I sleep") as some sort of life-affirming act. Frost himself was not particularly helpful in guiding his readers, often scoffing at those who had read too much metaphysical portent into such a simple lyric, although in other poems he presents objects such as a rock wall between neighboring farms or an abandoned woodpile in a manner that leads the reader to feel that they obviously possess some larger significance. Many modern poems remain so enigmatic that readers have consistently returned to them seeking new interpretations. Poems like these were to a degree influenced by the symbolists, a group of French poets of the late nineteenth century, who deliberately wrote poems filled with vague nuances subject to multiple interpretations. Such American attempts at symbolist experiments as Wallace Stevens's "Anecdote of the Jar" or "The Emperor of Ice-Cream" continue to perplex and fascinate readers, particularly those who are versed in recent schools of interpretation which focus on the indeterminacy of a poetic text.

Tone of Voice

Even the simplest statement is subject to multiple interpretations if it is delivered in several different tones of voice. Consider the shift in emphasis between saying "*I* gave you the money," "I *gave* you the money" and "I gave *you* the money." Even a seemingly innocent compliment like "You look lovely this morning" takes on a different meaning if it is delivered by a woman to her obviously hungover husband. Still, these variations in **tone,** the speaker's implied attitude toward the words he or she says, depend primarily on vocal inflection. Because a poet only rarely gets the opportunity to elucidate his tones in a public performance, it is possible that readers may have difficulties in grasping the tone of a poem printed on the page. Still, many poems establish their tone quite clearly from the outset. The opening of Milton's sonnet "On the Late Massacre in Piedmont" ("Avenge, O Lord, thy slaughtered saints . . .") establishes a tone of righteous anger that is consistent throughout the poem. Keats's initial apostrophe in "Ode on a Grecian Urn" ("Thou still unravished bride of quietness,/Thou foster-child of silence and slow time . . .") strikes the reader as both passionate and reverent in the poet's response to an undamaged artifact of the ancient past. Thus, in many cases we can relate the tone of voice in poems to the emotions we employ in our own speech, and we would have to violate quite a few rules of common sense to argue that Milton is being flippant or that Keats is speaking sarcastically.

Irony is the element of tone by which a poet may imply an attitude that is in fact contrary to what his words appear to say. Of course, the simplest form of irony is **sarcasm,** the wounding tone of voice we use to imply exactly the opposite of what we say: "That's really a *great* excuse!" or "What a *wonderful* performance!" For obvious reasons, sarcasm is appropriate primarily to spoken language. It has become almost universal to follow a bit of gentle sarcasm in an e-mail message with a symbolic :) to indicate that the remark is not to be taken "straight." **Verbal irony** is the conscious manipulation of tone by which the poet's actual attitude is the opposite of what he says. In a poem like Thomas Hardy's "The Ruined Maid," it is obvious that one speaker considers the meaning of "ruined" to be somewhat less severe than the other, and the whole poem hinges on this ironic counterpoint of definitions and the different moral and social attitudes they imply. Consider the opening lines of Oliver Wendell Holmes's "Old Ironsides," a piece of propaganda verse which succeeded in raising enough money to save the U.S.S. *Constitution* from the scrapyard: "Ay, tear her tattered ensign down!/Long has it waved on high,/And many an eye has danced to see/That banner in the sky. . . ." Because Holmes's poetic mission is to *save* the ship, it is obvious that he is speaking ironically in the opening line; he emphatically *does not* want the ship's flag stripped from her, an attitude that is made clear in the third and fourth lines. Verbal irony is also a conspicuous feature of **verse satire,** poetry that exists primarily to mock or ridicule, although often with serious intent. One famous example, in the form of a short satirical piece, or **epigram,** is Sarah N. Cleghorn's "The Golf Links," a poem written before the advent of child labor laws:

> The golf links lie so near the mill
>> That almost every day
> The laboring children can look out
>> And see the men at play.

Here the weight of the verbal irony falls on two words, "laboring" and "play," and the way each is incongruously applied to the wrong group of people.

"The Golf Links," taken as a whole, also represents a second form of irony, **situational irony,** in which the setting of the poem (laboring children watching playing adults) contains a built-in incongruity. One master of ironic situation is Thomas Hardy, who used the title "Satires of Circumstance" in a series of short poems illustrating this sort of irony. Hardy's "Ah, Are You Digging on My Grave?" hinges on this kind of irony, with a ghostly persona asking questions of living speakers who end up offering little comfort to the dead woman. **Dramatic irony,** the third type of irony, occurs when the persona of a poem is less aware of the full import of his or her words than is the reader. William Blake's "The Chimney Sweeper" (from *Songs of Innocence*) is spoken by a child who does not seem to fully realize how badly he is being exploited by his employer, who has apparently been using the promises of religion as a way of keeping his underage workers in line. A similar statement could be made of the persona of Walter Savage Landor's "Mother, I Cannot":

> Mother, I cannot mind my wheel;
>> My fingers ache, my lips are dry:
> Oh! if you felt the pain I feel!
>> But oh, who ever felt as I?

> No longer could I doubt him true;
>> All other men may use deceit:
> He always said my eyes were blue,
>> And often swore my lips were sweet.

The young woman who speaks here apparently has not realized (or is deliberately unwilling to admit) that she has been sexually deceived and deserted by a scoundrel; "All other men may use deceit" gives the measure of her tragic naïvete. Dramatic irony, as the term implies, is most often found in dramatic monologues, where the gap between the speaker's perception of the situation and the reader's may be wide indeed.

Repetition: Sounds and Schemes

Because poetry uses language at its most intense level, we are aware of the weight of individual words and phrases to a degree that is usually lacking when we read prose. Poets have long known that the meanings that they attempt to convey often depend as much on the sound of the words as their meaning. We have already mentioned one sound device, onomatopoeia. Consider how much richer the experience of "the murmuring of innumerable bees" is than a synonymous phrase, "the low sound of a lot of bees." It has often been said that all art aspires to the condition of music in the way that it affects an audience on some unconscious, visceral level. By carefully exploiting the repetition of sound devices, a poet may attempt to produce some of the same effects that the musical composer does.

Of course, much of this sonic level of poetry is subjective; what strikes one listener as pleasant may overwhelm the ear of another. Still, it is useful to distinguish between a poet's use of **euphony,** a series of pleasant sounds, and **cacophony,** sounds that are deliberately unpleasant. Note the following passages from Alexander Pope's "An Essay on Criticism," a didactic poem which attempts to illustrate many of the devices poets use:

> Soft is the strain when Zephyr gently blows,
> And the smooth stream in smoother numbers flows . . .

The repetition of the initial consonant sounds is called **alliteration,** and here Pope concentrates on the *s* sound. The vowel sounds are generally long: str*ai*n, bl*ow*s, sm*oo*th, and fl*ow*s. Here the description of the gentle west wind is assisted by the generally pleasing sense of euphony. But Pope, to illustrate the opposite quality, follows this couplet with a second:

> But when loud surges lash the sounding shore,
> The hoarse, rough verse should like the torrent roar.

Now the wind is anything but gentle, and the repetition of the *r* sounds in su*r*ges, sho*r*e, hoa*r*se, *r*ough, ve*r*se, to*r*rent, and *r*oar force the reader to speak from the back of the throat, making sounds that are anything but euphonious.

Repetition of sounds has no inherent meaning values (although some linguists may argue that certain sounds do stimulate particular emotions), but this repetition does call attention to itself and can be particularly effective when a poet wishes to emphasize a certain passage. We have already mentioned alliteration. Other sound patterns are **assonance,** the repetition of similar vowel sounds (st*ee*p, *e*ven, rec*ei*ve, v*ea*l), and consonance, the repetition of similar consonant sounds (du*ck*, tor*que*, stri*k*e, tri*ck*le). It should go without saying that spelling has little to do with any sound pattern; an initial *f* will alliterate with an initial *ph*.

Rhyme is the most important sound device, and our pleasure in deftly executed rhymes (consider the possibilities of rhyming "neighbor" with "sabre," as Richard Wilbur does in one of his translations) goes beyond mere sound to include the pleasure we take when an unexpected word is magically made to fit with another. There are several types of rhyme. **Masculine rhyme** occurs between single stressed syllables: *fleece, release, surcease, niece,* and so on. **Feminine rhyme,** also called **double rhyme,** matches two syllables, the first stressed and the second usually unstressed: *stinging, upbringing, flinging.* **Triple rhyme** goes further: *slithering, withering.* **Slant rhyme** (also called **near rhyme** and **off rhyme**) contains hints of sound repetition (sometimes related to assonance and consonance): *chill, dull,* and *sale* are possibilities, although poets often grant themselves considerable leeway in counting as rhyming words pairs that often have only the slightest similarity. When rhymes fall in a pattern in a poem and are **end rhymes,** occurring at the ends of lines, it is then convenient to assign letters to the sounds and speak of a **rhyme scheme.** Thus, a stanza of four lines ending with *heaven, hell, bell, eleven* would be said to have a rhyme scheme of *abba.* Rhymes may also occasionally be found in the interior of lines, which is called **internal rhyme.** Note how both end and internal rhymes work in the complex stanza which Poe uses in "The Raven."

More complicated patterns of repetition involve more than mere sounds but whole phrases and grammatical units. Ancient rhetoricians, teaching the art of public speaking, identified several of these, and they are also found in poetry. **Parallel structure** is simply the repetition of grammatically similar phrases or clauses: Tennyson's "To strive, to seek, to find, and not to yield." **Anaphora** and **epistrophe** are repeated words or phrases at, respectively, the beginning and end of lines. Walt Whitman uses these schemes extensively, often in the same lines. This passage from "Song of Myself" illustrates both anaphora and epistrophe:

> If they are not yours as much as mine they are nothing, or next to
>   nothing,
> If they are not the riddle and the untying of the riddle they are
>   nothing,
> If they are not just as close as they are distant they are nothing.

Antithesis is the matching of parallel units which contain contrasting meanings, such as Whitman's "I am of old and young, of the foolish as much as the wise./Regardless of others, ever regardful of others./ Maternal as well as paternal, a child as well as a man. . . ." Although the rhetorical schemes are perhaps more native to the orator, the poet can still make occasional effective use of them. Whitman's poetry was influenced by many sources but by none perhaps so powerfully as the heavily schematic language of the King James Bible.

Meter and Rhythm

The subject of poetic meter and rhythm can be a difficult one, to say the least, and it is doubtless true that such phrases as *trochaic octameter* or *spondaic substitution* have an intimidating quality. Still, discussions of meter need not be limited to experts, and even beginning readers should be able to apply a few of the metrical principles that are commonly found in poetry written in English.

First, let us distinguish between two terms that are often used synonymously: **poetry** and **verse.** Poetry refers to a whole genre of literature and thus stands with fiction and drama as one of the three major types of writing, whereas verse refers to a mode of writing in lines of a certain length; thus, many poets still retain the old practice of capitalizing the first word of each line to indicate its integrity as a unit of composition. Virtually any piece of writing can be versified (and sometimes rhymed as well). Especially useful are bits of **mnemonic verse,** in which information like the number of days in the months (thirty days has September . . .) or simple spelling rules ("I before E/Except after C . . .") is cast in a form that is easy to remember. Although it is not strictly accurate to do so, many writers use verse to denote metrical writing that somehow does not quite measure up to the level of true poetry; phrases like **light verse** or **occasional verse** (lines written for a specific occasion, like a birthday or anniversary) are often used in this manner.

If a writer is unconcerned about the length of individual lines and is governed only by the width of the paper being used, then he or she is not writing verse but **prose.** All verse is metrical writing; prose is not. Surprisingly enough, there is a body of writing called **prose poetry,** writing that uses language in a poetic manner but avoids any type of meter;

Carolyn Forché's "The Colonel" is one example. Perhaps the simplest way to think of **meter** in verse is to think of its synonym **measure** (think of the use of meter in words like odometer or kilometer). Thus, meter refers to the method by which a poet determines line length.

When we talk about meter in poetry we ordinarily mean that the poet is employing some kind of consistent **prosody** or system of measurement. There are many possible prosodies, depending on what the poet decides to count as the unit of measurement in the line, but only three of these systems are common in English poetry. Perhaps the simplest is **syllabic verse.** In verse of this type, the length of the line is determined by counting the total number of syllables the line contains (Sylvia Plath's "Metaphors," for one example, uses lines of nine syllables, a witty metaphor for the poem's subject, pregnancy). Much French poetry of the past was written in twelve-syllable lines, or **Alexandrines,** and in English a word like **octosyllabic** denotes a line of eight syllables. Because English is a language of strong stresses, most of our poets have favored other prosodic systems, but syllabic poetry has been attempted by many poets, among them Marianne Moore, Richard Wilbur, and Dylan Thomas. Moore, in particular, often wrote in **quantitative syllabics,** that is, stanzas containing the same number of lines with identical numbers of syllables in the corresponding lines of different stanzas. Moore's "The Fish" uses stanzas made of lines of one, three, nine, six, and nine syllables, respectively.

More natural to the English language is **accentual** verse, a prosodic system in which only accented or strongly stressed syllables are counted in a line, which can also contain a varying number of unaccented syllables. Much folk poetry, perhaps intended to be recited to the beat of a percussion instrument, retains this stress-based pattern, and the oldest verse in the British tradition, Anglo-Saxon poetry like *Beowulf*, is composed in four-stress lines which were recited to musical accompaniment. Many of the verses we recall from nursery rhymes, children's chanting games ("Red rover, red rover, / Send [any name from one to four syllables can be substituted here—*Bill, Susan, Latisha, Elizabeth*] right over") and sports cheers ("Two bits, four bits, six bits, a dollar! / All for the [*Owls, Cowboys, Cardinals, Thundering Herd*] stand up and holler!") retain the strong sense of rhythmical pulse that characterizes much accentual verse, a fact we recognize when we clap our hands and move rhythmically to the sound of the words. Indeed, the lyrics to much current rap music are actually composed to a four-stress accentual line, and the stresses or "beats" can be heard plainly when we listen or dance. Gerard Manley Hopkins, attempting to recapture some of the flavor of Anglo-Saxon verse, pioneered a type of accentual prosody that he called **sprung rhythm,** in which he counted only the strong stresses in his lines. Accentual meters still supply possibilities for contemporary poets; indeed, what often appears to be free verse is revealed, on closer inspection, to be a poem written in accentual meter. Richard Wilbur's "The Writer," for example, is written in a stanza containing lines of three, five, and three strong stresses, respectively, but the stresses do not overwhelm the reader insistently. Wilbur's "Junk" employs Anglo-Saxon meter, and his strong alliteration helps the reader hear the four strong stresses in each line.

Accentual-syllabic verse is the most important prosodic system in English, dominating our poetry for the five centuries from Chaucer's time down to the early years of the twentieth century. Even though in the last fifty years free verse has become the prevailing style in which poetry is written, accentual-syllabic verse still has many able practitioners. An accentual-syllabic prosody is somewhat more complicated than the two systems we have mentioned, because it requires that the poet count both the strongly stressed syllables and the total number of syllables in the line. Because stressed and unstressed syllables alternate fairly regularly in this system, four **metrical feet,** representing the most common patterns, designate the subdivisions of rhythm that make up the line (think of a yardstick divided into three feet). These feet are the **iamb** (or **iambic foot**), one unstressed and one stressed syllable; the **trochee** (or **trochaic foot**), one stressed and one unstressed syllable; the **anapest** (or **anapestic foot**), two unstressed syllables and one stressed syllable; and the **dactyl** (or **dactylic foot**), one stressed and two unstressed syllables. The first two of these, iambic and trochaic, are called **double meters;** the second two, **triple meters.** Iambic and anapestic meters are sometimes called **rising meters** because they "rise" toward the stressed syllable; trochaic and dactylic meters are called **falling meters** for the opposite reason. Simple repetition of words or phrases can give us the sense of how these lines sound in a purely schematic sense. The **breve** (◡) and **ictus** (′) are used to denote unstressed and stressed syllables, respectively.

Iambic:

release / release / release

to fall / into / despair

Marie / discov / ers candy

Trochaic:

melting / melting / melting / melting

Peter / disa / greed en / tirely

clever / writing / filled the / page

Anapestic:

to the top / to the top

a retriev / er appeared

and a ter / ri ble thunder

Dactylic:

shivering / shivering / shivering / shivering / shivering

terribly / ill with the / symptoms of / viral pneu / monia

note how the / minister / whispered at / Emily's / grave

Because each of these lines contains a certain number of feet, a second specialized term is used to denote how many times a pattern is repeated in a line:

one foot	**monometer**
two feet	**dimeter**
three feet	**trimeter**
four feet	**tetrameter**
five feet	**pentameter**
six feet	**hexameter**
seven feet	**heptameter**
eight feet	**octameter**

Thus, in the examples above, the first set of lines is iambic trimeter; the second, trochaic tetrameter; the third, anapestic dimeter; and the fourth, dactylic pentameter. The third lines in the iambic and anapestic examples are **hypermetrical;** that is, they contain an extra unstressed syllable or **feminine ending.** Conversely, the third lines in the trochaic and dactylic examples are missing one and two unstressed final syllables, respectively, a common practice called **catalexis.** Although over thirty combinations of foot type and number per line theoretically are possible, relatively few are ordinarily encountered in poetry. The iambic foot is most common in English, followed by the anapest and the trochee; the dactylic foot is relatively rare. Line lengths tend to be from three to five feet, with anything shorter or longer used only sparingly. Still, there are famous exceptions like Poe's "The Raven," which is composed in trochaic octameter, or Southwell's "The Burning Babe," written in iambic heptameter.

Meter denotes regularity, the "blueprint" for a line from which the poet works. Because iambic pentameter is the most common meter used in English poetry, our subsequent discussion will focus on poems written in it. Most poets quickly learn that a metronomic regularity, five iambic feet marching in lockstep line after line, is not a virtue and quickly becomes predictable. Thus, there are several ways by which poets can add variety to their lines so that the actual **rhythm** of the line, what is actually heard, plays a subtle counterpoint against the regularity of the meter. One way is to vary the placement of the **caesura** (‖) or pause within a line (usually indicated by a mark of punctuation). Another is by mixing **end-stopped lines,** which clearly pause at their conclusion, with **enjambed** lines, which run on into the next line with no pause. The following lines from Tennyson's "Ulysses" illustrate these techniques:

> This is my son, mine own Telemachus,
> To whom I leave the scepter and the isle,
> Well-loved of me, discerning to fulfill
> This labor, by slow prudence to make mild
> A rugged people, and through soft degrees
> Subdue them to the useful and the good.

Lines two and six have no caesurae; the others do, after either the third, fourth, or fifth syllable. Lines one, two, and six are end-stopped; the others are enjambed (or use *enjambment*).

Another technique of varying regularity is **metrical substitution,**
where feet of a different type are substituted for what the meter calls
for. In iambic meter, trochaic feet are often encountered at the beginnings of lines, or after a caesura. Two other feet, the **pyrrhic** (∪ ∪),
consisting of two unstressed syllables, and the **spondee** (′ ′), consisting of two stressed syllables, are also commonly substituted. Here are
Tennyson's lines with their scansion marked.

This is / my son, || / mine own / Telem / achus,

To whom / I leave / the scep / ter and / the isle,

Well-loved / of me, || / discern / ing to / fulfill

This la / bor, || by / slow pru / dence to / make mild

A rug / ged peo / ple, || and / through soft / degrees

Subdue / them to / the use / ful and / the good.

Even though these are fairly regular iambic pentameter lines, it should
be observed that no single line is without some substitution. Still, the
dominant pattern of five iambic feet per line should be apparent (out of
thirty total feet, about twenty are iambs); there is even a strong tendency on the reader's part to "promote" the middle syllable of three unstressed syllables ("Subdue / them *to* / the use / ful *and* / the good") to
keep the sense of the iambic rhythm.

How far can a poet depart from the pattern without losing contact
with the original meter? That is a question that is impossible to answer
in general terms. The following scansion will probably strike us at first
as a far departure from regular iambic pentameter:

′ || ′ / ∪ || ′ ′ / ∪ ∪ || / ′ ∪ / ∪ ′

Yet it is actually the opening line of one of Shakespeare's most often
quoted passages, Mark Antony's funeral oration from *Julius Caesar:*

Friends, || Ro / mans, || coun / trymen, || / lend me / your ears

Poets who have learned to use the full resources of meter do not
consider it a restraint; instead, they are able to stretch the pattern to its

limits without breaking it. A good analogy might be made between poetry and dance. Beginning dancers watch their feet and count the steps while making them; after considerable practice, the movements become second nature, and a skillful pair of partners can add dips and passes without losing the basic step of the music.

Free Verse, Open Form, and Closed Form

Nothing has been so exhaustively debated in English-language poetry as the exact nature of **free verse**. The simplest definition may be the best: free verse is verse with no consistent metrical pattern. In free verse, line length is a subjective decision made by the poet, and length may be determined by grammatical phrases, the poet's own sense of individual "breath-units," or even by the visual arrangement of lines on the page. Clearly, it is easier to speak of what free verse is not than to explain what it is. Even its practitioners do not seem very happy with the term free verse, which is derived from the French *vers libre*. The extensive use of free verse is a fairly recent phenomenon in the history of poetry. Even though there are many examples of free verse from the past (the Psalms, Ecclesiastes, and the Song of Solomon from the King James Bible), the modern history of free verse begins in 1855 with the publication of Walt Whitman's *Leaves of Grass*. Whitman, influenced by Ralph Waldo Emerson's statement that "it is not meters but meter-making argument that makes a poem," created a unique variety of long-line free verse based on grammatical units—phrases and clauses. Whitman's free verse is so distinctive that he has had few direct imitators (Robinson Jeffers is one from the twentieth century), and subsequent poets who have used free verse have written lines that vary widely in syllable count. Good free verse, as T. S. Eliot remarked, still contains some kind of "ghost of meter," and its rhythms can be as terse and clipped as those of Philip Levine or as lushly sensuous as those of Pattiann Rogers. The poet who claims that free verse is somehow easier to write than metrical verse would find many arguments to the contrary. As Eliot said, "No verse is free for the poet who wants to do a good job."

All poems have form, the arrangement of the poem on the page that differentiates it from prose. Sometimes this arrangement indicates that the poet is following a preconceived plan—a metrical pattern, a rhyme scheme, a purely visual design like that of **concrete** or **spatial**

poetry, or a scheme like that of **acrostic verse,** in which the first letters of the lines spell a message. An analysis of poetic form notes how the lines are arranged, how long they are, and how they are grouped into blocks or **stanzas.** Further analysis might reveal the existence of types of repetition, rhyme, or the use of a **refrain,** or a repeated line or groups of lines. A large number of the poems composed in the twentieth and twenty-first centuries have been written in **open form,** which simply means that there is no strict pattern of regularity in the elements mentioned above; that is, there is no consistent meter and no rhyme scheme. Still, even a famous poem in open form like William Carlos Williams's "The Red Wheelbarrow" can be described in formal terms:

> so much depends
> upon
>
> a red wheel
> barrow
>
> glazed with rain
> water
>
> beside the white
> chickens.

Here we observe that the eight-line poem is divided into **uniform stanzas** of two lines each (or couplets). Line length varies between four and two syllables per line. The odd-numbered lines each contain three words; the even, one. Although there is no apparent use of rhyme or repetition here, many poems in open form contain some rhyme and metrical regularity at their conclusions. Alan Dugan's "Love Song: I and Thou" falls into regular iambic tetrameter in its final lines, and a typical contemporary example of an open form poem, Naomi Shihab Nye's "The Traveling Onion," concludes with a closing rhyme on "career" and "disappear."

Closed form, unlike open form, denotes the existence of some kind of regular pattern of meter, stanza, rhyme, or repetition. **Stanza forms** are consistent patterns in the individual units of the poem (stanza means "room" in Italian); **fixed forms** are patterns that encompass a complete poem, for example, a sonnet or a villanelle. **Traditional**

forms are patterns that have been used for long periods of time and thus may be associated with certain subjects, themes, or types of poems; the sonnet is one example, for it has been used primarily (but by no means exclusively) for lyric poetry. **Nonce forms** are patterns that originate in an individual poem and have not been widely used by other poets. Of course, it goes without saying that every traditional form was at first a nonce form; the Italian poet (now lost to memory) who first wrote a lyric consisting of fourteen rhymed eleven-syllable lines could not have foreseen that in subsequent centuries poets the world over would produce literally millions of sonnets that are all variations on the original model. Some of the most common stanza and fixed forms are briefly discussed herein.

Stanza Forms

Blank verse is not, strictly speaking, a stanza form because it consists of individual lines of iambic pentameter that do not rhyme. However, long poems in blank verse may be arranged into **verse paragraphs** or stanzas with a varying number of lines. Blank verse originally appeared in English with the Earl of Surrey's translation of the *Aeneid* in the fifteenth century; it has been used extensively for narrative and dramatic purposes since then, particularly in epics like Milton's *Paradise Lost* and in Shakespeare's plays. Also written in stanzas of varying lengths is the **irregular ode,** a poem which employs lines of varying lengths (although usually of a regular rhythm that is iambic or matches one of the other feet) and an irregular rhyme scheme.

Paired rhyming lines *(aabbcc . . .)* are called **couplets,** although they are only rarely printed as separate stanzas. **Short couplets** have a meter of iambic tetrameter (and are sometimes called **octosyllabic couplets**). If their rhymes are predominantly feminine and seem chosen for comic effect, they may be called **Hudibrastic couplets** after Samuel Butler's satirical poem *Hudibras* of the late 1600s. **Heroic couplets** have a meter of iambic pentameter and take their name from John Dryden's translation of the *Aeneid* (1697) and Alexander Pope's hugely successful translation of Homer's *Iliad* and *Odyssey* (1720–1726); all three of these are "heroic" or epic poems. Heroic couplets have also been used effectively in satirical poems like Alexander Pope's "mock epic" *The Dunciad* and even in dramatic monologues like Robert Browning's "My Last

Duchess," where the rhymes are so effectively buried by enjambment that the poem approximates speech. Two other couplet forms, both rare, are **poulter's measure,** rhyming pairs of alternating lines of iambic hexameter and iambic heptameter, and **fourteeners,** pairs of iambic heptameter (fourteen-syllable) lines which, because a natural caesura usually falls after the fourth foot, closely resemble common meter (see below).

A three-line stanza is called a **tercet.** If it rhymes in an *aaa bbb* . . . pattern, it is a **triplet;** sometimes triplets appear in poems written in heroic couplets, especially at the end of sections or where special emphasis is desired. Iambic pentameter tercets rhyming *aba bcb cdc . . .* form **terza rima,** a pattern invented by Dante for *The Divine Comedy.*

A four-line stanza is known as a **quatrain.** Alternating lines of tetrameter and trimeter in any foot, rhyming *abcb* or *abab,* make up a **ballad stanza;** if the feet are strictly iambic, then the quatrain is called **common meter,** the form of many popular hymns like "Amazing Grace." **Long meter,** also widely used in hymns, consists of iambic tetrameter lines rhyming *abcb* or *abab;* **short meter** has a similar rhyme scheme but contains first, second, and fourth lines of iambic trimeter and a third line of iambic tetrameter. The *In Memoriam* **stanza,** named after Tennyson's long poetic sequence, is iambic tetrameter rhyming *abba.* The *Rubaiyat* **stanza,** an import from Persia, consists of lines of either iambic tetrameter or pentameter, rhyming *aaba bbcb . . .* ; Edward FitzGerald's translation *The Rubaiyat of Omar Khayyam* employs this form. Four lines of iambic pentameter rhyming *abab* are known as an **English quatrain,** also known as the **elegiac stanza** (after Thomas Gray's "Elegy Written in a Country Churchyard"). Lines of the same meter rhyming *abba* make up an **Italian quatrain.** One other unusual quatrain stanza is an import from ancient Greece, the **Sapphic stanza,** named after the poet Sappho. The Sapphic stanza consists of three **hendecasyllabic** (eleven-syllable) lines of this pattern:

/ ᴗ / / ᴗ / / ᴗ ᴗ / / ᴗ / / ᴗ

and a fourth line called an **Adonic,** which is five syllables long and consists of one dactylic foot and one trochaic foot. The Sapphic stanza is usually unrhymed. The quatrain stanza is also used in another import, the **pantoum,** a poem in which the second and fourth lines of the first stanza become the first and third of the second, and the second and fourth of the second become the first and third of the fourth, and so on. Pantoums may be written in any meter and may or may not employ rhyme.

A five-line stanza is known as a **quintet** and is relatively rare in English poetry. The **sestet,** or six-line stanza, can be found with a number of different meters and rhyme schemes. A seven-line stanza is called a **septet;** one septet stanza form is **rime royal,** seven lines of iambic pentameter rhyming *ababbcc.* An eight-line stanza is called an **octave;** one widely used stanza of this length is **ottava rima,** iambic pentameter lines rhyming *abababcc.* Another octave form is the **Monk's Tale stanza,** named after one of Chaucer's tales. It is iambic pentameter and rhymes *ababbcbc.* The addition of a ninth line, rhyming *c* and having a meter of iambic hexameter, makes a **Spenserian stanza,** named after Edmund Spenser, the poet who invented it for *The Faerie Queene,* a long metrical romance.

Fixed Forms

Fixed forms are combinations of meter, rhyme scheme, and repetition that comprise complete poems. One familiar three-line fixed form is the **haiku,** a Japanese import consisting of lines of five, seven, and five syllables, respectively. Related to the haiku is the **tanka,** which adds two additional seven-syllable lines.

Two five-line fixed forms are the **limerick** and the **cinquain.** The limerick consists of anapestic trimeter in lines one, two, and five, and anapestic dimeter in lines three and four. The rhymes, *aabba,* are usually double rhymes used for comic effect. In a brilliant bit of satire, the English poet Wendy Cope satirically reduces T. S. Eliot's "The Waste Land," a long modernist poem to which Eliot appended his own explanatory footnotes, to a set of five limericks. Cope concludes:

> No water. Dry rocks and dry throats,
> Then thunder, a shower of quotes
> From the Sanskrit and Dante.
> Da. Damyata. Shantih.
> I hope you'll make sense of the notes.

A cinquain, the invention of American poet Adelaide Crapsey (1878–1914), consists of five unrhymed lines of two, four, six, eight, and two syllables, respectively. The most important of the fixed forms is the **sonnet,** which consists of fourteen lines of rhymed iambic pentameter. The original form of the sonnet is called the **Italian sonnet** or the **Petrarchan sonnet** after the fourteenth-century poet who popularized it. An Italian sonnet is usually cast in two stanzas, an octave rhyming *abbaabba* and a sestet with a variable rhyme scheme; *cdcdcd, cdecde,* and *cddcee* are some of the possible patterns. A **volta** or "turn," usually a conjunction or conjunctive adverb like "but" or "then," may appear at the beginning of the sestet, signifying a slight change of direction in thought. Many Italian sonnets have a strong logical connection between octave and sestet problem/solution, cause/effect, question/answer and the volta helps to clarify the transition. The **English sonnet,** also known as the **Shakespearean sonnet** after its prime exemplar, was developed in the sixteenth century after the sonnet was imported to England and employs a different rhyme scheme that takes into consideration the relative scarcity of rhymes in English (compared with Italian). The English sonnet has a rhyme scheme of *ababcdcdefefgg* and is usually printed as a single stanza. The pattern of three English quatrains plus a heroic couplet often forces a slightly different organizational scheme on the poet, although many of Shakespeare's sonnets still employ a strong volta at the beginning of the ninth line. Other English sonnets may withhold the turn until the beginning of the closing couplet. A third sonnet type, relatively rare, is the **Spenserian sonnet,** named after Edmund Spenser, author of *Amoretti,* one of the earliest sonnet sequences in English. The Spenserian sonnet rhymes *ababbcbc-cdcdee.* Many other sonnets have been written over the years which have other rhyme schemes, often hybrids of the Italian and English types. These are usually termed **nonce sonnets;** Shelley's "Ozymandias," with its unusual rhyme scheme of *ababacdcedefef,* is one notable example. In "Ode to the West Wind," Shelley employs a fourteen-line stanza rhyming *aba bcb cdc ded ee,* which has been called a **terza rima sonnet.**

Several other fixed forms, all French imports, have appeared frequently in English poetry. The **rondeau** has fifteen lines of iambic tetrameter or pentameter arranged in three stanzas: *aabba aabR aabbaR;* the *R* here stands for the unrhymed refrain, which repeats the first few words of the poem's first line. A maddeningly complex variation is the thirty-one line **rondeau redoublé,** through which Wendy Cope wittily maneuvers in her poem of the same name. The **villanelle** is a nineteen-line poem, usually written in iambic pentameter, employing two refrain lines, A_1 and A_2, in a pattern of five tercets and a final quatrain: $A_1bA_2\ abA_1\ abA_2\ abA_1\ abA_2\ abA_1A_2$. A related form, also nineteen lines long, is the **terzanelle,** which uses several more repeating lines (capitalized here): $A_1BA_2\ bCB\ cDC\ dED$ $eFE\ f\ A_1FA_2$. The **ballade** is twenty-eight lines of iambic tetrameter employing a refrain that appears at the end of its three octaves and final quatrain, or **envoy:** *ababbcbC ababbcbC ababbcbC bcbC.* Obviously the rhyming demands of the villanelle, the terzanelle, and the ballade pose serious challenges to English-language poets. A final fixed form is the thirty-nine-line **sestina,** which may be either metered or in free verse and uses a complicated sequence repeating, in different order, the six words that end the lines of the initial stanza. The sequence for the first six sestets is *123456 615243 364125 532614 451362 246531.* A final tercet uses three words in the interior of the lines and three at the ends in the pattern *(2)5(4)3(6)1.* Many sestinas hinge on the poet's choice of six end words that have multiple meanings and can serve as more than one part of speech.

There are many other less familiar types of stanza forms and fixed forms. Lewis Turco's *The Book of Forms* and Miller Williams's *Patterns of Poetry* are two reference sources that are useful in identifying them.

Literary History and Poetic Conventions

What a poet attempts to do in any given poem is always governed by the tension that exists between originality and convention, or between the poet's desire, in Ezra Pound's famous phrase, to "make it new," and the various stylistic devices that other poets and readers are familiar with through their understanding of the poetic tradition. If we look at some of the most obscure passages of Pound's *Cantos* (a single page may contain passages in several foreign languages), we may think that the poet has departed about as far from conventional modes of expression as possible, leaving his audience far behind him. Yet it is important to keep two facts in mind. First, this style was not arrived at overnight; Pound's early poetry is relatively traditional and should present little difficulty to most readers. He arrived at the style of the *Cantos* after a twenty-year apprenticeship to the styles of writers as different as Li-Po, Robert Browning, and William Butler Yeats. Second, by the time Pound was writing his mature poetry the modernist movement was in full flower, forcing the public not only to read poems but also to look at paintings and sculpture and to listen to music in ways that would have been unimaginable only a decade or two earlier. When we talk about the stylistic conventions of any given literary period, we should keep in mind that poets are rarely willing to go much beyond what they have educated their audiences to understand. This mutual sense of agreement is the essence of poetic convention.

One should be wary of making sweeping generalizations about "schools" of poetry or the shared conventions of literary periods. In any era, there is always a significant amount of diversity among individual poets. Further, an anthology of this limited scope, which by its very nature must exclude most long poems, is likely to contribute to a misleading view of literary history and the development of poetry in English. When we read Shakespeare's or Milton's sonnets, we should not forget that their major reputations rest on poetry of a very different sort. The neoclassical era in English poetry, stretching from the late seventeenth century until almost the end of the eighteenth, is poorly represented in this anthology because the satires of John Dryden and Alexander Pope and long philosophical poems like Pope's *An Essay on Man* do not readily lend themselves to being excerpted (an exception is the section on meter from Pope's *An Essay on Criticism*). Edgar Allan Poe once claimed that a long poem is "simply a contradiction in terms," but the continued high reputations of *The Faerie Queene, Paradise Lost, Don Juan,* and even a modern verse-novella like Robinson Jeffers's "The Roan Stallion" demonstrate that Poe's was far from the last word on the subject.

The earliest poems in this volume, all anonymous, represent poetry's links to the oral folk tradition. The American folk songs that children learn to sing in elementary school represent our own inheritance of this rich legacy. The poets of the Tudor (1485–1558) and Elizabethan (1558–1603) eras excelled at lyric poetry; Sir Thomas Wyatt and Henry Howard, Earl of Surrey, had imported the sonnet form from Italy, and the form was perfected during this period. Much of the love poetry of the age is characterized by conventional imagery, so-called Petrarchan conceits, which even a later poet like Thomas Campion employs in "There Is a Garden in Her Face" and which Shakespeare satirizes brilliantly in his Sonnet 130 ("My mistress' eyes are nothing like the sun").

The poetry of the first half of the seventeenth century has several major schools: A smooth lyricism influenced by Ben Jonson that can be traced through the work of Robert Herrick, Edmund Waller, and Richard Lovelace; a serious body of devotional poetry by John Donne, George Herbert, and John Milton; and the metaphysical style, which uses complex extended metaphors or metaphysical conceits—Donne and Herbert are its chief exemplars, followed by the early American poets Anne Bradstreet and Edward Taylor. Shortly after the English Restoration in 1660, a profound period of conservatism began in the arts, and the neoclassical era, lasting through most of the eighteenth century, drew heavily on Greek and Roman models. Poetry written during this period—the age of Jonathan Swift, Alexander Pope, and Thomas Gray—was dominated by one form, the heroic couplet; the genres of epic and satire; and an emphasis on human reason as the poet's chief guide. Never has the private voice been so subordinated to the public as in this period when, as Pope put it, a poet's highest aspiration should be to utter "What oft was thought, but ne'er so well expressed."

The first inklings of the romantic era coincide with the American and French revolutions, and poets of the latter half of the eighteenth century like Philip Freneau and William Blake exhibit some of its characteristics. But it was not until the publication of *Lyrical Ballads*, a 1798 book containing the best early work of William Wordsworth and Samuel Taylor Coleridge, that the romantic era can be said to have truly flowered. Wordsworth's famous formulation of a poem as "the spontaneous overflow of powerful feeling recollected in tranquillity" remains one of romanticism's key definitions, with its emphasis on emotion and immediacy and reflection; Wordsworth's own poetry, with its focus on the natural world, was tremendously influential. Most of the English and American poets of the first half of the nineteenth century have ties to romanticism in its various guises, and even a poet as late as Walt Whitman (b. 1819) inherits many of its liberal, democratic attitudes. Poets of the Victorian era (1837–1901), such as Alfred, Lord Tennyson and Robert Browning, continued to explore many of the same themes and genres as their romantic forebears, but certainly much of the optimism of the early years of the century had dissipated by the time poets like Thomas Hardy, A. E. Housman, and William Butler Yeats, with their omnipresent irony and pessimism, arrived on the scene in the century's last decades.

The twentieth century and the beginning of the twenty-first have been ruled by the upheavals that modernism caused in every art form. If anything characterized the first half of the twentieth century, it was its tireless experimentation with the forms of poetry. There is a continuum in English-language poetry from Chaucer through Robert Frost and Edwin Arlington Robinson, but Ezra Pound, T. S. Eliot, William Carlos Williams, and e. e. cummings, to mention only four chief modernists, published poetry that would have totally mystified readers of their grandparents' day, just as Picasso and Matisse produced paintings that represented radical breaks with the visual forms of the past. Although many of the experiments of movements like imagism and surrealism seem not much more than historical curiosities today, they parallel the unusual directions that most of the other arts took during the same period.

For the sake of convenience more than anything else, it has been useful to refer to the era following the end of World War II as the postmodern era. Certainly many of the hard-won modernist gains—open form and increased candor in language and subject matter—have been taken for granted by poets writing in the contemporary period. The confessional poem, a frankly autobiographical narrative that reveals what poets in earlier ages might have striven desperately to conceal, surfaced in the late 1950s in the works of Robert Lowell, W. D. Snodgrass, Syliva Plath, and Anne Sexton, and remains one of the chief postmodern genres. Still, as the selections here will attest, there is considerable variety to be found in the contemporary scene, and it will perhaps be many years before critics have the necessary historical distance to assess the unique characteristics of the present period.

Introduction
to Drama

The Play's the Thing

The theater, located in the heart of a fading downtown business district, is a relic of the silent movie era that has been restored to something approaching its former glory. Although only a few members of tonight's audience can actually remember it in its heyday, the expertise of the organist seated at the antique Wurlitzer instills a sense of false nostalgia in the crowd, now settling by twos and threes into red, plush-covered seats and looking around in search of familiar faces. Just as the setting is somewhat out of the ordinary, so is this group. Unlike movie audiences, they are for the most part older and less casually dressed. Few small children are present, and even the teenagers seem to be on their best behavior. Oddly, no one is eating popcorn or noisily drawing on a soda straw. A mood of seriousness and anticipation hovers over the theater, and those who have lived in the town long enough can spot the spouse or companion of one of the principal actors nervously folding a program or checking a watch.

As the organ magically descends into the recesses of the orchestra pit, the lights dim, a hush falls over the crowd, and the curtain creakily rises. There is a general murmur of approval at the ingenuity and many hours of hard work that have transformed empty space into a remarkable semblance of a turn-of-the-century upper-class drawing room. Dressed as a domestic servant, a young woman, known by face to the audience from her frequent appearances in local television commercials, enters and begins to dust a table. She hums softly to herself. A tall young man, in reality a junior partner in a local law firm, wanders in, carrying a tennis racket. The maid turns, sees him, and catches her breath, startled. "Why Mr. Fenton!" she exclaims. . . .

And the world begins.

The full experience of drama—whether at an amateur production like the little theater performance described here or at a huge Broadway playhouse—is much more complex than that of any other form of literature. The word **drama** itself comes from a Greek word meaning "a thing that is done," and the roots of both **theater** and **audience** call to mind the acts of seeing and hearing, respectively. Like other communal public activities—such as religious services, sporting events, and meetings of political or fraternal organizations—drama's own set of customs, rituals, and rules has evolved over many centuries. The exact shape of these characteristics—**dramatic conventions**—may differ from country to country or from period to period, but they all have one aim in common, namely to define and govern an art form whose essence is to be found in public performances of written texts. No other form of literature shares this primary goal. Before we can discuss drama purely as literature, we should first ponder some aspects of its unique status as "a thing that is done."

It is worth noting that dramatists are also called playwrights. Note the spelling; a "wright" is a maker, as old family names like Cartwright or Boatwright attest. If a play is in fact *made* rather than written, then a playwright is similar to an architect who has designed a unique building. The concept may be his or hers, but the construction project requires the contributions of many other hands before the sparkling steel and glass tower alters the city's skyline. In the case of a new play, money must be raised by a producer, a director must be chosen, a cast and a crew found, a set designed and built, and many hours of rehearsal completed before the curtain can be raised for the first time. Along the way, modifications to the original play may become necessary, and it is possible that the author will listen to advice from the actors, director, or stage manager and incorporate these opinions into any revisions. Professional theater is, after all, a branch of show business, and no play will survive much beyond its premiere if it does not attract paying crowds. The dramatists we read and study so reverently today managed to reach large popular audiences in their time. Even ancient Greek playwrights like Sophocles and Euripides must have stood by surreptitiously "counting the house" as the open-air seats slowly filled, and Shakespeare prospered as part-owner of the Globe theater to the extent that he was able to retire to his hometown at the ripe old age of forty-seven.

When compared with this rich communal experience, the solitary act of reading a play seems a poor substitute, contrary to the play's very nature (only a small category known as **closet drama** comprises plays intended to be read instead of acted). Yet dramatists like Shakespeare and Ibsen are counted among the giants of world literature, and their works are annually read by far more people than actually see these plays performed. In reading a play, we are forced to pay close attention to such matters as **set description,** particularly with a playwright like Ibsen who lavishes great attention on the design of his set; references to **properties** or "props" that will figure in the action of the play; physical description of characters and costumes; **stage directions** indicating the movements and gestures made by actors in scenes; and any other **stage business,** that is, action without dialogue. Many modern dramatists are very scrupulous in detailing these matters; writers of earlier periods, however, provided little or no instruction. In reading Sophocles or Shakespeare, we are forced to concentrate on the characters' words to envision how actions and other characters were originally conceived. Reading aloud, alone or in a group, or following along in the text while listening to a recorded performance is particularly recommended for verse plays like *Oedipus the King* or *Othello.* Also, versions of many of the plays contained in this book are currently available on videotape. Although viewing a film is an experience of a different kind from seeing a live performance, film versions obviously provide a convenient insight into the ways in which great actors have interpreted their roles. Seeing the joy in the face of Laurence Fishburne when, as Othello, he lands triumphantly in Cyprus and rejoins his bride makes his tragic fall even more poignant.

Origins of Drama

No consensus exists about the exact date of the birth of drama but, according to most authorities, it originated in Greece over 2500 years ago as an outgrowth of the worship of the god Dionysus, who was associated with fertility, agriculture (especially the cultivation of vineyards), and seasonal renewal. In these Dionysian festivals, a group of fifty citizens of Athens, known as a **chorus,** outfitted and trained by a leader, or **choragos,** would perform hymns of praise to the god, known as **dithyrambic poetry.** The celebration concluded with the ritual sacrifice of a goat, or *tragos.* The two main genres of drama originally took their names from these rituals. The word comedy comes from *kômos,* the Greek term for a festivity. These primitive revels were invariably accompanied with a union of the sexes (*gamos* in Greek, a word that survives in English words like "monogamy"), perhaps in the symbolic form of a dance celebrating fertility and continuance of the race. This is an ancient custom still symbolically observed in the "fade-out kiss" that concludes most comedies. The word tragedy literally means "song of the goat," taking its name from the *tragos* that was killed on the altar *(thymele),* cooked, and shared by the celebrants with their god.

Around 600 BC certain refinements took place. In the middle of the sixth century BC an official springtime festival, known as the Greater or City Dionysia, was established in Athens, and prizes for the best dithyrambic poems were first awarded. At about the same time a special *orchestra,* or "dancing place," was constructed, a circular area surrounding the altar, and permanent seats, or a *theatron* ("seeing place"), arranged in a semicircle around the orchestra were added. At the back of the orchestra the facade of a temple (the *skene*) and a raised "porch" in front of it (the *proskenion,* in later theaters the **proscenium**) served as a backdrop, usually representing the palace of the ruler; walls extending to either side of the *skene,* the *parodoi,* served to conceal backstage activity from the audience. Behind the skene a crane-like device called a *mechane* could be used to lower a god from the heavens or represent a spectacular effect like the flying chariot drawn by dragons at the conclusion of Euripides's *Medea.*

In c. 535 BC a writer named Thespis won the annual competition with a startling innovation. Thespis separated one member of the chorus (called a *hypocrites,* or "actor") and had him engage in **dialogue,** spoken lines representing conversation, with the remaining members. If we define drama primarily as a story related through live action and recited dialogue, then Thespis may rightly be called the father of drama, and his name endures in "thespian," a synonym for actor.

The century after Thespis, from 500–400 BC, saw many refinements in the way tragedies were performed and is considered the golden age of Greek drama. In that century, the careers of the three great tragic playwrights—Aeschylus (525–456 BC), Sophocles (c. 496–406 BC), and Euripides (c. 485–408 BC)—and the greatest comic playwright, Aristophanes (448–380 BC), overlapped. It is no coincidence that in this remarkable period Athens, under the leadership of the general Pericles (d. 429 BC), reached the height of its wealth, influence, and cultural development and was home to the philosophers Socrates (470–399 BC) and Plato (427–327 BC). Aristotle (384–322 BC), the third of the great Athenian philosophers, was also a literary critic who wrote the first extended analysis of drama.

Aristotle on Tragedy

In our earlier discussions of fiction and poetry we made use of Aristotle's *Poetics*, the earliest work of literary criticism in western civilization. Aristotle attempts to define and classify the different literary **genres** that use rhythm, language, and harmony. He identifies four genres—epic poetry, dithyrambic poetry, comedy, and tragedy—which have in common their attempts at imitation, or *mimesis*, of various types of human activity.

Aristotle comments most fully on tragedy, and his definition of the genre demands close examination:

> *A tragedy, then, is the imitation of an action that is serious and also, as having magnitude, complete in itself; in language with pleasurable accessories, each kind brought in separately in the parts of the work; in a dramatic, not in a narrative form; with incidents arousing pity and fear, wherewith to accomplish its catharsis of such emotions.*

First we should note that the imitation here is of *action*. Later in the passage, when Aristotle differentiates between narrative and dramatic forms of literature, it is clear that he is referring to tragedy as a type of literature written primarily for public performance. Furthermore, tragedy must be serious and must have magnitude. By this, Aristotle implies that issues of life and death must be involved and that these issues must be of public import. In many Greek tragedies the fate of the *polis*, or city, of which the chorus is the voice, is bound up with the actions taken by the main character in the play. Despite their rudimentary form of democracy, the people of Athens would have been perplexed by a tragedy with an ordinary citizen at its center; the magnitude of tragedy demands that only the affairs of persons of high rank are of sufficient importance for tragedy. Aristotle further requires that this imitated action possess a sense of completeness. At no point does he say that a tragedy has to end with a death or even in a state of unhappiness; he does require, however, that the audience sense that after the last words are spoken no further story cries out to be told.

The next part of the passage may confuse the modern reader. By "language with pleasurable accessories" Aristotle means the poetic devices of rhythm and, in the choral parts of the tragedy, music and dance as well. Reading the choral passages in a Greek tragedy, we are likely to forget that these passages were intended to be chanted or sung ("chorus" and "choir" share the same root word in Greek) and danced ("choreography" comes from this root as well).

The rest of Aristotle's definition dwells on the emotional effects of tragedy on the audience. Pity and fear are to be evoked—pity because we must care for the characters and to some extent empathize with them, fear because we come to realize that the fate they endure involves actions that civilized men and women most abhor; in *Oedipus the King*, these actions involve murder, incest, suicide, and self-mutilation. Finally, Aristotle's word **catharsis** has proven controversial over the centuries. The word literally means "a purging," but readers have debated whether Aristotle is referring to a release of harmful emotions or a transformation of them. In either case, the implication is that viewing a tragedy has a beneficial effect on an audience, perhaps because the viewers' deepest fears are brought to light in a make-believe setting. How many of us, at the end of some particularly wrenching film, have turned to a companion and said, "Thank god, it was only a movie"? The sacrificial animal from whom tragedy took its name was, after all, only a stand-in whose blood was offered to the gods as a substitute for a human subject. The protagonist of a tragedy remains, in many ways, a "scapegoat" on whose head we project our own unconscious terrors.

Aristotle identifies six elements of a tragedy, and these elements are still useful in analyzing not only tragedies but other types of plays as well. In order of importance they are **plot, characterization, theme, diction, melody,** and **spectacle.** Despite the fact that *Poetics* is over two thousand years old, Aristotle's elements still provide a useful way of understanding how plays work.

Plot

Aristotle considers plot the chief element of a play, and it is easy to see this when we consider that in discussing a film with a friend we usually give a brief summary, or **synopsis,** of the plot, stopping just short of "giving it away" by telling how the story concludes. Aristotle defines plot as "the combination of incidents, or things done in the story," going on to give the famous formulation that a plot "is that which has beginning, middle, and end." Aristotle notes that the best plots are selective in their use of material and have an internal coherence and logic. Aristotle seems to favor plays with **unified plot,** that is, one that takes place in a single day; in a short play with a unified plot like Susan Glaspell's *Trifles,* the action is continuous and imitates the amount of time that the events would have taken in real life. By **episodic plot** we mean one that spreads its action out over a longer period of time; in the case of Wendy Wasserstein's long play *The Heidi Chronicles,* over twenty-five years. A play which has a unified plot, a single setting, and no subplots is said to observe the **three unities,** which critics in some past eras have virtually insisted on as ironclad rules. Although most plots are chronological, playwrights in the last half-century have experimented, sometimes radically, with such straightforward progression through time. Arthur Miller's *Death of a Salesman* effectively blends **flashbacks** to past events with his main action, and David Ives's *Sure Thing* plays havoc with chronology, allowing his protagonist to "replay" his previous scenes until he has learned the way to the "sure thing" of the title.

Two other important elements of plots that Aristotle considers most successful are **reversal** (*peripeteia* in Greek, also known as **peripety**), and **recognition** (*anagnorisis* in Greek, also known as **discovery**). By reversal he means a change "from one state of things within the play to its opposite." Aristotle cites one example from *Oedipus the King:* "the Messenger, who, coming to gladden Oedipus and to remove his fears as to his mother, reveals the secret of his birth"; but an earlier reversal in the same play occurs when Jocaste, attempting to alleviate Oedipus's fears of prophecies, inadvertently mentions the "place where three roads meet," where Oedipus killed a man he took as a stranger. Most plays have more than a single reversal; each episode or act builds on the main character's hopes that his or her problems will be dissolved, only to dash those expectations as the play proceeds. Recognition, the second term, is perhaps more properly an element of characterization because it involves a character's "change from ignorance to knowledge." If the events of the plot have not served to illuminate the character about his or her failings, then the audience is likely to feel that the story lacks depth. The kind of self-knowledge that tragedies provide is invariably accompanied by suffering and is won at great emotional cost, whereas in comedies reversals may bring relief to the characters, and recognition may bring about the happy conclusion of the play.

As earlier noted in the Introduction to Fiction, a typical plot may be broken down into several components. First comes the **exposition,** which provides the audience with essential information—who, what, when, where—that it needs to know before the play can continue. A novelist or short story writer can present information directly with some sort of variation on the "Once upon a time" opening. But dramatists have particular problems with exposition because facts must be presented in the form of dialogue and action. Greek dramatists used the first two parts of a tragedy, a prologue and the first appearance of the chorus, to refresh the audience's familiarity with the myths being retold and to set up the initial situation of the play. Other types of drama use a single character to provide expository material. Medieval morality plays often use a "heavenly messenger" to deliver the opening speech, and some of Shakespeare's plays employ a single character named "Chorus" who speaks an introductory prologue and sets the scene for later portions of the plays as well (the film *Shakespeare in Love* captures this memorably). In *The Glass Menagerie*, Tom Wingfield fulfills this role in an unusual manner, telling the audience at the beginning, "I am the narrator of the play, and also a character in it." Occasionally, we even encounter the least elegant solution to the problem of dramatic exposition, employing minor characters whose sole function is to provide background information in the play's opening scene. Countless drawing-room comedies have raised the curtain on a pair of servants in the midst of a gossipy conversation which catches the audience up on the doings of the family members who make up the rest of the cast.

The second part of a plot is called the **complication,** the interjection of some circumstance or event that shakes up the stable situation that has existed before the play's opening and begins the **rising action** of the play, during which the audience's tension and expectations become tightly intertwined and involved with the characters and the events they experience. Complication in a play may be both external and internal. A plague, a threatened invasion, or a conclusion of a war are typical examples of external complication, outside events which affect the characters' lives. However, many plays rely primarily on an internal complication, a single character's weakness in his or her personality. Often the complication is heightened by **conflict** between two characters whom events have forced into collision with each other. In Arthur Miller's *Death of a Salesman,* for example, the external complication stems from Willie's troubles with his boss, the internal complication is his growing depression and suicidal tendencies, and the chief conflict is with his son, Biff. No matter how it is presented, the complication of the plot usually introduces a problem that the characters cannot avoid. The rising action, which constitutes the body of the play, usually contains a number of moments of **crisis,** when solutions crop up momentarily but quickly disappear. These critical moments in the scenes may take the form of the kinds of reversals discussed above, and the audience's emotional involvement in the plot generally hinges on the characters' rising and falling hopes.

The central moment of crisis in the play is the **climax,** or the moment of greatest tension, which initiates the **falling action** of the plot. Perhaps "moments" of greatest tension would be a more exact phrase, for skillful playwrights know how to wring as much tension as possible from the audience. In the best plots everything in earlier parts of the play has pointed to this scene—a duel, a suicide, a murder—and the play's highest pitch of emotion.

The final part of a plot is the **dénouement, or resolution.** As noted in our discussion of plot in fiction, the French word literally refers to the untying of a knot, the release of the tension that has built up during the play. The dénouement returns the play and its characters to a stable situation, though not the same one that existed at the beginning of the play, and gives some indication of what the future holds for them. A dénouement may be either closed or open. A **closed dénouement** ties up everything neatly and explains all unanswered questions the audience might have; an **open dénouement** leaves a few tantalizing loose ends.

Several other plot terms should also be noted. Aristotle mentions, not altogether favorably, plots with "double issues." The most common word for this is **subplot**, a less important story involving minor characters which may mirror the main plot of the play. Some plays like Shakespeare's *A Midsummer Night's Dream* may even have more than one subplot. Occasionally, a playwright finds it necessary to drop hints about coming events in the plot, perhaps to keep the audience from complaining that certain incidents have happened "out of the blue." This is called **foreshadowing.** If a climactic incident that helps to resolve the plot has not been adequately prepared for, the playwright may be accused of having resorted to a ***deus ex machina*** ending, which takes its name from the *mechane* that once literally lowered a god or goddess into the midst of the dramatic proceedings. An ending of this sort, like that of an old western movie in which the cavalry arrives just as the wagon train is about to be annihilated, is rarely satisfactory.

Finally the difference between **suspense** and **dramatic irony** should be addressed. Both of these devices generate tension in the audience, although through opposite means—suspense when the audience does not know what is about to happen, dramatic irony, paradoxically, when it does. Much of our pleasure in reading a new play lies in speculating about what will happen next, but in Greek tragedy the original audience would be fully familiar with the basic outlines of the mythic story before the action even began. Dramatic irony, thus, occurs at moments when the audience is more knowledgeable about events than the on-stage characters are. In *Oedipus the King*, the audience knows who the murderer of Laius is, and in *Othello* we are continually reminded that Iago is lying to Othello. In some plays, our foreknowledge of certain events is so strong that we may want to cry out a warning to the characters.

Characterization

The Greek word *agon* means "debate," and refers to the central issue or conflict of a play. From *agon* we derive two words commonly used to denote the chief characters in a play: **protagonist**, literally the "first speaker," and **antagonist,** one who speaks against him. Often the word "hero" is used as a synonym for protagonist, and it is difficult not to think of Oedipus or Othello as tragic heroes. In many modern plays it may be more appropriate to speak of the protagonist as an **anti-hero** because he or she may possess few, if any, of the traditional attributes of a hero, a point that Arthur Miller discusses in his essay "Tragedy and the Common Man." Similarly, the word "villain" brings to mind a black-mustached, sneering character in a top hat and opera cloak from an old-fashioned **melodrama** (a play whose complications are solved happily at the last minute by the "triumph of good over evil") and usually has little application to the complex characters one encounters in a serious play.

Aristotle, in his discussion of characterization, stresses the complexity that marks the personages in the greatest plays. Nothing grows tiresome more quickly than a perfectly virtuous man or woman at the center of a play, and nothing is more offensive to the audience than seeing absolute innocence despoiled. Although Aristotle stresses that a successful protagonist must be better than ordinary men and women, he also insists that the protagonist be somewhat less than perfect:

> *There remains, then, the intermediate kind of personage, a man not preeminently virtuous and just, whose misfortune, however, is brought upon him not by vice and depravity but by some error of judgement. . . .*

Aristotle's word for this error is **hamartia,** which is commonly translated as "tragic flaw" but might more properly be termed a "great error." Whether he means some innate flaw, like a psychological defect, or simply a great mistake is open to question, but writers of tragedies have traditionally created deeply flawed protagonists. In ordinary circumstances, the protagonist's strength of character may allow him to prosper, but under the pressure of events he may crack as one small chink in his armor widens and leaves him vulnerable. A typical flaw in tragedies is **hybris,** arrogance or excessive pride, which leads the protagonist into errors that might have been avoided if he had listened to the advice of others. Oedipus, for example, is adequately warned by Tiresias not to pursue his investigation into Laius's death, but he is too stubborn to listen. Although he does not use the term himself, Aristotle touches here on the concept of **poetic justice,** the audience's sense that virtue and vice have been fairly dealt with in the play and that the protagonist's punishment is to some degree deserved.

We should bear in mind that the greatest burden of characterization in drama falls on the actor or actress who undertakes a role. No matter how well-written a part is, in the hands of an incompetent or inappropriate performer the character will not be credible. Vocal inflection, gesture, and even the strategic use of silence are the stock in trade of actors, for it is up to them to convince us that we are involved in the sufferings and joys of real human beings. No two actors will play the same part in the same manner. We are lucky to have two excellent film versions of Shakespeare's *Henry the Fifth* available. Comparing the cool elegance of Laurence Olivier with the rough and ready exuberance of Kenneth Branagh is a wonderful short course in the equal validity of two radically different approaches to the same role.

In reading, there are several points to keep in mind about main characters. Physical description, while it may be minimal at best, is worth paying close attention to. To cite one example from the plays contained in this edition, Shakespeare identifies Othello simply as a "Moor," a native of North Africa. Race and color are important causes of conflict in the play, to be sure, but through the years the part has been played with equal success by both black and white actors. The important issue in *Othello* is that the tragic hero is a cultural misfit in the Venetian society from which he takes a wife; he is a widely respected military leader but an outsider all the same. Shakespeare provides us with few other details of his appearance, but we can probably assume that he is a large and powerful warrior, capable of commanding men by his mere presence. Sometimes an author will give a character a name that is an indicator of his or her personality and appearance. Oedipus's name, in Greek, refers to his scarred feet. Willy Loman, the failed protagonist of Arthur Miller's *Death of a Salesman*, bears a surname ("low man") which contains a pun on his character, a device called a **characternym.**

Character motivation is another point of characterization to ponder. Why do characters act in a certain manner? What do they hope to gain from their actions? In some cases, these motives are clear enough and may be discussed openly by the characters. In other plays, motivation is more elusive, as the playwright deliberately mystifies the audience by presenting characters who perhaps are not fully aware of the reasons for their compulsions. Modern dramatists, influenced by advances in psychology, have often refused to reduce characters' actions to simple equations of cause and effect.

Two conventions that the playwright may employ in revealing motivation are **soliloquy** and **aside.** A soliloquy is a speech made by a single character on stage alone. Hamlet's soliloquies, among them some of the most famous passages in all drama, show us the process of his mind as he toys with various plans of revenge but delays putting them into action. The aside is a brief remark (traditionally delivered to the side of a raised hand) that an actor makes directly to the audience and that the other characters on stage cannot hear. Occasionally an aside reveals a reason for a character's behavior in a scene. Neither of these devices is as widely used in today's theatre as in earlier periods, but they remain part of the dramatist's collection of techniques.

Minor characters are also of great importance in a successful play, and several different traditional types exist. A **foil,** a minor character with whom a major character sharply contrasts, is used primarily as a sounding board for ideas, as in the way Iago banters with the foolish Roderigo. A **confidant,** like Nora Helmer's friend Dr. Rank in Ibsen's *A Doll House,* is a trusted friend or servant to whom a major character speaks frankly and openly; confidants fulfill in some respects one role that the chorus plays in Greek tragedy. **Stock characters** are stereotypes that are useful for advancing the plot and fleshing out the scenes, particularly in comedies. Hundreds of plays have employed a pair of innocent young lovers, sharp-tongued servants, and meddling mothers-in-law as part of their casts. **Allegorical characters** in morality plays like *Everyman* are clearly labeled by their names and, for the most part, are personifications of human attributes (Beauty, Good Deeds) or of theological concepts (Confession). **Comic relief** in a tragedy may be provided by minor characters like Shakespeare's fools or clowns.

Theme

Aristotle has relatively little to say about the theme of a play, simply noting that "Thought of the personages is shown in everything to be effected by their language." Because he focuses to such a large degree on the emotional side of tragedy—its stimulation of pity and fear—he seems to give less importance to the role of drama as a serious forum for the discussion of ideas, referring his readers to another of his works,

The Art of Rhetoric, where these matters have greater prominence. Nevertheless, **theme,** the central idea or ideas that a play discusses, is important in Greek tragedy and in the subsequent history of the theater. The trilogies of early playwrights were thematically unified around an *aition*, a Greek word for the origin of a custom, just as a typical elementary school Thanksgiving pageant portrays how the holiday traditions were first established in the Plymouth Colony.

Some dramas are explicitly **didactic** in their intent, existing with the specific aim of instructing the audience in ethical, religious, or political areas. A **morality play,** a popular type of drama in the late Middle Ages, is essentially a sermon on sin and redemption rendered in dramatic terms. More subtle in its didacticism is the **problem play** of the late nineteenth century, popularized by Ibsen, which uses the theatre as a forum for the serious debate of social issues like industrial pollution or women's rights. The **drama of ideas** of playwrights like George Bernard Shaw does not merely present social problems; it goes further, actually advancing programs of reform. In the United States during the Great Depression, Broadway theaters featured a great deal of **social drama,** in which radical social and political programs were openly propagandized. In the ensuing decades the theater has remained a popular forum for debating issues of race, class, and gender, as the success of *Fences* and many other plays will attest.

Keep in mind, however, that plays are not primarily religious or political forums. If we are not entertained and moved by a play's language, action, and plot, then it is unlikely that we will respond to its message. The author who must resort to long sermons from a *raisonneur* (like Cléante, the protagonist's brother-in-law in Molière's famous comedy *Tartuffe*) who serves primarily as the voice or reason, that is, the mouthpiece for the playwright's opinions, is not likely to hold the audience's sympathy or attention for long. The best plays are complex enough that they cannot be reduced to simple "thesis statements" which sum up their meaning in a few words.

Diction

Aristotle was also the author of the first important manual of public speaking, *The Art of Rhetoric*, so it should come as no surprise that he devotes considerable attention in the *Poetics* to the precise words, either alone or in combinations, that playwrights use. Instead of "diction," we would probably speak today of a playwright's "style" or discuss his or her handling of various levels of idiom in the dialogue. Although much of what Aristotle has to say about parts of speech and the sounds of words in Greek is of little interest to us, his emphasis on clarity and originality in the choice of words remains relevant. For Aristotle, the language of tragedy should be "poetic" in the best sense, somehow elevated above the level of ordinary speech but not so ornate that it loses the power to communicate feelings and ideas to an audience. Realism in speech is largely a matter of illusion, and close inspection of the actual lines of modern dramatists like Miller and Williams reveal a discrepancy between the carefully chosen words that characters speak in plays, often making up lengthy **monologues,** and the halting, often inarticulate ("Ya know what I mean?") manner in which we express ourselves in everyday life. The language of the theatre has always been an artificial one. The idiom of plays, whether by Shakespeare or by August Wilson, *imitates* the language of life; it does not duplicate it.

Ancient Greek is a language with a relatively small vocabulary and, even in translation, we encounter a great deal of repetition of key words. *Polis,* the Greek word for city, appears many times in Sophocles' plays, stressing the communal fate that the protagonist and the chorus, representing the citizens, share. Shakespeare's use of the full resources of the English language has been the standard against which all subsequent writers in the language have had to measure themselves. However, Shakespeare's language presents some special difficulties for the modern reader. His vocabulary is essentially the same as ours, but many words have changed in meaning or become obsolete over the last four hundred years. Shakespeare is also a master of different **levels of diction.** In the space of a few lines he can range from self-consciously flowery heights ("If after every tempest come such calms,/May the winds blow till they have waken'd death!/And let the labouring bark climb hills of seas/Olympus-high and duck again as low/As hell's to heaven!" exults Othello on being reunited with his bride in Cyprus) to the slangy level of the streets—he is a master of the off-color joke and the sarcastic put-down. Responding to Roderigo's threat to drown himself, Iago says, "Come, be a man. Drown thyself! drown cats and blind puppies." We should remember that Shakespeare's poetic drama lavishly uses figurative language; his lines abound with similes, metaphors, personifications, and hyperboles, all characteristic devices of the language of poetry. Shakespeare's theater had little in the way of scenery and no "special effects," so a passage from *Hamlet* like "But, look, the morn, in russet mantle clad/Walks o'er the dew of yon high eastward hill" is not merely pretty or picturesque; it has the dramatic function of helping the audience visualize the welcome end of a long, fearful night.

It is true that playwrights since the middle of the nineteenth century have striven for more fidelity to reality, more verisimilitude, in the language their characters use, but even realistic dramatists often rise to rhetorical peaks that have little relationship to the way people actually speak. Both Ibsen and Williams began their careers as poets and, surprisingly, the first draft of Arthur Miller's "realistic" tragedy *Death of a Salesman* was largely written in verse.

Melody

Greek tragedy was accompanied by music. None of this music survives, and we cannot be certain how it was integrated into the drama. Certainly the choral parts of the play were sung and danced, and it is likely that even the dialogue involved highly rhythmical chanting, especially in passages employing **stichomythia,** rapid alternation of single lines between two actors, a device often encountered during moments of high dramatic tension. In the original language, the different poetic rhythms used in Greek tragedy are still evident, although these are for the most part lost in English translation. At any rate, it is apparent that the skillful manipulation of a variety of **poetic meters,** combinations of line lengths and rhythms, for different types of scenes was an important part of the tragic poet's repertoire.

Both tragedies and comedies have been written in verse throughout the ages, often employing rhyme as well as rhythm. *Oedipus the King* is written in a variety of poetic meters, with some of them appropriate for dialogue between actors and others for the choral odes. Shakespeare's *Othello* is composed, like all of his plays, largely in **blank verse,** that is, unrhymed lines of iambic pentameter (lines of ten syllables, alternating unstressed and stressed syllables). He also uses rhymed pairs of lines called **couplets,** particularly for emphasis at the close of scenes; songs (there are three in *Othello*); and even prose passages, especially when dealing with comic or "low" characters. A study of Shakespeare's versification is beyond the scope of this discussion, but suffice it to say that a trained actor must be aware of the rhythmical patterns that Shakespeare utilized if he or she is to deliver the lines with anything approaching accuracy.

Of course, not only verse drama has rhythm. Tom Wingfield's last speech in Tennessee Williams's *The Glass Menagerie* can be broken into lines of fairly regular blank verse (Williams wrote a considerable amount of poetry):

> Then all at once my sister touches my shoulder.
> I turn around and look into her eyes . . .
> Oh, Laura, Laura, I tried to leave you behind me,
> but I am more faithful than I intended to be!
> I reach for a cigarette, I cross the street,
> I run into the movies or a bar,
> I buy a drink, I speak to the nearest stranger—
> anything that can blow your candles out!
> —for nowadays the world is lit by lightning!
> Blow your candles out, Laura—and so good-bye. . . .

The ancient verse heritage of tragedy lingers on in the modern theater and has proven resistant to even the prosaic rhythms of what Williams calls a "world lit by lightning."

Spectacle

Spectacle (sometimes called *mise en scène,* French for "putting on stage") is the last of Aristotle's elements of tragedy and, in his view, the least important. By spectacle we mean the purely visual dimension of a play; in ancient Greece, this meant costumes, a few props, and effects carried out by the use of the *mechane.* Costumes in Greek tragedy were simple but impressive. The tragic mask, or *persona,* and a high-heeled boot *(cothurnus),* were apparently designed to give characters a larger-than-life appearance. Historians also speculate that the mask might have additionally served as a crude megaphone to amplify the actors' voices, a necessary feature when we consider that the open air theater in Athens could seat over 10,000 spectators. Other elements of set decoration were kept to a minimum, although playwrights occasionally employed a few well-chosen spectacular effects like the triumphant entrance of the victorious king in Aeschylus's *Agamemnon,* which involves a horse-drawn chariot and brilliant red carpet on which Agamemnon walks to his death. Elizabethan drama likewise relied little on spectacular stage effects. Shakespeare's plays call for few props, and little attempt was made at historical accuracy in costumes, a noble patron's cast-off clothing dressing Caesar one week, Othello the next.

Advances in technology since Shakespeare's day have obviously facilitated more elaborate effects in what we now call **staging** than patrons of earlier centuries could have envisioned. In the nineteenth century, first gas and then electric lighting not only made effects like sunrises possible but also, through the use of different combinations of color, added atmosphere to certain scenes. By Ibsen's day, realistic **box sets** were designed to resemble, in the smallest details, interiors of houses and apartments with an invisible "fourth wall" nearest the audience. Modern theater has experimented in all directions with set design, from the bare stage to barely suggested walls and furnishings, from revolving stages to scenes that "break the plane" by involving the audience in the drama. *The Glass Menagerie* employs music, complicated lighting and sound effects, and semi-transparent **scrims** onto which images are projected, all to enhance the play's dream-like atmosphere. The most impressive uses of spectacle in today's Broadway productions may represent anything from the catacombs beneath the Paris Opera House in *Phantom of the Opera* to thirty-foot-high street barricades manned by soldiers firing muskets in *Les Misérables*. Modern technology can create virtually any sort of stage illusion; the only limitations in today's professional theater are imagination and budget.

Before we leave our preliminary discussion, one further element should be mentioned—**setting.** Particular locales—Thebes, Corinth, and Mycenæ—are the sites of different tragedies, and each city has its own history; in the case of Thebes, this history involves a family curse that touches the members of three generations. But for the most part specific locales in the greatest plays are less important than the universal currents that are touched. If we are interested in the particular features of middle-class marriage in Oslo in the late nineteenth century, we would perhaps do better going to sociology texts than to Ibsen's *A Doll House.*

Still, every play implies a larger sense of setting, a sense of history that is called the **enveloping action.** The "southern belle" youth of Amanda Wingfield in Williams's *The Glass Menagerie* is a fading dream as anachronistic as the "gentlemen callers" she still envisions knocking on her daughter's door. Even though a play from the past may still speak eloquently today, it also provides a "time capsule" whose contents tell us how people lived and what they most valued during the period when the play was written and first performed.

Brief History and Description of Dramatic Conventions

Greek Tragedy

By the time of Sophocles, tragedy had evolved into an art form with a complex set of conventions. Each playwright would submit a **tetralogy**, or set of four plays, to the yearly competition. The first three plays, or **trilogy**, would be tragedies, perhaps unified like those of Aeschylus's *Oresteia*, which deals with Agamemnon's tragic homecoming from the Trojan War. The fourth, called a **satyr-play**, was comic, with a chorus of goat-men engaging in bawdy revels that, oddly, mocked the serious content of the preceding tragedies. Only one complete trilogy, the *Oresteia* by Aeschylus, and one satyr-play, *The Cyclops* by Euripides, have survived. Three plays by Sophocles on the myths surrounding Oedipus and his family—*Oedipus the King, Oedipus at Colonus*, and *Antigone*—are still performed and read, but they were written at separate times and accompanied by other tragedies that are now lost. As tragedy developed in this period, it seems clear that playwrights thought increasingly of individual plays as complete in themselves; *Oedipus the King* does not leave the audience with the feeling that there is more to be told, even though Oedipus is still alive at the end of the play.

Each tragedy was composed according to a prescribed formula, as ritualized as the order of worship in a contemporary church service. The tragedy begins with a **prologue** *(prologos)*, "that which is said first." The prologue is an introductory scene that tells the audience important information about the play's setting, characters, and events immediately preceding the opening of the drama. The second part of the tragedy is called the *parodos,* the first appearance of the chorus in the play. As the members of chorus enter the orchestra, they dance and sing more generally of the situation in which the city finds itself. Choral parts in some translations are divided into sections called **strophes** and **antistrophes,** respectively, indicating choral movements to left and right. The body of the play is made up of two types of alternating scenes. The first, an episode *(episodos)* is a passage of dialogue between two or more actors or between actors and the chorus. Each of these "acts" of the tragedy is separated from the rest by a choral **ode** *(stasimon;* pl. *stasima)* during which the chorus is alone on the orchestra, commenting, as the voice of public opinion, about the course of action being taken by the main characters. Typically there are four pairs of episodes and odes in the play. The final scene of the play is called the *exodos.* During this part, the climax occurs out of sight of the audience, and a vivid description of this usually violent scene is sometimes given by a messenger or other witness. After the messenger's speech, the protagonist reappears and the resolution of his fate is determined. In some plays, a wheeled platform called an *eccyclema* was used to move this fatal tableau into the view of the spectators. A tragedy concludes with the exit of the main characters, sometimes leaving the chorus to deliver a brief speech or **epilogue,** a final summing up of the play's meaning.

Although we may at first find such complicated rituals bizarre, we should keep in mind that dramatic conventions are primarily customary and artificial and have little to do with "reality" as we usually experience it. The role of the chorus (set by the time of Sophocles at fifteen members) may seem puzzling to modern readers but in many ways, the conventions of Greek tragedy are no stranger than those of contemporary musical comedy like *Grease*, in which a pair of teenage lovers burst into a duet and dance, soon to be joined by a host of other cast members. What is most remarkable about the history of drama is not how much these conventions have changed but how remarkably similar they have remained for over twenty-five centuries.

Medieval Drama

Drama flourished during Greek and Roman times, but after the fall of the Roman Empire (AD 476) it went into four centuries of eclipse, kept alive throughout Europe only by wandering troupes of actors performing various types of **folk drama.** The "Punch and Judy" puppet show, still popular in parts of Europe, is a late survivor of this tradition, as are the ancient slapstick routines of circus clowns. Even though drama was officially discouraged by the Church for a long period, when it did reemerge it was as an outgrowth of the Roman Catholic mass, in the form of **liturgical drama.** Around the ninth century, short passages of sung dialogue between the priest and choir, called **tropes,** were added on special holidays to commemorate the event. These tropes grew more elaborate over the years until full-fledged religious pageants were being performed in front of the altar. In 1210, Pope Innocent III, wishing to restore the dignity of the services, banned such performances from the interior of the church. Moving them outside, first to the church porch and later entirely off church property, provided greater opportunity for inventiveness in action and staging.

In the fourteenth and fifteenth centuries, much of the work of putting on plays passed to the guilds, organizations of skilled craftsmen, and their productions became part of city-wide festivals in many continental and British cities. Several types of plays evolved. **Mystery plays** were derived from holy scripture. **Passion plays** (some of which survive unchanged today) focused on the crucifixion of Christ. **Miracle plays** dramatized the lives of the saints. The last and most complex, **morality plays,** were dramatized sermons with allegorical characters (Everyman, Death, Good Deeds) representing various generalized aspects of human life.

Elizabethan Drama

Although the older morality plays were still performed throughout the sixteenth century, during the time of Queen Elizabeth I (b. 1533, reigned 1558–1603) a new type of drama, typical in many ways of other innovative types of literature developed in the Renaissance, began to be produced professionally by companies of actors not affiliated with any religious institutions. This **secular drama,** beginning in short pieces called **interludes** that may have been designed for entertainment during banquets or other public celebrations, eventually evolved into full-length tragedies and comedies designed for performance in large outdoor theaters like Shakespeare's famous Globe.

A full history of this fertile period would take many pages, but a few of its dramatic conventions are worth noting. We have already mentioned blank verse, the poetic line perfected by Shakespeare's contemporary Christopher Marlowe (1564–1593). Shakespeare wrote tragedies, comedies, and historical dramas with equal success, all characterized by passages that remain the greatest examples of poetic expression in English.

The raised platform stage in an Elizabethan theater used little or no scenery, but relied on the author's descriptive talents to set the scene and indicate lighting and weather. The stage itself had two supporting columns, which might be used to represent trees or hiding places; a raised area at the rear, which could represent a balcony or upper story of a house; a small curtained alcove at its base; and a trap door, which could serve as a grave or hiding place. In contrast to the relatively bare stage, costumes were elaborate and acting was highly stylized, with the blank verse lines delivered at high volume and with broad gestures. Female roles were played by young boys, and the same actor might play several different minor roles in the same play.

A few more brief words about Shakespeare's plays may be in order. First, drama in Shakespeare's time was intended for performance, with publication being of only secondary importance. The text of many of Shakespeare's plays were published in cheap editions called **quartos,** which are full of misprints and often contain widely different versions of the same play. Any play by Shakespeare contains words and passages that different editors have trouble agreeing on. Second, originality, in the sense we prize it, meant little to a playwright in a time before copyright laws; virtually every one of Shakespeare's plays is derived from an earlier source—Greek myth, history, another play or, in the case of *Othello,* an Italian short story of questionable literary merit. The true test of Shakespeare's genius rests in his ability to transform these raw materials into art. Finally, we should keep in mind that Shakespeare's plays were designed to appeal to a wide audience—educated aristocrats and slovenly "groundlings" filled the theater—and this fact may account for the great diversity of tones and levels of language in the plays. Purists of later eras may have been dismayed by some of Shakespeare's wheezy clowns and bad puns, but for us the mixture of "high" and "low" elements gives his plays their remarkable texture.

The Comic Genres

Shakespeare's ability to move easily between "high" and "low," between tragic and comic, should be a reminder that comedy has developed along lines parallel to tragedy and never wholly separate from it. Most

of Aristotle's remarks on comedy are lost, but he does make the observation that comedy differs from tragedy in that comedy depicts men
and women as worse than they are, whereas tragedy generally stresses
their best qualities. During the great age of Greek tragedy, comedies
were regularly performed at Athenian festivals. The greatest of the early
comic playwrights was Aristophanes (c. 450–380 BC). The plays of
Aristophanes are classified as **Old Comedy** and shared many of the
same structural elements as tragedy, with scenes alternating with choral
parts. Old Comedy was always satirical and usually obscene; in
Lysistrata, written during the devastating Athenian wars with Sparta,
the men of both sides are brought to their knees by the women of the
two cities, who engage in a sex strike until the men relent. **New
Comedy,** which evolved in the century after Aristophanes, tended to
observe more traditional moral values and stressed romance. The New
Comedy of Greece greatly influenced the writings of Roman playwrights
like Plautus (254–184 BC) and Terence (190–59 BC). Plautus's *Miles
Gloriosus* still finds favor in its modern musical adaptation, *A Funny
Thing Happened on the Way to the Forum.*

Like other forms of drama, comedy virtually vanished during the
early Middle Ages. Its spirit was kept alive primarily by roving companies of actors who staged improvisational dramas in the squares of
towns throughout Europe. The popularity of these plays is evidenced by
certain elements in the religious dramas of the same period; the *Second
Shepherd's Play* (c. 1450) involves a sheep-rustler with three shepherds
in an uproarious parody of the Nativity that still evokes laughter today.
Even a serious play such as *Everyman* contains satirical elements in the
complicated excuses that Goods and other characters contrive for not
accompanying the protagonist on his journey with Death.

On the continent, a highly stylized form of improvisational drama
appeared in sixteenth century Italy, apparently an evolution from earlier
types of folk drama. ***Commedia dell'arte*** involved a cast of masked
stock characters (the miserly old man, the young wife, the ardent seducer) in situations involving mistaken identity and cuckoldry. Because
it was an improvisational form, *commedia dell'arte*, does not survive in
written texts, but its popularity influenced the direction that comedy
would take in the next century. The great French comic playwright
Molière (1622–1673) incorporated many of its elements into his own
plays, which combine elements of **farce,** a type of comedy which hinges

on broadly drawn characters and embarrassing situations usually involving sexual misconduct, with serious social satire. Comedy such as Molière's, which exposes the hypocrisy and pretensions of people in social situations, is called **comedy of manners;** as Molière put it, the main purpose of his plays was "the correction of mankind's vices."

Other types of comedy have also been popular in different eras. Shakespeare's comedies begin with the farcical complications of *The Comedy of Errors*, progress through romantic **pastoral** comedies such as *As You Like It*, which present an idealized view of rural life, and end with the philosophical comedies of his final period, of which *The Tempest* is the greatest example. His contemporary Ben Jonson (1572–1637) favored a type known as **comedy of humours,** a type of comedy of manners in which the conduct of the characters is determined by their underlying dominant trait (the four humours were thought to be bodily fluids whose proportions determined personality). English plays of the late seventeenth and early eighteenth centuries tended to combine the hard-edged satire of comedy of manners with varying amounts of sentimental romance. A play of this type, usually hinging on matters of inheritance and marriage, is known as a **drawing-room comedy,** and its popularity, while peaking in the mid-nineteenth century, endures today.

Modern comedy in English can be said to begin with Oscar Wilde (1854–1900) and George Bernard Shaw (1856–1950). Wilde's brilliant wit and skillful incorporation of paradoxical **epigrams,** witty sayings that have made him one of the most quoted authors of the nineteenth century, have rarely been equaled. Shaw, who began his career as a drama critic, admired both Wilde and Ibsen, and succeeded in combining the best elements of the comedy of manners and the problem play in his works. *Major Barbara* (1905), a typical **comedy of ideas,** frames serious discussion of war, religion, and poverty with a search for an heir to a millionaire's fortune and a suitable husband for one of his daughters. Most subsequent writers of comedy, from Neil Simon to Wendy Wasserstein, reveal their indebtedness to Wilde and Shaw.

One striking development of comedy in recent times lies in its deliberate harshness. So-called **black humor,** an extreme type of satire in which barriers of taste are assaulted and pain seems the constant companion of laughter, has characterized much of the work of playwrights like Samuel Beckett (1906–1989), Eugene Ionesco (1909–1994), and Edward Albee (b. 1928).

Realistic Drama, the Modern Stage, and Beyond

Realism is a term that is loosely employed as a synonym for "true to life," but in literary history it denotes a style of writing that developed in the mid-nineteenth century, first in the novels of such masters as Dickens, Flaubert, and Tolstoy, and later in the dramas of Ibsen and Chekhov. Many of the aspects of dramatic realism have to do with staging and acting. The box set, with its invisible "fourth wall" facing the audience, could, with the added subtleties of artificial lighting, successfully mimic the interior of a typical middle-class home. Realistic prose drama dropped devices like the soliloquy in favor of more natural means of acting such as those championed by Konstantin Stanislavsky (1863–1938). This Russian director worked closely with Anton Chekhov (1860–1904) to perfect a method whereby actors learned to identify with their characters' psychological problems from "inside out." This "method" acting often tries, as is the case in Chekhov's plays and, later, those of Tennessee Williams and Arthur Miller, to develop a play's **subtext,** the crucial issue in the play that no one can bear to address directly. Stanislavsky's theories have influenced several generations of actors and have become standard throughout the world of the theater. Ibsen's plays, which in fact ushered in the modern era of the theater, are often called **problem plays** because they deal with serious, even controversial or taboo issues, in society. Shaw said that Ibsen's great originality as a playwright lay in his ability to shock the members of the audience into thinking about their own lives. As the barriers of censorship have fallen over the years, the capacity of the theatre to shock has perhaps been diminished, but writers still find it a forum admirably suited for debating the controversial issues which divide society.

American and world drama in this century has gone far beyond realism to experiment with the dream-like atmosphere of **expressionism** (which, like the invisible walls in Miller's *Death of a Salesman*, employs distorted sets to mirror the troubled, perhaps even unbalanced, psyches of the play's characters) or **theater of the absurd,** which depicts a world without meaning in which everything seems ridiculous. Nevertheless, realism is still the dominant style of today's theatre, even if our definition of it has to be modified to take into account plays as diverse as *The Glass Menagerie, Death of a Salesman,* and *Fences.*

Film Versions: A Note

Nothing can equal the experience of an actual stage production, but the many fine film versions of the plays in this anthology offer instructors and students the opportunity, in some cases, to explore two or three different cinematic approaches to the same material. I regularly teach a course in drama and film, and I have found that the differences between print and film versions of plays offer students many challenging topics for discussion, analysis, and writing. Of course, the two media differ radically; in some cases noted below, the film versions, especially those from past decades, badly compromise the original plays. To cite one notorious instance regarding a play not in this anthology, Elia Kazan's celebrated film of Tennessee Williams's *A Streetcar Named Desire,* so wonderful in its sets, direction, and the performances of Marlon Brando and Vivien Leigh, tampers with the play's ending (on orders from the Hollywood Production Code office) to give the impression that Stella will take her child and leave Stanley. Williams himself wrote the screenplay, and he was aware of, if not exactly happy with, the moral standards of the times.

The late O. B. Hardison, director of the Folger Shakespeare Library, once observed two important differences between plays and films. The first is that attending a play is a social function; the audience members and the performers are aware of one another's presence, and laughter in the wrong place can signal the beginning of a disaster. But film is largely a private experience; it was with good reason that one film critic titled a collection of her reviews *A Year in the Dark.* The other chief difference, Hardison notes, is that drama is a realistic medium, whereas film is surrealistic. Watching a play, we see real persons who have a physical reality, and we see them from a uniform perspective. But film has conditioned us to its own complex vocabulary of close-ups, jump cuts, and panoramas, and we view the action from a variety of perspectives. These differences, as fundamental as they seem, are rarely noted by students (unless they have taken a film course) until they are pointed out. Still, film versions provide us with a wonderful time capsule in which many treasures of drama's past have been preserved. A reasoned list of some of these, most of them available on video, follows.

Oedipuſ the King

Tyrone Guthrie's 1957 version, *Oedipus Rex*, is a filmed record of his famous Statford, Ontario, production and retains the masks and choral movements of ancient Greek tragedy. Guthrie uses the William Butler Yeats translation, which sacrifices literal fidelity to poetic grandeur. Douglas Campbell and Eleanor Stuart are impressive as Oedipus and Jocasta, and the messenger is played by Douglas Rain, the voice of the HAL computer in *2001: A Space Odyssey*. The youthful William Shatner, hidden behind a mask, is a member of the chorus. Philip Savile's 1968 version, starring Christopher Plummer, is also worthwhile; this version opens up the play with scenes beautifully photographed in ancient settings. Orson Welles's performance as Tiresias is particularly striking, though some may protest at actually having to *watch* Oedipus blind himself while listening to the messenger's voiceover narration.

The Tragedy of Othello, the Moor of Venice

Othello has proved one of Shakespeare's most popular plays on film. Orson Welles's 1952 version, thought lost for many years, was lovingly restored by his daughter Rebecca Welles and features a remastered soundtrack that remedies most of the original complaints about the poor quality of sound in the film. A fascinating film-noir study in Shakespeare, it features a bravura performance by Welles and an affecting one by Suzanne Cloutier as Desdemona. Less successful is Laurence Olivier's 1966 version, essentially a filmed version of his acclaimed Royal Shakespeare Company production. Olivier's controversial performance, which mimics West Indian speech patterns, and that of Maggie Smith as Desdemona are worth seeing, but Olivier's stage make-up, unconvincing in film closeups, and minimal production values mar the effort. The 1980 version starring Anthony Hopkins as Othello and Bob Hoskins as Iago features interesting performances from the principals, despite Hopkins's distracting hairpiece. This uncut version was part of the PBS Shakespeare series and is widely available in libraries. The 1995 film, directed by Oliver Parker, has excellent performances by Laurence Fishburne and Kenneth Branagh and a sumptuous, erotic style. Contemporary students will probably find it the most satisfying of the four.

A Doll House

For some inexplicable reason *A Doll's House*, as it is titled in both films, was made into two films in the same year, 1973. Patrick Garland's version stars Clair Bloom as Nora and Anthony Hopkins as Torvald. Sir Ralph Richardson essays the role of Dr. Rank, and the reliable Denholm Elliott plays Krogstad. Joseph Losey's version features Jane Fonda as an energetic (and very young) Nora, David Warner as Torvald, and Trevor Howard as Dr. Rank. Most critics felt that the Losey version, which includes actual scenes which Ibsen only hints at, tried too obviously to make the play relevant to contemporary audiences.

The Glass Menagerie

The 1950 version, directed by Irving Rapper, has the advantage of Gertrude Lawrence, Arthur Kennedy, and Jane Wyman in the roles of the Wingfield family, but Kirk Douglas seems oddly out of place as Jim O'Connor. The film concludes with an absurd final shot of Amanda and Laura gleefully waving as a new gentleman caller approaches their door. The 1973 version, with Katharine Hepburn and Sam Waterston, surmounts the obvious problem of Hepburn, a New Englander if ever there was one, seeming plausible as a faded southern belle. In 1987 Paul Newman directed a well-received version with Joanne Woodward and John Malkovich in the leads.

Death of a Salesman

Miller was not pleased with the 1951 film, in which Fredric March overacted badly as Willy Loman. Still, Mildred Dunnock, Kevin McCarthy, and Cameron Mitchell provided excellent support. Volker Schlöndorff's 1985 version has been widely acclaimed, though some viewers have found Dustin Hoffman ill-suited to the role that Miller wrote with the large-boned Lee J. Cobb in mind. John Malkovich and Kate Reid are very good, and Schlöndorff's impressionistic set designs and seamless handling of flashbacks are very impressive. A videotape of the final performance of the award-winning 1999 Broadway revival, starring Brian Dennehy and Elizabeth Franz, aired on Showtime in 2000. Dennehy brought a magnitude to the role of Willy Loman that many critics found impressive.

Writing About Literature

First Considerations

You are in your first college-level literature class and you have probably already completed a composition course in which you used different organizational schemes—example and illustration, comparison and contrast, cause and effect—in writing 500-word essays that were largely drawn from your own personal experiences. When your first effort was returned by your instructor with a bewildering array of correction symbols and a grade that was lower than any you had ever received for your writing, you were at first discouraged. But then you noticed your classmates also shaking their heads in dismay, and you realized that there were certain skills you would have to learn if you were ever going to get out of English Composition I. You corrected your spelling errors, matched your instructor's grading symbols to those in your handbook, revised mistakes in usage, punctuation, and grammar, and polished your first draft and handed it in again. This time, when it was returned, you were pleased to find fewer correction marks and a couple of encouraging bits of praise in your margins. If you weren't exactly assured that you had permanently mastered every fine point of composition, at least you now had some hope that, with practice, hard work, and careful application of the skills you were learning, your writing would improve and the improvement would be rewarded.

Everyone has been there. Even your instructor was once a student in a freshman writing class, and very few instructors are candid enough to have preserved their own early writing efforts to display to their students. But the problem is no longer your instructor's. She has survived the process to acquire an advanced degree, and her job now is teach you the writing skills that she has acquired. You have some confidence in your own ability, but you also have begun to suspect that writing about literature is quite a bit more demanding than writing about your own life. An introduction to literature course places equal weight on your demonstrated skills as a writer and on your ability to go beyond what you have discussed in the classroom to formulate critical responses to the works that you have read. You may have written thesis papers and completed research projects that you were assigned in high school, but you still do not feel entirely confident about your ability to write about literature. You enjoy reading stories, poems, and plays, but you may find expressing your thoughts about their meaning or their literary merit intimidating. With these thoughts in mind, here are a few general strategies that may help you to write successful critical papers.

Topic into Thesis

Writing assignments differ greatly, and your instructions may range from general *(Discuss the roles of three minor characters in any of the plays we have read.)* to very specific *(Contrast, in at least 500 words, the major differences in the plot, characterization, and setting between Joyce Carol Oates's short story "Where Are You Going, Where Have You Been?" and Joyce Chopra's* Smooth Talk, *the 1985 film version of the story.)* In some cases, especially in essay-type examinations, your instructor may give the whole class the same topic; in others, you may be allowed considerable freedom in selecting one. Length requirements may range from a single paragraph to the standard 500-word thesis (in some cases written during a single class period) to a full-scale research paper of three or four times that length. The assignment will probably require that you support your assertions with quotes from the story, poem, or play; or it may require that you add further supporting evidence from secondary critical sources. There is no way to predict the precise kinds of papers you may have to write in a literature course; however, there are a few simple guidelines to remember that may help you make the prewriting process easier.

Consider a typical assignment for an essay on poetry: *Discuss any three poems in our textbook which share a similar theme.* Although this topic allows you some latitude in selecting the poems you wish to write about, paradoxically, it is just this type of assignment which may cause you the most distress. Why is this so? Simply because there are over three hundred poems in this book, and it is usually impossible for the typical class to cover more than a fraction of that number in the time allotted during the semester to the study of poetry. Before despairing, though, consider the different ways the topic could be limited. Instead of "three poems" you might narrow the field by selecting a more specific group, for example, "three ballads," "three war poems," or "three poems by contemporary African-American poets." Suppose you settle on a group that is limited, yet still allows some selection. Choosing "three sonnets by Shakespeare" would allow you to pick from a total of six sonnets included here. In the same way, the second half of the assignment—to find three sonnets with a similar theme—can be limited in various ways. After reading the sonnets, you might observe that sonnets 18, 20, and 30 deal with friendship; after further consideration you might decide that sonnet 116, because it deals with a "marriage of true minds," is also about a type of friendship. Reading the same group of sonnets a second time, you might be struck by how sonnets 18, 73, and 130 deal with physical beauty and its loss. Or, a third time, you might notice that sonnets 29, 30, and 73 all possess a depressed tone that sometimes verges on self-pity. After weighing your options and deciding which three sonnets you feel most comfortable discussing, you might formulate a thesis sentence: "In three of his sonnets, Shakespeare stresses that ideal love should be based on more than mere physical beauty." Always keep in mind that the process of choosing, limiting, and developing a topic and thesis sentence should follow the same steps that you practiced in earlier composition courses. To aid you in locating stories, poems, and plays that share similarities, the appendix at the end of this book groups works thematically.

What is next? A certain amount of informal preparation is always useful: It may be helpful to brainstorm by taking notes on random ideas and refining those ideas further through discussing them with your peers and instructor. Many composition and introduction to literature courses now include group discussion and peer review of rough drafts as part of the writing process. Even if your class does not use formal group discussion as part of its prewriting activities, there is still nothing to prevent you from talking over your ideas with your classmates or scheduling a conference with your instructor. The conference, especially, is a good idea because it allows you to get a clearer sense of what is expected from you. In many cases, after a conference with your instructor, you may discover that you could have limited your topic even further or that you could have selected other more pertinent examples to support your thesis.

Explication, Analysis, Reviewing

In general, writing assignments on literature fall into three broad categories: explication, analysis, and reviewing. Explication, which literally means "an unfolding" and is also known as "close reading," is a painstaking analysis of the details of a piece of writing. Because of its extremely limited focus—only on the specific words that the author uses—explication is a consistent favorite for writing assignments on individual poems. In such assignments, the writer attempts to discuss every possible nuance of meaning that a poet has employed. The most useful aid to explication is the dictionary; a full-scale assignment of this type may even involve using the multivolume *Oxford English Dictionary* to demonstrate how a word in a poem may have once possessed a meaning different from its present one or to support your contention that a phrase may have several possible meanings. Explication assignments are also possible in writing about fiction and drama. You might be expected to focus closely on a single short passage from a story, for example, explicating the passages describing Arnold Friend in Joyce Carol Oates's "Where Are You Going, Where Have You Been?"; or you might be limited to one scene from a play, being asked to discuss how Othello's speeches in Act I, Scene 3, reveal both his strengths of character and the weaknesses that will prove his undoing. Many useful critical sources are available to support assignments of this type, and some of them are mentioned later in the section on research methods.

Analysis uses the same general techniques of explication, that is, the use of specific details from the text to support your statements. But where explication attempts to exhaust the widest possible range of meanings, analysis is more selective in its focus, requiring that you examine how a single element—a theme, a technique, a structural device—functions in a single work or in a related group of works. Instead of being assigned to explicate Walt Whitman's "Crossing Brooklyn Ferry" (a formidable task given its length), you might be asked to analyze only the poet's use of various schemes of repetition or to examine his imagery or to focus exclusively on the structure of his free verse. Analysis assignments often take the form of comparison-contrast essays *(Compare and contrast the motivations and actions of the female protagonists of "Eveline" and "Where Are You Going, Where Have You Been?")* or essays which combine definition with example-illustration *(Define the ballad and discuss ballads written by three poets of this century, showing their links to the tradition of this type of poem.)* In the case of these examples, general reference books like William Harmon and C. Hugh Holman's *A Handbook to Literature* or the exhaustive *The New Princeton Encyclopedia of Poetry and Poetics* will help you to establish your definitions and an overall context for your examples.

The third category, reviewing, is less common in introductory literature courses. A review is a first-hand reaction to a performance or a publication and combines literary analysis with the techniques of journalism. A review of a play or film would evaluate the theatrical elements—acting, direction, sets, etc.—of the performance. Reviews are largely descriptive reporting, but they should also provide evaluation and recommendation. Many of the stories and plays in this volume have been filmed, and you could be asked to discuss how one of them has been adapted for a different medium. Even a local production of a play that you are reading in class is a possibility, and you might find yourself jotting down notes on how the quiet young woman who sits beside you in chemistry lab has transformed herself into the vibrant role of Ibsen's Nora. It is even possible that you might find yourself reviewing a public reading given by a poet or fiction writer whose works you first encountered in this book, and you may find yourself commenting on the distance between the image that the writer projects in the poems or stories and his or her actual "stage presence" as a performer. On the purely literary side, book reviews of new collections of stories and poems regularly appear in periodicals like the *Hudson Review* or the literary sections of major newspapers (the *New York Times Book Review*, published as a separate section of the Sunday *Times*, is the most comprehensive of these), and it is simple enough to find many excellent models should you be assigned to write a paper of this type.

One last word of warning: Note that nowhere above are primarily biographical essays about authors listed as possible writing assignments. Research assignments may ask you to discuss how the particular circumstances of a writer's life may have influenced his or her works, but for the most part biographical information should reside in the background, not the foreground, of literary analysis. An explication of a single poem that begins "Richard Wilbur was born in 1921 in New York City . . ." gives the erroneous impression that you are writing about the poet's life instead of about his work. Try to find a more direct (and original) way of opening your paper.

Critical Approaches

Although most instructors of introduction to literature classes stress a formalist approach (or "close reading") to literary works, other instructors may lecture from a distinct critical perspective and ask their students to employ these techniques in their writing. You might be encouraged to apply a certain kind of critical strategy—feminist criticism or a type of historical approach—to the works you have studied. An instructor might stress that you should emphasize the socioeconomic situation and concerns of a fiction writer and his characters. Or you may be asked to explore how female poets employ visual images that differ from those used by men. The appendix to this book, *Literature: Thematic and Critical Approaches*, provides suggestions about how works may be grouped together for analysis using various critical methods. Here you will find some brief notes on six of the most often used areas of literary criticism and some advice on how to use the thematic listings to find stories, poems, and plays that might best profit from analysis that employs a specific critical approach. Applying complicated critical theories to individual works is a demanding assignment, and frequent instructor-student conferences may not just be helpful—they may be essential.

Style and Content

Style is the major stumbling block that many students find in writing an effective piece of literary analysis. They may be aware that their vocabulary and sentence structure are less sophisticated than those found in the primary and secondary materials being discussed, and thus they sometimes try to overcompensate by adopting, usually without much success, the language of professional critics. This practice can result in garbled sentence and jargon-filled writing. It is much better to write simple, direct sentences, avoiding slang and contractions and using only words with which you are familiar.

Writing in a style with which you are comfortable allows you to make clear transitions between your own writing and the sources that you are citing for supporting evidence. In introducing a quote from a critic, use a phrase like "As [the critic's name] notes in his essay on . . ." to guide the reader from your own style into one that is very different. Never include a statement from a critical work that you do not understand yourself, and do not hesitate to go on for a sentence or two after a supporting quote to explain it in your own words. Remember that literary criticism has its own technical vocabulary and that many of these literary terms are discussed elsewhere in this book. Proper terminology should be used instead of homemade substitutes. Thus, to talk about the "high-point of the story-line" instead of "the climax of the plot" or the "style of the rhythm and rhyme" instead of "the formal strategies of the poem" is to invite an unfavorable response.

As far as the content of your paper is concerned, try to avoid eccentric personal responses for which you can find no critical support. This rule holds for all types of literature but is especially true if you are writing about poetry. Because poetry compresses language and detail, you may have to fill in more than a few blanks spaces to make sense of a poem. Good poems often *suggest* information instead of explicitly stating it; the shorter the poem, the more that may be suggested. If you do not begin by determining a poem's dramatic situation—the basic *who, what, where,* and *when* of a poem—you will not have established the basis on which your subsequent remarks must be anchored. It is possible for a student to go far astray on a poem as simple as A. E. Housman's "Eight O'Clock" because he or she failed to notice the poem's most important detail, that the only character in it has a *noose* around his neck.

In writing about other genres, you may have a brilliant intuition that Emily Grierson's servant Tobe is the real murderer of Homer Barron in Faulkner's "A Rose for Emily," but you may encounter difficulty in finding support for these conclusions in either the text or in the work of critics. Also, do not try, unless you are specifically asked to take a biographical approach, to make close connections between an author's work and the events of his or her life; literature and autobiography are not identical. Some perfectly decent people (Robert Browning is one example) have relished creating characters who are masterpieces of madness or evil, and some perfectly awful people have created beautiful works of literature. It may be the professional biographer's job to judge literary merit on the basis of what he or she perceives as the moral virtues or lack thereof of a writer, but unless you are specifically asked to take a biographical approach, you should probably limit your remarks to the text that you are analyzing.

Writing About Fiction

As mentioned previously, an explication assignment on a single short story demands close attention to detail because it focuses on the subtleties of a writer's language. "Close reading" means exactly that: You should carefully weigh every word in the passage you are explicating. Typically, an explication assignment might ask you to look carefully at a key section of a short story, explaining how it contains some element upon which the whole story hinges and without which it could not succeed. Suppose, for example, that you are asked to explicate the opening paragraph of Cheever's "Reunion" and are explicitly requested to explain what the paragraph conveys beyond obvious expository information. After poring over the paragraph several times, you might decide that it contains ample foreshadowing of the disastrous events that are about to occur. In particular you might cite such phrases as "his secretary wrote to say" or "my mother divorced him" as Cheever's way of dropping hints about the father's unstable personality. Then you might go on to mention Charlie's forebodings of his own "doom," all leading up to the aroma of prelunch cocktails that Charlie notices when he and his father embrace. Any explication demands that you quote extensively from the text, explaining why certain choices of words and details are important and speculating about why the writer made these choices.

A typical analysis assignment in short fiction might ask you to explain what a "rites of passage" story is and demonstrate that "Reunion" has most of the characteristics of the type. Here you might want to first define the initiation story, using your lecture notes, general literary reference books, and your familiarity with other stories from popular sources like fairy tales or motion pictures. After demonstrating that this type of story is indeed well-established and having described its chief characteristics, you might then focus on such matters in "Reunion" as Charlie's age, his naïve expectations, his disillusioning experience, and his eventual "passage" out of his father's life at the end of the story. A slightly more complicated analysis assignment might involve writing a comparison and contrast paper about two texts or performing a comparative analysis of more than two. Generally, comparison seeks out common ground between two subjects whereas contrast finds differences; most papers of this type will do both, first pointing out the similarities before going on to demonstrate how each story represents a variation on the theme. Comparison-contrast essays may examine a single story, analyzing two characters' approaches to a similar situation, or even a single character's "before and after" view of another character or event. Or these essays may compare and contrast two or more works that have common threads. If you are examining a single author in depth, you might be required to locate other stories which deal with similar themes. Because Cheever writes extensively about alcoholism, family tensions, and divorce, you might choose several of his stories that reflect the same basic themes as "Reunion." Even more demanding might be a topic asking you to find stories (or even poems or plays) by other authors to compare or contrast. Among the stories in this book, there are several examples of initiation stories and others which deal with tensions between parents and children. Assignments in comparative analysis require careful selection and planning, and it is essential to find significant examples of both similarities and differences to support your thesis.

Writing About Poetry

Because explication of a poem involves careful close reading on a line-by-line basis, an assignment of this type will usually deal with a relatively short poem or a passage from a longer one. Some poems yield most of their meaning on a single reading; others, however, may contain complexities and nuances that deserve a careful inspection of how the poet utilizes all of the resources at his or her command. A typical explication examines both form and content. Because assignments in analysis usually involve many of the same techniques as explication, we will look at explication more closely. Poetry explications usually require much more familiarity with the technical details of poems than do those about fiction and drama, so following is a checklist of questions that you might ask before explicating a poem. The answers apply to a poem from this book, Edwin Arlington Robinson's sonnet "Firelight."

Form

1. How many lines does the poem contain? How are they arranged into stanzas? Is either the whole poem or the stanza an example of a traditional poetic form?

> "Firelight" is an Italian sonnet. It is divided into two stanzas, an octave and sestet, and there is a shift, or what is known in sonnets as a "turn" or volta, at the beginning of line nine, though here there is no single word that signals the shift.

2. Is there anything worth noting in the visual arrangement of the poem—indentation, spacing, etc. Are capitalization and punctuation unusual?

> Capitalization and punctuation are standard in the poem, and Robinson follows the traditional practice of capitalizing the first word of each line.

3. What meter, if any, is the poem written in? Does the poet use any notable examples of substitution in the meter? Are the lines primarily end-stopped or enjambed?

> The meter is fairly regular iambic pentameter ("Her thoughts / a mo / ment since / of one / who shines") with occasional substitution of trochees ("Wiser / for si / lence") and spondees ("their joy / recalls / No snake, || / no sword").
> Enjambment, found at the ends of lines two, five, six, seven, nine, ten, twelve, and thirteen, has the effect of masking the regular meter and rhymes and enforcing a conversational tone, an effect that is assisted by the caesurae in lines six, seven,

nine, and (most importantly) fourteen. The caesura in
this last line calls attention to "Apart," which
ironically contrasts with the poem's opening phrase:
"Ten years together."

4. What is the rhyme scheme, if any, of the poem? What types of rhyme
are used?

The rhyme scheme of this poem is abbaabba cdecde.
Robinson uses exact masculine rhyme, with the rhyming
sounds falling on single stressed syllables; the only
possible exception is "intervals," where the meter
forces a secondary stress on the third syllable.

5. Are significant sound patterns evident? Is there any repetition of
whole lines, phrases, or words?

Alliteration is present in "firelight" and
"four" in line three and "wan" and "one" in line
eleven, and there are several instances of assonance
("Wiser for silence"; "endowed / And bowered") and
consonance ("Serenely and perennially endowed"; the
wan face of one somewhere alone"). However, these
sound patterns do not call excessive attention to
themselves and depart from the poem's relaxed, conversational sound. "Firelight" contains no prominent
use of repetition, with the possible exception of the
pronoun "they" and its variant forms "their" and
"them" and the related use of the third person singular pronouns "he" and "she" in the last five lines of
the poem. This pronoun usage, confusing at first
glance, indirectly carries the poem's theme of the
separateness of the lovers' thoughts. The only notable instance of parallel phrasing occurs in line
seven with "No snake, no sword."

Content

1. To what genre (lyric, narrative, dramatic) does the poem belong?
Does it contain elements of more than one genre?

"Firelight" is a short narrative poem. Even
though it has little plot in the conventional sense,
it contains two characters in a specific setting who
perform actions that give the reader insight into the
true nature of their relationship. The sonnet form
has traditionally been used for lyric poetry.

2. Who is the persona of the poem? Is there an auditor? If so, who?
What is the relationship between persona and auditor? Does the poem
have a specific setting? If so, where and when is it taking place? Is there
any action that has taken place before the poem opens? What actions
take place during the poem?

The persona here is a third-person omniscient
narrator such as might be encountered in a short
story; the narrator has the ability to read "Her
thoughts a moment since" and directly comments that
the couple is "Wiser for silence." The unnamed characters in the poem are a man and woman who have been
married for ten years. The poem is set in their home,
apparently in a comfortable room with a fireplace
where they are spending a quiet evening together.
Neither character speaks during the poem; the only
action is their looking at "each other's eyes are in-
tervals/Of gratefulness." Much of the poem's ironic
meaning hinges on the couple's silence: "what neither
says aloud."

3. Does the poem contain any difficulties with grammar or syntax?
What individual words or phrases are striking because of their denotation or connotation?

The syntax of "Firelight" is straightforward and
contains no inversions or ellipses. The poem's sentence structure is deceptively simple. The first four
lines make up a single sentence with one main clause;
the second four lines also make up a single sentence,
this time with two main clauses; the final six lines
also make up a single sentence, broken into two equal
parts by the semicolon, and consisting of both main

and dependent clauses. The poem's vocabulary is not
unusual, though "obliteration" (literally an <u>erasure</u>)
seems at first a curious choice to describe the effects of love. One should note the allusion implied
by "bowered," "snake," and "sword" in the octave and
the rather complicated use of the subjunctive "were"
in lines nine, ten, and twelve. Again, this slight
alteration in grammar bears indirectly on the theme
of the poem. "Yet" in the first line provides an interesting touch since it injects a slight negative
note into the picture of marital bliss.

4. Does the poem use any figures of speech? If so, how do they add to
the overall meaning? Is the action of the poem to be taken literally, symbolically, or both ways?

"Firelight" uses several figures of speech.
"Cloud" is a commonly employed metaphor for "foreboding." "Firelight" and "four walls" are a metonymy and
synecdoche, respectively, for the couple's comfortable home. The allusion to the "snake" and "sword"
direct the reader to the Garden of Eden story. "Wiser
for silence" is a slight paradox. "The graven tale of
lines / on the wan face" is an implied metaphor which
compares the lines on a person's face to the written
("graven") story of her life. To say that a person
"shines" instead of "excels" is another familiar
metaphor. "Firelight" is to be understood primarily
on the literal level. The characters are symbolic
only in that the man and woman are perhaps representative of many married couples, who outwardly express
happiness yet inwardly carry regrets and fantasies
from past relationships.

5. Is the title of the poem appropriate? What are its subject, tone of
voice, and theme? Is the theme stated or implied?

"Firelight" is a good title since it carries
both the connotation of domestic tranquility and a
hint of danger. "To bring to the light" means to re-

veal the truth, and the narrator in this poem does
this. Robinson's attitude toward the couple is
ironic. On the surface they seem to be the picture of
ideal happiness, but Robinson reveals that this happiness has been purchased, in the man's case, at the
expense of an earlier lover and, in the woman's, by
settling for someone who has achieved less than another man for whom she apparently had unrequited
love. Robinson's ironic view of marital stability is
summed up in the phrase "Wiser for silence." Several
themes are implied: the difference between surface
appearance and deeper insight; the cynical idea that
in love ignorance of what one's partner is thinking
may be the key to bliss; the sense that individual
happiness is not without its costs. All of these are
possible ways to state Robinson's bittersweet theme.

Your instructor may ask you to employ specific strategies in your explication and may require a certain type of organization for the paper. In
writing the body of the explication you will probably proceed through the
poem from beginning to end, summarizing and paraphrasing some lines
and quoting others fully when you feel an explanation is required. It
should be stressed that there are many ways, in theory, to approach a poem
and that no two explications of the same poem will agree in every detail.

A writing assignment in analysis might examine the way a single element—dramatic situation, meter, form, imagery, one or more figures
of speech, theme—functions in poetry. An analysis would probably require that you write about two or more poems, using the organizational
patterns of comparison-contrast or definition/example-illustration.
Such an assignment might examine two or more related poems by the
same poet, or it might inspect the way that several poets have used a
poetic device or theme. Comparison-contrast essays might explore both
similarities and differences found in two poems. Definition-illustration
papers usually begin with a general discussion of the topic, say, a popular theme like the *carpe diem* motif, and then go on to illustrate how
is may be found in several different poems. Assignments in analysis often lead to longer papers, which may require the use of secondary
sources.

Writing About Drama

A review of a play is an evaluation of an actual performance and will focus less on the text of the play itself (especially if it is a well-known one) than on the actors' performances, the overall direction of the production, and the elements of staging. Because reviews are, first, news stories, basic information about the time and place of production should be given at the beginning of the review. A short summary of the play's plot might follow, and subsequent paragraphs will evaluate the performers and the production. Remember that a review is chiefly a *recommendation*, either positive or negative, to readers. Films of most of the plays in this book are available on videotape, and you might also be asked to review one of these versions, paying attention to the ways in directors have "opened up" the action by utilizing the complex technical resources of motion pictures. Excellent examples of drama and film reviews can be found in almost any major newspaper or in the pages of popular magazines like *Time* or *The New Yorker*.

Explication assignments, like the examples from fiction and poetry given earlier, will probably require that you pay close attention to a selected passage, giving a detailed account of all the fine shadings of language in a scene or perhaps a single speech. Because Shakespeare's poetry is often full of figurative language that may not be fully understood until it has been subjected to explication, close reading of one of the monologues or soliloquies in *Othello* would be a likely choice for this type of writing assignment. Or you might be asked to explicate selected passages for a common thread of imagery, for example, identifying the various kinds of birds to which the condescending Helmer metaphorically compares his wife Nora throughout *A Doll House*.

Analysis assignments typically hinge on only one of the elements of the play like plot or characterization, or on a concept set forth by a critic. For example, you might be asked to explain Aristotle's statements about reversal and recognition and then apply his terminology to a modern play like *The Glass Menagerie*. Here you would attempt to locate relevant passages from the play to support Aristotle's contentions about the importance of these reversals in the best plots. Or you might be asked to provide a summary of his comments about the tragic hero and then apply this definition to a character like Othello. Again, comparison and contrast schemes are useful. You might be asked to contrast two or more characters in a single play (Nora and Mrs. Linde as examples of two kinds of feminine strength) or to compare characters in two different plays (Oedipus and Othello as undeserving victims of fate).

The Process of Research: The Library and the Internet

Research is a time-consuming and sometimes frustrating process, but a few general principles may help you to streamline it. First, bear in mind that about ninety percent of the time you spend on assembling research materials will take place in one section of the library, the reference room, and that a large amount of information about where to find certain materials is now available on computer databases. If you rush off to consult a book on the fifth-floor shelves every time you locate a mention of something that is potentially useful to you, you may gain more expertise in operating an elevator than in conducting effective research. Thus, use the reference room to assemble the "shopping list" of items you will have to find in other parts of the library. Also, remember that the CD-ROM reader and the online index have greatly enhanced the mechanics of research. It may be frustrating to learn that an article you spotted in a musty index and found, after a long search, in a bound volume of a journal could have been downloaded and printed out in seconds from a CD-ROM or electronic database.

Most contemporary students have literally grown up writing with computers and are familiar with the Internet. Still, a few words about the use of the Internet for online research may be helpful. In recent years, the Internet has facilitated the chores of research, and many online databases, reference works, and periodicals may be quickly located using search engines like Yahoo *(www.yahoo.com)* and Google *(www.google.com)*. The Internet also holds a wealth of information in the form of individual websites devoted to authors, many of which are run by universities or private organizations. Navigating the Internet can be a forbidding task, and a book like Lester Faigley's *The Longman Guide to the Web* is an invaluable traveler's companion. Students should be aware, however, that websites vary widely in quality. Some are legitimate sources displaying sound scholarship; others are little more than "fan pages" that may contain erroneous or misleading information. Online information, like any other kind of research material, should be carefully evaluated before using it.

Careful documentation of your sources is essential; if you use any material other than what is termed "common knowledge" you must cite it in your paper. Common knowledge includes biographical information, an author's publications, prizes and awards received, and other information that can be found in more than one reference book. Anything else—direct quotes or material you have put in your own words by paraphrasing—requires both a parenthetical citation in the body of your paper and an entry on your works cited pages.

The first step in successful research is very simple: Read the assigned text before looking for secondary sources. After you have read the story, poem, or play that you have been assigned, you may have already begun to formulate a workable thesis sentence. If you have done this before beginning your research, you will eliminate any number of missteps and repetitions. Next, perform a subject search for books that will be useful to you. If, for example, you are writing on one of Keats's odes, a subject search may reveal one or more books devoted solely to this single type of poem. Computerized library catalogs are set up in different configurations, but many of them allow multiple "keyword" searches; a command like FIND KEATS AND ODE might automatically cross-reference all books in the library that mention both subjects. If you are unfamiliar with your terminology and do not know, for example, how an ode differs from other kinds of poems, you should consult a reference book containing a discussion of literary terms. After you have located books and reference sources that will be of use, check the journals that publish literary criticism. The standard index for these is the *MLA International Bibliography*, which is available both in bound volumes and in CD-ROM and online versions. A reference librarian may also direct you to other indexes such as the *Literary Criticism Index* and the *Essay and General Literature Index*. It is a good idea to check indexes like these early in your research. No single college library carries all of the journals listed in the *MLA International Bibliography*, and you may discover that getting a reprint through interlibrary services can take a week or more.

Once you have located and assembled your sources, you can decide which of them will be most valuable to you. Again, if you have already formulated your thesis and perhaps completed a tentative outline as well, you can move more swiftly. One blessed addition to every library is the copying machine, which removes the tedious chore of taking notes by hand on 3″ × 5″ cards. Note cards may still be useful if you want to try different arrangements of your material, but most students have happily discarded them as relics of the distant past.

It is impossible to guess what research materials will be available in any given library, but most college libraries contain many different kinds of indexes and reference books for literary research. If you are writing about a living writer, particularly recommended are three popular reference sets published by Gale Research: *Dictionary of Literary Biography (DLB)*, *Contemporary Authors (CA)*, and *Contemporary Literary Criticism (CLC)*. Both of the latter two reference works are also available in editions which cover the nineteenth and twentieth centuries. These will provide you both with useful overviews of careers and with generous samples of criticism about the authors. *DLB* and *CA* articles also contain extensive bibliographies of other relevant sources; *CLC* contains reprints of book reviews and relevant passages from critical works. Similar to these reference works are those in the *Critical Survey* series from Magill Publishers, multivolume sets which focus on short and long fiction, poetry, drama, and film. Another reliable source of information on individual writers can be found in several series of critical books published by Twayne Publishers, which can be located in a subject search.

For locating explications, several indexes are available, including *Poetry Explication: A Checklist of Interpretations Since 1925 of British and American Poems Past and Present* and *The Explicator Cyclopedia*, which reprints explications originally appearing in the periodical of the same name. *Poetry Criticism* and *Short Story Criticism* are multivolume reference works which reprint excerpts from critical essays and books. There are several popular indexes of book reviews; one of these, the annual *Book Review Digest* reprints brief passages from the most representative reviews. Two reference sources providing, respectively, examples of professional drama and film reviews are *The New York Times Theater Reviews, 1920–1970* (and subsequent volumes) and *The New York*

Times Film Reviews. Popular magazines containing book, drama, and film reviews (and occasionally poetry reviews as well) include *Time*, *Newsweek*, and *The New Yorker*, and these reviews are indexed in the *Readers' Guide to Periodical Literature*, more recent volumes of which are available online. Also, yearbooks like *Theatre World* or the *Dictionary of Literary Biography Yearbook* provide a wealth of information about the literary activities of a given year.

Quotation and Citation

First, a warning about plagiarism. Few students knowingly plagiarize, and those who do usually are not successful at it. An instructor who has read four or five weak papers from a student is likely to be suspicious if the same student suddenly begins to sound like an officer of the Modern Language Association, writing, with no citations, about "paradigms" or "*différance*" in the "*texte.*" A definition of "common knowledge," the kind of information that does not require a citation, is given above. Otherwise, any *opinion* about a writer and his or her work must be followed by a citation indicating its source. If the opinion is directly quoted, paraphrased, or even summarized in passing, then you should still include a citation. Doing less than this is to commit an act of plagiarism, for which the penalties are usually severe. Internet materials, which are so easily cut and pasted into a manuscript, provide an easy temptation but are immediately noticeable. Nothing is easier to spot in a paper than an uncited "lift" from a source; in most cases the vocabulary and sentence structure will be radically different from the rest of the paper.

You should always support the general statements you make about a story, poem, or play by quoting directly from the text or, if required, by using secondary sources for additional critical opinion. The *MLA Handbook for Writers of Research Papers* (5th ed), which is found in the reference section of almost any library, contains standard formats for bibliographies and manuscripts; indeed, most of the writing handbooks used in college composition courses follow MLA style guidelines. However, if you have doubts or if you have not been directed to use a certain format, ask your instructor which one he or she prefers.

The type of parenthetical citation used in MLA-style format to indicate the source of quotations is simple to learn and dispenses with such

tedious and repetitive chores as footnotes and endnotes. In using parenthetical citations remember that your goal is to direct your reader from
the quoted passage in the paper to the corresponding entry on your
works cited pages and from there, if necessary, to the book or periodical
from which the quote was taken. A good parenthetical citation gives
only the *minimal* information needed to accomplish this task. Here are a
few typical examples from student papers on fiction, poetry, and drama.
The first discusses Cheever's "Reunion":

> Cheever moves very quickly to indicate that the
> "Reunion" may well be memorable but will not be
> happy. As soon as father and son enter the first
> restaurant and are seated, Charlie's father begins to
> act strangely: "We sat down, and my father hailed the
> waiter in a loud voice. 'Kellner!' he shouted.
> 'Garcon! Cameriere! You!' His boisterousness in the
> empty restaurant seemed out of place" (518).

Here you should note a couple of conventions of writing about fiction
and literature in general. One is that the present tense is used in speaking of the events of the story; in general, use the present tense throughout your critical writing, except when you are giving biographical or historical information. Second, note the use of single and double quotation
marks. Double quotes from the story are changed to single quotes here
because they appear within the writer's own quotation marks. The parenthetical citation lists only a page number, for earlier in this paper the
writer has mentioned Cheever by name and the context makes it clear
that the quotation comes from the story. Only one work by Cheever appears among the works cited entries. If several works by Cheever had
been listed there, the parenthetical citation would clarify which one was
being referred to by adding a shortened form of the book's title: (*Stories*
518). The reader finds the following entry among the sources:

> Cheever, John. The Stories of John Cheever. New York:
> Knopf, 1978.

Similarly, quotes and paraphrases from secondary critical sources
should follow the same rules of common sense:

> Cheever's daughter Susan, in her candid memoir
> of her father, observes that the author's alcoholism
> followed an increasingly destructive pattern:
>> Long before I was even aware that he was
>> alcoholic, there were bottles hidden all
>> over the house, and even outside in the
>> privet hedge and the garden shed. Drink was
>> his crucible, his personal hell. As early
>> as the 1950s [. . .] he spent a lot of en-
>> ergy trying not to drink before 4 p.m., and
>> then before noon, and then before 10 a.m.,
>> and then before breakfast. (43)
> But she goes on to observe that Cheever's drinking
> had not yet affected his skills as a writer.

This quotation is longer than four lines, so it is indented ten spaces. Indented quotes of this type do not require quotation marks. Also note how ellipses in square brackets are used to omit extraneous information. Because the author of the quotation is identified, only the page number is included in the parenthetical citation. The reader knows where to look among the sources:

> Cheever, Susan. <u>Home Before Dark</u>. Boston: Houghton,
>> 1984.

Notice that a paraphrase of the same passage requires the citation as well:

> Cheever's daughter Susan, in her candid memoir
> of her father, observes that the author's alcoholism
> followed an increasingly destructive pattern. She
> notes that as a child she found bottles hidden in the
> house, in outbuildings, and even in the hedge. She
> recalls that he spent a great deal of energy simply
> not trying to drink before a certain hour, at first
> before 4 p.m. but eventually before breakfast (43).

To simplify parenthetical citations, it is recommended that quotes from secondary sources be introduced, whenever possible, in a manner that identifies the author so that only the page number of the quote is needed inside of the parentheses.

Slightly different conventions govern quotations from poetry. Here are a few examples from papers on Edwin Arlington Robinson's poetry:

> Robinson's insights into character are never
> sharper than in "Miniver Cheevy," a portrait of a
> town drunk who loves "the days of old/When swords
> were bright and steeds were prancing" and dreams in-
> congruously "of Thebes and Camelot,/And Priam's
> neighbors" (347).

Note how only parts of lines are quoted here to support the sentence and how the parts fit smoothly into the writer's sentence structure. In general, bracketed ellipses [. . .] are not necessary at the beginning or end of these quotes since it is clear that they are quoted fragmentarily; they should, however, be used if something is omitted from the middle of a quote ("the days of old/When [. . .] steeds were prancing"). The virgule or slash (/) is used to indicate line breaks; a double slash (//) indicates stanza breaks. Quotes of up to three lines should be treated in this manner. If a quote is longer than three lines, it should be indented ten spaces (with no quotation marks) and printed as it appears in the original poem:

> Robinson opens one of his most effective and
> pitiless character sketches with an unsparing por-
> trait of failure and bitterness:
>> Miniver Cheevy, child of scorn,
>>> Grew lean while he assailed the seasons;
>> He wept that he was ever born,
>>> And he had reasons. (347)

As in the example from the Cheever story, the parenthetical citation here lists only a page number because only one work by Robinson appears in the bibliography. If you are dealing with a classic poem that can be found in many editions (an ode by Keats or a Shakespeare sonnet, for example), the *MLA Handbook* recommends using line numbers instead of page numbers inside the parentheses. This practice should also be followed if you have included a copy of the poem that you are explicating with the paper.

Quoting from a play follows similar procedures. These examples discuss *Othello:*

> In a disarming display of modesty before the
> Venetian senators, Othello states that his military
> background has not prepared him to act as an eloquent
> spokesman in his own defense, readily admitting that
> "little shall I grace my cause/In speaking for my-
> self" (1.3.90-91).

Classic poetic dramas like *Othello* may be cited by act, scene, and line numbers instead of by page numbers. The reader knows that Shakespeare is the author, so the citation here will simply direct him or her to the edition of Shakespeare listed in the works cited pages at the end of the paper. Also note that verse dramas should be quoted in the same manner as poems; quotations of more than three lines should be indented ten spaces. In this paper, a scene involving dialogue is quoted:

> In the climactic scene of <u>Othello</u>, Shakespeare's
> practice of fragmenting his blank verse lines into
> two or more parts emphasizes the violence that is
> about to occur:
> > OTHELLO.   He hath confessed.
> > DESDEMONA. What, my lord?
> > OTHELLO.   That he hath used thee.
> > DESDEMONA.   How?
> >   Unlawfully?
> > OTHELLO.   Ay.
> > DESDEMONA. He will not say so. (5.2.73-75)

If you are quoting from a prose drama, you would cite a page number from the edition of the play which you used:

> In <u>A Doll House</u> Ibsen wants to demonstrate imme-
> diately that Nora and Helmer share almost childlike
> attitudes toward each other. "Is that my little lark
> twittering out there?" is Helmer's initial line in
> the play (43).

Remember that common sense is the best test to apply to any parenthetical citation. Have you given the reader enough information in the citation to locate the source from which the quote was taken?

Sample Works Cited Entries

Here are formats for some of the most commonly accessed types of materials used in literary research. More detailed examples may be found in the *MLA Handbook for Writers of Research Papers*.

BOOK BY A SINGLE AUTHOR

Finch, Annie. The Ghost of Meter: Culture and Prosody
    in American Free Verse. Ann Arbor: U of Michigan
    P, 1993.
Ives, David. All in the Timing: Fourteen Plays. New
    York: Vintage, 1995.
Reynolds, Clay. Monuments. Lubbock: Texas Tech UP,
    2000.
Sanderson, Jim. Semi-Private Rooms. Youngstown: Pig
    Iron, 1994.
Wilbur, Richard. Mayflies. New York: Harcourt, 2000.

BOOK WITH AUTHOR AND EDITOR

Robinson, Edwin Arlington. Edwin Arlington Robinson's
    Letters to Edith Brower. Ed. Richard Cary.
    Cambridge: Harvard UP, 1968.

CASEBOOK OR EDITED COLLECTION OF CRITICAL ESSAYS

Dean, Leonard Fellows, ed. A Casebook on Othello. New
    York: Crowell, 1961.
Snyder, Susan, ed. Othello: Critical Essays. New
    York: Garland, 1988.

INDIVIDUAL SELECTION FROM A CASEBOOK OR EDITED COLLECTION

Urbanski, Marie Mitchell Oleson. "Existential
    Allegory: Joyce Carol Oates's 'Where Are You
    Going, Where Have You Been?'" "Where Are You
    Going, Where Have You Been?": Joyce Carol Oates.
    Ed. Elaine Showalter. New Brunswick: Rutgers UP,
    1994. 75-79.

Woodring, Carl R. "Once More The Windhover." <u>Gerard</u>
<u>Manley Hopkins: The Windhover</u>. Ed. John Pick.
Columbus: Merrill, 1969. 52–56.

STORY, POEM, OR PLAY REPRINTED IN ANTHOLOGY OR TEXTBOOK

Cheever, John. "The Swimmer." <u>The Longman Anthology</u>
<u>of Short Fiction: Stories and Authors in</u>
<u>Context</u>. Ed. Dana Gioia and R. S. Gwynn. New
York: Longman, 2001. 390–99.

Hansberry, Lorraine. <u>A Raisin in the Sun</u>. <u>Black</u>
<u>Theater: A Twentieth-Century Collection of the</u>
<u>Work of Its Best Playwrights</u>. Ed. Lindsay
Patterson. New York: Dodd, 1971. 221–76.

Robinson, Edwin Arlington. "Richard Cory."
<u>Literature: An Introduction to Poetry, Fiction,</u>
<u>and Drama</u>. 7th ed. Ed. X. J. Kennedy and Dana
Gioia. New York: Longman, 1999. 793.

ARTICLE IN REFERENCE BOOK

Johnson, Richard A. "Auden, W. H." <u>Academic American</u>
<u>Encyclopedia (Electronic Edition)</u>. 1993 ed. CD-
ROM. Danbury: Grolier, 1993.

"<u>Othello</u>." <u>The Oxford Companion to English</u>
<u>Literature</u>. Ed. Margaret Drabble. 5th ed. New
York: Oxford UP, 1985.

Seymour-Smith, Martin. "Cheever, John." <u>Who's Who in</u>
<u>Twentieth Century Literature</u>. New York: McGraw,
1976.

ARTICLE, BOOK REVIEW, STORY, OR POEM IN SCHOLARLY JOURNAL

Berry, Edward. "Othello's Alienation." <u>Studies in</u>
<u>English Literature, 1500–1900</u> 30 (1990): 315–33.

Horgan, Paul. "To Meet Mr. Eliot: Three Glimpses."
<u>American Scholar</u> 60 (1991): 407–13.

McDonald, Walter. "Sandstorms." <u>Negative Capability</u>
3.4 (1983): 93.

Read, Arthur M., II. "Robinson's 'The Man Against the
Sky.' " <u>Explicator</u> 26 (1968): 49.

Article, Book Review, Story, or Poem in Magazine

Becker, Alida. Rev. of <u>Morning, Noon, and Night</u>, by
    Sidney Sheldon. <u>New York Times Book Review</u> 15
    Oct. 1995: 20.
Iyer, Pico. "Magic Carpet Ride." Rev. of <u>The English
    Patient</u>, by Michael Ondattje. <u>Time</u> 2 Nov. 1992:
    71. <u>Time Man of the Year</u>. CD-ROM. Compact. 1993.
Jones, Rodney. "TV." <u>Atlantic Monthly</u> Jan. 1993: 52.
Spires, Elizabeth. "One Life, One Art: Elizabeth
    Bishop in Her Letters." Rev. of <u>One Art:
    Letters</u>, by Elizabeth Bishop. <u>New Criterion</u> May
    1994: 18–23.

Interview

Cheever, John. Interview. "John Cheever: The Art of
    Fiction LXII." By Annette Grant. <u>Paris Review</u> 17
    (1976): 39–66.

Review of Play Production

Evans, Everett. "Sturdy Staging of 'Equus' Raises
    Intriguing Issues." <u>Houston Chronicle</u> 19 Jan.
    2001: D1+.

Film, Video, or Audio Recording

Harjo, Joy, and Poetic Justice. <u>The Woman Who Fell
    from the Sky</u>. Audiocassette. Norton, 1994.
<u>Pygmalion</u>. Dir. Anthony Asquith and Leslie Howard.
    Perf. Leslie Howard and Wendy Hiller. Paschal,
    1938.

Online: Article or Review

Wasserstein, Wendy. "A Place They'd Never Been: The
    Theater." <u>Theater Development Fund</u>. 7 June 2000.
    1 Mar. 2001 <http://www.tdf.org/communications/
    wendy.htm>.

ONLINE: AUTHOR OR CRITICAL WEBSITE

"August Wilson." <u>Literature Online</u>. Rev. 12 May 2001.
    28 Feb. 2001 <http://longman.awl.com/kennedy/
    wilson/biography.html>.
"A Page for Edwin." 5 Feb. 1998. 12 Apr. 2001
    <http://www.du.edu/~dokonski/robin.html>.

ONLINE: PLAY PRODUCTION WEBSITE

"Death of a Salesman." 15 Nov. 2000. 12 Jan. 2001
    <http:www.deathofasalesman.com>.

ONLINE: REFERENCE WORK

"Sophocles." <u>Britannica Online</u>. 15 Feb. 2001
    <http://www.britannica.com/bcom/eb/article/0/
    0,5716,118260+1109862,00.html?query=sophocles>.

The Annotated Bibliography

Many instructors consider the research paper a semester-long project
and grade students' intermediate steps in the process—preliminary
research, mastery of MLA-style formats, rough drafts, etc. One of the
most popular types of intermediate assignments is to have students
assemble a preliminary bibliography of different types of research
materials—primary sources by the writer, reference book articles,
book reviews, critical essays on the writer's work, interviews, Internet
websites, and other materials. Although many of these sources may
not actually be used in the works cited section of the final paper, students can gain an overview of an author's career, his or her chief concerns, and the critical reaction to the work by assembling such a bibliography. Brief annotation of the sources, which follows each entry,
ensures that the students have inspected the material to see whether
or not it will be useful in the final paper. Below are the first six entries in a sample annotated bibliography on a fictitious poet, "Marion
Kirstein."

ANNOTATED BIBLIOGRAPHY

Cary, Jason. "Conspiracy Theories in Verse: Marion
     Kirstein on Form, Meter, and Rime." <u>Saturday</u>
     <u>Review</u> 5 May 1973: 14-15.

In this early article/interview, Kirstein argues that prevailing fashions in verse have made it almost impossible for older poets to publish work in many magazines. Kirstein stresses that his own magazine, <u>Inner Vision</u>, remains open to these poets.

Collins, Michael J. "The Poetry of Marion Kirstein."
     <u>World Literature Today</u> 61.1 (1997): 55-58.

A 1500-word overview of Kirstein's career. Collins draws special attention to his "unfashionable" use of traditional forms like the sonnet.

Goodman, Thomas. "Marion Kirstein." <u>American Poets</u>
     <u>Since World War II</u>. <u>Dictionary of Literary</u>
     <u>Biography</u>. Vol. 5. 1980. 294-97.

This critical and biographical essay contains photographs of Kirstein and sample manuscript pages. It pays particular attention to the influence of John Phillips, Kirstein's undergraduate creative writing teacher at Meridian College.

Hooper, Jeremy. "Marion Kirstein." <u>Critical Survey of</u>
     <u>Poetry</u>. 1982. 1167-76.

A 2500-word overview of Kirstein's career. Hooper is more interested in Kirstein's controversial political subject matter than in his poetic practices.

Kaye, Marilyn. Rev. of <u>The Forsaken Cry</u>, by Marion
     Kirstein. <u>New York Times Book Review</u> 22 Mar.
     1984: 24.

A 250-word review of Kirstein's third book of poetry. Kaye praises his formal technique but feels that his political sympathies are out of date.

Kirstein, Marion "Be Still." <u>New Poets of England and America: Second Selection</u>. Ed. Donald Hall and Robert Pack. New York: Meridian, 1962. 149–51.

This 300-line blank verse poem about the death of the poet's father appeared in Kirstein's first collection, *Afterglow*.

Final Considerations

Finally, some basic matters of common sense are worth pondering. Consider the first impression the paper which you are about to turn in will make on your instructor. He or she may teach as many as five composition classes and, with an average classroom load of thirty students writing six to eight essays per class, may have to read, mark, and grade something approaching a half-million words of student writing in a single semester. No instructor, with the clock ticking past midnight and the coffee growing cold, likes trying to read an essay in scrawled handwriting, with pieces of its torn edges, hastily ripped from a spiral notebook, drifting to the carpet. If your instructor does allow handwritten work, try to present a copy that can be read without extensive training in cryptographic analysis; in other words, make sure your writing is legible. But do not go to the opposite extreme and present a masterpiece of computer wizardry, complete with multiple sizes, shapes, and colors of fonts. In a word, plain vanilla is always the safest flavor to choose. Handwritten work should be done on one side of standard-ruled notebook paper, leaving generous margins on both the right-hand side and the bottom of the pages. In most cases, it will be required that your work be word-processed or typed. Your final copy should be double-spaced, using a letter-quality printer set at the highest resolution. Choose a standard typewriter-style font (Courier or Times Roman 12-point type are the most widely used), and do not expect a faint, smeared, draft-quality printout to receive as much attention as a readable manuscript printed on good-quality paper. Do not put your paper in any kind of folder or binder unless you are specifically asked to do so. You may have been given specific instructions about title pages and page numbering, so be sure to follow them.

It goes without saying that you should proofread your final draft carefully, paying particular attention to some of the special problems in writing mechanics (punctuation and verb tenses are two of the most common) that arise in critical papers. And, please, remember two things about the computer: First, a paper that has not been spell-checked is absolute proof of lack of diligence; second, even the most sophisticated spell-checker cannot distinguish between "there" and "their" or "it's" and "its." Errors in proper nouns, such as the names of authors or publishers, also must be checked manually. Writing assignments are graded both for content and for their demonstration that the writer knows the basics of composition. A spelling error on the title page is not the best introduction to the body of your paper, and even the most original insights into a literary work will not receive due credit if the rules of standard English are consistently ignored.

Effective writing requires a long process involving topic-selection, assembly of support, organization, rough drafts, and final adjustments. By the time you have finished printing out your final draft, you may feel that not only have you exhausted the topic, it has exhausted *you*. Still, the most important element that you can bring to any assignment is the simplest one: *care*. May your efforts be rewarded!

Fiction

Nathaniel Hawthorne (1804–1864) was born in Salem, Massachusetts, and could trace his heritage back to the earliest settlers of New England. He attended Bowdoin College, where his schoolmates included Henry Wadsworth Longfellow and future president Franklin Pierce, for whom Hawthorne later wrote an official campaign biography. For twelve years after his 1825 graduation Hawthorne lived at his parents' home, devoting himself solely to learning the craft of writing. An early novel, Fanshawe *(1828), attracted no attention, but a collection of short stories,* Twice-Told Tales *(1837), was the subject of an enthusiastic review by Edgar Allan Poe (see page 4 of the introduction). Hawthorne traveled in Europe in his later years and served as American consul at Liverpool during the Pierce administration. Unlike his friend Ralph Waldo Emerson, whose optimism was a constant in his transcendentalist credo, Hawthorne was a moralist who did not shrink from depicting the dark side of human nature, and his often painful examinations of American history and conscience have set the tone for many subsequent generations of writers. His ambivalent attitude toward his Puritan ancestors' religious beliefs (one of his forebears, John Hathorne, was a magistrate who assisted the prosecution during the infamous Salem witch trials) supplied material for his novel* The Scarlet Letter *(1850) and many of his short stories, including "Young Goodman Brown," which is set in roughly the same period as the trials.*

Nathaniel Hawthorne
Young Goodman Brown

Young Goodman Brown came forth, at sunset, into the street at Salem village;[1] but put his head back, after crossing the threshold, to exchange a parting kiss with his young wife. And Faith, as the wife was aptly named, thrust her pretty head into the street, letting the wind play with the pink ribbons of her cap while she called to Goodman Brown.

"Dearest heart," whispered she, softly and rather sadly, when her lips were close to his ear, "Prithee put off your journey until sunrise and sleep in your own bed to-night. A lone woman is troubled with such dreams and such thoughts that she's afeared of herself sometimes. Pray tarry with me this night, dear husband, of all nights in the year."

"My love and my Faith," replied young Goodman Brown, "of all nights in the year, this one night must I tarry away from thee. My journey, as thou callest it, forth and back again, must needs be done 'twixt

---

[1]The story takes place several years before the "witch trials" of 1692. Goody Cloyse and Martha Carrier were among the persons sentenced by the courts.

now and sunrise. What, my sweet, pretty wife, dost thou doubt me already, and we but three months married?"

"Then God bless you!" said Faith, with the pink ribbons; "and may you find all well when you come back."

"Amen!" cried Goodman Brown. "Say thy prayers, dear Faith, and go to bed at dusk, and no harm will come to thee."

So they parted; and the young man pursued his way until, being about to the corner by the meeting-house, he looked back and saw the head of Faith peeping after him with a melancholy air, in spite of her pink ribbons.

"Poor little Faith!" thought he, for his heart smote him. "What a wretch am I to leave her on such an errand! She talks of dreams, too. Methought as she spoke there was trouble in her face, as if a dream had warned her what work is to be done to-night. But no, no; 'twould kill her to think it. Well, she's a blessed angel on earth and after this one night, I'll cling to her skirts and follow her to heaven."

With this excellent resolve for the future, Goodman Brown felt himself justified in making more haste on his present evil purpose. He had taken a dreary road, darkened by all the gloomiest trees of the forest, which barely stood aside to let the narrow path creep through, and closed immediately behind. It was all as lonely as could be; and there is this peculiarity in such a solitude, that the traveller knows not who may be concealed by the innumerable trunks and the thick boughs overhead; so that with lonely footsteps he may yet be passing through an unseen multitude.

"There may be a devilish Indian behind every tree," said Goodman Brown to himself and he glanced fearfully behind him as he added, "What if the devil himself should be at my very elbow!"

His head being turned back, he passed a crook of the road, and, looking forward again, beheld the figure of a man, in grave and decent attire, seated at the foot of an old tree. He arose at Goodman Brown's approach and walked onward side by side with him.

"You are late, Goodman Brown," said he. "The clock of the Old South was striking as I came through Boston, and that is full fifteen minutes agone."

"Faith kept me back a while," replied the young man, with a tremor in his voice, caused by the sudden appearance of his companion, though not wholly unexpected.

It was now deep dusk in the forest, and deepest in that part of it where these two were journeying. As nearly as could be discerned, the second traveller was about fifty years old, apparently in the same rank of life as Goodman Brown, and bearing a considerable resemblance to him, though perhaps more in expression than features. Still they might have been taken for father and son. And yet, though the elder person was as simply clad as the younger, and as simple in manner too, he had an indescribable air of one who knew the world, and who would not have felt abashed at the governor's dinner table, or in King William's court, were it possible that his affairs should call him thither. But the only thing about him that could be fixed upon as remarkable was his staff, which bore the likeness of a great black snake, so curiously wrought that it might almost be seen to twist and wriggle itself like a living serpent. This, of course, must have been an ocular deception, assisted by uncertain light.

"Come, Goodman Brown," cried his fellow-traveller, "this is a dull pace for the beginning of a journey. Take my staff, if you are so soon weary."

"Friend," said the other, exchanging his slow pace for a full stop, "having kept covenant by meeting thee here, it is my purpose now to return whence I came. I have scruples touching the matter thou wot'st of."

"Sayest thou so?" replied he of the serpent, smiling apart. "Let us walk on, nevertheless, reasoning as we go; and if I convince thee not thou shalt turn back. We are but a little way in the forest yet."

"Too far! too far!" exclaimed the Goodman, unconsciously resuming his walk. "My father never went into the woods on such an errand, nor his father before him. We have been a race of honest men and good Christians since the days of the martyrs; and shall I be the first of the name of Brown that ever took this path and kept—"

"Such company, thou wouldst say," observed the elder person, interpreting his pause. "Well said, Goodman Brown! I have been as well acquainted with your family as with ever a one among the Puritans; and that's no trifle to say. I helped your grandfather, the constable, when he lashed the Quaker woman so smartly through the streets of Salem; and it was I that brought your father a pitch-pine knot, kindled at my own hearth, to set fire to an Indian village, in King Philip's war. They were my good friends, both; and many a pleasant walk have we had along this path, and returned merrily after midnight. I would fain be friends with you for their sake."

"If it be as thou sayest," replied Goodman Brown, "I marvel they never spoke of these matters, or, verily, I marvel not, seeing that the least rumor of the sort would have driven them from New England. We are a people of prayer, and good works to boot, and abide no such wickedness."

"Wickedness or not," said the traveller with the twisted staff, "I have a very general acquaintance here in New England. The deacons of many a church have drunk the communion wine with me; the selectmen of divers towns make me their chairman; and a majority of the Great and General Court are firm supporters of my interest. The governor and I, too—But these are state secrets."

"Can this be so!" cried Goodman Brown, with a stare of amazement at his undisturbed companion. "Howbeit, I have nothing to do with the governor and council; they have their own ways, and are no rule for a simple husbandman like me. But, were I to go on with thee, how should I meet the eye of that good old man, our minister, at Salem village? Oh, his voice would make me tremble both Sabbath day and lecture day!"

Thus far the elder traveller had listened with due gravity; but now burst into a fit of irrepressible mirth, shaking himself so violently that his snake-like staff actually seemed to wriggle in sympathy.

"Ha! ha! ha!" shouted he again and again; then composing himself, "Well, go on, Goodman Brown, go on; but, prithee, don't kill me with laughing."

"Well, then, to end the matter at once," said Goodman Brown, considerably nettled, "there is my wife, Faith. It would break her dear little heart; and I'd rather break my own."

"Nay, if that be the case," answered the other, "e'en go thy ways, Goodman Brown. I would not for twenty old women like the one hobbling before us that Faith should come to any harm."

As he spoke he pointed his staff at a female figure on the path, in whom Goodman Brown recognized a very pious and exemplary dame, who had taught him his catechism in youth, and was still his moral and spiritual adviser, jointly with the minister and Deacon Gookin.

"A marvel, truly, that Goody Cloyse should be so far in the wilderness at night fall," said he. "But with your leave, friend, I shall take a cut through the woods until we have left this Christian woman behind. Being a stranger to you, she might ask whom I was consorting with and whither I was going."

"Be it so," said his fellow-traveller. "Betake you the woods, and let me keep the path."

Accordingly the young man turned aside, but took care to watch his companion, who advanced softly along the road until he had come within a staff's length of the old dame. She, meanwhile, was making the best of her way, with singular speed for so aged a woman, and mumbling some indistinct words–a prayer, doubtless—as she went. The traveller put forth his staff and touched her withered neck with what seemed the serpent's tail.

"The devil!" screamed the pious old lady.

"Then Goody Cloyse knows her old friend?" observed the traveller, confronting her and leaning on his writhing stick.

"Ah, forsooth, and is it your worship indeed?" cried the good dame. "Yea, truly is it, and in the very image of my old gossip, Goodman Brown, the grandfather of the silly fellow that now is. But—would your worship believe it?—my broomstick hath strangely disappeared, stolen, as I suspect, by that unhanged witch, Goody Cory and that, too, when I was all anointed with the juice of smallage and cinquefoil and wolf's bane—"[2]

"Mingled with fine wheat and the fat of a new-born babe," said the shape of old Goodman Brown.

"Ah, your worship knows the recipe," cried the old lady, cackling aloud. "So, as I was saying, being all ready for the meeting, and no horse to ride on, I made up my mind to foot it; for they tell me there is a nice young man to be taken into communion to-night. But now your good worship will lend me your arm, and we shall be there in a twinkling."

"That can hardly be," answered her friend. "I may not spare you my arm, Goody Cloyse; but here is my staff, if you will."

So saying, he threw it down at her feet, where, perhaps, it assumed life, being one of the rods which its owner had formerly lent to the Egyptian magi. Of this fact, however, Goodman Brown could not take cognizance. He had cast up his eyes in astonishment, and, looking down again, beheld neither Goody Cloyse nor the serpentine staff but his fellow-traveller alone, who waited for him as calmly as if nothing had happened.

"That old woman taught me my catechism," said the young man; and there was a world of meaning in this simple comment.

---

[2]Wild plants and herbs.

They continued to walk onward, while the elder traveller exhorted his companion to make good speed and persevere in the path, discoursing so aptly that his arguments seemed rather to spring up in the bosom of his auditor than to be suggested by himself. As they went, he plucked a branch of maple to serve for a walking-stick, and began to strip it of the twigs and little boughs, which were wet with evening dew. The moment his fingers touched them they became strangely withered and dried up as with a week's sunshine. Thus the pair proceeded, at a good free pace, until suddenly, in a gloomy hollow of the road, Goodman Brown sat himself down on the stump of a tree and refused to go any farther.

"Friend," said he, stubbornly, "my mind is made up. Not another step will I budge on this errand. What if a wretched old woman do choose to go to the devil when I thought she was going to heaven: is that any reason why I should quit my dear Faith and go after her?"

"You will think better of this by and by," said his acquaintance, composedly. "Sit here and rest yourself a while; and when you feel like moving again, there is my staff to help you along."

Without more words, he threw his companion the maple stick, and was as speedily out of sight as if he had vanished into the deepening gloom. The young man sat a few moments by the roadside, applauding himself greatly, and thinking with how clear a conscience he should meet the minister in his morning walk, nor shrink from the eye of good old Deacon Gookin. And what calm sleep would be his that very night, which was to have been spent so wickedly, but so purely and sweetly now, in the arms of Faith! Amidst these pleasant and praiseworthy meditations, Goodman Brown heard the tramp of horses along the road, and deemed it advisable to conceal himself within the verge of the forest, conscious of the guilty purpose that had brought him thither, though now so happily turned from it.

On came the hoof-tramps and the voices of the riders, two grave old voices, conversing soberly as they drew near. These mingled sounds appeared to pass along the road, within a few yards of the young man's hiding-place; but, owing doubtless to the depth of the gloom at that particular spot, neither the travellers nor their steeds were visible. Though their figures brushed the small boughs by the wayside, it could not be seen that they intercepted, even for a moment, the faint gleam from the strip of bright sky athwart which they must have passed.

Goodman Brown alternately crouched and stood on tiptoe, pulling aside the branches and thrusting forth his head as far as he durst without discerning so much as a shadow. It vexed him the more, because he could have sworn, were such a thing possible, that he recognized the voices of the minister and Deacon Gookin, jogging along quietly, as they were wont to do, when bound to some ordination or ecclesiastical council. While yet within hearing, one of the riders stopped to pluck a switch.

"Of the two, reverend sir," said the voice like the deacon's, "I had rather miss an ordination dinner than to-night's meeting. They tell me that some of our community are to be here from Falmouth and beyond, and others from Connecticut and Rhode Island, besides several of the Indian powwows, who, after their fashion, know almost as much deviltry as the best of us. Moreover, there is a goodly young woman to be taken into communion."

"Mighty well, Deacon Gookin!" replied the solemn old tones of the minister. "Spur up, or we shall be late. Nothing can be done, you know, until I get on the ground."

The hoofs clattered again; and the voices, talking so strangely in the empty air, passed on through the forest, where no church had ever been gathered or solitary Christian prayed. Whither, then, could these holy men be journeying so deep into the heathen wilderness? Young Goodman Brown caught hold of a tree for support, being ready to sink down on the ground, faint and overburdened with the heavy sickness of his heart. He looked up to the sky, doubting whether there really was a heaven above him. Yet, there was the blue arch, and the stars brightening in it.

"With heaven above, and Faith below, I will yet stand firm against the devil," cried Goodman Brown.

While he still gazed upward into the deep arch of the firmament and had lifted his hands to pray, a cloud, though no wind was stirring, hurried across the zenith and hid the brightening stars. The blue sky was still visible, except directly overhead, where this black mass of cloud was sweeping swiftly northward. Aloft in the air, as if from the depths of the cloud, came a confused and doubtful sound of voices. Once the listener fancied that he could distinguish the accents of towns-people of his own, men and women, both pious and ungodly, many of whom he had met at the communion table, and had seen others rioting at the tavern. The next moment, so indistinct were the sounds, he doubted whether he had heard aught but the murmur of the old forest, whispering without a wind.Then came a stronger swell of those familiar tones, heard daily in the sunshine at Salem village, but never until now from a cloud of night. There was one voice, of a young woman, uttering lamentations, yet with an uncertain sorrow, and entreating for some favor, which, perhaps it would grieve her to obtain; and all the unseen multitude, both saints and sinners seemed to encourage her onward.

"Faith!" shouted Goodman Brown, in a voice of agony and desperation; and the echoes of the forest mocked him, crying, "Faith! Faith!" as if bewildered wretches were seeking her all through the wilderness.

The cry of grief, rage, and terror was yet piercing the night, when the unhappy husband held his breath for a response. There was a scream, drowned immediately in a louder murmur of voices, fading into far-off laughter, as the dark cloud swept away, leaving the clear and silent sky above Goodman Brown. But something fluttered lightly down through the air and caught on the branch of a tree. The young man seized it, and beheld a pink ribbon.

"My Faith is gone!" cried he, after one stupefied moment. "There is no good on earth; and sin is but a name. Come, devil; for to thee is this world given."

And, maddened with despair, so that he laughed loud and long, did Goodman Brown grasp his staff and set forth again, at such a rate that he seemed to fly along the forest path, rather than to walk or run. The road grew wilder and drearier and more faintly traced, and vanished at length, leaving him in the heart of the dark wilderness, still rushing onward with the instinct that guides mortal man to evil. The whole forest was peopled with frightful sounds—the creaking of the trees, the howling of wild beasts, and the yell of Indians; while sometimes the wind tolled like a distant church bell, and sometimes gave a broad roar around the traveller, as if all Nature were laughing him to scorn. But he was himself the chief horror of the scene, and shrank not from its other horrors.

"Ha! ha! ha!" roared Goodman Brown when the wind laughed at him. "Let us hear which will laugh loudest! Think not to frighten me with your deviltry! Come witch, come wizard, come Indian powwow, come devil himself, and here comes Goodman Brown. You may as well fear him as he fear you!"

In truth, all through the haunted forest there could be nothing more frightful than the figure of Goodman Brown. On he flew among the

black pines, brandishing his staff with frenzied gestures, now giving
vent to an inspiration of horrid blasphemy, and now shouting forth such
laughter as set all the echoes of the forest laughing like demons around
him. The fiend in his own shape is less hideous than when he rages in
the breast of man. Thus sped the demoniac on his course, until, quivering among the trees, he saw a red light before him, as when the felled
trunks and branches of a clearing have been set on fire, and throw up
their lurid blaze against the sky, at the hour of midnight. He paused, in
a lull of the tempest that had driven him onward, and heard the swell of
what seemed a hymn, rolling solemnly from a distance with the weight
of many voices. He knew the tune; it was a familiar one in the choir of
the village meeting-house. The verse died heavily away, and was length-
ened by a chorus, not of human voices, but of all the sounds of the be-
nighted wilderness pealing in awful harmony together. Goodman Brown
cried out; and his cry was lost to his own ear by its unison with the cry
of the desert.

In the interval of silence he stole forward until the light glared full
upon his eyes. At one extremity of an open space, hemmed in by the
dark wall of the forest, arose a rock, bearing some rude, natural resemblance either to an altar or a pulpit, and surrounded by four blazing
pines, their tops aflame, their stems untouched, like candles at an
evening meeting. The mass of foliage that had overgrown the summit of
the rock was all on fire, blazing high into the night and fitfully illuminating the whole field. Each pendent twig and leafy festoon was in a blaze.
As the red light arose and fell, a numerous congregation alternately
shone forth, then disappeared in shadow, and again grew, as it were, out
of the darkness, peopling the heart of the solitary woods at once.

"A grave and dark-clad company," quoth Goodman Brown.

In truth, they were such. Among them, quivering to-and-fro between gloom and splendor, appeared faces that would be seen next day
at the council board of the province, and others which, Sabbath after
Sabbath, looked devoutly heavenward, and benignantly over the
crowded pews, from the holiest pulpits in the land. Some affirm that the
lady of the governor was there. At least there were high dames well
known to her, and wives of honored husbands, and widows, a great
multitude, and ancient maidens, all of excellent repute, and fair young
girls, who trembled lest their mothers should espy them. Either the sudden gleams of light flashing over the obscure field bedazzled Goodman

Brown, or he recognized a score of the church-members of Salem village famous for their especial sanctity. Good old Deacon Gookin had arrived, and waited at the skirts of that venerable saint, his revered pastor. But, irreverently consorting with these grave, reputable, and pious people, these elders of the church, these chaste dames and dewy virgins, there were men of dissolute lives and women of spotted fame, wretches given over to all mean and filthy vice, and suspected even of horrid crimes. It was strange to see, that the good shrank not from the wicked, nor were the sinners abashed by the saints. Scattered also among their pale-faced enemies were the Indian priests, or powwows, who had often scared their native forest with more hideous incantations than any known to English witchcraft.

"But, where is Faith?" thought Goodman Brown; and, as hope came into his heart, he trembled.

Another verse of the hymn arose, a slow and mournful strain, such as the pious love, but joined to words which expressed all that our nature can conceive of sin, and darkly hinted at far more. Unfathomable to mere mortals is the lore of fiends. Verse after verse was sung; and still the chorus of the desert swelled between, like the deepest tone of a mighty organ; and, with the final peal of that dreadful anthem there came a sound, as if the roaring wind, the rushing streams, the howling beasts, and every other voice of the unconcerted wilderness were mingling and according with the voice of guilty man in homage to the prince of all. The four blazing pines threw up a loftier flame, and obscurely discovered shapes and visages of horror on the smoke wreaths above the impious assembly. At the same moment the fire on the rock shot redly forth and formed a glowing arch above its base, where now appeared a figure. With reverence be it spoken, the figure bore no slight similitude, both in garb and manner, to some grave divine of the New England church.

"Bring forth the converts!" cried a voice that echoed through the field and rolled into the forest.

At the word, Goodman Brown stepped forth from the shadow of the trees and approached the congregation, with whom he felt a loathful brotherhood by the sympathy of all that was wicked in his heart. He could have well nigh sworn that the shape of his own dead father beckoned him to advance, looking downward from a smoke wreath, while a woman, with dim features of despair, threw out her hand to warn him back. Was it his mother? But he had no power to retreat one step, nor to resist, even in thought, when the minister and good old Deacon Gookin seized his arms and led him to the blazing rock. Thither came also the slender form of a veiled female, led between Goody Cloyse, that pious teacher of the catechism, and Martha Carrier, who had received the devil's promise to be queen of hell. A rampant hag was she. And there stood the proselytes beneath the canopy of fire.

"Welcome, my children," said the dark figure, "to the communion of your race. Ye have found thus young your nature and your destiny. My children, look behind you!"

They turned; and flashing forth, as it were, in a sheet of flame, the fiend worshippers were seen; the smile of welcome gleamed darkly on every visage.

"There," resumed the sable form, "are all whom ye have reverenced from youth. Ye deemed them holier than yourselves, and shrank from your own sin, contrasting it with their lives of righteousness and prayerful aspirations heavenward. Yet here are they all in my worshipping assembly. This night it shall be granted you to know their secret deeds: how hoary-bearded elders of the church have whispered wanton words to the young maids of their households; how many a woman, eager for widow's weeds, has given her husband a drink at bedtime, and let him sleep his last sleep in her bosom; how beardless youths have made haste to inherit their fathers' wealth; and how fair damsels—blush not, sweet ones— have dug little graves in the garden, and bidden me, the sole guest, to an infant's funeral. By the sympathy of your human hearts for sin ye shall scent out all the places—whether in church, bed-chamber, street, field, or forest—where crime has been committed, and shall exult to behold the whole earth one stain of guilt, one mighty blood spot. Far more than this. It shall be yours to penetrate, in every bosom, the deep mystery of sin, the fountain of all wicked arts, and which inexhaustibly supplies more evil impulses than human power—than my power at its utmost—can make manifest in deeds. And now, my, children, look upon each other."

They did so; and, by the blaze of the hell-kindled torches, the wretched man beheld his Faith, and the wife her husband, trembling before that unhallowed altar.

"Lo, there ye stand, my children," said the figure, in a deep and solemn tone, almost sad with its despairing awfulness, as if his once angelic nature could yet mourn for our miserable race. "Depending upon one another's hearts, ye had still hoped that virtue were not all a dream. Now are ye undeceived. Evil is the nature of mankind. Evil must be your only happiness. Welcome, again, my children, to the communion of your race."

"Welcome," repeated the fiend worshippers, in one cry of despair and triumph.

And there they stood, the only pair, as it seemed, who were yet hesitating on the verge of wickedness in this dark world. A basin was hollowed, naturally, in the rock. Did it contain water, reddened by the lurid light? or was it blood? or, perchance, a liquid flame? Herein did the shape of evil dip his hand and prepare to lay the mark of baptism upon their foreheads, that they might be partakers of the mystery of sin, more conscious of the secret guilt of others, both in deed and thought, than they could now be of their own. The husband cast one look at his pale wife, and Faith at him. What polluted wretches would the next glance show them to each other, shuddering alike at what they disclosed and what they saw!

"Faith! Faith!" cried the husband, "look up to heaven, and resist the wicked one."

Whether Faith obeyed he knew not. Hardly had he spoken when he found himself amid calm night and solitude, listening to a roar of the wind which died heavily away through the forest. He staggered against the rock, and felt it chill and damp; while a hanging twig, that had been all on fire, besprinkled his cheek with the coldest dew.

The next morning young Goodman Brown came slowly into the street of Salem village, staring around him like a bewildered man. The good old minister was taking a walk along the graveyard to get an appetite for breakfast and meditate his sermon, and bestowed a blessing, as he passed, on Goodman Brown. He shrank from the venerable saint as if to avoid an anathema. Old Deacon Gookin was at domestic worship, and the holy words of his prayer were heard through the open window. "What God doth the wizard pray to?" quoth Goodman Brown. Goody Cloyse, that excellent old Christian, stood in the early sunshine at her own lattice, catechizing a little girl who had brought her a pint of morning's milk. Goodman Brown snatched away the child as from the grasp of the fiend himself. Turning the corner by the meeting-house, he spied the head of Faith, with the pink ribbons, gazing anxiously forth, and bursting into such joy at sight of him that she skipped along the street and almost kissed her husband before the whole village. But Goodman Brown looked sternly and sadly into her face, and passed on without a greeting.

Had Goodman Brown fallen asleep in the forest and only dreamed a wild dream of a witch-meeting?

Be it so, if you will; but, alas! it was a dream of evil omen for young Goodman Brown. A stern, a sad, a darkly meditative, a distrustful, if not a desperate man did he become from the night of that fearful dream. On the Sabbath day, when the congregation were singing a holy psalm, he could not listen because an anthem of sin rushed loudly upon his ear and drowned all the blessed strain. When the minister spoke from the pulpit with power and fervid eloquence, and, with his hand on the open Bible, of the sacred truths of our religion, and of saint-like lives and triumphant deaths, and of future bliss or misery unutterable, then did Goodman Brown turn pale, dreading lest the roof should thunder down upon the gray blasphemer and his hearers. Often, awakening suddenly at midnight, he shrank from the bosom of Faith; and at morning or eventide, when the family knelt down at prayer, he scowled and muttered to himself, and gazed sternly at his wife, and turned away. And when he had lived long, and was borne to his grave a hoary corpse, followed by Faith, an aged woman, and children and grandchildren, a goodly procession, besides neighbors, not a few, they carved no hopeful verse upon his tombstone, for his dying hour was gloom.

—1835

Edgar Allan Poe (1809–1849) has become so much the captive of his own legend that his name summons up visions of a mad genius who has little in common with the meticulous craftsman of criticism, fiction, and poetry whose influence on world literature has been immense. Born in Boston, Poe was the child of actors and orphaned at age two. Nevertheless, he lived a privileged childhood as the ward of John Allan, a wealthy Richmond merchant who gave Poe his middle name. After a profligate year at the University of Virginia, successful military service (under an assumed name), and an abortive stay at West Point, Poe broke with his foster father, married his young cousin, and set about a literary career, succeeding as editor of several prominent magazines. However, his irregular habits and a drinking problem, which grew more pronounced following the death of his wife in 1847, led to his mysterious death in Baltimore at the age of thirty-nine. Poe's poetry and short fiction have influenced writers as diverse as Charles Baudelaire and Stephen King; genres like the horror tale and the detective story must list Poe stories like "Ligeia" or "The Murders in the Rue Morgue" among their earliest important examples. Similarly, Poe's literary criticism has been extremely influential; his theory of the "single effect" is quoted and discussed in the introduction to this book. "The Fall of the House of Usher," one of Poe's most complex tales, employs the standard gothic trappings of an isolated mansion and family curses, but Poe never delved as deeply into the abyss of a tortured and doomed soul as he did with Roderick Usher. The story also contains one of Poe's finest poems, "The Haunted Palace," here cited by the narrator as an example of his host's gift of spontaneous lyrical improvisation. "The Fall of the House of Usher" is as well a revealing allegory of Usher's own increasing madness.

Edgar Allan Poe
The Fall of the House of Usher

> Son cœur est un luth suspendu;
> Sitôt qu'on le touche il résonne.
>
> —de Béranger[1]

During the whole of a dull, dark, and soundless day in the autumn of the year, when the clouds hung oppressively low in the heavens, I had been passing alone, on horseback, through a singularly dreary tract of country;

---

[1]Poe has adapted two famous lines from the French poet Pierre-Jean de Béranger (1780–1857). They translate as "His heart is a tightly strung lute; / As soon as one touches it, it resounds." Béranger's original reads "My heart. . . ."

and at length found myself, as the shades of the evening drew on, within view of the melancholy House of Usher. I know not how it was—but, with the first glimpse of the building, a sense of insufferable gloom pervaded my spirit. I say insufferable; for the feeling was unrelieved by any of that half-pleasurable, because poetic, sentiment, with which the mind usually receives even the sternest natural images of the desolate or terrible. I looked upon the scene before me—upon the mere house, and the simple landscape features of the domain—upon the bleak walls—upon the vacant eyelike windows—upon a few rank sedges—and upon a few white trunks of decayed trees—with an utter depression of soul which I can compare to no earthly sensation more properly than to the after-dream of the reveller upon opium—the bitter lapse into every-day life—the hideous dropping off of the veil. There was an iciness, a sinking, a sickening of the heart—an unredeemed dreariness of thought which no goading of the imagination could torture into aught of the sublime. What was it—I paused to think—what was it that so unnerved me in the contemplation of the House of Usher? It was a mystery all insoluble; nor could I grapple with the shadowy fancies that crowded upon me as I pondered. I was forced to fall back upon the unsatisfactory conclusion, that while, beyond doubt, there *are* combinations of very simple natural objects which have the power of thus affecting us, still the analysis of this power lies among considerations beyond our depth. It was possible, I reflected, that a mere different arrangement of the particulars of the scene, of the details of the picture, would be sufficient to modify, or perhaps to annihilate its capacity for sorrowful impression; and, acting upon this idea, I reined my horse to the precipitous brink of a black and lurid tarn that lay in unruffled luster by the dwelling, and gazed down—but with a shudder even more thrilling than before—upon the remodelled and inverted images of the gray sedge, and the ghastly tree-stems, and the vacant and eye-like windows.

Nevertheless, in this mansion of gloom I now proposed to myself a sojourn of some weeks. Its proprietor, Roderick Usher, had been one of my boon companions in boyhood; but many years had elapsed since our last meeting. A letter, however, had lately reached me in a distant part of the country—a letter from him—which, in its wildly importunate nature, had admitted of no other than a personal reply. The MS.[2] gave evidence of nervous agitation. The writer spoke of

---

[2]manuscript

acute bodily illness—of a mental disorder which oppressed him—and of an earnest desire to see me, as his best, and indeed his only personal friend, with a view of attempting, by the cheerfulness of my society, some alleviation of his malady. It was the manner in which all this, and much more, was said—it was the apparent *heart* that went with his request—which allowed me no room for hesitation; and I accordingly obeyed forthwith what I still considered a very singular summons.

Although, as boys, we had been even intimate associates, yet I really knew little of my friend. His reserve had been always excessive and habitual. I was aware, however, that his very ancient family had been noted, time out of mind, for a peculiar sensibility of temperament, displaying itself, through long ages, in many works of exalted art, and manifested, of late, in repeated deeds of munificent yet unobtrusive charity, as well as in a passionate devotion to the intricacies, perhaps even more than to the orthodox and easily recognizable beauties, of musical science. I had learned, too, the very remarkable fact, that the stem of the Usher race, all time-honored as it was, had put forth, at no period, any enduring branch; in other words, that the entire family lay in the direct line of descent, and had always, with very trifling and very temporary variation, so lain. It was this deficiency, I considered, while running over in thought the perfect keeping of the character of the premises with the accredited character of the people, and while speculating upon the possible influence which the one, in the long lapse of centuries, might have exercised upon the other—it was this deficiency, perhaps, of collateral issue, and the consequent undeviating transmission, from sire to son, of the patrimony with the name, which had, at length, so identified the two as to merge the original title of the estate in the quaint and equivocal appellation of the "House of Usher"—an appellation which seemed to include, in the minds of the peasantry who used it, both the family and the family mansion.

I have said that the sole effect of my somewhat childish experiment—that of looking down within the tarn—had been to deepen the first singular impression. There can be no doubt that the consciousness of the rapid increase of my superstition—for why should I not so term it?—served mainly to accelerate the increase itself. Such, I have long known, is the paradoxical law of all sentiments having terror as a basis. And it might have been for this reason only, that, when I again uplifted my eyes to the house itself, from its image in the pool, there grew in my mind a strange fancy—a fancy so ridiculous, indeed, that I but mention it to show the vivid force of the sensations which oppressed me. I had so worked upon my imagination as really to believe that about the whole mansion and domain there hung an atmosphere peculiar to themselves and their immediate vicinity—an atmosphere which had no affinity with the air of heaven, but which had reeked up from the decayed trees, and the gray wall, and the silent tarn—a pestilent and mystic vapor, dull, sluggish, faintly discernible, and leaden-hued.

Shaking off from my spirit what *must* have been a dream, I scanned more narrowly the real aspect of the building. Its principal feature seemed to be that of an excessive antiquity. The discoloration of ages had been great. Minute fungi overspread the whole exterior, hanging in a fine tangled web-work from the eaves. Yet all this was apart from any extraordinary dilapidation. No portion of the masonry had fallen; and there appeared to be a wild inconsistency between its still perfect adaptation of parts, and the crumbling condition of the individual stones. In this there was much that reminded me of the specious totality of old woodwork which has rotted for long years in some neglected vault, with no disturbance from the breath of the external air. Beyond this indication of extensive decay, however, the fabric gave little token of instability. Perhaps the eye of a scrutinizing observer might have discovered a barely perceptible fissure, which, extending from the roof of the building in front, made its way down the wall in a zigzag direction, until it became lost in the sullen waters of the tarn.

Noticing these things, I rode over a short causeway to the house. A servant in waiting took my horse, and I entered the Gothic archway of the hall. A valet, of stealthy step, thence conducted me, in silence, through many dark and intricate passages in my progress to the *studio* of his master. Much that I encountered on the way contributed, I know not how, to heighten the vague sentiments of which I have already spoken. While the objects around me—while the carvings of the ceilings, the somber tapestries of the walls, the ebon blackness of the floors, and the phantasmagoric armorial trophies which rattled as I strode, were but matters to which, or to such as which, I had been accustomed from my infancy—while I hesitated not to acknowledge how familiar was all this—I still wondered to find how unfamiliar were the fancies which ordinary images were stirring up. On one of the staircases, I met the physician of the family. His countenance, I thought, wore a mingled expression of low cunning and perplexity. He accosted me with trepidation and passed on. The valet now threw open a door and ushered me into the presence of his master.

The room in which I found myself was very large and lofty. The windows were long, narrow, and pointed, and at so vast a distance from the black oaken floor as to be altogether inaccessible from within. Feeble gleams of encrimsoned light made their way through the trellised panes, and served to render sufficiently distinct the more prominent objects around; the eye, however, struggled in vain to reach the remoter angles of the chamber, or the recesses of the vaulted and fretted ceiling. Dark draperies hung upon the walls. The general furniture was profuse, comfortless, antique, and tattered. Many books and musical instruments lay scattered about, but failed to give any vitality to the scene. I felt that I breathed an atmosphere of sorrow. An air of stern, deep, and irredeemable gloom hung over and pervaded all.

Upon my entrance, Usher arose from a sofa on which he had been lying at full length, and greeted me with a vivacious warmth which had much in it, I at first thought, of an overdone cordiality—of the constrained effort of the *ennuyé*[3] man of the world. A glance, however, at his countenance, convinced me of his perfect sincerity. We sat down; and for some moments, while he spoke not, I gazed upon him with a feeling half of pity, half of awe. Surely, man had never before so terribly altered, in so brief a period, as had Roderick Usher! It was with difficulty that I could bring myself to admit the identity of the wan being before me with the companion of my early boyhood. Yet the character of his face had been at all times remarkable. A cadaverousness of complexion; an eye large, liquid, and luminous beyond comparison; lips somewhat thin and very pallid, but of a surpassingly beautiful curve; a nose of a delicate Hebrew model, but with a breadth of nostril unusual in similar formations; a finely molded chin, speaking, in its want of prominence, of a want of moral energy; hair of a more than web-like softness and tenuity; these features, with an inordinate expansion above the regions of the temple, made up altogether a countenance not easily to be forgotten. And now in the mere exaggeration of the prevailing character of these features, and of the expression they were wont to con-

[3]*ennuyé:* world-weary

vey, lay so much of change that I doubted to whom I spoke. The now ghastly pallor of the skin, and the now miraculous luster of the eye, above all things startled and even awed me. The silken hair, too, had been suffered to grow all unheeded, and as, in its wild gossamer texture, it floated rather than fell about the face, I could not, even with effort, connect its Arabesque[4] expression with any idea of simple humanity.

In the manner of my friend I was at once struck with an incoherence—an inconsistency; and I soon found this to arise from a series of feeble and futile struggles to overcome an habitual trepidancy—an excessive nervous agitation. For something of this nature I had indeed been prepared, no less by his letter, than by reminiscences of certain boyish traits, and by conclusions deduced from his peculiar physical conformation and temperament. His action was alternately vivacious and sullen. His voice varied rapidly from a tremulous indecision (when the animal spirits seemed utterly in abeyance) to that species of energetic concision—that abrupt, weighty, unhurried, and hollow-sounding enunciation—that leaden, self-balanced and perfectly modulated guttural utterance, which may be observed in the lost drunkard, or the irreclaimable eater of opium, during the periods of his most intense excitement.

It was thus that he spoke of the object of my visit, of his earnest desire to see me, and of the solace he expected me to afford him. He entered, at some length, into what he conceived to be the nature of his malady. It was, he said, a constitutional and a family evil, and one for which he despaired to find a remedy—a mere nervous affection, he immediately added, which would undoubtedly soon pass off. It displayed itself in a host of unnatural sensations. Some of these, as he detailed them, interested and bewildered me; although, perhaps, the terms and the general manner of the narration had their weight. He suffered much from a morbid acuteness of the senses; the most insipid food was alone endurable; he could wear only garments of certain texture; the odors of all flowers were oppressive; his eyes were tortured by even a faint light; and there were but peculiar sounds, and these from stringed instruments, which did not inspire him with horror.

To an anomalous species of terror I found him a bounden slave. "I shall perish," said he, "I *must* perish in this deplorable folly. Thus, thus, and not otherwise, shall I be lost. I dread the events of the future,

[4]*Arabesque:* complex (in the Arab decorative manner)

not in themselves, but in their results. I shudder at the thought of any, even the most trivial, incident, which may operate upon this intolerable agitation of soul. I have, indeed, no abhorrence of danger, except in its absolute effect—in terror. In this unnerved—in this pitiable condition— I feel that the period will sooner or later arrive when I must abandon life and reason together, in some struggle with the grim phantasm, FEAR."

I learned, moreover, at intervals, and through broken and equivocal hints, another singular feature of his mental condition. He was enchained by certain superstitious impressions in regard to the dwelling which he tenanted, and whence, for many years, he had never ventured forth—in regard to an influence whose suppositious force was conveyed in terms too shadowy here to be restated—an influence which some peculiarities in the mere form and substance of his family mansion, had, by dint of long sufferance, he said, obtained over his spirit—an effect which the *physique* of the gray walls and turrets, and of the dim tarn into which they all looked down, had, at length, brought about upon the *morale* of his existence.

He admitted, however, although with hesitation, that much of the peculiar gloom which thus afflicted him could be traced to a more natural and far more palpable origin—to the severe and long-continued illness—indeed to the evidently approaching dissolution—of a tenderly beloved sister—his sole companion for long years—his last and only relative on earth. "Her decease," he said, with a bitterness which I can never forget, "would leave him (him the hopeless and the frail) the last of the ancient race of the Ushers." While he spoke, the lady Madeline (for so was she called) passed slowly through a remote portion of the apartment, and, without having noticed my presence, disappeared. I regarded her with an utter astonishment not unmingled with dread—and yet I found it impossible to account for such feelings. A sensation of stupor oppressed me, as my eyes followed her retreating steps. When a door, at length, closed upon her, my glance sought instinctively and eagerly the countenance of the brother—but he had buried his face in his hands, and I could only perceive that a far more than ordinary wanness had overspread the emaciated fingers through which trickled many passionate tears.

The disease of the lady Madeline had long baffled the skill of her physicians. A settled apathy, a gradual wasting away of the person, and frequent although transient affections of a partially cataleptical character, were the unusual diagnosis. Hitherto she had steadily borne up against the pressure of her malady, and had not betaken herself finally to bed; but, on the closing in of the evening of my arrival at the house, she succumbed (as her brother told me at night with inexpressible agitation) to the prostrating power of the destroyer; and I learned that the glimpse I had obtained of her person would thus probably be the last I should obtain—that the lady, at least while living, would be seen by me no more.

For several days ensuing, her name was unmentioned by either Usher or myself: and during this period I was busied in earnest endeavors to alleviate the melancholy of my friend. We painted and read together; or I listened, as if in a dream, to the wild improvisations of his speaking guitar. And thus, as a closer and still closer intimacy admitted me more unreservedly into the recesses of his spirit, the more bitterly did I perceive the futility of all attempt at cheering a mind from which darkness, as if an inherent positive quality, poured forth upon all objects of the moral and physical universe, in one unceasing radiation of gloom.

I shall ever bear about me a memory of the many solemn hours I thus spent alone with the master of the House of Usher. Yet I should fail in any attempt to convey an idea of the exact character of the studies, or of the occupations, in which he involved me, or led me the way. An excited and highly distempered ideality threw a sulphureous luster over all. His long improvised dirges will ring forever in my ears. Among other things, I hold painfully in mind a certain singular perversion and amplification of the wild air of the last waltz of Von Weber.[5] From the paintings over which his elaborate fancy brooded, and which grew, touch by touch, into vaguenesses at which I shuddered the more thrillingly, because I shuddered knowing not why;—from these paintings (vivid as their images now are before me) I would in vain endeavor to educe more than a small portion which should lie within the compass of merely written words. By the utter simplicity, by the nakedness of his designs, he arrested and overawed attention. If ever mortal painted an idea, that mortal was Roderick Usher. For me at least—in the circumstances then surrounding me—these arose out of the pure abstractions which the

---

[5]*last waltz of Von Weber:* waltz composed by Karl Gottlieb Reissiger (1798–1859) in honor of the composer Carl Maria von Weber (1786–1826).

hypochondriac contrived to throw upon his canvas, an intensity of intolerable awe, no shadow of which felt I ever yet in the contemplation of the certainly glowing yet too concrete reveries of Fuseli.[6]

One of the phantasmagoric conceptions of my friend, partaking not so rigidly of the spirit of abstraction, may be shadowed forth, although feebly, in words. A small picture presented the interior of an immensely long and rectangular vault or tunnel, with low walls, smooth, white, and without interruption or device. Certain accessory points of the design served well to convey the idea that this excavation lay at an exceeding depth below the surface of the earth. No outlet was observed in any portion of its vast extent, and no torch, or other artificial source of light was discernible; yet a flood of intense rays rolled throughout, and bathed the whole in a ghastly and inappropriate splendor.

I have just spoken of that morbid condition of the auditory nerve which rendered all music intolerable to the sufferer, with the exception of certain effects of stringed instruments. It was, perhaps, the narrow limits to which he thus confined himself upon the guitar, which gave birth, in great measure, to the fantastic character of his performances. But the fervid *facility* of his *impromptus* could not be so accounted for. They must have been, and were, in the notes, as well as in the words of his wild fantasias (for he not unfrequently accompanied himself with rhymed verbal improvisations), the result of that intense mental collectedness and concentration to which I have previously alluded as observable only in particular moments of the highest artificial excitement. The words of one of these rhapsodies I have easily remembered. I was, perhaps, the more forcibly impressed with it, as he gave it, because in the under or mystic current of its meaning, I fancied that I perceived, and for the first time, a full consciousness on the part of Usher, of the tottering of his lofty reason upon her throne. The verses, which were entitled "The Haunted Palace," ran very nearly, if not accurately, thus:

I.

> In the greenest of our valleys,
>   By good angels tenanted,
> Once a fair and stately palace—
>   Radiant palace—reared its head.

[6]*Fuseli:* Henry Fuseli (1742–1825), Swiss-born artist, who painted nightmarish scenes.

In the monarch Thought's dominion—
  It stood there!
Never seraph spread a pinion
  Over fabric half so fair.

II.

Banners yellow, glorious, golden,
  On its roof did float and flow;
(This—all this—was in the olden
  Time long ago)
And every gentle air that dallied,
  In that sweet day,
Along the ramparts plumed and pallid,
  A winged odor went away.

III.

Wanderers in that happy valley
  Through two luminous windows saw
Spirits moving musically
  To a lute's well-tunèd law,
Round about a throne, where sitting
  (Porphyrogene!)[7]
In state his glory well befitting,
  The ruler of the realm was seen.

IV.

And all with pearl and ruby glowing
  Was the fair palace door,
Through which came flowing, flowing, flowing
  And sparkling evermore,
A troop of Echoes whose sweet duty
  Was but to sing,
In voices of surpassing beauty,
  The wit and wisdom of their king.

V.

But evil things, in robes of sorrow,
  Assailed the monarch's high estate;
(Ah, let us mourn, for never morrow
  Shall dawn upon him, desolate!)
And, round about his home, the glory

---

[7]*Porphyrogene:* "born to the purple," that is, of aristocratic descent.

> *That blushed and bloomed*
> *Is but a dim-remembered story*
> *Of the old time entombed.*

VI.

> *And travelers now within that valley,*
> *Through the red-litten windows, see*
> *Vast forms that move fantastically*
> *To a discordant melody;*
> *While, like a rapid ghastly river,*
> *Through the pale door,*
> *A hideous throng rush out forever,*
> *And laugh—but smile no more.*

I well remember that suggestions arising from this ballad, led us into a train of thought wherein there became manifest an opinion of Usher's which I mention not so much on account of its novelty, (for other men have thought thus,) as on account of the pertinacity with which he maintained it. This opinion, in its general form, was that of the sentience of all vegetable things. But, in his disordered fancy, the idea had assumed a more daring character, and trespassed, under certain conditions, upon the kingdom of inorganization. I lack words to express the full extent, or the earnest *abandon* of his persuasion. The belief, however, was connected (as I have previously hinted) with the gray stones of the home of his forefathers. The conditions of the sentience had been here, he imagined, fulfilled in the method of collocation of these stones—in the order of their arrangement, as well as in that of the many *fungi* which overspread them, and of the decayed trees which stood around—above all, in the long undisturbed endurance of this arrangement, and in its reduplication in the still waters of the tarn. Its evidence—the evidence of the sentience—was to be seen, he said, (and I here started as he spoke,) in the gradual yet certain condensation of an atmosphere of their own about the waters and the walls. The result was discoverable, he added, in that silent, yet importunate and terrible influence which for centuries had molded the destinies of his family, and which made *him* what I now saw him—what he was. Such opinions need no comment, and I will make none.

Our books—the books which, for years, had formed no small portion of the mental existence of the invalid—were, as might be supposed, in strict keeping with this character of phantasm. We pored together over such works as the Ververt et Chartreuse of Gresset; the Belphegor of Machiavelli; the Heaven and Hell of Swedenborg; the Subterranean Voyage of Nicholas Klimm by Holberg; the Chiromancy of Robert Flud, of Jean D'Indaginé, and of De la Chambre; the Journey into the Blue Distance of Tieck; and the City of the Sun of Campanella. One favorite volume was a small octavo edition of the *Directorium Inquisitorum*, by the Dominican Eymeric de Gironne; and there were passages in Pomponius Mela, about the old African Satyrs and Ægipans, over which Usher would sit dreaming for hours. His chief delight, however, was found in the perusal of an exceedingly rare and curious book in quarto Gothic—the manual of a forgotten church—the *Vigiliae Mortuorum secundum Chorum Ecclesiae Maguntinae*.[8]

I could not help thinking of the wild ritual of this work, and of its probable influence upon the hypochondriac, when, one evening, having informed me abruptly that the lady Madeline was no more, he stated his intention of preserving her corpse for a fortnight, (previously to its final interment,) in one of the numerous vaults within the main walls of the building. The worldly reason, however, assigned for this singular proceeding, was one which I did not feel at liberty to dispute. The brother had been led to his resolution (so he told me) by consideration of the unusual character of the malady of the deceased, of certain obtrusive and eager inquiries on the part of her medical men, and of the remote and exposed situation of the burial-ground of the family. I will not deny that when I called to mind the sinister countenance of the person whom I met upon the staircase, on the day of my arrival at the house, I had no desire to oppose what I regarded as at best but a harmless, and by no means an unnatural, precaution.

At the request of Usher, I personally aided him in the arrangements for the temporary entombment. The body having been encoffined, we two alone bore it to its rest. The vault in which we placed it (and which had been so long unopened that our torches, half smothered in its oppressive atmosphere, gave us little opportunity for investigation) was small, damp, and entirely without means of admission for light; lying, at great depth, immediately beneath that portion of the building in which was my own sleeping apartment. It had been used, apparently, in remote feudal

---

[8]*We pored together over . . . Maguntinae:* these books of occult lore are real, with the exception of the last, *The Vigils of the Dead.*

times, for the worst purposes of a donjon-keep, and, in later days, as a place of deposit for powder, or some other highly combustible substance, as a portion of its floor, and the whole interior of a long archway through which we reached it, were carefully sheathed with copper. The door, of massive iron, had been, also, similarly protected. Its immense weight caused an unusually sharp grating sound, as it moved upon its hinges.

Having deposited our mournful burden upon tressels within this region of horror, we partially turned aside the yet unscrewed lid of the coffin, and looked upon the face of the tenant. A striking similitude between the brother and sister now first arrested my attention; and Usher, divining, perhaps, my thoughts, murmured out some few words from which I learned that the deceased and himself had been twins, and that sympathies of a scarcely intelligible nature had always existed between them. Our glances, however, rested not long upon the dead—for we could not regard her unawed. The disease which had thus entombed the lady in the maturity of youth, had left, as usual in all maladies of a strictly cataleptical character, the mockery of a faint blush upon the bosom and the face, and that suspiciously lingering smile upon the lip which is so terrible in death. We replaced and screwed down the lid, and, having secured the door of iron, made our way, with toil, into the scarcely less gloomy apartments of the upper portion of the house.

And now, some days of bitter grief having elapsed, an observable change came over the features of the mental disorder of my friend. His ordinary manner had vanished. His ordinary occupations were neglected or forgotten. He roamed from chamber to chamber with hurried, unequal, and objectless step. The pallor of his countenance had assumed, if possible, a more ghastly hue—but the luminousness of his eye had utterly gone out. The once occasional huskiness of his tone was heard no more; and a tremulous quaver, as if of extreme terror, habitually characterized his utterance. There were times, indeed, when I thought his unceasingly agitated mind was laboring with some oppressive secret, to divulge which he struggled for the necessary courage. At times, again, I was obliged to resolve all into the mere inexplicable vagaries of madness, for I beheld him gazing upon vacancy for long hours, in an attitude of the profoundest attention as if listening to some imaginary sound. It was no wonder that his condition terrified—that it infected me. I felt creeping upon me, by slow yet certain degrees, the wild influences of his own fantastic yet impressive superstitions.

It was, especially, upon retiring to bed late in the night of the seventh or eighth day after the placing of the lady Madeline within the donjon, that I experienced the full power of such feelings. Sleep came not near my couch—while the hours waned and waned away. I struggled to reason off the nervousness which had dominion over me. I endeavored to believe that much, if not all of what I felt, was due to the bewildering influence of the gloomy furniture of the room—of the dark and tattered draperies, which, tortured into motion by the breath of a rising tempest, swayed fitfully to and fro upon the walls, and rustled uneasily about the decorations of the bed. But my efforts were fruitless. An irrepressible tremor gradually pervaded my frame; and, at length, there sat upon my very heart an incubus of utterly causeless alarm. Shaking this off with a gasp and a struggle, I uplifted myself upon the pillows, and, peering earnestly within the intense darkness of the chamber, hearkened—I know not why, except that an instinctive spirit prompted me—to certain low and indefinite sounds which came, through the pauses of the storm, at long intervals, I knew not whence. Overpowered by an intense sentiment of horror, unaccountable yet unendurable, I threw on my clothes with haste (for I felt that I should sleep no more during the night), and endeavored to arouse myself from the pitiable condition into which I had fallen, by pacing rapidly to and fro through the apartment.

I had taken but few turns in this manner, when a light step on an adjoining staircase arrested my attention. I presently recognized it as that of Usher. In an instant afterward he rapped, with a gentle touch, at my door, and entered, bearing a lamp. His countenance was, as usual, cadaverously wan—but, moreover, there was a species of mad hilarity in his eyes—an evidently restrained *hysteria* in his whole demeanor. His air appalled me—but anything was preferable to the solitude which I had so long endured, and I even welcomed his presence as a relief.

"And you have not seen it?" he said abruptly, after having stared about him for some moments in silence—"you have not then seen it?—but, stay! you shall." Thus speaking, and having carefully shaded his lamp, he hurried to one of the casements, and threw it freely open to the storm.

The impetuous fury of the entering gust nearly lifted us from our feet. It was, indeed, a tempestuous yet sternly beautiful night, and one wildly singular in its terror and its beauty. A whirlwind had apparently collected its force in our vicinity; for there were frequent and violent alterations in the direction of the wind; and the exceeding density of the clouds (which hung so low as to press upon the turrets of the house) did not prevent our perceiving the life-like velocity with which they flew careering from all points against each other, without passing away into the distance. I say that even their exceeding density did not prevent our perceiving this—yet we had no glimpse of the moon or stars—nor was there any flashing forth of the lightning. But the under surfaces of the huge masses of agitated vapor, as well as all terrestrial objects immediately around us, were glowing in the unnatural light of a faintly luminous and distinctly visible gaseous exhalation which hung about and enshrouded the mansion.

"You must not—you shall not behold this!" said I, shudderingly, to Usher, as I led him, with a gentle violence, from the window to a seat. "These appearances, which bewilder you, are merely electrical phenomena not uncommon—or it may be that they have their ghastly origin in the rank miasma of the tarn. Let us close this casement;—the air is chilling and dangerous to your frame. Here is one of your favorite romances. I will read, and you shall listen;—and so we will pass away this terrible night together."

The antique volume which I had taken up was the "Mad Trist" of Sir Launcelot Canning;[9] but I had called it a favorite of Usher's more in sad jest than in earnest; for, in truth, there is little in its uncouth and unimaginative prolixity which could have had interest for the lofty and spiritual ideality of my friend. It was, however, the only book immediately at hand; and I indulged a vague hope that the excitement which now agitated the hypochondriac, might find relief (for the history of mental disorder is full of similar anomalies) even in the extremeness of the folly which I should read. Could I have judged, indeed, by the wild over-strained air of vivacity with which he hearkened, or apparently hearkened, to the words of the tale, I might well have congratulated myself upon the success of my design.

I had arrived at that well-known portion of the story where Ethelred, the hero of the Trist, having sought in vain for peaceable admission into the dwelling of the hermit, proceeds to make good an en-

---

[9] *"Mad Trist" of Sir Launcelot Canning:* a fictitious tale and author.

trance by force. Here, it will be remembered, the words of the narrative run thus:

"And Ethelred, who was by nature of a doughty heart, and who was now mighty withal, on account of the powerfulness of the wine which he had drunken, waited no longer to hold parley with the hermit, who, in sooth, was of an obstinate and maliceful turn, but, feeling the rain upon his shoulders, and fearing the rising of the tempest, uplifted his mace outright, and, with blows, made quickly room in the plankings of the door for his gauntleted hand; and now pulling therewith sturdily, he so cracked, and ripped, and tore all asunder, that the noise of the dry and hollow-sounding wood alarumed and reverberated throughout the forest."

At the termination of this sentence I started, and for a moment, paused; for it appeared to me (although I at once concluded that my excited fancy had deceived me)—it appeared to me that, from some very remote portion of the mansion, there came, indistinctly, to my ears, what might have been, in its exact similarity of character, the echo (but a stifled and dull one certainly) of the very cracking and ripping sound which Sir Launcelot had so particularly described. It was, beyond doubt, the coincidence alone which had arrested my attention; for, amid the rattling of the sashes of the casements, and the ordinary commingled noises of the still increasing storm, the sound, in itself, had nothing, surely, which should have interested or disturbed me. I continued the story:

"But the good champion Ethelred, now entering within the door, was sore enraged and amazed to perceive no signal of the maliceful hermit; but, in the stead thereof, a dragon of a scaly and prodigious demeanor, and of a fiery tongue, which sate in guard before a palace of gold, with a floor of silver; and upon the wall there hung a shield of shining brass with this legend enwritten—

> *Who entereth herein, a conqueror hath bin;*
> *Who slayeth the dragon, the shield he shall win;*

And Ethelred uplifted his mace, and struck upon the head of the dragon, which fell before him, and gave up his pesty breath, with a shriek so horrid and harsh, and withal so piercing, that Ethelred had fain to close his ears with his hands against the dreadful noise of it, the like whereof was never before heard."

Here again I paused abruptly, and now with a feeling of wild amazement—for there could be no doubt whatever that, in this instance, I did actually hear (although from what direction it proceeded I found it impossible to say) a low and apparently distant, but harsh, protracted, and most unusual screaming or grating sound—the exact counterpart of what my fancy had already conjured up for the dragon's unnatural shriek as described by the romancer.

Oppressed, as I certainly was, upon the occurrence of the second and most extraordinary coincidence, by a thousand conflicting sensations, in which wonder and extreme terror were predominant, I still retained sufficient presence of mind to avoid exciting, by any observation, the sensitive nervousness of my companion. I was by no means certain that he had noticed the sounds in question; although, assuredly, a strange alteration had, during the last few minutes, taken place in his demeanor. From a position fronting my own, he had gradually brought round his chair, so as to sit with his face to the door of the chamber; and thus I could but partially perceive his features, although I saw that his lips trembled as if he were murmuring inaudibly. His head had dropped upon his breast—yet I knew that he was not asleep, from the wide and rigid opening of the eye as I caught a glance of it in profile. The motion of his body, too, was at variance with this idea—for he rocked from side to side with a gentle yet constant and uniform sway. Having rapidly taken notice of all this, I resumed the narrative of Sir Launcelot, which thus proceeded:

"And now, the champion, having escaped from the terrible fury of the dragon, bethinking himself of the brazen shield, and of the breaking up of the enchantment which was upon it, removed the carcass from out of the way before him, and approached valorously over the silver pavement of the castle to where the shield was upon the wall; which in sooth tarried not for his full coming, but fell down at his feet upon the silver floor, with a mighty great and terrible ringing sound."

No sooner had these syllables passed my lips, than—as if a shield of brass had indeed, at the moment, fallen heavily upon a floor of silver—I became aware of a distinct, hollow, metallic, and clangorous, yet apparently muffled reverberation. Completely unnerved, I leaped to my feet; but the measured rocking movement of Usher was undisturbed. I rushed to the chair in which he sat. His eyes were bent fixedly before him, and throughout his whole countenance there reigned a stony rigidity. But, as I placed my hand upon his shoulder, there came a strong shudder over his whole person; a sickly smile quivered about his lips; and I saw that he spoke in a low, hurried, and gibbering murmur, as if unconscious of my presence. Bending closely over him, I at length drank in the hideous import of his words.

"Not hear it?—yes, I hear it, and *have* heard it. Long—long— long—many minutes, many hours, many days, have I heard it—yet I dared not—oh, pity me, miserable wretch that I am!—I dared not—I *dared* not speak! *We have put her living in the tomb!* Said I not that my senses were acute? I *now* tell you that I heard her first feeble movements in the hollow coffin. I heard them—many, many days ago—yet I dared not—*I dared not speak!* And now—to-night—Ethelred—ha! ha!—the breaking of the hermit's door, and the death-cry of the dragon, and the clangor of the shield! say, rather, the rending of her coffin, and the grating of the iron hinges of her prison, and her struggles within the coppered archway of the vault! Oh whither shall I fly? Will she not be here anon? Is she not hurrying to upbraid me for my haste? Have I not heard her footstep on the stair? Do I not distinguish that heavy and horrible beating of her heart? *Madman!*" here he sprang furiously to his feet, and shrieked out his syllables, as if in the effort he were giving up his soul—*"Madman! I tell you that she now stands without the door!"*

As if in the superhuman energy of his utterance there had been found the potency of a spell—the huge antique panels to which the speaker pointed, threw slowly back, upon the instant, their ponderous and ebony jaws. It was the work of the rushing gust—but then without those doors there *did* stand the lofty and enshrouded figure of the lady Madeline of Usher. There was blood upon her white robes, and the evidence of some bitter struggle upon every portion of her emaciated frame. For a moment she remained trembling and reeling to and fro upon the threshold, then, with a low moaning cry, fell heavily inward upon the person of her brother, and in her violent and now final death-agonies, bore him to the floor a corpse, and a victim to the terrors he had anticipated.

From that chamber, and from that mansion, I fled aghast. The storm was still abroad in all its wrath as I found myself crossing the old causeway. Suddenly there shot along the path a wild light, and I turned to see whence a gleam so unusual could have issued; for the vast house and its shadows were alone behind me. The radiance was that of the full, setting, and blood-red moon which now shone vividly through that once barely-discernible fissure of which I have before spoken as extending from the roof of the building, in a zigzag direction, to the base. While I gazed, this fissure rapidly widened—there came a fierce breath of the whirlwind—the entire orb of the satellite burst at once upon my sight—my brain reeled as I saw the mighty walls rushing asunder—there was a long tumultuous shouting sound like the voice of a thousand waters—and the deep and dank tarn at my feet closed sullenly and silently over the fragments of the *"House of Usher."*

—1839

Guy de Maupassant (1850–1893) did not consider a literary career until he was almost thirty years of age. After military service he worked as a French government clerk until 1882. The great influence on his development as a writer was the novelist Gustave Flaubert, who introduced him to other Parisian literary figures, including Émile Zola, the leader of the naturalists. "Boule-de-suif," the story of a prostitute (the title, literally "grease-ball," is her nickname) whose generosity is gratefully accepted by a group of war refugees until they reach safety and revert to their former contempt, made Maupassant a celebrity when it was published in 1880 in an anthology of stories about the Franco-Prussian War of 1870. This humiliating defeat for France also provides the background for "Mother Savage." Maupassant died young, a victim of a self-destructive lifestyle that led to syphilis, attempted suicide, and madness, but during his most productive decade (1880–1890) he produced over three hundred stories, six novels, poetry, travel writing, and a play. Like his American contemporary O. Henry (William Sidney Porter), Maupassant first reached a large popular audience through mass-circulation magazines. Maupassant's focus on the unglamourous realities of both rural and urban life mark him as one of the masters of literary naturalism, and his careful plot construction and attention to detail set high standards for later writers of short fiction.

Guy de Maupassant
Mother Savage

I

It had been fifteen years since I had visited Virelogne. One autumn I returned to do some hunting and stayed with my friend Serval, who had finally rebuilt the château that the Prussians had destroyed.

I was madly in love with the area. It is one of those delightful corners of the world that possess a sensual appeal for the eyes. This is almost a physical kind of love. Those of us who are easily seduced by landscapes retain fond memories of certain springs, certain woods, certain streams, and certain hills which have become familiar to us and which can move our hearts like happy events. Sometimes our day-dreams return to a wooded spot, or a riverbank, or an orchard bursting into blossom, seen only once on a lovely day but held in our hearts like images of women strolling the streets on a spring morning with fresh, clean faces, stirring

Translated by Lafcadio Hearn; edited and revised by R. S. Gwynn.

body and soul with unrequited desire, with the unforgettable sensation of fleeting joy.

At Virelogne, I loved the whole countryside, dotted with little woods and traversed by streams that course though the soil like veins carrying blood to the earth. We fished for crawfish, for trout and eels. Such blessed happiness! There were spots to swim, and we could flush snipe from the tall weeds that grew along the banks of these narrow ribbons of water.

I walked along, lightly as a goat, watching my two dogs range in front of me. Serval, a hundred meters to my right, beat through a field of high grass. As I came around the bushes that mark the border of the Saudres Forest, I saw a thatched cottage in ruins.

Suddenly I recalled that I had seen it before, the last time in 1869, well kept up, covered with vines, and with a few chickens around the front door. What can be sadder than a dead house with its skeleton still standing, ruined and sinister?

I also recalled that the good woman who lived there had asked me in, one day when I was bone-tired, for a glass of wine, and that Serval had later told me the family history. The father, an old poacher, had been shot by the police. The son, whom I had seen before, was a tall, wiry fellow who also had a reputation as a fierce killer of game. They were called the Savages.

Was this their name or nickname?

I called out to Serval. He walked over to me with his long, ambling stride.

I asked him:

"What's become of the people who lived here?"

And he told me this story.

II

When the war broke out, Mother Savage's son, who was then thirty-three years old, volunteered, leaving his mother all alone. However, no one felt sorry for the old woman because everybody knew that she had money.

So she lived by herself in her isolated cottage, far from the village at the edge of the forest. But she was not a bit afraid, being made of the same stuff as the men of the countryside—a hardy old woman, tall and gaunt, who seldom laughed and whom nobody dared to cross. The women of the countryside do not laugh much. That's the men's business! The souls of these women are melancholy and narrow, for their lives are dismal and rarely brightened by an hour of joy. The peasant husbands or sons enjoy a little noisy gaiety in taverns, but their wives or mothers remain serious, with perpetually severe expressions. The muscles of their faces have never learned the movements of laughter.

Mother Savage continued to live as she always had in her cottage, which was soon covered with snow. Once a week she used to come to the village to buy bread and a meat, after which she would return home. As there was quite a bit of talk about wolves, she never went out without a gun slung on her shoulder, her son's rifle, a rusty weapon whose stock was quite worn from the hands that had rubbed against it; she made a strange sight, that tall old woman, a little stooped by age, walking with slow steps through the snow with the barrel of the gun sticking up behind the black scarf which covered her head and concealed the white hair that no one had ever seen.

One day the Prussians came. They were billeted with the people of the area, according to the wealth and resources of each family. The old woman had to take four of them because she was known to have money.

These were four big fellows with fair skin, blond beards, and blue eyes who had not grown thin in spite of all the wear and tear they had endured; they seemed to be good boys, even though they were in a conquered country. Finding themselves alone with the old woman, they took pains to show her all possible consideration and did everything they could save her trouble or expense. You could see them every morning, all four of them, washing up at the well in their shirt sleeves, pouring great quantities of cold water over that fair, rosy Northern skin of theirs even on the days when it was snowing most heavily—while Mother Savage came and went, getting their soup ready. Later they could be seen cleaning up the kitchen, washing windows, chopping wood, peeling potatoes, washing linen—in short, doing all the chores like four good boys working for their own mother.

But the old woman was always thinking of her own son—her tall, gaunt boy with his hooked nose and brown eyes and thick mustache that seemed to cover his upper lip like a pelt of black fur. And every day she used to ask the four soldiers quartered in her home, "Do you know where that French regiment is, the 23rd of the line? My son is in it."

They would reply, "No, not know, not nothing." And sensing her pain and fear, they, who had mothers far away themselves, showed her a thousand little courtesies. She liked them well enough, too, those four enemies of hers; for country people do not as a rule feel patriotic hatred—those feelings are reserved for the upper classes. The humble folk—those who pay the most because they are poor and are always being weighed down with new burdens, those who are slaughtered wholesale, those who make up the real cannon fodder because there are so many of them, those who, to tell the truth, suffer most hideously from the miserable atrocities of war because they are the most vulnerable and the least powerful—such people do not understand war fever or the fine points of military honor or, even less, those so-called political necessities which exhaust two nations in six months, both victor and vanquished alike.

Speaking of Mother Savage's Germans, folks in the area would say, "Well, those four landed in a safe enough spot."

One morning while Mother Savage was at home alone, she caught sight of a man far off across the fields, hurrying towards her gate. He soon came near enough for her to recognize him: it was the rural postman. He handed her a sheet of folded paper, and she took her glasses, which she always wore when sewing, out of their case, and read:

> *Madam Savage,*
> *This letter has a sad story to tell you. Your boy Victor was killed yesterday by a cannonball, which cut him practically in two. I was right there when it happened, for we stood next to each other in line and he was always talking to me about you so that I could let you know at once if he had any bad luck.*
> *I took his watch out of his pocket to bring to you when the war is over.*
> *Cordially,*
>
> > *Césaire Rivot,*
> > *Private Second Class in the*
> > *Twenty-third Regiment of the Line*

The letter was dated three weeks earlier.

She did not cry. She remained motionless, so overwhelmed, so stupefied by the blow that she did not immediately feel anything. She thought, "There's Victor, and now he's been killed." Then, little by little, tears slowly rose in her eyes, and sorrow invaded her heart. Thoughts came to her, one after the other—frightful, torturing ones. She would never kiss him again, her only child, her big, tall boy—never! The police had killed his father, and now the Prussians had killed the son . . . he had been cut in two by a cannonball. And it seemed to her she could see it all, the whole horrible thing: his head falling with his eyes wide open, his teeth still gnawing the corners of his thick mustache the way he used to do when he was angry.

What had they done afterward with his body? Couldn't they have brought her son back the same way they brought her husband back to her, with a bullet hole in the middle of his forehead?

But then she heard the sound of loud voices. It was the Prussians returning from the village. Quickly she hid the letter in her pocket and met them very calmly with her usual expression, for she had managed to wipe her eyes.

All four of them were laughing, quite delighted that they had been able to bring home a fine rabbit—doubtless stolen—and they made signs to the old woman that they were all going to have something really good to eat.

She set to work at once to prepare their dinner, but when the time came to kill the rabbit she did not have the heart to do it. Yet surely this wasn't the first rabbit she had ever been given to kill! One of the soldiers knocked it out by striking it behind the ears with his hand. Once it was dead she pulled the red body out of its skin, but the sight of the blood she was handling, which covered her fingers—the warm blood that she could feel cooling and coagulating—made her tremble from head to toe; all the while she kept seeing her tall son, cut in two and all red just like the body of the still quivering animal.

She sat down at the table with her Prussians, but she could not eat, not so much as a mouthful. They devoured the rabbit without paying any attention to her. Meanwhile she watched them from the corners of her eyes, not speaking—turning an idea over and over in her head, but with such an impassive face that none of them noticed anything unusual.

All of a sudden she said, "I don't even know your names, and we've been together for a whole month." They understood, with some difficulty, what she wanted and told her their names. But that was not enough; she made them write them down on a piece of paper along with the addresses of their families, and, placing her reading glasses on her big nose, she looked over the foreign writing; then she folded up the paper and put it into her pocket, next to the letter which had told her about the death of her son.

When the meal was over she said to them:

"Now I'm going to do something for you."

And she started carrying straw up into the loft where they slept.

They thought this was rather strange, but when she explained to them that it would keep them warmer they helped her. They stacked the bales all the way up to the thatched ceiling and made themselves a sort of large room with four walls of forage, warm and fragrant, where they could sleep peacefully.

At supper one of them became worried that Mother Savage still had not eaten anything. She told him that she had stomach cramps. Then she lit a good fire to warm herself, and the four Germans climbed up into their loft on the ladder they used every evening.

As soon as they had closed the trapdoor, the old woman took away the ladder, and, going outside without a sound, she began to collect straw and filled her kitchen with it. She walked barefoot through the snow—so softly that no one could hear her. From time to time she heard the loud and fitful snoring of the four sleeping soldiers.

When she decided that her preparations were complete, she thrust one of the bundles of straw into the fire, then flung the burning handful on top of the others and went outside to watch.

In several seconds a fierce glare lit the inside of the cottage; then the whole thing became a terrible furnace, a gigantic oven whose violent light blazed through the single narrow window and sent a bright ray reflecting over the snow.

Loud cries rang out from the upper part of the house. Then they were followed by a clamor of human screams full of agony and terror. Then, the trapdoor having been lifted, a storm of flame roared up into the loft, burnt through the roof of straw, rose up to the heavens like a vast bonfire, and the whole cottage went up in flames.

Nothing could now be heard but the crackling of the fire, the crumbling of the walls, the falling of the beams. The last fragments of the roof fell in, and the red-hot shell of the dwelling flung a huge shower of sparks skyward through clouds of thick smoke.

The snow-covered fields, lit up by the fire, shone like a sheet of silver tinged with crimson.

Far away, a bell began to ring.

Old Mother Savage stood at attention in front of the ruins of her home, armed with a gun, her dead son's rifle, to make sure that none of them could escape.

When she saw that it was all over, she threw the weapon into the fire. A single shot rang out.

People came running to the scene—the neighbors, the Prussian soldiers.

They found the old woman sitting on a tree stump, calm and satisfied.

A German officer, who spoke French like a son of France, asked her: "Where are your soldiers?"

She stretched out her skinny arm towards the smoldering mass of ruins where the fire was dying down at last and answered in a strong voice:

"There! Inside!"

Everyone gathered around her. The Prussian asked:

"How did the fire start?"

She answered:

"I started it."

They could not believe her, and they thought that the disaster had driven her mad. Then, when everyone had moved closer to listen to her, she told the whole story from beginning to end—from the arrival of the letter down to the final screams of the burning men inside her house. She did not leave out a single detail of what she had felt and what she had done.

When she finished, she took two pieces of paper out of her pocket and, so she could tell one from the other by the last light of the fire, adjusted her glasses and announced, holding up one piece of paper, "This one is Victor's death." Holding up the other, she added, nodding her head towards the still-red ruins, "This one has their names on it so you can write home about them." She calmly handed the white sheet to the officer, who was now holding her by the shoulders, and she continued:

"You can write them how this all happened, and you can tell their parents that I was the one who did it—I, Victoire Simon, The Savage! Never forget it."

The officer screamed some orders in German. They seized her and pushed her up against the still-warm walls of her house. Then a dozen men lined up in front of her, twenty meters away. She never blinked an eye. She knew what was coming, and she waited.

An order rang out, followed by a loud volley. One shot echoed all by itself after the others.

The old woman did not fall. She sank straight down as though her legs had been cut away from under her.

The Prussian officer approached to look. She had been cut almost in two, and her stiffened fingers still clutched the letter, bathed in blood.

III

My friend Serval added, "In reprisal, the Germans destroyed the local château, which I owned."

For my own part, I thought about the mothers of those four poor boys who had burned inside, and of the terrible heroism of that other mother, shot dead against that wall.

And I picked up a little stone, which still bore the scorch marks of the fire.

—1884

Kate Chopin (1851–1904) *was virtually forgotten for most of the twentieth century. She was rarely mentioned in histories of American literature and was remembered primarily as a chronicler of life among the Louisiana Creoles and Cajuns. Her works had long been out of print, when they were rediscovered in recent decades, initially by feminist critics and subsequently by general readers. Her most important novel,* The Awakening *(1899), today appears frequently on college reading lists and was filmed in 1992 as* Grand Isle. *Born in St. Louis, Chopin spent the 1870s in rural Louisiana, the wife of Oscar Chopin, a cotton broker from New Orleans. Later she lived with her husband on a plantation near Natchitoches, an area that provides the setting of the stories collected in* Bayou Folk *(1894) and* A Night in Arcadie *(1897) and from which she absorbed a rich mixture of French and black cultures. After her husband's death in 1883, Chopin returned to St. Louis with her six children and began her literary career, placing stories and regional pieces in popular magazines. Much of her later work is remarkable for its frank depiction of women's sexuality, a subject rarely broached in the literature of the era, and Chopin became the subject of controversy after the appearance of* The Awakening. *The negative reception of that work caused Chopin to suffer social ostracism and effectively ended her active career as a writer.*

Kate Chopin
The Story of an Hour

Knowing that Mrs. Mallard was afflicted with a heart trouble, great care was taken to break to her as gently as possible the news of her husband's death.

It was her sister Josephine who told her, in broken sentences, veiled hints that revealed in half concealing. Her husband's friend Richards was there, too, near her. It was he who had been in the newspaper office when intelligence of the railroad disaster was received, with Brently Mallard's name leading the list of "killed." He had only taken the time to assure himself of its truth by a second telegram, and had hastened to forestall any less careful, less tender friend in bearing the sad message.

She did not hear the story as many women have heard the same, with a paralyzed inability to accept its significance. She wept at once, with sudden, wild abandonment, in her sister's arms. When the storm of grief had spent itself she went away to her room alone. She would have no one follow her.

There stood, facing the open window, a comfortable, roomy arm-chair. Into this she sank, pressed down by a physical exhaustion that haunted her body and seemed to reach into her soul.

She could see in the open square before her house the tops of trees that were all aquiver with the new spring life. The delicious breath of rain was in the air. In the street below a peddler was crying his wares. The notes of a distant song which some one was singing reached her faintly, and countless sparrows were twittering in the eaves.

There were patches of blue sky showing here and there through the clouds that had met and piled above the other in the west facing her window.

She sat with her head thrown back upon the cushion of the chair quite motionless, except when a sob came up into her throat and shook her, as a child who has cried itself to sleep continues to sob in its dreams.

She was young, with a fair, calm face, whose lines bespoke repression and even a certain strength. But now there was a dull stare in her eyes, whose gaze was fixed away off yonder on one of those patches of blue sky. It was not a glance of reflection, but rather indicated a suspension of intelligent thought.

There was something coming to her and she was waiting for it, fearfully. What was it? She did not know; it was too subtle and elusive to name. But she felt it, creeping out of the sky, reaching toward her through the sounds, the scents, the color that filled the air.

Now her bosom rose and fell tumultuously. She was beginning to recognize this thing that was approaching to possess her, and she was striving to beat it back with her will—as powerless as her two white slender hands would have been.

When she abandoned herself a little whispered word escaped her slightly parted lips. She said it over and over under her breath: "Free, free, free!" The vacant stare and the look of terror that had followed it went from her eyes. They stayed keen and bright. Her pulses beat fast, and the coursing blood warmed and relaxed every inch of her body.

She did not stop to ask if it were not a monstrous joy that held her. A clear and exalted perception enabled her to dismiss the suggestion as trivial.

She knew that she would weep again when she saw the kind, tender hands folded in death; the face that had never looked save with love upon her, fixed and gray and dead. But she saw beyond that bitter moment a long procession of years to come that would belong to her absolutely. And she opened and spread her arms out to them in welcome.

There would be no one to live for her during those coming years; she would live for herself. There would be no powerful will bending her in that blind persistence with which men and women believe they have a right to impose a private will upon a fellow creature. A kind intention or a cruel intention made the act seem no less a crime as she looked upon it in that brief moment of illumination.

And yet she had loved him—sometimes. Often she had not. What did it matter! What could love, the unsolved mystery, count for in face of this possession of self-assertion which she suddenly recognized as the strongest impulse of her being.

"Free! Body and soul free!" she kept whispering.

Josephine was kneeling before the closed door with her lips to the keyhole, imploring for admission. "Louise, open the door! I beg; open the door—you will make yourself ill. What are you doing, Louise? For heaven's sake open the door."

"Go away. I am not making myself ill." No; she was drinking in a very elixir of life through that open window.

Her fancy was running riot along those days ahead of her. Spring days and summer days, and all sorts of days that would be her own. She breathed a quick prayer that life might be long. It was only yesterday she had thought with a shudder that life might be long.

She arose at length and opened the door to her sister's importunities. There was a feverish triumph in her eyes, and she carried herself unwittingly like a goddess of Victory. She clasped her sister's waist, and together they descended the stairs. Richards stood waiting for them at the bottom.

Some one was opening the front door with a latchkey. It was Brently Mallard who entered, a little travel-stained, composedly carrying his grip-sack and umbrella. He had been far from the scene of the accident, and did not even know there had been one. He stood amazed at Josephine's piercing cry; at Richards' quick motion to screen him from the view of his wife.

But Richards was too late.

When the doctors came they said she had died of heart disease—of joy that kills.

—*1894*

Anton Chekhov (1860–1904) *was the grandchild of Russian serfs but showed great understanding of and sympathy for upper-class characters, like those in his masterpiece* The Cherry Orchard *(1904), who could see their world ending in the decades before the Russian Revolution. After early education in his native town of Taganrog, Chekhov entered the University of Moscow, where he took a medical degree in 1884. Except for occasional service during epidemics, Chekhov practiced only rarely, preferring to earn his living as a regular contributor of stories to humor magazines. His first play,* Ivanov, *was produced in 1887, beginning a career as a dramatist that flourished in the last decade of his life when he allied himself with the Moscow Art Theatre and its influential director, Konstantin Stanislavsky. Chekhov's early stories were primarily comic, but those of his mature period, like his plays, are remarkable for their emotional depth. Chekhov's objectivity and realism, qualities that he perhaps gained from his medical studies, continue to make him one of the most modern of nineteenth-century authors; there are rarely easy morals in Chekhov's works. The "unheroic heroes and heroines" whom he depicts with sympathy and gentle irony foreshadow many of the key literary themes of our century.*

Anton Chekhov
An Upheaval

Mashenka Pavletsky, a young girl who had only just finished her studies at a boarding school, returning from a walk to the house of the Kushkins, with whom she was living as a governess, found the household in a terrible turmoil. Mihailo, the porter who opened the door to her, was excited and red as a crab.

Translated by Constance Garnett.

Loud voices were heard from upstairs.

"Madame Kushkin is in a fit, most likely, or else she has quarrelled with her husband," thought Mashenka.

In the hall and in the corridor she met maidservants. One of them was crying. Then Mashenka saw, running out of her room, the master of the house himself, Nikolay Sergeitch, a little man with a flabby face and a bald head, though he was not old. He was red in the face and twitching all over. He passed the governess without noticing her, and throwing up his arms, exclaimed:

"Oh, how horrible it is! How tactless! How stupid! How barbarous! Abominable!"

Mashenka went into her room, and then, for the first time in her life, it was her lot to experience in all its acuteness the feeling that is so familiar to persons in dependent positions, who eat the bread of the rich and powerful, and cannot speak their minds. There was a search going on in her room. The lady of the house, Fedosya Vassilyevna, a stout, broad-shouldered, uncouth woman with thick black eyebrows, a faintly perceptible moustache, and red hands, who was exactly like a plain, illiterate cook in face and manners, was standing, without her cap on, at the table, putting back into Mashenka's work-bag balls of wool, scraps of materials, and bits of papers. . . . Evidently the governess's arrival took her by surprise, since, on looking round and seeing the girl's pale and astonished face, she was a little taken aback, and muttered:

"*Pardon*. I . . . I upset it accidentally. . . . My sleeve caught in it . . ."

And saying something more, Madame Kushkin rustled her long skirts and went out. Mashenka looked round her room with wondering eyes, and, unable to understand it, not knowing what to think, shrugged her shoulders, and turned cold with dismay. What had Fedosya Vassilyevna been looking for in her work-bag? If she really had, as she said, caught her sleeve in it and upset everything, why had Nikolay Sergeitch lashed out of her room so excited and red in the face? Why was one drawer of the table pulled out a little way? The money-box, in which the governess put away ten kopeck pieces and old stamps, was open. They had opened it, but did not know how to shut it, though they had scratched the lock all over. The whatnot with her books on it, the things on the table, the bed—all bore fresh traces of a search. Her linen-basket, too. The linen had been carefully folded, but it was not in the same order as Mashenka had left it when she went out. So the search had been thorough, most thorough. But what was it for? Why? What had happened? Mashenka remembered the excited porter, the general turmoil which was still going on, the weeping servant-girl; had it not all some connection with the search that had just been made in her room? Was she not mixed up in something dreadful? Mashenka turned pale, and feeling cold all over, sank on to her linen-basket.

A maidservant came into the room.

"Liza, you don't know why they have been rummaging in my room?" the governess asked her.

"Mistress has lost a brooch worth two thousand," said Liza.

"Yes, but why have they been rummaging in my room?"

"They've been searching every one, miss. They've searched all my things, too. They stripped us all naked and searched us. . . . God knows, miss, I never went near her toilet-table, let alone touching the brooch. I shall say the same at the police-station."

"But . . . why have they been rummaging here?" the governess still wondered.

"A brooch has been stolen, I tell you. The mistress has been rummaging in everything with her own hands. She even searched Mihailo, the porter, herself. It's a perfect disgrace! Nikolay Sergeitch simply looks on and cackles like a hen. But you've no need to tremble like that, miss. They found nothing here. You've nothing to be afraid of if you didn't take the brooch."

"But Liza, it's vile . . . it's insulting," said Mashenka, breathless with indignation. "It's so mean, so low! What right had she to suspect me and to rummage in my things?"

"You are living with strangers, miss," sighed Liza. "Though you are a young lady, still you are . . . as it were . . . a servant. . . . It's not like living with your papa and mamma."

Mashenka threw herself on the bed and sobbed bitterly. Never in her life had she been subjected to such an outrage, never had she been so deeply insulted. . . . She, well-educated, refined, the daughter of a teacher, was suspected of theft; she had been searched like a street-walker! She could not imagine a greater insult. And to this feeling of resentment was added an oppressive dread of what would come next. All sorts of absurd ideas came into her mind. If they could suspect her of theft, then they might arrest her, strip her naked, and search her, then lead her through the street with an escort of soldiers, cast her into a cold, dark cell with mice and wood lice, exactly like the dungeon in which Princess Tarakanov was imprisoned. Who would stand up for her? Her parents lived far away in the Provinces; they had not the money to come to her. In the capital she was as solitary as in a desert, without friends or kindred. They could do what they liked with her.

"I will go to all the courts and all the lawyers," Mashenka thought, trembling. "I will explain to them, I will take an oath. . . . They will believe that I could not be a thief!"

Mashenka remembered that under the sheets in her basket she had some sweetmeats, which, following the habits of her schooldays, she had put in her pocket at dinner and carried off to her room. She felt hot all over, and was ashamed at the thought that her little secret was known to the lady of the house; all this terror, shame, resentment, brought on an attack of palpitation of the heart, which set up a throbbing in her temples, in her heart, and deep down in her stomach.

"Dinner is ready," the servant summoned Mashenka.

"Shall I go, or not?"

Mashenka brushed her hair, wiped her face with a wet towel and went into the dining-room. There they had already begun dinner. At one end of the table sat Fedosya Vassilyevna with a stupid, solemn, serious face; at the other end Nikolay Sergeitch. At the sides there were the visitors and the children. The dishes were handed by two footmen in swallowtails and white gloves. Everyone knew that there was an upset in the house, that Madame Kushkin was in trouble, and everyone was silent. Nothing was heard but the sound of munching and the rattle of spoons on the plates.

The lady of the house, herself, was the first to speak.

"What is the third course?" she asked the footman in a weary, injured voice.

"*Esturgeon à la russe*,"[1] answered the footman.

"I ordered that, Fenya," Nikolay Sergeitch hastened to observe. "I wanted some fish. If you don't like it, *ma chère*, don't let them serve it. I just ordered it. . . ."

Fedosya Vassilyevna did not like dishes that she had not ordered herself, and now her eyes filled with tears.

"Come, don't let us agitate ourselves," Mamikov, her household doctor, observed in a honeyed voice, just touching her arm, with a smile as

---

[1]*Esturgeon à la russe:* sturgeon, cooked in the Russian manner.

honeyed. "We are nervous enough as it is. Let us forget the brooch! Health is worth more than two thousand roubles!"

"It's not the two thousand I regret," answered the lady, and a big tear rolled down her check. "It's the fact itself that revolts me! I cannot put up with thieves in my house. I don't regret it—I regret nothing; but to steal from me is such ingratitude! That's how they repay me for my kindness. . . ."

They all looked into their plates, but Mashenka fancied after the lady's words that every one was looking at her. A lump rose in her throat; she began crying and put her handkerchief to her lips.

"*Pardon,*" she muttered. "I can't help it. My head aches. I'll go away."

And she got up from the table, scraping her chair awkwardly, and went out quickly, still more overcome with confusion.

"It's beyond everything!" said Nikolay Sergeitch, frowning. "What need was there to search her room? How out of place it was!"

"I don't say she took the brooch," said Fedosya Vassilyevna, "but can you answer for her? To tell the truth, I haven't much confidence in these learned paupers."

"It really was unsuitable, Fenya. . . . Excuse me, Fenya, but you've no kind of legal right to make a search."

"I know nothing about your laws. All I know is that I've lost my brooch. And I will find the brooch!" She brought her fork down on the plate with a clatter, and her eyes flashed angrily. "And you eat your dinner, and don't interfere in what doesn't concern you!"

Nikolay Sergeitch dropped his eyes mildly and sighed. Meanwhile Mashenka, reaching her room, flung herself on her bed. She felt now neither alarm nor shame, but she felt an intense longing to go and slap the cheeks of this hard, arrogant, dull-witted, prosperous woman.

Lying on her bed she breathed into her pillow and dreamed of how nice it would be to go and buy the most expensive brooch and fling it into the face of this bullying woman. If only it were God's will that Fedosya Vassilyevna should come to ruin and wander about begging, and should taste all the horrors of poverty and dependence, and that Mashenka, whom she had insulted, might give her alms! Oh, if only she could come in for a big fortune, could buy a carriage, and could drive noisily past the windows so as to be envied by that woman!

But all these were only dreams, in reality there was only one thing left to do—to get away as quickly as possible, not to stay another hour in this place. It was true it was terrible to lose her place, to go back to her parents, who had nothing; but what could she do? Mashenka could not bear the sight of the lady of the house nor of her little room; she felt stifled and wretched here. She was so disgusted with Fedosya Vassilyevna, who was so obsessed by her illnesses and her supposed aristocratic rank, that everything in the world seemed to have become coarse and unattractive because this woman was living in it. Mashenka jumped up from the bed and began packing.

"May I come in?" asked Nikolay Sergeitch at the door; he had come up noiselessly to the door, and spoke in a soft, subdued voice. "May I?"

"Come in."

He came in and stood still near the door. His eyes looked dim and his red little nose was shiny. After dinner he used to drink beer, and the fact was perceptible in his walk, in his feeble, flabby hands.

"What's this?" he asked, pointing to the basket.

"I am packing. Forgive me, Nikolay Sergeitch, but I cannot remain in your house. I feel deeply insulted by this search!"

"I understand. . . . Only you are wrong to go. . . . Why should you? They've searched your things, but you . . . what does it matter to you? You will be none the worse for it."

Mashenka was silent and went on packing. Nikolay Sergeitch pinched his moustache, as though wondering what he should say next, and went on in an ingratiating voice:

"I understand, of course, but you must make allowances. You know my wife is nervous, headstrong; you mustn't judge her too harshly."

Mashenka did not speak.

"If you are so offended," Nikolay Sergeitch went on, "well, if you like, I'm ready to apologize. I ask your pardon."

Mashenka made no answer, but only bent lower over her box. This exhausted, irresolute man was of absolutely no significance in the household. He stood in the pitiful position of a dependent and hanger-on, even with the servants, and his apology meant nothing either.

"H'm . . . You say nothing! That's not enough for you. In that case, I will apologize for my wife. In my wife's name. . . . She behaved tactlessly, I admit it as a gentleman . . ."

Nikolay Sergeitch walked about the room, heaved a sigh, and went on:

"Then you want me to have it rankling here, under my heart. . . . You want my conscience to torment me. . . ."

"I know it's not your fault, Nikolay Sergeitch," said Mashenka, looking him full in the face with her big tear-stained eyes. "Why should you worry yourself?"

"Of course, no. . . . But still, don't you . . . go away. I entreat you."

Mashenka shook her head. Nikolay Sergeitch stopped at the window and drummed on a pane with his fingertips.

"Such misunderstandings are simply torture to me," he said. "Why, do you want me to go down on my knees to you, or what? Your pride is wounded, and here you've been crying and packing up to go; but I have pride, too, and you do not spare it! Or do you want me to tell you what I would not tell at Confession? Do you? Listen; you want me to tell you what I won't tell the priest on my deathbed?"

Mashenka made no answer.

"I took my wife's brooch," Nikolay Sergeitch said quickly. "Is that enough now? Are you satisfied? Yes, I . . . took it. . . . But, of course, I count on your discretion. . . . For God's sake, not a word, not half a hint to any one!"

Mashenka, amazed and frightened, went on packing; she snatched her things, crumpled them up, and thrust them anyhow into the box and the basket. Now, after this candid avowal on the part of Nikolay Sergeitch, she could not remain another minute, and could not understand how she could have gone on living in the house before.

"And it's nothing to wonder at," Nikolay Sergeitch went on after a pause. "It's an everyday story! I need money, and she . . . won't give it to me. It was my father's money that bought this house and everything, you know! It's all mine, and the brooch belonged to my mother, and . . . it's all mine! And she took it, took possession of everything. . . . I can't go to law with her, you'll admit. . . . I beg you most earnestly, overlook it . . . stay on. *Tout comprendre, tout pardonner.*[2] Will you stay?"

"No!" said Mashenka resolutely, beginning to tremble. "Let me alone, I entreat you!"

"Well, God bless you!" sighed Nikolay Sergeitch, sitting down on the stool near the box. "I must own I like people who still can feel resentment, contempt, and so on. I could sit here forever and look at your indignant face. . . . So you won't stay, then? I understand. . . . it's

[2]*Tout comprendre, tout pardonner:* all is understood, all is forgiven.

bound to be so. . . . Yes, of course. . . . It's all right for you, but for me—wo-o-o-o! . . . I can't stir a step out of this cellar. I'd go off to one of our estates, but in every one of them there are some of my wife's rascals . . . stewards, experts, damn them all! They mortgage and remortgage. . . . You mustn't catch fish, must keep off the grass, mustn't break the trees."

"Nikolay Sergeitch!" his wife's voice called from the drawing-room. "Agnia, call your master!"

"Then you won't stay?" asked Nikolay Sergeitch, getting up quickly and going toward the door. "You might as well stay, really. In the evenings I could come and have a talk with you. Eh? Stay! If you go, there won't be a human face left in the house. It's awful!"

Nikolay Sergeitch's pale, exhausted face besought her, but Mashenka shook her head, and with a wave of his hand he went out.

Half an hour later she was on her way.

—1917

Edith Jones Wharton (1862–1937) was born into a socially prominent New York family and was privately educated at home and in Europe. A writer from her adolescence, Wharton received little encouragement from her parents or her husband, Edward Wharton, whom she married in 1885. Wharton's marriage was never happy, although it lasted until 1912, when her husband's serious mental illness made divorce imperative. Wharton's first publication was a book on interior decorating, but near the turn of the century her short fiction began to appear in magazines and was first collected in The Greater Inclination *(1899). Novels such as* The House of Mirth *(1905) and* The Age of Innocence *(1920) proved popular and have both been recently made into successful film versions. Wharton was awarded the Pulitzer Prize for* The Age of Innocence, *and the stage adaptation of another of her works,* The Old Maid, *also won one in 1935. Following her divorce, Wharton lived in France and was made a member of the Legion of Honor for her relief work during World War I. A longtime friend of Henry James, she shares some of the elder writer's interests as a keen observer and chronicler of the comedies (and tragedies) of manners among the American upper class. It is somewhat ironic that one of her best known works today is the novella* Ethan Frome *(1911), a grimly naturalistic tale of a doomed love triangle set in rural New England.*

Edith Wharton

Roman Fever

I

From the table at which they had been lunching two American ladies of ripe but well-cared-for middle age moved across the lofty terrace of the Roman restaurant and, leaning on its parapet, looked first at each other, and then down on the outspread glories of the Palatine and the Forum, with the same expression of vague but benevolent approval.

As they leaned there a girlish voice echoed up gaily from the stairs leading to the court below. "Well, come along, then," it cried, not to them but to an invisible companion, "and let's leave the young things to their knitting" and a voice as fresh laughed back: "Oh, look here, Babs, not actually *knitting*—" "Well, I mean figuratively," rejoined the first. "After all, we haven't left our poor parents much else to do . . ." and at that point the turn of the stairs engulfed the dialogue.

The two ladies looked at each other again, this time with a tinge of smiling embarrassment, and the smaller and paler one shook her head and colored slightly.

"Barbara!" she murmured, sending an unheard rebuke after the mocking voice in the stairway.

The other lady, who was fuller, and higher in color, with a small determined nose supported by vigorous black eyebrows, gave a good-humored laugh. "That's what our daughters think of us!"

Her companion replied by a deprecating gesture. "Not of us individually. We must remember that. It's just the collective modern idea of Mothers. And you see—" Half guiltily she drew from her handsomely mounted black hand-bag a twist of crimson silk run through by two fine knitting needles. "One never knows," she murmured. "The new system has certainly given us a good deal of time to kill; and sometimes I get tired just looking—even at this." Her gesture was now addressed to the stupendous scene at their feet.

The dark lady laughed again, and they both relapsed upon the view, contemplating it in silence, with a sort of diffused serenity which might have been borrowed from the spring effulgence of the Roman skies. The luncheon hour was long past, and the two had their end of the vast terrace to themselves. At its opposite extremity a few groups, detained by a lingering look at the outspread city, were gathering up guide-books and fumbling for tips. The last of them scattered, and the two ladies were alone on the air-washed height.

"Well, I don't see why we shouldn't just stay here," said Mrs. Slade, the lady of the high color and energetic brows. Two derelict basket chairs stood near, and she pushed them into the angle of the parapet, and settled herself in one, her gaze upon the Palatine. "After all, it's still the most beautiful view in the world."

"It always will be, to me," assented her friend Mrs. Ansley, with so slight a stress on the "me" that Mrs. Slade, though she noticed it, wondered if it were not merely accidental, like the random underlinings of old-fashioned letter writers.

"Grace Ansley was always old-fashioned," she thought; and added aloud, with a retrospective smile: "It's a view we've both been familiar with for a good many years. When we first met here we were younger than our girls are now. You remember?"

"Oh, yes, I remember," murmured Mrs. Ansley, with the same undefinable stress—"There's that headwaiter wondering," she interpolated. She was evidently far less sure than her companion of herself and of her rights in the world.

"I'll cure him of wondering," said Mrs. Slade, stretching her hand toward a bag as discreetly opulent-looking as Mrs. Ansley's. Signing to the head-waiter, she explained that she and her friend were old lovers of Rome, and would like to spend the end of the afternoon looking down on the view—that is, if it did not disturb the service? The headwaiter, bowing over her gratuity, assured her that the ladies were most welcome, and would be still more so if they would condescend to remain for dinner. A full moon night, they would remember. . . .

Mrs. Slade's black brows drew together, as though references to the moon were out-of-place and even unwelcome. But she smiled away her frown as the headwaiter retreated. "Well, why not? We might do worse. There's no way of knowing, I suppose, when the girls will be back. Do you even know back from *where?* I don't!"

Mrs. Ansley again colored slightly. "I think those young Italian aviators we met at the Embassy invited them to fly to Tarquinia for tea. I suppose they'll want to wait and fly back by moonlight."

"Moonlight—moonlight! What a part it still plays. Do you suppose they're as sentimental as we were?"

"I've come to the conclusion that I don't in the least know what they are," said Mrs. Ansley. "And perhaps we didn't know much more about each other."

"No; perhaps we didn't."

Her friend gave her a shy glance. "I never should have supposed you were sentimental, Alida."

"Well, perhaps I wasn't." Mrs. Slade drew her lips together in retrospect; and for a few moments the two ladies, who had been intimate since childhood, reflected how little they knew each other. Each one, of course, had a label ready to attach to the other's name; Mrs. Delphin Slade, for instance, would have told herself, or any one who asked her, that Mrs. Horace Ansley, twenty-five years ago, had been exquisitely lovely—no, you wouldn't believe it, would you? . . . though, of course, still charming, distinguished. . . . Well, as a girl she had been exquisite; far more beautiful than her daughter Barbara, though certainly Babs, according to the new standards at any rate, was more effective—had more *edge*, as they say. Funny where she got it, with those two nullities as parents. Yes; Horace Ansley was—well, just the duplicate of his wife. Museum specimens of old New York. Good-looking, irreproachable, exemplary. Mrs. Slade and Mrs. Ansley had lived opposite each other—actually as well as figuratively—for years. When the drawing-room curtains in No. 20 East 73rd Street were renewed, No. 23, across the way, was always aware of it. And of all the movings, buyings, travels, anniversaries, illnesses—the tame chronicle of an estimable pair. Little of it escaped Mrs. Slade. But she had grown bored with it by the time her husband made his big *coup* in Wall Street, and when they bought in upper Park Avenue had already begun to think: "I'd rather live opposite a speakeasy for a change; at least one might see it raided." The idea of seeing Grace raided was so amusing that (before the move) she launched it at a women's lunch. It made a hit, and went the rounds—she sometimes wondered if it had crossed the street, and reached Mrs. Ansley. She hoped not, but didn't much mind. Those were the days when respectability was at a discount, and it did the irreproachable no harm to laugh at them a little.

A few years later, and not many months apart, both ladies lost their husbands. There was an appropriate exchange of wreaths and condolences, and a brief renewal of intimacy in the half-shadow of their mourning; and now, after another interval, they had run across each other in Rome, at the same hotel, each of them the modest appendage of a salient daughter. The similarity of their lot had again drawn them together, lending itself to mild jokes, and the mutual confession that, if in old days it must have been tiring to "keep up" with daughters, it was now, at times, a little dull not to.

No doubt, Mrs. Slade reflected, she felt her unemployment more than poor Grace ever would. It was a big drop from being the wife of Delphin Slade to being his widow. She had always regarded herself (with a certain conjugal pride) as his equal in social gifts, as contributing her full share to the making of the exceptional couple they were: but the difference after his death was irremediable. As the wife of the famous corporation lawyer, always with an international case or two on hand, every day brought its exciting and unexpected obligation: the impromptu entertaining of eminent colleagues from abroad, the hurried dashes on legal business to London, Paris or Rome, where the entertaining was so handsomely reciprocated; the amusement of hearing in her wake: "What, that handsome woman with the good clothes and the eyes is Mrs. Slade—*the* Slade's wife? Really? Generally the wives of celebrities are such frumps."

Yes; being *the* Slade's widow was a dullish business after that. In living up to such a husband all her faculties had been engaged; now she had only her daughter to live up to, for the son who seemed to have inherited his father's gifts had died suddenly in boyhood. She had fought through that agony because her husband was there, to be helped and to help; now, after the father's death, the thought of the boy had become unbearable. There was nothing left but to mother her daughter; and dear Jenny was such a perfect daughter that she needed no excessive mothering. "Now with Babs Ansley I don't know that I *should* be so quiet," Mrs. Slade sometimes half-enviously reflected; but Jenny, who was younger than her brilliant friend, was that rare accident, an extremely pretty girl who somehow made youth and prettiness seem as safe as their absence. It was all perplexing—and to Mrs. Slade a little boring. She wished that Jenny would fall in love— with the wrong man, even; that she might have to be watched, out-maneuvered, rescued. And instead, it was Jenny who watched her mother, kept her out of draughts, made sure that she had taken her tonic. . . .

Mrs. Ansley was much less articulate than her friend, and her mental portrait of Mrs. Slade was slighter, and drawn with fainter touches. "Alida Slade's awfully brilliant; but not as brilliant as she thinks," would have summed it up; though she would have added, for the enlightenment of strangers, that Mrs. Slade had been an extremely dashing girl; much more so than her daughter, who was pretty, of course, and clever in a way, but had none of her mother's—well "vividness," someone had once called it. Mrs. Ansley would take up current words like this, and cite them in quotation marks, as unheard-of audacities. No; Jenny was not like her mother. Sometimes Mrs. Ansley thought Alida Slade was disappointed; on the whole she had had a sad life. Full of failures and mistakes; Mrs. Ansley had always been rather sorry for her. . . .

So these two ladies visualized each other, each through the wrong end of her little telescope.

II

For a long time they continued to sit side by side without speaking. It seemed as though, to both, there was a relief in laying down their somewhat futile activities in the presence of the vast Memento Mori[1]

---

[1]*Memento Mori:* the Latin means "remember you must die": it applies to any object that reminds one of mortality.

which faced them. Mrs. Slade sat quite still, her eyes fixed on the golden slope of the Palace of the Caesars, and after a while Mrs. Ansley ceased to fidget with her bag, and she too sank into meditation. Like many intimate friends, the two ladies had never before had occasion to be silent together, and Mrs. Ansley was slightly embarrassed by what seemed, after so many years, a new stage in their intimacy, and one with which she did not yet know how to deal.

Suddenly the air was full of that deep clangor of bells which periodically covers Rome with a roof of silver. Mrs. Slade glanced at her wristwatch. "Five o'clock already," she said, as though surprised.

Mrs. Ansley suggested interrogatively: "There's bridge at the Embassy at five." For a long time Mrs. Slade did not answer. She appeared to be lost in contemplation, and Mrs. Ansley thought the remark had escaped her. But after a while she said, as if speaking out of a dream: "Bridge, did you say? Not unless you want to. . . . But I don't think I will, you know."

"Oh, no," Mrs. Ansley hastened to assure her. "I don't care to at all. It's so lovely here; and so full of old memories, as you say." She settled herself in her chair, and almost furtively drew forth her knitting. Mrs. Slade took sideway note of this activity, but her own beautifully cared-for hands remained motionless on her knee.

"I was just thinking," she said slowly, "what different things Rome stands for to each generation of travelers. To our grandmothers, Roman fever; to our mothers, sentimental danger—how we used to be guarded!—to our daughters, no more dangers than the middle of Main Street. They don't know it—but how much they're missing!"

The long golden light was beginning to pale, and Mrs. Ansley lifted her knitting a little closer to her eyes. "Yes; how we were guarded!"

"I always used to think," Mrs. Slade continued, "that our mothers had a much more difficult job than our grandmothers. When Roman fever stalked the streets it must have been comparatively easy to gather in the girls at the danger hour; but when you and I were young, with such beauty calling us, and the spice of disobedience thrown in, and no worse risk than catching cold during the cool hour after sunset, the mothers used to be put to it to keep us in—didn't they?"

She turned again toward Mrs. Ansley, but the latter had reached a delicate point in her knitting. "One, two, three—slip two; yes, they must have been," she assented, without looking up.

Mrs. Slade's eyes rested on her with a deepened attention. "She can knit—in the face of *this!* How like her. . . ."

Mrs. Slade leaned back, brooding, her eyes ranging from the ruins which faced her to the long green hollow of the Forum, the fading glow of the church fronts beyond it, and the outlying immensity of the Colosseum. Suddenly she thought: "It's all very well to say that our girls have done away with sentiment and moonlight. But if Babs Ansley isn't out to catch that young aviator—the one who's a Marchese—then I don't know anything. And Jenny has no chance beside her. I know that too. I wonder if that's why Grace Ansley likes the two girls to go everywhere together? My poor Jenny as a foil—!" Mrs. Slade gave a hardly audible laugh, and at the sound Mrs. Ansley dropped her knitting.

"Yes—?"

"I—oh, nothing. I was only thinking how your Babs carries everything before her. That Campolieri boy is one of the best matches in Rome. Don't look so innocent, my dear—you know he is. And I was wondering, ever so respectfully, you understand . . . wondering how two such exemplary characters as you and Horace had managed to produce anything quite so dynamic." Mrs. Slade laughed again, with a touch of asperity.

Mrs. Ansley's hands lay inert across her needles. She looked straight out at the accumulated wreckage of passion and splendor at her feet. But her small profile was almost expressionless. At length she said: "I think you overrate Babs, my dear."

Mrs. Slade's tone grew easier. "No; I don't. I appreciate her. And perhaps envy you. Oh, my girl's perfect; if I were a chronic invalid I'd—well, I think I'd rather be in Jenny's hands. There must be times . . . but there! I always wanted a brilliant daughter . . . and never quite understood why I got an angel instead."

Mrs. Ansley echoed her laugh in a faint murmur. "Babs is an angel too."

"Of course—of course! But she's got rainbow wings. Well, they're wandering by the sea with their young men; and here we sit . . . and it all brings back the past a little too acutely."

Mrs. Ansley had resumed her knitting. One might almost have imagined (if one had known her less well, Mrs. Slade reflected) that, for her also, too many memories rose from the lengthening shadows of those august ruins. But no; she was simply absorbed in her work.

What was there for her to worry about? She knew that Babs would almost certainly come back engaged to the extremely eligible Campolieri. "And she'll sell the New York house, and settle down near them in Rome, and never be in their way . . . she's much too tactful. But she'll have an excellent cook, and just the right people in for bridge and cocktails . . . and a perfectly peaceful old age among her grandchildren."

Mrs. Slade broke off this prophetic flight with a recoil of self-disgust. There was no one of whom she had less right to think unkindly than of Grace Ansley. Would she never cure herself of envying her? Perhaps she had begun too long ago.

She stood up and leaned against the parapet, filling her troubled eyes with the tranquilizing magic of the hour. But instead of tranquilizing her the sight seemed to increase her exasperation. Her gaze turned toward the Colosseum. Already its golden flank was drowned in purple shadow, and above it the sky curved crystal clear, without light or color. It was the moment when afternoon and evening hang balanced in mid-heaven.

Mrs. Slade turned back and laid her hand on her friend's arm. The gesture was so abrupt that Mrs. Ansley looked up, startled.

"The sun's set. You're not afraid, my dear?"

"Afraid—?"

"Of Roman fever or pneumonia? I remember how ill you were that winter. As a girl you had a very delicate throat, hadn't you?"

"Oh, we're all right up here. Down below, in the Forum, it does get deathly cold, all of a sudden . . . but not here."

"Ah, of course you know because you had to be so careful." Mrs. Slade turned back to the parapet. She thought: "I must make one more effort not to hate her." Aloud she said: "Whenever I look at the Forum from up here I remember that story about a great-aunt of yours, wasn't she? A dreadfully wicked great-aunt?"

"Oh yes; Great-aunt Harriet. The one who was supposed to have sent her young sister out to the Forum after sunset to gather a night-blooming flower for her album. All of our great-aunts and grandmothers used to have albums of dried flowers."

Mrs. Slade nodded. "But she really sent her because they were in love with the same man—"

"Well that was the family tradition. They said Aunt Harriet confessed it years afterward. At any rate, the poor little sister caught the fever and died. Mother used to frighten us with the story when we were children."

"And you frightened *me* with it, that winter when you and I were here as girls. The winter I was engaged to Delphin."

Mrs. Ansley gave a faint laugh. "Oh, did I? Really frightened you? I don't believe you're easily frightened."

"Not often; but I was then. I was easily frightened because I was too happy. I wonder if you know what that means?"

"I—yes. . . ." Mrs. Ansley faltered.

"Well, I suppose that was why the story of your wicked aunt made such an impression on me. And I thought: 'There's no more Roman fever, but the Forum is deathly cold after sunset—especially after a hot day. And the Colosseum's even colder and damper.'"

"The Colosseum—?"

"Yes. It wasn't easy to get in, after the gates were locked for the night. Far from easy. Still, in those days it could be managed; it was managed, often. Lovers met there who couldn't meet elsewhere. You knew that?"

"I—I daresay. I don't remember."

"You don't remember? You don't remember going to visit some ruins or other one evening, just after dark, and catching a bad chill? You were supposed to have gone to see the moon rise. People always said that expedition was what caused your illness."

There was a moment's silence; then Mrs. Ansley rejoined: "Did they? It was all so long ago."

"Yes. And you got well again—so it didn't matter. But I suppose it struck your friends—the reason given for your illness, I mean—because everybody knew you were so prudent on account of your throat, and your mother took such care of you. . . . You *had* been out late sightseeing, hadn't you, that night?"

"Perhaps I had. The most prudent girls aren't always prudent. What made you think of it now?"

Mrs. Slade seemed to have no answer ready. But after a moment she broke out: "Because I simply can't bear it any longer—!"

Mrs. Ansley lifted her head quickly. Her eyes were wide and very pale. "Can't bear what?"

"Why—your not knowing that I've always known why you went."

"Why I went—?"

"Yes. You think I'm bluffing, don't you? Well, you went to meet the man I was engaged to—and I can repeat every word of the letter that took you there."

While Mrs. Slade spoke Mrs. Ansley had risen unsteadily to her feet. Her bag, her knitting and gloves, slid in a panic-stricken heap to the ground. She looked at Mrs. Slade as though she were looking at a ghost.

"No, no—don't," she faltered out.

"Why not? Listen, if you don't believe me. 'My one darling, things can't go on like this. I must see you alone. Come to the Colosseum immediately after dark tomorrow. There will be somebody to let you in. No one whom you need fear will suspect'—but perhaps you've forgotten what the letter said?"

Mrs. Ansley met the challenge with unexpected composure. Steadying herself against the chair she looked at her friend, and replied: "No; I know it by heart too."

"And the signature? 'Only *your* D.S.' Was that it? I'm right, am I? That was the letter that took you out that evening after dark?"

Mrs. Ansley was still looking at her. It seemed to Mrs. Slade that a slow struggle was going on behind the voluntarily controlled mask of her small quiet face. "I shouldn't have thought she had herself so well in hand," Mrs. Slade reflected, almost resentfully. But at this moment Mrs. Ansley spoke. "I don't know how you knew. I burnt that letter at once."

"Yes; you would, naturally—you're so prudent!" The sneer was open now. "And if you burnt the letter you're wondering how on earth I know what was in it. That's it, isn't it?"

Mrs. Slade waited, but Mrs. Ansley did not speak.

"Well, my dear, I know what was in that letter because I wrote it!"

"You wrote it?"

"Yes."

The two women stood for a minute staring at each other in the last golden light. Then Mrs. Ansley dropped back into her chair. "Oh," she murmured, and covered her face with her hands.

Mrs. Slade waited nervously for another word or movement. None came, and at length she broke out: "I horrify you."

Mrs. Ansley's hands dropped to her knee. The face they uncovered was streaked with tears. "I wasn't thinking of you. I was thinking—it was the only letter I ever had from him!"

"And I wrote it. Yes; I wrote it! But I was the girl he was engaged to. Did you happen to remember that?"

Mrs. Ansley's head drooped again. "I'm not trying to excuse myself . . . I remembered. . . ."

"And still you went?"

"Still I went."

Mrs. Slade stood looking down on the small bowed figure at her side. The flame of her wrath had already sunk, and she wondered why she had ever thought there would be any satisfaction in inflicting so purposeless a wound on her friend. But she had to justify herself.

"You do understand? I'd found out—and I hated you, hated you. I knew you were in love with Delphin—and I was afraid; afraid of you, of your quiet ways, your sweetness . . . your . . . well, I wanted you out of the way, that's all. Just for a few weeks; just till I was sure of him. So in a blind fury I wrote that letter . . . I don't know why I'm telling you now."

"I suppose," said Mrs. Ansley slowly, "it's because you've always gone on hating me."

"Perhaps. Or because I wanted to get the whole thing off my mind." She paused. "I'm glad you destroyed the letter. Of course I never thought you'd die."

Mrs. Ansley relapsed into silence, and Mrs. Slade, leaning above her, was conscious of a strange sense of isolation, of being cut off from the warm current of human communion. "You think me a monster!"

"I don't know. . . . It was the only letter I had, and you say he didn't write it?"

"Ah, how you care for him still!"

"I cared for that memory," said Mrs. Ansley.

Mrs. Slade continued to look down on her. She seemed physically reduced by the blow—as if, when she got up, the wind might scatter her like a puff of dust. Mrs. Slade's jealousy suddenly leapt up again at the sight. All these years the woman had been living on that letter. How she must have loved him, to treasure the mere memory of its ashes! The letter of the man her friend was engaged to. Wasn't it she who was the monster?

"You tried your best to get him away from me, didn't you? But you failed; and I kept him. That's all."

"Yes. That's all."

"I wish now I hadn't told you. I've no idea you'd feel about it as you do; I thought you'd be amused. It all happened so long ago, as you say;

and you must do me the justice to remember that I had no reason to think you'd ever taken it seriously. How could I, when you were married to Horace Ansley two months afterward? As soon as you could get out of bed your mother rushed you off to Florence and married you. People were rather surprised—they wondered at its being done so quickly; but I thought I knew. I had an idea you did it out of *pique*—to be able to say you'd got ahead of Delphin and me. Girls have such silly reasons for doing the most serious things. And your marrying so soon convinced me that you'd never really cared."

"Yes. I suppose it would," Mrs. Ansley assented.

The clear heaven overhead was emptied of all its gold. Dusk spread over it, abruptly darkening the Seven Hills. Here and there lights began to twinkle through the foliage at their feet. Steps were coming and going on the deserted terrace—waiters looking out of the doorway at the head of the stairs, then reappearing with trays and napkins and flasks of wine. Tables were moved, chairs straightened. A feeble string of electric lights flickered out. Some vases of faded flowers were carried away, and brought back replenished. A stout lady in a dustcoat suddenly appeared, asking in broken Italian if anyone had seen the elastic band which held together her tattered Baedeker. She poked with her stick under the table at which she had lunched, the waiters assisting.

The corner where Mrs. Slade and Mrs. Ansley sat was still shadowy and deserted. For a long time neither of them spoke. At length Mrs. Slade began again: "I suppose I did it as a sort of joke—"

"A joke?"

"Well, girls are ferocious sometimes, you know. Girls in love especially. And I remember laughing to myself all that evening at the idea that you were waiting around there in the dark, dodging out of sight, listening for every sound, trying to get in—Of course I was upset when I heard you were so ill afterward."

Mrs. Ansley had not moved for a long time. But now she turned slowly toward her companion. "But I didn't wait. He'd arranged everything. He was there. We were let in at once," she said.

Mrs. Slade sprang up from her leaning position. "Delphin there? They let you in?—Ah, now you're lying!" she burst out with violence.

Mrs. Ansley's voice grew clearer, and full of surprise. "But of course he was there. Naturally he came—"

"Came? How did he know he'd find you there? You must be raving!"

Mrs. Ansley hesitated, as though reflecting. "But I answered the letter. I told him I'd be there. So he came."

Mrs. Slade flung her hands up to her face. "Oh, God—you answered! I never thought of your answering. . . ."

"It's odd you never thought of it, if you wrote the letter."

"Yes. I was blind with rage."

Mrs. Ansley rose, and drew her fur scarf about her. "It is cold here. We'd better go. . . . I'm sorry for you," she said, as she clasped the fur about her throat.

The unexpected words sent a pang through Mrs. Slade. "Yes; we'd better go." She gathered up her bag and cloak. "I don't know why you should be sorry for me," she muttered.

Mrs. Ansley stood looking away from her toward the dusky secret mass of the Colosseum. "Well—because I didn't have to wait that night."

Mrs. Slade gave an unquiet laugh. "Yes; I was beaten there. But I oughtn't to begrudge it to you, I suppose. At the end of all these years. After all, I had everything; I had him for twenty-five years. And you had nothing but that one letter that he didn't write."

Mrs. Ansley was again silent. At length she turned toward the door of the terrace. She took a step, and turned back, facing her companion.

"I had Barbara," she said, and began to move ahead of Mrs. Slade toward the stairway.

—*1936*

Willa Cather (1873–1947) *was born in rural Virginia but moved in childhood to the Nebraska farmlands. After graduating from the University of Nebraska she lived for a time in Pittsburgh (the hometown of the title character in "Paul's Case"), where she moved so that she, like Paul, could attend the theater and concerts. After some years as a drama critic for the Pittsburgh* Daily Leader *and a brief term as a high school English teacher, she moved to New York, where she eventually became managing editor of* McClure's Magazine, *a position she held from 1906 to 1912. Her novels about the settling of the Nebraska farmlands,* O Pioneers! *(1913) and* My Antonía *(1918), proved successful, and for the rest of her life Cather devoted her full energies to writing fiction. In her later years she ranged further for her subjects—New Mexico for the setting of* Death Comes to the Archbishop *(1927) and Quebec for* Shadows on the Rock *(1931). "Paul's Case," one of the stories that helped her obtain a position with* McClure's, *casts an almost clinical eye on heredity and environment as influences on the protagonist's personality. This deterministic view of character and Paul's desperate attempt to escape the dreary trap of his hometown reflect important themes of naturalism, a literary movement with which Cather would later express dissatisfaction but that dominated much fiction written near the turn of the century.*

Willa Cather
Paul's Case[1]

It was Paul's afternoon to appear before the faculty of the Pittsburgh High School to account for his various misdemeanors. He had been suspended a week ago, and his father had called at the Principal's office and confessed his perplexity about his son. Paul entered the faculty room suave and smiling. His clothes were a trifle outgrown and the tan velvet on the collar of his open overcoat was frayed and worn; but for all that there was something of the dandy about him, and he wore an opal pin in his neatly knotted black four-in-hand, and a red carnation in his buttonhole. This latter adornment the faculty somehow felt was not properly significant of the contrite spirit befitting a boy under the ban of suspension.

Paul was tall for his age and very thin, with high, cramped shoulders and a narrow chest. His eyes were remarkable for a certain hysterical brilliancy and he continually used them in a conscious, theatrical

---

[1]A Study in Temperament (Cather's subtitle).

sort of way, peculiarly offensive in a boy. The pupils were abnormally large, as though he were addicted to belladonna, but there was a glassy glitter about them which that drug does not produce.

When questioned by the Principal as to why he was there, Paul stated, politely enough, that he wanted to come back to school. This was a lie, but Paul was quite accustomed to lying; found it, indeed, indispensable for overcoming friction. His teachers were asked to state their respective charges against him, which they did with such a rancor and aggrieved-ness as evinced that this was not a usual case. Disorder and impertinence were among the offenses named, yet each of his instructors felt that it was scarcely possible to put into words the real cause of the trouble, which lay in a sort of hysterically defiant manner of the boy's; in the contempt which they all knew he felt for them, and which he seemingly made not the least effort to conceal. Once, when he had been making a synopsis of a paragraph at the blackboard, his English teacher had stepped to his side and attempted to guide his hand. Paul had started back with a shud-der and thrust his hands violently behind him. The astonished woman could scarcely have been more hurt and embarrassed had he struck at her. The insult was so involuntary and definitely personal as to be unfor-gettable. In one way and another, he had made all his teachers, men and women alike, conscious of the same feeling of physical aversion. In one class he habitually sat with his hand shading his eyes; in another he al-ways looked out of the window during the recitation; in another he made a running commentary on the lecture, with humorous intention.

His teachers felt this afternoon that his whole attitude was symbol-ized by his shrug and his flippantly red carnation flower, and they fell upon him without mercy, his English teacher leading the pack. He stood through it smiling, his pale lips parted over his white teeth. (His lips were continually twitching, and he had a habit of raising his eyebrows that was contemptuous and irritating to the last degree.) Older boys than Paul had broken down and shed tears under that baptism of fire, but his set smile did not once desert him, and his only sign of discomfort was the nervous trembling of the fingers that toyed with the buttons of his overcoat, and an occasional jerking of the other hand that held his hat. Paul was always smiling, always glancing about him, seeming to feel that people might be watching him and trying to detect something. This conscious expression, since it was as far as possible from boyish mirthfulness, was usually attributed to insolence or "smartness."

As the inquisition proceeded, one of his instructors repeated an impertinent remark of the boy's, and the Principal asked him whether he thought that a courteous speech to have made a woman. Paul shrugged his shoulders slightly and his eyebrows twitched.

"I don't know," he replied. "I didn't mean to be polite or impolite, either. I guess it's a sort of way I have of saying things regardless."

The Principal, who was a sympathetic man, asked him whether he didn't think that a way it would be well to get rid of. Paul grinned and said he guessed so. When he was told that he could go, he bowed gracefully and went out. His bow was but a repetition of the scandalous red carnation.

His teachers were in despair, and his drawing master voiced the feeling of them all when he declared there was something about the boy which none of them understood. He added: "I don't really believe that smile of his comes altogether from insolence; there's something sort of haunted about it. The boy is not strong, for one thing. I happen to know that he was born in Colorado, only a few months before his mother died out there of a long illness. There is something wrong about the fellow."

The drawing master had come to realize that, in looking at Paul, one saw only his white teeth and the forced animation of his eyes. One warm afternoon the boy had gone to sleep at his drawing-board, and his master had noted with amazement what a white, blue-veined face it was; drawn and wrinkled like an old man's about the eyes, the lips twitching even in his sleep, and stiff with a nervous tension that drew them back from his teeth.

His teachers left the building dissatisfied and unhappy; humiliated to have felt so vindictive toward a mere boy, to have uttered this feeling in cutting terms, and to have set each other on, as it were, in the gruesome game of intemperate reproach. Some of them remembered having seen a miserable street cat set at bay by a ring of tormentors.

As for Paul, he ran down the hill whistling the Soldiers' Chorus from *Faust* looking wildly behind him now and then to see whether some of his teachers were not there to writhe under his light-heartedness. As it was now late in the afternoon and Paul was on duty that evening as usher at Carnegie Hall, he decided that he would not go home to supper. When he reached the concert hall the doors were not yet open and, as it was chilly outside, he decided to go up into the picture gallery—always deserted at this hour—where there were some of Raffaelli's gay studies

of Paris streets and an airy blue Venetian scene or two that always exhilarated him. He was delighted to find no one in the gallery but the old
guard, who sat in one corner, a newspaper on his knee, a black patch
over one eye and the other closed. Paul possessed himself of the place
and walked confidently up and down, whistling under his breath. After
a while he sat down before a blue Rico and lost himself. When he
bethought him to look at his watch, it was after seven o'clock, and he
rose with a start and ran downstairs, making a face at Augustus, peering out from the cast-room, and an evil gesture at the Venus of Milo as
he passed her on the stairway.

When Paul reached the ushers' dressing-room half-a-dozen boys
were there already, and he began excitedly to tumble into his uniform. It
was one of the few that at all approached fitting, and Paul thought it
very becoming—though he knew that the tight, straight coat accentu-
ated his narrow chest, about which he was exceedingly sensitive. He was
always considerably excited while he dressed, twanging all over to the
tuning of the strings and the preliminary flourishes of the horns in the
music-room; but tonight he seemed quite beside himself, and he teased
and plagued the boys until, telling him that he was crazy, they put him
down on the floor and sat on him.

Somewhat calmed by his suppression, Paul dashed out to the front
of the house to seat the early comers. He was a model usher; gracious
and smiling he ran up and down the aisles; nothing was too much trouble for him; he carried messages and brought programmes as though it
were his greatest pleasure in life, and all the people in his section
thought him a charming boy, feeling that he remembered and admired
them. As the house filled, he grew more and more vivacious and animated, and the color came to his cheeks and lips. It was very much as
though this were a great reception and Paul were the host. Just as the
musicians came out to take their places, his English teacher arrived
with checks for the seats which a prominent manufacturer had taken
for the season. She betrayed some embarrassment when she handed
Paul the tickets, and a *hauteur* which subsequently made her feel very
foolish. Paul was startled for a moment, and had the feeling of wanting
to put her out; what business had she here among all these fine people
and gay colors? He looked her over and decided that she was not appro-
priately dressed and must be a fool to sit downstairs in such togs. The
tickets had probably been sent her out of kindness, he reflected as he

put down a seat for her, and she had about as much right to sit there as he had.

When the symphony began Paul sank into one of the rear seats with a long sigh of relief, and lost himself as he had done before the Rico. It was not that symphonies, as such, meant anything in particular to Paul, but the first sigh of the instruments seemed to free some hilarious and potent spirit within him; something that struggled there like the Genius in the bottle found by the Arab fisherman. He felt a sudden zest of life; the lights danced before his eyes and the concert hall blazed into unimaginable splendor. When the soprano soloist came on, Paul forgot even the nastiness of his teacher's being there and gave himself up to the peculiar stimulus such personages always had for him. The soloist chanced to be a German woman, by no means in her first youth, and the mother of many children; but she wore an elaborate gown and a tiara, and above all she had that indefinable air of achievement, that world-shine upon her, which, in Paul's eyes, made her a veritable queen of Romance.

After a concert was over Paul was always irritable and wretched until he got to sleep, and tonight he was even more than usually restless. He had the feeling of not being able to let down, of its being impossible to give up this delicious excitement which was the only thing that could be called living at all. During the last number he withdrew and, after hastily changing his clothes in the dressing-room, slipped out to the side door where the soprano's carriage stood. Here he began pacing rapidly up and down the walk, waiting to see her come out.

Over yonder the Schenley, in its vacant stretch, loomed big and square through the fine rain, the windows of its twelve stories glowing like those of a lighted cardboard house under a Christmas tree. All the actors and singers of the better class stayed there when they were in the city, and a number of the big manufacturers of the place lived there in the winter. Paul had often hung about the hotel, watching the people go in and out, longing to enter and leave school-masters and dull care behind him forever.

At last the singer came out, accompanied by the conductor, who helped her into her carriage and closed the door with a cordial *auf wiedersehen*[2] which set Paul to wondering whether she were not an old sweetheart of his. Paul followed the carriage over to the hotel, walking so rapidly as not to be far from the entrance when the singer alighted

---

[2]*auf wiedersehen*: good-bye.

and disappeared behind the swinging glass doors that were opened by a
negro in a tall hat and a long coat. In the moment that the door was ajar
it seemed to Paul that he, too, entered. He seemed to feel himself go after her up the steps, into the warm, lighted building, into an exotic, a
tropical world of shiny, glistening surfaces and basking ease. He reflected upon the mysterious dishes that were brought into the dining-
room, the green bottles in buckets of ice, as he had seen them in the
supper party pictures of the *Sunday World* supplement. A quick gust of
wind brought the rain down with sudden vehemence, and Paul was
startled to find that he was still outside in the slush of the gravel driveway; that his boots were letting in the water and his scanty overcoat was
clinging wet about him; that the lights in front of the concert hall were
out, and that the rain was driving in sheets between him and the orange
glow of the windows above him. There it was, what he wanted—tangi-
bly before him, like the fairy world of a Christmas pantomime, but
mocking spirits stood guard at the doors, and, as the rain beat in his
face, Paul wondered whether he were destined always to shiver in the
black night outside, looking up at it.

He turned and walked reluctantly toward the car tracks. The end
had to come sometime; his father in his night-clothes at the top of the
stairs, explanations that did not explain, hastily improvised fictions that
were forever tripping him up, his upstairs room and its horrible yellow
wall-paper, the creaking bureau with the greasy plush collar-box, and
over his painted wooden bed the pictures of George Washington and
John Calvin, and the framed motto, "Feed my Lambs," which had been
worked in red worsted by his mother.

Half an hour later, Paul alighted from his car and went slowly down
one of the side streets off the main thoroughfare. It was a highly respectable street, where all the houses were exactly alike, and where
businessmen of moderate means begot and reared large families of children, all of whom went to Sabbath-school and learned the shorter catechism, and were interested in arithmetic; all of whom were as exactly
alike as their homes, and of a piece with the monotony in which they
lived. Paul never went up Cordelia Street without a shudder of loathing.
His home was next to the house of the Cumberland[3] minister. He approached it tonight with the nerveless sense of defeat, the hopeless feeling of sinking back forever into ugliness and commonness that he had

---

[3]*Cumberland:* an offshoot of the Presbyterian Church.

always had when he came home. The moment he turned into Cordelia Street he felt the waters close above his head. After each of these orgies of living, he experienced all the physical depression which follows a debauch; the loathing of respectable beds, of common food, of a house penetrated by kitchen odors; a shuddering repulsion for the flavorless, colorless mass of everyday existence; a morbid desire for cool things and soft lights and fresh flowers.

The nearer he approached the house, the more absolutely unequal Paul felt to the sight of it all; his ugly sleeping chamber; the cold bathroom with the grimy zinc tub, the cracked mirror, the dripping spigots; his father, at the top of the stairs, his hairy legs sticking out from his night-shirt, his feet thrust into carpet slippers. He was so much later than usual that there would certainly be inquiries and reproaches. Paul stopped short before the door. He felt that he could not be accosted by his father tonight; that he could not toss again on that miserable bed. He would not go in. He would tell his father that he had no car fare, and it was raining so hard he had gone home with one of the boys and stayed all night.

Meanwhile, he was wet and cold. He went around to the back of the house and tried one of the basement windows, found it open, raised it cautiously, and scrambled down the cellar wall to the floor. There he stood, holding his breath, terrified by the noise he had made, but the floor above him was silent, and there was no creak on the stairs. He found a soap-box, and carried it over to the soft ring of light that streamed from the furnace door, and sat down. He was horribly afraid of rats, so he did not try to sleep, but sat looking distrustfully at the dark, still terrified lest he might have awakened his father. In such reactions, after one of the experiences which made days and nights out of the dreary blanks of the calendar, when his senses were deadened, Paul's head was always singularly clear. Suppose his father had heard him getting in at the window and had come down and shot him for a burglar? Then, again, suppose his father had come down, pistol in hand, and he had cried out in time to save himself, and his father had been horrified to think how nearly he had killed him? Then, again, suppose a day should come when his father would remember that night, and wish there had been no warning cry to stay his hand? With this last supposition Paul entertained himself until daybreak.

The following Sunday was fine; the sodden November chill was broken by the last flash of autumnal summer. In the morning Paul had to go to church and Sabbath-school, as always. On seasonable Sunday afternoons the burghers of Cordelia Street always sat out on their front "stoops," and talked to their neighbors on the next stoop, or called to those across the street in neighborly fashion. The men usually sat on gay cushions placed upon the steps that led down to the sidewalk, while the women, in their Sunday "waists,"[4] sat in rockers on the cramped porches, pretending to be greatly at their ease. The children played in the streets; there were so many of them that the place resembled the recreation grounds of a kindergarten. The men on the steps—all in their shirt sleeves, their vests unbuttoned—sat with their legs well apart, their stomachs comfortably protruding, and talked of the prices of things, or told anecdotes of the sagacity of their various chiefs and overlords. They occasionally looked over the multitude of squabbling children, listened affectionately to their high-pitched, nasal voices, smiling to see their own proclivities reproduced in their offspring, and interspersed their legends of the iron kings with remarks about their sons' progress at school, their grades in arithmetic, and the amounts they had saved in their toy banks.

On this last Sunday of November, Paul sat all the afternoon on the lowest step of his "stoop," staring into the street, while his sisters, in their rockers, were talking to the minister's daughters next door about how many shirt-waists they had made in the last week, and how many waffles some one had eaten at the last church supper. When the weather was warm, and his father was in a particularly jovial frame of mind, the girls made lemonade, which was always brought out in a red-glass pitcher, ornamented with forget-me-nots in blue enamel. This the girls thought very fine, and the neighbors always joked about the suspicious color of the pitcher.

Today Paul's father sat on the top step, talking to a young man who shifted a restless baby from knee to knee. He happened to be the young man who was daily held up to Paul as a model, and after whom it was his father's dearest hope that he would pattern. This young man was of a ruddy complexion, with a compressed, red mouth, and faded, near-sighted eyes, over which he wore thick spectacles, with gold bows that curved about his ears. He was clerk to one of the magnates of a great steel corporation, and was looked upon in Cordelia Street as a young

---

[4]*"waists"*: shirt waist dresses.

man with a future. There was a story that, some five years ago—he was now barely twenty-six—he had been a trifle dissipated but in order to curb his appetites and save the loss of time and strength that a sowing of wild oats might have entailed, he had taken his chief's advice, oft reiterated to his employees, and at twenty-one had married the first woman whom he could persuade to share his fortunes. She happened to be an angular schoolmistress, much older than he, who also wore thick glasses, and who had now borne him four children, all near-sighted, like herself.

The young man was relating how his chief, now cruising in the Mediterranean, kept in touch with all the details of the business, arranging his office hours on his yacht just as though he were at home, and "knocking off work enough to keep two stenographers busy." His father told, in turn, the plan his corporation was considering, of putting in an electric railway plant at Cairo. Paul snapped his teeth; he had an awful apprehension that they might spoil it all before he got there. Yet he rather liked to hear these legends of the iron kings, that were told and retold on Sundays and holidays; these stories of palaces in Venice, yachts on the Mediterranean, and high play at Monte Carlo appealed to his fancy, and he was interested in the triumphs of these cash boys who had become famous, though he had no mind for the cash-boy stage.

After supper was over, and he had helped to dry the dishes, Paul nervously asked his father whether he could go to George's to get some help in his geometry, and still more nervously asked for car fare. This latter request he had to repeat, as his father, on principle, did not like to hear requests for money, whether much or little. He asked Paul whether he could not go to some boy who lived nearer, and told him that he ought not to leave his school work until Sunday; but he gave him the dime. He was not a poor man, but he had a worthy ambition to come up in the world. His only reason for allowing Paul to usher was, that he thought a boy ought to be earning a little.

Paul bounded upstairs, scrubbed the greasy odor of the dish-water from his hands with the ill-smelling soap he hated, and then shook over his fingers a few drops of violet water from the bottle he kept hidden in his drawer. He left the house with his geometry conspicuously under his arm, and the moment he got out of Cordelia Street and boarded a downtown car, he shook off the lethargy of two deadening days, and began to live again.

The leading juvenile of the permanent stock company which played at one of the downtown theatres was an acquaintance of Paul's, and the boy had been invited to drop in at the Sunday-night rehearsals whenever he could. For more than a year Paul had spent every available moment loitering about Charley Edwards's dressing-room. He had won a place among Edwards's following not only because the young actor, who could not afford to employ a dresser, often found him useful, but because he recognized in Paul something akin to what churchmen term "vocation."

It was at the theatre and at Carnegie Hall that Paul really lived; the rest was but a sleep and a forgetting. This was Paul's fairy tale, and it had for him all the allurement of a secret love. The moment he inhaled the gassy, painty, dusty odor behind the scenes, he breathed like a prisoner set free, and felt within him the possibility of doing or saying splendid, brilliant, poetic things. The moment the cracked orchestra beat out the overture from *Martha*, or jerked at the serenade from *Rigoletto*, all stupid and ugly things slid from him, and his senses were deliciously, yet delicately fired.

Perhaps it was because, in Paul's world, the natural nearly always wore the guise of ugliness, that a certain element of artificiality seemed to him necessary in beauty. Perhaps it was because his experience of life elsewhere was so full of Sabbath-school picnics, petty economies, wholesome advice as to how to succeed in life, and the unescapable odors of cooking, that he found this existence so alluring, these smartly-clad men and women so attractive, that he was so moved by these starry apple orchards that bloomed perennially under the limelight.

It would be difficult to put it strongly enough how convincingly the stage entrance of that theatre was for Paul the actual portal of Romance. Certainly none of the company ever suspected it, least of all Charley Edwards. It was very like the old stories that used to float about London of fabulously rich Jews, who had subterranean halls there, with palms, and fountains, and soft lamps and richly apparelled women who never saw the disenchanting light of London day. So, in the midst of that smoke-palled city, enamored of figures and grimy toil, Paul had his secret temple, his wishing carpet, his bit of blue-and-white Mediterranean shore bathed in perpetual sunshine.

Several of Paul's teachers had a theory that his imagination had been perverted by garish fiction, but the truth was that he scarcely ever read at all. The books at home were not such as would either tempt or corrupt a youthful mind, and as for reading the novels that some of his friends urged upon him—well, he got what he wanted much more quickly from music; any sort of music, from an orchestra to a barrel organ. He needed only the spark, the indescribable thrill that made his imagination master of his senses, and he could make plots and pictures enough of his own. It was equally true that he was not stage struck— not, at any rate, in the usual acceptation of that expression. He had no desire to become an actor, any more than he had to become a musician. He felt no necessity to do any of these things; what he wanted was to see, to be in the atmosphere, float on the wave of it, to be carried out, blue league after blue league, away from everything.

After a night behind the scenes, Paul found the school room more than ever repulsive; the bare floors and naked walls; the prosy men who never wore frock coats, or violets in their button-holes; the women with their dull gowns, shrill voices, and pitiful seriousness about prepositions that govern the dative. He could not bear to have the other pupils think, for a moment, that he took these people seriously; he must convey to them that he considered it all trivial, and was there only by way of a jest, anyway. He had autographed pictures of all the members of the stock company which he showed his classmates, telling them the most incredible stories of his familiarity with these people, of his acquaintance with the soloists who came to Carnegie Hall, his suppers with them and the flowers he sent them. When these stories lost their effect, and his audience grew listless, he became desperate and would bid all the boys good-bye, announcing that he was going to travel for a while; going to Naples, to Venice, to Egypt. Then, next Monday, he would slip back, conscious and nervously smiling; his sister was ill, and he should have to defer his voyage until spring.

Matters went steadily worse with Paul at school. In the itch to let his instructors know how heartily he despised them and their homilies, and how thoroughly he was appreciated elsewhere, he mentioned once or twice that he had no time to fool with theorems; adding—with a twitch of the eyebrows and a touch of that nervous bravado which so perplexed them—that he was helping the people down at the stock company; they were old friends of his.

The upshot of the matter was that the Principal went to Paul's father, and Paul was taken out of school and put to work. The manager at Carnegie Hall was told to get another usher in his stead; the doorkeeper at the theatre was warned not to admit him to the house; and Charley Edwards remorsefully promised the boy's father not to see him again.

The members of the stock company were vastly amused when some of Paul's stories reached them—especially the women. They were hard-working women, most of them supporting indigent husbands or brothers, and they laughed rather bitterly at having stirred the boy to such fervid and florid inventions. They agreed with the faculty and with his father that Paul's was a bad case.

The east-bound train was ploughing through a January snowstorm; the dull dawn was beginning to show grey when the engine whistled a mile out of Newark. Paul started up from the seat where he had lain curled in uneasy slumber, rubbed the breath-misted window glass with his hand, and peered out. The snow was whirling in curling eddies above the white bottom lands, and the drifts lay already deep in the fields and along the fences, while here and there the long dead grass and dried weed stalks protruded black above it. Lights shone from the scattered houses, and a gang of laborers who stood beside the track waved their lanterns.

Paul had slept very little, and he felt grimy and uncomfortable. He had made the all-night journey in a day coach, partly because he was ashamed, dressed as he was, to go into a Pullman, and partly because he was afraid of being seen there by some Pittsburgh businessman, who might have noticed him in Denny & Carson's office. When the whistle awoke him, he clutched quickly at his breast pocket, glancing about him with an uncertain smile. But the little, clay-bespattered Italians were still sleeping, the slatternly women across the aisle were in open-mouthed oblivion, and even the crumby, crying babies were for the nonce stilled. Paul settled back to struggle with his impatience as best as he could.

When he arrived at the Jersey City station, he hurried through his breakfast manifestly ill at ease and keeping a sharp eye about him. After he reached the Twenty-third Street station, he consulted a cabman, and had himself driven to a men's furnishing establishment that was just opening for the day. He spent upward of two hours there, buying with endless reconsidering and great care. His new street suit he put on in the fitting-room; the frock coat and dress clothes he had bundled into the cab with his linen. Then he drove to a hatter's and a shoe house.

His next errand was at Tiffany's, where he selected his silver and a new scarf-pin. He would not wait to have his silver marked, he said. Lastly, he stopped at a trunk shop on Broadway, and had his purchases packed into various traveling bags.

It was a little after one o'clock when he drove up to the Waldorf, and after settling with the cabman, went into the office. He registered from Washington; said his mother and father had been abroad, and that he had come down to await the arrival of their steamer. He told his story plausibly and had no trouble, since he volunteered to pay for them in advance, in engaging his rooms; a sleeping-room, sitting-room and bath.

Not once, but a hundred times Paul had planned this entry into New York. He had gone over every detail of it with Charley Edwards, and in his scrap book at home there were pages of description about New York hotels, cut from the Sunday papers. When he was shown to his sitting-room on the eighth floor, he saw at a glance that everything was as it should be; there was but one detail in his mental picture that the place did not realize, so he rang for the bell boy and sent him down for flowers. He moved about nervously until the boy returned, putting away his new linen and fingering it delightedly as he did so. When the flowers came, he put them hastily into water, and then tumbled into a hot bath. Presently he came out of his white bathroom, resplendent in his new silk underwear, and playing with the tassels of his red robe. The snow was whirling so fiercely outside his windows that he could scarcely see across the street, but within the air was deliciously soft and fragrant. He put the violets and jonquils on the taboret beside the couch, and threw himself down, with a long sigh, covering himself with a Roman blanket. He was thoroughly tired; he had been in such haste, he had stood up to such a strain, covered so much ground in the last twenty-four hours, that he wanted to think how it had all come about. Lulled by the sound of the wind, the warm air, and the cool fragrance of the flowers, he sank into deep, drowsy retrospection.

It had been wonderfully simple; when they had shut him out of the theatre and concert hall, when they had taken away his bone, the whole thing was virtually determined. The rest was a mere matter of opportunity. The only thing that at all surprised him was his own courage—for he realized well enough that he had always been tormented by fear, a sort of apprehensive dread that, of late years, as the meshes of the lies he had told closed about him, had been pulling the muscles of his body tighter and tighter. Until now, he could not remember the time when he had not been dreading something. Even when he was a little boy, it was always there—behind him, or before, or on either side. There had always been the shadowed corner, the dark place into which he dared not look, but from which something seemed always to be watching him— and Paul had done things that were not pretty to watch, he knew.

But now he had a curious sense of relief, as though he had at last thrown down the gauntlet to the thing in the corner.

Yet it was but a day since he had been sulking in the traces; but yesterday afternoon that he had been sent to the bank with Denny & Carson's deposit, as usual—but this time he was instructed to leave the book to be balanced. There was above two thousand dollars in checks, and nearly a thousand in the bank notes which he had taken from the book and quietly transferred to his pocket. At the bank he had made out a new deposit slip. His nerves had been steady enough to permit of his returning to the office, where he had finished his work and asked for a full day's holiday tomorrow, Saturday, giving a perfectly reasonable pretext. The bank book, he knew, would not be returned before Monday or Tuesday, and his father would be out of town for the next week. From the time he slipped the bank notes into his pocket until he boarded the night train for New York, he had not known a moment's hesitation. It was not the first time Paul had steered through treacherous waters.

How astonishingly easy it had all been; here he was, the thing done; and this time there would be no awakening, no figure at the top of the stairs. He watched the snow flakes whirling by his window until he fell asleep.

When he awoke, it was three o'clock in the afternoon. He bounded up with a start; half of one of his precious days gone already! He spent more than an hour in dressing, watching every stage of his toilet carefully in the mirror. Everything was quite perfect; he was exactly the kind of boy he had always wanted to be.

When he went downstairs, Paul took a carriage and drove up Fifth Avenue toward the Park. The snow had somewhat abated; carriages and tradesmen's wagons were hurrying soundlessly to and fro in the winter twilight; boys in woollen mufflers were shovelling off the doorsteps; the avenue stages made fine spots of color against the white street. Here and there on the corners were stands, with whole flower gardens blooming under glass cases, against the sides of which the snow flakes stuck and melted; violets, roses, carnations, lilies of the valley—somehow vastly more lovely and alluring that they blossomed thus unnaturally in the snow. The Park itself was a wonderful stage winter-piece.

When he returned, the pause of the twilight had ceased, and the tune of the streets had changed. The snow was falling faster, lights streamed from the hotels that reared their dozen stories fearlessly up into the storm, defying the raging Atlantic winds. A long, black stream of carriages poured down the avenue, intersected here and there by other streams, tending horizontally. There were a score of cabs about the entrance of his hotel, and his driver had to wait. Boys in livery were running in and out of the awning stretched across the sidewalk, up and down the red velvet carpet laid from the door to the street. Above, about, within it all was the rumble and roar, the hurry and toss of thousands of human beings as hot for pleasure as himself, and on every side of him towered the glaring affirmation of the omnipotence of wealth.

The boy set his teeth and drew his shoulders together in a spasm of realization: the plot of all dramas, the text of all romances, the nerve-stuff of all sensations was whirling about him like the snow flakes. He burnt like a faggot in a tempest.

When Paul went down to dinner, the music of the orchestra came floating up the elevator shaft to greet him. His head whirled as he stepped into the thronged corridor, and he sank back into one of the chairs against the wall to get his breath. The lights, the chatter, the perfumes, the bewildering medley of color—he had, for a moment, the feeling of not being able to stand it. But only for a moment; these were his own people, he told himself. He went slowly about the corridors, through the writing-rooms, smoking-rooms, reception-rooms, as though he were exploring the chambers of an enchanted palace, built and peopled for him alone.

When he reached the dining-room he sat down at a table near a window. The flowers, the white linen, the many-colored wine glasses, the gay toilettes of the women, the low popping of corks, the undulating repetitions of the *Blue Danube* from the orchestra, all flooded Paul's dream with bewildering radiance. When the roseate tinge of his champagne was added—that cold, precious, bubbling stuff that creamed and foamed in his glass—Paul wondered that there were honest men in the world at all. This was what all the world was fighting for, he reflected; this was what all the struggle was about. He doubted the reality of his past. Had he ever known a place called Cordelia Street, a place where fagged-looking businessmen got on the early car; mere rivets in a machine they seemed to Paul—sickening men, with combings of children's hair always hanging to their coats, and the smell of cooking in their clothes. Cordelia Street—Ah! that belonged to another time and country; had he not always been thus, had he not sat here night after night, from as far back as he could remember, looking pensively over just such shimmering textures, and slowly twirling the stem of a glass like this one between his thumb and middle finger? He rather thought he had.

He was not in the least abashed or lonely. He had no especial desire to meet or to know any of these people; all he demanded was the right to look on and conjecture, to watch the pageant. The mere stage properties were all he contended for. Nor was he lonely later in the evening, in his loge at the Metropolitan. He was now entirely rid of his nervous misgivings, of his forced aggressiveness, of the imperative desire to show himself different from his surroundings. He felt now that his surroundings explained him. Nobody questioned the purple; he had only to wear it passively. He had only to glance down at his attire to reassure himself that here it would be impossible for anyone to humiliate him.

He found it hard to leave his beautiful sitting-room to go to bed that night, and sat long watching the raging storm from his turret window. When he went to sleep it was with the lights turned on in his bedroom; partly because of his old timidity, and partly so that, if he should wake in the night, there would be no wretched moment of doubt, no horrible suspicion of yellow wallpaper, or of Washington and Calvin above his bed.

Sunday morning the city was practically snowbound. Paul breakfasted late, and in the afternoon he fell in with a wild San Francisco boy, a freshman at Yale, who said he had run down for a "little flyer" over Sunday. The young man offered to show Paul the night side of the town, and the two boys went out together after dinner, not returning to the hotel until seven o'clock the next morning. They had started out in the confiding warmth of a champagne friendship, but their parting in the elevator was singularly cool. The freshman pulled himself together to make his train, and Paul went to bed. He awoke at two o'clock in the afternoon, very thirsty and dizzy, and rang for ice-water, coffee, and the Pittsburgh papers.

On the part of the hotel management, Paul excited no suspicion. There was this to be said for him, that he wore his spoils with dignity and in no way made himself conspicuous. Even under the glow of his wine he was never boisterous, though he found the stuff like a magician's wand for wonder-building. His chief greediness lay in his ears and eyes, and his excesses were not offensive ones. His dearest pleasures were the grey winter twilights in his sitting-room; his quiet enjoyment of his flowers, his clothes, his wide divan, his cigarette, and his sense of power. He could not remember a time when he had felt so at peace with himself. The mere release from the necessity of petty lying, lying every day and every day, restored his self-respect. He had never lied for pleasure, even at school; but to be noticed and admired, to assert his difference from other Cordelia Street boys; and he felt a good deal more manly, more honest, even, now that he had no need for boastful pretensions, now that he could, as his actor friends used to say, "dress the part." It was characteristic that remorse did not occur to him. His golden days went by without a shadow, and he made each as perfect as he could.

On the the eighth day after his arrival in New York, he found the whole affair exploited in the Pittsburgh papers, exploited with a wealth of detail which indicated that local news of a sensational nature was at a low ebb. The firm of Denny & Carson announced that the boy's father had refunded the full amount of the theft, and that they had no intention of prosecuting. The Cumberland minister had been interviewed, and expressed his hope of yet reclaiming the motherless lad, and his Sabbath-school teacher declared that she would spare no effort to that end. The rumor had reached Pittsburgh that the boy had been seen in a New York hotel, and his father had gone East to find him and bring him home.

Paul had just come in to dress for dinner; he sank into a chair, weak to the knees, and clasped his head in his hands. It was to be worse than jail, even; the tepid waters of Cordelia Street were to close over him finally and forever. The grey monotony stretched before him in hopeless, unrelieved years; Sabbath-school, Young People's Meeting, the yellow-papered room, the damp dishtowels; it all rushed back upon him with a sickening vividness. He had the old feeling that the orchestra had suddenly stopped, the sinking sensation that the play was over. The sweat broke out on his face, and he sprang to his feet, looked about him with his white, conscious smile, and winked at himself in the mirror. With something of the old childish belief in miracles with which he had so often gone to class, all his lessons unlearned, Paul dressed and dashed whistling down the corridor to the elevator.

He had no sooner entered the dining-room and caught the measure of the music than his remembrance was lightened by his old elastic power of claiming the moment, mounting with it, and finding it all sufficient. The glare and glitter about him, the mere scenic accessories had again, and for the last time, their old potency. He would show himself that he was game, he would finish the thing splendidly. He doubted, more than ever, the existence of Cordelia Street, and for the first time he drank his wine recklessly. Was he not, after all, one of those fortunate beings born to the purple, was he not still himself and in his own place? He drummed a nervous accompaniment to the Pagliacci music and looked about him, telling himself over and over that it had paid.

He reflected drowsily, to the swell of the music and the chill sweetness of his wine, that he might have done it more wisely. He might have caught an outboard steamer and been well out of their clutches before now. But the other side of the world had seemed too far away and too uncertain then; he could not have waited for it; his need had been too sharp. If he had to choose over again, he would do the same thing tomorrow. He looked affectionately about the dining-room, now gilded with a soft mist. Ah, it had paid indeed!

Paul was awakened next morning by a painful throbbing in his head and feet. He had thrown himself across the bed without undressing, and had slept with his shoes on. His limbs and hands were lead heavy, and his tongue and throat were parched and burnt. There came upon him one of those fateful attacks of clearheadedness that never occurred except when he was physically exhausted and his nerves hung loose. He lay still and closed his eyes and let the tide of things wash over him.

His father was in New York; "stopping at some joint or other," he told himself. The memory of successive summers on the front stoop fell upon him like a weight of black water. He had not a hundred dollars left; and he knew now, more than ever, that money was everything, the wall that stood between all he loathed and all he wanted. The thing was winding itself up; he had thought of that on his first glorious day in New York, and had even provided a way to snap the thread. It lay on his dressing-table now; he had got it out last night when he came blindly up from dinner, but the shiny metal hurt his eyes, and he disliked the looks of it.

He rose and moved about with a painful effort, succumbing now and again to attacks of nausea. It was the old depression exaggerated;

all the world had become Cordelia Street. Yet somehow he was not afraid of anything, was absolutely calm; perhaps because he had looked into the dark corner at last and knew. It was bad enough, what he saw there, but somehow not so bad as his long fear of it had been. He saw everything clearly now. He had a feeling that he had made the best of it, that he had lived the sort of life he was meant to live, and for half an hour he sat staring at the revolver. But he told himself that was not the way, so he went downstairs and took a cab to the ferry.

When Paul arrived at Newark, he got off the train and took another cab, directing the driver to follow the Pennsylvania tracks out of the town. The snow lay heavy on the roadways and had drifted deep in the open fields. Only here and there the dead grass or dried weed stalks projected, singularly black, above it. Once well into the country, Paul dismissed the carriage and walked, floundering along the tracks, his mind a medley of irrelevant things. He seemed to hold in his brain an actual picture of everything he had seen that morning. He remembered every feature of both his drivers, of the toothless old woman from whom he had bought the red flowers in his coat, the agent from whom he had got his ticket, and all of his fellow-passengers on the ferry. His mind, unable to cope with vital matters near at hand, worked feverishly and deftly at sorting and grouping these images. They made for him a part of the ugliness of the world, of the ache in his head, and the bitter burning on his tongue. He stooped and put a handful of snow into his mouth as he walked, but that, too, seemed hot. When he reached a little hillside, where the tracks ran through a cut some twenty feet below him, he stopped and sat down.

The carnations in his coat were drooping with the cold, he noticed; their red glory all over. It occurred to him that all the flowers he had seen in the glass cases that first night must have gone the same way, long before this. It was only one splendid breath they had, in spite of their brave mockery at the winter outside the glass; and it was a losing game in the end, it seemed, this revolt against the homilies by which the world is run. Paul took one of the blossoms carefully from his coat and scooped a little hole in the snow, where he covered it up. Then he dozed a while, from his weak condition, seemingly insensible to the cold.

The sound of an approaching train awoke him, and he started to his feet, remembering only his resolution, and afraid lest he should be too late. He stood watching the approaching locomotive, his teeth chattering, his lips drawn away from them in a frightened smile; once or twice he glanced nervously sidewise, as though he were being watched. When the right moment came, he jumped. As he fell, the folly of his haste occurred to him with merciless clearness, the vastness of what he had left undone. There flashed through his brain, clearer than ever before, the blue of Adriatic water, the yellow of Algerian sands.

He felt something strike his chest, and that his body was being thrown swiftly through the air, on and on, immeasurably far and fast, while his limbs were gently relaxed. Then, because the picture-making mechanism was crushed, the disturbing visions flashed into black, and Paul dropped back into the immense design of things.

—1904

James Joyce (1882–1941) is best known for his masterpiece Ulysses, *the difficult modernist novel of a single day in the life of Dublin that shortly after its appearance in 1922 became both a classic and the subject of a landmark censorship case, which its publishers eventually won. Joyce's lifelong quarrel with the provincial concerns of Irish religious, cultural, and literary life (all touched on in his long story "The Dead") led him to permanent continental self-exile in Zürich and Paris. Most readers would associate Joyce with his pioneering of experimental techniques such as the fragmentary observations found in his early* Epiphanies *(posthumously published in 1956), his use of interior monologue and stream of consciousness, and the complicated linguistic games of* Finnegan's Wake *(1939), forgetting that his earlier works lie squarely in the realm of traditional fiction.* Dubliners *(1914), his collection of short stories of life in his native city, remains an imposing achievement, as does his autobiographical novel* A Portrait of the Artist as a Young Man *(1916). "Eveline," in the surprising failure of its protagonist to free herself from an unhappy life, mirrors Joyce's own ambivalence toward his homeland, which he abandoned physically but never spiritually.*

James Joyce
Eveline

She sat at the window watching the evening invade the avenue. Her head was leaned against the window curtains and in her nostrils was the odour of dusty cretonne.[1] She was tired.

---

[1]*cretonne:* the cotton fabric of the curtains.

Few people passed. The man out of the last house passed on his way home; she heard his footsteps clacking along the concrete pavement and afterwards crunching on the cinder path before the new red houses. One time there used to be a field there in which they used to play every evening with other people's children. Then a man from Belfast bought the field and built houses in it—not like their little brown houses but bright brick houses with shining roofs. The children of the avenue used to play together in that field—the Devines, the Waters, the Dunns, little Keogh the cripple, she and her brothers and sisters. Ernest, however, never played: he was too grown up. Her father used often to hunt them in out of the field with his blackthorn stick; but usually little Keogh used to keep *nix* and call out when he saw her father coming. Still they seemed to have been rather happy then. Her father was not so bad then; and besides, her mother was alive. That was a long time ago; she and her brothers and sisters were all grown up; her mother was dead. Tizzie Dunn was dead, too, and the Waters had gone back to England. Everything changes. Now she was going to go away like the others, to leave her home.

Home! She looked round the room, reviewing all its familiar objects which she had dusted once a week for so many years, wondering where on earth all the dust came from. Perhaps she would never see again those familiar objects from which she had never dreamed of being divided. And yet during all those years she had never found out the name of the priest whose yellowing photograph hung on the wall above the broken harmonium beside the coloured print of the promises made to Blessed Margaret Mary Alacoque. He had been a school friend of her father. Whenever he showed the photograph to a visitor her father used to pass it with a casual word:

—He is in Melbourne now.

She had consented to go away, to leave her home. Was that wise? She tried to weigh each side of the question. In her home anyway she had shelter and food; she had those whom she had known all her life about her. Of course she had to work hard both in the house and at business. What would they say of her in the Stores when they found out that she had run away with a fellow? Say she was a fool, perhaps; and her place would be filled up by advertisement. Miss Gavan would be glad. She had always had an edge on her, especially whenever there were people listening.

—Miss Hill, don't you see these ladies are waiting?

—Look lively, Miss Hill, please.

She would not cry many tears at leaving the Stores.

But in her new home, in a distant unknown country, it would not be like that. Then she would be married—she, Eveline. People would treat her with respect then. She would not be treated as her mother had been. Even now, though she was over nineteen, she sometimes felt herself in danger of her father's violence. She knew it was that that had given her the palpitations. When they were growing up he had never gone for her, like he used to go for Harry and Ernest, because she was a girl; but latterly he had begun to threaten her and say what he would do to her only for her dead mother's sake. And now she had nobody to protect her. Ernest was dead and Harry, who was in the church decorating business, was nearly always down somewhere in the country. Besides, the invariable squabble for money on Saturday nights had begun to weary her unspeakably. She always gave her entire wages—seven shillings—and Harry always sent up what he could but the trouble was to get any money from her father. He said she used to squander the money, that she had no head, that he wasn't going to give her his hard-earned money to throw about the streets, and much more, for he was usually fairly bad of a Saturday night. In the end he would give her the money and ask her had she any intention of buying Sunday's dinner. Then she had to rush out as quickly as she could and do her marketing, holding her black leather purse tightly in her hand as she elbowed her way through the crowds and returning home late under her load of provisions. She had hard work to keep the house together and to see that the two young children who had been left to her charge went to school regularly and got their meals regularly. It was hard work—a hard life—but now that she was about to leave it she did not find it a wholly undesirable life.

She was about to explore another life with Frank. Frank was very kind, manly, open-hearted. She was to go away with him by the night-boat to be his wife and to live with him in Buenos Ayres where he had a home waiting for her. How well she remembered the first time she had seen him; he was lodging in a house on the main road where she used to visit. It seemed a few weeks ago. He was standing at the gate, his peaked cap pushed back on his head and his hair tumbled forward over a face of bronze. Then they had come to know each other. He used to meet her outside the Stores every evening and see her home. He took her to see *The Bohemian Girl* and she felt elated as she sat in an unaccustomed part of the theatre with him. He was awfully fond of music and sang a little. People knew that they were courting and, when he sang about the lass that loves a sailor, she always felt pleasantly confused. He used to call her Poppens out of fun. First of all it had been an excitement for her to have a fellow and then she had begun to like him. He had tales of distant countries. He had started as a deck boy at a pound a month on a ship of the Allan Line going out to Canada. He told her the names of the ships he had been on and the names of the different services. He had sailed through the Straits of Magellan and he told her stories of the terrible Patagonians. He had fallen on his feet in Buenos Ayres, he said, and had come over to the old country just for a holiday. Of course, her father had found out the affair and had forbidden her to have anything to say to him.

—I know these sailor chaps, he said.

One day he had quarrelled with Frank and after that she had to meet her lover secretly.

The evening deepened in the avenue. The white of two letters in her lap grew indistinct. One was to Harry; the other was to her father. Ernest had been her favourite but she liked Harry too. Her father was becoming old lately, she noticed; he would miss her. Sometimes he could be very nice. Not long before, when she had been laid up for a day, he had read her out a ghost story and made toast for her at the fire. Another day, when their mother was alive, they had all gone for a picnic to the Hill of Howth. She remembered her father putting on her mother's bonnet to make the children laugh.

Her time was running out but she continued to sit by the window, leaning her head against the window curtain, inhaling the odour of dusty cretonne. Down far in the avenue she could hear a street organ playing. She knew the air. Strange that it should come that very night to remind her of the promise to her mother, her promise to keep the home together as long as she could. She remembered the last night of her mother's illness; she was again in the close dark room at the other side of the hall and outside she heard a melancholy air of Italy. The organ-player had been ordered to go away and given sixpence. She remembered her father strutting back into the sickroom saying:

—Damned Italians! coming over here!

As she mused the pitiful vision of her mother's life laid its spell on the very quick of her being—that life of commonplace sacrifices closing in final craziness. She trembled as she heard again her mother's voice saying constantly with foolish insistence:

—Derevaun Seraun! Derevaun Seraun![2]

She stood up in a sudden impulse of terror. Escape! She must escape! Frank would save her. He would give her life, perhaps love, too. But she wanted to live. Why should she be unhappy? She had a right to happiness. Frank would take her in his arms, fold her in his arms. He would save her.

She stood among the swaying crowd in the station at the North Wall. He held her hand and she knew that he was speaking to her, saying something about the passage over and over again. The station was full of soldiers with brown baggages. Through the wide doors of the sheds she caught a glimpse of the black mass of the boat, lying in beside the quay wall, with illumined portholes. She answered nothing. She felt her cheek pale and cold and, out of a maze of distress, she prayed to God to direct her, to show her what was her duty. The boat blew a long mournful whistle into the mist. If she went, to-morrow she would be on the sea with Frank, steaming towards Buenos Ayres. Their passage had been booked. Could she still draw back after all he had done for her? Her distress awoke a nausea in her body and she kept moving her lips in silent fervent prayer.

A bell clanged upon her heart. She felt him seize her hand:

—Come!

All the seas of the world tumbled about her heart. He was drawing her into them: he would drown her. She gripped with both hands at the iron railing.

—Come!

No! No! No! It was impossible. Her hands clutched the iron in frenzy. Amid the seas she sent a cry of anguish!

—Eveline! Evvy!

He rushed beyond the barrier and called to her to follow. He was shouted at to go on but he still called to her. She set her white face to him, passive, like a helpless animal. Her eyes gave him no sign of love or farewell or recognition.

—1916

---

[2]*Derevaun Seraun:* apparently this is gibberish.

***D. H. Lawrence** (1885–1930) whose working-class origins in the English Midlands provided him with autobiographical subject matter for* Sons and Lovers *(1913) and also provided characters and setting for novels like* The Rainbow *(1915) and* Women in Love *(1920). Born in Nottinghamshire, the son of a coal miner and a teacher, Lawrence was encouraged in his reading by his mother. After receiving his teaching certificate from University College in Nottingham, Lawrence taught briefly, then began to publish poetry and fiction. His first novel,* The White Peacock, *appeared in 1911. Lawrence's long marriage to Frieda von Richtofen, a cousin of the German "Red Baron" of World War I fame, endured many strains but lasted until his death. His interest in Freudian psychology and the dynamics of human sexuality made him controversial during his career and perhaps still overshadows his skills as a chronicler of English life in villages forever altered by the Industrial Revolution. Still,* Lady Chatterley's Lover *(1928), with its frank language and depictions of sex, remains a landmark in the battle against literary censorship, and an unexpurgated edition did not appear in England until thirty years after the author's death. Lawrence has proved popular with filmmakers;* Lady Chatterley's Lover, Sons and Lovers, Women in Love, *and* The Rainbow *have been made into films, as has "The Rocking-Horse Winner." The tragedy of Paul's failed rites of passage contains a criticism of middle-class values that is a major theme of Lawrence's fiction.*

D. H. Lawrence
The Rocking-Horse Winner

There was a woman who was beautiful, who started with all the advantages, yet she had no luck. She married for love, and the love turned to dust. She had bonny children, yet she felt they had been thrust upon her, and she could not love them. They looked at her coldly, as if they were finding fault with her. And hurriedly she felt she must cover up some fault in herself. Yet what it was that she must cover up she never knew. Nevertheless, when her children were present, she always felt the center of her heart go hard. This troubled her, and in her manner she was all the more gentle and anxious for her children, as if she loved them very much. Only she herself knew that at the center of her heart was a hard little place that could not feel love, no, not for anybody. Everybody else said of her: "She is such a good mother. She adores her children." Only she herself, and her children themselves, knew it was not so. They read it in each other's eyes.

There were a boy and two little girls. They lived in a pleasant house, with a garden, and they had discreet servants, and felt themselves superior to anyone in the neighbourhood.

Although they lived in style, they always an anxiety in the house. There was never enough money. The mother had a small income, and the father had a small income, but not nearly enough for the social position which they had to keep up. The father went in to town to some office. But though he had good prospects, these prospects never materialized. There was always the grinding sense of the shortage of money, though the style was always kept up.

At last the mother said: "I will see if *I* can't make something." But she did not know where to begin. She racked her brains, and tried this thing and the other, but could not find anything successful. The failure made deep lines come into her face. Her children were growing up, they would have to go to school. There must be more money, there must be more money. The father, who was always very handsome and expensive in his tastes, seemed as if he never *would* be able to do anything worth doing. And the mother, who had a great belief in herself, did not succeed any better, and her tastes were just as expensive.

And so the house came to be haunted by the unspoken phrase: *There must be more money! There must be more money!* The children could hear it all the time, though nobody said it aloud. They heard it at Christmas, when the expensive and splendid toys filled the nursery. Behind the shining modern rocking-horse, behind the smart doll's house, a voice would start whispering: "There *must* be more money! There *must* be more money!" And the children would stop playing, to listen for a moment. They would look into each other's eyes, to see if they had all heard. And each one saw in the eyes of the other two that they too had heard. "There *must* be more money! There *must* be more money!"

It came whispering from the springs of the still-swaying rocking-horse, and even the horse, bending his wooden, champing head, heard it. The big doll, sitting so pink and smirking in her new pram, could hear it quite plainly, and seemed to be smirking all the more self-consciously because of it. The foolish puppy, too, that took the place of the teddy-bear, he was looking so extraordinarily foolish for no other reason but that he heard the secret whisper all over the house: "There *must* be more money!"

Yet nobody ever said it aloud. The whisper was everywhere, and therefore no one spoke it. Just as no one ever says: "We are breathing!" in spite of the fact that breath is coming and going all the time.

"Mother," said the boy Paul one day, "why don't we keep a car of our own? Why do we always use uncle's, or else a taxi?"

"Because we're the poor members of the family," said the mother.

"But why *are* we, mother?"

"Well—I suppose," she said slowly and bitterly, "it's because your father has no luck."

The boy was silent for some time.

"Is luck money, mother?" he asked, rather timidly.

"No, Paul. Not quite. It's what causes you to have money."

"Oh!" said Paul vaguely. "I thought when Uncle Oscar said *filthy lucker*, it meant money."

"*Filthy lucre* does mean money," said the mother. "But it's lucre, not luck."

"Oh!" said the boy. "Then what *is* luck, mother?"

"It's what causes you to have money. If you're lucky you have money. That's why it's better to be born lucky than rich. If you're rich, you may lose your money. But if you're lucky, you will always get more money."

"Oh! Will you? And is father not lucky?"

"Very unlucky, I should say," she said bitterly.

The boy watched her with unsure eyes.

"Why?" he asked.

"I don't know. Nobody ever knows why one person is lucky and another unlucky."

"Don't they? Nobody at all? Does *nobody* know?"

"Perhaps God. But He never tells."

"He ought to, then. And aren't you lucky either, mother?"

"I can't be, if I married an unlucky husband."

"But by yourself, aren't you?"

"I used to think I was, before I married. Now I think I am very unlucky indeed."

"Why?"

"Well—never mind! Perhaps I'm not really," she said.

The child looked at her, to see if she meant it. But he saw, by the lines of her mouth, that she was only trying to hide something from him.

"Well, anyhow," he said stoutly, "I'm a lucky person."

"Why?" said his mother, with a sudden laugh.

He stared at her. He didn't even know why he had said it.

"God told me," he asserted, brazening it out.

"I hope He did, dear!" she said, again with a laugh, but rather bitter.

"He did, mother!"

"Excellent!" said the mother, using one of her husband's exclamations.

The boy saw she did not believe him; or, rather, that she paid no attention to his assertion. This angered him somewhat, and made him want to compel her attention.

He went off by himself, vaguely, in a childish way, seeking for the clue to "luck." Absorbed, taking no heed of other people, he went about with a sort of stealth, seeking inwardly for luck. He wanted luck, he wanted it, he wanted it. When the two girls were playing dolls in the nursery, he would sit on his big rocking-horse, charging madly into space, with a frenzy that made the little girls peer at him uneasily. Wildly the horse careered, the waving dark hair of the boy tossed, his eyes had a strange glare in them. The little girls dared not speak to him.

When he had ridden to the end of his mad little journey, he climbed down and stood in front of his rocking-horse, staring fixedly into its lowered face. Its red mouth was slightly open, its big eye was wide and glassy-bright.

"Now!" he would silently command the snorting steed. "Now, take me to where there is luck! Now take me!"

And he would slash the horse on the neck with the little whip he had asked Uncle Oscar for. He *knew* the horse could take him to where there was luck, if only he forced it. So he would mount again, and start on his furious ride, hoping at last to get there. He knew he could get there.

"You'll break your horse, Paul!" said the nurse.

"He's always riding like that! I wish he'd leave off!" said his elder sister Joan.

But he only glared down on them in silence. Nurse gave him up. She could make nothing of him. Anyhow he was growing beyond her.

One day his mother and his Uncle Oscar came in when he was on one of his furious rides. He did not speak to them.

"Hallo, you young jockey! Riding a winner?" said his uncle.

"Aren't you growing too big for a rocking-horse? You're not a very little boy any longer, you know," said his mother.

But Paul only gave a blue glare from his big, rather close-set eyes. He would speak to nobody when he was in full tilt. His mother watched him with an anxious expression on her face.

At last he suddenly stopped forcing his horse into the mechanical gallop, and slid down.

"Well, I got there!" he announced fiercely, his blue eyes still flaring, and his sturdy long legs straddling apart.

"Where did you get to?" asked his mother.

"Where I wanted to go," he flared back at her.

"That's right, son!" said Uncle Oscar. "Don't you stop till you get there. What's the horse's name?"

"He doesn't have a name," said the boy.

"Gets on without all right?" asked the uncle.

"Well, he has different names. He was called Sansovino last week."

"Sansovino, eh? Won the Ascot. How did you know his name?"

"He always talks about horse-races with Bassett," said Joan.

The uncle was delighted to find that his small nephew was posted with all the racing news. Bassett, the young gardener, who had been wounded in the left foot in the war and had got his present job through Oscar Cresswell, whose batman[1] he had been, was a perfect blade of the "turf." He lived in the racing events, and the small boy lived with him.

Oscar Cresswell got it all from Bassett.

"Master Paul comes and asks me, so I can't do more than tell him, sir," said Bassett, his face terribly serious, as if he were speaking of religious matters.

"And does he ever put anything on a horse he fancies?"

"Well—I don't want to give him away—he's a young sport, a fine sport, sir. Would you mind asking him himself? He sort of takes a pleasure in it, and perhaps he'd feel I was giving him away, sir, if you don't mind."

Bassett was serious as a church.

The uncle went back to his nephew and took him off for a ride in the car.

"Say, Paul, old man, do you ever put anything on a horse?" the uncle asked.

The boy watched the handsome man closely.

---

[1]*batman:* an enlisted man who serves as valet to a cavalry officer.

"Why, do you think I oughtn't to?" he parried.

"Not a bit of it. I thought perhaps you might give me a tip for the Lincoln."

The car sped on into the country, going down to Uncle Oscar's place in Hampshire.

"Honor bright?" said the nephew.

"Honor bright, son!" said the uncle.

"Well, then, Daffodil."

"Daffodil! I doubt it, sonny. What about Mirza?"

"I only know the winner," said the boy. "That's Daffodil."

"Daffodil, eh?"

There was a pause. Daffodil was an obscure horse comparatively.

"Uncle!"

"Yes, son?"

"You won't let it go any further, will you? I promised Bassett."

"Bassett be damned, old man! What's he got to do with it?"

"We're partners. We've been partners from the first. Uncle, he lent me my first five shillings, which I lost. I promised him, honor bright, it was only between me and him; only you gave me that ten-shilling note I started winning with, so I thought you were lucky. You won't let it go any further, will you?"

The boy gazed at his uncle from those big, hot, blue eyes, set rather close together. The uncle stirred and laughed uneasily.

"Right you are, son! I'll keep your tip private. Daffodil, eh? How much are you putting on him?"

"All except twenty pounds," said the boy. "I keep that in reserve."

The uncle thought it a good joke.

"You keep twenty pounds in reserve, do you, you young romancer? What are you betting, then?"

"I'm betting three hundred," said the boy gravely. "But it's between you and me, Uncle Oscar! Honor bright?"

The uncle burst into a roar of laughter.

"It's between you and me all right, you young Nat Gould," he said, laughing. "But where's your three hundred?"

"Bassett keeps it for me. We're partners."

"You are, are you! And what is Bassett putting on Daffodil?"

"He won't go quite as high as I do, I expect. Perhaps he'll go a hundred and fifty."

"What, pennies?" laughed the uncle.

"Pounds," said the child, with a surprised look at his uncle. "Bassett keeps a bigger reserve than I do."

Between wonder and amusement Uncle Oscar was silent. He pursued the matter no further, but he determined to take his nephew with him to the Lincoln races.

"Now son," he said, "I'm putting twenty on Mirza, and I'll put five for you on any horse you fancy. What's your pick?"

"Daffodil, uncle."

"No, not the fiver on Daffodil!"

"I should if it was my own fiver," said the child.

"Good! Good! Right you are! A fiver for me and a fiver for you on Daffodil."

The child had never been to a race-meeting before, and his eyes were blue fire. He pursed his mouth tight, and watched. A Frenchman just in front had put his money on Lancelot. Wild with excitement, he flayed his arms up and down, yelling, "*Lancelot! Lancelot!*" in his French accent.

Daffodil came in first, Lancelot second, Mirza third. The child, flushed and with eyes blazing, was curiously serene. His uncle brought him four five-pound notes, four to one.

"What am I to do with these?" he cried, waving them before the boy's eyes.

"I suppose we'll talk to Bassett," said the boy. "I expect I have fifteen hundred now; and twenty in reserve; and this twenty."

His uncle studied him for some moments.

"Look here, son!" he said. "You're not serious about Bassett and that fifteen hundred, are you?"

"Yes, I am. But it's between you and me, uncle. Honor bright!"

"Honor bright all right, son! But I must talk to Bassett."

"If you'd like to be a partner, uncle, with Bassett and me, we could all be partners. Only, you'd have to promise, honor bright, uncle, not to let it go beyond us three. Bassett and I are lucky, and you must be lucky, because it was your ten shillings I started winning with. . . ."

Uncle Oscar took both Bassett and Paul into Richmond Park for an afternoon, and there they talked.

"It's like this, you see, sir," Bassett said. "Master Paul would get me talking about racing events, spinning yarns, you know, sir. And he was always keen on knowing if I'd made or if I'd lost. It's about a year since, now, that I put five shillings on Blush of Dawn for him—and we lost. Then the luck turned, and with that ten shillings he had from you: that we put on Singhalese. And since that time, it's been pretty steady, all things considering What do you say, Master Paul?"

"We're all right when we're sure," said Paul. "It's when we're not quite sure that we go down."

"Oh, but we're careful then," said Bassett.

"But when are you *sure?*" smiled Uncle Oscar.

"It's Master Paul, sir," said Bassett, in a secret, religious voice. "It's as if he had it from heaven. Like Daffodil, now, for the Lincoln. That was as sure as eggs."

"Did you put anything on Daffodil?" asked Oscar Cresswell.

"Yes, sir. I made my bit."

"And my nephew?"

Bassett was obstinately silent, looking at Paul.

"I made twelve hundred, didn't I, Bassett? I told uncle I was putting three hundred on Daffodil."

"That's right," said Bassett, nodding.

"But where's the money?" asked the uncle.

"I keep it safe locked up, sir. Master Paul he can have it any minute he likes to ask for it."

"What, fifteen hundred pounds?"

"And twenty! And *forty*; that is, with the twenty he made on the course."

"It's amazing!" said the uncle.

"If Master Paul offers you to be partners, sir, I would, if I were you; if you'll excuse me," said Bassett.

Oscar Cresswell thought about it.

"I'll see the money," he said.

They drove home again, and sure enough, Bassett came round to the garden-house with fifteen hundred pounds in notes. The twenty pounds reserve was left with Joe Glee, in the Turf Commission deposit.

"You see, it's all right, uncle, when I'm *sure!* Then we go strong, for all we're worth. Don't we, Bassett!"

"We do that, Master Paul."

"And when are you sure?" said the uncle, laughing.

"Oh, well, sometimes I'm *absolutely* sure, like about Daffodil," said the boy, "and sometimes I have an idea; and sometimes I haven't even an idea, have I, Bassett? Then we're careful, because we mostly go down."

"You do, do you! And when you're sure, like about Daffodil, what makes you sure, sonny?"

"Oh, well, I don't know," said the boy uneasily. "I'm sure, you know, uncle; that's all."

"It's as if he had it from heaven, sir," Bassett reiterated.

"I should say so!" said the uncle.

But he became a partner. And when the Leger was coming on, Paul was "sure" about Lively Spark, which was a quite inconsiderable horse. The boy insisted on putting a thousand on the horse, Bassett went for five hundred, and Oscar Cresswell two hundred. Lively Spark came in first, and the betting had been ten to one against him. Paul had made ten thousand.

"You see," he said, "I was absolutely sure of him."

Even Oscar Cresswell had cleared two thousand.

"Look here, son," he said, "this sort of thing makes me nervous."

"It needn't, uncle! Perhaps I shan't be sure again for a long time."

"But what are you going to do with your money?" asked the uncle.

"Of course," said the boy, "I started it for mother. She said she had no luck, because father is unlucky, so I thought if I was lucky, it might stop whispering."

"What might stop whispering?"

"Our house. I *hate* our house for whispering."

"What does it whisper?"

"Why—why"—the boy fidgeted—"why, I don't know. But it's always short of money, you know, uncle."

"I know it, son, I know it."

"You know people send mother writs, don't you, uncle?"

"I'm afraid I do," said the uncle.

"And then the house whispers, like people laughing at you behind your back. It's awful, that is! I thought if I was lucky. . . ."

"You might stop it," added the uncle.

The boy watched him with big blue eyes, that had an uncanny cold fire in them, and he said never a word.

"Well, then!" said the uncle. "What are we doing?"

"I shouldn't like mother to know I was lucky," said the boy.

"Why not, son?"

"She'd stop me."

"I don't think she would."

"Oh!"—and the boy writhed in an odd way—"I *don't* want her to know, uncle."

"All right, son! We'll manage it without her knowing."

They managed it very easily. Paul, at the other's suggestion, handed over five thousand pounds to his uncle, who deposited it with the family lawyer, who was then to inform Paul's mother that a relative had put five thousand pounds into his hands, which sum was to be paid out a thousand pounds at a time, on the mother's birthday, for the next five years.

"So she'll have a birthday present of a thousand pounds for five successive years," said Uncle Oscar. "I hope it won't make it all the harder for her later."

Paul's mother had her birthday in November. The house had been "whispering" worse than ever lately, and, even in spite of his luck, Paul could not bear up against it. He was very anxious to see the effect of the birthday letter, telling his mother about the thousand pounds.

When there were no visitors, Paul now took his meals with his parents, as he was beyond the nursery control. His mother went into town nearly every day. She had discovered that she had an odd knack of sketching furs and dress materials, so she worked secretly in the studio of a friend who was the chief "artist" for the leading drapers. She drew the figures of ladies in furs and ladies in silk and sequins for the newspaper advertisements. This young woman artist earned several thousand pounds a year, but Paul's mother only made several hundreds, and she was again dissatisfied. She so wanted to be first in something, and she did not succeed, even in making sketches for drapery advertisements.

She was down to breakfast on the morning of her birthday. Paul watched her face as she read the letters. He knew the lawyer's letter. As his mother read it, her face hardened and became more expressionless. Then a cold, determined look came on her mouth. She hid the letter under the pile of others, and said not a word about it.

"Didn't you have anything nice in the post for your birthday, mother?" said Paul.

"Quite moderately nice," she said, her voice cold and absent.

She went away to town without saying more.

But in the afternoon Uncle Oscar appeared. He said Paul's mother had had a long interview with the lawyer, asking if the whole five thousand could not be advanced at once, as she was in debt.

"What do you think, uncle?" said the boy.

"I leave it to you, son."

"Oh, let her have it, then! We can get some more with the other," said the boy.

"A bird in the hand is worth two in the bush, laddie!" said Uncle Oscar.

"But I'm sure to *know* for the Grand National; or the Lincolnshire; or else the Derby. I'm sure to know for *one* of them," said Paul.

So Uncle Oscar signed the agreement, and Paul's mother touched the whole five thousand. Then something very curious happened. The voices in the house suddenly went mad, like a chorus of frogs on a spring evening. There were certain new furnishings, and Paul had a tutor. He was *really* going to Eton, his father's school, in the following autumn. There were flowers in the winter, and a blossoming of the luxury Paul's mother had been used to. And yet the voices in the house, behind the sprays of mimosa and almond blossom, and from under the piles of iridescent cushions, simply trilled and screamed in a sort of ecstasy: "There *must* be more money! Oh-h-h; there *must* be more money. Oh, now, now-w! Now-w-w- —there *must* be more money—more than ever! More than ever!"

It frightened Paul terribly. He studied away at his Latin and Greek with his tutors. But his intense hours were spent with Bassett. The Grand National had gone by: he had not "known," and had lost a hundred pounds. Summer was at hand. He was in agony for the Lincoln. But even for the Lincoln he didn't "know," and he lost fifty pounds. He became wild-eyed and strange, as if something were going to explode in him.

"Let it alone, son! Don't you bother about it!" urged Uncle Oscar. But it was as if the boy couldn't really hear what his uncle was saying.

"I've got to know for the Derby! I've got to know for the Derby!" the child reiterated, his big blue eyes blazing with a sort of madness.

His mother noticed how overwrought he was.

"You'd better go to the seaside. Wouldn't you like to go now to the seaside, instead of waiting? I think you'd better," she said, looking down at him anxiously, her heart curiously heavy because of him.

But the child lifted his uncanny blue eyes.

"I couldn't possibly go before the Derby, mother!" he said. "I couldn't possibly!"

"Why not?" she said, her voice becoming heavy when she was opposed. "Why not? You can still go from the seaside to see the Derby with your Uncle Oscar, if that's what you wish. No need for you to wait here. Besides, I think you care too much about these races. It's a bad sign. My family has been a gambling family, and you won't know till you grow up how much damage it has done. But it has done damage. I shall have to send Bassett away, and ask Uncle Oscar not to talk racing to you, unless you promise to be reasonable about it; go away to the seaside and forget it. You're all nerves!"

"I'll do what you like, mother, so long as you don't send me away till after the Derby," the boy said.

"Send you away from where? Just from this house?"

"Yes," he said, gazing at her.

"Why, you curious child, what makes you care about this house so much, suddenly? I never knew you loved it."

He gazed at her without speaking. He had a secret within a secret, something he had not divulged, even to Bassett or to his Uncle Oscar.

But his mother, after standing undecided and a little bit sullen for some moments, said:

"Very well, then! Don't go to the seaside till after the Derby, if you don't wish it. But promise me you won't let your nerves go to pieces. Promise you won't think so much about horse-racing and *events*, as you call them!"

"Oh, no," said the boy casually. "I won't think much about them, mother. You needn't worry. I wouldn't worry, mother, if I were you."

"If you were me and I were you," said his mother, "I wonder what we *should* do!"

"But you know you needn't worry, mother, don't you?" the boy repeated.

"I should be awfully glad to know it," she said wearily.

"Oh, well, you *can*, you know. I mean, you *ought* to know you needn't worry," he insisted.

"Ought I? Then I'll see about it," she said.

Paul's secret of secrets was his wooden horse, that which had no name. Since he was emancipated from a nurse and a nursery-governess, he had had his rocking-horse removed to his own bedroom at the top of the house.

"Surely, you're too big for a rocking-horse!" his mother had remonstrated.

"Well, you see, mother, till I can have a *real* horse, I like to have *some* sort of animal about," had been his quaint answer.

"Do you feel he keeps you company?" she laughed.

"Oh, yes! He's very good, he always keeps me company, when I'm there," said Paul.

So the horse, rather shabby, stood in an arrested prance in the boy's bedroom.

The Derby was drawing near, and the boy grew more and more tense. He hardly heard what was spoken to him, he was very frail, and his eyes were really uncanny. His mother had sudden strange seizures of uneasiness about him. Sometimes, for half-an-hour, she would feel a sudden anxiety about him that was almost anguish. She wanted to rush to him at once, and know he was safe.

Two nights before the Derby, she was at a big party in town, when one of her rushes of anxiety about her boy, her first-born, gripped her heart till she could hardly speak. She fought with the feeling, might and main, for she believed in common-sense. But it was too strong. She had to leave the dance and go downstairs to telephone to the country. The children's nursery-governess was terribly surprised and startled at being rung up in the night.

"Are the children all right, Miss Wilmot?"

"Oh, yes, they are quite all right."

"Master Paul? Is he all right?"

"He went to bed as right as a trivet. Shall I run up and look at him?"

"No," said Paul's mother reluctantly. "No! Don't trouble. It's all right. Don't sit up. We shall be home fairly soon." She did not want her son's privacy intruded upon.

"Very good," said the governess.

It was about one-o'clock when Paul's mother and father drove up to their house. All was still. Paul's mother went to her room and slipped off her white fur cloak. She had told her maid not to wait up for her. She heard her husband downstairs, mixing a whisky-and-soda.

And then, because of the strange anxiety at her heart, she stole upstairs to her son's room. Noiselessly she went along the upper corridor. Was there a faint noise? What was it?

She stood, with arrested muscles, outside his door, listening. There was a strange, heavy, and yet not loud noise. Her heart stood still. It was a soundless noise, yet rushing and powerful. Something huge, in violent, hushed motion. What was it? What in God's name was it? She ought to know. She felt that she knew the noise. She knew what it was.

Yet she could not place it. She couldn't say what it was. And on and on it went, like a madness.

Softly, frozen with anxiety and fear, she turned the door-handle.

The room was dark. Yet in the space near the window, she heard and saw something plunging to and fro. She gazed in fear and amazement.

Then suddenly she switched on the light, and saw her son, in his green pajamas, madly surging on the rocking-horse. The blaze of light suddenly lit him up, as he urged the wooden horse, and lit her up, as she stood, blonde, in her dress of pale green and crystal, in the doorway.

"Paul!" she cried. "Whatever are you doing?"

"It's Malabar!" he screamed, in a powerful, strange voice. "It's Malabar!"

His eyes blazed at her for one strange and senseless second, as he ceased urging his wooden horse. Then he fell with a crash to the ground, and she, all her tormented motherhood flooding upon her, rushed to gather him up.

But he was unconscious, and unconscious he remained, with some brain fever. He talked and tossed, and his mother sat stonily by his side.

"Malabar! It's Malabar! Bassett, Bassett I *know!* It's Malabar!"

So the child cried, trying to get up and urge the rocking-horse that gave him his inspiration.

"What does he mean by Malabar?" asked the heart-frozen mother.

"I don't know," said the father stonily.

"What does he mean by Malabar?" she asked her brother Oscar.

"It's one of the horses running for the Derby," was the answer.

And, in spite of himself, Oscar Cresswell spoke to Bassett, and himself put a thousand on Malabar: at fourteen to one.

The third day of the illness was critical: they were waiting for a change. The boy, with his rather long, curly hair, was tossing ceaselessly on the pillow. He neither slept nor regained consciousness, and his eyes were like blue stones. His mother sat, feeling her heart had gone, turned actually into a stone.

In the evening, Oscar Cresswell did not come, but Bassett sent a message, saying could he come up for one moment, just one moment? Paul's mother was very angry at the intrusion, but on second thought she agreed. The boy was the same. Perhaps Bassett might bring him to consciousness.

The gardener, a shortish fellow with a little brown moustache, and sharp little brown eyes, tiptoed into the room, touched his imaginary cap to Paul's mother, and stole to the bedside, staring with glittering, smallish eyes, at the tossing, dying child.

"Master Paul!" he whispered. "Master Paul! Malabar came in first all right, a clean win. I did as you told me. You've made over seventy thousand pounds, you have; you've got over eighty thousand. Malabar came in all right, Master Paul."

"Malabar! Malabar! Did I say Malabar, mother? Did I say Malabar? Do you think I'm lucky, mother? I knew Malabar, didn't I? Over eighty thousand pounds! I call that lucky, don't you, mother? Over eighty thousand pounds! I knew, didn't I know I knew? Malabar came in all right. If I ride my horse till I'm sure, then I tell you, Bassett, you can go as high as you like. Did you go for all you were worth, Bassett?"

"I went a thousand on it, Master Paul."

"I never told you, mother, that if I can ride my horse, and *get there*, then I'm absolutely sure—oh, absolutely! Mother, did I ever tell you? I *am* lucky!"

"No, you never did," said the mother.

But the boy died in the night.

And even as he lay dead, his mother heard her brother's voice saying to her: "My God, Hester, you're eighty-odd thousand to the good, and a poor devil of a son to the bad. But, poor devil, poor devil, he's best gone out of a life where he rides his rocking-horse to find a winner."

—1933

Katherine Anne Porter (1890–1980) whose allegorical novel of a voyage to Germany at the beginning of the Nazi era, Ship of Fools, *was a great popular success in 1962, changed from a "writer's writer" known mainly for prestigious literary essays, book reviews, and short stories to an international celebrity. Born in Indian Creek, Texas, and educated in Catholic schools in the South, Porter's youth was a study in rebellion, with stints as a reporter and traveling singer and entertainer. The recipient of a Guggenheim Fellowship after the appearance of her first book, Porter subsequently traveled in Mexico and Europe, gathering further material for her stories, which were collected in* Flowering Judas *(1930),* Pale Horse, Pale Rider *(1939), and* The Leaning Tower *(1944). Porter's* Collected Stories *won both a Pulitzer Prize and a National Book Award in 1965, the same year in which Stanley Kramer's popular film version of* Ship of Fools *appeared. Although Porter is not primarily identified as a regional writer, "The Jilting of Granny Weatherall" draws on the rural landscapes of her youth and makes effective use of her upbringing as a southern Roman Catholic. It also makes effective use of stream of consciousness, a technique Porter often employs in her stories. "The Jilting of Granny Weatherall" was made into a film as part of the PBS* American Short Story *series.*

Katherine Anne Porter
The Jilting of Granny Weatherall

She flicked her wrist neatly out of Doctor Harry's pudgy careful fingers and pulled the sheet up to her chin. The brat ought to be in knee breeches. Doctoring around the country with spectacles on his nose! "Get along now, take your schoolbooks and go. There's nothing wrong with me."

Doctor Harry spread a warm paw like a cushion on her forehead where the forked green vein danced and made her eyelids twitch. "Now, now, be a good girl, and we'll have you up in no time."

"That's no way to speak to a woman nearly eighty years old just because she's down. I'd have you respect your elders, young man."

"Well, Missy, excuse me." Doctor Harry patted her cheek. "But I've got to warn you, haven't I? You're a marvel, but you must be careful or you're going to be good and sorry."

"Don't tell me what I'm going to be. I'm on my feet now, morally speaking. It's Cornelia. I had to go to bed to get rid of her."

Her bones felt loose, and floated around in her skin, and Doctor Harry floated like a balloon around the foot of the bed. He floated and pulled down his waistcoat and swung his glasses on a cord. "Well, stay where you are, it certainly can't hurt you."

"Get along and doctor your sick," said Granny Weatherall. "Leave a well woman alone. I'll call for you when I want you. . . . Where were you forty years ago when I pulled through milk-leg and double pneumonia? You weren't even born. Don't let Cornelia lead you on," she shouted, because Doctor Harry appeared to float up to the ceiling and out. "I pay my own bills, and I don't throw my money away on nonsense!"

She meant to wave good-bye, but it was too much trouble. Her eyes closed of themselves, it was like a dark curtain drawn around the bed. The pillow rose and floated under her, pleasant as a hammock in a light wind. She listened to the leaves rustling outside the window. No, somebody was swishing newspapers: no, Cornelia and Doctor Harry were whispering together. She leaped broad awake, thinking they whispered in her ear.

"She was never like this, *never* like this!" "Well, what can we expect?" "Yes, eighty years old . . ."

Well, and what if she was? She still had ears. It was like Cornelia to whisper around doors. She always kept things secret in such a public way. She was always being tactful and kind. Cornelia was dutiful; that was the trouble with her. Dutiful and good: "So good and dutiful," said Granny, "and I'd like to spank her." She saw herself spanking Cornelia and making a fine job of it.

"What'd you say, Mother?"

Granny felt her face tying up in hard knots.

"Can't a body think, I'd like to know?"

"I thought you might want something."

"I do. I want a lot of things. First off, go away and don't whisper."

She lay and drowsed, hoping in her sleep that the children would keep out and let her rest a minute. It had been a long day. Not that she was tired. It was always pleasant to snatch a minute now and then. There was always so much to be done, let me see: tomorrow.

Tomorrow was far away and there was nothing to trouble about. Things were finished somehow when the time came; thank God there was always a little margin over for peace: then a person could spread out the plan of life and tuck in the edges orderly. It was good to have everything clean and folded away, with the hair brushes and tonic bottles sitting straight on the white embroidered linen: the day started without fuss and the pantry shelves laid out with rows of jelly glasses and brown jugs and white stone-china jars with blue whirligigs and words painted on them: coffee, tea, sugar, ginger, cinnamon, allspice: and the bronze clock with the lion on top nicely dusted off. The dust that lion could collect in twenty-four hours! The box in the attic with all those letters tied up, she'd have to go through that tomorrow. All those letters—George's letters and John's letters and her letters to them both—lying around for the children to find afterwards made her uneasy. Yes, that would be tomorrow's business. No use to let them know how silly she had been once.

While she was rummaging around she found death in her mind and it felt clammy and unfamiliar. She had spent so much time preparing for death there was no need for bringing it up again. Let it take care of itself now. When she was sixty she had felt very old, finished, and went around making farewell trips to see her children and grandchildren, with a secret in her mind: This is the very last of your mother, children! Then she made her will and came down with a long fever. That was all just a notion like a lot of other things, but it was lucky too, for she had once for all got over the idea of dying for a long time. Now she couldn't be worried. She hoped she had better sense now. Her father had lived to be one hundred and two years old and had drunk a noggin of strong hot toddy on his last birthday. He told the reporters it was his daily habit, and he owed his long life to that. He had made quite a scandal and was very pleased about it. She believed she'd just plague Cornelia a little.

"Cornelia! Cornelia!" No footsteps, but a sudden hand on her cheek. "Bless you, where have you been?"

"Here, Mother."

"Well, Cornelia, I want a noggin of hot toddy."

"Are you cold, darling?"

"I'm chilly, Cornelia. Lying in bed stops the circulation. I must have told you that a thousand times."

Well, she could just hear Cornelia telling her husband that Mother was getting a little childish and they'd have to humor her. The thing that most annoyed her was that Cornelia thought she was deaf, dumb, and blind. Little hasty glances and tiny gestures tossed around her and over her head saying, "Don't cross her, let her have her way, she's eighty years old," and she sitting there as if she lived in a thin glass cage. Sometimes Granny almost made up her mind to pack up and move back to her own house where nobody could remind her every minute that she was old.

Wait, wait, Cornelia, till your own children whisper behind your back! In her day she had kept a better house and had got more work done. She wasn't too old yet for Lydia to be driving eighty miles for advice when one of the children jumped the track, and Jimmy still dropped in and talked things over: "Now, Mammy, you've a good business head, I want to know what you think of this? . . ." Old. Cornelia couldn't change the furniture around without asking. Little things, little things! They had been so sweet when they were little. Granny wished the old days were back again with the children young and everything to be done over. It had been a hard pull, but not too much for her. When she thought of all the food she had cooked, and all the clothes she had cut and sewed, and all the gardens she had made—well, the children showed it. There they were, made out of her, and they couldn't get away from that. Sometimes she wanted to see John again and point to them and say, Well, I didn't do so badly, did I? But that would have to wait. That was for tomorrow. She used to think of him as a man, but now all the children were older than their father, and he would be a child beside her if she saw him now. It seemed strange and there was something wrong in the idea. Why, he couldn't possibly recognize her. She had fenced in a hundred acres once, digging the post holes herself and clamping the wires with just a negro boy to help. That changed a woman. John would be looking for a young woman with the peaked Spanish comb in her hair and the painted fan. Digging post holes changed a woman. Riding country roads in the winter when women had their babies was another thing: sitting up nights with sick horses and sick negroes and sick children and hardly ever losing one. John, I hardly ever lost one of them! John would see that in a minute, that would be something he could understand, she wouldn't have to explain anything!

It made her feel like rolling up her sleeves and putting the whole place to rights again. No matter if Cornelia was determined to be everywhere at once, there were a great many things left undone on this place. She would start tomorrow and do them. It was good to be strong enough for everything, even if all you made melted and changed and slipped under your hands, so that by the time you finished you almost forgot what you were working for. What was it I set out to do? she asked herself intently, but she could not remember. A fog rose over the valley, she saw it marching across the creek swallowing the trees and moving up the hill like an army of ghosts. Soon it would be at the near edge of the orchard, and then it was time to go in and light the lamps. Come in, children, don't stay out in the night air.

Lighting the lamps had been beautiful. The children huddled up to her and breathed like little calves waiting at the bars in the twilight. Their eyes followed the match and watched the flame rise and settle in a blue curve, then they moved away from her. The lamp was lit, they didn't have to be scared and hang on to mother any more. Never, never, never more. God, for all my life I thank Thee. Without Thee, my God, I could never have done it. Hail, Mary, full of grace.

I want you to pick all the fruit this year and see that nothing is wasted. There's always someone who can use it. Don't let good things rot for want of using. You waste life when you waste good food. Don't let things get lost. It's bitter to lose things. Now, don't let me get to thinking, not when I am tired and taking a little nap before supper. . . .

The pillow rose about her shoulders and pressed against her heart and the memory was being squeezed out of it: oh, push down the pillow, somebody: it would smother her if she tried to hold it. Such a fresh breeze blowing and such a green day with no threats in it. But he had not come, just the same. What does a woman do when she has put on the white veil and set out the white cake for a man and he doesn't come? She tried to remember. No, I swear he never harmed me but in that. He never harmed me but in that . . . and what if he did? There was the day, the day, but a whirl of dark smoke rose and covered it, crept up and over into the bright field where everything was planted so carefully in orderly rows. That was hell, she knew hell when she saw it. For sixty years she had prayed against remembering him and against losing her soul in the deep pit of hell, and now the two things were mingled in one and the thought of him was a smoky cloud from hell that moved and crept in her head when she had just got rid of Doctor Harry and was trying to rest a minute. Wounded vanity, Ellen, said a sharp voice in the top of her mind. Don't let your wounded vanity get the upper hand of you. Plenty of girls get jilted. You were jilted, weren't you?

Then stand up to it. Her eyelids wavered and let in streamers of blue-gray light like tissue paper over her eyes. She must get up and pull the shades down or she'd never sleep. She was in bed again and the shades were not down. How could that happen? Better turn over, hide from the light, sleeping in the light gave you nightmares. "Mother, how do you feel now?" and a stinging wetness on her forehead. But I don't like having my face washed in cold water!

Hapsy? George? Lydia? Jimmy? No, Cornelia, and her features were swollen and full of little puddles. "They're coming, darling, they'll all be here soon." Go wash your face, child, you look funny.

Instead of obeying, Cornelia knelt down and put her head on the pillow. She seemed to be talking but there was no sound. "Well, are you tongue-tied? Whose birthday is it? Are you going to give a party?"

Cornelia's mouth moved urgently in strange shapes. "Don't do that, you bother me, daughter."

"Oh, no, Mother. Oh, no. . . ."

Nonsense. It was strange about children. They disputed your every word. "No what, Cornelia?"

"Here's Doctor Harry."

"I won't see that boy again. He just left five minutes ago."

"That was this morning, Mother. It's night now. Here's the nurse."

"This is Doctor Harry, Mrs. Weatherall. I never saw you look so young and happy!"

"Ah, I'll never be young again—but I'd be happy if they'd let me lie in peace and get rested."

She thought she spoke up loudly, but no one answered. A warm weight on her forehead, a warm bracelet on her wrist, and a breeze went on whispering, trying to tell her something. A shuffle of leaves in the everlasting hand of God. He blew on them and they danced and rattled. "Mother, don't mind, we're going to give you a little hypodermic." "Look here, daughter, how do ants get in this bed? I saw sugar ants yesterday." Did you send for Hapsy too?

It was Hapsy she really wanted. She had to go a long way back through a great many rooms to find Hapsy standing with a baby on her arm. She seemed to herself to be Hapsy also, and the baby on Hapsy's arm was Hapsy and himself and herself, all at once, and there was no surprise in the meeting. Then Hapsy melted from within and turned flimsy as gray gauze and the baby was a gauzy shadow, and Hapsy came up close and said, "I thought you'd never come," and looked at her very searchingly and said, "You haven't changed a bit!" They leaned forward to kiss, when Cornelia began whispering from a long way off, "Oh, is there anything you want to tell me? Is there anything I can do for you?"

Yes, she had changed her mind after sixty years and she would like to see George. I want you to find George. Find him and be sure to tell him I forgot him. I want him to know I had my husband just the same and my children and my house like any other woman. A good house too and a good husband that I loved and fine children out of him. Better than I hoped for even. Tell him I was given back everything he took away and more. Oh, no, oh, God, no, there was something else besides the house and the man and the children. Oh, surely they were not all? What was it? Something not given back . . . Her breath crowded down under her ribs and grew into a monstrous frightening shape with cutting edges; it bored up into her head, and the agony was unbelievable—Yes, John, get the doctor now, no more talk, my time has come.

When this one was born it should be the last. The last. It should have been born first, for it was the one she had truly wanted. Everything came in good time. Nothing left out, left over. She was strong, in three days she would be as well as ever. Better. A woman needed milk in her to have her full health.

"Mother, do you hear me?"

"I've been telling you—"

"Mother, Father Connolly's here."

"I went to Holy Communion only last week. Tell him I'm not so sinful as all that."

"Father just wants to speak to you."

He could speak as much as he pleased. It was like him to drop in and inquire about her soul as if it were a teething baby, and then stay on for a cup of tea and a round of cards and gossip. He always had a funny story of some sort, usually about an Irishman who made his little mistakes and confessed them, and the point lay in some absurd thing he would blurt out in the confessional showing his struggles between native piety and original sin. Granny felt easy about her soul. Cornelia, where are your manners? Give Father Connolly a chair. She had her secret comfortable understanding with a few favorite saints who cleared a straight road to God for her. All as surely signed and sealed as the papers for the new Forty Acres. Forever . . . heirs and assigns forever. Since the day the wedding cake was not cut, but thrown out and wasted. The whole bottom dropped out of the world, and there she was blind and sweating with nothing under her feet and walls falling away. His hand had caught her under the breast, she had not fallen, there was the freshly polished floor with the green rug on it, just as before. He had cursed like a sailor's parrot and said, "I'll kill him for you." Don't lay a hand on him, for my sake leave something to God. "Now, Ellen, you must believe what I tell you. . . ."

So there was nothing, nothing to worry about any more, except sometimes in the night one of the children screamed in a nightmare, and they both hustled out shaking and hunting for the matches and calling, "There, wait a minute, here we are!" John, get the doctor now, Hapsy's time has come. But there was Hapsy standing by the bed in a white cap. "Cornelia, tell Hapsy to take off her cap. I can't see her plain."

Her eyes opened very wide and the room stood out like a picture she had seen somewhere. Dark colors with the shadows rising towards the ceiling in long angles. The tall black dresser gleamed with nothing on it but John's picture, enlarged from a little one, with John's eyes very black when they should have been blue. You never saw him, so how do you know how he looked? But the man insisted the copy was perfect, it was very rich and handsome. For a picture, yes, but it's not my husband. The table by the bed had a linen cover and a candle and a crucifix. The light was blue from Cornelia's silk lampshades. No sort of light at all, just frippery. You had to live forty years with kerosene lamps to appreciate honest electricity. She felt very strong and she saw Doctor Harry with a rosy nimbus around him.

"You look like a saint, Doctor Harry, and I vow that's as near as you'll ever come to it."

"She's saying something."

"I heard you, Cornelia. What's all this carrying on?"

"Father Connolly's saying—"

Cornelia's voice staggered and bumped like a cart in a bad road. It rounded corners and turned back again and arrived nowhere. Granny stepped up in the cart very lightly and reached for the reins, but a man sat beside her and she knew him by his hands, driving the cart. She did not look in his face, for she knew without seeing, but looked instead down the road where the trees leaned over and bowed to each other and a thousand birds were singing a Mass. She felt like singing too, but she put her hand in the bosom of her dress and pulled out a rosary, and Father Connolly murmured Latin in a very solemn voice and tickled her feet. My God, will you stop that nonsense? I'm a married woman. What if he did run away and leave me to face the priest by myself? I found another a whole world better. I wouldn't have exchanged my husband for anybody except St. Michael himself, and you may tell him that for me with a thank you in the bargain.

Light flashed on her closed eyelids, and a deep roaring shook her. Cornelia, is that lightning? I hear thunder. There's going to be a storm. Close all the windows. Call the children in. . . . "Mother, here we are, all of us." "Is that you, Hapsy?" "Oh, no, I'm Lydia. We drove as fast as we could." Their faces drifted above her, drifted away. The rosary fell out of her hands and Lydia put it back. Jimmy tried to help, their hands fumbled together, and Granny closed two fingers around Jimmy's thumb. Beads wouldn't do, it must be something alive. She was so amazed her thoughts ran round and round. So, my dear Lord, this is my death and I wasn't even thinking about it. My children have come to see me die. But I can't, it's not time. Oh, I always hated surprises. I wanted to give Cornelia the amethyst set—Cornelia, you're to have the amethyst set, but Hapsy's to wear it when she wants, and, Doctor Harry, do shut up. Nobody sent for you. Oh, my dear Lord, do wait a minute. I meant to do something about the Forty Acres, Jimmy doesn't need it and Lydia will later on, with that worthless husband of hers. I meant to finish the altar cloth and send six bottles of wine to Sister Borgia for her dyspepsia. I want to send six bottles of wine to Sister Borgia, Father Connolly, now don't let me forget.

Cornelia's voice made short turns and tilted over and crashed, "Oh, Mother, oh, Mother, oh, Mother. . . ."

"I'm not going, Cornelia. I'm taken by surprise. I can't go."

You'll see Hapsy again. What about her? "I thought you'd never come." Granny made a long journey outward, looking for Hapsy. What if I don't find her? What then? Her heart sank down and down, there was no bottom to death, she couldn't come to the end of it. The blue light from Cornelia's lampshade drew into a tiny point in the center of her brain, it flickered and winked like an eye, quietly it fluttered and dwindled. Granny lay curled down within herself, amazed and watchful, staring at the point of light that was herself; her body was now only a deeper mass of shadow in an endless darkness and this darkness would curl around the light and swallow it up. God, give a sign!

For the second time there was no sign. Again no bridegroom and the priest in the house. She could not remember any other sorrow because this grief wiped them all away. Oh, no, there's nothing more cruel than this—I'll never forgive it. She stretched herself with a deep breath and blew out the light.

—1929

Zora Neale Hurston (1891–1960) was born in Eatonville, Florida, one of eight children of a father who was a carpenter and Baptist preacher and became mayor of the first all-black town incorporated in the United States. After her mother's death, Hurston moved north, eventually attending high school and taking courses at Howard University and Barnard College, where she earned a B.A. in anthropology, and Columbia University, where she did graduate work. Hurston published her first story while a student and became an important member of the Harlem Renaissance, a group of young black artists, musicians, and writers who explored African-American heritage and identity. Hurston's most famous story, "Sweat," appeared in the only issue of Fire!!, *a 1926 avant-garde magazine, and displays her unerring ear for the country speech of blacks in her native Florida. The expert handling of dialect would become a trademark of her style. Hurston achieved only modest success during her lifetime, despite the publication of her controversial novel,* Their Eyes Were Watching God *(1937). Hurston made many contributions to the study of African-American folklore, traveling through the Caribbean and the South to transcribe black myths, fables, and folk tales, which were collected in* Mules and Men *(1935). Hurston died in a Florida welfare home and was buried in an unmarked grave, with most of her works long out of print. In the 1970s the rebirth of her reputation began, spurred by novelist Alice Walker, and virtually all of her works have since been republished.*

Zora Neale Hurston

Sweat

I

It was eleven o'clock of a Spring night in Florida. It was Sunday. Any other night, Delia Jones would have been in bed for two hours by this time. But she was a washwoman, and Monday morning meant a great deal to her. So she collected the soiled clothes on Saturday when she returned the clean things. Sunday night after church, she sorted and put the white things to soak. It saved her almost a half-day's start. A great hamper in the bedroom held the clothes that she brought home. It was so much neater than a number of bundles lying around.

She squatted on the kitchen floor beside the great pile of clothes, sorting them into small heaps according to color, and humming a song in a mournful key, but wondering through it all where Sykes, her husband, had gone with her horse and buckboard.[1]

Just then something long, round, limp, and black fell upon her shoulders and slithered to the floor beside her. A great terror took hold of her. It softened her knees and dried her mouth so that it was a full minute before she could cry out or move. Then she saw that it was the big bull whip her husband liked to carry when he drove.

She lifted her eyes to the door and saw him standing there bent over with laughter at her fright. She screamed at him.

"Sykes, what you throw dat whip on me like dat? You know it would skeer me—looks just like a snake, an' you knows how skeered Ah is of snakes."

"Course Ah knowed it! That's how come Ah done it." He slapped his leg with his hand and almost rolled on the ground in his mirth. "If you such a big fool dat you got to have a fit over a earth worm or a string, Ah don't keer how bad Ah skeer you."

"You ain't got no business doing it. Gawd knows it's a sin. Some day Ah'm gointuh drop dead from some of yo' foolishness. 'Nother thing, where you been wid mah rig? Ah feeds dat pony. He ain't fuh you to be drivin' wid no bull whip."

"You sho' is one aggravatin' nigger woman!" he declared and stepped into the room. She resumed her work and did not answer him at once. "Ah done tole you time and again to keep them white folks' clothes outa dis house."

He picked up the whip and glared at her. Delia went on with her work. She went out into the yard and returned with a galvanized tub and set it on the washbench. She saw that Sykes had kicked all of the clothes together again, and now stood in her way truculently, his whole manner hoping, *praying*, for an argument. But she walked calmly around him and commenced to re-sort the things.

[1]*buckboard:* open wagon with a seat

"Next time, Ah'm gointer kick 'em outdoors," he threatened as he struck a match along the leg of his corduroy breeches.

Delia never looked up from her work, and her thin, stooped shoulders sagged further.

"Ah ain't for no fuss t'night Sykes. Ah just come from taking sacrament at the church house."

He snorted scornfully. "Yeah, you just come from de church house on a Sunday night, but heah you is gone to work on them clothes. You ain't nothing but a hypocrite. One of them amen-corner Christians—sing, whoop, and shout, then come home and wash white folks' clothes on the Sabbath."

He stepped roughly upon the whitest pile of things, kicking them helter-skelter as he crossed the room. His wife gave a little scream of dismay, and quickly gathered them together again.

"Sykes, you quit grindin' dirt into these clothes! How can Ah git through by Sat'day if Ah don't start on Sunday?"

"Ah don't keer if you never git through. Anyhow, Ah done promised Gawd and a couple of other men, Ah ain't gointer have it in mah house. Don't gimme no lip neither, else Ah'll throw 'em out and put mah fist up side yo' head to boot."

Delia's habitual meekness seemed to slip from her shoulders like a blown scarf. She was on her feet; her poor little body, her bare knuckly hands bravely defying the strapping hulk before her.

"Looka heah, Sykes, you done gone too fur. Ah been married to you fur fifteen years, and Ah been takin' in washin' fur fifteen years. Sweat, sweat, sweat! Work and sweat, cry and sweat, pray and sweat!"

"What's that got to do with me?" he asked brutally.

"What's it got to do with you, Sykes? Mah tub of suds is filled yo' belly with vittles more times than yo' hands is filled it. Mah sweat is done paid for this house and Ah reckon Ah kin keep on sweatin' in it."

She seized the iron skillet from the stove and struck a defensive pose, which act surprised him greatly, coming from her. It cowed him and he did not strike her as he usually did.

"Naw you won't," she panted, "that ole snaggle-toothed black woman you runnin' with ain't comin' heah to pile up on *mah* sweat and blood. You ain't paid for nothin' on this place, and Ah'm gointer stay right heah till Ah'm toted out foot foremost."

"Well, you better quit gittin' me riled up, else they'll be totin' you out sooner than you expect. Ah'm so tired of you Ah don't know whut to do. Gawd! How Ah hates skinny wimmen!"

A little awed by this new Delia, he sidled out of the door and slammed the back gate after him. He did not say where he had gone, but she knew too well. She knew very well that he would not return until nearly daybreak also. Her work over, she went on to bed but not to sleep at once. Things had come to a pretty pass!

She lay awake, gazing upon the debris that cluttered their matrimonial trail. Not an image left standing along the way. Anything like flowers had long ago been drowned in the salty stream that had been pressed from her heart. Her tears, her sweat, her blood. She had brought love to the union and he had brought a longing after the flesh. Two months after the wedding, he had given her the first brutal beating. She had the memory of his numerous trips to Orlando with all of his wages when he had returned to her penniless, even before the first year had passed. She was young and soft then, but now she thought of her knotty, muscled limbs, her harsh knuckly hands, and drew herself up into an unhappy little ball in the middle of the big feather bed. Too late now to hope for love, even if it were not Bertha it would be someone else. This case differed from the others only in that she was bolder than the others. Too late for everything except her little home. She had built it for her old days, and planted one by one the trees and flowers there. It was lovely to her, lovely.

Somehow, before sleep came, she found herself saying aloud: "Oh well, whatever goes over the Devil's back, is got to come under his belly. Sometime or ruther, Sykes, like everybody else, is gointer reap his sowing." After that she was able to build a spiritual earthworks against her husband. His shells could no longer reach her. AMEN. She went to sleep and slept until he announced his presence in bed by kicking her feet and rudely snatching the covers away.

"Gimme some kivah heah, an' git yo' damn foots over on yo' own side! Ah oughter mash you in yo' mouf fuh drawing dat skillet on me."

Delia went clear to the rail without answering him. A triumphant indifference to all that he was or did.

II

The week was full of work for Delia as all other weeks, and Saturday found her behind her little pony, collecting and delivering clothes.

It was a hot, hot day near the end of July. The village men on Joe Clarke's porch even chewed cane listlessly. They did not hurl the cane-knots as usual. They let them dribble over the edge of the porch. Even conversation had collapsed under the heat.

"Heah come Delia Jones," Jim Merchant said, as the shaggy pony came 'round the bend of the road toward them. The rusty buckboard was heaped with baskets of crisp, clean laundry.

"Yep," Joe Lindsay agreed. "Hot or col', rain or shine, jes' ez reg'lar ez de weeks rool roun' Delia carries 'em an' fetches 'em on Sat'day."

"She better if she wanter eat," said Moss. "Syke Jones ain't wuth de shot an' powder hit would tek tuh kill 'em. Not to *huh* he ain't."

"He sho' ain't," Walter Thomas chimed in. "It's too bad, too, cause she wuz a right pretty li'l trick when he got huh. Ah'd uh mah'ied huh mahself if he hadnter beat me to it."

Delia nodded briefly at the men as she drove past.

"Too much knockin' will ruin *any* 'oman. He done beat huh 'nough tuh kill three women, let 'lone change they looks," said Elijah Moseley. "How Syke kin stommuck dat big black greasy Mogul he's layin' roun' wid, gits me. Ah swear dat eight-rock couldn't kiss a sardine can Ah done thowed out de back do' 'way las' yeah."

"Aw, she's fat, thass how come. He's allus been crazy 'bout fat women," put in Merchant. "He'd a' been tied up wid one long time ago if he could a' found one tuh have him. Did Ah tell yuh 'bout him come sidlin' roun' *mah* wife—bringin' her a basket uh peecans outa his yard fuh a present? Yessir, mah wife! She tol' him tuh take 'em right straight back home, 'cause Delia works so hard ovah dat washtub she reckon everything on de place taste lak sweat an' soapsuds. Ah jus' wisht Ah'd a' caught 'im 'roun' dere! Ah'd a' made his hips ketch on fiah down dat shell road."

"Ah know he done it, too. Ah sees 'im grinnin' at every 'oman dat passes," Walter Thomas said. "But even so, he useter eat some mighty big hunks uh humble pie tuh git dat li'l 'oman he got. She wuz ez pretty ez a speckled pup! Dat wuz fifteen years ago. He useter be so skeered uh losin' huh, she could make him do some parts of a husband's duty. Dey never wuz de same in de mind."

"There oughter be a law about him," said Lindsay. "He ain't fit tuh carry guts tuh a bear."

Clarke spoke for the first time. "Tain't no law on earth dat kin make a man be decent if it ain't in 'im. There's plenty men dat takes a wife lak dey do a joint uh sugar-cane. It's round, juicy, an' sweet when dey gits it. But dey squeeze an' grind, squeeze an' grind an' wring tell dey wring every drop uh pleasure dat's in 'em out. When dey's satisfied dat dey is wrung dry, dey treats 'em jes' lak dey do a cane-chew. Dey thows 'em away. Dey knows whut dey is doin' while dey is at it, an' hates their-selves fuh it but they keeps on hangin' after huh tell she's empty. Den dey hates huh fuh bein' a cane-chew an' in de way."

"We oughter take Syke an' dat stray 'oman uh his'n down in Lake Howell swamp an' lay on de rawhide till they cain't say Lawd a' mussy. He allus wuz uh ovahbearin niggah, but since dat white 'oman from up north done teached 'im how to run a automobile, he done got too beggety to live—an' we oughter kill 'im," Old Man Anderson advised.

A grunt of approval went around the porch. But the heat was melting their civic virtue and Elijah Moseley began to bait Joe Clarke.

"Come on, Joe, git a melon outa dere an' slice it up for yo' customers. We'se all sufferin' wid de heat. De bear's done got *me!*"

"Thass right, Joe, a watermelon is jes' whut Ah needs tuh cure de eppizudicks," Walter Thomas joined forces with Moseley. "Come on dere, Joe. We all is steady customers an' you ain't set us up in a long time. Ah chooses dat long, bowlegged Floridy favorite."

"A god, an' be dough. You all gimme twenty cents and slice away," Clarke retorted. "Ah needs a col' slice m'self. Heah, everybody chip in. Ah'll lend y'all mah meat knife."

The money was all quickly subscribed and the huge melon brought forth. At that moment, Sykes and Bertha arrived. A determined silence fell on the porch and the melon was put away again.

Merchant snapped down the blade of his jackknife and moved toward the store door.

"Come on in, Joe, an' gimme a slab uh sow belly an' uh pound uh coffee—almost fuhgot 'twas Sat'day. Got to git on home." Most of the men left also.

Just then Delia drove past on her way home, as Sykes was ordering magnificently for Bertha. It pleased him for Delia to see.

"Git whutsoever yo' heart desires, Honey. Wait a minute, Joe. Give huh two bottles uh strawberry soda-water, uh quart parched ground-peas, an' a block uh chewin' gum."

With all this they left the store, with Sykes reminding Bertha that this was his town and she could have it if she wanted it.

The men returned soon after they left, and held their watermelon feast.

"Where did Syke Jones git da 'oman from nohow?" Lindsay asked.

"Ovah Apopka. Guess dey musta been cleanin' out de town when she lef'. She don't look lak a thing but a hunk uh liver wid hair on it."

"Well, she sho' kin squall," Dave Carter contributed. "When she gits ready tuh laff, she jes' opens huh mouf an' latches it back tuh de las' notch. No ole granpa alligator down in Lake Bell ain't got nothin' on huh."

III

Bertha had been in town three months now. Sykes was still paying her room-rent at Della Lewis'—the only house in town that would have taken her in. Sykes took her frequently to Winter Park to "stomps." He still assured her that he was the swellest man in the state.

"Sho' you kin have dat li'l ole house soon's Ah git dat 'oman out-adere. Everything b'longs tuh me an' you sho' kin have it. Ah sho' 'bominates uh skinny 'oman. Lawdy, you sho' is got one portly shape on you! You kin git *anything* you wants. Dis is *mah* town an' you sho' kin have it."

Delia's work-worn knees crawled over the earth in Gethsemane² and up the rocks of Calvary³ many, many times during these months. She avoided the villagers and meeting places in her efforts to be blind and deaf. But Bertha nullified this to a degree, by coming to Delia's house to call Sykes out to her at the gate.

Delia and Sykes fought all the time now with no peaceful interludes. They slept and ate in silence. Two or three times Delia had attempted a timid friendliness, but she was repulsed each time. It was plain that the breaches must remain agape.

The sun had burned July to August. The heat streamed down like a million hot arrows, smiting all things living upon the earth. Grass withered, leaves browned, snakes went blind in shedding, and men and dogs went mad. Dog days!

Delia came home one day and found Sykes there before her. She wondered, but started to go on into the house without speaking, even

---

²*Gethsemane:* the garden that was the scene of Jesus' arrest (see Matthew 26:36–57); hence, any scene of suffering.   ³*Calvary:* hill outside Jerusalem where Jesus was crucified.

though he was standing in the kitchen door and she must either stoop under his arm or ask him to move. He made no room for her. She noticed a soap box beside the steps, but paid no particular attention to it, knowing that he must have brought it there. As she was stooping to pass under his outstretched arm, he suddenly pushed her backward, laughingly.

"Look in de box dere Delia, Ah done brung yuh somethin'!"

She nearly fell upon the box in her stumbling, and when she saw what it held, she all but fainted outright.

"Syke! Syke, mah Gawd! You take dat rattlesnake 'way from heah! You *gottuh.* Oh, Jesus, have mussy!"

"Ah ain't got tuh do nuthin' uh de kin'—fact is Ah ain't got tuh do nothin' but die. Tain't no use uh you puttin' on airs makin' out lak you skeered uh dat snake—he's gointer stay right heah tell he die. He wouldn't bite me cause Ah knows how tuh handle 'im. Nohow he wouldn't risk breakin' out his fangs 'gin *yo* skinny laigs."

"Naw, now Syke, don't keep dat thing 'round tryin' tuh skeer me tuh death. You knows Ah'm even feared uh earth worms. Thass de biggest snake Ah evah did see. Kill 'im Syke, please."

"Doan ast me tuh do nothin' fuh yuh. Goin' 'round tryin' tuh be so damn asterperious.[4] Naw, Ah ain't gonna kill it. Ah think uh damn sight mo' uh him dan you! Dat's a nice snake an' anybody doan lak 'im kin jes' hit de grit."

The village soon heard that Sykes had the snake, and came to see and ask questions.

"How de hen-fire did you ketch dat six-foot rattler, Syke?" Thomas asked.

"He's full uh frogs so he cain't hardly move, thass how Ah eased up on 'm. But Ah'm a snake charmer an' knows how tuh handle 'em. Shux, dat ain't nothin'. Ah could ketch one eve'y day if Ah so wanted tuh."

"Whut he needs is a heavy hick'ry club leaned real heavy on his head. Dat's de bes' way tuh charm a rattlesnake."

"Naw, Walt, y'all jes' don't understand dese diamon' backs lak Ah do," said Sykes in a superior tone of voice.

The village agreed with Walter, but the snake stayed on. His box remained by the kitchen door with its screen wire covering. Two or three

---

[4]*asterperious:* haughty.

days later it had digested its meal of frogs and literally came to life. It rattled at every movement in the kitchen or the yard. One day as Delia came down the kitchen steps she saw his chalky-white fangs curved like scimitars hung in the wire meshes. This time she did not run away with averted eyes as usual. She stood for a long time in the doorway in a red fury that grew bloodier for every second that she regarded the creature that was her torment.

That night she broached the subject as soon as Sykes sat down to the table.

"Syke, Ah wants you tuh take dat snake 'way fum heah. You done starved me an' Ah put up widcher, you done beat me an Ah took dat, but you done kilt all mah insides bringin' dat varmint heah."

Sykes poured out a saucer full of coffee and drank it deliberately before he answered her.

"A whole lot Ah keer 'bout how you feels inside uh out. Dat snake ain't goin' no damn wheah till Ah gits ready fuh 'im tuh go. So fur as beatin' is concerned, yuh ain't took near all dat you gointer take ef yuh stay 'round *me*."

Delia pushed back her plate and got up from the table. "Ah hates you, Sykes," she said calmly. "Ah hates you tuh de same degree dat Ah useter love yuh. Ah done took an' took till mah belly is full up tuh mah neck. Dat's de reason Ah got mah letter fum de church an' moved mah membership tuh Woodbridge—so Ah don't haftuh take no sacrament wid yuh. Ah don't wantuh see yuh 'round me at all. Lay 'round wid dat 'oman all yuh wants tuh, but gwan 'way fum me an' mah house. Ah hates yuh lak uh suck-egg dog."

Sykes almost let the huge wad of corn bread and collard greens he was chewing fall out of his mouth in amazement. He had a hard time whipping himself up to the proper fury to try to answer Delia.

"Well, Ah'm glad you does hate me. Ah'm sho' tiahed uh you hangin' ontuh me. Ah don't want yuh. Look at yuh stringey ole neck! Yo' rawbony laigs an' arms is enough tuh cut uh man tuh death. You looks jes' lak de devvul's doll-baby tuh *me*. You cain't hate me no worse dan Ah hates you. Ah been hatin' *you* fuh years."

"Yo' ole black hide don't look lak nothin' tuh me, but uh passle uh wrinkled up rubber, wid yo' big ole yeahs flappin' on each side lak uh paih uh buzzard wings. Don't think Ah'm gointuh be run 'way fum mah house neither. Ah'm goin' tuh de white folks 'bout *you*, mah young man, de very nex' time you lay yo' han's on me. Mah cup is done run ovah." Delia said this with no signs of fear and Sykes departed from the house, threatening her, but made not the slightest move to carry out any of them.

That night he did not return at all, and the next day being Sunday, Delia was glad she did not have to quarrel before she hitched up her pony and drove the four miles to Woodbridge.

She stayed to the night service—"love feast"—which was very warm and full of spirit. In the emotional winds her domestic trials were borne far and wide so that she sang as she drove homeward,

> *Jurden water,*[5] *black an' col*
> *Chills de body, not de soul*
> *An' Ah wantah cross Jurden in uh calm time.*

She came from the barn to the kitchen door and stopped.

"Whut's de mattah, ol' Satan, you ain't kickin' up yo' racket?" She addressed the snake's box. Complete silence. She went on into the house with a new hope in its birth struggles. Perhaps her threat to go to the white folks had frightened Sykes! Perhaps he was sorry! Fifteen years of misery and suppression had brought Delia to the place where she would hope *anything* that looked towards a way over or through her wall of inhibitions.

She felt in the match-safe behind the stove at once for a match. There was only one there.

"Dat niggah wouldn't fetch nothin' heah tuh save his rotten neck, but he kin run thew whut Ah brings quick enough. Now he done toted off nigh on tuh haff uh box uh matches. He done had dat 'oman heah in mah house, too."

Nobody but a woman could tell how she knew this even before she struck the match. But she did and it put her into a new fury.

Presently she brought in the tubs to put the white things to soak. This time she decided she need not bring the hamper out of the bedroom; she would go in there and do the sorting. She picked up the pot-bellied lamp and went in. The room was small and the hamper stood hard by the foot of the white iron bed. She could sit and reach through the bedposts—resting as she worked.

[5]*Jurden water:* the River Jordan.

"*Ah wantah cross Jurden in uh calm time.*" She was singing again. The mood of the "love feast" had returned. She threw back the lid of the basket almost gaily. Then, moved by both horror and terror, she sprang back toward the door. *There lay the snake in the basket!* He moved sluggishly at first, but even as she turned round and round, jumped up and down in an insanity of fear, he began to stir vigorously. She saw him pouring his awful beauty from the basket upon the bed, then she seized the lamp and ran as fast as she could to the kitchen. The wind from the open door blew out the light and the darkness added to her terror. She sped to the darkness of the yard, slamming the door after her before she thought to set down the lamp. She did not feel safe even on the ground, so she climbed up in the hay barn.

There for an hour or more she lay sprawled upon the hay a gibbering wreck.

Finally she grew quiet, and after that came coherent thought. With this stalked through her a cold, bloody rage. Hours of this. A period of introspection, a space of retrospection, then a mixture of both. Out of this an awful calm.

"Well, Ah done de bes' Ah could. If things ain't right, Gawd knows tain't mah fault."

She went to sleep—a twitch sleep—and woke up to a faint gray sky. There was a loud hollow sound below. She peered out. Sykes was at the wood-pile, demolishing a wire-covered box.

He hurried to the kitchen door, but hung outside there some minutes before he entered, and stood some minutes more inside before he closed it after him.

The gray in the sky was spreading. Delia descended without fear now, and crouched beneath the low bedroom window. The drawn shade shut out the dawn, shut in the night. But the thin walls held back no sound.

"Dat ol' scratch[6] is woke up now!" She mused at the tremendous whirr inside, which every woodsman knows, is one of the sound illusions. The rattler is a ventriloquist. His whirr sounds to the right, to the left, straight ahead, behind, close under foot—everywhere but where it is. Woe to him who guesses wrong unless he is prepared to hold up his end of the argument! Sometimes he strikes without rattling at all.

---

[6]*scratch:* the devil.

Inside, Sykes heard nothing until he knocked a pot lid off the stove while trying to reach the match-safe in the dark. He had emptied his pockets at Bertha's.

The snake seemed to wake up under the stove and Sykes made a quick leap into the bedroom. In spite of the gin he had had, his head was clearing now.

"Mah Gawd!" he chattered, "ef Ah could on'y strack uh light!"

The rattling ceased for a moment as he stood paralyzed. He waited. It seemed that the snake waited also.

"Oh, fuh de light! Ah thought he'd be too sick"—Sykes was muttering to himself when the whirr began again, closer, right underfoot this time. Long before this, Sykes' ability to think had been flattened down to primitive instinct and he leaped—onto the bed.

Outside Delia heard a cry that might have come from a maddened chimpanzee, a stricken gorilla. All the terror, all the horror, all the rage that man possibly could express, without a recognizable human sound.

A tremendous stir inside there, another series of animal screams, the intermittent whirr of the reptile. The shade torn violently down from the window, letting in the red dawn, a huge brown hand seizing the window stick, great dull blows upon the wooden floor punctuating the gibberish of sound long after the rattle of the snake had abruptly subsided. All this Delia could see and hear from her place beneath the window, and it made her ill. She crept over to the four o'clocks and stretched herself on the cool earth to recover.

She lay there. "Delia, Delia!" She could hear Sykes calling in a most despairing tone as one who expected no answer. The sun crept on up, and he called. Delia could not move—her legs had gone flabby. She never moved, he called, and the sun kept rising.

"Mah Gawd!" She heard him moan, "Mah Gawd fum Heben!" She heard him stumbling about and got up from her flower-bed. The sun was growing warm. As she approached the door she heard him call out hopefully, "Delia, is dat you Ah heah?"

She saw him on his hands and knees as soon as she reached the door. He crept an inch or two toward her—all that he was able, and she saw his horribly swollen neck and his one open eye shining with hope. A surge of pity too strong to support bore her away from that eye that must, could not, fail to see the tubs. He would see the lamp. Orlando with its doctors was too far. She could scarcely reach the chinaberry tree, where she waited in the growing heat while inside she knew the cold river was creeping up and up to extinguish that eye which must know by now that she knew.

—*1926*

William Faulkner (1897–1962) came from a family whose name was originally spelled "Falkner," but a misprint in an early book led him to change it. Faulkner spent long periods of his adult life in Hollywood, where he had some success as a screenwriter (a 1991 film, Barton Fink, *has a character obviously modeled on him), but always returned to Oxford, Mississippi, the site of his fictional Jefferson and Yoknapatawpha County. With Thomas Wolfe and others, he was responsible for the flowering of southern fiction in the early decades of the century, though for Faulkner fame came relatively late in life. Despite the success of* Sanctuary (1931) *and the critical esteem in which other early works like* The Sound and the Fury (1929) *and* As I Lay Dying (1930) *were held, Faulkner proved too difficult for most readers and failed to attract large audiences for what are now considered his best novels. By the late 1940s most of his books were out of print. His reputation was revived when Malcolm Cowley's edition of* The Portable Faulkner *appeared in 1946, but despite the success of* Intruder in the Dust (1948) *he was not as well known as many of his contemporaries when he won the Nobel Prize in 1950. A brilliant innovator of unusual narrative techniques in his novels, Faulkner created complex genealogies of characters to inhabit the world of his mythical South.*

William Faulkner
A Rose for Emily

I

When Miss Emily Grierson died, our whole town went to her funeral: the men through a sort of respectful affection for a fallen monument, the women mostly out of curiosity to see the inside of her house, which no one save an old manservant—a combined gardener and cook—had seen in at least ten years.

It was a big, squarish frame house that had once been white, decorated with cupolas and spires and scrolled balconies in the heavily lightsome style of the seventies, set on what had once been our most select street. But garages and cotton gins had encroached and obliterated even the august names of that neighborhood; only Miss Emily's house was left, lifting its stubborn and coquettish decay above the cotton wagons and the gasoline pumps—an eyesore among eyesores. And now Miss Emily had gone to join the representatives of those august names where they lay in the cedar-bemused cemetery among the ranked and anonymous graves of Union and Confederate soldiers who fell at the battle of Jefferson.

Alive, Miss Emily had been a tradition, a duty, and a care; a sort of hereditary obligation upon the town, dating from that day in 1894 when Colonel Sartoris, the mayor—he who fathered the edict that no Negro woman should appear on the streets without an apron—remitted her taxes, the dispensation dating from the death of her father on into perpetuity. Not that Miss Emily would have accepted charity. Colonel Sartoris invented an involved tale to the effect that Miss Emily's father had loaned money to the town, which the town, as a matter of business, preferred this way of repaying. Only a man of Colonel Sartoris' generation and thought could have invented it, and only a woman could have believed it.

When the next generation, with its more modern ideas, became mayors and aldermen, this arrangement created some little dissatisfaction. On the first of the year they mailed her a tax notice. February came, and there was no reply. They wrote her a formal letter, asking her to call at the sheriff's office at her convenience. A week later the mayor wrote her himself, offering to call or to send his car for her, and received in reply a note on paper of an archaic shape, in a thin, flowing calligraphy in faded ink, to the effect that she no longer went out at all. The tax notice was also enclosed, without comment.

They called a special meeting of the Board of Aldermen. A deputation waited upon her, knocked at the door through which no visitor had passed since she ceased giving china-painting lessons eight or ten years earlier. They were admitted by the old Negro into a dim hall from which a staircase mounted into still more shadow. It smelled of dust and disuse—a close, dank smell. The Negro led them into the parlor. It was furnished in heavy, leather-covered furniture. When the Negro opened the blinds of one window, they could see that the leather was cracked; and when they sat down, a faint dust rose sluggishly about their thighs, spinning with slow motes in the single sunray. On a tarnished gilt easel before the fireplace stood a crayon portrait of Miss Emily's father.

They rose when she entered—a small, fat woman in black, with a thin gold chain descending to her waist and vanishing into her belt, leaning on an ebony cane with a tarnished gold head. Her skeleton was small and spare; perhaps that was why what would have been merely plumpness in another was obesity in her. She looked bloated, like a body long submerged in motionless water, and of that pallid hue. Her eyes, lost in the fatty ridges of her face, looked like two small pieces of coal pressed into a lump of dough as they moved from one face to another while the visitors stated their errand.

She did not ask them to sit. She just stood in the door and listened quietly until the spokesman came to a stumbling halt. Then they could hear the invisible watch ticking at the end of the gold chain.

Her voice was dry and cold. "I have no taxes in Jefferson. Colonel Sartoris explained it to me. Perhaps one of you can gain access to the city records and satisfy yourselves."

"But we have. We are the city authorities, Miss Emily. Didn't you get a notice from the sheriff, signed by him?"

"I received a paper, yes," Miss Emily said. "Perhaps he considers himself the sheriff. . . . I have no taxes in Jefferson."

"But there is nothing on the books to show that, you see. We must go by the—"

"See Colonel Sartoris. I have no taxes in Jefferson."

"But, Miss Emily—"

"See Colonel Sartoris." (Colonel Sartoris had been dead almost ten years.) "I have no taxes in Jefferson. Tobe!" The Negro appeared. "Show these gentlemen out."

II

So she vanquished them, horse and foot, just as she had vanquished their fathers thirty years before about the smell. That was two years after her father's death and a short time after her sweetheart—the one we believed would marry her—had deserted her. After her father's death she went out very little; after her sweetheart went away people hardly saw her at all. A few of the ladies had the temerity to call, but were not received, and the only sign of life about the place was the Negro man— a young man then—going in and out with a market basket.

"Just as if a man—any man—could keep a kitchen properly," the ladies said; so they were not surprised when the smell developed. It was another link between the gross, teeming world and the high and mighty Griersons.

A neighbor, a woman, complained to the mayor, Judge Stevens, eighty years old.

"But what will you have me do about it, madam?" he said.

"Why, send her word to stop it," the woman said. "Isn't there a law?"

"I'm sure that won't be necessary," Judge Stevens said. "It's probably just a snake or a rat that nigger of hers killed in the yard. I'll speak to him about it."

The next day he received two more complaints, one from a man who came in diffident deprecation. "We really must do something about it, Judge. I'd be the last one in the world to bother Miss Emily, but we've got to do something." That night the Board of Aldermen met—three gray-beards and one younger man, a member of the rising generation.

"It's simple enough," he said. "Send her word to have her place cleaned up. Give her a certain time to do it in, and if she don't. . . ."

"Dammit, sir," Judge Stevens said, "will you accuse a lady to her face of smelling bad?"

So the next night, after midnight, four men crossed Miss Emily's lawn and slunk about the house like burglars, sniffing along the base of the brickwork and at the cellar openings while one of them performed a regular sowing motion with his hand out of a sack slung from his shoulder. They broke open the cellar door and sprinkled lime there, and in all the outbuildings. As they recrossed the lawn, a window that had been dark was lighted and Miss Emily sat in it, the light behind her, and her upright torso motionless as that of an idol. They crept quietly across the lawn and into the shadow of the locusts that lined the street. After a week or two the smell went away.

That was when people had begun to feel really sorry for her. People in our town, remembering how old lady Wyatt, her great-aunt, had gone completely crazy at last, believed that the Griersons held themselves a little too high for what they really were. None of the young men were quite good enough for Miss Emily and such. We had long thought of them as a tableau; Miss Emily a slender figure in white in the background, her father a spraddled silhouette in the foreground, his back to her and clutching a horsewhip, the two of them framed by the back-flung front door. So when she got to be thirty and was still single, we were not pleased exactly, but vindicated; even with insanity in the family she wouldn't have turned down all of her chances if they had really materialized.

When her father died, it got about that the house was all that was left to her; and in a way, people were glad. At last they could pity Miss Emily. Being left alone, and a pauper, she had become humanized. Now she too would know the old thrill and the old despair of a penny more or less.

The day after his death all the ladies prepared to call at the house and offer condolence and aid, as is our custom. Miss Emily met them at the door, dressed as usual and with no trace of grief on her face. She told them that her father was not dead. She did that for three days, with the ministers calling on her, and the doctors, trying to persuade her to let them dispose of the body. Just as they were about to resort to law and force, she broke down, and they buried her father quickly.

We did not say she was crazy then. We believed she had to do that. We remembered all the young men her father had driven away, and we knew that with nothing left, she would have to cling to that which had robbed her, as people will.

III

She was sick for a long time. When we saw her again, her hair was cut short, making her look like a girl, with a vague resemblance to those angels in colored church windows—sort of tragic and serene.

The town had just let the contracts for paving the sidewalks, and in the summer after her father's death they began the work. The construction company came with niggers and mules and machinery, and a foreman named Homer Barron, a Yankee—a big, dark, ready man, with a big voice and eyes lighter than his face. The little boys would follow in groups to hear him cuss the niggers, and the niggers singing in time to the rise and fall of picks. Pretty soon he knew everybody in town. Whenever you heard a lot of laughing anywhere about the square, Homer Barron would be in the center of the group. Presently we began to see him and Miss Emily on Sunday afternoons driving in the yellow-wheeled buggy and the matched team of bays from the livery stable.

At first we were glad that Miss Emily would have an interest, because the ladies all said, "Of course a Grierson would not think seriously of a Northerner, a day laborer." But there were still others, older people, who said that even grief could not cause a real lady to forget *noblesse oblige*—without calling it *noblesse oblige*. They just said, "Poor Emily. Her kinsfolk should come to her." She had some kin in Alabama; but years ago her father had fallen out with them over the estate of old lady Wyatt, the crazy woman, and there was no communication between the two families. They had not even been represented at the funeral.

And as soon as the old people said, "Poor Emily," the whispering began. "Do you suppose it's really so?" they said to one another. "Of course it is. What else could . . ." This behind their hands; rustling of craned silk and satin behind jalousies closed upon the sun of Sunday afternoon as the thin, swift clop-clop-clop of the matched team passed: "Poor Emily."

She carried her head high enough—even when we believed that she was fallen. It was as if she demanded more than ever the recognition of her dignity as the last Grierson; as if it had wanted that touch of earthiness to reaffirm her imperviousness. Like when she bought the rat poison, the arsenic. That was over a year after they had begun to say "Poor Emily," and while the two female cousins were visiting her.

"I want some poison," she said to the druggist. She was over thirty then, still a slight woman, though thinner than usual, with cold, haughty black eyes in a face the flesh of which was strained across the temples and about the eyesockets as you imagine a lighthousekeeper's face ought to look. "I want some poison," she said.

"Yes, Miss Emily. What kind? For rats and such? I'd recom—"

"I want the best you have. I don't care what kind."

The druggist named several. "They'll kill anything up to an elephant. But what you want—"

"Arsenic," Miss Emily said. "Is that a good one?"

"Is . . . arsenic? Yes, ma'am. But what you want—"

"I want arsenic."

The druggist looked down at her. She looked back at him, erect, her face like a strained flag. "Why, of course," the druggist said. "If that's what you want. But the law requires you to tell what you are going to use it for."

Miss Emily just stared at him, her head tilted back in order to look him eye for eye, until he looked away and went and got the arsenic and wrapped it up. The Negro delivery boy brought her the package; the druggist didn't come back. When she opened the package at home there was written on the box, under the skull and bones—"For rats."

IV

So the next day we all said, "She will kill herself"; and we said it would be the best thing. When she had first begun to be seen with Homer Barron, we had said, "She will marry him." Then we said, "She will persuade him yet," because Homer himself had remarked—he liked men, and it was known that he drank with the younger men in the Elks' Club—that he was not a marrying man. Later we said, "Poor Emily" behind the jalousies as they passed on Sunday afternoon in the glittering buggy, Miss Emily with her head high and Homer Barron with his hat cocked and a cigar in his teeth, reins and whip in a yellow glove.

Then some of the ladies began to say that it was a disgrace to the town and a bad example to the young people. The men did not want to interfere, but at last the ladies forced the Baptist minister—Miss Emily's people were Episcopal—to call upon her. He would never divulge what happened during that interview, but he refused to go back again. The next Sunday they again drove about the streets, and the following day the minister's wife wrote to Miss Emily's relations in Alabama.

So she had blood-kin under her roof again and we sat back to watch developments. At first nothing happened. Then we were sure that they were to be married. We learned that Miss Emily had been to the jeweler's and ordered a man's toilet set in silver, with the letters H. B. on each piece. Two days later we learned that she had bought a complete outfit of men's clothing, including a nightshirt, and we said, "They are married." We were really glad. We were glad because the two female cousins were even more Grierson than Miss Emily had ever been.

So we were not surprised when Homer Barron—the streets had been finished some time since—was gone. We were a little disappointed that there was not a public blowing-off, but we believed that he had gone on to prepare for Miss Emily's coming, or to give her a chance to get rid of the cousins. (By that time it was a cabal, and we were all Miss Emily's allies to help circumvent the cousins.) Sure enough, after another week they departed. And, as we had expected all along, within three days Homer Barron was back in town. A neighbor saw the Negro man admit him at the kitchen door at dusk one evening.

And that was the last we saw of Homer Barron. And of Miss Emily for some time. The Negro man went in and out with the market basket, but the front door remained closed. Now and then we would see her at a window for a moment, as the men did that night when they sprinkled the lime, but for almost six months she did not appear on the streets. Then we knew that this was to be expected too; as if that quality of her father which had thwarted her woman's life so many times had been too virulent and too furious to die.

When we next saw Miss Emily, she had grown fat and her hair was turning gray. During the next few years it grew grayer and grayer until it attained an even pepper-and-salt iron-gray, when it ceased turning. Up to the day of her death at seventy-four it was still that vigorous iron-gray, like the hair of an active man.

From that time on her front door remained closed, save for a period of six or seven years, when she was about forty, during which she gave lessons in china painting. She fitted up a studio in one of the downstairs rooms, where the daughters and granddaughters of Colonel Sartoris' contemporaries were sent to her with the same regularity and in the same spirit that they were sent to church on Sundays with a twenty-five cent piece for the collection plate. Meanwhile her taxes had been remitted.

Then the newer generation became the backbone and the spirit of the town, and the painting pupils grew up and fell away and did not send their children to her with boxes of color and tedious brushes and pictures cut from the ladies' magazines. The front door closed upon the last one and remained closed for good. When the town got free postal delivery, Miss Emily alone refused to let them fasten the metal numbers above her door and attach a mailbox to it. She would not listen to them.

Daily, monthly, yearly we watched the Negro grow grayer and more stooped, going in and out with the market basket. Each December we sent her a tax notice, which would be returned by the post office a week later, unclaimed. Now and then we would see her in one of the downstairs windows—she had evidently shut up the top floor of the house—like the carven torso of an idol in a niche, looking or not looking at us, we could never tell which. Thus she passed from generation to generation—dear, inescapable, impervious, tranquil, and perverse.

And so she died. Fell ill in the house filled with dust and shadows, with only a doddering Negro man to wait on her. We did not even know she was sick; we had long since given up trying to get any information from the Negro. He talked to no one, probably not even to her, for his voice had grown harsh and rusty, as if from disuse.

She died in one of the downstairs rooms, in a heavy walnut bed with a curtain, her gray head propped on a pillow yellow and moldy with age and lack of sunlight.

V

The Negro met the first of the ladies at the front door and let them in, with their hushed, sibilant voices and their quick, curious glances, and then he disappeared. He walked right through the house and out the back and was not seen again.

The two female cousins came at once. They held the funeral on the second day, with the town coming to look at Miss Emily beneath a mass of bought flowers, with the crayon face of her father musing profoundly above the bier and the ladies sibilant and macabre; and the very old men—some in their brushed Confederate uniforms—on the porch and the lawn, talking of Miss Emily as if she had been a contemporary of theirs, believing that they had danced with her and courted her perhaps, confusing time with its mathematical progression, as the old do, to whom all the past is not a diminishing road but, instead, a huge meadow which no winter ever quite touches, divided from them now by the narrow bottleneck of the most recent decade of years.

Already we knew that there was one room in that region above stairs which no one had seen in forty years, and which would have to be forced. They waited until Miss Emily was decently in the ground before they opened it.

The violence of breaking down the door seemed to fill this room with pervading dust. A thin, acrid pall as of the tomb seemed to lie everywhere upon this room decked and furnished as for a bridal: upon the valance curtains of faded rose color, upon the rose-shaded lights, upon the dressing table, upon the delicate array of crystal and the man's toilet things backed with tarnished silver, silver so tarnished that the monogram was obscured. Among them lay collar and tie, as if they had just been removed, which, lifted, left upon the surface a pale crescent in the dust. Upon a chair hung the suit, carefully folded; beneath it the two mute shoes and the discarded socks.

The man himself lay in the bed.

For a long while we just stood there, looking down at the profound and fleshless grin. The body had apparently once lain in the attitude of an embrace, but now the long sleep that outlasts love, that conquers even the grimace of love, had cuckolded him. What was left of him, rotted beneath what was left of the nightshirt, had become inextricable from the bed in which he lay; and upon him and upon the pillow beside him lay that even coating of the patient and biding dust.

Then we noticed that in the second pillow was the indentation of a head. One of us lifted something from it, and leaning forward, that faint and invisible dust dry and acrid in the nostrils, we saw a long strand of iron-gray hair.

—1930

Ernest Hemingway (1899–1961) completely embodied the public image of the successful writer for so long that even today, three decades after his suicide, it is difficult to separate the celebrity from the serious artist, the sportsman and carouser from the stylist whose influence on the short story and novel continues to be felt. The complexity of his life and personality still fascinates biographers, even though a half-dozen major studies have already appeared. Born the son of a doctor in a middle-class suburb of Chicago, wounded as an volunteer ambulance driver in Italy during World War I, trained as a reporter on the Kansas City Star, *Hemingway moved to Paris in the early 1920s, where he was at the center of a brilliant generation of American expatriates that included Gertrude Stein and F. Scott Fitzgerald. His wide travels are reflected in his work. He spent much time in Spain, which provided material for his first novel,* The Sun Also Rises *(1926), and his many later articles on bullfighting. Stories like "Hills like White Elephants," in which the unspoken subject is an abortion, earned him a reputation for daring subject matter and made him one of the chief spokesmen for the so-called Lost Generation. In the 1930s he covered the Spanish Civil War, the backdrop for his most popular novel,* For Whom the Bell Tolls *(1940). His African safaris and residence in pre-Castro Cuba were also sources for his fiction. When all else is said, Hemingway's greatest contribution may lie in the terse, stripped-down quality of his early prose, which renders modern alienation with stark concrete details. Hemingway won the Nobel Prize in 1954. The decades since his death have seen the release of much unpublished material—a memoir of his Paris years,* A Moveable Feast *(1964); two novels,* Islands in the Stream *and* The Garden of Eden; *and a "fictional memoir" of his final African safari,* True at First Light *(1999). None of these posthumously published works has advanced his literary reputation.*

Ernest Hemingway
Hills Like White Elephants

The hills across the valley of the Ebro were long and white. On this side there was no shade and no trees and the station was between two lines of rails in the sun. Close against the side of the station there was the warm shadow of the building and a curtain, made of strings of bamboo beads, hung across the open door into the bar, to keep out flies. The American and the girl with him sat at a table in the shade, outside the building. It was very hot and the express from Barcelona would come in forty minutes. It stopped at this junction for two minutes and went on to Madrid.

"What should we drink?" the girl asked. She had taken off her hat and put it on the table.

"It's pretty hot," the man said.

"Let's drink beer."

"*Dos cervezas*," the man said into the curtain.

"Big ones?" a woman asked from the doorway.

"Yes. Two big ones."

The woman brought two glasses of beer and two felt pads. She put the felt pads and the beer glasses on the table and looked at the man and the girl. The girl was looking off at the line of hills. They were white in the sun and the country was brown and dry.

"They look like white elephants," she said.

"I've never seen one," the man drank his beer.

"No, you wouldn't have."

"I might have," the man said. "Just because you say I wouldn't have doesn't prove anything."

The girl looked at the bead curtain. "They've painted something on it," she said. "What does it say?"

"Anis del Toro. It's a drink."

"Could we try it?"

The man called "Listen" through the curtain. The woman came out from the bar.

"Four reales."

"We want two Anis del Toro."

"With water?"

"Do you want it with water?"

"I don't know," the girl said. "Is it good with water?"

"It's all right."

"You want them with water?" asked the woman.

"Yes, with water."

"It tastes like licorice," the girl said and put the glass down.

"That's the way with everything."

"Yes," said the girl. "Everything tastes of licorice. Especially all the things you've waited so long for, like absinthe."

"Oh, cut it out."

"You started it," the girl said. "I was being amused. I was having a fine time."

"Well, let's try and have a fine time."

"All right. I was trying. I said the mountains looked like white elephants. Wasn't that bright?"

"That was bright."

"I wanted to try this new drink: That's all we do, isn't it—look at things and try new drinks?"

"I guess so."

The girl looked across at the hills.

"They're lovely hills," she said. "They don't really look like white elephants. I just meant the coloring of their skin through the trees."

"Should we have another drink?"

"All right."

The warm wind blew the bead curtain against the table.

"The beer's nice and cool," the man said.

"It's lovely," the girl said.

"It's really an awfully simple operation, Jig," the man said. "It's not really an operation at all."

The girl looked at the ground the table legs rested on.

"I know you wouldn't mind it, Jig. It's really not anything. It's just to let the air in."

The girl did not say anything.

"I'll go with you and I'll stay with you all the time. They just let the air in and then it's all perfectly natural."

"Then what will we do afterward?"

"We'll be fine afterward. Just like we were before."

"What makes you think so?"

"That's the only thing that bothers us. It's the only thing that's made us unhappy."

The girl looked at the bead curtain, put her hand out and took hold of two of the strings of beads.

"And you think then we'll be all right and be happy."

"I know we will. You don't have to be afraid. I've known lots of people that have done it."

"So have I," said the girl. "And afterward they were all so happy."

"Well," the man said, "if you don't want to you don't have to. I wouldn't have you do it if you didn't want to. But I know it's perfectly simple."

"And you really want to?"

"I think it's the best thing to do. But I don't want you to do it if you don't really want to."

"And if I do it you'll be happy and things will be like they were and you'll love me?"

"I love you now. You know I love you."

"I know. But if I do it, then it will be nice again if I say things are like white elephants, and you'll like it?"

"I'll love it. I love it now but I just can't think about it. You know how I get when I worry."

"If I do it you won't ever worry?"

"I won't worry about that because it's perfectly simple."

"Then I'll do it. Because I don't care about me."

"What do you mean?"

"I don't care about me."

"Well, I care about you."

"Oh, yes. But I don't care about me. And I'll do it and then everything will be fine."

"I don't want you to do it if you feel that way."

The girl stood up and walked to the end of the station. Across, on the other side, were fields of grain and trees along the banks of the Ebro. Far away, beyond the river, were mountains. The shadow of a cloud moved across the field of grain and she saw the river through the trees.

"And we could have all this," she said. "And we could have everything and every day we make it more impossible."

"What did you say?"

"I said we could have everything."

"We can have everything."

"No, we can't."

"We can have the whole world."

"No, we can't."

"We can go everywhere."

"No, we can't. It isn't ours any more."

"It's ours."

"No, it isn't. And once they take it away, you never get it back."

"But they haven't taken it away."

"We'll wait and see."

"Come on back in the shade," he said. "You mustn't feel that way."

"I don't feel any way," the girl said. "I just know things."

"I don't want you to do anything that you don't want to do——"

"Nor that isn't good for me," she said. "I know. Could we have another beer?"

"All right. But you've got to realize——"

"I realize," the girl said. "Can't we maybe stop talking?"

They sat down at the table and the girl looked across at the hills on the dry side of the valley and the man looked at her and at the table.

"You've got to realize," he said, "that I don't want you to do it if you don't want to. I'm perfectly willing to go through with it if it means anything to you."

"Doesn't it mean anything to you? We could get along."

"Of course it does. But I don't want anybody but you. I don't want any one else. And I know it's perfectly simple."

"Yes, you know it's perfectly simple."

"It's all right for you to say that, but I do know it."

"Would you do something for me now?"

"I'd do anything for you."

"Would you please please please please please please please stop talking?"

He did not say anything but looked at the bags against the wall of the station. There were labels on them from all the hotels where they had spent nights.

"But I don't want you to," he said, "I don't care anything about it."

"I'll scream," the girl said.

The woman came out through the curtains with two glasses of beer and put them down on the damp felt pads. "The train comes in five minutes," she said.

"What did she say?" asked the girl.

"That the train is coming in five minutes."

The girl smiled brightly at the woman, to thank her.

"I'd better take the bags over to the other side of the station," the man said. She smiled at him.

"All right. Then come back and we'll finish the beer."

He picked up the two heavy bags and carried them around the station to the other tracks. He looked up the tracks but could not see the train. Coming back, he walked through the barroom, where people waiting for the train were drinking. He drank an Anis at the bar and looked at the people. They were all waiting reasonably for the train. He went out through the bead curtain. She was sitting at the table and smiled at him.

"Do you feel better?" he asked.

"I feel fine," she said. "There's nothing wrong with me. I feel fine."

—1927

Jorge Luis Borges (1899–1986) is perhaps the most original writer in Spanish of the twentieth century, and many of his experiments anticipate the "meta-fiction" and "cyberpunk" techniques of today's avant-garde. Born in Buenos Aires, Borges was caught with his parents in Switzerland during World War I, a circumstance that happily led to a multi-lingual education. Borges was equally fluent in English (he was an expert in Anglo-Saxon literature) and his native Spanish, and he also learned French, German, and Latin. In his early career he was associated with a group of avant-garde experimental poets who attempted, in the pages of literary magazines like Sur, *to connect the provincial Argentine reading public with the main currents of modernism. Borges himself translated the works of difficult American poets like e. e. cummings and Wallace Stevens into Spanish. Borges turned to fiction in his forties, and his paradoxical allegories of time and being, although widely discussed, were never aimed at large popular audiences. A vocal opponent of the Nazis (who had many supporters in Argentina) and of the Perón dictatorship, Borges was dismissed from several positions because of his politics. After the fall of Perón in 1955, Borges served a distinguished term as director of Argentina's national library, despite progressive deterioration of his sight, which left him almost totally blind. In his later years he traveled and lectured in the United States and oversaw the translation of his works into English.*

Jorge Luis Borges
The Gospel According to Mark

These events took place at La Colorada ranch, in the southern part of the township of Junín, during the last days of March 1928. The protagonist was a medical student named Baltasar Espinosa. We may describe him, for now, as one of the common run of young men from Buenos Aires, with nothing more noteworthy about him than an almost

Translated by Norman Thomas di Giovanni in collaboration with the author.

unlimited kindness and a capacity for public speaking that had earned him several prizes at the English school in Ramos Mejía. He did not like arguing, and preferred having his listener rather than himself in the right. Although he was fascinated by the probabilities of chance in any game he played, he was a bad player because it gave him no pleasure to win. His wide intelligence was undirected; at the age of thirty-three, he still had not qualified for graduation in the subject to which he was most drawn. His father, who was a freethinker[1] (like all the gentlemen of his day), had introduced him to the lessons of Herbert Spencer,[2] but his mother, before leaving on a trip for Montevideo, once asked him to say the Lord's Prayer and make the sign of the cross every night. Through the years, he had never gone back on that promise.

Espinosa was not lacking in spirit; one day, with more indifference than anger, he had exchanged two or three punches with a group of fellow-students who were trying to force him to take part in a university demonstration. Owing to an acquiescent nature, he was full of opinions, or habits of mind, that were questionable: Argentina mattered less to him than a fear that in other parts of the world people might think of us as Indians; he worshiped France but despised the French; he thought little of Americans but approved the fact that there were tall buildings, like theirs, in Buenos Aires; he believed the gauchos[3] of the plains to be better riders than those of hill or mountain country. When his cousin Daniel invited him to spend the summer months out at La Colorada, he said yes at once—not because he was really fond of the country, but more out of his natural complacency and also because it was easier to say yes than to dream up reasons for saying no.

The ranch's main house was big and slightly rundown; the quarters of the foreman, whose name was Gutre, were close by. The Gutres were three: the father, an unusually uncouth son, and a daughter of uncertain paternity. They were tall, strong, and bony, and had hair that was on the reddish side and faces that showed traces of Indian blood. They were barely articulate. The foreman's wife had died years before.

There in the country, Espinosa began learning things he never knew, or even suspected—for example, that you do not gallop a horse when approaching settlements, and that you never go out riding except for

---

[1]*freethinker:* i.e., agnostic.   [2]*Herbert Spencer:* a British philosopher (1820–1903) who championed the theories of Charles Darwin.   [3]*gauchos:* South American cowboys.

some special purpose. In time, he was to come to tell the birds apart by their calls.

After a few days, Daniel had to leave for Buenos Aires to close a deal on some cattle. At most, this bit of business might take him a week. Espinosa, who was already somewhat weary of hearing about his cousin's incessant luck with women and his tireless interest in the minute details of men's fashion, preferred staying on at the ranch with his textbooks. But the heat was unbearable, and even the night brought no relief. One morning at daybreak, thunder woke him. Outside, the wind was rocking the Australian pines. Listening to the first heavy drops of rain, Espinosa thanked God. All at once, cold air rolled in. That afternoon, the Salado overflowed its banks.

The next day, looking out over the flooded fields from the gallery of the main house, Baltasar Espinosa thought that the stock metaphor comparing the pampa to the sea was not altogether false—at least, not that morning—though W. H. Hudson[4] had remarked that the sea seems wider because we view it from a ship's deck and not from a horse or from eye level.

The rain did not let up. The Gutres, helped or hindered by Espinosa, the town dweller, rescued a good part of the livestock, but many animals were drowned. There were four roads leading to La Colorada; all of them were under water. On the third day, when a leak threatened the foreman's house, Espinosa gave the Gutres a room near the toolshed, at the back of the main house. This drew them all closer; they ate together in the big dining room. Conversation turned out to be difficult. The Gutres, who knew so much about country things, were hard put to it to explain them. One night, Espinosa asked them if people still remembered the Indian raids from back when the frontier command was located there in Junín. They told him yes, but they would have given the same answer to a question about the beheading of Charles I.[5] Espinosa recalled his father's saying that almost every case of longevity that was cited in the country was really a case of bad memory or of a dim notion of dates. Gauchos are apt to be ignorant of the year of their birth or of the name of the man who begot them.

In the whole house, there was apparently no other reading matter than a set of the *Farm Journal*, a handbook of veterinary medicine, a deluxe edition of the Uruguayan epic *Tabaré*, a history of shorthorn

---

[4]*W. H. Hudson:* English author (1841–1922) who wrote about South America.   [5]*Charles I:* King of England, beheaded in 1649.

cattle in Argentina, a number of erotic or detective stories, and a recent novel called *Don Segundo Sombra*. Espinosa, trying in some way to bridge the inevitable after-dinner gap, read a couple of chapters of this novel to the Gutres, none of whom could read or write. Unfortunately, the foreman had been a cattle drover, and the doings of the hero, another cattle drover, failed to whet his interest. He said that the work was light, that drovers always traveled with a packhorse that carried everything they needed, and that, had he not been a drover, he would never have seen such far-flung places as the Laguna de Gómez, the town of Bragado, and the spread of the Núñez family in Chacabuco. There was a guitar in the kitchen; the ranch hands, before the time of the events I am describing, used to sit around in a circle. Someone would tune the instrument without ever getting around to playing it. This was known as a guitarfest.

Espinosa, who had grown a beard, began dallying in front of the mirror to study his new face, and he smiled to think how, back in Buenos Aires, he would bore his friends by telling them the story of the Salado flood. Strangely enough, he missed places he never frequented and never would: a corner of Cabrera Street on which there was a mailbox; one of the cement lions of a gateway on Jujuy Street, a few blocks from the Plaza del Once; an old barroom with a tiled floor, whose exact whereabouts he was unsure of. As for his brothers and his father, they would already have learned from Daniel that he was isolated—etymologically, the word was perfect—by the floodwaters.

Exploring the house, still hemmed in by the watery waste, Espinosa came across an English Bible. Among the blank pages at the end, the Guthries—such was their original name—had left a handwritten record of their lineage. They were natives of Inverness;[6] had reached the New World, no doubt as common laborers, in the early part of the nineteenth century; and had intermarried with Indians. The chronicle broke off sometime during the 1870s, when they no longer knew how to write. After a few generations, they had forgotten English; their Spanish, at the time Espinosa knew them, gave them trouble. They lacked any religious faith, but there survived in their blood, like faint tracks, the rigid fanaticism of the Calvinist and the superstitions of the pampa Indian. Espinosa later told them of his find, but they barely took notice.

[6]*Inverness:* a county in Scotland.

Leafing through the volume, his fingers opened it at the beginning of the Gospel according to Saint Mark. As an exercise in translation, and maybe to find out whether the Gutres understood any of it, Espinosa decided to begin reading them that text after their evening meal. It surprised him that they listened attentively, absorbed. Maybe the gold letters on the cover lent the book authority. It's still there in their blood, Espinosa thought. It also occurred to him that the generations of men, throughout recorded time, have always told and retold two stories—that of a lost ship which searches the Mediterranean seas for a dearly loved island, and that of a god who is crucified on Golgotha. Remembering his lessons in elocution from his schooldays in Ramos Mejía, Espinosa got to his feet when he came to the parables.

The Gutres took to bolting their barbecued meat and their sardines so as not to delay the Gospel. A pet lamb that the girl adorned with a small blue ribbon had injured itself on a strand of barbed wire. To stop the bleeding, the three had wanted to apply a cobweb to the wound, but Espinosa treated the animal with some pills. The gratitude that this treatment awakened in them took him aback. (Not trusting the Gutres at first, he'd hidden away in one of his books the 240 pesos he had brought with him.) Now, the owner of the place away, Espinosa took over and gave timid orders, which were immediately obeyed. The Gutres, as if lost without him, liked following him from room to room and along the gallery that ran around the house. While he read to them, he noticed that they were secretly stealing the crumbs he had dropped on the table. One evening, he caught them unawares, talking about him respectfully, in very few words.

Having finished the Gospel according to Saint Mark, he wanted to read another of the three Gospels that remained, but the father asked him to repeat the one he had just read, so that they could understand it better. Espinosa felt that they were like children, to whom repetition is more pleasing than variations or novelty. That night—this is not to be wondered at—he dreamed of the Flood; the hammer blows of the building of the Ark woke him up, and he thought that perhaps they were thunder. In fact, the rain, which had let up, started again. The cold was bitter. The Gutres had told him that the storm had damaged the roof of the toolshed, and that they would show it to him when the beams were fixed. No longer a stranger now, he was treated by them with special attention, almost to the point of spoiling him. None of them liked coffee, but for him there was always a small cup into which they heaped sugar.

The new storm had broken out on a Tuesday. Thursday night, Espinosa was awakened by a soft knock at his door, which, just in case, he always kept locked. He got out of bed and opened it; there was the girl. In the dark he could hardly make her out, but by her footsteps he could tell she was barefoot, and moments later, in bed, that she must have come all the way from the other end of the house naked. She did not embrace him or speak a single word; she lay beside him, trembling. It was the first time she had known a man. When she left, she did not kiss him; Espinosa realized that he didn't even know her name. For some reason that he did not want to pry into, he made up his mind that upon returning to Buenos Aires he would tell no one about what had taken place.

The next day began like the previous ones, except that the father spoke to Espinosa and asked him if Christ had let Himself be killed so as to save all other men on earth. Espinosa, who was a freethinker but who felt committed to what he had read to the Gutres, answered, "Yes, to save everyone from Hell."

Gutre then asked, "What's Hell?"

"A place under the ground where souls burn and burn."

"And the Roman soldiers who hammered in the nails—were they saved, too?"

"Yes," said Espinosa, whose theology was rather dim.

All along, he was afraid that the foreman might ask him about what had gone on the night before with his daughter. After lunch, they asked him to read the last chapters over again.

Espinosa slept a long nap that afternoon. It was a light sleep, disturbed by persistent hammering and by vague premonitions. Toward evening, he got up and went out onto the gallery. He said, as if thinking aloud, "The waters have dropped. It won't be long now."

"It won't be long now," Gutre repeated, like an echo.

The three had been following him. Bowing their knees to the stone pavement, they asked his blessing. Then they mocked at him, spat on him, and shoved him toward the back part of the house. The girl wept. Espinosa understood what awaited him on the other side of the door. When they opened it, he saw a patch of sky. A bird sang out. A goldfinch, he thought. The shed was without a roof; they had pulled down the beams to make the cross.

—*1970*

John Steinbeck (1902–1968) was another American winner of the Nobel Prize. Steinbeck has not attracted as much biographical and critical attention as his contemporaries William Faulkner and Ernest Hemingway, but future generations may view The Grapes of Wrath *(1939), his epic novel of the Depression and the Oklahoma dust bowl, with the same reverence we reserve for nineteenth-century masterpieces of historical fiction like Thackeray's* Vanity Fair *or Tolstoy's* War and Peace. *If one measure of a great writer is how well he or she manages to capture the temper of the times, then Steinbeck stands as tall as any. Born in Salinas, California, he drew throughout his career on his familiarity with the farming country, ranches, and fishing communities of his native state, especially in novels like* Tortilla Flat *(1935),* Of Mice and Men *(1937), and* Cannery Row *(1945). Steinbeck's short fiction is less well known, although he excelled at the novella form in* The Pearl *(1947). "The Chrysanthemums" comes from* The Long Valley, *a collection of short stories set in the Salinas Valley. Like many of the best American writers of the century, Steinbeck was a humanitarian whose sympathies lay with the common man or woman, although he rarely indulged in the shallow propagandizing that characterized many so-called proletarian novels of the 1930s. Steinbeck was a lifelong student of marine biology, and his sensitivity to the effects of environment on organisms, both animal and human, is reflected in his scrupulous attention to setting.*

John Steinbeck

The Chrysanthemums

The high grey-flannel fog of winter closed off the Salinas Valley from the sky and from all the rest of the world. On every side it sat like a lid on the mountains and made of the great valley a closed pot. On the broad, level land floor the gang plows bit deep and left the black earth shining like metal where the shares had cut. On the foothill ranches across the Salinas River, the yellow stubble fields seemed to be bathed in pale cold sunshine, but there was no sunshine in the valley now in December. The thick willow scrub along the river flamed with sharp and positive yellow leaves.

It was a time of quiet and of waiting. The air was cold and tender. A light wind blew up from the southwest so that the farmers were mildly hopeful of a good rain before long; but fog and rain do not go together. Across the river, on Henry Allen's foothill ranch there was little work to be done, for the hay was cut and stored and the orchards were plowed up to receive the rain deeply when it should come. The cattle on the higher slopes were becoming shaggy and rough-coated.

Elisa Allen, working in her flower garden, looked down across the yard and saw Henry, her husband, talking to two men in business suits. The three of them stood by the tractor shed, each man with one foot on the side of the little Fordson. They smoked cigarettes and studied the machine as they talked.

Elisa watched them for a moment and then went back to her work. She was thirty-five. Her face was lean and strong and her eyes were as clear as water. Her figure looked blocked and heavy in her gardening costume, a man's black hat pulled low down over her eyes, clod-hopper shoes, a figured print dress almost completely covered by a big corduroy apron with four big pockets to hold the snips, the trowel and scratcher, the seeds and the knife she worked with. She wore heavy leather gloves to protect her hands while she worked.

She was cutting down the old year's chrysanthemum stalks with a pair of short and powerful scissors. She looked down toward the men by the tractor shed now and then. Her face was eager and mature and handsome; even her work with the scissors was over-eager, over-powerful. The chrysanthemum stems seemed too small and easy for her energy.

She brushed a cloud of hair out of her eyes with the back of her glove, and left a smudge of earth on her cheek in doing it. Behind her stood the neat white farm house with red geraniums close-banked around it as high as the windows. It was a hard-swept looking little house with hard-polished windows, and a clean mud-mat on the front steps.

Elisa cast another glance toward the tractor shed. The strangers were getting into their Ford coupe. She took off a glove and put her strong fingers down into the forest of new green chrysanthemum sprouts that were growing around the old roots. She spread the leaves and looked down among the close-growing stems. No aphids were there, no sowbugs or snails or cutworms. Her terrier fingers destroyed such pests before they could get started.

Elisa started at the sound of her husband's voice. He had come near quietly, and he leaned over the wire fence that protected her flower garden from cattle and dogs and chickens.

"At it again," he said. "You've got a strong new crop coming."

Elisa straightened her back and pulled on the gardening glove again. "Yes. They'll be strong this coming year." In her tone and on her face there was a little smugness.

"You've got a gift with things," Henry observed. "Some of those yellow chrysanthemums you had this year were ten inches across. I wish you'd work out in the orchard and raise some apples that big."

Her eyes sharpened. "Maybe I could do it, too. I've a gift with things, all right. My mother had it. She could stick anything in the ground and make it grow. She said it was having planters' hands that knew how to do it."

"Well, it sure works with flowers," he said.

"Henry, who were those men you were talking to?"

"Why, sure, that's what I came to tell you. They were from the Western Meat Company. I sold those thirty head of three-year-old steers. Got nearly my own price, too."

"Good," she said. "Good for you."

"And I thought," he continued, "I thought how it's Saturday afternoon, and we might go into Salinas for dinner at a restaurant, and then to a picture show—to celebrate, you see."

"Good," she repeated. "Oh, yes. That will be good."

Henry put on his joking tone. "There's fights tonight. How'd you like to go to the fights?"

"Oh, no," she said breathlessly. "No, I wouldn't like fights."

"Just fooling, Elisa. We'll go to a movie. Let's see. It's two now. I'm going to take Scotty and bring down those steers from the hill. It'll take us maybe two hours. We'll go in town about five and have dinner at the Cominos Hotel. Like that?"

"Of course I'll like it. It's good to eat away from home."

"All right, then. I'll go get up a couple of horses."

She said, "I'll have plenty of time to transplant some of these sets, I guess."

She heard her husband calling Scotty down by the barn. And a little later she saw the two men ride up the pale yellow hillside in search of the steers.

There was a little square sandy bed kept for rooting the chrysanthemums. With her trowel she turned the soil over and over, and smoothed it and patted it firm. Then she dug ten parallel trenches to receive the sets. Back at the chrysanthemum bed she pulled out the little crisp shoots, trimmed off the leaves of each one with her scissors and laid it on a small orderly pile.

A squeak of wheels and plod of hoofs came from the road. Elisa looked up. The country road ran along the dense bank of willows and cottonwoods that bordered the river, and up this road came a curious vehicle, curiously drawn. It was an old springwagon, with a round canvas top on it like the cover of a prairie schooner. It was drawn by an old bay horse and a little grey-and-white burro. A big stubble bearded man sat between the cover flaps and drove the crawling team. Underneath the wagon, between the hind wheels, a lean and rangy mongrel dog walked sedately. Words were painted on the canvas, in clumsy, crooked letters. "Pots, pans, knives, sisors, lawn mores, Fixed." Two rows of articles, and the triumphantly definitive "Fixed" below. The black paint had run down in little sharp-points beneath each letter.

Elisa, squatting on the ground, watched to see the crazy, loose-jointed wagon pass by. But it didn't pass. It turned into the farm road in front of her house, crooked old wheels skirling and squeaking. The rangy dog darted from between the wheels and ran ahead. Instantly the two ranch shepherds flew out at him. Then all three stopped, and with stiff and quivering tails, with taut straight legs, with ambassadorial dignity, they slowly circled, sniffing daintily. The caravan pulled up to Elisa's wire fence and stopped. Now the newcomer dog, feeling outnumbered, lowered his tail and retired under the wagon with raised hackles and bared teeth.

The man on the wagon seat called out, "That's a bad dog in a fight when he gets started."

Elisa laughed. "I see he is. How soon does he generally get started?"

The man caught up her laughter and echoed it heartily. "Sometimes not for weeks and weeks," he said. He climbed stiffly down, over the wheel. The horse and the donkey drooped like unwatered flowers.

Elisa saw that he was a very big man. Although his hair and beard were greying, he did not look old. His worn black suit was wrinkled and spotted with grease. The laughter had disappeared from his face and eyes the moment his laughing voice ceased. His eyes were dark, and they were full of the brooding that gets in the eyes of teamsters and of sailors. The calloused hands he rested on the wire fence were cracked, and every crack was a black line. He took off his battered hat.

"I'm off my general road, ma'am," he said. "Does this dirt road cut over across the river to the Los Angeles highway?"

Elisa stood up and shoved the thick scissors in her apron pocket. "Well, yes, it does, but it winds around and then fords the river. I don't think your team could pull through the sand."

He replied with some asperity. "It might surprise you what them beasts can pull through."

"When they get started?" she asked.

He smiled for a second. "Yes. When they get started."

"Well," said Elisa, "I think you'll save time if you go back to the Salinas road and pick up the highway there."

He drew a big finger down the chicken wire and made it sing. "I ain't in any hurry, ma'am. I go from Seattle to San Diego and back every year. Takes all my time. About six months each way. I aim to follow nice weather."

Elisa took off her gloves and stuffed them in the apron pocket with the scissors. She touched the under edge of her man's hat, searching for fugitive hairs. "That sounds like a nice kind of a way to live," she said.

He leaned confidentially over the fence. "Maybe you noticed the writing on my wagon. I mend pots and sharpen knives and scissors. You got any of them things to do?"

"Oh, no," she said quickly. "Nothing like that." Her eyes hardened with resistance.

"Scissors is the worst thing," he explained. "Most people just ruin scissors trying to sharpen 'em, but I know how. I got a special tool. It's a little bobbit kind of thing, and patented. But it sure does the trick."

"No. My scissors are all sharp."

"All right, then. Take a pot," he continued earnestly, "a bent pot, or a pot with a hole. I can make it like new so you don't have to buy no new ones. That's a saving for you."

"No," she said shortly. "I tell you I have nothing like that for you to do."

His face fell to an exaggerated sadness. His voice took on a whining undertone. "I ain't had a thing to do today. Maybe I won't have no supper tonight. You see I'm off my regular road. I know folks on the highway clear from Seattle to San Diego. They save their things for me to sharpen up because they know I do it so good and save them money."

"I'm sorry," Elisa said irritably. "I haven't anything for you to do."

His eyes left her face and fell to searching the ground. They roamed about until they came to the chrysanthemum bed where she had been working. "What's them plants, ma'am?"

The irritation and resistance melted from Elisa's face. "Oh, those are chrysanthemums, giant whites and yellows. I raise them every year, bigger than anybody around here."

"Kind of a long-stemmed flower? Looks like a quick puff of colored smoke?" he asked.

"That's it. What a nice way to describe them."

"They smell kind of nasty till you get used to them," he said.

"It's a good bitter smell," she retorted, "not nasty at all."

He changed his tone quickly. "I like the smell myself."

"I had ten-inch blooms this year," she said.

The man leaned farther over the fence. "Look. I know a lady down the road a piece, has got the nicest garden you ever seen. Got nearly every kind of flower but no chrysanthemums. Last time I was mending a copper bottom wash tub for her (that's a hard job but I do it good), she said to me, 'If you ever run acrost some nice chrysanthemums I wish you'd try to get me a few seeds.' That's what she told me."

Elisa's eyes grew alert and eager. "She couldn't have known much about chrysanthemums. You *can* raise them from seed, but it's much easier to root the little sprouts you see there."

"Oh," he said. "I s'pose I can't take none to her, then."

"Why yes you can," Elisa cried. "I can put some in damp sand, and you can carry them right along with you. They'll take root in the pot if you keep them damp. And then she can transplant them."

"She'd sure like to have some, ma'am. You say they're nice ones?"

"Beautiful," she said. "Oh, beautiful." Her eyes shone. She tore off the battered hat and shook out her dark pretty hair. "I'll put them in a flower pot, and you can take them right with you. Come into the yard."

While the man came through the picket gate Elisa ran excitedly along the geranium-bordered path to the back of the house. And she returned carrying a big red flower pot. The gloves were forgotten now. She kneeled on the ground by the starting bed and dug up the sandy soil with her fingers and scooped it into the bright new flower pot. Then she picked up the little pile of shoots she had prepared. With her strong fingers she pressed them into the sand and tamped around them with her knuckles. The man stood over her. "I'll tell you what to do," she said. "You remember so you can tell the lady."

"Yes, I'll try to remember."

"Well, look. These will take root in about a month. Then she must set them out, about a foot apart in good rich earth like this, see?" She lifted a handful of dark soil for him to look at. "They'll grow fast and tall. Now remember this: In July tell her to cut them down, about eight inches from the ground."

"Before they bloom?" he asked.

"Yes, before they bloom." Her face was tight with eagerness. "They'll grow right up again. About the last of September the buds will start."

She stopped and seemed perplexed. "It's the budding that takes the most care," she said hesitantly. "I don't know how to tell you." She looked deep into his eyes, searchingly. Her mouth opened a little, and she seemed to be listening. "I'll try to tell you," she said. "Did you ever hear of planting hands?"

"Can't say I have, ma'am."

"Well, I can only tell you what it feels like. It's when you're picking off the buds you don't want. Everything goes right down into your fingertips. You watch your fingers work. They do it themselves. You can feel how it is. They pick and pick the buds. They never make a mistake. They're with the plant. Do you see? Your fingers and the plant. You can feel that, right up your arm. They know. They never make a mistake. You can feel it. When you're like that you can't do anything wrong. Do you see that? Can you understand that?"

She was kneeling on the ground looking up at him. Her breast swelled passionately.

The man's eyes narrowed. He looked away self-consciously. "Maybe I know," he said. "Sometimes in the night in the wagon there—"

Elisa's voice grew husky. She broke in on him, "I've never lived as you do, but I know what you mean. When the night is dark—why, the stars are sharp-pointed, and there's quiet. Why, you rise up and up! Every pointed star gets driven into your body. It's like that. Hot and sharp and—lovely."

Kneeling there, her hand went out toward his legs in the greasy black trousers. Her hesitant fingers almost touched the cloth. Then her hand dropped to the ground. She crouched low like a fawning dog.

He said, "It's nice, just like you say. Only when you don't have no dinner, it ain't."

She stood up then, very straight, and her face was ashamed. She held the flower pot out to him and placed it gently in his arms. "Here. Put it in your wagon, on the seat, where you can watch it. Maybe I can find something for you to do."

At the back of the house she dug in the can pile and found two old and battered aluminum saucepans. She carried them back and gave them to him. "Here, maybe you can fix these."

His manner changed. He became professional. "Good as new I can fix them." At the back of his wagon he set a little anvil, and out of an oily tool box dug a small machine hammer. Elisa came through the gate to watch him while he pounded out the dents in the kettles. His mouth grew sure and knowing. At a difficult part of the work he sucked his under-lip.

"You sleep right in the wagon?" Elisa asked.

"Right in the wagon, ma'am. Rain or shine I'm dry as a cow in there."

"It must be nice," she said. "It must be very nice. I wish women could do such things."

"It ain't the right kind of a life for a woman."

Her upper lip raised a little, showing her teeth. "How do you know? How can you tell?" she said.

"I don't know, ma'am," he protested. "Of course I don't know. Now here's your kettles, done. You don't have to buy no new ones."

"How much?"

"Oh, fifty cents'll do. I keep my prices down and my work good. That's why I have all them satisfied customers up and down the highway."

Elisa brought him a fifty-cent piece from the house and dropped it in his hand. "You might be surprised to have a rival some time. I can sharpen scissors, too. And I can beat the dents out of little pots. I could show you what a woman might do."

He put his hammer back in the oily box and shoved the little anvil out of sight. "It would be a lonely life for a woman, ma'am, and a scarey life, too, with animals creeping under the wagon all night." He climbed over the singletree, steadying himself with a hand on the burro's white rump. He settled himself in the seat, picked up the lines. "Thank you kindly, ma'am," he said. "I'll do like you told me; I'll go back and catch the Salinas road."

"Mind," she called, "if you're long in getting there, keep the sand damp."

"Sand, ma'am? . . . Sand? Oh, sure. You mean around the chrysanthemums. Sure I will." He clucked his tongue. The beasts leaned luxuriously into their collars. The mongrel dog took his place between the back wheels. The wagon turned and crawled out the entrance road and back the way it had come, along the river.

Elisa stood in front of her wire fence watching the slow progress of the caravan. Her shoulders were straight, her head thrown back, her eyes half-closed, so that the scene came vaguely into them. Her lips moved silently, forming the words "Good-bye—good-bye." Then she whispered, "That's a bright direction. There's a glowing there." The sound of her whisper startled her. She shook herself free and looked about to see whether anyone had been listening. Only the dogs had heard. They lifted their heads toward her from their sleeping in the dust, and then stretched out their chins and settled asleep again. Elisa turned and ran hurriedly into the house.

In the kitchen she reached behind the stove and felt the water tank. It was full of hot water from the noonday cooking. In the bathroom she tore off her soiled clothes and flung them into the corner. And then she scrubbed herself with a little block of pumice, legs and thighs, loins and chest and arms, until her skin was scratched and red. When she had dried herself she stood in front of a mirror in her bedroom and looked at her body. She tightened her stomach and threw out her chest. She turned and looked over her shoulder at her back.

After a while she began to dress, slowly. She put on her newest underclothing and her nicest stockings and the dress which was the symbol of her prettiness. She worked carefully on her hair, penciled her eyebrows and rouged her lips.

Before she was finished she heard the little thunder of hoofs and the shouts of Henry and his helper as they drove the red steers into the corral. She heard the gate bang shut and set herself for Henry's arrival.

His step sounded on the porch. He entered the house calling, "Elisa, where are you?"

"In my room, dressing. I'm not ready. There's hot water for your bath. Hurry up. It's getting late."

When she heard him splashing in the tub, Elisa laid his dark suit on the bed, and shirt and socks and tie beside it. She stood his polished shoes on the floor beside the bed. Then she went to the porch and sat primly and stiffly down. She looked toward the river road where the willow-line was still yellow with frosted leaves so that under the high grey fog they seemed a thin band of sunshine. This was the only color in the grey afternoon. She sat unmoving for a long time. Her eyes blinked rarely.

Henry came banging out of the door shoving his tie inside his vest as he came. Elisa stiffened and her face grew tight. Henry stopped short and looked at her. "Why—why, Elisa. You look so nice!"

"Nice? You think I look nice? What do you mean by 'nice'?"

Henry blundered on. "I don't know. I mean you look different, strong and happy."

"I am strong? Yes, strong. What do you mean 'strong'?"

He looked bewildered. "You're playing some kind of a game," he said helplessly. "It's a kind of a play. You look strong enough to break a calf over your knee, happy enough to eat it like a watermelon."

For a second she lost her rigidity. "Henry! Don't talk like that. You didn't know what you said." She grew complete again. "I'm strong," she boasted. "I never knew before how strong."

Henry looked down toward the tractor shed, and when he brought his eyes back to her, they were his own again. "I'll get out the car. You can put on your coat while I'm starting."

Elisa went into the house. She heard him drive to the gate and idle down his motor, and then she took a long time to put on her hat. She pulled it here and pressed it there. When Henry turned the motor off she slipped into her coat and went out.

The little roadster bounced along on the dirt road by the river, raising the birds and driving the rabbits into the brush. Two cranes flapped heavily over the willow-line and dropped into the river-bed.

Far ahead on the road Elisa saw a dark speck. She knew.

She tried not to look as they passed it, but her eyes would not obey. She whispered to herself sadly, "He might have thrown them off the road. That wouldn't have been much trouble, not very much. But he kept the pot," she explained. "He had to keep the pot. That's why he couldn't get them off the road."

The roadster turned a bend and she saw the caravan ahead. She swung full around toward her husband so she could not see the little covered wagon and the mismatched team as the car passed them.

In a moment it was over. The thing was done. She did not look back.

She said loudly, to be heard above the motor, "It will be good, tonight, a good dinner."

"Now you're changed again," Henry complained. He took one hand from the wheel and patted her knee. "I ought to take you in to dinner oftener. It would be good for both of us. We get so heavy out on the ranch."

"Henry," she asked, "could we have wine at dinner?"

"Sure we could. Say! That will be fine."

She was silent for a while; then she said, "Henry, at those prize fights, do the men hurt each other very much?"

"Sometimes a little, not often. Why?"

"Well, I've read how they break noses, and blood runs down their chests. I've read how the fighting gloves get heavy and soggy with blood."

He looked around at her. "What's the matter, Elisa? I didn't know you read things like that." He brought the car to a stop, then turned to the right over the Salinas River bridge.

"Do any women ever go to the fights?" she asked.

"Oh, sure, some. What's the matter, Elisa? Do you want to go? I don't think you'd like it, but I'll take you if you really want to go."

She relaxed limply in the seat. "Oh, no. No. I don't want to go. I'm sure I don't." Her face was turned away from him. "It will be enough if we can have wine. It will be plenty." She turned up her coat collar so he could not see that she was crying weakly—like an old woman.

—1940

Richar∂ Wright (1908–1960) *was the son of a Mississippi farm worker and mill hand who abandoned the family when the writer was five and a mother who was forced by poverty to place her son in orphanages during part of his childhood. As he relates in his autobiography,* Black Boy *(1945), he was largely self-educated through extensive reading; while working for the post office in Memphis he discovered the essays of H. L. Mencken, whom he credited as the major influence on his decision to become a writer. In Chicago in the 1930s he became associated with the Federal Writers' Project and, briefly, with the Communist party. He later lived in New York and, for the last fifteen years of his life, Paris, where he was associated with French existentialist writers like Jean-Paul Sartre. Wright's first novel,* Native Son *(1940), based on an actual 1938 murder case, describes the chain of circumstances that lead to a black chauffeur's being tried and executed for the accidental slaying of a wealthy white woman. The success of that book established Wright as the leading black novelist of his generation, and while none of his subsequent works attracted the same level of attention, he nevertheless helped define many of the themes that African-American writers continue to explore today. "The Man Who Was Almost a Man" was filmed as part of the* PBS American Short Story *series.*

Richar∂ Wright
The Man Who Was Almost a Man

Dave struck out across the fields, looking homeward through paling light. Whut's the use talkin wid em niggers in the field? Anyhow, his mother was putting supper on the table. Them niggers can't understan nothing. One of these days he was going to get a gun and practice shooting, then they couldn't talk to him as though he were a little boy. He slowed, looking at the ground. Shucks, Ah ain scareda them even if they are biggern me! Aw, Ah know what Ahma do. Ahm going by ol Joe's sto n git that Sears Roebuck catlog n look at them guns. Mebbe Ma will lemme buy one when she gits mah pay from ol man Hawkins. Ahma beg her t gimme some money. Ahm ol ernough to hava gun. Ahm seventeen. Almost a man. He strode, feeling his long loose-jointed limbs. Shucks, a man oughta hava little gun aftah he done worked hard all day.

He came in sight of Joe's store. A yellow lantern glowed on the front porch. He mounted steps and went through the screen door, hearing it bang behind him. There was a strong smell of coal oil and mackerel fish. He felt very confident until he saw fat Joe walk in through the rear door, then his courage began to ooze.

"Howdy, Dave! Whutcha want?"

"How yuh, Mistah Joe? Aw, Ah don wanna buy nothing. Ah jus wanted t see ef yuhd lemme look at tha catlog erwhile."

"Sure! You wanna see it here?"

"Nawsuh. Ah wants t take it home wid me. Ah'll bring it back termorrow when Ah come in from the fiels."

"You plannin on buying something?"

"Yessuh."

"Your ma lettin you have your own money now?"

"Shucks. Mistah Joe, Ahm gittin t be a man like anybody else!"

Joe laughed and wiped his greasy white face with a red bandanna.

"Whut you plannin on buyin?"

Dave looked at the floor, scratched his head, scratched his thigh, and smiled. Then he looked up shyly.

"Ah'll tell yuh, Mistah Joe, ef yuh promise yuh won't tell."

"I promise."

"Waal, Ahma buy a gun."

"A gun? What you want with a gun?"

"Ah wanna keep it."

"You ain't nothing but a boy. You don't need a gun."

"Aw, lemme have the catlog, Mistah Joe. Ah'll bring it back."

Joe walked through the rear door. Dave was elated. He looked around at barrels of sugar and flour. He heard Joe coming back. He craned his neck to see if he were bringing the book. Yeah, he's got it. Gawddog, he's got it!

"Here, but be sure you bring it back. It's the only one I got."

"Sho, Mistah Joe."

"Say, if you wanna buy a gun, why don't you buy one from me? I gotta gun to sell."

"Will it shoot?"

"Sure it'll shoot."

"Whut kind is it?"

"Oh, it's kinda old . . . . a left-hand Wheeler. A pistol. A big one."

"Is it got bullets in it?"

"It's loaded."

"Kin Ah see it?"

"Where's your money?"

"Whut yuh wan fer it?"

"I'll let you have it for two dollars."

"Just two dollahs? Shucks, Ah could buy that when Ah git mah pay."

"I'll have it here when you want it."

"Awright, suh. Ah be in fer it."

He went through the door, hearing it slam again behind him. Ahma git some money from Ma n buy me a gun! Only two dollahs! He tucked the thick catalogue under his arm and hurried.

"Where yuh been, boy?" His mother held a steaming dish of black-eyed peas.

"Aw, Ma, Ah jus stopped down the road t talk wid the boys."

"Yuh know bettah t keep suppah waitin."

He sat down, resting the catalogue on the edge of the table.

"Yuh git up from there and git to the well n wash yosef! Ah ain feedin no hogs in mah house!"

She grabbed his shoulder and pushed him. He stumbled out of the room, then came back to get the catalogue.

"Whut this?"

"Aw, Ma, it's jusa catlog."

"Who yuh git it from?"

"From Joe, down at the sto."

"Waal, thas good. We kin use it in the outhouse."

"Naw, Ma." He grabbed for it. "Gimme ma catlog, Ma."

She held onto it and glared at him.

"Quit hollerin at me! Whut's wrong wid yuh? Yuh crazy?"

"But Ma, please. It ain mine! It's Joe's! He tol me t bring it back t im termorrow."

She gave up the book. He stumbled down the back steps, hugging the thick book under his arm. When he had splashed water on his face and hands, he groped back to the kitchen and fumbled in a corner for the towel. He bumped into a chair; it clattered to the floor. The catalogue sprawled at his feet. When he had dried his eyes he snatched up the book and held it again under his arm. His mother stood watching him.

"Now, ef yuh gonna act a fool over that ol book, Ah'll take it n burn it up."

"Naw, Ma, please."

"Waal, set down n be still!"

He sat down and drew the oil lamp close. He thumbed page after page, unaware of the food his mother set on the table. His father came in. Then his small brother.

"Whutcha got there, Dave?" his father asked.

"Jusa catlog," he answered, not looking up.

"Yeah, here they is!" His eyes glowed at blue-and-black revolvers. He glanced up, feeling sudden guilt. His father was watching him. He eased the book under the table and rested it on his knees. After the blessing was asked, he ate. He scooped up peas and swallowed fat meat without chewing. Buttermilk helped to wash it down. He did not want to mention money before his father. He would do much better by cornering his mother when she was alone. He looked at his father uneasily out of the edge of his eye.

"Boy, how come yuh don quit foolin wid tha book n eat yo suppah?"

"Yessuh."

"How you n ol man Hawkins gitten erlong?"

"Suh?"

"Can't yuh hear? Why don yuh lissen? Ah ast yu how wuz yuh n ol man Hawkins gittin erlong?"

"Oh, swell, Pa. Ah plows mo lan than anybody over there."

"Waal, yuh oughta keep you mind on what yuh doin."

"Yessuh."

He poured his plate full of molasses and sopped it up slowly with a chunk of cornbread. When his father and brother had left the kitchen, he still sat and looked again at the guns in the catalogue, longing to muster courage enough to present his case to his mother. Lawd, ef Ah only had tha pretty one! He could almost feel the slickness of the weapon with his fingers. If he had a gun like that he would polish it and keep it shining so it would never rust! N Ah'd keep it loaded, by Gawd!

"Ma?" His voice was hesitant.

"Hunh?"

"Ol man Hawkins give yuh mah money yit?"

"Yeah, but ain no usa yuh thinking bout throwin nona it erway. Ahm keeping tha money sos yuh kin have cloes t go to school this winter."

He rose and went to her side with the open catalogue in his palms. She was washing dishes, her head bent low over a pan. Shyly he raised the book. When he spoke, his voice was husky, faint.

"Ma, Gawd knows Ah wans one of these."

"One of whut?" she asked, not raising her eyes.

"One of these," he said again, not daring even to point. She glanced up at the page, then at him with wide eyes. "Nigger, is yuh gone plumb crazy?"

"Aw, Ma—"

"Git outta here! Don yuh talk t me bout no gun! Yuh a fool!"

"Ma, Ah kin buy one fer two dollahs."

"Not ef Ah knows it, yuh ain!"

"But yuh promised me one—"

"Ah don care what Ah promised! Yuh ain nothing but a boy yit!"

"Ma, ef yuh lemme buy one Ah'll *never* ast yuh fer nothing no mo."

"Ah tol yuh t git outta here! Yuh ain gonna toucha penny of tha money fer no gun! Thas how come Ah has Mistah Hawkins t pay yo wages t me, cause Ah knows yuh ain got no sense."

"But, Ma, we needa gun. Pa ain got no gun. We needa gun in the house. Yuh kin never tell whut might happen."

"Now don yuh try to maka fool outta me, boy! Ef we did hava gun, yuh wouldn't have it!"

He laid the catalogue down and slipped his arm around her waist.

"Aw, Ma, Ah done worked hard alla summer n ain ast yuh fer nothing, is Ah, now?"

"Thas what yuh spose t do!"

"But Ma, Ah wans a gun. Yuh kin lemme have two dollahs outta mah money. Please, Ma. I kin give it to Pa . . . Please, Ma! Ah loves yuh, Ma!"

When she spoke her voice came soft and low.

"What yu wan wida gun, Dave? Yuh don need no gun. Yuh'll git in trouble. N ef yo pa jus thought Ah let yuh have money t buy a gun he'd hava fit."

"Ah'll hide it, Ma. It ain but two dollahs."

"Lawd, chil, whut's wrong wid yuh?"

"Ain nothin wrong, Ma. Ahm almos a man now. Ah wans a gun."

"Who gonna sell yuh a gun?"

"Ol Joe at the sto."

"N it don cos but two dollahs?"

"Thas all, Ma. Jus two dollahs. Please, Ma."

She was stacking the plates away; her hands moved slowly, reflectively. Dave kept an anxious silence. Finally, she turned to him.

"Ah'll let yuh git tha gun if yuh promise me one thing."

"What's tha, Ma?"

"Yuh bring it straight back t me, yuh hear? It be fer Pa."

"Yessum! Lemme go now, Ma."

She stooped, turned slightly to one side, raised the hem of her dress, rolled down the top of her stocking, and came up with a slender wad of bills.

"Here," she said. "Lawd knows yuh don need no gun. But yer pa does. Yuh bring it right back t me, yuh hear? Ahma put it up. Now ef yuh don, Ahma have yuh pa lick yuh so hard yuh won fergit it."

"Yessum."

He took the money, ran down the steps, and across the yard.

"Dave! Yuuuuuh Daaaaave!"

He heard, but he was not going to stop now. "Naw, Lawd!"

The first movement he made the following morning was to reach under the pillow for the gun. In the gray light of dawn he held it loosely, feeling a sense of power. Could kill a man with a gun like this. Kill anybody, black or white. And if he were holding his gun in his hand, nobody could run over him; they would have to respect him. It was a big gun, with a long barrel and a heavy handle. He raised and lowered it in his hand, marveling at its weight.

He had not come straight home with it as his mother had asked; instead he had stayed out in the fields, holding the weapon in his hand, aiming it now and then at some imaginary foe. But he had not fired it; he had been afraid that his father might hear. Also he was not sure he knew how to fire it.

To avoid surrendering the pistol he had not come into the house until he knew that they were all asleep. When his mother had tiptoed to his bedside late that night and demanded the gun, he had first played possum; then he had told her that the gun was hidden outdoors, that he would bring it to her in the morning. Now he lay turning it slowly in his hands. He broke it, took out the cartridges, felt them, and then put them back.

He slid out of bed, got a long strip of old flannel from a trunk, wrapped the gun in it, and tied it to his naked thigh while it was still loaded. He did not go in to breakfast. Even though it was not yet daylight he started for Jim Hawkins' plantation. Just as the sun was rising he reached the barns where the mules and plows were kept.

"Hey! That you, Dave?"

He turned. Jim Hawkins stood eyeing him suspiciously.

"What're yuh doing here so early?"

"Ah didn't know Ah wuz gittin up so early, Mistah Hawkins. Ah was fixin t hitch up ol Jenny n take her t the fiels."

"Good. Since you're so early, how about plowing that stretch down by the woods?"

"Suits me, Mistah Hawkins."

"O.K. Go to it!"

He hitched Jenny to a plow and started across the fields. Hot dog! This was just what he wanted. If he could get down by the woods, he could shoot his gun and nobody would hear. He walked behind the plow, hearing the traces creaking, feeling the gun tied tight to his thigh.

When he reached the woods, he plowed two whole rows before he decided to take out the gun. Finally, he stopped, looked in all directions, then untied the gun and held it in his hand. He turned to the mule and smiled.

"Know whut this is, Jenny? Naw, yuh wouldn know! Yuhs jusa ol mule! Anyhow, this is a gun, n it kin shoot, by Gawd!"

He held the gun at arm's length. Whut t hell, Ahma shoot this thing! He looked at Jenny again.

"Lissen here, Jenny! When Ah pull this ol trigger, Ah don wan yuh t run n acka fool now!"

Jenny stood with head down, her short ears pricked straight. Dave walked off about twenty feet, held the gun far out from him at arm's length, and turned his head. Hell, he told himself, Ah ain afraid. The gun felt loose in his fingers; he waved it wildly for a moment. Then he shut his eyes and tightened his forefinger. Bloom! A report half deafened him and he thought his right hand was torn from his arm. He heard Jenny whinnying and galloping over the field, and he found himself on his knees, squeezing his fingers hard between his legs. His hand was numb; he jammed it into his mouth, trying to warm it, trying to stop the pain. The gun lay at his feet. He did not quite know what had happened. He stood up and stared at the gun as though it were a living thing. He gritted his teeth and kicked the gun. Yuh almos broke mah arm! He turned to look for Jenny; she was far over the fields, tossing her head and kicking wildly.

"Hol on there, ol mule!"

When he caught up with her she stood trembling, walling her big white eyes at him. The plow was far away; the traces had broken. Then Dave stopped short, looking, not believing. Jenny was bleeding. Her left side was red and wet with blood. He went closer. Lawd, have mercy! Wondah did Ah shoot this mule? He grabbed for Jenny's mane. She flinched, snorted, whirled, tossing her head.

"Hol on now! Hol on."

Then he saw the hole in Jenny's side, right between the ribs. It was round, wet, red. A crimson stream streaked down the front leg, flowing fast. Good Gawd! Ah wuzn't shootin at tha mule. He felt panic. He knew he had to stop that blood, or Jenny would bleed to death. He had never seen so much blood in all his life. He chased the mule for half a mile, trying to catch her. Finally she stopped, breathing hard, stumpy tail half arched. He caught her mane and led her back to where the plow and gun lay. Then he stopped and grabbed handfuls of damp black earth and tried to plug the bullet hole. Jenny shuddered, whinnied, and broke from him.

"Hol on! Hol on now!"

He tried to plug it again, but blood came anyhow. His fingers were hot and sticky. He rubbed dirt into his palms, trying to dry them. Then again he attempted to plug the bullet hole, but Jenny shied away, kicking her heels high. He stood helpless. He had to do something. He ran at Jenny; she dodged him. He watched a red stream of blood flow down Jenny's leg and form a bright pool at her feet.

"Jenny . . . Jenny," he called weakly.

His lips trembled. She's bleeding t death! He looked in the direction of home, wanting to go back, wanting to get help. But he saw the pistol lying in the damp black clay. He had a queer feeling that if he only did something, this would not be; Jenny would not be there bleeding to death.

When he went to her this time, she did not move. She stood with sleepy, dreamy eyes; and when he touched her she gave a low-pitched whinny and knelt to the ground, her front knees slopping in blood.

"Jenny . . . Jenny . . ." he whispered.

For a long time she held her neck erect; then her head sank, slowly. Her ribs swelled with a mighty heave and she went over.

Dave's stomach felt empty, very empty. He picked up the gun and held it gingerly between his thumb and forefinger. He buried it at the foot of a tree. He took a stick and tried to cover the pool of blood with dirt—but what was the use? There was Jenny lying with her mouth open and her eyes walled and glassy. He could not tell Jim Hawkins he had shot his mule. But he had to tell something. Yeah, Ah'll tell em Jenny started gittin wil n fell on the joint of the plow . . . But that would hardly happen to a mule. He walked across the field slowly, head down.

It was sunset. Two of Jim Hawkins' men were over near the edge of the woods digging a hole in which to bury Jenny. Dave was surrounded by a knot of people, all of whom were looking down at the dead mule.

"I don't see how in the world it happened," said Jim Hawkins for the tenth time.

The crowd parted and Dave's mother, father, and small brother pushed into the center.

"Where Dave?" his mother called.

"There he is," said Jim Hawkins.

His mother grabbed him.

"Whut happened, Dave? Whut yuh done?"

"Nothin."

"C mon, boy, talk," his father said.

Dave took a deep breath and told the story he knew nobody believed.

"Waal," he drawled. "Ah brung ol Jenny down here sos Ah could do mah plowin. Ah plowed bout two rows, just like yuh see." He stopped and pointed at the long rows of upturned earth. "Then somethin musta been wrong wid ol Jenny. She wouldn ack right a-tall. She started snortin n kickin her heels. Ah tried t hol her, but she pulled erway, rearin n goin in. Then when the point of the plow was stickin up in the air, she swung erroun n twisted herself back on it . . . She stuck herself n started t bleed. N fo Ah could do anything, she wuz dead."

"Did you ever hear anything like that in all your life?" asked Jim Hawkins.

There were white and black standing in the crowd. They murmured. Dave's mother came close to him and looked hard into his face. "Tell the truth, Dave," she said.

"Looks like a bullet hole to me," said one man.

"Dave, whut yuh do wid the gun?" his mother asked.

The crowd surged in, looking at him. He jammed his hands into his pockets, shook his head slowly from left to right, and backed away. His eyes were wide and painful.

"Did he hava gun?" asked Jim Hawkins.

"By Gawd, Ah tol yuh tha wuz a gun wound," said a man, slapping his thigh.

His father caught his shoulders and shook him till his teeth rattled. "Tell whut happened, yuh rascal! Tell whut . . ."

Dave looked at Jenny's stiff legs and began to cry.

"Whut yuh do wid tha gun?" his mother asked.

"What wuz he doin wida gun?" his father asked.

"Come on and tell the truth," said Hawkins. "Ain't nobody going to hurt . . ."

His mother crowded close to him.

"Did yuh shoot tha mule, Dave?"

Dave cried, seeing blurred white and black faces.

"Ahh ddinn gggo tt sshooot hher . . . Ah ssswear ffo Gawd Ahh ddin . . . Ah wuz a-tryin t sssee ef the old gggun would sshoot—"

"Where yuh git the gun from?" his father asked.

"Ah got it from Joe, at the sto."

"Where yuh git the money?"

"Ma give it t me."

"He kept worryin me, Bob. Ah had t. Ah tol im t bring the gun right back t me . . . It was fer yuh, the gun."

"But how yuh happen to shoot that mule?" asked Jim Hawkins.

"Ah wuzn shootin at the mule, Mistah Hawkins. The gun jumped when Ah pulled the trigger . . . N fo Ah knowed anythin Jenny was there a-bleedin."

Somebody in the crowd laughed. Jim Hawkins walked close to Dave and looked into his face.

"Well, looks like you have bought you a mule, Dave."

"Ah swear fo Gawd, Ah didn go t kill the mule, Mistah Hawkins!"

"But you killed her!"

All the crowd was laughing now. They stood on tiptoe and poked heads over one another's shoulders.

"Well, boy, looks like yuh done bought a dead mule! Hahaha!"

"Ain tha ershame."

"Hohohohoho."

Dave stood, head down, twisting his feet in the dirt.

"Well, you needn't worry about it, Bob," said Jim Hawkins to Dave's father. "Just let the boy keep on working and pay me two dollars a month."

"Whut yuh wan fer yo mule, Mistah Hawkins?"

Jim Hawkins screwed up his eyes.

"Fifty dollars."

"Whut yuh do wid tha gun?" Dave's father demanded.

Dave said nothing.

"Yuh wan me t take a tree n beat yuh till yuh talk!"

"Nawsuh!"

"Whut yuh do wid it?"

"Ah throwed it erway."

"Where?"

"Ah . . . Ah throwed it in the creek."

"Waal, c mon home. N firs thing in the mawnin git to tha creek n fin tha gun."

"Yessuh."

"Whut yuh pay fer it?"

"Two dollahs."

"Take tha gun n git yo money back n carry it to Mistah Hawkins, yuh hear? N don fergit Ahma lam you black bottom good fer this! Now march yosef on home, suh!"

Dave turned and walked slowly. He heard people laughing. Dave glared, his eyes welling with tears. Hot anger bubbled in him. Then he swallowed and stumbled on.

That night Dave did not sleep. He was glad that he had gotten out of killing the mule so easily, but he was hurt. Something hot seemed to turn over inside him each time he remembered how they had laughed. He tossed on his bed, feeling his hard pillow. *N Pa says he's gonna beat me . . .* He remembered other beatings, and his back quivered. *Naw, naw, Ah sho don wan im t beat me tha way no mo. Dam em all! Nobody ever gave him anything. All he did was work. They treat me like a mule, n then they beat me.* He gritted his teeth. *N Ma had t tell on me.*

Well, if he had to, he would take old man Hawkins that two dollars. But that meant selling the gun. And he wanted to keep that gun. Fifty dollars for a dead mule.

He turned over, thinking how he had fired the gun. He had an itch to fire it again. *Ef other men kin shoota gun, by Gawd, Ah kin!* He was still, listening. *Mebbe they all sleepin now.* The house was still. He heard the soft breathing of his brother. *Yes, now!* He would go down and get that gun and see if he could fire it! He eased out of bed and slipped into overalls.

The moon was bright. He ran almost all the way to the edge of the woods. He stumbled over the ground, looking for the spot where he had buried the gun. Yeah, here it is. Like a hungry dog scratching for a bone, he pawed it up. He puffed his black cheeks and blew dirt from the trigger and barrel. He broke it and found four cartridges unshot. He looked around; the fields were filled with silence and moonlight. He clutched the gun stiff and hard in his fingers. But, as soon as he wanted to pull the trigger, he shut his eyes and turned his head. Naw, Ah can't shoot wid mah eyes closed n mah head turned. With effort he held his eyes open; then he squeezed. *Blooooom!* He was stiff, not breathing. The gun was still in his hands. Dammit, he'd done it! He fired again. *Bloooom!* He smiled. *Bloooom! Bloooom! Click, click.* There! It was empty. If anybody could shoot a gun, he could. He put the gun into his hip pocket and started across the fields.

When he reached the top of a ridge he stood straight and proud in the moonlight, looking at Jim Hawkins' big white house, feeling the gun sagging in his pocket. Lawd, ef Ah had just one mo bullet Ah'd taka shot at tha house. Ah'd like t scare ol man Hawkins jusa little . . . . Jusa enough t let im know Dave Saunders is a man.

To his left the road curved, running to the tracks of the Illinois Central. He jerked his head, listening. From far off come a faint *hoooof-hoooof; hoooof-hoooof* . . . He stood rigid. Two dollahs a mont. Les see now . . . Tha means it'll take bout two years. Shucks! Ah'll be dam!

He started down the road, toward the tracks. Yeah, here she comes! He stood beside the track and held himself stiffly. Here she comes, er-roun the ben . . . C mon, yuh slow poke! C mon! He had his hand on his gun; something quivered in his stomach. Then the train thundered past, the gray and brown box cars rumbling and clinking. He gripped the gun tightly; then he jerked his hand out of his pocket. Ah betcha Bill wouldn't do it! Ah betcha . . . The cars slid past, steel grinding upon steel. Ahm ridin yuh ternight, so hep me Gawd! He was hot all over. He hesitated just a moment; then he grabbed, pulled atop of a car, and lay flat. He felt his pocket; the gun was still there. Ahead the long rails were glinting in the moonlight, stretching away, away to somewhere, some-where where he could be a man. . . .

—*1937*

Eudora Welty (b. 1909) bears a name that invariably surfaces when lists of both outstanding southern and major women writers are made. Born in Jackson, Mississippi, she was educated at Mississippi State College for Women and the University of Wisconsin. Except for a brief period in New York City, where she studied advertising, Welty has spent most of her life in her native state, which provides material for her most characteristic work, especially novels like Delta Wedding *(1946) and* The Ponder Heart *(1956). Like William Faulkner and Flannery O'Connor, Welty is a scrupulous craftsperson. She has managed to exploit fully both the comic and tragic possibilities of a region and at the same time achieve a national reputation that led to her appointment as writer-in-residence at Smith College in Massachusetts. Equally adept as a novelist and writer of short stories, Welty was awarded a Pulitzer Prize in 1973 for* The Optimist's Daughter. *"Livvie" is taken from her 1953 collection* The Wide Net, *which contains stories set in the rural areas along the Natchez Trace. Like her first novel,* The Robber Bridegroom *(1942), "Livvie" combines elements of both American and European folklore with the realistic setting of a farm in the backwoods where a "May-December" marriage comes to an end.* The Collected Stories of Eudora Welty *appeared in 1980.*

Eudora Welty
Livvie

Solomon carried Livvie twenty-one miles away from her home when he married her. He carried her away up on the Old Natchez Trace[1] into the deep country to live in his house. She was sixteen—an only girl, then. Once people said he thought nobody would ever come along there. He told her that it had been a long time, and a day she did not know about, since that road was a traveled road with *people* coming and going. He was good to her, but he kept her in the house. She had not thought that she could not get back. Where she came from, people said an old man did not want anybody in the world to ever find his wife, for fear they would steal her back from him. Solomon asked her before he took her, "Would she be happy?"—very dignified, for he was a colored man that owned his land and had it written down in the courthouse; and she said, "Yes, sir," since he was an old man and she was young and just listened and answered. He asked her, if she was choosing winter, would she pine for spring, and she said, "No indeed." Whatever

---

[1]*Old Natchez Trace:* ancient Indian travel route through western Tennessee and Mississippi.

she said, always, was because he was an old man . . . while nine years went by. All the time, he got old, and he got so old he gave out. At last he slept the whole day in bed, and she was young still.

It was a nice house, inside and outside both. In the first place, it had three rooms. The front room was papered in holly paper, with green palmettos from the swamp spaced at careful intervals over the walls. There was fresh newspaper cut with fancy borders on the mantleshelf, on which were propped photographs of old or very young men printed in faint yellow—Solomon's people. Solomon had a houseful of furniture. There was a double settee, a tall scrolled rocker and an organ in the front room, all around a three-legged table with a pink marble top, on which was set a lamp with three gold feet, beside a jelly glass with pretty hen feathers in it. Behind the front room, the other room had the bright iron bed with the polished knobs like a throne, in which Solomon slept all day. There were snow-white curtains of wiry lace at the window, and a lace bedspread belonged on the bed. But what old Solomon slept sound under was a big feather-stitched piece-quilt in the pattern "Trip Around the World," which had twenty-one different colors, four hundred and forty pieces, and a thousand yards of thread, and that was what Solomon's mother made in her life and old age. There was a table holding the Bible, and a trunk with a key. On the wall were two calendars, and a diploma from somewhere in Solomon's family, and under that Livvie's one possession was nailed, a picture of the little white baby of the family she worked for, back in Natchez before she was married. Going through that room and on to the kitchen, there was a big wood stove and a big round table always with a wet top and with the knives and forks in one jelly glass and the spoons in another, and a cut-glass vinegar bottle between, and going out from those, many shallow dishes of pickled peaches, fig preserves, watermelon pickles and blackberry jam always sitting there. The churn sat in the sun, the doors of the safe were always both shut, and there were four baited mouse-traps in the kitchen, one in every corner.

The outside of Solomon's house looked nice. It was not painted, but across the porch was an even balance. On each side there was one easy chair with high springs, looking out, and a fern basket hanging over it from the ceiling, and a dishpan of zinnia seedlings growing at its foot on the floor. By the door was a plow-wheel, just a pretty iron circle, nailed up on one wall and a square mirror on the other, a turquoise-blue comb stuck up in the frame, with the wash stand beneath it. On the door was a wooden knob with a pearl in the end, and Solomon's black hat hung on that, if he was in the house.

Out front was a clean dirt yard with every vestige of grass patiently uprooted and the ground scarred in deep whorls from the strike of Livvie's broom. Rose bushes with tiny blood-red roses blooming every month grew in threes on either side of the steps. On one side was a peach tree, on the other a pomegranate. Then coming around up the path from the deep cut of the Natchez Trace below was a line of bare crape-myrtle trees with every branch of them ending in a colored bottle, green or blue. There was no word that fell from Solomon's lips to say what they were for, but Livvie knew that there could be a spell put in trees, and she was familiar from the time she was born with the way bottle trees kept evil spirits from coming into the house—by luring them inside the colored bottles, where they cannot get out again. Solomon had made the bottle trees with his own hands over the nine years, in labor amounting to about a tree a year, and without a sign that he had any uneasiness in his heart, for he took as much pride in his precautions against spirits coming in the house as he took in the house, and sometimes in the sun the bottle trees looked prettier than the house did.

It was a nice house. It was in a place where the days would go by and surprise anyone that they were over. The lamplight and the firelight would shine out the door after dark, over the still and breathing country, lighting the roses and the bottle trees, and all was quiet there.

But there was nobody, nobody at all, not even a white person. And if there had been anybody, Solomon would not have let Livvie look at them, just as he would not let her look at a field hand, or a field hand look at her. There was no house near, except for the cabins of the tenants that were forbidden to her, and there was no house as far as she had been, stealing away down the still, deep Trace. She felt as if she waded a river when she went, for the dead leaves on the ground reached as high as her knees, and when she was all scratched and bleeding she said it was not like a road that went anywhere. One day, climbing up the high bank, she had found a graveyard without a church; with ribbon-grass growing about the foot of an angel (she had climbed up because she thought she saw angel wings), and in the sun, trees shining like burning flames through the great caterpillar nets which enclosed them. Scarey thistles stood looking like the prophets in the Bible in

Solomon's house. Indian paint brushes grew over her head, and the mourning dove made the only sound in the world. Oh for a stirring of the leaves, and a breaking of the nets! But not by a ghost, prayed Livvie, jumping down the bank. After Solomon took to his bed, she never went out, except one more time.

Livvie knew she made a nice girl to wait on anybody. She fixed things to eat on a tray like a surprise. She could keep from singing when she ironed, and to sit by a bed and fan away the flies, she could be so still she could not hear herself breathe. She could clean up the house and never drop a thing, and wash the dishes without a sound, and she would step outside to churn, for churning sounded too sad to her, like sobbing, and if it made her home-sick and not Solomon, she did not think of that.

But Solomon scarcely opened his eyes to see her, and scarcely tasted his food. He was not sick or paralyzed or in any pain that he mentioned, but he was surely wearing out in the body, and no matter what nice hot thing Livvie would bring him to taste, he would only look at it now, as if he was past seeing how he could add anything more to himself. Before she could beg him, he would go fast asleep. She could not surprise him any more, if he would not taste, and she was afraid that he was never in the world going to taste another thing she brought him—and so how could he last?

But one morning it was breakfast time and she cooked his eggs and grits, carried them in on a tray, and called his name. He was sound asleep. He lay in a dignified way with his watch beside him, on his back in the middle of the bed. One hand drew the quilt up high, though it was the first day of spring. Through the white lace curtains a little puffy wind was blowing as if it came from round cheeks. All night the frogs had sung out in the swamp, like a commotion in the room, and he had not stirred, though she lay wide awake and saying, "Shh, frogs!" for fear he would mind them.

He looked as if he would like to sleep a little longer, and so she put back the tray and waited a little. When she tiptoed and stayed so quiet, she surrounded her self with a little reverie, and sometimes it seemed to her when she was so stealthy that the quiet she kept was for a sleeping baby, and that she had a baby and was its mother. When she stood at Solomon's bed and looked down at him, she would be thinking, "He sleeps so well," and she would hate to wake him up. And in some other way, too, she was afraid to wake him up because even in his sleep he seemed to be such a strict man.

Of course, nailed to the wall over the bed—only she would forget who it was—there was a picture of him when he was young. Then he had a fan of hair over his forehead like a king's crown. Now his hair lay down on his head, the spring had gone out of it. Solomon had a lightish face, with eyebrows scattered but rugged, the way privet grows, strong eyes, with second sight, a strict mouth, and a little gold smile. This was the way he looked in his clothes, but in bed in the daytime he looked like a different and smaller man, even when he was wide awake, and holding the Bible. He looked like somebody kin to himself. And then sometimes when he lay in sleep and she stood fanning the flies away, and the light came in, his face was like new, so smooth and clear that it was like a glass of jelly held to the window, and she could almost look through his forehead and see what he thought.

She fanned him and at length he opened his eyes and spoke her name, but he would not taste the nice eggs she had kept warm under a pan.

Back in the kitchen she ate heartily, his breakfast and hers, and looked out the open door at what went on. The whole day, and the whole night before, she had felt the stir of spring close to her. It was as present in the house as a young man would be. The moon was in the last quarter and outside they were turning the sod and planting peas and beans. Up and down the red fields, over which smoke from the brush-burning hung showing like a little skirt of sky, a white horse and a white mule pulled the plow. At intervals hoarse shouts came through the air and roused her as if she dozed neglectfully in the shade, and they were telling her, "Jump up!" She could see how over each ribbon of field were moving men and girls, on foot and mounted on mules, with hats set on their heads and bright with tall hoes and forks as if they carried streamers on them and were going to some place on a journey—and how as if at a signal now and then they would all start at once shouting, hollering, cajoling, calling and answering back, running, being leaped on and breaking away, flinging to earth with a shout and lying motionless in the trance of twelve o'clock. The old women came out of the cabins and brought them food they had ready for them, and then all worked together, spread evenly out. The little children came too, like a bouncing stream overflowing the fields, and set upon the men, the women, the dogs, the rushing birds, and the wave-like rows of earth, their little voices almost too high to be heard. In the middle distance like some white-and-gold towers were the haystacks, with black cows coming around to eat their edges. High above everything, the wheel of fields, house, and cabins, and the deep road surrounding like a moat to keep them in, was the turning sky, blue with long, far-flung white mare's tail clouds, serene and still as high flames. And sound asleep while all this went around him that was his, Solomon was like a little still spot in the middle.

Even in the house the earth was sweet to breathe. Solomon had never let Livvie go any farther than the chicken house and the well. But what if she would walk now into the heart of the fields and take a hoe and work until she fell stretched out and drenched with her efforts, like other girls, and laid her cheek against the laid-open earth, and shamed the old man with her humbleness and delight? To shame him! A cruel wish would come in uninvited and so fast while she looked out the back door. She washed the dishes and scrubbed the table. She could hear the cries of the little lambs. Her mother, that she had not seen since her wedding day, had said one time, "I rather a man be anything, than a woman be mean."

So all morning she kept tasting the chicken broth on the stove, and when it was right she poured off a nice cupful. She carried it in to Solomon, and there he lay having a dream. Now what did he dream about? For she saw him sigh gently as if not to disturb some whole thing he held round in his mind, like a fresh egg. So even an old man dreamed about something pretty. Did he dream of her, while his eyes were shut and sunken, and his small hand with the wedding ring curled close in sleep around the quilt? He might be dreaming of what time it was, for even through his sleep he kept track of it like a clock, and knew how much of it went by, and waked up knowing where the hands were even before he consulted the silver watch that he never let go. He would sleep with the watch in his palm, and even holding it to his cheek like a child that loves a plaything. Or he might dream of journeys and travels on a steamboat to Natchez. Yet she thought he dreamed of her; but even while she scrutinized him, the rods of the foot of the bed seemed to rise up like a rail fence between them, and she could see that people never could be sure of anything as long as one of them was asleep and the other awake. To look at him dreaming of her when he might be going to die frightened her a little, as if he might carry her with him that way, and she wanted to run out of the room. She took hold of the bed and held on, and Solomon opened his eyes and called her name, but he did not want anything. He would not taste the good broth.

Just a little after that, as she was taking up the ashes in the front room for the last time in the year, she heard a sound. It was somebody coming. She pulled the curtains together and looked through the slit.

Coming up the path under the bottle trees was a white lady. At first she looked young, but then she looked old. Marvelous to see, a little car stood steaming like a kettle out in the field-track—it had come without a road.

Livvie stood listening to the long, repeated knockings at the door, and after a while she opened it just a little. The lady came in through the crack, though she was more than middle-sized and wore a big hat.

"My name is Miss Baby Marie," she said.

Livvie gazed respectfully at the lady and at the little suitcase she was holding close to her by the handle until the proper moment. The lady's eyes were running over the room, from palmetto to palmetto, but she was saying, "I live at home . . . out from Natchez . . . and get out and show these pretty cosmetic things to the white people and the colored people both . . . all around . . . years and years . . . Both shades of powder and rouge . . . It's the kind of work a girl can do and not go clear 'way from home. . . ." And the harder she looked, the more she talked. Suddenly she turned up her nose and said, "It's not Christian or sanitary to put feathers in a vase," and then she took a gold key out of the front of her dress and began unlocking the locks on her suitcase. Her face drew the light, the way it was covered with intense white and red, with a little patty-cake of white between the wrinkles by her upper lip. Little red tassels of hair bobbed under the rusty wires of her picture-hat, as with an air of triumph and secrecy she now drew open her little suitcase and brought out bottle after bottle and jar after jar, which she put down on the table, the mantlepiece, the settee, and the organ.

"Did you ever see so many cosmetics in your life?" cried Miss Baby Marie.

"No'm," Livvie tried to say, but the cat had her tongue.

"Have you ever applied cosmetics?" asked Miss Baby Marie next.

"No'm," Livvie tried to say.

"Then look!" she said, and pulling out the last thing of all, "Try this!" she said. And in her hand was unclenched a golden lipstick which popped open like magic. A fragrance came out of it like incense, and Livvie cried out suddenly, "Chinaberry flowers!"

Her hand took the lipstick, and in an instant she was carried away in the air through the spring, and looking down with a half-drowsy smile from a purple cloud she saw from above a chinaberry tree, dark and smooth and neatly leaved, neat as a guinea hen in the dooryard, and there was her home that she had left. On one side of the tree was her mama holding up her heavy apron, and she could see it was loaded with ripe figs, and on the other side was her papa holding a fish-pole over the pond, and she could see it transparently, the little clear fishes swimming up to the brim.

"Oh, no, not chinaberry flowers—secret ingredients," said Miss Baby Marie. "My cosmetics have secret ingredients—not chinaberry flowers."

"It's purple," Livvie breathed, and Miss Baby Marie said, "Use it freely. Rub it on."

Livvie tiptoed out to the wash stand on the front porch and before the mirror put the paint on her mouth. In the wavery surface her face danced before her like a flame. Miss Baby Marie followed her out, took a look at what she had done, and said, "That's it."

Livvie tried to say "Thank you" without moving her parted lips where the paint lay so new.

By now Miss Baby Marie stood behind Livvie and looked in the mirror over her shoulder, twisting up the tassels of her hair. "The lipstick I can let you have for only two dollars," she said, close to her neck.

"Lady, but I don't have no money, never did have," said Livvie.

"Oh, but you don't pay the first time. I make another trip, that's the way I do. I come back again—later."

"Oh," said Livvie, pretending she understood everything so as to please the lady.

"But if you don't take it now, this may be the last time I'll call at your house," said Miss Baby Marie sharply. "It's far away from anywhere, I'll tell you that. You don't live close to anywhere."

"Yes'm. My husband, he keep the *money*," said Livvie, trembling. "He is strict as he can be. He don't know *you* walk in here—Miss Baby Marie!"

"Where is he?"

"Right now, he in yonder sound asleep, an old man. I wouldn't ever ask him for anything."

Miss Baby Marie took back the lipstick and packed it up. She gathered up the jars for both black and white and got them all inside the suitcase, with the same little fuss of triumph with which she had brought them out. She started away.

"Goodbye," she said, making herself look grand from the back, but at the last minute she turned around in the door. Her old hat wobbled as she whispered, "Let me see your husband."

Livvie obediently went on tiptoe and opened the door to the other room. Miss Baby Marie came behind her and rose on her toes and looked in.

"My, what a little tiny old, old man!" she whispered, clasping her hands and shaking her head over them. "What a beautiful quilt! What a tiny old, old man!"

"He can sleep like that all day," whispered Livvie proudly.

They looked at him awhile so fast asleep, and then all at once they looked at each other. Somehow that was as if they had a secret, for he had never stirred. Livvie then politely, but all at once, closed the door.

"Well! I'd certainly like to leave you with a lipstick!" said Miss Baby Marie vivaciously. She smiled in the door.

"Lady, but I told you I don't have no money, and never did have."

"And never will?" In the air and all around, like a bright halo around the white lady's nodding head, it was a true spring day.

"Would you take eggs, lady?" asked Livvie softly.

"No, I have plenty of eggs—plenty," said Miss Baby Marie.

"I still don't have no money," said Livvie, and Miss Baby Marie took her suitcase and went on somewhere else.

Livvie stood watching her go, and all the time she felt her heart beating in her left side. She touched the place with her hand. It seemed as if her heart beat and her whole face flamed from the pulsing color of her lips. She went to sit by Solomon and when he opened his eyes he could not see a change in her. "He's fixin' to die," she said inside. That was the secret. That was when she went out of the house for a little breath of air.

She went down the path and down the Natchez Trace a way, and she did not know how far she had gone, but it was not far, when she saw a sight. It was a man, looking like a vision—she standing on one side of the Old Natchez Trace and he standing on the other.

As soon as this man caught sight of her, he began to look himself over. Starting at the bottom with his pointed shoes, he began to look up, lifting his peg-top pants the higher to see fully his bright socks. His coat long and wide and leaf-green he opened like doors to see his high-up tawny pants and his pants he smoothed downward from the points of his collar, and he wore a luminous baby-pink satin shirt. At the end, he reached gently above his wide platter-shaped round hat, the color of a plum, and one finger touched at the feather, emerald green, blowing in the spring winds.

No matter how she looked, she could never look so fine as he did, and she was not sorry for that, she was pleased.

He took three jumps, one down and two up, and was by her side.

"My name is Cash," he said.

He had a guinea pig in his pocket. They began to walk along. She stared on and on at him, as if he were doing some daring spectacular thing, instead of just walking beside her. It was not simply the city way he was dressed that made her look at him and see hope in its insolence looking back. It was not only the way he moved along kicking the flowers as if he could break through everything in the way and destroy anything in the world, that made her eyes grow bright. It might be, if he had not appeared the way he did appear that day she would never have looked so closely at him, but the time people come makes a difference.

They walked through the still leaves of the Natchez Trace, the light and the shade falling through trees about them, the white irises shining like candles on the banks and the new ferns shining like green stars up in the oak branches. They came out at Solomon's house, bottle trees and all. Livvie stopped and hung her head.

Cash began whistling a little tune. She did not know what it was, but she had heard it before from a distance, and she had a revelation. Cash was a field hand. He was a transformed field hand. Cash belonged to Solomon. But he had stepped out of his overalls into this. There in front of Solomon's house he laughed. He had a round head, a round face, all of him was young, and he flung his head up, rolled it against the mare's-tail sky in his round hat, and he could laugh just to see Solomon's house sitting there. Livvie looked at it, and there was Solomon's black hat hanging on the peg on the front door, the blackest thing in the world.

"I been to Natchez," Cash said, wagging his head around the sky. "*I taken a trip, I ready for Easter!*"

How was it possible to look so fine before the harvest? Cash must have stolen the money, stolen it from Solomon. He stood in the path and lifted his spread hand high and brought it down again and again in his laughter. He kicked up his heels. A little chill went through her. It was as if Cash was bringing that strong hand down to beat a drum or to rain blows upon a man, such an abandon and menace were in his laugh. Frowning, she went closer to him and his swinging arm drew her in at once and the fright was crushed from her body, as a little match-flame might be smothered out by what it lighted. She gathered the folds of his coat behind him and fastened her red lips to his mouth, and she was dazzled by herself then, the way he had been dazzled with himself to begin with.

In that instant she felt something that could not be told—that Solomon's death was at hand, that he was the same to her as if he were dead now. She cried out, and uttering little cries turned and ran for the house.

At once Cash was coming, following after, he was running behind her. He came close, and half-way up the path he laughed and passed her. He even picked up a stone and sailed it into the bottle trees. She put her hands over her head, and sounds clattered through the bottle trees like cries of outrage. Cash stamped and plunged zigzag up the front steps and in at the door.

When she got there, he had stuck his hands in his pockets and was turning slowly about in the front room. The little guinea pig peeped out. Around Cash, the pinned-up palmettos looked as if a lazy green monkey had walked up and down and around the walls leaving green prints of his hands and feet.

She got through the room and his hands were still in his pockets, and she fell upon the closed door to the other room and pushed it open. She ran to Solomon's bed, calling "Solomon! Solomon!" The little shape of the old man never moved at all, wrapped under the quilt as if it were winter still.

"Solomon!" She pulled the quilt away, but there was another one under that, and she fell on her knees beside him. He made no sound except a sigh, and then she could hear in the silence the light springy steps of Cash walking and walking in the front room, and the ticking of Solomon's silver watch, which came from the bed. Old Solomon was far away in his sleep, his face looked small, relentless, and devout, as if he were walking somewhere where she could imagine the snow falling.

Then there was a noise like a hoof pawing the floor, and the door gave a creak, and Cash appeared beside her. When she looked up, Cash's face was so black it was bright, and so bright and bare of pity that it looked sweet to her. She stood up and held up her head. Cash was so powerful that his presence gave her strength even when she did not need any.

Under their eyes Solomon slept. People's faces tell of things and places not known to the one who looks at them while they sleep, and while Solomon slept under the eyes of Livvie and Cash his face told them like a mythical story that all his life he had built, little scrap by little scrap, respect. A beetle could not have been more laborious or more ingenious in the task of its destiny. When Solomon was young, as he was in his picture overhead, it was the infinite thing with him, and he could see no end to the respect he would contrive and keep in a house. He had built a lonely house, the way he would make a cage, but it grew to be the same with him as a great monumental pyramid and sometimes in his absorption of getting it erected he was like the builder-slaves of Egypt who forgot or never knew the origin and meaning of the thing to which they gave all their strength of their bodies and used up all their days. Livvie and Cash could see that as a man might rest from a life-labor he lay in his bed, and they could hear how, wrapped in his quilt, he sighed to himself comfortably in sleep, while in his dreams he might have been an ant, a beetle, a bird, an Egyptian, assembling and carrying on his back and building with his hands, or he might have been an old man of India or a swaddled baby, about to smile and brush all away.

Then without warning old Solomon's eyes flew wide open under the hedgelike brows. He was wide awake.

And instantly Cash raised his quick arm. A radiant sweat stood on his temples. But he did not bring his arm down—it stayed in the air, as if something might have taken hold.

It was not Livvie—she did not move. As if something said "Wait," she stood waiting. Even while her eyes burned under motionless lids, her lips parted in a stiff grimace, and with her arms stiff at her sides she stood above the prone old man and the panting young one, erect and apart.

Movement when it came came in Solomon's face. It was an old and strict face, a frail face, but behind it, like a covered light, came an animation that could play hide and seek, that would dart and escape, had always escaped. The mystery flickered in him, and invited from his eyes. It was that very mystery that Cash with his quick arm would have to strike, and that Livvie could not weep for. But Cash only stood holding his arm in the air, when the gentlest flick of his great strength, almost a puff of his breath, would have been enough, if he had known how to give it, to send the old man over the obstruction that kept him away from death.

If it could not be that the tiny illumination in the fragile and ancient face caused a crisis, a mystery in the room that would not permit a blow to fall, at least it was certain that Cash, throbbing in his Easter clothes, felt a pang of shame that the vigor of a man would come to such an end that he could not be struck without warning. He took down his hand and stepped back behind Livvie, like a round-eyed schoolboy on whose unsuspecting head the dunce cap has been set.

"Young ones can't wait," said Solomon.

Livvie shuddered violently, and then in a gush of tears she stooped for a glass of water and handed it to him, but he did not see her.

"So here come the young man Livvie wait for. Was no prevention. No prevention. Now I lay eyes on young man and it come to be somebody I know all the time, and been knowing since he were born in a cotton patch, and watched grow up year to year, Cash McCord, growed to size, growed up to come in my house in the end—ragged and barefoot."

Solomon gave a cough of distaste. Then he shut his eyes vigorously, and his lips began to move like a chanter's.

"When Livvie married, her husband were already somebody. He had paid great cost for his land. He spread sycamore leaves over the ground from wagon to door, day he brought her home, so her foot would not have to touch ground. He carried her through his door. Then he growed old and could not lift her, and she were still young."

Livvie's sobs followed his words like a soft melody repeating each thing as he stated it. His lips moved for a little without sound, or she cried too fervently, and unheard he might have been telling his whole life and then he said, "God forgive Solomon for sins great and small. God forgive Solomon for carrying away too young girl for wife and keeping her away from her people and from all the young people would clamor for her back."

Then he lifted up his right hand toward Livvie where she stood by the bed and offered her his silver watch. He dangled it before her eyes, and she hushed crying; her tears stopped. For a moment the watch could be heard ticking as it always did, precisely in his proud hand. She lifted it away. Then he took hold of the quilt; then he was dead.

Livvie left Solomon dead and went out of the room. Stealthily, nearly without noise, Cash went beside her. He was like a shadow, but his shiny shoes moved over the floor in spangles, and the green downy feather shone like a light in his hat. As they reached the front door, he seized her deftly as a long black cat and dragged her hanging by the waist round and round him, while he turned in a circle, his face bent down to hers. The first moment, she kept one arm and its hand stiff and still, the one that held Solomon's watch. Then the fingers softly let go, all of her was limp, and the watch fell somewhere on the floor. It ticked away in the still room, and all at once there began outside the full song of a bird.

They moved around and around the room and into the brightness of the open door, then he stopped and shook her once. She rested in silence in his trembling arms, unprotesting as a bird on a nest. Outside the red-birds were flying and crisscrossing, the sun was in all the bottles on the prisoned trees, and the young peach was shining in the middle of them with the bursting light of spring.

—1943

John Cheever (1912–1982) was associated with The New Yorker *for most of his creative life. It was the magazine that first published most of his short stories. Cheever's examinations of the tensions of life in white-collar suburbia take many forms —from naturalism to outright fantasy —but virtually all of his fiction is suffused with a melancholy that is often fueled by marital tensions, failed social aspirations, and what one story aptly calls "the sorrows of gin." Born in Quincy, Massachusetts, Cheever was expelled from Thayer Academy at seventeen, an event that formed the subject of his first published story, and he worked almost exclusively as a writer of fiction for the rest of his life, with occasional periods spent teaching at universities and writing for television. His most original writing is arguably in his short stories, but novels like the National Book Award-winning* The Wapshot Chronicle *(1957),* The Wapshot Scandal *(1964),* Bullet Park *(1969), and* Falconer *(1977) brought him to the attention of large audiences.* The Stories of John Cheever *won the Pulitzer Prize in 1979. In recent years his daughter, Susan Cheever, has published a memoir,* Home Before Dark, *and an edition of her father's journals, both of which chronicle Cheever's long struggles with alcoholism and questions of sexual identity.*

John Cheever
Reunion

The last time I saw my father was in Grand Central Station. I was going from my grandmother's in the Adirondacks to a cottage on the Cape that my mother had rented, and I wrote my father that I would be in New York between trains for an hour and a half, and asked if we could have lunch together. His secretary wrote to say that he would meet me at the information booth at noon, and at twelve o'clock sharp I saw him coming through the crowd. He was a stranger to me—my mother divorced him three years ago and I hadn't been with him since—but as soon as I saw him I felt that he was my father, my flesh and blood, my future and my doom. I knew that when I was grown I would be something like him; I would have to plan my campaigns within his limitations. He was a big, good-looking man, and I was terribly happy to see him again. He struck me on the back and shook my hand. "Hi, Charlie," he said. "Hi, boy. I'd like to take you up to my club, but it's in the Sixties, and if you have to catch an early train I guess we'd better get something to eat around here." He put his arm around me, and I smelled my father the way my mother sniffs a rose. It was a rich compound of whiskey, after-shave lotion, shoe polish, woolens, and the rankness of a mature male. I hoped that someone would see us together. I wished that we could be photographed. I wanted some record of our having been together.

We went out of the station and up a side street to a restaurant. It was still early, and the place was empty. The bartender was quarreling with a delivery boy, and there was one very old waiter in a red coat down by the kitchen door. We sat down, and my father hailed the waiter in a loud voice. "*Kellner!*" he shouted. "*Garçon! Cameriere! You!*" His boisterousness in the empty restaurant seemed out of place. "Could we have a little service here!" he shouted. "Chop-chop." Then he clapped his hands. This caught the waiter's attention, and he shuffled over to our table.

"Were you clapping your hands at me?" he asked.

"Calm down, calm down, *sommelier*," my father said. "If it isn't too much to ask of you—if it wouldn't be too much above and beyond the call of duty, we would like a couple of Beefeater Gibsons."

"I don't like to be clapped at," the waiter said.

"I should have brought my whistle," my father said. "I have a whistle that is audible only to the ears of old waiters. Now, take out your little pad and your little pencil and see if you can get this straight: two Beefeater Gibsons. Repeat after me: two Beefeater Gibsons."

"I think you'd better go somewhere else," the waiter said quietly.

"That," said my father, "is one of the most brilliant suggestions I have ever heard. Come on, Charlie, let's get the hell out of here!"

I followed my father out of that restaurant into another. He was not so boisterous this time. Our drinks came, and he cross-questioned me about the baseball season. He then struck the edge of his empty glass with his knife and began shouting again. "*Garçon! Kellner! Cameriere! You!* Could we trouble you to bring us two more of the same."

"How old is the boy?" the waiter asked.

"That," my father said, "is none of your God-damned business."

"I'm sorry, sir," the waiter said, "but I won't serve the boy another drink."

"Well, I have some news for you," my father said. "I have some very interesting news for you. This doesn't happen to be the only restaurant in New York. They've opened another on the corner. Come on, Charlie."

He paid the bill, and I followed him out of that restaurant into another. Here the waiters wore pink jackets like hunting coats, and there was a lot of horse tack on the walls. We sat down, and my father began to shout again. "Master of the hounds! Tallyhoo and all that sort of thing. We'd like a little something in the way of a stirrup cup. Namely, two Bibson Geefeaters."

"Two Bibson Geefeaters?" the waiter asked, smiling.

"You know damned well what I want," my father said angrily. "I want two Beefeater Gibsons, and make it snappy. Things have changed in jolly old England. So my friend the duke tells me. Let's see what England can produce in the way of a cocktail."

"This isn't England," the waiter said.

"Don't argue with me," my father said. "Just do as you're told."

"I just thought you might like to know where you are," the waiter

"If there is one thing I cannot tolerate," my father said, "it is an impudent domestic. Come on, Charlie."

The fourth place we went to was Italian. "*Buon giorno,*" my father said. "*Per favore, possiamo avere due cocktail americani, forti, forti. Molto gin, poco vermut.*"[1]

"I don't understand Italian," the waiter said.

"Oh, come off it," my father said. "You understand Italian, and you know damned well you do. *Vogliamo due cocktail americani. Subito.*"

The waiter left us and spoke with the captain, who came over to our table and said, "I'm sorry, sir, but this table is reserved."

"All right," my father said. "Get us another table."

"All the tables are reserved," the captain said.

"I get it," my father said. "You don't desire our patronage. Is that it? Well, the hell with you. *Vada all' inferno.* Let's go, Charlie."

"I have to get my train," I said.

"I'm sorry, sonny," my father said. "I'm terribly sorry." He put his arm around me and pressed me against him. "I'll walk you back to the station. If there had only been time to go up to my club."

"That's all right, Daddy," I said.

"I'll get you a paper," he said. "I'll get you a paper to read on the train."

Then he went up to a newsstand and said, "Kind sir, will you be good enough to favor me with one of your God-damned, no-good, ten-cent afternoon papers?" The clerk turned away from him and stared at

---

[1]The father is ordering drinks in Italian.

a magazine cover. "Is it asking too much, kind sir," my father said, "is it asking too much for you to sell me one of your disgusting specimens of yellow journalism?"

"I have to go, Daddy," I said. "It's late."

"Now, just wait a second, sonny," he said. "I want to get a rise out of this chap."

"Goodbye, Daddy," I said, and I went down the stairs and got my train, and that was the last time I saw my father.

—*1962*

Albert Camus (1913–1960), *along with Jean Paul Sartre and Simone Beauvoir, was a leader of the brilliant literary movement that arose from the French defeat in World War II. He was associated with the philosophical school of existentialism, and the ironies of Camus's own life and premature death in an automobile accident only two years after winning the Nobel Prize mirror the "absurd" situations of his alienated protagonists. His nonfiction work* The Myth of Sisyphus *(1942) explores the futility of the individual's quest for meaning in life, but his existentialist ideas are best illustrated in novels like* The Stranger *(1942), in which a man is condemned not because he commits a murder in a moment of passion but because he fails to display proper emotion at his mother's funeral.* The Plague *(1947), set in Camus's native North Africa, can be read both as a realistic account of an epidemic and as an allegory of French occupation by the Nazis. "The Guest" takes place in Algeria during the waning years of French control there, when even the most fundamentally decent of civil servants is forced to share the blame for what is perceived by the Algerian rebels as a callous example of colonial injustice. Camus lived to witness the terrorism that swept Algeria and France in the 1950s but died before Algerian independence was proclaimed in 1962.*

Albert Camus
The Guest

The schoolmaster was watching the two men climb toward him. One was on horseback, the other on foot. They had not yet tackled the abrupt rise leading to the schoolhouse built on the hillside. They were toiling onward, making slow progress in the snow, among the stones, on the vast expanse of the high deserted plateau. From time to time the

Translated by Justin O'Brien.

horse stumbled. Without hearing anything yet, he could see the breath issuing from the horse's nostrils. One of the men, at least, knew the region. They were following the trail although it had disappeared days ago under a layer of dirty white snow. The schoolmaster calculated that it would take them half an hour to get onto the hill. It was cold; he went back into the school to get a sweater.

He crossed the empty, frigid classroom. On the blackboard the four rivers of France, drawn with four different colored chalks, had been flowing toward their estuaries for the past three days. Snow had suddenly fallen in mid-October after eight months of drought without the transition of rain, and the twenty pupils, more or less, who lived in the villages scattered over the plateau had stopped coming. With fair weather they would return. Daru now heated only the single room that was his lodging, adjoining the classroom and giving also onto the plateau to the east. Like the class windows, his window looked to the south. On that side the school was a few kilometers from the point where the plateau began to slope toward the south. In clear weather could be seen the purple mass of the mountain range where the gap opened onto the desert.

Somewhat warmed, Daru returned to the window from which he had first seen the two men. They were no longer visible. Hence they must have tackled the rise. The sky was not so dark, for the snow had stopped falling during the night. The morning had opened with a dirty light which had scarcely become brighter as the ceiling of clouds lifted. At two in the afternoon it seemed as if the day were merely beginning. But still this was better than those three days when the thick snow was falling amidst unbroken darkness with little gusts of wind that rattled the double door of the classroom. Then Daru had spent long hours in his room, leaving it only to go to the shed and feed the chickens or get some coal. Fortunately the delivery truck from Tadjid, the nearest village to the north, had brought his supplies two days before the blizzard. It would return in forty-eight hours.

Besides, he had enough to resist a siege, for the little room was cluttered with bags of wheat that the administration left as a stock to distribute to those of his pupils whose families had suffered from the drought. Actually they had all been victims because they were all poor. Every day Daru would distribute a ration to the children. They had missed it, he knew, during these bad days. Possibly one of the fathers or big brothers would come this afternoon and he could supply them with grain. It was just a matter of carrying them over to the next harvest. Now shiploads of wheat were arriving from France and the worst was over. But it would be hard to forget that poverty, that army of ragged ghosts wandering in the sunlight, the plateaus burned to a cinder month after month, the earth shriveled up little by little, literally scorched, every stone bursting into dust under one's foot. The sheep had died then by thousands and even a few men, here and there, sometimes without anyone's knowing.

In contrast with such poverty, he who lived almost like a monk in his remote schoolhouse, nonetheless satisfied with the little he had and with the rough life, had felt like a lord with his whitewashed walls, his narrow couch, his unpainted shelves, his well, and his weekly provision of water and food. And suddenly this snow, without warning, without the foretaste of rain. This is the way the region was, cruel to live in, even without men—who didn't help matters either. But Daru had been born here. Everywhere else, he felt exiled.

He stepped out onto the terrace in front of the schoolhouse. The two men were now halfway up the slope. He recognized the horseman as Balducci, the old gendarme[1] he had known for a long time. Balducci was holding on the end of a rope an Arab who was walking behind him with hands bound and head lowered. The gendarme waved a greeting to which Daru did not reply, lost as he was in contemplation of the Arab dressed in a faded blue jellaba,[2] his feet in sandals but covered with socks of heavy raw wool, his head surmounted by a narrow, short *chèche*.[3] They were approaching. Balducci was holding back his horse in order not to hurt the Arab, and the group was advancing slowly.

Within earshot, Balducci shouted: "One hour to do the three kilometers from El Ameur!" Daru did not answer. Short and square in his thick sweater, he watched them climb. Not once had the Arab raised his head. "Hello," said Daru when they got up onto the terrace. "Come and warm up." Balducci painfully got down from his horse without letting go of the rope. From under his bristling mustache he smiled at the schoolmaster. His little dark eyes, deep-set under a tanned forehead, and his mouth surrounded with wrinkles made him look attentive and studious. Daru took the bridle, led the horse to the shed, and came back

---

[1]*gendarme:* policeman. [2]*jellaba:* hooded cloak. [3]*chèche:* cap.

to the two men, who were now waiting for him in the school. He led them into his room. "I am going to heat up the classroom," he said. "We'll be more comfortable there." When he entered the room again Balducci was on the couch. He had undone the rope tying him to the Arab, who had squatted near the stove. His hands still bound, the *chèche* pushed back on his head, he was looking toward the window. At first Daru noticed only his huge lips, fat, smooth, almost Negroid; yet his nose was straight, his eyes were dark and full of fever. The *chèche* revealed an obstinate forehead and, under the weathered skin now rather discolored by the cold, the whole face had a restless and rebellious look that struck Daru when the Arab, turning his face toward him, looked him straight in the eyes. "Go into the other room," said the schoolmaster, "and I'll make you some mint tea." "Thanks," Balducci said. "What a chore! How I long for retirement." And addressing his prisoner in Arabic: "Come on, you." The Arab got up and, slowly, holding his bound wrists in front of him, went into the classroom.

With the tea, Daru brought a chair. But Balducci was already enthroned on the nearest pupil's desk and the Arab had squatted against the teacher's platform facing the stove, which stood between the desk and the window. When he held out the glass of tea to the prisoner, Daru hesitated at the sight of his bound hands. "He might perhaps be untied." "Sure," said Balducci. "That was for the trip." He started to get to his feet. But Daru, setting the glass on the floor, had knelt beside the Arab. Without saying anything, the Arab watched him with his feverish eyes. Once his hands were free, he rubbed his swollen wrists against each other, took the glass of tea, and sucked up the burning liquid in swift little sips.

"Good," said Daru. "And where are you headed?"

Balducci withdrew his mustache from the tea. "Here, son."

"Odd pupils! And you're spending the night?"

"No. I'm going back to El Ameur. And you will deliver this fellow to Tinguit. He is expected at police headquarters."

Balducci was looking at Daru with a friendly little smile.

"What's this story?" asked the schoolmaster. "Are you pulling my leg?"

"No, son. Those are the orders."

"The orders? I'm not..." Daru hesitated, not wanting to hurt the old Corsican. "I mean, that's not my job."

"What! What's the meaning of that? In wartime people do all kinds of jobs."

"Then I'll wait for the declaration of war!"

Balducci nodded.

"O.K. But the orders exist and they concern you too. Things are brewing, it appears. There is talk of a forthcoming revolt. We are mobilized, in a way."

Daru still had his obstinate look.

"Listen, son," Balducci said. "I like you and you must understand. There's only a dozen of us at El Ameur to patrol throughout the whole territory of a small department and I must get back in a hurry. I was told to hand this guy over to you and return without delay. He couldn't be kept there. His village was beginning to stir; they wanted to take him back. You must take him to Tinguit tomorrow before the day is over. Twenty kilometers shouldn't faze a husky fellow like you. After that, all will be over. You'll come back to your pupils and your comfortable life."

Behind the wall the horse could be heard snorting and pawing the earth. Daru was looking out the window. Decidedly, the weather was clearing and the light was increasing over the snowy plateau. When all the snow was melted, the sun would take over again and once more would burn the fields of stone. For days, still, the unchanging sky would shed its dry light on the solitary expanse where nothing had any connection with man.

"After all," he said, turning around toward Balducci, "what did he do?" And, before the gendarme had opened his mouth, he asked: "Does he speak French?"

"No, not a word. We had been looking for him for a month, but they were hiding him. He killed his cousin."

"Is he against us?"

"I don't think so. But you can never be sure."

"Why did he kill?"

"A family squabble, I think. One owed the other grain, it seems. It's not at all clear. In short, he killed his cousin with a billhook. You know, like a sheep, *kreezk!*"

Balducci made the gesture of drawing a blade across his throat and the Arab, his attention attracted, watched him with a sort of anxiety. Daru felt a sudden wrath against the man, against all men with their rotten spite, their tireless hates, their blood lust.

But the kettle was singing on the stove. He served Balducci more tea, hesitated, then served the Arab again, who, a second time, drank avidly. His raised arms made the jellaba fall open and the schoolmaster saw his thin, muscular chest.

"Thanks, kid," Balducci said. "And now, I'm off."

He got up and went toward the Arab, taking a small rope from his pocket.

"What are you doing?" Daru asked dryly.

Balducci, disconcerted, showed him the rope.

"Don't bother."

The old gendarme hesitated. "It's up to you. Of course, you are armed?"

"I have my shotgun."

"Where?"

"In the trunk."

"You ought to have it near your bed."

"Why? I have nothing to fear."

"You're crazy, son. If there's an uprising, no one is safe, we're all in the same boat."

"I'll defend myself. I'll have time to see them coming."

Balducci began to laugh, then suddenly the mustache covered the white teeth. "You'll have time? O.K. That's just what I was saying. You have always been a little cracked. That's why I like you, my son was like that."

At the same time he took out his revolver and put it on the desk.

"Keep it; I don't need two weapons from here to El Ameur."

The revolver shone against the black paint of the table. When the gendarme turned toward him, the schoolmaster caught the smell of leather and horseflesh.

"Listen, Balducci," Daru said suddenly, "every bit of this disgusts me, and first of all your fellow here. But I won't hand him over. Fight, yes, if I have to. But not that."

The old gendarme stood in front of him and looked at him severely.

"You're being a fool," he said slowly. "I don't like it either. You don't get used to putting a rope on a man even after years of it, and you're even ashamed—yes, ashamed. But you can't let them have their way."

"I won't hand him over," Daru said again.

"It's an order, son, and I repeat it."

"That's right. Repeat to them what I've said to you: I won't hand him over."

Balducci made a visible effort to reflect. He looked at the Arab and at Daru. At last he decided.

"No, I won't tell them anything. If you want to drop us, go ahead; I'll not denounce you. I have an order to deliver the prisoner and I'm doing so. And now you'll just sign this paper for me."

"There's no need. I'll not deny that you left him with me."

"Don't be mean with me. I know you'll tell the truth. You're from hereabouts and you are a man. But you must sign, that's the rule."

Daru opened his drawer, took out a little square bottle of purple ink, the red wooden penholder with the "sergeant-major" pen he used for making models of penmanship, and signed. The gendarme carefully folded the paper and put it into his wallet. Then he moved toward the door.

"I'll see you off," Daru said.

"No," said Balducci. "There's no use being polite. You insulted me."

He looked at the Arab, motionless in the same spot, sniffed peevishly, and turned away toward the door. "Good-by, son," he said. The door shut behind him. Balducci appeared suddenly outside the window and then disappeared. His footsteps were muffled by the snow. The horse stirred on the other side of the wall and several chickens fluttered in fright. A moment later Balducci reappeared outside the window leading the horse by the bridle. He walked toward the little rise without turning around and disappeared from sight with the horse following him. A big stone could be heard bouncing down. Daru walked back toward the prisoner, who, without stirring, never took his eyes off him. "Wait," the schoolmaster said in Arabic and went toward the bedroom. As he was going through the door, he had a second thought, went to the desk, took the revolver, and stuck it in his pocket. Then, without looking back, he went into his room.

For some time he lay on his couch watching the sky gradually close over, listening to the silence. It was this silence that had seemed painful to him during the first days here, after the war. He had requested a post in the little town at the base of the foothills separating the upper plateaus from the desert. There, rocky walls, green and black to the north, pink and lavender to the south, marked the frontier of eternal summer. He had been named to a post farther north, on the plateau itself. In the beginning, the solitude and the silence had been hard for him on these wastelands peopled only by stones. Occasionally, furrows suggested cultivation, but they had been dug to uncover a certain kind of stone good for building. The only plowing here was to harvest rocks. Elsewhere a thin layer of soil accumulated in the hollows would be scraped out to enrich paltry village gardens. This is the way it was: bare rock covered three quarters of the region. Towns sprang up, flourished, then disappeared; men came by, loved one another or fought bitterly, then died. No one in this desert, neither he nor his guest, mattered. And yet, outside this desert neither of them, Daru knew, could have really lived.

When he got up, no noise came from the classroom. He was amazed at the unmixed joy he derived from the mere thought that the Arab might have fled and that he would be alone with no decision to make. But the prisoner was there. He had merely stretched out between the stove and the desk. With eyes open, he was staring at the ceiling. In that position, his thick lips were particularly noticeable, giving him a pouting look. "Come," said Daru. The Arab got up and followed him. In the bedroom, the schoolmaster pointed to a chair near the table under the window. The Arab sat down without taking his eyes off Daru.

"Are you hungry?"

"Yes," the prisoner said.

Daru set the table for two. He took flour and oil, shaped a cake in a frying-pan, and lighted the little stove that functioned on bottled gas. While the cake was cooking, he went out to the shed to get cheese, eggs, dates, and condensed milk. When the cake was done he set it on the window sill to cool, heated some condensed milk diluted with water, and beat up the eggs into an omelette. In one of his motions he knocked against the revolver stuck in his right pocket. He set the bowl down, went into the classroom, and put the revolver in his desk drawer. When he came back to the room, night was falling. He put on the light and served the Arab. "Eat," he said. The Arab took a piece of the cake, lifted it eagerly to his mouth, and stopped short.

"And you?" he asked.

"After you. I'll eat too."

The thick lips opened slightly. The Arab hesitated, then bit into the cake determinedly.

The meal over, the Arab looked at the schoolmaster. "Are you the judge?"

"No, I'm simply keeping you until tomorrow."

"Why do you eat with me?"

"I'm hungry."

The Arab fell silent. Daru got up and went out. He brought back a folding bed from the shed, set it up between the table and the stove, perpendicular to his own bed. From a large suitcase which, upright in a corner, served as a shelf for papers, he took two blankets and arranged them on the camp bed. Then he stopped, felt useless, and sat down on his bed. There was nothing more to do or to get ready. He had to look at this man. He looked at him, therefore, trying to imagine his face bursting with rage. He couldn't do so. He could see nothing but the dark yet shining eyes and the animal mouth.

"Why did you kill him?" he asked in a voice whose hostile tone surprised him.

The Arab looked away. "He ran away. I ran after him."

He raised his eyes to Daru and they were full of a sort of woeful interrogation. "Now what will they do to me?"

"Are you afraid?"

He stiffened, turning his eyes away.

"Are you sorry?"

The Arab stared at him openmouthed. Obviously he did not understand. Daru's annoyance was growing. At the same time he felt awkward and self-conscious with his big body wedged between the two beds.

"Lie down there," he said impatiently. "That's your bed."

The Arab didn't move. He called to Daru:

"Tell me!"

The schoolmaster looked at him.

"Is the gendarme coming back tomorrow?"

"I don't know."

"Are you coming with us?"

"I don't know. Why?"

The prisoner got up and stretched out on top of the blankets, his feet toward the window. The light from the electric bulb shone straight into his eyes and he closed them at once.

"Why?" Daru repeated, standing beside the bed.

The Arab opened his eyes under the blinding light and looked at him, trying not to blink.

"Come with us," he said.

In the middle of the night, Daru was still not asleep. He had gone to bed after undressing completely; he generally slept naked. But when he suddenly realized that he had nothing on he hesitated. He felt vulnerable and the temptation came to him to put his clothes back on. Then he shrugged his shoulders; after all, he wasn't a child and, if need be, he could break his adversary in two. From his bed he could observe him, lying on his back, still motionless with his eyes closed under the harsh light. When Daru turned out the light, the darkness seemed to coagulate all of a sudden. Little by little, the night came back to life in the window where the starless sky was stirring gently. The schoolmaster soon made out the body lying at his feet. The Arab still did not move, but his eyes seemed open. A faint wind was prowling around the schoolhouse. Perhaps it would drive away the clouds and the sun would reappear.

During the night the wind increased. The hens fluttered a little and then were silent. The Arab turned over on his side with his back to Daru, who thought he heard him moan. Then he listened for his guest's breathing, become heavier and more regular. He listened to that breath so close to him and mused without being able to go to sleep. In this room where he had been sleeping alone for a year, this presence bothered him. But it bothered him also by imposing on him a sort of brotherhood he knew well but refused to accept in the present circumstances. Men who share the same rooms, soldiers or prisoners, develop a strange alliance as if, having cast off their armor with their clothing, they fraternized every evening, over and above their differences, in the ancient community of dream and fatigue. But Daru shook himself; he didn't like such musings, and it was essential to sleep.

A little later, however, when the Arab stirred slightly, the schoolmaster was still not asleep. When the prisoner made a second move, he stiffened, on the alert. The Arab was lifting himself slowly on his arms with almost the motion of a sleepwalker. Seated upright in bed, he waited motionless without turning his head toward Daru, as if he were listening attentively. Daru did not stir; it had just occurred to him that the revolver was still in the drawer of his desk. It was better to act at once. Yet he continued to observe the prisoner, who, with the same slithery motion, put his feet on the ground, waited again, then began to stand up slowly. Daru was about to call out to him when the Arab began to walk, in a quite natural but extraordinary silent way. He was heading toward the door at the end of the room that opened into the shed. He lifted the latch with precaution and went out, pushing the door behind him but without shutting it. Daru had not stirred. "He is running away," he merely thought. "Good riddance!" Yet he listened attentively. The hens were not fluttering; the guest must be on the plateau. A faint sound of water reached him, and he didn't know what it was until the Arab again stood framed in the doorway, closed the door carefully, and came back to bed without a sound. Then Daru turned his back on him and fell asleep. Still later he seemed, from the depths of his sleep, to hear furtive steps around the schoolhouse. "I'm dreaming! I'm dreaming!" he repeated to himself. And he went on sleeping.

When he awoke, the sky was clear; the loose window let in a cold, pure air. The Arab was asleep, hunched up under the blankets now, his mouth open, utterly relaxed. But when Daru shook him, he started dreadfully, staring at Daru with wild eyes as if he had never seen him and such a frightened expression that the schoolmaster stepped back. "Don't be afraid. It's me. You must eat." The Arab nodded and said yes. Calm had returned to his face, but his expression was vacant and listless.

The coffee was ready. They drank it seated together on the folding bed as they munched their pieces of the cake. Then Daru led the Arab under the shed and showed him the faucet where he washed. He went back into the room, folded the blankets and the bed, made his own bed and put the room in order. Then he went through the classroom and out onto the terrace. The sun was already rising in the blue sky; a soft bright light was bathing the deserted plateau. On the ridge the snow was melting in spots. The stones were about to reappear. Crouched on the edge of the plateau, the schoolmaster looked at the deserted expanse. He thought of Balducci. He had hurt him, for he had sent him off in a way as if he didn't want to be associated with him. He could hear the gendarme's farewell and, without knowing why, he felt strangely empty and vulnerable. At that moment, from the other side of the schoolhouse, the prisoner coughed. Daru listened to him almost despite himself and then, furious, threw a pebble that whistled through the air before sinking into the snow. That man's stupid crime revolted him, but to hand him over was contrary to honor. Merely thinking of it made him smart with humiliation. And he cursed at one and the same time his own people who had sent him this Arab and the Arab too who had dared to kill and not managed to get away. Daru got up, walked in a circle on the terrace, waited motionless, and then went back into the schoolhouse.

The Arab, leaning over the cement floor of the shed, was washing his teeth with two fingers. Daru looked at him and said: "Come." He went back into the room ahead of the prisoner. He slipped a hunting-jacket on over his sweater and put on walking-shoes. Standing, he waited until the Arab had put on his *chèche* and sandals. They went into the classroom and the schoolmaster pointed to the exit, saying: "Go ahead." The fellow didn't budge. "I'm coming," said Daru. The Arab went out. Daru went back into the room and made a package of pieces of rusk, dates, and sugar. In the classroom, before going out, he hesitated a second in front of his desk, then crossed the threshold and locked the door. "That's the way," he said. He started toward the east, followed by the prisoner. But, a short distance from the schoolhouse, he thought he heard a slight sound behind them. He retraced his steps and examined the surroundings of the house; there was no one there. The Arab watched him without seeming to understand. "Come on," said Daru.

They walked for an hour and rested beside a sharp peak of limestone. The snow was melting faster and faster and the sun was drinking up the puddles at once, rapidly cleaning the plateau, which gradually dried and vibrated like the air itself. When they resumed walking, the ground rang under their feet. From time to time a bird rent the space in front of them with a joyful cry. Daru breathed in deeply the fresh morning light. He felt a sort of rapture before the vast familiar expanse, now almost entirely yellow under its dome of blue sky. They walked an hour or more, descending toward the south. They reached a level height made up of crumbly rocks. From there on, the plateau sloped down, eastward toward a low plain where there were a few spindly trees and, to the south, toward outcroppings of rock that gave the landscape a chaotic look.

Daru surveyed the two directions. There was nothing but the sky on the horizon. Not a man could be seen. He turned toward the Arab, who was looking at him blankly. Daru held out the package to him. "Take it," he said. "There are dates, bread, and sugar. You can hold out for two days. Here are a thousand francs too." The Arab took the package and the money but kept his full hands at chest level as if he didn't know what to do with what was being given him. "Now look," the schoolmaster said as he pointed in the direction of the east, "there's the way to Tinguit. You have a two-hour walk. At Tinguit you'll find the administration and the police. They are expecting you." The Arab looked toward the east, still holding the package and the money against his chest. Daru took his elbow and turned him rather roughly toward the south. At the foot of the height on which they stood could be seen a faint path. "That's the trail across the plateau. In a day's walk from here you'll find pasturelands and the first nomads. They'll take you in and shelter you according to their law." The Arab had now turned toward Daru and a sort of panic was visible in his expression. "Listen," he said. Daru shook his head: "No, be quiet. Now I'm leaving you." He turned his back on him, took two long steps in the direction of the school, looked hesitantly at the motionless Arab, and started off again. For a few minutes he heard nothing but his own step resounding on the cold ground and did not turn his head. A moment later, however, he turned around. The Arab was still there on the edge of the hill, his arms hanging now, and he was looking at the schoolmaster. Daru felt something rise in his throat. But he swore with impatience, waved vaguely, and started off again. He had already gone some distance when he again stopped and looked. There was no longer anyone on the hill.

Daru hesitated. The sun was now rather high in the sky and was beginning to beat down on his head. The schoolmaster retraced his steps, at first somewhat uncertainly, then with decision. When he reached the little hill, he was bathed in sweat. He climbed it as fast as he could and stopped, out of breath, at the top. The rock-fields to the south stood out sharply against the blue sky, but on the plain to the east a steamy heat was already rising. And in that slight haze, Daru, with heavy heart, made out the Arab walking slowly on the road to prison.

A little later, standing before the window of the classroom, the schoolmaster was watching the clear light bathing the whole surface of the plateau, but he hardly saw it. Behind him on the blackboard, among the winding French rivers, sprawled the clumsily chalked-up words he had just read: "You handed over our brother. You will pay for this." Daru looked at the sky, the plateau, and, beyond, the invisible lands stretching all the way to the sea. In the vast landscape he had loved so much, he was alone.

—1957

*Ralph Ellison (1914–1995) was born in Oklahoma City, where his early inter-
ests were primarily musical; he played trumpet and knew many prominent jazz musicians of the depression era. In 1933 he attended Tuskegee Institute, intending to
study music, but he was drawn to literature through his study of contemporary writers (especially the poet T. S. Eliot). Ellison left school in 1936 for New York City,
where he found work for a time with the Federal Writers' Project and began to publish stories and reviews in the later 1930s in progressive magazines like* New
Masses. *Tuskegee and Harlem provided him with material for* Invisible Man
*(1952), a brilliant picaresque novel of black life that established him as a major
force in American fiction.* Invisible Man *won the National Book Award in 1953
and in 1965 was voted in a* Book Week *poll the most distinguished novel of the
postwar period. Ellison published little subsequently, with two collections of essays,*
Shadow and Act *(1964) and* Going to the Territory *(1986), a posthumous
volume of collected stories, and an unfinished novel,* Juneteenth *(1999), having to
suffice for readers who long anticipated a second novel that might somehow help to
define the changes four decades had wrought in the experience of black America. "A
Party Down at the Square," a brutally direct account of a lynching, is based on true
accounts of similar events that appeared primarily in African-American newspapers
in the 1920s and 1930s. Uncollected and almost forgotten at Ellison's death, it was
reprinted in* Esquire.

Ralph Ellison
A Party Down at the Square

I don't know what started it. A bunch of men came by my Uncle Ed's
place and said there was going to be a party down at the Square, and
my uncle hollered for me to come on and I ran with them through the
dark and rain and there we were at the Square. When we got there
everybody was mad and quiet and standing around looking at the nigger. Some of the men had guns, and one man kept goosing the nigger in
his pants with the barrel of a shotgun, saying he ought to pull the trigger, but he never did. It was right in front of the courthouse, and the old
clock in the tower was striking twelve. The rain was falling cold and
freezing as it fell. Everybody was cold, and the nigger kept wrapping his
arms around himself trying to stop the shivers.

Then one of the boys pushed through the circle and snatched off the
nigger's shirt, and there he stood, with his black skin all shivering in the

light from the fire, and looking at us with a scaired look on his face and putting his hands in his pants pockets. Folks started yelling to hurry up and kill the nigger. Somebody yelled: "Take your hands out of your pockets, nigger; we gonna have plenty heat in a minnit." But the nigger didn't hear him and kept his hands where they were.

I tell you the rain was cold. I had to stick my hands in my pockets they got so cold. The fire was pretty small, and they put some logs around the platform they had the nigger on and then threw on some gasoline, and you could see the flames light up the whole Square. It was late and the streetlights had been off for a long time. It was so bright that the bronze statue of the general standing there in the Square was like something alive. The shadows playing on his moldy green face made him seem to be smiling down at the nigger.

They threw on more gas, and it made the Square bright like it gets when the lights are turned on or when the sun is setting red. All the wagons and cars were standing around the curbs. Not like Saturday though—the niggers weren't there. Not a single nigger was there except this Bacote nigger and they dragged him there tied to the back of Jed Wilson's truck. On Saturday there's as many niggers as white folks.

Everybody was yelling crazy 'cause they were about to set fire to the nigger, and I got to the rear of the circle and looked around the Square to try to count the cars. The shadows of the folks was flickering on the trees in the middle of the Square. I saw some birds that the noise had woke up flying through the trees. I guess maybe they thought it was morning. The ice had started the cobblestones in the street to shine where the rain was falling and freezing. I counted forty cars before I lost count. I knew folks must have been there from Phenix City by all the cars mixed in with the wagons.

God, it was a hell of a night. It was some night all right. When the noise died down I heard the nigger's voice from where I stood in the back, so I pushed my way up front. The nigger was bleeding from his nose and ears, and I could see him all red where the dark blood was running down his black skin. He kept lifting first one foot and then the other, like a chicken on a hot stove. I looked down to the platform they had him on, and they had pushed a ring of fire up close to his feet. It must have been hot to him with the flames almost touching his big black toes. Somebody yelled for the nigger to say his prayers, but the nigger wasn't saying anything now. He just kinda moaned with his eyes shut and kept moving up and down on his feet, first one foot and then the other.

I watched the flames burning the logs up closer and closer to the nigger's feet. They were burning good now, and the rain had stopped and the wind was rising, making the flames flare higher. I looked, and there must have been thirty-five women in the crowd, and I could hear their voices clear and shrill mixed in with those of the men. Then it happened. I heard the noise about the same time everyone else did. It was like the roar of a cyclone blowing up from the gulf, and everyone was looking up into the air to see what it was. Some of the faces looked surprised and scaired, all but the nigger. He didn't even hear the noise. He didn't even look up. Then the roar came closer, right above our heads and the wind was blowing higher and higher and the sound seemed to be going in circles.

Then I saw her. Through the clouds and fog I could see a red and green light on her wings. I could see them just for a second; then she rose up into the low clouds. I looked out for the beacon over the tops of the buildings in the direction of the airfield that's forty miles away, and it wasn't circling around. You usually could see it sweeping around the sky at night, but it wasn't there. Then, there she was again, like a big bird lost in the fog. I looked for the red and green lights, and they weren't there anymore. She was flying even closer to the tops of the buildings than before. The wind was blowing harder, and leaves started flying about, making funny shadows on the ground, and tree limbs were cracking and falling.

It was a storm all right. The pilot must have thought he was over the landing field. Maybe he thought the fire in the Square was put there for him to land by. Gosh, but it scaired the folks. I was scaired too. They started yelling: "He's going to land. He's going to land." And: "He's going to fall." A few started for their cars and wagons. I could hear the wagons creaking and chains jangling and cars spitting and missing as they started the engines up. Off to my right, a horse started pitching and striking his hooves against a car.

I didn't know what to do. I wanted to run, and I wanted to stay and see what was going to happen. The plane was close as hell. The pilot must have been trying to see where he was at, and her motors were drowning out all the sounds. I could even feel the vibration, and my hair felt like it was standing up under my hat. I happened to look over at the statue of the general standing with one leg before the other and leaning back on a sword, and I was fixing to run over and climb between his legs and sit there and watch when the roar stopped some, and I looked up and she was gliding just over the top of the trees in the middle of the Square.

Her motors stopped altogether and I could hear the sound of branches cracking and snapping off below her landing gear. I could see her plain now, all silver and shining in the light of the fire with T.W.A. in black letters under her wings. She was sailing smoothly out of the Square when she hit the high power lines that follow the Birmingham highway through the town. It made a loud crash. It sounded like the wind blowing the door of a tin barn shut. She only hit with her landing gear, but I could see the sparks flying, and the wires knocked loose from the poles were spitting blue sparks and whipping around like a bunch of snakes and leaving circles of blue sparks in the darkness.

The plane had knocked five or six wires loose, and they were dangling and swinging, and every time they touched they threw off more sparks. The wind was making them swing, and when I got over there, there was a crackling and spitting screen of blue haze across the highway. I lost my hat running over, but I didn't stop to look for it. I was among the first and I could hear the others pounding behind me across the grass of the Square. They were yelling to beat all hell, and they came up fast, pushing and shoving, and someone got pushed against a swinging wire. It made a sound like when a blacksmith drops a red hot horseshoe into a barrel of water, and the steam comes up. I could smell the flesh burning. The first time I'd ever smelled it. I got up close and it was a woman. It must have killed her right off. She was lying in a puddle stiff as a board, with pieces of glass insulators that the plane had knocked off the poles lying all around her. Her white dress was torn, and I saw one of her tits hanging out in the water and her thighs. Some woman screamed and fainted and almost fell on a wire, but a man caught her. The sheriff and his men were yelling and driving folks back with guns shining in their hands, and everything was lit up blue by the sparks. The shock had turned the woman almost as black as the nigger. I was trying to see if she wasn't blue too, or if it was just the sparks, and the sheriff drove me away. As I backed off trying to see, I heard the motors of the plane start up again somewhere off to the right in the clouds.

The clouds were moving fast in the wind and the wind was blowing the smell of something burning over to me. I turned around, and the crowd was headed back to the nigger. I could see him standing there in the middle of the flames. The wind was making the flames brighter every minute. The crowd was running. I ran too. I ran back across the grass with the crowd. It wasn't so large now that so many had gone when the plane came. I tripped and fell over the limb of a tree lying in the grass and bit my lip. It ain't well yet I bit it so bad. I could taste the blood in my mouth as I ran over. I guess that's what made me sick. When I got there, the fire had caught the nigger's pants, and the folks were standing around watching, but not too close on account of the wind blowing the flames. Somebody hollered, "Well, nigger, it ain't so cold now, is it? You don't need to put your hands in your pockets now." And the nigger looked up with his great white eyes looking like they was 'bout to pop out of his head, and I had enough. I didn't want to see anymore. I wanted to run somewhere and puke, but I stayed. I stayed right there in the front of the crowd and looked.

The nigger tried to say something I couldn't hear for the roar of the wind in the fire, and I strained my ears. Jed Wilson hollered, "What you say there, nigger?" And it came back through the flames in his nigger voice: "Will one a you gentlemen please cut my throat?" he said. "Will somebody please cut my throat like a Christian?" And Jed hollered back, "Sorry, but ain't no Christians around tonight. Ain't no Jew-boys neither. We're just one hundred percent Americans."

Then the nigger was silent. Folks started laughing at Jed. Jed's right popular with the folks, and next year, my uncle says, they plan to run him for sheriff. The heat was too much for me, and the smoke was making my eyes to smart. I was trying to back away when Jed reached down and brought up a can of gasoline and threw it in the fire on the nigger. I could see the flames catching the gas in a puff as it went in in a silver sheet and some of it reached the nigger, making spurts of blue fire all over his chest.

Well, that nigger was tough. I have to give it to that nigger; he was really tough. He had started to burn like a house afire and was making the smoke smell like burning hides. The fire was up around his head, and the smoke was so thick and black we couldn't see him. And him not moving—we thought he was dead. Then he started out. The fire had burned the ropes they had tied him with, and he started jumping and kicking about like he was blind, and you could smell his skin burning. He kicked so hard that the platform, which was burning too, fell in, and he rolled out of the fire at my feet. I jumped back so he wouldn't get on me. I'll never forget it. Every time I eat barbeque I'll remember that nigger. His back was just like a barbecued hog. I could see the prints of his ribs where they start around from his backbone and curve down and around. It was a sight to see, that nigger's back. He was right at my feet, and somebody behind pushed me and almost made me step on him, and he was still burning.

I didn't step on him though, and Jed and somebody else pushed him back into the burning planks and logs and poured on more gas. I wanted to leave, but the folks were yelling and I couldn't move except to look around and see the statue. A branch the wind had broken was resting on his hat. I tried to push out and get away because my guts were gone, and all I got was spit and hot breath in my face from the woman and two men standing directly behind me. So I had to turn back around. The nigger rolled out of the fire again. He wouldn't stay put. It was on the other side this time. I couldn't see him very well through the flames and smoke. They got some tree limbs and held him there this time and he stayed there till he was ashes. I guess he stayed there. I know he burned to ashes because I saw Jed a week later, and he laughed and showed me some white finger bones still held together with little pieces of the nigger's skin. Anyway, I left when somebody moved around to see the nigger. I pushed my way through the crowd, and a woman in the rear scratched my face as she yelled and fought to get up close.

I ran across the Square to the other side, where the sheriff and his deputies were guarding the wires that were still spitting and making a blue fog. My heart was pounding like I had been running a long ways, and I bent over and let my insides go. Everything came up and spilled in a big gush over the ground. I was sick, and tired, and weak, and cold. The wind was still high, and large drops of rain were beginning to fall. I headed down the street to my uncle's place past a store where the wind had broken a window, and glass lay over the sidewalk. I kicked it as I went by. I remember somebody's fool rooster crowing like it was morning in all that wind.

The next day I was too weak to go out, and my uncle kidded me and called me "the gutless wonder from Cincinnati." I didn't mind. He said you get used to it in time. He couldn't go out himself. There was too much wind and rain. I got up and looked out of the window, and the rain was pouring down and dead sparrows and limbs of trees were scattered all over the yard. There had been a cyclone all right. It swept a path right through the county, and we were lucky we didn't get the full force of it.

It blew for three days steady, and put the town in a hell of a shape. The wind blew sparks and set fire to the white-and-green-rimmed house on Jackson Avenue that had the big concrete lions in the yard and burned it down to the ground. They had to kill another nigger who tried to run out of the county after they burned this Bacote nigger. My Uncle Ed said they always have to kill niggers in pairs to keep the other niggers in place. I don't know though, the folks seem a little skittish of the niggers. They all came back, but they act pretty sullen. They look mean as hell when you pass them down at the store. The other day I was down to Brinkley's store, and a white cropper said it didn't do no good to kill the niggers 'cause things don't get no better. He looked hungry as hell. Most of the croppers look hungry. You'd be surprised how hungry white folks can look. Somebody said that he'd better shut his damn mouth, and he shut up. But from the look on his face he won't stay shut long. He went out of the store muttering to himself and spit a big chew of tobacco right down on Brinkley's floor. Brinkley said he was sore 'cause he wouldn't let him have credit. Anyway, it didn't seem to help things. First it was the nigger and the storm, then the plane, then the woman and the wires, and now I hear the airplane line is investigating to find who set the fire that almost wrecked their plane. All that in one night, and all of it but the storm over one nigger. It was some night all right. It was some party too. I was right there, see. I was right there watching it all. It was my first party and my last. God, but that nigger was tough. That Bacote nigger was some nigger!

—*1996*

Shirley Jackson (1919–1965) was born in San Francisco and educated at Syracuse University. With her husband, the literary critic Stanley Edgar Hyman, she lived in Bennington, Vermont. There she produced three novels and the popular Life Among the Savages *(1953), a "disrespectful memoir" of her four children, and a sequel to it,* Raising Demons *(1957). "The Lottery," which created a sensation when it appeared in* The New Yorker *in 1948, remains a fascinating example of an allegory whose ultimate meaning is open to debate. Many readers at the time, for obvious reasons, associated it with the Holocaust, although it should not be approached in such a restrictive manner. "The Lottery" is the only one of Jackson's many short stories that has been widely reprinted (it was also dramatized for television), but she was a versatile writer of humorous articles for popular magazines, psychological novels, and a popular gothic horror novel,* The Haunting of Hill House *(1959), which was made into a motion picture called* The Haunting *(1963). Jackson published two collections of short stories,* The Lottery *(1949) and* The Magic of Shirley Jackson *(1966).*

Shirley Jackson
The Lottery

The morning of June 27th was clear and sunny, with the fresh warmth of a full-summer day; the flowers were blossoming profusely and the grass was richly green. The people of the village began to gather in the square, between the post office and the bank, around ten o'clock; in some towns there were so many people that the lottery took two days and had to be started on June 26th, but in this village, where there were only about three hundred people, the whole lottery took less than two hours, so it could begin at ten o'clock in the morning and still be through in time to allow the villagers to get home for noon dinner.

The children assembled first, of course. School was recently over for the summer, and the feeling of liberty sat uneasily on most of them; they tended to gather together quietly for a while before they broke into boisterous play, and their talk was still of the classroom and the teacher, of books and reprimands. Bobby Martin had already stuffed his pockets full of stones, and the other boys soon followed his example, selecting the smoothest and roundest stones; Bobby and Harry Jones and Dickie Delacroix—the villagers pronounced this name "Dellacroy"—eventually made a great pile of stones in one corner of the square and guarded it against the raids of the other boys. The girls stood aside, talking among themselves, looking over their shoulders at the boys, and the very small children rolled in the dust or clung to the hands of their older brothers or sisters.

Soon the men began to gather, surveying their own children, speaking of planting and rain, tractors and taxes. They stood together, away from the pile of stones in the corner, and their jokes were quiet and they smiled rather than laughed. The women, wearing faded house dresses and sweaters, came shortly after their menfolk. They greeted one another and exchanged bits of gossip as they went to join their husbands. Soon the women, standing by their husbands, began to call to their children, and the children came reluctantly, having to be called four or five times. Bobby Martin ducked under his mother's grasping hand and ran, laughing, back to the pile of stones. His father spoke up sharply, and Bobby came quickly and took his place between his father and his oldest brother.

The lottery was conducted—as were the square dances, the teenage club, the Halloween program—by Mr. Summers, who had time and energy to devote to civic activities. He was a roundfaced, jovial man and he ran the coal business, and people were sorry for him, because he had no children and his wife was a scold. When he arrived in the square, carrying the black wooden box, there was a murmur of conversation among the villagers and he waved and called, "Little late today, folks." The postmaster, Mr. Graves, followed him, carrying a three-legged stool, and the stool was put in the center of the square and Mr. Summers set the black box down on it. The villagers kept their distance, leaving a space between themselves and the stool, and when Mr. Summers said, "Some of you fellows want to give me a hand?" there was a hesitation before two men, Mr. Martin and his oldest son, Baxter, came forward to hold the box steady on the stool while Mr. Summers stirred up the papers inside it.

The original paraphernalia for the lottery had been lost long ago, and the black box now resting on the stool had been put into use even before Old Man Warner, the oldest man in town, was born. Mr. Summers spoke frequently to the villagers about making a new box, but no one liked to upset even as much tradition as was represented by the black box. There was a story that the present box had been made with some pieces of the box that had preceded it, the one that had been constructed when the first people settled down to make a village here.

Every year, after the lottery, Mr. Summers began talking again about a new box, but every year the subject was allowed to fade off without anything's being done. The black box grew shabbier each year; by now it was no longer completely black but splintered badly along one side to show the original wood color, and in some places faded or stained.

Mr. Martin and his oldest son, Baxter, held the black box securely on the stool until Mr. Summers had stirred the papers thoroughly with his hand. Because so much of the ritual had been forgotten or discarded, Mr. Summers had been successful in having slips of paper substituted for the chips of wood that had been used for generations. Chips of wood, Mr. Summers had argued, had been all very well when the village was tiny, but now that the population was more than three hundred and likely to keep on growing, it was necessary to use something that would fit more easily into the black box. The night before the lottery, Mr. Summers and Mr. Graves made up the slips of paper and put them in the box, and it was then taken to the safe of Mr. Summers's coal company and locked up until Mr. Summers was ready to take it to the square next morning. The rest of the year, the box was put away, sometimes one place, sometimes another; it had spent one year in Mr. Graves's barn and another year underfoot in the post office, and sometimes it was set on a shelf in the Martin grocery and left there.

There was a great deal of fussing to be done before Mr. Summers declared the lottery open. There were lists to make up—of heads of families, heads of households in each family, members of each household in each family. There was the proper swearing-in of Mr. Summers by the postmaster, as the official of the lottery; at one time, some people remembered, there had been a recital of some sort, performed by the official of the lottery, a perfunctory, tuneless chant that had been rattled off duly each year; some people believed that the official of the lottery used to stand just so when he said or sang it, others believed that he was supposed to walk among the people, but years and years ago this part of the ritual had been allowed to lapse. There had been, also, a ritual salute, which the official of the lottery had had to use in addressing each person who came up to draw from the box, but this also had changed with time, until now it was felt necessary only for the official to speak to each person approaching. Mr. Summers was very good at all this; in his clean white shirt and blue jeans, with one hand resting carelessly on the black box, he seemed very proper and important as he talked interminably to Mr. Graves and the Martins.

Just as Mr. Summers finally left off talking and turned to the assembled villagers, Mrs. Hutchinson came hurriedly along the path to the square, her sweater thrown over her shoulders, and slid into place in the back of the crowd. "Clean forgot what day it was," she said to Mrs. Delacroix, who stood next to her, and they both laughed softly. "Thought my old man was out back stacking wood," Mrs. Hutchinson went on, "and then I looked out the window and the kids were gone, and then I remembered it was the twenty-seventh and came a-running." She dried her hands on her apron, and Mrs. Delacroix said, "You're in time, though. They're still talking away up there."

Mrs. Hutchinson craned her neck to see through the crowd and found her husband and children standing near the front. She tapped Mrs. Delacroix on the arm as a farewell and began to make her way through the crowd. The people separated good-humoredly to let her through; two or three people said, in voices just loud enough to be heard across the crowd, "Here comes your Missus, Hutchinson," and "Bill, she made it after all." Mrs. Hutchinson reached her husband, and Mr. Summers, who had been waiting, said cheerfully, "Thought we were going to have to get on without you, Tessie." Mrs. Hutchinson said, grinning, "Wouldn't have me leave m'dishes in the sink, now would you, Joe?," and soft laughter ran through the crowd as the people stirred back into position after Mrs. Hutchinson's arrival.

"Well, now," Mr. Summers said soberly, "guess we better get started, get this over with, so's we can go back to work. Anybody ain't here?"

"Dunbar," several people said. "Dunbar, Dunbar."

Mr. Summers consulted his list. "Clyde Dunbar," he said. "That's right. He's broke his leg, hasn't he? Who's drawing for him?"

"Me, I guess," a woman said, and Mr. Summers turned to look at her. "Wife draws for her husband," Mr. Summers said. "Don't you have a grown boy to do it for you, Janey?" Although Mr. Summers and everyone else in the village knew the answer perfectly well, it was the business of the official of the lottery to ask such questions formally. Mr. Summers waited with an expression of polite interest while Mrs. Dunbar answered.

"Horace's not but sixteen yet," Mrs. Dunbar said regretfully. "Guess I gotta fill in for the old man this year."

"Right," Mr. Summers said. He made a note on the list he was holding. Then he asked, "Watson boy drawing this year?"

A tall boy in the crowd raised his hand. "Here," he said. "I'm drawing for m'mother and me." He blinked his eyes nervously and ducked his head as several voices in the crowd said things like "Good fellow, Jack," and "Glad to see your mother's got a man to do it."

"Well," Mr. Summers said, "guess that's everyone. Old Man Warner make it?"

"Here," a voice said, and Mr. Summers nodded.

A sudden hush fell on the crowd as Mr. Summers cleared his throat and looked at the list. "All ready?" he called. "Now, I'll read the names—heads of families first—and the men come up and take a paper out of the box. Keep the paper folded in your hand without looking at it until everyone has had a turn. Everything clear?"

The people had done it so many times that they only half listened to the directions; most of them were quiet, wetting their lips, not looking around. Then Mr. Summers raised one hand high and said, "Adams." A man disengaged himself from the crowd and came forward. "Hi, Steve," Mr. Summers said, and Mr. Adams said, "Hi, Joe." They grinned at one another humorlessly and nervously. Then Mr. Adams reached into the black box and took out a folded paper. He held it firmly by one corner as he turned and went hastily back to his place in the crowd, where he stood a little apart from his family, not looking down at his hand.

"Allen," Mr. Summers said. "Anderson . . . Bentham."

"Seems like there's no time at all between lotteries any more," Mrs. Delacroix said to Mrs. Graves in the back row. "Seems like we got through with the last one only last week."

"Time sure goes fast," Mrs. Graves said.

"Clark . . . Delacroix."

"There goes my old man," Mrs. Delacroix said. She held her breath while her husband went forward.

"Dunbar," Mr. Summers said, and Mrs. Dunbar went steadily to the box while one of the women said, "Go on, Janey," and another said, "There she goes."

"We're next," Mrs. Graves said. She watched while Mr. Graves came around from the side of the box, greeted Mr. Summers gravely, and selected a slip of paper from the box. By now, all through the crowd there were men holding the small folded papers in their large hands, turning them over and over nervously. Mrs. Dunbar and her two sons stood to-gether, Mrs. Dunbar holding the slip of paper.

"Harburt . . . Hutchinson."

"Get up there, Bill," Mrs. Hutchinson said, and the people near her laughed.

"Jones."

"They do say," Mr. Adams said to Old Man Warner, who stood next to him, "that over in the north village they're talking of giving up the lottery."

Old Man Warner snorted. "Pack of crazy fools," he said. "Listening to the young folks, nothing's good enough for *them*. Next thing you know, they'll be wanting to go back to living in caves, nobody work any more, live *that* way for a while. Used to be a saying about 'Lottery in June, corn be heavy soon.' First thing you know, we'd all be eating stewed chickweed and acorns. There's *always* been a lottery," he added petulantly. "Bad enough to see young Joe Summers up there joking with everybody."

"Some places have already quit lotteries," Mrs. Adams said.

"Nothing but trouble in *that*," Old Man Warner said stoutly. "Pack of young fools."

"Martin." And Bobby Martin watched his father go forward. "Overdyke . . . Percy."

"I wish they'd hurry," Mrs. Dunbar said to her older son. "I wish they'd hurry."

"They're almost through," her son said.

"You get ready to run tell Dad," Mrs. Dunbar said.

Mr. Summers called his own name and then stepped forward pre-cisely and selected a slip from the box. Then he called, "Warner."

"Seventy-seventh year I been in the lottery," Old Man Warner said as he went through the crowd. "Seventy-seventh time."

"Watson." The tall boy came awkwardly through the crowd. Someone said, "Don't be nervous, Jack," and Mr. Summers said, "Take your time, son."

"Zanini."

After that, there was a long pause, a breathless pause, until Mr. Summers, holding his slip of paper in the air, said, "All right, fellows." For a minute, no one moved, and then all the slips of paper were opened.

Suddenly, all women began to speak at once, saying, "Who is it?" "Who's got it?" "Is it the Dunbars?" "Is it the Watsons?" Then the voices began to say, "It's Hutchinson. It's Bill." "Bill Hutchinson's got it."

"Go tell your father," Mrs. Dunbar said to her older son.

People began to look around to see the Hutchinsons. Bill Hutchinson was standing quiet, staring down at the paper in his hand. Suddenly, Tessie Hutchinson shouted to Mr. Summers, "You didn't give him time enough to take any paper he wanted. I saw you. It wasn't fair!"

"Be a good sport, Tessie," Mrs. Delacroix called, and Mrs. Graves said, "All of us took the same chance."

"Shut up, Tessie," Bill Hutchinson said.

"Well, everyone," Mr. Summers said, "that was done pretty fast, and now we've got to be hurrying a little more to get done in time." He consulted his next list. "Bill," he said, "you draw for the Hutchinson family. You got any other households in the Hutchinsons?"

"There's Don and Eva," Mrs. Hutchinson yelled. "Make *them* take their chance!"

"Daughters draw with their husbands' families, Tessie," Mr. Summers said gently. "You know that as well as anyone else."

"It wasn't fair," Tessie said.

"I guess not, Joe," Bill Hutchinson said regretfully. "My daughter draws with her husband's family, that's only fair. And I've got no other family except the kids."

"Then, as far as drawing for families is concerned, it's you," Mr. Summers said in explanation, "and as far as drawing for households is concerned, that's you, too. Right?"

"Right," Bill Hutchinson said.

"How many kids, Bill?" Mr. Summers asked formally.

"Three," Bill Hutchinson said. "There's Bill, Jr., and Nancy, and little Dave. And Tessie and me."

"All right, then," Mr. Summers said. "Harry, you got their tickets back?"

Mr. Graves nodded and held up the slips of paper. "Put them in the box, then," Mr. Summers directed. "Take Bill's and put it in."

"I think we ought to start over," Mrs. Hutchinson said, as quietly as she could. "I tell you it wasn't *fair*. You didn't give him time enough to choose. *Every*body saw that."

Mr. Graves had selected the five slips and put them in the box, and he dropped all the papers but those onto the ground, where the breeze caught them and lifted them off.

"Listen, everybody," Mrs. Hutchinson was saying to the people around her.

"Ready, Bill?" Mr. Summers asked, and Bill Hutchinson, with one quick glance around at his wife and children, nodded.

"Remember," Mr. Summers said, "take the slips and keep them folded until each person has taken one. Harry, you help little Dave." Mr. Graves took the hand of the little boy, who came willingly with him up to the box. "Take a paper out of the box, Davy," Mr. Summers said. Davy put his hand into the box and laughed. "Take just *one* paper," Mr. Summers said. "Harry, you hold it for him." Mr. Graves took the child's hand and removed the folded paper from the tight fist and held it while little Dave stood next to him and looked up at him wonderingly.

"Nancy next," Mr. Summers said. Nancy was twelve, and her school friends breathed heavily as she went forward, switching her skirt, and took a slip daintily from the box. "Bill, Jr.," Mr. Summers said, and Billy, his face red and his feet overlarge, nearly knocked the box over as he got a paper out. "Tessie," Mr. Summers said. She hesitated for a minute, looking around defiantly, and then set her lips and went up to the box. She snatched a paper out and held it behind her.

"Bill," Mr. Summers said, and Bill Hutchinson reached into the box and felt around, bringing his hand out at last with the slip of paper in it.

The crowd was quiet. A girl whispered, "I hope it's not Nancy," and the sound of the whisper reached the edges of the crowd.

"It's not the way it used to be," Old Man Warner said clearly. "People ain't the way they used to be."

"All right," Mr. Summers said. "Open the papers. Harry, you open little Dave's."

Mr. Graves opened the slip of paper and there was a general sigh through the crowd as he held it up and everyone could see that it was blank. Nancy and Bill, Jr., opened theirs at the same time, and both beamed and laughed, turning around to the crowd and holding their slips of paper above their heads.

"Tessie," Mr. Summers said. There was a pause, and then Mr. Summers looked at Bill Hutchinson, and Bill unfolded his paper and showed it. It was blank.

"It's Tessie," Mr. Summers said, and his voice was hushed. "Show us her paper, Bill."

Bill Hutchinson went over to his wife and forced the slip of paper out of her hand. It had a black spot on it, the black spot Mr. Summers had made the night before with the heavy pencil in the coal-company office. Bill Hutchinson held it up, and there was a stir in the crowd.

"All right, folks," Mr. Summers said, "let's finish quickly."

Although the villagers had forgotten the ritual and lost the original black box, they still remembered to use stones. The pile of stones the boys had made earlier was ready; there were stones on the ground with the blowing scraps of paper that had come out of the box. Mrs. Delacroix selected a stone so large she had to pick it up with both hands and turned to Mrs. Dunbar. "Come on," she said. "Hurry up."

Mrs. Dunbar had small stones in both hands, and she said, gasping for breath, "I can't run at all. You'll have to go ahead and I'll catch up with you."

The children had stones already, and someone gave little Davy Hutchinson a few pebbles.

Tessie Hutchinson was in the center of a cleared space by now, and she held her hands out desperately as the villagers moved in on her. "It isn't fair," she said. A stone hit her on the side of the head.

Old Man Warner was saying, "Come on, come on, everyone." Steve Adams was in the front of the crowd of villagers, with Mrs. Graves beside him.

"It isn't fair, it isn't right," Mrs. Hutchinson screamed, and then they were upon her.

—1948

Flannery O'Connor (1925–1964) was one of the first of many important writers to emerge from the Writers' Workshop of the University of Iowa, where she received an M.F.A. in creative writing. Born in Savannah, Georgia, she attended Georgia State College for Women, graduating in 1945. Plagued by disseminated lupus, the same incurable illness that killed her father in 1941, O'Connor spent most of the last decade of her life living with her mother on a dairy farm near Milledgeville, Georgia, where she wrote and raised peacocks. Unusual among modern American writers in the seriousness of her Christianity (she was a devout Roman Catholic in the largely Protestant South), O'Connor focuses an uncompromising moral eye on the violence and spiritual disorder of the modern world. She is sometimes called a "southern gothic" writer because of her fascination with the grotesque, although today she seems far ahead of her time in depicting a region in which the social and religious certainties of the past are becoming extinct almost overnight. O'Connor's published work includes two short novels, Wise Blood *(1952) and* The Violent Bear It Away *(1960), and two collections of short stories,* A Good Man Is Hard To Find *(1955) and* Everything That Rises Must Converge, *published posthumously in 1965. A collection of essays and miscellaneous prose,* Mystery and Manners *(1961), and her selected letters,* The Habit of Being *(1979), reveal an engaging social side of her personality that is not always apparent in her fiction.*

Flannery O'Connor
A Good Man Is Hard to Find

The grandmother didn't want to go to Florida. She wanted to visit some of her connections in east Tennessee and she was seizing at every chance to change Bailey's mind. Bailey was the son she lived with, her only boy. He was sitting on the edge of his chair at the table, bent over the orange sports section of the *Journal.* "Now look here, Bailey," she said, "see here, read this," and she stood with one hand on her thin hip and the other rattling the newspaper at his bald head. "Here this fellow that calls himself The Misfit is aloose from the Federal Pen and headed toward Florida and you read here what it says he did to these people. Just you read it. I wouldn't take my children in any direction with a criminal like that aloose in it. I couldn't answer to my conscience if I did."

Bailey didn't look up from his reading so she wheeled around then and faced the children's mother, a young woman in slacks, whose face was as broad and innocent as a cabbage and was tied around with a green head-kerchief that had two points on the top like rabbit's ears. She was sitting on the sofa, feeding the baby his apricots out of a jar. "The children have been to Florida before," the old lady said. "You all ought to take them somewhere else for a change so they would see different parts of the world and be broad. They never have been to east Tennessee."

The children's mother didn't seem to hear her but the eight-year-old boy, John Wesley, a stocky child with glasses, said, "If you don't want to go to Florida, why dontcha stay at home?" He and the little girl, June Star, were reading the funny papers on the floor.

"She wouldn't stay at home to be queen for a day," June Star said without raising her yellow head.

"Yes and what would you do if this fellow, The Misfit, caught you?" the grandmother said.

"I'd smack his face," John Wesley said.

"She wouldn't stay at home for a million bucks," June Star said. "Afraid she'd miss something. She has to go everywhere we go."

"All right, Miss," the grandmother said. "Just remember that the next time you want me to curl your hair."

June Star said her hair was naturally curly.

The next morning the grandmother was the first one in the car, ready to go. She had her big black valise that looked like the head of a hippopotamus in one corner, and underneath it she was hiding a basket with Pitty Sing, the cat, in it. She didn't intend for the cat to be left alone in the house for three days because he would miss her too much and she was afraid he might brush against one of the gas burners and accidentally asphyxiate himself. Her son, Bailey, didn't like to arrive at a motel with a cat.

She sat in the middle of the back seat with John Wesley and June Star on either side of her. Bailey and the children's mother and the baby sat in front and they left Atlanta at eight forty-five with the mileage on the car at 55890. The grandmother wrote this down because she thought it would be interesting to say how many miles they had been when they got back. It took them twenty minutes to reach the outskirts of the city.

The old lady settled herself comfortably, removing her white cotton gloves and putting them up with her purse on the shelf in front of the back window. The children's mother still had on slacks and still had her hair tied up in a green kerchief, but the grandmother had on a navy blue straw sailor hat with a bunch of white violets on the brim and a navy blue dress with a small white dot in the print. Her collars and cuffs were white organdy trimmed with lace and at her neckline she had pinned a purple spray of cloth violets containing a sachet. In case of an accident, anyone seeing her dead on the highway would know at once that she was a lady.

She said she thought it was going to be a good day for driving, neither too hot nor too cold, and she cautioned Bailey that the speed limit was fifty-five miles an hour and that the patrolmen hid themselves behind billboards and small clumps of trees and sped out after you before you had a chance to slow down. She pointed out interesting details of the scenery: Stone Mountain; the blue granite that in some places came up to both sides of the highway; the brilliant red clay banks slightly streaked with purple; and the various crops that made rows of green lace-work on the ground. The trees were full of silver-white sunlight and the meanest of them sparkled. The children were reading comic magazines and their mother had gone back to sleep.

"Let's go through Georgia fast so we won't have to look at it much," John Wesley said.

"If I were a little boy," said the grandmother, "I wouldn't talk about my native state that way. Tennessee has the mountains and Georgia has the hills."

"Tennessee is just a hillbilly dumping ground," John Wesley said, "and Georgia is a lousy state too."

"You said it," June Star said.

"In my time," said the grandmother, folding her thin veined fingers, "children were more respectful of their native states and their parents and everything else. People did right then. Oh look at the cute little pickaninny!" she said and pointed to a Negro child standing in the door of a shack. "Wouldn't that make a picture, now?" she asked and they all turned and looked at the little Negro out of the back window. He waved.

"He didn't have any britches on," June Star said.

"He probably didn't have any," the grandmother explained. "Little niggers in the country don't have things like we do. If I could paint, I'd paint that picture," she said.

The children exchanged comic books.

The grandmother offered to hold the baby and the children's mother passed him over the front seat to her. She set him on her knee and bounced him and told him about the things they were passing. She rolled her eyes and screwed up her mouth and stuck her leathery thin face into his smooth bland one. Occasionally he gave her a faraway smile. They passed a large cotton field with five or six graves fenced in the middle of it, like a small island. "Look at the graveyard!" the grandmother said, pointing it out. "That was the old family burying ground. That belonged to the plantation."

"Where's the plantation?" John Wesley asked.

"Gone With the Wind," said the grandmother. "Ha. Ha."

When the children finished all the comic books they had brought, they opened the lunch and ate it. The grandmother ate a peanut butter sandwich and an olive and would not let the children throw the box and the paper napkins out the window. When there was nothing else to do they played a game by choosing a cloud and making the other two guess what shape it suggested. John Wesley took one the shape of a cow and June Star guessed a cow and John Wesley said, no, an automobile, and June Star said he didn't play fair, and they began to slap each other over the grandmother.

The grandmother said she would tell them a story if they would keep quiet. When she told a story, she rolled her eyes and waved her head and was very dramatic. She said once when she was a maiden lady she had been courted by a Mr. Edgar Atkins Teagarden from Jasper, Georgia. She said he was a very good-looking man and a gentleman and that he brought her a watermelon every Saturday afternoon with his initials cut in it, E. A. T. Well, one Saturday, she said, Mr. Teagarden brought the watermelon and there was nobody at home and he left it on the front porch and returned in his buggy to Jasper, but she never got the watermelon, she said, because a nigger boy ate it when he saw the initials, E. A. T.!

This story tickled John Wesley's funny bone and he giggled and giggled but June Star didn't think it was any good. She said she wouldn't marry a man that just brought her a watermelon on Saturday. The grandmother said she would have done well to marry Mr. Teagarden because he was a gentleman and had bought Coca-Cola stock when it first came out and that he had died only a few years ago, a very wealthy man.

They stopped at The Tower for barbecued sandwiches. The Tower was a part stucco and part wood filling station and dance hall set in a clearing outside of Timothy. A fat man named Red Sammy Butts ran it and there were signs stuck here and there on the building and for miles up and down the highway saying, TRY RED SAMMY'S FAMOUS BARBEQUE. NONE LIKE FAMOUS RED SAMMY'S! RED SAM! THE FAT BOY WITH THE HAPPY LAUGH. A VETERAN! RED SAMMY'S YOUR MAN!

Red Sammy was lying on the bare ground outside The Tower with his head under a truck while a gray monkey about a foot high, chained to a small chinaberry tree, chattered nearby. The monkey sprang back into the tree and got on the highest limb as soon as he saw the children jump out of the car and run toward him.

Inside, The Tower was a long dark room with a counter at one end and tables at the other and dancing space in the middle. They all sat down at a board table next to the nickelodeon and Red Sam's wife, a tall burnt-brown woman with hair and eyes lighter than her skin, came and took their order. The children's mother put a dime in the machine and played "The Tennessee Waltz," and the grandmother said that tune always made her want to dance. She asked Bailey if he would like to dance but he only glared at her. He didn't have a naturally sunny disposition like she did and trips made him nervous. The grandmother's brown eyes were very bright. She swayed her head from side to side and pretended she was dancing in her chair. June Star said play something she could tap to so the children's mother put in another dime and played a fast number and June Star stepped out onto the dance floor and did her tap routine.

"Ain't she cute?" Red Sam's wife said, leaning over the counter. "Would you like to come be my little girl?"

"No I certainly wouldn't," June Star said. "I wouldn't live in a broken-down place like this for a million bucks!" and she ran back to the table.

"Ain't she cute?" the woman repeated, stretching her mouth politely.

"Ain't you ashamed?" hissed the grandmother.

Red Sam came in and told his wife to quit lounging on the counter and hurry up with these people's order. His khaki trousers reached just to his hip bones and his stomach hung over them like a sack of meal swaying under his shirt. He came over and sat down at a table nearby and let out a combination sigh and yodel. "You can't win," he said. "You can't win," and he wiped his sweating red face off with a gray handkerchief. "These days you don't know who to trust," he said. "Ain't that the truth?"

"People are certainly not nice like they used to be," said the grandmother.

"Two fellers come in here last week," Red Sammy said, "driving a Chrysler. It was a old beat-up car but it was a good one and these boys looked all right to me. Said they worked at the mill and you know I let them fellers charge the gas they bought? Now why did I do that?"

"Because you're a good man!" the grandmother said at once.

"Yes'm, I suppose so," Red Sam said as if he were struck with this answer.

His wife brought the orders, carrying the five plates all at once without a tray, two in each hand and one balanced on her arm. "It isn't a soul in this green world of God's that you can trust," she said. "And I don't count nobody out of that, not nobody," she repeated, looking at Red Sammy.

"Did you read about that criminal, The Misfit, that's escaped?" asked the grandmother.

"I wouldn't be a bit surprised if he didn't attact this place right here," said the woman. "If he hears about it being here, I wouldn't be none surprised to see him. If he hears it's two cent in the cash register, I wouldn't be a-tall surprised if he . . ."

"That'll do," Red Sam said. "Go bring these people their Co'-Colas," and the woman went off to get the rest of the order.

"A good man is hard to find," Red Sammy said. "Everything is getting terrible. I remember the day you could go off and leave your screen door unlatched. Not no more."

He and the grandmother discussed better times. The old lady said that in her opinion Europe was entirely to blame for the way things were now. She said the way Europe acted you would think we were made of money and Red Sam said it was no use talking about it, she was exactly right. The children ran outside into the white sunlight and looked at the monkey in the lacy chi-naberry tree. He was busy catching fleas on himself and biting each one carefully between his teeth as if it were a delicacy.

They drove off again into the hot afternoon. The grandmother took cat naps and woke up every five minutes with her own snoring. Outside of Toombsboro she woke up and recalled an old plantation that she had visited in this neighborhood once when she was a young lady. She said the house had six white columns across the front and that there was an

avenue of oaks leading up to it and two little wooden trellis arbors on either side in front where you sat down with your suitor after a stroll in
the garden. She recalled exactly which road to turn off to get to it. She
knew that Bailey would not be willing to lose any time looking at an old
house, but the more she talked about it, the more she wanted to see it
once again and find out if the little twin arbors were still standing.
"There was a secret panel in this house," she said craftily, not telling the
truth but wishing that she were, "and the story went that all the family
silver was hidden in it when Sherman[1] came through but it was never
found . . ."

"Hey!" John Wesley said. "Let's go see it! We'll find it! We'll poke
all the woodwork and find it! Who lives there? Where do you turn off
at? Hey, Pop, can't we turn off there?"

"We never have seen a house with a secret panel!" June Star
shrieked. "Let's go to the house with the secret panel! Hey Pop, can't we
go see the house with the secret panel!"

"It's not far from here, I know," the grandmother said. "It wouldn't
take over twenty minutes."

Bailey was looking straight ahead. His jaw was as rigid as a horseshoe. "No," he said.

The children began to yell and scream that they wanted to see the
house with the secret panel. John Wesley kicked the back of the front
seat and June Star hung over her mother's shoulder and whined desperately into her ear that they never had any fun even on their vacation,
that they could never do what THEY wanted to do. The baby began to
scream and John Wesley kicked the back of the seat so hard that his father could feel the blows in his kidney.

"All right!" he shouted and drew the car to a stop at the side of the
road. "Will you all shut up? Will you all just shut up for one second? If
you don't shut up, we won't go anywhere."

"It would be very educational for them," the grandmother murmured.

"All right," Bailey said, "but get this: this is the only time we're going to stop for anything like this. This is the one and only time."

"The dirt road that you have to turn down is about a mile back," the
grandmother directed. "I marked it when we passed."

---

[1]*Sherman:* General William Tecumseh Sherman, whose Union troops burned Atlanta in 1864, then
marched across Georgia to the sea.

"A dirt road," Bailey groaned.

After they had turned around and were headed toward the dirt road, the grandmother recalled other points about the house, the beautiful glass over the front doorway and the candle-lamp in the hall. John Wesley said that the secret panel was probably in the fireplace.

"You can't go inside this house," Bailey said. "You don't know who lives there."

"While you all talk to the people in front, I'll run around behind and get in a window," John Wesley suggested.

"We'll all stay in the car," his mother said.

They turned onto the dirt road and the car raced roughly along in a swirl of pink dust. The grandmother recalled the times when there were no paved roads and thirty miles was a day's journey. The dirt road was hilly and there were sudden washes in it and sharp curves on dangerous embankments. All at once they would be on a hill, looking down over the blue tops of trees for miles around, then the next minute, they would be in a red depression with the dust-coated trees looking down on them.

"This place had better turn up in a minute," Bailey said, "or I'm going to turn around."

The road looked as if no one had traveled on it for months.

"It's not much farther," the grandmother said and just as she said it, a horrible thought came to her. The thought was so embarrassing that she turned red in the face and her eyes dilated and her feet jumped up, upsetting her valise in the corner. The instant the valise moved, the newspaper top she had over the basket under it rose with a snarl and Pitty Sing, the cat, sprang onto Bailey's shoulder.

The children were thrown to the floor and their mother, clutching the baby, was thrown out the door onto the ground; the old lady was thrown into the front seat. The car turned over once and landed right-side-up in a gulch off the side of the road. Bailey remained in the driver's seat with the cat—gray-striped with a broad white face and an orange nose—clinging to his neck like a caterpillar.

As soon as the children saw they could move their arms and legs, they scrambled out of the car, shouting, "We've had an ACCIDENT!" The grandmother was curled up under the dashboard, hoping she was injured so that Bailey's wrath would not come down on her all at once. The horrible thought she had had before the accident was that the house she had remembered so vividly was not in Georgia but in Tennessee.

Bailey removed the cat from his neck with both hands and flung it out the window against the side of a pine tree. Then he got out of the car and started looking for the children's mother. She was sitting against the side of the red gutted ditch, holding the screaming baby, but she only had a cut down her face and a broken shoulder. "We've had an ACCIDENT!" the children screamed in a frenzy of delight.

"But nobody's killed," June Star said with disappointment as the grandmother limped out of the car, her hat still pinned to her head but the broken front brim standing up at a jaunty angle and the violet spray hanging off the side. They all sat down in the ditch, except the children, to recover from the shock. They were all shaking.

"Maybe a car will come along," said the children's mother hoarsely.

"I believe I have injured an organ," said the grandmother, pressing her side, but no one answered her. Bailey's teeth were clattering. He had on a yellow sport shirt with bright blue parrots designed in it and his face was as yellow as the shirt. The grandmother decided that she would not mention that the house was in Tennessee.

The road was about ten feet above and they could see only the tops of the trees on the other side of it. Behind the ditch they were sitting in there were more woods, tall and dark and deep. In a few minutes they saw a car some distance away on top of a hill, coming slowly as if the occupants were watching them. The grandmother stood up and waved both her arms dramatically to attract their attention. The car continued to come on slowly, disappeared around a bend and appeared again, moving even slower, on top of the hill they had gone over. It was a big black battered hearse-like automobile. There were three men in it.

It came to a stop just over them and for some minutes, the driver looked down with a steady expressionless gaze to where they were sitting, and didn't speak. Then he turned his head and muttered something to the other two and they got out. One was a fat boy in black trousers and a red sweat shirt with a silver stallion embossed on the front of it. He moved around on the right side of them and stood staring, his mouth partly open in a kind of loose grin. The other had on khaki pants and a blue striped coat and a gray hat pulled down very low, hiding most of his face. He came around slowly on the left side. Neither spoke.

The driver got out of the car and stood by the side of it, looking down at them. He was an older man than the other two. His hair was just beginning to gray and he wore silver-rimmed spectacles that gave him a scholarly look. He had a long creased face and didn't have on any shirt or undershirt. He had on blue jeans that were too tight for him and was holding a black hat and a gun. The two boys also had guns.

"We've had an ACCIDENT!" the children screamed.

The grandmother had the peculiar feeling that the bespectacled man was someone she knew. His face was as familiar to her as if she had known him all her life but she could not recall who he was. He moved away from the car and began to come down the embankment, placing his feet carefully so that he wouldn't slip. He had on tan and white shoes and no socks, and his ankles were red and thin. "Good afternoon," he said. "I see you all had you a little spill."

"We turned over twice!" said the grandmother.

"Oncet," he corrected. "We seen it happen. Try their car and see will it run, Hiram," he said quietly to the boy with the gray hat.

"What you got that gun for?" John Wesley asked. "Whatcha gonna do with that gun?"

"Lady," the man said to the children's mother, "would you mind calling them children to sit down by you? Children make me nervous. I want all you all to sit down right together there where you're at."

"What are you telling US what to do for?" June Star asked.

Behind them the line of woods gaped like a dark open mouth. "Come here," said their mother.

"Look here now," Bailey began suddenly, "we're in a predicament! We're in . . . ."

The grandmother shrieked. She scrambled to her feet and stood staring. "You're The Misfit!" she said. "I recognized you at once!"

"Yes'm," the man said, smiling slightly as if he were pleased in spite of himself to be known, "but it would have been better for all of you, lady, if you hadn't of reckernized me."

Bailey turned his head sharply and said something to his mother that shocked even the children. The old lady began to cry and The Misfit reddened.

"Lady," he said, "don't you get upset. Sometimes a man says things he don't mean. I don't reckon he meant to talk to you thataway."

"You wouldn't shoot a lady, would you?" the grandmother said and removed a clean handkerchief from her cuff and began to slap at her eyes with it.

The Misfit pointed the toe of his shoe into the ground and made a little hole and then covered it up again. "I would hate to have to," he said.

"Listen," the grandmother almost screamed, "I know you're a good man. You don't look a bit like you have common blood. I know you must come from nice people!"

"Yes ma'am," he said, "finest people in the world." When he smiled he showed a row of strong white teeth. "God never made a finer woman than my mother and my daddy's heart was pure gold," he said. The boy with the red sweat shirt had come around behind them and was standing with his gun at his hip. The Misfit squatted down on the ground. "Watch them children, Bobby Lee," he said. "You know they make me nervous." He looked at the six of them huddled together in front of him and he seemed to be embarrassed as if he couldn't think of anything to say. "Ain't a cloud in the sky," he remarked, looking up at it. "Don't see no sun but don't see no cloud neither."

"Yes, it's a beautiful day," said the grandmother. "Listen," she said, "you shouldn't call yourself The Misfit because I know you're a good man at heart. I can just look at you and tell."

"Hush!" Bailey yelled. "Hush! Everybody shut up and let me handle this!" He was squatting in the position of a runner about to sprint forward but he didn't move.

"I pre-chate that, lady," The Misfit said and drew a little circle in the ground with the butt of his gun.

"It'll take a half a hour to fix this here car," Hiram called, looking over the raised hood of it.

"Well, first you and Bobby Lee get him and that little boy to step over yonder with you," The Misfit said, pointing to Bailey and John Wesley. "The boys want to ast you something," he said to Bailey. "Would you mind stepping back in them woods there with them?"

"Listen," Bailey began, "we're in a terrible predicament! Nobody realizes what this is," and his voice cracked. His eyes were as blue and intense as the parrots in his shirt and he remained perfectly still.

The grandmother reached up to adjust her hat brim as if she were going to the woods with him but it came off in her hand. She stood staring at it and after a second she let it fall on the ground. Hiram pulled Bailey up by the arm as if he were assisting an old man. John Wesley caught hold of his father's hand and Bobby Lee followed. They went off toward the woods and just as they reached the dark edge, Bailey turned and supporting himself against a gray naked pine trunk, he shouted, "I'll be back in a minute, Mamma, wait on me!"

"Come back this instant!" his mother shrilled but they all disappeared into the woods.

"Bailey Boy!" the grandmother called in a tragic voice but she found she was looking at The Misfit squatting on the ground in front of her. "I just know you're a good man," she said desperately. "You're not a bit common!"

"Nome, I ain't a good man," The Misfit said after a second as if he had considered her statement carefully, "but I ain't the worst in the world neither. My daddy said I was a different breed of dog from my brothers and sisters. 'You know,' Daddy said, 'it's some that can live their whole life out without asking about it and it's others has to know why it is, and this boy is one of the latters. He's going to be into everything!'" He put on his black hat and looked up suddenly and then away deep into the woods as if he were embarrassed again. "I'm sorry I don't have on a shirt before you ladies," he said, hunching his shoulders slightly. "We buried our clothes that we had on when we escaped and we're just making do until we can get better. We borrowed these from some folks we met," he explained.

"That's perfectly all right," the grandmother said. "Maybe Bailey has an extra shirt in his suitcase."

"I'll look and see terrectly," The Misfit said.

"Where are they taking him?" the children's mother screamed.

"Daddy was a card himself," The Misfit said. "You couldn't put anything over on him. He never got in trouble with the Authorities though. Just had the knack of handling them."

"You could be honest too if you'd only try," said the grandmother. "Think how wonderful it would be to settle down and live a comfortable life and not have to think about somebody chasing you all the time."

The Misfit kept scratching in the ground with the butt of his gun as if he were thinking about it. "Yes'm, somebody is always after you," he murmured.

The grandmother noticed how thin his shoulder blades were just behind his hat because she was standing up looking down on him. "Do you ever pray?" she asked.

He shook his head. All she saw was the black hat wiggle between his shoulder blades. "Nome," he said.

There was a pistol shot from the woods, followed closely by another. Then silence. The old lady's head jerked around. She could hear the wind move through the tree tops like a long satisfied insuck of breath. "Bailey Boy!" she called.

"I was a gospel singer for a while," The Misfit said. "I been most everything. Been in the arm service, both land and sea, at home and abroad, been twict married, been an undertaker, been with the railroads, plowed Mother Earth, been in a tornado, seen a man burnt alive oncet," and he looked up at the children's mother and the little girl who were sitting close together, their faces white and their eyes glassy; "I even seen a woman flogged," he said.

"Pray, pray," the grandmother began, "pray, pray. . ."

"I never was a bad boy that I remember of," The Misfit said in an almost dreamy voice, "but somewheres along the line I done something wrong and got sent to the penitentiary. I was buried alive," and he looked up and held her attention to him by a steady stare.

"That's when you should have started to pray," she said. "What did you do to get sent to the penitentiary that first time?"

"Turn to the right, it was a wall," The Misfit said, looking up again at the cloudless sky. "Turn to the left, it was a wall. Look up it was a ceiling, look down it was a floor. I forget what I done, lady. I set there and set there, trying to remember what it was I done and I ain't recalled it to this day. Oncet in a while, I would think it was coming to me, but it never come."

"Maybe they put you in by mistake," the old lady said vaguely.

"Nome," he said. "It wasn't no mistake. They had the papers on me."

"You must have stolen something," she said.

The Misfit sneered slightly. "Nobody had nothing I wanted," he said. "It was a head-doctor at the penitentiary said what I had done was kill my daddy but I known that for a lie. My daddy died in nineteen ought nineteen of the epidemic flu and I never had a thing to do with it. He was buried in the Mount Hopewell Baptist churchyard and you can go there and see for yourself."

"If you would pray," the old lady said, "Jesus would help you."

"That's right," The Misfit said.

"Well then, why don't you pray?" she asked trembling with delight suddenly.

"I don't want no hep," he said. "I'm doing all right by myself."

Bobby Lee and Hiram came ambling back from the woods. Bobby Lee was dragging a yellow shirt with bright blue parrots in it.

"Thow me that shirt, Bobby Lee," The Misfit said. The shirt came flying at him and landed on his shoulder and he put it on. The grandmother couldn't name what the shirt reminded her of. "No, lady," The Misfit said while he was buttoning it up, "I found out the crime don't matter. You can do one thing or you can do another, kill a man or take a tire off his car, because sooner or later you're going to forget what it was you done and just be punished for it."

The children's mother had begun to make heaving noises as if she couldn't get her breath. "Lady," he asked, "would you and that little girl like to step off yonder with Bobby Lee and Hiram and join your husband?"

"Yes, thank you," the mother said faintly. Her left arm dangled helplessly and she was holding the baby, who had gone to sleep, in the other. "Hep that lady up, Hiram," The Misfit said as she struggled to climb out of the ditch, "and Bobby Lee, you hold onto that little girl's hand."

"I don't want to hold hands with him," June Star said. "He reminds me of a pig."

The fat boy blushed and laughed and caught her by the arm and pulled her off into the woods after Hiram and her mother.

Alone with The Misfit, the grandmother found that she had lost her voice. There was not a cloud in the sky nor any sun. There was nothing around her but woods. She wanted to tell him that he must pray. She opened and closed her mouth several times before anything came out. Finally she found herself saying, "Jesus. Jesus," meaning, Jesus will help you, but the way she was saying it, it sounded as if she might be cursing.

"Yes'm," The Misfit said as if he agreed. "Jesus thown everything off balance. It was the same case with Him as with me except He hadn't committed any crime and they could prove I had committed one because they had the papers on me. Of course," he said, "they never shown me my papers. That's why I sign myself now. I said long ago, you get you a signature and sign everything you do and keep a copy of it. Then you'll know what you done and you can hold up the crime to the punishment and see do they match and in the end you'll have something to prove you ain't been treated right. I call myself The Misfit," he said, "because I can't make what all I done wrong fit what all I gone through in punishment."

There was a piercing scream from the woods, followed closely by a pistol report. "Does it seem right to you, lady, that one is punished a heap and another ain't punished at all?"

"Jesus!" the old lady cried. "You've got good blood! I know you wouldn't shoot a lady! I know you come from nice people! Pray! Jesus, you ought not to shoot a lady. I'll give you all the money I've got!"

"Lady," The Misfit said, looking beyond her far into the woods, "there never was a body that give the undertaker a tip."

There were two more pistol reports and the grandmother raised her head like a parched old turkey hen crying for water and called, "Bailey Boy, Bailey Boy!" as if her heart would break.

"Jesus was the only One that ever raised the dead," The Misfit continued, "and He shouldn't have done it. He thown everything off balance. If He did what He said, then it's nothing for you to do but thow away everything and follow Him, and if He didn't, then it's nothing for you to do but enjoy the few minutes you got left the best way you can—by killing somebody or burning down his house or doing some other meanness to him. No pleasure but meanness," he said and his voice had become almost a snarl.

"Maybe He didn't raise the dead," the old lady mumbled, not knowing what she was saying and feeling so dizzy that she sank down in the ditch with her legs twisted under her.

"I wasn't there so I can't say He didn't," The Misfit said. "I wisht I had of been there," he said, hitting the ground with his fist. "It ain't right I wasn't there because if I had of been there I would of known. Listen lady," he said in a high voice, "if I had of been there I would of known and I wouldn't be like I am now." His voice seemed about to crack and the grandmother's head cleared for an instant. She saw the man's face twisted close to her own as if he were going to cry and she murmured, "Why you're one of my babies. You're one of my own children!" She reached out and touched him on the shoulder. The Misfit sprang back as if a snake had bitten him and shot her three times through the chest. Then he put his gun down on the ground and took off his glasses and began to clean them.

Hiram and Bobby Lee returned from the woods and stood over the ditch, looking down at the grandmother who half sat and half lay in a puddle of blood with her legs crossed under her like a child's and her face smiling up at the cloudless sky.

Without his glasses, The Misfit's eyes were red-rimmed and pale and defenseless-looking. "Take her off and thow her where you thown the others," he said, picking up the cat that was rubbing itself against his leg.

"She was a talker, wasn't she?" Bobby Lee said, sliding down the ditch with a yodel.

"She would of been a good woman," The Misfit said, "if it had been somebody there to shoot her every minute of her life."

"Some fun!" Bobby Lee said.

"Shut up, Bobby Lee," The Misfit said. "It's no real pleasure in life."

—1955

Gabriel García Márquez (b. 1928) is the author of a brilliant serio-comic historical novel, One Hundred Years of Solitude *(1967). It is one of the landmarks of contemporary fiction, and rapidly became an international bestseller. "Magic realism" is the term that is often used to describe the author's unique blend of folklore, historical fact, naturalism, and fantasy, much of it occurring in the fictional village of Macondo. A native of Colombia, García Márquez, the eldest of twelve children, was born in Aracéataca, a small town that is the model for the isolated, decaying settlements found in his fiction. García Márquez was trained as a journalist, first coming to public attention in 1955 with his investigative reporting about the government cover-up that followed the sinking of a Colombian navy vessel. After residence in Paris during the late 1950s, he worked for a time as a correspondent for Fidel Castro's official news agency. He has also lived in Mexico and Spain. Other works include the short story collections* No One Writes to the Colonel *(1968),* Leaf Storm and Other Stories *(1972), and* Innocent Eréndira and Other Stories *(1978). His novel* Love in the Time of Cholera *was a major success in 1988. He was awarded the Nobel Prize in 1982. In recent years García Márquez has focused on nonfiction.* News of a Kidnapping *(1997) tells the true story of how Colombian drug kingpins took ten citizens hostage to extort favors from their government.*

Gabriel García Márquez

A Very Old Man with Enormous Wings

On the third day of rain they had killed so many crabs inside the house that Pelayo had to cross his drenched courtyard and throw them into the sea, because the newborn child had a temperature all night and they thought it was due to the stench. The world had been sad since Tuesday. Sea and sky were a single ash-gray thing and the sands of the beach, which on March nights glimmered like powdered light, had become a stew of mud and rotten shellfish. The light was so weak at noon that when Pelayo was coming back to the house after throwing away the crabs, it was hard for him to see what it was that was moving and groaning in the rear of the courtyard. He had to go very close to see that it was an old man, a very old man, lying face down in the mud, who, in spite of his tremendous efforts, couldn't get up, impeded by his enormous wings.

Translated by Gregory Rabassa.

Frightened by that nightmare, Pelayo ran to get Elisenda, his wife, who was putting compresses on the sick child, and he took her to the rear of the courtyard. They both looked at the fallen body with mute stupor. He was dressed like a ragpicker. There were only a few faded hairs left on his bald skull and very few teeth in his mouth, and his pitiful condition of a drenched great-grandfather had taken away any sense of grandeur he might have had. His huge buzzard wings, dirty and half-plucked, were forever entangled in the mud. They looked at him so long and so closely that Pelayo and Elisenda very soon overcame their surprise and in the end found him familiar. Then they dared speak to him, and he answered in an incomprehensible dialect with a strong sailor's voice. That was how they skipped over the inconvenience of the wings and quite intelligently concluded that he was a lonely castaway from some foreign ship wrecked by the storm. And yet, they called in a neighbor woman who knew everything about life and death to see him, and all she needed was one look to show them their mistake.

"He's an angel," she told them. "He must have been coming for the child, but the poor fellow is so old that the rain knocked him down."

On the following day everyone knew that a flesh-and-blood angel was held captive in Pelayo's house. Against the judgment of the wise neighbor woman, for whom angels in those times were the fugitive survivors of a celestial conspiracy, they did not have the heart to club him to death. Pelayo watched over him all afternoon from the kitchen, armed with his bailiff's club, and before going to bed he dragged him out of the mud and locked him up with the hens in the wire chicken coop. In the middle of the night, when the rain stopped, Pelayo and Elisenda were still killing crabs. A short time afterward the child woke up without a fever and with a desire to eat. Then they felt magnanimous and decided to put the angel on a raft with fresh water and provisions for three days and leave him to his fate on the high seas. But when they went out into the courtyard with the first light of dawn, they found the whole neighborhood in front of the chicken coop having fun with the angel, without the slightest reverence, tossing him things to eat through the openings in the wire as if he weren't a supernatural creature but a circus animal.

Father Gonzaga arrived before seven o'clock, alarmed at the strange news. By that time onlookers less frivolous than those at dawn had already arrived and they were making all kinds of conjectures concerning the captive's future. The simplest among them thought that he should be named mayor of the world. Others of sterner mind felt that he should be promoted to the rank of five-star general in order to win all wars. Some visionaries hoped that he could be put to stud in order to implant on earth a race of winged wise men who could take charge of the universe. But Father Gonzaga, before becoming a priest, had been a robust woodcutter. Standing by the wire, he reviewed his catechism in an instant and asked them to open the door so that he could take a close look at that pitiful man who looked more like a huge decrepit hen among the fascinated chickens. He was lying in a corner drying his open wings in the sunlight among the fruit peels and breakfast leftovers that the early risers had thrown him. Alien to the impertinences of the world, he only lifted his antiquarian eyes and murmured something in his dialect when Father Gonzaga went into the chicken coop and said good morning to him in Latin. The parish priest had his first suspicion of an impostor when he saw that he did not understand the language of God or know how to greet His ministers. Then he noticed that seen close up he was much too human: he had an unbearable smell of the outdoors, the back side of his wings was strewn with parasites and his main feathers had been mistreated by terrestrial winds, and nothing about him measured up to the proud dignity of angels. Then he came out of the chicken coop and in a brief sermon warned the curious against the risks of being ingenuous. He reminded them that the devil had the bad habit of making use of carnival tricks in order to confuse the unwary. He argued that if wings were not the essential element in determining the difference between a hawk and an airplane, they were even less so in the recognition of angels. Nevertheless, he promised to write a letter to his bishop so that the latter would write to his primate so that the latter would write to the Supreme Pontiff in order to get the final verdict from the highest courts.

His prudence fell on sterile hearts. The news of the captive angel spread with such rapidity that after a few hours the courtyard had the bustle of a marketplace and they had to call in troops with fixed bayonets to disperse the mob that was about to knock the house down. Elisenda, her spine all twisted from sweeping up so much marketplace trash, then got the idea of fencing in the yard and charging five cents admission to see the angel.

The curious came from far away. A traveling carnival arrived with a flying acrobat who buzzed over the crowd several times, but no one paid any attention to him because his wings were not those of an angel but, rather, those of a sidereal[1] bat. The most unfortunate invalids on earth came in search of health: a poor woman who since childhood had been counting her heartbeats and had run out of numbers, a Portuguese man who couldn't sleep because the noise of the stars disturbed him, a sleep-walker who got up at night to undo the things he had done while awake; and many others with less serious ailments. In the midst of that ship-wreck disorder that made the earth tremble, Pelayo and Elisenda were happy with fatigue, for in less than a week they had crammed their rooms with money and the line of pilgrims waiting their turn to enter still reached beyond the horizon.

The angel was the only one who took no part in his own act. He spent his time trying to get comfortable in his borrowed nest, befuddled by the hellish heat of the oil lamps and sacramental candles that had been placed along the wire. At first they tried to make him eat some mothballs, which according to the wisdom of the wise neighbor woman, were the food prescribed for angels. But he turned them down, just as he turned down the papal lunches that the penitents brought him, and they never found out whether it was because he was an angel or because he was an old man that in the end he ate nothing but eggplant mush. His only super-natural virtue seemed to be patience. Especially during the first days, when the hens pecked at him, searching for the stellar parasites that proliferated in his wings, and the cripples pulled out feathers to touch their defective parts with, and even the most merciful threw stones at him, trying to get him to rise so they could see him standing. The only time they succeeded in arousing him was when they burned his side with an iron for branding steers, for he had been mo-tionless for so many hours that they thought he was dead. He awoke with a start, ranting in his hermetic language and with tears in his eyes, and he flapped his wings a couple of times, which brought on a whirl-wind of chicken dung and lunar dust and a gale of panic that did not seem to be of this world. Although many thought that his reaction had been one not of rage but of pain, from then on they were careful not to annoy him, because the majority understood that his passivity was not that of a hero taking his ease but that of a cataclysm in repose.

Father Gonzaga held back the crowd's frivolity with formulas of maidservant inspiration while awaiting the arrival of a final judgment

---

[1]*sidereal:* coming from the stars.

on the nature of the captive. But the mail from Rome showed no sense of urgency. They spent their time finding out if the prisoner had a navel, if his dialect had any connection with Aramaic, how many times he could fit on the head of a pin, or whether he wasn't just a Norwegian with wings. Those meager letters might have come and gone until the end of time if a providential event had not put an end to the priest's tribulations.

It so happened that during those days, among so many other carnival attractions, there arrived in town the traveling show of the woman who had been changed into a spider for having disobeyed her parents. The admission to see her was not only less than the admission to see the angel, but people were permitted to ask her all manner of questions about her absurd state and to examine her up and down so that no one would ever doubt the truth of her honor. She was a frightful tarantula the size of a ram and with the head of a sad maiden. What was most heart-rending, however, was not her outlandish shape but the sincere affliction with which she recounted the details of her misfortune. While still practically a child she had sneaked out of her parents' house to go to a dance, and while she was coming back through the woods after having danced all night without permission, a fearful thunderclap rent the sky in two and through the crack came the lightning bolt of brimstone that changed her into a spider. Her only nourishment came from the meatballs that charitable souls chose to toss into her mouth. A spectacle like that, full of so much human truth and with such a fearful lesson, was found to defeat without even trying that of a haughty angel who scarcely deigned to look at mortals. Besides, the few miracles attributed to the angel showed a certain mental disorder, like the blind man who didn't recover his sight but grew three new teeth, or the paralytic who didn't get to walk, but almost won the lottery, and the leper whose sores sprouted sunflowers. Those consolation miracles, which were more like mocking fun, had already ruined the angel's reputation when the woman who had been changed into a spider finally crushed him completely. That was how Father Gonzaga was cured forever of his insomnia and Pelayo's courtyard went back to being as empty as during the time it had rained for three days and crabs walked through the bedrooms.

The owners of the house had no reason to lament. With the money they saved they built a two-story mansion with balconies and gardens and high netting so that crabs wouldn't get in during the winter, and with iron bars on the windows so that angels wouldn't get in. Pelayo also set up a rabbit warren close to town and gave up his job as bailiff for good, and Elisenda bought some satin pumps with high heels and many dresses of iridescent silk, the kind worn on Sunday by the most desirable women in those times. The chicken coop was the only thing that didn't receive any attention. If they washed it down with creolin and burned tears of myrrh inside it every so often, it was not in homage to the angel but to drive away the dungheap stench that still hung everywhere like a ghost and was turning the new house into an old one. At first, when the child learned to walk, they were careful that he not get too close to the chicken coop. But then they began to lose their fears and got used to the smell, and before the child got his second teeth he'd gone inside the chicken coop to play, where the wires were falling apart. The angel was no less standoffish with him than with other mortals, but he tolerated the most ingenious infamies with the patience of a dog who had no illusions. They both came down with chicken pox at the same time. The doctor who took care of the child couldn't resist the temptation to listen to the angel's heart, and he found so much whistling in the heart and so many sounds in his kidneys that it seemed impossible for him to be alive. What surprised him most, however, was the logic of his wings. They seemed so natural on that completely human organism that he couldn't understand why other men didn't have them too.

When the child began school it had been some time since the sun and rain had caused the collapse of the chicken coop. The angel went dragging himself about here and there like a stray dying man. They would drive him out of the bedroom with a broom and a moment later find him in the kitchen. He seemed to be in so many places at the same time that they grew to think that he'd been duplicated, that he was reproducing himself all through the house, and the exasperated and unhinged Elisenda shouted that it was awful living in that hell full of angels. He could scarcely eat and his antiquarian eyes had also become so foggy that he went about bumping into posts. All he had left were the bare cannulae[2] of his last feathers. Pelayo threw a blanket over him and extended him the charity of letting him sleep in the shed, and only then did they notice that he had a temperature at night, and was delirious with the tongue twisters of an old Norwegian. That was one of the few times they became alarmed, for they thought he was going to die and

[2]*cannulae:* the tubular pieces by which feathers are attached to a body.

not even the wise neighbor woman had been able to tell them what to do with dead angels.

And yet he not only survived his worst winter, but seemed improved with the first sunny days. He remained motionless for several days in the farthest corner of the courtyard, where no one would see him, and at the beginning of December some large, stiff feathers began to grow on his wings, the feathers of a scarecrow, which looked more like another misfortune of decrepitude. But he must have known the reason for those changes, for he was quite careful that no one should notice them, that no one should hear the sea chanteys that he sometimes sang under the stars. One morning Elisenda was cutting some bunches of onions for lunch when a wind that seemed to come from the high seas blew into the kitchen. Then she went to the window and caught the angel in his first attempts at flight. They were so clumsy that his fingernails opened a furrow in the vegetable patch and he was on the point of knocking the shed down with the ungainly flapping that slipped on the light and he couldn't get a grip on the air. But he did manage to gain altitude. Elisenda let out a sigh of relief, for herself and for him, when she saw him pass over the last houses, holding himself up in some way with the risky flapping of a senile vulture. She kept watching him even when she was through cutting the onions and she kept on watching until it was no longer possible for her to see him, because then he was no longer an annoyance in her life but an imaginary dot on the horizon of the sea.

—*1968*

Chinua Achebe (b. 1930) was born in Ogidi, Nigeria, and, after graduation from University College in Ibadan and study at London University, was employed by the Nigerian Broadcasting Service, where he served for years as a producer. After the appearance of his first novel, Things Fall Apart, *in 1958 (the title is taken from William Butler Yeats's apocalyptic poem "The Second Coming") he became one of the most widely acclaimed writers to emerge from the former British colonies of Africa. The author of several novels as well as a collection of short stories, Achebe has taught in the United States at the University of California, Los Angeles, Stanford University, and the University of Massachusetts—Amherst. One of his chief services to contemporary literature was his editorship of the African Writers Series, which sponsored the first publications of many of his fellow Nigerian writers. Achebe draws heavily on the oral traditions of his native country, but he has been successful in adapting European fictional techniques to deal with subjects like the degradations imposed by colonialism and the relative failure of most post-colonial governments to materially improve on the past for the betterment of the lives of their citizens.*

Chinua Achebe

Dead Men's Path

Michael Obi's hopes were fulfilled much earlier than he had expected. He was appointed headmaster of Ndume Central School in January 1949. It had always been an unprogressive school, so the Mission authorities decided to send a young and energetic man to run it. Obi accepted this responsibility with enthusiasm. He had many wonderful ideas and this was an opportunity to put them into practice. He had had sound secondary school education which designated him a "pivotal teacher" in the official records and set him apart from the other headmasters in the mission field. He was outspoken in his condemnation of the narrow views of these older and often less-educated ones.

"We shall make a good job of it, shan't we?" he asked his young wife when they first heard the joyful news of his promotion.

"We shall do our best," she replied. "We shall have such beautiful gardens and everything will be just *modern* and delightful. . . ." In their two years of married life she had become completely infected by his passion for "modern methods" and his denigration of "these old and superannuated people in the teaching field who would be better employed as traders in the Onitsha market." She began to see herself already as the admired wife of the young headmaster, the queen of the school.

The wives of the other teachers would envy her position. She would set the fashion in everything. . . . Then, suddenly, it occurred to her that there might not be other wives. Wavering between hope and fear, she asked her husband, looking anxiously at him.

"All our colleagues are young and unmarried," he said with enthusiasm which for once she did not share. "Which is a good thing," he continued.

"Why?"

"Why? They will give all their time and energy to the school."

Nancy was downcast. For a few minutes she became skeptical about the new school; but it was only for a few minutes. Her little personal misfortune could not blind her to her husband's happy prospects. She looked at him as he sat folded up in a chair. He was stoop-shouldered and looked frail. But he sometimes surprised people with sudden bursts of physical energy. In his present posture, however, all his bodily strength seemed to have retired behind his deep-set eyes, giving them an extraordinary power of penetration. He was only twenty-six, but looked thirty or more. On the whole, he was not unhandsome.

"A penny for your thoughts, Mike," said Nancy after a while, imitating the woman's magazine she read.

"I was thinking what a grand opportunity we've got at last to show these people how a school should be run."

Ndume School was backward in every sense of the word. Mr. Obi put his whole life into the work, and his wife hers too. He had two aims. A high standard of teaching was insisted upon, and the school compound was to be turned into a place of beauty. Nancy's dream-gardens came to life with the coming of the rains, and blossomed. Beautiful hibiscus and allamanda hedges in brilliant red and yellow marked out the carefully tended school compound from the rank neighborhood bushes.

One evening as Obi was admiring his work he was scandalized to see an old woman from the village hobble right across the compound, through a marigold flower-bed and the hedges. On going up there he found faint signs of an almost disused path from the village across the school compound to the bush on the other side.

"It amazes me," said Obi to one of his teachers who had been three years in the school, "that you people allowed the villagers to make use of this footpath. It is simply incredible." He shook his head.

"The path," said the teacher apologetically, "appears to be very important to them. Although it is hardly used, it connects the village shrine with their place of burial."

"And what has that got to do with the school?" asked the headmaster.

"Well, I don't know," replied the other with a shrug of the shoulders. "But I remember there was a big row some time ago when we attempted to close it."

"That was some time ago. But it will not be used now," said Obi as he walked away. "What will the Government Education Officer think of this when he comes to inspect the school next week? The villagers might, for all I know, decide to use the schoolroom for a pagan ritual during the inspection."

Heavy sticks were planted closely across the path at the two places where it entered and left the school premises. These were further strengthened with barbed wire.

Three days later the village priest of *Ani* called on the headmaster. He was an old man and walked with a slight stoop. He carried a stout walking-stick which he usually tapped on the floor, by way of emphasis, each time he made a new point in his argument.

"I have heard," he said after the usual exchange of cordialities, "that our ancestral footpath has recently been closed. . . ."

"Yes," replied Mr. Obi. "We cannot allow people to make a highway of our school compound."

"Look here, my son," said the priest bringing down his walking-stick, "this path was here before you were born and before your father was born. The whole life of this village depends on it. Our dead relatives depart by it and our ancestors visit us by it. But most important, it is the path of children coming in to be born. . . ."

Mr. Obi listened with a satisfied smile on his face.

"The whole purpose of our school," he said finally, "is to eradicate just such beliefs as that. Dead men do not require footpaths. The whole idea is just fantastic. Our duty is to teach your children to laugh at such ideas."

"What you say may be true," replied the priest, "but we follow the practices of our fathers. If you reopen the path we shall have nothing to quarrel about. What I always say is: let the hawk perch and let the eagle perch." He rose to go.

"I am sorry," said the young headmaster. "But the school compound cannot be a thoroughfare. It is against our regulations. I would suggest your constructing another path, skirting our premises. We can even get our boys to help in building it. I don't suppose the ancestors will find the little detour too burdensome."

"I have no more words to say," said the old priest, already outside.

Two days later a young woman in the village died in childbed. A diviner was immediately consulted and he prescribed heavy sacrifices to propitiate ancestors insulted by the fence.

Obi woke up next morning among the ruins of his work. The beautiful hedges were torn up not just near the path but right round the school, the flowers trampled to death and one of the school buildings pulled down. . . That day, the white Supervisor came to inspect the school and wrote a nasty report on the state of the premises but more seriously about the "tribal-war situation developing between the school and the village, arising in part from the misguided zeal of the new headmaster."

—1953

Alice Munro (b. 1931) was born on a farm in Wingham, Ontario, and educated at the University of Ontario, where she received her degree in 1952. Her first book, Dance of the Happy Shades, *appeared in 1968, and she has continued regularly to publish collections of short stories. Asked about her devotion to short fiction, Munro told* Contemporary Authors: *"I never intended to be a short story writer — I started writing them because I didn't have time to write anything else — I had three children. And then I got used to writing short stories, so I see my materials that way, and now I don't think I'll ever write a novel." Parent-child relations and the discovery of personal freedom are constant themes in Munro's work, especially in* The Beggar Maid: Stories of Rose and Flo *(1982), a series of stories about a woman and her stepdaughter. Munro has won both the Governor General's Literary Award and the Canadian Booksellers' award, befitting her status as one of her country's most distinguished writers.* Selected Stories *appeared in 1996, and* The Love of a Good Woman *was published in 1998.*

Alice Munro
Vandals

I

"Liza, my dear, I have never written you yet to thank you for going out to our house (poor old Dismal, I guess it really deserves the name now) in the teeth or anyway the aftermath of the storm last February and for letting me know what you found there. Thank your husband, too, for taking you there on his snowmobile, also if as I suspect he was the one to board up the broken window to keep out the savage beasts, etc. Lay not up treasure on earth where moth and dust not to mention teenagers doth corrupt. I hear you are a Christian now, Liza, what a splendid thing to be! Are you born again? I always liked the sound of that!

"Oh, Liza, I know it's boring of me but I still think of you and poor little Kenny as pretty sunburned children slipping out from behind the trees to startle me and leaping and diving in the pond.

"Ladner had not the least premonition of death on the night before his operation—or maybe it was the night before that, whenever I phoned you. It is not very often nowadays that people die during a simple by-pass and also he really did not think about being mortal. He was just worried about things like whether he had turned the water off. He was obsessed more and more by that sort of detail. The one way his age showed. Though I suppose it is not such a detail if you consider the pipes bursting, that would be a calamity. But a calamity occurred anyway. I have been out there just once to look at it and the odd thing was it just looked natural to me. On top of Ladner's death, it seemed almost the right way for things to be. What would seem unnatural would be to get to work and clean it up, though I suppose I shall have to do that, or hire somebody. I am tempted just to light a match and let everything go up in smoke, but I imagine that if I did that I would find myself locked up.

"I wish in a way that I had had Ladner cremated, but I didn't think of it. I just put him here in the Doud plot to surprise my father, and my stepmother. But now I must tell you, the other night I had a dream! I dreamed that I was around behind the Canadian Tire Store and they had the big plastic tent up as they do when they are selling bedding-plants in the spring. I went and opened up the trunk of my car, just as if I were getting my annual load of salvia or impatiens. Other people were waiting as well and men in green aprons were going back and forth from the tent. A woman said to me, "Seven years sure goes by in a hurry!" She seemed to know me but I didn't know her and I thought, Why is this always happening? Is it because I did a little schoolteaching? Is it because of what you might politely call the conduct of my life?

"Then the significance of the seven years struck me and I knew what I was doing there and what the other people were doing there. They had come for the bones. I had come for Ladner's bones, in the dream it was seven years since he had been buried. But I thought, Isn't this what they do in Greece or somewhere, why are we doing it here? I said to some people, Are the graveyards getting overcrowded? What have we taken up this custom for? Is it pagan or Christian or what? The people I spoke to looked rather sullen and offended and I thought, What have I done now. I've lived around here all my life but I can still get this look—is it the word 'pagan'? Then one of the men handed me a plastic bag and I took it gratefully and held it, thinking of Ladner's strong leg bones and wide shoulder bones and intelligent skull all washed and polished by some bath-and-brush apparatus no doubt concealed in the plastic tent. This seemed to have something to do with my feelings for him and his for me being purified but the idea was more interesting and subtle than that. I was so happy, though, to receive my load and other people were happy too. In fact some of them became quite jolly and were tossing their plastic bags in the air. Some of the bags were bright blue, but most were green, and mine was one of the regular green ones.

"'Oh,' someone said to me. 'Did you get the little girl?'

"I understood what was meant. The little girl's bones. I saw that my bag was really quite small and light, to contain Ladner. I mean, Ladner's bones. What little girl? I thought, but I was already getting confused about everything and had a suspicion that I might be dreaming. It came into my mind, Do they mean the little boy? Just as I woke up I was thinking of Kenny and wondering, Was it seven years since the accident? (I hope it doesn't hurt you, Liza, that I mention this—also I know that Kenny was no longer little when the accident happened.) I woke up and thought that I must ask Ladner about this. I always know even before I am awake that Ladner's body is not beside me and that the sense of him I have, of his weight and heat and smell, are memories. But I still have the feeling—when I wake—that he is in the next room and I can call him and tell him my dream or whatever. Then I have to realize that isn't so, every morning, and I feel a chill. I feel a shrinking. I feel as if I had a couple of wooden planks lying across my chest, which doesn't incline me to get up. A common experience I'm having. But at the moment I'm not having it, just describing it, and in fact I am rather happy sitting here with my bottle of red wine."

This was a letter Bea Doud never sent and in fact never finished. In her big, neglected house in Carstairs, she had entered a period of musing and drinking, of what looked to everybody else like a slow decline, but to her seemed, after all, sadly pleasurable, like a convalescence.

Bea Doud had met Ladner when she was out for a Sunday drive in the country with Peter Parr. Peter Parr was a science teacher, also the principal of the Carstairs High School, where Bea had for a while done some substitute teaching. She did not have a teacher's certificate, but she had an M.A. in English and things were more lax in those days. Also, she would be called upon to help with school excursions, herding a class to the Royal Ontario Museum or to Stratford for their annual dose of Shakespeare. Once she became interested in Peter Parr, she tried to keep clear of such involvements. She wished things to be seemly, for his sake. Peter Parr's wife was in a nursing home—she had multiple sclerosis, and he visited her faithfully. Everyone thought he was an admirable man, and most understood his need to have a steady girlfriend (a word Bea said she found appalling), but some perhaps thought that his choice was a pity. Bea had had what she herself referred to as a checkered career. But she settled down with Peter—his decency and good faith and good humor had brought her into an orderly life, and she thought that she enjoyed it.

When Bea spoke of having had a checkered career, she was taking a sarcastic or disparaging tone that did not reflect what she really felt about her life of love affairs. That life had started when she was married. Her husband was an English airman stationed near Walley during the Second World War. After the war she went to England with him, but they were soon divorced. She came home and did various things, such as keeping house for her stepmother, and getting her M.A. But love affairs were the main content of her life, and she knew that she was not being honest when she belittled them. They were sweet, they were sour; she was happy in them, she was miserable. She knew what it was to wait in a bar for a man who never showed up. To wait for letters, to cry in public, and on the other hand to be pestered by a man she no longer wanted. (She had been obliged to resign from the Light Opera Society because of a fool who directed baritone solos at her.) But still she felt the first signal of a love affair like the warmth of the sun on her skin, like music through a doorway, or the moment, as she had often said, when the black-and-white television commercial bursts into color. She did not think that her time was being wasted. She did not think it had been wasted.

She did think, she did admit, that she was vain. She liked tributes and attention. It irked her, for instance, when Peter Parr took her for a drive in the country, that he never did it for the sake of her company alone. He was a well-liked man and he liked many people, even people that he had just met. He and Bea would always end up dropping in on somebody, or talking for an hour with a former student now working at a gas station, or joining an expedition that had been hatched up with some people they had run into when they stopped at a country store for ice-cream cones. She had fallen in love with him because of his sad situation and his air of gallantry and loneliness and his shy, thin-lipped smile, but in fact he was compulsively sociable, the sort of person who could not pass a family volleyball game in somebody's front yard without wanting to leap out of the car and get into the action.

On a Sunday afternoon in May, a dazzling, freshly green day, he said to her that he wanted to drop in for a few minutes on a man named Ladner. (With Peter Parr, it was always a few minutes.) Bea thought that he had already met this man somewhere, since he called him by a single name and seemed to know a great deal about him. He said that Ladner had come out here from England soon after the war, that he had served in the Royal Air Force (yes, like her husband!), had been shot down and had received burns all down one side of his body. So he had decided to live like a hermit. He had turned his back on corrupt and warring and competitive society, he had bought up four hundred acres of unproductive land, mostly swamp and bush, in the northern part of the county, in Stratton Township, and he had created there a remarkable sort of nature preserve, with bridges and trails and streams dammed up to make ponds, and exhibits along the trails of lifelike birds and animals. For he made his living as a taxidermist, working mostly for museums. He did not charge people anything for walking along his trails and looking at the exhibits. He was a man who had been wounded and disillusioned in the worst way and had withdrawn from the world, yet gave all he could back to it in his attention to nature.

Much of this was untrue or only partly true, as Bea discovered. Ladner was not at all a pacifist—he supported the Vietnam War and believed that nuclear weapons were a deterrent. He favored a competitive society. He had been burned only on the side of his face and neck, and that was from an exploding shell during the ground fighting (he was in the Army) near Caen. He had not left England immediately but had worked for years there, in a museum, until something happened—Bea never knew what—that soured him on the job and the country.

It was true about the property and what he had done with it. It was true that he was a taxidermist.

Bea and Peter had some trouble finding Ladner's house. It was just a basic A-frame in those days, hidden by the trees. They found the driveway at last and parked there and got out of the car. Bea was expecting to be introduced and taken on a tour and considerably bored for an hour or two, and perhaps to have to sit around drinking beer or tea while Peter Parr consolidated a friendship.

Ladner came around the house and confronted them. It was Bea's impression that he had a fierce dog with him. But this was not the case. Ladner did not own a dog. He was his own fierce dog.

Ladner's first words to them were "What do you want?"

Peter Parr said that he would come straight to the point. "I've heard so much about this wonderful place you've made here," he said. "And I'll tell you right off the bat, I am an educator. I educate high-school kids, or try to. I try to give them a few ideas that will keep them from mucking up the world or blowing it up altogether when their time comes. All around them what do they see but horrible examples? Hardly one thing that is positive. And that's where I'm bold enough to approach you, sir. That's what I've come here to ask you to consider."

Field trips. Selected students. See the difference one individual can make. Respect for nature, cooperation with the environment, opportunity to see at first hand.

"Well, I am not an educator," said Ladner. "I do not give a fuck about your teenagers, and the last thing I want is a bunch of louts shambling around my property smoking cigarettes and leering like half-wits. I don't know where you got the impression that what I've done here I've done as a public service, because that is something in which I have zero interest. Sometimes I let people go through but they're the people I decide on."

"Well, I wonder just about us," said Peter Parr. "Just us, today—would you let us have a look?"

"Out of bounds today," said Ladner. "I'm working on the trail."

Back in the car, heading down the gravel road, Peter Parr said to Bea, "Well, I think that's broken the ice, don't you?"

This was not a joke. He did not make that sort of joke. Bea said something vaguely encouraging. But she realized—or had realized some minutes before, in Ladner's driveway—that she was on the wrong track with Peter Parr. She didn't want any more of his geniality, his good intentions, his puzzling and striving. All the things that had appealed to her and comforted her about him were now more or less dust and ashes. Now that she had seen him with Ladner.

She could have told herself otherwise, of course. But such was not her nature. Even after years of good behavior, it was not her nature.

She had a couple of friends then, to whom she wrote and actually sent letters that tried to investigate and explain this turn in her life. She wrote that she would hate to think she had gone after Ladner because he was rude and testy and slightly savage, with the splotch on the side of his face that shone like metal in the sunlight coming through the trees. She would hate to think so, because wasn't that the way in all the dreary romances—some brute gets the woman tingling and then it's goodbye to Mr. Fine-and-Decent?

No, she wrote, but what she did think—and she knew that this was very regressive and bad form—what she did think was that some

women, women like herself, might be always on the lookout for an insanity that could contain them. For what was living with a man if it
wasn't living inside his insanity? A man could have a very ordinary, a
very unremarkable, insanity, such as his devotion to a ball team. But
that might not be enough, not big enough—and an insanity that was
not big enough simply made a woman mean and discontented. Peter
Parr, for instance, displayed kindness and hopefulness to a fairly fanat-
ical degree. But in the end, for me, Bea wrote, that was not a suitable
insanity.

What did Ladner offer her then, that she could live inside? She
didn't mean just that she would be able to accept the importance of
learning the habits of porcupines and writing fierce letters on the
subject to journals that she, Bea, had never before heard of. She
meant also that she would be able to live surrounded by implacabil-
ity, by ready doses of indifference which at times might seem like
scorn.

So she explained her condition, during the first half-year.

Several other women had thought themselves capable of the same
thing. She found traces of them. A belt—size 26—a jar of cocoa butter,
fancy combs for the hair. He hadn't let any of them stay. Why them and
not me? Bea asked him.

"None of them had any money," said Ladner.

A joke. *I am slit top to bottom with jokes.* (Now she wrote her letters
only in her head.)

But driving out to Ladner's place during the school week, a few days after she had first met him, what was her state? Lust and terror. She had
to feel sorry for herself, in her silk underwear. Her teeth chattered. She
pitied herself for being a victim of such wants. Which she had felt before—she would not pretend she hadn't. This was not yet so different
from what she had felt before.

She found the place easily. She must have memorized the route well.
She had thought up a story: She was lost. She was looking for a place up
here that sold nursery shrubs. That would suit the time of year. But
Ladner was out in front of his trees working on the road culvert, and he
greeted her in such a matter-of-fact way, without surprise or displeasure, that it was not necessary to trot out this excuse.

"Just hang on until I get this job done," he said. "It'll take me about ten minutes."

For Bea there was nothing like this—nothing like watching a man work at some hard job, when he is forgetful of you and works well, in a way that is tidy and rhythmical, nothing like it to heat the blood. There was no waste about Ladner, no extra size or unnecessary energy and certainly no elaborate conversation. His gray hair was cut very short, in the style of his youth—the top of his head shone silver like the metallic-looking patch of skin.

Bea said that she agreed with him about the students. "I've done some substitute teaching and taken them on treks," she said. "There have been times when I felt like setting Dobermans on them and driving them into a cesspit.

"I hope you don't think I'm here to persuade you of anything," she said. "Nobody knows I'm here."

He took his time answering her. "I expect you'd like a tour," he said when he was ready. "Would you? Would you like a tour of the place yourself?"

That was what he said and that was what he meant. A tour. Bea was wearing the wrong shoes—at that time in her life she did not own any shoes that would have been right. He did not slow down for her or help her in any way to cross a creek or climb a bank. He never held out a hand, or suggested that they might sit and rest on any appropriate log or rock or slope.

He led her first on a boardwalk across a marsh to a pond, where some Canada geese had settled and a pair of swans were circling each other, their bodies serene but their necks mettlesome, their beaks letting out bitter squawks. "Are they mates?" said Bea.

"Evidently."

Not far from these live birds was a glass-fronted case containing a stuffed golden eagle with its wings spread, a gray owl, and a snow owl. The case was an old gutted freezer, with a window set in its side and a camouflage of gray and green swirls of paint.

"Ingenious," said Bea.

Ladner said, "I use what I can get."

He showed her the beaver meadow, the pointed stumps of the trees the beavers had chewed down, their heaped, untidy constructions, the two richly furred beavers in their case. Then in turn she looked at a red fox, a golden mink, a white ferret, a dainty family of skunks, a porcupine, and a fisher, which Ladner told her was intrepid enough to kill porcupines. Stuffed and lifelike raccoons clung to a tree trunk, a wolf stood poised to howl, and a black bear had just managed to lift its big soft head, its melancholy face. Ladner said that was a small bear. He couldn't afford to keep the big ones, he said—they brought too good a price.

Many birds as well. Wild turkeys, a pair of ruffled grouse, a pheasant with a bright-red ring around its eye. Signs told their habitat, their Latin names, food preferences, and styles of behavior. Some of the trees were labelled too. Tight, accurate, complicated information. Other signs presented quotations.

> Nature does nothing uselessly.
>
> —*Aristotle*

> Nature never deceives us; it is always we who deceive ourselves.
>
> —*Rousseau*

When Bea stopped to read these, it seemed to her that Ladner was impatient, that he scowled a little. She no longer made comments on anything she saw.

She couldn't keep track of their direction or get any idea of the layout of the property. Did they cross different streams, or the same stream several times? The woods might stretch for miles, or only to the top of a near hill. The leaves were new and couldn't keep out the sun. Trilliums abounded. Ladner lifted a Mayapple leaf to show her the hidden flower. Fat leaves, ferns just uncurling, yellow skunk cabbage bursting out of bogholes, all the sap and sunshine around, and the treacherous tree rot underfoot, and then they were in an old apple orchard, enclosed by woods, and he directed her to look for mushrooms—morels. He himself found five, which he did not offer to share. She confused them with last year's rotted apples.

A steep hill rose up in front of them, cluttered with little barbed hawthorn trees in bloom. "The kids call this Fox Hill," he said. "There's a den up here."

Bea stood still. "You have children?"

He laughed. "Not to my knowledge. I mean the kids from across the road. Mind the branches, they have thorns."

By this time lust was lost to her altogether, though the smell of the hawthorn blossoms seemed to her an intimate one, musty or yeasty. She had long since stopped fixing her eyes on a spot between his shoulder blades and willing him to turn around and embrace her. It occurred to her that this tour, so strenuous physically and mentally, might be a joke on her, a punishment for being, after all, such a tiresome vamp and fraud. So she roused her pride and acted as if it were exactly what she had come for. She questioned, she took an interest, she showed no fatigue. As later on—but not on this day—she would learn to match him with some of the same pride in the hard-hearted energy of sex.

She did not expect him to ask her into the house. But he said, "Would you like a cup of tea? I can make you a cup of tea," and they went inside. A smell of hides greeted her, of Borax soap, wood shavings, turpentine. Skins lay in piles, folded flesh-side out. Heads of animals, with empty eyeholes and mouth holes, were set on stands. What she thought at first was the skinned body of a deer turned out to be only a wire armature with bundles of what looked like glued straw tied to it. He told her the body would be built up with papier-mâché.

There were books in the house—a small section of books on taxidermy, the others mostly in sets. The History of the Second World War. The History of Science. The History of Philosophy. The History of Civilization. The Peninsular War. The Peloponnesian Wars. The French and Indian Wars. Bea thought of his long evenings in the winter—his orderly solitude, his systematic reading and barren contentment.

He seemed a little nervous, getting the tea. He checked the cups for dust. He forgot that he had already taken the milk out of the refrigerator, and he forgot that she had already said she did not take sugar. When she tasted the tea, he watched her, asked her if it was all right. Was it too strong, would she like a little hot water? Bea reassured him and thanked him for the tour and mentioned things about it that she had particularly appreciated. Here is this man, she was thinking, not so strange a man after all, nothing so very mysterious about him, maybe nothing even so very interesting. The layers of information. The French and Indian Wars.

She asked for a bit more milk in her tea. She wanted to drink it down faster and be on her way.

He said that she must drop in again if she was ever out in this part of the country with nothing particular to do. "And feel the need of a little exercise," he said. "There is always something to see, whatever the time of year." He spoke of the winter birds and the tracks on the snow and asked if she had skis. She saw that he did not want her to go. They stood in the open doorway and he told her about skiing in Norway, about the tramcars with ski racks on top of them and the mountains at the edge of town.

She said that she had never been to Norway but she was sure she would like it.

She looked back on this moment as their real beginning. They both seemed uneasy and subdued, not reluctant so much as troubled, even sorry for each other. She asked him later if he had felt anything important at the time, and he said yes—he had realized that she was a person he could live with. She asked him if he couldn't say wanted to live with, and he said yes, he could say that. He could say it, but he didn't.

She had many jobs to learn which had to do with the upkeep of this place and also with the art and skill of taxidermy. She would learn, for instance, how to color lips and eyelids and the ends of noses with a clever mixture of oil paint and linseed and turpentine. Other things she had to learn concerned what he would say and wouldn't say. It seemed that she had to be cured of all her froth and vanity and all her old notions of love.

> *One night I got into his bed and he did not take his eyes from his book or move or speak a word to me even when I crawled out and returned to my own bed, where I fell asleep almost at once because I think I could not bear the shame of being awake.*
>
> *In the morning he got into my bed and all went as usual.*
>
> *I come up against blocks of solid darkness.*

She learned, she changed. Age was a help to her. Drink also.

And when he got used to her, or felt safe from her, his feelings took a turn for the better. He talked to her readily about what he was interested in and took a kinder comfort from her body.

On the night before the operation they lay side by side on the strange bed, with all available bare skin touching—legs, arms, haunches.

II

Liza told Warren that a woman named Bea Doud had phoned from Toronto and asked if they—that is, Warren and Liza—could go out and check on the house in the country, where Bea and her husband lived. They wanted to make sure that the water had been turned off. Bea and

Ladner (not actually her husband, said Liza) were in Toronto waiting for Ladner to have an operation. A heart bypass. "Because the pipes might burst," said Liza. This was on a Sunday night in February during the worst of that winter's storms.

"You know who they are," said Liza. "Yes, you do. Remember that couple I introduced you to? One day last fall on the square outside of Radio Shack? He had a scar on his cheek and she had long hair, half black and half gray. I told you he was a taxidermist, and you said, 'What's that?'"

Now Warren remembered. An old—but not too old—couple in flannel shirts and baggy pants. His scar and English accent, her weird hair and rush of friendliness. A taxidermist stuffs dead animals. That is, animal skins. Also dead birds and fish.

He had asked Liza, "What happened to the guy's face?" and she had said, "W.W. Two."

"I know where the key is—that's why she called me," Liza said. "This is up in Stratton Township. Where I used to live."

"Did they go to your same church or something?" Warren said.

"Bea and *Ladner*? Let's not be funny. They just lived across the road.

"It was her gave me some money." Liza continued, as if it was something he ought to know, "To go to college. I never asked her. She just phones up out of the blue and says she wants to. So I think, Okay, she's got lots."

• • •

When she was little, Liza had lived in Stratton Township with her father and her brother Kenny, on a farm. Her father wasn't a farmer. He just rented the house. He worked as a roofer. Her mother was already dead. By the time Liza was ready for high school—Kenny was a year younger and two grades behind her—her father had moved them to Carstairs. He met a woman there who owned a trailer home, and later on he married her. Later still, he moved with her to Chatham. Liza wasn't sure where they were now—Chatham or Wallaceburg or Sarnia. By the time they moved, Kenny was dead—he had been killed when he was fifteen, in one of the big teenage car crashes that seemed to happen every spring, involving drunk, often unlicensed drives, temporarily stolen cars, fresh gravel on the country roads, crazy speeds. Liza finished high school and went to college in Guelph for one year. She didn't like college, didn't like the people there. By that time she had become a Christian.

That was how Warren met her. His family belonged to the Fellowship of the Saviour Bible Chapel, in Walley. He had been going to the Bible Chapel all his life. Liza started going there after she moved to Walley and got a job in the government liquor store. She still worked there, though she worried about it and sometimes thought that she should quit. She never drank alcohol now, she never even ate sugar. She didn't want Warren eating a Danish on his break, so she packed him oat muffins that she made at home. She did the laundry every Wednesday night and counted the strokes when she brushed her teeth and got up early in the morning to do knee bends and read Bible verses.

She thought she should quit, but they needed the money. The small-engines shop where Warren used to work had closed down, and he was retraining so that he could sell computers. They had been married a year.

• • •

In the morning, the weather was clear, and they set off on the snowmobile shortly before noon. Monday was Liza's day off. The plows were working on the highway, but the back roads were still buried in snow. Snowmobiles had been roaring through the town streets since before dawn and had left their tracks across the inland fields and on the frozen river.

Liza told Warren to follow the river track as far as Highway 86, then head northeast across the fields so as to half-circle the swamp. All over the river there were animal tracks in straight lines and loops and circles. The only ones that Warren knew for sure were dog tracks. The river with its three feet of ice and level covering of snow made a wonderful road. The storm had come from the west, as storms usually did in that country, and the trees along the eastern bank were all plastered with snow, clotted with it, their branches spread out like wicker snow baskets. On the western bank, drifts curled like waves stopped, like huge lappings of cream. It was exciting to be out in this, with all the other snowmobiles carving the trails and assaulting the day with such roars and swirls of noise.

The swamp was black from a distance, a long smudge on the northern horizon. But close up, it too was choked with snow. Black trunks against the snow flashed by in a repetition that was faintly sickening. Liza directed Warren with light blows of her hand on his leg to a back road full as a bed, and finally hit him hard to stop him. The change of noise for silence and speed for stillness made it seem as if they had dropped out of streaming clouds into something solid. They were stuck in the solid middle of the winter day.

On one side of the road was a broken-down barn with old gray hay bulging out of it. "Where we used to live," said Liza. "No, I'm kidding. Actually, there was a house. It's gone now."

On the other side of the road was a sign, "Lesser Dismal," with trees behind it, and an extended A-frame house painted a light gray. Liza said that there was a swamp somewhere in the United States called Great Dismal Swamp, and that was what the name referred to. A joke.

"I never heard of it," said Warren.

Other signs said "No Trespassing," "No Hunting," "No Snowmobiling," "Keep Out."

The key to the back door was in an odd place. It was in a plastic bag inside a hole in a tree. There were several old bent trees—fruit trees, probably—close to the back steps. The hole in the tree had tar around it—Liza said that was to keep out squirrels. There was tar around other holes in other trees, so the hole for the key didn't in any way stand out. "How did you find it, then?" Liza pointed out a profile—easy to see, when you looked closely—emphasized by a knife following cracks in the bark. A long nose, a down-slanting eye and mouth, and a big drop—that was the tarred hole—right at the end of the nose.

"Pretty funny?" said Liza, stuffing the plastic bag in her pocket and turning the key in the back door. "Don't stand there," she said. "Come on in. Jeepers, it's cold as the grave in here." She was always very conscientious about changing the exclamation "Jesus" to "Jeepers" and "Hell" to "help," as they were supposed to do in the Fellowship.

She went around twirling thermostats to get the baseboard heating going.

Warren said, "We aren't going to hang around here, are we?"

"Hang around till we get warmed up," said Liza.

Warren was trying the kitchen taps. Nothing came out. "Water's off," he said. "It's O.K."

Liza had gone into the front room. "What?" she called. "What's O.K.?"

"The water. It's turned off."

"Oh, is it? Good."

Warren stopped in the front-room doorway. "Shouldn't we ought to take our boots off?" he said. "Like, if we're going to walk around?"

"Why?" said Liza, stomping on the rug. "What's the matter with good clean snow?"

Warren was not a person who noticed much about a room and what was in it, but he did see that this room had some things that were usual and some that were not. It had rugs and chairs and a television and a sofa and books and a big desk. But it also had shelves of stuffed and mounted birds, some quite tiny and bright, and some large and suitable for shooting. Also a sleek brown animal—a weasel?—and a beaver, which he knew by its paddle tail.

Liza was opening the drawers of the desk and rummaging in the paper she found there. He thought that she must be looking for something the woman had told her to get. Then she started pulling the drawers all the way out and dumping them and their contents on the floor. She made a funny noise—an admiring cluck of her tongue, as if the drawers had done this on their own.

"Christ!" he said. (Because he had been in the Fellowship all his life, he was not nearly so careful as Liza about his language.) "Liza? What do you think you're doing?"

"Nothing that is remotely any of your business," said Liza. But she spoke cheerfully, even kindly. "Why don't you relax and watch TV or something?"

She was picking up the mounted birds and animals and throwing them down one by one, adding them to the mess she was making on the floor. "He uses balsa wood," she said. "Nice and light."

Warren did go and turn on the television. It was a black-and-white set, and most of its channels showed nothing but snow or ripples. The only thing he could get clear was a scene from the old series with the blond girl in the harem outfit—she was a witch—and the J.R. Ewing actor when he was so young he hadn't yet become J.R.

"Look at this," he said. "Like going back in time."

Liza didn't look. He sat down on a hassock with his back to her. He was trying to be like a grownup who won't watch. Ignore her and she'll quit. Nevertheless he could hear behind him the ripping of books and paper. Books were being scooped off the shelves, torn apart, tossed on the floor. He heard her go out to the kitchen and yank out drawers, slam cupboard doors, smash dishes. She came back to the front room after a while, and a white dust began to fill the air. She must have dumped out flour. She was coughing.

Warren had to cough, too, but he did not turn around. Soon he heard stuff being poured out of bottles—thin, splashing liquid and thick glug-glug-glugs. He could smell vinegar and maple syrup and whisky. That was what she was pouring over the flour and the books and the rugs and the feathers and fur of the bird and animal bodies. Something shattered against the stove. He bet it was the whisky bottle.

"Bull's-eye!" said Liza.

Warren wouldn't turn. His whole body felt as if it was humming, with the effort to be still and make this be over.

Once, he and Liza had gone to a Christian rock concert and dance in St. Thomas. There was a lot of controversy about Christian rock in the Fellowship—about whether there could even be such a thing. Liza was bothered by this question. Warren wasn't. He had gone a few times to rock concerts and dances that didn't even call themselves Christian. But when they started to dance, it was Liza who slid under, right away, it was Liza who caught the eye—the vigilant, unhappy eye—of the Youth Leader, who was grinning and clapping uncertainly on the sidelines. Warren had never seen Liza dance, and the crazy, slithery spirit that possessed her amazed him. He felt proud rather than worried, but he knew that whatever he felt did not make the least difference. There was Liza, dancing, and the only thing he could do was wait it out while she tore her way through the music, supplicated and curled around it, kicked loose, and blinded herself to everything around her.

That's what she's got in her, he felt like saying to them all. He thought that he had known it. He had known something the first time he had seen her at the Fellowship. It was summer and she was wearing the little summer straw hat and the dress with sleeves that all the Fellowship girls had to wear, but her skin was too golden and her body too slim for a Fellowship girl's. Not that she looked like a girl in a magazine, a model or a show-off. Not Liza, with her high, rounded forehead and deep-set brown eyes, her expression that was both childish and fierce. She looked unique, and she was. She was a girl who wouldn't say, "Jesus!" but who would, in moments of downright contentment and meditative laziness, say, "Well, *fuck!*"

She said she had been wild before becoming a Christian. "Even when I was a kid," she said.

"Wild in what way?" he had asked her. "Like, with guys?"

She gave him a look, as if to say, Don't be dumb.

Warren felt a trickle now, down one side of his scalp. She had sneaked up behind him. He put a hand to his head and it came away green and sticky and smelling of peppermint.

"Have a sip," she said, handing him a bottle. He took a gulp, and the strong mint drink nearly strangled him. Liza took back the bottle and threw it against the big front window. It didn't go through the window but it cracked the glass. The bottle hadn't broken—it fell to the floor, and a pool of beautiful liquid streamed out from it. Dark-green blood. The window glass had filled with thousands of radiating cracks, and turned as white as a halo. Warren was standing up, gasping from the liquor. Waves of heat were rising through his body. Liza stepped delicately among the torn, spattered books and broken glass, the smeared, stomped birds, the pools of whisky and maple syrup and the sticks of charred wood dragged from the stove to make black tracks on the rugs, the ashes and gummed flour and feathers. She stepped delicately, even in her snowmobile boots, admiring what she'd done, what she'd managed so far.

Warren picked up the hassock he had been sitting on and flung it at the sofa. It toppled off; it didn't do any damage, but the action had put him in the picture. This was not the first time he'd been involved in trashing a house. Long ago, when he was nine or ten years old, he and a friend had got into a house on their way home from school. It was his friend's aunt who lived in this house. She wasn't home—she worked in a jewelry store. She lived by herself. Warren and his friend broke in because they were hungry. They made themselves soda-cracker-and-jam sandwiches and drank some ginger ale. But then something took over. They dumped a bottle of ketchup on the table-cloth and dipped their fingers in, and wrote on the wallpaper, *"Beware! Blood!"* They broke plates and threw some food around.

They were strangely lucky. Nobody had seen them getting into the house and nobody saw them leaving. The aunt herself put the blame on some teenagers whom she had recently ordered out of the store.

Recalling this, Warren went to the kitchen looking for a bottle of ketchup. There didn't seem to be any, but he found and opened a can of tomato sauce. It was thinner than ketchup and didn't work as well, but he tried to write with it on the wooden kitchen wall. *"Beware! This is your blood!"*

The sauce soaked into or ran down the boards. Liza came up close to read the words before they blotted themselves out. She laughed. Somewhere in the rubble she found a Magic Marker. She climbed up on a chair and wrote above the fake blood, "*The Wages of Sin is Death.*"

"I should have got out more stuff," she said. "Where he works is full of paint and glue and all kinds of crap. In that side room."

Warren said, "Want me to get some?"

"Not really," she said. She sank down on the sofa—one of the few places in the front room where you could still sit down. "Liza Minnelli," she said peacefully. "Liza Minnelli, stick it in your belly!"

Was that something kids at school sang at her? Or something she made up for herself?

Warren sat down beside her. "So what did they do?" he said. "What did they do that made you so mad?"

"Who's mad?" said Liza, and hauled herself up and went to the kitchen. Warren followed, and saw that she was punching out a number on the phone. She had to wait a little. Then she said, "Bea?" in a soft, hurt, hesitant voice. "Oh, Bea!" She waved at Warren to turn off the television.

He heard her saying, "The window by the kitchen door. . . . I think so. Even maple syrup, you wouldn't believe it. . . . Oh, and the beautiful big front window, they threw something at that, and they got sticks out of the stove and the ashes and those birds that were sitting around and the big beaver. I can't tell you what it looks like. . . ."

He came back into the kitchen, and she made a face at him, raising her eyebrows and setting her lips blubbering as she listened to the voice on the other end of the phone. Then she went on describing things, commiserating, making her voice quiver with misery and indignation. Warren didn't like watching her. He went around looking for their helmets.

When she had hung up the phone, she came and got him. "It was her," she said. "I already told you what she did to me. She sent me to college!" That started them both laughing.

But Warren was looking at a bird in the mess on the floor. Its soggy feathers, its head hanging loose, showing one bitter red eye. "It's weird doing that for a living," he said. "Always having dead stuff around."

"They're weird," Liza said.

Warren said, "Do you care if he croaks?"

Liza made croaking noises to stop him being thoughtful. Then she touched her teeth, her pointed tongue to his neck.

III

Bea asked Liza and Kenny a lot of questions. She asked them what their favorite TV shows and colors and ice-cream flavors were, and what kind of animals they would be if they could turn into animals, and what was the earliest thing they remembered. "Eating boogers," said Kenny. He did not mean to be funny.

Ladner and Liza and Bea all laughed—Liza the loudest. Then Bea said, "You know, that's one of the earliest things I can remember myself!"

She's lying, Liza thought. Lying for Kenny's sake, and he doesn't even know it.

"This is Miss Doud," Ladner had told them. "Try to be decent to her."

"Miss Doud," said Bea, as if she had swallowed something surprising. "Bea. Bzzz. My name is Bea."

"Who is that?" Kenny said to Liza, when Bea and Ladner were walking ahead of them. "Is she going to live with him?"

"It's his girlfriend," Liza said. "They are probably going to get married." By the time Bea had been at Ladner's place for a week, Liza could not stand the thought of her ever going away.

• • •

The first time that Liza and Kenny had ever been on Ladner's property, they had sneaked in under a fence, as all the signs and their own father had warned them not to do. When they had got so far into the trees that Liza was not sure of the way out, they heard a sharp whistle.

Ladner called them: "You two!" He came out like a murderer on television, with a little axe, from behind a tree. "Can you two read?"

They were about six and seven at this time. Liza said, "Yes."

"So did you read my signs?"

Kenny said faintly, "A fox run in here." When they were driving with their father, one time, they had seen a red fox run across to the road and disappear into the trees here. Their father had said, "Bugger's living in Ladner's bush."

Foxes do not live in the bush, Ladner told them. He took them to see where the fox did live. A den, he called it. There was a pile of sand beside a hole on a hillside covered with dry, tough grass and little white flowers. "Pretty soon those are going to turn into strawberries," Ladner said.

"What will?" said Liza.

"You are a pair of dumb kids," Ladner said. "What do you do all day—watch TV?"

That was the beginning of their spending Saturdays—and, when summer came, nearly all days—with Ladner. Their father said it was all right, if Ladner was fool enough to put up with them. "But you better not cross him or he'll skin you alive," their father said. "Like he does with his other stuff. You know that?"

They knew what Ladner did. He had let them watch. They had seen him clean out a squirrel's skull and fix a bird's feathers to best advantage with delicate wire and pins. Once he was sure that they would be careful enough, he let them fit the glass eyes in place. They had watched him skin animals, scrape the skins and salt them, and set them to dry inside out before he sent them to the tanner's. Tanning put a poison in them so they would never crack, and the fur would never fall out.

Ladner fitted the skin around a body in which nothing was real. A bird's body could be all of one piece, carved of wood, but an animal's larger body was a wonderful construction of wires and burlap and glue and mushed-up paper and clay.

Liza and Kenny had picked up skinned bodies that were tough as rope. They had touched guts that looked like plastic tubing. They had squished eyeballs to jelly. They told their father about that. "But we won't get any diseases," Liza said. "We wash our hands in Borax soap."

Not all the information they had was about dead things: What does the red-winged blackbird say? *Compan-ee!* What does the Jenny wren say? *Pleasa-pleasa-please, can I have a piece of cheese?*

"Oh, can it!" said their father.

Soon they knew much more. At least Liza did. She knew birds, trees, mushrooms, fossils, the solar system. She knew where certain rocks came from and that the swelling on a goldenrod stem contains a little white worm that can live nowhere else in the world.

She knew not to talk so much about all she knew.

Bea was standing on the bank of the pond, in her Japanese kimono. Liza was already swimming. She called to Bea, "Come on in, come in!" Ladner was working on the far side of the pond, cutting reeds and clearing the weeds that clogged the water. Kenny was supposed to be helping him. Liza thought, Like a family.

Bea dropped her kimono and stood in her yellow, silky bathing suit. She was a small woman with dark hair, lightly grayed, falling heavily around her shoulders. Her eyebrows were thick and dark and their arched shape, like the sweet sulky shape of her mouth, entreated kindness and consolation. The sun had covered her with dim freckles, and she was just a bit too soft all over. When she lowered her chin, little pouches collected along her jaw and under her eyes. She was prey to little pouches and sags, dents and ripples in the skin or flesh, sunbursts of tiny purplish veins, faint discolorations in the hollows. And it was in fact this collection of flaws, this shadowy damage, that Liza especially loved. Also she loved the dampness that was often to be seen in Bea's eyes, the tremor and teasing and playful pleading in Bea's voice, its huskiness and artificiality. Bea was not measured or judged by Liza in the way that other people were. But this did not mean that Liza's love for Bea was easy or restful—her love was one of expectation, but she did not know what it was that she expected.

Now Bea entered the pond. She did this in stages. A decision, a short run, a pause. Knee-high in the water, she hugged herself and squealed.

"It's not cold," said Liza.

"No, no, I love it!" Bea said. And she continued, with noises of appreciation, to a spot where the water was up to her waist. She turned around to face Liza, who had swum around behind her with the intention of splashing.

"Oh, no, you don't!" Bea cried. And she began to jump in place, to pass her hands through the water, fingers spread, gathering it as if it were flower petals. Ineffectually, she splashed Liza.

Liza turned over and floated on her back and gently kicked a little water toward Bea's face. Bea kept rising and falling and dodging the water Liza kicked, and as she did so she set up some sort of happy silly chant. *Oh-woo, oh-woo, oh-woo.* Something like that.

Even though she was lying on her back, floating on the water, Liza could see that Ladner had stopped working. He was standing in waist-deep water on the other side of the pond, behind Bea's back. He was watching Bea. Then he, too, started jumping up and down in the water. His body was stiff but he turned his head sharply from side to side, skimming or patting the water with fluttery hands. Preening, twitching, as if carried away with admiration for himself.

He was imitating Bea. He was doing what she was doing but in a sillier, ugly way. He was most intentionally and insistently making a fool of her. See how vain she is, said Ladner's angular prancing. See what a fake. Pretending not to be afraid of the deep water, pretending to be happy, pretending not to know how we despise her.

This was thrilling and shocking. Liza's face was trembling with her need to laugh. Part of her wanted to make Ladner stop, to stop at once, before the damage was done, and part of her longed for that very damage, the damage Ladner could do, the ripping open, the final delight of it.

Kenny whooped out loud. He had no sense.

Bea had already seen the change in Liza's face, and now she heard Kenny. She turned to see what was behind her. But Ladner had dropped into the water again, he was pulling up weeds.

Liza at once kicked up a distracting storm. When Bea didn't respond to this, she swam out into the deep part of the pond and dived down. Deep, deep, to where it's dark, where the carp live, in the mud. She stayed down there as long as she could. She swam so far that she got tangled in the weeds near the other bank and came up gasping, only a yard or so away from Ladner.

"I got caught in the reeds," she said. "I could have drowned."

"No such luck," said Ladner. He made a pretend grab at her, to get her between the legs. At the same time he made a pious, shocked face, as if the person in his head was having a fit at what his hand might do.

Liza pretended not to notice. "Where's Bea?" she said.

Ladner looked at the opposite bank. "Maybe up to the house," he said. "I didn't see her go." He was quite ordinary again, a serious workman, slightly fed up with all their foolishness. Ladner could do that. He could switch from one person to another and make it your fault if you remembered.

Liza swam in a straight line as hard as she could across the pond. She splashed her way out and heavily climbed the bank. She passed the owls and the eagle staring from behind glass. The "Nature does nothing uselessly" sign.

She didn't see Bea anywhere. Not ahead on the boardwalk over the marsh. Not in the open space under the pine trees. Liza took the path to the back door of the house. In the middle of the path was a beech tree you had to go around, and there were initials carved in the smooth bark. One "L" for Ladner, another for Liza, a "K" for Kenny. A foot or so below were the letters "P.D.P." When Liza had first shown Bea the initials, Kenny had banged his fist against P.D.P. "Pull down pants!" he shouted, hopping up and down. Ladner gave him a serious pretend-rap on the head. "Proceed down path," he said, and pointed out the arrow scratched in the bark, curving around the trunk. "Pay no attention to the dirty-minded juveniles," he said to Bea.

Liza could not bring herself to knock on the door. She was full of guilt and foreboding. It seemed to her that Bea would have to go away. How could she stay after such an insult—how could she put up with any of them? Bea did not understand about Ladner. And how could she? Liza herself couldn't have described to anybody what he was like. In the secret life she had with him, what was terrible was always funny, badness was mixed up with silliness, you always had to join in with dopey faces and voices and pretending he was a cartoon monster. You couldn't get out of it, or even want to, any more than you could stop an invasion of pins and needles.

Liza went around the house and out of the shade of the trees. Barefoot, she crossed the hot gravel road. There was her own house sitting in the middle of a cornfield at the end of a short lane. It was a wooden house with the top half painted white and the bottom half a glaring pink, like lipstick. That had been Liza's father's idea. Maybe he thought it would perk the place up. Maybe he thought pink would make it look as if it had a woman inside it.

There is a mess in the kitchen—spilled cereal on the floor, puddles of milk souring on the counter. A pile of clothes from the Laundromat overflowing the corner armchair, and the dishcloth—Liza knows this without looking—all wadded up with the garbage in the sink. It is her job to clean all this up, and she had better do it before her father gets home.

She doesn't worry about it yet. She goes upstairs where it is baking hot under the sloping roof and gets out her little bag of precious things. She keeps this bag stuffed in the toe of an old rubber boot that is too small for her. Nobody knows about it. Certainly not Kenny.

In the bag there is a Barbie-doll evening dress, stolen from a girl
Liza used to play with (Liza doesn't much like the dress anymore, but
it has an importance because it was stolen), a blue snap-shut case with
her mother's glasses inside, a painted wooden egg that was her prize for
an Easter picture-drawing contest in Grade 2 (with a smaller egg inside
it and a still smaller egg inside that). And the one rhinestone earring
that she found on the road. For a long time she believed the rhinestones to be diamonds. The design of the earring is complicated and
graceful, with teardrop rhinestones dangling from loops and scallops of
smaller stones, and when hung from Liza's ear it almost brushes her
shoulders.

She is wearing only her bathing suit, so she has to carry the earring curled up in her palm, a blazing knot. Her head feels swollen
with the heat, with leaning over her secret bag, with her resolution.
She thinks with longing of the shade under Ladner's trees, as if that
were a black pond.

There is not one tree anywhere near this house, and the only bush is
a lilac with curly, brown-edged leaves, by the back steps. Around the
house nothing but corn, and at a distance the leaning old barn that Liza
and Kenny are forbidden to go into, because it might collapse at any
time. No divisions over here, no secret places—everything is bare and
simple.

But when you cross the road—as Liza is doing now, trotting on the
gravel—when you cross into Ladner's territory, it's like coming into a
world of different and distinct countries. There is the marsh country,
which is deep and jungly, full of botflies and jewelweed and skunk cabbage. A sense there of tropical threats and complications. Then the pine
plantation, solemn as a church, with its high boughs and needled carpet, inducing whispering. And the dark rooms under the down-swept
branches of the cedars—entirely shaded and secret rooms with a bare
earth floor. In different places the sun falls differently and in some
places not at all. In some places the air is thick and private, and in other
places you feel an energetic breeze. Smells are harsh or enticing. Certain
walks impose decorum and certain stones are set a jump apart so that
they call out for craziness. Here are the scenes of serious instruction
where Ladner taught them how to tell a hickory tree from a butternut
and a star from a planet, and places also where they have run and
hollered and hung from branches and performed all sorts of rash stunts.

And places where Liza thinks there is a bruise on the ground, a tickling and shame in the grass.

P.D.P.
Squeegey-boy.
Rub-a-dub-dub.

When Ladner grabbed Liza and squashed himself against her, she had a sense of danger deep inside him, a mechanical sputtering, as if he would exhaust himself in one jab of light, and nothing would be left of him but black smoke and burnt smells and frazzled wires. Instead, he collapsed heavily, like the pelt of an animal flung loose from its flesh and bones. He lay so heavy and useless that Liza and even Kenny felt for a moment that it was a transgression to look at him. He had to pull his voice out of his groaning innards, to tell them they were bad.

He clucked his tongue faintly and his eyes shone out of ambush, hard and round as the animals' glass eyes.

Bad-bad-bad.

"The loveliest thing," Bea said. "Liza, tell me—was this your mother's?"

Liza said yes. She could see now that this gift of a single earring might be seen as childish and pathetic—perhaps intentionally pathetic. Even keeping it as a treasure could seem stupid. But if it was her mother's, that would be understandable, and it would be a gift of some importance. "You could put it on a chain," she said. "If you put it on a chain you could wear it around your neck."

"But I was just thinking that!" Bea said. "I was just thinking it would look lovely on a chain. A silver chain—don't you think? Oh, Liza, I am just so proud you gave it to me!"

"You could wear it in your nose," said Ladner. But he said this without any sharpness. He was peaceable now—played out, peaceable. He spoke of Bea's nose as if it might be a pleasant thing to contemplate.

Ladner and Bea were sitting under the plum trees right behind the house. They sat in the wicker chairs that Bea had brought out from town. She had not brought much—just enough to make islands here and there among Ladner's skins and instruments. These chairs, some cups, a cushion. The wineglasses they were drinking out of now.

Bea had changed into a dark-blue dress of very thin and soft material. It hung long and loose from her shoulders. She trickled the rhinestones through her fingers, she let them fall and twinkle in the folds of her blue dress. She had forgiven Ladner, after all, or made a bargain not to remember.

Bea could spread safety, if she wanted to. Surely she could. All that is needed is for her to turn herself into a different sort of woman, a hard-and-fast, draw-the-line sort, clean-sweeping, energetic, and intolerant. *None of that. Not allowed. Be good.* The woman who could rescue them—who could make them all, keep them all, good.

What Bea has been sent to do, she doesn't see.

Only Liza sees.

IV

Liza locked the door as you had to, from the outside. She put the key in the plastic bag and the bag in the hole in the tree. She moved towards the snowmobile, and when Warren didn't do the same she said, "What's the matter with you?"

Warren said, "What about the window by the back door?"

Liza breathed out noisily. "Ooh, I'm an idiot!" she said. "I'm an idiot ten times over!"

Warren went back to the window and kicked at the bottom pane. Then he got a stick of firewood from the pile by the tin shed and was able to smash the glass out. "Big enough so a kid could get in," he said.

"How could I be so stupid?" Liza said. "You saved my life."

"Our life," Warren said.

The tin shed wasn't locked. Inside it he found some cardboard boxes, bits of lumber, simple tools. He tore off a piece of cardboard of a suitable size. He took great satisfaction in nailing it over the pane that he had just smashed out. "Otherwise animals could get in," he said to Liza.

When he was all finished with this job, he found that Liza had walked down into the snow between the trees. He went after her.

"I was wondering if the bear was still in there," she said.

He was going to say that he didn't think bears came this far south, but she didn't give him the time. "Can you tell what the trees are by their bark?" she said.

Warren said he couldn't even tell from their leaves. "Well, maples,"
he said. "Maples and pines."
"Cedar," said Liza. "You've got to know cedar. There's a cedar.
There's a wild cherry. Down there's birch. The white ones. And that one
with the bark like gray skin? That's a beech. See, it had letters carved
on it, but they've spread out, they just look like any old blotches now."
Warren wasn't interested. He only wanted to get home. It wasn't
much after three o'clock, but you could feel the darkness collecting, rising among the trees, like cold smoke coming off the snow.

—1995

---

*John Updike (b. 1932) is a writer whose novels so consistently appear on the best-
seller lists that his brilliant forays into light verse, serious poetry, the literary essay,
and the short story are often overshadowed by his achievement in longer forms.
Born in Shillingford, in rural Pennsylvania, he attended Harvard, where he con-
tributed humor and cartoons to the* Lampoon, *and he later studied art in England.
After his return to the United States, he worked for three years for* The New
Yorker, *to which he remains a regular contributor of book reviews on a wide range
of subjects. Updike is a prolific writer who has won many awards, including the
National Book Award in 1963 and both the Pulitzer Prize and an American Book
Award in 1982, yet he remains a talent so protean that he is difficult to classify.
Still, his bestselling novels about the life of a contemporary American "everyman,"
Harry "Rabbit" Anngstrom—*Rabbit, Run *(1960),* Rabbit Redux *(1971),*
Rabbit Is Rich *(1981), and* Rabbit at Rest *(1990), for which he received his sec-
ond Pulitzer Prize—have solidified his reputation as one of the most astute observers
of the American middle class. In recent years, his novel,* The Witches of Eastwick
*(1984) was made into a popular motion picture starring Jack Nicholson, Cher, and
Michelle Pfeiffer. "A & P," one of his most widely reprinted works, comes from his
1962 collection of short stories,* Pigeon Feathers.

John Updike
A & P

In walks three girls in nothing but bathing suits. I'm in the third check-
out slot, with my back to the door, so I don't see them until they're over
by the bread. The one that caught my eye first was the one in the plaid
green two-piece. She was a chunky kid, with a good tan and a sweet

broad soft-looking can with those two crescents of white just under it, where the sun never seems to hit, at the top of the backs of her legs. I stood there with my hand on a box of HiHo crackers trying to remember if I rang it up or not. I ring it up again and the customer starts giving me hell. She's one of these cash-register-watchers, a witch about fifty with rouge on her cheekbones and no eyebrows, and I know it made her day to trip me up. She'd been watching cash registers for fifty years and probably never seen a mistake before.

By the time I got her feathers smoothed and her goodies into a bag— she gives me a little snort in passing, if she'd been born at the right time they would have burned her over in Salem—by the time I get her on her way the girls had circled around the bread and were coming back, without a pushcart, back my way along the counters, in the aisle between the check-outs and the Special bins. They didn't even have shoes on. There was this chunky one, with the two-piece—it was bright green and the seams on the bra were still sharp and her belly was still pretty pale so I guessed she just got it (the suit)—there was this one, with one of those chubby berry-faces, the lips all bunched together under her nose, this one, and a tall one, with black hair that hadn't quite frizzed right, and one of these sunburns right across under the eyes, and a chin that was too long—you know, the kind of girl other girls think is very "striking" and "attractive" but never quite makes it, as they very well know, which is why they like her so much—and then the third one, that wasn't quite so tall. She was the queen. She kind of led them, the other two peeking around and making their shoulders round. She didn't look around, not this queen, she just walked straight on slowly, on these long white prima-donna legs. She came down a little hard on her heels, as if she didn't walk in her bare feet that much, putting down her heels and then letting the weight move along to her toes as if she was testing the floor with every step, putting a little deliberate extra action into it. You never know for sure how girls' minds work (do you really think it's a mind in there or just a little buzz like a bee in a glass jar?) but you got the idea she had talked the other two into coming in here with her, and now she was showing them how to do it, walk slow and hold yourself straight.

She had on a kind of dirty-pink—beige maybe, I don't know— bathing suit with a little nubble all over it and, what got me, the straps were down. They were off her shoulders looped loose around the cool tops of her arms, and I guess as a result the suit had slipped a little on her, so all around the top of the cloth there was this shining rim. If it hadn't been there you wouldn't have known there could have been anything whiter than those shoulders. With the straps pushed off, there was nothing between the top of the suit and the top of her head except just *her*, this clean bare plane of the top of her chest down from the shoulder bones like a dented sheet of metal tilted in the light. I mean, it was more than pretty.

She had sort of oaky hair that the sun and salt had bleached, done up in a bun that was unravelling, and a kind of prim face. Walking into the A & P with your straps down, I suppose it's the only kind of face you *can* have. She held her head so high her neck, coming up out of those white shoulders, looked kind of stretched, but I didn't mind. The longer her neck was, the more of her there was.

She must have felt in the corner of her eye me and over my shoulder Stokesie in the second slot watching, but she didn't tip. Not this queen. She kept her eyes moving across the racks, and stopped, and turned so slow it made my stomach rub the inside of my apron, and buzzed to the other two, who kind of huddled against her for relief, and then they all three of them went up the cat and dog food-breakfast-cereal-macaroni-rice-raisins-seasonings-spreads-spaghetti-soft   drinks-crackers-and-cookies aisle. From the third slot I look straight up this aisle to the meat counter, and I watched them all the way. The fat one with the tan sort of fumbled with the cookies, but on second thought she put the packages back. The sheep pushing their carts down the aisle—the girls were walking against the usual traffic (not that we have one-way signs or anything)—were pretty hilarious. You could see them, when Queenie's white shoulders dawned on them, kind of jerk, or hop, or hiccup, but their eyes snapped back to their own baskets and on they pushed. I bet you could set off dynamite in an A & P and the people would by and large keep reaching and checking oatmeal off their lists and muttering "Let me see, there was a third thing, began with A, asparagus, no, ah, yes, applesauce!" or whatever it is they do mutter. But there was no doubt, this jiggled them. A few house slaves in pin curlers even look around after pushing their carts past to make sure what they had seen was correct.

You know, it's one thing to have a girl in a bathing suit down on the beach, where what with the glare nobody can look at each other much anyway, and another thing in the cool of the A & P, under the fluorescent lights, against all those stacked packages, with her feet padding along naked over our checker-board green-and-cream rubber-tile floor.

"Oh, Daddy," Stokesie said beside me. "I feel so faint."

"Darling," I said. "Hold me tight." Stokesie's married, with two babies chalked up on his fuselage already, but as far as I can tell that's the only difference. He's twenty-two, and I was nineteen this April.

"Is it done?" he asks, the responsible married man finding his voice. I forgot to say he thinks he's going to be manager some sunny day, maybe in 1990 when it's called the Great Alexandrov and Petrooshki Tea Company or something.

What he meant was, our town is five miles from a beach, with a big summer colony out on the Point, but we're right in the middle of town, and the women generally put on a shirt or shorts or something before they get out of the car into the street. And anyway these are usually women with six children and varicose veins mapping their legs and nobody, including them, could care less. As I say, we're right in the middle of town, and if you stand at our front doors you can see two banks and the Congregational church and the newspaper store and three real estate offices and about twenty-seven old freeloaders tearing up Central Street because the sewer broke again. It's not as if we're on the Cape; we're north of Boston and there's people in this town haven't seen the ocean for twenty years.

The girls had reached the meat counter and were asking McMahon something. He pointed, they pointed, and they shuffled out of sight behind a pyramid of Diet Delight peaches. All that was left for us to see was old McMahon patting his mouth and looking after them sizing up their joints. Poor kids, I began to feel sorry for them, they couldn't help it.

Now here comes the sad part of the story, at least my family says it's sad, but I don't think it's so sad myself. The store's pretty empty, it being Thursday afternoon, so there was nothing much to do except lean on the register and wait for the girls to show up again. The whole store was like a pinball machine and I didn't know which tunnel they'd come out of. After a while they come around out of the far aisle, around the light bulbs, records at discount of the Caribbean Six or Tony Martin Sings or some such gunk you wonder they waste the wax on, sixpacks of candy bars, and plastic toys done up in cellophane that fall apart when a kid looks at them anyway. Around they come, Queenie still leading the way, and holding a little gray jar in her hand. Slots Three through Seven are unmanned and I could see her wondering between Stokes and me, but Stokesie with his usual luck draws an old party in baggy gray pants who stumbles up with four giant cans of pineapple juice (what do these bums *do* with all that pineapple juice? I've often asked myself) so the girls come to me. Queenie puts down the jar and I take it into my fingers icy cold. Kingfish Fancy Herring Snacks in Pure Sour Cream: 49¢. Now her hands are empty, not a ring or a bracelet, bare as God made them, and I wonder where the money's coming from. Still with that prim look she lifts a folded dollar bill out of the hollow at the center of her nubbled pink top. The jar went heavy in my hand. Really, I thought that was so cute.

Then everybody's luck begins to run out. Lengel comes in from haggling with a truck full of cabbages on the lot and is about to scuttle into that door marked MANAGER behind which he hides all day when the girls touch his eye. Lengel's pretty dreary, teaches Sunday school and the rest, but he doesn't miss that much. He comes over and says, "Girls, this isn't the beach."

Queenie blushes, though maybe it's just a brush of sunburn I was noticing for the first time, now that she was so close. "My mother asked me to pick up a jar of herring snacks." Her voice kind of startled me, the way voices do when you see the people first, coming out so flat and dumb yet kind of tony, too, the way it ticked over "pick up" and "snacks." All of a sudden I slid right down her voice into her living room. Her father and the other men were standing around in ice-cream coats and bow ties and the women were in sandals picking up herring snacks on toothpicks off a big glass plate and they were all holding drinks the color of water with olives and sprigs of mint in them. When my parents have somebody over they get lemonade and if it's a real racy affair Schlitz in tall glasses with "They'll Do It Every Time" cartoons stencilled on.

"That's all right," Lengel said. "But this isn't the beach." His repeating this struck me as funny, as if it had just occurred to him, and he had been thinking all these years the A & P was a great big dune and he was the head lifeguard. He didn't like my smiling—as I say he doesn't miss much—but he concentrates on giving the girls that sad Sunday-school-superintendent stare.

Queenie's blush is no sunburn now, and the plump one in plaid, that I liked better from the back—a really sweet can—pipes up, "We weren't doing any shopping. We just came in for the one thing."

"That makes no difference," Lengel tells her, and I could see from the way his eyes went that he hadn't noticed she was wearing a two-piece before. "We want you decently dressed when you come in here."

"We *are* decent," Queenie says suddenly, her lower lip pushing, getting sore now that she remembers her place, a place from which the crowd that runs the A & P must look pretty crummy. Fancy Herring Snacks flashed in her very blue eyes.

"Girls, I don't want to argue with you. After this come in here with your shoulders covered. It's our policy." He turns his back. That's policy for you. Policy is what the kingpins want. What the others want is juvenile delinquency.

All this while, the customers had been showing up with their carts but, you know, sheep, seeing a scene, they had all bunched up on Stokesie, who shook open a paper bag as gently as peeling a peach, not wanting to miss a word. I could feel in the silence everybody getting nervous, most of all Lengel, who asks me, "Sammy, have you rung up this purchase?"

I thought and said "No" but it wasn't about that I was thinking. I go through the punches, 4, 9, GROC, TOT—it's more complicated than you think, and after you do it often enough, it begins to make a little song, that you hear words to, in my case "Hello *(bing)* there, you *(gung)* hap-py *peepul (splat)!*"—the splat being the drawer flying out. I un-crease the bill, tenderly as you may imagine, it just having come from between the two smoothest scoops of vanilla I had ever known were there, and pass a half and a penny into her narrow pink palm, and nestle the herrings in a bag and twist its neck and hand it over, all the time thinking.

The girls, and who'd blame them, are in a hurry to get out, so I say "I quit" to Lengel quick enough for them to hear, hoping they'll stop and watch me, their unsuspected hero. They keep right on going, into the electric eye; the door flies open and they flicker across the lot to their car, Queenie and Plaid and Big Tall Goony-Goony (not that as raw material she was so bad), leaving me with Lengel and a kink in his eyebrow.

"Did you say something, Sammy?"

"I said I quit."

"I thought you did."

"You didn't have to embarrass them."

"It was they who were embarrassing us."

I started to say something that came out "Fiddle-de-doo." It's a saying of my grandmother's, and I know she would have been pleased.

"I don't think you know what you're saying," Lengel said.

"I know you don't," I said. "But I do." I pull the bow at the back of my apron and start shrugging it off my shoulders. A couple customers that had been heading for my slot begin to knock against each other, like scared pigs in a chute.

Lengel sighs and begins to look very patient and old and gray. He's been a friend of my parents for years. "Sammy, you don't want to do this to your Mom and Dad," he tells me. It's true, I don't. But it seems to me that once you begin a gesture it's fatal not to go through with it. I fold the apron, "Sammy" stitched in red on the pocket, and put it on the counter, and drop the bow tie on top of it. The bow tie is theirs, if you've ever wondered. "You'll feel this for the rest of your life," Lengel says, and I know that's true, too, but remembering how he made that pretty girl blush makes me so scrunchy inside I punch the No Sale tab and the machine whirs "pee-pul" and the drawer splats out. One advantage to this scene taking place in summer, I can follow this up with a clean exit, there's no fumbling around getting your coat and galoshes, I just saunter into the electric eye in my white shirt that my mother ironed the night before, and the door heaves itself open, and outside the sunshine is skating around on the asphalt.

I look around for my girls, but they're gone, of course. There wasn't anybody but some young married screaming with her children about some candy they didn't get by the door of a powder-blue Falcon station wagon. Looking back in the big windows, over the bags of peat moss and aluminum lawn furniture stacked on the pavement, I could see Lengel in my place in the slot, checking the sheep through. His face was dark gray and his back stiff, as if he'd just had an injection of iron, and my stomach kind of fell as I felt how hard the world was going to be to me hereafter.

—*1962*

Raymond Carver (1938–1988) built a reputation as a master of the contemporary short story that was still growing at the end of his life, which came prematurely after a long struggle with cancer. A native of Clatskanie, Oregon, Carver worked at a number of unskilled jobs in his early years. Married and the father of two before he was twenty, he knew the working class more intimately than have most American writers. Carver worked his way through Humboldt State College (now the University of California—Humboldt) and, like many major figures in contemporary American writing, was a graduate of the Writers' Workshop of the University of Iowa. Carver's publishing career is bracketed by collections of poetry; his earliest publications were poems, and A New Path to the Waterfall appeared posthumously in 1989. The compression of language he learned as a poet may in part account for the lean quality of his prose, which has been called, perhaps unfairly and inaccurately, "minimalist." Carver's last years were spent with his second wife, poet Tess Gallagher, and he taught at a number of universities. His personal victory over alcoholism paralleled the remarkable triumphs of his final years, which included receipt of a prestigious MacArthur Foundation Fellowship. Where I'm Calling From: New and Selected Stories was prepared by Carver shortly before his death and appeared in 1988, and Call If You Need Me, a volume of his uncollected stories and prose, was published in 2001. "A Small, Good Thing" was one of the Carver stories filmed by Robert Altman in his 1993 movie Short Cuts.

Raymond Carver
A Small, Good Thing

Saturday afternoon she drove to the bakery in the shopping center. After looking through a loose-leaf binder with photographs of cakes taped onto the pages, she ordered chocolate, the child's favorite. The cake she chose was decorated with a spaceship and launching pad under a sprinkling of white stars, and a planet made of red frosting at the other end. His name, SCOTTY, would be in green letters beneath the planet. The baker, who was an older man with a thick neck, listened without saying anything when she told him the child would be eight years old next Monday. The baker wore a white apron that looked like a smock. Straps cut under his arms, went around in back and then to the front again, where they were secured under his heavy waist. He wiped his hands on his apron as he listened to her. He kept his eyes down on the photographs and let her talk. He let her take her time. He'd just come to work and he'd be there all night, baking, and he was in no real hurry.

She gave the baker her name, Ann Weiss, and her telephone number. The cake would be ready on Monday morning, just out of the oven, in plenty of time for the child's party that afternoon. The baker was not jolly. There were no pleasantries between them, just the minimum exchange of words, the necessary information. He made her feel uncomfortable, and she didn't like that. While he was bent over the counter with the pencil in his hand, she studied his coarse features and wondered if he'd ever done anything else with his life besides be a baker. She was a mother and thirty-three years old, and it seemed to her that everyone, especially someone the baker's age—a man old enough to be her father—must have children who'd gone through this special time of cakes and birthday parties. There must be that between them, she thought. But he was abrupt with her—not rude, just abrupt. She gave up trying to make friends with him. She looked into the back of the bakery and could see a long, heavy wooden table with aluminum pie pans stacked at one end; and beside the table a metal container filled with empty racks. There was an enormous oven. A radio was playing country-western music.

The baker finished printing the information on the special order card and closed up the binder. He looked at her and said, "Monday morning." She thanked him and drove home.

On Monday morning, the birthday boy was walking to school with another boy. They were passing a bag of potato chips back and forth and the birthday boy was trying to find out what his friend intended to give him for his birthday that afternoon. Without looking, the birthday boy stepped off the curb at an intersection and was immediately knocked down by a car. He fell on his side with his head in the gutter and his legs out in the road. His eyes were closed, but his legs moved back and forth as if he were trying to climb over something. His friend dropped the potato chips and started to cry. The car had gone a hundred feet or so and stopped in the middle of the road. The man in the driver's seat looked back over his shoulder. He waited until the boy got unsteadily to his feet. The boy wobbled a little. He looked dazed, but okay. The driver put the car into gear and drove away.

The birthday boy didn't cry, but he didn't have anything to say about anything either. He wouldn't answer when his friend asked him what it felt like to be hit by a car. He walked home, and his friend went on to school. But after the birthday boy was inside his house and was telling his mother about it—she sitting beside him on the sofa, holding his hands in her lap, saying, "Scotty, honey, are you sure you feel all right, baby?" thinking she would call the doctor anyway—he suddenly lay back on the sofa, closed his eyes, and went limp. When she couldn't wake him up, she hurried to the telephone and called her husband at work. Howard told her to remain calm, remain calm, and then he called an ambulance for the child and left for the hospital himself.

Of course, the birthday party was canceled. The child was in the hospital with a mild concussion and suffering from shock. There'd been vomiting, and his lungs had taken in fluid which needed pumping out that afternoon. Now he simply seemed to be in a very deep sleep—but no coma, Dr. Francis had emphasized, no coma, when he saw the alarm in the parents' eyes. At eleven o'clock that night, when the boy seemed to be resting comfortably enough after the many X-rays and the lab work, and it was just a matter of his waking up and coming around, Howard left the hospital. He and Ann had been at the hospital with the child since that afternoon, and he was going home for a short while to bathe and change clothes. "I'll be back in an hour," he said. She nodded. "It's fine," she said. "I'll be right here." He kissed her on the forehead, and they touched hands. She sat in the chair beside the bed and looked at the child. She was waiting for him to wake up and be all right. Then she could begin to relax.

Howard drove himself home from the hospital. He took the wet, dark streets very fast, then caught himself and slowed down. Until now, his life had gone smoothly and to his satisfaction—college, marriage, another year of college for the advanced degree in business, a junior partnership in an investment firm. Fatherhood. He was happy and, so far, lucky—he knew that. His parents were still living, his brothers and his sister were established, his friends from college had gone out to take their places in the world. So far, he had kept away from any real harm, from those forces he knew existed and that could cripple or bring down a man if the luck went bad, if things suddenly turned. He pulled into the driveway and parked. His left leg began to tremble. He sat in the car for a minute and tried to deal with the present situation in a rational manner. Scotty had been hit by a car and was in the hospital, but he was going to be all right. Howard closed his eyes and ran his hand over his face. He got out of the car and went up to the front door. The dog was barking inside the house. The telephone rang and rang while he unlocked the door and fumbled for the light switch. He shouldn't have left the hospital, he shouldn't have. "Goddamn it!" he said. He picked up the receiver and said, "I just walked in the door!"

"There's a cake here that wasn't picked up," the voice on the other end of the line said.

"What are you saying?" Howard asked.

"A cake," the voice said. "A sixteen-dollar cake."

Howard held the receiver against his ear, trying to understand. "I don't know anything about a cake," he said. "Jesus, what are you talking about?"

"Don't hand me that," the voice said.

Howard hung up the telephone. He went into the kitchen and poured himself some whiskey. He called the hospital. But the child's condition remained the same; he was still sleeping and nothing had changed there. While water poured into the tub, Howard lathered his face and shaved. He'd just stretched out in the tub and closed his eyes when the telephone rang again. He hauled himself out, grabbed a towel, and hurried through the house, saying, "Stupid, stupid," for having left the hospital. But when he picked up the receiver and shouted, "Hello!" there was no sound at the other end of the line. Then the caller hung up.

He arrived back at the hospital a little after midnight. Ann still sat in the chair beside the bed. She looked up at Howard, and then she looked back at the child. The child's eyes stayed closed, the head was still wrapped in bandages. His breathing was quiet and regular. From an apparatus over the bed hung a bottle of glucose with a tube running from the bottle to the boy's arm.

"How is he?" Howard said, "What's all this?" waving at the glucose and the tube.

"Dr. Francis's orders," she said. "He needs nourishment. He needs to keep up his strength. Why doesn't he wake up, Howard? I don't understand, if he's all right."

Howard put his hand against the back of her head. He ran his fingers through her hair. "He's going to be all right. He'll wake up in a little while. Dr. Francis knows what's what."

After a time, he said, "Maybe you should go home and get some rest. I'll stay here. Just don't put up with this creep who keeps calling. Hang up right away."

"Who's calling?" she asked.

"I don't know, just somebody with nothing better to do than call up people. You go on now."

She shook her head. "No," she said, "I'm fine."

"Really," he said. "Go home for a while, and then come back and spell me in the morning. It'll be all right. What did Dr. Francis say? He said Scotty's going to be all right. We don't have to worry. He's just sleeping now, that's all."

A nurse pushed the door open. She nodded at them as she went to the bedside. She took the left arm out from under the covers and put her fingers on the wrist, found the pulse, then consulted her watch. In a little while, she put the arm back under the covers and moved to the foot of the bed, where she wrote something on a clipboard attached to the bed.

"How is he?" Ann said. Howard's hand was a weight on her shoulder. She was aware of the pressure from his fingers.

"He's stable," the nurse said. Then she said, "Doctor will be in again shortly. Doctor's back in the hospital. He's making rounds right now."

"I was saying maybe she'd want to go home and get a little rest," Howard said. "After the doctor comes," he said.

"She could do that," the nurse said. "I think you should both feel free to do that, if you wish." The nurse was a big Scandinavian woman with blond hair. There was the trace of an accent in her speech.

"We'll see what the doctor says," Ann said. "I want to talk to the doctor. I don't think he should keep sleeping like this. I don't think that's a good sign." She brought her hand up to her eyes and let her head come forward a little. Howard's grip tightened on her shoulder, and then his hand moved up to her neck, where his fingers began to knead the muscles there.

"Dr. Francis will be here in a few minutes," the nurse said. Then she left the room.

Howard gazed at his son for a time, the small chest quietly rising and falling under the covers. For the first time since the terrible minutes after Ann's telephone call to him at his office, he felt a genuine fear starting in his limbs. He began shaking his head. Scotty was fine, but instead of sleeping at home in his own bed, he was in a hospital bed with bandages around his head and a tube in his arm. But this help was what he needed right now.

Dr. Francis came in and shook hands with Howard, though they'd just seen each other a few hours before. Ann got up from the chair. "Doctor?"

"Ann," he said and nodded. "Let's just first see how he's doing," the doctor said. He moved to the side of the bed and took the boy's pulse. He peeled back one eyelid and then the other. Howard and Ann stood beside the doctor and watched. Then the doctor turned back the covers and listened to the boy's heart and lungs with his stethoscope. He pressed his fingers here and there on the abdomen. When he was finished, he went to the end of the bed and studied the chart. He noted the time, scribbled something on the chart, and then looked at Howard and Ann.

"Doctor, how is he?" Howard said. "What's the matter with him exactly?"

"Why doesn't he wake up?" Ann said.

The doctor was a handsome, big-shouldered man with a tanned face. He wore a three-piece suit, a striped tie, and ivory cuff links. His gray hair was combed along the sides of his head, and he looked as if he had just come from a concert. "He's all right," the doctor said. "Nothing to shout about, he could be better, I think. But he's all right. Still, I wish he'd wake up. He should wake up pretty soon." The doctor looked at the boy again. "We'll know some more in a couple of hours, after the results of a few more tests are in. But he's all right, believe me, except for the hairline fracture of the skull. He does have that."

"Oh, no," Ann said.

"And a bit of a concussion, as I said before. Of course, you know he's in shock," the doctor said. "Sometimes you see this in shock cases. This sleeping."

"But he's out of any real danger?" Howard said. "You said before he's not in a coma. You wouldn't call this a coma, then—would you, doctor?" Howard waited. He looked at the doctor.

"No, I don't want to call it a coma," the doctor said and glanced over at the boy once more. "He's just in a very deep sleep. It's a restorative measure the body is taking on its own. He's out of any real danger, I'd say that for certain, yes. But we'll know more when he wakes up and the other tests are in," the doctor said.

"It's a coma," Ann said. "Of sorts."

"It's not a coma yet, not exactly," the doctor said. "I wouldn't want to call it coma. Not yet, anyway. He's suffered shock. In shock cases, this kind of reaction is common enough; it's a temporary reaction to bodily trauma. Coma. Well, coma is a deep, prolonged unconsciousness, something that could go on for days, or weeks even. Scotty's not in that area, not as far as we can tell. I'm certain his condition will show improvement by morning. I'm betting that it will. We'll know more when he wakes up, which shouldn't be long now. Of course, you may do as you like, stay here or go home for a time. But by all means feel free to leave the hospital for a while if you want. This is not easy, I know." The doctor gazed at the boy again, watching him, and then he turned to Ann and said, "You try not to worry, little mother. Believe me, we're doing all that can be done. It's just a question of a little more time now." He nodded at her, shook hands with Howard again, and then he left the room.

Ann put her hand over the child's forehead. "At least he doesn't have a fever," she said. Then she said, "My God, he feels so cold, though. Howard? Is he supposed to feel like this? Feel his head."

Howard touched the child's temples. His own breathing had slowed. "I think he's supposed to feel this way right now," he said. "He's in shock, remember? That's what the doctor said. The doctor was just in here. He would have said something if Scotty wasn't okay."

Ann stood there a while longer, working her lip with her teeth. Then she moved over to her chair and sat down.

Howard sat in the chair next to her chair. They looked at each other. He wanted to say something else and reassure her, but he was afraid, too. He took her hand and put it in his lap, and this made him feel better, her hand being there. He picked up her hand and squeezed it. Then he just held her hand. They sat like that for a while, watching the boy and not talking. From time to time, he squeezed her hand. Finally, she took her hand away.

"I've been praying," she said.

He nodded.

She said, "I almost thought I'd forgotten how, but it came back to me. All I had to do was close my eyes and say, 'Please God, help us—help Scotty,' and then the rest was easy. The words were right there. Maybe if you prayed, too," she said to him.

"I've already prayed," he said. "I prayed this afternoon—yesterday afternoon, I mean—after you called, while I was driving to the hospital. I've been praying," he said.

"That's good," she said. For the first time, she felt they were together in it, this trouble. She realized with a start that, until now, it had only been happening to her and to Scotty. She hadn't let Howard into it, though he was there and needed all along. She felt glad to be his wife.

The same nurse came in and took the boy's pulse again and checked the flow from the bottle hanging above the bed.

In an hour, another doctor came in. He said his name was Parsons, from Radiology. He had a bushy moustache. He was wearing loafers, a Western shirt, and a pair of jeans.

"We're going to take him downstairs for more pictures," he told them. "We need to do some more pictures, and we want to do a scan."

"What's that?" Ann said. "A scan?" She stood between this new doctor and the bed. "I thought you'd already taken all your X-rays."

"I'm afraid we need some more," he said. "Nothing to be alarmed about. We just need some more pictures, and we want to do a brain scan on him."

"My God," Ann said.

"It's perfectly normal procedure in cases like this," this new doctor said. "We just need to find out for sure why he isn't back awake yet. It's normal medical procedure, and nothing to be alarmed about. We'll be taking him down in a few minutes," this doctor said.

In a little while, two orderlies came into the room with a gurney. They were black-haired, dark-complexioned men in white uniforms, and they said a few words to each other in a foreign tongue as they unhooked the boy from the tube and moved him from his bed to the gurney. Then they wheeled him from the room. Howard and Ann got on the same elevator. Ann gazed at the child. She closed her eyes as the elevator began its descent. The orderlies stood at either end of the gurney without saying anything, though once one of the men made a comment to the other in their own language, and the other man nodded slowly in response.

Later that morning, just as the sun was beginning to lighten the windows in the waiting room outside the X-ray department, they brought the boy out and moved him back up to his room. Howard and Ann rode up on the elevator with him once more, and once more they took up their places beside the bed.

They waited all day, but still the boy did not wake up. Occasionally, one of them would leave the room to go downstairs to the cafeteria to drink coffee and then, as if suddenly remembering and feeling guilty, get up from the table and hurry back to the room. Dr. Francis came again that afternoon and examined the boy once more and then left after telling them he was coming along and could wake up at any minute now. Nurses, different nurses from the night before, came in from time to time. Then a young woman from the lab knocked and entered the room. She wore white slacks and a white blouse and carried a little tray of things which she put on the stand beside the bed. Without a word to them, she took blood from the boy's arm. Howard closed his eyes as the woman found the right place on the boy's arm and pushed the needle in.

"I don't understand this," Ann said to the woman.

"Doctor's orders," the young woman said. "I do what I'm told. They say draw that one, I draw. What's wrong with him, anyway?" she said. "He's a sweetie."

"He was hit by a car," Howard said. "A hit-and-run."

The young woman shook her head and looked again at the boy. Then she took her tray and left the room.

"Why won't he wake up?" Ann said. "Howard? I want some answers from these people."

Howard didn't say anything. He sat down again in the chair and crossed one leg over the other. He rubbed his face. He looked at his son and then he settled back in the chair, closed his eyes and went to sleep.

Ann walked to the window and looked out at the parking lot. It was night, and cars were driving into and out of the parking lot with their lights on. She stood at the window with her hands gripping the sill, and knew in her heart that they were into something now, something hard. She was afraid, and her teeth began to chatter until she tightened her jaws. She saw a big car stop in front of the hospital and someone, a woman in a long coat, get into the car. She wished she were that woman and somebody, anybody, was driving her away from here to somewhere else, a place where she would find Scotty waiting for her when she stepped out of the car, ready to say *Mom* and let her gather him in her arms.

In a little while, Howard woke up. He looked at the boy again. Then he got up from the chair, stretched, and went over to stand beside her at the window. They both stared out at the parking lot. They didn't say anything. But they seemed to feel each other's insides now, as though the worry had made them transparent in a perfectly natural way.

The door opened and Dr. Francis came in. He was wearing a different suit and tie this time. His gray hair was combed along the sides of his head, and he looked as if he had just shaved. He went straight to the bed and examined the boy. "He ought to have come around by now. There's just no good reason for this," he said. "But I can tell you we're all convinced he's out of any danger. We'll just feel better when he wakes up. There's no reason, absolutely none, why he shouldn't come around. Very soon. Oh, he'll have himself a dilly of a headache when he does, you can count on that. But all of his signs are fine. They're as normal as can be."

"It is a coma, then?" Ann said.

The doctor rubbed his smooth cheek. "We'll call it that for the time being, until he wakes up. But you must be worn out. This is hard. I know this is hard. Feel free to go out for a bite," he said. "It would do you good. I'll put a nurse in here while you're gone if you'll feel better about going. Go and have yourselves something to eat."

"I couldn't eat anything," Ann said.

"Do what you need to do, of course," the doctor said. "Anyway, I wanted to tell you that all the signs are good, the tests are negative, nothing showed up at all, and just as soon as he wakes up he'll be over the hill."

"Thank you, doctor," Howard said. He shook hands with the doctor again. The doctor patted Howard's shoulder and went out.

"I suppose one of us should go home and check on things," Howard said. "Slug needs to be fed, for one thing."

"Call one of the neighbors," Ann said. "Call the Morgans. Anyone will feed a dog if you ask them to."

"All right," Howard said. After a while, he said, "Honey, why don't *you* do it? Why don't you go home and check on things, and then come back? It'll do you good. I'll be right here with him. Seriously," he said. "We need to keep up our strength on this. We'll want to be here for a while even after he wakes up."

"Why don't *you* go?" she said. "Feed Slug. Feed yourself."

"I already went," he said. "I was gone for exactly an hour and fifteen minutes. You go home for an hour and freshen up. Then come back."

She tried to think about it, but she was too tired. She closed her eyes and tried to think about it again. After a time, she said, "Maybe I *will* go home for a few minutes. Maybe if I'm not just sitting right here watching him every second, he'll wake up and be all right. You know? Maybe he'll wake up if I'm not here. I'll go home and take a bath and put on clean clothes. I'll feed Slug. Then I'll come back."

"I'll be right here," he said. "You go on home, honey. I'll keep an eye on things here." His eyes were bloodshot and small, as if he'd been drinking for a long time. His clothes were rumpled. His beard had come out again. She touched his face, and then she took her hand back. She understood he wanted to be by himself for a while, not have to talk or share his worry for a time. She picked her purse up from the nightstand, and he helped her into her coat.

"I won't be gone long," she said.

"Just sit and rest for a little while when you get home," he said. "Eat something. Take a bath. After you get out of the bath, just sit for a while and rest. It'll do you a world of good, you'll see. Then come back," he said. "Let's try not to worry. You heard what Dr. Francis said."

She stood in her coat for a minute trying to recall the doctor's exact words, looking for any nuances, any hint of something behind his words other than what he had said. She tried to remember if his expression had changed any when he bent over to examine the child. She remembered the way his features had composed themselves as he rolled back the child's eyelids and then listened to his breathing.

She went to the door, where she turned and looked back. She looked at the child, and then she looked at the father. Howard nodded. She stepped out of the room and pulled the door closed behind her.

She went past the nurses' station and down to the end of the corridor, looking for the elevator. At the end of the corridor, she turned to her right and entered a little waiting room where a Negro family sat in wicker chairs. There was a middle-aged man in a khaki shirt and pants, a baseball cap pushed back on his head. A large woman wearing a housedress and slippers was slumped in one of the chairs. A teenaged girl in jeans, hair done in dozens of little braids, lay stretched out in one of the chairs smoking a cigarette, her legs crossed at the ankles. The family swung their eyes to Ann as she entered the room. The little table was littered with hamburger wrappers and Styrofoam cups.

"Franklin," the large woman said as she roused herself. "Is it about Franklin?" Her eyes widened. "Tell me now, lady," the woman said. "Is it about Franklin?" She was trying to rise from her chair, but the man had closed his hand over her arm.

"Here, here," he said. "Evelyn."

"I'm sorry," Ann said. "I'm looking for the elevator. My son is in the hospital, and now I can't find the elevator."

"Elevator is down that way, turn left," the man said as he aimed a finger.

The girl drew on her cigarette and stared at Ann. Her eyes were narrowed to slits, and her broad lips parted slowly as she let the smoke escape. The Negro woman let her head fall on her shoulder and looked away from Ann, no longer interested.

"My son was hit by a car," Ann said to the man. She seemed to need to explain herself. "He has a concussion and a little skull fracture, but he's going to be all right. He's in shock now, but it might be some kind of coma, too. That's what really worries us, the coma part. I'm going out for a little while, but my husband is with him. Maybe he'll wake up while I'm gone."

"That's too bad," the man said and shifted in the chair. He shook his head. He looked down at the table, and then he looked back at Ann. She was still standing there. He said, "Our Franklin, he's on the operating table. Somebody cut him. Tried to kill him. There was a fight where he was at. At this party. They say he was just standing and watching. Not bothering nobody. But that don't mean nothing these days. Now he's on the operating table. We're just hoping and praying, that's all we can do now." He gazed at her steadily.

Ann looked at the girl again, who was still watching her, and at the older woman, who kept her head down, but whose eyes were now closed. Ann saw the lips moving silently, making words. She had an urge to ask what those words were. She wanted to talk more with these people who were in the same kind of waiting she was in. She was afraid, and they were afraid. They had that in common. She would have liked to have said something else about the accident, told them more about Scotty, that it had happened on the day of his birthday, Monday, and that he was still unconscious. Yet she didn't know how to begin. She stood looking at them without saying anything more.

She went down the corridor the man had indicated and found the elevator. She waited a minute in front of the closed doors, still wondering if she was doing the right thing. Then she put out her finger and touched the button.

She pulled into the driveway and cut the engine. She closed her eyes and leaned her head against the wheel for minute. She listened to the ticking sounds the engine made as it began to cool. Then she got out of the car. She could hear the dog barking inside the house. She went to the front door, which was unlocked. She went inside and turned on lights and put on a kettle of water for tea. She opened some dog food and fed Slug on the back porch. The dog ate in hungry little smacks. It kept running into the kitchen to see that she was going to stay. As she sat down on the sofa with her tea, the telephone rang.

"Yes!" she said as she answered. "Hello!"

"Mrs. Weiss," a man's voice said. It was five o'clock in the morning, and she thought she could hear machinery or equipment of some kind in the background.

"Yes, yes! What is it?" she said. "This is Mrs. Weiss. This is she. What is it, please?" She listened to whatever it was in the background. "Is it Scotty, for Christ's sake?"

"Scotty," the man's voice said. "It's about Scotty, yes. It has to do with Scotty, that problem. Have you forgotten about Scotty?" the man said. Then he hung up.

She dialed the hospital's number and asked for the third floor. She demanded information about her son from the nurse who answered the telephone. Then she asked to speak to her husband. It was, she said, an emergency.

She waited, turning the telephone cord in her fingers. She closed her eyes and felt sick at her stomach. She would have to make herself eat. Slug came in from the back porch and lay down near her feet. He wagged his tail. She pulled at his ear while he licked her fingers. Howard was on the line.

"Somebody just called here," she said. She twisted the telephone cord. "He said it was about Scotty," she cried.

"Scotty's fine," Howard told her. "I mean, he's still sleeping. There's been no change. The nurse has been in twice since you've been gone. A nurse or else a doctor. He's all right."

"This man called. He said it was about Scotty," she told him.

"Honey, you rest for a little while, you need the rest. It must be that same caller I had. Just forget it. Come back down here after you've rested. Then we'll have breakfast or something."

"Breakfast," she said. "I don't want any breakfast."

"You know what I mean," he said. "Juice, something. I don't know. I don't know anything, Ann. Jesus, I'm not hungry, either. Ann, it's hard to talk now. I'm standing here at the desk. Dr. Francis is coming again at eight o'clock this morning. He's going to have something to tell us then, something more definite. That's what one of the nurses said. She didn't know any more than that. Ann? Honey, maybe we'll know something more then. At eight o'clock. Come back here before eight. Meanwhile, I'm right here and Scotty's all right. He's still the same," he added.

"I was drinking a cup of tea," she said, "when the telephone rang. They said it was about Scotty. There was a noise in the background. Was there a noise in the background on that call you had, Howard?"

"I don't remember," he said. "Maybe the driver of the car, maybe he's a psychopath and found out about Scotty somehow. But I'm here with him. Just rest like you were going to do. Take a bath and come back by seven or so, and we'll talk to the doctor together when he gets here. It's going to be all right, honey. I'm here, and there are doctors and nurses around. They say his condition is stable."

"I'm scared to death," she said.

She ran water, undressed, and got into the tub. She washed and dried quickly, not taking the time to wash her hair. She put on clean underwear, wool slacks, and a sweater. She went into the living room, where the dog looked up at her and let its tail thump once against the floor. It was just starting to get light outside when she went out to the car.

She drove into the parking lot of the hospital and found a space close to the front door. She felt she was in some obscure way responsible for what had happened to the child. She let her thoughts move to the Negro family. She remembered the name Franklin and the table that was covered with hamburger papers, and the teenaged girl staring at her as she drew on her cigarette. "Don't have children," she told the girl's image as she entered the front door of the hospital. "For God's sake, don't."

She took the elevator up to the third floor with two nurses who were just going on duty. It was Wednesday morning, a few minutes before seven. There was a page for a Dr. Madison as the elevator doors slid open on the third floor. She got off behind the nurses, who turned in the other direction and continued the conversation she had interrupted when she'd gotten into the elevator. She walked down the corridor to the little alcove where the Negro family had been waiting. They were gone now, but the chairs were scattered in such a way that it looked as if people had just jumped up from them the minute before. The tabletop was cluttered with the same cups and papers, the ashtray was filled with cigarette butts.

She stopped at the nurses' station. A nurse was standing behind the counter, brushing her hair and yawning.

"There was a Negro boy in surgery last night," Ann said. "Franklin was his name. His family was in the waiting room. I'd like to inquire about his condition."

A nurse who was sitting at a desk behind the counter looked up from a chart in front of her. The telephone buzzed and she picked up the receiver, but she kept her eyes on Ann.

"He passed away," said the nurse at the counter. The nurse held the hairbrush and kept looking at her. "Are you a friend of the family or what?"

"I met the family last night," Ann said. "My own son is in the hospital. I guess he's in shock. We don't know for sure what's wrong. I just wondered about Franklin, that's all. Thank you." She moved down the corridor. Elevator doors the same color as the walls slid open and a gaunt, bald man in white pants and white canvas shoes pulled a heavy cart off the elevator. She hadn't noticed these doors last night. The man wheeled the cart out into the corridor and stopped in front of the room nearest the elevator and consulted a clipboard. Then he reached down and slid a tray out of the cart. He rapped lightly on the door and entered the room. She could smell the unpleasant odors of warm food as she passed the cart. She hurried on without looking at any of the nurses and pushed open the door to the child's room.

Howard was standing at the window with his hands behind his back. He turned around as she came in.

"How is he?" she said. She went over to the bed. She dropped her purse on the floor beside the nightstand. It seemed to her she had been gone a long time. She touched the child's face. "Howard?"

"Dr. Francis was here a little while ago," Howard said. She looked at him closely and thought his shoulders were bunched a little.

"I thought he wasn't coming until eight o'clock this morning," she said quickly.

"There was another doctor with him. A neurologist."

"A neurologist," she said.

Howard nodded. His shoulders were bunching, she could see that. "What'd they say, Howard? For Christ's sake, what'd they say? What is it?"

"They said they're going to take him down and run more tests on him, Ann. They think they're going to operate, honey. Honey, they *are* going to operate. They can't figure out why he won't wake up. It's more than just shock or concussion, they know that much now. It's in his skull, the fracture, it has something, something to do with that, they think. So they're going to operate. I tried to call you, but I guess you'd already left the house."

"Oh, God," she said. "Oh, please, Howard, please," she said, taking his arms.

"Look!" Howard said. "Scotty! Look, Ann!" He turned her toward the bed.

The boy had opened his eyes, then closed them. He opened them again now. The eyes stared straight ahead for a minute, then moved slowly in his head until they rested on Howard and Ann, then traveled away again.

"Scotty," his mother said, moving to the bed.

"Hey, Scott," his father said. "Hey, son."

They leaned over the bed. Howard took the child's hand in his hands and began to pat and squeeze the hand. Ann bent over the boy and kissed his forehead again and again. She put her hands on either side of his face. "Scotty, honey, it's Mommy and Daddy," she said. "Scotty?"

They boy looked at them, but without any sign of recognition. Then his mouth opened, his eyes scrunched closed, and he howled until he had no more air in his lungs. His face seemed to relax and soften then. His lips parted as his last breath was puffed through his throat and exhaled gently through the clenched teeth.

The doctors called it a hidden occlusion and said it was a one-in-a-million circumstance. Maybe if it could have been detected somehow and surgery undertaken immediately, they could have saved him. But more than likely not. In any case, what would they have been looking for? Nothing had shown up in the tests or in the X-rays.

Dr. Francis was shaken. "I can't tell you how badly I feel. I'm so very sorry, I can't tell you," he said as he led them into the doctors' lounge. There was a doctor sitting in a chair with his legs hooked over the back of another chair, watching an early-morning TV show. He was wearing a green delivery-room outfit, loose green pants and green blouse, and a green cap that covered his hair. He looked at Howard and Ann and then looked at Dr. Francis. He got to his feet and turned off the set and went out of the room. Dr. Francis guided Ann to the sofa, sat down beside her, and began to talk in a low, consoling voice. At one point, he leaned over and embraced her. She could feel his chest rising and falling evenly against her shoulder. She kept her eyes open and let him hold her. Howard went into the bathroom, but he left the door open. After a violent fit of weeping, he ran water and washed his face. Then he came out and sat down at the little table that held a telephone. He looked at the telephone as though deciding what to do first. He made some calls. After a time, Dr. Francis used the telephone.

"Is there anything else I can do for the moment?" he asked them.

Howard shook his head. Ann stared at Dr. Francis as if unable to comprehend his words.

The doctor walked them to the hospital's front door. People were entering and leaving the hospital. It was eleven o'clock in the morning. Ann was aware of how slowly, almost reluctantly, she moved her feet. It seemed to her that Dr. Francis was making them leave when she felt they should stay, when it would be more the right thing to do to stay. She gazed out into the parking lot and then turned around and looked back at the front of the hospital. She began shaking her head. "No, no," she said. "I can't leave him here, no." She heard herself say that and thought how unfair it was that the only words that came out were the sort of words used on TV shows where people were stunned by violent or sudden deaths. She wanted her words to be her own. "No," she said, and for some reason the memory of the Negro woman's head lolling on the woman's shoulder came to her. "No," she said again.

"I'll be talking to you later in the day," the doctor was saying to Howard. "There are still some things that have to be done, things that have to be cleared up to our satisfaction. Some things that need explaining."

"An autopsy," Howard said.

Dr. Francis nodded.

"I understand," Howard said. Then he said, "Oh, Jesus. No, I don't understand, doctor. I can't, I can't. I just can't."

Dr. Francis put his arm around Howard's shoulders. "I'm sorry. God, how I'm sorry." He let go of Howard's shoulders and held out his hand. Howard looked at the hand, and then he took it. Dr. Francis put his arms around Ann once more. He seemed full of some goodness she didn't understand. She let her head rest on his shoulder, but her eyes stayed open. She kept looking at the hospital. As they drove out of the parking lot, she looked back at the hospital.

At home, she sat on the sofa with her hands in her coat pockets. Howard closed the door to the child's room. He got the coffee-maker going and then he found an empty box. He had thought to pick up some of the child's things that were scattered around the living room. But instead he sat down beside her on the sofa, pushed the box to one side, and leaned forward, arms between his knees. He began to weep. She pulled his head over into her lap and patted his shoulder. "He's gone," she said. She kept patting his shoulder. Over his sobs, she could hear the coffee-maker hissing in the kitchen. "There, there," she said tenderly. "Howard, he's gone. He's gone and now we'll have to get used to that. To being alone."

In a little while, Howard got up and began moving aimlessly around the room with the box, not putting anything into it, but collecting some things together on the floor at one end of the sofa. She continued to sit with her hands in her coat pockets. Howard put the box down and brought coffee into the living room. Later, Ann made calls to relatives. After each call had been placed and the party had answered, Ann would blurt out a few words and cry for a minute. Then she would quietly explain, in a measured voice, what had happened and tell them about arrangements. Howard took the box out to the garage, where he saw the child's bicycle. He dropped the box and sat down on the pavement beside the bicycle. He took hold of the bicycle awkwardly so that it leaned against his chest. He held it, the rubber pedal sticking into his chest. He gave the wheel a turn.

Ann hung up the telephone after talking to her sister. She was looking up another number when the telephone rang. She picked it up on the first ring.

"Hello," she said, and she heard something in the background, a humming noise. "Hello!" she said. "For God's sake," she said. "Who is this? What is it you want?"

"Your Scotty, I got him ready for you," the man's voice said. "Did you forget him?"

"You evil bastard!" she shouted into the receiver. "How can you do this, you evil son of a bitch!"

"Scotty," the man said. "Have you forgotten about Scotty?" Then the man hung up on her.

Howard heard the shouting and came in to find her with her head on her arms over the table, weeping. He picked up the receiver and listened to the dial tone.

Much later, just before midnight, after they had dealt with many things, the telephone rang again.

"You answer it," she said. "Howard, it's him, I know." They were sitting at the kitchen table with coffee in front of them. Howard had a small glass of whiskey beside his cup. He answered on the third ring.

"Hello," he said. "Who is this? Hello! Hello!" The line went dead. "He hung up," Howard said. "Whoever it was."

"It was him," she said. "That bastard, I'd like to kill him," she said. "I'd like to shoot him and watch him kick," she said.

"Ann, my God," he said.

"Could you hear anything?" she said. "In the background? A noise, machinery, something humming?"

"Nothing, really. Nothing like that," he said. "There wasn't much time. I think there was some radio music. Yes, there was a radio going, that's all I could tell. I don't know what in God's name is going on," he said.

She shook her head. "If I could, could get my hands on him." It came to her then. She knew who it was. Scotty, the cake, the telephone number. She pushed the chair away from the table and got up. "Drive me down to the shopping center," she said. "Howard."

"What are you saying?"

"The shopping center. I know who it is who's calling. I know who it is. It's the baker, the son-of-a-bitching baker, Howard. I had him bake a cake for Scotty's birthday. That's who's calling. That's who has the number and keeps calling us. To harass us about that cake. The baker, that bastard."

They drove down to the shopping center. The sky was clear and stars were out. It was cold, and they ran the heater in the car. They parked in front of the bakery. All of the shops and stores were closed, but there were cars at the far end of the lot in front of the movie theater.

The bakery windows were dark, but when they looked through the glass they could see a light in the back room and, now and then, a big man in an apron moving in and out of the white, even light. Through the glass, she could see the display cases and some little tables with chairs. She tried the door. She rapped on the glass. But if the baker heard them, he gave no sign. He didn't look in their direction.

They drove around behind the bakery and parked. They got out of the car. There was a lighted window too high up for them to see inside. A sign near the back door said THE PANTRY BAKERY, SPECIAL ORDERS. She could hear faintly a radio playing inside and something creak—an oven door as it was pulled down? She knocked on the door and waited. Then she knocked again, louder. The radio was turned down and there was a scraping sound now, the distinct sound of something, a drawer, being pulled open and then closed.

Someone unlocked the door and opened it. The baker stood in the light and peered out at them. "I'm closed for business," he said. "What do you want at this hour? It's midnight. Are you drunk or something?"

She stepped into the light that fell through the open door. He blinked his heavy eyelids as he recognized her. "It's you," he said.

"It's me," she said. "Scotty's mother. This is Scotty's father. We'd like to come in."

The baker said, "I'm busy now. I have work to do."

She had stepped inside the doorway anyway. Howard came in behind her. The baker moved back. "It smells like a bakery in here. Doesn't it smell like a bakery in here, Howard?"

"What do you want?" the baker said. "Maybe you want your cake? That's it, you decided you want your cake. You ordered a cake, didn't you?"

"You're pretty smart for a baker," she said. "Howard, this is the man who's been calling us." She clenched her fists. She stared at him fiercely. There was a deep burning inside her, an anger that made her feel larger than herself, larger than either of these men.

"Just a minute here," the baker said. "You want to pick up your three-day-old cake? That it? I don't want to argue with you, lady. There it sits over there, getting stale. I'll give it to you for half of what I quoted you. No. You want it? You can have it. It's no good to me, no good to anyone now. It cost me time and money to make that cake. If you want it, okay, if you don't, that's okay, too. I have to get back to work." He looked at them and rolled his tongue behind his teeth.

"More cakes," she said. She knew she was in control of it, of what was increasing in her. She was calm.

"Lady, I work sixteen hours a day in this place to earn a living," the baker said. He wiped his hands on his apron. "I work night and day in here, trying to make ends meet." A look crossed Ann's face that made the baker move back and say, "No trouble, now." He reached to the counter and picked up a rolling pin with his right hand and began to tap it against the palm of his other hand. "You want the cake or not? I have to get back to work. Bakers work at night," he said again. His eyes were small, mean-looking, she thought, nearly lost in the bristly flesh around his cheeks. His neck with thick with fat.

"I know bakers work at night," Ann said. "They make phone calls at night, too. You bastard," she said.

The baker continued to tap the rolling pin against his hand. He glanced at Howard. "Careful, careful," he said to Howard.

"My son's dead," she said with a cold, even finality. "He was hit by a car Monday morning. We've been waiting with him until he died. But, of course, you couldn't be expected to know that, could you? Bakers can't know everything—can they, Mr. Baker? But he's dead. He's dead, you bastard!" Just as suddenly as it had welled in her, the anger dwindled, gave way to something else, a dizzy feeling of nausea. She leaned against the wooden table that was sprinkled with flour, put her hands over her face, and began to cry, her shoulders rocking back and forth. "It isn't fair," she said. "It isn't, isn't fair."

Howard put his hand at the small of her back and looked at the baker. "Shame on you," Howard said to him. "Shame."

The baker put the rolling pin back on the counter. He undid his apron and threw it on the counter. He looked at them, and then he shook his head slowly. He pulled a chair out from under the card table that held papers and receipts, an adding machine, and a telephone directory. "Please sit down," he said. "Let me get you a chair," he said to Howard. "Sit down, now, please." The baker went into the front of the shop and returned with two little wrought-iron chairs. "Please sit down, you people."

Ann wiped her eyes and looked at the baker. "I wanted to kill you," she said. "I wanted you dead."

The baker had cleared a space for them at the table. He shoved the adding machine to one side, along with the stacks of notepaper and receipts. He pushed the telephone directory onto the floor, where it landed with a thud. Howard and Ann sat down and pulled their chairs up to the table. The baker sat down, too.

"Let me say how sorry I am," the baker said, putting his elbows on the table. "God alone knows how sorry. Listen to me. I'm just a baker. I don't claim to be anything else. Maybe once, maybe years ago, I was a different kind of human being. I've forgotten, I don't know for sure. But I'm not any longer, if I ever was. Now I'm just a baker. That don't excuse my doing what I did, I know. But I'm deeply sorry. I'm sorry for your son, and sorry for my part in this," the baker said. He spread his hands out on the table and turned them over to reveal his palms. "I don't have any children myself, so I can only imagine what you must be feeling. All I can say to you now is that I'm sorry. Forgive me, if you can," the baker said. "I'm not an evil man, I don't think. Not evil, like you said on the phone. You got to understand what it comes down to is I don't know how to act anymore, it would seem. Please," the man said, "let me ask you if you can find it in your hearts to forgive me?"

It was warm inside the bakery. Howard stood up from the table and took off his coat. He helped Ann from her coat. The baker looked at them for a minute and then nodded and got up from the table. He went to the oven and turned off some switches. He found cups and poured coffee from an electric coffee-maker. He put a carton of cream on the table, and a bowl of sugar.

"You probably need to eat something," the baker said. "I hope you'll eat some of my hot rolls. You have to eat and keep going. Eating is a small, good thing in a time like this," he said.

He served them warm cinnamon rolls just out of the oven, the icing still runny. He put butter on the table and knives to spread the butter. Then the baker sat down at the table with them. He waited. He waited until they each took a roll from the platter and began to eat. "It's good to eat something," he said, watching them. "There's more. Eat up. Eat all you want. There's all the rolls in the world in here."

They ate rolls and drank coffee. Ann was suddenly hungry, and the rolls were warm and sweet. She ate three of them, which pleased the baker. Then he began to talk. They listened carefully. Although they were tired and in anguish, they listened to what the baker had to say.

They nodded when the baker began to speak of loneliness, and of the sense of doubt and limitation that had come to him in his middle years. He told them what it was like to be childless all these years. To repeat the days with the ovens endlessly full and endlessly empty. The party food, the celebrations he'd worked over. Icing knuckle-deep. The tiny wedding couples stuck into cakes. Hundreds of them, no, thousands by now. Birthdays. Just imagine all those candles burning. He had a necessary trade. He was a baker. He was glad he wasn't a florist. It was better to be feeding people. This was a better smell anytime than flowers.

"Smell this," the baker said, breaking open a dark loaf. "It's a heavy bread, but rich." They smelled it, then he had them taste it. It had the taste of molasses and coarse grains. They listened to him. They ate what they could. They swallowed the dark bread. It was like daylight under the fluorescent trays of light. They talked on into the early morning, the high, pale cast of light in the windows, and they did not think of leaving.

—1983

Joyce Carol Oates (b. 1938) is a prolific writer who has published over sixty books since her first appeared in 1963, and she shows few signs of slowing her output. Her new books — whether novels, books of poems, collections of stories, or nonfiction memoirs on subjects like boxing — always draw serious critical attention and more often than not land on the bestseller lists, and she has even written suspense novels pseudonymously as Rosamond Smith. Born in Lockport, New York, she holds degrees from Syracuse and the University of Wisconsin, and she is writer-in-residence at Princeton University, where she also codirects, with her husband, the Ontario Review Press. *Oates's work is often violent, a fact for which she has been criticized on numerous occasions. In response, she has remarked that these comments are "always ignorant, always sexist," implying that different standards are often applied to the work of women authors whose realism may be too strong for some tastes. Few readers would argue that her stories and novels exceed the violence of the society they depict.* Them, *a novel of African-American life in Detroit, won a National Book Award in 1970, and Oates has since garnered many other honors. "Where Are You Going, Where Have You Been?" is based on a* Life *magazine story about a serial rapist and killer known as "The Pied Piper of Tucson." In 1985 Oates's story was filmed by Joyce Chopra as* Smooth Talk, *starring Laura Dern and Treat Williams. Indicating the long popularity of this story, Oates published a collection of prose pieces in 1999 titled* Where I've Been, and Where I'm Going. *Her thirtieth novel,* Blonde *(2000), took as its subject the life of Marilyn Monroe.*

Joyce Carol Oates
Where Are You Going, Where Have You Been?

To Bob Dylan

Her name was Connie. She was fifteen and she had a quick nervous giggling habit of craning her neck to glance into mirrors or checking other people's faces to make sure her own was all right. Her mother, who noticed everything and knew everything and who hadn't much reason any longer to look at her own face, always scolded Connie about it. "Stop gawking at yourself, who are you? You think you're so pretty?" she would say. Connie would raise her eyebrows at these familiar complaints and look right through her mother, into a shadowy vision of herself as she was right at that moment: she knew she was pretty and that was everything. Her mother had been pretty once too, if you could believe those old snapshots in the album, but now her looks were gone and that was why she was always after Connie.

"Why don't you keep your room clean like your sister? How've you got your hair fixed—what the hell stinks? Hair spray? You don't see your sister using that junk."

Her sister June was twenty-four and still lived at home. She was a secretary in the high school Connie attended, and if that wasn't bad enough—with her in the same building—she was so plain and chunky and steady that Connie had to hear her praised all the time by her mother and her mother's sisters. June did this, June did that, she saved money and helped clean the house and cooked and Connie couldn't do a thing, her mind was all filled with trashy daydreams. Their father was away at work most of the time and when he came home he wanted supper and he read the newspaper at supper and after supper he went to bed. He didn't bother talking much to them, but around his bent head Connie's mother kept picking at her until Connie wished her mother was dead and she herself was dead and it was all over. "She makes me want to throw up sometimes," she complained to her friends. She had a high, breathless, amused voice which made everything she said sound a little forced, whether it was sincere or not.

There was one good thing: June went places with girlfriends of hers, girls who were just as plain and steady as she, and so when Connie wanted to do that her mother had no objections. The father of Connie's best girlfriend drove the girls the three miles to town and left them off at a shopping plaza, so that they could walk through the stores or go to a movie, and when he came to pick them up again at eleven he never bothered to ask what they had done.

They must have been familiar sights, walking around that shopping plaza in their shorts and flat ballerina slippers that always scuffed the sidewalk, with charm bracelets jingling on their thin wrists; they would lean together to whisper and laugh secretly if someone passed by who amused or interested them. Connie had long dark blond hair that drew anyone's eye to it, and she wore part of it pulled up on her head and puffed out and the rest of it she let fall down her back. She wore a pull over jersey blouse that looked one way when she was at home and another way when she was away from home. Everything about her had two sides to it, one for home and one for anywhere that was not home: her walk that could be childlike and bobbing, or languid enough to make anyone think she was hearing music in her head, her mouth which was pale and smirking most of the time, but bright and pink on these evenings out, her laugh which was cynical and drawling at home—"Ha, ha, very funny"—but high-pitched and nervous anywhere else, like the jingling of the charms on her bracelet.

Sometimes they did go shopping or to a movie, but sometimes they went across the highway, ducking fast across the busy road, to a drive-in restaurant where older kids hung out. The restaurant was shaped like a big bottle, though squatter than a real bottle, and on its cap was a revolving figure of a grinning boy who held a hamburger aloft. One night in midsummer they ran across, breathless with daring, and right away someone leaned out a car window and invited them over, but it was just a boy from high school they didn't like. It made them feel good to be able to ignore him. They went up through the maze of parked and cruising cars to the bright-lit, fly-infested restaurant, their faces pleased and expectant as if they were entering a sacred building that loomed out of the night to give them what haven and what blessing they yearned for. They sat at the counter and crossed their legs at the ankles, their thin shoulders rigid with excitement, and listened to the music that made everything so good: the music was always in the background like music at a church service, it was something to depend upon.

A boy named Eddie came in to talk with them. He sat backward on his stool, turning himself jerkily around in semicircles and then stopping and turning again, and after a while he asked Connie if she would like something to eat. She said she did and so she tapped her friend's arm on her way out—her friend pulled her face up into a brave droll look—and Connie said she would meet her at eleven, across the way. "I just hate to leave her like that," Connie said earnestly, but the boy said that she wouldn't be alone for long. So they went out to his car and on the way Connie couldn't help but let her eyes wander over the windshields and faces all around her, her face gleaming with a joy that had nothing to do with Eddie or even this place; it might have been the music. She drew her shoulders up and sucked in her breath with the pure pleasure of being alive, and just at that moment she happened to glance at a face just a few feet from hers. It was a boy with shaggy black hair, in a convertible jalopy painted gold. He stared at her and then his lips widened into a grin. Connie slit her eyes at him and turned away, but she couldn't help glancing back and there he was still watching her. He wagged a finger and laughed and said, "Gonna get you, baby," and Connie turned away again without Eddie noticing anything.

She spent three hours with him, at the restaurant where they ate hamburgers and drank Cokes in wax cups that were always sweating, and then down an alley a mile or so away, and when he left her off at five to eleven only the movie house was still open at the plaza. Her girlfriend was there, talking with a boy. When Connie came up the two girls smiled at each other and Connie said, "How was the movie?" and the girl said, "You should know." They rode off with the girl's father, sleepy and pleased, and Connie couldn't help but look at the darkened shopping plaza with its big empty parking lot and its signs that were faded and ghostly now, and over at the drive-in restaurant where cars were still circling tirelessly. She couldn't hear the music at this distance.

Next morning June asked her how the movie was and Connie said, "So-so."

She and that girl and occasionally another girl went out several times a week that way, and the rest of the time Connie spent around the house—it was summer vacation—getting in her mother's way and thinking, dreaming, about the boys she met. But all the boys fell back and dissolved into a single face that was not even a face, but an idea, a feeling, mixed up with the urgent insistent pounding of the music and the humid night air of July. Connie's mother kept dragging her back to the daylight by finding things for her to do or saying, suddenly, "What's this about the Pettinger girl?"

And Connie would say nervously, "Oh, her. That dope." She always drew thick clear lines between herself and such girls, and her mother was simple and kindly enough to believe her. Her mother was so simple, Connie thought, that it was maybe cruel to fool her so much. Her mother went scuffling around the house in old bedroom slippers and complained over the telephone to one sister about the other, then the other called up and the two of them complained about the third one. If June's name was mentioned her mother's tone was approving, and if Connie's name was mentioned it was disapproving. This did not really mean she disliked Connie and actually Connie thought that her mother preferred her to June because she was prettier, but the two of them kept up a pretense of exasperation, a sense that they were tugging and struggling over something of little value to either of them. Sometimes, over coffee, they were almost friends, but something would come up—some vexation that was like a fly buzzing suddenly around their heads—and their faces went hard with contempt.

One Sunday Connie got up at eleven—none of them bothered with church—and washed her hair so that it could dry all day long, in the sun. Her parents and sister were going to a barbecue at an aunt's house and Connie said no, she wasn't interested, rolling her eyes to let her mother know just what she thought of it. "Stay home alone then," her mother said sharply. Connie sat out back in a lawn chair and watched them drive away, her father quiet and bald, hunched around so that he could back the car out, her mother with a look that was still angry and not at all softened through the windshield, and in the back seat poor old June all dressed up as if she didn't know what a barbecue was, with all the running yelling kids and the flies. Connie sat with her eyes closed in the sun, dreaming and dazed with the warmth about her as if this were a kind of love, the caresses of love, and her mind slipped over onto thoughts of the boy she had been with the night before and how nice he had been, how sweet it always was, not the way someone like June would suppose but sweet, gentle, the way it was in movies and promised in songs; and when she opened her eyes she hardly knew where she was, the back yard ran off into weeds and a fence line of trees and behind it the sky was perfectly blue and still. The asbestos "ranch house" that was now three years old startled her—it looked small. She shook her head as if to get awake.

It was too hot. She went inside the house and turned on the radio to drown out the quiet. She sat on the edge of her bed, barefoot, and listened for an hour and a half to a program called XYZ Sunday Jamboree, record after record of hard, fast, shrieking songs she sang along with, interspersed by exclamations from "Bobby King": "An' look here you girls at Napoleon's—Son and Charley want you to pay real close attention to this song coming up!"

And Connie paid close attention herself, bathed in a glow of slow-pulsed joy that seemed to rise mysteriously out of the music itself and lay languidly about the airless little room, breathed in and breathed out with each gentle rise and fall of her chest.

After a while she heard a car coming up the drive. She sat up at once, startled, because it couldn't be her father so soon. The gravel kept crunching all the way in from the road—the driveway was long—and Connie ran to the window. It was a car she didn't know. It was an open jalopy, painted a bright gold that caught the sunlight opaquely. Her heart began to pound and her fingers snatched at her hair, checking it, and she whispered "Christ, Christ," wondering how bad she looked. The car came to a stop at the side door and the horn sounded four short taps as if this were a signal Connie knew.

She went into the kitchen and approached the door slowly, then hung out the screen door, her bare toes curling down off the step. There were two boys in the car and now she recognized the driver: he had shaggy, shabby black hair that looked crazy as a wig and he was grinning at her.

"I ain't late, am I?" he said.

"Who the hell do you think you are?" Connie said.

"Toldja I'd be out, didn't I?"

"I don't even know who you are."

She spoke sullenly, careful to show no interest or pleasure, and he spoke in a fast bright monotone. Connie looked past him to the other boy, taking her time. He had fair brown hair, with a lock that fell onto his forehead. His sideburns gave him a fierce, embarrassed look, but so far he hadn't even bothered to glance at her. Both boys wore sunglasses. The driver's glasses were metallic and mirrored everything in miniature.

"You wanta come for a ride?" he said.

Connie smirked and let her hair fall loose over one shoulder.

"Don'tcha like my car? New paint job," he said. "Hey."

"What?"

"You're cute."

She pretended to fidget, chasing flies away from the door.

"Don'tcha believe me, or what?" he said.

"Look, I don't even know who you are," Connie said in disgust.

"Hey, Ellie's got a radio, see. Mine's broke down." He lifted his friend's arm and showed her the little transistor the boy was holding, and now Connie began to hear the music. It was the same program that was playing inside the house.

"Bobby King?" she said.

"I listen to him all the time. I think he's great."

"He's kind of great," Connie said reluctantly.

"Listen, that guy's *great*. He knows where the action is."

Connie blushed a little, because the glasses made it impossible for her to see just what this boy was looking at. She couldn't decide if she liked him or if he was just a jerk, and so she dawdled in the doorway and wouldn't come down or go back inside. She said, "What's all that stuff painted on your car?"

"Can'tcha read it?" He opened the door very carefully, as if he was afraid it might fall off. He slid out just as carefully, planting his feet firmly on the ground, the tiny metallic world in his glasses slowing down like gelatine hardening and in the midst of it Connie's bright green blouse. "This here is my name, to begin with," he said. ARNOLD FRIEND was written in tarlike black letters on the side, with a drawing of a round grinning face that reminded Connie of a pumpkin, except it wore sunglasses. "I wanta introduce myself, I'm Arnold Friend and that's my real name and I'm gonna be your friend, honey, and inside the car's Ellie Oscar, he's kinda shy." Ellie brought his transistor radio up to his shoulder and balanced it there. "Now these numbers are a secret code, honey," Arnold Friend explained. He read off the numbers 33, 19, 17 and raised his eyebrows at her to see what she thought of that, but she didn't think much of it. The left rear fender had been smashed and around it was written, on the gleaming gold background—DONE BY CRAZY WOMAN DRIVER. Connie had to laugh at that. Arnold Friend was pleased at her laughter and looked up at her. "Around the other side's a lot more—you wanta come and see them?"

"No."

"Why not?"

"Why should I?"

"Don'tcha wanta see what's on the car? Don'tcha wanta go for a ride?"

"I don't know."

"Why not?"

"I got things to do."

"Like what?"

"Things."

He laughed as if she had said something funny. He slapped his thighs. He was standing in a strange way, leaning back against the car as if he were balancing himself. He wasn't tall, only an inch or so taller than she would be if she came down to him. Connie liked the way he was dressed, which was the way all of them dressed: tight faded jeans stuffed into black, scuffed boots, a belt that pulled his waist in and showed how lean he was, and a white pullover shirt that was a little soiled and showed the hard small muscles of his arms and shoulders. He looked as if he probably did hard work, lifting and carrying things. Even his neck looked muscular. And his face was a familiar face, somehow—the jaw and chin and cheeks slightly darkened, because he hadn't shaved for a day or two, and the nose long and hawklike, sniffing as if she were a treat he was going to gobble up and it was all a joke.

"Connie, you ain't telling the truth. This is your day set aside for a ride with me and you know it," he said, still laughing. The way he straightened and recovered from his fit of laughing showed that it had been all fake.

"How do you know what my name is?" she said suspiciously.

"It's Connie."

"Maybe and maybe not."

"I know my Connie," he said, wagging his finger. Now she remembered him even better, back at the restaurant, and her cheeks warmed at the thought of how she sucked in her breath just at the moment she passed him—how she must have looked to him. And he had remembered her. "Ellie and I come out here especially for you," he said. "Ellie can sit in back. How about it?"

"Where?"

"Where what?"

"Where're we going?"

He looked at her. He took off the sunglasses and she saw how pale the skin around his eyes was, like holes that were not in shadow but instead in light. His eyes were like chips of broken glass that catch the light in an amiable way. He smiled. It was as if the idea of going for a ride somewhere, to some place, was a new idea to him.

"Just for a ride, Connie sweetheart."

"I never said my name was Connie," she said.

"But I know what it is. I know your name and all about you, lots of things," Arnold Friend said. He had not moved yet but stood still leaning back against the side of his jalopy. "I took a special interest in you, such a pretty girl, and found out all about you like I know your parents and sister are gone somewheres and I know where and how long they're going to be gone, and I know who you were with last night, and your best girlfriend's name is Betty. Right?"

He spoke in a simple lilting voice, exactly as if he were reciting the words to a song. His smile assured her that everything was fine. In the

car Ellie turned up the volume on his radio and did not bother to look
around at them.

"Ellie can sit in the back seat," Arnold Friend said. He indicated his
friend with a casual jerk of his chin, as if Ellie did not count and she
should not bother with him.

"How'd you find out all that stuff?" Connie said.

"Listen: Betty Schultz and Tony Fitch and Jimmy Pettinger and
Nancy Pettinger," he said, in a chant. "Raymond Stanley and Bob
Hutter—"

"Do you know all those kids?"

"I know everybody."

"Look, you're kidding. You're not from around here."

"Sure."

"But—how come we never saw you before?"

"Sure you saw me before," he said. He looked down at his boots, as
if he were a little offended. "You just don't remember."

"I guess I'd remember you," Connie said.

"Yeah?" He looked up at this, beaming. He was pleased. He began
to mark time with the music from Ellie's radio, tapping his fists lightly
together. Connie looked away from his smile to the car, which was
painted so bright it almost hurt her eyes to look at it. She looked at that
name, ARNOLD FRIEND. And up at the front fender was an expression
that was familiar—MAN THE FLYING SAUCERS. It was an expression kids
had used the year before, but didn't use this year. She looked at it for a
while as if the words meant something to her that she did not yet know.

"What're you thinking about? Huh?" Arnold Friend demanded.
"Not worried about your hair blowing around in the car, are you?"

"No."

"Think I maybe can't drive good?"

"How do I know?"

"You're a hard girl to handle. How come?" he said. "Don't you
know I'm your friend? Didn't you see me put my sign in the air when
you walked by?"

"What sign?"

"My sign." And he drew an X in the air, leaning out toward her.
They were maybe ten feet apart. After his hand fell back to his side the
X was still in the air, almost visible. Connie let the screen door close and
stood perfectly still inside it, listening to the music from her radio and

the boy's blend together. She stared at Arnold Friend. He stood there so stiffly relaxed, pretending to be relaxed, with one hand idly on the door handle as if he were keeping himself up that way and had no intention of ever moving again. She recognized most things about him, the tight jeans that showed his thighs and buttocks and the greasy leather boots and the tight shirt, and even that slippery friendly smile of his, that sleepy dreamy smile that all the boys used to get across ideas they didn't want to put into words. She recognized all this and also the singsong way he talked, slightly mocking, kidding, but serious and a little melancholy, and she recognized the way he tapped one fist against the other in homage to the perpetual music behind him. But all these things did not come together.

She said suddenly, "Hey, how old are you?"

His smile faded. She could see then that he wasn't a kid, he was much older—thirty, maybe more. At this knowledge her heart began to pound faster.

"That's a crazy thing to ask. Can'tcha see I'm your own age?"

"Like hell you are."

"Or maybe a coupla years older, I'm eighteen."

"Eighteen?" she said doubtfully.

He grinned to reassure her and lines appeared at the corners of his mouth. His teeth were big and white. He grinned so broadly his eyes became slits and she saw how thick the lashes were, thick and black as if painted with a black tarlike material. Then he seemed to become embarrassed, abruptly, and looked over his shoulder at Ellie. "*Him*, he's crazy," he said. "Ain't he a riot, he's a nut, a real character." Ellie was still listening to the music. His sunglasses told nothing about what he was thinking. He wore a bright orange shirt unbuttoned halfway to show his chest, which was a pale, bluish chest and not muscular like Arnold Friend's. His shirt collar was turned up all around and the very tips of the collar pointed out past his chin as if they were protecting him. He was pressing the transistor radio up against his ear and sat there in a kind of daze, right in the sun.

"He's kinda strange," Connie said.

"Hey, she says you're kinda strange! Kinda strange!" Arnold Friend cried. He pounded on the car to get Ellie's attention. Ellie turned for the first time and Connie saw with shock that he wasn't a kid either—he had a fair, hairless face, cheeks reddened slightly as if the veins grew too close to the surface of his skin, the face of a forty-year-old baby. Connie felt a wave of dizziness rise in her at this sight and she stared at him as if waiting for something to change the shock of the moment, make it all right again. Ellie's lips kept shaping words, mumbling along, with the words blasting in his ear.

"Maybe you two better go away," Connie said faintly.

"What? How come?" Arnold Friend cried. "We come out here to take you for a ride. It's Sunday." He had the voice of the man on the radio now. It was the same voice, Connie thought. "Don'tcha know it's Sunday all day and honey, no matter who you were with last night today you're with Arnold Friend and don't you forget it!—Maybe you better step out here," he said, and this last was in a different voice. It was a little flatter, as if the heat was finally getting to him.

"No. I got things to do."

"Hey."

"You two better leave."

"We ain't leaving until you come with us."

"Like hell I am—"

"Connie, don't fool around with me. I mean, I mean, don't fool *around*," he said, shaking his head. He laughed incredulously. He placed his sunglasses on top of his head, carefully, as if he were indeed wearing a wig, and brought the stems down behind his ears. Connie stared at him, another wave of dizziness and fear rising in her so that for a moment he wasn't even in focus but was just a blur, standing there against his gold car, and she had the idea that he had driven up the driveway all right but had come from nowhere before that and belonged nowhere and that everything about him and even about the music that was so familiar to her was only half real.

"If my father comes and sees you—"

"He ain't coming. He's at the barbecue."

"How do you know that?"

"Aunt Tillie's. Right now they're—uh—they're drinking. Sitting around," he said vaguely, squinting as if he were staring all the way to town and over to Aunt Tillie's back yard. Then the vision seemed to get clear and he nodded energetically. "Yeah. Sitting around. There's your sister in a blue dress, huh? And high heels, the poor sad bitch—nothing like you, sweetheart! And your mother's helping some fat woman with the corn, they're cleaning the corn—husking the corn—"

"What fat woman?" Connie cried.

"How do I know what fat woman. I don't know every goddam fat woman in the world!" Arnold Friend laughed.

"Oh, that's Mrs. Hornby . . . Who invited her?" Connie said. She felt a little light-headed. Her breath was coming quickly.

"She's too fat. I don't like them fat. I like them the way you are, honey," he said, smiling sleepily at her. They stared at each other for a while, through the screen door. He said softly, "Now what you're going to do is this: you're going to come out that door. You're going to sit up front with me and Ellie's going to sit in the back, the hell with Ellie, right? This isn't Ellie's date. You're my date. I'm your lover, honey."

"What? You're crazy—"

"Yes, I'm your lover. You don't know what that is but you will," he said. "I know that too. I know all about you. But look: it's real nice and you couldn't ask for nobody better than me, or more polite. I always keep my word. I'll tell you how it is, I'm always nice at first, the first time. I'll hold you so tight you won't think you have to try to get away or pretend anything because you'll know you can't. And I'll come inside you where it's all secret and you'll give in to me and you'll love me—"

"Shut up! You're crazy!" Connie said. She backed away from the door. She put her hands against her ears as if she'd heard something terrible, something not meant for her. "People don't talk like that, you're crazy," she muttered. Her heart was almost too big now for her chest and its pumping made sweat break out all over her. She looked out to see Arnold Friend pause and then take a step toward the porch lurching. He almost fell. But, like a clever drunken man, he managed to catch his balance. He wobbled in his high boots and grabbed hold of one of the porch posts.

"Honey?" he said. "You still listening?"

"Get the hell out of here!"

"Be nice, honey. Listen."

"I'm going to call the police—"

He wobbled again and out of the side of his mouth came a fast spat curse, an aside not meant for her to hear. But even this "Christ!" sounded forced. Then he began to smile again. She watched this smile come, awkward as if he were smiling from inside a mask. His whole face was a mask, she thought wildly, tanned down onto his throat but then running out as if he had plastered makeup on his face but had forgotten about his throat.

"Honey—? Listen, here's how it is. I always tell the truth and I promise you this: I ain't coming in that house after you."

"You better not! I'm going to call the police if you—if you don't—"

"Honey," he said, talking right through her voice, "honey, I'm not coming in there but you are coming out here. You know why?"

She was panting. The kitchen looked like a place she had never seen before, some room she had run inside but which wasn't good enough, wasn't going to help her. The kitchen window had never had a curtain, after three years, and there were dishes in the sink for her to do—prob- ably—and if you ran your hand across the table you'd probably feel something sticky there.

"You listening, honey? Hey?"

"—going to call the police—"

"Soon as you touch the phone I don't need to keep my promise and can come inside. You won't want that."

She rushed forward and tried to lock the door. Her fingers were shaking. "But why lock it," Arnold Friend said gently, talking right into her face. "It's just a screen door. It's just nothing." One of his boots was at a strange angle, as if his foot wasn't in it. It pointed out to the left, bent at the ankle. "I mean, anybody can break through a screen door and glass and wood and iron or anything else if he needs to, any- body at all and specially Arnold Friend. If the place got lit up with a fire honey you'd come runnin' out into my arms, right into my arms an' safe at home—like you knew I was your lover and'd stopped fool- ing around. I don't mind a nice shy girl but I don't like no fooling around." Part of those words were spoken with a slight rhythmic lilt, and Connie somehow recognized them—the echo of a song from last year, about a girl rushing into her boyfriend's arms and coming home again—

Connie stood barefoot on the linoleum floor, staring at him. "What do you want?" she whispered.

"I want you," he said.

"What?"

"Seen you that night and thought, that's the one, yes sir. I never needed to look any more."

"But my father's coming back. He's coming to get me. I had to wash my hair first—" She spoke in a dry, rapid voice, hardly raising it for him to hear.

"No, your Daddy is not coming and yes, you had to wash your hair and you washed it for me. It's nice and shining and all for me, I thank you, sweetheart," he said, with a mock bow, but again he almost lost his balance. He had to bend and adjust his boots. Evidently his feet did not go all the way down; the boots must have been stuffed with something so that he would seem taller. Connie stared out at him and behind him Ellie in the car, who seemed to be looking off toward Connie's right, into nothing. This Ellie said, pulling the words out of the air one after another as if he were just discovering them, "You want me to pull out the phone?"

"Shut your mouth and keep it shut," Arnold Friend said, his face red from bending over or maybe from embarrassment because Connie had seen his boots. "This ain't none of your business."

"What—what are you doing? What do you want?" Connie said. "If I call the police they'll get you, they'll arrest you—"

"Promise was not to come in unless you touch that phone, and I'll keep that promise," he said. He resumed his erect position and tried to force his shoulders back. He sounded like a hero in a movie, declaring something important. He spoke too loudly and it was as if he were speaking to someone behind Connie. "I ain't made plans for coming in that house where I don't belong but just for you to come out to me, the way you should. Don't you know who I am?"

"You're crazy," she whispered. She backed away from the door but did not want to go into another part of the house, as if this would give him permission to come through the door. "What do you . . . You're crazy, you . . ."

"Huh? What're you saying, honey?"

Her eyes darted everywhere in the kitchen. She could not remember what it was, this room.

"This is how it is, honey: you come out and we'll drive away, have a nice ride. But if you don't come out we're gonna wait till your people come home and then they're all going to get it."

"You want that telephone pulled out?" Ellie said. He held the radio away from his ear and grimaced, as if without the radio the air was too much for him.

"I toldja shut up, Ellie," Arnold Friend said, "you're deaf, get a hearing aid, right? Fix yourself up. This little girl's no trouble and's gonna be nice to me, so Ellie keep to yourself, this ain't your date— right? Don't hem in on me. Don't hog. Don't crush. Don't bird dog. Don't trail me," he said in a rapid meaningless voice, as if he were running through all the expressions he'd learned but was no longer sure which one of them was in style, then rushing on to new ones, making them up with his eyes closed, "Don't crawl under my fence, don't squeeze in my chipmunk hole, don't sniff my glue, suck my popsicle, keep your own greasy fingers on yourself!" He shaded his eyes and peered in at Connie, who was backed against the kitchen table. "Don't mind him honey he's just a creep. He's a dope. Right? I'm the boy for you and like I said you come out here nice like a lady and give me your hand, and nobody else gets hurt, I mean, your nice old bald-headed daddy and your mummy and your sister in her high heels. Because listen: why bring them in this?"

"Leave me alone," Connie whispered.

"Hey, you know that old woman down the road, the one with the chickens and stuff—you know her?"

"She's dead!"

"Dead? What? You know her?" Arnold Friend said.

"She's dead—"

"Don't you like her?"

"She's dead—she's—she isn't here any more—"

"But don't you like her, I mean, you got something against her? Some grudge or something?" Then his voice dipped as if he were conscious of a rudeness. He touched the sunglasses perched on top of his head as if to make sure they were still there. "Now you be a good girl."

"What are you going to do?"

"Just two things, or maybe three," Arnold Friend said. "But I promise it won't last long and you'll like me the way you get to like people you're close to. You will. It's all over for you here, so come on out. You don't want your people in any trouble, do you?"

She turned and bumped against a chair or something, hurting her leg, but she ran into the back room and picked up the telephone. Something roared in her ear, a tiny roaring, and she was so sick with fear that she could do nothing but listen to it—the telephone was clammy and very heavy and her fingers groped down to the dial but were too weak to touch it. She began to scream into the phone, into the roaring. She cried out, she cried for her mother, she felt her breath start jerking back and forth in her lungs as if it were something Arnold Friend were stabbing her with again and again with no tenderness. A noisy sorrowful wailing rose all about her and she was locked inside it the way she was locked inside the house.

After a while she could hear again. She was sitting on the floor with her wet back against the wall.

Arnold Friend was saying from the door, "That's a good girl. Put the phone back."

She kicked the phone away from her.

"No, honey. Pick it up. Put it back right."

She picked it up and put it back. The dial tone stopped.

"That's a good girl. Now come outside."

She was hollow with what had been fear, but what was now just an emptiness. All that screaming had blasted it out of her. She sat, one leg cramped under her, and deep inside her brain was something like a pinpoint of light that kept going and would not let her relax. She thought, I'm not going to see my mother again. She thought, I'm not going to sleep in my bed again. Her bright green blouse was all wet.

Arnold Friend said, in a gentle-loud voice that was like a stage voice, "The place where you came from ain't there any more, and where you had in mind to go is canceled out. This place you are now—inside your daddy's house—is nothing but a cardboard box I can knock down any time. You know that and always did know it. You hear me?"

She thought, I have got to think. I have to know what to do.

"We'll go out to a nice field, out in the country here where it smells so nice and it's sunny," Arnold Friend said. "I'll have my arms tight around you so you won't need to try to get away and I'll show you what love is like, what it does. The hell with this house! It looks solid all right," he said. He ran a fingernail down the screen and the noise did not make Connie shiver, as it would have the day before. "Now put your hand on your heart, honey. Feel that? That feels solid too but we know better, be nice to me, be sweet like you can because what else is there for a girl like you but to be sweet and pretty and give in?—and get away before her people come back?"

She felt her pounding heart. Her hand seemed to enclose it. She thought for the first time in her life that it was nothing that was hers, that belonged to her, but just a pounding, living thing inside this body that wasn't really hers either.

"You don't want them to get hurt," Arnold Friend went on. "Now get up, honey. Get up all by yourself."

She stood up.

"Now turn this way. That's right. Come over here to me—Ellie, put that away, didn't I tell you? You dope. You miserable creepy dope," Arnold Friend said. His words were not angry but only part of an incantation. The incantation was kindly. "Now come out through the kitchen to me honey, and let's see a smile, try it, you're a brave sweet little girl and now they're eating corn and hot dogs cooked to bursting over an outdoor fire, and they don't know one thing about you and never did and honey you're better than them because not a one of them would have done this for you."

Connie felt the linoleum under her feet; it was cool. She brushed her hair back out of her eyes. Arnold Friend let go of the post tentatively and opened his arms for her, his elbows pointing in toward each other and his wrists limp, to show that this was an embarrassed embrace and a little mocking, he didn't want to make her self-conscious.

She put out her hand against the screen. She watched herself push the door slowly open as if she were safe back somewhere in the other doorway, watching this body and this head of long hair moving out into the sunlight where Arnold Friend waited.

"My sweet little blue-eyed girl," he said, in a half-sung sigh that had nothing to do with her brown eyes but was taken up just the same by the vast sunlit reaches of the land behind him and on all sides of him, so much land that Connie had never seen before and did not recognize except to know that she was going to it.

—1966

Margaret Atwood (b. 1939) is a leading figure among Canadian writers, and she is equally skilled as a poet and fiction writer. She is also an internationally known feminist spokesperson in great demand for appearances at symposia on women's issues, and she was named by Ms. magazine *as* Woman of the Year *for 1986. Born in Ottawa, Ontario, she graduated from University of Toronto in 1962, the same year that her first book appeared, and she later did graduate work at Radcliffe and Harvard. She has published two volumes of selected poems, over a dozen novels and collections of short stories, and a book of literary criticism. In addition, she served as editor of two anthologies of Canadian literature and wrote* Survival: A Thematic Guide to Canadian Literature *(1972), an influential work that challenged Canadian writers to explore their own unique cultural heritage. Atwood has served as writer in residence at universities in Canada, the United States, and abroad. The* Handmaid's Tale *(1985), a work that presents a future dystopia controlled by a fundamentalist patriarchy, was a bestseller and was filmed in 1990.* The Blind Assassin, *a complex, multilayered novel, was published in 2000.*

Margaret Atwood

Happy Endings

> John and Mary meet.
> What happens next?
> If you want a happy ending, try A.

A

John and Mary fall in love and get married. They both have worthwhile and remunerative jobs which they find stimulating and challenging. They buy a charming house. Real estate values go up. Eventually, when they can afford live-in help, they have two children, to whom they are devoted. The children turn out well. John and Mary have a stimulating and challenging sex life and worthwhile friends. They go on fun vacations together. They retire. They both have hobbies which they find stimulating and challenging. Eventually they die. This is the end of the story.

B

Mary falls in love with John but John doesn't fall in love with Mary. He merely uses her body for selfish pleasure and ego gratification of a tepid kind. He comes to her apartment twice a week and she cooks him dinner, you'll notice that he doesn't even consider her worth the price of a dinner out, and after he's eaten the dinner he fucks her and after that he falls asleep, while she does the dishes so he won't think she's untidy, having all those dirty dishes lying around, and puts on fresh lipstick so she'll look good when he wakes up, but when he wakes up he doesn't even notice, he puts on his socks and his shorts and his pants and his shirt and his tie and his shoes, the reverse order from the one in which he took them off. He doesn't take off Mary's clothes, she takes them off herself, she acts as if she's dying for it every time, not because she likes sex exactly, she doesn't, but she wants John to think she does because if they do it often enough surely he'll get used to her, he'll come to depend on her and they will get married, but John goes out the door with hardly so much as a good-night and three days later he turns up at six o'clock and they do the whole thing over again.

Mary gets run-down. Crying is bad for your face, everyone knows that and so does Mary but she can't stop. People at work notice. Her friends tell her John is a rat, a pig, a dog, he isn't good enough for her, but she can't believe it. Inside John, she thinks, is another John, who is much nicer. This other John will emerge like a butterfly from a cocoon, a Jack from a box, a pit from a prune, if the first John is only squeezed enough.

One evening John complains about the food. He has never complained about the food before. Mary is hurt.

Her friends tell her they've seen him in a restaurant with another woman, whose name is Madge. It's not even Madge that finally gets to Mary: it's the restaurant. John has never taken Mary to a restaurant. Mary collects all the sleeping pills and aspirins she can find, and takes them and a half a bottle of sherry. You can see what kind of a woman she is by the fact that it's not even whiskey. She leaves a note for John. She hopes he'll discover her and get her to the hospital in time and repent and then they can get married, but this fails to happen and she dies.

John marries Madge and everything continues as in A.

C

John, who is an older man, falls in love with Mary, and Mary, who is only twenty-two, feels sorry for him because he's worried about his hair falling out. She sleeps with him even though she's not in love with him. She met him at work. She's in love with someone called James, who is twenty-two also and not yet ready to settle down.

John on the contrary settled down long ago: this is what is bothering him. John has a steady, respectable job and is getting ahead in his field, but Mary isn't impressed by him, she's impressed by James, who has a motorcycle and a fabulous record collection. But James is often away on his motorcycle, being free. Freedom isn't the same for girls, so in the meantime Mary spends Thursday evenings with John. Thursdays are the only days John can get away.

John is married to a woman called Madge and they have two children, a charming house which they bought just before the real estate values went up, and hobbies which they find stimulating and challenging, when they have the time. John tells Mary how important she is to him, but of course he can't leave his wife because a commitment is a commitment. He goes on about this more than is necessary and Mary finds it boring, but older men can keep it up longer so on the whole she has a fairly good time.

One day James breezes in on his motorcycle with some top-grade California hybrid and James and Mary get higher than you'd believe possible and they climb into bed. Everything becomes very underwater, but along comes John, who has a key to Mary's apartment. He finds them stoned and entwined. He's hardly in any position to be jealous, considering Madge, but nevertheless he's overcome with despair. Finally he's middle-aged, in two years he'll be bald as an egg and he can't stand it. He purchases a handgun, saying he needs it for target practice—this is the thin part of the plot, but it can be dealt with later—and shoots the two of them and himself.

Madge, after a suitable period of mourning, marries an understanding man called Fred and everything continues as in A, but under different names.

D

Fred and Madge have no problems. They get along exceptionally well and are good at working out any little difficulties that may arise. But their charming house is by the seashore and one day a giant tidal wave approaches. Real estate values go down. The rest of the story is about what caused the tidal wave and how they escape from it. They do, though thousands drown, but Fred and Madge are virtuous and lucky. Finally on high ground they clasp each other, wet and dripping and grateful, and continue as in A.

E

Yes, but Fred has a bad heart. The rest of the story is about how kind and understanding they both are until Fred dies. Then Madge devotes herself to charity work until the end of A. If you like, it can be "Madge," "cancer," "guilty and confused," and "bird watching."

F

If you think this is all too bourgeois, make John a revolutionary and Mary a counterespionage agent and see how far that gets you. Remember, this is Canada. You'll still end up with A, though in between you may get a lustful brawling saga of passionate involvement, a chronicle of our times, sort of.

You'll have to face it, the endings are the same however you slice it. Don't be deluded by any other endings, they're all fake, either deliberately fake, with malicious intent to deceive, or just motivated by excessive optimism if not by downright sentimentality.

The only authentic ending is the one provided here:

John and Mary die. John and Mary die. John and Mary die.

So much for endings. Beginnings are always more fun. True connoisseurs, however, are known to favor the stretch in between, since it's the hardest to do anything with.

That's about all that can be said for plots, which anyway are just one thing after another, a what and a what and a what.

Now try How and Why.

—1983

Bobbie Ann Mason (b. 1940) was born in Mayfield, Kentucky, and grew up on a dairy farm run by her parents. The rural background of her youth figures in many of her best stories, and one of Mason's favorite subjects is the assimilation of the countryside and the South into a larger American culture. Mason's characters may dream of living in log cabins, but they also take adult education courses, watch TV talk shows, and shop in supermarkets and malls. After taking degrees from the University of Kentucky and the University of Connecticut, Mason published her first two books, both works of literary criticism, in the mid 1970s. One of them, The Girl Sleuth, *was a feminist guide to the exploits of fictional detectives like Nancy Drew that Mason read as a child. After years of attempts, Mason's stories began to appear in prestigious magazines, most prominently* The New Yorker, *and the publication of* Shiloh and Other Stories *(1982) established her as an important new voice in American fiction. She has since published a second collection of short stories and two novels, one of which,* In Country *(1985), was filmed in 1989. "Shiloh," like several of the stories in the collection from which it is taken, gains considerable immediacy from Mason's use of present tense and her sure sense of regional speech patterns. In recent years, Mason has published a novel,* Feather Crowns *(1993), and a memoir of her Kentucky childhood,* Clear Springs *(1999).*

Bobbie Ann Mason
Shiloh

Leroy Moffitt's wife, Norma Jean, is working on her pectorals. She lifts three-pound dumbbells to warm up, then progresses to a twenty-pound barbell. Standing with her legs apart, she reminds Leroy of Wonder Woman.

"I'd give anything if I could just get these muscles to where they're real hard," says Norma Jean. "Feel this arm. It's not as hard as the other one."

"That's 'cause you're right-handed," says Leroy, dodging as she swings the barbell in an arc.

"Do you think so?"

"Sure."

Leroy is a truckdriver. He injured his leg in a highway accident four months ago, and his physical therapy which involves weights and a pulley, prompted Norma Jean to try building herself up. Now she is attending a body-building class. Leroy has been collecting temporary disability since his tractor-trailer jackknifed in Missouri, badly twisting his left leg in its socket. He has a steel pin in his hip. He will probably not be able to drive his rig again. It sits in the backyard, like a gigantic bird that has flown home to roost. Leroy has been home in Kentucky for three months, and his leg is almost healed, but the accident frightened him and he does not want to drive any more long hauls. He is not sure what to do next. In the meantime, he makes things from craft kits. He started by building a miniature log cabin from notched Popsicle sticks. He varnished it and place it on the TV set, where it remains. It reminds him of a rustic Nativity scene. Then he tried string art (sailing ships on black velvet), a macramé owl kit, a snap-together B-17 Flying Fortress, and a lamp made out of a model truck, with a light fixture screwed in the top of the cab. At first the kits were diversions, something to kill time, but now he is thinking about building a full-scale log house from a kit. It would be considerably cheaper than building a regular house, and besides, Leroy has grown to appreciate how things are put together. He has begun to realize that in all the years he was on the road he never took time to examine anything. He was always flying past scenery.

"They won't let you build a log cabin in any of the new subdivisions," Norma Jean tells him.

"They will if I tell them it's for you," he says, teasing her. Ever since they were married, he has promised Norma Jean he would build her a new home one day. They have always rented, and the house they live in is small and nondescript. It does not even feel like a home, Leroy realizes now.

Norma Jean works at the Rexall drugstore, and she has acquired an amazing amount of information about cosmetics. When she explains to Leroy the three stages of complexion care, involving creams, toners, and moisturizers, he thinks happily of other petroleum products—axle grease, diesel fuel. This is a connection between him and Norma Jean. Since he has been home, he has felt unusually tender about his wife and guilty over his long absences. But he can't tell what she feels about him. Norma Jean has never complained about his traveling; she has never made hurt remarks, like calling his truck a "widow-maker." He is reasonably certain she has been faithful to him, but he wishes she would celebrate his permanent home-coming more happily. Norma Jean is often startled to find Leroy at home, and he thinks she seems a little disappointed about it. Perhaps he reminds her too much of the early days of their marriage, before he went on the road. They had a child who died as an infant, years ago. They never speak about their memories of Randy, which have almost faded, but now that Leroy is home all the time, they sometimes feel awkward around each other, and Leroy wonders if one of them should mention the child. He has the feeling that they are waking up out of a dream together—that they must create a new marriage, start afresh. They are lucky they are still married. Leroy has read that for most people losing a child destroys the marriage—or else he heard this on *Donahue*. He can't always remember where he learns things anymore.

At Christmas, Leroy bought an electric organ for Norma Jean. She used to play the piano when she was in high school. "It don't leave you," she told him once. "It's like riding a bicycle."

The new instrument had so many keys and buttons that she was bewildered by it at first. She touched the keys tentatively, pushed some buttons, then pecked out "Chopsticks." It came out in an amplified foxtrot rhythm, with marimba sounds.

"It's an orchestra!" she cried.

The organ had a pecan-look finish and eighteen preset chords, with optional flute, violin, trumpet, clarinet, and banjo accompaniments. Norma Jean mastered the organ almost immediately. At first she played Christmas songs. Then she bought *The Sixties Songbook* and learned every tune in it, adding variations to each with the rows of brightly colored buttons.

"I didn't like these old songs back then," she said. "But I have this crazy feeling I missed something."

"You didn't miss a thing," said Leroy.

Leroy likes to lie on the couch and smoke a joint and listen to Norma Jean play "Can't Take My Eyes Off You" and "I'll Be Back." He is back again. After fifteen years on the road, he is finally settling down with the woman he loves. She is still pretty. Her skin is flawless. Her frosted curls resemble pencil trimmings.

Now that Leroy has come home to stay, he notices how much the town has changed. Subdivisions are spreading across western Kentucky like an oil slick. The sign at the edge of town says "Pop: 11,500"—only seven hundred more than it said twenty years before. Leroy can't figure out who is living in all the new houses. The farmers who used to gather around the courthouse square on Saturday afternoons to play checkers and spit tobacco juice have gone. It has been years since Leroy has thought about the farmers, and they have disappeared without his noticing.

Leroy meets a kid named Stevie Hamilton in the parking lot at the new shopping center. While they pretend to be strangers meeting over a stalled car, Stevie tosses an ounce of marijuana under the front seat of Leroy's car. Stevie is wearing orange jogging shoes and a T-shirt that says CHATTAHOOCHEE SUPER RAT. His father is a prominent doctor who lives in one of the expensive subdivisions in a new white-columned brick house that looks like a funeral parlor. In the phone book under his name there is a separate number, with the listing "Teenagers."

"Where do you get this stuff?" asks Leroy. "From your pappy?"

"That's for me to know and you to find out," Stevie says. He is slit-eyed and skinny.

"What else you got?"

"What you interested in?"

"Nothing special. Just wondered."

Leroy used to take speed on the road. Now he has to go slowly. He needs to be mellow. He leans back against the car and says, "I'm aiming to build me a log house, soon as I get time. My wife, though, I don't think she likes the idea."

"Well, let me know when you want me again," Stevie says. He has a cigarette in his cupped palm, as though sheltering it from the wind. He takes a long drag, then stomps it on the asphalt and slouches away.

Stevie's father was two years ahead of Leroy in high school. Leroy is thirty-four. He married Norma Jean when they were both eighteen, and their child Randy was born a few months later, but he died at the age of four months and three days. He would be about Stevie's age now. Norma Jean and Leroy were at the drive-in, watching a double feature *(Dr. Strangelove* and *Lover Come Back)*, and the baby was sleeping in the back seat. When the first movie ended, the baby was dead. It was the sudden infant death syndrome. Leroy remembers handing Randy to a nurse at the emergency room, as though he were offering her a large doll as a present. A dead baby feels like a sack of flour. "It just happens sometimes," said the doctor, in what Leroy always recalls as a nonchalant tone. Leroy can hardly remember the child anymore, but he still sees vividly a scene from *Dr. Strangelove* in which the President of the United States was talking in a folksy voice on the hot line to the Soviet premier about the bomber accidentally headed toward Russia. He was in the War Room, and the world map was lit up. Leroy remembers

Norma Jean standing catatonically beside him in the hospital and himself thinking: Who is this strange girl? He had forgotten who she was. Now scientists are saying that crib death is caused by a virus. Nobody knows anything, Leroy thinks. The answers are always changing.

When Leroy gets home from the shopping center, Norma Jean's mother, Mabel Beasley, is there. Until this year, Leroy has not realized how much time she spends with Norma Jean. When she visits, she inspects the closets and then the plants, informing Norma Jean when a plant is droopy or yellow. Mabel calls the plants "flowers," although there are never any blooms. She also notices if Norma Jean's laundry is piling up. Mabel is a short, overweight woman whose tight, brown-dyed curls look more like a wig than the actual wig she sometimes wears. Today she has brought Norma Jean an off-white dust ruffle she made for the bed; Mabel works in a custom upholstery shop.

"This is the tenth one I made this year," Mabel says. "I got started and couldn't stop."

"It's real pretty," says Norma Jean.

"Now we can hide things under the bed," says Leroy, who gets along with his mother-in-law primarily by joking with her. Mabel has never really forgiven him for disgracing her by getting Norma Jean pregnant. When the baby died, she said that fate was mocking her.

"What's that thing?" Mabel says to Leroy in a loud voice, pointing to a tangle of yarn on a piece of canvas.

Leroy holds it up for Mabel to see. "It's my needlepoint," he explains. "This is a *Star Trek* pillow cover."

"That's what a woman would do," says Mabel. "Great day in the morning!"

"All the big football players on TV do it," he says.

"Why, Leroy, you're always trying to fool me. I don't believe you for one minute. You don't know what to do with yourself—that's the whole trouble. Sewing!"

"I'm aiming to build us a log house," says Leroy. "Soon as my plans come."

"Like *heck* you are," says Norma Jean. She takes Leroy's needlepoint and shoves it into a drawer. "You have to find a job first. Nobody can afford to build now anyway."

Mabel straightens her girdle and says, "I still think before you get tied down y'all ought to take a little run to Shiloh."

"One of these days, Mama," Norma Jean says impatiently.

Mabel is talking about Shiloh, Tennessee. For the past few years, she has been urging Leroy and Norma Jean to visit the Civil War battle-ground there. Mabel went there on her honeymoon—the only real trip she ever took. Her husband died of a perforated ulcer when Norma Jean was ten, but Mabel, who was accepted into the United Daughters of the Confederacy in 1975, is still preoccupied with going back to Shiloh.

"I've been to kingdom come and back in that truck out yonder," Leroy says to Mabel, "but we never yet set foot in that battleground. Ain't that something? How did I miss it?"

"It's not even that far," Mabel says.

After Mabel leaves, Norma Jean reads to Leroy from a list she has made. "Things you could do," she announces. "You could get a job as a guard at Union Carbide, where they'd let you set on a stool. You could get on at the lumberyard. You could do a little carpenter work, if you want to build so bad. You could—"

"I can't do something where I'd have to stand up all day."

"You ought to try standing up all day behind a cosmetics counter. It's amazing that I have strong feet, coming from two parents that never had strong feet at all." At the moment Norma Jean is holding on to the kitchen counter, raising her knees one at a time as she talks. She is wearing two-pound ankle weights.

"Don't worry," says Leroy. "I'll do something."

"You could truck calves to slaughter for somebody. You wouldn't have to drive any big old truck for that."

"I'm going to build you this house," says Leroy. "I want to make you a real home."

"I don't want to live in any log cabin."

"It's not a cabin. It's a house."

"I don't care. It looks like a cabin."

"You and me together could lift those logs. It's just like lifting weights."

Norma Jean doesn't answer. Under her breath, she is counting. Now she is marching through the kitchen. She is doing goose steps.

Before his accident, when Leroy came home he used to stay in the house with Norma Jean, watching TV in bed and playing cards. She would cook fried chicken, picnic ham, chocolate pie—all his favorites. Now he is home alone much of the time. In the mornings, Norma Jean disappears, leaving a cooling place in the bed. She eats a cereal called Body Buddies, and she leaves the bowl on the table, with the soggy tan balls floating in a milk puddle. He sees things about Norma Jean that he never realized before. When she chops onions, she stares off into a corner, as if she can't bear to look. She puts on her house slippers almost precisely at nine o'clock every evening and nudges her jogging shoes under the couch. She saves bread heels for the birds. Leroy watches the birds at the feeder. He notices the peculiar way goldfinches fly past the window. They close their wings, then fall, then spread their wings to catch and lift themselves. He wonders if they close their eyes when they fall. Norma Jean closes her eyes when they are in bed. She wants the lights turned out. Even then, he is sure she closes her eyes.

He goes for long drives around town. He tends to drive a car rather carelessly. Power steering and an automatic shift make a car feel so small and inconsequential that his body is hardly involved in the driving process. His injured leg stretches out comfortably. Once or twice he has almost hit something, but even the prospect of an accident seems minor in a car. He cruises the new subdivisions, feeling like a criminal rehearsing for a robbery. Norma Jean is probably right about a log house being inappropriate here in the new subdivision. All the houses look grand and complicated. They depress him.

One day when Leroy comes home from a drive he finds Norma Jean in tears. She is in the kitchen making a potato and mushroom-soup casserole, with grated cheese topping. She is crying because her mother caught her smoking.

"I didn't hear her coming. I was standing here puffing away pretty as you please," Norma Jean says, wiping her eyes.

"I knew it would happen sooner or later," says Leroy, putting his arm around her.

"She don't know the meaning of the word 'knock,'" says Norma Jean. "It's a wonder she hadn't caught me years ago."

"Think of it this way," Leroy says. "What if she caught me with a joint?"

"You better not let her!" Norma Jean shrieks. "I'm warning you, Leroy Moffitt!"

"I'm just kidding. Here, play me a tune. That'll help you relax."

Norma Jean puts the casserole in the oven and sets the timer. Then she plays a ragtime tune, with horns and banjo, as Leroy lights up a joint and lies on the couch, laughing to himself about Mabel's catching him at it. He thinks of Stevie Hamilton—a doctor's son pushing grass. Everything is funny. The whole town seems crazy and small. He is reminded of Virgil Mathis, a boastful policeman Leroy used to shoot pool with. Virgil recently led a drug bust in a back room at a bowling alley, where he seized ten thousand dollars' worth of marijuana. The newspaper had a picture of him holding up the bags of grass and grinning widely. Right now, Leroy can imagine Virgil breaking down the door and arresting him with a lungful of smoke. Virgil would probably have been alerted to the scene because of all the racket Norma Jean is making. Now she sounds like a hard-rock band. Norma Jean is terrific. When she switches to a Latin-rhythm version of "Sunshine Superman," Leroy hums along. Norma Jean's foot goes up and down, up and down.

"Well, what do you think?" Leroy says, when Norma Jean pauses to search through her music.

"What do I think about what?"

His mind has gone blank. Then he says, "I'll sell my rig and build us a house." That wasn't what he wanted to say. He wanted to know what she thought—what she *really* thought—about them.

"Don't start in on that again," says Norma Jean. She begins playing "Who'll Be the Next in Line?"

Leroy used to tell hitchhikers his whole life story—about his travels, his hometown, the baby. He would end with a question: "Well, what do you think?" It was just a rhetorical question. In time, he had the feeling that he'd been telling the same story over and over to the same hitchhikers. He quit talking to hitchhikers when he realized how his voice sounded—whining and self-pitying, like some teenage-tragedy song. Now Leroy has the sudden impulse to tell Norma Jean about himself, as if he had just met her. They have known each other so long they have forgotten a lot about each other. They could become reacquainted. But when the oven timer goes off and she runs to the kitchen, he forgets why he wants to do this.

The next day, Mabel drops by. It is Saturday and Norma Jean is cleaning. Leroy is studying the plans of his log house, which have finally come in the mail. He has them spread out on the table—big sheets of stiff blue paper, with diagrams and numbers printed in white. While Norma Jean runs the vacuum, Mabel drinks coffee. She sets her coffee cup on a blueprint.

"I'm just waiting for time to pass," she says to Leroy, drumming her fingers on the table.

As soon as Norma Jean switches off the vacuum, Mabel says in a loud voice, "Did you hear about the datsun dog that killed the baby?"

Norma Jean says, "The word is 'dachshund.'"

"They put the dog on trial. It chewed the baby's legs off. The mother was in the next room all the time." She raises her voice. "They thought it was neglect."

Norma Jean is holding her ears. Leroy manages to open the refrigerator and get some Diet Pepsi to offer Mabel. Mabel still has some coffee and she waves away the Pepsi.

"Datsuns are like that," Mabel says. "They're jealous dogs. They'll tear a place to pieces if you don't keep an eye on them."

"You better watch out what you're saying, Mabel," says Leroy.

"Well, facts is facts."

Leroy looks out the window at his rig. It is like a huge piece of furniture gathering dust in the backyard. Pretty soon it will be an antique. He hears the vacuum cleaner. Norma Jean seems to be cleaning the living room rug again.

Later, she says to Leroy, "She just said that about the baby because she caught me smoking. She's trying to pay me back."

"What are you talking about?" Leroy says, nervously shuffling blueprints.

"You know good and well," Norma Jean says. She is sitting in a kitchen chair with her feet up and her arms wrapped around her knees. She looks small and helpless. She says, "The very idea, her bringing up a subject like that! Saying it was neglect."

"She didn't mean that," Leroy says.

"She might not have *thought* she meant it. She always says things like that. You don't know how she goes on."

"But she didn't really mean it. She was just talking."

Leroy opens a king-sized bottle of beer and pours it into two glasses, dividing it carefully. He hands a glass to Norma Jean and she takes it from him mechanically. For a long time, they sit by the kitchen window watching the birds at the feeder.

• • •

Something is happening. Norma Jean is going to night school. She has graduated from her six-week body-building course and now she is taking an adult-education course in composition at Paducah Community College. She spends her evenings outlining paragraphs.

"First, you have a topic sentence," she explains to Leroy. "Then you divide it up. Your secondary topic has to be connected to your primary topic."

To Leroy, this sounds intimidating. "I never was any good in English," he says.

"It makes a lot of sense."

"What are you doing this for, anyhow?"

She shrugs. "It's something to do." She stands up and lifts her dumbbells a few times.

"Driving a rig, nobody cared about my English."

"I'm not criticizing your English."

Norma Jean used to say, "If I lose ten minutes' sleep, I just drag all day." Now she stays up late, writing compositions. She got a B on her first paper—a how-to theme on soup-based casseroles. Recently Norma Jean has been cooking unusual foods—tacos, lasagna, Bombay chicken. She doesn't play the organ anymore, though her second paper was called "Why Music Is Important to Me." She sits at the kitchen table, concentrating on her outlines, while Leroy plays with his log house plans, practicing with a set of Lincoln Logs. The thought of getting a truckload of notched, numbered logs scares him, and he wants to be prepared. As he and Norma Jean work together at the kitchen table, Leroy has the hopeful thought that they are sharing something, but he knows he is a fool to think this. Norma Jean is miles away. He knows he is going to lose her. Like Mabel, he is just waiting for time to pass.

One day, Mabel is there before Norma Jean gets home from work, and Leroy finds himself confiding in her. Mabel, he realizes, must know Norma Jean better than he does.

"I don't know what's got into that girl," Mabel says. "She used to go to bed with the chickens. Now you say she's up all hours. Plus her a-smoking. I like to died."

"I want to make her this beautiful home," Leroy says, indicating the Lincoln Logs. "I don't think she even wants it. Maybe she was happier with me gone."

"She don't know what to make of you, coming home like this."

"Is that it?"

Mabel takes the roof off his Lincoln Log cabin. "You couldn't get me in a log cabin," she says. "I was raised in one. It's no picnic, let me tell you."

"They're different now," says Leroy.

"I tell you what," Mabel says, smiling oddly at Leroy.

"What?"

"Take her on down to Shiloh. Y'all need to get out together, stir a little. Her brain's all balled up over them books."

Leroy can see traces of Norma Jean's features in her mother's face. Mabel's worn face has the texture of crinkled cotton, but suddenly she looks pretty. It occurs to Leroy that Mabel has been hinting all along that she wants them to take her with them to Shiloh.

"Let's all go to Shiloh," he says. "You and me and her. Come Sunday."

Mabel throws up her hand in protest. "Oh, no, not me. Young folks want to be by theirselves."

When Norma Jean comes in with groceries, Leroy says excitedly, "Your mama here's been dying to go to Shiloh for thirty-five years. It's about time we went, don't you think?"

"I'm not going to butt in on anybody's second honeymoon," Mabel says.

"Who's going on a honeymoon, for Christ's sake?" Norma Jean says loudly.

"I never raised no daughter of mine to talk that-a-way," Mabel says.

"You ain't seen nothing yet," says Norma Jean. She starts putting away boxes and cans, slamming cabinet doors.

"There's a log cabin at Shiloh," Mabel says. "It was there during the battle. There's bullet holes in it."

"When are you going to *shut up* about Shiloh, Mama?" asks Norma Jean.

"I always thought Shiloh was the prettiest place, so full of history," Mabel goes on. "I just hoped y'all could see it once before I die, so you could tell me about it." Later, she whispers to Leroy, "You do what I said. A little change is what she needs."

"Your name means 'the king,'" Norma Jean says to Leroy that evening. He is trying to get her to go to Shiloh, and she is reading a book about another century.

"Well, I reckon I ought to be right proud."

"I guess so."

"Am I still king around here?"

Norma Jean flexes her biceps and feels them for hardness. "I'm not fooling around with anybody, if that's what you mean," she says.

"Would you tell me if you were?"

"I don't know."

"What does *your* name mean?"

"It was Marilyn Monroe's real name."

"No kidding!"

"Norma comes from the Normans. They were invaders," she says. She closes her book and looks hard at Leroy. "I'll go to Shiloh with you if you'll stop staring at me."

On Sunday, Norma Jean packs a picnic and they go to Shiloh. To Leroy's relief Mabel says she does not want to come with them. Norma Jean drives, and Leroy, sitting beside her, feels like some boring hitchhiker she has picked up. He tries some conversation, but she answers him in monosyllables. At Shiloh, she drives aimlessly through the park, past bluffs and trails and steep ravines. Shiloh is an immense place, and Leroy cannot see it as a battleground. It is not what he expected. He thought it would look like a golf course. Monuments are everywhere, showing through the thick clusters of trees. Norma Jean passes the log cabin Mabel mentioned. It is surrounded by tourists looking for bullet holes.

"That's not the kind of log house I've got in mind," says Leroy apologetically.

"I know *that*."

"This is a pretty place. Your mama was right."

"It's O.K.," says Norma Jean. "Well, we've seen it. I hope she's satisfied."

They burst out laughing together.

At the park museum, a movie on Shiloh is shown every half hour, but they decide that they don't want to see it. They buy a souvenir Confederate flag for Mabel, and then they find a picnic spot near the cemetery. Norma Jean has brought a picnic cooler, with pimiento sandwiches, soft drinks, and Yodels. Leroy eats a sandwich and then smokes a joint, hiding it behind the picnic cooler. Norma Jean has quit smoking altogether. She is picking cake crumbs from the cellophane wrapper, like a fussy bird.

Leroy says, "So the boys in gray ended up in Corinth. The Union soldiers zapped 'em finally. April 7, 1862."

They both know that he doesn't know any history. He is just talking about some of the historical plaques they have read. He feels awkward, like a boy on a date with an older girl. They are still just making conversation.

"Corinth is where Mama eloped to," says Norma Jean.

They sit in silence and stare at the cemetery for the Union dead and, beyond, at a tall cluster of trees. Campers are parked nearby, bumper to bumper, and small children in bright clothing are cavorting and squealing. Norma Jean wads up the cake wrapper and squeezes it tightly in her hand. Without looking at Leroy, she says, "I want to leave you."

Leroy takes a bottle of Coke out of the cooler and flips off the cap. He holds the bottle poised near his mouth but cannot remember to take a drink. Finally he says, "No, you don't."

"Yes, I do."

"I won't let you."

"You can't stop me."

"Don't do me that way."

Leroy knows Norma Jean will have her own way. "Didn't I promise to be home from now on?" he says.

"In some ways, a woman prefers a man who wanders," says Norma Jean. "That sounds crazy, I know."

"You're not crazy." Leroy remembers to drink from his Coke. Then he says, "Yes, you *are* crazy. You and me could start all over again. Right back at the beginning."

"We *have* started all over again," says Norma Jean. "And this is how it turned out."

"What did I do wrong?"

"Nothing."

"Is this one of those women's lib things?" Leroy asks.

"Don't be funny."

The cemetery, a green slope dotted with white markers, looks like a subdivision site. Leroy is trying to comprehend that his marriage is breaking up, but for some reason he is wondering about white slabs in a graveyard.

"Everything was fine till Mama caught me smoking," says Norma Jean, standing up. "That set something off."

"What are you talking about?"

"She won't leave me alone—*you* won't leave me alone." Norma Jean seems to be crying, but she is looking away from him. "I feel eighteen again. I can't face that all over again." She starts walking away. "No, it *wasn't* fine. I don't know what I'm saying. Forget it."

Leroy takes a lungful of smoke and closes his eyes as Norma Jean's words sink in. He tries to focus on the fact that thirty-five hundred soldiers died on the grounds around him. He can only think of that war as a board game with plastic soldiers. Leroy almost smiles, as he compares the Confederates' daring attack on the Union camps and Virgil Mathis's raid on the bowling alley. General Grant, drunk and furious, shoved the Southerners back to Corinth, where Mabel and Jet Beasley were married years later, when Mabel was still thin and good-looking. The next day, Mabel and Jet visited the battleground, and then Norma Jean was born, and then she married Leroy and they had a baby, which they lost, and now Leroy and Norma Jean are here at the same battleground. Leroy knows he is leaving out a lot. He is leaving out the insides of history. History was always just names and dates to him. It occurs to him that building a house of logs is similarly empty—too simple. And the real inner workings of a marriage, like most of history, have escaped him. Now he sees that building a log house is the dumbest idea he could have had. It was clumsy of him to think Norma Jean would want a log house. It was a crazy idea. He'll have to think of something else, quickly. He will wad the blueprints into tight balls and fling them into the lake. Then he'll get moving again. He opens his eyes. Norma Jean has moved away and is walking through the cemetery, following a serpentine brick path.

Leroy gets up to follow his wife, but his good leg is asleep and his bad leg still hurts him. Norma Jean is far away, walking rapidly toward the bluff by the river, and he tries to hobble toward her. Some children run past him, screaming noisily. Norma Jean has reached the bluff, and she is looking out over the Tennessee River. Now she turns toward Leroy and waves her arms. Is she beckoning to him? She seems to be doing an exercise for her chest muscles. The sky is unusually pale—the color of the dust ruffle Mabel made for their bed.

—1982

Alice Walker (b. 1944) wrote the Pulitzer Prize-winning epistolary novel, The Color Purple *(1982). The book and its 1985 film version have made her the most famous living African-American woman writer, perhaps the most widely read of any American woman of color. A native of Eatonton, Georgia, Walker was the eighth child of an impoverished farm couple. She attended Spelman College in Atlanta and Sarah Lawrence College on scholarships, graduating in 1965. Walker began her literary career as a poet, eventually publishing six volumes of verse. Walker's short story collections and novels, including* The Temple of My Familiar *(1989) and* Possessing the Secret of Joy *(1992), which takes as its subject the controversial practice of female circumcision among African tribes, have continued to reach large audiences and have solidified her reputation as one of the major figures in contemporary literature. Walker has coined the term "womanist" to stand for the black feminist concerns of much of her fiction. "Everyday Use," a story from the early 1970s, is simultaneously a satisfying piece of realistic social commentary and a subtly satirical variation on the ancient fable of "The City Mouse and the Country Mouse." Her most recent collection of stories,* The Way Forward Is with a Broken Heart *(2000), was described by* Booklist *as "part memoir, part fiction, and part bibliotherapy."*

Alice Walker
Everyday Use

For your grandmama

I will wait for her in the yard that Maggie and I made so clean and wavy yesterday afternoon. A yard like this is more comfortable than most people know. It is not just a yard. It is like an extended living room. When the hard clay is swept clean as a floor and the fine sand around the edges lined with tiny, irregular grooves anyone can come and sit and look up into the elm tree and wait for the breezes that never come inside the house.

Maggie will be nervous until after her sister goes: she will stand hopelessly in corners homely and ashamed of the burn scars down her arms and legs, eyeing her sister with a mixture of envy and awe. She thinks her sister has held life always in the palm of one hand, that "no" is a word the world never learned to say to her.

You've no doubt seen those TV shows where the child who has "made it" is confronted, as a surprise, by her own mother and father, tottering in weakly from backstage. (A pleasant surprise, of course: What would they do if parent and child came on the show only to curse out and insult each other?) On TV mother and child embrace and smile into each other's faces. Sometimes the mother and father weep, the child wraps them in her arms and leans across the table to tell how she would not have made it without their help. I have seen these programs.

Sometimes I dream a dream in which Dee and I are suddenly brought together on a TV program of this sort. Out of a dark and soft-seated limousine I am ushered into a bright room filled with many people. There I meet a smiling, gray, sporty man like Johnny Carson who shakes my hand and tells me what a fine girl I have. Then we are on the stage and Dee is embracing me with tears in her eyes. She pins on my dress a large orchid, even though she has told me once that she thinks orchids are tacky flowers.

In real life I am a large, big-boned woman with rough, man-working hands. In the winter I wear flannel nightgowns to bed and overalls during the day. I can kill and clean a hog as mercilessly as a man. My fat keeps me hot in zero weather. I can work outside all day, breaking ice to get water for washing. I can eat pork liver cooked over the open fire minutes after it comes steaming from the hog. One winter I knocked a bull calf straight in the brain between the eyes with a sledge hammer and had the meat hung up to chill before nightfall. But of course all this does not show on television. I am the way my daughter would want me to be: a hundred pounds lighter, my skin like an uncooked barley pancake. My hair glistens in the hot bright lights. Johnny Carson has much to do to keep up with my quick and witty tongue.

But that is a mistake. I know even before I wake up. Who ever knew a Johnson with a quick tongue? Who can even imagine me looking a strange white man in the eye? It seems to me I have talked to them always with one foot raised in flight, with my head turned in whichever way is farthest from them. Dee, though. She would always look anyone in the eye. Hesitation was no part of her nature.

"How do I look, Mama?" Maggie says, showing just enough of her thin body enveloped in pink skirt and red blouse for me to know she's there, almost hidden by the door.

"Come out into the yard," I say.

Have you ever seen a lame animal, perhaps a dog run over by some careless person rich enough to own a car, sidle up to someone who is ignorant enough to be kind to him? That is the way my Maggie walks.

She has been like this, chin on chest, eyes on ground, feet in shuffle, ever since the fire that burned the other house to the ground.

Dee is lighter than Maggie, with nicer hair and a fuller figure. She's a woman now, though sometimes I forget. How long ago was it that the other house burned? Ten, twelve years? Sometimes I can still hear the flames and feel Maggie's arms sticking to me, her hair smoking and her dress falling off her in little black papery flakes. Her eyes seemed stretched open, blazed open by the flames reflected in them. And Dee. I see her standing off under the sweet gum tree she used to dig gum out of; a look of concentration on her face as she watched the last dingy gray board of the house fall in toward the red-hot brick chimney. Why don't you do a dance around the ashes? I'd wanted to ask her. She had hated the house that much.

I used to think she hated Maggie, too. But that was before we raised the money, the church and me, to send her to Augusta to school. She used to read to us without pity; forcing words, lies, other folks' habits, whole lives upon us two, sitting trapped and ignorant underneath her voice. She washed us in a river of make-believe, burned us with a lot of knowledge we didn't necessarily need to know. Pressed us to her with the serious way she read, to shove us away at just the moment, like dimwits, we seemed about to understand.

Dee wanted nice things. A yellow organdy dress to wear to her graduation from high school; black pumps to match a green suit she'd made from an old suit somebody gave me. She was determined to stare down any disaster in her efforts. Her eyelids would not flicker for minutes at a time. Often I fought off the temptation to shake her. At sixteen she had a style of her own: and knew what style was.

I never had an education myself. After second grade the school was closed down. Don't ask me why: in 1927 colored asked fewer questions than they do now. Sometimes Maggie reads to me. She stumbles along good-naturedly but can't see well. She knows she is not bright. Like good looks and money, quickness passed her by. She will marry John Thomas (who has mossy teeth in an earnest face) and then I'll be free to sit here and I guess just sing church songs to myself. Although I never was a good singer. Never could carry a tune. I was always better at a man's job. I used to love to milk till I was hoofed in the side in '49. Cows are soothing and slow and don't bother you, unless you try to milk them the wrong way.

I have deliberately turned my back on the house. It is three rooms, just like the one that burned, except the roof is tin; they don't make shingle roofs any more. There are no real windows, just some holes cut in the sides, like the portholes in a ship, but not round and not square, with rawhide holding the shutters up on the outside. This house is in a pasture, too, like the other one. No doubt when Dee sees it she will want to tear it down. She wrote me once that no matter where we "choose" to live, she will manage to come see us. But she will never bring her friends. Maggie and I thought about this and Maggie asked me, "Mama, when did Dee ever *have* any friends?"

She had a few. Furtive boys in pink shirts hanging about on washday after school. Nervous girls who never laughed. Impressed with her they worshiped the well-turned phrase, the cute shape, the scalding humor that erupted like bubbles in lye. She read to them.

When she was courting Jimmy T she didn't have much time to pay to us, but turned all her faultfinding power on him. He *flew* to marry a cheap gal from a family of ignorant flashy people. She hardly had time to recompose herself.

When she comes I will meet—but there they are!

Maggie attempts to make a dash for the house, in her shuffling way, but I stay her with my hand. "Come back here," I say. And she stops and tries to dig a well in the sand with her toe.

It is hard to see them clearly through the strong sun. But even the first glimpse of leg out of the car tells me it is Dee. Her feet were always neat-looking, as if God himself had shaped them with a certain style. From the other side of the car comes a short, stocky man. Hair is all over his head a foot long and hanging from his chin like a kinky mule tail. I hear Maggie suck in her breath. "Uhnnnh," is what it sounds like. Like when you see the wriggling end of a snake just in front of your foot on the road. "Uhnnnh."

Dee next. A dress down to the ground, in this hot weather. A dress so loud it hurts my eyes. There are yellows and oranges enough to throw back the light of the sun. I feel my whole face warming from the heat waves it throws out. Earrings, too, gold and hanging down to her shoulders. Bracelets dangling and making noises when she moves her arm up to shake the folds of the dress out of her armpits. The dress is loose and flows, and as she walks closer, I like it. I hear Maggie go "Uhnnnh" again. It is her sister's hair. It stands straight up like the wool on a sheep. It is black as night and around the edges are two long pigtails that rope about like small lizards disappearing behind her ears.

"Wa-su-zo-Tean-o!" she says, coming on in that gliding way the dress makes her move. The short stocky fellow with the hair to his navel is all grinning and he follows up with "Asalamalakim, my mother and sister!" He moves to hug Maggie but she falls back, right up against the back of my chair. I feel her trembling there and when I look up I see the perspiration falling off her chin.

"Don't get up," says Dee. Since I am stout it takes something of a push. You can see me trying to move a second or two before I make it. She turns, showing white heels through her sandals, and goes back to the car. Out she peeks next with a Polaroid. She stoops down quickly and lines up picture after picture of me sitting there in front of the house with Maggie cowering behind me. She never takes a shot without making sure the house is included. When a cow comes nibbling around the edge of the yard she snaps it and me and Maggie and the house. Then she puts the Polaroid in the back seat of the car, and comes up and kisses me on the forehead.

Meanwhile Asalamalakim is going through the motions with Maggie's hand. Maggie's hand is as limp as a fish, and probably as cold, despite the sweat, and she keeps trying to pull it back. It looks like Asalamalakim wants to shake hands but wants to do it fancy. Or maybe he don't know how people shake hands. Anyhow, he soon gives up on Maggie.

"Well," I say. "Dee."

"No, Mama," she says. "Not 'Dee,' Wangero Leewanika Kemanjo!"

"What happened to 'Dee'?" I wanted to know.

"She's dead," Wangero said. "I couldn't bear it any longer being named after the people who oppress me."

"You know as well as me you was named after your aunt Dicie," I said. Dicie is my sister. She named Dee. We called her "Big Dee" after Dee was born.

"But who was *she* named after?" asked Wangero.

"I guess after Grandma Dee," I said.

"And who was she named after?" asked Wangero.

"Her mother," I said, and saw Wangero was getting tired. "That's about as far back as I can trace it," I said. Though, in fact, I probably could have carried it back beyond the Civil War through the branches.

"Well," said Asalamalakim, "there you are."

"Uhnnnh," I heard Maggie say.

"There I was not," I said, "before 'Dicie' cropped up in our family, so why should I try to trace it that far back?"

He just stood there grinning, looking down on me like somebody inspecting a Model A car. Every once in a while he and Wangero sent eye signals over my head.

"How do you pronounce this name?" I asked.

"You don't have to call me by it if you don't want to," said Wangero.

"Why shouldn't I?" I asked. "If that's what you want us to call you, we'll call you."

"I know it might sound awkward at first," said Wangero.

"I'll get used to it," I said. "Ream it out again."

Well, soon we got the name out of the way. Asalamalakim had a name twice as long and three times as hard. After I tripped over it two or three times he told me to just to call him Hakim-a-barber. I wanted to ask him was he a barber, but I didn't really think he was, so I didn't ask.

"You must belong to those beef-cattle peoples down the road," I said. They said "Asalamalakim" when they met you, too, but they didn't shake hands. Always too busy: feeding the cattle, fixing the fences, putting up salt-lick shelters, throwing down hay. When the white folks poisoned some of the herd the men stayed up all night with rifles in their hands. I walked a mile and a half just to see the sight.

Hakim-a-barber said, "I accept some of their doctrines, but farming and raising cattle is not my style." (They didn't tell me, and I didn't ask, whether Wangero [Dee] had really gone and married him.)

We sat down to eat and right away he said he didn't eat collards and pork was unclean. Wangero, though, went on through the chitlins and corn bread, the greens and everything else. She talked a blue streak over the sweet potatoes. Everything delighted her. Even the fact that we still used the benches her daddy made for the table when we couldn't afford to buy chairs.

"Oh, Mama!" she cried. Then turned to Hakim-a-barber. "I never knew how lovely these benches are. You can feel the rump prints," she said, running her hands underneath her and along the bench. Then she gave a sigh and her hand closed over Grandma Dee's butter dish. "That's it!" she said. "I knew there was something I wanted to ask you if I could have." She jumped up from the table and went over in the corner where the churn stood, the milk in it clabber by now. She looked at the churn and looked at it.

"This churn top is what I need," she said. "Didn't Uncle Buddy whittle it out of a tree you all used to have?"

"Yes," I said.

"Uh huh," she said happily. "And I want the dasher, too."

"Uncle Buddy whittle that, too?" asked the barber.

Dee (Wangero) looked up at me.

"Aunt Dee's first husband whittled the dash," said Maggie so low you almost couldn't hear her. "His name was Henry, but they called him Stash."

"Maggie's brain is like an elephant's," Wangero said, laughing. "I can use the churn top as a centerpiece for the alcove table," she said, sliding a plate over the churn, "and I'll think of something artistic to do with the dasher."

When she finished wrapping the dasher the handle stuck out. I took it for a moment in my hands. You didn't even have to look close to see where hands pushing the dasher up and down to make butter had left a kind of sink in the wood. In fact, there were a lot of small sinks; you could see where thumbs and fingers had sunk into the wood. It was beautiful light yellow wood, from a tree that grew in the yard where Big Dee and Stash had lived.

After dinner Dee (Wangero) went to the trunk at the foot of my bed and started rifling through it. Maggie hung back in the kitchen over the dishpan. Out came Wangero with two quilts. They had been pieced by Grandma Dee and then Big Dee and me had hung them on the quilt frames on the front porch and quilted them. One was in the Lone Star pattern. The other was Walk Around the Mountain. In both of them were scraps of dresses Grandma Dee had worn fifty and more years ago. Bits and pieces of Grandpa Jarrell's paisley shirts. And one teeny faded blue piece, about the piece of a penny matchbox, that was from Great Grandpa Ezra's uniform that he wore in the Civil War.

"Mama," Wangero said sweet as a bird. "Can I have these old quilts?"

I heard something fall in the kitchen, and a minute later the kitchen door slammed.

"Why don't you take one or two of the others?" I asked. "These old things was just done by me and Big Dee from some tops your grandma pieced before she died."

"No," said Wangero. "I don't want those. They are stitched around the borders by machine."

"That's make them last better," I said.

"That's not the point," said Wangero. "These are all pieces of dresses Grandma used to wear. She did all this stitching by hand. Imagine!" She held the quilts securely in her arms, stroking them.

"Some of the pieces, like those lavender ones, come from old clothes her mother handed down to her," I said, moving up to touch the quilts. Dee (Wangero) moved back just enough so that I couldn't reach the quilts. They already belonged to her.

"Imagine!" she breathed again, clutching them closely to her bosom.

"The truth is," I said, "I promised to give them quilts to Maggie, for when she marries John Thomas."

She gasped like a bee had stung her.

"Maggie can't appreciate these quilts!" she said. "She'd probably be backward enough to put them to everyday use."

"I reckon she would," I said. "God knows I been saving 'em for long enough with nobody using 'em. I hope she will!" I didn't want to bring up how I had offered Dee (Wangero) a quilt when she went away to college. Then she had told me they were old-fashioned, out of style.

"But they're *priceless!*" she was saying now, furiously; for she has a temper. "Maggie would put them on the bed and in five years they'd be in rags. Less than that!"

"She can always make some more," I said. "Maggie knows how to quilt."

Dee (Wangero) looked at me with hatred. "You just will not understand. The point is these quilts, *these* quilts!"

"Well," I said, stumped. "What would *you* do with them?"

"Hang them," she said. As if that was the only thing you *could* do with quilts.

Maggie by now was standing in the door. I could almost hear the sound her feet made as they scraped over each other.

"She can have them, Mama," she said, like somebody used to never winning anything, or having anything reserved for her. "I can 'member Grandma Dee without the quilts."

I looked at her hard. She had filled her bottom lip with checkerberry snuff and it gave her face a kind of dopey, hangdog look. It was Grandma Dee and Big Dee who taught her how to quilt herself. She stood there with her scarred hands hidden in the folds of her skirt. She looked at her sister with something like fear but she wasn't mad at her. This was Maggie's portion. This was the way she knew God to work.

When I looked at her like that something hit me in the top of my head and ran down to the soles of my feet. Just like when I'm in church and the spirit of God touches me and I get happy and shout. I did something I never had done before: hugged Maggie to me, then dragged her on into the room, snatched the quilts out of Miss Wangero's hands and dumped them into Maggie's lap. Maggie just sat there on my bed with her mouth open.

"Take one or two of the others," I said to Dee.

But she turned without a word and went out to Hakim-a-barber.

"You just don't understand," she said, as Maggie and I came out to the car.

"What don't I understand?" I wanted to know.

"Your heritage," she said. And then she turned to Maggie, kissed her, and said, "You ought to try to make something of yourself, too, Maggie. It's really a new day for us. But from the way you and Mama still live you'd never know it."

She put on some sunglasses that hid everything above the tip of her nose and her chin.

Maggie smiled; maybe at the sunglasses. But a real smile, not scared. After we watched the car dust settle I asked Maggie to bring me a dip of snuff. And then the two of us sat there just enjoying, until it was time to go in the house and go to bed.

—*1973*

Tim Gautreaux (b. 1947) was born in Morgan City, Louisiana, a port that grew prosperous in the early days of the offshore oil industry and declined as the industry waned. "Died and Gone to Vegas," which was originally published in The Atlantic Monthly, *captures the regional speech patterns and "American dreams" of working-class members of the Cajun (Acadian) culture of southern Louisiana. Educated at Nicholls State University and the University of South Carolina, Gautreaux is a professor of English at Southeastern Louisiana University in Hammond. "Died and Gone to Vegas," a witty contemporary revision of the frame-tale structure of Chaucer's* Canterbury Tales, *appeared in* Same Place, Same Things *(1996), Gautreaux's first collection of short fiction. He has since published a second collection,* Welding with Children *(1999), and a first novel,* The Next Step in the Dance *(1998).*

Tim Gautreaux
Died and Gone to Vegas

Raynelle Bullfinch told the young oiler that the only sense of mystery in her life was provided by a deck of cards. As she set up the table in the engine room of the *Leo B. Canterbury*, a government steam dredge anchored in a pass at the mouth of the Mississippi River, she lectured him. "Nick, you're just a college boy sitting out a bit until you get money to go back to school, but for me, this is it." She pulled a coppery braid from under her overalls strap, looked around at the steam chests and piping and sniffed at the smell of heat-proof red enamel. In the glass of a steam gauge she checked her round, bright cheeks for grease and ran a white finger over the blue arcs of her eyebrows. She was the cook on the big boat, which was idle for a couple of days because of high winter winds. "My big adventure is cards. One day I'll save up enough to play with the skill boys in Vegas. Set up those folding chairs," she told him. "Seven in all."

"I don't know how to play bourrée, ma'am." Nick Montalbano ran a hand through long hair shiny with dressing. "I only had one semester of college." He looked sideways at the power straining the bronze buckles of the tall woman's bib and avoided her green eyes, which were deep-set and full of intense judgment.

"Bullshit. A pet rat can play bourrée. Sit down." She pointed to a metal chair, and the oiler, a thin boy wearing an untucked plaid flannel shirt and a baseball cap, obeyed. "Pay attention here. I deal out five cards to everybody, and I turn up the last card. Whatever suit it is, that's trumps. Then you discard all your nontrumps and draw replacements. Remember, trumps beat all other suits, high trumps beat low trumps. Whatever card is led, you follow suit." She ducked her head under the bill of his cap, looking for his eyes. "This ain't too hard for you is it? Ain't college stuff more complicated than this?"

"Sure, sure. I understand. But what if you can't follow suit?"

"If nontrumps is led, put a trump on it. If you ain't got no more trumps, just throw your lowest card. Trust me—you'll catch on quick."

"How do you win?" The oiler turned his cap around.

"Every hand has five tricks to take. If you take three tricks, you win the pot, unless only two decide to play that hand after the draw. Then you need four tricks. If you got any questions, ask Sidney there."

Sidney, the chief engineer, a little fireplug of a man who would wear a white T-shirt in a blizzard, sat down heavily with a whistle. "Oh, boy. Fresh meat." He squeezed the oiler's neck.

The steel door next to the starboard triple-expansion engine opened, letting in a wash of frigid air around the day fireman, pilot, deckhand, and welder, who came into the big room cursing and clapping the cold out of their clothes. Through the door the angry whitecaps of Southwest Pass raced down the Mississippi, bucking into the tarnished Gulf sky.

"Close that damned pneumonia-hole," Raynelle cried, sailing cards precisely before the seven chairs. "Sit down, worms. Usual game: dollar ante, five-dollar rip if you don't take a trick." After the rain of halves and dollars came discards, more dealing, and then a flurry of cards ending with a rising snowstorm of curses as no one took three tricks and the pot rolled over to the next hand. Three players took no tricks and put up the five-dollar rip.

The engineer unrolled a pack of Camels from his T-shirt sleeve and cursed loudest. "I heard of a bourrée game on a offshore rig where the pot didn't clear for eighty-three passes. By the time somebody won that bitch, it had seventeen hundred dollars in it. The next day the genius what took it got a wrench upside the head in a Morgan City bar and woke up with his pockets inside out and the name Conchita tattooed around his left nipple."

Pig, the day fireman, put up his ante and collected the next hand. "That ain't nothin'." He touched three discards to the top of his bald head and threw them down. "A ol' boy down at the dock told me the other day that he heard about a fellow got hit in the head over in Orange,

Texas, and didn't know who he was when he looked at his driver's license. Had amnesia. That sorry-ass seaman's hospital sent him home to his scuzz-bag wife, and he didn't know her from Adam's house cat."

"That mighta been a blessing," Raynelle said, sending him three cards in a flock. She rolled left on her ample bottom.

"No it wasn't," the day fireman said, unzipping his heavy green field jacket. "That gal told him she was his sister, gave him a remote control and a color TV; he was happy as a fly on a pie. She started bringin' boyfriends in at night, and that fool waved them into the house. Fixed 'em drinks. Figured any old dude good enough for Sis was good enough for him. The neighbors got to lookin' at her like they was smellin' somethin' dead, so she and her old man moved to a better trailer park where nobody knew he lost his memory. She started into cocaine, and hookin' for fun on the side. Her husband's settlement money he got from the company what dropped a thirty-six-inch Stillson wrench on his hard hat began to shrink up a bit, but that old boy just sat there dizzy on some cheap pills she told him was a prescription. He'd channel surf all day, greet the johns like one of those old dried-up coots at Wal-Mart, and was the happiest son of a bitch in Orange, Texas." The day fireman spread wide his arms. "Was he glad to see Sis come home every day. He was proud she had more friends than a postman with a bag full of welfare checks. And then his memory came back."

"Ho, ho, the *merde*[1] hit the blower," the engineer said, slamming a queen down and raking in a trick.

"Nope. That poor bastard remembered every giggle in the rear bedroom and started feelin' lower than a snake's nuts. He tried to get his old woman straight, but the dyed-over tramp just laughed in his face and moved out on him. He got so sorry he went to a shrink, but that just cost him more bucks. Finally, you know what the old dude wound up doin'? He looked for someone would hit him in the head again—you know, so he could get back the way he was. He offered a hundred dollars a pop, and in them Orange bars most people will whack on you for free, so you can imagine what kind of service he bought hisself. After nearly gettin' killed four or five times, he gave up and spent the rest of his settlement money on a hospital stay for a concussion. After that he held up a Pac-a-Bag for enough money to get himself hypnotized back

---

[1] *merde:* shit (French).

to like he was after he got hit the first time. Wound up in the pen doin' twenty hard ones."

They played three hands of cards while the day fireman finished the story, and then the deckhand in the game, a thick blond man in a black cotton sweater, threw back his head and laughed, *ha ha*, as if he were only pretending. "If that wadn' so funny, it'd be sad. It reminds me of this dumb-ass peckerwood kid lived next to me in Kentucky, built like a stringbean. He was a few thimbles shy of a quart, but he sort of knew he wadn' no nuclear-power-plant repairman and he got along with everybody. Then he started hangin' with these bad-ass kids—you know, the kind that carry spray paint, wear their hats backward, and stuff live rats in your mailbox. Well, they told the poor bastard he was some kind of Jesse James and got him into stealin' hubcaps and electric drills. He started struttin' around the neighborhood like he was bad news at midnight, and soon the local deputies had him in the back seat for runnin' off with a lawn mower. Dummy stole it in December."

"What's wrong with that?" the day fireman asked, pitching in a dollar.

"Who's gonna buy a used mower in winter, you moron? Anyway, the judge had pity on him, gave him a two-bit fine and sent him to bed with a sugar-tit. Said he was a good boy who ought to be satisfied to be simple and honest. But Stringbean hung out on the street corner crowin'. He was proud now. A real gangster, happy as Al Capone, his head pumped full of swamp gas by these losers he's hangin' around with. Finally one night he breaks into the house of a gun collector. Showin' how smart he is, he chooses only one gun to take from the rack—an engraved Purdy double-barrel, mint condition, with gold and ivory inlays all over, a twenty-thousand-dollar gun. Stringbean took it home and with a two-dollar hacksaw cut the stock off and then most of the barrel. He went out and held up a taco joint and got sixteen dollars and thirteen cents. Was arrested when he walked out the door. This time a hard-nut judge sent him up on a multiple bill and he got two hundred ninety-seven years in Bisley."

"All right," Raynelle sang. "Better than death."

"He did ten years before the weepy-ass parole board noticed the sentence and pulled him in for review. Asked him did he get rehabilitated and would he go straight if he got out, and he spit on their mahogany table. He told them he wadn' no dummy and would be the richest bank robber in Kentucky if he got half a chance." The deckhand laughed, *ha ha*. "That give everybody an ice-cream headache, and the meetin' came to a vote right quick. Even the American Civil Liberties lesbo lawyers on the parole board wanted to weld the door shut on him. It was somethin'."

The pilot, a tall man wearing a pea jacket and a sock cap, raised a new hand to his sharp blue eyes and winced, keeping one trump and asking for four cards. "Gentlemen, that reminds me of a girl in Kentucky I knew at one time."

"Why? Did she get sent up two hundred ninety-seven years in Bisley?" the deckhand asked.

"No, she was from Kentucky, like that crazy fellow you just lied to us about. By the way that king won't walk," he said, laying down an ace of diamonds. "This woman was a nurse at the VA hospital in Louisville and fell in love with one of her patients, a good-looking, mild-mannered fellow with a cyst in his brain that popped and gave him amnesia."

"Now, there's something you don't hear every day," the engineer said, trumping the ace with a bang.

"He didn't know what planet he came from," the pilot said stiffly. "A few months later they got married and he went to work in a local iron plant. After a year he began wandering away from work at lunchtime. So they fired him. He spent a couple of weeks walking up and down his street and all over Louisville looking into people's yards and checking passing buses for the faces in the windows. It was like he was looking for someone, but he couldn't remember who. One day he didn't come home at all. For eighteen months this pretty little nurse was beside herself with worry. Then her nephew was at a rock concert downtown and spotted a shaggy guy who looked familiar in the mosh pit, just standing there like he was watching a string quartet. Between songs the nephew asked the shaggy guy if he had amnesia, which is a rather odd question, considering, and the man almost started crying, because he figured he'd been recognized."

"That's a sweet story," the day fireman said, rubbing his eyes with his bear-paw-sized-hands. "Sidney, could you loan me your handkerchief? I'm all choked up."

"Choke this," the pilot said, trumping the fireman's jack. "Anyway, the little nurse gets attached to the guy again and is glad to have him back. She refreshes his memory about their marriage and all that and starts over with him. Things are better than ever, as far as she is concerned. Well, about a year of marital bliss goes by, and one evening there is a knock at the door. She gets up off the sofa where the amnesia guy is, opens it, and it's her husband, whose memory came back."

"Wait a minute," the deckhand said. "I thought that was her husband on the sofa."

"I never said it was her husband. She just thought it was her husband. It turns out that the guy on the sofa she's been living with for a year is the identical twin to the guy on the doorstep. Got an identical popped cyst, too."

"Aw, bullshit," the day fireman bellowed.

The engineer leaned back and put his hand on a valve handle. "I better pump this place out."

"Hey," the pilot yelled above the bickering. "I knew this girl. Her family lived across the street from my aunt. Anyway after all the explanations were made, the guy who surfaced at the rock concert agreed it would be best if he moved on, and the wandering twin started back where he left off with his wife. Got his job back at the iron plant. But the wife wasn't happy anymore."

"Why the hell not?" the engineer asked, dealing the next hand. "She had two for the price of one."

"Yeah, well, even though those guys were identical in every way, something was different. We'll never know what it was, but she couldn't get over the second twin. Got so she would wander around herself, driving all over town looking for him."

"What the hell?" The deckhand threw down his cards. "She had her husband back, didn't she?"

"Oh, it was bad," the pilot continued. "She's driving down the street one day and sees the rock-concert twin, gets out of her car, runs into a park yelling and sobbing, and throws her arms around him, crying, 'I found you at last, I found you at last.' Only it wasn't him."

"Jeez," the engineer said. "Triplets."

"No," The pilot shook his had. "It was worse than that. It was her husband, who was out on a delivery for the iron plant, taking a break in the park after shucking his coveralls. Mild-mannered amnesiac or not, he was pretty put out at the way she was carrying on. But he didn't show it. He pretended to be his twin and asked her why she liked him better than her husband. And she told him. Now, don't ask me what it was.

The difference was in her mind, the way I heard it. But that guy disappeared again the next morning, and that was five years ago. They say you can go down in east Louisville and see her driving around today in a ratty green Torino, looking for one of those twins, this scared look in her eyes like she'll find one and never be sure which one she got hold of."

Raynelle pulled a pecan out of her bib pocket and cracked it between her thumb and forefinger. "That story's sadder'n a armless old man in a room full of skeeters. You sorry sons of bitches tell the depressingest lies I ever heard."

The deckhand lit up an unfiltered cigarette. "Well, sweet thing, why don't you cheer us up with one of your own?"

Raynelle looked up at a brass steam gauge bolted to an I beam. "I did know a fellow worked in an iron foundry, come to think of it. His whole family worked the same place, which is a pain in the butt if you've ever done that, what with your uncle giving you wet willies and your cousin bumming money. This fellow drove a gray Dodge Dart, the kind with the old slant-six engine that'll carry you to hell and back, slow. His relatives made fun of him for it, said he was cheap and wore plastic shoes and ate Spam—that kind of thing." She turned the last card to show trumps, banging up a king. "Sidney, you better not bourrée again. You're in this pot for thirty dollars."

The engineer swept up his hand, pressing it against his T-shirt. "I can count."

"Anyway, this boy thought he'd show his family a thing or two and went out and proposed to the pretty girl who keyed in the invoices in the office. He bought her a diamond ring that would choke an elephant, on time. It was a *nice* ring." Raynelle looked at the six men around the table as if none of them would ever buy such a ring. "He was gonna give it to her on her birthday, right before they got married in three weeks, and meantime he showed it around at the iron foundry figuring it would make 'em shut up, which basically it did."

"They was probably speechless at how dumb he was," the deckhand said out of the side of his mouth.

"But don't you know that before he got to give it to her, that girl hit her head on the edge of her daddy's swimming pool and drowned. The whole foundry went into mourning, as did those kids' families and the little town in general. She had a big funeral and she was laid out in her wedding dress in a white casket surrounded by every carnation in four counties. Everybody was crying, and the funeral parlor had this lovely music playing. I guess the boy got caught up in the feeling, because he walked over to the coffin right before they were gonna screw down the lid and he put that engagement ring on that girl's finger."

"Naw," the engineer said breathlessly, playing a card without looking at it.

"Yes, he did. And he felt proud that he had done it. At least for a month or two. Then he began to have eyes for a dental hygienist, and that little romance took off hot as a bottle rocket. He courted her for six months and decided to pop the question. But he started thinking about the monthly payments he was making on that ring and how they would go on for four and a half more years, keeping him from affording a decent ring for this living girl."

"Oh, no," The pilot said, as the hand split again and the pot rolled over yet another time.

"That's right. He got some tools and after midnight went down to the Heavenly Oaks Mausoleum and unscrewed the marble door on her drawer, slid out the coffin, and opened it up. I don't know how he could stand to rummage around in whatever was left in the box, but damned if he didn't get that ring and put the grave back together as slick as a whistle. So the next day he give it to the hygienist and everything's okay. A bit later they get married and are doing the lovebird bit in a trailer down by the foundry." Raynelle cracked another pecan against the edge of the table, crushing it with the pressure of her palm in a way that made the welder and the oiler look at each other. "But there is a big blue blowfly in the ointment. She was showing off that ring by the minute, and someone recogized the damned thing and told her. Well, she had a thirty-megaton double-PMS hissy fit and told him straight up that she she won't wear no dead woman's ring, and throws it in his face. Said the thing gave her the willies. He told her it's that or a King Edward cigar band, because he won't get out from under the payments until the twenty-first century. It went back and forth like that for a month, with the neighbors up and down the road, including my aunt Tammy, calling the police to come get them to shut up. Finally the hygienist told him she'd wear the ring."

"Well, that's a happy ending," the deckhand said.

Raynelle popped half a pecan into her red mouth. "Shut up, Jack, I ain't finished. This hygienist began to wear cowboy blouses and jean miniskirts just like the girl in the foundry office did. The old boy kind of liked it at first, but when she dyed her hair the same color as the first girl, it gave him the shakes. She said she was dreaming of that dead girl at least twice a week and saw her in her dresser mirror when she woke up. Then she began to talk like the foundry girl did, with a snappy Arkansas twang. And the dead girl was a country-music freak—liked the old stuff, too. Damned if in the middle of the night the guy wasn't waked up by his wife singing in her sleep all eleven verses of 'El Paso,' the Marty Robbins tune.

"He figured it was the ring causing all the trouble, so he got his wife drunk and while she was asleep slipped that sucker off and headed to the graveyard to put it back on that bone where he took it. Soon as he popped the lid, the cops was on him asking him what the living hell he was doing. He told them he was putting a diamond ring back in the coffin, and they said Sure, buddy. Man, he got charged with six or eight nasty things perverts do to dead bodies, and then the dead girl's family filed six or eight civil suits, and believe me there was mental anguish, pain, and suffering enough to feed the whole county. A local judge who was the dead girl's uncle sent him up for six years, and the hygienist divorced him. Strange thing was that she kept her new hair color and way of dressing, began going to George Jones concerts, and last I heard had quit her job at the dentist and was running the computers down at the foundry."

"Raynelle, *chère*,[2] I wish you wouldn't of said that one." Simoneaux, the welder, never spoke much until late in the game. He was a thin Cajun, seldom without a Camel in the corner of his mouth and a high-crowned, polka-dotted welder's cap turned backward on his head. He shrugged off a violent chill. "That story gives me *les frissons*[3] up and down my back." A long stick of beef jerky jutted from the pocket of his flannel shirt. He pulled it out, plucked a lint ball from the bottom, and bit off a small knob of meat. "But that diamond shit reminds me of a old boy I knew down in Grand Crapaud who was workin' on Pancho Oil number six offshore from Point au Fer. The driller was puttin' down the pipe hard one day and my frien' the mud engineer was takin' a dump on the engine-room toilet. All at once they hit them a gas pocket at five t'ousand feet and drill pipe came back up that hole like drinkin' straws, knockin' out the top of

---

[2] *chère:* term of endearment (French).   [3] *les frissons:* cold chills.

the rig, flyin' up in the sky, and breakin' apart at the joints. Well, my frien', he had a magazine spread out across his lap when a six-inch drill pipe hit the roof like a spear and went through-and-through the main diesel engine. About a half second later another one passed between his knees, through the Playmate of the Month and the steel deck both, yeah. He could hear the iron comin' down all over the rig, but he couldn't run because his pants was around his ankles on the other side of the drill column between his legs. He figured he was goin' to glory before he could get some toilet paper, but a worm[4] run in the engine room and cut him loose with a jackknife, and then they both took off over the side and hit the water. My frien' rolled through them breakers holdin' on to a drum of mineral spirits, floppin' around until a bad-ass fish gave him a bite on his giblets, and that was the only injury he had."

"Ouch, man." The deckhand crossed his legs.

"What?" Raynelle looked up while posting her five-dollar bourrée.

The welder threw in yet another ante, riffling the dollar bills in the pot as though figuring how much it weighed. "Well, he was hurt enough to get the company to pay him a lump sum after he got a four-by-four lawyer to sue their two-by-four insurance company. That's for true. My frien', he always said he wanted a fancy car. The first t'ing he did was to drive to Lafayette and buy a sixty-five-t'ousand-dollar Mercedes, yeah. He put new mud-grip tires on that and drove it down to the Church Key Lounge, in Morgan City, where all his mud-pumpin' buddies hung out, and it didn't take long to set off about half a dozen of them hard hats, no." The welder shook his narrow head. "He was braggin' bad, yeah."

The engineer opened his cards on his belly and rolled his eyes. "A new Mercedes in Morgan City? Whew."

"*Mais oui*,[5] you can say that again. About two, t'ree o'clock in the mornin' my frien', he come out and what he saw woulda made a muskrat cry. Somebody took a number two ball-peen hammer and dented everythin' on that car that would take a dent. That t'ing looked like it got caught in a cue-ball tornado storm. Next day he brought it by the insurance people and they told him the policy didn't cover vandalism. Told him he would have to pay to get it fixed or drive it like that.

"But my frien', he had blew most all his money on the car to begin with. When he drove it, everybody looked at him like he was some kind

---

[4]*worm:* inexperienced oil rig worker.   [5]*Mais oui:* But yes (French).

of freak. You know, he wanted people to look at him, that's why he bought the car, but they was lookin' at him the wrong way, like 'You mus' be some prime jerk to have someone mess with you car like that.' So after a week of havin' people run off the road turnin' their necks to look at that new Mercedes, he got drunk, went to the store and bought twenty cans of Bondo, tape, and cans of spray paint."

"Don't say it," the deckhand cried.

"No, no," the engineer said to his cards.

"What?" Raynelle asked.

"Yeah, the po' bastard couldn't make a snake out of Play-Doh and is gonna try and restore a fine European se-dan. He filed and sanded on that poor car for a week, and then hit it with that dollar-a-can paint. When he finished up, that Mercedes looked like it was battered for fryin'. He drove it around Grand Crapaud, and people just pointed and doubled over. He kept it outside his trailer at night, and people would drive up and park, just to look at it. Phone calls started comin', the hang-up kind that said things like 'You look like your car,' click, or 'What kind of icin' did you use?' click. My frien' finally took out his insurance policy and saw what it did cover—theft.

"So he started leavin' the keys in it parked down by the abandoned lumber yard, but nobody in Grand Crapaud would steal it. He drove to Lafayette, rented a motel room, yeah, and parked it outside that bad housin' project with keys in it." The welder threw in another hand and watched the cards fly. "Next night he left the windows down with the keys in it." He pulled off his polka-dotted cap and ran his fingers through his dark hair. "Third night he left the motor runnin' and the lights on with the car blockin' the driveway of a crack house. Next mornin' he found it twenty feet away, idled out of diesel with a dead battery. It was that ugly."

"What happened next?" The pilot trumped an ace as if he were killing a bug.

"My frien', he called me up you know. Said he wished he had a used standard-shift Ford pick-up and the money in the bank. His wife left him, his momma made him take a cab to come see her, and all he could stand to do was drink and stay in his trailer. I didn't know what to tell him. He said he was gonna read his policy some more."

"Split pot again," the deckhand shouted. "I can't get out this game. I feel like my nuts is hung up in a fan belt."

"Shut your trap and deal," Raynelle said, sailing a loose wad of cards in the deckhand's direction. "What happened to the Mercedes guy?"

The welder put his cap back on and pulled up the crown. "Well, his policy said it covered all kinds of accidents, you know, so he parked it in back next to a big longleaf pine and cut that sucker down, only it was a windy day and as soon as he got through that tree with the saw, a gust come up and pushed it the other way from where he wanted it to fall."

"What'd it hit?"

"It mashed his trailer like a cockroach, yeah. The propane stove blew up, and by the time the Grand Crapaud fire truck come around, all they could do was break out coat hangers and mushmellas. His wife what lef' ain't paid the insurance on the double-wide, no, so now he got to get him a camp stove and a picnic table, so he can shack up in the Mercedes."

"He lived in the car?"

The welder nodded glumly. "Po' bastard wouldn't do nothin' but drink up the few bucks he had lef' and lie in the back seat. One night last fall we had that cold snap, you remember? It got so cold around Grand Crapaud you could hear the sugarcane stalks poppin' out in the fields like firecrackers. They found my frien' froze to death sittin' up behind the steerin' wheel. T-nook, the paramedic, said his eyes was open, starin' over the hood like he was goin' for a drive." The welder pushed his downturned hand out slowly like a big sedan driving toward the horizon. Everybody's eyes followed it for a long moment.

"New deck," the engineer cried, throwing in his last trump and watching it get swallowed by a jack. "Nick, you little dago, give me that blue deck." The oiler, a quiet, olive-skinned boy from New Orleans's west bank, pushed the new box over. "New deck, new luck," the engineer told him. "You know, I used to date this old fat gal lived in a double-wide north of Biloxi. God, that woman liked to eat. When I called it off, she asked me why, and I told her I was afraid she was going to get thirteen inches around the ankles. That must of got her attention, because she went on some kind of fat-killer diet and exercise program that about wore out the floor beams in that trailer. But she got real slim, I heard. She had a pretty face, I'll admit that. She started hittin' the bars and soon had her a cow farmer ask her to marry him, which she did."

"Is a cow farmer like a rancher?" Raynelle asked, her tongue in her cheek like a jaw breaker.

"It's what I said it was. Who the hell ever heard of a ranch in Biloxi? Anyway, this old gal developed a fancy for steaks, since her man got meat reasonable, bein' a cow farmer and all. She started puttin' away the T-bones and swellin' like a sow on steroids. After a year she blowed up to her fightin' weight and then some. I heard she'd eat up about half the cows on the farm before he told her he wanted a divorce. She told him she'd sue to get half the farm, and he said go for it—it'd be worth it if someone would just roll her off his half. She hooked up with this greasy little lawyer from Waveland, and sure enough, he got half the husband's place. After the court dealings he took this old gal out to supper to celebrate and one thing led to another and they wound up at her apartment for a little slap-and-tickle. I'll be damned if they didn't fall out of bed together with her on top, and he broke three ribs and ruined a knee on a night table. After a year of treatments he sued her good and got her half of the farm."

The deckhand threw his head back, *ha ha*. "That's a double screwin' if ever there was one."

"Hey, it don't stop there. The little lawyer called up the farmer and said, 'Since we gonna be neighbors, why don't you tell me a good spot to build a house?' They got together and hit it off real good, like old drinkin' buddies. After a couple of months the lawyer went into business with the farmer and together they doubled the cattle production, 'specially since they got rid of the critters' worst predator."

Raynelle's eyebrows came together like a small thunderhead. "Well?"

"Well what?" The engineer scratched an armpit.

"What happened to that poor girl?"

All the men looked around uneasily. Raynelle had permanently disabled a boilermaker on the *St. Genevieve* with a cornbread skillet.

"She got back on her diet, I heard. Down to one hundred twenty pounds again."

"That's the scary thing about women," the day fireman volunteered, putting up three fingers to ask for his draw. "Marryin' 'em is just like cuttin' the steel bands on a bale of cotton. First thing you know, you've got a roomful of woman."

Raynelle glowered. "Careful I don't pour salt on you and watch you melt."

The engineer released a sigh. "Okay, Nick, you the only one ain't told a lie yet."

The young oiler ducked his head. "Don't know none."

"Haw," Raynelle said. "A man without bullshit. Check his drawers, Simoneaux, see if he ain't Nancy instead of Nicky."

Reddening, the oiler frowned at his hand. "Well, the cows remind me of somethin' I heard while I was playin' the poker machines over in Port Allen the other day," he said, a long strand of black hair falling in his eyes. "There was this Mexican guy named Gonzales who worked with cows in Matamoros."

"Another cow farmer," the deckhand said with a groan.

"Shut up," Raynelle said. "Was that his first name or second name?"

"Well, both."

"What?" She pitched a card at him.

"Aw, Miss Raynelle, you know how those Mexicans are with their names. This guy's name was Gonzales Gonzales, with a bunch of names in between." Raynelle cocked her ear whenever she heard the oiler speak. She had a hard time with his New Orleans accent, which she found to be Bronxlike. "He was a pretty smart fella and got into Texas legal, worked a few years, and became a naturalized citizen, him and his wife both."

"What was his wife's name?" the pilot asked. "Maria Maria?"

"Come on, now, do you want to hear this or don'tcha?" The oiler pushed the hair out of his eyes. "The cattle industry shrunk up where he was at and he looked around for another place to try and settle. He started to go to Gonzales, Texas, but there ain't no work there, so he gets out a map and spots Gonzales, Louisiana."

"That rough place with all the jitterbug joints?"

"Yep. Lots of blacks and roughnecks, but they ain't no Mexicans. Must have been settled a million years ago by a family of Gonzaleses who probably speak French and eat gumbo nowadays. So Gonzales Gonzales gets him a job for two local lawyers who run a horse farm on the side. He gets an apartment on Gonzales Street down by the train station." The oiler looked at a new hand, fanning the cards out slowly. "You know how hard-nosed the Airline Highway cops are through there? Well, this Gonzales was dark, and his car was a beat-up smoker, so they pulled him one day on his way to Baton Rouge. The cop stands outside his window and says, 'Lemme see your license'; Gonzales says he forgot it at home on the dresser. The cop pulls out a ticket book and says, 'What's your last name?' He says, 'Gonzales.' The cop says,

'What's your first name?' and he tells him. That officer leans in the window and sniffs his breath. 'Okay, Gonzales Gonzales,' he says real nasty, 'where you live?' 'Gonzales,' he says. 'Okay, boy. Get out the car,' the cop says. He throws him against the door, hard. 'And who do you work for?' Gonzales looks him in the eye and says, 'Gonzales and Gonzales.' The cop turns him around and slams his head against the roof and says, 'Yeah, and you probably live on Gonzales Street, huh, you slimy son of a bitch.' 'At one-two-two-six, Apartment E,' Gonzales says."

The deckhand puts his cards over his eyes. "The poor bastard."

"Yeah," the oiler said, and sighed. "He got beat up and jailed that time until the Gonzales lawyers went up and sprung him. About once a month some cop would pull him over and give him hell. When he applied for a little loan at the bank, they threw him in the street. When he tried to get a credit card, the company called the feds, who investigated him for fraud. Nobody would cash his checks, and the first year he filed state and federal taxes, three government cars stayed in his driveway for a week. Nobody believed who he was."

"That musta drove him nuts," the welder said, drawing four cards.

"I don't think so, man. He knew who he was. Gonzales Gonzales knew he was in America and you could control what you was, unlike in Mexico. So, when the traffic cops beat him up, he sold his car and got a bike. When the banks wouldn't give him no checks, he used cash. When the tax people refused to admit he existed, he stopped payin' taxes. Man, he worked hard and saved every penny. One day it was real hot, and he was walkin' into Gonzales because his bike had a flat. He stopped in the Rat's Nest Lounge to get a root beer, and they was this drunk from west Texas in there makin' life hard for the barmaid. He come over to Gonzales and asked him would he have a drink. He said sure, and the bartender set up a whiskey and a root beer. The cowboy was full of Early Times and pills, and you coulda lit a blowtorch off his eyeballs. He put his arm around Gonzales and asked him what his name was, you know. When he heard it, he got all serious, like he was bein' made fun of or somethin'. He asked a couple more questions and started struttin' and cussin'. He pulled an engraved Colt out from under a cheesy denim jacket and stuck it in Gonzales's mouth. 'You jerkin' me around, man,' that cowboy told him. 'You tellin' me you're Gonzales Gonzales from Gonzales who lives on Gonzales Street and works for Gonzales and Gonzales?' That Mexican looked at the gun, and I don't know what was goin' through his head, but he nodded. And the cowboy pulled back the hammer."

"Damn," the welder said.

"I don't want to hear this." Raynelle clapped the cards to her ears.

"Hey," the oiler said. "Like I told you, he knew who he was. He pointed to the phone book by the register, and after a minute the bartender had it open and held it out to the cowboy. Sure enough, old Ma Bell had come through for the American way, and Gonzales was listed, with the street and all. The cowboy took the gun out of Gonzales's mouth and started cryin' like the crazy snail he was. He told Gonzales that he was sorry and gave him the Colt. Said that his girlfriend left him and his dog died, or maybe it was the other way around. Gonzales went down the street and called the cops. In two months he got a six-thousand-dollar reward for turnin' in the guy, who, it turns out, had killed his girlfriend and his dog, too, over in Laredo. He got five hundred for the Colt and moved to Baton Rouge, where he started a postage stamp of a used-car lot. Did well, too. Got a dealership now."

The day fireman snapped his fingers. "G. Gonzales Buick-Olds?"

"That's it, man," the oiler said.

"The smilin' rich dude in the commercials?"

"Like I said," the oiler told the table. "He knew who he was."

"Mary and Joseph, everybody is in this hand," the pilot yelled. "Spades is trumps."

"*Laissez les bons temps rouler,*"[6] the welder sang, laying an eight of spades on a pile of diamonds and raking in the trick.

"That's your skinny ass," Raynelle said, playing a ten of spades last, taking the second trick.

"Do I smell the ten millionth rollover pot?" the engineer asked. "There must be six hundred fifty dollars in that pile." He threw down a nine and covered the third trick.

"Coming gitcha." Raynelle raised her hand high, plucked a card, and slammed a jack to win the fourth trick.

That was two. She led the king of spades and watched the cards follow.

The pilot put his hands together and prayed. "Please, somebody, have the ace." He played his card and sat up to watch as each man threw his last card in, no one able to beat the king, and then Raynelle

[6]*Laissez les bons temps rouler:* Cajun French for "let the good times roll."

jumped in the air like a hooked marlin, nearly upsetting the table, screaming and waving her meaty arms through the steamy engine-room air. "I never won so much money in my life," she cried, falling from the waist onto the pile of bills and coins and raking it beneath her.

"Whatcha gonna do with all that money?" the welder asked, turning his hat around in disbelief.

She began stuffing the bib pocket on her overalls with half dollars. "I'm gonna buy me a silver lamé dress and one of those cheap tickets to Las Vegas, where I can do some high-class gambling. No more of this penny-ante stuff with old men and worms."

Four of the men got up to relieve their bladders or get cigarettes or grab something to drink. The pilot leaned against a column of insulated pipe. "Hell, we all want to go to Las Vegas. Don't you want to take one of us along to the holy land?"

"Man, I'm gonna gamble with gentlemen. Ranchers, not cow farmers either." She folded a wad of bills into a hip pocket.

Nick, the young oiler, laced his fingers behind his head, leaned back, and closed his eyes. He wondered what Raynelle would do in such a glitzy place as Las Vegas. He imagined her wearing a Sears gown in a casino full of tourists dressed in shorts and sneakers. She would be drinking too much and eating too much, and the gown would look like it was crammed with rising dough. She would get in a fight with a blackjack dealer after she'd lost all her money and would be thrown out on the street. After selling her plane ticket, she would be back at the slot machines until she was completely broke, and then she would be on a neon-infested boulevard, her tiny silver purse hanging from her shoulder on a long spaghetti strap, one heel broken off a silver shoe. He saw her walking at last across the desert through the waves of heat, mountains in front and the angry snarl of cross-country traffic in the rear, until she sobered up and began to hitch, and was picked up by a carload of Jehovah's Witnesses driving to a convention in Baton Rouge in an un-air-conditioned compact stuck in second gear. Every thirty miles the car would overheat and they would all get out, stand among the cactus, and pray. Raynelle would curse them, and they would pray harder for the big sunburned woman sweating in the metallic dress. The desert would spread before her as far as the end of the world, a hot and rocky place empty of mirages and dreams. She might not live to get out of it.

—1995

Dagoberto Gilb (b. 1950) crafts terse, plain-spoken cadences of prose that belie his undergraduate training in philosophy, but his knowledge of blue-collar life is strictly firsthand, firmly grounded in his work experiences as a day-laborer and carpenter in Los Angeles and El Paso. "Look on the Bright Side," originally published in The Threepenny Review, *appears in Gilb's 1993 collection* The Magic of Blood, *which was a recipient of the PEN/Hemingway Award for First Fiction. A novel,* The Last Known Residence of Mickey Acuña, *appeared in 1994 from Grove Press and was chosen a Notable Book of the Year by the* New York Times Book Review. *Gilb has served as visiting professor of writing at the Universities of Texas, Arizona, and Wyoming, and he is currently a member of the creative writing faculty at Southwest Texas State University.* Woodcuts of Women, *a new collection of stories, appeared in 2001.*

Dagoberto Gilb
Look on the Bright Side

The way I see it, a man can have all the money in the world but if he can't keep his self-respect, he don't have shit. A man has to stand up for things even when it may not be very practical. A man can't have pride and give up his rights.

This is exactly what I told my wife when Mrs. Kevovian raised our rent illegally. I say illegally because, well aside from it being obviously unfriendly and greedy whenever a landlord or lady wants money above the exceptional amount she wanted when you moved in not so long ago, here in this enlightened city of Los Angeles it's against the law to raise it above a certain percentage and then only once every twelve months, which is often enough. Now the wife argued that since Mrs. Kevovian was a little ignorant, nasty, and hard to communicate with, we should have gone ahead and paid the increase—added up it was only sixty some-odd bones, a figure the landlady'd come up with getting the percentage right, but this time she tried to get it two months too early. My wife told me to pay it and not have the hassle. She knew me better than this. We'd already put up with the cucarachas and rodents, I fixed the plumbing myself, and our back porch was screaming to become dust and probably would just when one of our little why nots—we have three of them—snuck onto it. People don't turn into dust on the way down, they splat first. One time I tried to explain this to Mrs. Kevovian, without success. You think I was going to pay more rent when I shouldn't have to?

My wife offered the check for the right amount to the landlady when she came to our door for her money and wouldn't take it. My wife tried to explain how there was a mistake, but when I got home from work the check was still on the mantle where it sat waiting. Should I have called her and talked it over? Not me. This was her problem and she could call. In the meantime, I could leave the money in the bank and feel that much richer for that much longer, and if she was so stupid I could leave it in the savings and let it earn interest. And the truth was that she was stupid enough, and stubborn, and mean. I'd talked to the other tenants, and I'd talked to tenants that'd left before us, so I wasn't at all surprised about the Pay or Quit notice we finally got. To me, it all seemed kind of fun. This lady wasn't nice, as God Himself would witness, and maybe, since I learned it would take about three months before we'd go to court, maybe we'd get three free months. We hadn't stopped talking about moving out since we unpacked.

You'd probably say that this is how things always go, and you'd probably be right. Yeah, about this same time I got laid off. I'd been laid off lots of times so it was no big deal, but the circumstances—well, the company I was working for went bankrupt and a couple of my paychecks bounced and it wasn't the best season of the year in what were not the best years for working people. Which could have really set me off, made me pretty unhappy, but that's not the kind of man I am. I believe in making whatever you have the right situation for you at the right moment for you. And look, besides the extra money from not paying rent, I was going to get a big tax return, and we also get unemployment compensation in this great country. It was a good time for a vacation, so I bunched the kids in the car with the old lady and drove to Baja. I deserved it, we all did.

Like my wife said, I should have figured how things were when we crossed back to come home. I think we were in the slowest line on the border. Cars next to us would pull up and within minutes be at that redlight green-light signal. You know how it is when you pick the worst line to wait in. I was going nuts. A poor dude in front of us idled so long that his radiator overheated and he had to push the old heap forward by himself. My wife told me to settle down and wait because if we changed lanes then it would stop moving. I turned the ignition off then on again when we moved a spot. When we did get there I felt a lot better, cheerful even. There's no prettier place for a vacation than Baja and we really had a good time. I smiled forgivingly at the customs guy who looked as kind as Captain Stubbing on the TV show "Love Boat."

"I'm American," I said, prepared like the sign told us to be. My wife said the same thing. I said, "The kids are American too. Though I haven't checked out the backseat for a while."

Captain Stubbing didn't think that was very funny. "What do you have to declare?"

"Let's see. A six-pack of Bohemia beer. A blanket. Some shells we found. A couple holy pictures. Puppets for the kids. Well, two blankets."

"No other liquor? No fruits? Vegetables? No animal life?"

I shook my head to each of them.

"So what were you doing in Mexico?"

"Sleeping on the beach, swimming in the ocean. Eating the rich folks's lobster." It seemed like he didn't understand what I meant. "Vacation. We took a vacation."

"How long were you in Mexico?" He made himself comfortable on the stool outside his booth after he'd run a license plate check through the computer.

"Just a few days," I said, starting to lose my good humor.

"How many days?"

"You mean exactly?"

"Exactly."

"Five days. Six. Five nights and six days."

"Did you spend a lot of money in Mexico?"

I couldn't believe this, and someone else in a car behind us couldn't either because he blasted the horn. Captain Stubbing made a mental note of him. "We spent some good money there. Not that much though. Why?" My wife grabbed my knee.

"Where exactly did you stay?"

"On the beach. Near Estero Beach."

"Don't you work?"

I looked at my wife. She was telling me to go along with it without saying so. "Of course I work."

"Why aren't you at work now?"

"Cuz I got laid off, man!"

"Did you do something wrong?"

"I said I got *laid off*; not *fired!*"

"What do you do?"

"Laborer!"

"What kind of laborer?"

"Construction!"

"And there's no other work? Where do you live?"

"No! Los Angeles!"

"Shouldn't you be looking for a job? Isn't that more important than taking a vacation?"

I was so hot I think my hair was turning red. I just glared at this guy.

"Are you receiving unemployment benefits?"

"Yeah I am."

"You're receiving unemployment and you took a vacation?"

"That's it! I ain't listening to this shit no more!"

"You watch your language, sir." He filled out a slip of paper and slid it under my windshield wiper. "Pull over there."

My wife was a little worried about the two smokes I never did and still had stashed in my wallet. She was wanting to tell me to take it easy as they went through the car, but that was hard for her because our oldest baby was crying. All I wanted to do was put in a complaint about that jerk to somebody higher up. As a matter of fact I wanted him fired, but anything to make him some trouble. I felt like they would've listened better if they hadn't found those four bottles of rum I was trying to sneak over. At that point I lost some confidence, though not my sense of being right. When this other customs man suggested that I might be detained further if I pressed the situation, I paid the penalty charges for the confiscated liquor and shut up. It wasn't worth a strip search, or finding out what kind of crime it was crossing the border with some B-grade marijuana.

Time passed back home and there was still nothing coming out of the union hall. There were a lot of men worried but at least I felt like I had the unpaid rent money to wait it out. I was fortunate to have a landlady like Mrs. Kevovian helping us through these bad times. She'd gotten a real smart lawyer for me too. He'd attached papers on his Unlawful Detainer to prove my case, which seemed so ridiculous that I called the city housing department just to make sure I couldn't be wrong about it all. I wasn't. I rested a lot easier without a rent payment, even took some guys out for some cold ones when I got the document with the official court date stamped on it, still more than a month away.

I really hadn't started out with any plan. But now that I was unemployed there were all these complications. I didn't have all the money it took to get into another place, and our rent, as much as it had been, was in comparison to lots still cheap, and rodents and roaches weren't that bad a problem to me. Still, I took a few ugly pictures like I was told to and had the city inspect the hazardous back porch and went to court on the assigned day hoping for something to ease our bills.

Her lawyer was Yassir Arafat without the bedsheet. He wore this suit with a vest that was supposed to make him look cool, but I've seen enough Ziedler & Ziedler commercials to recognize discount fashion. Mrs. Kevovian sat on that hard varnished bench with that wrinkled forehead of hers. Her daughter translated whatever she didn't understand when the lawyer discussed the process. I could hear every word even though there were all these other people because the lawyer's voice carried in the long white hall and polished floor of justice. He talked as confidently as a dude with a sharp blade.

"You're the defendant?" he asked five minutes before court was to be in session.

"That's me, and that's my wife," I pointed. "We're both defendants."

"I'm Mr. Villalobos, attorney representing the plaintiff."

"All right! Law school, huh? You did the people proud, eh? So how come you're working for the wrong side? That ain't a nice lady you're helping to evict us, man."

"You're the one who refuses to pay the rent."

"I'm disappointed in you, compa. You should know I been trying to pay the rent. You think I should beg her to take it? She wants more money than she's supposed to get, and because I wanna pay her what's right, she's trying to throw us onto the streets."

Yassir Villalobos scowled over my defense papers while I gloated. I swore it was the first time he saw them or the ones he turned in. "Well, I'll do this. Reimburse Mrs. Kevovian for the back rent and I'll drop the charges."

"You'll drop the charges? Are you making a joke, man? You talk like I'm the one who done something wrong. I'm *here* now. Unless you wanna say drop what I owe her, something like that, then I won't let the judge see how you people tried to harass me unlawfully."

Villalobos didn't like what I was saying, and he didn't like my attitude one bit.

"I'm the one who's right," I emphasized. "I know it, and you know it too." He was squirming mad. I figured he was worried about looking like a fool in the court. "Unless you offer me something better, I'd just as soon see what that judge has to say."

"There's no free rent," he said finally. "I'll just drop these charges and re-serve you." He said that as an ultimatum, real pissed.

I smiled. "You think I can't wait another three months?"

That did it. He stir-armed the swinging door and made arrangements with the court secretary, and my old lady and me picked the kids up from the babysitter's a lot earlier than we'd planned. The truth was I was relieved. I did have the money, but now that I'd been out of work so long it was getting close. If I didn't get some work soon we wouldn't have enough to pay it all. I'd been counting on that big income tax check, and when the government decided to take all of it except nine dollars and some change, what remained of a debt from some other year and the penalties it included, I was almost worried. I wasn't happy with the US Govt and I tried to explain to it on the phone how hard I worked and how it was only that I didn't understand those letters they sent me and couldn't they show some kindness to the unemployed, to a family that obviously hadn't planned to run with that tax advantage down to Costa Rica and hire bodyguards to watch over an estate. The thing is, it's no use being right when the US Govt thinks it's not wrong.

Fortunately, we still had Mrs. Kevovian as our landlady. I don't know how we'd have lived without her. Unemployment money covers things when you don't have to pay rent. And I didn't want to for as long as possible. The business agent at the union hall said there was supposed to be a lot of work breaking soon, but in the meantime I told everyone in our home who talked and didn't crawl to lay low and not answer any doors to strangers with summonses. My wife didn't like peeking around corners when she walked the oldest to school, though the oldest liked it a mess. We waited and waited but nobody came. Instead it got nailed to the front door very impolitely.

So another few months had passed and what fool would complain about that? Not this one. Still, I wanted justice. I wanted The Law to hand down fair punishment to these evil people who were conspiring to take away my family's home. Man, I wanted that judge to be so pissed that he'd pound that gavel and it'd ring in my ears like a Vegas jackpot. I didn't want to pay any money back. And not because I didn't have the money, or I didn't have a job, or that pretty soon they'd be cutting off my unemployment. I'm not denying their influence on my thinking, but mostly it was the principle of the thing. It seemed to me if I had so much to lose for being wrong, I should have something equal to win for being right.

"There's no free rent," Villalobos told me again five minutes before we were supposed to swing through those doors and please rise. "You don't have the money, do you?"

"Of course I have the money. But I don't see why I should settle this with you now and get nothing out of it. Seems like I had to go outa my way to come down here. It ain't easy finding a babysitter for our kids, who you wanna throw on the streets, and we didn't, and we had to pay that expensive parking across the street. This has been a mess of trouble for me to go, sure, I'll pay what I owe without the mistaken rent increase, no problem."

"The judge isn't going to offer you free rent."

"I'd rather hear what he has to say."

Villalobos was some brother, but I guess that's what happens with some education and a couple of cheap suits and ties. I swore right then that if I ever worked again I wasn't paying for my kids' college education.

The judge turned out to be a sister whose people hadn't gotten much justice either and that gave me hope. And I was real pleased we were the first case because the kids were fidgeting like crazy and my wife was miserable trying to keep them settled down. I wanted the judge to see what a big happy family we were so I brought them right up to our assigned "defendant" table.

"I think it would be much easier if your wife took your children out to the corridor," the judge told me.

"She's one of the named defendants, your honor."

"I'm sure you can represent your case adequately without the baby crying in your wife's arms."

"Yes ma'am, your honor."

The first witness for the plaintiff was this black guy who looked like they pulled a bottle away from the night before, who claimed to have come by my place to serve me all these times but I wouldn't answer the door. The sleaze was all lie up until when he said he attached it to my door, which was a generous exaggeration. Then Mrs. Kevovian took the witness stand. Villalobos asked her a couple of unimportant questions, and then I got to ask questions. I've watched enough lawyer shows and I was ready.

I heard the gavel but it didn't tinkle like a line of cherries.

"You can state your case in the witness stand at the proper moment," the judge said.

"But your honor, I just wanna show how this landlady . . ."

"You don't have to try your case through this witness."

"Yes ma'am, your honor."

So when that moment came all I could do was show her those polaroids of how bad things got and tell her about roaches and rats and fire hazards and answer oh yes, your honor, I've been putting that money away, something which concerned the judge more than anything else did.

I suppose that's the way of swift justice. Back at home, my wife, pessimistic as always, started packing the valuable stuff into the best boxes. She couldn't believe that anything good was going to come from the verdict in the mail. The business agent at the hall was still telling us about all the work about to break any day now, but I went ahead and started reading the help wanted ads in the newspaper.

A couple of weeks later the judgment came in an envelope. We won. The judge figured up all the debt and then cut it by twenty percent. Victory is sweet, probably, when there's a lot of coins clinking around the pants' pockets, but I couldn't let up. Now that I was proven right I figured we could do some serious negotiating over payment. A little now and a little later and a little bit now and again. That's what I'd offer when Mrs. Kevovian came for the money, which she was supposed to do the next night by 5 p.m., according to the legal document. "The money to be collected by the usual procedure," were the words, which meant Mrs. Kevovian was supposed to knock on the door and, knowing her, at five o'clock exactly.

Maybe I was a tiny bit worried. What if she wouldn't take anything less than all of it? Then I'd threaten to give her nothing and to disappear into the mounds of other uncollected debts. Mrs. Kevovian needed this money, I knew that. Better all of it over a long period than none of it over a longer one, right? That's what I'd tell her, and I'd be standing there with my self confidence more muscled-up than ever.

Except she never came. There was no knock on the door. A touch nervous, I started calling lawyers. I had a stack of junk mail letters from all these legal experts advising me that for a small fee they'd help me with my eviction procedure. None of them seemed to understand my problem over the phone, though maybe if I came by their office. One of them did seem to catch enough though. He said if the money wasn't collected by that time then the plaintiff had the right to reclaim the premises. Actually the lawyer didn't say that, the judgment paper did, and I'd read it to him over the phone. All the lawyer said was, "The marshall will physically evict you in ten days." He didn't charge a fee for the information.

We had a garage sale. You know, miscellaneous things, things easy to replace, that you could buy anywhere when the time was right again, like beds and lamps and furniture. We stashed the valuables in the trunk of the car—a perfect fit—and Greyhound was having a special sale which made it an ideal moment for a visit to the abuelitos back home, who hadn't been able to see their grandkids and daughter in such a long time. You have to look on the bright side. I wouldn't have to pay any of that money back, and there was the chance to start a new career, just like they say, and I'd been finding lots of opportunities from reading the newspaper. Probably any day I'd be going back to work at one of those jobs about to break. Meanwhile, we left a mattress in the apartment for me to sleep on so I could have the place until a marshal beat on the door. Or soon I'd send back for the family from a house with a front and backyard I promised I'd find and rent. However it worked out. Or there was always the car with that big backseat.

One of those jobs I read about in the want ads was as a painter for the city. I applied, listed all this made-up experience I had, but I still had to pass some test. So I went down to the library to look over one of those books on the subject. I guess I didn't think much about the hours libraries keep, and I guess I was a few hours early, and so I took a seat next to this pile of newspapers on this cement bench not that far from the front doors. The bench smelled like piss, but since I was feeling pretty open minded about things I didn't let it bother me. I wanted to enjoy all the scenery, which was nice for the big city, with all the trees and dewy grass, though the other early risers weren't so involved with the love of nature. One guy not so far away was rolling from one side of his body to the other, back and forth like that, from under a tree. He just went on and on. This other man, or maybe woman—wearing a sweater on top that was too baggy to make chest impressions on and another sweater below that, wrapped around like a skirt, and pants under that, cords, and unisex homemade sandals made out of old tennis shoes and leather, and finally, on the head, long braided hair which wasn't braided too good—this person was foraging off the cement path, digging through the trash for something. I thought aluminum too but there were about five empty beer cans nearby and the person kicked those away. It was something that this person knew by smell, because that's how he or she tested whether it was the right thing or not. I figured this was someone to keep my eye on.

Then without warning came a monster howl, and those pigeons bundled-up on the lawn scattered to the trees. I swore somebody took a shot at me. "Traitor! You can't get away with it!" Those were the words I got out of the tail end of the loud speech from this dude who came out of nowhere, who looked pretty normal, hip even if it weren't for the clothes. He had one of those great, long graying beards and hair, like some wise man, some Einstein. I was sure a photographer would be along to take his picture if they hadn't already. You know how Indians and winos make the most interesting photographs. His clothes were bad though, took away from his cool. Like he'd done caca and spilled his spaghetti and rolled around in the slime for a lot of years since mama'd washed a bagful of the dirties. The guy really had some voice, and just when it seemed like he'd settled back into a stroll like anyone else, just when those pigeons trickled back down onto the lawn into a coo-cooing lump, he cut loose again. It was pretty hard to understand, even with his volume so high, but I figured it out to be about patriotism, justice, and fidelity.

"That guy's gone," John said when he came up to me with a bag of groceries he dropped next to me. He'd told me his name right off. "John. John. The name's John, they call me John." He pulled out a loaf of white bread and started tearing up the slices into big and little chunks and throwing them onto the grass. The pigeons picked up on this quick. "Look at 'em, they act like they ain't eaten in weeks, they're eatin like vultures, like they're starvin, like vultures, good thing I bought three loafs of bread, they're so hungry, but they'll calm down, they'll calm down after they eat some." John was blond and could almost claim to have a perm if you'd asked me. He'd shaven some days ago so the stubble on his face wasn't so bad. He'd never have much of a beard anyway. "They can't get enough, look at 'em, look at 'em, good thing I bought three loafs, I usually buy two." He moved like he talked—nervously, in jerks, and without pausing—and, when someone passed by, his conversation didn't break up. "Hey good morning, got any spare change for some food? No? So how ya gonna get to Heaven?" A man in a business suit turned his head with a smile, but didn't change direction. "I'll bury you deeper in Hell then, I'll dig ya deeper!" John went back to feeding the birds, who couldn't get enough. "That's how ya gotta talk to 'em," he told me. "Ya gotta talk to 'em like that and like ya can back it up, like ya can back it up."

I sort of got to liking John. He reminded me of a hippie, and it was sort of nice to see hippies again. He had his problems, of course, and he told me about them too, about how a dude at the hotel he stayed at kept his SSI check, how he called the police but they wouldn't pay attention, that his hotel was just a hangout for winos and hypes and pimps and he was gonna move out, turn that guy in and go to court and testify or maybe he'd get a gun and blow the fucker away, surprise him. He had those kind of troubles but seemed pretty intelligent otherwise to me. Even if he was a little wired, he wasn't like the guy who was still rolling around under the tree or the one screaming at the top of his lungs.

While we both sat at the bench watching those pigeons clean up what became only visible to them in the grass, one of the things John said before he took off was this: "Animals are good people. They're not like people, people are no good, they don't care about nobody. People won't do nothing for ya. That's the age we live in, that's how it is. Hitler had that plan. I think it was Hitler, maybe it was somebody else, it coulda been somebody else." We were both staring at this pigeon with only one foot, the other foot being a balled-up red stump, hopping around, pecking at the lawn. "I didn't think much of him gettin rid of the cripples and the mentals and the old people. That was no good, that was no good. It musta been Hitler, or Preacher Jobe. It was him, or it musta been somebody else I heard. Who was I thinkin of? Hey you got any change? How ya gonna getto Heaven? I wish I could remember who it was I was thinkin of."

I sure didn't know, but I promised John that if I thought of it, or if something else came up, I'd look him up at the address he gave me and filed in my pocket. I had to show him a couple of times it was still there. I was getting a little tired from such a long morning already, and I wished that library would hurry up and open so I could study for the test. I didn't have the slightest idea what they could ask me on a test for painting either. But then jobs at the hall were bound to break and probably I wouldn't have to worry too much anyway.

I was really sleepy by now, and I was getting used to the bench, even when I did catch that whiff of piss. I leaned back and closed the tired eyes and it wasn't so bad. I thought I'd give it a try—you know, why not?—and I scooted over and nuzzled my head into that stack of newspapers and tucked my legs into my chest. I shut them good this time and yawned. I didn't see why I should fight it, and it was just until the library opened.

—*1993*

Amy Tan (b. 1952) is the only child of Chinese immigrants and grew up in Oakland, California. Her hugely successful first novel, The Joy Luck Club *(1989), from which "Two Kinds" is taken, is an example of frame-tale fiction, telling sixteen interconnected stories of four Chinese-American mothers and their daughters as they adjust to the cultural mixture of life in San Francisco. The Joy Luck Club was made into a successful film. Tan's other books include two novels,* The Kitchen God's Wife *and* The Hundred Secret Senses, *and two books for children,* The Moon Lady *and* The Chinese Siamese Cat. *A new novel set in China and the United States,* The Bonesetter's Daughter, *appeared in 2001.*

Amy Tan
Two Kinds

My mother believed you could be anything you wanted to be in America. You could open a restaurant. You could work for the government and get good retirement. You could buy a house with almost no money down. You could become rich. You could become instantly famous.

"Of course you can be prodigy, too," my mother told me when I was nine. "You can be best anything. What does Auntie Lindo know? Her daughter, she is only best tricky."

America was where all my mother's hopes lay. She had come here in 1949 after losing everything in China: her mother and father, her family home, her first husband, and two daughters, twin baby girls. But she never looked back with regret. There were so many ways for things to get better.

We didn't immediately pick the right kind of prodigy. At first my mother thought I could be a Chinese Shirley Temple. We'd watch Shirley's old movies on TV as though they were training films. My mother would poke my arm and say, *"Ni kan."* You watch. And I would see Shirley tapping her feet, or singing a sailor song, or pursing her lips into a very round O while saying, "Oh, my goodness."

"Ni kan," said my mother as Shirley's eyes flooded with tears. "You already know how. Don't need talent for crying!"

Soon after my mother got this idea about Shirley Temple, she took me to a beauty training school in the Mission district and put me in the hands of a student who could barely hold the scissors without shaking. Instead of getting big fat curls, I emerged with an uneven mass of crinkly black fuzz. My mother dragged me off to the bathroom and tried to wet down my hair.

"You look like Negro Chinese," she lamented, as if I had done this on purpose.

The instructor of the beauty training school had to lop off these soggy clumps to make my hair even again. "Peter Pan is very popular these days," the instructor assured my mother. I now had hair the length of a boy's, with straight-across bangs that hung at a slant two inches above my eyebrows. I liked the haircut and it made me actually look forward to my future fame.

In fact, in the beginning, I was just as excited as my mother, maybe even more so. I pictured this prodigy part of me as many different images, trying each one on for size. I was a dainty ballerina girl standing by the curtains, waiting to hear the right music that would send me floating on my tiptoes. I was like the Christ child lifted out of the straw manger, crying with holy indignity. I was Cinderella stepping from her pumpkin carriage with sparkly cartoon music filling the air.

In all of my imaginings, I was filled with a sense that I would soon become *perfect.* My mother and father would adore me. I would be beyond reproach. I would never feel the need to sulk for anything.

But sometimes the prodigy in me became impatient. "If you don't hurry up and get me out of here, I'm disappearing for good," it warned. "And then you'll always be nothing."

Every night after dinner, my mother and I would sit at the Formica kitchen table. She would present new tests, taking her examples from stories of amazing children she had read in *Ripley's Believe It or Not*, or *Good Housekeeping, Reader's Digest*, and a dozen other magazines she kept in a pile in our bathroom. My mother got these magazines from people whose houses she cleaned. And since she cleaned many houses each week, we had a great assortment. She would look through them all, searching for stories about remarkable children.

The first night she brought out a story about a three-year-old boy who knew the capitals of all the states and even most of the European countries. A teacher was quoted as saying the little boy could also pronounce the names of the foreign cities correctly.

"What's the capital of Finland?" my mother asked me, looking at the magazine story.

All I knew was the capital of California, because Sacramento was the name of the street we lived on in Chinatown. "Nairobi!" I guessed, saying the most foreign word I could think of. She checked to see if that was possibly one way to pronounce "Helsinki" before showing me the answer.

The tests got harder—multiplying numbers in my head, finding the queen of hearts in a deck of cards, trying to stand on my head without using my hands, predicting the daily temperatures in Los Angeles, New York, and London. One night I had to look at a page from the Bible for three minutes and then report everything I could remember. "Now Jehoshaphat had riches and honor in abundance and . . . that's all I remember, Ma," I said.

And after seeing my mother's disappointed face once again, something inside of me began to die. I hated the tests, the raised hopes and failed expectations. Before going to bed that night, I looked in the mirror above the bathroom sink and when I saw only my face staring back—and that it would always be this ordinary face—I began to cry. Such a sad, ugly girl! I made high-pitched noises like a crazed animal, trying to scratch out the face in the mirror.

And then I saw what seemed to be the prodigy side of me—because I had never seen that face before. I looked at my reflection, blinking so I could see more clearly. The girl staring back at me was angry, powerful. This girl and I were the same. I had new thoughts, willful thoughts, or rather thoughts filled with lots of won'ts. I won't let her change me, I promised myself. I won't be what I'm not.

So now on nights when my mother presented her tests, I performed listlessly, my head propped on one arm. I pretended to be bored. And I was. I got so bored I started counting the bellows of the foghorns out on the bay while my mother drilled me in other areas. The sound was comforting and reminded me of the cow jumping over the moon. And the next day, I played a game with myself, seeing if my mother would give up on me before eight bellows. After a while I usually counted only one, maybe two bellows at most. At last she was beginning to give up hope.

Two or three months had gone by without any mention of my being a prodigy again. And then one day my mother was watching *The Ed Sullivan Show* on TV. The TV was old and the sound kept shorting out. Every time my mother got halfway up from the sofa to adjust the set, the sound would go back on and Ed would be talking. As soon as she sat down, Ed would go silent again. She got up—the TV broke into loud piano music. She sat down—silence. Up and down, back and forth, quiet and loud. It was like a stiff embraceless dance between her and the TV set. Finally she stood by the set with her hand on the sound dial.

She seemed entranced by the music, a little frenzied piano piece with this mesmerizing quality, sort of quick passages and then teasing lilting ones before it returned to the quick playful parts.

"*Ni kan,*" my mother said, calling me over with hurried hand gestures. "Look here."

I could see why my mother was fascinated by the music. It was being pounded out by a little Chinese girl, about nine years old, with a Peter Pan haircut. The girl had the sauciness of a Shirley Temple. She was proudly modest like a proper Chinese child. And she also did this fancy sweep of a curtsy, so that the fluffy skirt of her white dress cascaded slowly to the floor like the petals of a large carnation.

In spite of these warning signs, I wasn't worried. Our family had no piano and we couldn't afford to buy one, let alone reams of sheet music and piano lessons. So I could be generous in my comments when my mother bad-mouthed the little girl on TV.

"Play note right, but doesn't sound good! No singing sound," complained my mother.

"What are you picking on her for?" I said carelessly. "She's pretty good. Maybe she's not the best, but she's trying hard." I knew almost immediately I would be sorry I said that.

"Just like you," she said. "Not the best. Because you not trying." She gave a little huff as she let go of the sound dial and sat down on the sofa.

The little Chinese girl sat down also to play an encore of "Anitra's Dance" by Grieg. I remember the song, because later on I had to learn how to play it.

Three days after watching *The Ed Sullivan Show*, my mother told me what my schedule would be for piano lessons and piano practice. She had talked to Mr. Chong, who lived on the first floor of our apartment building. Mr. Chong was a retired piano teacher and my mother had traded housecleaning services for weekly lessons and a piano for me to practice on every day, two hours a day, from four until six.

When my mother told me this, I felt as though I had been sent to hell. I whined and then kicked my foot a little when I couldn't stand it anymore.

"Why don't you like me the way I am? I'm *not* a genius! I can't play the piano. And even if I could, I wouldn't go on TV if you paid me a million dollars!" I cried.

My mother slapped me. "Who ask you be genius?" she shouted. "Only ask you be your best. For you sake. You think I want you be genius? Hnnh! What for! Who ask you!"

"So ungrateful," I heard her mutter in Chinese. "If she had as much talent as she has temper, she would be famous now."

Mr. Chong, whom I secretly nicknamed Old Chong, was very strange, always tapping his fingers to the silent music of an invisible orchestra. He looked ancient in my eyes. He had lost most of the hair on top of his head and he wore thick glasses and had eyes that always looked tired and sleepy. But he must have been younger than I thought, since he lived with his mother and was not yet married.

I met Old Lady Chong once and that was enough. She had this peculiar smell like a baby that had done something in its pants. And her fingers felt like a dead person's, like an old peach I once found in the back of the refrigerator; the skin just slid off the meat when I picked it up.

I soon found out why Old Chong had retired from teaching piano. He was deaf. "Like Beethoven!" he shouted to me. "We're both listening only in our head!" And he would start to conduct his frantic silent sonatas.

Our lessons went like this. He would open the book and point to different things, explaining their purpose: "Key! Treble! Bass! No sharps or flats! So this is C major! Listen now and play after me!"

And then he would play the C scale a few times, a simple chord, and then, as if inspired by an old, unreachable itch, he gradually added more notes and running trills and a pounding bass until the music was really something quite grand.

I would play after him, the simple scale, the simple chord, and then I just played some nonsense that sounded like a cat running up and down on top of garbage cans. Old Chong smiled and applauded and then said, "Very good! But now you must learn to keep time!"

So that's how I discovered that Old Chong's eyes were too slow to keep up with the wrong notes I was playing. He went through the motions in half-time. To help me keep rhythm, he stood behind me, pushing down on my right shoulder for every beat. He balanced pennies on top of my wrists so I would keep them still as I slowly played scales and arpeggios. He had me curve my hand around an apple and keep that shape when playing chords. He marched stiffly to show me how to make each finger dance up and down, staccato like an obedient little soldier.

He taught me all these things, and that was how I also learned I could be lazy and get away with mistakes, lots of mistakes. If I hit the wrong notes because I hadn't practiced enough, I never corrected myself. I just kept playing in rhythm. And Old Chong kept conducting his own private reverie.

So maybe I never really gave myself a fair chance. I did pick up the basics pretty quickly, and I might have become a good pianist at that young age. But I was so determined not to try, not to be anybody different, that I learned to play only the most ear-splitting preludes, the most discordant hymns.

Over the next year, I practiced like this, dutifully in my own way. And then one day I heard my mother and her friend Lindo Jong both talking in a loud bragging tone of voice so others could hear. It was after church, and I was leaning against the brick wall wearing a dress with stiff white petticoats. Auntie Lindo's daughter, Waverly, who was about my age, was standing farther down the wall about five feet away. We had grown up together and shared all the closeness of two sisters squabbling over crayons and dolls. In other words, for the most part, we hated each other. I thought she was snotty. Waverly Jong had gained a certain amount of fame as "Chinatown's Littlest Chinese Chess Champion."

"She bring home too many trophy," lamented Auntie Lindo that Sunday. "All day she play chess. All day I have no time do nothing but dust off her winnings." She threw a scolding look at Waverly, who pretended not to see her.

"You lucky you don't have this problem," said Auntie Lindo with a sigh to my mother.

And my mother squared her shoulders and bragged: "Our problem worser than yours. If we ask Jing-mei wash dish, she hear nothing but music. It's like you can't stop this natural talent."

And right then, I was determined to put a stop to her foolish pride.

A few weeks later, Old Chong and my mother conspired to have me play in a talent show which would be held in the church hall. By then, my parents had saved up enough to buy me a secondhand piano, a black Wurlitzer spinet with a scarred bench. It was the showpiece of our living room.

For the talent show, I was to play a piece called "Pleading Child" from Schumann's *Scenes from Childhood.* It was a simple, moody piece that sounded more difficult than it was. I was supposed to memorize the whole thing, playing the repeat parts twice to make the piece sound longer. But I dawdled over it, playing a few bars and then cheating, looking up to see what notes followed. I never really listened to what I was playing. I daydreamed about being somewhere else, about being someone else.

The part I liked to practice best was the fancy curtsy: right foot out, touch the rose on the carpet with a pointed foot, sweep to the side, left leg bends, look up and smile.

My parents invited all the couples from the Joy Luck Club to witness my debut. Auntie Lindo and Uncle Tin were there. Waverly and her two older brothers had also come. The first two rows were filled with children both younger and older than I was. The littlest ones got to go first. They recited simple nursery rhymes, squawked out tunes on miniature violins, twirled Hula Hoops, pranced in pink ballet tutus, and when they bowed or curtsied, the audience would sigh in unison, "Awww," and then clap enthusiastically.

When my turn came, I was very confident. I remember my childish excitement. It was as if I knew, without a doubt, that the prodigy side of me really did exist. I had no fear whatsoever, no nervousness. I remember thinking to myself, This is it! This is it! I looked out over the audience, at my mother's blank face, my father's yawn, Auntie Lindo's stiff-lipped smile, Waverly's sulky expression. I had on a white dress layered with sheets of lace, and a pink bow in my Peter Pan haircut. As I sat down I envisioned people jumping to their feet and Ed Sullivan rushing up to introduce me to everyone on TV.

And I started to play. It was so beautiful. I was so caught up in how lovely I looked that at first I didn't worry how I would sound. So it was a surprise to me when I hit the first wrong note and I realized something didn't sound quite right. And then I hit another and another followed that. A chill started at the top of my head and began to trickle down. Yet I couldn't stop playing, as though my hands were bewitched. I kept thinking my fingers would adjust themselves back, like a train switching to the right track. I played this strange jumble through two repeats, the sour notes staying with me all the way to the end.

When I stood up, I discovered my legs were shaking. Maybe I had just been nervous and the audience, like Old Chong, had seen me go through the right motions and had not heard anything wrong at all. I swept my right foot out, went down on my knee, looked up and smiled. The room was quiet, except for Old Chong, who was beaming and shouting, "Bravo! Bravo! Well done!" But then I saw my mother's face, her stricken face. The audience clapped weakly, and as I walked back to my chair, with my whole face quivering as I tried not to cry, I heard a little boy whisper loudly to his mother, "That was awful," and the mother whispered back, "Well, she certainly tried."

And now I realized how many people were in the audience—the whole world it seemed. I was aware of eyes burning into my back. I felt the shame of my mother and father as they sat stiffly throughout the rest of the show.

We could have escaped during intermission. Pride and some strange sense of honor must have anchored my parents to their chairs. And so we watched it all: the eighteen-year-old boy with a fake mustache who did a magic show and juggled flaming hoops while riding a unicycle. The breasted girl with white makeup who sang from *Madama Butterfly* and got honorable mention. And the eleven-year-old boy who won first prize playing a tricky violin song that sounded like a busy bee.

After the show, the Hsus, the Jongs, and the St. Clairs from the Joy Luck Club came up to my mother and father.

"Lots of talented kids," Auntie Lindo said vaguely, smiling broadly.

"That was somethin' else," said my father, and I wondered if he was referring to me in a humorous way, or whether he even remembered what I had done.

Waverly looked at me and shrugged her shoulders. "You aren't a genius like me," she said matter-of-factly. And if I hadn't felt so bad, I would have pulled her braids and punched her stomach.

But my mother's expression was what devastated me: a quiet, blank look that said she had lost everything. I felt the same way, and it seemed as if everybody were now coming up, like gawkers at the scene of an accident, to see what parts were actually missing. When we got on the bus to go home, my father was humming the busy-bee tune and my mother was silent. I kept thinking she wanted to wait until we got home before shouting at me. But when my father unlocked the door to our apartment, my mother walked in and then went to the back, into the bedroom. No accusations. No blame. And in a way, I felt disappointed. I had been waiting for her to start shouting, so I could shout back and cry and blame her for all my misery.

I assumed my talent-show fiasco meant I never had to play the piano again. But two days later, after school, my mother came out of the kitchen and saw me watching TV.

"Four clock," she reminded me as if it were any other day. I was stunned, as though she were asking me to go through the talent-show torture again. I wedged myself more tightly in front of the TV.

"Turn off TV," she called from the kitchen five minutes later.

I didn't budge. And then I decided. I didn't have to do what my mother said anymore. I wasn't her slave. This wasn't China. I had listened to her before and look what happened. She was the stupid one.

She came out from the kitchen and stood in the arched entryway of the living room. "Four clock," she said once again, louder.

"I'm not going to play anymore," I said nonchalantly. "Why should I? I'm not a genius."

She walked over and stood in front of the TV. I saw her chest was heaving up and down in an angry way.

"No!" I said, and I now felt stronger, as if my true self had finally emerged. So this was what had been inside me all along.

"No! I won't!" I screamed.

She yanked me by the arm, pulled me off the floor, snapped off the TV. She was frighteningly strong, half pulling, half carrying me toward the piano as I kicked the throw rugs under my feet. She lifted me up and onto the hard bench. I was sobbing by now, looking at her bitterly.

Her chest was heaving even more and her mouth was open, smiling crazily as if she were pleased I was crying.

"You want me to be someone that I'm not!" I sobbed. "I'll never be the kind of daughter you want me to be!"

"Only two kinds of daughters," she shouted in Chinese. "Those who are obedient and those who follow their own mind! Only one kind of daughter can live in this house. Obedient daughter!"

"Then I wish I wasn't your daughter. I wish you weren't my mother," I shouted. As I said these things I got scared. It felt like worms and toads and slimy things crawling out of my chest, but it also felt good, as if this awful side of me had surfaced, at last.

"Too late change this," said my mother shrilly.

And I could sense her anger rising to its breaking point. I wanted to see it spill over. And that's when I remembered the babies she had lost in China, the ones we never talked about. "Then I wish I'd never been born!" I shouted. "I wish I were dead! Like them."

It was as if I had said the magic words. Alakazam!—and her face went blank, her mouth closed, her arms went slack, and she backed out of the room, stunned, as if she were blowing away like a small brown leaf, thin, brittle, lifeless.

It was not the only disappointment my mother felt in me. In the years that followed, I failed her so many times, each time asserting my own will, my right to fall short of expectations. I didn't get straight As. I didn't become class president. I didn't get into Stanford. I dropped out of college.

For unlike my mother, I did not believe I could be anything I wanted to be. I could only be me.

And for all those years, we never talked about the disaster at the recital or my terrible accusations afterward at the piano bench. All that remained unchecked, like a betrayal that was now unspeakable. So I never found a way to ask her why she had hoped for something so large that failure was inevitable.

And even worse, I never asked her what frightened me the most: Why had she given up hope? For after our struggle at the piano, she never mentioned my playing again. The lessons stopped. The lid to the piano was closed, shutting out the dust, my misery, and her dreams.

So she surprised me. A few years ago, she offered to give me the piano, for my thirtieth birthday. I had not played in all those years. I saw the offer as a sign of forgiveness, a tremendous burden removed.

"Are you sure?" I asked shyly. "I mean, won't you and Dad miss it?"

"No, this your piano," she said firmly. "Always your piano. You only one can play."

"Well, I probably can't play anymore," I said. "It's been years."

"You pick up fast," said my mother, as if she knew this was certain. "You have natural talent. You could been genius if you want to."

"No I couldn't."

"You just not trying," said my mother. And she was neither angry nor sad. She said it as if to announce a fact that could never be disproved. "Take it," she said.

But I didn't at first. It was enough that she had offered it to me. And after that, every time I saw it in my parents' living room, standing in front of the bay windows, it made me feel proud, as if it were a shiny trophy I had won back.

Last week I sent a tuner over to my parents' apartment and had the piano reconditioned, for purely sentimental reasons. My mother had died a few months before and I had been getting things in order for my father, a little bit at a time. I put the jewelry in special silk pouches. The sweaters she had knitted in yellow, pink, bright orange—all the colors I hated—I put those in moth-proof boxes. I found some old Chinese silk dresses, the kind with little slits up the sides. I rubbed the old silk against my skin, then wrapped them in tissue and decided to take them home with me.

After I had the piano tuned, I opened the lid and touched the keys. It sounded even richer than I remembered. Really, it was a very good piano. Inside the bench were the same exercise notes with handwritten scales, the same secondhand music books with their covers held together with yellow tape.

I opened up the Schumann book to the dark little piece I had played at the recital. It was on the left-hand side of the page, "Pleading Child." It looked more difficult than I remembered. I played a few bars, surprised at how easily the notes came back to me.

And for the first time, or so it seemed, I noticed the piece on the right-hand side. It was called "Perfectly Contented." I tried to play this one as well. It had a lighter melody but the same flowing rhythm and turned out to be quite easy. "Pleading Child" was shorter but slower; "Perfectly Contented" was longer, but faster. And after I played them both a few times, I realized they were two halves of the same song.

—*1989*

Sandra Cisneros (b. 1954) received a MacArthur Foundation Fellowship in 1995. A native of Chicago and longtime resident of San Antonio, she is a graduate of the University of Iowa Writers' Workshop. My Wicked, Wicked Ways *(1987), a collection of poetry which contains several poems about Cisnero's experiences as the only daughter among her parents' seven children, has gone through several editions and was followed by a second collection,* Loose Woman *(1994). The compressed style of short pieces life "Barbie-Q" owes much to her background as a poet. Her two collections of short fiction are* The House on Mango Street *(1984) and* Woman Hollering Creek *(1991), which is named after a real creek in the Texas Hill Country. Two nonfiction books on which Cisneros collaborated with other writers,* Days and Nights of Love and War *and* The Future is Mestizo: Life Where Cultures Meet, *were published in 2000.*

Sandra Cisneros

Barbie-Q

for Licha

Yours is the one with mean eyes and a ponytail. Striped swimsuit, stilettos, sunglasses, and gold hoop earrings. Mine is the one with bubble hair. Red swimsuit, stilettos, pearl earrings, and a wire stand. But that's all we can afford, besides one extra outfit apiece. Yours, "Red Flair," sophisticated A-line coatdress with a Jackie Kennedy pillbox hat, white gloves, handbag, and heels included. Mine, "Solo in the Spotlight," evening elegance in black glitter strapless gown with a puffy skirt at the bottom like a mermaid tail, formal-length gloves, pink chiffon scarf, and mike included. From so much dressing and undressing, the black glitter wears off where her titties stick out. This and a dress invented from an old sock when we cut holes here and here and here, the cuff rolled over for the glamorous, fancy-free, off-the-shoulder look.

Every time the same story. Your Barbie is roommates with my Barbie, and my Barbie's boyfriend comes over and your Barbie steals him, okay? Kiss kiss kiss. Then the two Barbies fight. You dumbbell! He's mine. Oh no he's not, you stinky! Only Ken's invisible, right? Because we don't have money for a stupid-looking boy doll when we'd both rather ask for a new Barbie outfit next Christmas. We have to make do with your mean-eyed Barbie and my bubblehead Barbie and our one outfit apiece not including the sock dress.

Until next Sunday when we are walking through the flea market on Maxwell Street and *there!* Lying on the street next to some tool bits, and platform shoes with the heels all squashed, and a fluorescent green wicker wastebasket, and aluminum foil, and hubcaps, and a pink shag rug, and windshield wiper blades, and dusty mason jars, and a coffee can full of rusty nails. *There!* Where? Two Mattel boxes. One with the "Career Gal" ensemble, snappy black-and-white business suit, three-quarter-length sleeve jacket with kick-pleat skirt, red sleeveless shell, gloves, pumps, and matching hat included. The other, "Sweet Dreams," dreamy pink-and-white plaid nightgown and matching robe, lace-trimmed slippers, hairbrush and hand mirror included. How much? Please, please, please, please, please, please, please, until they say okay.

On the outside you and me skipping and humming but inside we are doing loopity-loops and pirouetting. Until at the next vendor's stand, next to boxed pies, and bright orange toilet brushes, and rubber gloves, and wrench sets, and bouquets of feather flowers, and glass towel racks, and steel wool, and Alvin and the Chipmunks records, *there!* And *there!* And *there!* And *there!* and *there!* and *there!* and *there!* Bendable legs Barbie with her new page-boy hairdo. Midge, Barbie's best friend. Ken, Barbie's boyfriend. Skipper, Barbie's little sister. Tutti and Todd, Barbie and Skipper's tiny twin sister and brother. Skipper's friends, Scooter and Ricky. Alan, Ken's buddy. And Francie, Barbie's MOD'ern cousin.

Everybody today selling toys, all of them damaged with water and smelling of smoke. Because a big toy warehouse on Halsted Street burned down yesterday—see there?—the smoke still rising and drifting across the Dan Ryan expressway. And now there is a big fire sale at Maxwell Street, today only.

So what if we didn't get our new Bendable Legs Barbie and Midge and Ken and Skipper and Tutti and Todd and Scooter and Ricky and Alan and Francie in nice clean boxes and had to buy them on Maxwell

Street, all water-soaked and sooty. So what if our Barbies smell like smoke when you hold them up to your nose even after you wash and wash and wash them. And if the prettiest doll, Barbie's MOD'ern cousin Francie with real eyelashes, eyelash brush included, has a left foot that's melted a little—so? If you dress her in her new "Prom Pinks" outfit, satin splendor with matching coat, gold belt, clutch, and hair bow included, so long as you don't lift her dress, right?—who's to know.

—1991

Louise Erdrich (b. 1954) *was born in Little Falls, Minnesota, and grew up in North Dakota. Her father was a teacher with the Bureau of Indian Affairs, and both he and her mother encouraged her to write stories from an early age. Erdrich holds degrees from Dartmouth College and Johns Hopkins University, where she studied creative writing. Her novel* Love Medicine, *from which "The Red Convertible" is taken, is a sequence of fourteen connected stories told by seven narrators.* Love Medicine *won the National Book Critics Circle Award for 1984. Much of Erdrich's fiction draws on her childhood on the Great Plains and her mixed cultural heritage (her ancestry is German American and Chippewa). In addition to* Love Medicine *she has published two other novels,* The Beet Queen *(1986) and* Tracks *(1988), several prize-winning short stories, and two books of poetry. Erdrich and her late husband Michael Dorris, another Native American writer, appeared in two documentary films shown on PBS and collaborated on a novel,* The Crown of Columbus *(1991). Along with James Welch and Leslie Marmon Silko, Erdrich has helped to redefine Native American fiction. According to the* Columbia Literary History of the United States, *"These authors have had to resist the formulaic approaches favored by the publishing industry, which has its own opinions about what constitutes the 'proper' form and content of minority fiction."* The Birchbark House, *a novel for young readers, and* The Antelope Wife, *a novel employing the techniques of magic realism, both appeared in 1999.*

Louise Erdrich

The Red Convertible

Lyman Lamartine

I was the first one to drive a convertible on my reservation. And of course it was red, a red Olds. I owned that car along with my brother Henry Junior. We owned it together until his boots filled with water on a windy night and he bought out my share. Now Henry owns the whole car, and his younger brother Lyman (that's myself), Lyman walks everywhere he goes.

How did I earn enough money to buy my share in the first place? My one talent was I could always make money. I had a touch for it, unusual in a Chippewa. From the first I was different that way, and everyone recognized it. I was the only kid they let in the American Legion Hall to shine shoes, for example, and one Christmas I sold spiritual bouquets for the mission door to door. The nuns let me keep a percentage. Once I started, it seemed the more money I made the easier the money came. Everyone encouraged it. When I was fifteen I got a job washing dishes at the Joliet Cafe, and that was where my first big break happened.

It wasn't long before I was promoted to bussing tables, and then the short-order cook quit and I was hired to take her place. No sooner than you know it I was managing the Joliet. The rest is history. I went on managing. I soon become part owner, and of course there was no stopping me then. It wasn't long before the whole thing was mine.

After I'd owned the Joliet for one year, it blew over in the worst tornado ever seen around here. The whole operation was smashed to bits. A total loss. The fryalator was up in a tree, the grill torn in half like it was paper. I was only sixteen. I had it all in my mother's name, and I lost it quick, but before I lost it I had every one of my relatives, and their relatives, to dinner, and I also bought that red Olds I mentioned, along with Henry.

The first time we saw it! I'll tell you when we first saw it. We had gotten a ride up to Winnipeg, and both of us had money. Don't ask me why, because we never mentioned a car or anything, we just had all our money. Mine was cash, a big bankroll from the Joliet's insurance. Henry had two checks—a week's extra pay for being laid off, and his regular check from the Jewel Bearing Plant.

We were walking down Portage anyway, seeing the sights, when we saw it. There it was, parked, large as life. Really as *if* it was alive. I thought of the word *repose*, because the car wasn't simply stopped, parked, or whatever. That car reposed, calm and gleaming, a FOR SALE sign in its left front window. Then, before we had thought it over at all, the car belonged to us and our pockets were empty. We had just enough money for gas back home.

We went places in that car, me and Henry. We took off driving all one whole summer. We started off toward the Little Knife River and Mandaree in Fort Berthold and then we found ourselves down in Wakpala somehow, and then suddenly we were over in Montana on the Rocky Boys, and yet the summer was not even half over. Some people hang on to details when they travel, but we didn't let them bother us and just lived our everyday lives here to there.

I do remember this one place with willows. I remember I laid under those trees and it was comfortable. So comfortable. The branches bent down all around me like a tent or a stable. And quiet, it was quiet, even though there was a powwow close enough so I could see it going on. The air was not too still, not too windy either. When the dust rises up and hangs in the air around the dancers like that, I feel good. Henry was asleep with his arms thrown wide. Later on, he woke up and we started driving again. We were somewhere in Montana, or maybe on the Blood Reserve— it could have been anywhere. Anyway it was where we met the girl.

All her hair was in buns around her ears, that's the first thing I noticed about her. She was posed alongside the road with her arm out, so we stopped. That girl was short, so short her lumber shirt looked comical on her, like a nightgown. She had jeans on and fancy moccasins and she carried a little suitcase.

"Hop on in," says Henry. So she climbs in between us.

"We'll take you home," I says. "Where do you live?"

"Chicken," she says.

"Where the hell's that?" I ask her.

"Alaska."

"Okay," says Henry, and we drive.

We got up there and never wanted to leave. The sun doesn't truly set there in summer, and the night is more a soft dusk. You might doze off, sometimes, but before you know it you're up again, like an animal in nature. You never feel like you have to sleep hard or put away the world. And things would grow up there. One day just dirt or moss, the next day flowers and long grass. The girl's name was Susy. Her family really took to us. They fed us and put us up. We had our own tent to live in by their house, and the kids would be in and out of there all day and night. They couldn't get over me and Henry being brothers, we looked so different. We told them we knew we had the same mother, anyway.

One night Susy came in to visit us. We sat around in the tent talking of this thing and that. The season was changing. It was getting darker by that time, and the cold was even getting just a little mean. I told her it was time for us to go. She stood up on a chair.

"You never seen my hair," Susy said.

That was true. She was standing on a chair, but still, when she unclipped her buns the hair reached all the way to the ground. Our eyes opened. You couldn't tell how much hair she had when it was rolled up so neatly. Then my brother Henry did something funny. He went up to the chair and said, "Jump on my shoulders." So she did that, and her hair reached down past his waist, and he started twirling, this way and that, so her hair was flung out from side to side.

"I always wondered what it was like to have long pretty hair," Henry says. Well we laughed. It was a funny sight, the way he did it. The next morning we got up and took leave of those people.

On to greener pastures, as they say. It was down through Spokane and across Idaho then Montana and very soon we were racing the weather right along under the Canadian border through Columbus, Des Lacs, and then we were in Bottineau County and soon home. We'd made most of the trip, that summer, without putting up the car hood at all. We got home just in time, it turned out, for the army to remember Henry had signed up to join it.

I don't wonder that the army was so glad to get my brother that they turned him into a Marine. He was built like a brick outhouse anyway. We liked to tease him that they really wanted him for his Indian nose. He had a nose big and sharp as a hatchet, like the nose on Red Tomahawk, the Indian who killed Sitting Bull, whose profile is on signs all along the North Dakota highways. Henry went off to training camp, came home once during Christmas, then the next thing you know we got an overseas letter from him. It was 1970, and he said he was stationed up in the northern hill country. Whereabouts I did not know. He wasn't such a hot letter writer, and only got off two before the enemy caught him. I could never keep it straight, which direction those good Vietnam soldiers were from.

I wrote him back several times, even though I didn't know if those letters would get through. I kept him informed all about the car. Most of the time I had it up on blocks in the yard or half taken apart, because that long trip did a hard job on it under the hood.

I always had good luck with numbers, and never worried about the draft myself. I never even had to think about what my number was. But Henry was never lucky in the same way as me. It was at least three years before Henry came home. By then I guess the whole war was solved in the government's mind, but for him it would keep on going. In those years I'd put his car into almost perfect shape. I always thought of it as his car while he was gone, even though when he left he said, "Now it's yours," and threw me his key.

"Thanks for the extra key," I'd said. "I'll put it up in your drawer just in case I need it." He laughed.

When he came home, though, Henry was very different, and I'll say this: the change was no good. You could hardly expect him to change for the better, I know. But he was quiet, so quiet, and never comfortable sitting still anywhere but always up and moving around. I thought back to times we'd sat still for whole afternoons, never moving a muscle, just shifting our weight along the ground, talking to whoever sat with us, watching things. He'd always had a joke, then, too, and now you couldn't get him to laugh, or when he did it was more the sound of a man choking, a sound that stopped up the throats of other people around him. They got to leaving him alone most of the time, and I didn't blame them. It was a fact: Henry was jumpy and mean.

I'd bought a color TV set for my mom and the rest of us while Henry was away. Money still came very easy. I was sorry I'd ever bought it though, because of Henry. I was also sorry I'd bought color, because with black-and-white the pictures seem older and farther away. But what are you going to do? He sat in front of it, watching it, and that was the only time he was completely still. But it was the kind of stillness that you see in a rabbit when it freezes and before it will bolt. He was not easy. He sat in his chair gripping the armrests with all his might, as if the chair itself was moving at a high speed and if he let go at all he would rocket forward and maybe crash right through the set.

Once I was in the room watching TV with Henry and I heard his teeth click at something. I looked over, and he'd bitten through his lip. Blood was going down his chin. I tell you right then I wanted to smash that tube to pieces. I went over to it but Henry must have known what I was up to. He rushed from his chair and shoved me out of the way, against the wall. I told myself he didn't know what he was doing.

My mom came in, turned the set off real quiet, and told us she had made something for supper. So we went and sat down. There was still blood going down Henry's chin, but he didn't notice it and no one said anything, even though every time he took a bite of his bread his blood fell onto it until he was eating his own blood mixed in with the food.

While Henry was not around we talked about what was going to happen to him. There were no Indian doctors on the reservation, and my mom was afraid of trusting Old Man Pillager because he courted her long ago and was jealous of her husbands. He might take revenge through her son. We were afraid that if we brought Henry to a regular hospital they would keep him.

"They don't fix them in those places," Mom said; "they just give them drugs."

"We wouldn't get him there in the first place," I agreed, "so let's just forget about it."

Then I thought about the car.

Henry had not even looked at the car since he'd gotten home, though like I said it was in tip-top condition and ready to drive. I thought the car might bring the old Henry back somehow. So I bided my time and waited for my chance to interest him in the vehicle.

One night Henry was off somewhere. I took myself a hammer. I went out to that car and I did a number on its underside. Whacked it up. Bent the tail pipe double. Ripped the muffler loose. By the time I was done with the car it looked worse than any typical Indian car that has been driven all its life on reservation roads, which they always say are like government promises—full of holes. It just about hurt me, I'll tell you that! I threw dirt in the carburetor and I ripped all the electric tape off the seats. I made it look just as beat up as I could. Then I sat back and waited for Henry to find it.

Still, it took him over a month. That was all right, because it was just getting warm enough, not melting, but warm enough to work outside.

"Lyman," he says, walking in one day, "that red car looks like shit."

"Well it's old," I says. "You got to expect that."

"No way!" says Henry. "That car's a classic! But you went and ran the piss right out of it, Lyman, and you know it don't deserve that. I kept that car in A-one shape. You don't remember. You're too young. But when I left, that car was running like a watch. Now I don't even know if I can get it to start again, let alone get it anywhere near its old condition."

"Well you try," I said, like I was getting mad, "but I say it's a piece of junk."

Then I walked out before he could realize I knew he'd strung together more than six words at once.

After that I thought he'd freeze himself to death working on that car. He was out there all day, and at night he rigged up a little lamp, ran a cord out the window, and had himself some light to see by while he worked. He was better than he had been before, but that's still not saying much. It was easier for him to do the things the rest of us did. He ate more slowly and didn't jump up and down during the meal to get this or that or look out the window. I put my hand in the back of the TV set, I admit, and fiddled around with it good, so that it was almost impossible now to get a clear picture. He didn't look at it very often anyway. He was always out with that car or going off to get parts for it. By the time it was really melting outside, he had it fixed.

I had been feeling down in the dumps about Henry around this time. We had always been together before. Henry and Lyman. But he was such a loner now that I didn't know how to take it. So I jumped at the chance one day when Henry seemed friendly. It's not that he smiled or anything. He just said, "Let's take that old shitbox for a spin." Just the way he said it made me think he could be coming around.

We went out to the car. It was spring. The sun was shining very bright. My only sister, Bonita, who was just eleven years old, came out and made us stand together for a picture. Henry leaned his elbow on the red car's windshield, and he took his other arm and put it over my shoulder, very carefully, as though it was heavy for him to lift and he didn't want to bring the weight down all at once.

"Smile," Bonita said, and he did.

That picture. I never look at it anymore. A few months ago, I don't know why, I got his picture out and tacked it on the wall. I felt good about Henry at the time, close to him. I felt good having his picture on the wall, until one night when I was looking at television. I was a little drunk and stoned. I looked up at the wall and Henry was staring at me. I don't know what it was, but his smile had changed, or maybe it was gone. All I know is I couldn't stay in the same room with that picture. I was shaking. I got up, closed the door, and went into the kitchen. A little later my friend Ray came over and we both went back into that room. We put the picture in a brown bag, folded the bag over and over tightly, then put it way back in a closet.

I still see that picture now, as if it tugs at me, whenever I pass that closet door. The picture is very clear in my mind. It was so sunny that day Henry had to squint against the glare. Or maybe the camera Bonita held flashed like a mirror, blinding him, before she snapped the picture. My face is right out in the sun, big and round. But he might have drawn back, because the shadows on his face are deep as holes. There are two shadows curved like little hooks around the ends of his smile, as if to frame it and try to keep it there—that one, first smile that looked like it might have hurt his face. He has his field jacket on and the worn-in clothes he'd come back in and kept wearing ever since. After Bonita took the picture, she went into the house and we got into the car. There was a full cooler in the trunk. We started off, east, toward Pembina and the Red River because Henry said he wanted to see the high water.

The trip over there was beautiful. When everything starts changing, drying up, clearing off, you feel like your whole life is starting. Henry felt it, too. The top was down and the car hummed like a top. He'd really put it back in shape, even the tape on the seats was very carefully put down and glued back in layers. It's not that he smiled again or even joked, but his face looked to me as if it was clear, more peaceful. It looked as though he wasn't thinking of anything in particular except the bare fields and windbreaks and houses we were passing.

The river was high and full of winter trash when we got there. The sun was still out, but it was colder by the river. There were still little clumps of dirty snow here and there on the banks. The water hadn't gone over the banks yet, but it would, you could tell. It was just at its limit, hard swollen, glossy like an old gray scar. We made ourselves a fire, and we sat down and watched the current go. As I watched it I felt something squeezing inside me and tightening and trying to let go all at the same time. I knew I was not just feeling it myself; I knew I was feeling what Henry was going through at that moment. Except that I couldn't stand it, the closing and opening. I jumped to my feet. I took

Henry by the shoulders and I started shaking him. "Wake up," I says, "wake up, wake up, wake up!" I didn't know what had come over me. I sat down beside him again.

His face was totally white and hard. Then it broke, like stones break all of a sudden when water boils up inside them.

"I know it," he says. "I know it. I can't help it. It's no use."

We start talking. He said he knew what I'd done with the car. It was obvious it had been whacked out of shape and not just neglected. He said he wanted to give the car to me for good now, it was no use. He said he'd fixed it just to give it back and I should take it.

"No way," I says, "I don't want it."

"That's okay," he says, "you take it."

"I don't want it, though," I says back to him, and then to emphasize, just to emphasize, you understand, I touch his shoulder. He slaps my hand off.

"Take that car," he says.

"No," I say, "make me," I say, and then he grabs my jacket and rips the arm loose. That jacket is a class act, suede with tags and zippers. I push Henry backwards, off the log. He jumps up and bowls me over. We go down in a clinch and come up swinging hard, for all we're worth, with our fists. He socks my jaw so hard I feel like it swings loose. Then I'm at his ribcage and land a good one under his chin so his head snaps back. He's dazzled. He looks at me and I look at him and then his eyes are full of tears and blood and at first I think he's crying. But no, he's laughing. "Ha! Ha!" he says. "Ha! Ha! Take good care of it."

"Okay," I says, "okay, no problem. Ha! Ha!"

I can't help it, and I start laughing, too. My face feels fat and strange, and after a while I get a beer from the cooler in the trunk, and when I hand it to Henry he takes his shirt and wipes my germs off. "Hoof-and-mouth disease," he says. For some reason this cracks me up, and so we're really laughing for a while, and then we drink all the rest of the beers one by one and throw them in the river and see how far, how fast, the current takes them before they fill up and sink.

"You want to go on back?" I ask after a while. "Maybe we could snag a couple nice Kashpaw girls."

He says nothing. But I can tell his mood is turning again.

"They're all crazy, the girls up here, every damn one of them."

"You're crazy too," I say, to jolly him up. "Crazy Lamartine boys!" He looks as though he will take this wrong at first. His face twists, then clears, and he jumps up on his feet. "That's right!" he says. "Crazier 'n hell. Crazy Indians!"

I think it's the old Henry again. He throws off his jacket and starts swinging his legs out from the knees like a fancy dancer. He's down doing something between a grouse dance and a bunny hop, no kind of dance I ever saw before, but neither has anyone else on all this green growing earth. He's wild. He wants to pitch whoopee! He's up and at me and all over. All this time I'm laughing so hard, so hard my belly is getting tied up in a knot.

"Got to cool me off!" he shouts all of a sudden. Then he runs over to the river and jumps in.

There's boards and other things in the current. It's so high. No sound comes from the river after the splash he makes, so I run right over. I look around. It's getting dark. I see he's halfway across the water already, and I know he didn't swim there but the current took him. It's far. I hear his voice, though, very clearly across it.

"My boots are filling," he says.

He says this in a normal voice, like he just noticed and he doesn't know what to think of it. Then he's gone. A branch comes by. Another branch. And I go in.

By the time I get out of the river, off the snag I pulled myself onto, the sun is down. I walk back to the car, turn on the high beams, and drive it up the bank. I put it in first gear and then I take my foot off the clutch. I get out, close the door, and watch it plow softly into the water. The headlights reach in as they go down, searching, still lighted even after the water swirls over the back end. I wait. The wires short out. It is all finally dark. And then there is only the water, the sound of it going and running and going and running and running.

—1984

Lorrie Moore (b. 1954) was born in Glens Falls in upstate New York, the child of parents who, according to the author, "both have a little of the writing gene." After graduating from St. Lawrence College, Moore spent two years in New York City as a paralegal. She did graduate work in creative writing at Cornell University, submitting a thesis that became her first collection of short stories, Self-Help *(1985). After her novel* Anagrams *was published the following year, she took a position in the English department at the University of Wisconsin, where she currently teaches. Many of the stories in* Self-Help, *from which "How to Talk to Your Mother" is taken, use what has been called "recipe fiction," or what Moore describes as "second person, mock-imperative narratives." Moore has also published a book of juvenile fiction,* The Forgotten Helper *(1987), edited* I Know Some Things: Stories about Childhood by Contemporary Writers *(1992), and written a short coming-of-age novel,* Who Will Run the Frog Hospital? *(1994), which recalls her own adolescence in Glens Falls in the early 1970s. Her most recent collection of short fiction,* Birds of America *(1998), spent several weeks on the bestseller lists.*

Lorrie Moore
How to Talk to Your Mother (Notes)

1982. Without her, for years now, murmur at the defrosting refrigerator, "What?" "Huh?" "Shush now," as it creaks, aches, groans, until the final ice block drops from the ceiling of the freezer like something vanquished.

Dream, and in your dreams babies with the personalities of dachshunds, fat as Macy balloons, float by the treetops.

The first permanent polyurethane heart is surgically implanted.

Someone upstairs is playing "You'll Never Walk Alone" on the recorder. Now it's "Oklahoma!" They must have a Rodgers and Hammerstein book.

1981. On public transportation, mothers with soft, soapy, corduroyed seraphs glance at you, their faces dominoes of compassion. Their seraphs are small and quiet or else restlessly counting bus-seat colors: "Blue-blue-blue, red-red-red, lullow-lullow-lullow." The mothers see you eyeing their children. They smile sympathetically. They believe you envy them. They believe you are childless. They believe they know why. Look quickly away, out the smudge of the window.

1980. The hum, rush, clack of things in the kitchen. These are some of the sounds that organize your life. The clink of the silverware inside the drawer, piled like bones in a mass grave. Your similes grow grim, grow tired.

Reagan is elected President, though you distributed donuts and brochures for Carter.

Date an Italian. He rubs your stomach and says, "These are marks of stretch, no? Marks of stretch?" and in your dizzy mind you think: Marks of Harpo, Ideas of Marx, Ides of March, Beware. He plants kisses on the sloping ramp of your neck, and you fall asleep against him, your underpants peeled and rolled around one thigh like a bride's garter.

1979. Once in a while take evening trips past the old unsold house you grew up in, that haunted rural crossroads two hours from where you now live. It is like Halloween: the raked, moonlit lawn, the mammoth, tumid trees, arms and fingers raised into the starless wipe of sky like burns, cracks, map rivers. Their black shadows rock against the side of the east porch. There are dream shadows, other lives here. Turn the corner slowly but continue to stare from the car window. This house is embedded in you deep, something still here you know, you think you know, a voice at the top of those stairs, perhaps, a figure on the porch, an odd apron caught high in the twigs, in the too-warm-for-a-fall-night breeze, something not right, that turret window you can still see from here, from outside, but which can't be reached from within. (The ghostly brag of your childhood: "We have a mystery room. The window shows from the front, but you can't go in, there's no door. A doctor lived there years ago and gave secret operations, and now it's blocked off.") The window sits like a dead eye in the turret.

You see a ghost, something like a spinning statue by a shrub.

1978. Bury her in the cold south sideyard of that Halloweenish house. Your brother and his kids are there. Hug. The minister in a tweed sportscoat, the neighborless fields, the crossroads, are all like some stark Kansas. There is praying, then someone shoveling. People walk toward the cars and hug again. Get inside your car with your niece. Wait. Look up through the windshield. In the November sky a wedge of wrens moves south, the lines of their formation, the very sides and vertices mysteriously choreographed, shifting, flowing, crossing like a skater's legs. "They'll descend instinctively upon a tree somewhere," you say, "but not for miles yet." You marvel, watch, until, amoebaslow, they are dark, faraway stitches in the horizon. You do not start the car. The quiet niece next to you finally speaks: "Aunt Ginnie, are we going to the restaurant with the others?" Look at her. Recognize her: nine in a pile parka. Smile and start the car.

1977. She ages, rocks in your rocker, noiseless as wind. The front strands of her white hair dangle yellow at her eyes from too many cigarettes. She smokes even now, her voice husky with phlegm. Sometimes at dinner in your tiny kitchen she will simply stare, rheumy-eyed, at you, then burst into a fit of coughing that racks her small old man's body like a storm.

Stop eating your baked potato. Ask if she is all right.

She will croak: "Do you remember, Ginnie, your father used to say that one day, with these cigarettes, I was going to have to 'face the mucus'?" At this she chuckles, chokes, gasps again.

Make her stand up.

Lean her against you.

Slap her lightly on the curved mound of her back.

Ask her for chrissakes to stop smoking.

She will smile and say: "For chrissakes? Is that any way to talk to your mother?"

At night go in and check on her. She lies there awake, her lips apart, open and drying. Bring her some juice. She murmurs, "Thank you, honey." Her mouth smells, swells like a grave.

1976. The Bicentennial. In the laundromat, you wait for the time on your coins to run out. Through the porthole of the dryer, you watch your bedeviled towels and sheets leap and fall. The radio station piped in from the ceiling plays slow, sad Motown; it encircles you with the desperate hopefulness of a boy at a dance, and it makes you cry. When you get back to your apartment, dump everything on your bed. Your mother is knitting crookedly: red, white, and blue. Kiss her hello. Say: "Sure was warm in that place." She will seem not to hear you.

1975. Attend poetry readings alone at the local library. Find you don't really listen well. Stare at your crossed thighs. Think about your mother. Sometimes you confuse her with the first man you ever loved, who ever loved you, who buried his head in the pills of your sweater and said magnificent things like "Oh god, oh god," who loved you unconditionally, terrifically, like a mother.

The poet loses his nerve for a second, a red flush through his neck and ears, but he regains his composure. When he is finished, people clap. There is wine and cheese.

Leave alone, walk home alone. The downtown streets are corridors of light holding you, holding you, past the church, past the community center. March, like Stella Dallas, spine straight, through the melodrama of street lamps, phone posts, toward the green house past Borealis Avenue, toward the rear apartment with the tilt and the squash on the stove.

Your horoscope says: Be kind, be brief.

You are pregnant again. Decide what you must do.

1974. She will have bouts with a mad sort of senility. She calls you at work. "There's no food here! Help me! I'm starving!" although you just bought forty dollars' worth of groceries yesterday. "Mom, there is too food there!"

When you get home the refrigerator is mostly empty. "Mom, where did you put all the milk and cheese and stuff?" Your mother stares at you from where she is sitting in front of the TV set. She has tears leaking out of her eyes. "There's no food here, Ginnie."

There is a rustling, scratching noise in the dishwasher. You open it up, and the eyes of a small rodent glint back at you. It scrambles out, off to the baseboards behind the refrigerator. Your mother, apparently, has put all the groceries inside the dishwasher. The milk is spilled, a white pool against blue, and things like cheese and bologna and apples have been nibbled at.

1973. At a party when a woman tells you where she bought some wonderful pair of shoes, say that you believe shopping for clothes is like masturbation—everyone does it, but it isn't very interesting and therefore should be done alone, in an embarrassed fashion, and never be the topic of party conversation. The woman will tighten her lips and eyebrows and say, "Oh, I suppose you have something more fascinating to talk about." Grow clumsy and uneasy. Say, "No," and head for the ginger ale. Tell the person next to you that your insides feel sort of sinking

and vinyl like a Claes Oldenburg toilet. They will say, "Oh?" and point
out that the print on your dress is one of paisleys impregnating paisleys.
Pour yourself more ginger ale.

1972. Nixon wins by a landslide.

Sometimes your mother calls you by her sister's name. Say, "No,
Mom, it's me. Virginia." Learn to repeat things. Learn that you have a
way of knowing each other which somehow slips out and beyond the
ways you have of not knowing each other at all.

Make apple crisp for the first time.

1971. Go for long walks to get away from her. Walk through wooded
areas; there is a life there you have forgotten. The smells and sounds
seem sudden, unchanged, exact, the papery crunch of the leaves, the
mouldering sachet of the mud. The trees are crooked as backs, the fence
posts splintered, trusting and precarious in their solid grasp of arms, the
asters spindly, dry, white, havishammed (Havishammed!) by frost. Find
a beautiful reddish stone and bring it home for your mother. Kiss her.
Say: "This is for you." She grasps it and smiles. "You were always such
a sensitive child," she says.

Say: "Yeah, I know."

1970. You are pregnant again. Try to decide what you should do. Get
your hair chopped, short as a boy's.

1969. Mankind leaps upon the moon.

Disposable diapers are first sold in supermarkets.

Have occasional affairs with absurd, silly men who tell you to grow
your hair to your waist and who, when you are sad, tickle your ribs to
cheer you up. Moonlight through the blinds stripes you like zebras. You
laugh. You never marry.

1968. Do not resent her. Think about the situation, for instance, when
you take the last trash bag from its box: you must throw out the box by
putting it in that very trash bag. What was once contained, now must
contain. The container, then, becomes the contained, the enveloped, the
held. Find more and more that you like to muse over things like this.

1967. Your mother is sick and comes to live with you. There is no place else for her to go. You feel many different emptinesses.

The first successful heart transplant is performed in South Africa.

1966. You confuse lovers, mix up who had what scar, what car, what mother.

1965. Smoke marijuana. Try to figure out what has made your life go wrong. It is like trying to figure out what is stinking up the refrigerator. It could be anything. The lid off the mayonnaise, Uncle Ron's honey wine four years in the left corner. Broccoli yellowing, flowering fast. They are all metaphors. They are all problems. Your horoscope says: Speak gently to a loved one.

1964. Your mother calls long distance and asks whether you are coming home for Thanksgiving, your brother and the baby will be there. Make excuses.

"As a mother gets older," your mother says, "these sorts of holidays become increasingly important."

Say: "I'm sorry, Mom."

1963. Wake up one morning with a man you had thought you'd spend your life with, and realize, a rock in your gut, that you don't even like him. Spend a weepy afternoon in his bathroom, not coming out when he knocks. You can no longer trust your affections. People and places you think you love may be people and places you hate.

Kennedy is shot.

Someone invents a temporary artificial heart, for use during operations.

1962. Eat Chinese food for the first time, with a lawyer from California. He will show you how to hold the chopsticks. He will pat your leg. Attack his profession. Ask him whether he feels the law makes large spokes out of the short stakes of men.

1961. Grandma Moses dies.

You are a zoo of insecurities. You take to putting brandy in your morning coffee and to falling in love too easily. You have an abortion.

1960. There is money from your father's will and his life insurance. You buy a car and a green velvet dress you don't need. You drive two hours to meet your mother for lunch on Saturdays. She suggests things for you to write about, things she's heard on the radio: a woman with telepathic twins, a woman with no feet.

1959. At the funeral she says: "He had his problems, but he was a generous man," though you know he was tight as a scout knot, couldn't listen to anyone, the only time you remember loving him being that once when he got the punchline of one of your jokes before your mom did and looked up from his science journal and guffawed loud as a giant, the two of you, for one split moment, communing like angels in the middle of that room, in that warm, shared light of mind.

Say: "He was okay."

"You shouldn't be bitter," your mother snaps. "He financed you and your brother's college educations." She buttons her coat. "He was also the first man to isolate a particular isotope of helium, I forget the name, but he should have won the Nobel Prize." She dabs at her nose.

Say: "Yeah, Mom."

1958. At your brother's wedding, your father is taken away in an ambulance. A tiny cousin whispers loudly to her mother, "Did Uncle Will have a hard attack?" For seven straight days say things to your mother like: "I'm sure it'll be okay," and "I'll stay here, why don't you go home and get some sleep."

1957. Dance the calypso with boys from a different college. Get looped on New York State burgundy, lose your virginity, and buy one of the first portable electric typewriters.

1956. Tell your mother about all the books you are reading at college. This will please her.

1955. Do a paint-by-numbers of Elvis Presley. Tell your mother you are in love with him. She will shake her head.

1954. Shoplift a cashmere sweater.

1953. Smoke a cigarette with Hillary Swedelson. Tell each other your crushes. Become blood sisters.

1952. When your mother asks you if there are any nice boys in junior high, ask her how on earth would you ever know, having to come in at nine! every night. Her eyebrows will lift like theater curtains. "You poor, abused thing," she will say.

Say, "Don't I know it," and slam the door.

1951. Your mother tells you about menstruation. The following day you promptly menstruate, your body only waiting for permission, for a signal. You wake up in the morning and feel embarrassed.

1949. You learn how to blow gum bubbles and to add negative numbers.

1947. The Dead Sea Scrolls are discovered.

You have seen too many Hollywood musicals. You have seen too many people singing in public places and you assume you can do it, too. Practice. Your teacher asks you a question. You warble back: "The answer to number two is twelve." Most of the class laughs at you, though some stare, eyes jewel-still, fascinated. At home your mother asks you to dust your dresser. Work up a vibrato you could drive a truck through. Sing: "Why do I have to do it now?" and tap your way through the dining room. Your mother requests that you calm down and go take a nap. Shout: "You don't care about me! You don't care about me at all!"

1946. Your brother plays "Shoofly Pie" all day long on the Victrola.

Ask your mother if you can go to Ellen's for supper. She will say, "Go ask your father," and you, pulling at your fingers, walk out to the living room and whimper by his chair. He is reading. Tap his arm. "Dad? Daddy? Dad?" He continues reading his science journal. Pull harder on your fingers and run back to the kitchen to tell your mother, who storms into the living room, saying, "Why don't you ever listen to your children when they try to talk to you?" You hear them arguing. Press your face into a kitchen towel, ashamed, the hum of the refrigerator motor, the drip in the sink scaring you.

1945. Your father comes home from his war work. He gives you a piggyback ride around the broad yellow thatch of your yard, the dead window in the turret, dark as a wound, watching you. He gives you wordless pushes on the swing.

Your brother has new friends, acts older and distant, even while you wait for the school bus together.

You spend too much time alone. You tell your mother that when you grow up you will bring your babies to Australia to see the kangaroos.

Forty thousand people are killed in Nagasaki.

1944. Dress and cuddle a tiny babydoll you have named "the Sue." Bring her everywhere. Get lost in the Wilson Creek fruit market, and call softly, "Mom, where are you?" Watch other children picking grapes, but never dare yourself. Your eyes are small, dark throats, your hand clutches the Sue.

1943. Ask your mother about babies. Have her read to you only the stories about babies. Ask her if she is going to have a baby. Ask her about the baby that died. Cry into her arm.

1940. Clutch her hair in your fist. Rub it against your cheek.

1939. As through a helix, as through an ear, it is here you are nearer the dream flashes, the other lives.

There is a tent of legs, a sundering of selves, as you both gasp blindly for breath. Across the bright and cold, she knows it when you try to talk to her, though this is something you never really manage to understand.

Germany invades Poland.

The year's big song is "Three Little Fishies" and someone, somewhere, is playing it.

—*1985*

Poetry

Some of the popular ballads and lyrics of England and Scotland, composed for the most part between 1300 and 1500, were first collected in their current forms by Thomas Percy, whose Reliques of Ancient English Poetry *(1765) helped to revive interest in folk poetry. Francis James Child (1825–1896), an American, gathered over a thousand variant versions of the three hundred-odd core of poems. The Romantic poets of the early nineteenth century showed their debt to the folk tradition by writing imitative "art ballads" (see Keats's "La Belle Dame sans Merci" or Burns's "John Barleycorn"), which incorporate many of their stylistic devices.*

Anonymous
Western Wind

Western wind, when will thou blow,
    The small rain down can rain?
Christ, if my love were in my arms
    And I in my bed again!

                                               —*1450?*

Bonny Barbara Allan

It was in and about the Martinmas° time,
    When the green leaves were a falling,
That Sir John Græme, in the West Country,
    Fell in love with Barbara Allan.

He sent his men down through the town,   5
    To the place where she was dwelling.
"O haste and come to my master dear,
    Gin° ye be Barbara Allan."

O hooly,° hooly rose she up,
    To the place where he was lying,   *10*
And when she drew the curtain by:
    "Young man, I think you're dying."

1 Martinmas November 11   **8 Gin** if   **9 hooly** slowly

"O it's I'm sick, and very, very sick,
    And 'tis a'° for Barbara Allan."
"O the better for me ye s'° never be,   15
    Though your heart's blood were a-spilling.

"O dinna° ye mind, young man," said she,
    "When ye was in the tavern a drinking,
That ye made the healths gae° round and round,
    And slighted Barbara Allan?"   20

He turned his face unto the wall,
    And death was with him dealing:
"Adieu, adieu, my dear friends all,
    And be kind to Barbara Allan."

And slowly, slowly raise she up,   25
    And slowly, slowly left him,
And sighing said she could not stay,
    Since death of life had reft him.

She had not gane° a mile but twa,°
    When she heard the dead-bell ringing,   30
And every jow° that the dead-bell geid,°
    It cried, "Woe to Barbara Allan!"

"O mother, mother, make my bed!
    O make it saft° and narrow!
Since my love died for me to-day,   35
    I'll die for him to-morrow."

                                                                —*1500?*

Sir Patrick Spens

The king sits in Dumferling town,
    Drinking the blude-reid° wine:
"O whar will I get guid sailor,
    To sail this ship of mine?"

---

14 a' all   **15 s'** shall   **17 dinna** do not   **19 gae** go   **29 gane** gone   **twa** two   **31 jow** stroke   **geid**
gave   **34 saft** soft
2 blude-reid blood-red

Up and spak an eldern knicht,°   5
    Sat at the king's richt° knee:
"Sir Patrick Spens is the best sailor
    That sails upon the sea."

The king has written a braid° letter,
    And signed it wi' his hand,   10
And sent it to Sir Patrick Spens,
    Was walking on the sand.

The first line that Sir Patrick read,
    A loud lauch° lauched he;
The next line that Sir Patrick read,   15
    The tear blinded his ee.°

"O wha is this has done this deed,
    This ill deed done to me,
To send me out this time o' the year,
    To sail upon the sea?   20

"Mak haste, mak haste, my mirry men all,
    Our guid ship sails the morn."
"O say na sae,° my master dear,
    For I fear a deadly storm.

"Late, late yestre'en° I saw the new moon,   25
    Wi' the auld moon in hir arm,
And I fear, I fear, my dear master,
    That we will come to harm."

O our Scots nobles wer richt laith°
    To weet° their cork-heeled shoon,°   30
But lang or a'° the play were played,
    Their hats they swam aboon.°

O lang, lang may their ladies sit,
    Wi' their fans into their hand,
Or ere they see Sir Patrick Spens   35
    Come sailing to the land.

---

5 eldern knicht elderly knight   **6 richt** right   **9 braid** long   **14 lauch** laugh   **16 ee** eye   **23 na sae** not so   **25 yestre'en** last evening   **29 laith** loath   **30 weet** wet   **shoon** shoes   **31 lang or a'** long before   **32 Their hats they swam aboon** their hats swam above them

O lang, lang may the ladies stand,
    Wi' their gold kems° in their hair,
Waiting for their ain dear lords,
    For they'll see them na mair.   *40*

Half o'er, half o'er to Aberdour
    It's fifty fadom deep,
And there lies guid Sir Patrick Spens
    Wi' the Scots lords at his feet.

                                           —*1500?*

Sir Thomas Wyatt (1503?–1542) served Henry VIII as a diplomat in Italy. Wyatt read the love poetry of Petrarch (1304–1374) and is generally credited with having imported both the fashions of these lyrics—hyperbolic "conceits" or metaphorical descriptions of the woman's beauty and the lover's suffering—and their form, the sonnet, to England. "They Flee from Me," an example of one of his original lyrics, displays Wyatt's unique grasp of the rhythms of speech.

Sir Thomas Wyatt
They Flee from Me

They flee from me, that sometime did me seek,
With naked foot stalking in my chamber.
I have seen them gentle, tame and meek,
That now are wild, and do not remember
That sometime they put themself in danger   *5*
To take bread at my hand; and now they range,
Busily seeking with a continual change.

Thanked be Fortune it hath been otherwise,
Twenty times better; but once in special,
In thin array, after a pleasant guise,°   *10*
When her loose gown from her shoulders did fall,
And she me caught in her arms long and small,

---

38 kems combs
10 guise appearance

And therewith all sweetly did me kiss
And softly said, "Dear heart, how like you this?"

It was no dream, I lay broad waking.   15
But all is turned, thorough° my gentleness,
Into a strange fashion of forsaking;
And I have leave to go, of her goodness,
And she also to use newfangleness.
But since that I so kindely° am served,   20
I fain° would know what she hath deserved.

                                                                —1557

Queen Elizabeth I (1533–1603) *was an amateur poet who drew praise from
the members of her court, many of whom were also versifiers. A few of her lyrics survive, as do translations she made from the Roman writers Seneca and Horace. Her
reign (1558–1603) established England as a world power and also nurtured the talents of Edmund Spenser, William Shakespeare, Christopher Marlowe, and Ben
Jonson.*

Queen Elizabeth I
When I Was Fair
and Young

When I was fair and young, and favor gracèd me,
Of many was I sought, their mistress for to be;
But I did scorn them all, and answered them therefore,
    "Go, go, go seek some otherwhere!
                Importune me no more!"   5

How many weeping eyes I made to pine with woe,
How many sighing hearts, I have no skill to show;
Yet I the prouder grew, and answered them therefore,
    "Go, go, go seek some otherwhere!
                Importune me no more!"   10

---

16 thorough through   **20 kindely** in this manner   **21 fain** gladly

Then spake fair Venus' son,° that proud victorious boy,
And said, "Fine dame, since that you be so coy,
I will so pluck your plumes that you shall say no more,
   'Go, go, go seek some otherwhere!

Importune me no more!'"   15

When he had spake these words, such change grew in my breast
That neither night nor day since that, I could take any rest.
Then lo! I did repent that I had said before,
   "Go, go, go seek some otherwhere!

Importune me no more!"   20

—1585

Edmund Spenser (1552–1599) was born in London, and spent most of his adult life in Ireland, where he held a variety of minor government posts. The Faerie Queene, *a long allegorical romance about Elizabethan England, was uncompleted at his death. The eighty-odd sonnets that make up the sequence called* Amoretti *are generally thought to detail his courtship of his second wife, Elizabeth Boyle, whom he married in 1594.*

Edmund Spenser
Amoretti: Sonnet 75

One day I wrote her name upon the strand,
But came the waves and washèd it away:
Agayne I wrote it with a second hand,°
But came the tyde, and made my paynes his pray.
"Vayne man," sayd she, "that doest in vaine assay,°   5
A mortall thing so to immortalize,
For I my selve shall lyke° to this decay
And eek° my name bee wypèd out lykewize."
"Not so," quod° I, "let baser things devize
To dy in dust, but you shall live by fame: 10
My verse your vertues rare shall eternize,

---

11 Venus' son Eros or Cupid, god of love
3 second hand second time **5 assay** attempt **7 lyke** be similar to **8 eek** also **9 quod** said

And in the hevens wryte your glorious name.
Where whenas death shall all the world subdew
Our love shall live, and later life renew."

—*1595*

Sir Philip Sidney (1554–1586) embodied many of the aspects of the ideal man of the Renaissance; he was a courtier, scholar, patron of the arts, and soldier who died of wounds received at the battle of Zutphen. His sonnet sequence Astrophel and Stella *appeared in 1591, several years before Spenser's* Amoretti, *and helped to precipitate the fashion for sonnets that lasted in England well into the next century.*

Sir Philip Sidney

Astrophel and Stella: Sonnet 1

1

Loving in truth, and fain° in verse my love to show,
That she dear she might take some pleasure of my pain,
Pleasure might cause her read, reading might make her know,
Knowledge might pity win, and pity grace obtain,
I sought fit words to paint the blackest face of woe: 5
Studying inventions fine, her wits to entertain,
Oft turning others' leaves,° to see if thence would flow
Some fresh and fruitful showers upon my sunburned brain.
But words came halting forth, wanting Invention's stay;
Invention, Nature's child, fled stepdame Study's blows;   10
And others' feet° still seemed but strangers in my way.
Thus, great with child to speak, and helpless in my throes,
Biting my truant pen, beating myself for spite:
"Fool," said my Muse to me, "look in thy heart, and write."

—*1582*

1 fain glad   **7 leaves** pages   **11 feet** metrical feet in poetry

Robert Southwell (1561?–1595) *was a Roman Catholic priest in Elizabeth's Protestant England, who was executed for his religious beliefs. His devotional poems, most of them on the subject of spiritual love, were largely written during his three years in prison. Southwell was declared a saint in the Roman Catholic Church in 1970.*

Robert Southwell
The Burning Babe

As I in hoary winter's night stood shivering in the snow,
Surprised I was with sudden heat which made my heart to glow;
And lifting up a fearful eye to view what fire was near,
A pretty babe all burning bright did in the air appear;
Who, scorchèd with excessive heat, such floods of tears did shed   5
As though his floods should quench his flames which with his
    tears were fed.
"Alas," quoth he, "but newly born in fiery heats I fry,
Yet none approach to warm their hearts or feel my fire but I!
My faultless breast the furnace is, the fuel wounding thorns,
Love is the fire, and sighs the smoke, the ashes shame and
    scorns;   10
The fuel justice layeth on, and mercy blows the coals,
The metal in this furnace wrought are men's defilèd souls,
For which, as now on fire I am to work them to their good,
So will I melt into a bath to wash them in my blood."
With this he vanished out of sight and swiftly shrunk away,   15
And straight I callèd unto mind that it was Christmas day.

—1602

Michael Drayton (1563–1631), like his contemporary, Shakespeare, excelled in several literary genres. He collaborated on plays with Thomas Dekker and wrote long poems on English history, biography, and topography. Drayton labored almost three decades on the sixty-three sonnets in Idea, *publishing them in their present form in 1619.*

Michael Drayton

Idea: Sonnet 61

Since there's no help, come let us kiss and part;
Nay, I have done, you get no more of me,
And I am glad, yea glad with all my heart
That thus so cleanly I myself can free;
Shake hands forever, cancel all our vows,   5
And when we meet at any time again,
Be it not seen in either of our brows
That we one jot of former love retain.
Now at the last gasp of love's latest breath,
When, his pulse failing, passion speechless lies,   10
When faith is kneeling by his bed of death,
And innocence is closing up his eyes,
> Now if thou wouldst, when all have given him over,
> From death to life thou mightst him yet recover.

—*1619*

William Shakespeare (1564–1616) first printed his sonnets in 1609, during the last years of his active career as a playwright, but they had circulated privately a dozen years before. Given the lack of concrete details about Shakespeare's life outside the theatre, critics have found the sonnets fertile ground for biographical speculation, and the sequence of 154 poems does contain distinct characters—a handsome youth to whom most of the first 126 sonnets are addressed, a "Dark Lady" who figures strongly in the remaining poems, and the poet himself, whose name is the source of many puns in the poems. There is probably no definitive "key" to the sonnets, but there is also little doubt that their place is secure among the monuments of English lyric verse. Shakespeare's other nondramatic poems include narratives, allegories, and songs, of which "When Daisies Pied," the companion pieces from his early comedy Love's Labour's Lost, *are perhaps the best examples.*

William Shakespeare
Sonnet 18

Shall I compare thee to a summer's day?
Thou art more lovely and more temperate:
Rough winds do shake the darling buds of May,
And summer's lease hath all too short a date:
Sometimes too hot the eye of heaven shines,   5
And often is his gold complexion dimmed;
And every fair from fair° sometimes declines,
By chance or nature's changing course untrimmed:°
But thy eternal summer shall not fade,
Nor lose possession of that fair thou ow'st;°   10
Nor shall death brag thou wander'st in his shade,
When in eternal lines to time thou grow'st:
So long as men can breathe, or eyes can see,
So long lives this, and this gives life to thee.

—*1609*

7 fair from fair every fair thing from its fairness   **8 untrimmed** stripped   **10 ow'st** ownest

Sonnet 20

A woman's face, with nature's own hand painted,
Hast thou, the master mistress of my passion—
A woman's gentle heart, but not acquainted
With shifting change, as is false women's fashion;
An eye more bright than theirs, less false in rolling,°   *5*
Gilding the object whereupon it gazeth;
A man in hue all hues in his controlling,
Which steals men's eyes and women's souls amazeth.
And for a woman wert thou first created,
Till nature as she wrought thee fell a-doting,   *10*
And by addition me of thee defeated,
By adding one thing to my purpose nothing.
    But since she pricked thee out for women's pleasure,
    Mine be thy love and thy love's use their treasure.

—1609

Sonnet 30

When to the sessions° of sweet silent thought
I summon up remembrance of things past,
I sigh the lack of many a thing I sought,
And with old woes new wail my dear time's waste:
Then can I drown an eye, unused to flow,   *5*
For precious friends hid in death's dateless° night,
And weep afresh love's long since canceled woe,
And moan the expense of many a vanished sight:
Then can I grieve at grievances foregone,
And heavily from woe to woe tell o'er   *10*
The sad account of fore-bemoanèd moan,
Which I new pay as if not paid before.
But if the while I think on thee, dear friend,
All losses are restored and sorrows end.

—1609

5 rolling wandering
1 sessions as in sessions of a court of law   **6 dateless** endless

Sonnet 73

That time of year thou mayst in me behold
When yellow leaves, or none, or few, do hang
Upon those boughs which shake against the cold,
Bare ruined choirs, where late the sweet birds sang.
In me thou see'st the twilight of such day   5
As after sunset fadeth in the west;
Which by and by black night doth take away,
Death's second self, that seals up all in rest.
In me thou see'st the glowing of such fire,
That on the ashes of his youth doth lie,   10
As the deathbed whereon it must expire,
Consumed with that which it was nourished by.
This thou perceiv'st, which makes thy love more strong,
To love that well which thou must leave ere long.

                                                        —*1609*

Sonnet 116

Let me not to the marriage of true minds
Admit impediments. Love is not love
Which alters when it alteration finds,
Or bends with the remover to remove:
Oh, no! it is an ever-fixèd mark,   5
That looks on tempests and is never shaken:
It is the star to every wandering bark,
Whose worth's unknown, although his height be taken.°
Love's not Time's fool, though rosy lips and cheeks
Within his bending sickle's compass° come;   10
Love alters not with his brief hours and weeks,
But bears it out even to the edge of doom.
If this be error and upon me proved,
I never writ, nor no man ever loved.

                                                        —*1609*

8 **height be taken** elevation be measured   10 **compass** range

Sonnet 130

My mistress' eyes are nothing like the sun;
Coral is far more red than her lips' red;
If snow be white, why then her breasts are dun;
If hairs be wires, black wires grow on her head.
I have seen roses damasked,° red and white,   *5*
But no such roses see I in her cheeks;
And in some perfumes is there more delight
Than in the breath that from my mistress reeks.
I love to hear her speak, yet well I know
That music hath a far more pleasing sound;   *10*
I grant I never saw a goddess go;
My mistress, when she walks, treads on the ground.
And yet, by heaven, I think my love as rare
As any she belied° with false compare.°

—*1609*

When Daisies Pied°

SPRING

When daisies pied and violets blue
    And ladysmocks all silver-white
And cuckoobuds of yellow hue
    Do paint the meadows with delight,
The cuckoo then, on every tree,   *5*
Mocks married men;° for thus sings he,
            Cuckoo;
Cuckoo, cuckoo: Oh word of fear,
Unpleasing to a married ear!
When shepherds pipe on oaten straws,   *10*
    And merry larks are plowmen's clocks,

---

5 damasked multi-colored   **14 belied** lied about   **compare** comparisons
Pied multi-colored   **6 Mocks married men** The pun is on the similarity between "cuckoo" and "cuckold."

When turtles tread,° and rooks, and daws,
   And maidens bleach their summer smocks,
The cuckoo then, on every tree,
Mocks married men; for thus sings he,   15
             Cuckoo:
Cuckoo, cuckoo: Oh word of fear,
Unpleasing to a married ear!

WINTER

When icicles hang by the wall
And Dick the shepherd blows his nail°   20
And Tom bears logs into the hall,
   And milk comes frozen home in pail,
When blood is nipped and ways be foul,
Then nightly sings the staring owl,
            Tu-who;   25
Tu-whit, tu-who: a merry note,
While greasy Joan doth keel° the pot.

When all aloud the wind doth blow,
   And coughing drowns the parson's saw,°
And birds sit brooding in the snow,   30
   And Marian's nose looks red and raw,
When roasted crabs° hiss in the bowl,
Then nightly sings the staring owl,
            Tu-who;
Tu-whit, tu-who: a merry note   35
While greasy Joan doth keel the pot.

—*1598*

---

12 turtles tread turtledoves mate   **20 nail** fingernails   **27 keel** stir   **29 saw** saying   **32 crabs** crabapples

Thomas Campion (1567–1620) was a poet and physician who wrote music and lyrics in a manner that was "chiefly aimed to couple my words and notes lovingly together." The imagery in "There Is a Garden in Her Face" represents a late flowering of the conceits of Petrarchan love poetry, so wittily mocked by Shakespeare in "Sonnet 130."

Thomas Campion

There Is a Garden in Her Face

There is a garden in her face,
Where roses and white lilies grow,
A heavenly paradise is that place,
Wherein all pleasant fruits do flow.
There cherries grow which none may buy   5
Till "Cherry-ripe!" themselves do cry.

Those cherries fairly do enclose
Of orient pearl a double row,
Which when her lovely laughter shows,
They look like rosebuds filled with snow.   10
Yet them nor peer nor prince can buy,
Till "Cherry-ripe!" themselves do cry.

Her eyes like angels watch them still;
Her brows like bended bows do stand,
Threatening with piercing frowns to kill   15
All that attempt with eye or hand
Those sacred cherries to come nigh,
Till "Cherry-ripe!" themselves do cry.

—*1617*

John Donne (1572–1631) was trained in the law for a career in government service, but Donne became the greatest preacher of his day, ending his life as dean of St. Paul's Cathedral in London. Only two of Donne's poems and a handful of his sermons were printed during his life, but both circulated widely in manuscript and his literary reputation among his contemporaries was considerable. His poetry falls into two distinct periods: the witty love poetry of his youth and the sober religious meditations of his maturity. In both, however, Donne shows remarkable originality in rhythm, diction, and the use of metaphor and conceit, which marks him as the chief poet of what has become commonly known as the metaphysical style.

John Donne

The Canonization

For God's sake hold your tongue, and let me love,
    Or chide my palsy, or my gout,
My five gray hairs, or ruined fortune, flout,
    With wealth your state, your mind with arts improve,
        Take you a course, get you a place,   *5*
        Observe His Honor, or His Grace,
Or the king's real,° or his stampèd face
    Contèmplate; what you will, approve,°
    So you will let me love.

Alas, alas, who's injured by my love?   *10*
    What merchant's ships have my sighs drowned?
Who says my tears have overflowed his ground?
    When did my colds a forward° spring remove?
        When did the heats which my veins fill
        Add one more to the plaguy bill?°   *15*
Soldiers find wars, and lawyers find out still
    Litigious men, which quarrels move,
    Though she and I do love.

Call us what you will, we're made such by love;
    Call her one, me another fly,   *20*

---

7 real coinage   **8 approve** attempt   **13 forward** early   **15 plaguy bill** list of dead by plague

We're tapers too, and at our own cost die,°
 And we in us find th' eagle and the dove.
  The phoenix° riddle hath more wit
  By us: we two being one, are it.
So, to one neutral thing both sexes fit,   25
 We die and rise the same, and prove
 Mysterious by this love.

We can die by it, if not live by love,
 And if unfit for tomb and hearse
Our legend be, it will be fit for verse;   30
  And if no piece of chronicle° we prove,
   We'll build in sonnets pretty rooms;
   As well a well-wrought urn becomes
The greatest ashes, as half-acre tombs;
  And by these hymns, all shall approve   35
  Us canonized for love:

And thus invoke us, "You whom reverend love
 Made one another's hermitage;
You, to whom love was peace, that now is rage;
  Who did the whole world's soul contract, and drove   40
   Into the glasses of your eyes
   (So made such mirrors, and such spies,°
That they did all to you epitomize)
  Countries, towns, courts: Beg from above
  A pattern of your love!"   45

             —*1633*

The Flea

Mark but this flea, and mark in this,
How little that which thou deniest me is;
Me it sucked first, and now sucks thee,
And in this flea our two bloods mingled be;

---

21 die i.e., to have sexual intercourse   **23 phoenix** legendary bird which is reborn from its own ashes   **31 chronicle** history   **42 spies** telescopes

Thou know'st that this cannot be said   5
A sin, or shame, or loss of maidenhead,
    Yet this enjoys before it woo,
    And pampered swells with one blood made of two,
    And this, alas, is more than we would do.

Oh stay, three lives in one flea spare,   10
Where we almost, nay more than married are.
This flea is you and I, and this
Our marriage bed and marriage temple is;
Though parents grudge, and you, we are met,
And cloistered in these living walls of jet.°   15
    Though use° make you apt to kill me
    Let not to that, self-murder added be,
    And sacrilege, three sins in killing three.

Cruel and sudden, hast thou since
Purpled thy nail° in blood of innocence?   20
Wherein could this flea guilty be,
Except in that drop which it sucked from thee?
Yet thou triumph'st, and say'st that thou
Find'st not thy self nor me the weaker now;
    'Tis true; then learn how false fears be: 25
    Just so much honor, when thou yield'st to me,
    Will waste, as this flea's death took life from thee.

—1633

Holy Sonnet 10

Death, be not proud, though some have callèd thee
Mighty and dreadful, for thou art not so;
For those whom thou think'st thou dost overthrow
Die not, poor Death, nor yet canst thou kill me.
From rest and sleep, which but thy pictures be,   5
Much pleasure; then from thee much more must flow,

---

15 jet black   **16 use** familiarity, especially in the sexual sense   **20 Purpled thy nail** bloodied your fingernail

And soonest our best men with thee do go,
Rest of their bones, and soul's delivery.
Thou'art slave to fate, chance, kings, and desperate men,
And dost with poison, war, and sickness dwell,   *10*
And poppy° or charms can make us sleep as well
And better than thy stroke; why swell'st thou then?
One short sleep past, we wake eternally,
And death shall be no more; Death, thou shalt die.

—*1633*

Holy Sonnet 14

Batter my heart, three-personed God; for You
As yet but knock, breathe, shine, and seek to mend;
That I may rise, and stand, o'erthrow me, and bend
Your force to break, blow, burn, and make me new.
I, like an usurped town, to another due,   *5*
Labor to admit You, but O, to no end;
Reason, Your viceroy in me, me should defend,
But is captived, and proves weak or untrue.
Yet dearly I love You, and would be lovèd fain,°
But am betrothed unto Your enemy.   *10*
Divorce me, untie or break that knot again;
Take me to You, imprison me, for I,
Except You enthrall me, never shall be free,
Nor ever chaste, except You ravish me.

—*1633*

11 poppy opium
9 fain gladly

A Valediction:°
Forbidding Mourning

As virtuous men pass mildly away,
    And whisper to their souls to go,
Whilst some of their sad friends do say
    The breath goes now, and some say, No;

So let us melt, and make no noise,   5
    No tear-floods, nor sigh-tempests move,
'Twere profanation of our joys
    To tell the laity our love.

Moving of th' earth brings harms and fears,
    Men reckon what it did and meant;   10
But trepidation of the spheres,°
    Though greater far, is innocent.

Dull sublunary° lovers' love,
    (Whose soul is sense) cannot admit
Absence, because it doth remove   15
    Those things which elemented it.
But we by a love so much refined
    That our selves know not what it is,
Inter-assurèd of the mind,
    Care less, eyes, lips, and hands to miss.   20

Our two souls therefore, which are one,
    Though I must go, endure not yet
A breach, but an expansion,
    Like gold to airy thinness beat.

If they be two, they are two so   25
    As stiff twin compasses° are two;

Valediction farewell speech; Donne is addressing his wife before leaving on a diplomatic mission.
11 trepidation of the spheres natural trembling of the heavenly spheres, a concept of Ptolemaic astronomy   **13 sublunary** under the moon, hence, changeable (a Ptolemaic concept)   **26 stiff twin compasses** drafting compasses

Thy soul, the fixed foot, makes no show
   To move, but doth, if th' other do.

And though it in the center sit,
   Yet when the other far doth roam,   30
It leans and hearkens after it,
   And grows erect, as that comes home.

Such wilt thou be to me, who must
   Like th' other foot, obliquely run;
Thy firmness makes my circle just,°   35
   And makes me end where I begun.

—*1633*

Ben Jonson (1573–1637) was Shakespeare's chief rival on the stage, and their contentious friendship has been the subject of much speculation. Jonson became England's first unofficial poet laureate, receiving a royal stipend from James I, and was a great influence of a group of younger poets who became known as the "Tribe of Ben." His tragedies are little regarded today, and his comedies, while still performed occasionally, have nevertheless failed to hold the stage as brilliantly as Shakespeare's. Still, he was a poet of considerable talents, particularly in short forms. His elegy on Shakespeare contains a famous assessment: "He was not of an age, but for all time!"

Ben Jonson
On My First Son

Farewell, thou child of my right hand,° and joy;
My sin was too much hope of thee, loved boy:
Seven years thou'wert lent to me, and I thee pay,
Exacted by thy fate, on the just day.°
Oh, could I lose all father now! for why   5
Will man lament the state he should envy,
To have so soon 'scaped world's and flesh's rage,

---

35 just complete
1 child of my right hand Benjamin, the child's name, means this in Hebrew.   **4 the just day** Jonson's son died on his seventh birthday.

And, if no other misery, yet age?
Rest in soft peace, and asked, say, "Here doth lie
Ben Jonson his best piece of poetry."   *10*
For whose sake henceforth all his vows be such
As what he loves may never like too much.

                                        —*1616*

Slow, Slow, Fresh Fount

From Cynthia's Revels°
Slow, slow, fresh fount, keep time with my salt tears;
Yet slower, yet, O faintly, gentle springs!
List to the heavy part the music bears,
Woe weeps out her division,° when she sings.
    Droop herbs and flowers;   *5*
    Fall grief in showers;
Our beauties are not ours. O, I could still,
Like melting snow upon some craggy hill,
    Drop, drop, drop, drop,
Since nature's pride is now a withered daffodil.   *10*

                                        —*1600*

Slow, Slow, Fresh Fount: From Cynthia's Revels spoken in this masque by the nymph Echo to the dead Narcissus   **4 division** part of a song

Mary Wroth (1587?–1651) was the niece of Sir Philip Sidney and the cousin of Sir Walter Raleigh, both distinguished poets and courtiers. A friend of poet Ben Jonson, who dedicated The Alchemist *to her, she was prominent in the court of King James I. Her prose romance,* Urania *(1621), stirred controversy because of its similarities to actual people and events. Wroth may have fallen into disfavor at court after the publication of* Urania, *and few facts are known about her later life.*

Mary Wroth

In This Strange Labyrinth How Shall I Turn

In this strange labyrinth how shall I turn,
Ways° are on all sides, while the way I miss:
If to the right hand, there in love I burn,
Let me go forward, therein danger is.

If to the left, suspicion hinders bliss: 5
Let me turn back, shame cries I ought return:
Nor faint, though crosses° with my fortunes kiss.
Stand still is harder, although sure to mourn.
Thus let me take the right, or left hand way,
Go forward, or stand still, or back retire: 10
I must these doubts endure without allay°
Or help, but travail find for my best hire
Yet that which most my troubled sense doth move,
Is to leave all and take the thread of Love°

---

2 ways paths   **7 crosses** troubles   **11 allay** alleviation   **14 Love** an allusion to the myth of Theseus, who, with the help of Ariddne, unrolled a thread behind him as he entered the labyrinth of Crete.

Robert Herrick (1591–1674) *was the most distinguished member of the "Tribe of Ben." Herrick is grouped with the Cavalier poets, whose graceful lyrics are marked by wit and gentle irony. Surprisingly, Herrick was a minister; his Royalist sympathies during the English Civil War caused him hardship during the Puritan era, but his position in the church was returned to him by Charles II after the Restoration.*

Robert Herrick
To the Virgins, to Make Much of Time

Gather ye rosebuds while ye may,
    Old time is still a-flying;
And this same flower that smiles today
    Tomorrow will be dying.

The glorious lamp of heaven, the sun,   5
    The higher he's a-getting,
The sooner will his race be run,
    And nearer he's to setting.

That age is best which is the first,
    When youth and blood are warmer;   10
But being spent, the worse, and worst
    Times still succeed the former.

Then be not coy, but use your time,
    And, while ye may, go marry;
For, having lost but once your prime,   15
    You may forever tarry.

—1648

George Herbert (1593–1633) was the great master of the English devotional lyric. Herbert was born into a distinguished family which included his mother, the formidable literary patroness Lady Magdalen Herbert, and his brother, the poet and statesman Edward, Lord Herbert of Cherbury. Like John Donne, with whom he shares the metaphysical label, Herbert early aimed at a political career but turned to the clergy, spending several happy years as rector of Bemerton before his death at age 40. The Temple, *which contains most of his poems, was published posthumously in 1633.*

George Herbert
Easter Wings

Lord, who createdst man in wealth and store,°
Though foolishly he lost the same,
Decaying more and more
Till he became
Most poor: 5
With Thee
O let me rise
As larks, harmoniously,
And sing this day Thy victories:
Then shall the fall further the flight in me.   10

My tender age in sorrow did begin;
And still with sicknesses and shame
Thou didst so punish sin,
That I became
Most thin.   15
With Thee
Let me combine,
And feel this day thy victory;
For, if I imp my wing on thine,°
Affliction shall advance the flight in me.   20

—*1633*

---

1 store abundance   **19 imp my wing on thine** to graft feathers from a strong wing onto a weak one, a term from falconry

Love (III)

Love bade me welcome: yet my soul drew back,
    Guilty of dust and sin.
But quick-eyed Love, observing me grow slack
    From my first entrance in,
Drew nearer to me, sweetly questioning   5
    If I lacked anything.

"A guest," I answered, "worthy to be here":
    Love said, "You shall be he."
"I, the unkind, ungrateful? Ah, my dear,
    I cannot look on thee."   10
Love took my hand, and smiling did reply,
    "Who made the eyes but I?"

"Truth, Lord, but I have marred them; let my shame
    Go where it doth deserve."
"And know you not," says Love, "who bore the blame?"   15
    "My dear, then I will serve."
"You must sit down," says Love, "and taste my meat."
    So I did sit and eat.

—*1633*

The Pulley

    When God at first made man,
Having a glass of blessings standing by,
    "Let us," said he, "pour on him all we can.
Let the world's riches, which dispersèd lie,
    Contract into a span."°   5

    So strength first made a way;
Then beauty flowed, then wisdom, honor, pleasure.
    When almost all was out, God made a stay,

5 span the distance between thumb tip and the tip of the little finger

Perceiving that, alone of all his treasure,
    Rest in the bottom lay.   *10*

    "For if I should," said he,
"Bestow this jewel also on my creature,
    He would adore my gifts instead of me,
And rest in Nature, not the God of Nature;
    So both should losers be.   *15*

    "Yet let him keep the rest,
But keep them with repining restlessness.
    Let him be rich and weary, that at least,
If goodness lead him not, yet weariness
    May toss him to my breast."   *20*

                           —1633

Redemption

Having been tenant long to a rich lord,
    Not thriving, I resolvèd to be bold,
    And make a suit° unto him, to afford°
A new small-rented lease, and cancel the old.
In heaven at his manor I him sought;   *5*
    They told me there that he was lately gone
    About some land, which he had dearly bought
Long since on earth, to take possession.

I straight returned, and knowing his great birth,
    Sought him accordingly in great resorts;   *10*
    In cities, theaters, gardens, parks, and courts;
At length I heard a ragged noise and mirth
    Of thieves and murderers; there I him espied,°
    Who straight, Your suit is granted, said, and died.

                           —1633

---

3 make a suit formally request   **afford** grant (me)   **13 him espied** saw him

Edmund Waller (1606–1687) was another Royalist sympathizer who suffered after the English Civil War, during Oliver Cromwell's protectorate. Waller is noted for having pioneered the use of the heroic couplet as a popular verse form. He has been often praised for the smoothness of his rhythms and sound patterns.

Edmund Waller

Song

Go, lovely rose!
Tell her that wastes her time and me
   That now she knows,
When I resemble° her to thee,
How sweet and fair she seems to be.   5

   Tell her that's young,
And shuns to have her graces spied,
   That hadst thou sprung
In deserts, where no men abide,
Thou must have uncommended died.   10

   Small is the worth
Of beauty from the light retired;
   Bid her come forth,
Suffer herself to be desired,
And not blush so to be admired.   15

   Then die! that she
The common fate of all things rare
   May read in thee;
How small a part of time they share
That are so wondrous sweet and fair!   20

—1645

---

4 resemble compare

John Milton (1608–1674) is best known as the author of Paradise Lost, *the greatest English epic poem. His life included service in the Puritan government of Cromwell, pamphleteering for liberal political causes, and brief imprisonment after the Restoration. Milton suffered from blindness in his later years. He excelled in the sonnet, a form to which he returned throughout his long literary life.*

John Milton
How Soon Hath Time

How soon hath Time, the subtle thief of youth,
    Stol'n on his wing my three and twentieth year!
    My hasting days fly on with full career,
    But my late spring no bud or blossom shew'th.°
Perhaps my semblance might deceive the truth,   5
    That I to manhood am arrived so near,
    And inward ripeness doth much less appear,
    That some more timely-happy spirits endu'th.°
Yet be it less or more, or soon or slow,
    It shall be still in strictest measure even°   10
    To that same lot, however mean or high,
Toward which Time leads me, and the will of Heaven;
    All is, if I have grace to use it so,
    As ever in my great Taskmaster's eye.

                       —*1645*

On the Late Massacre in Piedmont°

Avenge, O Lord, thy slaughtered saints, whose bones
    Lie scattered on the Alpine mountains cold,
    Even them who kept thy truth so pure of old
    When all our fathers worshiped stocks and stones,°

---

4 shew'th shows   **8 endu'th** endows   **10 even** equal
Massacre in Piedmont 1700 Protestants from this North Italian state were massacred by Papal forces on Easter Day, 1655.   **4 stocks and stones** idols

Forget not: in thy book record their groans   5
    Who were thy sheep and in their ancient fold
    Slain by the bloody Piedmontese that rolled
    Mother with infant down the rocks. Their moans
The vales redoubled to the hills, and they
    To Heaven. Their martyred blood and ashes sow   10
    O'er all th'Italian fields where still doth sway
The triple tyrant:° that from these may grow
    A hundredfold, who having learnt thy way
    Early may fly the Babylonian woe.°

—*1655*

When I Consider How My Light Is Spent

When I consider how my light is spent
    Ere half my days, in this dark world and wide,
    And that one talent which is death to hide°
    Lodged with me useless, though my soul more bent
To serve therewith my Maker, and present   5
    My true account, lest he returning chide;
    "Doth God exact day-labor, light denied?"
    I fondly° ask; but Patience to prevent
That murmur, soon replies, "God doth not need
    Either man's work or his own gifts; who best   10
    Bear his mild yoke, they serve him best. His state
Is kingly. Thousands at his bidding speed
    And post o'er land and ocean without rest:
    They also serve who only stand and wait."

—*1673*

---

12 triple tyrant the Pope   **14 Babylonian woe** Early Protestants often linked ancient Babylon to modern Rome as centers of vice.
3 talent which is death to hide See the Parable of the Talents, Matthew 25:14–30.   **8 fondly** foolishly

Anne Bradstreet (1612–1672) was an American Puritan who was one of the first settlers of the Massachusetts Bay Colony, along with her husband Simon, later governor of the colony. The Tenth Muse Lately Sprung Up in America, *published abroad by a relative without her knowledge, was the first American book of poetry published in England, and the circumstances of its appearance lie behind the witty tone of "The Author to Her Book."*

Anne Bradstreet

The Author to Her Book

Thou ill-formed offspring of my feeble brain,
Who after birth didst by my side remain,
Till snatched from thence by friends, less wise than true,
Who thee abroad, exposed to public view,
Made thee in rags, halting to th' press° to trudge,   5
Where errors were not lessened (all may judge).
At thy return my blushing was not small,
My rambling brat (in print) should mother call,
I cast thee by as one unfit for light,
Thy visage was so irksome in my sight;   10
Yet being mine own, at length affection would
Thy blemishes amend, if so I could:
I washed thy face, but more defects I saw,
And rubbing off a spot still made a flaw.
I stretched thy joints to make thee even feet,°   15
Yet still thou run'st more hobbling than is meet;
In better dress to trim thee was my mind,
But nought save homespun cloth i' th' house I find.
In this array 'mongst vulgars° may'st thou roam.
In critic's hands beware thou dost not come,   20
And take thy way where yet thou art not known;
If for thy father asked, say thou hadst none;
And for thy mother, she alas is poor,
Which caused her thus to send thee out of door.

—*1678*

5 press printing press; also a clothes closet or chest   **15 even feet** a pun on metrical feet
19 vulgars common people, i.e., average readers

Richard Lovelace (1618–1658) was another Cavalier lyricist who was a staunch supporter of Charles I, serving as a soldier in Scotland and France. He composed many of his poems in prison following the English Civil War.

Richard Lovelace
To Lucasta, Going to the Wars

Tell me not, sweet, I am unkind
That from the nunnery
Of thy chaste breast and quiet mind,
To war and arms I fly.

True, a new mistress now I chase,   5
The first foe in the field;
And with a stronger faith embrace
A sword, a horse, a shield.

Yet this inconstancy is such
As you too shall adore;   10
I could not love thee, dear, so much,
Loved I not honor more.

—1649

Andrew Marvell (1621–1678) was widely known for the playful sexual wit of this most famous example of the carpé diem *poem in English. Marvell was a learned Latin scholar who moved in high circles of government under both the Puritans and Charles II, serving as a member of parliament for two decades. Oddly, Marvell was almost completely forgotten as a lyric poet for almost two hundred years after his death, although today he is considered the last of the great exemplars of the metaphysical style.*

Andrew Marvell
To His Coy Mistress

Had we but world enough, and time,
This coyness,° lady, were no crime.
We would sit down, and think which way
To walk, and pass our long love's day.
Thou by the Indian Ganges' side   5
Shouldst rubies find; I by the tide
Of Humber° would complain. I would
Love you ten years before the flood,
And you should, if you please, refuse
Till the conversion of the Jews.°   10
My vegetable° love should grow
Vaster than empires, and more slow;
An hundred years should go to praise
Thine eyes, and on thy forehead gaze;
Two hundred to adore each breast,   15
But thirty thousand to the rest;
An age at least to every part,
And the last age should show your heart.
For, lady, you deserve this state,°
Nor would I love at lower rate.   20
      But at my back I always hear
Time's wingèd chariot hurrying near;
And yonder all before us lie

---

2 coyness here, artificial sexual reluctance   **7 Humber** an English river near Marvell's home
10 conversion of the Jews at the end of time   **11 vegetable** flourishing   **19 state** estate

Deserts of vast eternity.
Thy beauty shall no more be found;   25
Nor, in thy marble vault, shall sound
My echoing song; then worms shall try°
That long-preserved virginity,
And your quaint° honor turn to dust,
And into ashes all my lust: 30
The grave's a fine and private place,
But none, I think, do there embrace.
    Now therefore, while the youthful hue
Sits on thy skin like morning glow,
And while thy willing soul transpires   35
At every pore with instant fires,
Now let us sport us while we may,
And now, like amorous birds of prey,
Rather at once our time devour
Than languish in his slow-chapped° power.   40
Let us roll all our strength and all
Our sweetness up into one ball,
And tear our pleasures with rough strife
Thorough the iron gates of life:
Thus, though we cannot make our sun   45
Stand still, yet we will make him run.

—*1681*

---

27 try test   **29 quaint** too subtle   **40 chapped** jawed

John Dryden (1631–1700) excelled at long forms — verse dramas like All for
Love, *his version of Shakespeare's* Antony and Cleopatra, *his translation of*
Virgil's Aeneid, *political allegories like* Absalom and Achitophel, *and*
MacFlecknoe, *the first great English literary satire. Dryden's balance and for-*
mal conservatism introduced the neoclassical style to English poetry, a manner
that prevailed for a century after his death. He became poet laureate of England
in 1668.

John Dryden

To the Memory of Mr. Oldham°

Farewell, too little, and too lately known,
Whom I began to think and call my own:
For sure our souls were near allied, and thine
Cast in the same poetic mold with mine.
One common note on either lyre did strike,   5
And knaves and fools we both abhorred alike.
To the same goal did both our studies drive;
The last set out the soonest did arrive.
Thus Nisus° fell upon the slippery place,
While his young friend performed and won the race.   10
O early ripe! to thy abundant store
What could advancing age have added more?
It might (what nature never gives the young)
Have taught the numbers° of thy native tongue.
But satire needs not those, and wit will shine   15
Through the harsh cadence of a rugged line:
A noble error, and but seldom made,
When poets are by too much force betrayed.
Thy generous fruits, though gathered ere their prime,
Still showed a quickness, and maturing time   20
But mellows what we write to the dull sweets of rhyme.
Once more, hail and farewell; farewell, thou young,

John Oldham (1653–1683) was a poet and a satirist.   **9 Nisus** In Virgil's *Aeneid* he is defeated in a
footrace by Euryalus, his friend.   **14 numbers** poetic meters

But ah too short, Marcellus° of our tongue;
Thy brows with ivy, and with laurels bound
But fate and gloomy night encompass thee around.   25

—1684

Epigram on Milton

Three poets, in three distant ages born,
Greece,° Italy,° and England did adorn.
The first in loftiness of thought surpassed,
The next in majesty, in both the last:
The force of Nature could no farther go;   5
To make a third, she joined the former two.

—1688

Edward Taylor (1642–1729) was a Calvinist minister in a village outside of Boston whose eccentric religious poems (obviously influenced by Donne and Herbert) remained in manuscript for over two centuries after his death, when they were discovered in the Yale University Library. Taylor was a true amateur, writing in isolation and apparently intending his poems as meditative exercises to assist him in his clerical duties. Taylor's poems were not published until the twentieth century.

Edward Taylor
Huswifery

Make me, O Lord, thy spinning wheel complete.
    Thy holy word my distaff° make for me.
Make mine affections thy swift flyers° neat,
    And make my soul thy holy spool° to be.
    My conversation make to be thy reel,°   5
    And reel the yarn thereon spun of thy wheel.

---

23 Marcellus Roman military leader who died at age twenty
2 Greece i.e., Homer   **Italy** i.e., Virgil
2 distaff part of a spinning wheel that holds raw material   **3 flyers** impart twist to yarn   **4 spool** collects spun yarn   **5 reel** receives finished thread

Make me thy loom then, knit therein this twine;
    And make thy holy spirit, Lord, wind quills.°
Then weave the web thyself. The yarn is fine.
    Thine ordinances make my fulling mills.°   *10*
    Then dye the same in heavenly colors choice,
    All pinked° with varnished° flowers of paradise.

Then clothe therewith mine understanding, will,
    Affections, judgment, conscience, memory,
My words, and actions, that their shine may fill   *15*
    My ways with glory and thee glorify.
    Then mine apparel shall display before ye
    That I am clothed in holy robes for glory.

                                                  —1685?

Jonathan Swift (1667–1745), the author of Gulliver's Travels, *stands unchallenged as the greatest English prose satirist, but his poetry too is remarkable in the unsparing realism of its best passages. Like many poets of the neoclassical era, Swift adds tension to his poetry by ironically emphasizing parallels between the heroic past and the familiar characters and scenes of contemporary London. A native of Dublin, Swift returned to Ireland in his maturity as dean of St. Patrick's Cathedral.*

Jonathan Swift

A Description of a City Shower

    Careful observers may foretell the hour
(By sure prognostics)° when to dread a shower:
While rain depends,° the pensive cat gives o'er
Her frolics, and pursues her tail no more.
Returning home at night, you'll find the sink°   *5*
Strike your offended sense with double stink.

---

8 quills spools   **10 fulling mills** where cloth is cleaned after weaving   **12 pinked** decorated
varnished shiny
2 prognostics forecasts   **3 depends** is imminent   **5 sink** sewer

If you be wise, then go not far to dine;
You'll spend in coach hire more than save in wine.
A coming shower your shooting corns presage,
Old aches throb, your hollow tooth will rage.   *10*
Sauntering in coffeehouse is Dulman° seen;
He damns the climate and complains of spleen.°
   Meanwhile the South, rising with dabbled wings,
A sable cloud athwart the welkin° flings,
That swilled more liquor than it could contain,   *15*
And, like a drunkard, gives it up again.
Brisk Susan whips her linen from the rope,
While the first drizzling shower is borne aslope:
Such is that sprinkling which some careless quean°
Flirts on you from her mop, but not so clean: *20*
You fly, invoke the gods; then turning, stop
To rail; she singing, still whirls on her mop.
Not yet the dust had shunned the unequal strife,
But, aided by the wind, fought still for life,
And wafted with its foe by violent gust,   *25*
'Twas doubtful which was rain and which was dust.
Ah! where must needy poet seek for aid,
When dust and rain at once his coat invade?
Sole coat, where dust cemented by the rain
Erects the nap, and leaves a mingled stain.   *30*
   Now in contiguous drops the flood comes down,
Threatening with deluge this devoted° town.
To shops in crowds the daggled° females fly,
Pretend to cheapen° goods, but nothing buy.
The Templar° spruce, while every spout's abroach,°   *35*
Stays till 'tis fair, yet seems to call a coach.
The tucked-up sempstress walks with hasty strides,
While streams run down her oiled umbrella's sides.
Here various kinds, by various fortunes led,
Commence acquaintance underneath a shed.   *40*

---

11 Dulman i.e., dull man   **12 spleen** mental depression   **14 welkin** sky   **19 quean** ill-mannered woman   **32 devoted** doomed   **33 daggled** spattered   **34 cheapen** inspect prices of   **35 Templar** law student   **abroach** pouring

Triumphant Tories and desponding Whigs°
Forget their feuds, and join to save their wigs.
Boxed in a chair° the beau impatient sits,
While spouts run clattering o'er the roof by fits,
And ever and anon with frightful din   *45*
The leather sounds; he trembles from within.
So when Troy chairmen bore the wooden steed,
Pregnant with Greeks impatient to be freed
(Those bully Greeks, who, as the moderns do,
Instead of paying chairmen, run them through),   *50*
Laocoön° struck the outside with his spear,
And each imprisoned hero quaked for fear.
      Now from all parts the swelling kennels° flow,
And bear their trophies with them as they go:
Filth of all hues and odors seem to tell   *55*
What street they sailed from, by their sight and smell.
They, as each torrent drives with rapid force,
From Smithfield° or St. Pulchre's shape their course,
And in huge confluence joined at Snow Hill ridge,
Fall from the conduit prone to Holborn Bridge.   *60*
Sweepings from butchers' stalls, dung, guts, and blood,
Drowned puppies, stinking sprats,° all drenched in mud,
Dead cats, and turnip tops, come tumbling down the flood.

—1710

---

41 Tories . . . Whigs rival political factions   **43 chair** sedan chair   **51 Laocoön** For his attempt to
warn the Trojans, he was crushed by sea serpents sent by Poseidon.   **53 kennels** storm drains
58 Smithfield site of London cattle exchange   **62 sprats** small fish

Alexander Pope (1688–1744) was a tiny man who was afflicted in childhood by a crippling disease. Pope was the dominant poet of eighteenth-century England, particularly excelling as a master of mock-epic satire in "The Rape of the Lock" and "The Dunciad." His translations of the Iliad *and the* Odyssey *made him famous and financially independent and remained the standard versions of Homer for almost two hundred years. "An Essay on Criticism," a long didactic poem modeled on Horace's* Ars Poetica, *remains the most complete statement of the neoclassical aesthetic.*

Alexander Pope

from An Essay on Criticism

But most by numbers judge a poet's song,
And smooth or rough with them is right or wrong.
In the bright Muse though thousand charms conspire,
Her voice is all these tuneful fools admire,
Who haunt Parnassus° but to please their ear,   5
Not mend their minds; as some to church repair,
Not for the doctrine, but the music there.
These equal syllables alone require,
Though oft the ear the open vowels tire,
While expletives° their feeble aid do join,   10
And ten low words oft creep in one dull line:
While they ring round the same unvaried chimes,
With sure returns of still expected rhymes;
Where'er you find "the cooling western breeze,"
In the next line, it "whispers through the trees";   15
If crystal streams "with pleasing murmurs creep,"
The reader's threatened (not in vain) with "sleep";
Then, at the last and only couplet fraught
With some unmeaning thing they call a thought,
A needless Alexandrine° ends the song   20
That, like a wounded snake, drags its slow length along.
Leave such to tune their own dull rhymes, and know
What's roundly smooth or languishingly slow;

---

5 Parnassus mountain of the Muses   **10 expletives** unnecessary filler words   **20 Alexandrine** line
of six iambic feet (as in the next line)

And praise the easy vigor of a line
Where Denham's strength and Waller's° sweetness join.   *25*
True ease in writing comes from art, not chance,
As those move easiest who have learned to dance.
'Tis not enough no harshness gives offense,
The sound must seem an echo to the sense.
Soft is the strain when Zephyr° gently blows,   *30*
And the smooth stream in smoother numbers flows;
But when loud surges lash the sounding shore,
The hoarse, rough verse should like the torrent roar.
When Ajax° strives some rock's vast weight to throw,
The line too labors, and the words move slow;   *35*
Not so when swift Camilla° scours the plain,
Flies o'er the unbending corn, and skims along the main.
Hear how Timotheus'° varied lays surprise,
And bid alternate passions fall and rise!
While at each change the son of Libyan Jove°   *40*
Now burns with glory, and then melts with love;
Now his fierce eyes with sparkling fury glow,
Now sighs steal out, and tears begin to flow:
Persians and Greeks like turns of nature found
And the world's victor stood subdued by sound!   *45*
The power of music all our hearts allow,
And what Timotheus was is Dryden now.
        Avoid extremes; and shun the fault of such
Who still are pleased too little or too much.
At every trifle scorn to take offense: *50*
That always shows great pride, or little sense.
Those heads, as stomachs, are not sure the best,
Which nauseate all, and nothing can digest.
Yet let not each gay turn thy rapture move;
For fools admire, but men of sense approve: *55*
As things seem large which we through mists descry,
Dullness is ever apt to magnify.

—1711

---

25 Denham's . . . Waller's earlier English poets praised by Pope   **30 Zephyr** the west wind
34 Ajax legendary strong man of the *Iliad*   **36 Camilla** messenger of the goddess Diana
38 Timotheus a legendary musician   **40 son of Libyan Jove** Alexander the Great

Ode on Solitude

Happy the man whose wish and care
    A few paternal acres bound,
Content to breathe his native air,
       In his own ground.

Whose herds with milk, whose fields with bread,   5
    Whose flocks supply him with attire,
Whose trees in summer yield him shade,
       In winter fire.

Blest, who can unconcernedly find
    Hours, days, and years slide soft away,   10
In health of body, peace of mind,
       Quiet by day,

Sound sleep by night; study and ease,
    Together mixed; sweet recreation;
And innocence, which most does please   15
       With meditation.

Thus let me live, unseen, unknown;
    Thus unlamented let me die;
Steal from the world, and not a stone
       Tell where I lie.   20

—1736

Thomas Gray (1716–1771) possesses a contemporary reputation that rests primarily on a single poem, but it remains one of the most often quoted in the whole English canon, and the quatrain stanza is often called "elegiac" in its honor. Gray lived almost all of his adult life at Cambridge University, where he was a professor of history and languages. He declined the poet laureateship of England in 1757.

Thomas Gray

Elegy Written in a Country Churchyard

The curfew tolls the knell of parting day,
    The lowing herd wind slowly o'er the lea,
The plowman homeward plods his weary way,
    And leaves the world to darkness and to me.

Now fades the glimmering landscape on the sight,   5
    And all the air a solemn stillness holds,
Save where the beetle wheels his droning flight,
    And drowsy tinklings lull the distant folds;

Save that from yonder ivy-mantled tower
    The moping owl does to the moon complain   10
Of such, as wandering near her secret bower,
    Molest her ancient solitary reign.

Beneath those rugged elms, that yew tree's shade,
    Where heaves the turf in many a moldering heap,
Each in his narrow cell forever laid,   15
    The rude° forefathers of the hamlet sleep.

The breezy call of incense-breathing morn,
    The swallow twittering from the straw-built shed,
The cock's shrill clarion, or the echoing horn,
    No more shall rouse them from their lowly bed.   20

For them no more the blazing hearth shall burn,
    Or busy housewife ply her evening care;

16 rude unlearned

No children run to lisp their sire's return,
    Or climb his knees the envied kiss to share.

Oft did the harvest to their sickle yield,   *25*
    Their furrow oft the stubborn glebe° has broke;
How jocund did they drive their team afield!
    How bowed the woods beneath their sturdy stroke!

Let not Ambition mock their useful toil,
    Their homely joys, and destiny obscure;   *30*
Nor Grandeur hear with a disdainful smile
    The short and simple annals of the poor.

The boast of heraldry, the pomp of power,
    And all that beauty, all that wealth e'er gave,
Awaits alike the inevitable hour.   *35*
    The paths of glory lead but to the grave.

Nor you, ye proud, impute to these the fault,
    If Memory o'er their tomb no trophies raise,
Where through the long-drawn aisle and fretted° vault
    The pealing anthem swells the note of praise.   *40*

Can storied urn or animated bust
    Back to its mansion call the fleeting breath?
Can Honor's voice provoke the silent dust,
    Or Flattery soothe the dull cold ear of Death?

Perhaps in this neglected spot is laid   *45*
    Some heart once pregnant with celestial fire;
Hands that the rod of empire might have swayed,
    Or waked to ecstasy the living lyre.

But Knowledge to their eyes her ample page
    Rich with the spoils of time did ne'er unroll;   *50*
Chill Penury repressed their noble rage,
    And froze the genial current of the soul.

Full many a gem of purest ray serene,
    The dark unfathomed caves of ocean bear:

26 glebe plot of farmland   **39 fretted** carved

Full many a flower is born to blush unseen,   55
    And waste its sweetness on the desert air.

Some village Hampden,° that with dauntless breast
    The little tyrant of his field withstood;
Some mute inglorious Milton here may rest,
    Some Cromwell° guiltless of his country's blood.   60

The applause of listening senates to command,
    The threats of pain and ruin to despise,
To scatter plenty o'er a smiling land,
    And read their history in a nation's eyes,

Their lot forbade: nor circumscribed alone   65
    Their growing virtues, but their crimes confined;
Forbade to wade through slaughter to a throne,
    And shut the gates of mercy on mankind,

The struggling pangs of conscious truth to hide,
    To quench the blushes of ingenuous shame,   70
Or heap the shrine of Luxury and Pride
    With incense kindled at the Muse's flame.

Far from the madding° crowd's ignoble strife,
    Their sober wishes never learned to stray;
Along the cool sequestered vale of life   75
    They kept the noiseless tenor of their way.

Yet even these bones from insult to protect
    Some frail memorial still erected nigh,
With uncouth rhymes and shapeless sculpture decked,
    Implores the passing tribute of a sigh.   80

Their name, their years, spelt by the unlettered Muse,
    The place of fame and elegy supply:
And many a holy text around she strews,
    That teach the rustic moralist to die.

57 Hampden hero of the English Civil War   **60 Cromwell** Lord Protector of England from 1653 to 1658   **73 madding** frenzied

For who to dumb Forgetfulness a prey,   85
    This pleasing anxious being e'er resigned,
Left the warm precincts of the cheerful day,
    Nor cast one longing lingering look behind?

On some fond breast the parting soul relies,
    Some pious drops the closing eye requires;   90
Even from the tomb the voice of Nature cries,
    Even in our ashes live their wonted fires.

For thee, who mindful of the unhonored dead
    Dost in these lines their artless tale relate;
If chance, by lonely contemplation led,   95
    Some kindred spirit shall inquire thy fate,

Haply some hoary°-headed swain° may say,
    "Oft have we seen him at the peep of dawn
Brushing with hasty steps the dews away
    To meet the sun upon the upland lawn.   100

"There at the foot of yonder nodding beech
    That wreathes its old fantastic roots so high,
His listless length at noontide would he stretch,
    And pore upon the brook that babbles by.

"Hard by yon wood, now smiling as in scorn,   105
    Muttering his wayward fancies he would rove,
Now drooping, woeful wan, like one forlorn,
    Or crazed with care, or crossed in hopeless love.

"One morn I missed him on the customed hill,
    Along the heath and near his favorite tree;   110
Another came; nor yet beside the rill,
    Nor up the lawn, nor at the wood was he;

"The next with dirges due in sad array
    Slow through the churchway path we saw him borne.
Approach and read (for thou canst read) the lay,   115
    Graved on the stone beneath yon aged thorn."

97 hoary frosty, white   **swain** peasant

The Epitaph

Here rests his head upon the lap of Earth
    A youth to Fortune and to Fame unknown.
Fair Science frowned not on his humble birth,
    And Melancholy marked him for her own.   120

Large was his bounty, and his soul sincere,
    Heaven did a recompense as largely send:
He gave to Misery all he had, a tear,
    He gained from Heaven ('twas all he wished) a friend.

No farther seek his merits to disclose,   125
    Or draw his frailties from their dread abode
(There they alike in trembling hope repose),
    The bosom of his Father and his God.

          —1751

Christopher Smart (1722–1771) was educated, like Thomas Gray, at Cambridge, but fell victim to religious mania and insanity yet continued to write throughout his life. Jubilate Agno ("Rejoice in the Lamb") is a long meditation on the immanence of God, even in such insignificant forms as Gray's cat Jeoffry. The poem is one of the earliest examples of free verse in English.

Christopher Smart
from Jubilate Agno

For I will consider my Cat Jeoffry.
For he is the servant of the Living God, duly and daily serving him.
For at the first glance of the glory of God in the East he worships in
    his way.
For is this done by wreathing his body seven times round with
    elegant quickness.
For then he leaps up to catch the musk,° which is the blessing of
    God upon his prayer.   5
For he rolls upon prank to work it in.

5 musk scented object or toy

For having done duty and received blessing he begins to
    consider himself.

For this he performs in ten degrees.

For first he looks upon his forepaws to see if they are clean.

For secondly he kicks up behind to clear away there.   *10*

For thirdly he works it upon stretch with the forepaws
    extended.

For fourthly he sharpens his paws by wood.

For fifthly he washes himself.

For sixthly he rolls upon wash.

For seventhly he fleas himself, that he may not be
    interrupted upon the beat.°   *15*

For eighthly he rubs himself against a post.

For ninthly he looks up for his instructions.

For tenthly he goes in quest of food.

For having considered God and himself he will consider his
    neighbor.

For if he meets another cat he will kiss her in kindness.   *20*

For when he takes his prey he plays with it to give it a chance.

For one mouse in seven escapes by his dallying.

For when his day's work is done his business more properly
    begins.

For he keeps the Lord's watch in the night against the
    adversary.°

For he counteracts the powers of darkness by his electrical
    skin and glaring eyes.   *25*

For he counteracts the Devil, who is death, by brisking about
    the life.

For in his morning orisons he loves the sun and the sun loves
    him.

For he is of the tribe of Tiger.

For the Cherub Cat is a term° of the Angel Tiger.

For he has the subtlety and hissing of a serpent, which in
    goodness he suppresses.   *30*

For he will not do destruction if he is well-fed, neither will he
    spit without provocation.

---

15 beat accustomed path   **24 adversary** i.e., Satan   **29 term** immature version

For he purrs in thankfulness when God tells him he's a good Cat.

For he is an instrument for the children to learn benevolence
upon.

For every house is incomplete without him, and a blessing is
lacking in the spirit.

For the Lord commanded Moses concerning the cats at the
departure of the Children of Israel from Egypt.   35

For every family had one cat at least in the bag.

For the English Cats are the best in Europe.

For he is the cleanest in the use of his forepaws of any quadruped.

For the dexterity of his defense is an instance of the love of
God to him exceedingly.

For he is the quickest to his mark of any creature.   40

For he is tenacious of his point.

For he is a mixture of gravity and waggery.

For he knows that God is his Saviour.

For there is nothing sweeter than his peace when at rest.

For there is nothing brisker than his life when in motion.   45

For he is of the Lord's poor, and so indeed is he called by
benevolence perpetually—Poor Jeoffry! poor Jeoffry! the
rat has bit thy throat.

For I bless the name of the Lord Jesus that Jeoffry is better.

For the divine spirit comes about his body to sustain it in
complete cat.

For his tongue is exceeding pure so that it has in purity what
it wants in music.

For he is docile and can learn certain things.   50

For he can sit up with gravity, which is patience upon
approbation.

For he can fetch and carry, which is patience in employment.

For he can jump over a stick, which is patience upon proof
positive.

For he can spraggle upon waggle at the word of command.

For he can jump from an eminence into his master's bosom.   55

For he can catch the cork and toss it again.

For he is hated by the hypocrite and miser.

For the former is afraid of detection.

For the latter refuses the charge.

For he camels his back to bear the first notion of business. 60
For he is good to think on, if a man would express himself
    neatly.
For he made a great figure in Egypt for his signal services.
For he killed the Icneumon° rat, very pernicious by land.
For his ears are so acute that they sting again.
For from this proceeds the passing quickness of his attention. 65
For by stroking of him I have found out electricity.
For I perceived God's light about him both wax and fire.
For the electrical fire is the spiritual substance which God
    sends from heaven to sustain the bodies both of man and
    beast.
For God has blessed him in the variety of his movements.
For, though he cannot fly, he is an excellent clamberer. 70
For his motions upon the face of the earth are more than
    any other quadruped.
For he can tread to all the measures upon the music.
For he can swim for life.
For he can creep.

                           —*ca. 1760*

Philip Freneau (1752–1832) *was a friend and political ally of Thomas Jefferson. Freneau was a popular journalist and writer whose patriotic verse earned him the moniker "Poet of the Revolution." This reputation has unfortunately overshadowed his considerable talents as a lyric poet whose fine eye for nature prefigures the next generation of American romantics.*

Philip Freneau
The Wild Honey Suckle

Fair flower, that dost so comely grow,
Hid in this silent, dull retreat,
Untouched thy honied blossoms blow,
Unseen thy little branches greet:

---

63 Icneumon resembling the mongoose *(Herpestes ichneumon)*

No roving foot shall crush thee here,   5
No busy hand provoke a tear.°

By Nature's self in white arrayed,
She bade thee shun the vulgar° eye,
And planted here the guardian shade,
And sent soft waters murmuring by;   10
    Thus quietly thy summer goes,
    Thy days declining to repose.

Smit with those charms, that must decay,
I grieve to see your future doom;
They died—nor were those flowers more gay,   15
The flowers that did in Eden bloom;
    Unpitying frosts, and Autumn's power
    Shall leave no vestige of this flower.

From morning suns and evening dews
At first thy little being came: 20
If nothing once, you nothing lose,
For when you die you are the same;
    The space between, is but an hour,
    The frail duration of a flower.

                        —*1788*

---

6 provoke a tear i.e., the nectar of the flower   **8 vulgar** common

William Blake (1757–1827) was a poet, painter, engraver, and visionary. Blake does not fit easily into any single category, although his political sympathies link him to the later romantic poets. His first book, Poetical Sketches, *attracted little attention, but his mature works, starting with* Songs of Innocence *and* Songs of Experience, *combine poetry with his own remarkable illustrations and are unique in English literature. Thought mad by many in his own day, Blake anticipated many future directions of both literature and modern psychology.*

William Blake
The Chimney Sweeper

When my mother died I was very young,
And my father sold me while yet my tongue
Could scarcely cry "'weep! 'weep! 'weep! 'weep!"
So your chimneys I sweep & in soot I sleep.

There's little Tom Dacre, who cried when his head   5
That curl'd like a lamb's back, was shav'd, so I said,
"Hush, Tom! never mind it, for when your head's bare,
You know that the soot cannot spoil your white hair."

And so he was quiet, & that very night,
As Tom was a-sleeping, he had such a sight!   10
That thousands of sweepers, Dick, Joe, Ned, & Jack,
Were all of them lock'd up in coffins of black;

And by came an Angel who had a bright key,
And he open'd the coffins & set them all free;
Then down a green plain, leaping, laughing, they run,   15
And wash in a river and shine in the Sun.

Then naked & white, all their bags left behind,
They rise upon clouds, and sport in the wind.
And the Angel told Tom, if he'd be a good boy,
He'd have God for his father, & never want joy.   20

And so Tom awoke; and we rose in the dark,
And got with our bags & our brushes to work.
Tho' the morning was cold, Tom was happy & warm;
So if all do their duty, they need not fear harm.

—1789

The Little Black° Boy

My mother bore me in the southern wild,
And I am black, but O! my soul is white;
White as an angel is the English child:
But I am black as if bereav'd of light.

My mother taught me underneath a tree,   5
And sitting down before the heat of day,
She took me on her lap and kissèd me,
And pointing to the east, began to say:

"Look on the rising sun: there God does live,
And gives his light, and gives his heat away;   10
And flowers and trees and beasts and men receive
Comfort in morning, joy in the noon day.

"And we are put on earth a little space,
That we may learn to bear the beams of love,
And these black bodies and this sun-burnt face   15
Is but a cloud, and like a shady grove.

"For when our souls have learn'd the heat to bear,
The cloud will vanish; we shall hear his voice,
Saying: 'Come out from the grove, my love & care,
And round my golden tent like lambs rejoice.'"   20

Thus did my mother say, and kissèd me;
And thus I say to little English boy:
When I from black and he from white cloud free,
And round the tent of God like lambs we joy,

I'll shade him from the heat till he can bear   25
To lean in joy upon our father's knee:
And then I'll stand and stroke his silver hair,
And be like him, and he will then love me.

—*1789*

Black probably Indian rather than African

A Poison Tree

I was angry with my friend:
I told my wrath, my wrath did end.
I was angry with my foe:
I told it not, my wrath did grow.

And I water'd it in fears,   5
Night & morning with my tears;
And I sunnèd it with smiles,
And with soft deceitful wiles.

And it grew both day and night,
Till it bore an apple bright;   10
And my foe beheld it shine,
And he knew that it was mine,

And into my garden stole
When the night had veil'd the pole;
In the morning glad I see   15
My foe outstretch'd beneath the tree.

—*1794*

The Tyger

Tyger! Tyger! burning bright
In the forests of the night,
What immortal hand or eye
Could frame thy fearful symmetry?

In what distant deeps or skies   5
Burnt the fire of thine eyes?
On what wings dare he aspire?
What the hand, dare seize the fire?

And what shoulder, & what art,
Could twist the sinews of thy heart?   10
And when thy heart began to beat,
What dread hand? & what dread feet?

What the hammer? what the chain?
In what furnace was thy brain?
What the anvil? what dread grasp   15
Dare its deadly terrors clasp?

When the stars threw down their spears,
And water'd heaven with their tears,
Did he smile his work to see?
Did he who made the Lamb make thee?   20

Tyger! Tyger! burning bright
In the forests of the night,
What immortal hand or eye,
Dare frame thy fearful symmetry?

—1794

Robert Burns (1759–1796) was a Scot known in his day as the "Ploughman Poet" and was one of the first English poets to put dialect to serious literary purpose. Chiefly known for his realistic depictions of peasant life, he was also an important lyric poet who prefigured many of the later concerns of the romantic era.

Robert Burns

A Red, Red Rose

O my luve's like a red, red rose,
　　That's newly sprung in June;
O my luve's like the melodie
　　That's sweetly played in tune.

As fair art thou, my bonnie lass,   5
　　So deep in luve am I;
And I will luve thee still, my dear,
　　Till a' the seas gang° dry.

Till a' the seas gang dry, my dear,
　　And the rocks melt wi' the sun;   10

8 gang go

O I will luve thee still, my dear,
    While the sands o' life shall run.

And fare thee weel, my only luve,
    And fare thee weel awhile!
And I will come again, my luve   *15*
    Though it were ten thousand mile.

—1791

John Barleycorn

There were three kings into the east,
Three kings both great and high;
And they has sworn a solemn oath
John Barleycorn should die.

They took a plough and plough'd him down,   *5*
Put clods upon his head;
And they hae sworn a solemn oath
John Barleycorn was dead.

But the cheerful spring came kindly on,
And showers began to fall;   *10*
John Barleycorn got up again,
And sore surprised them all.

The sultry suns of summer came,
And he grew thick and strong;
His head well armed wi' point'd spears,   *15*
That no one should him wrong.

The sober autumn enter'd mild,
When he grew wan and pale;
His bending joints and drooping head
Show'd he began to fail.   *20*

His colour sicken'd more and more
He faded into age;

And then his enemies began
To show their deadly rage.

They've ta'en a weapon long and sharp,   25
And cut him by the knee;
Then tied him fast upon a cart,
Like a rogue for forgery.

They laid him down upon his back,
And cudgell'd him full sore;   30
They hung him up before the storm,
And turn'd him o'er and o'er.

They fill'd up a darksome pit
With water to the brim;
They heaved in John Barleycorn,   35
There let him sink or swim.

They laid him out upon the floor,
To work him further woe;
And still as signs of life appear'd,
They toss'd him to and fro.   40

They wasted o'er a scorching flame
The marrow of his bones;
But a miller used him worst of all
He crushed him 'tween two stones.

And they has ta'en his very heart's blood,   45
And drank it round and round,
And still the more and more they drank,
Their joy did more abound.

John Barleycorn was a hero bold,
Of noble enterprise;   50
For if you do but taste his blood,
'Twill make your courage rise.

'Twill make a man forget his woe;
'Twill heighten all his joy;

'Twill make the widow's heart to sing,   55
Though the tear were in her eye.

Then let us toast John Barleycorn,
Each man a glass in hand;
And may his great posterity
Ne'er fail in old Scotland!   60

—1786

William Wordsworth (1770–1850) *is generally considered the first of the
English romantics.* Lyrical Ballads, *the 1798 volume that introduced both his poetry and Samuel Taylor Coleridge's to a wide readership, remains one of the most influential collections of poetry ever published. Wordsworth's preface to the revised edition of 1800 contains the famous Romantic formulation of poetry as the
"spontaneous overflow of powerful feelings," a theory exemplified in short lyrics like
"I Wandered Lonely as a Cloud" and in longer meditative pieces like "Tintern
Abbey" (the title by which "Lines" is commonly known). Wordsworth served as poet
laureate from 1843 to his death.*

William Wordsworth
I Wandered Lonely as a Cloud

I wandered lonely as a cloud
That floats on high o'er vales and hills,
When all at once I saw a crowd,
A host, of golden daffodils;
Beside the lake, beneath the trees,   5
Fluttering and dancing in the breeze.

Continuous as the stars that shine
And twinkle on the milky way,
They stretched in never-ending line
Along the margin of a bay: 10
Ten thousand saw I at a glance,
Tossing their heads in sprightly dance.

The waves beside them danced, but they
Outdid the sparkling waves in glee;
A poet could not but be gay,   15
In such a jocund company;
I gazed—and gazed—but little thought
What wealth the show to me had brought:

For oft, when on my couch I lie
In vacant or in pensive mood,   20
They flash upon that inward eye
Which is the bliss of solitude;
And then my heart with pleasure fills,
And dances with the daffodils.

—1807

It Is a Beauteous Evening

It is a beauteous evening, calm and free,
The holy time is quiet as a Nun
Breathless with adoration; the broad sun
Is sinking down in its tranquillity;
The gentleness of heaven broods o'er the Sea: 5
Listen! the mighty Being is awake,
And doth with his eternal motion make
A sound like thunder—everlastingly.
Dear Child! dear Girl!° that walkest with me here,
If thou appear untouched by solemn thought,   10
Thy nature is not therefore less divine:
Thou liest in Abraham's bosom° all the year,
And worship'st at the Temple's inner shrine,
God being with thee when we know it not.

—1807

---

9 Dear Child! dear Girl! the poet's daughter   **12 Abraham's bosom** where souls rest in Heaven

Lines

*Composed a Few Miles Above Tintern Abbey on Revisiting the Banks of
the Wye During a Tour. July 13, 1798*

    Five years have passed; five summers, with the length
Of five long winters! and again I hear
These waters, rolling from their mountain-springs
With a sweet inland murmur.—Once again
Do I behold these steep and lofty cliffs,   5
That on a wild secluded scene impress
Thoughts of more deep seclusion; and connect
The landscape with the quiet of the sky.
The day is come when I again repose
Here, under this dark sycamore, and view   10
These plots of cottage ground, these orchard tufts,
Which at this season, with their unripe fruits,
Are clad in one green hue, and lose themselves
'Mid groves and copses. Once again I see
These hedgerows, hardly hedgerows, little lines   15
Of sportive wood run wild; these pastoral farms,
Green to the very door; and wreaths of smoke
Sent up, in silence, from among the trees!
With some uncertain notice, as might seem
Of vagrant dwellers in the houseless woods,   20
Or of some Hermit's cave, where by his fire
The Hermit sits alone.

                      These beauteous forms,
Through a long absence, have not been to me
As is a landscape to a blind man's eye;
But oft, in lonely rooms, and 'mid the din   25
Of towns and cities, I have owed to them,
In hours of weariness, sensations sweet,
Felt in the blood, and felt along the heart;
And passing even into my purer mind,
With tranquil restoration:—feelings too   30
Of unremembered pleasure; such, perhaps,
As have no slight or trivial influence

On that best portion of a good man's life,
His little, nameless, unremembered, acts
Of kindness and of love. Nor less, I trust,   35
To them I may have owed another gift,
Of aspect more sublime; that blessed mood,
In which the burthen° of the mystery,
In which the heavy and the weary weight
Of all this unintelligible world,   40
Is lightened—that serene and blessed mood,
In which the affections gently lead us on—
Until, the breath of this corporeal frame
And even the motion of our human blood
Almost suspended, we are laid asleep   45
In body, and become a living soul;
While with an eye made quiet by the power
Of harmony, and the deep power of joy,
We see into the life of things.

                                      If this
Be but a vain belief, yet, oh! how oft—   50
In darkness and amid the many shapes
Of joyless daylight; when the fretful stir
Unprofitable, and the fever of the world,
Have hung upon the beatings of my heart—
How oft, in spirit, have I turned to thee,   55
O sylvan Wye! Thou wanderer through the woods,
How often has my spirit turned to thee!

      And now, with gleams of half-extinguished thought,
With many recognitions dim and faint,
And somewhat of a sad perplexity,   60
The picture of the mind revives again:
While here I stand, not only with the sense
Of present pleasure, but with pleasing thoughts
That in this moment there is life and food
For future years. And so I dare to hope,   65
Though changed, no doubt, from what I was when first

38 burthen burden

I came among these hills; when like a roe
I bounded o'er the mountains, by the sides
Of the deep rivers, and the lonely streams,
Wherever nature led—more like a man   70
Flying from something that he dreads than one
Who sought the thing he loved. For nature then
(The coarser pleasures of my boyish days,
And their glad animal movements all gone by)
To me was all in all.—I cannot paint   75
What then I was. The sounding cataract
Haunted me like a passion: the tall rock,
The mountain, and the deep and gloomy wood,
Their colours and their forms, were then to me
An appetite: a feeling and a love,   80
That had no need of a remoter charm,
By thought supplied, or any interest
Unborrowed from the eye.—That time is past,
And all its aching joys are now no more,
And all its dizzy raptures. Not for this   85
Faint I, nor mourn nor murmur: other gifts
Have followed; for such loss, I would believe,
Abundant recompense. For I have learned
To look on nature, not as in the hour
Of thoughtless youth; but hearing oftentimes   90
The still, sad music of humanity,
Nor harsh nor grating, though of ample power
To chasten and subdue. And I have felt
A presence that disturbs me with the joy
Of elevated thoughts; a sense sublime   95
Of something far more deeply interfused,
Whose dwelling is the light of setting suns,
And the round ocean and the living air,
And the blue sky, and in the mind of man:
A motion and a spirit, that impels   100
All thinking things, all objects of all thought,
And rolls through all things. Therefore am I still
A lover of the meadows and the woods,
And mountains; and of all that we behold

From this green earth; of all the mighty world   *105*
Of eye, and ear—both what they half create,
And what perceive; well pleased to recognize
In nature and the language of the sense
The anchor of my purest thoughts, the nurse,
The guide, the guardian of my heart, and soul   *110*
Of all my moral being.

                        Nor, perchance,
If I were not thus taught, should I the more
Suffer my genial spirits° to decay:
For thou art with me, here, upon the banks
Of this fair river; thou, my dearest Friend,°   *115*
My dear, dear Friend; and in thy voice I catch
The language of my former heart, and read
My former pleasures in the shooting lights
Of thy wild eyes. Oh! yet a little while
May I behold in thee what I was once,   *120*
My dear, dear Sister! And this prayer I make,
Knowing that Nature never did betray
The heart that loved her; 'tis her privilege,
Through all the years of this our life, to lead
From joy to joy: for she can so inform   *125*
The mind that is within us, so impress
With quietness and beauty, and so feed
With lofty thoughts, that neither evil tongues,
Rash judgments, nor the sneers of selfish men,
Nor greetings where no kindness is, nor all   *130*
The dreary intercourse of daily life,
Shall e'er prevail against us, or disturb
Our cheerful faith, that all which we behold
Is full of blessings. Therefore let the moon
Shine on thee in thy solitary walk;   *135*
And let the misty mountain winds be free
To blow against thee: and, in after years,
When these wild ecstasies shall be matured

113 genial spirits natural abilities   **115 Friend** the poet's sister Dorothy (1771–1855)

Into a sober pleasure; when thy mind
Shall be a mansion for all lovely forms,   140
Thy memory be as a dwelling place
For all sweet sounds and harmonies; oh! then,
If solitude, or fear, or pain, or grief,
Should be thy portion, with what healing thoughts
Of tender joy wilt thou remember me,   145
And these my exhortations! Nor, perchance—
If I should be, where I no more can hear
Thy voice, nor catch from thy wild eyes these gleams
Of past existence—wilt thou then forget
That on the banks of this delightful stream   150
We stood together; and that I, so long
A worshipper of Nature, hither came,
Unwearied in that service: rather say
With warmer love,—oh! with far deeper zeal
Of holier love. Nor wilt thou then forget,   155
That after many wanderings, many years
Of absence, these steep woods and lofty cliffs,
And this green pastoral landscape, were to me
More dear, both for themselves and for thy sake!

—*1798*

Nuns Fret Not at Their Convent's Narrow Room

Nuns fret not at their convent's narrow room;
And hermits are contented with their cells;
And students with their pensive citadels;
Maids at the wheel, the weaver at his loom,
Sit blithe and happy; bees that soar for bloom,   5
High as the highest Peak of Furness-fells,°
Will murmur by the hour in foxglove bells:
In truth the prison, into which we doom
Ourselves, no prison is: and hence for me,

6 **Furness-fells** mountains located in the English Lake District

In sundry moods, 'twas pastime to be bound   *10*
Within the Sonnet's scanty plot of ground;
Pleased if some Souls (for such there needs must be)
Who have felt the weight of too much liberty,
Should find brief solace there, as I have found.

—*1807*

Ode

*Intimations of Immortality
from Recollections of Early Childhood*

The Child is Father of the Man;
And I could wish my days to be
Bound each to each by natural piety.°

1

There was a time when meadow, grove, and stream,
The earth, and every common sight,
     To me did seem
     Appareled in celestial light,
The glory and the freshness of a dream.   *5*
It is not now as it hath been of yore;—
     Turn wheresoe'er I may,
     By night or day,
The things which I have seen I now can see no more.

2

     The Rainbow comes and goes,   *10*
     And lovely is the Rose,
     The Moon doth with delight
Look round her when the heavens are bare,
     Waters on a starry night
     Are beautiful and fair;   *15*
   The sunshine is a glorious birth;
   But yet I know, where'er I go,
That there hath past away a glory from the earth.

The Child . . . natural piety last three lines of the poet's "My Heart Leaps Up"

3

Now, while the birds thus sing a joyous song,
    And while the young lambs bound   *20*
       As to the tabor's° sound,
To me alone there came a thought of grief:
A timely utterance gave that thought relief,
       And I again am strong:
The cataracts blow their trumpets from the steep;   *25*
No more shall grief of mine the season wrong;
I hear the Echoes through the mountains throng,
The Winds come to me from the fields of sleep,
       And all the earth is gay;
         Land and sea   *30*
       Give themselves up to jollity,
       And with the heart of May
       Doth every Beast keep holiday;—
        Thou Child of Joy,
Shout round me, let me hear thy shouts, thou happy
    Shepherd-boy!   *35*

4

Ye blessèd Creatures, I have heard the call
    Ye to each other make; I see
The heavens laugh with you in your jubilee;
    My heart is at your festival,   *40*
    My head hath its coronal,°
The fulness of your bliss, I feel—I feel it all.
       Oh evil day! if I were sullen
       While Earth herself is adorning,
        This sweet May-morning,   *45*
       And the Children are culling
        On every side,
       In a thousand valleys far and wide,
       Fresh flowers; while the sun shines warm,
And the Babe leaps up on his Mother's arm:—   *50*

---

21 tabor's small drum's   **41 coronal** floral crown

I hear, I hear, with joy I hear!
—But there's a Tree, of many, one,
A single Field which I have looked upon,
Both of them speak of something that is gone:
      The Pansy at my feet   55
      Doth the same tale repeat:
Whither is fled the visionary gleam?
Where is it now, the glory and the dream?

5

Our birth is but a sleep and a forgetting:
The Soul that rises with us, our life's Star,   60
      Hath had elsewhere its setting,
         And cometh from afar:
      Not in entire forgetfulness,
      And not in utter nakedness,
But trailing clouds of glory do we come   65
      From God, who is our home:
Heaven lies about us in our infancy!
Shades of the prison-house begin to close
      Upon the growing Boy,
But he beholds the light, and whence it flows,   70
      He sees it in his joy;
The Youth, who daily farther from the east
      Must travel, still is Nature's Priest,
      And by the vision splendid
      Is on his way attended;   75
At length the Man perceives it die away,
And fade into the light of common day.

6

Earth fills her lap with pleasures of her own;
Yearnings she hath in her own natural kind,
And, even with something of a Mother's mind,   80
      And no unworthy aim,
      The homely Nurse doth all she can
To make her Foster-child, her Inmate Man,
      Forget the glories he hath known,

7

Behold the Child among his new-born blisses,
A six years' Darling of a pigmy size!
See where 'mid work of his own hand he lies,
Fretted° by sallies of his mother's kisses,
With light upon him from his father's eyes!   90
See, at his feet, some little plan or chart,
Some fragment from his dream of human life,
Shaped by himself with newly-learnèd art;
     A wedding or a festival,
     A mourning or a funeral;   95
       And this hath now his heart,
     And unto this he frames his song:
     Then will he fit his tongue
To dialogues of business, love, or strife;
     But it will not be long   100
     Ere this be thrown aside,
     And with new joy and pride
The little Actor cons another part;
Filling from time to time his "humorous stage"°
With all the Persons, down to palsied Age,   105
That Life brings with her in her equipage;
     As if his whole vocation
     Were endless imitation.

8

Thou whose exterior semblance doth belie
     Thy Soul's immensity;   110
Thou best Philosopher, who yet dost keep
Thy heritage, thou Eye among the blind,
That, deaf and silent, read'st the eternal deep,
Haunted for ever by the eternal mind,—
     Mighty Prophet! Seer blest!   115
     On whom those truths do rest,
Which we are toiling all our lives to find,
In darkness lost, the darkness of the grave;

---

89 fretted annoyed or marked   **104 "humorous stage"** phrase from poet Samuel Daniel
(1563–1619)

Thou, over whom thy Immortality
Broods like the Day, a Master o'er a Slave,   *120*
A Presence which is not to be put by;
Thou little Child, yet glorious in the might
Of heaven-born freedom on thy being's height,
Why with such earnest pains dost thou provoke
The years to bring the inevitable yoke,   *125*
Thus blindly with thy blessedness at strife?
Full soon thy Soul shall have her earthly freight,
And custom lie upon thee with a weight,
Heavy as frost, and deep almost as life!

    9

      O joy! that in our embers   *130*
      Is something that doth live,
      That nature yet remembers
        What was so fugitive!
The thought of our past years in me doth breed
Perpetual benediction: not indeed   *135*
For that which is most worthy to be blest;
Delight and liberty, the simple creed
Of Childhood, whether busy or at rest,
With new-fledged hope still fluttering in his breast:—
      Not for these I raise   *140*
      The song of thanks and praise;
      But for those obstinate questionings
      Of sense and outward things,
      Fallings from us, vanishings;
      Blank misgivings of a Creature   *145*
Moving about in worlds not realized,
High instincts before which our mortal Nature
Did tremble like a guilty Thing surprised:
      But for those first affections,
      Those shadowy recollections,   *150*
      Which, be they what they may,
Are yet the fountain light of all our day,
Are yet a master light of all our seeing;
      Uphold us, cherish, and have power to make
Our noisy years seem moments in the being   *155*

Of the eternal Silence: truths that wake,
      To perish never;
Which neither listlessness, nor mad endeavour,
      Nor Man nor Boy,
Nor all that is at enmity with joy,   *160*
Can utterly abolish or destroy!
   Hence in a season of calm weather
      Though inland far we be,
Our Souls have sight of that immortal sea
      Which brought us hither,   *165*
    Can in a moment travel thither,
And see the Children sport upon the shore,
And hear the mighty waters rolling evermore.

    10

Then sing, ye Birds, sing, sing a joyous song!
      And let the young Lambs bound   *170*
      As to the tabor's sound!
We in thought will join your throng,
      Ye that pipe and ye that play,
      Ye that through your hearts to-day
      Feel the gladness of the May!   *175*
What though the radiance which was once so bright
Be now for ever taken from my sight,
      Though nothing can bring back the hour
Of splendour in the grass, of glory in the flower;
      We will grieve not, rather find   *180*
      Strength in what remains behind;
      In the primal sympathy
      Which having been must ever be;
      In the soothing thoughts that spring
      Out of human suffering;   *185*
      In the faith that looks through death,
In years that bring the philosophic mind.

    11

And O, ye Fountains, Meadows, Hills, and Groves,
Forbode not any severing of our loves!

Yet in my heart of hearts I feel your might;   *190*
I only have relinquished one delight
To live beneath your more habitual sway.
I love the Brooks which down their channels fret,
Even more than when I tripped lightly as they;
The innocent brightness of a new-born Day   *195*
      Is lovely yet;
The Clouds that gather round the setting sun
Do take a sober colouring from an eye
That hath kept watch o'er man's mortality;
Another race hath been, and other palms are won.   *200*
Thanks to the human heart by which we live,
Thanks to its tenderness, its joys, and fears,
To me the meanest° flower that blows can give
Thoughts that do often lie too deep for tears.

                                                     —*1807*

Samuel Taylor Coleridge (1772–1834), inspired but erratic, did his best work, like Wordsworth, during the great first decade of their friendship, the period that produced Lyrical Ballads. *Coleridge's later life is a tragic tale of financial and marital problems, unfinished projects, and a ruinous addiction to opium. A brilliant critic, Coleridge lectured on Shakespeare and other writers and wrote the* Biographia Literaria, *perhaps the greatest literary autobiography ever written.*

Samuel Taylor Coleridge
Frost at Midnight

    The Frost performs its secret ministry,
Unhelped by any wind. The owlet's cry
Came loud—and hark, again! loud as before.
The inmates of my cottage, all at rest,
Have left me to that solitude, which suits   *5*
Abstruser musings: save that at my side
My cradled infant° slumbers peacefully.

203 meanest least significant
7 My cradled infant the poet's son Hartley (1796–1849)

'Tis calm indeed! so calm, that it disturbs
And vexes meditation, with its strange
And extreme silentness. Sea, hill, and wood,   *10*
This populous village! Sea, and hill, and wood,
With all the numberless goings-on of life,
Inaudible as dreams! the thin blue flame
Lies on my low-burnt fire, and quivers not;
Only that film,° which fluttered on the grate,   *15*
Still flutters there, the sole unquiet thing.
Methinks its motion in this hush of nature
Gives it dim sympathies with me who live,
Making it a companionable form,
Whose puny flaps and freaks the idling Spirit   *20*
By its own moods interprets, everywhere
Echo or mirror seeking of itself,
And makes a toy of Thought.

                But O! how oft,
How oft, at school, with most believing mind,
Presageful,° have I gazed upon the bars,   *25*
To watch that fluttering *stranger!* and as oft
With unclosed lids, already had I dreamt
Of my sweet birthplace, and the old church tower,
Whose bells, the poor man's only music, rang
From morn to evening, all the hot Fair-day,   *30*
So sweetly, that they stirred and haunted me
With a wild pleasure, falling on mine ear
Most like articulate sounds of things to come!
So gazed I, till the soothing things, I dreamt,
Lulled me to sleep, and sleep prolonged my dreams!   *35*
And so I brooded all the following morn,
Awed by the stern preceptor's° face, mine eye
Fixed with mock study on my swimming book:
Save if the door half opened, and I snatched
A hasty glance, and still my heart leaped up,   *40*
For still I hoped to see the *stranger's* face,

---

15 film a piece of ash   **25 Presageful** with hints of the future   **37 preceptor** teacher

Townsman, or aunt, or sister more beloved,
My playmate when we both were clothed alike!

   Dear Babe, that sleepest cradled by my side,
Whose gentle breathings, heard in this deep calm,   45
Fill up the interspersèd vacancies
And momentary pauses of the thought!
My babe so beautiful! it thrills my heart
With tender gladness, thus to look at thee,
And think that thou shalt learn far other lore,   50
And in far other scenes! For I was reared
In the great city, pent 'mid cloisters dim,
And saw nought lovely but the sky and stars.
But *thou*, my babe! shalt wander like a breeze
By lakes and sandy shores, beneath the crags   55
Of ancient mountain, and beneath the clouds,
Which image in their bulk both lakes and shores
And mountain crags: so shalt thou see and hear
The lovely shapes and sounds intelligible
Of that eternal language, which thy God   60
Utters, who from eternity doth teach
Himself in all, and all things in himself.
Great universal Teacher! he shall mold
Thy spirit, and by giving make it ask.

   Therefore all seasons shall be sweet to thee,   65
Whether the summer clothe the general earth
With greenness, or the redbreast sit and sing
Betwixt the tufts of snow on the bare branch
Of mossy apple tree, while the nigh thatch
Smokes in the sun-thaw; whether the eave-drops fall   70
Heard only in the trances of the blast,
Or if the secret ministry of frost
Shall hang them up in silent icicles,
Quietly shining to the quiet Moon.

—1798

Kubla Khan°

<small>OR A VISION IN A DREAM,° A FRAGMENT</small>

In Xanadu did Kubla Khan
A stately pleasure-dome decree:
Where Alph, the sacred river, ran
Through caverns measureless to man
    Down to a sunless sea.   5
So twice five miles of fertile ground
With walls and towers were girdled round:
And there were gardens bright with sinuous rills,
Where blossomed many an incense-bearing tree;
And here were forests ancient as the hills,   10
Enfolding sunny spots of greenery.

But oh! that deep romantic chasm which slanted
Down the green hill athwart a cedarn cover!
A savage place! as holy and enchanted
As e'er beneath a waning moon was haunted   15
By woman wailing for her demon lover!
And from this chasm, with ceaseless turmoil seething,
As if this earth in fast thick pants were breathing,
A mighty fountain momently was forced:
Amid whose swift half-intermitted burst   20
Huge fragments vaulted like rebounding hail,
Or chaffy grain beneath the thresher's flail:
And 'mid these dancing rocks at once and ever
It flung up momently the sacred river.
Five miles meandering with a mazy motion   25
Through wood and dale the sacred river ran,
Then reached the caverns measureless to man,

Kubla Khan ruler of China (1216–1294)   **vision in a dream** Coleridge's own account tells how he took opium for an illness and slept for three hours, during which time he envisioned a complete poem of some 300 lines. When he awoke, he began to write down the details of his dream. "At this moment he was unfortunately called out by a person on business from Porlock, and detained by him above an hour, and on his return to the room found, to his no small surprise and mortification, that though he still retained some vague and dim recollection of the general purport of the vision, yet, with the exception of some eight or ten scattered lines and images on the surface of a stream into which a stone has been cast . . ." [Coleridge's note]

And sank in tumult to a lifeless ocean:
And 'mid this tumult Kubla heard from far
Ancestral voices prophesying war!   *30*

 The shadow of the dome of pleasure
 Floated midway on the waves;
 Where was heard the mingled measure
 From the fountain and the caves.
It was a miracle of rare device,   *35*
A sunny pleasure-dome with caves of ice!

 A damsel with a dulcimer
 In a vision once I saw:
 It was an Abyssinian maid,
 And on her dulcimer she played,   *40*
 Singing of Mount Abora.
 Could I revive within me
 Her symphony and song,
 To such a deep delight 'twould win me,
That with music loud and long,   *45*
I would build that dome in air,
That sunny dome! those caves of ice!
And all who heard should see them there,
And all should cry, Beware! Beware!
His flashing eyes, his floating hair!   *50*
Weave a circle round him thrice,
And close your eyes with holy dread,
For he on honey-dew hath fed,
And drunk the milk of Paradise.

           —1797–98

Work Without Hope

Lines Composed 21st February 1825

All Nature seems at work. Slugs leave their lair—
The bees are stirring—birds are on the wing—
And Winter slumbering in the open air

Wears on his smiling face a dream of Spring!
And I the while, the sole unbusy thing,   5
Nor honey make, nor pair, nor build, nor sing.

Yet well I ken° the banks where amaranths° blow,
Have traced the fount whence streams of nectar flow.
Bloom, O ye amaranths! bloom for whom ye may,
For me ye bloom not! Glide, rich streams, away!   10
With lips unbrightened, wreathless brow, I stroll:
And would you learn the spells that drowse my soul?
Work without Hope draws° nectar in a sieve,
And Hope without an object cannot live.

—*1828*

George Gordon, Lord Byron (1788–1824) attained flamboyant celebrity status, leading an unconventional lifestyle that contributed to his notoriety. Byron was the most widely read of all the English romantic poets, but his verse romances and mock-epic poems like Don Juan *have not proved as popular in this century. An English aristocrat who was committed to revolutionary ideals, Byron died while lending military assistance to the cause of Greek freedom.*

George Gordon, Lord Byron

Stanzas

When A Man Hath No Freedom To Fight For At Home

When a man hath no freedom to fight for at home,
    Let him combat for that of his neighbors;
Let him think of the glories of Greece and of Rome,
    And get knocked on his head for his labors.

To do good to mankind is the chivalrous plan,   5
    And is always as nobly requited:
Then battle for freedom wherever you can,
    And, if not shot or hanged, you'll get knighted.

—*1824*

---

7 ken know   **amaranths** legendary flowers that never fade   **13 draws** dips

When We Two Parted

When we two parted
  In silence and tears,
Half broken-hearted
  To sever for years,
Pale grew thy cheek and cold,   5
  Colder thy kiss;
Truly that hour foretold
  Sorrow to this.

The dew of the morning
  Sunk chill on my brow—   10
It felt like the warning
  Of what I feel now.
Thy vows are all broken,
  And light is thy fame;
I hear thy name spoken,   15
  And share in its shame.

They name thee before me,
  A knell to mine ear;
A shudder comes o'er me—
  Why wert thou so dear?   20
They know not I knew thee,
  Who knew thee too well:—
Long, long shall I rue thee,
  Too deeply to tell.

In secret we met—   25
  In silence I grieve
That thy heart could forget,
  Thy spirit deceive.
If I should meet thee
  After long years,   30
How should I greet thee?—
  With silence and tears.

—1813

Percy Bysshe Shelley (1792–1822), *like his friend Byron, has not found as much favor in recent eras as the other English romantics, although his political liberalism anticipates many currents of our own day. Perhaps his unbridled emotionalism is sometimes too intense for modern readers. His wife, Mary Wollstonecraft Shelley, will be remembered as the author of the classic horror novel* Frankenstein.

Percy Bysshe Shelley
Ode to the West Wind

1

O wild West Wind, thou breath of Autumn's being,
Thou, from whose unseen presence the leaves dead
Are driven, like ghosts from an enchanter fleeing,

Yellow, and black, and pale, and hectic red,
Pestilence-stricken multitudes: O thou,   5
Who chariotest to their dark wintry bed

The wingèd seeds, where they lie cold and low,
Each like a corpse within its grave, until
Thine azure sister of the Spring° shall blow

Her clarion o'er the dreaming earth, and fill   10
(Driving sweet buds like flocks to feed in air)
With living hues and odors plain and hill:

Wild Spirit, which art moving everywhere;
Destroyer and preserver; hear, oh, hear!

2

Thou on whose stream, mid the steep sky's commotion,   15
Loose clouds like earth's decaying leaves are shed,
Shook from the tangled boughs of Heaven and Ocean,

Angels of rain and lightning: there are spread
On the blue surface of thine aëry surge,
Like the bright hair uplifted from the head   20

---

9 azure sister of the Spring i.e., the South Wind

Of some fierce Mænad,° even from the dim verge
Of the horizon to the zenith's height,
The locks of the approaching storm. Thou dirge

Of the dying year, to which this closing night
Will be the dome of a vast sepulcher,   25
Vaulted with all thy congregated might

Of vapors, from whose solid atmosphere
Black rain, and fire, and hail will burst: oh, hear!

3

Thou who didst waken from his summer dreams
The blue Mediterranean, where he lay,   30
Lulled by the coil of his crystàlline streams,

Beside a pumice isle in Baiae's bay,°
And saw in sleep old palaces and towers
Quivering within the wave's intenser day,

All overgrown with azure moss and flowers   35
So sweet, the sense faints picturing them! Thou
For whose path the Atlantic's level powers

Cleave themselves into chasms, while far below
The sea-blooms and the oozy woods which wear
The sapless foliage of the ocean, know   40

Thy voice, and suddenly grow gray with fear,
And tremble and despoil themselves: oh, hear!

4

If I were a dead leaf thou mightest bear;
If I were a swift cloud to fly with thee;
A wave to pant beneath thy power, and share   45

The impulse of thy strength, only less free
Than thou, O uncontrollable! If even
I were as in my boyhood, and could be

---

21 Mænad female worshipper of Bacchus, god of wine   **32 Baiae's bay** near Naples

The comrade of thy wanderings over Heaven,
As then, when to outstrip thy skyey speed   50
Scarce seemed a vision; I would ne'er have striven

As thus with thee in prayer in my sore need.
Oh, lift me as a wave, a leaf, a cloud!
I fall upon the thorns of life! I bleed!

A heavy weight of hours has chained and bowed   55
One too like thee: tameless, and swift, and proud.

      5

Make me thy lyre, even as the forest is:
What if my leaves are falling like its own!
The tumult of thy mighty harmonies

Will take from both a deep, autumnal tone,   60
Sweet though in sadness. Be thou, Spirit fierce,
My spirit! Be thou me, impetuous one!

Drive my dead thoughts over the universe
Like withered leaves to quicken a new birth!
And, by the incantation of this verse,   65

Scatter, as from an unextinguished hearth
Ashes and sparks, my words among mankind!
Be through my lips to unawakened earth

The trumpet of a prophecy! O Wind,
If Winter comes, can Spring be far behind?   70

                                           —*1820*

Ozymandias°

I met a traveler from an antique land
Who said: Two vast and trunkless legs of stone
Stand in the desert. . . . Near them, on the sand,
Half sunk, a shattered visage lies, whose frown,

Ozymandias Ramses II of Egypt (c. 1250 B.C.)

And wrinkled lip, and sneer of cold command,   5
Tell that its sculptor well those passions read
Which yet survive, stamped on these lifeless things,
The hand that mocked them, and the heart that fed:
And on the pedestal these words appear:
"My name is Ozymandias, king of kings: 10
Look on my works, ye Mighty, and despair!"
Nothing beside remains. Round the decay
Of that colossal wreck, boundless and bare
The lone and level sands stretch far away.

—*1818*

William Cullen Bryant (1794–1878) *was often called "the American Wordsworth" for his adaptation of the techniques of English romanticism to the American landscape. Bryant's observations of nature have rarely been equaled.*

William Cullen Bryant
To the Fringed Gentian

Thou blossom bright with autumn dew,
And colored with the heaven's own blue,
That openest when the quiet light
Succeeds the keen and frosty night—

Thou comest not when violets lean   5
O'er wandering brooks and springs unseen,
Or columbines, in purple dressed,
Nod o'er the ground-bird's hidden nest.

Thou waitest late and com'st alone,
When woods are bare and birds are flown,   10
And frosts and shortening days portend
The aged year is near his end.

Then doth thy sweet and quiet eye
Look through its fringes to the sky,
Blue—blue—as if that sky let fall   15
A flower from its cerulean wall.

I would that thus, when I shall see
The hour of death draw near to me,
Hope, blossoming within my heart,
May look to heaven as I depart.   20

—*1829*

---

*John Keats (1795–1821) is now perhaps the most admired of all the major roman-
tics. Certainly his tragic death from tuberculosis in his twenties gives poignancy to
thoughts of the doomed young poet writing feverishly in a futile race against time; "Here
lies one whose name was writ in water" are the words he chose for his own epitaph. Many
of Keats's poems are concerned with glimpses of the eternal, whether a translation of an
ancient epic poem or a pristine artifact of a vanished civilization.*

John Keats

La Belle Dame sans Merci°

O what can ail thee, Knight at arms,
    Alone and palely loitering?
The sedge has withered from the Lake
    And no birds sing!

O what can ail thee, Knight at arms,   5
    So haggard, and so woebegone?
The squirrel's granary is full
    And the harvest's done.

I see a lily on thy brow
    With anguish moist and fever dew,   10
And on thy cheeks a fading rose
    Fast withereth too.

"I met a Lady in the Meads,
    Full beautiful, a faery's child,
Her hair was long, her foot was light,   15
    And her eyes were wild.

La Belle Dame sans Merci "the beautiful lady without pity"

"I made a Garland for her head,
    And bracelets too, and fragrant Zone;°
She looked at me as she did love
    And made sweet moan.   *20*

"I set her on my pacing steed
    And nothing else saw all day long,
For sidelong would she bend and sing
    A faery's song.

"She found me roots of relish sweet,   *25*
    And honey wild, and manna dew,
And sure in language strange she said
    'I love thee true.'

"She took me to her elfin grot°
    And there she wept and sighed full sore,   *30*
And there I shut her wild wild eyes
    With kisses four.

"And there she lullèd me asleep,
    And there I dreamed, Ah Woe betide!
The latest dream I ever dreamt   *35*
    On the cold hill side.

"I saw pale Kings, and Princes too,
    Pale warriors, death-pale were they all;
They cried, 'La belle Dame sans merci
    Hath thee in thrall!'   *40*

"I saw their starved lips in the gloam
    With horrid warning gapèd wide,
And I awoke, and found me here
    On the cold hill's side.

"And this is why I sojourn here   *45*
    Alone and palely loitering;
Though the sedge is withered from the Lake,
    And no birds sing."

—1819

18 Zone belt   **29 grot** cave

Ode on a Grecian Urn

1

Thou still unravished bride of quietness,
    Thou foster-child of silence and slow time,
Sylvan historian, who canst thus express
    A flowery tale more sweetly than our rhyme:
What leaf-fringed legend haunts about thy shape   5
    Of deities or mortals, or of both,
        In Tempe or the dales of Arcady?°
    What men or gods are these? What maidens loath?°
What mad pursuit? What struggle to escape?
        What pipes and timbrels?° What wild ecstasy?   10

2

Heard melodies are sweet, but those unheard
    Are sweeter; therefore, ye soft pipes, play on;
Not to the sensual ear, but, more endeared,
    Pipe to the spirit ditties of no tone:
Fair youth, beneath the trees, thou canst not leave   15
    Thy song, nor ever can those trees be bare;
        Bold Lover, never, never canst thou kiss,
Though winning near the goal—yet, do not grieve;
        She cannot fade, though thou hast not thy bliss,
    Forever wilt thou love, and she be fair!   20

3

Ah, happy, happy boughs! that cannot shed
    Your leaves, nor ever bid the Spring adieu;
And, happy melodist, unwearièd,
    Forever piping songs forever new;
More happy love! more happy, happy love!   25
    Forever warm and still to be enjoyed,
        Forever panting, and forever young;
All breathing human passion far above,

---

7 Tempe or the dales of Arcady idealized Greek settings   **8 loath** reluctant   **10 timbrels** tambourines

That leaves a heart high-sorrowful and cloyed,
　　A burning forehead, and a parching tongue.　　*30*

　　4

Who are these coming to the sacrifice?
　　To what green altar, O mysterious priest,
Lead'st thou that heifer lowing at the skies,
　　And all her silken flanks with garlands dressed?
What little town by river or sea shore,　　*35*
　　Or mountain-built with peaceful citadel,
　　　　Is emptied of this folk, this pious morn?
And, little town, thy streets forevermore
　　Will silent be; and not a soul to tell
　　　　Why thou art desolate, can e'er return.　　*40*

　　5

O Attic° shape! Fair attitude! with brede°
　　Of marble men and maidens overwrought,
With forest branches and the trodden weed;
　　Thou, silent form, dost tease us out of thought
As doth eternity: Cold Pastoral!　　*45*
　　When old age shall this generation waste,
　　　　Thou shalt remain, in midst of other woe
Than ours, a friend to man, to whom thou say'st,
"Beauty is truth, truth beauty,"—that is all
　　　　Ye know on earth, and all ye need to know.　　*50*

　　　　　　　　　　　　　　　　—1819

Ode to a Nightingale

　　1

My heart aches, and a drowsy numbness pains
　　My sense, as though of hemlock° I had drunk,
Or emptied some dull opiate to the drains

---

41 Attic Greek　　**brede** ornamental pattern
2 hemlock a deadly poison

One minute past, and Lethe-wards° had sunk.
'Tis not through envy of thy happy lot,   5
  But being too happy in thine happiness—
    That thou, light-wingèd Dryad° of the trees,
      In some melodious plot
Of beechen green, and shadows numberless,
    Singest of summer in full-throated ease.   10

  2

O, for a draught of vintage! that hath been
  Cooled a long age in the deep-delvèd earth,
Tasting of Flora° and the country green,
  Dance, and Provençal° song, and sunburnt mirth!
O for a beaker full of the warm South,   15
  Full of the true, the blushful Hippocrene,°
    With beaded bubbles winking at the brim,
      And purple-stainèd mouth;
That I might drink, and leave the world unseen,
    And with thee fade away into the forest dim: 20

  3

Fade far away, dissolve, and quite forget
  What thou among the leaves hast never known,
The weariness, the fever, and the fret
  Here, where men sit and hear each other groan;
Where palsy shakes a few, sad, last gray hairs,   25
  Where youth grows pale, and specter-thin, and dies;
    Where but to think is to be full of sorrow
      And leaden-eyed despairs,
  Where Beauty cannot keep her lustrous eyes,
    Or new Love pine at them beyond tomorrow.   30

  4

Away! away! for I will fly to thee,
  Not charioted by Bacchus° and his pards,°

4 Lethe-wards toward the waters of forgetfulness   **7 Dryad** tree nymph   **13 Flora** Roman goddess
of spring   **14 Provençal** of Provence, in South of France   **16 Hippocrene** fountain of the Muses
32 Bacchus Roman god of wine   **pards** leopards

But on the viewless wings of Poesy,°
   Though the dull brain perplexes and retards:
Already with thee! tender is the night,   *35*
     And haply the Queen-Moon is on her throne,
        Clustered around by all her starry Fays;°
           But here there is no light,
     Save what from heaven is with the breezes blown
        Through verdurous glooms and winding mossy ways.   *40*

   5

I cannot see what flowers are at my feet,
   Nor what soft incense hangs upon the boughs,
But, in embalmèd darkness, guess each sweet
   Wherewith the seasonable month endows
The grass, the thicket, and the fruit-tree wild;   *45*
     White hawthorn, and the pastoral eglantine;
        Fast fading violets covered up in leaves;
           And mid-May's eldest child,
     The coming musk-rose, full of dewy wine,
        The murmurous haunt of flies on summer eves.   *50*

   6

Darkling° I listen; and for many a time
   I have been half in love with easeful Death,
Called him soft names in many a musèd rhyme,
   To take into the air my quiet breath;
Now more than ever seems it rich to die,   *55*
     To cease upon the midnight with no pain,
        While thou art pouring forth thy soul abroad
           In such an ecstasy!
     Still wouldst thou sing, and I have ears in vain—
        To thy high requiem become a sod.   *60*

   7

Thou wast not born for death, immortal Bird!
   No hungry generations tread thee down;

33 Poesy poetry   **37 Fays** fairies   **51 Darkling** in the dark

The voice I hear this passing night was heard
    In ancient days by emperor and clown;
Perhaps the selfsame song that found a path   65
      Through the sad heart of Ruth, when, sick for home,
          She stood in tears amid the alien corn;°
            The same that ofttimes hath
      Charmed magic casements, opening on the foam
          Of perilous seas, in faery lands forlorn.   70

8

Forlorn! the very word is like a bell
    To toll me back from thee to my sole self!
Adieu! the fancy cannot cheat so well
    As she is famed to do, deceiving elf.
Adieu! adieu! thy plaintive anthem fades   75
      Past the near meadows, over the still stream,
          Up the hill side; and now 'tis buried deep
            In the next valley-glades:
      Was it a vision, or a waking dream?
          Fled is that music:—Do I wake or sleep?   *80*

                            —1819

On First Looking into Chapman's Homer°

Much have I traveled in the realms of gold,
    And many goodly states and kingdoms seen;
    Round many western islands have I been
Which bards in fealty to Apollo° hold.
Oft of one wide expanse had I been told   5
    That deep-browed Homer ruled as his demesne;
    Yet did I never breathe its pure serene

66-67 Ruth . . . alien corn in the Old Testament she is a stranger working in the grain fields of Judah

Chapman's Homer translation of the *Iliad* and *Odyssey* by George Chapman (1559–1634)
4 Apollo here, the god of poetry

Till I heard Chapman speak out loud and bold:
Then felt I like some watcher of the skies
    When a new planet swims into his ken;   *10*
Or like stout Cortez° when with eagle eyes
    He stared at the Pacific—and all his men
Looked at each other with a wild surmise—
    Silent, upon a peak in Darien.°

                                    —1816

When I Have Fears

When I have fears that I may cease to be
    Before my pen has gleaned my teeming brain,
Before high-pilèd books, in charact'ry,°
    Hold like rich garners the full-ripened grain;
When I behold, upon the night's starred face,   *5*
    Huge cloudy symbols of a high romance,
And think that I may never live to trace
    Their shadows, with the magic hand of chance;
And when I feel, fair creature of an hour,
    That I shall never look upon thee more,   *10*
Never have relish in the faery power
    Of unreflecting love!—then on the shore
Of the wide world I stand alone, and think
Till Love and Fame to nothingness do sink.

                                      —1818

11 Cortez Balboa was actually the first European to see the Pacific   **14 Darien** in modern-day Panama
3 charact'ry writing

Elizabeth Barrett Browning (1806–1861) *was already a famous poet when she met her husband-to-be, Robert Browning, who had been corresponding with her on literary matters. She originally published her famous sonnet sequence, written in the first years of her marriage, in the guise of a translation of Portuguese poems, perhaps to mask their personal revelations.*

Elizabeth Barrett Browning
Sonnets from the Portuguese, 43

How do I love thee? Let me count the ways.
I love thee to the depth and breadth and height
My soul can reach, when feeling out of sight
For the ends of Being and ideal Grace.
I love thee to the level of everyday's   5
Most quiet need, by sun and candle-light.
I love thee freely, as men strive for Right;
I love thee purely, as they turn from Praise.
I love thee with the passion put to use
In my old griefs, and with my childhood's faith.   10
I love thee with a love I seemed to lose
With my lost saints—I love thee with the breath,
Smiles, tears, of all my life!—and, if God choose,
I shall but love thee better after death.

—*1845–46*

Henry Wadsworth Longfellow (1807–1882) was by far the most prominent nineteenth-century American poet, and his international fame led to his bust being placed in Westminster Abbey after his death. The long epic poems like Evangeline *and* Hiawatha *that were immensely popular among contemporary readers are seldom read today, but his shorter poems reveal a level of craftsmanship that few poets have equaled.*

Henry Wadsworth Longfellow
The Arsenal at Springfield

This is the Arsenal. From floor to ceiling,
    Like a huge organ, rise the burnished arms;
But from their silent pipes no anthem pealing
    Startles the villages with strange alarms.

Ah! what a sound will rise, how wild and dreary,   5
    When the death-angel touches those swift keys!
What loud lament and dismal Miserere°
    Will mingle with their awful symphonies!

I hear even now the infinite fierce chorus,
    The cries of agony, the endless groan,   10
Which, through the ages that have gone before us,
    In long reverberations reach our own.

On helm and harness rings the Saxon hammer,
    Through Cimbric° forest roars the Norseman's song,
And loud, amid the universal clamor,   15
    O'er distant deserts sounds the Tartar gong.

I hear the Florentine, who from his palace
    Wheels out his battle-bell with dreadful din,
And Aztec priests upon their teocallis°
    Beat the wild war-drums made of serpent's skin;   20

7 Miserere Latin hymn from Psalm 1: "Have mercy on me, Lord."   **14 Cimbric** in Denmark
19 teocallis temples atop pyramids

The tumult of each sacked and burning village;
    The shout that every prayer for mercy drowns;
The soldiers' revels in the midst of pillage;
    The wail of famine in beleaguered towns;

The bursting shell, the gateway wrenched asunder,   25
    The rattling musketry, the clashing blade;
And ever and anon, in tones of thunder
    The diapason° of the cannonade.

Is it, O man, with such discordant noises,
    With such accursed instruments as these,   30
Thou drownest Nature's sweet and kindly voices,
    And jarrest the celestial harmonies?

Were half the power, that fills the world with terror,
    Were half the wealth bestowed on camps and courts,
Given to redeem the human mind from error,   35
    There were no need of arsenals or forts:

The warrior's name would be a name abhorred!
    And every nation, that should lift again
Its hand against a brother, on its forehead
    Would wear forevermore the curse of Cain!   40

Down the dark future, through long generations,
    The echoing sounds grow fainter and then cease;
And like a bell, with solemn, sweet vibrations,
    I hear once more the voice of Christ say, "Peace!"

Peace! and no longer from its brazen portals   45
    The blast of War's great organ shakes the skies!
But beautiful as songs of the immortals,
    The holy melodies of love arise.

—1846

---

28 diapason full range of pipe organ

The Cross of Snow

In the long, sleepless watches of the night,
    A gentle face—the face of one long dead—
    Looks at me from the wall, where round its head
    The night-lamp casts a halo of pale light.
Here in this room she died; and soul more white   5
    Never through martyrdom of fire° was led
    To its repose; nor can in books be read
    The legend of a life more benedight.°
There is a mountain in the distant West
    That, sun-defying, in its deep ravines   10
    Displays a cross of snow upon its side.
Such is the cross I wear upon my breast
    These eighteen years, through all the changing scenes
    And seasons, changeless since the day she died.

                                 —1886

Edgar Allan Poe (1809–1849) has survived his own myth as a deranged, drug-crazed genius, despite the wealth of evidence to the contrary that can be gleaned from his brilliant, though erratic, career as a poet, short-story writer, critic, and editor. Poe's brand of romanticism seems at odds with that of other American poets of his day, and is perhaps more in keeping with the spirit of Coleridge than that of Wordsworth. "The Raven" has been parodied perhaps more than any other American poem, yet it still retains a powerful hold on its audience.

Edgar Allan Poe
The Haunted Palace

In the greenest of our valleys,
    By good angels tenanted,
Once a fair and stately palace—
    Radiant palace—reared its head.

---

6 martyrdom of fire Longfellow's second wife, Frances, died as the result of a household fire in 1861. **8 benedight** blessed

In the monarch Thought's dominion—   *5*
    It stood there!
Never seraph spread a pinion
    Over fabric half so fair!

Banners yellow, glorious, golden,
    On its roof did float and flow,   *10*
(This—all this—was in the olden
    Time long ago,)
And every gentle air that dallied,
    In that sweet day,
Along the ramparts plumed and pallid,   *15*
    A wingéd odor went away.

Wanderers in that happy valley,
    Through two luminous windows, saw
Spirits moving musically
    To a lute's well-tunéd law,   *20*
Round about a throne where, sitting,
    Porphyrogene!°
In state his glory well befitting,
    The ruler of the realm was seen.

And all with pearl and ruby glowing   *25*
    Was the fair palace door,
Through which came flowing, flowing, flowing,
    And sparkling evermore,
A troop of Echoes, whose sweet duty
    Was but to sing,   *30*
In voices of surpassing beauty,
    The wit and wisdom of their king.

But evil things, in robes of sorrow,
    Assailed the monarch's high estate.
(Ah, let us mourn!—for never morrow   *35*
    Shall dawn upon him, desolate!)
And round about his home the glory
    That blushed and bloomed,

---

22 Porphyrogene born to the purple, i.e., royal

Is but a dim-remembered story
Of the old time entombed.   *40*

and travellers, now, within that valley,
Through the red-litten windows see
Vast forms that move fantastically
To a discordant melody,
While, like a ghastly rapid river,   *45*
Through the pale door
A hideous throng rush out forever,
And laugh—but smile no more.

                                                                  —*1845*

The Raven

Once upon a midnight dreary, while I pondered, weak and weary,
Over many a quaint and curious volume of forgotten lore—
While I nodded, nearly napping, suddenly there came a tapping,
As of some one gently rapping, rapping at my chamber door.
"'Tis some visitor," I muttered, "tapping at my chamber door—   *5*
            Only this and nothing more."

Ah, distinctly I remember it was in the bleak December;
And each separate dying ember wrought its ghost upon the floor.
Eagerly I wished the morrow;—vainly I had sought to borrow
From my books surcease of sorrow—sorrow for the lost Lenore—   *10*
For the rare and radiant maiden whom the angels name Lenore—
            Nameless *here* for evermore.

And the silken, sad, uncertain rustling of each purple curtain
Thrilled me—filled me with fantastic terrors never felt before;
So that now, to still the beating of my heart, I stood repeating   *15*
"'Tis some visitor entreating entrance at my chamber door;—
Some late visitor entreating entrance at my chamber door;—
            This it is and nothing more."

Presently my soul grew stronger; hesitating then no longer,
"Sir," said I, "or Madam, truly your forgiveness I implore;   *20*
But the fact is I was napping, and so gently you came rapping,

And so faintly you came tapping, tapping at my chamber door,
That I scarce was sure I heard you"—here I opened wide the door;—
Darkness there and nothing more.

Deep into that darkness peering, long I stood there wondering, fearing,   25
Doubting, dreaming dreams no mortal ever dared to dream before;
But the silence was unbroken, and the stillness gave no token,
And the only word there spoken was the whispered word, "Lenore?"
This I whispered, and an echo murmured back the word, "Lenore!"
Merely this and nothing more.   30

Back into the chamber turning, all my soul within me burning,
Soon again I heard a tapping somewhat louder than before.
"Surely," said I, "surely that is something at my window lattice;
Let me see, then, what thereat is, and this mystery explore—
Let my heart be still a moment and this mystery explore;—   35
'Tis the wind and nothing more!"

Open here I flung the shutter, when, with many a flirt and flutter,
In there stepped a stately Raven of the saintly days of yore;
Not the least obeisance made he; not a minute stopped or stayed he;
But, with mien of lord or lady, perched above my chamber door—   40
Perched upon a bust of Pallas° just above my chamber door—
Perched, and sat, and nothing more.

Then this ebony bird beguiling my sad fancy into smiling,
By the grave and stern decorum of the countenance it wore,
"Though thy crest be shorn and shaven, thou," I said, "art sure no craven,
45
Ghastly grim and ancient Raven wandering from the Nightly shore—
Tell me what thy lordly name is on the Night's Plutonian° shore!"
Quoth the Raven, "Nevermore."

Much I marvelled this ungainly fowl to hear discourse so plainly,
Though its answer little meaning—little relevancy bore;   50
For we cannot help agreeing that no living human being

41 Pallas Athena, goddess of wisdom   **47 Plutonian** after Pluto, Roman god of the underworld

Ever yet was blessed with seeing bird above his chamber door—
Bird or beast upon the sculptured bust above his chamber door,
                    With such name as "Nevermore."

But the Raven, sitting lonely on the placid bust, spoke only   55
That one word, as if his soul in that one word he did outpour.
Nothing farther then he uttered—not a feather then he fluttered—
Till I scarcely more than muttered, "Other friends have flown
    before—
On the morrow *he* will leave me, as my Hopes have flown before."
                    Then the bird said, "Nevermore."   60

Startled at the stillness broken by reply so aptly spoken,
"Doubtless," said I, "what it utters is its only stock and store
Caught from some unhappy master whom unmerciful Disaster
Followed fast and followed faster till his songs one burden bore—
Till the dirges of his Hope that melancholy burden bore   65
                    Of 'Never—nevermore.'"

But the Raven still beguiling all my sad fancy into smiling,
Straight I wheeled a cushioned seat in front of bird and bust and
    door;
Then, upon the velvet sinking, I betook myself to linking
Fancy unto fancy, thinking what this ominous bird of yore—   70
What this grim, ungainly, ghastly, gaunt, and ominous bird of yore
                    Meant in croaking "Nevermore."

This I sat engaged in guessing, but no syllable expressing
To the fowl whose fiery eyes now burned into my bosom's core;
This and more I sat divining, with my head at ease reclining   75
On the cushion's velvet lining that the lamp-light gloated o'er,
But whose velvet-violet lining with the lamp-light gloating o'er,
                    She shall press, ah, nevermore!

Then, methought, the air grew denser, perfumed from an unseen
    censer
Swung by seraphim whose foot-falls tinkled on the tufted floor.   80
"Wretch," I cried, "thy God hath lent thee—by these angels he
    hath sent thee.

Respite—respite and nepenthe° from thy memories of Lenore;
Quaff, oh quaff this kind nepenthe and forget this lost Lenore!"
Quoth the Raven, "Nevermore."

"Prophet!" said I, "thing of evil!—prophet still, if bird or devil!—   85
Whether Tempter sent, or whether tempest tossed thee here ashore,
Desolate yet all undaunted, on this desert land enchanted—
On this home by Horror haunted—tell me truly, I implore—
Is there—*is* there balm in Gilead?—tell me—tell me, I implore!"
Quoth the Raven, "Nevermore."   90

"Prophet!" said I, "thing of evil!—prophet still, if bird or devil!
By that Heaven that bends above us—by that God we both adore—
Tell this soul with sorrow laden if, within the distant Aidenn,°
It shall clasp a sainted maiden whom the angels name Lenore—
Clasp a rare and radiant maiden whom the angels name Lenore."   95
Quoth the Raven, "Nevermore."

"Be that word our sign of parting, bird or fiend!" I shrieked,
    upstarting—
"Get thee back into the tempest and the Night's Plutonian shore!
Leave no black plume as a token of that lie thy soul hath spoken!
Leave my loneliness unbroken!—quit the bust above my door!   100
Take thy beak from out my heart, and take thy form from off my
    door!"
Quoth the Raven, "Nevermore."

And the Raven, never flitting, still is sitting, *still* is sitting
On the pallid bust of Pallas just above my chamber door;
And his eyes have all the seeming of a demon's that is dreaming,   105
And the lamp-light o'er him streaming throws his shadow on the floor;
And my soul from out that shadow that lies floating on the floor
Shall be lifted—nevermore!

—*1845*

---

82 nepenthe drug causing forgetfulness   **93 Aidenn** Eden

To Helen

Helen, thy beauty is to me
   Like those Nicean° barks of yore,
That gently, o'er a perfumed sea
   The weary, way-worn wanderer bore
   To his own native shore.   5

On desperate seas long wont to roam,
   Thy hyacinth° hair, thy classic face
Thy Naiad° airs have brought me home
   To the glory that was Greece
And the grandeur that was Rome.   10

Lo! in yon brilliant window-niche
   How statue-like I see thee stand!
   The agate lamp within thy hand,
Ah! Psyche,° from the regions which
   Are Holy Land!   15

—1831

---

2 Nicean possibly of Nice (in the South of France); or Phoenician   **7 hyacinth** reddish, like the flower of Greek myth   **8 Naiad** water nymph   **14 Psyche** the soul

Alfred, Lord Tennyson (1809–1892) became the most famous English poet with the 1850 publication of In Memoriam, *a sequence of poems on the death of his friend A. H. Hallam. In the same year he became poet laureate. Modern critical opinion has focused more favorably on Tennyson's lyrical gifts than on his talents for narrative or drama. T. S. Eliot and W. H. Auden, among other critics, praised Tennyson's rhythms and sound patterns but had reservations about his depth of intellect, especially when he took on the role of official apologist for Victorian England.*

Alfred, Lord Tennyson

The Eagle

FRAGMENT

He clasps the crag with crooked hands;
Close to the sun in lonely lands,
Ringed with the azure world, he stands.

The wrinkled sea beneath him crawls;
He watches from his mountain walls,   5
And like a thunderbolt he falls.

—*1851*

In Memoriam A. H. H.,° 54

O, yet we trust that somehow good
   Will be the final goal of ill,
   To pangs of nature, sins of will,
Defects of doubt, and taints of blood;

That nothing walks with aimless feet;   5
   That not one life shall be destroyed,
   Or cast as rubbish to the void,
When God hath made the pile complete;

A. H. H. the poet's college friend Arthur Henry Hallam (1811–1833)

That not a worm is cloven in vain;
    That not a moth with vain desire   *10*
    Is shriveled in a fruitless fire,
Or but subserves another's gain.

Behold, we know not anything;
    I can but trust that good shall fall
    At last—far off—at last, to all,   *15*
And every winter change to spring.

So runs my dreams; but what am I?
    An infant crying in the night;
    An infant crying for the light,
And with no language but a cry.   *20*

—1833

Tears, Idle Tears

FROM *THE PRINCESS*

    Tears, idle tears, I know not what they mean,
Tears from the depth of some divine despair
Rise in the heart, and gather to the eyes,
In looking on the happy autumn-fields,
And thinking of the days that are no more.   *5*

    Fresh as the first beam glittering on a sail,
That brings our friends up from the underworld,
Sad as the last which reddens over one
That sinks with all we love below the verge;
So sad, so fresh, the days that are no more.   *10*

    Ah, sad and strange as in dark summer dawns
The earliest pipe of half-awakened birds
To dying ears, when unto dying eyes
The casement slowly grows a glimmering square;
So sad, so strange, the days that are no more.   *15*

Dear as remembered kisses after death,
And sweet as those by hopeless fancy feigned
On lips that are for others; deep as love,
Deep as first love, and wild with all regret;
O Death in Life, the days that are no more!   20

—*1847*

Ulysses°

It little profits that an idle king,
By this still hearth, among these barren crags,
Matched with an aged wife, I mete and dole
Unequal laws unto a savage race,
That hoard, and sleep, and feed, and know not me.   5
I cannot rest from travel; I will drink
Life to the lees. All times I have enjoyed
Greatly, have suffered greatly, both with those
That loved me, and alone; on shore, and when
Through scudding drifts the rainy Hyades°   10
Vexed the dim sea. I am become a name;
For always roaming with a hungry heart
Much have I seen and known—cities of men
And manners, climates, councils, governments,
Myself not least, but honored of them all—   15
And drunk delight of battle with my peers,
Far on the ringing plains of windy Troy.
I am a part of all that I have met;
Yet all experience is an arch wherethrough
Gleams that untraveled world whose margin fades   20
For ever and for ever when I move.
How dull it is to pause, to make an end,
To rust unburnished, not to shine in use!
As though to breathe were life! Life piled on life

Ulysses Homer's *Odyssey* ends with the return of Odysseus (Ulysses) to his island kingdom, Ithaca. Tennyson's poem takes place some years later.   **10 Hyades** a constellation thought to predict rain

Were all too little, and of one to me   25
Little remains; but every hour is saved
From that eternal silence, something more,
A bringer of new things; and vile it were
For some three suns to store and hoard myself,
And this gray spirit yearning in desire   30
To follow knowledge like a sinking star,
Beyond the utmost bound of human thought.
　　This is my son, mine own Telemachus,
To whom I leave the scepter and the isle,
Well-loved of me, discerning to fulfill   35
This labor, by slow prudence to make mild
A rugged people, and through soft degrees
Subdue them to the useful and the good.
Most blameless is he, centered in the sphere
Of common duties, decent not to fail   40
In offices of tenderness, and pay
Meet adoration to my household gods,
When I am gone. He works his work, I mine.
　　There lies the port; the vessel puffs her sail;
There gloom the dark, broad seas. My mariners,   45
Souls that have toiled, and wrought, and thought with me,
That ever with a frolic welcome took
The thunder and the sunshine, and opposed
Free hearts, free foreheads—you and I are old;
Old age hath yet his honor and his toil.   50
Death closes all; but something ere the end,
Some work of noble note, may yet be done,
Not unbecoming men that strove with gods.
The lights begin to twinkle from the rocks;
The long day wanes; the low moon climbs; the deep   55
Moans round with many voices. Come, my friends,
'Tis not too late to seek a newer world.
Push off, and sitting well in order smite
The sounding furrows; for my purpose holds
To sail beyond the sunset, and the baths   60
Of all the western stars, until I die.
It may be that the gulfs will wash us down;

It may be we shall touch the Happy Isles,°
And see the great Achilles, whom we knew.
Though much is taken, much abides; and though   65
We are not now that strength which in old days
Moved earth and heaven, that which we are, we are,
One equal temper of heroic hearts,
Made weak by time and fate, but strong in will
To strive, to seek, to find, and not to yield.   70

—*1833*

Robert Browning (1812–1889) wrote many successful dramatic monologues that are his lasting legacy, for he brings the genre to a level of achievement rarely equaled. Less regarded during his lifetime than his contemporary Tennyson, he has consistently risen in the esteem of modern readers. Often overlooked in his gallery of often grotesque characters are his considerable metrical skills and ability to simulate speech while working in demanding poetic forms.

Robert Browning
My Last Duchess

FERRARA°

That's my last duchess painted on the wall,
Looking as if she were alive. I call
That piece a wonder, now: Frà Pandolf's° hands
Worked busily a day, and there she stands.
Will't please you sit and look at her? I said   5
"Frà Pandolf" by design, for never read
Strangers like you that pictured countenance,
The depth and passion of its earnest glance,
But to myself they turned (since none puts by

---

63 Happy Isles Elysium, the resting place of dead heroes
Ferrara The speaker is probably Alfonso II d'Este, Duke of Ferrara (1533–158?)   **3 Frà Pandolf** an imaginary painter

The curtain I have drawn for you, but I)   10
And seemed as they would ask me, if they durst,
How such a glance came there; so, not the first
Are you to turn and ask thus. Sir, 'twas not
Her husband's presence only, called that spot
Of joy into the Duchess' cheek: perhaps   15
Frà Pandolf chanced to say "Her mantle laps
Over my lady's wrist too much," or "Paint
Must never hope to reproduce the faint
Half-flush that dies along her throat": such stuff
Was courtesy, she thought, and cause enough   20
For calling up that spot of joy. She had
A heart—how shall I say?—too soon made glad,
Too easily impressed; she liked whate'er
She looked on, and her looks went everywhere.
Sir, 'twas all one! My favor at her breast,   25
The dropping of the daylight in the West,
The bough of cherries some officious fool
Broke in the orchard for her, the white mule
She rode with round the terrace—all and each
Would draw from her alike the approving speech,   30
Or blush, at least. She thanked men—good! but thanked
Somehow—I know not how—as if she ranked
My gift of a nine-hundred-years-old name
With anybody's gift. Who'd stoop to blame
This sort of trifling? Even had you skill   35
In speech—which I have not—to make your will
Quite clear to such an one, and say, "Just this
Or that in you disgusts me; here you miss,
Or there exceed the mark"—and if she let
Herself be lessoned so, nor plainly set   40
Her wits to yours, forsooth, and made excuse,
—E'en then would be some stooping; and I choose
Never to stoop. Oh sir, she smiled, no doubt,
Whene'er I passed her; but who passed without
Much the same smile? This grew; I gave commands;   45

Then all smiles stopped together. There she stands
As if alive. Will't please you rise? We'll meet
The company below, then. I repeat,
The Count your master's° known munificence
Is ample warrant that no just pretense   *50*
Of mine for dowry will be disallowed;
Though his fair daughter's self, as I avowed
At starting, is my object. Nay, we'll go
Together down, sir. Notice Neptune, though,
Taming a sea horse, thought a rarity,   *55*
Which Claus of Innsbruck cast in bronze for me!

—1842

Porphyria's° Lover

The rain set early in tonight,
    The sullen wind was soon awake,
It tore the elm-tops down for spite,
    And did its worst to vex the lake:
        I listened with heart fit to break.   *5*
When glided in Porphyria; straight
    She shut the cold out and the storm,
And kneeled and made the cheerless grate
    Blaze up, and all the cottage warm;
        Which done, she rose, and from her form   *10*
Withdrew the dripping cloak and shawl,
    And laid her soiled gloves by, untied
Her hat and let the damp hair fall,
    And, last, she sat down by my side
        And called me. When no voice replied,   *15*
She put my arm about her waist,
    And made her smooth white shoulder bare,

---

49 Count your master's The auditor is apparently an envoy sent to arrange a marriage between the Duke of Ferrara and a count's daughter
Porphyria name suggesting purple, the color of nobility and royalty

And all her yellow hair displaced,
    And, stooping, made my cheek lie there,
    And spread, o'er all, her yellow hair,   *20*
Murmuring how she loved me—she
    Too weak, for all her heart's endeavor,
To set its struggling passion free
    From pride, and vainer ties dissever,
    And give herself to me forever.   *25*
But passion sometimes would prevail,
    Nor could tonight's gay feast restrain
A sudden thought of one so pale
    For love of her, and all in vain:
    So, she was come through wind and rain.   *30*
Be sure I looked up at her eyes
    Happy and proud; at last I knew
Porphyria worshipped me; surprise
    Made my heart swell, and still it grew
    While I debated what to do.   *35*
That moment she was mine, mine, fair,
    Perfectly pure and good: I found
A thing to do, and all her hair
    In one long yellow string I wound
    Three times her little throat around,   *40*
And strangled her. No pain felt she;
    I am quite sure she felt no pain.
As a shut bud that holds a bee,
    I warily oped her lids: again
    Laughed the blue eyes without a stain.   *45*
And I untightened next the tress
    About her neck; her cheek once more
Blushed bright beneath my burning kiss:
    I propped her head up as before,
    Only, this time my shoulder bore   *50*
Her head, which droops upon it still:
    The smiling rosy little head
So glad it has its utmost will,
    That all it scorned at once is fled,
    And I, its love, am gained instead!   *55*

Porphyria's love: she guessed not how
    Her darling one wish would be heard.
And thus we sit together now,
    And all night long we have not stirred,
    And yet God has not said a word!   *60*

—1842

Walt Whitman (1819–1892) pioneered the use of free verse, which established him as one of the forebears of modern poetry, but his subject matter, often dealing with sexual topics, and his unsparing realism were equally controversial in his day. An admirer of Emerson, he adapted many of the ideas of transcendentalism in Song of Myself, *his first major sequence, and also incorporated many of Emerson's calls for poets to use American subjects and patterns of speech.* Leaves of Grass, *which he revised from 1855 until his death, expanded to include virtually all of his poems, including the graphic poems he wrote while serving as a volunteer in Civil War army hospitals.*

Walt Whitman
A Sight in Camp in the Daybreak Gray and Dim

A sight in camp in the daybreak gray and dim,
As from my tent I emerge so early sleepless,
As slow I walk in the cool fresh air the path near by the hospital
    tent,
Three forms I see on stretchers lying, brought out there untended
    lying,
Over each the blanket spread, ample brownish woolen blanket,   *5*
Gray and heavy blanket, folding, covering all.

Curious I halt and silent stand,
Then with light fingers I from the face of the nearest the first just
    lift the blanket;
Who are you elderly man so gaunt and grim, with well-gray'd
    hair, and flesh all sunken about the eyes?
Who are you my dear comrade?   *10*

Then to the second I step—and who are you my child and darling?
Who are you sweet boy with cheeks yet blooming?

Then to the third—a face nor child nor old, very calm, as of
    beautiful yellow-white ivory;
Young man I think I know you—I think this face is the face of
    the Christ himself,
Dead and divine and brother of all, and here again he lies.   15

—1867

Crossing Brooklyn Ferry

1

Flood-tide below me! I see you face to face!
Clouds of the west—sun there half an hour high—I see you also
    face to face.

Crowds of men and women attired in the usual costumes, how
    curious you are to me!
On the ferry-boats the hundreds and hundreds that cross,
    returning home, are more curious to me than you suppose,
And you that shall cross from shore to shore years hence are
    more to me, and more in my meditations, than you might
    suppose.   5

2

The impalpable sustenance of me from all things at all hours of
    the day,
The simple, compact, well-join'd scheme, myself disintegrated,
    every one disintegrated yet part of the scheme,
The similitudes of the past and those of the future,
The glories strung like beads on my smallest sights and hearings,
    on the walk in the street and the passage over the river,
The current rushing so swiftly and swimming with me
    far away,   10
The others that are to follow me, the ties between me and them,
The certainty of others, the life, love, sight, hearing of others.

Others will enter the gates of the ferry and cross from shore to shore,
Others will watch the run of the flood-tide,
Others will see the shipping of Manhattan north and west, and
    the heights of Brooklyn to the south and east,   *15*
Others will see the islands large and small;
Fifty years hence, others will see them as they cross, the sun
    half an hour high,
A hundred years hence, or ever so many hundred years hence,
    others will see them,
Will enjoy the sunset, the pouring-in of the flood-tide, the
    falling-back to the sea of the ebb-tide.

3

It avails not, time nor place—distance avails not,   *20*
I am with you, you men and women of a generation, or ever so
    many generations hence,
Just as you feel when you look on the river and sky, so I felt,
Just as any of you is one of a living crowd, I was one of a crowd,
Just as you are refresh'd by the gladness of the river and the
    bright flow, I was refresh'd,
Just as you stand and lean on the rail, yet hurry with the swift
    current, I stood yet was hurried,   *25*
Just as you look on the numberless masts of ships and the
    thick-stemm'd pipes of steamboats, I look'd.

I too many and many a time cross'd the river of old,
Watched the Twelfth-month° sea-gulls, saw them high in the
    air floating with motionless wings, oscillating their bodies,
Saw how the glistening yellow lit up parts of their bodies and
    left the rest in strong shadow,
Saw the slow-wheeling circles and the gradual edging toward
    the south,   *30*
Saw the reflection of the summer sky in the water,
Had my eyes dazzled by the shimmering track of beams,
Look'd at the fine centrifugal spokes of light round the shape
    of my head in the sunlit water,

---

28 Twelfth-month Whitman's mother was a Quaker, hence this phrase for December.

Look'd on the haze on the hills southward and south-westward,
Look'd on the vapor as it flew in fleeces tinged with violet,   35
Look'd toward the lower bay to notice the vessels arriving,
Saw their approach, saw aboard those that were near me,
Saw the white sails of schooners and sloops, saw the ships at
    anchor,
The sailors at work in the rigging or out astride the spars,
The round masts, the swinging motion of the hulls, the slender
    serpentine pennants,   40
The large and small steamers in motion, the pilots in their
    pilothouses,
The white wake left by the passage, the quick tremulous whirl
    of the wheels,
The flags of all nations, the falling of them at sunset,
The scallop-edged waves in the twilight, the ladled cups, the
    frolicsome crests and glistening,
The stretch afar growing dimmer and dimmer, the gray walls
    of the granite storehouses by the docks,   45
On the river the shadowy group, the big steam-tug closely
    flank'd on each side by the barges, the hay-boat, the belated
    lighter,
On the neighboring shore the fires from the foundry chimneys
    burning high and glaringly into the night,
Casting their flicker of black contrasted with wild red and yellow
    light over the tops of houses, and down into the clefts of streets.

4

These and all else were to me the same as they are to you,
I loved well those cities, loved well the stately and rapid river,   50
The men and women I saw were all near to me,
Others the same—others who look back on me because I look'd
    forward to them,
(The time will come, though I stop here to-day and to-night.)

5

What is it then between us?
What is the count of the scores or hundreds of years between us?   55

Whatever it is, it avails not—distance avails not, and place avails not,
I too lived, Brooklyn of ample hills was mine,
I too walk'd the streets of Manhattan island, and bathed in the
    waters around it,
I too felt the curious abrupt questionings stir within me,
In the day among crowds of people sometimes they came
    upon me,   60
In my walks home late at night or as I lay in my bed they came
    upon me,
I too had been struck from the float forever held in solution,
I too had receiv'd identity by my body,
That I was I knew was of my body, and what I should be I
    knew I should be of my body.

6

It is not upon you alone the dark patches fall,   65
The dark threw its patches down upon me also,
The best I had done seem'd to me blank and suspicious,
My great thoughts as I supposed them, were they not in reality
    meagre?
Nor is it you alone who know what it is to be evil,
I am he who knew what it was to be evil,   70
I too knitted the old knot of contrariety,
Blabb'd, blush'd, resented, lied, stole, grudg'd,
Had guile, anger, lust, hot wishes I dared not speak,
Was wayward, vain, greedy, shallow, sly, cowardly, malignant,
The wolf, the snake, the hog, not wanting in me,   75
The cheating look, the frivolous word, the adulterous wish,
    not wanting,
Refusals, hates, postponements, meanness, laziness, none of
    these wanting,
Was one with the rest, the days and haps of the rest,
Was call'd by my nighest name by clear loud voices of young
    men as they saw me approaching or passing,
Felt their arms on my neck as I stood, or the negligent leaning
    of their flesh against me as I sat,   80
Saw many I loved in the street or ferry-boat or public
    assembly, yet never told them a word,

Lived the same life with the rest, the same old laughing, gnawing,
    sleeping,
Play'd the part that still looks back on the actor or actress,
The same old role, the role that is what we make it, as great as
    we like,
Or as small as we like, or both great and small.   85

7

Closer yet I approach you,
What thought you have of me now, I had as much of you—I laid
    in my stores in advance,
I consider'd long and seriously of you before you were born.

Who was to know what should come home to me?
Who knows but I am enjoying this?   90
Who knows, for all the distance, but I am as good as looking
    at you now, for all you cannot see me?

8

Ah, what can ever be more stately and admirable to me than
    mast-hemm'd Manhattan?
River and sunset and scallop-edg'd waves of flood-tide?
The sea-gulls oscillating their bodies, the hay-boat in the twilight,
    and the belated lighter?
What gods can exceed these that clasp me by the hand, and
    with voices I love call me promptly and loudly by my
    nighest name as I approach?   95
What is more subtle than this which ties me to the woman or
    man that looks in my face?
Which fuses me into you now, and pours my meaning into you?

We understand then do we not?
What I promis'd without mentioning it, have you not accepted?
What the study could not teach—what the preaching could not
    accomplish is accomplish'd, is it not?   100

9

Flow on, river! flow with the flood-tide, and ebb with the ebbtide!
Frolic on, crested and scallop-edg'd waves!

Gorgeous clouds of the sunset! drench with your splendor me, or
    the men and women generations after me!
Cross from shore to shore, countless crowds of passengers!
Stand up, tall masts of Mannahatta! stand up, beautiful hills
    of Brooklyn!   *105*
Throb, baffled and curious brain! throw out questions and
    answers!
Suspend here and everywhere, eternal float of solution!
Gaze, loving and thirsting eyes, in the house or street or public
    assembly!
Sound out, voices of young men! loudly and musically call me
    by my nighest name!
Live, old life! play the part that looks back on the actor or
    actress!   *110*
Play the old role, the role that is great or small according as one
    makes it!
Consider, you who peruse me, whether I may not in unknown
    ways be looking upon you;
Be firm, rail over the river, to support those who lean idly, yet
    haste with the hasting current;
Fly on, sea-birds! fly sideways, or wheel in large circles high in
    the air;
Receive the summer sky, you water, and faithfully hold it till
    all downcast eyes have time to take it from you!   *115*
Diverge, fine spokes of light, from the shape of my head, or
    any one's head, in the sunlit water!
Come on, ships from the lower bay! pass up or down, white-sail'd
    schooners, sloops, lighters!
Flaunt away, flags of all nations! be duly lower'd at sunset!
Burn high your fires, foundry chimneys! cast black shadows at
    nightfall! cast red and yellow light over the tops of the
    houses!
Appearances, now or henceforth, indicate what you are,   *120*
You necessary film, continue to envelop the soul,
About my body for me, and your body for you, be hung our
    divinest aromas,
Thrive, cities—bring your freight, bring your shows, ample and
    sufficient rivers,

Expand, being than which none else is perhaps more
    spiritual,
Keep your places, objects than which none else is more l
    asting.   *125*

You have waited, you always wait, you dumb, beautiful
    ministers,
We receive you with free sense at last, and are insatiate hence-
    forward,
Not you any more shall be able to foil us, or withhold yourselves
    from us,
We use you, and do not cast you aside—we plant you
    permanently within us,
We fathom you not—we love you—there is perfection in you
    also,   *130*
You furnish your parts toward eternity,
Great or small, you furnish your parts toward the soul.

                         —1881–82

A Noiseless Patient Spider

A noiseless patient spider,
I mark'd where on a little promontory it stood isolated,
Mark'd how to explore the vacant vast surrounding,
It launch'd forth filament, filament, filament, out of itself,
Ever unreeling them, ever tirelessly speeding them.   *5*

And you O my soul where you stand,
Surrounded, detached, in measureless oceans of space,
Ceaselessly musing, venturing, throwing, seeking the spheres to
    connect them,
Till the bridge you will need be form'd, till the ductile anchor
    hold,
Till the gossamer thread you fling catch somewhere, O my
    soul.   *10*

                         —1876

Out of the Cradle Endlessly Rocking

Out of the cradle endlessly rocking,
Out of the mocking-bird's throat, the musical shuttle,
Out of the Ninth-month° midnight,
Over the sterile sands and the fields beyond, where the child
    leaving his bed wander'd alone, bareheaded, barefoot,
Down from the shower'd halo,   5
Up from the mystic play of shadows twining and twisting as if
    they were alive,
Out from the patches of briers and blackberries,
From the memories of the bird that chanted to me,
From your memories sad brother, from the fitful risings and
    fallings I heard,
From under that yellow half-moon late-risen and swollen as if
    with tears,   10
From those beginning notes of yearning and love there in the
    mist,
From the thousand responses of my heart never to cease,
From the myriad thence-arous'd words,
From the word stronger and more delicious than any,
From such as now they start the scene revisiting,   15
As a flock, twittering, rising, or overhead passing,
Borne hither, ere all eludes me, hurriedly,
A man, yet by these tears a little boy again,
Throwing myself on the sand, confronting the waves,
I, chanter of pains and joys, uniter of here and hereafter,   20
Taking all hints to use them, but swiftly leaping beyond them,
A reminiscence sing.

Once Paumanok,°
When the lilac-scent was in the air and Fifth-month° grass was
    growing,

---

3 Ninth-month Quaker term for September   **23 Paumanok** Indian name for Long Island
24 Fifth-month May (Quaker)

Up this seashore in some briers,   25
Two feather'd guests from Alabama, two together,
And their nest, and four light-green eggs spotted with brown,
And every day the he-bird to and fro near at hand,
And every day the she-bird crouch'd on her nest, silent, with
    bright eyes,
And every day I, a curious boy, never too close, never
    disturbing them,   30
Cautiously peering, absorbing, translating.

Shine! shine! shine!
Pour down your warmth, great sun!
While we bask, we two together.

Two together!   35
Winds blow south, or winds blow north,
Day come white, or night come black,
Home, or rivers and mountains from home,
Singing all time, minding no time,
While we two keep together.   40

Till of a sudden,
May-be kill'd, unknown to her mate,
One forenoon the she-bird crouch'd not on the nest,
Nor return'd that afternoon, nor the next,
Nor ever appear'd again.   45

And thenceforward all summer in the sound of the sea,
And at night under the full of the moon in calmer weather,
Over the hoarse surging of the sea,
Or flitting from brier to brier by day,
I saw, I heard at intervals the remaining one, the he-bird,   50
The solitary guest from Alabama.

Blow! blow! blow!
Blow up sea-winds along Paumanok's shore;
I wait and I wait till you blow my mate to me.

Yes, when the stars glisten'd,   55
All night long on the prong of a moss-scallop'd stake,
Down almost amid the slapping waves,
Sat the lone singer wonderful causing tears.

He call'd on his mate,
He pour'd forth the meaning which I of all men know.   60
Yes my brother I know,
The rest might not, but I have treasur'd every note,
For more than once dimly down to the beach gliding,
Silent, avoiding the moonbeams, blending myself with the
    shadows,
Recalling now the obscure shapes, the echoes, the sounds and
    sights after their sorts,   65
The white arms out in the breakers tirelessly tossing,
I, with bare feet, a child, the wind wafting my hair,
Listen'd long and long.

Listen'd to keep, to sing, now translating the notes,
Following you my brother.   70

Soothe! soothe! soothe!
Close on its wave soothes the wave behind,
And again another behind embracing and lapping, every one
    close,
But my love soothes not me, not me.

Low hangs the moon, it rose late,   75
It is lagging—O I think it is heavy with love, with love.

O madly the sea pushes upon the land,
With love, with love.

O night! do I not see my love fluttering out among the breakers?
What is that little black thing I see there in the white?   80

Loud! loud! loud!
Loud I call to you, my love!

High and clear I shoot my voice over the waves,
Surely you must know who is here, is here,
You must know who I am, my love.   85

Low-hanging moon!
What is that dusky spot in your brown yellow?
O it is the shape, the shape of my mate!
O moon do not keep her from me any longer.

Land! land! O land! 90
Whichever way I turn, O I think you could give me my mate
  back again if you only would,
For I am almost sure I see her dimly whichever way I look.

O rising stars!
Perhaps the one I want so much will rise, will rise with some
  of you.

O throat! O trembling throat! 95
Sound clearer through the atmosphere!
Pierce the woods, the earth,
Somewhere listening to catch you must be the one I want.

Shake out carols!
Solitary here, the night's carols! 100
Carols of lonesome love! death's carols!
Carols under that lagging, yellow, waning moon!
O under that moon where she droops almost down into the sea!
O reckless despairing carols.

But soft! sink low! 105
Soft! let me just murmur,
And do you wait a moment you husky-nois'd sea,
For somewhere I believe I heard my mate responding to me,
So faint, I must be still, be still to listen,
But not altogether still, for then she might not come
  immediately to me. 110

Hither my love!
Here I am! here!
With this just-sustain'd note I announce myself to you,
This gentle call is for you my love, for you.

Do not be decoy'd elsewhere, 115
That is the whistle of the wind, it is not my voice,
That is the fluttering, the fluttering of the spray,
Those are the shadows of leaves.

O darkness! O in vain!
O I am very sick and sorrowful. 120

O brown halo in the sky near the moon, drooping upon the sea!
O troubled reflection in the sea!
O throat! O throbbing heart!
And I singing uselessly, uselessly all the night.

O past! O happy life! O songs of joy!   125
In the air, in the woods, over fields,
Loved! loved! loved! loved! loved!
But my mate no more, no more with me!
We two together no more.

The aria sinking,   130
All else continuing, the stars shining,
The winds blowing, the notes of the bird continuous echoing,
With angry moans the fierce old mother incessantly moaning,
On the sands of Paumanok's shore gray and rustling,
The yellow half-moon enlarged, sagging down, drooping, the
      face of the sea almost touching,   135
The boy ecstatic, with his bare feet the waves, with his hair
      the atmosphere dallying,
The love in the heart long pent, now loose, now at last
      tumultuously bursting,
The aria's meaning, the ears, the soul, swiftly depositing,
The strange tears down the cheeks coursing,
The colloquy there, the trio, each uttering,   140
The undertone, the savage old mother incessantly crying,
To the boy's soul's questions sullenly timing, some drown'd
      secret hissing,
To the outsetting bard.

Demon or bird! (said the boy's soul,)
Is it indeed toward your mate you sing? or is it really to me?   145
For I, that was a child, my tongue's use sleeping, now I have
      heard you,
Now in a moment I know what I am for, I awake,
And already a thousand singers, a thousand songs, clearer,
      louder and more sorrowful than yours,
A thousand warbling echoes have started to life within me,
      never to die.

O you singer solitary, singing by yourself, projecting me,   *150*
O solitary me listening, never more shall I cease perpetuating
    you,
Never more shall I escape, never more the reverberations,
Never more the cries of unsatisfied love be absent from me,
Never again leave me to be the peaceful child I was before what
    there in the night,
By the sea under the yellow and sagging moon,   *155*
The messenger there arous'd, the fire, the sweet hell within,
The unknown want, the destiny of me.

O give me the clew!° (it lurks in the night here somewhere,)
O if I am to have so much, let me have more!

A word then, (for I will conquer it,)   *160*
The word final, superior to all,
Subtle, sent up—what is it?—I listen;
Are you whispering it, and have been all the time, you sea waves?
Is that it from your liquid rims and wet sands?

Whereto answering, the sea,   *165*
Delaying not, hurrying not,
Whisper'd me through the night, and very plainly before
    daybreak,
Lisp'd to me the low and delicious word death,
And again death, death, death, death,
Hissing melodious, neither like the bird nor like my arous'd
    child's heart,   *170*
But edging near as privately for me rustling at my feet,
Creeping thence steadily up to my ears and laving me softly
    all over,
Death, death, death, death, death.

Which I do not forget,
But fuse the song of my dusky demon and brother,   *175*
That he sang to me in the moonlight on Paumanok's gray
    beach,

158 clew clue

With the thousand responsive songs at random,
My own songs awaked from that hour,
And with them the key, the word up from the waves,
The word of the sweetest song and all songs,   *180*
That strong and delicious word which, creeping to my feet,
(Or like some old crone rocking the cradle, swathed in sweet
    garments, bending aside,)
The sea whisper'd me.

                                                        —*1881–82*

Song of Myself, 6

A child said *What is the grass?* fetching it to me with full hands;
How could I answer the child? I do not know what it is any more
    than he.

I guess it must be the flag of my disposition, out of hopeful green
    stuff woven.

Or I guess it is the handkerchief of the Lord,
A scented gift and remembrancer designedly dropped,   *5*
Bearing the owner's name someway in the corners, that we may
    see and remark, and say *Whose?*

Or I guess the grass is itself a child, the produced babe of the
    vegetation.

Or I guess it is a uniform hieroglyphic,
And it means, Sprouting alike in broad zones and narrow
    zones,
Growing among black folks as among white,   *10*
Kanuck,° Tuckahoe,° Congressman, Cuff,° I give them the
    same, I receive them the same.

And now it seems to me the beautiful uncut hair of graves.

Tenderly will I use you curling grass,
It may be you transpire from the breasts of young men,

---

11 Kanuck French-Canadian   **Tuckahoe** coastal Virginian   **Cuff** a black slave

It may be if I had known them I would have loved them,   15
It may be you are from old people, or from offspring taken
     soon out of their mothers' laps,
And here you are the mothers' laps.

This grass is very dark to be from the white heads of old mothers,
Darker than the colorless beards of old men,
Dark to come from under the faint red roofs of mouths.   20

O I perceive after all so many uttering tongues,
And I perceive they do not come from the roofs of mouths for
     nothing.

I wish I could translate the hints about the dead young men
     and women,
And the hints about old men and mothers, and the offspring
     taken soon out of their laps.

What do you think has become of the young and old men?   25
And what do you think has become of the women and
     children?

They are alive and well somewhere,
The smallest sprout shows there is really no death,
And if ever there was it led forward life, and does not wait at
     the end to arrest it,
And ceased the moment life appeared.   30

All goes onward and outward, nothing collapses,
And to die is different from what anyone supposed, and luckier.

—1855

When I Heard the Learn'd Astronomer

When I heard the learn'd astronomer,
When the proofs, the figures, were ranged in columns before me,
When I was shown the charts and diagrams, to add, divide, and
     measure them,

When I sitting heard the astronomer where he lectured with much
    applause in the lecture-room,
How soon unaccountable I became tired and sick,   5
Till rising and gliding out I wander'd off by myself,
In the mystical moist night-air, and from time to time,
Look'd up in perfect silence at the stars.

                        —*1865*

---

*Matthew Arnold (1822–1888) was the son of the headmaster of Rugby School
and himself served as an inspector of schools during much of his adult life. An influential essayist as well as a poet, Arnold was unsparing in his criticism of middle-
class "Philistinism." At least part of "Dover Beach" is thought to date from his honeymoon in 1851.*

Matthew Arnold
Dover Beach

The sea is calm tonight.
The tide is full, the moon lies fair
Upon the straits; on the French coast the light
Gleams and is gone; the cliffs of England stand,
Glimmering and vast, out in the tranquil bay.   5
Come to the window, sweet is the night-air!
Only, from the long line of spray
Where the sea meets the moon-blanched land,
Listen! you hear the grating roar
Of pebbles which the waves draw back, and fling,   10
At their return, up the high strand,
Begin, and cease, and then again begin,
With tremulous cadence slow, and bring
The eternal note of sadness in.

Sophocles° long ago   15
Heard it on the Aegean, and it brought

---

15 Sophocles Athenian tragic poet (496–406 B.C.)

Into his mind the turbid ebb and flow
Of human misery; we
Find also in the sound a thought,
Hearing it by this distant northern sea.   20

The Sea of Faith
Was once, too, at the full, and round earth's shore
Lay like the folds of a bright girdle° furled.
But now I only hear
Its melancholy, long, withdrawing roar,   25
Retreating, to the breath
Of the night-wind, down the vast edges drear
And naked shingles° of the world.

Ah, love, let us be true
To one another! for the world, which seems   30
To lie before us like a land of dreams,
So various, so beautiful, so new,
Hath really neither joy, nor love, nor light,
Nor certitude, nor peace, nor help for pain;
And we are here as on a darkling plain   35
Swept with confused alarms of struggle and flight,
Where ignorant armies clash by night.

—1867

---

23 girdle sash   **28 shingles** beach pebbles

Emily Dickinson (1830–1886) *has been reinvented with each generation, and readers' views of her have ranged between two extremes — one perceiving her as the abnormally shy "Belle of Amherst" making poetry out of her own neuroses and another seeing her as a proto-feminist carving out a world of her own in self-willed isolation. What remains is her brilliant poetry — unique, original, and marked with the stamp of individual talent. Dickinson published only seven poems during her lifetime, but left behind hundreds of poems in manuscript at her death. Published by her relatives, they were immediately popular, but it was not until the edition of Thomas Johnson in 1955 that they were read with Dickinson's eccentric punctuation and capitalization intact.*

Emily Dickinson
Because I Could Not Stop for Death

Because I could not stop for Death—
He kindly stopped for me—
The Carriage held but just Ourselves—
And Immortality.

We slowly drove—He knew no haste   5
And I had put away
My labor and my leisure too,
For His Civility—

We passed the School, where Children strove
At Recess—in the Ring—   10
We passed the Fields of Gazing Grain—
We passed the Setting Sun—

Or rather—He passed Us—
The Dews drew quivering and chill—
For only Gossamer, my Gown—   15
My Tippet°—only Tulle°—

We paused before a House that seemed
A Swelling of the Ground—

16 Tippet shawl   **Tulle** net-like fabric

The Roof was scarcely visible—
The Cornice—in the Ground—   20

Since then—'tis Centuries—and yet
Feels shorter than the Day
I first surmised the Horses' Heads
Were toward Eternity—

—*1890*

I Died for Beauty—But Was Scarce

I died for Beauty—but was scarce
Adjusted in the Tomb
When One who died for Truth, was lain
In an adjoining Room—

He questioned softly "Why I failed?"   5
"For Beauty," I replied—
"And I—for Truth—Themself are One—
We Brethren, are," He said—

And so, as Kinsmen, met a Night—
We talked between the Rooms—   10
Until the Moss had reached our lips—
And covered up—our names—

—*1890*

I Heard a Fly Buzz— When I Died—

I heard a Fly buzz—when I died—
The Stillness in the Room
Was like the Stillness in the Air—
Between the Heaves of Storm—

The Eyes around—had wrung them dry—   5
And Breaths were gathering firm
For that last Onset—when the King
Be witnessed—in the Room—

I willed my Keepsakes—Signed away
What portion of me be   10
Assignable—and then it was
There interposed a Fly—

With Blue—uncertain stumbling Buzz—
Between the light—and me—
And then the Windows failed—and then   15
I could not see to see—

                                                                  —1896

My Life Closed Twice Before Its Close

My life closed twice before its close;
It yet remains to see
If Immortality unveil
A third event to me

So huge, so hopeless to conceive   5
As these that twice befell.
Parting is all we know of heaven,
And all we need of hell.

                                                                  —1896

A Narrow Fellow in the Grass

A narrow Fellow in the Grass
Occasionally rides—
You may have met Him—did you not
His notice sudden is—

The Grass divides as with a Comb—   5
A spotted shaft is seen—
And then it closes at your feet
And opens further on—

He likes a Boggy Acre
A Floor to cool for Corn—   10
Yet when a Boy, and Barefoot—
I more than once at Noon
Have passed, I thought, a Whip lash
Unbraiding in the Sun
When stooping to secure it   15
It wrinkled, and was gone—

Several of Nature's People
I know, and they know me—
I feel for them a transport
Of cordiality—   20

But never met this Fellow
Attended, or alone
Without a tighter breathing
And Zero at the Bone—

                                          —1866

The Soul Selects Her Own Society—

The Soul selects her own Society—
Then—shuts the Door—
To her divine Majority—
Present no more—

Unmoved—she notes the Chariots—pausing—   5
At her low Gate—
Unmoved—an Emperor be kneeling
Upon her Mat—

I've known her—from an ample nation—
Choose One—   10
Then—close the Valves° of her attention—
Like Stone—

—*1890*

Christina Rossetti (1830–1894) was the younger sister of Dante Gabriel and William, also distinguished writers, and was the author of numerous devotional poems and prose works. Her collected poems, edited by her brother William, appeared posthumously in 1904.

Christina Rossetti
Up-Hill

Does the road wind up-hill all the way?
   Yes, to the very end.
Will the day's journey take the whole long day?
   From morn to night, my friend.

But is there for the night a resting-place?   5
   A roof for when the slow dark hours begin.
May not the darkness hide it from my face?
   You cannot miss that inn.

Shall I meet other wayfarers at night?
   Those who have gone before.   10
Then must I knock, or call when just in sight?
   They will not keep you waiting at that door.

Shall I find comfort, travel-sore and weak?
   Of labor you shall find the sum.
Will there be beds for me and all who seek?   15
   Yea, beds for all who come.

—*1858*

---

11 Valves sliding doors

Thomas Hardy (1840–1928), after the disappointing response to his novel Jude the Obscure *in 1895, returned to his first love, writing poetry for the last thirty years of his long life. The language and life of Hardy's native Wessex inform both his novels and poems. His subject matter is very much of the nineteenth century, but his ironic, disillusioned point of view marks him as one of the chief predecessors of modernism.*

Thomas Hardy
Ah, Are You Digging on My Grave?

"Ah, are you digging on my grave
    My loved one?—planting rue?"°
—"No: yesterday he went to wed
One of the brightest wealth has bred.
'It cannot hurt her now,' he said,   5
    'That I should not be true.'"

"Then who is digging on my grave?
    My nearest dearest kin?"
—"Ah, no; they sit and think, 'What use!
What good will planting flowers produce?   10
No tendance of her mound can loose
    Her spirit from Death's gin.'"

"But some one digs upon my grave?
    My enemy?—prodding sly?"
—"Nay: when she heard you had passed the Gate   15
That shuts on all flesh soon or late.
She thought you no more worth her hate,
    And cares not where you lie."

"Then who is digging on my grave?
Say—since I have not guessed!"   20
—"O it is I, my mistress dear,
Your little dog, who still lives near,
And much I hope my movements here
    Have not disturbed your rest?"

2 rue yellow flower traditionally associated with sadness

"Ah, yes! *You* dig upon my grave . . .   25
          Why flashed it not on me
That one true heart was left behind!
What feeling do we ever find
To equal among human kind
          A dog's fidelity!"   30

"Mistress, I dug upon your grave
          To bury a bone, in case
I should be hungry near this spot
When passing on my daily trot.
I am sorry, but I quite forgot   35
          It was your resting-place."

                                        —*1914*

The Convergence of the Twain

Lines on the Loss of the Titanic

          1

          In a solitude of the sea
          Deep from human vanity,
And the Pride of Life that planned her, stilly couches she.

          2

          Steel chambers, late the pyres
          Of her salamadrine fires,°
Cold currents thrid,° and turn to rhythmic tidal lyres.   5

          3

          Over the mirrors meant
          To glass the opulent
The sea-worm crawls—grotesque, slimed, dumb, indifferent.

---

5 salamandrine fires The salamander, according to legend, could live in fire   **6 thrid** thread

4

   Jewels in joy designed   *10*
   To ravish the sensuous mind
Lie lightless, all their sparkles bleared and black and blind.

5

   Dim moon-eyed fishes near
   Gaze at the gilded gear
And query: "What does this vaingloriousness down here?"   *15*

6

   Well: while was fashioning
   This creature of cleaving wing,
The Immanent Will° that stirs and urges everything

7

   Prepared a sinister mate
   For her—so gaily great—   *20*
A Shape of Ice, for the time far and dissociate.

8

   And as the smart ship grew
   In stature, grace, and hue,
In shadowy silent distance grew the Iceberg too.

9

   Alien they seemed to be: *25*
   No mortal eye could see
The intimate welding of their later history,

10

   Or sign that they were bent
   By paths coincident
On being anon twin halves of one august event,   *30*

---

18 Immanent Will Term used by Hardy for fate

11

    Till the Spinner of the Years
    Said "Now!" And each one hears,
And consummation comes, and jars two hemispheres.

—*1912*

Neutral Tones

We stood by a pond that winter day,
And the sun was white, as though chidden of God,
And a few leaves lay on the starving sod;
    —They had fallen from an ash, and were gray.

Your eyes on me were as eyes that rove   *5*
Over tedious riddles of years ago;
And some words played between us to and fro
    On which lost the more by our love.

The smile on your mouth was the deadest thing
Alive enough to have strength to die;   *10*
And a grin of bitterness swept thereby
    Like an ominous bird a-wing . . .

Since then, keen lessons that love deceives,
And wrings with wrong, have shaped to me
Your face, and the God-curst sun, and a tree,   *15*
    And a pond edged with grayish leaves.

—*1898*

The Ruined Maid

"O 'Melia, my dear, this does everything crown!
Who could have supposed I should meet you in Town?
And whence such fair garments, such prosperi-ty?"
"O didn't you know I'd been ruined?" said she.

"You left us in tatters, without shoes or socks,   5
Tired of digging potatoes, and spudding up docks;°
And now you've gay bracelets and bright feathers three!"
"Yes: that's how we dress when we're ruined," said she.

"At home in the barton° you said 'thee' and 'thou,'
And 'thik oon,' and 'theäs oon,'° and 't'other'; but now   10
Your talking quite fits 'ee for high compa-ny!"
"Some polish is gained with one's ruin," said she.

"Your hands were like paws then, your face blue and bleak
But now I'm bewitched by your delicate cheek,
And your little gloves fit as on any la-dy!"   15
"We never do work when we're ruined," said she.

"You used to call home-life a hag-ridden dream,
And you'd sigh, and you'd sock; but at present you seem
To know not of megrims° or melancho-ly!"
"True. One's pretty lively when ruined," said she.   20

"I wish I had feathers, a fine sweeping gown,
And a delicate face, and could strut about Town!"
"My dear—a raw country girl, such as you be,
Cannot quite expect that. You ain't ruined," said she.

—*1866*

6 docks weeds **9 barton** barnyard **10 thik oon and theäs oon** dialect: "that one and this one"
19 megrims migraines

Gerard Manley Hopkins (1844–1889) was an English Jesuit priest who developed elaborate theories of poetic meter (what he called "sprung rhythm") and language to express his own spiritual ardor. Most of his work was posthumously printed through the efforts of his Oxford friend and later correspondent Robert Bridges, who was poet laureate.

Gerard Manley Hopkins

God's Grandeur

The world is charged with the grandeur of God.
  It will flame out, like shining from shook foil;°
  It gathers to a greatness, like the ooze of oil
Crushed.° Why do men then now not reck his rod?
Generations have trod, have trod, have trod;   5
  And all is seared with trade; bleared, smeared with toil;
  And wears man's smudge and shares man's smell: the soil
Is bare now, nor can foot feel, being shod.

And for all this, nature is never spent;
  There lives the dearest freshness deep down things;   10
And though the last lights off the black West went
  Oh, morning, at the brown brink eastward, springs—
Because the Holy Ghost over the bent
  World broods with warm breast and with ah! bright wings.

                          —1877

Pied Beauty

Glory be to God for dappled things—
  For skies of couple-color as a brinded° cow;
    For rose-moles all in stipple upon trout that swim;
Fresh-firecoal chestnut-falls;° finches' wings;
  Landscape plotted and pieced—fold, fallow, and plough;   5
    And all trades, their gear and tackle and trim.

---

2 foil gold leaf   **4 Crushed** Hopkins is referring to olive oil
2 brinded streaked   **4 Fresh-firecoal chestnut-falls** according to the poet, chestnuts have a red color

All things counter, original, spare, strange;
    Whatever is fickle, freckled (who knows how?)
        With swift, slow; sweet, sour; adazzle, dim;
He fathers-forth whose beauty is past change: *10*
        Praise him.

                               —1877

A. E. Housman (1859–1936) was educated in the classics at Oxford and was almost forty before he began to write verse seriously. His ballad-like poems of Shropshire (an area in which he never actually lived) have proved some of the most popular lyrics in English, despite their pervasive mood of bittersweet pessimism.

A. E. Housman

Eight O'Clock

He stood, and heard the steeple
    Sprinkle the quarters° on the morning town.
One, two, three, four, to market-place and people
    It tossed them down.

Strapped, noosed, nighing his hour,   *5*
    He stood and counted them and cursed his luck;
And then the clock collected in the tower
    Its strength, and struck.

                               —1922

Loveliest of Trees, the Cherry Now

Loveliest of trees, the cherry now
Is hung with bloom along the bough,
And stands about the woodland ride
Wearing white for Eastertide.

2 quarters quarter hours

Now, of my threescore years and ten,   5
Twenty will not come again,
And take from seventy springs a score,
It only leaves me fifty more.

And since to look at things in bloom
Fifty springs are little room,   10
About the woodlands I will go
To see the cherry hung with snow.

—1896

Stars, I Have Seen
Them Fall

Stars, I have seen them fall,
    But when they drop and die
No star is lost at all
    From all the star-sown sky.
The toil of all that be   5
    Helps not the primal fault;
It rains into the sea
    And still the sea is salt.

—1936

"Terence, This Is Stupid
Stuff . . ."

"Terence, this is stupid stuff:
You eat your victuals fast enough;
There can't be much amiss, 'tis clear,
To see the rate you drink your beer.
But oh, good Lord, the verse you make,   5
It gives a chap the belly-ache.
The cow, the old cow, she is dead;
It sleeps well, the hornèd head:

We poor lads, 'tis our turn now
To hear such tunes as killed the cow.   10
Pretty friendship 'tis to rhyme
Your friends to death before their time
Moping melancholy mad:
Come, pipe a tune to dance to, lad."

     Why, if 'tis dancing you would be,   15
There's brisker pipes than poetry.
Say, for what were hop-yards meant,
Or why was Burton built on Trent?°
Oh many a peer of England brews
Livelier liquor than the Muse,   20
And malt does more than Milton can
To justify God's ways to man.
Ale, man, ale's the stuff to drink
For fellows whom it hurts to think:
Look into the pewter pot   25
To see the world as the world's not.
And faith, 'tis pleasant till 'tis past:
The mischief is that 'twill not last.
Oh I have been to Ludlow fair
And left my necktie God knows where,   30
And carried halfway home, or near,
Pints and quarts of Ludlow beer:
Then the world seemed none so bad,
And I myself a sterling lad;
And down in lovely muck I've lain,   35
Happy till I woke again.
Then I saw the morning sky:
Heigho, the tale was all a lie;
The world, it was the old world yet,
I was I, my things were wet,   40
And nothing now remained to do
But begin the game anew.

18 Burton built on Trent site of breweries

Therefore, since the world has still
Much good, but much less good than ill,
And while the sun and moon endure   45
Luck's a chance, but trouble's sure,
I'd face it as a wise man would,
And train for ill and not for good.
'Tis true, the stuff I bring for sale
Is not so brisk a brew as ale: 50
Out of a stem that scored the hand
I wrung it in a weary land.
But take it: if the smack is sour,
The better for the embittered hour;
It should do good to heart and head   50
When your soul is in my soul's stead;
And I will friend you, if I may,
In the dark and cloudy day.

There was a king reigned in the East:
There, when kings will sit to feast,   60
They get their fill before they think
With poisoned meat and poisoned drink.
He gathered all that springs to birth
From the many-venomed earth;
First a little, thence to more,   65
He sampled all her killing store;
And easy, smiling, seasoned sound,
Sate the king when healths went round.
They put arsenic in his meat
And stared aghast to watch him eat;   70
They poured strychnine in his cup
And shook to see him drink it up:
They shook, they stared as white's their shirt:
Them it was their poison hurt.
—I tell the tale that I heard told.   75
Mithridates,° he died old.

—*1896*

---

76 Mithridates legendary King of Pontus, he protected himself from poisons by taking small doses
regularly

To an Athlete Dying Young

The time you won your town the race
We chaired you through the market-place;
Man and boy stood cheering by,
And home we brought you shoulder-high.

Today, the road all runners come,   5
Shoulder-high we bring you home,
And set you at your threshold down,
Townsman of a stiller town.

Smart lad, to slip betimes° away
From fields where glory does not stay   10
And early though the laurel grows
It withers quicker than the rose.

Eyes the shady night has shut
Cannot see the record cut,
And silence sounds no worse than cheers   15
After earth has stopped the ears:

Now you will not swell the rout
Of lads that wore their honours out,
Runners whom renown outran
And the name died before the man.   20

So set, before its echoes fade,
The fleet foot on the sill of shade,
And hold to the low lintel up
The still-defended challenge-cup.

And round that early-laurelled head   25
Will flock to gaze the strengthless dead,
And find unwithered on its curls
The garland briefer than a girl's.

—1896

9 betimes early

William Butler Yeats (1865–1939) is considered the greatest Irish poet and provides an important link between the late romantic era and early modernism. His early poetry, focusing on Irish legend and landscape, is regional in the best sense of the term, but his later work, with its prophetic tone and symbolist texture, moves on a larger stage. Yeats lived in London for many years and was at the center of British literary life. He was awarded the Nobel Prize in 1923.

William Butler Yeats
The Lake Isle of Innisfree

I will arise and go now, and go to Innisfree,
And a small cabin build there, of clay and wattles° made:
Nine bean-rows will I have there, a hive for the honey-bee,
And live alone in the bee-loud glade.

And I shall have some peace there, for peace comes dropping slow, 5
Dropping from the veils of the morning to where the cricket sings;
There midnight's all a glimmer, and noon a purple glow,
And evening full of the linnet's wings.

I will arise and go now, for always night and day
I hear lake water lapping with low sounds by the shore; 10
While I stand on the roadway, or on the pavements gray,
I hear it in the deep heart's core.

—*1892*

Leda° and the Swan

A sudden blow: the great wings beating still
Above the staggering girl, her thighs caressed
By the dark webs, her nape caught in his bill,
He holds her helpless breast upon his breast.

How can those terrified vague fingers push 5
The feathered glory from her loosening thighs?

---

2 wattles woven poles and reeds
Leda mortal mother of Helen of Troy and Clytemnestra, wife and assassin of Agamemnon

And how can body, laid in that white rush,
But feel the strange heart beating where it lies?

A shudder in the loins engenders there
The broken wall, the burning roof and tower   10
And Agamemnon dead.°
      Being so caught up,
So mastered by the brute blood of the air,
Did she put on his knowledge with his power
Before the indifferent beak could let her drop?

                                       —*1923*

Sailing to Byzantium°

1

That is no country for old men. The young
In one another's arms, birds in the trees
—Those dying generations—at their song,
The salmon-falls, the mackerel-crowded seas,
Fish, flesh, or fowl, commend all summer long   5
Whatever is begotten, born, and dies.
Caught in that sensual music all neglect
Monuments of unaging intellect.

2

An aged man is but a paltry thing,
A tattered coat upon a stick, unless   10
Soul clap its hands and sing, and louder sing
For every tatter in its mortal dress,
Nor is there singing school but studying
Monuments of its own magnificence;
And therefore I have sailed the seas and come   15
To the holy city of Byzantium.

10–11 The broken wall . . . Agamemnon dead events that occurred during and after the
Trojan War
Byzantium Constantinople or Istanbul, capital of the Eastern Roman Empire

3

O sages standing in God's holy fire
As in the gold mosaic of a wall,
Come from the holy fire, perne in a gyre,°
And be the singing-masters of my soul.
Consume my heart away; sick with desire   20
And fastened to a dying animal
It knows not what it is; and gather me
Into the artifice of eternity.

4

Once out of nature I shall never take   25
My bodily form from any natural thing,
But such a form as Grecian goldsmiths make
Of hammered gold and gold enameling
To keep a drowsy Emperor awake;
Or set upon a golden bough to sing   30
To lords and ladies of Byzantium
Of what is past, or passing, or to come.

—*1927*

The Second Coming

Turning and turning in the widening gyre°
The falcon cannot hear the falconer;
Things fall apart; the center cannot hold;
Mere anarchy is loosed upon the world,
The blood-dimmed tide is loosed, and everywhere   5
The ceremony of innocence is drowned;
The best lack all conviction, while the worst
Are full of passionate intensity.

Surely some revelation is at hand;
Surely the Second Coming is at hand.   10
The Second Coming! Hardly are those words out

---

19 perne in a gyre descend in a spiral; the gyre for Yeats was a private symbol of historical cycles
1 gyre see note to "Sailing to Byzantium"

When a vast image out of *Spiritus Mundi*°
Troubles my sight: somewhere in the sands of the desert
A shape with lion body and the head of a man,
A gaze blank and pitiless as the sun,   15
Is moving its slow thighs, while all about it
Reel shadows of the indignant desert birds.
The darkness drops again; but now I know
That twenty centuries of stony sleep
Were vexed to nightmare by a rocking cradle,   20
And what rough beast, its hour come round at last,
Slouches towards Bethlehem to be born?

—*1921*

The Song of Wandering Aengus°

I went out to the hazel wood,
Because a fire was in my head,
And cut and peeled a hazel wand,
And hooked a berry to a thread;
And when white moths were on the wing,   5
And moth-like stars were flickering out,
I dropped the berry in a stream
And caught a little silver trout.

When I had laid it on the floor
I went to blow the fire aflame,   10
But something rustled on the floor,
And some one called me by my name:
It had become a glimmering girl
With apple blossom in her hair
Who called me by my name and ran   15
And faded through the brightening air.

---

12 Spiritus Mundi World-Spirit
Aengus Among the Sidhe (native Irish deities), the god of youth, love, beauty, and poetry. Yeats once also called him the "Master of Love." Here, however, he seems mortal.

Though I am old with wandering
Through hollow lands and hilly lands,
I will find out where she has gone,
And kiss her lips and take her hands;   20
And walk among long dappled grass,
And pluck till time and times are done
The silver apples of the moon,
The golden apples of the sun.

—*1899*

Edwin Arlington Robinson (1869–1935) wrote many poems set in "Tilbury," a recreation of his hometown of Gardiner, Maine. These poems continue to present readers with a memorable cast of eccentric characters who somehow manifest universal human desires. Robinson languished in poverty and obscurity for many years before his reputation began to flourish as a result of the interest taken in his work by President Theodore Roosevelt, who obtained a government job for Robinson and wrote a favorable review of one of his books.

Edwin Arlington Robinson

Firelight

Ten years together without yet a cloud,
They seek each other's eyes at intervals
Of gratefulness to firelight and four walls
For love's obliteration of the crowd.
Serenely and perennially endowed   5
And bowered as few may be, their joy recalls
No snake, no sword, and over them there falls
The blessing of what neither says aloud.

Wiser for silence, they were not so glad
Were she to read the graven° tale of lines   10
On the wan face of one somewhere alone;

---

10 graven engraved

Nor were they more content could he have had
Her thoughts a moment since of one who shines
Apart, and would be hers if he had known.

—1920

Eros Turannos°

She fears him, and will always ask
    What fated her to choose him;
She meets in his engaging mask
    All reasons to refuse him
But what she meets and what she fears   5
Are less than are the downward years,
Drawn slowly to the foamless weirs
    Of age, were she to lose him.

Between a blurred sagacity
    That once had power to sound him,   10
And Love, that will not let him be
    The Judas that she found him,
Her pride assuages her almost,
As if it were alone the cost.—
He sees that he will not be lost,   15
    And waits and looks around him.

A sense of ocean and old trees
    Envelops and allures him;
Tradition, touching all he sees,
    Beguiles and reassures him;   20
And all her doubts of what he says
Are dimmed with what she knows of days—
Till even prejudice delays
    And fades, and she secures him.

The falling leaf inaugurates   25
    The reign of her confusion;

Eros Turannos "Love, the Tyrant"

The pounding wave reverberates
    The dirge of her illusion;
And home, where passion lived and died
Becomes a place where she can hide,   30
While all the town and harbor side
    Vibrate with her seclusion.

We tell you, tapping on our brows,
    The story as it should be,—
As if the story of a house   35
    Were told, or ever could be;
We'll have no kindly veil between
Her visions and those we have seen,—
As if we guessed what hers have been,
    Or what they are or would be.   40

Meanwhile we do no harm; for they
    That with a god have striven,
Not hearing much of what we say
    Take what the god has given;
Though like waves breaking it may be   45
Or like a changed familiar tree,
Or like a stairway to the sea
    Where down the blind are driven.

                                       —*1916*

The Mill

The miller's wife had waited long,
    The tea was cold, the fire was dead;
And there might yet be nothing wrong
    In how he went and what he said:
"There are no millers any more,"   5
    Was all that she had heard him say;
And he had lingered at the door
    So long that it seemed yesterday.

Sick with a fear that had no form
    She knew that she was there at last;   10

And in the mill there was a warm
    And mealy fragrance of the past.
What else there was would only seem
    To say again what he had meant;
And what was hanging from a beam   *15*
    Would not have heeded where she went.

And if she thought it followed her,
    She may have reasoned in the dark
That one way of the few there were
    Would hide her and would leave no mark: *20*
Black water, smooth above the weir
    Like starry velvet in the night,
Though ruffled once, would soon appear
    The same as ever to the sight.

          —1920

Richard Cory

Whenever Richard Cory went down town,
We people on the pavement looked at him:
He was a gentleman from sole to crown,
Clean favored, and imperially slim.

And he was always quietly arrayed,   *5*
And he was always human when he talked;
But still he fluttered pulses when he said,
"Good-morning," and he glittered when he walked.

And he was rich—yes, richer than a king—
And admirably schooled in every grace: *10*
In fine, we thought that he was everything
To make us wish that we were in his place.

So on we worked, and waited for the light,
And went without the meat, and cursed the bread;
And Richard Cory, one calm summer night,   *15*
Went home and put a bullet through his head.

          —1896

Stephen Crane (1871–1900) was the brilliant young journalist who wrote The Red Badge of Courage *and was also an unconventional poet whose skeptical epigrams and fables today seem far ahead of their time. In many ways he mirrors the cosmic pessimism of contemporaries like Hardy, Housman, and Robinson, all of whom were influenced by the currents of determinism that ran so strongly at the end of the nineteenth century.*

Stephen Crane

The Black Riders

VI

God fashioned the ship of the world carefully.
With the infinite skill of an All-Master
Made He the hull and the sails,
Held He the rudder
Ready for adjustment.   5
Erect stood He, scanning His work proudly.
Then—at fateful time—a wrong called,
And God turned, heeding.
Lo, the ship, at this opportunity, slipped slyly,
Making cunning noiseless travel down the ways.   10
So that, for ever rudderless, it went upon the seas
Going ridiculous voyages,
Making quaint progress,
Turning as with serious purpose
Before stupid winds.   15
And there were many in the sky
Who laughed at this thing.

—*1895*

War Is Kind

XXI

A man said to the universe:
"Sir, I exist!"
"However," replied the universe,
"The fact has not created in me
A sense of obligation."   5

—*1899*

---

*Paul Laurence Dunbar (1872–1906), a native of Dayton, Ohio, was one of the
first black poets to make a mark in American literature. Many of his dialect poems
reflect a sentimentalized view of life in the South, which he did not know directly.
However, he was also capable of powerful expressions of racial protest.*

Paul Laurence Dunbar
We Wear the Mask

We wear the mask that grins and lies,
It hides our cheeks and shades our eyes,—
This debt we pay to human guile;
With torn and bleeding hearts we smile,
And mouth with myriad subtleties.   5

Why should the world be over-wise,
In counting all our tears and sighs?
Nay, let them only see us, while
        We wear the mask.

We smile, but, O great Christ, our cries   10
To thee from tortured souls arise.
We sing, but oh the clay is vile
Beneath our feet, and long the mile;
But let the world dream otherwise,
        We wear the mask!   15

—*1896*

Robert Frost (1874–1963), during the second half of his long life, was a public figure who attained a popularity unmatched by any American poet of the last century. His reading at the inauguration of John F. Kennedy in 1961 capped an impressive career that included four Pulitzer Prizes. Unattracted by the more exotic aspects of modernism, Frost nevertheless remains a poet who speaks eloquently to contemporary uncertainties about humanity's place in a universe that does not seem to care much for its existence. While Frost is rarely directly an autobiographical poet ("Home Burial" may reflect the death of Frost's son Elliot at age three), his work always bears the stamp of his powerful personality and identification with the New England landscape.

Robert Frost

Acquainted with the Night

I have been one acquainted with the night.
I have walked out in rain—and back in rain.
I have outwalked the furthest city light.

I have looked down the saddest city lane.
I have passed by the watchman on his beat   5
And dropped my eyes, unwilling to explain.

I have stood still and stopped the sound of feet
When far away an interrupted cry
Came over houses from another street,

But not to call me back or say good-bye;   10
And further still at an unearthly height
One luminary clock against the sky

Proclaimed the time was neither wrong nor right.
I have been one acquainted with the night.

—1928

After Apple-Picking

My long two-pointed ladder's sticking through a tree
Toward heaven still,
And there's a barrel that I didn't fill
Beside it, and there may be two or three

Apples I didn't pick upon some bough.   5
But I am done with apple-picking now.
Essence of winter sleep is on the night,
The scent of apples: I am drowsing off.
I cannot rub the strangeness from my sight
I got from looking through a pane of glass   10
I skimmed this morning from the drinking trough
And held against the world of hoary grass.
It melted, and I let it fall and break.
But I was well
Upon my way to sleep before it fell,   15
And I could tell
What form my dreaming was about to take.
Magnified apples appear and disappear,
Stem end and blossom end,
And every fleck of russet showing clear.   20
My instep arch not only keeps the ache,
It keeps the pressure of a ladder-round.
I feel the ladder sway as the boughs bend.
And I keep hearing from the cellar bin
The rumbling sound   25
Of load on load of apples coming in.
For I have had too much
Of apple-picking: I am overtired
Of the great harvest I myself desired.
There were ten thousand thousand fruit to touch,   30
Cherish in hand, lift down, and not let fall.
For all
That struck the earth,
No matter if not bruised or spiked with stubble,
Went surely to the cider-apple heap   35
As of no worth.
One can see what will trouble
This sleep of mine, whatever sleep it is.
Were he not gone,
The woodchuck could say whether it's like his   40
Long sleep, as I describe its coming on,
Or just some human sleep.

—*1914*

Design

I found a dimpled spider, fat and white,
On a white heal-all,° holding up a moth
Like a white piece of rigid satin cloth—
Assorted characters of death and blight
Mixed ready to begin the morning right,   5
Like the ingredients of a witches' broth—
A snow-drop spider, a flower like a froth,
And dead wings carried like a paper kite.

What had that flower to do with being white,
The wayside blue and innocent heal-all?   10
What brought the kindred spider to that height,
Then steered the white moth thither in the night?
What but design of darkness to appall?—
If design govern in a thing so small.

—1936

Home Burial

He saw her from the bottom of the stairs
Before she saw him. She was starting down,
Looking back over her shoulder at some fear.
She took a doubtful step and then undid it
To raise herself and look again. He spoke   5
Advancing toward her: "What is it you see
From up there always?—for I want to know."
She turned and sank upon her skirts at that,
And her face changed from terrified to dull.
He said to gain time: "What is it you see?"   10
Mounting until she cowered under him.
"I will find out now—you must tell me, dear."
She, in her place, refused him any help,
With the least stiffening of her neck and silence.

2 **heal-all** a wildflower, usually blue

She let him look, sure that he wouldn't see,   15
Blind creature; and awhile he didn't see.
But at last he murmured, "Oh," and again, "Oh."

"What is it—what?" she said.

                                "Just that I see."

"You don't," she challenged. "Tell me what it is."

"The wonder is I didn't see at once   20
I never noticed it from here before.
I must be wonted to it—that's the reason.
The little graveyard where my people are!
So small the window frames the whole of it.
Not so much larger than a bedroom, is it?   25
There are three stones of slate and one of marble,
Broad-shouldered little slabs there in the sunlight
On the sidehill. We haven't to mind *those*.
But I understand: it is not the stones,
But the child's mound—"

                     "Don't, don't, don't, don't," she cried.   30

She withdrew, shrinking from beneath his arm
That rested on the banister, and slid downstairs;
And turned on him with such a daunting look,
He said twice over before he knew himself:
"Can't a man speak of his own child he's lost?"   35

"Not you!—Oh, where's my hat? Oh, I don't need it!
I must get out of here. I must get air.—
I don't know rightly whether any man can."

"Amy! Don't go to someone else this time.
Listen to me. I won't come down the stairs."   40
He sat and fixed his chin between his fists.
"There's something I should like to ask you, dear."

"You don't know how to ask it."

                         "Help me, then."

Her fingers moved the latch for all reply.

"My words are nearly always an offense.   45
I don't know how to speak of anything
So as to please you. But I might be taught,
I should suppose. I can't say I see how.
A man must partly give up being a man
With womenfolk. We could have some arrangement   50
By which I'd bind myself to keep hands off
Anything special you're a-mind to name.
Though I don't like such things 'twixt those that love.
Two that don't love can't live together without them.
But two that do can't live together with them."   55
She moved the latch a little. "Don't—don't go.
Don't carry it to someone else this time.
Tell me about it if it's something human.
Let me into your grief. I'm not so much
Unlike other folks as your standing there   60
Apart would make me out. Give me my chance.
I do think, though, you overdo it a little.
What was it brought you up to think it the thing
To take your mother-loss of a first child
So inconsolably—in the face of love.   65
You'd think his memory might be satisfied—"

"There you go sneering now!"

                              "I'm not, I'm not!
You make me angry. I'll come down to you.
God, what a woman! And it's come to this,
A man can't speak of his own child that's dead."   70

"You can't because you don't know how to speak.
If you had any feelings, you that dug
With your own hand—how could you?—his little grave;
I saw you from that very window there,
Making the gravel leap and leap in air,   75
Leap up, like that, like that, and land so lightly
And roll back down the mound beside the hole.
I thought, Who is that man? I didn't know you.
And I crept down the stairs and up the stairs
To look again, and still your spade kept lifting.   80

Then you came in. I heard your rumbling voice
Out in the kitchen, and I don't know why,
But I went near to see with my own eyes.
You could sit there with the stains on your shoes
Of the fresh earth from your own baby's grave   *85*
And talk about your everyday concerns.
You had stood the spade up against the wall
Outside there in the entry, for I saw it."

"I shall laugh the worst laugh I ever laughed.
I'm cursed. God, if I don't believe I'm cursed."   *90*
"I can repeat the very words you were saying:
'Three foggy mornings and one rainy day
Will rot the best birch fence a man can build.'
Think of it, talk like that at such a time!
What had how long it takes a birch to rot   *95*
To do with what was in the darkened parlor?
You *couldn't* care! The nearest friends can go
With anyone to death, comes so far short
They might as well not try to go at all.
No, from the time when one is sick to death,   *100*
One is alone, and he dies more alone.
Friends make pretense of following to the grave,
But before one is in it, their minds are turned
And making the best of their way back to life
And living people, and things they understand.   *105*
But the world's evil. I won't have grief so
If I can change it. Oh, I won't, I won't!"

"There, you have said it all and you feel better.
You won't go now. You're crying. Close the door.
The heart's gone out of it: why keep it up?   *110*
Amy! There's someone coming down the road!"

"*You*—oh, you think the talk is all. I must go—
Somewhere out of this house. How can I make you—"

"If—you—do!" She was opening the door wider.
"Where do you mean to go? First tell me that.   *115*
I'll follow and bring you back by force. I *will!*—"

—*1914*

The Need of Being Versed in Country Things

The house had gone to bring again
To the midnight sky a sunset glow.
Now the chimney was all of the house that stood,
Like a pistil after the petals go.

The barn opposed across the way,   5
That would have joined the house in flame
Had it been the will of the wind, was left
To bear forsaken the place's name.

No more it opened with all one end
For teams that came by the stony road   10
To drum on the floor with scurrying hoofs
And brush the mow with the summer load.

The birds that came to it through the air
At broken windows flew out and in,
Their murmur more like the sigh we sigh   15
From too much dwelling on what has been.

Yet for them the lilac renewed its leaf,
And the aged elm, though touched with fire;
And the dry pump flung up an awkward arm;
And the fence post carried a strand of wire.   20

For them there was really nothing sad.
But though they rejoiced in the nest they kept,
One had to be versed in country things
Not to believe the phoebes wept.

—*1923*

Stopping by Woods on a Snowy Evening

Whose woods these are I think I know.
His house is in the village though;
He will not see me stopping here
To watch his woods fill up with snow.

My little horse must think it queer   5
To stop without a farmhouse near
Between the woods and frozen lake
The darkest evening of the year.

He gives his harness bells a shake
To ask if there is some mistake.   10
The only other sound's the sweep
Of easy wind and downy flake.

The woods are lovely, dark and deep,
But I have promises to keep,
And miles to go before I sleep,   15
And miles to go before I sleep.

—1923

Wallace Stevens (1879–1955) *was a lawyer specializing in surety bonds and rose to be a vice-president of the Hartford Accident and Indemnity Company. His poetry was collected for the first time in* Harmonium *when he was forty-five, and while he published widely during his lifetime, his poetry was only slowly recognized as the work of a major modernist whose originality has not been surpassed. Stevens's idea of poetry as a force taking the place of religion has had a profound influence on poets and critics of this century.*

Wallace Stevens

Anecdote of the Jar

I placed a jar in Tennessee,
And round it was, upon a hill.
It made the slovenly wilderness
Surround that hill.

The wilderness rose up to it,   5
And sprawled around, no longer wild.
The jar was round upon the ground
And tall and of a port in air.

It took dominion everywhere.
The jar was gray and bare.   10
It did not give of bird or bush,
Like nothing else in Tennessee.

—1923

Disillusionment of Ten O'Clock

The houses are haunted
By white night-gowns.
None are green,
Or purple with green rings,
Or green with yellow rings,
Or yellow with blue rings.   5
None of them are strange,

With socks of lace
And beaded ceintures.°
People are not going   10
To dream of baboons and periwinkles.°
Only, here and there, an old sailor,
Drunk and asleep in his boots,
Catches tigers
In red weather.   15

—*1923*

The Snow Man

One must have a mind of winter
To regard the frost and the boughs
Of the pine-trees crusted with snow;

And have been cold a long time
To behold the junipers shagged with ice,   5
The spruces rough in the distant glitter

Of the January sun; and not to think
Of any misery in the sound of the wind,
In the sound of a few leaves,

Which is the sound of the land   10
Full of the same wind
That is blowing in the same bare place

For the listener, who listens in the snow,
And, nothing himself, beholds
Nothing that is not there and the nothing that is.   15

—*1923*

9 ceintures sashes   **11 periwinkles** either wildflowers or small mollusks

Sunday Morning

I

Complacencies of the peignoir,° and late
Coffee and oranges in a sunny chair,
And the green freedom of a cockatoo
Upon a rug mingle to dissipate
The holy hush of ancient sacrifice.   5
She dreams a little, and she feels the dark
Encroachment of that old catastrophe,
As a calm darkens among water-lights.
The pungent oranges and bright, green wings
Seem things in some procession of the dead,   10
Winding across wide water, without sound.
The day is like wide water, without sound,
Stilled for the passing of her dreaming feet
Over the seas, to silent Palestine,
Dominion of the blood and sepulchre.   15

II

Why should she give her bounty to the dead?
What is divinity if it can come
Only in silent shadows and in dreams?
Shall she not find in comforts of the sun,
In pungent fruit and bright, green wings, or else   20
In any balm or beauty of the earth,
Things to be cherished like the thought of heaven?
Divinity must live within herself:
Passions of rain, or moods in falling snow;
Grievings in loneliness, or unsubdued   25
Elations when the forest blooms; gusty
Emotions on wet roads on autumn nights;
All pleasures and all pains, remembering
The bough of summer and the winter branch.
These are the measures destined for her soul.   30

---

1 peignoir woman's dressing gown

III

Jove° in the clouds had his inhuman birth.
No mother suckled him, no sweet land gave
Large-mannered motions to his mythy mind.
He moved among us, as a muttering king,
Magnificent, would move among his hinds,°   *35*
Until our blood, commingling, virginal,
With heaven, brought such requital to desire
The very hinds discerned it, in a star.
Shall our blood fail? Or shall it come to be
The blood of paradise? And shall the earth   *40*
Seem all of paradise that we shall know?
The sky will be much friendlier then than now,
A part of labor and a part of pain,
And next in glory to enduring love,
Not this dividing and indifferent blue.   *45*

IV

She says, "I am content when wakened birds,
Before they fly, test the reality
Of misty fields, by their sweet questionings;
But when the birds are gone, and their warm fields
Return no more, where, then, is paradise?"   *50*
There is not any haunt of prophecy,
Nor any old chimera° of the grave,
Neither the golden underground, nor isle
Melodious, where spirits gat them home,
Nor visionary south, nor cloudy palm   *55*
Remote on heaven's hill, that has endured
As April's green endures; or will endure
Like her remembrance of awakened birds,
Or her desire for June and evening, tipped
By the consummation of the swallow's wings.   *60*

---

31 Jove Roman name of Zeus   **35 hinds** inferiors or shepherds who saw the star of the nativity
52 chimera imagined monster

V

She says, "But in contentment I still feel
The need of some imperishable bliss."
Death is the mother of beauty; hence from her,
Alone, shall come fulfilment to our dreams
And our desires. Although she strews the leaves   65
Of sure obliteration on our paths,
The path sick sorrow took, the many paths
Where triumph rang its brassy phrase, or love
Whispered a little out of tenderness,
She makes the willow shiver in the sun   70
For maidens who were wont to sit and gaze
Upon the grass, relinquished to their feet.
She causes boys to pile new plums and pears
On disregarded plate. The maidens taste
And stray impassioned in the littering leaves.   75

VI

Is there no change of death in paradise?
Does ripe fruit never fall? Or do the boughs
Hang always heavy in that perfect sky,
Unchanging, yet so like our perishing earth,
With rivers like our own that seek for seas   80
They never find, the same receding shores
That never touch with inarticulate pang?
Why set the pear upon those river-banks
Or spice the shores with odors of the plum?
Alas, that they should wear our colors there,   85
The silken weavings of our afternoons,
And pick the strings of our insipid lutes!
Death is the mother of beauty, mystical,
Within whose burning bosom we devise
Our earthly mothers waiting, sleeplessly.   90

VII

Supple and turbulent, a ring of men
Shall chant in orgy on a summer morn
Their boisterous devotion to the sun,

Not as a god, but as a god might be,
Naked among them, like a savage source. 95
Their chant shall be a chant of paradise,
Out of their blood, returning to the sky;
And in their chant shall enter, voice by voice,
The windy lake wherein their lord delights,
The trees, like serafin,° and echoing hills, 100
That choir among themselves long afterward.
They shall know well the heavenly fellowship
Of men that perish and of summer morn.
And whence they came and whither they shall go
The dew upon their feet shall manifest. 105

VIII

She hears, upon that water without sound,
A voice that cries, "The tomb in Palestine
Is not the porch of spirits lingering.
It is the grave of Jesus, where he lay."
We live in an old chaos of the sun, 110
Or old dependency of day and night,
Or island solitude, unsponsored, free,
Of that wide water, inescapable.
Deer walk upon our mountains, and the quail
Whistle about us their spontaneous cries; 115
Sweet berries ripen in the wilderness;
And, in the isolation of the sky,
At evening, casual flocks of pigeons make
Ambiguous undulations as they sink,
Downward to darkness, on extended wings. 120

—*1923*

100 **serafin** seraphim, a type of angel

William Carlos Williams (1883–1963), like his friend Wallace Stevens, followed an unconventional career for a poet, working until his death as a pediatrician in Rutherford, New Jersey. Williams is modern poetry's greatest proponent of the American idiom. His plainspoken poems have been more widely imitated than those of any other American poet of this century, perhaps because he represents a home-grown modernist alternative to the intellectualized Europeanism of Eliot and Ezra Pound (a friend of his from college days). In his later years, Williams assisted many younger poets, among them Allen Ginsberg, for whose controversial book Howl *he wrote an introduction.*

William Carlos Williams

The Last Words of My English Grandmother

There were some dirty plates
and a glass of milk
beside her on a small table
near the rank, disheveled bed—

Wrinkled and nearly blind   5
she lay and snored
rousing with anger in her tones
to cry for food,

Gimme something to eat—
They're starving me—   10
I'm all right—I won't go
to the hospital. No, no, no

Give me something to eat!
Let me take you
to the hospital, I said   15
and after you are well

you can do as you please.
She smiled, Yes
you do what you please first
then I can do what I please—   20

Oh, oh, oh! she cried
as the ambulance men lifted
her to the stretcher—
Is this what you call

making me comfortable?   25
By now her mind was clear—
Oh you think you're smart
you young people,

she said, but I'll tell you
you don't know anything.   30
Then we started.
On the way

We passed a long row
of elms. She looked at them
awhile out of   35
the ambulance window and said,

What are all those
fuzzy-looking things out there?
Trees? Well, I'm tired
of them and rolled her head away.   40

—1920

The Red Wheelbarrow

so much depends
upon

a red wheel
barrow

glazed with rain   5
water

beside the white
chickens.

—1923

Spring and All

By the road to the contagious hospital°
under the surge of the blue
mottled clouds driven from the
northeast—a cold wind. Beyond, the
waste of broad, muddy fields   5
brown with dried weeds, standing and fallen

patches of standing water
the scattering of tall trees

All along the road the reddish
purplish, forked, upstanding, twiggy   10
stuff of bushes and small trees
with dead, brown leaves under them
leafless vines—

Lifeless in appearance, sluggish
dazed spring approaches—   15

They enter the new world naked,
cold, uncertain of all
save that they enter. All about them
the cold, familiar wind—

Now the grass, tomorrow   20
the stiff curl of wildcarrot leaf
One by one objects are defined—
It quickens: clarity, outline of leaf

But now the stark dignity of
entrance—Still, the profound change   25
has come upon them: rooted, they
grip down and begin to awaken

—*1923*

---

1 contagious hospital a hospital for quarantined patients

Ezra Pound (1885–1972) was the greatest international proponent of modern poetry. Born in Idaho and reared in Philadelphia, he emigrated to England in 1909, where he befriended Yeats, promoted the early work of Frost, and discovered Eliot. Pound's early promotion of the imagist movement assisted a number of important poetic principles and reputations, including those of H. D. (Hilda Doolittle) and, later, William Carlos Williams. Pound's support of Mussolini during World War II, expressed in controversial radio broadcasts, caused him to be held for over a decade after the war as a mental patient in the United States, after which he returned to Italy for the final years of his long and controversial life.

Ezra Pound

In a Station of the Metro

The apparition of these faces in the crowd;
Petals on a wet, black bough.

—1916

Portrait d'une Femme°

Your mind and you are our Sargasso Sea,°
London has swept about you this score years
And bright ships left you this or that in fee:
Ideas, old gossip, oddments of all things,
Strange spars of knowledge and dimmed wares of price.   5
Great minds have sought you—lacking someone else.
You have been second always. Tragical?
No. You preferred it to the usual thing:
One dull man, dulling and uxorious,°
One average mind—with one thought less, each year   10
Oh, you are patient, I have seen you sit
Hours, where something might have floated up.
And now you pay one. Yes, you richly pay.

Portrait d'une Femme Portrait of a Lady   **1 Sargasso Sea** area of seaweed in the mid-Atlantic where flotsam accumulates   **9 uxorious** doting and submissive

You are a person of some interest, one comes to you
And takes strange gain away: *15*
Trophies fished up; some curious suggestion;
Fact that leads nowhere; and a tale or two,
Pregnant with mandrakes,° or with something else
That might prove useful and yet never proves,
That never fits a corner or shows use,   *20*
Or finds its hour upon the loom of days:
That tarnished, gaudy, wonderful old work;
Idols and ambergris° and rare inlays,
These are your riches, your great store; and yet
For all this sea-hoard of deciduous things,   *25*
Strange woods half sodden, and new brighter stuff:
In the slow float of differing light and deep,
No! there is nothing! In the whole and all,
Nothing that's quite your own.
                Yet this is you

                                  —1912

The River-Merchant's Wife: A Letter°

While my hair was still cut straight across my forehead
I played about the front gate, pulling flowers.
You came by on bamboo stilts, playing horse,
You walked about my seat, playing with blue plums.
And we went on living in the village of Chokan: *5*
Two small people, without dislike or suspicion.
At fourteen I married My Lord you.
I never laughed, being bashful.
Lowering my head, I looked at the wall.
Called to, a thousand times, I never looked back.   *10*

---

18 mandrakes plants with roots shaped like the lower half of the human body   **23 ambergris** intestinal secretion of the sperm whale; valuable and used in making perfumes
The River-Merchant's Wife: A Letter imitation of a poem by Li-Po (A.D. 701–762)

At fifteen I stopped scowling,
I desired my dust to be mingled with yours
Forever and forever and forever.
Why should I climb the lookout?

At sixteen you departed,   15
You went into far Ku-to-yen, by the river of swirling eddies,
And you have been gone five months.
The monkeys make sorrowful noise overhead.

You dragged your feet when you went out.
By the gate now, the moss is grown, the different mosses,   20
Too deep to clear them away!
The leaves fall early this autumn, in wind.
The paired butterflies are already yellow with August
Over the grass in the West garden;
They hurt me. I grow older.   25
If you are coming down through the narrows of the river Kiang,
Please let me know beforehand,
And I will come out to meet you
    As far as Cho-Fu-Sa.

—*1915*

Elinor Wylie (1885–1928), whose considerable lyrical skills found wide popularity during her relatively brief career, has recently come to the notice of the present generation. For many readers in the post-World War I era, Wylie, along with her slightly younger contemporary Edna St. Vincent Millay, helped to define the literary role of the New Woman of the 1920s. A poetic traditionalist whose lifestyle was thoroughly modern, Wylie now seems overdue for a serious reassessment of her place in the development of twentieth-century women's poetry.

Elinor Wylie
Let No Charitable Hope

Now let no charitable hope
Confuse my mind with images
Of eagle and of antelope:
I am in nature none of these.

I was, being human, born alone;   5
I am, being woman, hard beset;
I live by squeezing from a stone
The little nourishment I get.

In masks outrageous and austere
The years go by in single file;   10
But none has merited my fear,
And none has quite escaped my smile.

—*1923*

H. D. (Hilda Doolittle) (1886–1961) *was born in Bethlehem, Pennsylvania.
Hilda Doolittle was a college friend of both Williams and Pound and moved to
Europe permanently in 1911. With her husband Richard Aldington, H. D. was an
important member of the imagist group promoted by Pound.*

H. D. (Hilda Doolittle)
Pear Tree

Silver dust,
lifted from the earth,
higher than my arms reach,
you have mounted,
O, silver,   5
higher than my arms reach,
you front us with great mass;

no flower ever opened
so staunch a white leaf,
no flower ever parted silver   10
from such rare silver;

O, white pear,
your flower-tufts
thick on the branch
bring summer and ripe fruits   15
in their purple hearts.

—*1916*

Sea Rose

Rose, harsh rose,
marred and with stint of petals,
meager flower, thin,
sparse of leaf,

more precious   5
than a wet rose
single on a stem—
you are caught in the drift.

Stunted, with small leaf,
you are flung on the sand,   10
you are lifted
in the crisp sand
that drives in the wind.

Can the spice-rose
drip such acrid fragrance   15
hardened in a leaf?

—*1916*

---

*Siegfried Sassoon (1886–1967) was a decorated hero who publicly denounced
World War I and became a friend and supporter of other British war poets, including
Robert Graves and Wilfred Owen. His sardonic, anti-heroic war poems owe much to
Thomas Hardy, whom he acknowledged as his chief poetic influence.*

Siegfried Sassoon
Dreamers

Soldiers are citizens of death's grey land,
    Drawing no dividend from time's tomorrows.
In the great hour of destiny they stand,
    Each with his feuds, and jealousies, and sorrows.
Soldiers are sworn to action; they must win   5
    Some flaming, fatal climax with their lives.
Soldiers are dreamers, when the guns begin
    They think of firelit homes, clean beds, and wives.

I see them in foul dug-outs, gnawed by rats,
  And in the ruined trenches, lashed with rain,   *10*
Dreaming of things they did with balls and bats,
  And mocked by hopeless longing to regain
Bank-holidays, and picture shows, and spats,
  And going to the office in the train.

                                                            —1918

Robinson Jeffers (1887–1962) *lived with his wife and children for many years in
Carmel, California, in a rock house that he built himself by the sea. Many of his
ideas about man's small place in the larger world of nature have gained in relevance
through the years since his death. Largely forgotten for many years, his poetry, particularly his book-length verse narratives, is once more regaining the attention of
serious readers.*

Robinson Jeffers
The Purse-Seine°

Our sardine fishermen work at night in the dark of the moon; daylight
    or moonlight
They could not tell where to spread the net, unable to see the
    phosphorescence of the shoals of fish.
They work northward from Monterey, coasting Santa Cruz; off New
    Year's Point or off Pigeon Point
The look-out man will see some lakes of milk-color light on the
    sea's night-purple; he points, and the helmsman
Turns the dark prow, the motorboat circles the gleaming shoal
    and drifts out her seine-net. They close the circle   5
and purse the bottom of the net, then with great labor haul it in.

                                          I cannot tell you
How beautiful the scene is, and a little terrible, then, when the
    crowded fish
Know they are caught, and wildly beat from one wall to the other of
    their closing destiny the phosphorescent

Purse-Seine large circular fishing net; the bottom is closed (or pursed) before it is hauled in

Water to a pool of flame, each beautiful slender body sheeted
    with flame, like a live rocket   *10*
A comet's tail wake of clear yellow flame; while outside the
    narrowing
Floats and cordage of the net great sea-lions come up to watch,
    sighing in the dark; the vast walls of night
Stand erect to the stars.

                        Lately I was looking from a night mountain-top
On a wide city, the colored splendor, galaxies of light: how could
    I help but recall the seine-net   *15*
Gathering the luminous fish? I cannot tell you how beautiful the
    city appeared, and a little terrible.
I thought, We have geared the machines and locked all together
    into interdependence; we have built the great cities; now
There is no escape. We have gathered vast populations incapable
    of free survival, insulated
From the strong earth, each person in himself helpless, on all
    dependent. The circle is closed, and the net
Is being hauled in. They hardly feel the cords drawing, yet they
    shine already. The inevitable mass-disasters   *20*
Will not come in our time nor in our children's, but we and our
    children
Must watch the net draw narrower, government take all powers—
    or revolution, and the new government
Take more than all, add to kept bodies kept souls—or anarchy,
    the mass-disasters.

                              These things are Progress;
Do you marvel our verse is troubled or frowning, while it keeps
    its reason? Or it lets go, lets the mood flow   *25*
In the manner of the recent young men into mere hysteria,
    splintered gleams, crackled laughter. But they are quite wrong.
There is no reason for amazement: surely one always knew that
    cultures decay, and life's end is death.

                                        —1937

Marianne Moore (1887–1972) called her own work poetry—unconventional and marked with the stamp of a rare personality—because, as she put it, there was no other category for it. For four years she was editor of the Dial, *one of the chief modernist periodicals. Moore's wide range of reference, which can leap from the commonplace to the wondrous within a single poem, reflects her unique set of personal interests—which range from exotic natural species to baseball.*

Marianne Moore
The Fish

wade
through black jade.
    Of the crow-blue mussel-shells, one keeps
    adjusting the ash-heaps;
        opening and shutting itself like   5

an
injured fan.
    The barnacles which encrust the side
    of the wave, cannot hide
        there for the submerged shafts of the   10

sun,
split like spun
    glass, move themselves with spotlight swiftness
    into the crevices—
        in and out, illuminating   15

the
turquoise sea
of bodies. The water drives a wedge
of iron through the iron edge
        of the cliff; whereupon the stars,   20

pink
rice-grains, ink-
    bespattered jelly-fish, crabs like green
    lilies, and submarine
        toadstools, slide each on the other.   25

All
external
    marks of abuse are present on this
    defiant edifice—
        all the physical features of   *30*
ac-
cident—lack
    of cornice, dynamite grooves, burns, and
    hatchet strokes, these things stand
        out on it; the chasm-side is   *35*
dead.
Repeated
    evidence has proved that it can live
    on what can not revive
        its youth. The sea grows old in it.

                                    —1921

Silence

My father used to say,
"Superior people never make long visits,
have to be shown Longfellow's grave
or the glass flowers at Harvard.
Self-reliant like the cat—   *5*
that takes its prey to privacy,
the mouse's limp tail hanging like a shoelace from its mouth—
they sometimes enjoy solitude
and can be robbed of speech
by speech which has delighted them.   *10*
The deepest feeling always shows itself in silence;
not in silence, but restraint."
Nor was he insincere in saying, "Make my house your inn."
Inns are not residences.

                                    —1935

T. S. Eliot (1888–1965) *was the author of* The Waste Land, *one of the most famous and difficult modernist poems, and became an international figure. Born in St. Louis and educated at Harvard, he moved to London in 1914, where he remained for the rest of his life, becoming a British subject in 1927. This chief prophet of modern despair turned to the Church of England in later life, and wrote successful dramas on religious themes. As a critic and influential editor, Eliot dominated poetic taste in England and America for over twenty-five years. He was awarded the Nobel Prize in 1948.*

T. S. Eliot
Journey of the Magi°

'A cold coming we had of it,
Just the worst time of the year
For a journey, and such a long journey:
The ways deep and the weather sharp,
The very dead of winter.'°   5
And the camels galled, sore-footed, refractory,
Lying down in the melting snow.
There were times we regretted
The summer palaces on slopes, the terraces,
And the silken girls bringing sherbet.   10
Then the camel men cursing and grumbling
And running away, and wanting their liquor and women,
And the night-fires going out, and the lack of shelters,
And the cities hostile and the towns unfriendly
And the villages dirty and charging high prices: 15
A hard time we had of it.
At the end we preferred to travel all night,
Sleeping in snatches,
With the voices singing in our ears, saying
That this was all folly.   20

Then at dawn we came down to a temperate valley,
Wet, below the snow line, smelling of vegetation;
With a running stream and a water-mill beating the darkness,

Magi Wise Men mentioned in Matthew 2:1-2   **1–5 'A cold . . . winter'** The quotation marks indicated Eliot's source, a sermon by Lancelot Andrewes (1555–1626).

And three trees on the low sky.
And an old white horse galloped away in the meadow.   25
Then we came to a tavern with vine-leaves over the lintel,
Six hands at an open door dicing for pieces of silver,
And feet kicking the empty wine-skins.
But there was no information, and so we continued
And arrived at evening, not a moment too soon   30
Finding the place; it was (you may say) satisfactory.

All this was a long time ago, I remember,
And I would do it again, but set down
This° set down
This: were we led all that way for   35
Birth or Death? There was a Birth, certainly,
We had evidence and no doubt. I had seen birth and death,
But had thought they were different; this Birth was
Hard and bitter agony for us, like Death, our death.
We returned to our places, these Kingdoms,   40
But no longer at ease here, in the old dispensation,°
With an alien people clutching their gods.
I should be glad of another death.

—*1927*

The Love Song of J. Alfred Prufrock

> S'io credesse che mia risposta fosse
> A persona che mai tornasse al mondo,
> Questa fiamma staria senza più scosse.
> Ma perciocche giammai di questo fondo
> Non tornò vivo alcun, s'i'odo il vero,
> Senza tema d'infamia ti rispondo.°

33-34 set down . . . This The Magus is dictating his memoirs to a scribe   **41 old dispensation** world before the birth of Christ

S'io credesse . . . rispondo From Dante's *Inferno* (Canto 27). The speaker is Guido da Montefeltro: "If I thought I spoke to someone who would return to the world, this flame would tremble no longer. But, if what I hear is true, since no one has ever returned alive from this place I can answer you without fear of infamy."

Let us go then, you° and I,
When the evening is spread out against the sky
Like a patient etherised upon a table;
Let us go, through certain half-deserted streets,
The muttering retreats   5
Of restless nights in one-night cheap hotels
And sawdust restaurants with oyster-shells:
Streets that follow like a tedious argument
Of insidious intent
To lead you to an overwhelming question . . .   10
Oh, do not ask, "What is it?"
Let us go and make our visit.

In the room the women come and go
Talking of Michelangelo.°

The yellow fog that rubs its back upon the window-panes,   15
The yellow smoke that rubs its muzzle on the window-panes,
Licked its tongue into the corners of the evening,
Lingered upon the pools that stand in drains,
Let fall upon its back the soot that falls from chimneys,
Slipped by the terrace, made a sudden leap,   20
And seeing that it was a soft October night,
Curled once about the house, and fell asleep.

And indeed there will be time
For the yellow smoke that slides along the street,
Rubbing its back upon the window-panes;   25
There will be time, there will be time
To prepare a face to meet the faces that you meet;
There will be time to murder and create,
And time for all the works and days of hands
That lift and drop a question on your plate: 30
Time for you and time for me,
And time yet for a hundred indecisions,
And for a hundred visions and revisions,
Before the taking of a toast and tea.

---

1 you Eliot said that the auditor of the poem was a male friend of Prufrock.   **14 Michelangelo**
Italian painter and sculptor (1475–1564)

In the room the women come and go   35
Talking of Michelangelo.

And indeed there will be time
To wonder, "Do I dare?" and, "Do I dare?"—
Time to turn back and descend the stair,
With a bald spot in the middle of my hair—   40
(They will say: "How his hair is growing thin!")
My morning coat, my collar mounting firmly to the chin,
My necktie rich and modest, but asserted by a simple pin—
(They will say: "But how his arms and legs are thin!")
Do I dare   45
Disturb the universe?
In a minute there is time
For decisions and revisions which a minute will reverse.

For I have known them all already, known them all:
Have known the evenings, mornings, afternoons,   50
I have measured out my life with coffee spoons;
I know the voices dying with a dying fall
Beneath the music from a farther room.
          So how should I presume?

And I have known the eyes already, known them all—   55
The eyes that fix you in a formulated phrase,
And when I am formulated, sprawling on a pin,
When I am pinned and wriggling on the wall,
Then how should I begin
To spit out all the butt-ends of my days and ways?   60
          And how should I presume?

And I have known the arms already, known them all—
Arms that are braceleted and white and bare
(But in the lamplight, downed with light brown hair!)
Is it perfume from a dress   65
That makes me so digress?
Arms that lie along a table, or wrap about a shawl.
          And should I then presume?
          And how should I begin?

          . . . . .

Shall I say, I have gone at dusk through narrow streets,   70
And watched the smoke that rises from the pipes
Of lonely men in shirtsleeves, leaning out of windows? . . .

I should have been a pair of ragged claws
Scuttling across the floors of silent seas.

. . . . .

And the afternoon, the evening, sleeps so peacefully!   75
Smoothed by long fingers,
Asleep . . . tired . . . or it malingers,
Stretched on the floor, here beside you and me.
Should I, after tea and cakes and ices,
Have the strength to force the moment to its crisis?   80
But though I have wept and fasted, wept and prayed,
Though I have seen my head (grown slightly bald) brought in
    upon a platter,
I am no prophet°—and here's no great matter;
I have seen the moment of my greatness flicker,
And I have seen the eternal Footman hold my coat, and
    snicker,   85
        And in short, I was afraid.

And would it have been worth it, after all,
After the cups, the marmalade, the tea,
Among the porcelain, among some talk of you and me,
Would it have been worth while,   90
To have bitten off the matter with a smile,
To have squeezed the universe into a ball
To roll it towards some overwhelming question,
To say: "I am Lazarus,° come from the dead,
Come back to tell you all, I shall tell you all"—   95
If one, settling a pillow by her head,
        Should say: "That is not what I meant at all;
        That is not it, at all."

82-83 my head . . . no prophet allusion to John the Baptist   **94 Lazarus** raised from the dead in
John 11:1-44

And would it have been worth it, after all,
Would it have been worth while,   *100*
After the sunsets and the dooryards and the sprinkled streets,
After the novels, after the teacups, after the skirts that trail
   along the floor—
And this, and so much more?—
It is impossible to say just what I mean!
But as if a magic lantern° threw the nerves in patterns on
   a screen: *105*
Would it have been worth while
If one, settling a pillow or throwing off a shawl,
And turning toward the window, should say:
   "That is not it at all,
   That is not what I meant, at all."   *110*

     . . . . .

No! I am not Prince Hamlet, nor was meant to be;
Am an attendant lord, one that will do
To swell a progress, start a scene or two,
Advise the prince; no doubt, an easy tool,
Deferential, glad to be of use,   *115*
Politic, cautious, and meticulous;
Full of high sentence, but a bit obtuse;
At times, indeed, almost ridiculous—
Almost, at times, the Fool.°

I grow old . . . I grow old . . .   *120*
I shall wear the bottoms of my trousers rolled.

Shall I part my hair behind? Do I dare to eat a peach?
I shall wear white flannel trousers, and walk upon the beach.
I have heard the mermaids singing, each to each.

I do not think that they will sing to me.   *125*

I have seen them riding seaward on the waves
Combing the white hair of the waves blown back

---

105 magic lantern old-fashioned slide projector   **111-119 not Prince Hamlet . . . the Fool** The
allusion is probably to Polonius, a character in *Hamlet.*

When the wind blows the water white and black.
We have lingered in the chambers of the sea
By sea-girls wreathed with seaweed red and brown   130
Till human voices wake us, and we drown.

—*1917*

John Crowe Ransom (1888–1974), as a professor at Vanderbilt University in Nashville, began a little magazine called the Fugitive, *which lent its name to a group of young southern poets who published in it. Later he moved to Kenyon College, where he was editor of the* Kenyon Review *for many years. Ransom was influential as both a poet and a critic.*

John Crowe Ransom

Bells for John Whiteside's Daughter

There was such speed in her little body,
And such lightness in her footfall,
It is no wonder her brown study°
Astonishes us all.

Her wars were bruited° in our high window.   5
We looked among orchard trees and beyond
Where she took arms against her shadow,
Or harried unto the pond

The lazy geese, like a snow cloud
Dripping their snow on the green grass,   10
Tricking and stopping, sleepy and proud,
Who cried in goose, Alas,

For the tireless heart within the little
Lady with rod that made them rise
From their noon apple-dreams and scuttle   15
Goose-fashion under the skies!

---

3 brown study appearance of deep concentration   **5 bruited** shouted

But now go the bells, and we are ready,
In one house we are sternly stopped
To say we are vexed at her brown study,
Lying so primly propped.   20

—*1924*

Piazza° Piece

—I am a gentleman in a dustcoat° trying
To make you hear. Your ears are soft and small
And listen to an old man not at all.
They want the young men's whispering and sighing.
But see the roses on your trellis dying   5
And hear the spectral singing of the moon;
For I must have my lovely lady soon,
I am a gentleman in a dustcoat trying.

—I am a lady young in beauty waiting
Until my truelove comes, and then we kiss.   10
But what grey man among the vines is this
Whose words are dry and faint as in a dream?
Back from my trellis, Sir, before I scream!
I am a lady young in beauty waiting.

—*1927*

Piazza courtyard   **1 dustcoat** old-fashioned coat worn while driving an open car

Edna St. Vincent Millay (1892–1950) was extremely popular in the 1920s, when her sonnets seemed the ultimate expression of the liberated sexuality of what was then called the New Woman. Neglected for many years, her poems have recently generated renewed interest, and it seems likely that she will eventually regain her status as one of the most important female poets of the twentieth century.

Edna St. Vincent Millay
If I Should Learn, in Some Quite Casual Way

If I should learn, in some quite casual way,
That you were gone, not to return again—
Read from the back-page of a paper, say,
Held by a neighbor in a subway train,
How at the corner of this avenue   5
And such a street (so are the papers filled)
A hurrying man, who happened to be you,
At noon today had happened to be killed—
I should not cry aloud—I could not cry
Aloud, or wring my hands in such a place—   10
I should but watch the station lights rush by
With a more careful interest on my face;
Or raise my eyes and read with greater care
Where to store furs and how to treat the hair.

—1917

Not in a Silver Casket

Not in a silver casket cool with pearls
Or rich with red corundum° or with blue,
Locked, and the key withheld, as other girls
Have given their loves, I give my love to you;

---

2 red corundum ruby-like gemstone

Not in a lovers'-knot, not in a ring   5
Worked in such fashion, and the legend plain—
Semper fidelis,° where a secret spring
Kennels a drop of mischief for the brain:
Love in the open hand, no thing but that,
Ungemmed, unhidden, wishing not to hurt,   10
As one should bring you cowslips in a hat
Swung from the hand, or apples in her skirt,
I bring you, calling out as children do:
"Look what I have!—And these are all for you."

—*1931*

Oh, Oh, You Will Be Sorry for that Word

Oh, oh, you will be sorry for that word!
Give back my book and take my kiss instead.
Was it my enemy or my friend I heard,
"What a big book for such a little head!"
Come, I will show you now my newest hat,   5
And you may watch me purse my mouth and prink!°
Oh, I shall love you still, and all of that.
I never again shall tell you what I think.
I shall be sweet and crafty, soft and sly;
You will not catch me reading any more: 10
I shall be called a wife to pattern by;
And some day when you knock and push the door,
Some sane day, not too bright and not too stormy,
I shall be gone, and you may whistle for me.

—*1923*

7 *Semper fidelis* always faithful
6 **prink** primp

What Lips My Lips Have Kissed, and Where, and Why

What lips my lips have kissed, and where, and why,
I have forgotten, and what arms have lain
Under my head till morning; but the rain
Is full of ghosts tonight, that tap and sigh
Upon the glass and listen for reply,   5
And in my heart there stirs a quiet pain
For unremembered lads that not again
Will turn to me at midnight with a cry.
Thus in the winter stands the lonely tree,
Nor knows what birds have vanished one by one,   10
Yet knows its boughs more silent than before:
I cannot say what loves have come and gone,
I only know that summer sang in me
A little while, that in me sings no more.

—*1923*

Wilfred Owen (1893–1918) was killed in the trenches only a few days before the armistice that ended World War I. Owen showed more promise than any other English poet of his generation. A decorated officer whose nerves broke down after exposure to battle, he met Siegfried Sassoon at Craiglockhart military hospital. His work was posthumously collected by his friend. A novel by Pat Barker, Regeneration (also made into a film), deals with their poetic and personal relationship.

Wilfred Owen
Dulce et Decorum Est°

Bent double, like old beggars under sacks,
Knock-kneed, coughing like hags, we cursed through sludge,
Till on the haunting flares we turned our backs

Dulce et Decorum Est (pro patria mori) from the Roman poet Horace: "It is sweet and proper to die for one's country"

And towards our distant rest began to trudge.
Men marched asleep. Many had lost their boots   5
But limped on, blood-shod. All went lame; all blind;
Drunk with fatigue; deaf even to the hoots
Of tired, outstripped Five-Nines° that dropped behind.

Gas! Gas! Quick, boys!—An ecstasy of fumbling
Fitting the clumsy helmets just in time;   10
But someone still was yelling out and stumbling
And flound'ring like a man in fire or lime . . .
Dim, through the misty panes and thick green light,°
As under a green sea, I saw him drowning.

In all my dreams, before my helpless sight,   15
He plunges at me, guttering, choking, drowning.

If in some smothering dreams you too could pace
Behind the wagon that we flung him in,
And watch the white eyes writhing in his face,
His hanging face, like a devil's sick of sin;   20
If you could hear, at every jolt, the blood
Come gargling from the froth-corrupted lungs,
Obscene as cancer, bitter as the cud
Of vile, incurable sores on innocent tongues,—
My friend,° you would not tell with such high zest   25
To children ardent for some desperate glory,
The old Lie: Dulce et decorum est
Pro patria mori.

—1920

---

8 Five-Nines German artillery shells (59 mm)   **13 misty panes and thick green light** i.e., through
the gas mask   **25 my friend** The poem was originally addressed to Jessie Pope, a writer of patriotic
verse.

Dorothy Parker (1893–1967), *as a humorist, journalist, and poet, was for many years associated with* The New Yorker *as both author and critic. Along with Robert Benchley, James Thurber, and E. B. White, she epitomizes the hard-edged humor that made that magazine unique among American periodicals.*

Dorothy Parker
One Perfect Rose

A single flow'r he sent me, since we met.
All tenderly his messenger he chose;
Deep-hearted, pure, with scented dew still wet—
One perfect rose.

I knew the language of the floweret;   5
"My fragile leaves," it said, "his heart enclose."
Love long has taken for his amulet
One perfect rose.

Why is it no one sent me yet
One perfect limousine, do you suppose?   10
Ah no, it's always just my luck to get
One perfect rose.

—1926

Résumé

Razors pain you;
Rivers are damp;
Acids stain you;
And drugs cause cramp.
Guns aren't lawful;   5
Nooses give;
Gas smells awful;
You might as well live.

—1926

e. e. cummings (1894–1962) was the son of a Harvard professor and Unitarian clergyman. Edward Estlin Cummings served as a volunteer ambulance driver in France during World War I. cummings's experimentation with the typographical aspects of poetry reveals his serious interest in cubist painting, which he studied in Paris in the 1920s. A brilliant satirist, he also excelled as a writer of lyrical poems whose unusual appearance and idiosyncratic grammar, spelling, and punctuation often overshadow their traditional themes.

e. e. cummings
nobody loses all the time

i had an uncle named
Sol who was a born failure and
nearly everybody said he should have gone
into vaudeville perhaps because my Uncle Sol could
sing McCann He Was a Diver on Xmas Eve like Hell Itself which   5
may or may not account for the fact that my Uncle

Sol indulged in that possibly most inexcusable
of all to use a highfalootin phrase
luxuries that is or to
wit farming and be   10
it needlessly
added

my Uncle Sol's farm
failed because the chickens
ate the vegetables so   15
my Uncle Sol had a
chicken farm till the
skunks ate the chickens when

my Uncle Sol
had a skunk farm but   20
the skunks caught cold and
died and so
my Uncle Sol imitated the
skunks in a subtle manner

or by drowning himself in the watertank   25
but somebody who'd given my Uncle Sol a Victor
Victrola and records while he lived presented to
him upon the auspicious occasion of his decrease a
scrumptious not to mention splendiferous funeral with
tall boys in black gloves and flowers and everything and   30

i remember we all cried like the Missouri
when my Uncle Sol's coffin lurched because
somebody pressed a button
(and down went
my Uncle   35
Sol

and started a worm farm)

—*1926*

pity this busy monster,manunkind

pity this busy monster,manunkind,

not. Progress is a comfortable disease:
your victim (death and life safely beyond)

plays with the bigness of his littleness
—electrons° deify one razorblade   5
into a mountainrange; lenses extend

unwish through curving wherewhen till unwish
returns on its unself.
                              A world of made
is not a world of born—pity poor flesh

and trees,poor stars and stones,but never this   10
fine specimen of hypermagical

---

5 **electrons** in an electron microscope

ultraomnipotence. We doctors know

a hopeless case if—listen: there's a hell
of a good universe next door; let's go

—*1944*

r-p-o-p-h-e-s-s-a-g-r

r-p-o-p-h-e-s-s-a-g-r

                    who
a)s w(e loo)k
upnowgath
            PPEGORHRASS   5
                    eringint(o-
aThe):l
    eA
    !p:
S   a   10
                (r
rIvInG   .gRrEaPsPhOs)
                            to
rea(be)rran(com)gi(e)ngly
.grasshopper;   15

—*1932*

Jean Toomer (1894–1967) *was born in Washington, D.C., the grandson of a black man who served as governor of Louisiana during Reconstruction. His book* Cane *(1923) is a mixed collection of prose and verse based on his observations of life in rural Georgia, where he was a schoolteacher. A complete edition of his poetry, most of it unpublished during his life, was assembled over twenty years after his death.*

Jean Toomer
Reapers

Black reapers with the sound of steel on stones
Are sharpening scythes. I see them place the hones
In their hip-pockets as a thing that's done,
And start their silent swinging, one by one.
Black horses drive a mower through the weeds,   5
And there, a field rat, startled, squealing bleeds,
His belly close to ground. I see the blade,
Blood-stained, continue cutting weeds and shade.

—1923

Louise Bogan (1897–1970) *was for many years the poetry editor and resident critic of* The New Yorker, *and the opinions expressed in her many book reviews have held up well in the years since her death. In her later years Bogan suffered from severe bouts of clinical depression and wrote little poetry, but her relatively slim output reveals a unique poetic voice.*

Louise Bogan
Women

Women have no wilderness in them,
They are provident instead,
Content in the tight hot cell of their hearts
To eat dusty bread.

They do not see cattle cropping red winter grass,   5
They do not hear

Snow water going down under culverts
Shallow and clear.

They wait, when they should turn to journeys,
They stiffen, when they should bend.   *10*
They use against themselves that benevolence
To which no man is friend.

They cannot think of so many crops to a field
Or of clean wood cleft by an axe.
Their love is an eager meaninglessness   *15*
Too tense, or too lax.

They hear in every whisper that speaks to them
A shout and a cry.
As like as not, when they take life over their door-sills
They should let it go by.   *20*

—*1923*

---

*Hart Crane (1899–1933) is one of the first modernists to make extensive poetic
use of the artifacts — advertising slogans, motion picture lore, trade names — of
American popular culture. Much of this material surfaces in* The Bridge *(1930),
his book-length attempt to write an epic sequence about modern America. Crane
committed suicide by leaping from a ship returning from the Yucatán, where he spent
his last year on a Guggenheim Fellowship attempting to write an epic poem about
the conquest of Mexico.*

Hart Crane

Chaplinesque°

We make our meek adjustments,
Contented with such random consolations
As the wind deposits
In slithered and too ample pockets.

Chaplinesque after Charlie Chaplin, silent-film comedian

For we can still love the world, who find   5
A famished kitten on the step, and know
Recesses for it from the fury of the street,
Or warm torn elbow coverts.

We will sidestep, and to the final smirk
Dally the doom of that inevitable thumb   10
That slowly chafes its puckered index toward us,
Facing the dull squint with what innocence
And what surprise!

And yet these fine collapses are not lies
More than the pirouettes of any pliant cane;   15
Our obsequies are in a way, no enterprise.
We can evade you, and all else but the heart:
What blame to us if the heart live on.

The game enforces smirks; but we have seen
The moon in lonely alleys make   20
A grail of laughter of an empty ash can,
And through all sound of gaiety and quest
Have heard a kitten in the wilderness.

—*1926*

Langston Hughes (1902–1967) was a leading figure in the Harlem Renaissance of the 1920s, and he became the most famous black writer of his day. Phrases from his poems and other writings have become deeply ingrained in the American consciousness. An important experimenter with poetic form, Hughes is credited with incorporating the rhythms of jazz into poetry.

Langston Hughes
Dream Boogie

Good morning, daddy!
Ain't you heard
The boogie-woogie rumble
Of a dream deferred?

Listen closely: 5
You'll hear their feet
Beating out and beating out a—

    You think
    It's a happy beat?

Listen to it closely: 10
Ain't you heard
something underneath
like a—

    What did I say?
Sure,   15
I'm happy!
Take it away!

    Hey, pop!
    Re-bop!
    Mop!   20

       Y-e-a-h!

                                         —*1951*

Theme for English B

The instructor said,

    Go home and write
    a page tonight.
    And let that page come out of you—
    Then, it will be true.   5

I wonder if it's that simple?
I am twenty-two, colored, born in Winston-Salem.
I went to school there, then Durham, then here
to this college on the hill above Harlem.
I am the only colored student in my class.   10
The steps from the hill lead down into Harlem,
through a park, then I cross St. Nicholas,

Eighth Avenue, Seventh, and I come to the Y,
the Harlem Branch Y, where I take the elevator
up to my room, sit down, and write this page: 15

It's not easy to know what is true for you or me
at twenty-two, my age. But I guess I'm what
I feel and see and hear, Harlem, I hear you:
hear you, hear you—we two—you, me, talk on this page.
(I hear New York, too.) Me—who?   20
Well, I like to eat, sleep, drink, and be in love.
I like to work, read, learn, and understand life.
I like a pipe for a Christmas present,
or records—Bessie,° bop, or Bach.
I guess being colored doesn't make me *not* like   25
the same things other folks like who are other races.
So will my page be colored that I write?
Being me, it will not be white.
But it will be
a part of you, instructor.   30
You are white—
yet a part of me, as I am a part of you.
That's American.
Sometimes perhaps you don't want to be a part of me.
Nor do I often want to be a part of you.   35
But we are, that's true!
I guess you learn from me—
although you're older—and white—
and somewhat more free.

This is my page for English B.   40

—*1951*

24 **Bessie** Bessie Smith (1898–1937), blues singer

*Countee Cullen (1903–1946), among black writers of the first half of the twenti-
eth century, crafted poetry representing a more conservative style than that of his
contemporary, Hughes. Although he wrote a number of lyrics on standard poetic
themes, he is best remembered for his eloquent poems on racial subjects.*

Countee Cullen
Incident

Once riding in old Baltimore,
    Heart-filled, head-filled with glee,
I saw a Baltimorean
    Keep looking straight at me.

Now I was eight and very small,   *5*
    And he was no whit bigger,
And so I smiled, but he poked out
    His tongue, and called me, "Nigger."

I saw the whole of Baltimore
    From May until December;   *10*
Of all the things that happened there
    That's all that I remember.

                —*1963*

Yet Do I Marvel

I doubt not God is good, well-meaning, kind,
And did He stoop to quibble could tell why
The little buried mole continues blind,
Why flesh that mirrors Him must some day die,
Make plain the reason tortured Tantalus°   *5*
Is baited by the fickle fruit, declare
If merely brute caprice dooms Sisyphus°
To struggle up a never-ending stair.
Inscrutable His ways are, and immune

5 Tantalus mythological character tortured by unreachable fruit   **7 Sisyphus** figure in myth who
endlessly rolls a boulder uphill

To catechism by a mind too strewn   10
With petty cares to slightly understand
What awful brain compels His awful hand.
Yet do I marvel at this curious thing:
To make a poet black and bid him sing!

—*1963*

Stanley Kunitz (b. 1905) *witnessed the approach of Halley's Comet as a child of five and wrote his poem about it seventy-five years later on the comet's next visit. Kunitz won the Pulitzer Prize for his* Selected Poems: 1928–1958, *and also was awarded the National Book Award for* Passing Through *in 1995. In 2000, at the age of ninety-five, Kunitz was appointed poet laureate of the United States.*

Stanley Kunitz
Halley's Comet

Miss Murphy in first grade
wrote its name in chalk
across the board and told us
it was roaring down the stormtracks
of the Milky Way at frightful speed   5
and if it wandered off its course
and smashed into the earth
there'd be no school tomorrow.
A red-bearded preacher from the hills
with a wild look in his eyes   10
stood in the public square
at the playground's edge
proclaiming he was sent by God
to save every one of us,
even the little children.   15
"Repent, ye sinners!" he shouted,
waving his hand-lettered sign.
At supper I felt sad to think
that it was probably
the last meal I'd share   20

with my mother and my sisters;
but I felt excited too
and scarcely touched my plate.
So mother scolded me
and sent me early to my room.   25
The whole family's asleep
except for me. They never heard me steal
into the stairwell hall and climb
the ladder to the fresh night air.
Look for me, Father, on the roof   30
of the red brick building
at the foot of Green Street—
that's where we live, you know, on the top floor.
I'm the boy in the white flannel gown
sprawled on this coarse gravel bed   35
searching the starry sky,
waiting for the world to end.

—*1995*

A. D. Hope (1907–2000) *was the first unquestionably major poet to emerge from Australia. Hope waited until he was almost fifty to publish his first collection of poetry. Even then, the sexual frankness of poems like "Imperial Adam" proved controversial in the conservative climate of mid-1950s Australia. A poet who strongly rejects most of the tendencies of modernism (most prominently free verse), Hope seems closer in spirit to eighteenth-century satirists like Swift and Pope, whom he obviously admires, and to his exact contemporary, W. H. Auden.*

A. D. Hope
Imperial Adam

Imperial Adam, naked in the dew,
Felt his brown flanks and found the rib was gone.
Puzzled he turned and saw where, two and two,
The mighty spoor of Jahweh marked the lawn.

Then he remembered through mysterious sleep   5
The surgeon fingers probing at the bone,

The voice so far away, so rich and deep:
"It is not good for him to live alone."

Turning once more he found Man's counterpart
In tender parody breathing at his side.   10
He knew her at first sight, he knew by heart
Her allegory of sense unsatisfied.

The pawpaw drooped its golden breasts above
Less generous than the honey of her flesh;
The innocent sunlight showed the place of love;   15
The dew on its dark hairs winked crisp and fresh.

This plump gourd severed from his virile root,
She promised on the turf of Paradise
Delicious pulp of the forbidden fruit;
Sly as the snake she loosed her sinuous thighs,   20

And waking, smiled up at him from the grass;
Her breasts rose softly and he heard her sigh—
From all the beasts whose pleasant task it was
In Eden to increase and multiply

Adam had learned the jolly deed of kind: 25
He took her in his arms and there and then,
Like the clean beasts, embracing from behind,
Began in joy to found the breed of men.

Then from the spurt of seed within her broke
Her terrible and triumphant female cry,   30
Split upward by the sexual lightning stroke.
It was the beasts now who stood watching by:

The gravid elephant, the calving hind,
The breeding bitch, the she-ape big with young
Were the first gentle midwives of mankind;   35
The teeming lioness rasped her with her tongue;

The proud vicuña nuzzled her as she slept
Lax on the grass; and Adam watching too
Saw how her dumb breasts at their ripening wept,
The great pod of her belly swelled and grew,   40

And saw its water break, and saw, in fear,
Its quaking muscles in the act of birth,
Between her legs a pigmy face appear,
And the first murderer lay upon the earth.

—*1955*

W. H. Auden (1907–1973) was already established as an important younger British poet before he moved to America in 1939 (he later became a U.S. citizen). As an important transatlantic link between two literary cultures, Auden was one of the most important literary figures and cultural spokespersons in the English-speaking world for almost forty years, giving a name to the postwar era when he dubbed it "The Age of Anxiety" in a poem. In his last years he returned briefly to Oxford, where he occupied the poetry chair.

W. H. Auden

As I Walked Out One Evening

As I walked out one evening,
   Walking down Bristol Street,
The crowds upon the pavement
   Were fields of harvest wheat.

And down by the brimming river   5
   I heard a lover sing
Under an arch of the railway:
   "Love has no ending.

"I'll love you, dear, I'll love you
   Till China and Africa meet,   10
And the river jumps over the mountain
   And the salmon sing in the street.

"I'll love you till the ocean
   Is folded and hung up to dry,
And the seven stars go squawking   15
   Like geese about the sky.

"The years shall run like rabbits,
 For in my arms I hold
The Flower of the Ages,
 And the first love of the world."   *20*

But all the clocks in the city
 Began to whirr and chime:
"O let not Time deceive you,
 You cannot conquer Time.

"In the burrows of the Nightmare   *25*
 Where Justice naked is,
Time watches from the shadow
 And coughs when you would kiss.

"In headaches and in worry
 Vaguely life leaks away,   *30*
And Time will have his fancy
 Tomorrow or to-day.

"Into many a green valley
 Drifts the appalling snow;
Time breaks the threaded dances   *35*
 And the diver's brilliant bow.

"O plunge your hands in water,
 Plunge them in up to the wrist;
Stare, stare in the basin
 And wonder what you've missed.   *40*

"The glacier knocks in the cupboard,
 The desert sighs in the bed,
And the crack in the tea-cup opens
 A lane to the land of the dead.

"Where the beggars raffle the banknotes   *45*
 And the Giant is enchanting to Jack,
And the Lily-white Boy is a Roarer,
 And Jill goes down on her back.

"O look, look in the mirror,
 O look in your distress;   *50*

Life remains a blessing
    Although you cannot bless.

"O stand, stand at the window
    As the tears scald and start;
You shall love your crooked neighbor   55
    With your crooked heart."

It was late, late in the evening,
    The lovers they were gone;
The clocks had ceased their chiming,
    And the deep river ran on.   60

            —1940

Musée des Beaux Arts°

About suffering they were never wrong,
The Old Masters: how well they understood
Its human position; how it takes place
While someone else is eating or opening a window or just
    walking dully along;
How, when the aged are reverently, passionately waiting   5
For the miraculous birth, there always must be
Children who did not specially want it to happen, skating
On a pond at the edge of the wood:
They never forgot
That even the dreadful martyrdom must run its course   10
Anyhow in a corner, some untidy spot
Where the dogs go on with their doggy life and the torturer's
    horse
Scratches its innocent behind on a tree.

In Brueghel's *Icarus,*° for instance: how everything turns away
Quite leisurely from the disaster; the ploughman may   15
Have heard the splash, the forsaken cry,

Musée des Beaux Arts Museum of Fine Arts   **14 Brueghel's *Icarus*** In this painting (c. 1550) the famous event from Greek myth is almost inconspicuous among the other details Auden mentions.

But for him it was not an important failure; the sun shone
As it had to on the white legs disappearing into the green
Water; and the expensive delicate ship that must have seen
Something amazing, a boy falling out of the sky,   *20*
Had somewhere to get to and sailed calmly on.

—1938

The Unknown Citizen

To JS/07/M/378
This Marble Monument Is Erected by the State

He was found by the Bureau of Statistics to be
One against whom there was no official complaint,
And all the reports on his conduct agree
That, in the modern sense of an old-fashioned word, he was a
     saint,
For in everything he did he served the Greater Community.   *5*
Except for the War till the day he retired
He worked in a factory and never got fired,
But satisfied his employers, Fudge Motors Inc.
Yet he wasn't a scab or odd in his views,
For his Union reports that he paid his dues,   *10*
(Our report on his Union shows it was sound)
And our Social Psychology workers found
That he was popular with his mates and liked a drink.
The Press are convinced that he bought a paper every day
And that his reactions to advertisements were normal in every
     way.   *15*
Policies taken out in his name prove that he was fully insured,
And his Health-card shows he was once in hospital but left it cured.
Both Producers Research and High-Grade Living declare
He was fully sensible to the advantages of the Installment Plan
And had everything necessary to the Modern Man,   *20*
A phonograph, a radio, a car and a frigidaire.
Our researchers into Public Opinion are content
That he held the proper opinions for the time of year;
When there was peace, he was for peace; when there was war,
     he went.

He was married and added five children to the population,   25
Which our Eugenist says was the right number for a parent of
  his generation,
And our teachers report that he never interfered with their
  education.
Was he free? Was he happy? The question is absurd:
Had anything been wrong, we should certainly have heard.

—*1939*

Theodore Roethke (1908–1963) was born in Michigan. Roethke was an influential teacher of poetry at the University of Washington for many years. His father was the owner of a greenhouse, and Roethke's childhood closeness to nature was an important influence on his mature poetry. His periodic nervous breakdowns, the result of bipolar manic-depression, presaged his early death.

Theodore Roethke
Dolor°

I have known the inexorable sadness of pencils,
Neat in their boxes, dolor of pad and paper-weight,
All of the misery of manilla folders and mucilage,
Desolation in immaculate public places,
Lonely reception room, lavatory, switchboard,   5
The unalterable pathos of basin and pitcher,
Ritual of multigraph, paper-clip, comma,
Endless duplication of lives and objects.
And I have seen dust from the walls of institutions,
Finer than flour, alive, more dangerous than silica,°   10
Sift, almost invisible, through long afternoons of tedium,
Dropping a fine film on nails and delicate eyebrows,
Glazing the pale hair, the duplicate grey standard faces.

—*1948*

Dolor sadness   **10 silica** rock dust, a cause of silicosis, an occupational disease of miners and quarry workers

My Papa's Waltz

The whiskey on your breath
Could make a small boy dizzy;
But I hung on like death:
Such waltzing was not easy.

We romped until the pans   5
Slid from the kitchen shelf;
My mother's countenance
Could not unfrown itself.

The hand that held my wrist
Was battered on one knuckle;   10
At every step you missed
My right ear scraped a buckle.

You beat time on my head
With a palm caked hard by dirt,
Then waltzed me off to bed   15
Still clinging to your shirt.

—*1948*

Root Cellar

Nothing would sleep in that cellar, dank as a ditch,
Bulbs broke out of boxes hunting for chinks in the dark,
Shoots dangled and drooped,
Lolling obscenely from mildewed crates,
Hung down long yellow evil necks, like tropical snakes.   5
And what a congress of stinks!—
Roots ripe as old bait,
Pulpy stems, rank, silo-rich,
Leaf-mold, manure, lime, piled against slippery planks.
Nothing would give up life: 10
Even the dirt kept breathing a small breath.

—*1948*

Elizabeth Bishop (1911–1979) for most of her life was highly regarded as a "poet's poet," winning the Pulitzer Prize for North and South *in 1956, but in the years since her death she has gained a wider readership. She traveled widely and lived in Brazil for a number of years before returning to the United States to teach at Harvard during the last years of her life.*

Elizabeth Bishop

The Fish

I caught a tremendous fish
and held him beside the boat
half out of water, with my hook
fast in a corner of his mouth.
He didn't fight.   5
He hadn't fought at all.
He hung a grunting weight,
battered and venerable
and homely. Here and there
his brown skin hung in strips   10
like ancient wallpaper,
and its pattern of darker brown
was like wallpaper:
shapes like full-blown roses
stained and lost through age.   15
He was speckled with barnacles,
fine rosettes of lime,
and infested
with tiny white sea-lice,
and underneath two or three   20
rags of green weed hung down.
While his gills were breathing in
the terrible oxygen
—the frightening gills,
fresh and crisp with blood,   25
that can cut so badly—
I thought of the coarse white flesh
packed in like feathers,

the big bones and the little bones,
the dramatic reds and blacks   30
of his shiny entrails,
and the pink swim-bladder
like a big peony.
I looked into his eyes
which were far larger than mine   35
but shallower, and yellowed,
the irises backed and packed
with tarnished tinfoil
seen through the lenses
of old scratched isinglass.°   40
They shifted a little, but not
to return my stare.
—It was more like the tipping
of an object toward the light.
I admired his sullen face,   45
the mechanism of his jaw,
and then I saw
that from his lower lip
—if you could call it a lip—
grim, wet, and weapon-like,   50
hung five old pieces of fish-line,
or four and a wire leader
with the swivel still attached,
with all their five big hooks
grown firmly in his mouth.   55
A green line, frayed at the end
where he broke it, two heavier lines,
and a fine black thread
still crimped from the strain and snap
when it broke and he got away.   60
Like medals with their ribbons
frayed and wavering,
a five-haired beard of wisdom
trailing from his aching jaw.

40 isinglass semi-transparent material made from fish bladders

I stared and stared   65
and victory filled up
the little rented boat,
from the pool of bilge
where oil had spread a rainbow
around the rusted engine   70
to the bailer° rusted orange,
the sun-cracked thwarts,
the oarlocks on their strings,
the gunnels°—until everything
was rainbow, rainbow, rainbow!   75
and I let the fish go.

—1946

One Art

The art of losing isn't hard to master;
so many things seem filled with the intent
to be lost that their loss is no disaster.

Lose something every day. Accept the fluster
of lost door keys, the hour badly spent.   5
The art of losing isn't hard to master.

Then practice losing farther, losing faster:
places, and names, and where it was you meant
to travel. None of these will bring disaster.

I lost my mother's watch. And look! my last, or   10
next-to-last, of three loved houses went.
The art of losing isn't hard to master.

I lost two cities, lovely ones. And, vaster,
some realms I owned, two rivers, a continent.
I miss them, but it wasn't a disaster.   15

---

71 bailer bucket   **74 gunnels** gunwales

—Even losing you (the joking voice, a gesture
I love) I shan't have lied. It's evident
the art of losing's not too hard to master
though it may look like *(Write* it!) like disaster.

—*1976*

May Sarton (1912–1995) *was born in Belgium. Sarton succeeded equally in poetry and prose. The journals and memoirs she produced in her last two decades added
considerably to the literature of aging and won her readers perhaps more numerous
than the many admirers of her poetry. Her feminism and lesbianism, made public
long before doing so was either fashionable or prudent, rarely overshadow her skills
at evoking the New England landscape she passionately loved.*

May Sarton
A Guest

My woods belong to woodcock and to deer;
For them, it is an accident I'm here.

If, for the plump raccoon, I represent
An ash can that was surely heaven-sent,

The bright-eyed mask, the clever little paws   5
Obey not mine, but someone else's laws.

The young buck takes me in with a long glance
That says that I, not he, am here by chance.

And they all go their ways, as I must do,
Up through the green and down again to snow,   10

No one of us responsible or near,
But each himself and in the singular.

When we do meet, I am the one to stare
As if an angel had me by the hair,

As I am flooded by some ancient bliss   15
Before all I possess and can't possess.

So when a stranger knocks hard at the door,
He cannot know what I am startled for—

To see before me an unfurry face,
A creature like myself in this wild place.   20

Our wilderness gets wilder every day
And we intend to keep the tamed at bay.

Robert Hayden (1913–1980) named Countee Cullen as one of the chief early influences on his poetry. A native of Michigan, he taught for many years at Fisk University in Nashville and at the University of Michigan. Although many of Hayden's poems are on African American subjects, he wished to be considered a poet with strong links to the mainstream English tradition.

Robert Hayden

Those Winter Sundays

Sundays too my father got up early
and put his clothes on in the blueblack cold,
then with cracked hands that ached
from labor in the weekday weather made
banked fires blaze. No one ever thanked him.   5

I'd wake and hear the cold splintering, breaking.
When the rooms were warm, he'd call,
and slowly I would rise and dress,
fearing the chronic angers of that house,

Speaking indifferently to him,   10
who had driven out the cold
and polished my good shoes as well.
What did I know, what did I know
of love's austere and lonely offices?°

                                                                        —*1962*

14 offices daily religious ceremonies

Dudley Randall (1914—2000) was the founder of Broadside Press, a black-owned publishing firm that eventually attracted important writers like Gwendolyn Brooks and Don L. Lee. For most of his life a resident of Detroit, Randall spent many years working in that city's library system before taking a similar position at the University of Detroit.

Dudley Randall
Ballad of Birmingham

(On the Bombing of a Church in
Birmingham, Alabama, 1963)°

"Mother dear, may I go downtown
Instead of out to play,
And march the streets of Birmingham
In a Freedom March today?"

"No, baby, no, you may not go,   5
For the dogs are fierce and wild,
And clubs and hoses, guns and jail
Aren't good for a little child."

"But, mother, I won't be alone.
Other children will go with me,   10
And march the streets of Birmingham
To make our country free."

"No, baby, no, you may not go,
For I fear those guns will fire.
But you may go to church instead   15
And sing in the children's choir."

She has combed and brushed her night-dark hair,
And bathed rose petal sweet,
And drawn white gloves on her small brown hands,
And white shoes on her feet.   20

Birmingham, Alabama, 1963 during the height of the civil rights movement

The mother smiled to know her child
Was in the sacred place,
But that smile was the last smile
To come upon her face.

For when she heard the explosion,   25
Her eyes grew wet and wild.
She raced through the streets of Birmingham
Calling for her child.

She clawed through bits of glass and brick,
Then lifted out a shoe.   30
"O, here's the shoe my baby wore,
But, baby, where are you?"

—*1969*

William Stafford *(1914–1993) was one of the most prolific poets of the postwar era. Stafford published in virtually every magazine in the United States. Raised in Kansas as a member of the pacifist Church of the Brethren, Stafford served in a camp for conscientious objectors during World War II. His first book did not appear until he was in his forties, but he published over thirty collections before his death at age seventy nine.*

William Stafford
Traveling Through the Dark

Traveling through the dark I found a deer
dead on the edge of the Wilson River road.
It is usually best to roll them into the canyon:
that road is narrow; to swerve might make more dead.

By glow of the tail-light I stumbled back of the car   5
and stood by the heap, a doe, a recent killing;
she had stiffened already, almost cold.
I dragged her off; she was large in the belly.

My fingers touching her side brought me the reason—
her side was warm; her fawn lay there waiting,   10
alive, still, never to be born.
Beside that mountain road I hesitated.

The car aimed ahead its lowered parking lights;
under the hood purred the steady engine.
I stood in the glare of the warm exhaust turning red;   15
around our group I could hear the wilderness listen.

I thought hard for us all—my only swerving—
then pushed her over the edge into the river.

—*1960*

---

*Dylan Thomas (1914–1953) was a legendary performer of his and others' poetry.
His popularity in the United States led to several collegiate reading tours, punctu-
ated with outrageous behavior and self-destructive drinking that led to his early
death in New York City, the victim of what the autopsy report labeled "insult to the
brain." The Wales of his childhood remained a constant source of inspiration for his
poetry and for radio dramas like Under Milk Wood, which was turned into a film
by fellow Welshman Richard Burton and his then-wife, Elizabeth Taylor.*

Dylan Thomas
Do Not Go Gentle into That Good Night

Do not go gentle into that good night,
Old age should burn and rave at close of day;
Rage, rage against the dying of the light.

Though wise men at their end know dark is right,
Because their words had forked no lightning they   5
Do not go gentle into that good night.

Good men, the last wave by, crying how bright
Their frail deeds might have danced in a green bay,
Rage, rage against the dying of the light.

Wild men who caught and sang the sun in flight,   10
And learn, too late, they grieved it on its way,
Do not go gentle into that good night.

Grave men, near death, who see with blinding sight
Blind eyes could blaze like meteors and be gay,
Rage, rage against the dying of the light.   15

And you, my father, there on the sad height,
Curse, bless, me now with your fierce tears, I pray,
Do not go gentle into that good night.
Rage, rage against the dying of the light.

—1952

Fern Hill

Now as I was young and easy under the apple boughs
About the lilting house and happy as the grass was green,
    The night above the dingle starry,
        Time let me hail and climb
      Golden in the heydays of his eyes,   5
And honored among wagons I was prince of the apple towns
And once below a time I lordly had the trees and leaves
        Trail with daisies and barley
      Down the rivers of the windfall light.

And as I was green and carefree, famous among the barns   10
About the happy yard and singing as the farm was home,
    In the sun that is young once only,
        Time let me play and be
      Golden in the mercy of his means,
And green and golden I was huntsman and herdsman, the calves 15
Sang to my horn, the foxes on the hills barked clear and cold,
        And the sabbath rang slowly
      In the pebbles of the holy streams.

All the sun long it was running, it was lovely, the hay
Fields high as the house, the tunes from the chimneys, it was air 20
        And playing, lovely and watery

       And fire green as grass.
    And nightly under the simple stars
As I rode to sleep the owls were bearing the farm away,
All the moon long I heard, blessed among stables, the night-jars   25
      Flying with the ricks, and the horses
         Flashing into the dark.

And then to awake, and the farm, like a wanderer white
With the dew, come back, the cock on his shoulder: it was all
      Shining, it was Adam and maiden,   30
         The sky gathered again
      And the sun grew round that very day.
So it must have been after the birth of the simple light
In the first, spinning place, the spellbound horses walking warm
      Out of the whinnying green stable   35
         On to the fields of praise.

And honored among foxes and pheasants by the gay house
Under the new made clouds and happy as the heart was long,
      In the sun born over and over,
         I ran my heedless ways,   40
      My wishes raced through the house high hay
And nothing I cared, at my sky blue trades, that time allows
In all his tuneful turning so few and such morning songs
      Before the children green and golden
         Follow him out of grace,   45

Nothing I cared, in the lamb white days, that time would take me
Up to the swallow thronged loft by the shadow of my hand,
      In the moon that is always rising,
        Nor that riding to sleep
      I should hear him fly with the high fields   50
And wake to the farm forever fled from the childless land.
Oh as I was young and easy in the mercy of his means,
      Time held me green and dying
    Though I sang in my chains like the sea.

                        —*1946*

Weldon Kees (1914–1955) was a multitalented poet, painter, jazz musician, and filmmaker who went from the University of Nebraska to New York to California. His reputation, aided by posthumous publication of his stories, criticism, letters, and novels, has grown steadily since his apparent suicide by leaping from the Golden Gate Bridge.

Weldon Kees

For My Daughter

Looking into my daughter's eyes I read
Beneath the innocence of morning flesh
Concealed, hintings of death she does not heed.
Coldest of winds have blown this hair, and mesh
Of seaweed snarled these miniatures of hands;   5
The night's slow poison, tolerant and bland,
Has moved her blood. Parched years that I have seen
That may be hers appear; foul, lingering
Death in certain war, the slim legs green.
Or, fed on hate, she relishes the sting   10
Of others' agony; perhaps the cruel
Bride of a syphilitic or a fool.
These speculations sour in the sun.
I have no daughter. I desire none.

—1943

Randall Jarrell (1914–1965) excelled as both a poet and a (sometimes brutally honest) reviewer of poetry. Ironically, the author of what is perhaps the best-known poem to have emerged from World War II did not see combat during the war: he served as a control tower officer in stateside bases. A native of Nashville, Kentucky, Jarrell studied at Vanderbilt University and followed his mentor, John Crowe Ransom, to Kenyon College in 1937, where he befriended another student, Robert Lowell.

Randall Jarrell
The Death of the Ball Turret° Gunner

From my mother's sleep I fell into the State,
And I hunched in its belly till my wet fur froze.
Six miles from earth, loosed from its dream of life,
I woke to black flak and the nightmare fighters.
When I died they washed me out of the turret with a hose.   5

—*1945*

Margaret Walker (1915–1998), as a female African-American poet, was perhaps overshadowed by Gwendolyn Brooks, even though Walker's receipt of the Yale Younger Poets Award in 1942 for For My People *came some years before Brooks's own recognition. A longtime teacher at Jackson State University, she influenced several generations of young writers.*

Margaret Walker
For Malcolm X

All you violated ones with gentle hearts;
You violent dreamers whose cries shout heartbreak;
Whose voices echo clamors of our cool capers,
And whose black faces have hollowed pits for eyes.
All you gambling sons and hooked children and bowery bums   5

Ball Turret A Plexiglas sphere set into the belly of a heavy bomber; Jarrell noted the similarity between the gunner and a fetus in the womb.

Hating white devils and black bourgeoisie,
Thumbing your noses at your burning red suns,
Gather round this coffin and mourn your dying swan.

Snow-white moslem head-dress around a dead black face!
Beautiful were your sand-papering words against our skins!   10
Our blood and water pour from your flowing wounds.
You have cut open our breasts and dug scalpels in our brains.
When and Where will another come to take your holy place?
Old man mumbling in his dotage, or crying child, unborn?

—1970

Gwendolyn Brooks (1917–2000) was the first African American to win a Pulitzer Prize for poetry. Brooks reflected many changes in black culture during her long career, and she wrote about the stages of her own life candidly in From the Mecca, *her literary autobiography. Brooks was the last poetry consultant of the Library of Congress before that position became poet laureate of the United States. At the end of her life Brooks was one of the most honored and beloved of American poets.*

Gwendolyn Brooks
the mother

Abortions will not let you forget.
You remember the children you got that you did not get,
The damp small pulps with a little or with no hair,
The singers and workers that never handled the air.
You will never neglect or beat   5
them, or silence or buy with a sweet.
You will never wind up the sucking-thumb
Or scuttle off ghosts that come.
You will never leave them, controlling your luscious sigh,
Return for a snack of them, with gobbling mother-eye.   10

I have heard in the voices of the wind the voices of my dim killed
    children.
I have contracted. I have eased
My dim dears at the breasts they could never suck.
I have said, Sweets, if I sinned, if I seized

Your luck   *15*
And your lives from your unfinished reach,
If I stole your births and your names,
Your straight baby tears and your games,
Your stilted or lovely loves, your tumults, your marriages, aches, and
    your deaths,
If I poisoned the beginnings of your breaths,   *20*
Believe that even in my deliberateness I was not deliberate.
Though why should I whine,
Whine that the crime was other than mine?—
Since anyhow you are dead.
Or rather, or instead,   *25*
You were never made.
But that too, I am afraid,
Is faulty: oh, what shall I say, how is the truth to be said?
You were born, you had body, you died.
It is just that you never giggled or planned or cried.   *30*
Believe me, I loved you all.
Believe me, I knew you, though faintly, and I loved, I loved you
All.

                                                  —1945

We Real Cool

        The Pool Players.
        Seven at the Golden Shovel.

We real cool. We
Left school. We

Lurk late. We
Strike straight. We

Sing sin. We   *5*
Thin gin. We

Jazz June. We
Die soon.

                                                  —1960

Robert Lowell (1917–1977) is noted as one of the chief confessional poets because of the immense influence of his nakedly autobiographical collection of 1959, Life Studies. *His literary career covered many bases —complex, formal early work; poetic dramas and translations; public figure —and he had, as the scion of one of Boston's oldest families, a ready-made stature that made him a public figure for most of his adult life.*

Robert Lowell

For the Union Dead

"Relinquunt Omnia Servare Rem Publicam"°

The old South Boston Aquarium stands
in a Sahara of snow now. Its broken windows are boarded.
The bronze weathervane cod has lost half its scales.
The airy tanks are dry.

Once my nose crawled like a snail on the glass;   5
my hand tingled
to burst the bubbles
drifting from the noses of the cowed, compliant fish.

My hand draws back. I often sigh still
for the dark downward and vegetating kingdom   10
of the fish and reptile. One morning last March,
I pressed against the new barbed and galvanized

fence on the Boston Common. Behind their cage,
yellow dinosaur steamshovels were grunting
as they cropped up tons of mush and grass   15
to gouge their underworld garage.

Parking spaces luxuriate like civic
sandpiles in the heart of Boston.
A girdle of orange, Puritan-pumpkin colored girders
braces the tingling Statehouse,   20

Relinquunt . . . Publicam "They sacrificed everything to serve the state"

shaking over the excavations, as it faces Colonel Shaw°
and his bell-cheeked Negro infantry
on St. Gaudens'° shaking Civil War relief,
propped by a plank splint against the garage's earthquake.

Two months after marching through Boston,   25
half the regiment was dead;
at the dedication,
William James° could almost hear the bronze Negroes breathe.

Their monument sticks like a fishbone
in the city's throat.   30
Its Colonel is as lean
as a compass-needle.

He has an angry wrenlike vigilance,
a greyhound's gentle tautness;
he seems to wince at pleasure,   35
and suffocate for privacy.

He is out of bounds now. He rejoices in man's lovely,
peculiar power to choose life and die—
when he leads his black soldiers to death,
he cannot bend his back.   40

On a thousand small town New England greens,
the old white churches hold their air
of sparse, sincere rebellion; frayed flags
quilt the graveyards of the Grand Army of the Republic.

The stone statues of the abstract Union Soldier   45
grow slimmer and younger each year—
wasp-waisted, they doze over muskets
and muse through their sideburns . . .

Shaw's father wanted no monument
except the ditch,   50
where his son's body was thrown
and lost with his "niggers."

---

21 Colonel Shaw Robert Gould Shaw (1837–1863) led the black troops of the Massachusetts 54th
regiment and died with many of them during the attack on Fort Wagner, S.C. *Glory*, a recent film,
was based on these events.   **23 St. Gaudens** American sculptor (1848–1907)   **28 William James**
American philosopher (1842–1910) who gave a dedication speech for the monument

The ditch is nearer.
There are no statues for the last war here;
on Boylston Street, a commercial photograph   55
shows Hiroshima boiling

over a Mosler Safe, the "Rock of Ages"
that survived the blast. Space is nearer.
When I crouch to my television set,
the drained faces of Negro school-children° rise like balloons.   60

Colonel Shaw
is riding on his bubble,
he waits
for the blessèd break.

The Aquarium is gone. Everywhere,   65
giant finned cars nose forward like fish;
a savage servility
slides by on grease.

                                                              —1959

---

*Lawrence Ferlinghetti (b. 1919), first owner of a literary landmark, San
Francisco's City Lights Bookstore, has promoted and published the voice of the
American avant-garde since the early 1950s. His own output has been relatively
small, but Ferlinghetti's* A Coney Island of the Mind *remains one of the quintes-
sential documents of the Beat Generation.*

Lawrence Ferlinghetti

A Coney Island of the Mind, #15

Constantly risking absurdity
                    and death
        whenever he performs
                above the heads
                        of his audience   5

---

60 Negro school-children refers to protesters during the early days of the civil rights movement

the poet like an acrobat
                climbs on rime
                        to a high wire of his own making
and balancing on eyebeams
                        above a sea of faces   *10*
        paces his way
                to the other side of day
      performing entrechats
                  and sleight-of-foot tricks
and other high theatrics   *15*
                  and all without mistaking
        any thing
                for what it may not be

   For he's the super realist
                  who must perforce perceive   *20*
      taut truth
              before the taking of each stance or step
in his supposed advance
               toward that still higher perch
where Beauty stands and waits   *25*
            with gravity
             to start her death-defying leap
   And he
     a little charleychaplin man
              who may or may not catch   *30*
her fair eternal form
        spreadeagled in the empty air
  of existence

                                —1958

May Swenson (1919–1989) displayed an inventiveness in poetry that ranges from traditional formalism to many spatial or concrete poems. A careful observer of the natural world, Swenson often attempts to mimic directly the rhythms of the physical universe in her self-labeled "iconographs."

May Swenson
How Everything Happens

(BASED ON A STUDY OF THE WAVE)

```
                                                    happen.
                                               to
                                         up
                                   stacking
                              is
                        something
When nothing is happening
When it happens
                   something
                        pulls
                            back
                                not
                                   to
                                      happen.
When                              has happened.
      pulling back        stacking up
                  happens
      has happened                          stacks up.
When it           something          nothing
                        pulls back while

Then nothing is happening
                                    happens.
                                 and
                          forward
                       pushes
                    up
             stacks
        something
Then                                        —1967
```

Howard Nemerov (1920–1991) *served as poet laureate of the United States during 1988 and 1989. A poet of brilliant formal inventiveness, he was also a skilled satirist and observer of the American scene. His sister, Diane Arbus, was a famous photographer. His* Collected Poems *won the Pulitzer Prize in 1978.*

Howard Nemerov
A Primer of the Daily Round

A peels an apple, while B kneels to God,
C telephones to D, who has a hand
On E's knee, F coughs, G turns up the sod
For H's grave, I do not understand
But J is bringing one clay pigeon down   5
While K brings down a nightstick on L's head,
And M takes mustard, N drives into town,
O goes to bed with P, and Q drops dead,
R lies to S, but happens to be heard
By T, who tells U not to fire V   10
For having to give W the word
That X is now deceiving Y with Z,
    Who happens just now to remember A
    Peeling an apple somewhere far away.

—*1958*

Richard Wilbur (b. 1921) will be remembered by posterity as perhaps the most skillful metricist and exponent of wit that American poetry has produced. His highly polished poetry—against the grain of much contemporary writing—is a monument to his craftsmanship and intelligence. Perhaps the most honored of all living American poets, Wilbur served as poet laureate of the United States in 1987. His translations of the verse dramas of Molière and Racine are regularly performed throughout the world.

Richard Wilbur

Junk

Huru Welandes
                        wore ne geswiceσ
monna a'nigum
                      σara σe Mimming can
heardne gehealdan.
                            —Waldere°

An axe angles
               from my neighbor's ashcan;
It is hell's handiwork,
                  the wood not hickory,
The flow of the grain
                  not faithfully followed.
The shivered shaft
            rises from a shellheap
Of plastic playthings,
                paper plates,   5
And the sheer shards
              of shattered tumblers
That were not annealed
              for the time needful.
At the same curbside,
            a cast-off cabinet
Of wavily-warped
           unseasoned wood
Waits to be trundled
            in the trash-man's truck.   10
Haul them off! Hide them!
             The heart winces

The epigraph, taken from a fragmentary Anglo-Saxon poem, concerns the legendary smith Wayland, and may roughly be translated: "Truly, Wayland's handiwork—the sword Mimming which he made—will never fail any man who knows how to use it bravely. [Wilbur's note]

For junk and gimcrack,
                    for jerrybuilt things
And the men who make them
                    for a little money,
Bartering pride
                    like the bought boxer
Who pulls his punches,
                    or the paid-off jockey   15
Who in the home stretch
                    holds in his horse.
Yet the things themselves
                    in thoughtless honor
Have kept composure,
                    like captives who would not
Talk under torture.
                    Tossed from a tailgate
Where the dump displays
                    its random dolmens,   20
Its black barrows
                    and blazing valleys,
They shall waste in the weather
                    toward what they were.
The sun shall glory
                    in the glitter of glass-chips,
Foreseeing the salvage
                    of the prisoned sand,
And the blistering paint
                    peel off in patches,   25
That the good grain
                    be discovered again.
Then burnt, bulldozed,
                    they shall all be buried
To the depth of diamonds,
                    in the making dark
Where halt Hephaestus
                    keeps his hammer
And Wayland's work
                    is worn away.   30

                                        —*1961*

Playboy

High on his stockroom ladder like a dunce
The stock-boy sits, and studies like a sage
The subject matter of one glossy page,
As lost in curves as Archimedes° once.

Sometimes, without a glance, he feeds himself.   *5*
The left hand, like a mother-bird in flight,
Brings him a sandwich for a sidelong bite,
And then returns it to a dusty shelf.

What so engrosses him? The wild décor
Of this pink-papered alcove into which   *10*
A naked girl has stumbled, with its rich
Welter of pelts and pillows on the floor,

Amidst which, kneeling in a supple pose,
She lifts a goblet in her farther hand,
As if about to toast a flower-stand   *15*
Above which hovers an exploding rose

Fired from a long-necked crystal vase that rests
Upon a tasseled and vermillion cloth
One taste of which would shrivel up a moth?
Or is he pondering her perfect breasts?   *20*

Nothing escapes him of her body's grace
Or of her floodlit skin, so sleek and warm
And yet so strangely like a uniform,
But what now grips his fancy is her face.

And how the cunning picture holds her still   *25*
At just that smiling instant when her soul,
Grown sweetly faint, and swept beyond control,
Consents to his inexorable will.

—1969

---

4 Archimedes Greek mathematician (287–212 B.C.)

The Writer

In her room at the prow of the house
Where light breaks, and the windows are tossed with linden,
My daughter is writing a story.

I pause in the stairwell, hearing
From her shut door a commotion of typewriter-keys   5
Like a chain hauled over a gunwale.

Young as she is, the stuff
Of her life is a great cargo, and some of it heavy:
I wish her a lucky passage.

But now it is she who pauses,   10
As if to reject my thought and its easy figure.
A stillness greatens, in which

The whole house seems to be thinking,
And then she is at it again with a bunched clamor
Of strokes, and again is silent.   15

I remember the dazed starling
Which was trapped in that very room, two years ago;
How we stole in, lifted a sash

And retreated, not to affright it;
And how for a helpless hour, through the crack of the door, 20
We watched the sleek, wild, dark

And iridescent creature
Batter against the brilliance, drop like a glove
To the hard floor, or the desk-top,

And wait then, humped and bloody,   25
For the wits to try it again; and how our spirits
Rose when, suddenly sure,

It lifted off from a chair-back,
Beating a smooth course for the right window
And clearing the sill of the world.   30

It is always a matter, my darling,
Of life or death, as I had forgotten. I wish
What I wished you before, but harder.

—*1976*

Year's End

Now winter downs the dying of the year,
And night is all a settlement of snow;
From the soft street the rooms of houses show
A gathered light, a shapen atmosphere,
Like frozen-over lakes whose ice is thin   5
And still allows some stirring down within.

I've known the wind by water banks to shake
The late leaves down, which frozen where they fell
And held in ice as dancers in a spell
Fluttered all winter long into a lake;   10
Graved on the dark in gestures of descent,
They seemed their own most perfect monument.

There was perfection in the death of ferns
Which laid their fragile cheeks against the stone
A million years. Great mammoths overthrown   15
Composedly have made their long sojourns,
Like palaces of patience, in the gray
And changeless lands of ice. And at Pompeii°

The little dog lay curled and did not rise
But slept the deeper as the ashes rose   20
And found the people incomplete, and froze
The random hands, the loose unready eyes
Of men expecting yet another sun
To do the shapely thing they had not done.

18 Pompeii Roman city destroyed by volcanic eruption in A.D. 79

These sudden ends of time must give us pause.   25
We fray into the future, rarely wrought
Save in the tapestries of afterthought.
More time, more time. Barrages of applause
Come muffled from a buried radio.
The New-year bells are wrangling with the snow.   30

—1950

Philip Larkin (1922–1985) *was perhaps the last British poet to establish a significant body of readers in the United States. The general pessimism of his work is mitigated by a wry sense of irony and brilliant formal control. For many years he was a librarian at the University of Hull, and he was also a dedicated fan and critic of jazz.*

Philip Larkin
Next, Please

Always too eager for the future, we
Pick up bad habits of expectancy.
Something is always approaching; every day
Till then we say,

Watching from a bluff the tiny, clear,   5
Sparkling armada of promises draw near.
How slow they are! And how much time they waste,
Refusing to make haste!

Yet still they leave us holding wretched stalks
Of disappointment, for, though nothing balks   10
Each big approach, leaning with brasswork prinked,
Each rope distinct,

Flagged, and the figurehead with golden tits
Arching our way, it never anchors; it's
No sooner present than it turns to past.   15
Right to the last

We think each one will heave to and unload
All good into our lives, all we are owed
For waiting so devoutly and so long.
But we are wrong: 20

Only one ship is seeking us, a black-
Sailed unfamiliar, towing at her back
A huge and birdless silence. In her wake
No waters breed or break.

                                                —*1951*

Aubade

I work all day, and get half drunk at night.
Waking at four to soundless dark, I stare.
In time the curtain-edges will grow light.
Till then I see what's really always there:
Unresting death, a whole day nearer now,   5
Making all thought impossible but how
And where and when I shall myself die.
Arid interrogation: yet the dread
Of dying, and being dead,
Flashes afresh to hold and horrify.   10

The mind blanks at the glare. Not in remorse
—The good not done, the love not given, time
Torn off unused—nor wretchedly because
An only life can take so long to climb
Clear of its wrong beginnings, and may never;   15
But at the total emptiness for ever,
The sure extinction that we travel to
And shall be lost in always. Not to be here,
Not to be anywhere,
And soon; nothing more terrible, nothing more true.   20

This is a special way of being afraid
No trick dispels. Religion used to try,
That vast moth-eaten musical brocade

Created to pretend we never die,
And specious stuff that says *No rational being*   25
Can fear a thing it will not feel, not seeing
That this is what we fear—no sight, no sound,
No touch or taste or smell, nothing to think with,
Nothing to love or link with,
The anaesthetic from which none come round.   30

And so it stays just on the edge of vision,
A small unfocused blur, a standing chill
That slows each impulse down to indecision.
Most things may never happen: this one will,
And realization of it rages out   35
In furnace-fear when we are caught without
People or drink. Courage is no good:
It means not scaring others. Being brave
Lets no one off the grave.
Death is no different whined at than withstood.   40

Slowly light strengthens, and the room takes shape.
It stands plain as a wardrobe, what we know,
Have always known, know that we can't escape,
Yet can't accept. One side will have to go.
Meanwhile telephones crouch, getting ready to ring   45
In locked-up offices, and all the uncaring
Intricate rented world begins to rouse.
The sky is white as clay, with no sun.
Work has to be done.
Postmen like doctors go from house to house.   50

—*1977*

This Be The Verse

They fuck you up, your mum and dad.
    They may not mean to, but they do.
They fill you with the faults they had
    And add some extra, just for you.

But they were fucked up in their turn   *5*
   By fools in old-style hats and coats,
Who half the time were soppy-stern
   And half at one another's throats.

Man hands on misery to man.
   It deepens like a coastal shelf.   *10*
Get out as early as you can,
   And don't have any kids yourself.

—1971

James Dickey (1923–1997) became a national celebrity with the success of his novel Deliverance *(1970) and the celebrated film version. There was a long background to Dickey's success, with years spent in the advertising business before he devoted himself fully to writing. Born in Atlanta and educated at Clemson, Vanderbilt, and Rice Universities, Dickey rarely strayed long from the South and taught at the University of South Carolina for over two decades.*

James Dickey
The Heaven of Animals

Here they are. The soft eyes open
If they have lived in a wood
It is a wood.
If they have lived on plains
It is grass rolling
Under their feet forever.   *5*

Having no souls, they have come,
Anyway, beyond their knowing.
Their instincts wholly bloom
And they rise.
The soft eyes open.   *10*

To match them, the landscape flowers,
Outdoing, desperately
Outdoing what is required:

The richest wood,
The deepest field.   *15*

For some of these,
It could not be the place
It is, without blood.
These hunt, as they have done,
But with claws and teeth grown perfect,   *20*

More deadly than they can believe.
They stalk more silently,
And crouch on the limbs of trees,
And their descent
Upon the bright backs of their prey   *25*

May take years
In a sovereign floating of joy.
And those that are hunted
Know this as their life,
Their reward: to walk   *30*

Under such trees in full knowledge
Of what is in glory above them,
And to feel no fear,
But acceptance, compliance.
Fulfilling themselves without pain   *35*

At the cycle's center,
They tremble, they walk
Under the tree,
They fall, they are torn,
They rise, they walk again.   *40*

—1962

Alan Dugan (b. 1923) received the 1961 Yale Younger Poets Award, leading to the publication of his first collection as he neared forty. His plainspoken poetic voice, often with sardonic overtones, is appropriate for the anti-romantic stance of his most characteristic poems. For many years Dugan has been associated with the Fine Arts Work Center in Provincetown, Massachusetts, on Cape Cod.

Alan Dugan

Love Song: I and Thou

Nothing is plumb, level or square:
    the studs are bowed, the joists
are shaky by nature, no piece fits
    any other piece without a gap
or pinch, and bent nails   5
    dance all over the surfacing
like maggots. By Christ
    I am no carpenter. I built
the roof for myself, the walls
    for myself, the floors   10
for myself, and got
    hung up in it myself. I
danced with a purple thumb
    at this house-warming, drunk
with my prime whiskey: rage.   15
    Oh I spat rage's nails
into the frame-up of my work:
    it held. It settled plumb,
level, solid, square and true
    for that great moment. Then   20
it screamed and went on through,
    skewing as wrong the other way.
God damned it. This is hell,
    but I planned it, I sawed it,
I nailed it, and I   25
    will live in it until it kills me.
I can nail my left palm
    to the left-hand cross-piece but

I can't do everything myself.
  I need a hand to nail the right,   *30*
a help, a love, a you, a wife.

                                                              —1961

Anthony Hecht (b. 1923) *is most often linked with Richard Wilbur as one of the American poets of the postwar era who have most effectively utilized traditional poetic forms. The brilliance of Hecht's technique, however, must be set beside the powerful moral intelligence that informs his poetry.* The Hard Hours, *his second collection, won the Pulitzer Prize in 1968.*

Anthony Hecht
"More Light! More Light!"°

          For Heinrich Blücher and Hannah Arendt°

Composed in the Tower before his° execution
These moving verses, and being brought at that time
Painfully to the stake, submitted, declaring thus:
"I implore my God to witness that I have made no crime."

Nor was he forsaken of courage, but the death was horrible,   *5*
The sack of gunpowder failing to ignite.
His legs were blistered sticks on which the black sap
Bubbled and burst as he howled for the Kindly Light.

And that was but one, and by no means one of the worst;
Permitted at least his pitiful dignity;   *10*
And such as were by made prayers in the name of Christ,
That shall judge all men, for his soul's tranquillity.

"More Light! More Light!" reputed last words of Johann Wolfgang von Goethe (1749–1832), greatest German poet   **Heinrich Blücher and Hannah Arendt** husband and wife who escaped from Germany in 1941; Arendt wrote several books on the Holocaust   **1 his** a fictional English religious martyr (c. 1550), a composite of several actual cases

We move now to outside a German wood.°
Three men are there commanded to dig a hole
In which the two Jews are ordered to lie down   15
And be buried alive by the third, who is a Pole.

Not light from the shrine at Weimar° beyond the hill
Nor light from heaven appeared. But he did refuse.
A Lüger° settled back deeply in its glove.
He was ordered to change places with the Jews.   20

Much casual death had drained away their souls.
The thick dirt mounted toward the quivering chin.
When only the head was exposed the order came
To dig him out again and to get back in.

No light, no light in the blue Polish eye.   25
When he finished a riding boot packed down the earth.
The Lüger hovered lightly in its glove.
He was shot in the belly and in three hours bled to death.

No prayers or incense rose up in those hours
Which grew to be years, and every day came mute   30
Ghosts from the ovens, sifting through crisp air,
And settled upon his eyes in a black soot.

—1967

---

13 **German wood** Buchenwald ("beechen wood") was the site of a concentration camp.   **17 shrine at Weimar** Goethe's home   **19 Lüger** German military pistol

Denise Levertov (1923–1999) was as an outspoken opponent of U.S. involvement in the Vietnam War, an activity that has tended to overshadow her accomplishments as a lyric poet. Born of Jewish and Welsh parents in England, she emigrated to the United States during World War II.

Denise Levertov
The Ache of Marriage

The ache of marriage:

thigh and tongue, beloved,
are heavy with it,
it throbs in the teeth

We look for communion   5
and are turned away, beloved,
each and each

It is leviathan° and we
in its belly
looking for joy, some joy   10
not to be known outside it

two by two in the ark of
the ache of it.

—1964

---

8 leviathan great sea-creature mentioned in book of Job

Louis Simpson (b. 1923) was born in Jamaica to a colonial lawyer father and an American mother. Simpson came to the United States in his teens and served in the U.S. Army in World War II. He won the Pulitzer Prize in 1964 for At the End of the Open Road, *a volume that attempts to reexamine Walt Whitman's nineteenth-century definitions of the American experience. Subsequent collections have continued to demonstrate Simpson's unsentimental view of American suburban life.*

Louis Simpson
American Classic

It's a classic American scene—
a car stopped off the road
and a man trying to repair it.

The woman who stays in the car
in the classic American scene   5
stares back at the freeway traffic.

They look surprised, and ashamed
to be so helpless . . .
let down in the middle of the road!

To think that their car would do this!   10
They look like mountain people
whose son has gone against the law.

But every night they set out food
and the robber goes skulking back to the trees.
That's how it is with the car . . .   15

it's theirs, they're stuck with it.
Now they know what it's like to sit
and see the world go whizzing by.

In the fume of carbon monoxide and dust
they are not such good Americans   20
as they thought they were.

The feeling of being left out
through no fault of your own, is common.
That's why I say, an American classic.

—*1980*

My Father in the Night Commanding No

My father in the night commanding No
Has work to do. Smoke issues from his lips;
    He reads in silence.
The frogs are croaking and the street lamps glow.

And then my mother winds the gramophone: 5
The Bride of Lammermoor° begins to shriek—
    Or reads a story
About a prince, a castle, and a dragon.

The moon is glittering above the hill.
I stand before the gateposts of the King—   10
    So runs the story—
Of Thule, at midnight when the mice are still.

And I have been in Thule! It has come true—
The journey and the danger of the world,
    All that there is   15
To bear and to enjoy, endure and do.

Landscapes, seascapes . . . Where have I been led?
The names of cities—Paris, Venice, Rome—
    Held out their arms.
A feathered god, seductive, went ahead.   20

Here is my house. Under a red rose tree
A child is swinging; another gravely plays.
    They are not surprised
That I am here; they were expecting me.

And yet my father sits and reads in silence,   25
My mother sheds a tear, the moon is still,
    And the dark wind
Is murmuring that nothing ever happens.

---

6 **Bride of Lammermoor** *Lucia di Lammermoor*, opera by Donizetti

Beyond his jurisdiction as I move,
Do I not prove him wrong? And yet, it's true   30
    They will not change
There, on the stage of terror and of love.

The actors in that playhouse always sit
In fixed positions—father, mother, child
    With painted eyes.   35
How sad it is to be a little puppet!

Their heads are wooden. And you once pretended
To understand them! Shake them as you will,
    They cannot speak.
Do what you will, the comedy is ended.   40

Father, why did you work? Why did you weep,
Mother? Was the story so important?
    "Listen!" the wind
Said to the children, and they fell asleep.

                                         —*1963*

Vassar Miller (1924–1997) was a lifelong resident of Houston born with cerebral palsy. Miller published both traditional devotional verse and a large body of autobiographical poetry in open forms. If I Had Wheels or Love, *her collected poems, appeared in 1990.*

Vassar Miller

Subterfuge

I remember my father, slight,
staggering in with his Underwood,°
bearing it in his arms like an awkward bouquet

for his spastic child who sits down
on the floor, one knee on the frame   5
of the typewriter, and holding her left wrist

2 Underwood popular brand of manual typewriter

with her right hand, in that precision known
to the crippled, pecks at the keys
with a sparrow's preoccupation.

Falling by chance on rhyme, novel and curious bubble   *10*
blown with a magic pipe, she tries them over and over,
spellbound by life's clashing in accord or against itself,

pretending pretense and playing at playing,
she does her childhood backward as children do,
her fun a delaying action against what she knows.   *15*

My father must lose her, his runaway on her treadmill,
will lose the terrible favor that life has done him
as she toils at tomorrow, tensed at her makeshift toy.

—*1981*

Donald Justice (b. 1925) has published more selectively than most of his contemporaries. His Pulitzer Prize–winning volume of selected poems displays considerable literary sophistication and reveals the poet's familiarity with the traditions of contemporary European and Latin American poetry. As an editor, he is responsible for rescuing the important work of Weldon Kees from obscurity.

Donald Justice
Counting the Mad

This one was put in a jacket,
This one was sent home,
This one was given bread and meat
But would eat none,
And this one cried No No No No   *5*
All day long.

this one looked at the window
As though it were a wall,
This one saw things that were not there,
This one things that were,   *10*
And this one cried No No No No
All day long.

This one thought himself a bird,
This one a dog,
And this one thought himself a man,   *15*
An ordinary man,
And this one cried No No No No
All day long.

                                                                —1960

---

*Carolyn Kizer (b. 1925) has led a fascinating career that includes a year's study
in Taiwan and another year in Pakistan, where she worked for the U.S. State
Department. Her first collection,* The Ungrateful Garden *(1961), demonstrates
an equal facility with formal and free verse, but her subsequent books (including the
Pulitzer Prize–winning* Yin *of 1985) have tended more toward the latter. A committed feminist, Kizer anticipated many of today's women's issues as early as the mid-
1950s, just as the poem "The Ungrateful Garden" was published a decade before
"ecology" became a household word.*

Carolyn Kizer
The Ungrateful Garden

Midas watched the golden crust
That formed over his streaming sores,
Hugged his agues, loved his lust,
But damned to hell the out-of-doors

Where blazing motes of sun impaled   5
The serried° roses, metal-bright.
"Those famous flowers," Midas wailed,
"Have scorched my retina with light."

This gift, he'd thought, would gild his joys,
Silt up the waters of his grief;   10
His lawns a wilderness of noise,
The heavy clang of leaf on leaf.

Within, the golden cup is good
To heft, to sip the yellow mead.

6 serried crowded in rows

Outside, in summer's rage, the rude   15
Gold thorn has made his fingers bleed.

"I strolled my halls in golden shift,
As ruddy as a lion's meat.
Then I rushed out to share my gift,
And golden stubble cut my feet."   20

Dazzled with wounds, he limped away
To climb into his golden bed.
Roses, roses can betray.
"Nature is evil," Midas said.

—*1961*

Maxine Kumin (b. 1925) was born in Philadelphia and educated at Radcliffe. Kumin was an early literary ally and friend of Anne Sexton, with whom she co-authored several children's books. The winner of the 1973 Pulitzer Prize, Kumin has preferred a rural life raising horses for some years. Her increased interest in the natural world has paralleled the environmental awareness of many of her readers.

Maxine Kumin

Noted in the *New York Times*

Lake Buena Vista, Florida, June 16, 1987

Death claimed the last pure dusky seaside sparrow
today, whose coastal range was narrow,
as narrow as its two-part buzzy song.
From hummocks lost to Cape Canaveral
this mouselike skulker in the matted grass,   5
a six-inch bird, plain brown, once thousands strong,
sang *toodle-raeee azhee*, ending on a trill
before the air gave way to rocket blasts.

It laid its dull white eggs (brown specked) in small
neat cups of grass on plots of pickleweed,   10
bulrushes, or salt hay. It dined

on caterpillars, beetles, ticks, the seeds
of sedges. Unremarkable
the life it led with others of its kind.

Tomorrow we can put it on a stamp,   15
a first-day cover with Key Largo rat,
Schaus swallowtail, Florida swamp
crocodile, and fading cotton mouse.
How simply symbols replace habitat!
The tower frames of Aerospace   20
quiver in the flush of another shot
where, once indigenous, the dusky sparrow
soared trilling twenty feet above its burrow.

—1989

Robert Creeley (b. 1926) *was educated at Harvard, and is one of several important contemporary poets (Denise Levertov is another) to be associated with Black Mountain College, a small experimental school in North Carolina that attracted writers and artists during the 1950s.*

Robert Creeley
I Know a Man

As I sd to my
friend, because I am
always talking,—John, I

sd, which was not his
name, the darkness sur-   5
rounds us, what

can we do against
it, or else, shall we &
why not, buy a goddamn big car,

drive, he sd, for   10
christ's sake, look
out where yr going.

—1962

Oh No

If you wander far enough
you will come to it
and when you get there
they will give you a place to sit

for yourself only, in a nice chair,   5
and all your friends will be there
with smiles on their faces
and they will likewise all have places.

—*1962*

Allen Ginsberg (1926–1997) became the chief poetic spokesman of the Beat Generation. He was a force—as poet and celebrity—who continued to outrage and delight four decades after the appearance of Howl, *the monumental poem describing how Ginsberg saw: "the best minds of my generation destroyed by madness." Ginsberg's poems are cultural documents that provide a key to understanding the radical changes in American life, particularly among youth, that began in the mid-1950s.*

Allen Ginsberg
A Supermarket in California

What thoughts I have of you tonight, Walt Whitman, for I walked
down the sidestreets under the trees with a headache self-conscious
looking at the full moon.

In my hungry fatigue, and shopping for images, I went into
the neon fruit supermarket, dreaming of your enumerations!

What peaches and what penumbras?° Whole families shopping at
night! Aisles full of husbands! Wives in the avocados, babies
in the tomatoes!—and you, García Lorca,° what were you doing down
by the watermelons?

---

3 penumbras shadows   **3 García Lorca** Federico García Lorca, Spanish poet (1899–1936)

I saw you, Walt Whitman, childless, lonely old grubber, poking among the meats in the refrigerator and eyeing the grocery boys.

I heard you asking questions of each: Who killed the pork chops? What price bananas? Are you my Angel?   5

I wandered in and out of the brilliant stacks of cans following you, and followed in my imagination by the store detective.

We strode down the open corridors together in our solitary fancy tasting artichokes, possessing every frozen delicacy, and never passing the cashier.

Where are we going, Walt Whitman? The doors close in an hour. Which way does your beard point tonight?

(I touch your book and dream of our odyssey in the super- market and feel absurd.)

Will we walk all night through solitary streets? The trees add shade to shade, lights out in the houses, we'll both be lonely.   10

Will we stroll dreaming of the lost America of love past blue automobiles in driveways, home to our silent cottage?

Ah, dear father, graybeard, lonely old courage-teacher, what America did you have when Charon° quit poling his ferry and you got out on a smoking bank and stood watching the boat disappear on the black waters of Lethe?°

—1956

---

12 **Charon** ferryman of Hades   **Lethe** river in Hades, means forgetfulness

James Merrill (1926–1995) wrote "The Changing Light at Sandover," a long poem that resulted from many years of sessions with a Ouija board. The book became his major work and, among many other things, a remarkable memoir of a long-term gay relationship. Merrill's shorter poems, collected in 2001, reveal meticulous craftsmanship and a play of wit unequaled among contemporary American poets.

James Merrill

Casual Wear

Your average tourist: Fifty. 2.3
Times married. Dressed, this year, in Ferdi Plinthbower°
Originals. Odds 1 to 9^{10}°
Against her strolling past the Embassy

Today at noon. Your average terrorist: 5
Twenty-five. Celibate. No use for trends,
At least in clothing. Mark, though, where it ends.
People have come forth made of colored mist

Unsmiling on one hundred million screens
To tell of his prompt phone call to the station,   *10*
"Claiming responsibility"—devastation
Signed with a flourish, like the dead wife's jeans.

                                          —1984

Charles on Fire

Another evening we sprawled about discussing
Appearances. And it was the consensus
That while uncommon physical good looks
Continued to launch one, as before, in life
(Among its vaporous eddies and false calms),   5
Still, as one of us said into his beard,
"Without your intellectual and spiritual
Values, man, you are sunk." No one but squared

2 Ferdi Plinthbower a fictional designer   **3 1 to 9**^{10} pronounced "one to nine to the tenth power"

The shoulders of his own unloveliness.
Long-suffering Charles, having cooked and served the meal,   10
Now brought out little tumblers finely etched
He filled with amber liquor and then passed.
"Say," said the same young man, "in Paris, France,
They do it this way"—bounding to his feet
And touching a lit match to our host's full glass.   15
A blue flame, gentle, beautiful, came, went
Above the surface. In a hush that fell
We heard the vessel crack. The contents drained
As who should step down from a crystal coach.
Steward of spirits, Charles's glistening hand   20
All at once gloved itself in eeriness.
The moment passed. He made two quick sweeps and
Was flesh again. "It couldn't matter less,"
He said, but with a shocked, unconscious glance
Into the mirror. Finding nothing changed,   25
He filled a fresh glass and sank down among us.

—1966

W. D. Snodgrass (b. 1926) *won the Pulitzer Prize for his first collection,* Heart's Needle *(1959), and is generally considered one of the first important confessional poets. However, in his later career he has turned away from autobiographical subjects, writing, among other poems, a long sequence of dramatic monologues spoken by leading Nazis during the final days of the Hitler regime.*

W. D. Snodgrass
Mementos, I

Sorting out letters and piles of my old
   Canceled checks, old clippings, and yellow note cards
That meant something once, I happened to find
   Your picture. *That* picture. I stopped there cold,
Like a man raking piles of dead leaves in his yard   5
     Who has turned up a severed hand.

Still, that first second, I was glad: you stand
   Just as you stood—shy, delicate, slender,
In that long gown of green lace netting and daisies
   That you wore to our first dance. The sight of you stunned   *10*
Us all. Well, our needs were different, then,
       And our ideals came easy.

Then through the war and those two long years
   Overseas, the Japanese dead in their shacks
Among dishes, dolls, and lost shoes; I carried   *15*
   This glimpse of you, there, to choke down my fear,
Prove it had been, that it might come back.
       That was before we got married.

—Before we drained out one another's force
   With lies, self-denial, unspoken regret   *20*
And the sick eyes that blame; before the divorce
   And the treachery. Say it: before we met. Still,
I put back your picture. Someday, in due course,
       I will find that it's still there.

                         —1968

---

*Frank O'Hara (1926–1966) suffered an untimely death in a dune buggy acci-
dent on Fire Island that robbed American poetry of one its most refreshing talents.
An authority on modern art, O'Hara incorporates many of the spontaneous techniques of abstract painting in his own poetry, which was often written as an immediate reaction to the events of his daily life.*

Frank O'Hara
The Day Lady° Died

It is 12:20 in New York a Friday
three days after Bastille day,° yes
it is 1959 and I go get a shoeshine
because I will get off the 4:19 in Easthampton

Lady Billie Holiday (1915–1959), blues singer   **2 Bastille day** July 14

at 7:15 and then go straight to dinner 5
and I don't know the people who will feed me

I walk up the muggy street beginning to sun
and have a hamburger and a malted and buy
an ugly NEW WORLD WRITING to see what the poets
in Ghana are doing these days 10
                           I go on to the bank
and Miss Stillwagon (first name Linda I once heard)
doesn't even look up my balance for once in her life
and in the GOLDEN GRIFFIN I get a little Verlaine
for Patsy with drawings by Bonnard although I do 15
think of Hesiod, trans. Richard Lattimore or
Brendan Behan's new play or *Le Balcon* or *Les Nègres*
of Genet, but I don't, I stick with Verlaine
after practically going to sleep with quandariness

and for Mike I just stroll into the PARK LANE 20
Liquor Store and ask for a bottle of Strega and
then I go back where I came from to 6th Avenue
and the tobacconist in the Ziegfeld Theatre and
casually ask for a carton of Gauloises and a carton
of Picayunes, and a NEW YORK POST with her face on it 25

and I am sweating a lot by now and thinking of
leaning on the john door in the 5 SPOT
while she whispered a song along the keyboard
to Mal Waldron° and everyone and I stopped breathing.

                              —*1964*

---

29 Mal Waldron Holiday's accompanist.

John Ashbery (b. 1927) was born in upstate New York and educated at Harvard University. His first full-length book, Some Trees, was chosen by W. H. Auden as winner of the Yale Younger Poets Award in 1956. His enigmatic poems have intrigued readers for so long that much contemporary literary theory seems to have been created expressly for explicating his poems. Impossible to dismiss, Ashbery is now seen as the chief inheritor of the symbolist tradition brought to American locales by Wallace Stevens.

John Ashbery
Farm Implements and Rutabagas in a Landscape

The first of the undecoded messages read: "Popeye sits in thunder,
Unthought of. From that shoebox of an apartment,
From livid curtain's hue, a tangram emerges: a country."
Meanwhile the Sea Hag was relaxing on a green couch: "How
    pleasant
To spend one's vacation *en la casa de Popeye*," she scratched   5
Her cleft chin's solitary hair. She remembered spinach

And was going to ask Wimpy if he had bought any spinach.
"M'love," he intercepted, "the plains are decked out in thunder
Today, and it shall be as you wish." He scratched
The part of his head under his hat. The apartment   10
Seemed to grow smaller. "But what if no pleasant
Inspiration plunge us now to the stars? *For this is my country.*"

Suddenly they remembered how it was cheaper in the country.
Wimpy was thoughtfully cutting open a number 2 can of
    spinach
When the door opened and Swee'pea crept in. "How
    pleasant!"   15
But Swee'pea looked morose. A note was pinned to his bib.
    "Thunder
And tears are unavailing," it read. "Henceforth shall Popeye's
    apartment
Be but remembered space, toxic or salubrious, whole or scratched."

Olive came hurtling through the window; its geraniums scratched
Her long thigh. "I have news!" she gasped. "Popeye, forced as you
    know to flee the country   20
One musty gusty evening, by the schemes of his wizened, duplicate
    father, jealous of the apartment
And all that it contains, myself and spinach
In particular, heaves bolts of loving thunder
At his own astonished becoming, rupturing the pleasant

Arpeggio of our years. No more shall pleasant   25
Rays of the sun refresh your sense of growing old, nor the scratched
Tree-trunks and mossy foliage, only immaculate darkness and thunder."
She grabbed Swee'pea. "I'm taking the brat to the country."
"But you can't do that—he hasn't even finished his spinach,"
Urged the Sea Hag, looking fearfully around at the apartment.   30

But Olive was already out of earshot. Now the apartment
Succumbed to a strange new hush. "Actually it's quite pleasant
Here," thought the Sea Hag. "If this is all we need fear from spinach
Then I don't mind so much. Perhaps we could invite Alice the Goon
    over"—she scratched
One dug pensively—"but Wimpy is such a country   35
Bumpkin, always burping like that." Minute at first, the thunder

Soon filled the apartment. It was domestic thunder,
The color of spinach. Popeye chuckled and scratched
His balls: it sure was pleasant to spend a day in the country.

                                       —*1966*

Paradoxes and Oxymorons

The poem is concerned with language on a very plain level.
Look at it talking to you. You look out a window
Or pretend to fidget. You have it but you don't have it.
You miss it, it misses you. You miss each other.

The poem is sad because it wants to be yours, and cannot.   5
What's a plain level? It is that and other things,

Bringing a system of them into play. Play?
Well, actually, yes, but I consider play to be

A deeper outside thing, a dreamed role-pattern,
As in the division of grace these long August days   10
Without proof. Open-ended. And before you know
It gets lost in the steam and chatter of typewriters.

It has been played once more. I think you exist only
To tease me into doing it, on your level, and then you aren't there
Or have adopted a different attitude. And the poem   15
Has set me softly down beside you. The poem is you.

—*1981*

W. S. Merwin (b. 1927) often displays environmental concerns that have moti-
vated much poetry in recent years. Even in earlier work his fears of the results of un-
controlled destruction of the environment are presented allegorically. Born in New
York City, he currently resides in Hawaii.

W. S. Merwin
For the Anniversary of My Death

Every year without knowing it I have passed the day
When the last fires will wave to me
And the silence will set out
Tireless traveller
Like the beam of a lightless star   5

Then I will no longer
find myself in life as in a strange garment
surprised at the earth
And the love of one woman
And the shamelessness of men   10
As today writing after three days of rain
Hearing the wren sing and the falling cease
And bowing not knowing to what

—*1969*

The Last One

Well they'd make up their minds to be everywhere because why not.
Everywhere was theirs because they thought so.
They with two leaves they whom the birds despise.
In the middle of stones they made up their minds.
They started to cut.   5

Well they cut everything because why not.
Everything was theirs because they thought so.
It fell into its shadows and they took both away.
Some to have some for burning.

Well cutting everything they came to the water.   10
They came to the end of the day there was one left standing.
They would cut it tomorrow they went away.
The night gathered in the last branches.
The shadow of the night gathered in the shadow on the water.
The night and the shadow put on the same head.   15
And it said Now.

Well in the morning they cut the last one.
Like the others the last one fell into its shadow.
It fell into its shadow on the water.
They took it away its shadow stayed on the water.   20

Well they shrugged they started trying to get the shadow away.
They cut right to the ground the shadow stayed whole.
They laid boards on it the shadow came out on top.
They shone lights on it the shadow got blacker and clearer.
They exploded the water the shadow rocked.   25
They built a huge fire on the roots.
They sent up black smoke between the shadow and the sun.
The new shadow flowed without changing the old one.
They shrugged they went away to get stones.

They came back the shadow was growing.   30
They started setting up stones it was growing.
They looked the other way it went on growing.
They decided they would make a stone out of it.
They took stones to the water they poured them into the shadow.

They poured them in they poured them in the stones vanished.   35
The shadow was not filled it went on growing.
That was one day.

The next day was just the same it went on growing.
They did all the same things it was just the same.
They decided to take its water from under it.   40
They took away water they took it away the water went down.
The shadow stayed where it was before.
It went on growing it grew onto the land.
They started to scrape the shadow with machines.
When it touched the machines it stayed on them.   45
They started to beat the shadow with sticks.
Where it touched the sticks it stayed on them.
They started to beat the shadow with hands.
Where it touched the hands it stayed on them.
That was another day.   50

Well the next day started about the same it went on growing.
They pushed lights into the shadow.
Where the shadow got onto them they went out.
They began to stomp on the edge it got their feet.
And when it got their feet they fell down.   55
It got into eyes the eyes went blind.
The ones that fell down it grew over and they vanished.
The ones that went blind and walked into it vanished.
The ones that could see and stood still
It swallowed their shadows.   60
Then it swallowed them too and they vanished.
Well the others ran.

The ones that were left went away to live if it would let them.
They went as far as they could.
The lucky ones with their shadows.   65

—*1969*

James Wright (1927–1980) showed compassion for losers and underdogs of all types, an attitude evident everywhere in his poetry. A native of Martins Ferry, Ohio, he often described lives of quiet desperation in the blue-collar towns of his youth. Like many poets of his generation, Wright wrote formal verse in his early career and shifted to open forms during the 1960s.

James Wright

A Blessing

Just off the highway to Rochester, Minnesota,
Twilight bounds softly forth on the grass.
And the eyes of those two Indian ponies
Darken with kindness.
They have come gladly out of the willows   5
To welcome my friend and me.
We step over the barbed wire into the pasture
Where they have been grazing all day, alone.
They ripple tensely, they can hardly contain their happiness
That we have come.   10
They bow shyly as wet swans. They love each other.
There is no loneliness like theirs.
At home once more,
They begin munching the young tufts of spring in the darkness.
I would like to hold the slenderer one in my arms,   15
For she has walked over to me
And nuzzled my left hand.
She is black and white,
Her mane falls wild on her forehead,
And the light breeze moves me to caress her long ear   20
That is delicate as the skin over a girl's wrist.
Suddenly I realize
That if I stepped out of my body I would break
Into blossom.

—1963

Saint Judas

When I went out to kill myself, I caught
A pack of hoodlums beating up a man.
Running to spare his suffering, I forgot
My name, my number, how my day began,
How soldiers milled around the garden stone   5
And sang amusing songs; how all that day
Their javelins measured crowds; how I alone
Bargained the proper coins, and slipped away.

Banished from heaven, I found this victim beaten,
Stripped, kneed, and left to cry. Dropping my rope   10
Aside, I ran, ignored the uniforms:
Then I remembered bread my flesh had eaten,
The kiss that ate my flesh. Flayed without hope,
I held the man for nothing in my arms.

—1959

Philip Levine (b. 1928) *was born in Detroit, Michigan. He is one of many contemporary poets to hold a degree from the University of Iowa Writers' Workshop. The gritty urban landscapes and characters trapped in dead-end industrial jobs that provide Levine subjects for many poems match exactly with his unadorned, informal idiom. Like the deceptively simple William Carlos Williams, Levine has influenced many younger poets.*

Philip Levine
Genius

Two old dancing shoes my grandfather
gave the Christian Ladies,
an unpaid water bill, the rear license
of a dog that messed on your lawn,
a tooth I saved for the good fairy   5
and which is stained with base metals

and plastic filler. With these images
and your black luck and my bad breath
a bright beginner could make a poem
in fourteen rhyming lines about the purity   *10*
of first love or the rose's many thorns
or dew that won't wait long enough
to stand my little gray wren a drink.

—1981

---

*Anne Sexton (1928–1974) lived a tortured life of mental illness and family trou-
bles, becoming the model of the confessional poet. A housewife with two small daughters, she began writing poetry as the result of a program on public television, later taking a workshop from Robert Lowell in which Sylvia Plath was a fellow student. For
fifteen years until her suicide, she was a vibrant, exciting presence in American poetry.
A controversial biography of Sexton by Diane Wood Middlebrook appeared in 1991.*

Anne Sexton
Cinderella

You always read about it:
the plumber with twelve children
who wins the Irish Sweepstakes.
From toilets to riches.
That story.   *5*

Or the nursemaid,
some luscious sweet from Denmark
who captures the oldest son's heart.
From diapers to Dior.
That story.   *10*

Or a milkman who serves the wealthy,
eggs, cream, butter, yogurt, milk,
the white truck like an ambulance
who goes into real estate
and makes a pile.   *15*
From homogenized to martinis at lunch.

Or the charwoman
who is on the bus when it cracks up
and collects enough from the insurance.
From mops to Bonwit Teller.   *20*
That story.

Once
the wife of a rich man was on her deathbed
and she said to her daughter Cinderella:
Be devout. Be good. Then I will smile   *25*
down from heaven in the seam of a cloud.
The man took another wife who had
two daughters, pretty enough
but with hearts like blackjacks.
Cinderella was their maid.   *30*
She slept on the sooty hearth each night
and walked around looking like Al Jolson.
Her father brought presents home from town,
jewels and gowns for the other women
but the twig of a tree for Cinderella.   *35*
She planted that twig on her mother's grave
and it grew to a tree where a white dove sat.
Whenever she wished for anything the dove
would drop it like an egg upon the ground.
The bird is important, my dears, so heed him.   *40*

Next came the ball, as you all know.
It was a marriage market.
The prince was looking for a wife.
All but Cinderella were preparing
and gussying up for the big event.   *45*
Cinderella begged to go too.
Her stepmother threw a dish of lentils
into the cinders and said: Pick them
up in an hour and you shall go.
The white dove brought all his friends;   *50*
all the warm wings of the fatherland came,
and picked up the lentils in a jiffy.
No, Cinderella, said the stepmother,

you have no clothes and cannot dance.
That's the way with stepmothers. 55

Cinderella went to the tree at the grave
and cried forth like a gospel singer:
Mama! Mama! My turtledove,
send me to the prince's ball!
The bird dropped down a golden dress 60
and delicate little gold slippers.
Rather a large package for a simple bird.
So she went. Which is no surprise.
Her stepmother and sisters didn't
recognize her without her cinder face 65
and the prince took her hand on the spot
and danced with no other the whole day.

As nightfall came she thought she'd
better get home. The prince walked her home
and she disappeared into the pigeon house 70
and although the prince took an axe and broke
it open she was gone. Back to her cinders.
These events repeated themselves for three days.
However on the third day the prince
covered the palace steps with cobbler's wax 75
And Cinderella's gold shoe stuck upon it.
Now he would find whom the shoe fit
and find his strange dancing girl for keeps.
He went to their house and the two sisters
were delighted because they had lovely feet. 80
The eldest went into a room to try the slipper on
but her big toe got in the way so she simply
sliced it off and put on the slipper.
The prince rode away with her until the white dove
told him to look at the blood pouring forth. 85
That is the way with amputations.
They don't just heal up like a wish.
The other sister cut off her heel
but the blood told as blood will.
The prince was getting tired. 90

He began to feel like a shoe salesman.
But he gave it one last try.
This time Cinderella fit into the shoe
like a love letter into its envelope.

At the wedding ceremony   95
the two sisters came to curry favor
and the white dove pecked their eyes out.
Two hollow spots were left
like soup spoons.

Cinderella and the prince   100
lived, they say, happily ever after,
like two dolls in a museum case
never bothered by diapers or dust,
never arguing over the timing of an egg,
never telling the same story twice,   105
never getting a middle-aged spread,
their darling smiles pasted on for eternity
Regular Bobbsey Twins.
That story.

                                                                —*1970*

The Truth the Dead Know

> For my mother, born March 1902, died March
> 1959, and my father, born February 1900, died
> June 1959

Gone, I say and walk from church,
refusing the stiff procession to the grave,
letting the dead ride alone in the hearse.
It is June. I am tired of being brave.

We drive to the Cape. I cultivate   5
myself where the sun gutters from the sky,
where the sea swings in like an iron gate
and we touch. In another country people die.

My darling, the wind falls in like stones
from the whitehearted water and when we touch   10
we enter touch entirely. No one's alone.
Men kill for this, or for as much

And what of the dead? They lie without shoes
in their stone boats. They are more like stone
than the sea would be if it stopped. They refuse   15
to be blessed, throat, eye and knucklebone.

—*1962*

Thom Gunn (b. 1929) is a British expatriate who has lived in San Francisco for
over four decades. Gunn has managed to retain his ties to the traditions of British
literature while writing about motorcycle gangs, surfers, gay bars, and drug experiences. The Man with Night Sweats, his 1992 collection, contains a number of
forthright poems on AIDS, of which "Terminal" is one.

Thom Gunn
From the Wave

It mounts at sea, a concave wall
      Down-ribbed with shine,
And pushes forward, building tall
      Its steep incline.

Then from their hiding rise to sight   5
      Black shapes on boards
Bearing before the fringe of white
      It mottles towards.

Their pale feet curl, they poise their weight
      With a learn'd skill.   10
It is the wave they imitate
      Keeps them so still.

The marbling bodies have become
      Half wave, half men,

Grafted it seems by feet of foam 15
    Some seconds, then,

Late as they can, they slice the face
    In timed procession:
Balance is triumph in this place,
    Triumph possession. 20

The mindless heave of which they rode
    A fluid shelf
Breaks as they leave it, falls and, slowed,
    Loses itself.

Clear, the sheathed bodies slick as seals 25
    Loosen and tingle;
And by the board the bare foot feels
    The suck of shingle.

They paddle in the shallows still;
    Two splash each other; 30
Then all swim out to wait until
    The right waves gather.

—*1971*

Terminal

The eight years difference in age seems now
Disparity so wide between the two
That when I see the man who armoured stood
Resistant to all help however good
Now helped through day itself, eased into chairs, 5
Or else led step by step down the long stairs
With firm and gentle guidance by his friend,
Who loves him, through each effort to descend,
Each wavering, each attempt made to complete
An arc of movement and bring down the feet 10
As if with that spare strength he used to enjoy,
I think of Oedipus, old, led by a boy.

—*1992*

John Hollander (b. 1929) is a prolific author of poetry and criticism. Hollander's wit and formal originality mark him as one of the chief contemporary heirs of W. H. Auden. A native of New York City, he was educated at Columbia University and served as a Junior Fellow at Harvard University. He has taught at Yale University for many years.

John Hollander
Adam's Task

> *"And Adam gave names to all cattle, and to the fowl of the air, and to every beast of the field . . ."—Genesis 2:20*

Thou, paw-paw-paw; thou, glurd; thou, spotted
    Glurd; thou, whitestap, lurching through
The high-grown brush; thou, pliant-footed,
    Implex; thou, awagabu.

Every burrower, each flier   5
    Came for the name he had to give:
Gay, first work, ever to be prior,
    Not yet sunk to primitive.

Thou, verdle; thou, McFleery's pomma;
    Thou; thou; thou—three types of grawl;   10
Thou, flisket; thou, kabasch; thou, comma-
    Eared mashawk; thou, all; thou, all.

Were, in a fire of becoming,
    Laboring to be burned away,
Then work, half-measuring, half-humming,   15
    Would be as serious as play.

Thou, pambler; thou, rivarn; thou, greater
    Wherret, and thou, lesser one;
Thou, sproal; thou, zant; thou, lily-eater.
    Naming's over. Day is done.   20

—1971

X. J. Kennedy (b. 1929) is one the few contemporary American poets who has not been attracted by free verse, preferring to remain what he calls a "dinosaur," one of those poets who continue to write in meter. He is also rare among his contemporaries in his commitment to writing poems with strong ties to song. Kennedy is also the author of Literature: An Introduction to Fiction, Poetry, and Drama, *perhaps the most widely used college literature text ever written.*

X. J. Kennedy
In a Prominent Bar in Secaucus One Day

To the tune of "The Old Orange Flute" or the
tune of "Sweet Betsy from Pike"

In a prominent bar in Secaucus one day
Rose a lady in skunk with a topheavy sway,
Raised a knobby red finger—all turned from their beer—
While with eyes bright as snowcrust she sang high and clear:

"Now who of you'd think from an eyeload of me   5
That I once was a lady as proud as could be?
Oh I'd never sit down by a tumbledown drunk
If it wasn't, my dears, for the high cost of junk.

"All the gents used to swear that the white of my calf
Beat the down of the swan by a length and a half.   10
In the kerchief of linen I caught to my nose
Ah, there never fell snot, but a little gold rose.

"I had seven gold teeth and a toothpick of gold,
My Virginia cheroot° was a leaf of it rolled
And I'd light it each time with a thousand in cash—   15
Why the bums used to fight if I flicked them an ash.

"Once the toast of the Biltmore, the belle of the Taft,
I would drink bottle beer at the Drake, never draft,

14 **cheroot** a thin cigar

And dine at the Astor on Salisbury steak
With a clean tablecloth for each bite I did take.   *20*

"In a car like the Roxy I'd roll to the track,
A steel-guitar trio, a bar in the back,
And the wheels made no noise, they turned over so fast,
Still it took you ten minutes to see me go past.

"When the horses bowed down to me that I might choose,   *25*
I bet on them all, for I hated to lose.
Now I'm saddled each night for my butter and eggs
And the broken threads race down the backs of my legs.

"Let you hold in mind, girls, that your beauty must pass
Like a lovely white clover that rusts with its grass.   *30*
Keep your bottoms off barstools and marry you young
Or be left—an old barrel with many a bung.

"For when time takes you out for a spin in his car
You'll be hard-pressed to stop him from going too far
And be left by the roadside, for all your good deeds,   *35*
Two toadstools for tits and a face full of weeds."

All the house raised a cheer, but the man at the bar
Made a phonecall and up pulled a red patrol car
And she blew us a kiss as they copped her away
From that prominent bar in Secaucus, N.J.   *40*

—1961

Adrienne Rich *Adrienne Rich's most recent books of poetry are* Dark Fields of the Republic (Poems 1991–1995) *and* Midnight Salvage (Poems 1995–1998). *A new selection of her essays,* Art of the Possible: Essays and Conversations, *and a new volume of poems,* Fox (Poems 1998–2000), *will be published in 2001. She has recently been the recipient of the Dorothea Tanning Prize and of the Lannan Foundation Lifetime Achievement Award. She lives in California.*

Adrienne Rich

Aunt Jennifer's Tigers

Aunt Jennifer's tigers prance across a screen,
Bright topaz denizens of a world of green.
They do not fear the men beneath the tree;
They pace in sleek chivalric certainty.

Aunt Jennifer's fingers fluttering through her wool   5
Find even the ivory needle hard to pull.
The massive weight of Uncle's wedding band
Sits heavily upon Aunt Jennifer's hand.

When Aunt is dead, her terrified hands will lie
Still ringed with ordeals she was mastered by.   10
The tigers in the panel that she made
Will go on prancing, proud and unafraid.

—1950

Diving into the Wreck

First having read the book of myths,
and loaded the camera,
and checked the edge of the knife-blade,
I put on
the body-armor of black rubber   5
the absurd flippers
the grave and awkward mask.
I am having to do this

not like Cousteau° with his
assiduous team   *10*
aboard the sun-flooded schooner
but here alone.

There is a ladder.
The ladder is always there
hanging innocently   *15*
close to the side of the schooner.
We know what it is for,
we who have used it.
Otherwise
it is a piece of maritime floss   *20*
some sundry equipment.

I go down.
Rung after rung and still
the oxygen immerses me
the blue light   *25*
the clear atoms
of our human air.
I go down.
My flippers cripple me,
I crawl like an insect down the ladder   *30*
and there is no one
to tell me when the ocean
will begin.

First the air is blue and then
it is bluer and then green and then   *35*
black I am blacking out and yet
my mask is powerful
it pumps my blood with power
the sea is another story
the sea is not a question of power   *40*
I have to learn alone

9 Cousteau Jacques-Yves Cousteau (1910–1997), underwater explorer and inventor of the scuba
tank

to turn my body without force
in the deep element.

And now: it is easy to forget
what I came for   45
among so many who have always
lived here
swaying their crenellated fans
between the reefs
and besides   50
you breathe differently down here.

I came to explore the wreck.
The words are purposes.
The words are maps.
I came to see the damage that was done   55
and the treasures that prevail.
I stroke the beam of my lamp
slowly along the flank
of something more permanent
than fish or weed   60

the thing I came for:
the wreck and not the story of the wreck
the thing itself and not the myth
the drowned face always staring
toward the sun   65
the evidence of damage
worn by salt and sway into this threadbare beauty
the ribs of the disaster
curving their assertion
among the tentative haunters.   70

This is the place.
And I am here, the mermaid whose dark hair
streams black, the merman in his armored body.
We circle silently
about the wreck   75
we dive into the hold.
I am she: I am he

whose drowned face sleeps with open eyes
whose breasts still bear the stress
whose silver, copper, vermeil cargo lies   80
obscurely inside barrels
half-wedged and left to rot
we are the half-destroyed instruments
that once held to a course
the water-eaten log   85
the fouled compass

We are, I am, you are
by cowardice or courage
the one who find our way
back to this scene   90
carrying a knife, a camera
a book of myths
in which
our names do not appear.

                                                      —*1972*

Rape

There is a cop who is both prowler and father:
he comes from your block, grew up with your brothers,
had certain ideals.
You hardly know him in his boots and silver badge,
on horseback, one hand touching his gun.   5

You hardly know him but you have to get to know him:
he has access to machinery that could kill you.
He and his stallion clop like warlords among the trash,
his ideals stand in the air, a frozen cloud
from between his unsmiling lips.   10

And so, when the time comes, you have to turn to him,
the maniac's sperm still greasing your thighs,
your mind whirling like crazy. You have to confess
to him, you are guilty of the crime
of having been forced.   15

And you see his blue eyes, the blue eyes of all the family
whom you used to know, grow narrow and glisten,
his hand types out the details
and he wants them all
but the hysteria in your voice pleases him best.   20

You hardly know him but now he thinks he knows you:
he has taken down your worst moment
on a machine and filed it in a file.
He knows, or thinks he knows, how much you imagined;
he knows, or thinks he knows, what you secretly wanted.   25

He has access to machinery that could get you put away;
and if, in the sickening light of the precinct,
and if, in the sickening light of the precinct,
your details sound like a portrait of your confessor,
will you swallow, will you deny them, will you lie your way home? 30

                                                        —1972

Ted Hughes (1930–1998) *was a native of Yorkshire, England. Hughes never ven-tured far from the natural world of his childhood for his subject matter. Hughes was married to Sylvia Plath until her death in 1963;* Birthday Letters, *a book of po-ems about their troubled relationship, appeared in 1998. At the time of his death, Hughes was the British poet laureate.*

Ted Hughes
Pike

Pike, three inches long, perfect
Pike in all parts, green tigering the gold.
Killers from the egg: the malevolent aged grin.
They dance on the surface among the flies.

Or move, stunned by their own grandeur,   5
Over a bed of emerald, silhouette
Of submarine delicacy and horror.
A hundred feet long in their world.

In ponds, under the heat-struck lily pads—
Gloom of their stillness: *10*
Logged on last year's black leaves, watching upwards.
Or hung in an amber cavern of weeds

The jaw's hooked clamp and fangs
Not to be changed at this date;
A life subdued to its instrument;   *15*
The gills kneading quietly, and the pectorals.

Three we kept behind glass,
Jungled in weed: three inches, four,
And four and a half: fed fry to them—
Suddenly there were two. Finally one   *20*

With a sag belly and the grin it was born with.
And indeed they spare nobody.
Two, six pounds each, over two feet long,
High and dry and dead in the willow-herb—

One jammed past its gills down the other's gullet: *25*
The outside eye stared: as a vice locks—
The same iron in this eye
Though its film shrank in death.

A pond I fished, fifty yards across,
Whose lilies and muscular tench°   *30*
Had outlasted every visible stone
Of the monastery that planted them—

Stilled legendary depth:
It was as deep as England. It held
Pike too immense to stir, so immense and old   *35*
That past nightfall I dared not cast

But silently cast and fished
With the hair frozen on my head
For what might move, for what eye might move.
The still splashes on the dark pond,   *40*

30 **tench** European freshwater fish

Owls hushing the floating woods
Frail on my ear against the dream
Darkness beneath night's darkness had freed,
That rose slowly towards me, watching.

—1960

Gary Snyder (b. 1930) *was deeply involved in poetic activity in his hometown, San Francisco, when that city became the locus of the Beat Generation in the mid-1950s. Yet Snyder, whose studies in Zen Buddhism and Oriental cultures preceded his acquaintance with Allen Ginsberg and Jack Kerouac, has always exhibited a seriousness of purpose that sets him apart from his peers. His long familiarity with the mountains of the Pacific Northwest dates from his jobs with logging crews during his college days.*

Gary Snyder
A Walk

Sunday the only day we don't work:
Mules farting around the meadow,
     Murphy fishing,
The tent flaps in the warm
Early sun: I've eaten breakfast and I'll   5
     take a walk
To Benson Lake. Packed a lunch,
Goodbye. Hopping on creekbed boulders
Up the rock throat three miles
     Piute Creek—   10
In steep gorge glacier-slick rattlesnake country
Jump, land by a pool, trout skitter,
The clear sky. Deer tracks.
Bad place by a falls, boulders big as houses,
Lunch tied to belt,   15
I stemmed up a crack and almost fell
But rolled out safe on a ledge
     and ambled on.
Quail chicks freeze underfoot, color of stone

Then run cheep! away, hen quail fussing.   *20*
Craggy west end of Benson Lake—after edging
Past dark creek pools on a long white slope—
Lookt down in the ice-black lake
  lined with cliff
From far above: deep shimmering trout.   *25*
A lone duck in a gunsightpass
  steep side hill
Through slide-aspen and talus, to the east end
Down to grass, wading a wide smooth stream
Into camp. At last.   *30*
 By the rusty three-year-
Ago left-behind cookstove
Of the old trail crew,
Stoppt and swam and ate my lunch.

             —*1968*

Derek Walcott (b. 1930) is a native of the tiny Caribbean island of St. Lucia in the West Indies. Walcott combines a love of the tradition of English poetry with the exotic surfaces of tropical life. In many ways, his life and career have constituted a study in divided loyalties, which are displayed in his ambivalent poems about life in the United States, where he has lived and taught for many years. Walcott was awarded the Nobel Prize in 1992.

Derek Walcott
Central America

Helicopters are cutlassing the wild bananas.
Between a nicotine thumb and forefinger
brittle faces crumble like tobacco leaves.
Children waddle in vests, their legs bowed,
little shrimps curled under their navels.   *5*
The old men's teeth are stumps in a charred forest.
Their skins grate like the iguana's.
Their gaze like slate stones.
Women squat by the river's consolations

where children wade up to their knees,   10
and a stick stirs up a twinkling of butterflies.
Up there, in the blue acres
of forest, flies circle their fathers.
In spring, in the upper provinces
of the Empire, yellow tanagers   15
float up through the bare branches.
There is no distinction in these distances.

—*1987*

Miller Williams (b. 1930) won the Poets' Prize in 1990 for Living on the
Surface, *a volume of selected poems. A skillful translator of both Giuseppe Belli, a
Roman poet of the early nineteenth century, and of Nicanor Parra, a contemporary
Chilean, Williams has written many poems about his travels throughout the world
yet has retained the relaxed idiom of his native Arkansas. He read a poem at the
1997 presidential inauguration.*

Miller Williams
The Book

I held it in my hands while he told the story.

He had found it in a fallen bunker,
a book for notes with all the pages blank.
He took it to keep for a sketchbook and diary.

He learned years later, when he showed the book   5
to an old bookbinder, who paled, and stepped back
a long step and told him what he held,
what he had laid the days of his life in.
It's bound, the binder said, in human skin.

I stood turning it over in my hands,   10
turning it in my head. Human skin.

What child did this skin fit? What man, what woman?
Dragged still full of its flesh from what dream?

Who took it off the meat? Some other one
who stayed alive by knowing how to do this?   15

I stared at the changing book and a horror grew,
I stared and a horror grew, which was, which is,
how beautiful it was until I knew.

—*1989*

Linda Pastan (b. 1932) served as poet laureate of Maryland, where she has lived and taught for many years. Her first book, A Perfect Circle of Sun, *appeared in 1971, and five more collections have been published since.*

Linda Pastan
Crocuses

They come
by stealth, spreading
the rumor of spring—
near the hedge . . .
by the gate . . .   5
at our chilly feet . . .
mothers of saffron, fathers
of insurrection, purple
and yellow scouts
of an army still massing   10
just to the south.

—*1991*

*Sylvia Plath (1932–1963), whose troubled personal life is often difficult to sepa-
rate from her poetry, is almost always read as an autobiographical and confessional
poet. Brilliant and precocious, she served a long apprenticeship to the tradition of
modern poetry before attaining her mature style in the final two years of her life.
Only one collection,* The Colossus, *appeared in her lifetime, and her fame has
mainly rested on her posthumous books of poetry and the success of her lone novel,*
The Bell Jar. *She committed suicide in 1963. Plath has been the subject of a half-
dozen biographical studies, reflecting the intense interest that readers, especially
women, have in her life and work.*

Sylvia Plath
Daddy

You do not do, you do not do
Any more, black shoe
In which I have lived like a foot
For thirty years, poor and white,
Barely daring to breathe or Achoo.   5

Daddy, I have had to kill you.
You died before I had time—
Marble-heavy, a bag full of God,
Ghastly statue with one gray toe
Big as a Frisco seal   10

And a head in the freakish Atlantic
Where it pours bean green over blue
In the waters off beautiful Nauset.
I used to pray to recover you.
Ach, du.°   15

In the German tongue, in the Polish town
Scraped flat by the roller
Of wars, wars, wars.
But the name of the town is common.
My Polack friend   20

---

15 Ach, du "Oh, you"

Says there are a dozen or two.
So I never could tell where you
Put your foot, your root,
I never could talk to you.
The tongue stuck in my jaw.   25

It stuck in a barb wire snare.
Ich, ich, ich, ich,°
I could hardly speak.
I thought every German was you.
And the language obscene   30

An engine, an engine
Chuffing me off like a Jew.
A Jew to Dachau, Auschwitz, Belsen.°
I began to talk like a Jew.
I think I may well be a Jew.   35

The snows of the Tyrol, the clear beer of Vienna
Are not very pure or true.
With my gypsy ancestress and my weird luck
And my Taroc pack and my Taroc pack
I may be a bit of a Jew.   40

I have always been scared of *you*,
With your Luftwaffe,° your gobbledygoo.
And your neat mustache
And your Aryan eye, bright blue.
Panzer-man, panzer-man, O You—   45

Not God but a swastika
So black no sky could squeak through.
Every woman adores a Fascist,
The boot in the face, the brute
Brute heart of a brute like you.   50

---

27 **Ich, ich, ich, ich** "I, I, I, I"   33 **Dachau, Auschwitz, Belsen** German concentration camps
42 **Luftwaffe** German Air Force

You stand at the blackboard, daddy,
In the picture I have of you,
A cleft in your chin instead of your foot
But no less a devil for that, no not
Any less the black man who   55

Bit my pretty red heart in two.
I was ten when they buried you.
At twenty I tried to die
And get back, back, back to you.
I thought even the bones would do.   60

But they pulled me out of the sack,
And they stuck me together with glue.
And then I knew what to do.
I made a model of you,
A man in black with a Meinkampf° look   65

And a love of the rack and the screw.
And I said I do, I do.
So daddy, I'm finally through.
The black telephone's off at the root,
The voices just can't worm through.   70

If I've killed one man, I've killed two—
The vampire who said he was you
And drank my blood for a year,
Seven years, if you want to know.
Daddy, you can lie back now.   75

There's a stake in your fat black heart
And the villagers never liked you.
They are dancing and stamping on you.
They always *knew* it was you.
Daddy, daddy, you bastard, I'm through.   80

—*1966*

---

65 Meinkampf title of Hitler's autobiography ("My Struggle")

Edge

The woman is perfected.
Her dead

Body wears the smile of accomplishment,
The illusion of a Greek necessity

Flows in the scrolls of her toga,   *5*
Her bare

Feet seem to be saying:
We have come so far, it is over.

Each dead child coiled, a white serpent,
One at each little   *10*

Pitcher of milk, now empty.
She has folded

Them back into her body as petals
Of a rose close when the garden

Stiffens and odors bleed   *15*
From the sweet, deep throats of the night flower.

The moon has nothing to be sad about,
Staring from her hood of bone.

She is used to this sort of thing.
Her blacks crackle and drag.   *20*

         —*1965*

Metaphors

I'm a riddle in nine syllables,
An elephant, a ponderous house,
A melon strolling on two tendrils.
O red fruit, ivory, fine timbers!
This loaf's big with its yeasty rising.   *5*

Money's new-minted in this fat purse.
I'm a means, a stage, a cow in calf.
I've eaten a bag of green apples,
Boarded the train there's no getting off.

—*1960*

Gerald Barrax (b. 1933) *served as the editor of* Obsidian II: Black Literature
in Review, *one of the most influential journals of African-American writing. The
author of five collections of poetry, he taught at North Carolina State University.*

Gerald Barrax
Strangers Like Us:
Pittsburgh, Raleigh,
1945–1985

The sounds our parents heard echoing over
housetops while listening to evening radios
were the uninterrupted cries running and cycling
we sent through the streets and yards, where spring summer
fall we were entrusted to the night, boys   5
and girls together, to send us home for bath
and bed after the dark had drifted down and eased
contests between pitcher and batter, hider and seeker.

Our own children live imprisoned in light.
They are cycloned into our yards and hearts,   10
whose gates flutter shut on unfamiliar smiles.
At the rumor of a moon, we call them in
before the monsters who hunt, who hurt, who haunt
us, rise up from our own dim streets.

—*1992*

Anne Stevenson (b. 1933) is perhaps best known as the author of a controversial biography of Sylvia Plath. Stevenson was born in England of American parents and educated at the University of Michigan. She has lived in England since her twenties. Her Selected Poems *appeared in 1987.*

Anne Stevenson

Sous-Entendu°

Don't think

that I don't know
that as you talk to me
the hand of your mind
is inconspicuously   5
taking off my stocking,
moving in resourceful blindness
up along my thigh.
Don't think
that I don't know   10
that you know
everything I say
is a garment.

—1969

Sous-Entendu "hidden meaning"

Mark Strand (b. 1934) displays a simplicity in his best poems that reveals the influence of Spanish-language poets like Nicanor Parra, the father of "anti-poetry," and Rafael Alberti, whom Strand has translated. Strand was named U.S. poet laureate in 1990.

Mark Strand

The Tunnel

A man has been standing
in front of my house
for days. I peek at him
from the living room
window and at night,   5
unable to sleep,
I shine my flashlight
down on the lawn.
He is always there.

After a while   10
I open the front door
just a crack and order
him out of my yard.
He narrows his eyes
and moans. I slam   15
the door and dash back
to the kitchen, then up
to the bedroom, then down.

I weep like a schoolgirl
and make obscene gestures   20
through the window. I
write large suicide notes
and place them so he
can read them easily.
I destroy the living   25
room furniture to prove
I own nothing of value.

When he seems unmoved
I decide to dig a tunnel
to a neighboring yard.   *30*
I seal the basement off
from the upstairs with
a brick wall. I dig hard
and in no time the tunnel
is done. Leaving my pick   *35*
and shovel below,

I come out in front of a house
and stand there too tired to
move or even speak, hoping
someone will help me.   *40*
I feel I'm being watched
and sometimes I hear
a man's voice,
but nothing is done
and I have been waiting for days.   *45*

—1968

Mary Oliver (b. 1935) was born in Cleveland, Ohio, and educated at Ohio State University and Vassar College. She has served as a visiting professor at a number of universities and at the Fine Arts Center in Provincetown, Massachusetts. She has won both the Pulitzer Prize and the National Book Award for her work, which first appeared in No Voyage and Other Poems *in 1965.*

Mary Oliver
The Black Walnut Tree

My mother and I debate:
we could sell
the black walnut tree
to the lumberman,
and pay off the mortgage.   *5*
Likely some storm anyway

will churn down its dark boughs,
smashing the house. We talk
slowly, two women trying
in a difficult time to be wise.
Roots in the cellar drains,   10
I say, and she replies
that the leaves are getting heavier
every year, and the fruit
harder to gather away.
But something brighter than money   15
moves in our blood—an edge
sharp and quick as a trowel
that wants us to dig and sow.
So we talk, but we don't do
anything. That night I dream   20
of my fathers out of Bohemia
filling the blue fields
of fresh and generous Ohio
with leaves and vines and orchards.
What my mother and I both know   25
is that we'd crawl with shame
in the emptiness we'd made
in our own and our fathers' backyard.
So the black walnut tree   30
swings through another year
of sun and leaping winds,
of leaves and bounding fruit,
and, month after month, the whip-
crack of the mortgage.   35

—*1979*

Fred Chappell (b. 1936) wrote the epic-length poem Midquest *(1981), and his achievement was recognized when he was awarded the Bollingen Prize in 1985. A four-part poem written over a decade,* Midquest *uses the occasion of the poet's thirty-fifth birthday as a departure for a complex sequence of autobiographical poems that are heavily indebted to Dante for their formal structure. A versatile writer of both poetry and prose, Chappell displays his classical learning brilliantly and in unusual contexts.*

Fred Chappell
Narcissus and Echo°

Shall the water not remember *Ember*
my hand's slow gesture, tracing above *of*
its mirror my half-imaginary *airy*
portrait? My only belonging *longing*
is my beauty, which I take *ache*   5
away and then return as love *of*
teasing playfully the one being *unbeing.*

whose gratitude I treasure *Is your*
moves me. I live apart *heart*
from myself, yet cannot *not*   10
live apart. In the water's tone, *stone?*
that brilliant silence, a flower *Hour,*
whispers my name with such slight *light,*
moment, it seems filament of air, *fare*
the world become cloudswell. *well.*   15

—*1985*

Narcissus and Echo In the myth, the vain Narcissus drowned attempting to embrace his own reflection in the water. Echo, a nymph who loved him, pined away until only her voice remained.

Lucille Clifton (b. 1936), a native of Depew, New York, was educated at SUNY—Fredonia and Howard University, and has taught at several colleges, including the American University in Washington, D.C. About her own work, she has commented succinctly, "I am a Black woman poet, and I sound like one." Clifton won a National Book Award in 2000.

Lucille Clifton

to my last period

well girl, goodbye,
after thirty-eight years.
thirty-eight years and you
never arrived
splendid in your red dress   5
without trouble for me
somewhere, somehow.

now it is done,
and i feel just like
the grandmothers who,   10
after the hussy has gone,
sit holding her photograph
and sighing, *wasn't she
beautiful? wasn't she beautiful?*

—*1991*

Marge Piercy (b. 1936) was *a political radical during her student days at the University of Michigan. Piercy has continued to be outspoken on political, cultural, and sexual issues. Her phrase "to be of use" has become a key measure by which feminist writers and critics have gauged the meaning of their own life experiences.*

Marge Piercy

Barbie Doll

This girlchild was born as usual
and presented dolls that did pee-pee
and miniature GE stoves and irons
and wee lipsticks the color of cherry candy.
Then in the magic of puberty, a classmate said: 5
You have a great big nose and fat legs.

She was healthy, tested intelligent
possessed strong arms and back,
abundant sexual drive and manual dexterity.
She went to and fro apologizing.   10
Everyone saw a fat nose on thick legs.

She was advised to play coy,
exhorted to come on hearty,
exercise, diet, smile and wheedle.
Her good nature wore out   15
like a fan belt.
So she cut off her nose and her legs
and offered them up.

In the casket displayed on satin she lay
with the undertaker's cosmetics painted on,   20
a turned-up putty nose,
dressed in a pink and white nightie.
Doesn't she look pretty? everyone said.
Consummation at last.
To every woman a happy ending.   25

—*1982*

Nancy Willard (b. 1936) is the author of nine collections of poetry. Willard has also written a novel and an award-winning book of poems for children, A Visit to William Blake's Inn. *About her whimsical work Donald Hall has said, "She imagines with a wonderful concreteness. But also, she takes real language and by literal-mindedness turns it into the structure of dream."*

Nancy Willard

A Hardware Store as Proof of the Existence of God

I praise the brightness of hammers pointing east
like the steel woodpeckers of the future,
and dozens of hinges opening brass wings,
and six new rakes shyly fanning their toes,
and bins of hooks glittering into bees,   5

and a rack of wrenches like the long bones of horses,
and mailboxes sowing rows of silver chapels,
and a company of plungers waiting for God
to claim their thin legs in their big shoes
and put them on and walk away laughing.   10

In a world not perfect but not bad either
let there be glue, glaze, gum, and grabs,
caulk also, and hooks, shackles, cables, and slips,
and signs so spare a child may read them,
Men, Women, In, Out, No Parking, Beware the Dog.   15

In the right hands, they can work wonders.

—*1989*

Betty Adcock (b. 1938) was born in San Augustine, Texas. Adcock has lived for many years in Raleigh, North Carolina, where she is poet-in-residence at Meredith College. Her volume of selected poems, Interuale, *appeared in 2001.*

Betty Adcock

Digression on the Nuclear Age

In some difficult part of Africa, a termite tribe
builds elaborate tenements that might be called
cathedrals, were they for anything so terminal
as Milton's God. Who was it said
the perfect arch will always separate   5
the civilized from the not? Never mind.

These creatures are quite blind and soft
and hard at labor chemically induced.
Beginning with a dish-like hollow, groups
of workers pile up earthen pellets.   10
A few such piles will reach a certain height;
fewer still, a just proximity.
That's when direction changes, or a change
directs: the correct two bands of laborers
will make their towers bow toward each other.   15
Like saved and savior, they will meet in air.
It is unambiguously an arch and it will serve,
among the others rising and the waste,
an arch's purposes. Experts are sure
a specific moment comes when the very structure   20
triggers the response that will perfect it.

I've got this far and don't know what
termites can be made to mean. Or this poem:
a joke, a play on arrogance, nothing
but language? Untranslated, the world gets on   25

with dark, flawless constructions rising,
rising even where we think we are. And think
how we must hope convergences will fail this time,
that whatever it is we're working on won't work.

—*1988*

---

*Gary Gildner (b. 1938) was born in West Branch, Michigan, and attended
Michigan State University. He lives on a ranch in the Clearwater Mountains of
Idaho. "First Practice" is the title poem of his first collection, published in 1969, and
a volume of Gildner's selected poems appeared in 1984.*

Gary Gildner

First Practice

After the doctor checked to see
we weren't ruptured,
the man with the short cigar took us
under the grade school,
where we went in case of attack   5
or storm, and said
he was Clifford Hill, he was
a man who believed dogs
ate dogs, he had once killed
for his country, and if   10
there were any girls present
for them to leave now.
          No one
left. OK, he said, he said I take
that to mean you are hungry   15
men who hate to lose as much
as I do. OK. Then
he made two lines of us
facing each other,
and across the way, he said,   20

is the man you hate most
in the world,
and if we are to win
that title I want to see how.
But I don't want to see   25
any marks when you're dressed,
he said. He said, *Now.*

—*1969*

---

*Robert Phillips (b. 1938) labored for over thirty years as a New York advertising
executive, a remarkable fact when one considers his many books of poetry, fiction,
and criticism and the numerous books he has edited. He currently lives in Houston,
where he teaches in the creative writing program at the University of Houston.*

Robert Phillips
Compartments

Which shall be final?
        Pine box in a concrete vault,
urn on a mantel?

Last breath a rattle,
        stuffed in a black body bag,   5
he's zipped head to toe.

At the nursing home,
        side drawn to prevent a fall—
in a crib again.

His dead wife's false teeth   10
        underfoot in their bedroom.
Feel the piercing chill.

Pink flamingo lawn,
        a Florida trailer park:
one space he'll avoid.   15

The box they gave him
     on retirement held a watch
that measures decades.

The new bifocals
     rest in their satin-lined case,   20
his body coffined.

Move to the suburbs.
     Crowded train at seven-oh-two,
empty head at night.

New playpen, new crib,   25
     can't compete with the newness
of the newborn child.

Oak four-poster bed
     inherited from family—
Jack Frost defrosted.   30

Once he was pink-slipped.
     Dad helped out: "A son's a son,
Son, from womb to tomb."

Fourteen-foot ceilings,
     parquet floors, marble fireplace,   35
proud first apartment.

The Jack Frost Motel,
     its very name a portent
for their honeymoon.

Backseat of a car,   40
     cursing the inventor of
nylon pantyhose.

First-job cubicle.
     Just how many years before
a window office?   45

College quad at noon,
     chapel bells, frat men, coeds,
no pocket money.

his grandfather's barn.
    After it burned to the ground,   *50*
the moon filled its space.

His favorite tree—
    the leaves return to branches?
No, butterflies light.

Closet where he hid   *55*
    to play with himself. None knew?
Mothball orgasms.

Chimney that he scaled
    naked to sweep for his Dad:
Blake's soot-black urchin.   *60*

The town's swimming pool
    instructor, throwing him in
again and again . . .

Kindergarten play
    ground: swings, slides, rings, jungle gym.   *65*
Scraped knees, molester.

Red, blue and green birds
    mobilize over his crib,
its sides a tall fence.

Two months premature,   *70*
    he incubates by light bulbs,
like a baby chick.

He is impatient,
    curled in foetal position,
floating in darkness.   *75*

—2000

Charles Simic (b. 1938) *was born in Yugoslavia and came with his parents to Chicago in 1949. Educated at New York University, he teaches at the University of New Hampshire.* The World Doesn't End, *a collection of prose poems, won the Pulitzer Prize in 1990.*

Charles Simic

Stone

Go inside a stone
That would be my way.
Let somebody else become a dove
Or gnash with a tiger's tooth.
I am happy to be a stone.   5

From the outside the stone is a riddle:
No one knows how to answer it.
Yet within, it must be cool and quiet
Even though a cow steps on it full weight,
Even though a child throws it in a river;   10
The stone sinks, slow, unperturbed
To the river bottom
Where the fishes come to knock on it
And listen.

I have seen sparks fly out   15
When two stones are rubbed,
So perhaps it is not dark inside after all;
Perhaps there is a moon shining
From somewhere, as though behind a hill—
Just enough light to make out   20
The strange writings, the star-charts
On the inner walls.

—*1971*

Dabney Stuart (b. 1938) has written many poems populated by the supporting cast of the American family romance—parents, wives and ex-wives, and children. A Virginian who has taught for many years at Washington and Lee University, Stuart published Light Years, *a volume of selected poems, in 1995.*

D a b n e y S t u a r t
Discovering My Daughter

Most of your life we have kept our separate places:
After I left your mother you knew an island,
Rented rooms, a slow coastal slide northward
To Boston, and, in summer, another island
Hung at the country's tip. Would you have kept going   5
All the way off the map, an absolute alien?

Sometimes I shiver, being almost forgetful enough
To have let that happen. We've come the longer way
Under such pressure, from one person to
Another. Our trip proves again the world is   10
Round, a singular island where people may come
Together, as we have, making a singular place.

            —1987

Margaret Atwood (b. 1939) is the leading woman writer of Canada. Atwood excels at both poetry and prose fiction. Among her six novels, The Handmaid's Tale *is perhaps the best known, becoming a bestseller in the United States and the subject of a motion picture. Atwood's* Selected Poems *appeared in 1976.*

M a r g a r e t A t w o o d
Siren° Song

This is the one song everyone
would like to learn: the song
that is irresistible:

Siren in Greek myth, one of the women whose irresistible song lured sailors onto the rocks

the song that forces men
to leap overboard in squadrons   5
even though they see the beached skulls

the song nobody knows
because anyone who has heard it
is dead, and the others can't remember.

Shall I tell you the secret   10
and if I do, will you get me
out of this bird suit?

I don't enjoy it here
squatting on this island
looking picturesque and mythical   15

with these two feathery maniacs,
I don't enjoy singing
this trio, fatal and valuable.

I will tell the secret to you,
to you, only to you.   20
Come closer. This song

is a cry for help: Help me!
Only you, only you can,
you are unique

at last. Alas   25
it is a boring song
but it works every time.

—*1974*

Stephen Dunn (b. 1939) *is a graduate of the creative writing program at Syracuse University. Dunn teaches at Stockton State College in Pomona, New Jersey. His attempt to blend ordinary experience with larger significance is illustrated in the duality of his book titles like* Full of Lust and Good Usage, Work and Love, *and* Between Angels. *Dunn was awarded the Pulitzer Prize in 2001.*

Stephen Dunn
The Sacred

After the teacher asked if anyone had
    a sacred place
and the students fidgeted and shrank

in their chairs, the most serious of them all
    said it was his car,   5
being in it alone, his tape deck playing

things he'd chosen, and others knew the truth
    had been spoken
and began speaking about their rooms,

their hiding places, but the car kept coming up,   10
    the car in motion,
music filling it, and sometimes one other person

who understood the bright altar of the dashboard
    and how far away
a car could take him from the need   15

to speak, or to answer, the key
    in having a key
and putting it in, and going.

—1989

Seamus Heaney (b. 1939) was born in the troubled country of Northern Ireland. Heaney has largely avoided the type of political divisions that have divided his homeland. Instead, he has chosen to focus on the landscape of the rural Ireland he knew while growing up as a farmer's son. Since 1982, Heaney has taught part of the year at Harvard University. He was awarded the Nobel Prize for Literature in 1995.

Seamus Heaney
Bogland

for T. P. Flanagan

We have no prairies
To slice a big sun at evening—
Everywhere the eye concedes to
Encroaching horizon,

Is wooed into the cyclops' eye   5
Of a tarn. Our unfenced country
Is bog that keeps crusting
Between the sights of the sun.

They've taken the skeleton
Of the Great Irish Elk   10
Out of the peat, set it up
An astounding crate full of air.

Butter sunk under
More than a hundred years
Was recovered salty and white.   15
The ground itself is kind, black butter

Melting and opening underfoot,
Missing its last definition
By millions of years.
They'll never dig coal here,   20

Only the waterlogged trunks
Of great firs, soft as pulp.
Our pioneers keep striking
Inwards and downwards,

Every layer they strip   25
Seems camped on before.
The bogholes might be Atlantic seepage.
The wet centre is bottomless.

—1969

Digging

Between my finger and my thumb
The squat pen rests; snug as a gun.

Under my window, a clean rasping sound
When the spade sinks into gravelly ground:
My father, digging. I look down   5

Till his straining rump among the flowerbeds
Bends low, comes up twenty years away
Stooping in rhythm through potato drills°
Where he was digging.

The coarse boot nestled on the lug, the shaft   10
Against the inside knee was levered firmly.
He rooted out tall tops, buried the bright edge deep
To scatter new potatoes that we picked
Loving their cool hardness in our hands.

By God, the old man could handle a spade.   15
Just like his old man.

My grandfather cut more turf in a day
Than any other man on Toner's bog.
Once I carried him milk in a bottle
Corked sloppily with paper. He straightened up   20
To drink it, then fell to right away

Nicking and slicing neatly, heaving sods
Over his shoulder, going down and down
For the good turf. Digging.

8 drills furrows

The cold smell of potato mould, the squelch and slap   25
Of soggy peat, the curt cuts of an edge
Through living roots awaken in my head.
But I've no spade to follow men like them.

Between my finger and my thumb
The squat pen rests.   30
I'll dig with it.

                   —*1980*

Punishment

I can feel the tug
of the halter at the nape
of her neck, the wind
on her naked front.

It blows her nipples   5
to amber beads,
it shakes the frail rigging
of her ribs.

I can see her drowned
body in the bog,   10
the weighing stone,
the floating rods and boughs.

Under which at first
she was a barked sapling
that is dug up   15
oak-bone, brain-firkin:°

her shaved head
like a stubble of black corn,
her blindfold a soiled bandage,
her noose a ring   20

to store
the memories of love.

16 firkin a small barrel

Little adulteress,
before they punished you

you were flaxen-haired,   25
undernourished, and your
tar-black face was beautiful.
My poor scapegoat,

I almost love you
but would have cast, I know,   30
the stones of silence.
I am the artful voyeur

of your brain's exposed
and darkened combs,
your muscles' webbing   35
and all your numbered bones:

I who have stood dumb
when your betraying sisters,
cauled in tar,
wept by the railings,   40

who would connive
in civilized outrage
yet understand the exact
and tribal, intimate revenge.

—1975

Tom Disch (b. 1940) is a science-fiction writer, author of interactive computer fiction, resident critic for magazines as diverse as Playboy *and* The Nation, *and poet. Disch is possibly the most brilliant satirist in contemporary American poetry.* Yes, Let's, *a collection of his selected poems, appeared in 1989.*

Ballade of the New God

I have decided I'm divine.
Caligula and Nero knew
A godliness akin to mine,
But they are strictly hitherto.

They're dead, and what can dead gods do?   *5*
I'm here and now. I'm dynamite.
I'd worship me if I were you.
A new religion starts tonight!

No booze, no pot, no sex, no swine:
I have decreed them all taboo.   *10*
My words will be your only wine,
The thought of me your honeydew.
All other thoughts you will eschew
And call yourself a Thomasite
And hymn my praise with loud yahoo.   *15*
A new religion starts tonight.

But (you might think) that's asinine!
I'm just as much a god as you.
You may have built yourself a shrine
But I won't bend my knee. Who   *20*
Asked you to be my god? I do,
Who am, as god, divinely right.
Now you must join my retinue:
A new religion starts tonight.

All that I have said is true.   *25*
I'm god and you're my acolyte.
Surrender's bliss: I envy you
A new religion starts tonight

—1995

Florence Cassen Mayers (b. 1940) is a widely published poet and children's au-thor. Her "ABC" books include children's guides to baseball and to the National Basketball Association.

Florence Cassen Mayers
All-American Sestina

One nation, indivisible
two-car garage
three strikes you're out
four-minute mile
five-cent cigar   5
six-string guitar

six-pack Bud
one-day sale
five-year warranty
two-way street   10
fourscore and seven years ago
three cheers

three-star restaurant
sixty-
four-dollar question   15
one-night stand
two-pound lobster
five-star general

five-course meal
three sheets to the wind   20
two bits
six-shooter
one-armed bandit
four-poster

four-wheel drive   25
five-and-dime
hole in one
three-alarm fire

sweet sixteen
two-wheeler   *30*

two-tone Chevy
four rms, hi flr, w/vu
six-footer
high five
three-ring circus   *35*
one-room schoolhouse

two thumbs up, five-karat diamond
Fourth of July, three-piece suit
six feet under, one-horse town

—*1996*

Pattiann Rogers (b. 1940) *is the foremost naturalist among contemporary American poets. Her poems resound with the rich names of unfamiliar species of plants and animals, most of which she seems to know on intimate terms.* Collected Poems *was published in 2001.*

Pattiann Rogers
Foreplay

When it first begins, as you might expect,
the lips and thin folds are closed, the pouting
layers pressed, lapped lightly,
almost languidly, against one another
in a sealed bud.   *5*

However, with certain prolonged
and random strokings of care
along each binding line, with soft
intrusions traced beneath each pursed
gathering and edge, with inquiring   *10*
intensities of gesture—as the sun
swinging slowly from winter back
to spring, touches briefly,

between moments of moon and masking
clouds, certain stunning points   *15*
and inner nubs of earth—so
with such ministrations, a slight
swelling, a quiver of reaching,
a tendency toward space,
might be noticed to commence.   *20*

Then with dampness from the dark,
with moisture from the falling
night of morning, from hidden places
within the hills, each seal begins
to loosen, each recalcitrant clasp   *25*
sinks away into itself, and every tucked
grasp, every silk tack willingly relents,
releases, gives way, proclaims a turning,
declares a revolution, assumes,
in plain sight, a surging position   *30*
that offers, an audacious offering
that beseeches, every petal parted wide.

Remember the spiraling, blue
valerian, remember the violet, sucking
larkspur, the laurel and rosebay   *35*
and pea cockle flung backwards, remember
the fragrant, funnelling lily, the lifted
honeysuckle, the sweet, open pucker
of the ground ivy blossom?

Now even the darkest crease possessed,   *40*
the most guarded, pulsing, least drop
of pearl bead, moon grain trembling
deep within is fully revealed, fully exposed
to any penetrating wind or shaking fur
or mad hunger or searing, plunging surprise   *45*
the wild descending sky in delirium
has to offer.

—1994

Robert Hass (b. 1941) was born and reared in San Francisco, and teaches at U. C. Berkeley. His first book, Field Guide, *was chosen for the Yale Series of Younger Poets in 1973. Recently he has collaborated with Nobel Prize–winner Czeslaw Milosz on English translations of the latter's poetry. He was appointed U.S. poet laureate in 1995.*

Robert Hass
Picking Blackberries with a Friend Who Has Been Reading Jacques Lacan°

August dust is here. Drought
stuns the road,
but juice gathers in the berries.

We pick them in the hot
slow-motion of midmorning.   5
Charlie is exclaiming:

for him it is twenty years ago
and raspberries and Vermont.
We have stopped talking

about *L'Histoire de la vérité,*°   10
about subject and object
and the mediation of desire.

Our ears are stoppered
in the bee-hum. And Charlie,
laughing wonderfully,   15

beard stained purple
by the word *juice,*
goes to get a bigger pot.

—*1979*

Jacques Lacan French psychoanalyst and literary theorist   **10** *L'Histoire de la vérité The History of Truth,* by Lacan

Simon J. Ortiz (b. 1941) *was born in the Pueblo of Acoma, near Albuquerque, New Mexico. Ortiz has explained why he writes: "Because Indians always tell a story. The only way to continue is to tell a story." The author of collections of poetry and prose and of several children's books, Ortiz has taught creative writing and Native American literature at many universities.*

Simon J. Ortiz
The Serenity in Stones

I am holding this turquoise
in my hands.
My hands hold the sky
wrought in this little stone.
There is a cloud   5
at the furthest boundary.
The world is somewhere underneath.

I turn the stone, and there is more sky.
This is the serenity possible in stones,
the place of a feeling to which one belongs.   10
I am happy as I hold this sky
in my hands, in my eyes, and in myself.

—*1975*

Gibbons Ruark (b. 1941) *is a native of North Carolina. Ruark is the author of five collections of poetry.* Passing through Customs, *a volume of new and selected poems, appeared in 1999. He teaches at the University of Delaware.*

Gibbons Ruark
The Visitor

Holding the arm of his helper, the blind
Piano tuner comes to our piano.
He hesitates at first, but once he finds
The keyboard, his hands glide over the slow
Keys, ringing changes finer than the eye   5

Can see. The dusty wires he touches, row
On row, quiver like bowstrings as he
Twists them one notch tighter. He runs his
Finger along a wire, touches the dry
Rust to his tongue, breaks into a pure bliss   10
And tells us, "One year more of damp weather
Would have done you in, but I've saved it this
Time. Would one of you play now, please? I hear
It better at a distance." My wife plays
Stardust. The blind man stands and smiles in her   15
Direction, then disappears into the blaze
Of new October. Now the afternoon,
The long afternoon that blurs in a haze
Of music . . . Chopin nocturnes, *Clair de Lune,*
All the old familiar, unfamiliar   20
Music-lesson pieces, *Papa's Haydn's*
Dead and gone, gently down the stream . . . Hours later,
After the latest car has doused its beams,
Has cooled down and stopped its ticking, I hear
Our cat, with the grace of animals free   25
To move in darkness, strike one key only,
And a single lucid drop of water stars my dream.

                                                   —1971

Benjamin Alire Sáenz (b. 1954) *is a native of New Mexico. Sáenz spoke only Spanish as a child, a background that lies behind lines like "I want to feel words / swimming in my throat / like fighting fish / that refuse to be hooked / on a line." His book,* Dark and Perfect Angels, *contains poems about the landscape of the Southwest and about Sáenz's three years as a Roman Catholic priest.*

Benjamin Alire Sáenz
To the Desert

I came to you one rainless August night.
You taught me how to live without the rain.
You are thirst and thirst is all I know.

You are sand, wind, sun, and burning sky,
The hottest blue. You blow a breeze and brand   5
Your breath into my mouth. You reach—then *bend*
Your force, to break, blow, burn, and make me new.
You wrap your name tight around my ribs
And keep me warm. I was born for you.
Above, below, by you, by you surrounded.   10
I wake to you at dawn. Never break your
Knot. Reach, rise, blow, *Sálvame, mi dios,*
Trágame, mi tierra. Salva, traga, Break me,
I am bread. I will be the water for your thirst.

—*1995*

Gladys Cardiff (b. 1942) is a member of the Cherokee nation. "Combing" is taken from her first collection, To Frighten a Storm, *which was originally published in 1976.*

Gladys Cardiff
Combing

Bending, I bow my head
And lay my hand upon
Her hair, combing, and think
How women do this for
Each other. My daughter's hair   5
Curls against the comb,
Wet and fragrant—orange
Parings. Her face, downcast,
Is quiet for one so young.

I take her place. Beneath   10
My mother's hands I feel
The braids drawn up tight
As a piano wire and singing,
Vinegar-rinsed. Sitting
Before the oven I hear   15

The orange coils tick
The early hour before school.

She combed her grandmother
Mathilda's hair using
A comb made out of bone.   20
Mathilda rocked her oak wood
Chair, her face downcast,
Intent on tearing rags
In strips to braid a cotton
Rug from bits of orange   25
and brown. A simple act,

Preparing hair. Something
Women do for each other,
Plaiting the generations.

—1976

---

*Charles Martin (b. 1942) is a lifelong resident of New York City. Martin has
taught English as a second language for many years at Queensborough College.
"E.S.L." appeared as a prefatory poem to Martin's sequence "Passages from
Friday," an ironic retelling of the Robinson Crusoe story from his servant's point of
view.*

Charles Martin
E.S.L.°

My frowning students carve
Me monsters out of prose:
This one—a gargoyle—thumbs its contemptuous nose
At how, in English, subject must agree
With verb—for any such agreement shows   5
    Too great a willingness to serve,
        A docility

E.S.L. English as a Second Language

Which wiry Miss Choi
Finds un-American.
She steals a hard look at me. I wink. Her grin   *10*
Is my reward. *In his will, our peace, our Pass:*
Gargoyle erased, subject and verb now in
    Agreement, reach object, enjoy
        Temporary truce.

    Tonight my students must   *15*
    Agree or disagree:
America is still a land of opportunity.
The answer is always, uniformly, *Yes*—even though
"It has no doubt that here were to much free,"
    As Miss Torrico will insist.   *20*
        She and I both know

    That Language binds us fast,
    And those of us without
Are bound and gagged by those within. Each fledgling
Polyglot must shake old habits: tapping her sneakered feet,   *25*
Miss Choi exorcises incensed ancestors, flout-
    ing the ghosts of her Chinese past.
        Writhing in the seat

    Next to Miss Choi, Mister
    Fedakis, in anguish   *30*
Labors to express himself in a tongue which
Proves *Linear B* to me, when I attempt to read it
Later. They're here for English as a Second Language,
    Which I'm teaching this semester.
        God knows they need it,   *35*

    And so, thank God, do they.
    The night's made easier
By our agreement: I am here to help deliver
Them into the good life they write me papers about.
English is pre-requisite for that endeavor,   *40*
    Explored in their nightly essays
        Boldly setting out

To reconnoiter the fair
New World they would enter:
Suburban Paradise, the endless shopping center   45
Where one may browse for hours before one chooses
Some new necessity—gold-flecked magenta
    Wallpaper to re-do the spare
        Bath no one uses,

    Or a machine which can,   50
    In seven seconds, crush
A newborn calf into such seamless mush
As a *mousse* might be made of—or our true sublime:
The gleaming counters where frosted cosmeticians brush
    Decades from the allotted span,   55
        Abrogating Time

    As the spring tide brushes
    A single sinister
Footprint from the otherwise unwrinkled shore
Of America the Blank. In absolute confusion   60
Poor Mister Fedakis rumbles with despair
    And puts the finishing smutches
        To his conclusion

    While Miss Choi erases:
    One more gargoyle routed.   65
Their pure, erroneous lines yield an illuminated
Map of the new found land. We will never arrive there,
Since it exists only in what we say about it,
    As all the rest of my class is
        Bound to discover.   70

—1987

Sharon Olds (b. 1942) displays a candor in dealing with the intimacies of family romance covering three generations that has made her one of the chief contemporary heirs to the confessional tradition. A powerful and dramatic reader, she is much in demand on the lecture circuit. Born in San Francisco, she currently resides in New York City.

Sharon Olds

The One Girl at the Boys Party

When I take my girl to the swimming party
I set her down among the boys. They tower and
bristle, she stands there smooth and sleek,
her math scores unfolding in the air around her.
They will strip to their suits, her body hard and   5
indivisible as a prime number,
they'll plunge into the deep end, she'll subtract
her height from ten feet, divide it into
hundreds of gallons of water, the numbers
bouncing in her mind like molecules of chlorine   10
in the bright blue pool. When they climb out,
her ponytail will hang its pencil lead
down her back, her narrow silk suit
with hamburgers and french fries printed on it
will glisten in the brilliant air, and they will   15
see her sweet face, solemn and
sealed, a factor of one, and she will
see their eyes, two each,
their legs, two each, and the curves of their sexes,
one each, and in her head she'll be doing her   20
wild multiplying, as the drops
sparkle and fall to the power of a thousand from her body.

—1983

James Tate (b. 1943) writes a unique brand of comic surrealism that has remained constant throughout his career. The Lost Pilot won the Yale Younger Poets Award in 1966. Tate's Selected Poems was the recipient of the Pulitzer Prize in 1992.

James Tate
Teaching the Ape to Write Poems

They didn't have much trouble
teaching the ape to write poems:
first they strapped him into the chair,
then tied the pencil around his hand
(the paper had already been nailed down).   5
Then Dr. Bluespire leaned over his shoulder
and whispered into his ear:
"You look like a god sitting there.
Why don't you try writing something?"

—1991

Ellen Bryant Voight (b. 1943) is a native of Virginia. Voight was trained as a concert pianist before earning her creative writing degree from the University of Iowa. She has taught poetry at a number of colleges in New England and the South.

Ellen Bryant Voight
Daughter

There is one grief worse than any other.

When your small feverish throat clogged, and quit,
I knelt beside the chair on the green rug
and shook you and shook you,
but the only sound was mine shouting you back,   5
the delicate curls at your temples,
the blue wool blanket,

your face blue,
your jaw clamped against remedy—

how could I put a knife to that white neck?   10
With you in my lap,
my hands fluttering like flags,
I bend instead over your dead weight
to administer a kiss so urgent, so ruthless,
pumping breath into your stilled body,   15
counting out the rhythm for how long until
the second birth, the second cry
oh Jesus that sudden noisy musical inhalation
that leaves me stunned
by your survival.   20

—1983

Robert Morgan (b. 1944) *is a native of the mountains of North Carolina, and has retained a large measure of regional ties in his poetry. One of his collections,* Sigodlin, *takes its title from an Appalachian word for things that are built slightly out of square.* Gap Creek: The Story of a Marriage, *a novel of turn-of-the-century mountain life, was a bestseller in 2000.*

Robert Morgan

Mountain Bride

They say Revis found a flatrock
on the ridge just
perfect for a natural hearth,
and built his cabin with a stick

and clay chimney right over it.   5
On their wedding night he lit
the fireplace to dry away the mountain
chill of late spring, and flung on

applewood to dye
the room with molten color while   10

he and Martha that was a Parrish
warmed the sheets between the tick

stuffed with leaves and its feather
cover. Under that wide hearth
a nest of rattlers,   15
they'll knot a hundred together,

had wintered and were coming awake.
The warming rock
flushed them out early.
It was she   20

who wakened to their singing near
the embers and roused him to go look.
Before he reached the fire
more than a dozen struck

and he died yelling her to stay   25
on the big four-poster.
Her uncle coming up the hollow
with a gift bearham two days later

found her shivering there
marooned above a pool   30
of hungry snakes,
and the body beginning to swell.

—*1979*

Craig Raine (b. 1944) early in his career displayed a comic surrealism that was responsible for so many imitations that critic James Fenton dubbed him the founder of the "Martian School" of contemporary poetry. Born in Bishop Auckland, England, and educated at Oxford, Raine is an editor with the prestigious publishing firm of Faber & Faber.

Craig Raine
A Martian Sends a Postcard Home

Caxtons° are mechanical birds with many wings
and some are treasured for their markings—

they cause the eyes to melt
or the body to shriek without pain.

I have never seen one fly, but   5
sometimes they perch on the hand.

Mist is when the sky is tired of flight
and rests its soft machine on ground:

then the world is dim and bookish
like engravings under tissue paper.   10

Rain is when the earth is television.
It has the property of making colours darker.

Model T is a room with the lock inside—
a key is turned to free the world

for movement, so quick there is a film   15
to watch for anything missed.

But time is tied to the wrist
or kept in a box, ticking with impatience.

In homes, a haunted apparatus sleeps,
that snores when you pick it up.   20

1 **Caxtons** i.e., books; after William Caxton (1422–1491), first English printer

If the ghost cries, they carry it
to their lips and soothe it to sleep

with sounds. And yet, they wake it up
deliberately, by tickling with a finger.

Only the young are allowed to suffer   25
openly. Adults go to a punishment room

with water but nothing to eat.
They lock the door and suffer the noises

alone. No one is exempt
and everyone's pain has a different smell.   30

At night, when all the colours die,
they hide in pairs

and read about themselves—
in colour, with their eyelids shut.

—1978

Eniд Shomer (b. 1944) *grew up in Washington, D.C., and lived for a number of years in Florida. Her first collection,* Stalking the Florida Panther *(1987), explored both the Jewish traditions of her childhood and her adult attachment to her adopted state. In recent years she has published* Imaginary Men, *a collection of short stories, and* Black Drums, *a collection of poetry.*

Eniд Shomer
Women Bathing at Bergen-Belsen°

April 24, 1945

Twelve hours after the Allies arrive
there is hot water, soap. Two women bathe
in a makeshift, open-air shower while nearby
fifteen thousand are flung naked into mass graves

Bergen-Belsen German concentration camp in WWII

by captured SS guards. Clearly legs and arms   5
are the natural handles of a corpse. The bathers,
taken late in the war, still have flesh
on their bones, still have breasts. Though nudity was
a death sentence here, they have undressed,
oblivious to the soldiers and the cameras.   10
The corpses push through the limed earth like upended
headstones. The bathers scrub their feet, bending
in beautiful curves, mapping the contours
of the body, that kingdom to which they've returned.

—1987

Alice Walker (b. 1944), the author of The Color Purple *and other novels, is a leading African-American writer. Less well known as a poet, she won the Pulitzer Prize for fiction in 1983. Her most recent novels combine her concerns with both racial and feminist issues.*

Alice Walker

Even as I Hold You

Even as I hold you
I think of you as someone gone
far, far away. Your eyes the color
of pennies in a bowl of dark honey
bringing sweet light to someone else   5
your black hair slipping through my fingers
is the flash of your head going
around a corner
your smile, breaking before me,
the flippant last turn   10
of a revolving door,
emptying you out, changed,
away from me.

Even as I hold you
I am letting go.   15

—1979

Wendy Cope (b. 1945) says, "I hardly ever tire of love or rhyme. / That's why I'm Poor and have a rotten time." Her first collection, Making Cocoa for Kingsley Amis *(1986), was a bestseller in England. Whether reducing T. S. Eliot's modernist classic "The Waste Land" to a set of five limericks or chronicling the life and loves of Jason Strugnell, her feckless poetic alter-ego, Cope remains one of the wisest and wittiest poets writing today. "I dislike the term 'light verse' because it is used as a way of dismissing poets who allow humor into their work. I believe that a humorous poem can also be 'serious'; deeply felt and saying something that matters." She lives in Winchester, England.*

Wendy Cope
Rondeau Redoublé

There are so many kinds of awful men—
One can't avoid them all. She often said
She'd never make the same mistake again:
She always made a new mistake instead.

The chinless type who made her feel ill-bred;   5
The practised charmer, less than charming when
He talked about the wife and kids and fled—
There are so many kinds of awful men.

The half-crazed hippy, deeply into Zen,
Whose cryptic homilies she came to dread;   10
The fervent youth who worshipped Tony Benn—
'One can't avoid them all,' she often said.

The ageing banker, rich and overfed,
who held forth on the dollar and the yen—
Though there were many more mistakes ahead,   15
She'd never make the same mistake again.

The budding poet, scribbling in his den
Odes not to her but to his pussy, Fred;
The drunk who fell asleep at nine or ten—
She always made a new mistake instead.   20

And so the gambler was at least unwed
And didn't preach or sneer or wield a pen
Or hoard his wealth or take the Scotch to bed.

She'd lived and learned and lived and learned but then
There are so many kinds.   25

                                                              —*1986*

B. H. Fairchild (b. 1945) grew up in Liberal, Kansas, and his father's machine shop provides the title and the setting for his prize-winning collection, The Art of the Lathe. *Fairchild teaches at the California State University, San Bernardino. His first two collections of poetry, both from small presses, have recently been published by alicejames books.*

B. H. Fairchild
Body and Soul

Half-numb, guzzling bourbon and Coke from coffee mugs,
our fathers fall in love with their own stories, nuzzling
the facts but mauling the truth, and my friend's father begins
to lay out with the slow ease of a blues ballad a story
about sandlot baseball in Commerce, Oklahoma decades ago.   5
These were men's teams, grown men, some in their thirties
and forties who worked together in zinc mines or on oil rigs,
sweat and khaki and long beers after work, steel guitar music
whanging in their ears, little white rent houses to return to
where their wives complained about money and broken
       Kenmores   10
and then said the hell with it and sang *Body and Soul*
in the bathtub and later that evening with the kids asleep
lay in bed stroking their husband's wrist tattoo and smoking
Chesterfields from a fresh pack until everything was O.K.
Well, you get the idea. Life goes on, the next day is Sunday,   15
another ball game, and the other team shows up one man short.

They say, we're one man short, but can we use this boy,
he's only fifteen years old, and at least he'll make a game.
They take a look at the kid, muscular and kind of knowing
the way he holds his glove, with the shoulders loose,   20
the thick neck, but then with that boy's face under
a clump of angelic blonde hair, and say, oh, hell, sure,

let's play ball. So it all begins, the men loosening up,
joking about the fat catcher's sex life, it's so bad
last night he had to hump his wife, that sort of thing,   25
pairing off into little games of catch that heat up into
throwing matches, the smack of the fungo bat, lazy jogging
into right field, big smiles and arcs of tobacco juice,
and the talk that gives a cool, easy feeling to the air,
talk among men normally silent, normally brittle and a little   30
angry with the empty promise of their lives. But they chatter
and say rock and fire, babe, easy out, and go right ahead
and pitch to the boy, but nothing fancy, just hard fastballs
right around the belt, and the kid takes the first two
but on the third pops the bat around so quick and sure   35
that they pause a moment before turning around to watch
the ball still rising and finally dropping far beyond
the abandoned tractor that marks left field. Holy shit.
They're pretty quiet watching him round the bases,
but then, what the hell, the kid knows how to hit a ball,   40
so what, let's play some goddamned baseball here.
And so it goes. The next time up, the boy gets a look
at a very nifty low curve, then a slider, and the next one
is the curve again, and he sends it over the Allis Chalmers,
high and big and sweet. The left fielder just stands there,
    frozen.   45
As if this isn't enough, the next time up he bats left-handed.
They can't believe it, and the pitcher, a tall, mean-faced
man from Okarche who just doesn't give a shit anyway
because his wife ran off two years ago leaving him with
three little ones and a rusted-out Dodge with a cracked block,   50
leans in hard, looking at the fat catcher like he was the
    sonofabitch
who ran off with his wife, leans in and throws something
out of the dark, green hell of forbidden fastballs, something
that comes in at the knees and then leaps viciously towards
the kid's elbow. He swings exactly the way he did
    right-handed,   55
and they all turn like a chorus line toward deep right field
where the ball loses itself in sagebrush and the sad burnt
dust of dustbowl Oklahoma. It is something to see.

But why make a long story long: runs pile up on both sides,
the boy comes around five times, and five times the pitcher   *60*
is cursing both God and His mother as his chew of tobacco
    sours
into something resembling horse piss, and a ragged and bruised
Spalding baseball disappears into the far horizon. Goodnight,
Irene. They have lost the game and some painful side bets
and they have been suckered. And it means nothing to them   *65*
though it should to you when they are told the boy's name is
Mickey Mantle. And that's the story and those are the facts.
But the facts are not the truth. I think, though, as I scan
the faces of these old men now lost in the innings of their
    youth,
I think I know what the truth of this story is, and I imagine   *70*
it lying there in the weeds behind that Allis Chalmers
just waiting for the obvious question to be asked: why, oh
why in hell didn't they just throw around the kid, walk him,
after he hit the third homer? Anybody would have,
especially nine men with disappointed wives and dirty socks   *75*
and diminishing expectations for whom winning at anything
meant everything. Men who know how to play the game,
who had talent when the other team had nothing except this
    ringer
who without a pitch to hit was meaningless, and they could go
    home
with their little two-dollar side bets and stride into the house   *80*
singing *If You've Got the Money, Honey, I've Got the Time*
with a bottle of Southern Comfort under their arms and grab
Dixie or May Ella up and dance across the gray linoleum
as if it were V-Day all over again. But they did not.
And they did not because they were men, and this was a boy.   *85*
And they did not because sometimes after making love,
after smoking their Chesterfields in the cool silence and
listening to the big bands on the radio that sounded so glamorous,
so distant, they glanced over at their wives and noticed the lines
growing heavier around the eyes and mouth, felt what their
    wives
    felt   *90*
felt: that Les Brown and Glenn Miller and all those dancing
    couples

and in fact all possibility of human gaiety and light-heartedness
were as far away and unreachable as Times Square or the Avalon
ballroom. They did not because of the gray linoleum lying there
in the half-dark, the free calendar from the local mortuary   95
that siad one day was pretty much like another, the work gloves
looped over the doorknob like dead squirrels. And they did not
because they had gone through a depression and a war that had left
them with the idea that being a man in the eyes of their fathers
and everyone else had cost them just too goddamned much to
     lay it   100
at the feet of a fifteen year-old boy. And so they did not walk
     him,
and lost, but at least had some ragged remnant of themselves
to take back home. But there is one thing more, though it is not
a fact. When I see my friend's father staring hard into the bottomless
well of home plate as Mantle's fifth homer heads toward
     Arkansas,   105
I know that this man with the half-orphaned children and
worthless Dodge has also encountered for his first and possibly
only time that vast gap between talent and genius, has seen
as few have in the harsh light of an Oklahoma Sunday, the blonde
and blue-eyed bringer of truth, who will not easily be
     forgiven.   110

—*1998*

---

*Leon Stokesbury (b. 1945), as an undergraduate at Lamar State College of
Technology (now Lamar Univesity), was acquainted with the legendary singer Janis
Joplin, the subject of "Evening's End." The author of three collections of poetry, including* Autumn Rhythm: New and Selected Poems, *Stokesbury has also
edited anthologies of contemporary Southern poetry and the poetry of World War II.*

Leon Stokesbury
Evening's End 1943–1970

For the first time in what must be
the better part of two years now
I happened to hear Janis

in her glory—
all that tinctured syrup   5
dripping off
a razorblade—
on the radio today singing "Summertime."

And it took me back to this girl I knew,
a woman really, my first year   10
writing undergraduate poetry
at the Mirabeau B. Lamar
State College of Technology
in Beaumont, Texas,
back in 1966.   15

This woman was the latest in a line,
the latest steady
of my friend John Coyle that spring—
and I remember she was plain:
she was short: and plain   20
and wore her brown hair up
in a sort of bun in back
that made her plainer still.

I don't know where John met her,
but word went round   25
she had moved back in with Mom and Dad
down in Port Arthur
to get her head straight,
to attend Lamar,
to study History,   30
after several years in San Francisco
where she had drifted
into a "bad scene"
taking heroin.

I was twenty,   35
still lived with Mom and Dad myself,
and so knew nothing
about "bad scenes,"
but I do remember once or twice
each month that spring   40

John would give a party
with this woman always there.
And always as the evening's end came on
this woman, silent for hours,
would reveal, from thin air,   45
her guitar,
settle in a chair,
release her long hair
from the bun it was in,
and begin.   50

Her hair flowed over her shoulders,
and the ends of the strands of hair
like tarnished brass in lamplight
would brush and drag across
the sides of the guitar   55
as this woman bent
over it.

How low and guttural, how
slow and torchlit, how
amber her song, how absolutely   60
unlike the tiny nondescript
a few minutes before.

And I remember also,
from later on that spring,
from May of that year,   65
two nights in particular.

The first night was a party
this woman gave
at her parents' home.
Her parents' home   70
was beige:
the bricks the parents' home
was built with
were beige.
The entire house was carpeted   75
in beige.

John's girl greeted everyone at the door,
a martini in one hand
and a lit cigarette
in an Oriental   *80*
ivory cigarette holder in the other,
laughing
for once, and tossing back
her long brown hair.

All the women wore
black full-length party dresses—
and I remember the young woman's father,
how odd he seemed
in his charcoal suit and tie,
his gray hair—   *90*
how unamused.

Then John Coyle was drunk.
He spilled his beer
across the beige frontroom carpet:
that darker dampness sinking in,   *95*
the father vanished
from the scene.

The next week we double-dated.
I convinced John and his girl
to see a double feature,   *100*
Irma La Douce and *Tom Jones*,
at the Pines Theatre.

And I can recall John's girl
saying just one thing that night.

After the films, John was quizzical,   *105*
contentious, full of ridicule
for movies I had guaranteed he would enjoy.
He turned and asked her
what she thought—
and in the softest   *110*
of tones, a vague rumor
of honeysuckle in the air,
she almost whispered,

"I thought they were beautiful."

That was the last time I saw her,   *115*
the last thing that I heard her say.

A few weeks later,
she drove over to John's house
in the middle of the afternoon,
and caught him in bed   *120*
with Suzanne Morain,
a graduate assistant
from the English Department at Lamar.

John told me later
that when she saw them in the bedroom   *125*
she ran into the kitchen,
picked up a broom,
and began to sweep the floor—
weeping.

When John sauntered in   *130*
she threw the broom at him,
ran out the door,
got in her car and drove away.
And from that day on,
no one ever saw that woman   *135*
in Beaumont again.

The next day she moved to Austin.
And later on, I heard,
back to San Francisco.
And I remember when John told me this,   *140*
with a semi-shocked expression
on his face, he turned
and looked up, and said, "You know,
I guess she must have really *loved* me."

I was twenty years old.   *145*
What did I know?
What could I say?

I could not think
of anything to say,
except, "Yes,   150
I guess so."

It was summertime.

Thus runs the world away.

—*1996*

Marilyn Nelson (b. 1946) is the author of The Homeplace, *a sequence of poems on family history. The* Homeplace *is remarkable for its sensitive exploration of the mixed white and black bloodlines in the poet's family history.* Carver: A Life in Poems, *a poetic biography of George Washington Carver, appeared in 2001.*

Marilyn Nelson
The Ballad of Aunt Geneva

Geneva was the wild one.
Geneva was a tart.
Geneva met a blue-eyed boy
and gave away her heart.

Geneva ran a roadhouse.   5
Geneva wasn't sent
to college like the others:
Pomp's pride her punishment.

She cooked out on the river,
watching the shore slide by,   10
her lips pursed into hardness,
her deep-set brown eyes dry.

They say she killed a woman
over a good black man
by braining the jealous heifer   15

with an iron frying pan.

They say, when she was eighty,
she got up late at night
and sneaked her old, white lover in
to make love, and to fight.   20

First, they heard the tell-tale
singing of the springs,
then Geneva's voice rang out:
I need to buy some things,

So next time, bring more money.   25
And bring more moxie, too.
I ain't got no time to waste
on limp white mens like you.

Oh yeah? Well, Mister White Man,
it sure might be stone-white,   30
but my thing's white as it is.
And you know damn well I'm right.

Now listen: take your heart pills
and pay the doctor mind.
If you up and die on me,   35
I'll whip your white behind.

They tiptoed through the parlor
on heavy, time-slowed feet.
She watched him, from her front door,
walk down the dawnlit street.   40

Geneva was the wild one.
Geneva was a tart.
Geneva met a blue-eyed boy
and gave away her heart.

—1990

Ai (b. 1947) has written a number of realistic dramatic monologues that often reveal the agonies of characters trapped in unfulfilling or even dangerous lives. With her gallery of social misfits, she is the contemporary heir to the tradition begun by Robert Browning.

Ai

Child Beater

Outside, the rain, pinafore of gray water, dresses the town
and I stroke the leather belt,
as she sits in the rocking chair,
holding a crushed paper cup to her lips.
I yell at her, but she keeps rocking;   5
back, her eyes open, forward, they close.
Her body, somehow fat, though I feed her only once a day,
reminds me of my own just after she was born.
It's been seven years, but I still can't forget how I felt.
How heavy it feels to look at her.   10

I lay the belt on a chair
and get her dinner bowl.
I hit the spoon against it, set it down
and watch her crawl to it,
pausing after each forward thrust of her legs   15
and when she takes her first bite,
I grab the belt and beat her across the back
until her tears, beads of salt-filled glass, falling,
shatter on the floor.

I move off. I let her eat,   20
while I get my dog's chain leash from the closet.
I whirl it around my head.
O daughter, so far, you've only had a taste of icing,
are you ready now for some cake?

—1973

Jim Hall (b. 1947) *is one of the most brilliantly inventive comic poets in recent years. He has also written a successful series of crime novels set in his native south Florida, beginning with* Under Cover of Daylight *in 1987.*

Jim Hall
Maybe Dats Your Pwoblem Too

All my pwoblems,
who knows, maybe evwybody's pwoblems
is due to da fact, due to da awful twuth
dat I am SPIDERMAN.

I know, I know. All da dumb jokes: 5
No flies on you, ha ha,
and da ones about what do I do wit all
doze extwa legs in bed. Well, dat's funny yeah.
But you twy being
SPIDERMAN for a month or two. Go ahead.   10

You get doze cwazy calls fwom da
Gubbener askin you to twap some booglar who's
only twying to wip off color T.V. sets.
Now, what do I cawre about T.V. sets?
But I pull on da suit, da stinkin suit,   15
wit da sucker cups on da fingers,
and get my wopes and wittle bundle of
equipment and den I go flying like cwazy
acwoss da town fwom woof top to woof top.

Till der he is. Some poor dumb color T.V. slob   20
and I fall on him and we westle a widdle

until I get him all woped. So big deal.

You tink when you SPIDERMAN
der's sometin big going to happen to you.
Well, I tell you what. It don't happen dat way.   25
Nuttin happens. Gubbener calls, I go.
Bwing him to powice, Gubbener calls again,
like dat over and over.

I tink I twy sometin diffunt. I tink I twy
sometin excitin like wacing cawrs. Sometin to make   30
my heart beat at a difwent wate.
But den you just can't quit being sometin like
SPIDERMAN.
You SPIDERMAN for life. Fowever. I can't even
buin my suit. It won't buin. It's fwame wesistent.   35
So maybe dat's youwr pwoblem too, who knows.
Maybe dat's da whole pwoblem wif evwytin.
Nobody can buin der suits, dey all fwame wesistent.
Who knows?

—1980

---

*Yusef Komunyakaa (b. 1947) is a native of Bogulusa, Louisiana. Komunyakaa
has written memorably on a wide range of subjects, including jazz and his service
during the Vietnam War.* Neon Vernacular: New and Selected Poems *(1993)
won the Pulitzer Prize in 1994, and* Pleasure Dome: New and Collected
Poems *appeared in 2001.*

Yusef Komunyakaa
Facing It

My black face fades,
hiding inside the black granite.

I said I wouldn't,
dammit: No tears.
I'm stone. I'm flesh.   5
My clouded reflection eyes me
like a bird of prey, the profile of night
slanted against morning. I turn
this way—the stone lets me go.
I turn this way—I'm inside   10
the Vietnam Veterans Memorial
again, depending on the light
to make a difference.
I go down the 58,022 names,
half-expecting to find   15
my own in letters like smoke.
I touch the name Andrew Johnson;
I see the booby trap's white flash.
Names shimmer on a woman's blouse
but when she walks away   20
the names stay on the wall.
Brushstrokes flash, a red bird's
wings cutting across my stare.
The sky. A plane in the sky.
A white vet's image floats   25
closer to me, then his pale eyes
look through mine. I'm a window.
He's lost his right arm
inside the stone. In the black mirror
a woman's trying to erase names: 30
No, she's brushing a boy's hair.

—1988

R. S. Gwynn (b. 1948) *is the editor of this volume and (with Dana Gioia) of* The Longman Anthology of Short Fiction. *He teaches at Lamar University* . No Word of Farewell: Selected Poems 1970–2000 *appeared in 2001.*

R. S. Gwynn

Approaching a Significant Birthday, He Peruses *The Norton Anthology of Poetry*

All human things are subject to decay.
Beauty is momentary in the mind.
The curfew tolls the knell of parting day.
If Winter comes, can Spring be far behind?

Forlorn! the very word is like a bell   5
And somewhat of a sad perplexity.
Here, take my picture, though I bid farewell;
In a dark time the eye begins to see

The woods decay, the woods decay and fall—
Bare ruined choirs where late the sweet birds sing.   10
What but design of darkness to appall?
An aged man is but a paltry thing.

If I should die, think only this of me:
Crass casualty obstructs the sun and rain
When I have fears that I may cease to be,   15
To cease upon the midnight with no pain

And hear the spectral singing of the moon
And strictly meditate the thankless muse.
The world is too much with us, late and soon.
It gathers to a greatness, like the ooze.   20

Do not go gentle into the good night.
Fame is no plant that grows on mortal soil.

Again he raised the jug up to the light:
Old age hath yet his honor and his toil.

Downward to darkness on extended wings,   25
Break, break, break, on thy cold gray stones, O Sea,
and tell sad stories of the death of kings.
I do not think that they will sing to me.

—1990

Timothy Steele (b. 1948) *has written a successful scholarly study of the rise of free verse,* Missing Measures, *and is perhaps the most skillful craftsman of the contemporary New Formalist poets. Born in Vermont, he has lived for a number of years in Los Angeles, where he teaches at California State University, Los Angeles.*

Timothy Steele

Sapphics° Against Anger

Angered, may I be near a glass of water;
May my first impulse be to think of Silence,
Its deities (who are they? do, in fact, they
        Exist? etc.).

May I recall what Aristotle says of   5
The subject: to give vent to rage is not to
Release it but to be increasingly prone
        To its incursions.

May I imagine being in the Inferno,
Hearing it asked: "Virgilio mio,° who's   10
That sulking with Achilles there?" and hearing
        Virgil say: "Dante,

That fellow, at the slightest provocation,
Slammed phone receivers down, and waved his arms like
A madman. What Attila did to Europe,   15
        What Genghis Khan did

To Asia, that poor dope did to his marriage."
May I, that is, put learning to good purpose,
Mindful that melancholy is a sin, though
        Stylish at present.   20

Better than rage is the post-dinner quiet,
The sink's warm turbulence, the streaming platters,
The suds rehearsing down the drain in spirals
        In the last rinsing.

For what is, after all, the good life save that   25
Conducted thoughtfully, and what is passion
If not the holiest of powers, sustaining
        Only if mastered.

        —1986

David Bottoms (b. 1949) was born in Canton, Georgia. Bottoms is the author both of collections of poetry and successful novels. His first book, Shooting Rats at Bibb County Dump, *was a winner of the Walt Whitman Award of the Academy of American Poets. He is the co-editor, with Dave Smith, of* The Morrow Anthology of Younger American Poets.

David Bottoms
Sign for My Father, Who Stressed the Bunt

On the rough diamond,
the hand-cut field below the dog lot and barn,
we rehearsed the strict technique
of bunting. I watched from the infield,
the mound, the backstop   5
as your left hand climbed the bat, your legs
and shoulders squared toward the pitcher.
You could drop it like a seed
down either base line. I admired your style,

but not enough to take my eyes off the bank   10
that served as our center-field fence.

Years passed, three leagues of organized ball,
no few lives. I could homer
into the garden beyond the bank,
into the left-field lot of Carmichael Motors,   15
and still you stressed the same technique,
the crouch and spring, the lead arm absorbing
just enough impact. That whole tiresome pitch
about basics never changing,
and I never learned what you were laying down.   20

Like a hand brushed across the bill of a cap,
let this be the sign
I'm getting a grip on the sacrifice.

—*1983*

James Fenton (b. 1949) was born in Lincoln, England, and educated at Oxford. Fenton has worked extensively as a book and drama critic. A brilliant satirical poet, he has also written lyrics for Les Misérables, *the musical version of Victor Hugo's novel, and has served as a journalist in Asia.*

James Fenton
God, a Poem

A nasty surprise in a sandwich,
A drawing-pin caught in your sock,
The limpest of shakes from a hand which
You'd thought would be firm as a rock,

A serious mistake in a nightie,   5
A grave disappointment all around
Is all that you'll get from th'Almighty.

Sapphics stanza form named after Sappho (c. 650 B.C.)   **10 Virgilio mio** Dante is addressing Virgil, his guide through hell.

Is all that you'll get underground.

Oh, he *said:* 'If you lay off the crumpet°
I'll see you alright in the end.   10
Just hang on until the last trumpet.
Have faith in me, chum—I'm your friend.'

But if you remind him, he'll tell you:
'I'm sorry, I must have been pissed—°
Though your name rings a sort of a bell. You   15
Should have guessed that I do not exist.

'I didn't exist at Creation,
I didn't exist at the Flood.
And I won't be around for Salvation
To sort out the sheep from the cud—   20

'Or whatever the phrase is. The fact is
In soteriological° terms
I'm a crude existential malpractice
And you are a diet of worms.

'You're a nasty surprise in a sandwich.   25
You're a drawing-pin caught in my sock.
You're the limpest of shakes from a hand which
I'd have thought would be firm as a rock,

'You're a serious mistake in a nightie,
You're a grave disappointment all round—   30
'That's all that you are,' says th'Almighty,
'And that's all that you'll be underground.'

                                                                        —1983

---

9 crumpet vulgar British slang for women   **14 pissed** drunk   **22 soteriological** relation to salvation

Sarah Cortez (b. 1950) grew up in Houston, Texas, and holds degrees in psychology and religion, classical studies, and accounting. She also serves as Visiting Scholar at the University of Houston's Center for Mexican-American Studies. She is a deputy constable in Harris County, Texas.

Sarah Cortez
Tu Negrito

She's got to bail me out,
he says into the phone outside the holding cell.
She's going there tomorrow anyway for Mikey.
Tell her she's got to do this for me.

He says into the phone outside the holding cell,   5
Make sure she listens. Make her feel guilty, man.
Tell her she's got to do this for me.
She can have all my money, man.

Make sure she listens. Make her feel guilty, man.
Tell her she didn't bail me out the other times.   10
She can have all my money, man.
She always bails out Mikey.

Tell her she didn't bail me out the other times.
I don't got no one else to call, cousin.
She always bails out Mikey.   15
Make sure you write all this down, cousin.

I don't got no one else to call, cousin.
I really need her now.
Make sure you write this all down, cousin.
Page her. Put in code 333. That's me.   20

I really need her now.
Write down "Mommie." Change it from "Mom."
Page her. Put in code 333. That's me.
Write down *"Tu Negrito."* Tell her I love her.

Write down "Mommie." Change it from "Mom."   25
I'm her littlest. Remind her.

Write down *"Tu Negrito."*
Tell her I love her. She's got to bail me out.

—2000

Carolyn Forché (b. 1950) won the Yale Younger Poets Award for her first collection, Gathering the Tribes *(1975).* The Country Between Us, *Forché's second collection, contains poems based on the poet's experiences in the war-torn country of El Salvador in the early 1980s.*

Carolyn Forché
The Colonel

What you have heard is true. I was in his house.° His wife carried a tray of coffee and sugar. His daughter filed her nails, his son went out for the night. There were daily papers, pet dogs, a pistol on the cushion beside him. The moon swung bare on its black cord over the house. On the television was a cop show. It was in English. Broken bottles were embedded in the walls around the house to scoop the kneecaps from a man's legs or cut his hands to lace. On the windows there were gratings like those in liquor stores. We had dinner, rack of lamb, good wine, a gold bell was on the table for calling the maid. The maid brought green mangoes, salt, a type of bread. I was asked how I enjoyed the country. There was a brief commercial in Spanish. His wife took everything away. There was some talk then of how difficult it had become to govern. The parrot said hello on the terrace. The colonel told it to shut up, and pushed himself from the table. My friend said to me with his eyes: say nothing. The colonel returned with a sack used to bring groceries home. He spilled many human ears on the table. They were like dried peach halves. There is no other way to say this. He took one of them in his hands, shook it in our faces, dropped it into a water glass. It came alive there. I am tired of fooling around he said. As for the rights of anyone, tell your people they can go fuck themselves. He swept the ears to the floor with his arm and held the last of his wine in the air. Something for your poetry, no? he said. Some of the ears on the floor caught this

---

1 his house in El Salvador

scrap of his voice. Some of the ears on the floor were pressed to the ground.

—1978

Dana Gioia (b. 1950) grew up in the suburbs of Los Angeles. He took a graduate degree in English from Harvard but made a successful career in business before devoting his full time to writing. The editor of several textbooks and anthologies, he is also an influential critic whose essay "Can Poetry Matter?" stimulated much discussion when it appeared in The Atlantic. Interrogations at Noon, *his third collection of poetry, appeared in 2001.*

Dana Gioia
Planting a Sequoia

All afternoon my brothers and I have worked in the orchard,
Digging this hole, laying you into it, carefully packing the soil.
Rain blackened the horizon, but cold winds kept it over the Pacific,
And the sky above us stayed the dull gray
Of an old year coming to an end.   5

In Sicily a father plants a tree to celebrate his first son's birth—
An olive or a fig tree—a sign that the earth has one more life to bear.
I would have done the same, proudly laying new stock into my father's
    orchard,
A green sapling rising among the twisted apple boughs,
A promise of new fruit in other autumns.   10

But today we kneel in the cold planting you, our native giant,
Defying the practical custom of our fathers,
Wrapping in your roots a lock of hair, a piece of an infant's birth cord,
All that remains above earth of a first-born son,
A few stray atoms brought back to the elements.   15

We will give you what we can—our labor and our soil,
Water drawn from the earth when the skies fail,
Nights scented with the ocean fog, days softened by the circuit of bees.
We plant you in the corner of the grove, bathed in western light,
A slender shoot against the sunset.   20

And when our family is no more, all of his unborn brothers dead,
Every niece and nephew scattered, the house torn down,
His mother's beauty ashes in the air,
I want you to stand among strangers, all young and ephemeral to you,
Silently keeping the secret of your birth.   25

—*1991*

Rodney Jones (b. 1950) *was born in Alabama and received important national
attention when* Transparent Gestures *won the Poets' Prize in 1990. Like many
younger southern poets, he often deals with the difficult legacy of racism and the adjustments that a new era have forced on both whites and blacks.*

Rodney Jones

Winter Retreat: Homage to Martin Luther King, Jr.

There is a hotel in Baltimore where we came together,
we black and white educated and educators,
for a week of conferences, for important counsel
sanctioned by the DOE° and the Carter administration,
to make certain difficult inquiries, to collate notes   5
on the instruction of the disabled, the deprived,
the poor, who do not score well on entrance tests,
who, failing school, must go with mop and pail
skittering across the slick floors of cafeterias,
or climb dewy girders to balance high above cities,   10
or, jobless, line up in the bone cold. We felt
substantive burdens lighter if we stated it right.
Very delicately, we spoke in turn. We walked
together beside the still waters of behaviorism.
Armed with graphs and charts, with new strategies   15
to devise objectives and determine accountability,
we empathetic black and white shone in seminar rooms.

4 DOE Department of Education

We enunciated every word clearly and without accent.
We moved very carefully in the valley of the shadow
of the darkest agreement error. We did not digress.   20
We ascended the trunk of that loftiest cypress
of Latin grammar the priests could never
successfully graft onto the rough green chestnut
of the English language. We extended ourselves
with that sinuous motion of the tongue that is half   25
pain and almost eloquence. We black and white
politely reprioritized the parameters of our agenda
to impact equitably on the Seminole and the Eskimo.
We praised diversity and involvement, the sacrifices
of fathers and mothers. We praised the next white   30
Gwendolyn Brooks° and the next black Robert Burns.°
We deep made friends. In that hotel we glistened
over the *pommes au gratin*° and the *poitrine de veau.*°
The morsels of lamb flamed near where we talked.
The waiters bowed and disappeared among the ferns.   35
And there is a bar there, there is a large pool.
Beyond the tables of the drinkers and raconteurs,
beyond the hot tub brimming with Lebanese tourists
and the women in expensive bathing suits doing laps,
if you dive down four feet, swim out far enough,   40
and emerge on the other side, it is sixteen degrees.
It is sudden and very beautiful and colder
than thought, though the air frightens you at first,
not because it is cold, but because it is visible,
almost palpable, in the fog that rises from difference.   45
While I stood there in the cheek-numbing snow,
all Baltimore was turning blue. And what I remember
of that week of talks is nothing the record shows,
but the revelation outside, which was the city
many came to out of the fields, then the thought   50
that we had wanted to make the world kinder,
but, in speaking proudly, we had failed a vision.

—1989

---

31 Gwendolyn Brooks black American poet (1917–2000)   **Robert Burns** Scottish poet
(1759–1796)   **33 pommes au gratin** potatoes baked with cheese   **poitrine de veau** brisket of veal

Timothy Murphy (b. 1950), a former student of Robert Penn Warren at Yale, returned to his native North Dakota to make a career as a venture capitalist in the agricultural field. Unpublished until his mid-forties, Murphy brought four collections to print during the 1990s.

Timothy Murphy
The Track of a Storm

Bastille Day, 1995

We grieve for the twelve trees we lost last night,
pillars of our community, old friends
and confidants dismembered in our sight,
stripped of their crowns by the unruly winds.
There were no baskets to receive their heads,   5
no women knitting by the guillotines,
only two sleepers rousted from their beds
by fusillades of hailstones on the screens.
Her nest shattered, her battered hatchlings drowned,
a stunned and silent junko watches me   10
chainsawing limbs from corpses of the downed,
clearing the understory of debris
while supple saplings which survived the blast
lay claim to light and liberty at last.

—*1998*

Joy Harjo (b. 1951), a member of the Creek tribe, is one of the leading voices of contemporary Native American poetry. She is a powerful performer and was one of the poets featured on Bill Moyers's television series, The Power of the Word.

Joy Harjo
Song for the Deer and Myself to Return On

This morning when I looked out the roof window
before dawn and a few stars were still caught
in the fragile weft of ebony night
I was overwhelmed. I sang the song Louis taught me:
a song to call the deer in Creek,° when hunting,   5
and I am certainly hunting something as magic as deer
in this city far from the hammock of my mother's belly.
It works, of course, and deer came into this room
and wondered at finding themselves
in a house near downtown Denver.   10
Now the deer and I are trying to figure out a song
to get them back, to get all of us back,
because if it works I'm going with them.
And it's too early to call Louis
and nearly too late to go home.   15

—*1990*

---

5 Creek Native American tribal language

Garrett Hongo (b. 1951), who is of Japanese ancestry, was born in Hawaii and educated at Pomona College and the University of California at Irvine. His books include Yellow Light *(1982) and* The River of Heaven *(1988).*

Garrett Hongo

Crossing Ka'ū Desert°

from under the harpstring shade of tree ferns
and the blue trumpets of morning glories
     beside the slick road,
the green creep of davallia and club moss
       (their tiny hammers   5
       staffed quarter-notes
        and fiddlenecks on the forest floor),
spider lilies and ginger flowers like paper cranes
     furling in the tongues of overgrowth,
       in the sapphired arpeggios of rain   *10*

to the frozen, shale-colored sea,
     froth, swirls, bleak dithyrambs of glass,
a blizzard of cinderrock and singed amulets,
warty spires and pipelines,
       threnodies of surf whirling on the lava land—   *15*
our blue car the last note of color
driving a black channel
       through hymnless ground

                             —*1988*

Ka´ū Desert on the island of Hawaii

Andrew Hudgins (b. 1951), reared in Montgomery, Alabama, has demonstrated his poetic skills in a wide variety of poems, including a book-length sequence of dramatic monologues, After the Lost War, *in the voice of Sidney Lanier, the greatest Southern poet of the late nineteenth century.*

Andrew Hudgins
Air View of an Industrial Scene

There is a train at the ramp, unloading people
who stumble from the cars and toward the gate.
The building's shadows tilt across the ground
and from each shadow juts a longer one
and from that shadow crawls a shadow of smoke   5
black as just-plowed earth. Inside the gate
is a small garden and someone on his knees.
Perhaps he's fingering the yellow blooms
to see which ones have set and will soon wither,
clinging to a green tomato as it swells.   10
The people hold back, but are forced to the open gate,
and when they enter they will see the garden
and some, gardeners themselves, will yearn
to fall to their knees there, untangling vines,
plucking at weeds, cooling their hands in damp earth. 15
They're going to die soon, a matter of minutes.
Even from our height, we see in the photograph
the shadow of the plane stamped dark and large
on Birkenau,° one black wing shading the garden.
We can't tell which are guards, which prisoners.   20
We're watchers. But if we had bombs we'd drop them.

—1985

---

19 **Birkenau** German concentration camp in World War II

Rita Dove (b. 1952) *won the Pulitzer Prize in 1987 for* Thomas and Beulah, *a sequence of poems about her grandparents' lives in Ohio. She is one of the most important voices of contemporary African-American poetry and served as poet laureate of the United States from 1993 to 1995.*

Rita Dove
Adolescence—III

With Dad gone, Mom and I worked
The dusky rows of tomatoes.
As they glowed orange in sunlight
And rotted in shadow, I too
Grew orange and softer, swelling out   5
Starched cotton slips.

The texture of twilight made me think of
Lengths of Dotted Swiss.° In my room
I wrapped scarred knees in dresses
That once went to big-band dances;   10
I baptized my earlobes with rosewater.
Along the window-sill, the lipstick stubs
Glittered in their steel shells.

Looking out at the rows of clay
And chicken manure, I dreamed how it would happen: 15
He would meet me by the blue spruce,
A carnation over his heart, saying,
"I have come for you, Madam;
I have loved you in my dreams."
At his touch, the scabs would fall away.   20
Over his shoulder, I see my father coming toward us:
He carries his tears in a bowl,
And blood hangs in the pine-soaked air.

—1980

8 **Dotted Swiss** type of sheer fabric

Mark Jarman (b. 1952) *was born in Kentucky and has lived in California and Tennessee, where he currently teaches at Vanderbilt University. With Robert McDowell, he edited* the Reaper, *a magazine specializing in narrative poetry. His most recent collection is* Unholy Sonnets, *released in 2000.*

Mark Jarman

After Disappointment

To lie in your child's bed when she is gone
Is calming as anything I know. To fall
Asleep, her books arranged above your head,
Is to admit that you have never been
So tired, so enchanted by the spell   5
Of your grown body. To feel small instead
Of blocking out the light, to feel alone,
Not knowing what you should or shouldn't feel,
Is to find out, no matter what you've said
About the cramped escapes and obstacles   10
You plan and face and have to call the world,
That there remain these places, occupied
By children, yours if lucky, like the girl
Who finds you here and lies down by your side.

—*1997*

Naomi Shihab Nye (b. 1952), a dedicated world traveler and humanitarian, has read her poetry in Bangladesh and the Middle East. Many of her poems are informed by her Palestinian ancestry, and she has translated contemporary Arabic poetry.

Naomi Shihab Nye
The Traveling Onion

> It is believed that the onion originally came from India. In Egypt it was an object of worship—why I haven't been able to find out. From Egypt the onion entered Greece and on to Italy, thence into all of Europe.
>
> —*Better Living Cookbook*

When I think how far the onion has traveled
just to enter my stew today, I could kneel and praise
all small forgotten miracles,
crackly paper peeling on the drainboard,
pearly layers in smooth agreement,   5
the way knife enters onion, straight
and onion falls apart on the chopping block,
a history revealed.

And I would never scold the onion
for causing tears.   10
It is right that tears fall
for something small and forgotten.
How at meal, we sit to eat,
commenting on texture of meat or herbal aroma
but never on the translucence of onion,   15
now limp, now divided,
or its traditionally honorable career:
For the sake of others,
disappear.

—*1986*

Alberto Ríos (b. 1952) *was born in Nogales, Arizona, the son of a Mexican-American father and an English-born mother. He won the Walt Whitman Award of the Academy of American Poets for his first book,* Whispering to Fool the Wind *(1982). He has also written a collection of short stories,* The Iguana Killer: Twelve Stories of the Heart, *which won the Western States Book Award in 1984.*

Alberto Ríos

The Purpose of Altar Boys

Tonio told me at catechism
the big part of the eye
admits good, and the little
black part is for seeing
evil—his mother told him   5
who was a widow and so
an authority on such things.
That's why at night
the black part gets bigger.
That's why kids can't go out   10
at night, and at night
girls take off their clothes
and walk around their
bedrooms or jump on their
beds or wear only sandals   15
and stand in their windows.
I was the altar boy
who knew about these things,
whose mission on some Sundays
was to remind people of   20
the night before as they
knelt for Holy Communion.
To keep Christ from falling
I held the metal plate under chins,
while on the thick   25
red carpet of the altar
I dragged my feet
and waited for the precise
moment: plate to chin

I delivered without expression   *30*
the Holy Electric Shock,
the kind that produces
a really large swallowing
and makes people think.
I thought of it as justice.   *35*
But on other Sundays the fire
in my eyes was different,
my mission somehow changed.
I would hold the metal plate
a little too hard   *40*
against those certain same
nervous chins, and I
I would look
with authority down
the tops of white dresses.   *45*

                                                        —*1982*

Gary Soto (b. 1952), *a professor of Chicano studies at the University of California at Berkeley, grew up in Fresno, California. His poetry collections include* The Elements of San Joaquin *(1977) and* The Tale of Sunlight *(1978). A prose book,* Living Up the Street *(1984), is a memoir of his urban childhood.*

Gary Soto
The Skeptics

Pyrrho of Elis and Sextus Empiricus were Skeptics,
Two big-shot thinkers who argued
Over figs, wine, and the loveliness of their sex.
I crowed to my brother about them,
And one evening, with Fig Newton crumbs in our mouths,   *5*
I was Pyrrho and Rick was Sextus,
Both of us skeptical about getting good jobs.
I said, "Brother Sextus, what will you render on the canvas
When you're all grown up?" He chewed
On his Fig Newton and answered, "Pyrrho,   *10*
My young flame, I will draw the reality

Of dead dogs with their feet in the air."
I crowed, "Wow, Rick—I mean Sextus—that's pretty good."
In sandals, we went down to the liquor store,
Each of us in our imaginary Greek robes,   15
And stole a quart of beer. Neither of us was a skeptic
When we swigged on that quart
And walked by the house with a woman hammering walnuts,
The rise and fall of her buttery hand quivering
The two hairs on my chest. We had our figs and wine,   20
And what we Skeptics needed,
Or at least I, was three strokes of that hammering.
I flowed over in my robe and said, "We're Brothers Skeptic,
Ruled by cautious truths." She smiled,
Hammer raised, and said, "Sure you are."   25
Right away we got along, a womanly skeptic
With a nice swing. I sat on the steps,
A young man with his figs, his wine,
And, with my Greek name shed,
A reverent believer in a woman with hammer in hand.   30

—*1995*

Julia Alvarez (b. 1953) published her first collection, Homecoming, *in 1984. It contained both free verse and "33," a sequence of 33 sonnets on the occasion of the poet's thirty-third birthday. She has gained acclaim for* In the Time of the Butterflies, *a work of fiction, and* The Other Side/El Otro Lado, *a collection of poems.*

Julia Alvarez
Bilingual Sestina

Some things I have to say aren't getting said
in this snowy, blond, blue-eyed, gum-chewing English:
dawn's early light sifting through *persianas* closed
the night before by dark-skinned girls whose words
evoke *cama, aposento, sueños* in *nombres*   5
from that first world I can't translate from Spanish.

Gladys, Rosario, Altagracia—the sounds of Spanish
wash over me like warm island waters as I say
your soothing names: a child again learning the *nombres*
of things you point to in the world before English   *10*
turned *sol, sierra, cielo, luna* to vocabulary words—
sun, earth, sky, moon. Language closed

like the touch-sensitive *morivivi* whose leaves closed
when we kids poked them, astonished. Even Spanish
failed us back then when we saw how frail a word is   *15*
when faced with the thing it names. How saying
its name won't always summon up in Spanish or English
the full blown genie from the bottled *nombre.*

Gladys, I summon you back by saying your *nombre.*
Open up again the house of slatted windows closed   *20*
since childhood, where *palabras* left behind for English
stand dusty and awkward in neglected Spanish.
Rosario, muse of *el patio,* sing in me and through me say
that world again, begin first with those first words

you put in my mouth as you pointed to the world—   *25*
not Adam, not God, but a country girl numbering
the stars, the blades of grass, warming the sun by saying,
¡Qué calor! as you opened up the morning closed
inside the night until you sang in Spanish,
Estas son las mañanitas, and listening in bed, no English   *30*

yet in my head to confuse me with translations, no English
doubling the world with synonyms, no dizzying array of words
—the world was simple and intact in Spanish—
luna, sol, casa, luz, flor, as if the *nombres*
were the outer skin of things, as if words were so close   *35*
one left a mist of breath on things by saying

their names, an intimacy I now yearn for in English—
words so close to what I mean that I almost hear my Spanish
heart beating, beating inside what I say *en inglés.*

—1995

David Mason (b. 1954) *is best known for the title poem of* The Country I Remember, *a long narrative about the life of a Civil War veteran and his daughter. The poem has been performed in a theatrical version. Mason edited, with Mark Jarman,* The Rebel Angels, *an anthology of recent poetry written in traditional forms.*

David Mason
Song of the Powers

Mine, said the stone,
mine is the hour.
I crush the scissors,
such is my power.
Stronger than wishes,   5
my power, alone.

Mine, said the paper,
mine are the words
that smother the stone
with imagined birds,   10
reams of them, flown
from the mind of the shaper.

Mine, said the scissors,
mine all the knives
gashing through paper's   15
ethereal lives;
nothing's so proper
as tattering wishes.

As stone crushes scissors,
as paper snuffs stone   20
and scissors cut paper,
all end alone.
So heap up your paper
and scissor your wishes
and uproot the stone   25
from the top of the hill.
They all end alone
as you will, you will.

—1996

Mary Jo Salter (b. 1954) has traveled widely with her husband, poet and novelist Brad Leithauser, and has lived in Japan, Italy, and Iceland. A student of Elizabeth Bishop at Harvard, Salter brings to her art a devotion to the poet's craft that mirrors that of her mentor. She has published four collections of poetry and The Moon Comes Home, *a children's book.*

Mary Jo Salter

Welcome to Hiroshima

is what you first see, stepping off the train:
a billboard brought to you in living English
by Toshiba Electric. While a channel
silent in the TV of the brain

projects those flickering re-runs of a cloud   5
that brims its risen columnful like beer
and, spilling over, hangs its foamy head,
you feel a thirst for history: what year

it started to be safe to breathe the air,
and when to drink the blood and scum afloat   10
on the Ohta River. But no, the water's clear,
they pour it for your morning cup of tea

in one of the countless sunny coffee shops
whose plastic dioramas advertise
mutations of cuisine behind the glass: 15
a pancake sandwich; a pizza someone tops

with a maraschino cherry. Passing by
the Peace Park's floral hypocenter (where
how bravely, or with what mistaken cheer,
humanity erased its own erasure),   20

you enter the memorial museum
and through more glass are served, as on a dish
of blistered grass, three mannequins. Like gloves
a mother clips to coatsleeves, strings of flesh

hang from their fingertips; or as if tied   25
to recall a duty for us, *Reverence*
the dead whose mourners too shall soon be dead,
but all commemoration's swallowed up

in questions of bad taste, how re-created
horror mocks the grim original,   30
and thinking at last *They should have left it all*
you stop. This is the wristwatch of a child.

Jammed on the moment's impact, resolute
to communicate some message, although mute,
it gestures with its hands at eight-fifteen   35
and eight-fifteen and eight-fifteen again

while tables of statistics on the wall
update the news by calling on a roll
of tape, death gummed on death, and in the case
adjacent, an exhibit under glass   40

is glass itself: a shard the bomb slammed in
a woman's arm at eight-fifteen, but some
three decades on—as if to make it plain
hope's only as renewable as pain,

and as if all the unsung   45
debasements of the past may one day come
rising to the surface once again—
worked its filthy way out like a tongue.

—1985

Cathy Song (b. 1955) was born in Honolulu, Hawaii, and holds degrees from Wellesley College and Boston University. Her first book, Picture Bride, *won the Yale Series of Younger Poets Award in 1983.* School Figures, *her third collection, appeared in 1995.*

Cathy Song
Stamp Collecting

The poorest countries
have the prettiest stamps
as if impracticality were a major export
shipped with the bananas, t-shirts, and coconuts.
Take Tonga, where the tourists,   5
expecting a dramatic waterfall replete with birdcalls
are taken to see the island's peculiar mystery:
hanging bats with collapsible wings
like black umbrellas swing upside down from fruit trees.
The Tongan stamp is a fruit.   10
The banana stamp is scalloped like a butter-varnished seashell.
The pineapple resembles a volcano, a spout of green on top,
and the papaya, a tarnished goat skull.

They look impressive,
these stamps of countries without a thing to sell   15
except for what is scraped, uprooted and hulled
from their mule-scratched hills.
They believe in postcards,
in portraits of progress: the new dam;
a team of young native doctors   20
wearing stethoscopes like exotic ornaments;
the recently constructed "Facultad de Medicina,"°
a building as lack-lustre as an American motel.

The stamps of others are predictable.
Lucky is the country that possesses indigenous beauty.   25

22 **Facultad de Medicina** Medical Faculty (building)

Say a tiger or a queen.
The Japanese can display to the world
their blossoms: a spray of pink on green.
Like pollen, they drift, airborne.
But pity the country that is bleak and stark.   30

Beauty and whimsey are discouraged as indiscreet.
Unbreakable as their climate, a monument of ice,
they issue serious statements, commemorating
factories, tramways and aeroplanes;
athletes marbled into statues.   35
They turn their noses upon the world, these countries,
and offer this: an unrelenting procession
of a grim, historic profile.

—*1988*

Janet Holmes (b. 1956) published a first collection, The Physicist at the Mall,
which contained several poems about her work experiences as a technical writer. The
Green Tuxedo, *a second collection, appeared in 1999. Holmes teaches at Boise*
State University in Idaho.

Janet Holmes
Cinquains for Rocky

You want
a word that means
separating two things
by bringing them closer. "What for?"
she asks.   5

"Doesn't
make sense." It does,
you tell her, when one speaks
about relationships—about
you two.   10

—*1993*

Catherine Tufariello (b. 1963) grew up in upstate New York and holds a Ph.D. from Cornell University. Her first two collections of poetry appeared in 2001. A translator of the sonnets of Petrarch, she has taught at the University of Miami.

Catherine Tufariello
Useful Advice

You're 37? Don't you think that maybe
It's time you settled down and had a baby?

No wine? You're pregnant, aren't you? I knew it!

Hey, are you sure you two know how to do it?

All Dennis has to do is look at me   5
And I'm knocked up.

                Some things aren't meant to be.
It's sad, but try to see this as God's will.

I've heard that sometimes when you take the Pill . . .

Does he wear boxers? Briefs are bad for sperm.

A former partner at my husband's firm   10
Who tried for years got pregnant when she stopped
Working so hard.

              Why don't you two adopt?
You'll have one of your own then, like my niece.

At work I heard about this herb from Greece—

My sister swears by dong quai. Want to try it?   15

Forget the high-tech stuff. Just change your diet.

Yoga is good for that. My cousin Carol—

It's true! Too much caffeine can make you sterile.

They have these ceremonies in Peru—

You mind my asking, is it him or you?   20

Have you tried acupuncture? Meditation?

It's in your head. Relax! Take a vacation
And have some fun. You think too much. Stop trying.

Did I say something wrong? Why are you crying?

—2000

Drama

Sophocles (496?–406 B.C.) lived in Athens in the age of Pericles, during the city's greatest period of culture, power, and influence. Sophocles distinguished himself as an athlete, a musician, a military advisor, a politician and, most important, a dramatist. At sixteen, he was chosen to lead a chorus in reciting a poem on the Greek naval victory over the Persians at Salamis, and he won his first prizes as a playwright before he was thirty. Although both Aeschylus, his senior, and Euripides, his younger rival, have their champions, Sophocles, whose career spanned so long a period that he competed against both of them, is generally considered to be the most important Greek writer of tragedies; his thirty victories in the City Dionysia surpass the combined totals of his two great colleagues. Of his 123 plays, only seven survive intact, including two other plays relating to Oedipus and his children, Antigone *and* Oedipus at Colonus, *which was produced after Sophocles' death by his grandson. He is generally credited with expanding the technical possibilities of drama by introducing a third actor in certain scenes (Aeschylus used only two) and by both reducing the number of lines given to the chorus and increasing its integration into his plays. Sophocles was intimately involved in both civic and military affairs, twice serving as a chief advisor to Pericles, and his sense of duty to the* polis *(Greek for city) is apparent in many of his plays.* Oedipus the King *was first performed in Athens in about 430 B.C. Its importance can be judged by the many references that Aristotle makes to it in his discussion of tragedy in the* Poetics.

Sophocles
Oedipus the King

CHARACTERS°

Oedipus
A Priest
Creon
Teiresias
Iocastê
Messenger
Shepherd of Laïos
Second Messenger
Chorus of Theban Elders

Characters: Some of the characters' names are usually Anglicized: Jocasta, Laius. This translation uses spelling that reflects the original Greek.

Translated by Dudley Fitts and Robert Fitzgerald

Scene: *Before the palace of Oedipus, King of Thebes. A central door and two lateral doors open onto a platform which runs the length of the façade. On the platform, right and left, are altars; and three steps lead down into the "orchestra," or chorus-ground. At the beginning of the action these steps are crowded by suppliants° who have brought branches and chaplets of olive leaves and who lie in various attitudes of despair. Oedipus enters.*

PROLOGUE°

OEDIPUS: My children, generations of the living
In the line of Kadmos,° nursed at his ancient hearth:
Why have you strewn yourself before these altars
In supplication, with your boughs and garlands?
The breath of incense rises from the city   5
With a sound of prayer and lamentation.
                                        Children,
I would not have you speak through messengers,
And therefore I have come myself to hear you—
I, Oedipus, who bear the famous name.
(*To a Priest.*) You, there, since you are eldest in the company,   10
Speak for them all, tell me what preys upon you,
Whether you come in dread, or crave some blessing:
Tell me, and never doubt that I will help you
In every way I can; I should be heartless
Were I not moved to find you suppliant here.   15
PRIEST: Great Oedipus, O powerful King of Thebes!
You see how all the ages of our people
Cling to your altar steps: here are boys
Who can barely stand alone, and here are priests
By weight of age, as I am a priest of God,   20
And young men chosen from those yet unmarried;
As for the others, all that multitude,

---

suppliants persons who come to ask a favor.   **Prologue** first part of a tragedy, containing the exposition.   **2 line of Kadmos** Thebes had been founded by Cadmus.

They wait with olive chaplets in the squares,
At the two shrines of Pallas,° and where Apollo°
Speaks in the glowing embers.

Your own eyes   25

Must tell you: Thebes is tossed on a murdering sea
And can not lift her head from the death surge.
A rust consumes the buds and fruits of the earth;
The herds are sick; children die unborn,
And labor is vain. The god of plague and pyre   30
Raids like detestable lightning through the city,
And all the house of Kadmos is laid waste,
All emptied, and all darkened: Death alone
Battens upon the misery of Thebes.
You are not one of the immortal gods, we know;   35
Yet we have come to you to make our prayer
As to the man surest in mortal ways
And wisest in the ways of God. You saved us
From the Sphinx, that flinty singer, and the tribute
We paid to her so long; yet you were never   40
Better informed than we, nor could we teach you:
It was some god breathed in you to set us free.
Therefore, O mighty King, we turn to you:
Find us our safety, find us a remedy,
Whether by counsel of the gods or men.   45
A king of wisdom tested in the past
Can act in a time of troubles, and act well.
Noblest of men, restore
Life to your city! Think how all men call you
Liberator for your triumph long ago;   50
Ah, when your years of kingship are remembered,
Let them not say *We rose, but later fell*—
Keep the State from going down in the storm!
Once, years ago, with happy augury,
You brought us fortune; be the same again!   55

---

24 Pallas Athena, goddess of wisdom.   **Apollo** here the god of prophecy. At his shrine at Delphi, the future could be divined.

No man questions your power to rule the land:
But rule over men, not over a dead city!
Ships are only hulls, citadels are nothing,
When no life moves in the empty passageways.

OEDIPUS: Poor children! You may be sure I know   60
All that you longed for in your coming here.
I know that you are deathly sick; and yet,
Sick as you are, not one is as sick as I.
Each of you suffers in himself alone
His anguish, not another's; but my spirit   65
Groans for the city, for myself, for you.
I was not sleeping, you are not waking me.
No, I have been in tears for a long while
And in my restless thought walked many ways.
In all my search, I found one helpful course,   70
And that I have taken: I have sent Creon,
Son of Menoikeus, brother of the Queen,
To Delphi, Apollo's place of revelation,
To learn there, if he can,
What act or pledge of mine may save the city.   75
I have counted the days, and now, this very day,
I am troubled, for he has overstayed his time.
What is he doing? He has been gone too long.
Yet whenever he comes back, I should do ill
To scant whatever duty God reveals.   80

PRIEST: It is a timely promise. At this instant
They tell me Creon is here.

OEDIPUS: O Lord Apollo!
May his news be fair as his face is radiant!

PRIEST: It could not be otherwise: he is crowned with bay,
The chaplet is thick with berries.

OEDIPUS: We shall soon know;   85
He is near enough to hear us now.

Enter Creon.

O Prince:

Brother: son of Menoikeus:
What answer do you bring us from the god?
CREON: A strong one. I can tell you, great afflictions
Will turn out well, if they are taken well.   90
OEDIPUS: What was the oracle? These vague words
Leave me still hanging between hope and fear.
CREON: Is it your pleasure to hear me with all these
Gathered around us? I am prepared to speak,
But should we not go in?
OEDIPUS: Let them all hear it   95
It is for them I suffer, more than for myself.
CREON: Then I will tell you what I heard at Delphi.
In plain words
The god commands us to expel from the land of Thebes
An old defilement we are sheltering.   100
It is a deathly thing, beyond cure.
We must not let it feed upon us longer.
OEDIPUS: What defilement? How shall we rid ourselves of it?
CREON: By exile or death, blood for blood. It was
Murder that brought the plague-wind on the city.   105
OEDIPUS: Murder of whom? Surely the god has named him?
CREON: My lord: long ago Laïos was our king,
Before you came to govern us.
OEDIPUS: I know;
I learned of him from others; I never saw him.
CREON: He was murdered; and Apollo commands us now   110
To take revenge upon whoever killed him.
OEDIPUS: Upon whom? Where are they? Where shall we
find a clue
To solve that crime, after so many years?
CREON: Here in this land, he said.
                        If we make enquiry,
We may touch things that otherwise escape us.   115
OEDIPUS: Tell me: Was Laïos murdered in his house,
Or in the fields, or in some foreign country?
CREON: He said he planned to make a pilgrimage.
He did not come home again.

OEDIPUS: And was there no one,
No witness, no companion, to tell what happened? *120*
CREON: They were all killed but one, and he got away
So frightened that he could remember one thing only.
OEDIPUS: What was that one thing? One may be the key
To everything, if we resolve to use it.
CREON: He said that a band of highwaymen attacked them, *125*
Outnumbered them, and overwhelmed the King.
OEDIPUS: Strange, that a highwayman should be so daring—
Unless some faction here bribed him to do it.
CREON: We thought of that. But after Laïos' death
New troubles arose and we had no avenger. *130*
OEDIPUS: What troubles could prevent your hunting down the
killers?
CREON: The riddling Sphinx's song
Made us deaf to all mysteries but her own.
OEDIPUS: Then once more I must bring what is dark to light.
It is most fitting that Apollo shows, *135*
As you do, this compunction for the dead.
You shall see how I stand by you, as I should,
To avenge the city and the city's god,
And not as though it were for some distant friend,
But for my own sake, to be rid of evil. *140*
Whoever killed King Laïos might—who knows?—
Decide at any moment to kill me as well.
By avenging the murdered king I protect myself.
Come, then, my children: leave the altar steps,
Lift up your olive boughs!
One of you go *145*
And summon the people of Kadmos to gather here.
I will do all that I can; you may tell them that.

Exit a Page.

So, with the help of God,
We shall be saved—or else indeed we are lost.
PRIEST: Let us rise, children. It was for this we came, *150*
And now the King has promised it himself.

Phoibos° has sent us an oracle; may he descend
Himself to save us and drive out the plague.

Exeunt Oedipus and Creon into the palace by the central
door. The Priest and the Suppliants disperse right and left.
After a short pause the Chorus enters the orchestra.

PÁRODOS °

STROPHE° 1

CHORUS: What is God singing in his profound
Delphi of gold and shadow?
What oracle for Thebes, the sunwhipped city?
Fear unjoints me, the roots of my heart tremble.
Now I remember, O Healer, your power, and wonder: 5
Will you send doom like a sudden cloud, or weave it
Like nightfall of the past?
Speak, speak to us, issue of holy sound:
Dearest to our expectancy: be tender!

ANTISTROPHE° 1

Let me pray to Athenê, the immortal daughter of Zeus,   10
And to Artemis her sister
Who keeps her famous throne in the market ring,
And to Apollo, bowman at the far butts of heaven—
O gods, descend! Like three streams leap against
The fires of our grief, the fires of darkness;   15
Be swift to bring us rest!
As in the old time from the brilliant house
Of air you stepped to save us, come again!

---

152 Phoibos that is, Apollo.
Párodos chanted by the chorus on its first entrance.   A **strophe** was chanted while the chorus
danced from stage right to stage left.   An **antistrophe** was chanted while the chorus danced from
left to right.

STROPHE 2

Now our afflictions have no end,
Now all our stricken host lies down   *20*
And no man fights off death with his mind;
The noble plowland bears no grain,
And groaning mothers can not bear—
See, how our lives like birds take wing,
Like sparks that fly when a fire soars,   *25*
To the shore of the god of evening.

ANTISTROPHE 2

The plague burns on, it is pitiless,
Though pallid children laden with death
Lie unwept in the stony ways,
And old gray women by every path   *30*
Flock to the strand about the altars
There to strike their breasts and cry
Worship of Phoibos in wailing prayers:
Be kind, God's golden child!

STROPHE 3

There are no swords in this attack by fire,   *35*
No shields, but we are ringed with cries.
Send the besieger plunging from our homes
Into the vast sea-room of the Atlantic
Or into the waves that foam eastward of Thrace—
For the day ravages what the night spares—   *40*
Destroy our enemy, lord of the thunder!
Let him be riven by lightning from heaven!

ANTISTROPHE 3

Phoibos Apollo, stretch the sun's bowstring,
That golden cord, until it sing for us,
Flashing arrows in heaven!
                              Artemis,° Huntress,   *45*
Race with flaring lights upon our mountains!

45 Artemis goddess of the hunt and female chastity.

O scarlet god, O golden-banded brow,
O Theban Bacchos in a storm of Maenads,°

Enter Oedipus, center.

Whirl upon Death, that all the Undying hate!
Come with blinding torches, come in joy! 50

SCENE I°

OEDIPUS: Is this your prayer? It may be answered. Come,
Listen to me, act as the crisis demands,
And you shall have relief from all these evils.
Until now I was a stranger to this tale,
As I had been a stranger to the crime. 5
Could I track down the murderer without a clue?
But now, friends,
As one who became a citizen after the murder,
I make this proclamation to all Thebans:
If any man knows by whose hand Laïos, son of Labdakos, 10
Met his death, I direct that man to tell me everything,
No matter what he fears for having so long withheld it.
Let it stand as promised that no further trouble
Will come to him, but he may leave the land in safety.
Moreover: If anyone knows the murderer to be foreign, 15
Let him not keep silent: he shall have his reward from me.
However, if he does conceal it; if any man
Fearing for his friend or for himself disobeys this edict,
Hear what I propose to do:
I solemnly forbid the people of this country, 20
Where power and throne are mine, ever to receive that man
Or speak to him, no matter who he is, or let him
Join in sacrifice, lustration, or in prayer.
I decree that he be driven from every house,
Being, as he is, corruption itself to us: the Delphic 25
Voice of Zeus has pronounced this revelation.
Thus I associate myself with the oracle

---

48 Bacchos . . . Maenads god of wine and his priestesses.   **Scene** in Greek, *episodos*

And take the side of the murdered king.
As for the criminal, I pray to God—
Whether it be a lurking thief, or one of a number—   30
I pray that that man's life be consumed in evil and
wretchedness.
And as for me, this curse applies no less
If it should turn out that the culprit is my guest here,
Sharing my hearth.
              You have heard the penalty.
I lay it on you now to attend to this   35
For my sake, for Apollo's, for the sick
Sterile city that heaven has abandoned.
Suppose the oracle had given you no command:
Should this defilement go uncleansed for ever?
You should have found the murderer: your king,   40
A noble king, had been destroyed!
            Now I,
Having the power that he held before me,
Having his bed, begetting children there
Upon his wife, as he would have, had he lived—
Their son would have been my children's brother,   45
If Laïos had had luck in fatherhood!
(But surely ill luck rushed upon his reign)—
I say I take the son's part, just as though
I were his son, to press the fight for him
And see it won! I'll find the hand that brought   50
Death to Labdakos' and Polydoros' child,
Heir of Kadmos' and Agenor's line.
And as for those who fail me,
May the gods deny them the fruit of the earth,
Fruit of the womb, and may they rot utterly!   55
Let them be wretched as we are wretched, and worse!
For you, for loyal Thebans, and for all
Who find my actions right, I pray the favor
Of justice, and of all the immortal gods.

CHORAGOS°:   Since I am under oath, my lord, I swear   60
    I did not do the murder, I can not name

---

60 **Choragos** leader of the chorus.

The murderer. Might not the oracle
That has ordained the search tell where to find him?
OEDIPUS: An honest question. But no man in the world
Can make the gods do more than the gods will.   65
CHORAGOS: There is one last expedient—
OEDIPUS: Tell me what it is.
Though it seem slight, you must not hold it back.
CHORAGOS: A lord clairvoyant to the lord Apollo,
As we all know, is the skilled Teiresias.
One might learn much about this from him, Oedipus.   70
OEDIPUS: I am not wasting time:
Creon spoke of this, and I have sent for him—
Twice, in fact; it is strange that he is not here.
CHORAGOS: The other matter—that old report—seems useless.
OEDIPUS: Tell me. I am interested in all reports.   75
CHORAGOS: The King was said to have been killed by
highwaymen.
OEDIPUS: I know. But we have no witnesses to that.
CHORAGOS: If the killer can feel a particle of dread,
Your curse will bring him out of hiding!
OEDIPUS: No.
The man who dared that act will fear no curse.   80

Enter the blind seer Teiresias, led by a Page.

CHORAGOS: But there is one man who may detect the criminal.
This is Teiresias, this is the holy prophet
In whom, alone of all men, truth was born.
OEDIPUS: Teiresias: seer: student of mysteries,
Of all that's taught and all that no man tells,   85
Secrets of Heaven and secrets of the earth:
Blind though you are, you know the city lies
Sick with plague; and from this plague, my lord,
We find that you alone can guard or save us.
Possibly you did not hear the messengers?   90
Apollo, when we sent to him,
Sent us back word that this great pestilence
Would lift, but only if we established clearly
The identity of those who murdered Laïos.
They must be killed or exiled.

Can you use   95
Birdflight or any art of divination
To purify yourself, and Thebes, and me
From this contagion? We are in your hands.
There is no fairer duty
Than that of helping others in distress.   100
TEIRESIAS: How dreadful knowledge of the truth can be
When there's no help in truth! I knew this well,
But made myself forget. I should not have come.
OEDIPUS: What is troubling you? Why are your eyes so cold?
TEIRESIAS: Let me go home. Bear your own fate, and I'll   105
Bear mine. It is better so: trust what I say.
OEDIPUS: What you say is ungracious and unhelpful
To your native country. Do not refuse to speak.
TEIRESIAS: When it comes to speech, your own is neither
temperate
Nor opportune. I wish to be more prudent.   110
OEDIPUS: In God's name, we all beg you—
TEIRESIAS: You are all ignorant.
No; I will never tell you what I know.
Now it is my misery; then, it would be yours.
OEDIPUS: What! You do know something, and will not
tell us?
You would betray us all and wreck the State?   115
TEIRESIAS: I do not intend to torture myself, or you.
Why persist in asking? You will not persuade me.
OEDIPUS: What a wicked old man you are! You'd try a stone's
Patience! Out with it! Have you no feeling at all?
TEIRESIAS: You call me unfeeling. If you could only see   120
The nature of your own feelings . . .
OEDIPUS: Why,
Who would not feel as I do? Who could endure
Your arrogance toward the city?
TEIRESIAS: What does it matter!
Whether I speak or not; it is bound to come.
OEDIPUS: Then, if "it" is bound to come, you are bound to
tell me.   125
TEIRESIAS: No, I will not go on. Rage as you please.

OEDIPUS: Rage? Why not!

And I'll tell you what I think:
You planned it, you had it done, you all but
Killed him with your own hands: if you had eyes,
I'd say the crime was yours, and yours alone.   *130*

TEIRESIAS: So? I charge you, then,
Abide by the proclamation you have made:
From this day forth
Never speak again to these men or to me;
You yourself are the pollution of this country.   *135*

OEDIPUS: You dare say that! Can you possibly think you have
Some way of going free, after such insolence?

TEIRESIAS: I have gone free. It is the truth sustains me.

OEDIPUS: Who taught you shamelessness? It was not your
craft.

TEIRESIAS: You did. You made me speak. I did not want to.   *140*

OEDIPUS: Speak what? Let me hear it again more clearly.

TEIRESIAS: Was it not clear before? Are you tempting me?

OEDIPUS: I did not understand it. Say it again.

TEIRESIAS: I say that you are the murderer whom you seek.

OEDIPUS: Now twice you have spat out infamy. You'll pay
for it!   *145*

TEIRESIAS: Would you care for more? Do you wish to be really
angry?

OEDIPUS: Say what you will. Whatever you say is worthless.

TEIRESIAS: I say you live in hideous shame with those
Most dear to you. You can not see the evil.

OEDIPUS: It seems you can go on mouthing like this for ever.   *150*

TEIRESIAS: I can, if there is power in truth.

OEDIPUS: There is:
But not for you, not for you,
You sightless, witless, senseless, mad old man!

TEIRESIAS: You are the madman. There is no one here
Who will not curse you soon, as you curse me.   *155*

OEDIPUS: You child of endless night! You can not hurt me
Or any other man who sees the sun.

TEIRESIAS: True: it is not from me your fate will come.
That lies within Apollo's competence,

As it is his concern.

OEDIPUS: Tell me: *160*
   Are you speaking for Creon, or for yourself?

TEIRESIAS: Creon is no threat. You weave your own doom.

OEDIPUS: Wealth, power, craft of statesmanship!
   Kingly position, everywhere admired!
   What savage envy is stored up against these,   *165*
   If Creon, whom I trusted, Creon my friend,
   For this great office which the city once
   Put in my hands unsought—if for this power
   Creon desires in secret to destroy me!
   He has brought this decrepit fortune-teller, this   *170*
   Collector of dirty pennies, this prophet fraud—
   Why, he is no more clairvoyant than I am!
                                    Tell us:
   Has your mystic mummery ever approached the truth?
   When that hellcat the Sphinx was performing here,
   What help were you to these people?   *175*
   Her magic was not for the first man who came along:
   It demanded a real exorcist. Your birds—
   What good were they? or the gods, for the matter of that?
   But I came by,
   Oedipus, the simple man, who knows nothing—   *180*
   I thought it out for myself, no birds helped me!
   And this is the man you think you can destroy,
   That you may be close to Creon when he's king!
   Well, you and your friend Creon, it seems to me,
   Will suffer most. If you were not an old man,   *185*
   You would have paid already for your plot.

CHORAGOS: We can not see that his words or yours
   Have been spoken except in anger, Oedipus,
   And of anger we have no need. How can God's will
   Be accomplished best? That is what most concerns us.   *190*

TEIRESIAS: You are a king. But where argument's concerned
   I am your man, as much a king as you.
   I am not your servant, but Apollo's.
   I have no need of Creon to speak for me.
   Listen to me. You mock my blindness, do you?   *195*

But I say that you, with both your eyes, are blind:
You can not see the wretchedness of your life,
Nor in whose house you live, no, nor with whom.
Who are your father and mother? Can you tell me?
You do not even know the blind wrongs   *200*
That you have done them, on earth and in the world below.
But the double lash of your parents' curse will whip you
Out of this land some day, with only night
Upon your precious eyes.
Your cries then—where will they not be heard?   *205*
What fastness of Kithairon° will not echo them?
And that bridal-descant of yours—you'll know it then,
The song they sang when you came here to Thebes
And found your misguided berthing.
All this, and more, that you can not guess at now, *210*
Will bring you to yourself among your children.
Be angry, then. Curse Creon. Curse my words.
I tell you, no man that walks upon the earth
Shall be rooted out more horribly than you.

OEDIPUS: Am I to bear this from him?—Damnation *215*
 Take you! Out of this place! Out of my sight!

TEIRESIAS: I would not have come at all if you had not
 asked me.

OEDIPUS: Could I have told that you'd talk nonsense, that
 You'd come here to make a fool of yourself, and of me?

TEIRESIAS: A fool? Your parents thought me sane enough. *220*

OEDIPUS: My parents again!—Wait: who were my parents?

TEIRESIAS: This day will give you a father, and break your
 heart.

OEDIPUS: Your infantile riddles! Your damned abracadabra!

TEIRESIAS: You were a great man once at solving riddles.

OEDIPUS: Mock me with that if you like; you will find it true. *225*

TEIRESIAS: It was true enough. It brought about your ruin.

OEDIPUS: But if it saved this town?

TEIRESIAS (*to the Page*): Boy, give me your hand.

OEDIPUS: Yes, boy; lead him away.

---

206 Kithairon a mountain near Thebes.

—While you are here
We can do nothing. Go; leave us in peace.

TEIRESIAS: I will go when I have said what I have to say.⁣ 230
How can you hurt me? And I tell you again:
The man you have been looking for all this time,
The damned man, the murderer of Laïos,
That man is in Thebes. To your mind he is foreignborn,
But it will soon be shown that he is a Theban,⁣ 235
A revelation that will fail to please.

⁣ A blind man,
Who has his eyes now; a penniless man, who is rich now;
And he will go tapping the strange earth with his staff;
To the children with whom he lives now he will be
Brother and father—the very same; to her⁣ 240
Who bore him, son and husband—the very same
Who came to his father's bed, wet with his father's blood.
Enough. Go think that over.
If later you find error in what I have said,
You may say that I have no skill in prophecy.⁣ 245

Exit Teiresias, led by his Page.
Oedipus goes into the palace.

ODE° I

STROPHE 1

CHORUS: The Delphic stone of prophecies
⁣ Remembers ancient regicide
⁣ And a still bloody hand.
⁣ That killer's hour of flight has come.
⁣ He must be stronger than riderless⁣ 5
⁣ Coursers of untiring wind,
⁣ For the son of Zeus° armed with his father's thunder
⁣ Leaps in lightning after him;
⁣ And the Furies° follow him, the sad Furies.

Ode also known as *stasimon*, a choral interlude.   **7 son of Zeus** Apollo.   **9 Furies** three female
spirits who punished evildoers.

Antistrophe 1

Holy Parnassos' peak of snow   *10*
Flashes and blinds that secret man,
That all shall hunt him down:
Though he may roam the forest shade
Like a bull gone wild from pasture
To rage through glooms of stone.   *15*
Doom comes down on him; flight will not avail him;
For the world's heart calls him desolate,
And the immortal Furies follow, for ever follow.

Strophe 2

But now a wilder thing is heard
From the old man skilled at hearing Fate in the wingbeat
of a bird.   *20*
Bewildered as a blown bird, my soul hovers and can not find
Foothold in this debate, or any reason or rest of mind.
But no man ever brought—none can bring
Proof of strife between Thebes' royal house,
Labdakos' line,° and the son of Polybos;°   *25*
And never until now has any man brought word
Of Laïos' dark death staining Oedipus the King.

Antistrophe 2

Divine Zeus and Apollo hold
Perfect intelligence alone of all tales ever told;
And well though this diviner works, he works in his own night;   *30*
No man can judge that rough unknown or trust in second sight,
For wisdom changes hands among the wise.
Shall I believe my great lord criminal
At a raging word that a blind old man let fall?
I saw him, when the carrion woman faced him of old,   *35*
Prove his heroic mind! These evil words are lies.

---

25 Labdakos' line descendants of Laïos.   **Polybos** king of Corinth who adopted Oedipus.

SCENE II

CREON: Men of Thebes:
    I am told that heavy accusations
    Have been brought against me by King Oedipus.
    I am not the kind of man to bear this tamely.
    If in these present difficulties   *5*
    He holds me accountable for any harm to him
    Through anything I have said or done—why, then,
    I do not value life in this dishonor.
    It is not as though this rumor touched upon
    Some private indiscretion. The matter is grave.   *10*
    The fact is that I am being called disloyal
    To the State, to my fellow citizens, to my friends.
CHORAGOS: He may have spoken in anger, not from his mind.
CREON: But did you not hear him say I was the one
    Who seduced the old prophet into lying?   *15*
CHORAGOS: The thing was said; I do not know how seriously.
CREON: But you were watching him! Were his eyes steady?
    Did he look like a man in his right mind?
CHORAGOS: I do not know.
    I can not judge the behavior of great men.
    But here is the King himself.

Enter Oedipus.

OEDIPUS: So you dared come back.   *20*
    Why? How brazen of you to come to my house,
    You murderer!
               Do you think I do not know
    That you plotted to kill me, plotted to steal my throne?
    Tell me, in God's name: am I coward, a fool,
    That you should dream you could accomplish this?   *25*
    A fool who could not see your slippery game?
    A coward, not to fight back when I saw it?
    You are the fool, Creon, are you not? hoping
    Without support or friends to get a throne?
    Thrones may be won or bought: you could do neither.   *30*
CREON: Now listen to me. You have talked; let me talk, too.

You can not judge unless you know the facts.

OEDIPUS: You speak well: there is one fact; but I find it hard
To learn from the deadliest enemy I have.

CREON: That above all I must dispute with you. 35

OEDIPUS: That above all I will not hear you deny.

CREON: If you think there is anything good in being stubborn
Against all reason, then I say you are wrong.

OEDIPUS: If you think a man can sin against his own kind
And not be punished for it, I say you are mad. 40

CREON: I agree. But tell me: what have I done to you?

OEDIPUS: You advised me to send for that wizard, did you not?

CREON: I did. I should do it again.

OEDIPUS: Very well. Now tell me:
How long has it been since Laïos—

CREON: What of Laïos?

OEDIPUS: Since he vanished in that onset by the road? 45

CREON: It was long ago, a long time.

OEDIPUS: And this prophet,
Was he practicing here then?

CREON: He was; and with honor, as now.

OEDIPUS: Did he speak of me at that time?

CREON: He never did;
At least, not when I was present.

OEDIPUS: But . . . the enquiry?
I suppose you held one?

CREON: We did, but we learned nothing. 50

OEDIPUS: Why did the prophet not speak against me then?

CREON: I do not know; and I am the kind of man
Who holds his tongue when he has no facts to go on.

OEDIPUS: There's one fact that you know, and you could tell it.

CREON: What fact is that? If I know it, you shall have it. 55

OEDIPUS: If he were not involved with you, he could not say
That it was I who murdered Laïos.

CREON: If he says that, you are the one that knows it!—
But now it is my turn to question you.

OEDIPUS: Put your questions. I am no murderer. 60

CREON: First then: You married my sister?

OEDIPUS: I married your sister.

CREON: And you rule the kingdom equally with her?
OEDIPUS: Everything that she wants she has from me.
CREON: And I am the third, equal to both of you?
OEDIPUS: That is why I call you a bad friend.   65
CREON: No. Reason it out, as I have done.
  Think of this first: Would any sane man prefer
  Power, with all a king's anxieties,
  To that same power and the grace of sleep?
  Certainly not I.   70
  I have never longed for the king's power—only his rights.
  Would any wise man differ from me in this?
  As matters stand, I have my way in everything
  With your consent, and no responsibilities.
  If I were king, I should be a slave to policy.   75
  How could I desire a scepter more
  Than what is now mine—untroubled influence?
  No, I have not gone mad; I need no honors,
  Except those with the perquisites I have now.
  I am welcome everywhere; every man salutes me,   80
  And those who want your favor seek my ear,
  Since I know how to manage what they ask.
  Should I exchange this ease for that anxiety?
  Besides, no sober mind is treasonable.
  I hate anarchy   85
  And never would deal with any man who likes it.
  Test what I have said. Go to the priestess
  At Delphi, ask if I quoted her correctly.
  And as for this other thing: if I am found
  Guilty of treason with Teiresias,   90
  Then sentence me to death! You have my word
  It is a sentence I should cast my vote for—
  But not without evidence!
                              You do wrong
  When you take good men for bad, bad men for good.
  A true friend thrown aside—why, life itself   95
  Is not more precious!
                              In time you will know this well:
  For time, and time alone, will show the just man,

Though scoundrels are discovered in a day.

CHORAGOS: This is well said, and a prudent man would
 ponder it.

 Judgments too quickly formed are dangerous.   *100*

OEDIPUS: But is he not quick in his duplicity?

 And shall I not be quick to parry him?

 Would you have me stand still, hold my peace, and let

 This man win everything, through my inaction?

CREON: And you want—what is it, then? To banish me?   *105*

OEDIPUS: No, not exile. It is your death I want,

 So that all the world may see what treason means.

CREON: You will persist, then? You will not believe me?

OEDIPUS: How can I believe you?

CREON: Then you are a fool.

OEDIPUS: To save myself?

CREON: In justice, think of me.   *110*

OEDIPUS: You are evil incarnate.

CREON: But suppose that you are
 wrong?

OEDIPUS: Still I must rule.

CREON: But not if you rule badly.

OEDIPUS: O city, city!

CREON: It is my city, too!

CHORAGOS: Now, my lords, be still. I see the Queen,

 Iocastê, coming from her palace chambers;   *115*

 And it is time she came, for the sake of you both.

 This dreadful quarrel can be resolved through her.

Enter Iocastê.

IOCASTÊ: Poor foolish men, what wicked din is this?

 With Thebes sick to death, is it not shameful

 That you should rake some private quarrel up?   *120*

 (*To Oedipus.*) Come into the house.

        —And you, Creon,

 go now:

 Let us have no more of this tumult over nothing.

CREON: Nothing? No, sister: what your husband plans for me

 Is one of two great evils: exile or death.

OEDIPUS: He is right.

Why, woman, I have caught him squarely   *125*

Plotting against my life.

CREON: No! Let me die

Accurst if ever I have wished you harm!

IOCASTÊ: Ah, believe it, Oedipus!

In the name of the gods, respect this oath of his

For my sake, for the sake of these people here!   *130*

STROPHE 1

CHORAGOS: Open your mind to her, my lord. Be ruled by her, I

beg you!

OEDIPUS: What would you have me do?

CHORAGOS: Respect Creon's word. He has never spoken like

a fool,

And now he has sworn an oath.

OEDIPUS: You know what you ask?

CHORAGOS: I do.

OEDIPUS: Speak on, then.

CHORAGOS: A friend so sworn should not be baited so,   *135*

In blind malice, and without final proof.

OEDIPUS: You are aware, I hope, that what you say

Means death for me, or exile at the least.

STROPHE 2

CHORAGOS: No, I swear by Helios, first in Heaven!

May I die friendless and accurst,   *140*

The worst of deaths, if ever I meant that!

It is the withering fields

That hurt my sick heart:

Must we bear all these ills,

And now your bad blood as well?   *145*

OEDIPUS: Then let him go. And let me die, if I must,

Or be driven by him in shame from the land of Thebes.

It is your unhappiness, and not his talk,

That touches me.

As for him—
Wherever he goes, hatred will follow him.   *150*

CREON: Ugly in yielding, as you were ugly in rage!
Natures like yours chiefly torment themselves.

OEDIPUS: Can you not go? Can you not leave me?

CREON: I can.
You do not know me; but the city knows me,
And in its eyes I am just, if not in yours.   *155*

Exit Creon.

ANTISTROPHE 1

CHORAGOS: Lady Iocastê, did you not ask the King to go to his
chambers?

IOCASTÊ: First tell me what has happened.

CHORAGOS: There was suspicion without evidence; yet it rankled
As even false charges will.

IOCASTÊ: On both sides?

CHORAGOS: On both.

IOCASTÊ: But what was said?

CHORAGOS: Oh let it rest, let it be done with!   *160*
Have we not suffered enough?

OEDIPUS: You see to what your decency has brought you:
You have made difficulties where my heart saw none.

ANTISTROPHE 2

CHORAGOS: Oedipus, it is not once only I have told you—
You must know I should count myself unwise   *165*
To the point of madness, should I now forsake you—
You, under whose hand,
In the storm of another time,
Our dear land sailed out free.
But now stand fast at the helm!   *170*

IOCASTÊ: In God's name, Oedipus, inform your wife as well:
Why are you so set in this hard anger?

OEDIPUS: I will tell you, for none of these men deserves
My confidence as you do. It is Creon's work,

His treachery, his plotting against me.   *175*

IOCASTÊ: Go on, if you can make this clear to me.

OEDIPUS: He charges me with the murder of Laïos.

IOCASTÊ: Has he some knowledge? Or does he speak from
hearsay?

OEDIPUS: He would not commit himself to such a charge,
But he has brought in that damnable soothsayer   *180*
To tell his story.

IOCASTÊ: Set your mind at rest.
If it is a question of soothsayers, I tell you
That you will find no man whose craft gives knowledge
Of the unknowable.

                 Here is my proof:
An oracle was reported to Laïos once   *185*
(I will not say from Phoibos himself, but from
His appointed ministers, at any rate)
That his doom would be death at the hands of his own son—
His son, born of his flesh and of mine!

Now, you remember the story: Laïos was killed   *190*
By marauding strangers where three highways meet;
But his child had not been three days in this world
Before the King had pierced the baby's ankles
And left him to die on a lonely mountainside.

Thus, Apollo never caused that child   *195*
To kill his father, and it was not Laïos' fate
To die at the hands of his son, as he had feared.
This is what prophets and prophecies are worth!
Have no dread of them.

                 It is God himself
Who can show us what he wills, in his own way.   *200*

OEDIPUS: How strange a shadowy memory crossed my mind,
Just now while you were speaking; it chilled my heart.

IOCASTÊ: What do you mean? What memory do you speak of?

OEDIPUS: If I understand you, Laïos was killed
At a place where three roads meet.

IOCASTÊ: So it was said;   *205*
We have no later story.

OEDIPUS: Where did it happen?

IOCASTÊ: Phokis, it is called: at a place where the Theban Way
Divides into the roads toward Delphi and Daulia.

OEDIPUS: When?

IOCASTÊ: We had the news not long before you came
And proved the right to your succession here.   *210*

OEDIPUS: Ah, what net has God been weaving for me?

IOCASTÊ: Oedipus! Why does this trouble you?

OEDIPUS: Do not ask
me yet.
First, tell me how Laïos looked, and tell me
How old he was.

IOCASTÊ: He was tall, his hair just touched
With white; his form was not unlike your own.   *215*

OEDIPUS: I think that I myself may be accurst
By my own ignorant edict.

IOCASTÊ: You speak strangely.
It makes me tremble to look at you, my King.

OEDIPUS: I am not sure that the blind man can not see.
But I should know better if you were to tell me—   *220*

IOCASTÊ: Anything—though I dread to hear you ask it.

OEDIPUS: Was the King lightly escorted, or did he ride
With a large company, as a ruler should?

IOCASTÊ: There were five men with him in all: one was a
herald,
And a single chariot, which he was driving.   *225*

OEDIPUS: Alas, that makes it plain enough!

                                            But who—
Who told you how it happened?

IOCASTÊ: A household servant,
The only one to escape.

OEDIPUS: And is he still
A servant of ours?

IOCASTÊ: No; for when he came back at last
And found you enthroned in the place of the dead king,   *230*
He came to me, touched my hand with his, and begged
That I would send him away to the frontier district
Where only the shepherds go—
As far away from the city as I could send him.

I granted his prayer; for although the man was a slave,   *235*
He had earned more than this favor at my hands.
OEDIPUS: Can he be called back quickly?
IOCASTÊ: Easily.
   But why?
OEDIPUS: I have taken too much upon myself
Without enquiry; therefore I wish to consult him.
IOCASTÊ: Then he shall come.
                        But am I not one also   *240*
To whom you might confide these fears of yours?
OEDIPUS: That is your right; it will not be denied you,
Now least of all; for I have reached a pitch
Of wild foreboding. Is there anyone
To whom I should sooner speak?   *245*
Polybos of Corinth is my father.
My mother is a Dorian: Meropê.
I grew up chief among the men of Corinth
Until a strange thing happened—
Not worth my passion, it may be, but strange.   *250*
At a feast, a drunken man maundering in his cups
Cries out that I am not my father's son!
I contained myself that night, though I felt anger
And a sinking heart. The next day I visited
My father and mother, and questioned them. They stormed,   *255*
Calling it all the slanderous rant of a fool;
And this relieved me. Yet the suspicion
Remained always aching in my mind;
I knew there was talk; I could not rest;
And finally, saying nothing to my parents,   *260*
I went to the shrine at Delphi.
The god dismissed my question without reply;
He spoke of other things.
                        Some were clear,
Full of wretchedness, dreadful, unbearable:
As, that I should lie with my own mother, breed   *265*
Children from whom all men would turn their eyes;
And that I should be my father's murderer.
I heard all this, and fled. And from that day

Corinth to me was only in the stars
Descending in that quarter of the sky,   270
As I wandered farther and farther on my way
To a land where I should never see the evil
Sung by the oracle. And I came to this country
Where, so you say, King Laïos was killed.
I will tell you all that happened there, my lady.   275
There were three highways
Coming together at a place I passed;
And there a herald came towards me, and a chariot
Drawn by horses, with a man such as you describe
Seated in it. The groom leading the horses   280
Forced me off the road at his lord's command;
But as this charioteer lurched over towards me
I struck him in my rage. The old man saw me
And brought his double goad down upon my head
As I came abreast.

              He was paid back, and more!   285
Swinging my club in this right hand I knocked him
Out of his car, and he rolled on the ground.

                         I killed him.
I killed them all.
Now if that stranger and Laïos were—kin,
Where is a man more miserable than I?   290
More hated by the gods? Citizen and alien alike
Must never shelter me or speak to me—
I must be shunned by all.

                And I myself
Pronounced this malediction upon myself!
Think of it: I have touched you with these hands,   295
These hands that killed your husband. What defilement!
Am I all evil, then? It must be so,
Since I must flee from Thebes, yet never again
See my own countrymen, my own country,
For fear of joining my mother in marriage   300
And killing Polybos, my father.

                   Ah,
If I was created so, born to this fate,

Who could deny the savagery of God?
O holy majesty of heavenly powers!
May I never see that day! Never!   305
Rather let me vanish from the race of men
Than know the abomination destined me!

CHORAGOS: We too, my lord, have felt dismay at this.
But there is hope: you have yet to hear the shepherd.

OEDIPUS: Indeed, I fear no other hope is left me.   310

IOCASTÊ: What do you hope from him when he
comes?

OEDIPUS: This much:
If his account of the murder tallies with yours,
Then I am cleared.

IOCASTÊ: What was it that I said
Of such importance?

OEDIPUS: Why, "marauders," you said,
Killed the King, according to this man's story.   315
If he maintains that still, if there were several,
Clearly the guilt is not mine: I was alone.
But if he says one man, singlehanded, did it,
Then the evidence all points to me.

IOCASTÊ: You may be sure that he said there were several;   320
And can he call back that story now? He cannot.
The whole city heard it as plainly as I.
But suppose he alters some detail of it:
He can not ever show that Laïos' death
Fulfilled the oracle: for Apollo said   325
My child was doomed to kill him; and my child—
Poor baby!—it was my child that died first.
No. From now on, where oracles are concerned,
I would not waste a second thought on any.

OEDIPUS: You may be right.
                                But come: let someone go   330
For the shepherd at once. This matter must be settled.

IOCASTÊ: I will send for him.
I would not wish to cross you in anything,
And surely not in this.—Let us go in.

Exeunt into the palace.

ODE II

STROPHE 1

CHORUS: Let me be reverent in the ways of right,
Lowly the paths I journey on;
Let all my words and actions keep
The laws of the pure universe
From highest Heaven handed down.   *5*
For Heaven is their bright nurse,
Those generations of the realms of light;
Ah, never of mortal kind were they begot,
Nor are they slaves of memory, lost in sleep:
Their Father is greater than Time, and ages not.   *10*

ANTISTROPHE 1

The tyrant is a child of Pride
Who drinks from his great sickening cup
Recklessness and vanity,
Until from his high crest headlong
He plummets to the dust of hope.   *15*
That strong man is not strong.
But let no fair ambition be denied;
May God protect the wrestler for the State
In government, in comely policy,
Who will fear God, and on His ordinance wait.   *20*

STROPHE 2

Haughtiness and the high hand of disdain
Tempt and outrage God's holy law;
And any mortal who dares hold
No immortal Power in awe
Will be caught up in a net of pain: *25*
The price for which his levity is sold.
Let each man take due earnings, then,
And keep his hands from holy things,
And from blasphemy stand apart—
Else the crackling blast of heaven   *30*
Blows on his head, and on his desperate heart;

Though fools will honor impious men,
In their cities no tragic poet sings.

ANTISTROPHE 2

Shall we lose faith in Delphi's obscurities,
We who have heard the world's core   35
Discredited, and the sacred wood
Of Zeus at Elis praised no more?
The deeds and the strange prophecies
Must make a pattern yet to be understood.
Zeus, if indeed you are lord of all,   40
Throned in light over night and day,
Mirror this in your endless mind:
Our masters call the oracle
Words on the wind, and the Delphic vision blind!
Their hearts no longer know Apollo,   45
And reverence for the gods has died away.

SCENE *III*

Enter Iocastê.

IOCASTÊ: Princes of Thebes, it has occurred to me
To visit the altars of the gods, bearing
These branches as a suppliant, and this incense.
Our King is not himself: his noble soul
Is overwrought with fantasies of dread,   5
Else he would consider
The new prophecies in the light of the old.
He will listen to any voice that speaks disaster,
And my advice goes for nothing.

She approaches the altar, right.

                              To you, then, Apollo,
Lycean lord, since you are nearest, I turn in prayer.   10
Receive these offerings, and grant us deliverance
From defilement. Our hearts are heavy with fear
When we see our leader distracted, as helpless sailors

Are terrified by the confusion of their helmsman.

Enter Messenger.

MESSENGER: Friends, no doubt you can direct me: 15
Where shall I find the house of Oedipus,
Or, better still, where is the King himself?
CHORAGOS: It is this very place, stranger; he is inside.
This is his wife and mother of his children.
MESSENGER: I wish her happiness in a happy house,   20
Blest in all the fulfillment of her marriage.
IOCASTÊ: I wish as much for you: your courtesy
Deserves a like good fortune. But now, tell me:
Why have you come? What have you to say to us?
MESSENGER: Good news, my lady, for your house and your
husband.   25
IOCASTÊ: What news? Who sent you here?
MESSENGER: I am from Corinth.
The news I bring ought to mean joy for you,
Though it may be you will find some grief in it.
IOCASTÊ: What is it? How can it touch us in both ways?
MESSENGER: The word is that the people of the Isthmus   30
Intend to call Oedipus to be their king.
IOCASTÊ: But old King Polybos—is he not reigning still?
MESSENGER: No. Death holds him in his sepulchre.
IOCASTÊ: What are you saying? Polybos is dead?
MESSENGER: If I am not telling the truth, may I die myself.   35
IOCASTÊ (*to a Maidservant*):   Go in, go quickly; tell this to your
master.
O riddlers of God's will, where are you now!
This was the man whom Oedipus, long ago,
Feared so, fled so, in dread of destroying him—
But it was another fate by which he died.   40

Enter Oedipus, center.

OEDIPUS: Dearest Iocastê, why have you sent for me?
IOCASTÊ: Listen to what this man says, and then tell me
What has become of the solemn prophecies.
OEDIPUS: Who is this man? What is his news for me?

IOCASTÊ: He has come from Corinth to announce your father's
   death!   *45*
OEDIPUS: Is it true, stranger? Tell me in your own words.
MESSENGER: I can not say it more clearly: the King is dead.
OEDIPUS: Was it by treason? Or by an attack of illness?
MESSENGER: A little thing brings old men to their rest.
OEDIPUS: It was sickness, then?
MESSENGER: Yes, and his many years.   *50*
OEDIPUS: Ah!
   Why should a man respect the Pythian hearth,° or
   Give heed to the birds that jangle above his head?
   They prophesied that I should kill Polybos,
   Kill my own father; but he is dead and buried,   *55*
   And I am here—I never touched him, never,
   Unless he died of grief for my departure,
   And thus, in a sense, through me. No. Polybos
   Has packed the oracles off with him underground.
   They are empty words.
IOCASTÊ: Had I not told you so?   *60*
OEDIPUS: You had; it was my faint heart that betrayed me
IOCASTÊ: From now on never think of those things again.
OEDIPUS: And yet—must I not fear my mother's bed?
IOCASTÊ: Why should anyone in this world be afraid,
   Since Fate rules us and nothing can be foreseen?   *65*
   A man should live only for the present day.
   Have no more fear of sleeping with your mother:
   How many men, in dreams, have lain with their mothers!
   No reasonable man is troubled by such things.
OEDIPUS: That is true; only—   *70*
   If only my mother were not still alive!
   But she is alive. I can not help my dread.
IOCASTÊ: Yet this news of your father's death is wonderful.
OEDIPUS: Wonderful. But I fear the living woman.
MESSENGER: Tell me, who is this woman that you fear?   *75*
OEDIPUS: It is Meropê, man; the wife of King Polybos.
MESSENGER: Meropê? Why should you be afraid of her?

---

52 Pythian hearth where burnt offerings were made at Delphi.

OEDIPUS: An oracle of the gods, a dreadful saying.

MESSENGER: Can you tell me about it or are you sworn to
silence?

OEDIPUS: I can tell you, and I will.   *80*

Apollo said through his prophet that I was the man

Who should marry his own mother, shed his father's blood

With his own hands. And so, for all these years

I have kept clear of Corinth, and no harm has come—

Though it would have been sweet to see my parents again.   *85*

MESSENGER: And is this the fear that drove you out of
Corinth?

OEDIPUS: Would you have me kill my father?

MESSENGER: As for that

You must be reassured by the news I gave you.

OEDIPUS: If you could reassure me, I would reward you.

MESSENGER: I had that in mind, I will confess: I thought   *90*

I could count on you when you returned to Corinth.

OEDIPUS: No: I will never go near my parents again.

MESSENGER: Ah, son, you still do not know what you are
doing—

OEDIPUS: What do you mean? In the name of God tell me!

MESSENGER: —If these are your reasons for not going home.   *95*

OEDIPUS: I tell you, I fear the oracle may come true.

MESSENGER: And guilt may come upon you through your
parents?

OEDIPUS: That is the dread that is always in my heart.

MESSENGER: Can you not see that all your fears are
groundless?

OEDIPUS: How can you say that? They are my parents, surely?   *100*

MESSENGER: Polybos was not your father.

OEDIPUS: Not my father?

MESSENGER: No more your father than the man speaking to
you.

OEDIPUS: But you are nothing to me!

MESSENGER: Neither was he.

OEDIPUS: Then why did he call me son?

MESSENGER: I will tell you:

Long ago he had you from my hands, as a gift.   *105*

OEDIPUS: Then how could he love me so, if I was not his?

MESSENGER: He had no children, and his heart turned to you.

OEDIPUS: What of you? Did you buy me? Did you find me by chance?

MESSENGER: I came upon you in the crooked pass of Kithairon.

OEDIPUS: And what were you doing there?

MESSENGER: Tending my flocks. *110*

OEDIPUS: A wandering shepherd?

MESSENGER: But your savior, son, that day.

OEDIPUS: From what did you save me?

MESSENGER: Your ankles should tell you that.

OEDIPUS: Ah, stranger, why do you speak of that childhood pain?

MESSENGER: I cut the bonds that tied your ankles together.

OEDIPUS: I have had the mark as long as I can remember. *115*

MESSENGER: That was why you were given the name you bear.

OEDIPUS: God! Was it my father or my mother who did it? Tell me!

MESSENGER: I do not know. The man who gave you to me Can tell you better than I. *120*

OEDIPUS: It was not you that found me, but another?

MESSENGER: It was another shepherd gave you to me.

OEDIPUS: Who was he? Can you tell me who he was?

MESSENGER: I think he was said to be one of Laïos' people.

OEDIPUS: You mean the Laïos who was king here years ago? *125*

MESSENGER: Yes; King Laïos; and the man was one of his herdsmen.

OEDIPUS: Is he still alive? Can I see him?

MESSENGER: These men here Know best about such things.

OEDIPUS: Does anyone here Know this shepherd that he is talking about? Have you seen him in the fields, or in the town? *130* If you have, tell me. It is time things were made plain.

CHORAGOS: I think the man he means is that same shepherd

You have already asked to see. Iocastê perhaps
Could tell you something.

OEDIPUS: Do you know anything
About him, Lady? Is he the man we have summoned?   *135*
Is that the man this shepherd means?

IOCASTÊ: Why think of him?
Forget this herdsman. Forget it all.
This talk is a waste of time.

OEDIPUS: How can you say that,
When the clues to my true birth are in my hands?

IOCASTÊ: For God's love, let us have no more questioning!   *140*
Is your life nothing to you?
My own is pain enough for me to bear.

OEDIPUS: You need not worry. Suppose my mother a slave,
And born of slaves: no baseness can touch you.

IOCASTÊ: Listen to me, I beg you: do not do this thing!   *145*

OEDIPUS: I will not listen; the truth must be made known.

IOCASTÊ: Everything that I say is for your own good!

OEDIPUS: My own
good
Snaps my patience, then; I want none of it.

IOCASTÊ: You are fatally wrong! May you never learn who
you are!

OEDIPUS: Go, one of you, and bring the shepherd here.   *150*
Let us leave this woman to brag of her royal name.

IOCASTÊ: Ah, miserable!
That is the only word I have for you now.
That is the only word I can ever have.

                                        Exit into the palace.

CHORAGOS: Why has she left us, Oedipus? Why has she gone   *155*
In such a passion of sorrow? I fear this silence:
Something dreadful may come of it.

OEDIPUS: Let it come!
However base my birth, I must know about it.
The Queen, like a woman, is perhaps ashamed
To think of my low origin. But I   *160*
Am a child of Luck; I can not be dishonored.

Luck is my mother; the passing months, my brothers,
Have seen me rich and poor.
                              If this is so,
How could I wish that I were someone else?
How could I not be glad to know my birth?   *165*

ODE III

STROPHE

CHORUS: If ever the coming time were known
          To my heart's pondering,
          Kithairon, now by Heaven I see the torches
          At the festival of the next full moon,
          And see the dance, and hear the choir sing   *5*
          A grace to your gentle shade:
          Mountain where Oedipus was found,
          O mountain guard of a noble race!
          May the god who heals us lend his aid,
          And let that glory come to pass   *10*
          For our king's cradling-ground.

ANTISTROPHE

          Of the nymphs that flower beyond the years,
          Who bore you, royal child,
          To Pan of the hills or the timberline Apollo,
          Cold in delight where the upland clears,   *15*
          Or Hermês for whom Kyllenê's° heights are piled?
          Or flushed as evening cloud,
          Great Dionysos, roamer of mountains,
          He—was it he who found you there,
          And caught you up in his own proud   *20*
          Arms from the sweet god-ravisher
          Who laughed by the Muses' fountains?

16 Kyllenê a sacred mountain of Hermês, the messenger of the gods.

Scene IV

OEDIPUS: Sirs: though I do not know the man,
I think I see him coming, this shepherd we want:
He is old, like our friend here, and the men
Bringing him seem to be servants of my house.
But you can tell, if you have ever seen him.   *5*

Enter Shepherd escorted by servants.

CHORAGOS: I know him, he was Laïos' man. You can trust
him.

OEDIPUS: Tell me first, you from Corinth: is this the shepherd
We were discussing?

MESSENGER: This is the very man.

OEDIPUS (*to Shepherd*):   Come here. No, look at me. You must
answer
Everything I ask.—You belonged to Laïos?   *10*

SHEPHERD: Yes: born his slave, brought up in his house.

OEDIPUS: Tell me: what kind of work did you do for him?

SHEPHERD: I was a shepherd of his, most of my life.

OEDIPUS: Where mainly did you go for pasturage?

SHEPHERD: Sometimes Kithairon, sometimes the hills near-by.   *15*

OEDIPUS: Do you remember ever seeing this man out there?

SHEPHERD: What would he be doing there? This man?

OEDIPUS: This man standing here. Have you ever seen him
before?

SHEPHERD: No. At least, not to my recollection.

MESSENGER: And that is not strange, my lord. But I'll refresh   *20*
His memory: he must remember when we two
Spent three whole seasons together, March to September,
On Kithairon or thereabouts. He had two flocks;
I had one. Each autumn I'd drive mine home
And he would go back with his to Laïos' sheepfold.—   *25*
Is this not true, just as I have described it?

SHEPHERD: True, yes; but it was all so long ago.

MESSENGER: Well, then: do you remember, back in those days
That you gave me a baby boy to bring up as my own?

SHEPHERD: What if I did? What are you trying to say?   *30*

MESSENGER: King Oedipus was once that little child.

SHEPHERD: Damn you, hold your tongue!

OEDIPUS: No more of that!

It is your tongue needs watching, not this man's.

SHEPHERD: My King, my Master, what is it I have done wrong?

OEDIPUS: You have not answered his question about the boy.   *35*

SHEPHERD: He does not know . . . He is only making

trouble . . .

OEDIPUS: Come, speak plainly, or it will go hard with you.

SHEPHERD: In God's name, do not torture an old man!

OEDIPUS: Come here, one of you; bind his arms behind him.

SHEPHERD: Unhappy king! What more do you wish to learn?   *40*

OEDIPUS: Did you give this man the child he speaks of?

SHEPHERD: I did.

And I would to God I had died that very day.

OEDIPUS: You will die now unless you speak the truth.

SHEPHERD: Yet if I speak the truth, I am worse than dead.

OEDIPUS: Very well; since you insist upon delaying—   *45*

SHEPHERD: No! I have told you already that I gave him the

boy.

OEDIPUS: Where did you get him? From your house? From

somewhere else?

SHEPHERD: Not from mine, no. A man gave him to me.

OEDIPUS: Is that man here? Do you know whose slave he was?

SHEPHERD: For God's love, my King, do not ask me any more!   *50*

OEDIPUS: You are a dead man if I have to ask you again.

SHEPHERD: Then . . . Then the child was from the palace of

Laïos.

OEDIPUS: A slave child? or a child of his own line?

SHEPHERD: Ah, I am on the brink of dreadful speech!

OEDIPUS: And I of dreadful hearing. Yet I must hear.   *55*

SHEPHERD: If you must be told, then . . .

                              They said it was

Laïos' child;

But it is your wife who can tell you about that.

OEDIPUS: My wife!—Did she give it to you?

SHEPHERD: My lord, she did.

OEDIPUS: Do you know why?

SHEPHERD: I was told to get rid of it.

OEDIPUS: An unspeakable mother!

SHEPHERD: There had been

prophecies . . .   *60*

OEDIPUS: Tell me.

SHEPHERD: It was said that the boy would kill his own father.

OEDIPUS: Then why did you give him over to this old man?

SHEPHERD: I pitied the baby, my King,

And I thought that this man would take him far away   *65*

To his own country.

He saved him—but for what a fate!

For if you are what this man says you are,

No man living is more wretched than Oedipus.

OEDIPUS: Ah God!

It was true!

All the prophecies!

—Now,   *70*

O Light, may I look on you for the last time!

I, Oedipus,

Oedipus, damned in his birth, in his marriage damned,

Damned in the blood he shed with his own hand!

                              He rushes into the palace.

ODE IV

STROPHE 1

CHORUS: Alas for the seed of men.

What measure shall I give these generations

That breathe on the void and are void

And exist and do not exist?

Who bears more weight of joy   *5*

Than mass of sunlight shifting in images,

Or who shall make his thought stay on

That down time drifts away?

Your splendor is all fallen.

O naked brow of wrath and tears,   *10*

O change of Oedipus!

I who saw your days call no man blest—

Your great days like ghosts gone.

ANTISTROPHE 1

That mind was a strong bow.
Deep, how deep you drew it then, hard archer,   15
At a dim fearful range,
And brought dear glory down!
You overcame the stranger—
The virgin with her hooking lion claws—
And though death sang, stood like a tower   20
To make pale Thebes take heart.
Fortress against our sorrow!
True king, giver of laws,
Majestic Oedipus!
No prince in Thebes had ever such renown,   25
No prince won such grace of power.

STROPHE 2

And now of all men ever known
Most pitiful is this man's story:
His fortunes are most changed, his state
Fallen to a low slave's   30
Ground under bitter fate.
O Oedipus, most royal one!
The great door that expelled you to the light
Gave at night—ah, gave night to your glory:
As to the father, to the fathering son.   35
All understood too late.
How could that queen whom Laïos won,
The garden that he harrowed at his height,
Be silent when that act was done?

ANTISTROPHE 2

But all eyes fail before time's eye,   40
All actions come to justice there.
Though never willed, though far down the deep past,
Your bed, your dread sirings,
Are brought to book at last.
Child by Laïos doomed to die,   45

Then doomed to lose that fortunate little death,
Would God you never took breath in this air
That with my wailing lips I take to cry:
For I weep the world's outcast.
I was blind, and now I can tell why: 50
Asleep, for you had given ease of breath
To Thebes, while the false years went by.

ÉXODOS°

Enter, from the palace, Second Messenger.

SECOND MESSENGER: Elders of Thebes, most honored in this
    land,
    What horrors are yours to see and hear, what weight
    Of sorrow to be endured, if, true to your birth,
    You venerate the line of Labdakos!
    I think neither Istros nor Phasis, those great rivers,   5
    Could purify this place of the corruption
    It shelters now, or soon must bring to light—
    Evil not done unconsciously, but willed.
    The greatest griefs are those we cause ourselves.
CHORAGOS: Surely, friend, we have grief enough already;   10
    What new sorrow do you mean?
SECOND MESSENGER: The Queen is dead.
CHORAGOS: Iocastê? Dead? But at whose hand?
SECOND MESSENGER: Her own.
    The full horror of what happened, you can not know,
    For you did not see it; but I, who did, will tell you
    As clearly as I can how she met her death.   15

    When she had left us,
    In passionate silence, passing through the court,
    She ran to her apartment in the house,
    Her hair clutched by the fingers of both hands.
    She closed the doors behind her; then, by that bed   20

Éxodos final scene (or *episodos*).

Where long ago the fatal son was conceived—
That son who should bring about his father's death—
We heard her call upon Laïos, dead so many years,
And heard her wail for the double fruit of her marriage,
A husband by her husband, children by her child.   25

Exactly how she died I do not know:
For Oedipus burst in moaning and would not let us
Keep vigil to the end: it was by him
As he stormed about the room that our eyes were caught.
From one to another of us he went, begging a sword,   30
Cursing the wife who was not his wife, the mother
Whose womb had carried his own children and himself.
I do not know: it was none of us aided him,
But surely one of the gods was in control!
For with a dreadful cry   35
He hurled his weight, as though wrenched out of himself,
At the twin doors: the bolts gave, and he rushed in.
And there we saw her hanging, her body swaying
From the cruel cord she had noosed about her neck.
A great sob broke from him, heartbreaking to hear,   40
As he loosed the rope and lowered her to the ground.

I would blot out from my mind what happened next!
For the King ripped from her gown the golden brooches
That were her ornament, and raised them, and plunged
them down
Straight into his own eyeballs, crying, "No more,   45
No more shall you look on the misery about me,
The horrors of my own doing! Too long you have known
The faces of those whom I should never have seen,
Too long been blind to those for whom I was searching!
From this hour, go in darkness!" And as he spoke,   50
He struck at his eyes—not once, but many times;
And the blood spattered his beard,
Bursting from his ruined sockets like red hail.

So from the unhappiness of two this evil has sprung,
A curse on the man and woman alike. The old   55
Happiness of the house of Labdakos

Was happiness enough: where is it today?
It is all wailing and ruin, disgrace, death—all
The misery of mankind that has a name—
And it is wholly and for ever theirs.   60
CHORAGOS: Is he in agony still? Is there no rest for him?
SECOND MESSENGER: He is calling for someone to lead him
   to the gates
So that all the children of Kadmos may look upon
His father's murderer, his mother's—no,
I can not say it!
             And then he will leave Thebes,   65
Self-exiled, in order that the curse
Which he himself pronounced may depart from the house.
He is weak, and there is none to lead him,
So terrible is his suffering.
             But you will see:
Look, the doors are opening; in a moment   70
You will see a thing that would crush a heart of stone.

The central door is opened; Oedipus, blinded, is led in.

CHORAGOS: Dreadful indeed for men to see.
   Never have my own eyes
   Looked on a sight so full of fear.
   Oedipus!   75
   What madness came upon you, what daemon
   Leaped on your life with heavier
   Punishment than a mortal man can bear?
   No: I can not even
   Look at you, poor ruined one.   80
   And I would speak, question, ponder,
   If I were able. No.
   You make me shudder.
OEDIPUS: God. God.
   Is there a sorrow greater?   85
   Where shall I find harbor in this world?
   My voice is hurled far on a dark wind.
   What has God done to me?
CHORAGOS: Too terrible to think of, or to see.

STROPHE 1

OEDIPUS: O cloud of night,   *90*
    Never to be turned away: night coming on,
    I can not tell how: night like a shroud!
    My fair winds brought me here.
                                  Oh God. Again
    The pain of the spikes where I had sight,
    The flooding pain   *95*
    Of memory, never to be gouged out.
CHORAGOS: This is not strange.
    You suffer it all twice over, remorse in pain,
    Pain in remorse.

ANTISTROPHE 1

OEDIPUS: Ah dear friend   *100*
    Are you faithful even yet, you alone?
    Are you still standing near me, will you stay here,
    Patient, to care for the blind?
                              The blind man!
    Yet even blind I know who it is attends me,
    By the voice's tone—   *105*
    Though my new darkness hide the comforter.
CHORAGOS: Oh fearful act!
    What god was it drove you to rake black
    Night across your eyes?

STROPHE 2

OEDIPUS: Apollo. Apollo. Dear   *110*
    Children, the god was Apollo.
    He brought my sick, sick fate upon me.
    But the blinding hand was my own!
    How could I bear to see
    When all my sight was horror everywhere?   *115*
CHORAGOS: Everywhere; that is true.
OEDIPUS: And now what is left?
    Images? Love? A greeting even,
    Sweet to the senses? Is there anything?

Ah, no, friends: lead me away. 120
Lead me away from Thebes.
            Lead the great wreck
And hell of Oedipus, whom the gods hate.
CHORAGOS: Your fate is clear, you are not blind to that.
Would God you had never found it out!

ANTISTROPHE 2

OEDIPUS: Death take the man who unbound 125
    My feet on that hillside
    And delivered me from death to life! What life?
    If only I had died,
    This weight of monstrous doom
    Could not have dragged me and my darlings down. 130
CHORAGOS: I would have wished the same.
OEDIPUS: Oh never to have come here
    With my father's blood upon me! Never
    To have been the man they call his mother's husband!
    Oh accurst! Oh child of evil, 135
    To have entered that wretched bed—
                the selfsame one!
    More primal than sin itself, this fell to me.
CHORAGOS: I do not know how I can answer you.
    You were better dead than alive and blind.
OEDIPUS: Do not counsel me any more. This punishment 140
    That I have laid upon myself is just.
    If I had eyes,
    I do not know how I could bear the sight
    Of my father, when I came to the house of Death,
    Or my mother: for I have sinned against them both 145
    So vilely that I could not make my peace
    By strangling my own life.
                Or do you think my children,
    Born as they were born, would be sweet to my eyes?
    Ah never, never! Nor this town with its high walls,
    Nor the holy images of the gods.
                For I, 150
    Thrice miserable!—Oedipus, noblest of all the line

Of Kadmos, have condemned myself to enjoy
These things no more, by my own malediction
Expelling that man whom the gods declared
To be a defilement in the house of Laïos.   155
After exposing the rankness of my own guilt,
How could I look men frankly in the eyes?
No, I swear it,
If I could have stifled my hearing at its source,
I would have done it and made all this body   160
A tight cell of misery, blank to light and sound:
So I should have been safe in a dark agony
Beyond all recollection.
                              Ah Kithairon!
Why did you shelter me? When I was cast upon you,
Why did I not die? Then I should never   165
Have shown the world my execrable birth.
Ah Polybos! Corinth, city that I believed
The ancient seat of my ancestors: how fair
I seemed, your child! And all the while this evil
Was cancerous within me!
                              For I am sick   170
In my daily life, sick in my origin.
O three roads, dark ravine, woodland and way
Where three roads met: you, drinking my father's blood,
My own blood, spilled by my own hand: can you remember
The unspeakable things I did there, and the things   175
I went on from there to do?
                              O marriage, marriage!
The act that engendered me, and again the act
Performed by the son in the same bed—
                              Ah, the net
Of incest, mingling fathers, brothers, sons,
With brides, wives, mothers: the last evil   180
That can be known by men: no tongue can say
How evil!
            No. For the love of God, conceal me
Somewhere far from Thebes; or kill me; or hurl me
Into the sea, away from men's eyes for ever.

Come, lead me. You need not fear to touch me. 185
Of all men, I alone can bear this guilt.

Enter Creon.

CHORAGOS: We are not the ones to decide; but Creon here
May fitly judge of what you ask. He only
Is left to protect the city in your place.
OEDIPUS: Alas, how can I speak to him? What right have I 190
To beg his courtesy whom I have deeply wronged?
CREON: I have not come to mock you, Oedipus,
Or to reproach you, either.
(*To Attendants.*) —You, standing there:
If you have lost all respect for man's dignity,
At least respect the flame of Lord Helios: 195
Do not allow this pollution to show itself
Openly here, an affront to the earth
And Heaven's rain and the light of day. No, take him
Into the house as quickly as you can.
For it is proper 200
That only the close kindred see his grief.
OEDIPUS: I pray you in God's name, since your courtesy
Ignores my dark expectation, visiting
With mercy this man of all men most execrable:
Give me what I ask—for your good, not for mine. 205
CREON: And what is it that you would have me do?
OEDIPUS: Drive me out of this country as quickly as may be
To a place where no human voice can ever greet me.
CREON: I should have done that before now—only,
God's will had not been wholly revealed to me. 210
OEDIPUS: But his command is plain: the parricide
Must be destroyed. I am that evil man.
CREON: That is the sense of it, yes; but as things are,
We had best discover clearly what is to be done.
OEDIPUS: You would learn more about a man like me? 215
CREON: You are ready now to listen to the god.
OEDIPUS: I will listen. But it is to you
That I must turn for help. I beg you, hear me.
The woman in there—

Give her whatever funeral you think proper: 220
She is your sister.
        —But let me go, Creon!
Let me purge my father's Thebes of the pollution
Of my living here, and go out to the wild hills,
To Kithairon, that has won such fame with me,
The tomb my mother and father appointed for me, 225
And let me die there, as they willed I should.
And yet I know
Death will not ever come to me through sickness
Or in any natural way: I have been preserved
For some unthinkable fate. But let that be. 230
As for my sons, you need not care for them.
They are men, they will find some way to live.
But my poor daughters, who have shared my table,
Who never before have been parted from their father—
Take care of them, Creon; do this for me. 235
And will you let me touch them with my hands
A last time, and let us weep together?
Be kind, my lord,
Great prince, be kind!
             Could I but touch them,
They would be mine again, as when I had my eyes. 240

Enter Antigonê and Ismene, attended.

Ah, God!
Is it my dearest children I hear weeping?
Has Creon pitied me and sent my daughters?

CREON: Yes, Oedipus: I knew that they were dear to you
In the old days, and know you must love them still. 245

OEDIPUS: May God bless you for this—and be a friendlier
Guardian to you than he has been to me!
Children, where are you?
Come quickly to my hands: they are your brother's—
Hands that have brought your father's once clear eyes 250
To this way of seeing—
               Ah dearest ones,
I had neither sight nor knowledge then, your father

By the woman who was the source of his own life!
And I weep for you—having no strength to see you—,
I weep for you when I think of the bitterness   255
That men will visit upon you all your lives.
What homes, what festivals can you attend
Without being forced to depart again in tears?
And when you come to marriageable age,
Where is the man, my daughters, who would dare   260
Risk the bane that lies on all my children?
Is there any evil wanting? Your father killed
His father; sowed the womb of her who bore him;
Engendered you at the fount of his own existence!
That is what they will say of you.

                                Then, whom   265
Can you ever marry? There are no bridegrooms for you,
And your lives must wither away in sterile dreaming.
O Creon, son of Menoikeus!
You are the only father my daughters have,
Since we, their parents, are both of us gone for ever.   270
They are your own blood: you will not let them
Fall into beggary and loneliness;
You will keep them from the miseries that are mine!
Take pity on them; see, they are only children,
Friendless except for you. Promise me this,   275
Great Prince, and give me your hand in token of it.

Creon clasps his right hand.

Children:
I could say much, if you could understand me,
But as it is, I have only this prayer for you:
Live where you can, be as happy as you can—   280
Happier, please God, than God has made your father!
CREON: Enough. You have wept enough. Now go within.
OEDIPUS: I must; but it is hard.
CREON: Time eases all things.
OEDIPUS: But you must promise—
CREON: Say what you desire.
OEDIPUS: Send me from Thebes!

CREON: God grant that I may!   *285*
OEDIPUS: But since God hates me . . .
CREON: No, he will grant your
wish.
OEDIPUS: You promise?
CREON: I cannot speak beyond my knowledge.
OEDIPUS: Then lead me in.
CREON: Come now, and leave your children.
OEDIPUS: No! Do not take them from me!
CREON: Think no longer
That you are in command here, but rather think   *290*
How, when you were, you served your own destruction.

*Exeunt into the house all but the Chorus; the Choragos
chants directly to the audience.*

CHORAGOS: Men of Thebes: look upon Oedipus.
This is the king who solved the famous riddle
And towered up, most powerful of men.
No mortal eyes but looked on him with envy,   *295*
Yet in the end ruin swept over him.
Let every man in mankind's frailty
Consider his last day; and let none
Presume on his good fortune until he find
Life, at his death, a memory without pain.   *300*

William Shakespeare (1564–1616), the supreme writer of English, was born, baptized, and buried in the market town of Stratford-on-Avon, eighty miles from London. Son of a glove maker and merchant who was high bailiff (or mayor) of the town, he probably attended grammar school and learned to read Latin authors in the original. At eighteen he married Anne Hathaway, twenty-six, by whom he had three children, including twins. By 1592 he had become well-known and envied as an actor and playwright in London. From 1594 until he retired, he belonged to the same theatrical company, the Lord Chamberlain's Men (later renamed the King's Men in honor of their patron, James I), for whom he wrote thirty-six plays—some of them, such as Hamlet *and* King Lear, *profound reworkings of old plays. As an actor, Shakespeare is believed to have played supporting roles, such as Hamlet's father's ghost. The company prospered, moved into the Globe Theater in 1599, and in 1608 bought the fashionable Blackfriars as well; Shakespeare owned an interest in both theaters. When plagues shut down the theaters from 1592 to 1594, Shakespeare turned to story poems; his great* sonnets *(published only in 1609) probably also date from the 1590s. Plays were regarded as entertainments of little literary merit and Shakespeare did not bother to supervise their publication. After* The Tempest *(1611), the last play entirely from his hand, he retired to Stratford, where since 1597 he had owned the second largest house in town. Most critics agree that when he wrote* Othello *(c. 1604), Shakespeare was at the height of his powers.*

William Shakespeare

The Tragedy of Othello, The Moor of Venice

CHARACTERS

Othello, the Moor
Brabantio, [a senator,] father to Desdemona
Cassio, an honorable lieutenant [to Othello]
Iago, [Othello's ancient,] a villain

NOTE ON THE TEXT: This text of *Othello* is based on that of the First Folio, or large collection, of Shakespeare's plays (1623). But there are many differences between the Folio text and that of the play's first printing in the Quarto, or small volume, of 1621 (eighteen or nineteen years after the play's first performance). Some readings from the Quarto are included. For the reader's convenience, some material has been added by the editor, David Bevington (some indications of scene, some stage directions). Such additions are enclosed in brackets. Mr. Bevington's text and notes were prepared for his book, *The Complete Works of Shakespeare*, 4th ed. (New York: HarperCollins, 1992).

Edited by David Bevington

Roderigo, a gulled gentleman
Duke of Venice
Senators [of Venice]
Montano, governor of Cyprus
Gentlemen of Cyprus
Lodovico and Gratiano, [kinsmen to Brabantio,] two noble Venetians
Sailors
Clown
Desdemona, [daughter to Brabantio and] wife to Othello
Emilia, wife to Iago
Bianca, a courtesan [and mistress to Cassio]
[*A Messenger*
A Herald
A Musician
Servants, Attendants, Officers, Senators, Musicians, Gentlemen]

[Scene: *Venice; a seaport in Cyprus*]

ACT I

SCENE I [VENICE. A STREET.]

Enter Roderigo and Iago.

RODERIGO: Tush, never tell me!° I take it much unkindly
    That thou, Iago, who hast had my purse
    As if the strings were thine, shouldst know of this.°
IAGO: 'Sblood,° but you'll not hear me.
    If ever I did dream of such a matter,   5
    Abhor me.
RODERIGO: Thou toldst me thou didst hold him in thy hate.
IAGO: Despise me
    If I do not. Three great ones of the city,
    In personal suit to make me his lieutenant,   10
    Off-capped to him;° and by the faith of man,

---

1 never tell me (An expression of incredulity, like "tell me another one.")   **3 this** i.e., Desdemona's elopement   **4 'Sblood** by His (Christ's) blood   **11 him** i.e., Othello

I know my price, I am worth no worse a place.
But he, as loving his own pride and purposes,
Evades them with a bombast circumstance°
Horribly stuffed with epithets of war,°   15
And, in conclusion,
Nonsuits° my mediators. For, "Certes,"° says he,
"I have already chose my officer."
And what was he?
Forsooth, a great arithmetician,°   20
One Michael Cassio, a Florentine,
A fellow almost damned in a fair wife,°
That never set a squadron in the field
Nor the division of a battle° knows
More than a spinster°—unless the bookish theoric,°   25
Wherein the togaed° consuls° can propose°
As masterly as he. Mere prattle without practice
Is all his soldiership. But he, sir, had th' election;
And I, of whom his° eyes had seen the proof
At Rhodes, at Cyprus, and on other grounds   30
Christened° and heathen, must be beeled and calmed°
By debitor and creditor.° This countercaster,°
He, in good time,° must his lieutenant be,
And I—God bless the mark!°—his Moorship's ancient.°
RODERIGO: By heaven, I rather would have been his hangman.°   35
IAGO: Why, there's no remedy. 'Tis the curse of service;
Preferment° goes by letter and affection,°

---

14 bombast circumstance wordy evasion. (Bombast is cotton padding.)   **15 epithets of war** military expressions   **17 Nonsuits** rejects the petition of.   **Certes** certainly   **20 arithmetician** i.e., a man whose military knowledge is merely theoretical, based on books of tactics   **22 A . . . wife** (Cassio does not seem to be married, but his counterpart in Shakespeare's source does have a woman in his house. See also Act IV, Scene i, line 127.)   **24 division of a battle** disposition of a military unit   **25 a spinster** i.e., a housewife, one whose regular occupation is spinning.   **theoric** theory   **26 togaed** wearing the toga.   **consuls** counselors, senators.   **propose** discuss   **29 his** i.e., Othello's   **31 Christened** Christian.   **beeled and calmed** left to leeward without wind, becalmed. (A sailing metaphor.)   **32 debitor and creditor** (A name for a system of bookkeeping, here used as a contemptuous nickname for Cassio.)   **countercaster** i.e., bookkeeper, one who tallies with *counters*, or "metal disks." (Said contemptuously.)   **33 in good time** opportunely, i.e., forsooth   **34 God bless the mark** (Perhaps originally a formula to ward off evil; here an expression of impatience.)   **ancient** standard-bearer, ensign   **35 his hangman** the executioner of him   **37 Preferment** promotion.   **letter and affection** personal influence and favoritism

And not by old gradation,° where each second
Stood heir to th' first. Now, sir, be judge yourself
Whether I in any just term° am affined°   *40*
To love the Moor.

RODERIGO: I would not follow him then.

IAGO: O sir, content you.°
I follow him to serve my turn upon him.
We cannot all be masters, nor all masters   *45*
Cannot be truly° followed. You shall mark
Many a duteous and knee-crooking knave
That, doting on his own obsequious bondage,
Wears out his time, much like his master's ass,
For naught but provender, and when he's old, cashiered.° *50*
Whip me° such honest knaves. Others there are
Who, trimmed in forms and visages of duty,°
Keep yet their hearts attending on themselves,
And, throwing but shows of service on their lords,
Do well thrive by them, and when they have lined their coats,° *55*
Do themselves homage.° These fellows have some soul,
And such a one do I profess myself. For, sir,
It is as sure as you are Roderigo,
Were I the Moor I would not be Iago.°
In following him, I follow but myself—   *60*
Heaven is my judge, not I for love and duty,
But seeming so for my peculiar° end.
For when my outward action doth demonstrate
The native° act and figure° of my heart
In compliment extern,° 'tis not long after   *65*
But I will wear my heart upon my sleeve
For daws° to peck at. I am not what I am.°

---

38 old gradation step-by-step seniority, the traditional way **40 term** respect. **affined** bound
43 content you don't you worry about that **46 truly** faithfully **50 cashiered** dismissed from service **51 Whip me** whip, as far as I'm concerned **52 trimmed . . . duty** dressed up in the mere
form and show of dutifulness **55 lined their coats** i.e., stuffed their purses **56 Do themselves
homage** i.e., attend to self-interest solely **59 Were . . . Iago** i.e., if I were able to assume command, I certainly would not choose to remain a subordinate, or, I would keep a suspicious eye on a
flattering subordinate **62 peculiar** particular, personal **64 native** innate. **figure** shape, intent
65 compliment extern outward show. (Conforming in this case to the inner workings and intention
of the heart.) **67 daws** small crowlike birds, proverbially stupid and avaricious. **I am not what I
am** i.e., I am not one who wears his heart on his sleeve

RODERIGO: What a full° fortune does the thick-lips° owe°
If he can carry 't thus!°

IAGO: Call up her father.
Rouse him, make after him, poison his delight,   70
Proclaim him in the streets; incense her kinsmen,
And, though he in a fertile climate dwell,
Plague him with flies.° Though that his joy be joy,°
Yet throw such changes of vexation° on 't
As it may° lose some color.°   75

RODERIGO: Here is her father's house. I'll call aloud.

IAGO: Do, with like timorous° accent and dire yell
As when, by night and negligence,° the fire
Is spied in populous cities.

RODERIGO: What ho, Brabantio! Signor Brabantio, ho!   80

IAGO: Awake! What ho, Brabantio! Thieves, thieves, thieves!
Look to your house, your daughter, and your bags!
Thieves, thieves!

Brabantio [enters] above [at a window].°

BRABANTIO: What is the reason of this terrible summons?
What is the matter° there?   85

RODERIGO: Signor, is all your family within?

IAGO: Are your doors locked?

BRABANTIO: Why, wherefore ask you this?

IAGO: Zounds,° sir, you're robbed. For shame, put on your gown!
Your heart is burst; you have lost half your soul.
Even now, now, very now, an old black ram   90
Is tupping° your white ewe. Arise, arise!
Awake the snorting° citizens with the bell,
Or else the devil° will make a grandsire of you.
Arise, I say!

---

68 full swelling.   **thick-lips** (Elizabethans often applied the term "Moor" to Negroes.)   **owe** own
69 carry 't thus carry this off   **72-73 though . . . flies** though he seems prosperous and happy
now, vex him with misery   **73 Though . . . be joy** although he seems fortunate and happy.
(Repeats the idea of line 72.)   **74 changes of vexation** vexing changes   **75 As it may** that may
cause it to.   **some color** some of its fresh gloss   **77 timorous** frightening   **78 and negligence**
i.e., by negligence   **83 [s.d.] at a window** (This stage direction, from the Quarto, probably calls for
an appearance on the gallery above and rearstage.)   **85 the matter** your business   **88 Zounds** by
His (Christ's) wounds   **91 tupping** covering, copulating with. (Said of sheep.)   **92 snorting** snoring   **93 the devil** (The devil was conventionally pictured as black.)

BRABANTIO: What, have you lost your wits?

RODERIGO: Most reverend signor, do you know my voice?   95

BRABANTIO: Not I. What are you?

RODERIGO: My name is Roderigo.

BRABANTIO: The worser welcome.
I have charged thee not to haunt about my doors.
In honest plainness thou hast heard me say   100
My daughter is not for thee; and now, in madness,
Being full of supper and distempering° drafts,
Upon malicious bravery° dost thou come
To start° my quiet.

RODERIGO: Sir, sir, sir—

BRABANTIO: But thou must needs be sure   105
My spirits and my place° have in° their power
To make this bitter to thee.

RODERIGO: Patience, good sir.

BRABANTIO: What tell'st thou me of robbing? This is Venice;
My house is not a grange.°

RODERIGO: Most grave Brabantio,
In simple° and pure soul I come to you.   110

IAGO: Zounds, sir, you are one of those that will not serve God
if the devil bid you. Because we come to do you service and
you think we are ruffians, you'll have your daughter covered
with a Barbary° horse; you'll have your nephews° neigh to
you; you'll have coursers° for cousins° and jennets° for germans.°   115

BRABANTIO: What profane wretch art thou?

IAGO: I am one, sir, that comes to tell you your daughter and
the Moor are now making the beast with two backs.

BRABANTIO: Thou art a villain.

IAGO: You are—a senator.°

BRABANTIO: This thou shalt answer.° I know thee, Roderigo.

---

102 distempering intoxicating   **103 Upon malicious bravery** with hostile intent to defy me
104 start startle, disrupt   **106 My spirits and my place** my temperament and my authority of office.   **have in** have it in   **109 grange** isolated country house   **110 simple** sincere   **113 Barbary**
from northern Africa (and hence associated with Othello).   **nephews** i.e., grandsons
114 coursers powerful horses.   **cousins** kinsmen.   **jennets** small Spanish horses.   **germans** near
relatives   **118 a senator** (Said with mock politeness, as though the word itself were an insult.)
119 answer be held accountable for

RODERIGO: Sir, I will answer anything. But I beseech you,   120
  If't be your pleasure and most wise° consent—
  As partly I find it is—that your fair daughter,
  At this odd-even° and dull watch o' the night,
  Transported with° no worse nor better guard
  But with a knave° of common hire, a gondolier,   125
  To the gross clasps of a lascivious Moor—
  If this be known to you and your allowance°
  We then have done you bold and saucy° wrongs.
  But if you know not this, my manners tell me
  We have your wrong rebuke. Do not believe   130
  That, from° the sense of all civility,°
  I thus would play and trifle with your reverence.°
  Your daughter, if you have not given her leave,
  I say again, hath made a gross revolt,
  Tying her duty, beauty, wit,° and fortunes   135
  In an extravagant° and wheeling° stranger°
  Of here and everywhere. Straight° satisfy yourself.
  If she be in her chamber or your house,
  Let loose on me the justice of the state
  For thus deluding you.   140
BRABANTIO: Strike on the tinder,° ho!
  Give me a taper! Call up all my people!
  This accident° is not unlike my dream.
  Belief of it oppresses me already.
  Light, I say, light!   *Exit* [*above*].
IAGO: Farewell, for I must leave you.   145
  It seems not meet° nor wholesome to my place°
  To be producted°—as, if I stay, I shall—
  Against the Moor. For I do know the state,
  However this may gall° him with some check,°

---

121 **wise** well-informed   123 **odd-even** between one day and the next, i.e., about midnight
124 **with** by   125 **But with a knave** than by a low fellow, a servant   127 **allowance** permission
128 **saucy** insolent   131 **from** contrary to.   **civility** good manners, decency   132 **your reverence**
the respect due to you   135 **wit** intelligence   136 **extravagant** expatriate, wandering far from
home.   **wheeling** roving about, vagabond.   **stranger** foreigner   137 **Straight** straightway
141 **tinder** charred linen ignited by a spark from flint and steel, used to light torches or tapers (lines
142, 167)   143 **accident** occurrence, event   146 **meet** fitting.   **place** position (as ensign)
147 **producted** produced (as a witness)   149 **gall** rub; oppress.   **check** rebuke

Cannot with safety cast° him, for he's embarked° 150
With such loud reason° to the Cyprus wars,
Which even now stands in act,° that, for their souls,°
Another of his fathom° they have none
To lead their business; in which regard,°
Though I do hate him as I do hell pains, 155
Yet for necessity of present life°
I must show out a flag and sign of love,
Which is indeed but sign. That you shall surely find him,
Lead to the Sagittary° the raisèd search,°
And there will I be with him. So farewell.   *Exit.* 160

*Enter [below] Brabantio [in his nightgown°] with servants
and torches.*

BRABANTIO: It is too true an evil. Gone she is;
And what's to come of my despisèd time°
Is naught but bitterness. Now, Roderigo,
Where didst thou see her?—O unhappy girl!—
With the Moor, sayst thou?—Who would be a father!— 165
How didst thou know 'twas she?—O, she deceives me
Past thought!—What said she to you?—Get more tapers.
Raise all my kindred.—Are they married, think you?
RODERIGO: Truly, I think they are.
BRABANTIO: O heaven! How got she out? O treason of the
blood! 170
Fathers, from hence trust not your daughters' minds
By what you see them act. Is there not charms°
By which the property° of youth and maidhood
May be abused?° Have you not read, Roderigo,
Of some such thing?
RODERIGO: Yes, sir, I have indeed. 175

---

150 cast dismiss.   embarked engaged   151 loud reason unanimous shout of confirmation (in the
Senate)   152 stands in act are going on.   for their souls to save themselves   153 fathom i.e.,
ability, depth of experience   154 in which regard out of regard for which   156 life livelihood
159 Sagittary (An inn or house where Othello and Desdemona are staying, named for its sign of
Sagittarius, or Centaur.)   raisèd search search party roused out of sleep   160 [s.d.] nightgown
dressing gown. (This costuming is specified in the Quarto text.)   162 time i.e., remainder of life
172 charms spells   173 property special quality, nature   174 abused deceived

BRABANTIO: Call up my brother.—O, would you had had her!—
　Some one way, some another.—Do you know
　Where we may apprehend her and the Moor?
RODERIGO: I think I can discover° him, if you please
　To get good guard and go along with me.　　　　　　*180*
BRABANTIO: Pray you, lead on. At every house I'll call;
　I may command° at most.—Get weapons, ho!
　And raise some special officers of night.—
　On, good Roderigo. I will deserve° your pains.

　　　　　　　　　　　　　　　　　　Exeunt.

SCENE II [VENICE. ANOTHER STREET, BEFORE
OTHELLO'S LODGINGS.]

　Enter Othello, Iago, attendants with torches.

IAGO: Though in the trade of war I have slain men,
　Yet do I hold it very stuff° o' the conscience
　To do no contrived° murder. I lack iniquity
　Sometimes to do me service. Nine or ten times
　I had thought t' have yerked° him° here under the ribs.　　*5*
OTHELLO: 'Tis better as it is.
IAGO:　　　　　　　　　　Nay, but he prated,
　And spoke such scurvy and provoking terms
　Against your honor
　That, with the little godliness I have,
　I did full hard forbear him.° But, I pray you, sir,　　　　*10*
　Are you fast married? Be assured of this,
　That the magnifico° is much beloved,
　And hath in his effect° a voice potential°
　As double as the Duke's. He will divorce you,
　Or put upon you what restraint or grievance　　　　　*15*
　The law, with all his might to enforce it on,
　Will give him cable.°

---

179 **discover** reveal, uncover　　182 **command** demand assistance　　184 **deserve** show gratitude for
2 **very stuff** essence, basic material (continuing the metaphor of *trade* from line 1)　　3 **contrived**
premeditated　　5 **yerked** stabbed.　**him** i.e., Roderigo　　10 **I . . . him** I restrained myself with
great difficulty from assaulting him　　12 **magnifico** Venetian grandee, i.e., Brabantio　　13 **in his ef-**
fect at his command.　**potential** powerful　　17 **cable** i.e., scope

OTHELLO: Let him do his spite.
My services which I have done the seigniory°
Shall out-tongue his complaints. 'Tis yet to know°—
Which, when I know that boasting is an honor,   *20*
I shall promulgate—I fetch my life and being
From men of royal siege,° and my demerits°
May speak unbonneted° to as proud a fortune
As this that I have reached. For know, Iago,
But that I love the gentle Desdemona,   *25*
I would not my unhousèd° free condition
Put into circumscription and confine°
For the sea's worth.° But look, what lights come yond?

Enter Cassio [and certain officers°] with torches.

IAGO: Those are the raisèd father and his friends.
You were best go in.
OTHELLO: Not I. I must be found.   *30*
My parts, my title, and my perfect soul°
Shall manifest me rightly. Is it they?
IAGO: By Janus,° I think no.
OTHELLO: The servants of the Duke? And my lieutenant?
The goodness of the night upon you, friends!   *35*
What is the news?
CASSIO: The Duke does greet you, General,
And he requires your haste-post-haste appearance
Even on the instant.
OTHELLO: What is the matter,° think you?
CASSIO: Something from Cyprus, as I may divine.°
It is a business of some heat.° The galleys   *40*
Have sent a dozen sequent° messengers
This very night at one another's heels,

---

18 **seigniory** Venetian government   19 **yet to know** not yet widely known   22 **siege** i.e., rank.
(Literally, a seat used by a person of distinction.)   **demerits** deserts   23 **unbonneted** without removing the hat, i.e., on equal terms (? Or "with hat off," "in all due modesty.")   26 **unhousèd** un-
confined, undomesticated   27 **circumscription and confine** restriction and confinement   28 **the
sea's worth** all the riches at the bottom of the sea.   [**s.d.**] **officers** (The Quarto text calls for "Cassio
with lights, officers with torches.")   31 **My . . . soul** my natural gifts, my position or reputation,
and my unflawed conscience   33 **Janus** Roman two-faced god of beginnings   38 **matter** business
39 **divine** guess   40 **heat** urgency   41 **sequent** successive

And many of the consuls,° raised and met,
Are at the Duke's already. You have been hotly called for;
When, being not at your lodging to be found,   45
The Senate hath sent about° three several° quests
To search you out.
OTHELLO: 'Tis well I am found by you.
I will but spend a word here in the house
And go with you.   [*Exit.*]
CASSIO: Ancient, what makes° he here?
IAGO: Faith, he tonight hath boarded° a land carrack.°   50
If it prove lawful prize,° he's made forever.
CASSIO: I do not understand.
IAGO: He's married.
CASSIO: To who?

[*Enter Othello.*]

IAGO: Marry,° to—Come, Captain, will you go?
OTHELLO: Have with you.°
CASSIO: Here comes another troop to seek for you.   55

Enter Brabantio, Roderigo, with officers and torches.°

IAGO: It is Brabantio. General, be advised.°
He comes to bad intent.
OTHELLO: Holla! Stand there!
RODERIGO: Signor, it is the Moor.
BRABANTIO: Down with him, thief!

[*They draw on both sides.*]

IAGO: You, Roderigo! Come, sir, I am for you.
OTHELLO: Keep up° your bright swords, for the dew will rust
them.   60
Good signor, you shall more command with years
Than with your weapons.

---

43 consuls senators   **46 about** all over the city.   **several** separate   **49 makes** does
50 boarded gone aboard and seized as an act of piracy (with sexual suggestion).   **carrack** large
merchant ship   **51 prize** booty   **53 Marry** (An oath, originally "by the Virgin Mary"; here used
with wordplay on *married.*)   **54 Have with you** i.e., let's go   **55 [s.d.] officers and torches** (The
Quarto text calls for "others with lights and weapons.")   **56 be advised** be on your guard
60 Keep up keep in the sheath

BRABANTIO: O thou foul thief, where hast thou stowed my
    daughter?
    Damned as thou art, thou hast enchanted her!
    For I'll refer me° to all things of sense,°   65
    If she in chains of magic were not bound
    Whether a maid so tender, fair, and happy,
    So opposite to marriage that she shunned
    The wealthy curlèd darlings of our nation,
    Would ever have, t' incur a general mock,   70
    Run from her guardage° to the sooty bosom
    Of such a thing as thou—to fear, not to delight.
    Judge me the world if 'tis not gross in sense°
    That thou hast practiced on her with foul charms,
    Abused her delicate youth with drugs or minerals°   75
    That weakens motion.° I'll have 't disputed on;°
    'Tis probable and palpable to thinking.
    I therefore apprehend and do attach° thee
    For an abuser of the world, a practicer
    Of arts inhibited° and out of warrant.°—   80
    Lay hold upon him! If he do resist,
    Subdue him at his peril.

OTHELLO: Hold your hands,
    Both you of my inclining° and the rest.
    Were it my cue to fight, I should have known it
    Without a prompter.—Whither will you that I go   85
    To answer this your charge?

BRABANTIO: To prison, till fit time
    Of law and course of direct session°
    Call thee to answer.

OTHELLO: What if I do obey?
    How may the Duke be therewith satisfied,   90
    Whose messengers are here about my side
    Upon some present business of the state

---

65 refer me submit my case.   **things of sense** commonsense understandings, or, creatures possessing common sense   **71 her guardage** my guardianship of her   **73 gross in sense** obvious   **75 minerals** i.e., poisons   **76 weakens motion** impair the vital faculties.   **disputed on** argued in court by professional counsel, debated by experts   **78 attach** arrest   **80 arts inhibited** prohibited arts, black magic.   **out of warrant** illegal   **83 inclining** following, party   **88 course of direct session** regular or specially convened legal proceedings

To bring me to him?

OFFICER: 'Tis true, most worthy signor.
The Duke's in council, and your noble self,
I am sure, is sent for.

BRABANTIO: How? The Duke in council? 95
In this time of the night? Bring him away.°
Mine's not an idle° cause. The Duke himself,
Or any of my brothers of the state,
Cannot but feel this wrong as 'twere their own;
For if such actions may have passage free,° 100
Bondslaves and pagans shall our statesmen be.

Exeunt.

SCENE III [VENICE. A COUNCIL CHAMBER.]

*Enter Duke [and] Senators [and sit at a table, with lights],
and Officers.° [The Duke and Senators are reading dispatches.]*

DUKE: There is no composition° in these news
That gives them credit.

FIRST SENATOR: Indeed, they are disproportioned.°
My letters say a hundred and seven galleys.

DUKE: And mine, a hundred forty.

SECOND SENATOR: And mine, two hundred. 5
But though they jump° not on a just° account—
As in these cases, where the aim° reports
'Tis oft with difference—yet do they all confirm
A Turkish fleet, and bearing up to Cyprus.

DUKE: Nay, it is possible enough to judgment. 10
I do not so secure me in the error
But the main article I do approve°
In fearful sense.

SAILOR (*within*): What ho, what ho, what ho!

---

96 away right along   **97 idle** trifling   **100 have passage free** are allowed to go unchecked
[s.d.] Enter . . . Officers (The Quarto text calls for the Duke and senators to "sit at a table with
lights and attendants.")
1 composition consistency   **3 disproportioned** inconsistent   **6 jump** agree.   **just** exact   **7 the
aim** conjecture   **11-12 I do not . . . approve** I do not take such (false) comfort in the discrepancies
that I fail to perceive the main point, i.e., that the Turkish fleet is threatening

Enter Sailor.

OFFICER: A messenger from the galleys.
DUKE: Now, what's the business?   15
SAILOR: The Turkish preparation° makes for Rhodes.
   So was I bid report here to the state
   By Signor Angelo.
DUKE: How say you by° this change?
FIRST SENATOR: This cannot be
   By no assay° of reason. 'Tis a pageant°   20
   To keep us in false gaze.° When we consider
   Th' importancy of Cyprus to the Turk,
   And let ourselves again but understand
   That, as it more concerns the Turk than Rhodes,
   So may he with more facile question bear it,°   25
   For that° it stands not in such warlike brace,°
   But altogether lacks th' abilities°
   That Rhodes is dressed in°—if we make thought of this,
   We must not think the Turk is so unskillful°
   To leave that latest° which concerns him first,   30
   Neglecting an attempt of ease and gain
   To wake° and wage° a danger profitless.
DUKE: Nay, in all confidence, he's not for Rhodes.
OFFICER: Here is more news.

Enter a Messenger.

MESSENGER: The Ottomites, reverend and gracious,   35
   Steering with due course toward the isle of Rhodes,
   Have there injointed them° with an after° fleet.
FIRST SENATOR: Ay, so I thought. How many, as you guess?
MESSENGER: Of thirty sail; and now they do restem
   Their backward course,° bearing with frank appearance°   40
   Their purposes toward Cyprus. Signor Montano,

---

16 **preparation** fleet prepared for battle   19 **by** about   20 **assay** test.   **pageant** mere show
21 **in false gaze** looking the wrong way   25 **So may . . . it** so also he (the Turk) can more easily
capture it (Cyprus)   26 **For that** since.   **brace** state of defense   27 **abilities** means of self-
defense   28 **dressed in** equipped with   29 **unskillful** deficient in judgment   30 **latest** last
32 **wake** stir up.   **wage** risk   37 **injointed them** joined themselves.   **after** second, following
39-40 **restem . . . course** retrace their original course   40 **frank appearance** undisguised intent

Your trusty and most valiant servitor,°
With his free duty° recommends° you thus,
And prays you to believe him.

DUKE: 'Tis certain then for Cyprus.   *45*
Marcus Luccicos, is not he in town?

FIRST SENATOR: He's now in Florence.

DUKE: Write from us to him, post-post-haste. Dispatch.

FIRST SENATOR: Here comes Brabantio and the valiant Moor.

Enter Brabantio, Othello, Cassio, Iago, Roderigo, and offi-
cers.

DUKE: Valiant Othello, we must straight° employ you   *50*
Against the general enemy° Ottoman.
[*To Brabantio.*] I did not see you; welcome, gentle° signor.
We lacked your counsel and your help tonight.

BRABANTIO: So did I yours. Good Your Grace, pardon me;
Neither my place° nor aught I heard of business   *55*
Hath raised me from my bed, nor doth the general care
Take hold on me, for my particular° grief
Is of so floodgate° and o'erbearing nature
That it engluts° and swallows other sorrows
And it is still itself.°

DUKE: Why, what's the matter?   *60*

BRABANTIO: My daughter! O, my daughter!

DUKE AND SENATORS: Dead?

BRABANTIO: Ay, to me.
She is abused,° stol'n from me, and corrupted
By spells and medicines bought of mountebanks;
For nature so preposterously to err,
Being not deficient,° blind, or lame of sense,°   *65*
Sans° witchcraft could not.

DUKE: Whoe'er he be that in this foul proceeding
Hath thus beguiled your daughter of herself,

---

42 servitor officer under your command   **43 free duty** freely given and loyal service.
recommends commends himself and reports to 50   **straight** straightway   **51 general enemy** universal enemy to all Christendom   **52 gentle** noble   **55 place** official position   **57 particular** personal   **58 floodgate** i.e., overwhelming (as when floodgates are opened)   **59 engluts** engulfs
60 is still itself remains undiminished   **62 abused** deceived   **65 deficient** defective.   **lame of
sense** deficient in sensory perception   **66 Sans** without

And you of her, the bloody book of law
You shall yourself read in the bitter letter   70
After your own sense°—yea, though our proper° son
Stood in your action.°
BRABANTIO: Humbly I thank Your Grace.
Here is the man, this Moor, whom now it seems
Your special mandate for the state affairs
Hath hither brought.
ALL: We are very sorry for 't.   75
DUKE [*to Othello*]: What, in your own part, can you say to
  this?
BRABANTIO: Nothing, but this is so.
OTHELLO: Most potent, grave, and reverend signors,
  My very noble and approved° good masters:
  That I have ta'en away this old man's daughter,   80
  It is most true; true, I have married her.
  The very head and front° of my offending
  Hath this extent, no more. Rude° am I in my speech,
  And little blessed with the soft phrase of peace;
  For since these arms of mine had seven years' pith,°   85
  Till now some nine moons wasted,° they have used
  Their dearest° action in the tented field;
  And little of this great world can I speak
  More than pertains to feats of broils and battle,
  And therefore little shall I grace my cause   90
  In speaking for myself. Yet, by your gracious patience,
  I will a round° unvarnished tale deliver
  Of my whole course of love—what drugs, what charms,
  What conjuration, and what mighty magic,
  For such proceeding I am charged withal,°   95
  I won his daughter.
BRABANTIO: A maiden never bold;
  Of spirit so still and quiet that her motion

---

71 **After . . . sense** according to your own interpretation.   **our proper** my own   72 **Stood . . .
action** were under your accusation   79 **approved** proved, esteemed   82 **head and front** height
and breadth, entire extent   83 **Rude** unpolished   85 **since . . . pith** i.e., since I was seven.   **pith**
strength, vigor   86 **Till . . . wasted** until some nine months ago (since when Othello has evidently
not been on active duty, but in Venice)   87 **dearest** most valuable   92 **round** plain   95 **withal**
with

Blushed at herself;° and she, in spite of nature,
Of years,° of country, credit,° everything,
To fall in love with what she feared to look on!   *100*
It is a judgment maimed and most imperfect
That will confess° perfection so could err
Against all rules of nature, and must be driven
To find out practices° of cunning hell
Why this should be. I therefore vouch° again   *105*
That with some mixtures powerful o'er the blood,°
Or with some dram conjured to this effect,°
He wrought upon her.

DUKE: To vouch this is no proof,
Without more wider° and more overt test°
Than these thin habits° and poor likelihoods°   *110*
Of modern seeming° do prefer° against him.

FIRST SENATOR: But Othello, speak.
Did you by indirect and forcèd courses°
Subdue and poison this young maid's affections?
Or came it by request and such fair question°   *115*
As soul to soul affordeth?

OTHELLO: I do beseech you,
Send for the lady to the Sagittary
And let her speak of me before her father.
If you do find me foul in her report,
The trust, the office I do hold of you   *120*
Not only take away, but let your sentence
Even fall upon my life.

DUKE: Fetch Desdemona hither.

OTHELLO: Ancient, conduct them. You best know the place.

[Exeunt Iago and attendants.]

And, till she come, as truly as to heaven

97-98 her . . . herself i.e., she blushed easily at herself. (*Motion* can suggest the impulse of the soul or of the emotions, or physical movement.)   **99 years** i.e., difference in age.   **credit** virtuous reputation   **102 confess** concede (that)   **104 practices** plots   **105 vouch** assert   **106 blood** passions   **107 dram . . . effect** dose made by magical spells to have this effect   **109 more wider** fuller.   **test** testimony   **110 habits** garments, i.e., appearances.   **poor likelihoods** weak inferences   **111 modern seeming** commonplace assumption.   **prefer** bring forth   **113 forcèd courses** means used against her will   **115 question** conversation

I do confess the vices of my blood,° 125
So justly° to your grave ears I'll present
How I did thrive in this fair lady's love,
And she in mine.
DUKE: Say it, Othello.
OTHELLO: Her father loved me, oft invited me, 130
Still° questioned me the story of my life
From year to year—the battles, sieges, fortunes
That I have passed.
I ran it through, even from my boyish days
To th' very moment that he bade me tell it, 135
Wherein I spoke of most disastrous chances,
Of moving accidents° by flood and field,
Of hairbreadth scapes i' th' imminent deadly breach,°
Of being taken by the insolent foe
And sold to slavery, of my redemption thence, 140
And portance° in my travels' history,
Wherein of antres° vast and deserts idle,°
Rough quarries,° rocks, and hills whose heads touch
heaven,
It was my hint° to speak—such was my process—
And of the Cannibals that each other eat, 145
The Anthropophagi,° and men whose heads
Do grow beneath their shoulders. These things to hear
Would Desdemona seriously incline;
But still the house affairs would draw her thence,
Which ever as she could with haste dispatch 150
She'd come again, and with a greedy ear
Devour up my discourse. Which I, observing,
Took once a pliant° hour, and found good means
To draw from her a prayer of earnest heart
That I would all my pilgrimage dilate,° 155
Whereof by parcels° she had something heard,

---

125 blood passions, human nature   **126 justly** truthfully, accurately   **131 Still** continually
137 moving accidents stirring happenings   **138 imminent . . . breach** death-threatening gaps
made in a fortification   **141 portance** conduct   **142 antres** caverns.   **idle** barren, desolate
143 Rough quarries rugged rock formations   **144 hint** occasion, opportunity
146 Anthropophagi man-eaters. (A term from Pliny's *Natural History*.)   **153 pliant** well-suiting
155 dilate relate in detail   **156 by parcels** piecemeal

But not intentively.° I did consent,
And often did beguile her of her tears,
When I did speak of some distressful stroke
That my youth suffered. My story being done, 160
She gave me for my pains a world of sighs.
She swore, in faith, 'twas strange, 'twas passing° strange,
'Twas pitiful, 'twas wondrous pitiful.
She wished she had not heard it, yet she wished
That heaven had made her° such a man. She thanked me, 165
And bade me, if I had a friend that loved her,
I should but teach him how to tell my story,
And that would woo her. Upon this hint° I spake.
She loved me for the dangers I had passed,
And I loved her that she did pity them. 170
This only is the witchcraft I have used.
Here comes the lady. Let her witness it.

Enter Desdemona, Iago, [and] attendants.

DUKE: I think this tale would win my daughter too.
Good Brabantio,
Take up this mangled matter at the best.° 175
Men do their broken weapons rather use
Than their bare hands.
BRABANTIO: I pray you, hear her speak.
If she confess that she was half the wooer,
Destruction on my head if my bad blame
Light on the man!—Come hither, gentle mistress. 180
Do you perceive in all this noble company
Where most you owe obedience?
DESDEMONA: My noble Father,
I do perceive here a divided duty.
To you I am bound for life and education;°
My life and education both do learn° me 185
How to respect you. You are the lord of duty;°

---

157 **intentively** with full attention, continuously   162 **passing** exceedingly   165 **made her** created her to be   168 **hint** opportunity. (Othello does not mean that she was dropping hints.)
175 **Take . . . best** make the best of a bad bargain   184 **education** upbringing   185 **learn** teach
186 **of duty** to whom duty is due

I am hitherto your daughter. But here's my husband,
And so much duty as my mother showed
To you, preferring you before her father,
So much I challenge° that I may profess   *190*
Due to the Moor my lord.

BRABANTIO: God be with you! I have done.
Please it Your Grace, on to the state affairs.
I had rather to adopt a child than get° it.
Come hither, Moor.   *195*

[He joins the hands of Othello and Desdemona.]

I here do give thee that with all my heart°
Which, but thou hast already, with all my heart°
I would keep from thee.—For your sake,° jewel,
I am glad at soul I have no other child,
For thy escape° would teach me tyranny,   *200*
To hang clogs° on them.—I have done, my lord.

DUKE: Let me speak like yourself,° and lay a sentence°
Which, as a grece° or step, may help these lovers
Into your favor.
When remedies° are past, the griefs are ended   *205*
By seeing the worst, which late on hopes depended.°
To mourn a mischief° that is past and gone
Is the next° way to draw new mischief on.
What° cannot be preserved when fortune takes,
Patience her injury a mockery makes.°   *210*
The robbed that smiles steals something from the thief;
He robs himself that spends a bootless grief.°

BRABANTIO: So let the Turk of Cyprus us beguile,
We lose it not, so long as we can smile.
He bears the sentence well that nothing bears   *215*

---

190 **challenge** claim   194 **get** beget   196 **with all my heart** wherein my whole affection has been engaged   197 **with all my heart** willingly, gladly   198 **For your sake** on your account
200 **escape** elopement   201 **clogs** (Literally, blocks of wood fastened to the legs of criminals or convicts to inhibit escape.)   202 **like yourself** i.e., as you would, in your proper temper.   **lay a sentence** apply a maxim   203 **grece** step   205 **remedies** hopes of remedy   206 **which . . . depended** which griefs were sustained until recently by hopeful anticipation   207 **mischief** misfortune, injury   208 **next** nearest   209 **What** whatever   210 **Patience . . . makes** patience laughs at the injury inflicted by fortune (and thus eases the pain)   212 **spends a bootless grief** indulges in unavailing grief

But the free comfort which from thence he hears,
But he bears both the sentence and the sorrow
That, to pay grief, must of poor patience borrow.°
These sentences, to sugar or to gall,
Being strong on both sides, are equivocal.°   220
But words are words. I never yet did hear
That the bruisèd heart was piercèd through the ear.°
I humbly beseech you, proceed to th' affairs of state.

DUKE: The Turk with a most mighty preparation makes for
Cyprus. Othello, the fortitude° of the place is best known to   225
you; and though we have there a substitute° of most al-
lowed° sufficiency, yet opinion, a sovereign mistress of effects, throws a more safer voice on you.° You must therefore
be content to slubber° the gloss of your new fortunes with
this more stubborn° and boisterous expedition.

OTHELLO: The tyrant custom, most grave senators,   230
Hath made the flinty and steel couch of war
My thrice—driven° bed of down. I do agnize°
A natural and prompt alacrity
I find in hardness,° and do undertake
These present wars against the Ottomites.   235
Most humbly therefore bending to your state,°
I crave fit disposition for my wife,
Due reference of place and exhibition,°
With such accommodation° and besort°
As levels° with her breeding.°   240

DUKE: Why, at her father's.

BRABANTIO: I will not have it so.

OTHELLO: Nor I.

215-218 He bears . . . borrow a person well bears out your maxim who can enjoy its platitudinous
comfort, free of all genuine sorrow, but anyone whose grief bankrupts his poor patience is left with
your saying and his sorrow, too. (*Bears the sentence* also plays on the meaning, "receives judicial sentence.")   **219-220 These . . . equivocal** these fine maxims are equivocal, either sweet or bitter in
their application   **222 piercèd . . . ear** i.e., surgically lanced and cured by mere words of advice
225 fortitude strength   **226 substitute** deputy.   **allowed** acknowledged   **226-227 opinion . . .
on you** general opinion, an important determiner of affairs, chooses you as the best man
228 slubber soil, sully.   **stubborn** harsh, rough   **232 thrice-driven** thrice sifted, winnowed.
agnize know in myself, acknowledge   **234 hardness** hardship   **236 bending . . . state** bowing or
kneeling to your authority   **238 reference . . . exhibition** provision of appropriate place to live
and allowance of money   **239 accommodation** suitable provision.   **besort** attendance
240 levels equals, suits.   **breeding** social position, upbringing

DESDEMONA: Nor I. I would not there reside,
To put my father in impatient thoughts
By being in his eye. Most gracious Duke,
To my unfolding° lend your prosperous° ear,   *245*
And let me find a charter° in your voice,
T' assist my simpleness.

DUKE: What would you, Desdemona?

DESDEMONA: That I did love the Moor to live with him,
My downright violence and storm of fortunes°   *250*
May trumpet to the world. My heart's subdued
Even to the very quality of my lord.°
I saw Othello's visage in his mind,
And to his honors and his valiant parts°
Did I my soul and fortunes consecrate.   *255*
So that, dear lords, if I be left behind
A moth° of peace, and he go to the war,
The rites° for why I love him are bereft me,
And I a heavy interim shall support
By his dear° absence. Let me go with him.   *260*

OTHELLO: Let her have your voice.°
Vouch with me, heaven, I therefor beg it not
To please the palate of my appetite,
Nor to comply with heat°—the young affects°
In me defunct—and proper° satisfaction,   *265*
But to be free° and bounteous to her mind.
And heaven defend° your good souls that you think°
I will your serious and great business scant
When she is with me. No, when light-winged toys
Of feathered Cupid seel° with wanton dullness   *270*
My speculative and officed instruments,°

---

245 unfolding explanation, proposal.   **prosperous** propitious   **246 charter** privilege, authorization   **250 My . . . fortunes** my plain and total breach of social custom, taking my future by storm and disrupting my whole life   **251-252 My heart's . . . lord** my heart is brought wholly into accord with Othello's virtues; I love him for his virtues   **254 parts** qualities   **257 moth** i.e., one who consumes merely   **258 rites** rites of love (with a suggestion, too, of "rights," sharing)   **260 dear** (1) heartfelt (2) costly   **261 voice** consent   **264 heat** sexual passion.   **young affects** passions of youth, desires   **265 proper** personal   **266 free** generous   **267 defend** forbid.   **think** should think   **270 seel** i.e., make blind (as in falconry, by sewing up the eyes of the hawk during training)   **271 speculative . . . instruments** eyes and other faculties used in the performance of duty

That° my disports° corrupt and taint° my business,
Let huswives make a skillet of my helm,
And all indign° and base adversities
Make head° against my estimation!°   275
DUKE: Be it as you shall privately determine,
   Either for her stay or going. Th' affair cries haste,
   And speed must answer it.
A SENATOR: You must away tonight.
DESDEMONA: Tonight, my lord?
DUKE: This night.
OTHELLO: With all my heart.
DUKE: At nine i' the morning here we'll meet again.   280
   Othello, leave some officer behind,
   And he shall our commission bring to you,
   With such things else of quality and respect°
   As doth import° you.
OTHELLO: So please Your Grace, my ancient;
   A man he is of honesty and trust.   285
   To his conveyance I assign my wife,
   With what else needful Your Good Grace shall think
   To be sent after me.
DUKE: Let it be so.
   Good night to everyone. [*To Brabantio.*] And, noble signor,
   If virtue no delighted° beauty lack,   290
   Your son-in-law is far more fair than black.
FIRST SENATOR: Adieu, brave Moor. Use Desdemona well.
BRABANTIO: Look to her, Moor, if thou hast eyes to see.
   She has deceived her father, and may thee.

   Exeunt [*Duke, Brabantio, Cassio, Senators, and officers*].

OTHELLO: My life upon her faith! Honest Iago,   295
   My Desdemona must I leave to thee.
   I prithee, let thy wife attend on her,
   And bring them after in the best advantage.°

---

272 That so that.   **disports** sexual pastimes.   **taint** impair   **274 indign** unworthy, shameful
275 Make head raise an army.   **estimation** reputation   **283 of quality and respect** of importance and relevance   **284 import** concern   **290 delighted** capable of delighting   **298 in . . . advantage** at the most favorable opportunity

Come, Desdemona. I have but an hour
Of love, of worldly matters and direction,°   *300*
To spend with thee. We must obey the time.°

> *Exit [with Desdemona].*

RODERIGO: Iago—

IAGO: What sayst thou, noble heart?

RODERIGO: What will I do, think'st thou?

IAGO: Why, go to bed and sleep.   *305*

RODERIGO: I will incontinently° drown myself.

IAGO: If thou dost, I shall never love thee after. Why, thou silly gentleman?

RODERIGO: It is silliness to live when to live is torment; and then have we a prescription° to die when death is our physician.

IAGO: O villainous!° I have looked upon the world for four times seven years, and, since I could distinguish betwixt a   *310* benefit and an injury, I never found man that knew how to love himself. Ere I would say I would drown myself for the love of a guinea hen,° I would change my humanity with a baboon.

RODERIGO: What should I do? I confess it is my shame to be so fond,° but it is not in my virtue° to amend it.   *315*

IAGO: Virtue? A fig!° 'Tis in ourselves that we are thus or thus. Our bodies are our gardens, to the which our wills are gardeners; so that if we will plant nettles or sow lettuce, set hyssop° and weed up thyme, supply it with one gender° of herbs or distract it with° many, either to have it sterile with idleness° or manured with industry—why, the power and corrigible authority° of this lies in our wills. If the beam° of our   *320* lives had not one scale of reason to poise° another of sensu-

---

300 direction instructions   **301 the time** the urgency of the present crisis   **306 incontinently** immediately, without self-restraint   **308–309 prescription** (1) right based on long-established custom (2) doctor's prescription   **310 villainous** i.e., what perfect nonsense   **313 guinea hen** (A slang term for a prostitute.)   **314 fond** infatuated   **315 virtue** strength, nature   **316 fig** (To give a fig is to thrust the thumb between the first and second fingers in a vulgar and insulting gesture.)
318 hyssop an herb of the mint family   **319 gender** kind.   **distract it with** divide it among.
320 idleness want of cultivation.   **corrigible authority** power to correct   **321 beam** balance.
322 poise counterbalance.

ality, the blood° and baseness of our natures would conduct
us to most preposterous conclusions. But we have reason to
cool our raging motions,° our carnal stings, our unbitted°
lusts, whereof I take this that you call love to be a sect or
scion.°   325

RODERIGO: It cannot be.

IAGO: It is merely a lust of the blood and a permission of the
will. Come, be a man. Drown thyself? Drown cats and blind
puppies. I have professed me thy friend, and I confess me
knit to thy deserving with cables of perdurable° toughness. I
could never better stead° thee than now. Put money in thy
purse. Follow thou the wars; defeat thy favor° with an   330
usurped° beard. I say, put money in thy purse. It cannot be
long that Desdemona should continue her love to the Moor—
put money in thy purse—nor he his to her. It was a violent
commencement in her, and thou shalt see an answerable se-
questration°—put but money in thy purse. These Moors are
changeable in their wills°—fill thy purse with money. The   335
food that to him now is as luscious as locusts° shall be to him
shortly as bitter as coloquintida.° She must change for
youth; when she is sated with his body, she will find the error
of her choice. She must have change, she must. Therefore
put money in thy purse. If thou wilt needs damn thyself, do
it a more delicate way than drowning. Make° all the money   340
thou canst. If sanctimony° and a frail vow betwixt an erring°
barbarian and a supersubtle Venetian be not too hard for my
wits and all the tribe of hell, thou shalt enjoy her. Therefore
make money. A pox of drowning thyself! It is clean out of the
way.° Seek thou rather to be hanged in compassing° thy joy
than to be drowned and go without her.   345

---

blood natural passions   **324 motions** appetites.   **unbitted** unbridled, uncontrolled   **325 sect or
scion** cutting or offshoot   **329 perdurable** very durable   **330 stead** assist   **331 defeat thy favor**
disguise your face.   **usurped** (The suggestion is that Roderigo is not man enough to have a beard of
his own.)   **334-335 an answerable sequestration** a corresponding separation or estrangement
336 wills carnal appetites   **337 locusts** fruit of the carob tree (see Matthew 3:4), or perhaps honeysuckle.   **coloquintida** colocynth or bitter apple, a purgative   **341 Make** raise, collect.
sanctimony sacred ceremony   **342 erring** wandering, vagabond, unsteady   **344 clean . . . way**
entirely unsuitable as a course of action   **compassing** encompassing, embracing

RODERIGO: Wilt thou be fast° to my hopes if I depend on the issue?°

IAGO: Thou art sure of me. Go, make money. I have told thee often, and I retell thee again and again, I hate the Moor. My cause is hearted;° thine hath no less reason. Let us be conjunctive° in our revenge against him. If thou canst cuckold him, thou dost thyself a pleasure, me a sport. There are many events in the womb of time which will be delivered.   *350* Traverse,° go, provide thy money. We will have more of this tomorrow. Adieu.

RODERIGO: Where shall we meet i' the morning?

IAGO: At my lodging.

RODERIGO: I'll be with thee betimes.° [*He starts to leave.*]   *355*

IAGO: Go to, farewell.—Do you hear, Roderigo?

RODERIGO: What say you?

IAGO: No more of drowning, do you hear?

RODERIGO: I am changed.

IAGO: Go to, farewell. Put money enough in your purse.   *360*

RODERIGO: I'll sell all my land.   *Exit.*

IAGO: Thus do I ever make my fool my purse;
   For I mine own gained knowledge should profane
   If I would time expend with such a snipe°
   But for my sport and profit. I hate the Moor;   *365*
   And it is thought abroad° that twixt my sheets
   He's done my office.° I know not if 't be true;
   But I, for mere suspicion in that kind,
   Will do as if for surety.° He holds me well;°
   The better shall my purpose work on him.   *370*
   Cassio's a proper° man. Let me see now:
   To get his place and to plume up° my will
   In double knavery—How, how?—Let's see:
   After some time, to abuse° Othello's ear
   That he° is too familiar with his wife.   *375*

---

346 fast true.   **issue** (successful) outcome   **348 hearted** fixed in the heart, heartfelt
349 conjunctive united   **351 Traverse** (A military marching term.)   **355 betimes** early
364 snipe woodcock, i.e., fool   **366 it is thought abroad** it is rumored   **367 my office** i.e., my
sexual function as husband   **369 do . . . surety** act as if on certain knowledge.   **holds me well**
regards me favorably   **371 proper** handsome   **372 plume up** put a feather in the cap of, i.e., glo-
rify, gratify   **374 abuse** deceive   **375 he** i.e., Cassio

He hath a person and a smooth dispose°
To be suspected, framed to make women false.
The Moor is of a free° and open° nature,
That thinks men honest that but seem to be so,
And will as tenderly° be led by the nose   380
As asses are.
I have 't. It is engendered. Hell and night
Must bring this monstrous birth to the world's light.

[Exit.]

ACT II

SCENE I [A SEAPORT IN CYPRUS. AN OPEN PLACE
NEAR THE QUAY.]

Enter Montano and two Gentlemen.

MONTANO: What from the cape can you discern at sea?
FIRST GENTLEMAN: Nothing at all. It is a high-wrought
flood.°
I cannot, twixt the heaven and the main,°
Descry a sail.
MONTANO: Methinks the wind hath spoke aloud at land;   5
A fuller blast ne'er shook our battlements.
If it hath ruffianed° so upon the sea,
What ribs of oak, when mountains° melt on them,
Can hold the mortise?° What shall we hear of this?
SECOND GENTLEMAN: A segregation° of the Turkish fleet.   10
For do but stand upon the foaming shore,
The chidden° billow seems to pelt the clouds;
The wind-shaked surge, with high and monstrous mane,°
Seems to cast water on the burning Bear°

---

376 dispose disposition   **378 free** frank, generous.   **open** unsuspicious   **380 tenderly** readily
2 high-wrought flood very agitated sea   **3 main** ocean (also at line 41)   **7 ruffianed** raged
8 mountains i.e., of water   **9 hold the mortise** hold their joints together. (A *mortise* is the socket
hollowed out in fitting timbers.)   **10 segregation** dispersal   **12 chidden** i.e., rebuked, repelled (by
the shore), and thus shot into the air   **13 monstrous mane** (The surf is like the mane of a wild
beast.)   **14 the burning Bear** i.e., the constellation Ursa Minor or the Little Bear, which includes
the polestar (and hence regarded as the guards of *th' ever-fixèd pole* in the next line; sometimes the
term *guards* is applied to the two "pointers" of the Big Bear or Dipper, which may be intended here.)

And quench the guards of th' ever-fixèd pole.   *15*
I never did like molestation° view
On the enchafèd° flood.
MONTANO: If that° the Turkish fleet
Be not ensheltered and embayed,° they are drowned;
It is impossible to bear it out.°   *20*

Enter a [Third] Gentleman.

THIRD GENTLEMAN: News, lads! Our wars are done.
The desperate tempest hath so banged the Turks
That their designment° halts.° A noble ship of Venice
Hath seen a grievous wreck° and sufferance°
On most part of their fleet.   *25*
MONTANO: How? Is this true?
THIRD GENTLEMAN: The ship is here put in,
A Veronesa;° Michael Cassio,
Lieutenant to the warlike Moor Othello,
Is come on shore; the Moor himself at sea,   *30*
And is in full commission here for Cyprus.
MONTANO: I am glad on 't. 'Tis a worthy governor.
THIRD GENTLEMAN: But this same Cassio, though he speak
of comfort
Touching the Turkish loss, yet he looks sadly°
And prays the Moor be safe, for they were parted   *35*
With foul and violent tempest.
MONTANO: Pray heaven he be,
For I have served him, and the man commands
Like a full° soldier. Let's to the seaside, ho!
As well to see the vessel that's come in
As to throw out our eyes for brave Othello,
Even till we make the main and th' aerial blue°   *40*
An indistinct regard.°
THIRD GENTLEMAN: Come, let's do so,

---

16 **like molestation** comparable disturbance   17 **enchafèd** angry   18 **If that** if   19 **embayed**
sheltered by a bay   20 **bear it out** survive, weather the storm   23 **designment** design, enterprise.
halts is lame   24 **wreck** shipwreck.   **sufferance** damage, disaster   28 **Veronesa** i.e., fitted out in
Verona for Venetian service, or possibly *Verennessa* (the Folio spelling), i.e., *verrinessa*, a cutter (from
verrinare, "to cut through")   34 **sadly** gravely   38 **full** perfect   41 **the main . . . blue** the sea
and the sky   42 **An indistinct regard** indistinguishable in our view

For every minute is expectancy°
Of more arrivance.°

Enter Cassio.

CASSIO: Thanks, you the valiant of this warlike isle,   *45*
That so approve° the Moor! O, let the heavens
Give him defense against the elements,
For I have lost him on a dangerous sea.
MONTANO: Is he well shipped?
CASSIO: His bark is stoutly timbered, and his pilot   *50*
Of very expert and approved allowance;°
Therefore my hopes, not surfeited to death,°
Stand in bold cure.°
                    [*A cry*] *within*: "A sail, a sail, a sail!"
CASSIO: What noise?
A GENTLEMAN: The town is empty. On the brow o' the sea°   *55*
Stand ranks of people, and they cry "A sail!"
CASSIO: My hopes do shape him for° the governor.

                              [*A shot within.*]

SECOND GENTLEMAN: They do discharge their shot of
courtesy;°
Our friends at least.
CASSIO: I pray you, sir, go forth,
And give us truth who 'tis that is arrived.   *60*
SECOND GENTLEMAN: I shall.   *Exit.*
MONTANO: But, good Lieutenant, is your general wived?
CASSIO: Most fortunately. He hath achieved a maid
That paragons° description and wild fame,°
One that excels the quirks° of blazoning° pens,   *65*
And in th' essential vesture of creation

---

43 is expectancy gives expectation   **44 arrivance** arrival   **46 approve** admire, honor
51 approved allowance tested reputation   **52 surfeited to death** i.e., overextended, worn thin
through repeated application or delayed fulfillment   **53 in bold cure** in strong hopes of fulfillment
55 brow o' the sea cliff-edge   **57 My . . . for** I hope it is   **58 discharge . . . courtesy** fire a
salute in token of respect and courtesy   **64 paragons** surpasses.   **wild fame** extravagant report
65 quirks witty conceits.   **blazoning** setting forth as though in heraldic language

Does tire the enginer.°

Enter [Second] Gentleman.°

How now? Who has put in?°

SECOND GENTLEMAN: 'Tis one Iago, ancient to the General.

CASSIO: He's had most favorable and happy speed.
Tempests themselves, high seas, and howling winds,   70
The guttered° rocks and congregated sands—
Traitors ensteeped° to clog the guiltless keel—
As° having sense of beauty, do omit°
Their mortal° natures, letting go safely by
The divine Desdemona.

MONTANO: What is she?   75

CASSIO: She that I spake of, our great captain's captain,
Left in the conduct of the bold Iago,
Whose footing° here anticipates our thoughts
A sennight's° speed. Great Jove, Othello guard,
And swell his sail with thine own powerful breath,   80
That he may bless this bay with his tall° ship,
Make love's quick pants in Desdemona's arms,
Give renewed fire to our extinced spirits,
And bring all Cyprus comfort!

Enter Desdemona, Iago, Roderigo, and Emilia.

                                   O, behold,
The riches of the ship is come on shore!   85
You men of Cyprus, let her have your knees.

[The gentlemen make curtsy to Desdemona.]

Hail to thee, lady! And the grace of heaven
Before, behind thee, and on every hand
Enwheel thee round!

DESDEMONA: I thank you, valiant Cassio.

66–67 **in . . . enginer** in her real, God-given, beauty, (she) defeats any attempt to praise her.
enginer engineer, i.e., poet, one who devises.   **[s.d.]** *Second Gentleman* (So identified in the Quarto
text here and in lines 58, 61, 68, and 96; the Folio calls him a gentleman.)   67 **put in** i.e., to harbor
71 **guttered** jagged, trenched   72 **ensteeped** lying under water   73 **As** as if.   **omit** forbear to exercise   74 **mortal** deadly   78 **footing** landing   79 **sennight's** week's   81 **tall** splendid, gallant

What tidings can you tell me of my lord? 90
CASSIO: He is not yet arrived, nor know I aught
But that he's well and will be shortly here.
DESDEMONA: O, but I fear—How lost you company?
CASSIO: The great contention of the sea and skies
Parted our fellowship.
(*Within*) "A sail, a sail!" [*A shot.*]
But hark. A sail! 95
SECOND GENTLEMAN: They give their greeting to the citadel.
This likewise is a friend.
CASSIO: See for the news.

[*Exit Second Gentleman.*]

Good Ancient, you are welcome. [*Kissing Emilia.*] Welcome,
mistress.
Let it not gall your patience, good Iago,
That I extend° my manners; 'tis my breeding° 100
That gives me this bold show of courtesy.
IAGO: Sir, would she give you so much of her lips
As of her tongue she oft bestows on me,
You would have enough.
DESDEMONA: Alas, she has no speech!° 105
IAGO: In faith, too much.
I find it still,° when I have list° to sleep.
Marry, before your ladyship, I grant,
She puts her tongue a little in her heart
And chides with thinking.°
EMILIA: You have little cause to say so. 110
IAGO: Come on, come on. You are pictures out of doors,°
Bells° in your parlors, wildcats in your kitchens,°
Saints° in your injuries, devils being offended,
Players° in your huswifery,° and huswives° in your beds.

---

100 **extend** give scope to. **breeding** training in the niceties of etiquette 105 **she has no speech**
i.e., she's not a chatterbox, as you allege 107 **still** always. **list** desire 110 **with thinking** i.e., in
her thoughts only 111 **pictures out of doors** i.e., silent and well-behaved in public 112 **Bells**
i.e., jangling, noisy, and brazen. **in your kitchens** i.e., in domestic affairs. (Ladies would not do
the cooking.) 113 **Saints** martyrs 114 **Players** idlers, triflers, or deceivers. **huswifery** housekeeping. **huswives** hussies (i.e., women are "busy" in bed, or unduly thrifty in dispensing sexual
favors)

DESDEMONA: O, fie upon thee, slanderer!   *115*
IAGO: Nay, it is true, or else I am a Turk.°
  You rise to play, and go to bed to work.
EMILIA: You shall not write my praise.
IAGO: No, let me not.
DESDEMONA: What wouldst write of me, if thou shouldst
  praise me?
IAGO: O gentle lady, do not put me to 't,   *120*
  For I am nothing if not critical.°
DESDEMONA: Come on, essay.°—There's one gone to the
  harbor?
IAGO: Ay, madam.
DESDEMONA: I am not merry, but I do beguile
  The thing I am° by seeming otherwise.   *125*
  Come, how wouldst thou praise me?
IAGO: I am about it, but indeed my invention
  Comes from my pate as birdlime° does from frieze°—
  It plucks out brains and all. But my Muse labors,°
  And thus she is delivered: *130*
  If she be fair and wise, fairness and wit,
  The one's for use, the other useth it.°
DESDEMONA: Well praised! How if she be black° and witty?
IAGO: If she be black, and thereto have a wit,
  She'll find a white° that shall her blackness fit.°   *135*
DESDEMONA: Worse and worse.
EMILIA: How if fair and foolish?
IAGO: She never yet was foolish that was fair,
  For even her folly° helped her to an heir.°
DESDEMONA: These are old fond° paradoxes to make fools
  laugh i' th' alehouse.
  What miserable praise hast thou for her that's foul and
  foolish?   *140*

---

116 a Turk an infidel, not to be believed   **121 critical** censorious   **122 essay** try   **125 The thing
I am** i.e., my anxious self   **128 birdlime** sticky substance used to catch small birds.   **frieze** coarse
woolen cloth   **129 labors** (1) exerts herself (2) prepares to deliver a child (with a following pun on
delivered in line 130)   **132 The one's . . . it** i.e., her cleverness will make use of her beauty
133 black dark-complexioned, brunette   **135 a white** a fair person (with word-play on "wight," a
person).   **fit** (with sexual suggestion of mating)   **138 folly** (with added meaning of "lechery, wantonness").   **to an heir** i.e., to bear a child   **139 fond** foolish

IAGO: There's none so foul° and foolish thereunto,°
　　　But does foul° pranks which fair and wise ones do.

DESDEMONA: O heavy ignorance! Thou praisest the worst
　　　best. But what praise couldst thou bestow on a deserving
　　　woman indeed, one that, in the authority of her merit, did
　　　justly put on the vouch° of very malice itself?　　　　　　　　*145*

IAGO: She that was ever fair, and never proud,
　　　Had tongue at will, and yet was never loud,
　　　Never lacked gold and yet went never gay,°
　　　Fled from her wish, and yet said, "Now I may,"°
　　　She that being angered, her revenge being nigh,　　　　　　　*150*
　　　Bade her wrong stay° and her displeasure fly,
　　　She that in wisdom never was so frail
　　　To change the cod's head for the salmon's tail,°
　　　She that could think and ne'er disclose her mind,
　　　See suitors following and not look behind,　　　　　　　　　*155*
　　　She was a wight, if ever such wight were—

DESDEMONA: To do what?

IAGO: To suckle fools° and chronicle small beer.°

DESDEMONA: O most lame and impotent conclusion! Do not
　　　learn of him, Emilia, though he be thy husband. How say　　*160*
　　　you, Cassio? Is he not a most profane° and liberal° coun-
　　　selor?

CASSIO: He speaks home,° madam. You may relish° him more
　　　in° the soldier than in the scholar.

[*Cassio and Desdemona stand together, conversing intimately.*]

IAGO [*aside*]:   He takes her by the palm. Ay, well said,° whisper.
　　　With as little a web as this will I ensnare as great a fly as　　*165*
　　　Cassio. Ay, smile upon her, do; I will gyve° thee in thine own

---

141 foul ugly.　　**thereunto** in addition　　**142 foul** sluttish　　**145 put . . . vouch** compel the approval　　**148 gay** extravagantly clothed　　**149 Fled . . . may** avoided temptation where the choice
was hers　　**151 Bade . . . stay** i.e., resolved to put up with her injury patiently　　**153 To . . . tail**
i.e., to exchange a lackluster husband for a sexy lover (?) (**Cod's head** is slang for "penis," and tail,
for "pudendum.")　　**158 suckle fools** breastfeed babies.　　**chronicle small beer** i.e., keep petty
household accounts, keep track of trivial matters　　**161 profane** irreverent, ribald.　　**liberal** licentious, free-spoken　　**162 home** right to the target. (A term from fencing.)　　**relish** appreciate　　**in** in
the character of　　**164 well said** well done　　**166 gyve** fetter, shackle.

courtship.° You say true;° 'tis so, indeed. If such tricks as
these strip you out of your lieutenantry, it had been better
you had not kissed your three fingers so oft, which now
again you are most apt to play the sir° in. Very good; well
kissed! An excellent courtesy! 'Tis so, indeed. Yet again your
fingers to your lips? Would they were clyster pipes° for your   *170*
sake! [*Trumpet within.*] The Moor! I know his trumpet.
CASSIO: 'Tis truly so.
DESDEMONA: Let's meet him and receive him.
CASSIO: Lo, where he comes!

Enter Othello and attendants.

OTHELLO: O my fair warrior!
DESDEMONA: My dear Othello!   *175*
OTHELLO: It gives me wonder great as my content
To see you here before me. O my soul's joy,
If after every tempest come such calms,
May the winds blow till they have wakened death,
And let the laboring bark climb hills of seas   *180*
Olympus-high, and duck again as low
As hell's from heaven! If it were now to die,
'Twere now to be most happy, for I fear
My soul hath her content so absolute
That not another comfort like to this   *185*
Succeeds in unknown fate.°
DESDEMONA: The heavens forbid
But that our loves and comforts should increase
Even as our days do grow!
OTHELLO: Amen to that, sweet powers!
I cannot speak enough of this content.   *190*
It stops me here; it is too much of joy.
And this, and this, the greatest discords be

[*They kiss.*]°

---

courtship courtesy, show of courtly manners.   **You say true** i.e., that's right, go ahead   **169 the
sir** i.e., the fine gentleman   **170 clyster pipes** tubes used for enemas and douches   **186 Succeeds
. . . fate** i.e., can follow in the unknown future   **192 [s.d.] They kiss** (The direction is from the
Quarto.)

That e'er our hearts shall make!

IAGO [*aside*]:   O, you are well tuned now!

But I'll set down° the pegs that make this music,   *195*

As honest as I am.°

OTHELLO: Come, let us to the castle.

News, friends! Our wars are done, the Turks are drowned.

How does my old acquaintance of this isle?—

Honey, you shall be well desired° in Cyprus;   *200*

I have found great love amongst them. O my sweet,

I prattle out of fashion,° and I dote

In mine own comforts.—I prithee, good Iago,

Go to the bay and disembark my coffers.°

Bring thou the master° to the citadel;   *205*

He is a good one, and his worthiness

Does challenge° much respect.—Come, Desdemona.—

Once more, well met at Cyprus!

> *Exeunt Othello and Desdemona [and all*
> *but Iago and Roderigo].*

IAGO [*to an attendant*]:   Do thou meet me presently at the harbor. [*To Roderigo.*] Come hither. If thou be'st valiant—as, they say, base men° being in love have then a nobility in   *210* their natures more than is native to them—list° me. The Lieutenant tonight watches on the court of guard.° First, I must tell thee this: Desdemona is directly in love with him.

RODERIGO: With him? Why, 'tis not possible.

IAGO: Lay thy finger thus,° and let thy soul be instructed.   *215* Mark me with what violence she first loved the Moor, but° for bragging and telling her fantastical lies. To love him still for prating? Let not thy discreet heart think it. Her eye must be fed; and what delight shall she have to look on the devil? When the blood is made dull with the act of sport,° there

---

195 set down loosen (and hence untune the instrument)   **196 As . . . I am** for all my supposed honesty   **200 desired** welcomed   **202 out of fashion** irrelevantly, incoherently (?)   **204 coffers** chests, baggage   **205 master** ship's captain   **207 challenge** lay claim to, deserve   **210 base men** even lowly born men   **211 list** listen to   **212 court of guard** guardhouse. (Cassio is in charge of the watch.)   **215 thus** i.e., on your lips   **216 but** only   **219 the act of sport** sex

should be, again to inflame it and to give satiety a fresh appetite, loveliness in favor,° sympathy° in years, manners,   *220*
and beauties—all which the Moor is defective in. Now, for
want of these required conveniences,° her delicate tenderness will find itself abused,° begin to heave the gorge,° dis-
relish and abhor the Moor. Very nature° will instruct her in it
and compel her to some second choice. Now, sir, this
granted—as it is a most pregnant° and unforced position—   *225*
who stands so eminent in the degree of° this fortune as
Cassio does? A knave very voluble,° no further conscion-
able° than in putting on the mere form of civil and humane°
seeming for the better compassing of his salt° and most hidden loose affection.° Why, none, why, none. A slipper° and
subtle knave, a finder out of occasions, that has an eye can
stamp° and counterfeit advantages,° though true advantage   *230*
never present itself; a devilish knave. Besides, the knave is
handsome, young, and hath all those requisites in him that
folly° and green° minds look after. A pestilent complete
knave, and the woman hath found him° already.

RODERIGO: I cannot believe that in her. She's full of most
blessed condition.°   *235*

IAGO: Blessed fig's end!° The wine she drinks is made of
grapes. If she had been blessed, she would never have loved
the Moor. Blessed pudding!° Didst thou not see her paddle
with the palm of his hand? Didst not mark that?

RODERIGO: Yes, that I did; but that was but courtesy.

IAGO: Lechery, by this hand. An index° and obscure° prologue   *240*
to the history of lust and foul thoughts. They met so near
with their lips that their breaths embraced together.
Villainous thoughts, Roderigo! When these mutualities° so

---

220 **favor** appearance.   **sympathy** correspondence, similarity   222 **required conveniences** things
conducive to sexual compatibility   223 **abused** cheated, revolted.   **heave the gorge** experience
nausea   224 **Very nature** her very instincts   225 **pregnant** evident, cogent   226 **in . . . of** as
next in line for   227 **voluble** facile, glib.   **conscionable** conscientious, conscience-bound
228 **humane** polite, courteous.   **salt** licentious   229 **affection** passion.   **slipper** slippery
230 **an eye can stamp** an eye that can coin, create   231 **advantages** favorable opportunities
233 **folly** wantonness.   **green** immature   234 **found him** sized him up, perceived his intent
235 **condition** disposition   236 **fig's end** (See Act I, Scene iii, line 316 for the vulgar gesture of the
fig.)   237 **pudding** sausage   240 **index** table of contents.   **obscure** (i.e., the *lust and foul
thoughts* in line 241 are secret, hidden from view)   243 **mutualities** exchanges, intimacies.

marshal the way, hard at hand° comes the master and main exercise, th' incorporate° conclusion. Pish! But, sir, be you ruled by me. I have brought you from Venice. Watch you° tonight; for the command, I'll lay 't upon you.° Cassio knows you not. I'll not be far from you. Do you find some occasion to anger Cassio, either by speaking too loud, or tainting° his discipline, or from what other course you please, which the time shall more favorably minister.° 245

RODERIGO: Well. 250

IAGO: Sir, he's rash and very sudden in choler,° and haply° may strike at you. Provoke him that he may, for even out of that will I cause these of Cyprus to mutiny,° whose qualification° shall come into no true taste° again but by the displanting of Cassio. So shall you have a shorter journey to your desires by the means I shall then have to prefer° them, and the impediment most profitably removed, without the which there were no expectation of our prosperity. 255

RODERIGO: I will do this, if you can bring it to any opportunity.

IAGO: I warrant° thee. Meet me by and by° at the citadel. I must fetch his necessaries ashore. Farewell. 260

RODERIGO: Adieu. *Exit.*

IAGO: That Cassio loves her, I do well believe 't;
That she loves him, 'tis apt° and of great credit.°
The Moor, howbeit that I endure him not,
Is of a constant, loving, noble nature, 265
And I dare think he'll prove to Desdemona
A most dear husband. Now, I do love her too,
Not out of absolute lust—though peradventure
I stand accountant° for as great a sin—
But partly led to diet° my revenge 270
For that I do suspect the lusty Moor
Hath leaped into my seat, the thought whereof

---

hard at hand closely following   **244 incorporate** carnal   **245 Watch you** stand watch   **245-246 for the command . . . you** I'll arrange for you to be appointed, given orders   **247 tainting** disparaging   **249 minister** provide   **251 choler** wrath   **haply** perhaps   **253 mutiny** riot. **qualification** appeasement.   **true taste** i.e., acceptable state   **255 prefer** advance   **259 warrant** assure.   **by and by** immediately   **263 apt** probable.   **credit** credibility   **269 accountant** accountable   **270 diet** feed

Doth, like a poisonous mineral, gnaw my innards;
And nothing can or shall content my soul
Till I am evened with him, wife for wife,   275
Or failing so, yet that I put the Moor
At least into a jealousy so strong
That judgment cannot cure. Which thing to do,
If this poor trash of Venice, whom I trace°
For° his quick hunting, stand the putting on,°   280
I'll have our Michael Cassio on the hip,°
Abuse° him to the Moor in the rank garb—°
For I fear Cassio with my nightcap° too—
Make the Moor thank me, love me, and reward me
For making him egregiously an ass   285
And practicing upon° his peace and quiet
Even to madness. 'Tis here, but yet confused.
Knavery's plain face is never seen till used.

                                                                   Exit.

SCENE II [CYPRUS. A STREET.]

Enter Othello's Herald with a proclamation.

HERALD: It is Othello's pleasure, our noble and valiant general, that, upon certain tidings now arrived, importing the
mere perdition° of the Turkish fleet, every man put himself
into triumph:° some to dance, some to make bonfires, each
man to what sport and revels his addiction° leads him. For,
besides these beneficial news, it is the celebration of his nup-
tial. So much was his pleasure should be proclaimed. All of-   5
fices° are open, and there is full liberty of feasting from this

---

279 trace i.e., train, or follow (?), or perhaps *trash,* a hunting term, meaning to put weights on a
hunting dog in order to slow him down   **280 For** to make more eager.   **stand . . . on** respond
properly when I incite him to quarrel   **281 on the hip** at my mercy, where I can throw him. (A
wrestling term.)   **282 Abuse** slander.   **rank garb** coarse manner, gross fashion   **283 with my
nightcap** i.e., as a rival in my bed, as one who gives me cuckold's horns   **286 practicing upon**
plotting against
2 mere perdition complete destruction   **3 triumph** public celebration   **4 addiction** inclination
6 offices rooms where food and drink are kept

present hour of five till the bell have told eleven. Heaven
bless the isle of Cyprus and our noble general Othello!

Exit.

Scene III [Cyprus. The Citadel.]

Enter Othello, Desdemona, Cassio, and attendants.

OTHELLO: Good Michael, look you to the guard tonight.
Let's teach ourselves that honorable stop°
Not to outsport° discretion.
CASSIO: Iago hath direction what to do,
But notwithstanding, with my personal eye   5
Will I look to 't.
OTHELLO: Iago is most honest.
Michael, good night. Tomorrow with your earliest°
Let me have speech with you. [*To Desdemona.*]
     Come, my dear love,
The purchase made, the fruits are to ensue;
That profit's yet to come 'tween me and you.°—   10
Good night.

Exit [Othello, with Desdemona and attendants].

Enter Iago.

CASSIO: Welcome, Iago. We must to the watch.
IAGO: Not this hour,° Lieutenant; 'tis not yet ten o' the clock.
Our general cast° us thus early for the love of his
Desdemona; who° let us not therefore blame. He hath not yet
made wanton the night with her, and she is sport for Jove.   15
CASSIO: She's a most exquisite lady.
IAGO: And, I'll warrant her, full of game.
CASSIO: Indeed, she's a most fresh and delicate creature.
IAGO: What an eye she has! Methinks it sounds a parley° to
provocation.

---

2 stop restraint   **3 outsport** celebrate beyond the bounds of   **7 with your earliest** at your earliest
convenience   **9-10 The purchase . . . you** i.e., though married, we haven't yet consummated our
love   **13 Not this hour** not for an hour yet.   **cast** dismissed   **14 who** i.e., Othello   **19 sounds a
parley** calls for a conference, issues an invitation

CASSIO: An inviting eye, and yet methinks right modest. 20
IAGO: And when she speaks, is it not an alarum° to love?
CASSIO: She is indeed perfection.
IAGO: Well, happiness to their sheets! Come, Lieutenant, I have
a stoup° of wine, and here without° are a brace° of Cyprus
gallants that would fain have a measure° to the health of 25
black Othello.
CASSIO: Not tonight, good Iago. I have very poor and unhappy
brains for drinking. I could well wish courtesy would invent
some other custom of entertainment.
IAGO: O, they are our friends. But one cup! I'll drink for you.°
CASSIO: I have drunk but one cup tonight, and that was
craftily qualified° too, and behold what innovation° it makes 30
here.° I am unfortunate in the infirmity and dare not task
my weakness with any more.
IAGO: What, man? 'Tis a night of revels. The gallants desire it.
CASSIO: Where are they?
IAGO: Here at the door. I pray you, call them in.
CASSIO: I'll do 't, but it dislikes me.°   *Exit.* 35
IAGO: If I can fasten but one cup upon him,
With that which he hath drunk tonight already,
He'll be as full of quarrel and offense°
As my young mistress' dog. Now, my sick fool Roderigo,
Whom love hath turned almost the wrong side out, 40
To Desdemona hath tonight caroused°
Potations pottle-deep;° and he's to watch.°
Three lads of Cyprus—noble swelling° spirits,
That hold their honors in a wary distance,°
The very elements° of this warlike isle— 45
Have I tonight flustered with flowing cups,
And they watch° too. Now, 'mongst this flock of drunkards

---

21 **alarum** signal calling men to arms (continuing the military metaphor of *parley,* line 19)
23 **stoup** measure of liquor, two quarts   24 **without** outside.   **brace** pair   24-25 **fain have a**
measure gladly drink a toast   28 **for you** in your place. (Iago will do the steady drinking to keep
the gallants company while Cassio has only one cup.)   29 **qualified** diluted   30 **innovation** disturbance, insurrection.   **here** i.e., in my head   35 **it dislikes me** i.e., I'm reluctant   38 **offense**
readiness to take offense   41 **caroused** drunk off   42 **pottle-deep** to the bottom of the tankard.
watch stand watch   43 **swelling** proud   44 **hold . . . distance** i.e., are extremely sensitive of
their honor   45 **very elements** typical sort   47 **watch** are members of the guard

Am I to put our Cassio in some action
That may offend the isle.—But here they come.

*Enter Cassio, Montano, and gentlemen; [servants following
with wine].*

If consequence do but approve my dream,°   50
My boat sails freely both with wind and stream.°
CASSIO: 'Fore God, they have given me a rouse° already.
MONTANO: Good faith, a little one; not past a pint, as I am a
soldier.
IAGO: Some wine, ho! [He *sings.*]

    "And let me the cannikin° clink, clink,   55
       And let me the cannikin clink.
    A soldier's a man,
    O, man's life's but a span;°
    Why, then, let a soldier drink."

Some wine, boys!   60
CASSIO: 'Fore God, an excellent song.
IAGO: I learned it in England, where indeed they are most po-
tent in potting.° Your Dane, your German, and your swag-
bellied Hollander—drink, ho!—are nothing to your English.
CASSIO: Is your Englishman so exquisite in his drinking?   65
IAGO: Why, he drinks you,° with facility, your Dane° dead
drunk; he sweats not° to overthrow your Almain;° he gives
your Hollander a vomit ere the next pottle can be filled.
CASSIO: To the health of our general!
MONTANO: I am for it, Lieutenant, and I'll do you justice.°   70
IAGO: O sweet England! [*He sings.*]

    "King Stephen was and—a worthy peer,
       His breeches cost him but a crown;
    He held them sixpence all too dear,
       With that he called the tailor lown.°   75

---

50 If . . . dream if subsequent events will only substantiate my scheme   **51 stream** current
52 rouse full draft of liquor   **55 cannikin** small drinking vessel   **58 span** brief span of time.
(Compare Psalm 39:6 as rendered in the 1928 *Book of Common Prayer:* "Thou hast made my days as
it were a span long.")   **62 potting** drinking   **66 drinks you** drinks.   **your Dane** your typical
Dane.   **sweats not** i.e., need not exert himself   **67 Almain** German   **70 I'll . . . justice** i.e., I'll
drink as much as you   **75 lown** lout, rascal

> He was a wight of high renown,
>   And thou art but of low degree.
> 'Tis pride° that pulls the country down;
>   Then take thy auld° cloak about thee."

Some wine, ho!   80

CASSIO: 'Fore God, this is a more exquisite song than the
other.

IAGO: Will you hear 't again?

CASSIO: No, for I hold him to be unworthy of his place that
does those things. Well, God's above all; and there be souls
must be saved, and there be souls must not be saved.   85

IAGO: It's true, good Lieutenant.

CASSIO: For mine own part—no offense to the General, nor
any man of quality°—I hope to be saved.

IAGO: And so do I too, Lieutenant.

CASSIO: Ay, but, by your leave, not before me; the lieutenant is
to be saved before the ancient. Let's have no more of this;   90
let's to our affairs.—God forgive us our sins!—Gentlemen,
let's look to our business. Do not think, gentlemen, I am
drunk. This is my ancient; this is my right hand, and this is
my left. I am not drunk now. I can stand well enough, and
speak well enough.

GENTLEMEN: Excellent well.   95

CASSIO: Why, very well then; you must not think then that I
am drunk.   *Exit.*

MONTANO: To th' platform, masters. Come, let's set the
watch.°

> [*Exeunt Gentlemen.*]

IAGO: You see this fellow that is gone before.
He's a soldier fit to stand by Caesar
And give direction; and do but see his vice.   100
'Tis to his virtue a just equinox,°
The one as long as th' other. 'Tis pity of him.

---

78 pride i.e., extravagance in dress   **79 auld** old   **88 quality** rank   **97 set the watch** mount the
guard   **101 just equinox** exact counterpart. (*Equinox* is a day on which daylight and nighttime
hours are equal.)

I fear the trust Othello puts him in,
On some odd time of his infirmity,
Will shake this island.

MONTANO: But is he often thus?   *105*

IAGO: 'Tis evermore the prologue to his sleep.
He'll watch the horologe a double set,°
If drink rock not his cradle.

MONTANO: It were well
The General were put in mind of it.
Perhaps he sees it not, or his good nature   *110*
Prizes the virtue that appears in Cassio
And looks not on his evils. Is not this true?

Enter Roderigo.

IAGO [aside to him]:   How now, Roderigo?
I pray you, after the Lieutenant; go.   [*Exit Roderigo.*]

MONTANO: And 'tis great pity that the noble Moor   *115*
Should hazard such a place as his own second
With° one of an engraffed° infirmity.
It were an honest action to say so
To the Moor.

IAGO: Not I, for this fair island.
I do love Cassio well and would do much   *120*
To cure him of this evil.   [*Cry within:* "Help! Help!"]
But, hark! What noise?

Enter Cassio, pursuing° Roderigo.

CASSIO: Zounds, you rogue! You rascal!

MONTANO: What's the matter, Lieutenant?

CASSIO: A knave teach me my duty? I'll beat the knave into a
twiggen° bottle.

RODERIGO: Beat me?   *125*

CASSIO: Dost thou prate, rogue? [*He strikes Roderigo.*]

---

107 watch . . . set stay awake twice around the clock or *horologe*   **116-117 hazard . . . With** risk
giving such an important position as his second in command to   **117 engraffed** engrafted, inveterate
121 s.d.pursuing (The Quarto text reads, "driving in.")   **124 twiggen** wicker-covered. (Cassio
vows to assail Roderigo until his skin resembles wickerwork or until he has driven Roderigo through
the holes in a wickerwork.)

MONTANO: Nay, good Lieutenant. [*Restraining him.*] I pray
you, sir, hold your hand.

CASSIO: Let me go, sir, or I'll knock you o'er the mazard.°

MONTANO: Come, come, you're drunk.

CASSIO: Drunk?   [*They fight.*]   130

IAGO [*aside to Roderigo*]:   Away, I say. Go out and cry a
mutiny.°

                                    [*Exit Roderigo.*]

Nay, good Lieutenant—God's will, gentlemen—
Help, ho!—Lieutenant—sir—Montano—sir—
Help, masters!°—Here's a goodly watch indeed!

[*A bell rings.*]°

Who's that which rings the bell?—Diablo,° ho!   135
The town will rise.° God's will, Lieutenant, hold!
You'll be ashamed forever.

Enter Othello and attendants [with weapons].

OTHELLO: What is the matter here?

MONTANO: Zounds, I bleed still.
I am hurt to th' death. He dies! [*He thrusts at Cassio.*]

OTHELLO: Hold, for your lives!

IAGO: Hold, ho! Lieutenant—sir—Montano—gentlemen—   140
Have you forgot all sense of place and duty?
Hold! The General speaks to you. Hold, for shame!

OTHELLO: Why, how now, ho! From whence ariseth this?
Are we turned Turks, and to ourselves do that
Which heaven hath forbid the Ottomites?°   145
For Christian shame, put by this barbarous brawl!
He that stirs next to carve for° his own rage
Holds his soul light;° he dies upon his motion.°
Silence that dreadful bell. It frights the isle

---

128 mazard i.e., head. (Literally, a drinking vessel.)   **131 mutiny** riot   **134 masters** sirs.   **s.d. A
bell rings** (This direction is from the Quarto, as are *Exit Roderigo* at line 114, *They fight* at line 130,
and *with weapons* at line 137.)   **135 Diablo** the devil   **136 rise** grow riotous   **144-145 to ourselves . . . Ottomites** inflict on ourselves the harm that heaven has prevented the Turks from doing
(by destroying their fleet)   **147 carve for** i.e., indulge, satisfy with his sword   **148 Holds . . .
light** i.e., places little value on his life.   **upon his motion** if he moves

From her propriety.° What is the matter, masters?   *150*
Honest Iago, that looks dead with grieving,
Speak. Who began this? On thy love, I charge thee.

IAGO: I do not know. Friends all but now, even now,
In quarter° and in terms° like bride and groom
Devesting them° for bed; and then, but now—   *155*
As if some planet had unwitted men—
Swords out, and tilting one at others' breasts
In opposition bloody. I cannot speak°
Any beginning to this peevish odds;°
And would in action glorious I had lost   *160*
Those legs that brought me to a part of it!

OTHELLO: How comes it, Michael, you are thus forgot?°

CASSIO: I pray you, pardon me. I cannot speak.

OTHELLO: Worthy Montano, you were wont be° civil;
The gravity and stillness° of your youth   *165*
The world hath noted, and your name is great
In mouths of wisest censure.° What's the matter
That you unlace° your reputation thus
And spend your rich opinion° for the name
Of a night-brawler? Give me answer to it.   *170*

MONTANO: Worthy Othello, I am hurt to danger.
Your officer, Iago, can inform you—
While I spare speech, which something° now offends° me—
Of all that I do know; nor know I aught
By me that's said or done amiss this night,   *175*
Unless self-charity be sometimes a vice,
And to defend ourselves it be a sin
When violence assails us.

OTHELLO: Now, by heaven,
My blood° begins my safer guides° to rule,
And passion, having my best judgment collied,°   *180*

---

150 propriety proper state or condition   **154 In quarter** in friendly conduct, within bounds.   **in terms** on good terms   **155 Devesting them** undressing themselves   **158 speak** explain
159 peevish odds childish quarrel   **162 are thus forgot** have forgotten yourself thus   **164 wont be** accustomed to be   **165 stillness** sobriety   **167 censure** judgment   **168 unlace** undo, lay open (as one might loose the strings of a purse containing reputation)   **169 opinion** reputation
173 something somewhat.   **offends** pains   **179 blood** passion (of anger).   **guides** i.e., reason
180 collied darkened

Essays° to lead the way. Zounds, if I stir,
Or do but lift this arm, the best of you
Shall sink in my rebuke. Give me to know
How this foul rout° began, who set it on;
And he that is approved in° this offense,   *185*
Though he had twinned with me, both at a birth,
Shall lose me. What? In a town of° war
Yet wild, the people's hearts brim full of fear,
To manage° private and domestic quarrel?
In night, and on the court and guard of safety?°   *190*
'Tis monstrous. Iago, who began 't?

MONTANO [*to Iago*]:   If partially affined,° or leagued in office,°
Thou dost deliver more or less than truth,
Thou art no soldier.

IAGO: Touch me not so near.
I had rather have this tongue cut from my mouth   *195*
Than it should do offense to Michael Cassio;
Yet, I persuade myself, to speak the truth
Shall nothing wrong him. Thus it is, General.
Montano and myself being in speech,
There comes a fellow crying out for help,   *200*
And Cassio following him with determined sword
To execute° upon him. Sir, this gentleman

[*indicating Montano*]

Steps in to Cassio and entreats his pause.°
Myself the crying fellow did pursue,
Lest by his clamor—as it so fell out—   *205*
The town might fall in fright. He, swift of foot,
Outran my purpose, and I returned, the rather°
For that I heard the clink and fall of swords
And Cassio high in oath, which till tonight
I ne'er might say before. When I came back—   *210*

---

181 Essays undertakes   **184 rout** riot   **185 approved in** found guilty of   **187 town of** town garrisoned for   **189 manage** undertake   **190 on . . . safety** at the main guardhouse or headquarters and on watch   **192 partially affined** made partial by some personal relationship.   **leagued in office** in league as fellow officers   **202 execute** give effect to (his anger)   **203 his pause** him to stop   **207 rather** sooner

For this was brief—I found them close together
At blow and thrust, even as again they were
When you yourself did part them.
More of this matter cannot I report.
But men are men; the best sometimes forget.° 215
Though Cassio did some little wrong to him,
As men in rage strike those that wish them best,°
Yet surely Cassio, I believe, received
From him that fled some strange indignity,
Which patience could not pass.°

OTHELLO: I know, Iago, 220
Thy honesty and love doth mince this matter,
Making it light to Cassio. Cassio, I love thee,
But nevermore be officer of mine.

Enter Desdemona, attended.

Look if my gentle love be not raised up.
I'll make thee an example. 225

DESDEMONA: What is the matter, dear?

OTHELLO: All's well now,
sweeting;
Come away to bed. [*To Montano.*] Sir, for your hurts,
Myself will be your surgeon.°—Lead him off.

[*Montano is led off.*]

Iago, look with care about the town
And silence those whom this vile brawl distracted. 230
Come, Desdemona. 'Tis the soldiers' life
To have their balmy slumbers waked with strife.

Exit [*with all but Iago and Cassio*].

IAGO: What, are you hurt, Lieutenant?

CASSIO: Ay, past all surgery.

IAGO: Marry, God forbid! 235

---

215 forget forget themselves   **217 those . . . best** i.e., even those who are well disposed   **220 pass** pass over, overlook   **228 be your surgeon** i.e., make sure you receive medical attention

CASSIO: Reputation, reputation, reputation! O, I have lost my reputation! I have lost the immortal part of myself, and what remains is bestial. My reputation, Iago, my reputation!

IAGO: As I am an honest man, I thought you had received some bodily wound; there is more sense in that than in reputation. 240 Reputation is an idle and most false imposition,° oft got without merit and lost without deserving. You have lost no reputation at all, unless you repute yourself such a loser. What, man, there are more ways to recover° the General again. You are but now cast in his mood°—a punishment more in policy° than in malice, even so as one would beat his offenseless dog to affright an imperious lion.° Sue° to him 245 again and he's yours.

CASSIO: I will rather sue to be despised than to deceive so good a commander with so slight,° so drunken, and so indiscreet an officer. Drunk? And speak parrot?° And squabble? Swagger? Swear? And discourse fustian with one's own shadow? O thou invisible spirit of wine, if thou hast no name to be 250 known by, let us call thee devil!

IAGO: What was he that you followed with your sword? What had he done to you?

CASSIO: I know not.

IAGO: Is 't possible?

CASSIO: I remember a mass of things, but nothing distinctly; a 255 quarrel, but nothing wherefore.° O God, that men should put an enemy in their mouths to steal away their brains! That we should, with joy, pleasance, revel, and applause° transform ourselves into beasts!

IAGO: Why, but you are now well enough. How came you thus recovered?

CASSIO: It hath pleased the devil drunkenness to give place to the devil wrath. One unperfectness shows me another, to 260 make me frankly despise myself.

---

241 false imposition thing artificially imposed and of no real value   **243 recover** regain favor with   **244 cast in his mood** dismissed in a moment of anger.   **in policy** done for expediency's sake and as a public gesture   **245 would . . . lion** i.e., would make an example of a minor offender in order to deter more important and dangerous offenders   **246 Sue** petition   **248 slight** worthless   **248-249 speak parrot** talk nonsense, rant   **256 wherefore** why   **258 applause** desire for applause

IAGO: Come, you are too severe a moraler.° As the time, the place, and the condition of this country stands, I could heartily wish this had not befallen; but since it is as it is, mend it for your own good.

CASSIO: I will ask him for my place again; he shall tell me I am 265 a drunkard. Had I as many mouths as Hydra,° such an answer would stop them all. To be now a sensible man, by and by a fool, and presently a beast! O, strange! Every inordinate cup is unblessed, and the ingredient is a devil.

IAGO: Come, come, good wine is a good familiar creature, if it be well used. Exclaim no more against it. And, good Lieu- 270 tenant, I think you think I love you.

CASSIO: I have well approved° it, sir. I drunk!

IAGO: You or any man living may be drunk at a time,° man. I'll tell you what you shall do. Our general's wife is now the general—I may say so in this respect, for that° he hath devoted and given up himself to the contemplation, mark, and de- 275 notement° of her parts° and graces. Confess yourself freely to her; importune her help to put you in your place again. She is of so free,° so kind, so apt, so blessed a disposition, she holds it a vice in her goodness not to do more than she is requested. This broken joint between you and her husband entreat her to splinter;° and, my fortunes against any lay° worth naming, 280 this crack of your love shall grow stronger than it was before.

CASSIO: You advise me well.

IAGO: I protest,° in the sincerity of love and honest kindness.

CASSIO: I think it freely;° and betimes in the morning I will beseech the virtuous Desdemona to undertake for me. I am 285 desperate of my fortunes if they check° me here.

IAGO: You are in the right. Good night, Lieutenant. I must to the watch.

CASSIO: Good night, honest Iago. *Exit Cassio.*

IAGO: And what's he then that says I play the villain,

---

262 moraler moralizer   **266 Hydra** the Lernaean Hydra, a monster with many heads and the ability to grow two heads when one was cut off, slain by Hercules as the second of his twelve labors   **272 approved** proved   **273 at a time** at one time or another   **274-275 in . . . that** in view of this fact, that   **275-276 mark, and denotement** (Both words mean "observation.")   **276 parts** qualities   **277 free** generous   **280 splinter** bind with splints.   **lay** stake, wager   **283 protest** insist, declare   **284 freely** unreservedly   **286 check** repulse

When this advice is free° I give, and honest,   *290*
Probal° to thinking, and indeed the course
To win the Moor again? For 'tis most easy
Th' inclining° Desdemona to subdue°
In any honest suit; she's framed as fruitful°
As the free elements.° And then for her   *295*
To win the Moor—were 't to renounce his baptism,
All seals and symbols of redeemèd sin—
His soul is so enfettered to her love
That she may make, unmake, do what she list,
Even as her appetite° shall play the god   *300*
With his weak function.° How am I then a villain,
To counsel Cassio to this parallel° course
Directly to his good? Divinity of hell!°
When devils will the blackest sins put on,°
They do suggest° at first with heavenly shows,   *305*
As I do now. For whiles this honest fool
Plies Desdemona to repair his fortune,
And she for him pleads strongly to the Moor,
I'll pour this pestilence into his ear,
That she repeals him° for her body's lust;   *310*
And by how much she strives to do him good,
She shall undo her credit with the Moor.
So will I turn her virtue into pitch,°
And out of her own goodness make the net
That shall enmesh them all.

Enter Roderigo.

                                 How now, Roderigo?   *315*
RODERIGO: I do follow here in the chase, not like a hound that
    hunts, but one that fills up the cry.° My money is almost

---

290 free (1) free from guile (2) freely given   **291 Probal** probable, reasonable   **293 inclining** favorably disposed.   **subdue** persuade   **294 framed as fruitful** created as generous   **295 free elements** i.e., earth, air, fire, and water, unrestrained and spontaneous   **300 her appetite** her desire, or, perhaps, his desire for her   **301 function** exercise of faculties (weakened by his fondness for her)   **302 parallel** corresponding to these facts and to his best interests   **303 Divinity of hell** inverted theology of hell (which seduces the soul to its damnation)   **304 put on** further, instigate   **305 suggest** tempt   **310 repeals him** attempts to get him restored   **313 pitch** i.e., (1) foul blackness (2) a snaring substance   **317 fills up the cry** merely takes part as one of the pack

spent; I have been tonight exceedingly well cudgeled; and I
think the issue will be I shall have so much° experience for
my pains, and so, with no money at all and a little more wit,
return again to Venice.   *320*

IAGO: How poor are they that have not patience!
What wound did ever heal but by degrees?
Thou know'st we work by wit, and not by witchcraft,
And wit depends on dilatory time.
Does 't not go well? Cassio hath beaten thee,   *325*
And thou, by that small hurt, hast cashiered° Cassio.
Though other things grow fair against the sun,
Yet fruits that blossom first will first be ripe.°
Content thyself awhile. By the Mass, 'tis morning!
Pleasure and action make the hours seem short.   *330*
Retire thee; go where thou art billeted.
Away, I say! Thou shalt know more hereafter.
Nay, get thee gone.   *Exit Roderigo.*
                    Two things are to be done.
My wife must move° for Cassio to her mistress;
I'll set her on;   *335*
Myself the while to draw the Moor apart
And bring him jump° when he may Cassio find
Soliciting his wife. Ay, that's the way.
Dull not device° by coldness° and delay.   *Exit.*

ACT III

SCENE I [BEFORE THE CHAMBER OF OTHELLO AND DESDEMONA.]

Enter Cassio [and] Musicians.

CASSIO: Masters, play here—I will content your pains°—
Something that's brief, and bid "Good morrow, General."
[*They play.*]

---

318 so much just so much and no more   **326 cashiered** dismissed from service   **327-328 Though
. . . ripe** i.e., plans that are well-prepared and set expeditiously in motion will soonest ripen into success   **334 move** plead   **337 jump** precisely   **339 device** plot.   **coldness** lack of zeal
1 content your pains reward your efforts

[*Enter*] *Clown.*

CLOWN: Why, masters, have your instruments been in Naples,
  that they speak i' the nose° thus?

A MUSICIAN: How, sir, how?   5

CLOWN: Are these, I pray you, wind instruments?

A MUSICIAN: Ay, marry, are they, sir.

CLOWN: O, thereby hangs a tail.

A MUSICIAN: Whereby hangs a tale, sir?

CLOWN: Marry, sir, by many a wind instrument° that I know.   10
  But, masters, here's money for you. [*He gives money.*] And
  the General so likes your music that he desires you, for love's
  sake,° to make no more noise with it.

A MUSICIAN: Well, sir, we will not.

CLOWN: If you have any music that may not° be heard, to 't
  again; but, as they say, to hear music the General does not
  greatly care.   15

A MUSICIAN: We have none such, sir.

CLOWN: Then put up your pipes in your bag, for I'll away.°
  Go, vanish into air, away!   *Exeunt Musicians.*

CASSIO: Dost thou hear, mine honest friend?

CLOWN: No, I hear not your honest friend; I hear you.   20

CASSIO: Prithee, keep up° thy quillets.° There's a poor piece of
  gold for thee. [*He gives money.*] If the gentle-woman that at-
  tends the General's wife be stirring, tell her there's one
  Cassio entreats her a little favor of speech.° Wilt thou do
  this?

CLOWN: She is stirring, sir. If she will stir° hither, I shall seem°
  to notify unto her.   25

CASSIO: Do, good my friend.   *Exit Clown.*

Enter Iago.

3-4 speak i' the nose (1) sound nasal (2) sound like one whose nose has been attacked by syphilis.
(Naples was popularly supposed to have a high incidence of venereal disease.)   **10 wind instrument**
(With a joke on flatulence. The *tail*, line 8, that hangs nearby the *wind instrument* suggests the penis.)
12 for love's sake (1) out of friendship and affection (2) for the sake of lovemaking in Othello's marriage   **14 may not** cannot   **17 I'll away** (Possibly a misprint, or a snatch of song?)   **21 keep up**
do not bring out, do not use.   **quillets** quibbles, puns   **23 a little . . . speech** the favor of a brief
talk   **25 stir** bestir herself (with a play on *stirring,* "rousing herself from rest")   **seem** deem it
good, think fit

In happy time,° Iago.

IAGO: You have not been abed, then?

CASSIO: Why, no. The day had broke
Before we parted. I have made bold, Iago,
To send in to your wife. My suit to her   30
Is that she will to virtuous Desdemona
Procure me some access.

IAGO: I'll send her to you presently;
And I'll devise a means to draw the Moor
Out of the way, that your converse and business   35
May be more free.

CASSIO: I humbly thank you for 't.   *Exit* [*Iago*].
                              I never knew
A Florentine° more kind and honest.

Enter Emilia.

EMILIA: Good morrow, good Lieutenant. I am sorry
For your displeasure;° but all will sure be well.   40
The General and his wife are talking of it,
And she speaks for you stoutly.° The Moor replies
That he you hurt is of great fame° in Cyprus
And great affinity,° and that in wholesome wisdom
He might not but refuse you; but he protests° he loves you   45
And needs no other suitor but his likings
To take the safest occasion by the front°
To bring you in again.

CASSIO: Yet I beseech you,
If you think fit, or that it may be done,
Give me advantage of some brief discourse   50
With Desdemon alone.

EMILIA: Pray you, come in.
I will bestow you where you shall have time
To speak your bosom° freely.

CASSIO: I am much bound to you.   [*Exeunt.*]

---

26 In happy time i.e., well-met   **38 Florentine** i.e., even a fellow Florentine. (Iago is a Venetian; Cassio is a Florentine.)   **40 displeasure** fall from favor   **42 stoutly** spiritedly   **43 fame** reputation, importance   **44 affinity** kindred, family connection   **45 protests** insists   **47 occasion . . . front** opportunity by the forelock   **53 bosom** inmost thoughts

SCENE II [THE CITADEL.]

Enter Othello, Iago, and Gentlemen.

OTHELLO [*giving letters*]: These letters give, Iago, to the pilot,
And by him do my duties° to the Senate.
That done, I will be walking on the works;°
Repair° there to me.

IAGO: Well, my good lord, I'll do 't.

OTHELLO: This fortification, gentlemen, shall we see 't?   5

GENTLEMEN: We'll wait upon° your lordship.   *Exeunt.*

SCENE III [THE GARDEN OF THE CITADEL.]

Enter Desdemona, Cassio, and Emilia.

DESDEMONA: Be thou assured, good Cassio, I will do
All my abilities in thy behalf.

EMILIA: Good madam, do. I warrant it grieves my husband
As if the cause were his.

DESDEMONA: O, that's an honest fellow. Do not doubt, Cassio,   5
But I will have my lord and you again
As friendly as you were.

CASSIO: Bounteous madam,
Whatever shall become of Michael Cassio,
He's never anything but your true servant.

DESDEMONA: I know 't. I thank you. You do love my lord;   10
You have known him long, and be you well assured
He shall in strangeness° stand no farther off
Than in a politic° distance.

CASSIO: Ay, but, lady,
That policy may either last so long,
Or feed upon such nice and waterish diet,°   15
Or breed itself so out of circumstance,°
That, I being absent and my place supplied,°

2 do my duties convey my respects   **3 works** breastworks, fortifications   **4 Repair** return, come
6 wait upon attend
12 strangeness aloofness   **13 politic** required by wise policy   **15 Or . . . diet** or sustain itself at
length upon such trivial and meager technicalities   **16 breed . . . circumstance** continually renew
itself so out of chance events, or yield so few chances for my being pardoned   **17 supplied** filled by
another person

My general will forget my love and service.

DESDEMONA: Do not doubt° that. Before Emilia here
I give thee warrant° of thy place. Assure thee,   20
If I do vow a friendship I'll perform it
To the last article. My lord shall never rest.
I'll watch him tame° and talk him out of patience;°
His bed shall seem a school, his board° a shrift;°
I'll intermingle everything he does   25
With Cassio's suit. Therefore be merry, Cassio,
For thy solicitor° shall rather die
Than give thy cause away.°

Enter Othello and Iago [at a distance].

EMILIA: Madam, here comes my lord.

CASSIO: Madam, I'll take my leave.   30

DESDEMONA: Why, stay, and hear me speak.

CASSIO: Madam, not now. I am very ill at ease,
Unfit for mine own purposes.

DESDEMONA: Well, do your discretion.°   *Exit Cassio.*

IAGO: Ha? I like not that.   35

OTHELLO: What dost thou say?

IAGO: Nothing, my lord; or if—I know not what.

OTHELLO: Was not that Cassio parted from my wife?

IAGO: Cassio, my lord? No, sure, I cannot think it,
That he would steal away so guiltylike,   40
Seeing you coming.

OTHELLO: I do believe 'twas he.

DESDEMONA: How now, my lord?
I have been talking with a suitor here,
A man that languishes in your displeasure.   45

OTHELLO: Who is 't you mean?

DESDEMONA: Why, your lieutenant, Cassio. Good my lord,
If I have any grace or power to move you,
His present reconciliation take;°

---

19 doubt fear   **20 warrant** guarantee   **23 watch him tame** tame him by keeping him from sleeping. (A term from falconry.)   **out of patience** past his endurance   **24 board** dining table.   **shrift** confessional   **27 solicitor** advocate   **28 away** up   **34 do your discretion** act according to your own discretion   **49 His . . . take** let him be reconciled to you right away

For if he be not one that truly loves you,   *50*
That errs in ignorance and not in cunning,°
I have no judgment in an honest face.
I prithee, call him back.

OTHELLO: Went he hence now?

DESDEMONA: Yes, faith, so humbled   *55*
That he hath left part of his grief with me
To suffer with him. Good love, call him back.

OTHELLO: Not now, sweet Desdemon. Some other time.

DESDEMONA: But shall 't be shortly?

OTHELLO: The sooner, sweet, for you.   *60*

DESDEMONA: Shall 't be tonight at supper?

OTHELLO: No, not tonight.

DESDEMONA: Tomorrow dinner,° then?

OTHELLO: I shall not dine at home.
I meet the captains at the citadel.   *65*

DESDEMONA: Why, then, tomorrow night, or Tuesday morn,
On Tuesday noon, or night, on Wednesday morn.
I prithee, name the time, but let it not
Exceed three days. In faith, he's penitent;
And yet his trespass, in our common reason°—   *70*
Save that, they say, the wars must make example
Out of her best°—is not almost° a fault
T' incur a private check.° When shall he come?
Tell me, Othello. I wonder in my soul
What you would ask me that I should deny,   *75*
Or stand so mammering on.° What? Michael Cassio,
That came a-wooing with you, and so many a time,
When I have spoke of you dispraisingly,
Hath ta'en your part—to have so much to do
To bring him in!° By 'r Lady, I could do much—   *80*

OTHELLO: Prithee, no more. Let him come when he will;
I will deny thee nothing.

---

51 in cunning wittingly   **63 dinner** (The noontime meal.)   **70 common reason** everyday judgments   **71-72 Save . . . best** were it not that, as the saying goes, military discipline requires making an example of the very best men. (*Her* refers to wars as a singular concept.)   **72 not almost** scarcely   **73 private check** even a private reprimand   **76 mammering on** wavering about   **80 bring him in** restore him to favor

DESDEMONA: Why, this is not a boon.
'Tis as I should entreat you wear your gloves,
Or feed on nourishing dishes, or keep you warm,   *85*
Or sue to you to do a peculiar° profit
To your own person. Nay, when I have a suit
Wherein I mean to touch° your love indeed,
It shall be full of poise° and difficult weight,
And fearful to be granted.   *90*

OTHELLO: I will deny thee nothing.
Whereon,° I do beseech thee, grant me this,
To leave me but a little to myself.

DESDEMONA: Shall I deny you? No. Farewell, my lord.

OTHELLO: Farewell, my Desdemona. I'll come to thee straight.°   *95*

DESDEMONA: Emilia, come.—Be as your fancies° teach you;
Whate'er you be, I am obedient.   *Exit [with Emilia].*

OTHELLO: Excellent wretch!° Perdition catch my soul
But I do love thee! And when I love thee not,
Chaos is come again.°   *100*

IAGO: My noble lord—

OTHELLO: What dost thou say, Iago?

IAGO: Did Michael Cassio, when you wooed my lady,
Know of your love?

OTHELLO: He did, from first to last. Why dost thou ask?   *105*

IAGO: But for a satisfaction of my thought;
No further harm.

OTHELLO: Why of thy thought, Iago?

IAGO: I did not think he had been acquainted with her.

OTHELLO: O, yes, and went between us very oft.

IAGO: Indeed?   *110*

OTHELLO: Indeed? Ay, indeed. Discern'st thou aught in that?
Is he not honest?

IAGO: Honest, my lord?

OTHELLO: Honest. Ay, honest.

---

86 peculiar particular, personal   **88 touch** test   **89 poise** weight, heaviness; or equipoise, delicate balance involving hard choice   **92 Whereon** in return for which   **95 straight** straightway   **96 fancies** inclinations   **98 wretch** (A term of affectionate endearment.)   **99-100 And . . . again** i.e., my love for you will last forever, until the end of time when chaos will return. (But with an unconscious, ironic suggestion that, if anything should induce Othello to cease loving Desdemona, the result would be chaos.)

IAGO: My lord, for aught I know. 115

OTHELLO: What dost thou think?

IAGO: Think, my lord?

OTHELLO: "Think, my lord?" By heaven, thou echo'st me,
As if there were some monster in thy thought
Too hideous to be shown. Thou dost mean something. 120
I heard thee say even now, thou lik'st not that,
When Cassio left my wife. What didst not like?
And when I told thee he was of my counsel°
In my whole course of wooing, thou criedst "Indeed?"
And didst contract and purse° thy brow together 125
As if thou then hadst shut up in thy brain
Some horrible conceit.° If thou dost love me,
Show me thy thought.

IAGO: My lord, you know I love you.

OTHELLO: I think thou dost; 130
And, for° I know thou'rt full of love and honesty,
And weigh'st thy words before thou giv'st them breath,
Therefore these stops° of thine fright me the more;
For such things in a false disloyal knave
Are tricks of custom,° but in a man that's just 135
They're close dilations,° working from the heart
That passion cannot rule.°

IAGO: For° Michael Cassio,
I dare be sworn I think that he is honest.

OTHELLO: I think so too.

IAGO: Men should be what they seem;
Or those that be not, would they might seem none!° 140

OTHELLO: Certain, men should be what they seem.

IAGO: Why, then, I think Cassio's an honest man.

OTHELLO: Nay, yet there's more in this.
I prithee, speak to me as to thy thinkings,
As thou dost ruminate, and give thy worst of thoughts 145

---

123 of my counsel in my confidence   **125 purse** knit   **127 conceit** fancy   **131 for** because
133 stops pauses   **135 of custom** customary   **136 close dilations** secret or involuntary expressions or delays   **137 That passion cannot rule** i.e., that are too passionately strong to be restrained (referring to the workings), or . . . that cannot rule its own passions (referring to the heart).
137 For as for   **140 none** i.e., not to be men, or not seem to be honest

The worst of words.

IAGO: Good my lord, pardon me.
Though I am bound to every act of duty,
I am not bound to that° all slaves are free to.°
Utter my thoughts? Why, say they are vile and false,
As where's the palace whereinto foul things   *150*
Sometimes intrude not? Who has that breast so pure
But some uncleanly apprehensions
Keep leets and law days,° and in sessions sit
With° meditations lawful?°

OTHELLO: Thou dost conspire against thy friend,° Iago,   *155*
If thou but think'st him wronged and mak'st his ear
A stranger to thy thoughts.

IAGO: I do beseech you,
Though I perchance am vicious° in my guess—
As I confess it is my nature's plague
To spy into abuses, and oft my jealousy°   *160*
Shapes faults that are not—that your wisdom then,°
From one° that so imperfectly conceits,°
Would take no notice, nor build yourself a trouble
Out of his scattering° and unsure observance.
It were not for your quiet nor your good,   *165*
Nor for my manhood, honesty, and wisdom,
To let you know my thoughts.

OTHELLO: What dost thou mean?

IAGO: Good name in man and woman, dear my lord,
Is the immediate° jewel of their souls;
Who steals my purse steals trash; 'tis something, nothing;   *170*
'Twas mine, 'tis his, and has been slave to thousands;
But he that filches from me my good name
Robs me of that which not enriches him
And makes me poor indeed.

OTHELLO: By heaven, I'll know thy thoughts.   *175*

---

148 that that which.   **free to** free with respect to   **153 Keep leets and law days** i.e., hold court,
set up their authority in one's heart. (*Leets* are a kind of manor court; *law days* are the days courts sit
in session, or those sessions.)   **154 With** along with.   **lawful** innocent   **155 thy friend** i.e.,
Othello   **158 vicious** wrong   **160 jealousy** suspicious nature   **161 then** on that account
162 one i.e., myself, Iago.   **conceits** judges, conjectures   **164 scattering** random
169 immediate essential, most precious

IAGO: You cannot, if° my heart were in your hand,
　　Nor shall not, whilst 'tis in my custody.
OTHELLO: Ha?
IAGO: O, beware, my lord, of jealousy.
　　It is the green-eyed monster which doth mock
　　The meat it feeds on.° That cuckold lives in bliss　　　　　　*180*
　　Who, certain of his fate, loves not his wronger;°
　　But O, what damnèd minutes tells° he o'er
　　Who dotes, yet doubts, suspects, yet fondly loves!
OTHELLO: O misery!
IAGO: Poor and content is rich, and rich enough,°　　　　　　*185*
　　But riches fineless° is as poor as winter
　　To him that ever fears he shall be poor.
　　Good God, the souls of all my tribe defend
　　From jealousy!
OTHELLO: Why, why is this?　　　　　　*190*
　　Think'st thou I'd make a life of jealousy,
　　To follow still the changes of the moon
　　With fresh suspicions?° No! To be once in doubt
　　Is once° to be resolved.° Exchange me for a goat
　　When I shall turn the business of my soul　　　　　　*195*
　　To such exsufflicate and blown° surmises
　　Matching thy inference.° 'Tis not to make me jealous
　　To say my wife is fair, feeds well, loves company,
　　Is free of speech, sings, plays, and dances well;
　　Where virtue is, these are more virtuous.　　　　　　*200*
　　Nor from mine own weak merits will I draw
　　The smallest fear or doubt of her revolt,°
　　For she had eyes, and chose me. No, Iago,
　　I'll see before I doubt; when I doubt, prove;
　　And on the proof, there is no more but this—　　　　　　*205*

---

176 if even if　**179-180 doth mock . . . on** mocks and torments the heart of its victim, the man who suffers jealousy　**181 his wronger** i.e., his faithless wife. (The unsuspecting cuckold is spared the misery of loving his wife only to discover she is cheating on him.)　**182 tells** counts　**185 Poor . . . enough** to be content with what little one has is the greatest wealth of all. (Proverbial.)
186 fineless boundless　**192-193 To follow . . . suspicions** to be constantly imagining new causes for suspicion, changing incessantly like the moon　**194 once** once and for all.　**resolved** free of doubt, having settled the matter　**196 exsufflicate and blown** inflated and blown up, rumored about, or, spat out and flyblown, hence, loathsome, disgusting　**197 inference** description or allegation　**202 doubt . . . revolt** fear of her unfaithfulness

Away at once with love or jealousy.

IAGO: I am glad of this, for now I shall have reason
To show the love and duty that I bear you
With franker spirit. Therefore, as I am bound,
Receive it from me. I speak not yet of proof.   *210*
Look to your wife; observe her well with Cassio.
Wear your eyes thus, not° jealous nor secure.°
I would not have your free and noble nature,
Out of self-bounty,° be abused.° Look to 't.
I know our country disposition well;   *215*
In Venice they do let God see the pranks
They dare not show their husbands; their best conscience
Is not to leave 't undone, but keep 't unknown.
Othello: Dost thou say so?

IAGO: She did deceive her father, marrying you;   *220*
And when she seemed to shake and fear your looks,
She loved them most.

OTHELLO: And so she did.

IAGO: Why, go to,° then!
She that, so young, could give out such a seeming,°
To seel° her father's eyes up close as oak,°
He thought 'twas witchcraft! But I am much to blame.   *225*
I humbly do beseech you of your pardon
For too much loving you.

OTHELLO: I am bound° to thee forever.

IAGO: I see this hath a little dashed your spirits.

OTHELLO: Not a jot, not a jot.

IAGO: I' faith, I fear it has.   *230*
I hope you will consider what is spoke
Comes from my love. But I do see you're moved.
I am to pray you not to strain my speech
To grosser issues° nor to larger reach°
Than to suspicion.   *235*

OTHELLO: I will not.

---

212 not neither. **secure** free from uncertainty   **214 self-bounty** inherent or natural goodness and
generosity. **abused** deceived   **222 go to** (An expression of impatience.)   **223 seeming** false appearance   **224 seel** blind. (A term from falconry.)   **oak** (A close-grained wood.)   **228 bound** indebted (but perhaps with ironic sense of "tied")   **234 issues** significances.   **reach** meaning, scope

IAGO: Should you do so, my lord,
    My speech should fall into such vile success°
    Which my thoughts aimed not. Cassio's my worthy friend.
    My lord, I see you're moved.

OTHELLO: No, not much moved.   *240*
    I do not think but Desdemona's honest.°

IAGO: Long live she so! And long live you to think so!

OTHELLO: And yet, how nature erring from itself—

IAGO: Ay, there's the point! As—to be bold with you—
    Not to affect° many proposèd matches   *245*
    Of her own clime, complexion, and degree,°
    Whereto we see in all things nature tends—
    Foh! One may smell in such a will° most rank,
    Foul disproportion,° thoughts unnatural.
    But pardon me. I do not in position°   *250*
    Distinctly speak of her, though I may fear
    Her will, recoiling° to her better° judgment,
    May fall to match you with her country forms°
    And happily° repent.

OTHELLO: Farewell, farewell!
    If more thou dost perceive, let me know more.   *255*
    Set on thy wife to observe. Leave me, Iago.

IAGO [*going*]: My lord, I take my leave.

OTHELLO: Why did I marry? This honest creature doubtless
    Sees and knows more, much more, than he unfolds.

IAGO [*returning*]: My Lord, I would I might entreat your honor   *260*
    To scan° this thing no farther. Leave it to time.
    Although 'tis fit that Cassio have his place—
    For, sure, he fills it up with great ability—
    Yet, if you please to hold him off awhile,
    You shall by that perceive him and his means.°   *265*
    Note if your lady strain his entertainment°
    With any strong or vehement importunity;

---

238 **success** effect, result   241 **honest** chaste   245 **affect** prefer, desire   246 **clime . . . degree**
country, color, and social position   248 **will** sensuality, appetite   249 **disproportion** abnormality
250 **position** argument, proposition   252 **recoiling** reverting. **better** i.e., more natural and re-
considered   253 **fall . . . forms** undertake to compare you with Venetian norms of handsomeness
254 **happily repent** haply repent her marriage   261 **scan** scrutinize   265 **his means** the method
he uses (to regain his post)   266 **strain his entertainment** urge his reinstatement

Much will be seen in that. In the meantime,
Let me be thought too busy° in my fears—
As worthy cause I have to fear I am—   270
And hold her free,° I do beseech your honor.

OTHELLO: Fear not my government.°

IAGO: I once more take my leave.   *Exit.*

OTHELLO: This fellow's of exceeding honesty,
And knows all qualities,° with a learnèd spirit,   275
Of human dealings. If I do prove her haggard,°
Though that her jesses° were my dear heartstrings,
I'd whistle her off and let her down the wind°
To prey at fortune.° Haply, for° I am black
And have not those soft parts of conversation°   280
That chamberers° have, or for I am declined
Into the vale of years—yet that's not much—
She's gone. I am abused,° and my relief
Must be to loathe her. O curse of marriage,
That we can call these delicate creatures ours   285
And not their appetites! I had rather be a toad
And live upon the vapor of a dungeon
Than keep a corner in the thing I love
For others' uses. Yet, 'tis the plague of great ones;
Prerogatived° are they less than the base.°   290
'Tis destiny unshunnable, like death.
Even then this forkèd° plague is fated to us
When we do quicken.° Look where she comes.

Enter Desdemona and Emilia.

If she be false, O, then heaven mocks itself!
I'll not believe 't.

---

269 busy interfering   **271 hold her free** regard her as innocent   **272 government** self-control,
conduct   **275 qualities** natures, types   **276 haggard** wild (like a wild female hawk)   **277 jesses**
straps fastened around the legs of a trained hawk   **278 I'd . . . wind** i.e., I'd let her go forever. (To
release a hawk downwind was to invite it not to return.)   **279 prey at fortune** fend for herself in the
wild.   **Haply, for** perhaps because   **280 soft . . . conversation** pleasing graces of social behavior
281 chamberers gallants   **283 abused** deceived   **290 Prerogatived** privileged (to have honest
wives).   **the base** ordinary citizens. (Socially prominent men are especially prone to the unavoidable
destiny of being cuckolded and to the public shame that goes with it.)   **292 forkèd** (An allusion to
the horns of the cuckold.)   **293 quicken** receive life. (Quicken may also mean to swarm with maggots as the body festers, as in Act IV, Scene ii, line 69, in which case lines 292-293 suggest that *even
then*, in death, we are cuckolded by *forkèd* worms.)

DESDEMONA: How now, my dear Othello?   *295*
  Your dinner, and the generous° islanders
  By you invited, do attend° your presence.
OTHELLO: I am to blame.
DESDEMONA: Why do you speak so faintly?
  Are you not well?
OTHELLO: I have a pain upon my forehead here.   *300*
DESDEMONA: Faith, that's with watching.° 'Twill away again.

[*She offers her handkerchief.*]

  Let me but bind it hard, within this hour
  It will be well.
OTHELLO: Your napkin° is too little.
  Let it alone.° Come, I'll go in with you.

[*He puts the handkerchief from him, and it drops.*]

DESDEMONA: I am very sorry that you are not well.   *305*

                            Exit [*with Othello*].

EMILIA [*picking up the handkerchief*]:   I am glad I have found
  this napkin.
  This was her first remembrance from the Moor.
  My wayward° husband hath a hundred times
  Wooed me to steal it, but she so loves the token—
  For he conjured her she should ever keep it—   *310*
  That she reserves it evermore about her
  To kiss and talk to. I'll have the work ta'en out,°
  And give 't Iago. What he will do with it
  Heaven knows, not I;
  I nothing but to please his fantasy.°   *315*

  Enter Iago.

IAGO: How now? What do you here alone?
EMILIA: Do not you chide. I have a thing for you.

---

296 generous noble   **297 attend** await   **301 watching** too little sleep   **303 napkin** handkerchief
304 Let it alone i.e., never mind   **308 wayward** capricious   **312 work ta'en out** design of the
embroidery copied   **315 fantasy** whim

IAGO: You have a thing for me? It is a common thing°—
EMILIA: Ha?
IAGO: To have a foolish wife.   *320*
EMILIA: O, is that all? What will you give me now
For that same handkerchief?
IAGO: What handkerchief?
EMILIA: What handkerchief?
Why, that the Moor first gave to Desdemona;   *325*
That which so often you did bid me steal.
IAGO: Hast stolen it from her?
EMILIA: No, faith. She let it drop by negligence,
And to th' advantage° I, being here, took 't up.
Look, here 'tis.
IAGO: A good wench! Give it me.   *330*
EMILIA: What will you do with 't, that you have been so
earnest
To have me filch it?
IAGO [*snatching it*]:   Why, what is that to you?
EMILIA: If it be not for some purpose of import,
Give 't me again. Poor lady, she'll run mad
When she shall lack° it.
IAGO: Be not acknown on 't.°   *335*
I have use for it. Go, leave me.   *Exit Emilia.*
I will in Cassio's lodging lose° this napkin
And let him find it. Trifles light as air
Are to the jealous confirmations strong
As proofs of Holy Writ. This may do something.   *340*
The Moor already changes with my poison.
Dangerous conceits° are in their natures poisons,
Which at the first are scarce found to distaste,°
But with a little act° upon the blood
Burn like the mines of sulfur.

Enter Othello.

---

318 common thing (With bawdy suggestion; *common* suggests coarseness and availability to all comers, and *thing* is a slang term for the pudendum.)   **329 to th' advantage** taking the opportunity
335 lack miss.   **Be . . . on't** do not confess knowledge of it   **337 lose** (The Folio spelling, *loose*, is a normal spelling for "lose," but it may also contain the idea of "let go," "release.")   **342 conceits** fancies, ideas   **343 distaste** be distasteful   **344 act** action, working

I did say so.   *345*
Look where he comes! Not poppy nor mandragora°
Nor all the drowsy syrups of the world
Shall ever medicine thee to that sweet sleep
Which thou owedst° yesterday.
OTHELLO: Ha, ha, false to me?
IAGO: Why, how now, General? No more of that.   *350*
OTHELLO: Avaunt! Begone! Thou hast set me on the rack.
I swear 'tis better to be much abused
Than but to know 't a little.
IAGO: How now, my lord?
OTHELLO: What sense had I of her stolen hours of lust?
I saw 't not, thought it not, it harmed not me.   *355*
I slept the next night well, fed well, was free° and merry;
I found not Cassio's kisses on her lips.
He that is robbed, not wanting° what is stolen,
Let him not know 't and he's not robbed at all.
IAGO: I am sorry to hear this.   *360*
OTHELLO: I had been happy if the general camp,
Pioners° and all, had tasted her sweet body,
So° I had nothing known. O, now, forever
Farewell the tranquil mind! Farewell content!
Farewell the plumèd troops and the big° wars   *365*
That makes ambition virtue! O, farewell!
Farewell the neighing steed and the shrill trump,
The spirit-stirring drum, th' ear-piercing fife,
The royal banner, and all quality,°
Pride,° pomp, and circumstance° of glorious war!   *370*
And O, you mortal engines,° whose rude throats
Th' immortal Jove's dread clamors° counterfeit,
Farewell! Othello's occupation's gone.
IAGO: Is 't possible, my lord?
OTHELLO: Villain, be sure thou prove my love a whore!   *375*

---

346 **mandragora** an opiate made of the mandrake root   349 **thou owedst** you did own   356 **free** carefree   358 **wanting** missing   362 **Pioners** diggers of mines, the lowest grade of soldiers   363 **So** provided   365 **big** stately   369 **quality** character, essential nature   370 **Pride** rich display.   **circumstance** pageantry   371 **mortal engines** i.e., cannon. (*Mortal* means "deadly.")   372 **Jove's dread clamors** i.e., thunder

Be sure of it. Give me the ocular proof,
Or, by the worth of mine eternal soul,
Thou hadst been better have been born a dog
Than answer my waked wrath!

IAGO: Is 't come to this?

OTHELLO: Make me to see 't, or at the least so prove it   *380*
That the probation° bear no hinge nor loop
To hang a doubt on, or woe upon thy life!

IAGO: My noble lord—

OTHELLO: If thou dost slander her and torture me,
Never pray more; abandon all remorse;°   *385*
On horror's head horrors accumulate;°
Do deeds to make heaven weep, all earth amazed;°
For nothing canst thou to damnation add
Greater than that.

IAGO: O grace! O heaven forgive me!
Are you a man? Have you a soul or sense?   *390*
God b' wi' you; take mine office. O wretched fool,°
That lov'st to make thine honesty a vice!°
O monstrous world! Take note, take note, O world,
To be direct and honest is not safe.
I thank you for this profit,° and from hence°   *395*
I'll love no friend, sith° love breeds such offense.°

OTHELLO: Nay, stay. Thou shouldst be° honest.

IAGO: I should be wise, for honesty's a fool
And loses that° it works for.

OTHELLO: By the world,
I think my wife be honest and think she is not;   *400*
I think that thou art just and think thou art not.
I'll have some proof. My name, that was as fresh
As Dian's° visage, is now begrimed and black
As mine own face. If there be cords, or knives,
Poison, or fire, or suffocating streams,   *405*

---

381 probation proof   **385 remorse** pity, penitent hope for salvation   **386 horrors accumulate**
add still more horrors   **387 amazed** confounded with horror   **391 O wretched fool** (Iago addresses himself as a fool for having carried honesty too far.)   **392 vice** failing, something overdone
395 profit profitable instruction.   **hence** henceforth   **396 sith** since.   **offense** i.e., harm to the
one who offers help and friendship   **397 Thou shouldst be** it appears that you are. (But Iago replies
in the sense of "ought to be.")   **399 that** what   **403 Dian** Diana, goddess of the moon and of
chastity

I'll not endure it. Would I were satisfied!

IAGO: I see, sir, you are eaten up with passion.

I do repent me that I put it to you.

You would be satisfied?

OTHELLO: Would? Nay, and I will.

IAGO: And may; but how? How satisfied, my lord?   *410*

Would you, the supervisor,° grossly gape on?

Behold her topped?

OTHELLO: Death and damnation! O!

IAGO: It were a tedious difficulty, I think,

To bring them to that prospect. Damn them then,°

If ever mortal eyes do see them bolster°   *415*

More° than their own.° What then? How then?

What shall I say? Where's satisfaction?

It is impossible you should see this,

Were they as prime° as goats, as hot as monkeys,

As salt° as wolves in pride,° and fools as gross   *420*

As ignorance made drunk. But yet I say,

If imputation and strong circumstances°

Which lead directly to the door of truth

Will give you satisfaction, you might have 't.

OTHELLO: Give me a living reason she's disloyal.   *425*

IAGO: I do not like the office.

But sith° I am entered in this cause so far,

Pricked° to 't by foolish honesty and love,

I will go on. I lay with Cassio lately,

And being troubled with a raging tooth   *430*

I could not sleep. There are a kind of men

So loose of soul that in their sleeps will mutter

Their affairs. One of this kind is Cassio.

In sleep I heard him say, "Sweet Desdemona,

Let us be wary, let us hide our loves!"   *435*

And then, sir, would he grip and wring my hand,

Cry "O sweet creature!", then kiss me hard,

---

411 supervisor onlooker   **414 Damn them then** i.e., they would have to be really incorrigible
415 bolster go to bed together, share a bolster   **416 More** other.   **own** own eyes   **419 prime**
lustful   **420 salt** wanton, sensual.   **pride** heat   **422 imputation . . . circumstances** strong cir-
cumstantial evidence   **427 sith** since   **428 Pricked** spurred

As if he plucked up kisses by the roots
That grew upon my lips; then laid his leg
Over my thigh, and sighed, and kissed, and then   440
Cried, "Cursèd fate that gave thee to the Moor!"

OTHELLO: O monstrous! Monstrous!

IAGO: Nay, this was but his
dream.

OTHELLO: But this denoted a foregone conclusion.°
'Tis a shrewd doubt,° though it be but a dream.

IAGO: And this may help to thicken other proofs   445
That do demonstrate thinly.

OTHELLO: I'll tear her all to pieces.

IAGO: Nay, but be wise. Yet we see nothing done;
She may be honest yet. Tell me but this:
Have you not sometimes seen a handkerchief
Spotted with strawberries° in your wife's hand?   450

OTHELLO: I gave her such a one. 'Twas my first gift.

Iago: I know not that; but such a handkerchief—
I am sure it was your wife's—did I today
See Cassio wipe his beard with.

OTHELLO: If it be that—

IAGO: If it be that, or any that was hers,   455
It speaks against her with the other proofs.

OTHELLO: O, that the slave° had forty thousand lives!
One is too poor, too weak for my revenge.
Now do I see 'tis true. Look here, Iago,
All my fond° love thus do I blow to heaven.   460
'Tis gone.
Arise, black vengeance, from the hollow hell!
Yield up, O love, thy crown and hearted° throne
To tyrannous hate! Swell, bosom, with thy freight,°
For 'tis of aspics'° tongues!   465

IAGO: Yet be content.°

OTHELLO: O, blood, blood, blood!

---

443 foregone conclusion concluded experience or action   **444 shrewd doubt** suspicious circumstance   **450 Spotted with strawberries** embroidered with a strawberry pattern   **457 the slave** i.e., Cassio   **460 fond** foolish (but also suggesting "affectionate")   **463 hearted** fixed in the heart   **464 freight** burden   **465 aspics'** venomous serpents'   **466 content** calm

IAGO: Patience, I say. Your mind perhaps may change.

OTHELLO: Never, Iago. Like to the Pontic Sea,°
    Whose icy current and compulsive course   470
    Ne'er feels retiring ebb, but keeps due on
    To the Propontic° and the Hellespont,°
    Even so my bloody thoughts with violent pace
    Shall ne'er look back, ne'er ebb to humble love,
    I that a capable° and wide revenge   475
    Swallow them up. Now, by yond marble° heaven,
    [*Kneeling*] In the due reverence of a sacred vow
    I here engage my words.

IAGO: Do not rise yet.
    [*He kneels.*]° Witness, you ever-burning lights above,
    You elements that clip° us round about,   480
    Witness that here Iago doth give up
    The execution° of his wit,° hands, heart,
    To wronged Othello's service. Let him command,
    And to obey shall be in me remorse,°
    What bloody business ever.° [*They rise.*]

OTHELLO: I greet thy love,   485
    Not with vain thanks, but with acceptance bounteous,
    And will upon the instant put thee to 't.°
    Within these three days let me hear thee say
    That Cassio's not alive.

IAGO: My friend is dead;
    'Tis done at your request. But let her live.   490

OTHELLO: Damn her, lewd minx!° O, damn her, damn her!
    Come, go with me apart. I will withdraw
    To furnish me with some swift means of death
    For the fair devil. Now art thou my lieutenant.

IAGO: I am your own forever.   *Exeunt.*   495

---

469 Pontic Sea Black Sea   **472 Propontic** Sea of Marmara, between the Black Sea and the Aegean.
Helllespont Dardanelles, straits where the Sea of Marmara joins with the Aegean   **475 capable**
ample, comprehensive   **476 marble** i.e., gleaming like marble and unrelenting   **479 [s.d.] He
kneels** (In the Quarto text, Iago kneels here after Othello has knelt at line 477.)   **480 clip** encompass   **482 execution** exercise, action.   **wit** mind   **484 remorse** pity (for Othello's wrongs)
485 ever soever   **487 to 't** to the proof   **491 minx** wanton

Scene IV [Before the Citadel.]

Enter Desdemona, Emilia, and Clown.

DESDEMONA: Do you know, sirrah,° where Lieutenant Cassio
lies?°

CLOWN: I dare not say he lies anywhere.

DESDEMONA: Why, man?

CLOWN: He's a soldier, and for me to say a soldier lies, 'tis
stabbing.

DESDEMONA: Go to. Where lodges he?   5

CLOWN: To tell you where he lodges is to tell you where I lie.

DESDEMONA: Can anything be made of this?

CLOWN: I know not where he lodges, and for me to devise a
lodging and say he lies here, or he lies there, were to lie in
mine own throat.°

DESDEMONA: Can you inquire him out, and be edified by report?   10

CLOWN: I will catechize the world for him; that is, make questions, and by them answer.

DESDEMONA: Seek him, bid him come hither. Tell him I have
moved° my lord on his behalf and hope all will be well.

CLOWN: To do this is within the compass of man's wit, and
therefore I will attempt the doing it.   *Exit Clown.*   15

DESDEMONA: Where should I lose that handkerchief, Emilia?

EMILIA: I know not, madam.

DESDEMONA: Believe me, I had rather have lost my purse
Full of crusadoes;° and but my noble Moor   20
Is true of mind and made of no such baseness
As jealous creatures are, it were enough
To put him to ill thinking.

EMILIA: Is he not jealous?

DESDEMONA: Who, he? I think the sun where he was born
Drew all such humors° from him.

EMILIA: Look where he comes.   25

---

1 sirrah (A form of address to an inferior.)   **lies** lodges. (But the Clown makes the obvious pun.)
9 lie . . . throat (1) lie egregiously and deliberately (2) use the windpipe to speak a lie   **13 moved**
petitioned   **20 crusadoes** Portuguese gold coins   **25 humors** (Refers to the four bodily fluids
thought to determine temperament.)

Enter Othello.

DESDEMONA: I will not leave him now till Cassio
    Be called to him.—How is 't with you, my lord?
OTHELLO: Well, my good lady. [*Aside.*] O, hardness to
    dissemble!—
    How do you, Desdemona?
DESDEMONA: Well, my good lord.
OTHELLO: Give me your hand. [*She gives her hand.*] This hand is
    moist, my lady.   *30*
DESDEMONA: It yet hath felt no age nor known no sorrow.
OTHELLO: This argues° fruitfulness° and liberal° heart.
    Hot, hot, and moist. This hand of yours requires
    A sequester° from liberty, fasting and prayer,
    Much castigation,° exercise devout;°   *35*
    For here's a young and sweating devil here
    That commonly rebels. 'Tis a good hand,
    A frank° one.
DESDEMONA: You may indeed say so,
    For 'twas that hand that gave away my heart.
OTHELLO: A liberal hand. The hearts of old gave hands,°   *40*
    But our new heraldry is hands, not hearts.°
DESDEMONA: I cannot speak of this. Come now, your
    promise.
OTHELLO: What promise, chuck?°
DESDEMONA: I have sent to bid Cassio come speak with you.
OTHELLO: I have a salt and sorry rheum° offends me;   *45*
    Lend me thy handkerchief.
DESDEMONA: Here, my lord. [*She offers a handkerchief.*]
OTHELLO: That which I gave you.
DESDEMONA: I have it not about me.
OTHELLO: Not?

---

32 argues gives evidence of. **fruitfulness** generosity, amorousness, and fecundity. **liberal** generous and sexually free **34 sequester** separation, sequestration **35 castigation** corrective discipline. **exercise devout** i.e., prayer, religious meditation, etc. **38 frank** generous, open (with sexual suggestion) **40 The hearts . . . hands** i.e., in former times, people would give their hearts
when they gave their hands to something **41 But . . . hearts** i.e., in our decadent times, the joining
of hands is no longer a badge to signify the giving of hearts **43 chuck** (A term of endearment.)
45 salt . . . rheum distressful head cold or watering of the eyes

DESDEMONA: No, faith, my lord.   50
OTHELLO: That's a fault. That handkerchief
Did an Egyptian to my mother give.
She was a charmer,° and could almost read
The thoughts of people. She told her, while she kept it
'Twould make her amiable° and subdue my father   55
Entirely to her love, but if she lost it
Or made a gift of it, my father's eye
Should hold her loathèd and his spirits should hunt
After new fancies.° She, dying, gave it me,
And bid me, when my fate would have me wived,   60
To give it her.° I did so; and take heed on 't;
Make it a darling like your precious eye.
To lose 't or give 't away were such perdition°
As nothing else could match.
DESDEMONA: Is 't possible?
OTHELLO: 'Tis true. There's magic in the web° of it.   65
A sibyl, that had numbered in the world
The sun to course two hundred compasses,°
In her prophetic fury° sewed the work;°
The worms were hallowed that did breed the silk,
And it was dyed in mummy° which the skillful   70
Conserved of° maidens' hearts.
DESDEMONA: I' faith! Is 't true?
OTHELLO: Most veritable. Therefore look to 't well.
DESDEMONA: Then would to God that I had never seen 't!
OTHELLO: Ha? Wherefore?
DESDEMONA: Why do you speak so startingly and rash?°   75
OTHELLO: Is 't lost? Is 't gone? Speak, is 't out o' the way?°
DESDEMONA: Heaven bless us!
OTHELLO: Say you?
DESDEMONA: It is not lost; but what an if° it were?
OTHELLO: How?   80

---

53 charmer sorceress   **55 amiable** desirable   **59 fancies** loves   **61 her** i.e., to my wife
63 perdition loss   **65 web** fabric, weaving   **67 compasses** annual circlings. (The *sibyl*, or
prophetess, was two-hundred years old.)   **68 prophetic fury** frenzy of prophetic inspiration.
work embroidered pattern   **70 mummy** medicinal or magical preparation drained from mummified
bodies   **71 Conserved of** prepared or preserved out of   **75 startingly and rash** disjointedly and
impetuously, excitedly   **76 out o' the way** lost, misplaced   **79 an if** if

DESDEMONA: I say it is not lost.
OTHELLO: Fetch 't, let me see 't.
DESDEMONA: Why, so I can, sir, but I will not now.
　　This is a trick to put me from my suit.
　　Pray you, let Cassio be received again.
OTHELLO: Fetch me the handkerchief! My mind misgives.   *85*
DESDEMONA: Come, come,
　　You'll never meet a more sufficient° man.
OTHELLO: The handkerchief!
DESDEMONA: I pray, talk° me of Cassio.
OTHELLO: The handkerchief!
DESDEMONA: A man that all his time°
　　Hath founded his good fortunes on your love,   *90*
　　Shared dangers with you—
OTHELLO: The handkerchief!
DESDEMONA: I' faith, you are to blame.
OTHELLO: Zounds!   *Exit Othello.*
EMILIA: Is not this man jealous?   *95*
DESDEMONA: I ne'er saw this before.
　　Sure, there's some wonder in this handkerchief.
　　I am most unhappy in the loss of it.
EMILIA: 'Tis not a year or two shows us a man.°
　　They are all but stomachs, and we all but° food;   *100*
　　They eat us hungerly,° and when they are full
　　They belch us.

Enter Iago and Cassio.

　　　　　　　Look you, Cassio and my husband.
IAGO [*to Cassio*]:   There is no other way; 'tis she must do 't.
　　And, lo, the happiness!° Go and importune her.
DESDEMONA: How now, good Cassio? What's the news with
　　you?
CASSIO: Madam, my former suit. I do beseech you
　　That by your virtuous° means I may again

---

87 **sufficient** able, complete   88 **talk** talk to   89 **all his time** throughout his career   99 **'Tis . . .
man** i.e., you can't really know a man even in a year or two of experience (?), or, real men come
along seldom (?)   100 **but** nothing but   101 **hungerly** hungrily   104 **the happiness** in happy
time, fortunately met   107 **virtuous** efficacious

Exist and be a member of his love
Whom I, with all the office° of my heart,
Entirely honor. I would not be delayed.   *110*
If my offense be of such mortal° kind
That nor my service past, nor° present sorrows,
Nor purposed merit in futurity
Can ransom me into his love again,
But to know so must be my benefit;°   *115*
So shall I clothe me in a forced content,
And shut myself up in° some other course,
To fortune's alms.°

DESDEMONA: Alas, thrice-gentle Cassio,
My advocation° is not now in tune.
My lord is not my lord; nor should I know him,   *120*
Were he in favor° as in humor° altered.
So help me every spirit sanctified
As I have spoken for you all my best
And stood within the blank° of his displeasure
For my free speech! You must awhile be patient.   *125*
What I can do I will, and more I will
Than for myself I dare. Let that suffice you.

IAGO: Is my lord angry?

EMILIA: He went hence but now,
And certainly in strange unquietness.

IAGO: Can he be angry? I have seen the cannon   *130*
When it hath blown his ranks into the air,
And like the devil from his very arm
Puffed his own brother—and is he angry?
Something of moment° then. I will go meet him.
There's matter in 't indeed, if he be angry.   *135*

DESDEMONA: I prithee, do so.   *Exit [Iago].*
          Something, sure, of state,°

---

109 office loyal service   **111 mortal** fatal   **112 nor . . . nor** neither . . . nor   **115 But . . .
benefit** merely to know that my case is hopeless will have to content me (and will be better than uncertainty)   **117 shut . . . in** confine myself to   **118 To fortune's alms** throwing myself on the
mercy of fortune   **119 advocation** advocacy   **121 favor** appearance.   **humor** mood
124 within the blank within point-blank range. (The *blank* is the center of the target.)   **134 of
moment** of immediate importance, momentous   **136 of state** concerning state affairs

Either from Venice, or some unhatched practice°
Made demonstrable here in Cyprus to him,
Hath puddled° his clear spirit; and in such cases
Men's natures wrangle with inferior things,   140
Though great ones are their object. 'Tis even so;
For let our finger ache, and it indues°
Our other, healthful members even to a sense
Of pain. Nay, we must think men are not gods,
Nor of them look for such observancy°   145
As fits the bridal.° Beshrew me° much, Emilia,
I was, unhandsome° warrior as I am,
Arraigning his unkindness with° my soul;
But now I find I had suborned the witness,°
And he's indicted falsely.

EMILIA: Pray heaven it be   150
State matters, as you think, and no conception
Nor no jealous toy° concerning you.

DESDEMONA: Alas the day! I never gave him cause.

EMILIA: But jealous souls will not be answered so;
They are not ever jealous for the cause,   155
But jealous for° they're jealous. It is a monster
Begot upon itself,° born on itself.

DESDEMONA: Heaven keep that monster from Othello's mind!

EMILIA: Lady, amen.

DESDEMONA: I will go seek him. Cassio, walk hereabout.   160
If I do find him fit, I'll move your suit
And seek to effect it to my uttermost.

CASSIO: I humbly thank your ladyship.

Exit [Desdemona with Emilia].

Enter Bianca.

BIANCA: Save° you, friend Cassio!

---

137 unhatched practice as yet unexecuted or undiscovered plot   **139 puddled** muddied
142 indues brings to the same condition   **145 observancy** attentiveness   **146 bridal** wedding
(when a bridegroom is newly attentive to his bride).   **Beshrew me** (A mild oath.)
147 unhandsome insufficient, unskillful   **148 with** before the bar of   **149 suborned the witness**
induced the witness to give false testimony   **152 toy** fancy   **156 for** because   **157 Begot upon itself** generated solely from itself   **164 Save** God save.

CASSIO: What make° you from home?
How is 't with you, my most fair Bianca?   *165*
I' faith, sweet love, I was coming to your house.
BIANCA: And I was going to your lodging, Cassio.
What, keep a week away? Seven days and nights?
Eightscore-eight° hours? And lovers' absent hours
More tedious than the dial° eightscore times?   *170*
O weary reckoning!
CASSIO: Pardon me, Bianca.
I have this while with leaden thoughts been pressed;
But I shall, in a more continuate° time,
Strike off this score° of absence. Sweet Bianca,

[*giving her Desdemona's handkerchief*]

Take me this work out.°
BIANCA: O Cassio, whence came this?   *175*
This is some token from a newer friend.°
To the felt absence now I feel a cause.
Is 't come to this? Well, well.
CASSIO: Go to, woman!
Throw your vile guesses in the devil's teeth,
From whence you have them. You are jealous now   *180*
That this is from some mistress, some remembrance.
No, by my faith, Bianca.
BIANCA: Why, whose is it?
CASSIO: I know not, neither. I found it in my chamber.
I like the work well. Ere it be demanded°—
As like° enough it will—I would have it copied.   *185*
Take it and do 't, and leave me for this time.
BIANCA: Leave you? Wherefore?
CASSIO: I do attend here on the General,
And think it no addition,° nor my wish,
To have him see me womaned.   *190*
BIANCA: Why, I pray you?

---

make do   **169 Eightscore-eight** one hundred sixty-eight, the number of hours in a week   **170 the dial** a complete revolution of the clock   **173 continuate** uninterrupted   **174 Strike . . . score** settle this account   **175 Take . . . out** copy this embroidery for me   **176 friend** mistress   **184 demanded** inquired for   **185 like** likely   **189 addition** i.e., addition to my reputation

CASSIO: Not that I love you not.

BIANCA: But that you do not love me.
I pray you, bring° me on the way a little,
And say if I shall see you soon at night.   *195*

CASSIO: 'Tis but a little way that I can bring you,
For I attend here; but I'll see you soon.

BIANCA: 'Tis very good. I must be circumstanced.°

Exeunt omnes.

ACT IV

SCENE I [BEFORE THE CITADEL.]

Enter Othello and Iago.

IAGO: Will you think so?

OTHELLO: Think so, Iago?

IAGO: What,
To kiss in private?

OTHELLO: An unauthorized kiss!

IAGO: Or to be naked with her friend in bed
An hour or more, not meaning any harm?

OTHELLO: Naked in bed, Iago, and not mean harm?   *5*
It is hypocrisy against the devil.
They that mean virtuously and yet do so,
The devil their virtue tempts, and they tempt heaven.

IAGO: If they do nothing, 'tis a venial° slip.
But if I give my wife a handkerchief—   *10*

OTHELLO: What then?

IAGO: Why then, 'tis hers, my lord, and being hers,
She may, I think, bestow 't on any man.

OTHELLO: She is protectress of her honor too.
May she give that?   *15*

IAGO: Her honor is an essence that's not seen;
They have it° very oft that have it not.

---

194 bring accompany   **198 be circumstanced** be governed by circumstance, yield to your conditions
9 venial pardonable   **17 They have it** i.e., they enjoy a reputation for it

But, for the handkerchief—

OTHELLO: By heaven, I would most gladly have forgot it.

Thou saidst—O, it comes o'er my memory   *20*
As doth the raven o'er the infectious house,°
Boding to all—he had my handkerchief.

IAGO: Ay, what of that?

OTHELLO: That's not so good now.

IAGO: What
If I had said I had seen him do you wrong?
Or heard him say—as knaves be such abroad,°   *25*
Who having, by their own importunate suit,
Or voluntary dotage° of some mistress,
Convincèd or supplied° them, cannot choose
But they must blab—

OTHELLO: Hath he said anything?

IAGO: He hath, my lord; but, be you well assured,   *30*
No more than he'll unswear.

OTHELLO: What hath he said?

IAGO: Faith, that he did—I know not what he did.

OTHELLO: What? What?

IAGO: Lie—

OTHELLO: With her?

IAGO: With her, on her; what you will.

OTHELLO: Lie with her? Lie on her? We say "lie on her" when
they belie° her. Lie with her? Zounds, that's fulsome.°—   *35*
Handkerchief—confessions—handkerchief!—To confess and
be hanged for his labor—first to be hanged and then to confess.°—I tremble at it. Nature would not invest herself in
such shadowing passion without some instruction.° It is not
words° that shakes me thus. Pish! Noses, ears, and lips.—Is
't possible?—Confess—handkerchief!—O devil!   *40*

---

21 raven . . . house (Allusion to the belief that the raven hovered over a house of sickness or infec-
tion, such as one visited by the plague.)   **25 abroad** around about   **27 voluntary dotage** willing
infatuation   **28 Convincèd or supplied** seduced or sexually gratified   **35 belie** slander
36 fulsome foul   **37-38 first . . . to confess** (Othello reverses the proverbial *confess* and *be
hanged*; Cassio is to be given no time to confess before he dies.)   **38-39 Nature . . . instruction**
i.e., without some foundation in fact, nature would not have dressed herself in such an overwhelming
passion that comes over me now and fills my mind with images, or in such a lifelike fantasy as Cassio
had in his dream of lying with Desdemona   **39 words** mere words

Falls in a trance.

IAGO: Work on,
My medicine, work! Thus credulous fools are caught,
And many worthy and chaste dames even thus,
All guiltless, meet reproach.—What, ho! My lord!   45
My lord, I say! Othello!

Enter Cassio.

How now, Cassio?
CASSIO: What's the matter?
IAGO: My lord is fall'n into an epilepsy.
This is his second fit. He had one yesterday.
CASSIO: Rub him about the temples.
IAGO: No, forbear.   50
The lethargy° must have his° quiet course.
If not, he foams at mouth, and by and by
Breaks out to savage madness. Look, he stirs.
Do you withdraw yourself a little while.
He will recover straight. When he is gone,   55
I would on great occasion° speak with you.

                                   [*Exit Cassio.*]

How is it, General? Have you not hurt your head?
OTHELLO: Dost thou mock me?°
IAGO: I mock you not, by heaven.
Would you would bear your fortune like a man!
OTHELLO: A hornèd man's a monster and a beast.   60
IAGO: There's many a beast then in a populous city,
And many a civil° monster.
OTHELLO: Did he confess it?
IAGO: Good sir, be a man.
Think every bearded fellow that's but yoked°   65
May draw with you.° There's millions now alive

---

51 lethargy coma.   **his** its   **56 on great occasion** on a matter of great importance   **58 mock me** (Othello takes Iago's question about hurting his head to be a mocking reference to the cuckold's horns.)   **62 civil** i.e., dwelling in a city   **65 yoked** (1) married (2) put into the yoke of infamy and cuckoldry   **66 draw with you** pull as you do, like oxen who are yoked, i.e., share your fate as cuckold

That nightly lie in those unproper° beds
Which they dare swear peculiar.° Your case is better.°
O, 'tis the spite of hell, the fiend's arch-mock,
To lip° a wanton in a secure° couch   70
And to suppose her chaste! No, let me know,
And knowing what I am,° I know what she shall be.°

OTHELLO: O, thou art wise. 'Tis certain.

IAGO: Stand you awhile apart;
Confine yourself but in a patient list.°   75
Whilst you were here o'erwhelmèd with your grief—
A passion most unsuiting such a man—
Cassio came hither. I shifted him away,°
And laid good 'scuse upon your ecstasy,°
Bade him anon return and here speak with me,   80
The which he promised. Do but encave° yourself
And mark the fleers,° the gibes, and notable° scorns
That dwell in every region of his face;
For I will make him tell the tale anew,
Where, how, how oft, how long ago, and when   85
He hath and is again to cope° your wife.
I say, but mark his gesture. Marry, patience!
Or I shall say you're all-in-all in spleen,°
And nothing of a man.

OTHELLO: Dost thou hear, Iago?
I will be found most cunning in my patience;   90
But—dost thou hear?—most bloody.

IAGO: That's not amiss;
But yet keep time° in all. Will you withdraw?

[*Othello stands apart.*]

Now will I question Cassio of Bianca,
A huswife° that by selling her desires
Buys herself bread and clothes. It is a creature   95

---

67 unproper not exclusively their own   **68 peculiar** private, their own.   **better** i.e., because you
know the truth   **70 lip** kiss.   **secure** free from suspicion   **72 what I am** i.e., a cuckold.   **she
shall be** will happen to her   **75 in . . . list** within the bounds of patience   **78 shifted him away**
used a dodge to get rid of him   **79 ecstasy** trance   **81 encave** conceal   **82 fleers** sneers.
notable obvious   **86 cope** encounter with, have sex with   **88 all-in-all in spleen** utterly governed
by passionate impulses   **92 keep time** keep yourself steady (as in music)   **94 huswife** hussy

That dotes on Cassio—as 'tis the strumpet's plague
To beguile many and be beguiled by one.
He, when he hears of her, cannot restrain°
From the excess of laughter. Here he comes.

Enter Cassio.

As he shall smile, Othello shall go mad;   *100*
And his unbookish° jealousy must conster°
Poor Cassio's smiles, gestures, and light behaviors
Quite in the wrong.—How do you now, Lieutenant?

CASSIO: The worser that you give me the addition°
Whose want° even kills me.   *105*

IAGO: Ply Desdemona well and you are sure on 't.
[*Speaking lower.*] Now, if this suit lay in Bianca's power,
How quickly should you speed!

CASSIO [*laughing*]: Alas, poor caitiff!°

OTHELLO [*aside*]: Look how he laughs already!   *110*

IAGO: I never knew a woman love man so.

CASSIO: Alas, poor rogue! I think, i' faith, she loves me.

OTHELLO: Now he denies it faintly, and laughs it out.

IAGO: Do you hear, Cassio?

OTHELLO: Now he importunes him
To tell it o'er. Go to!° Well said,° well said.   *115*

IAGO: She gives it out that you shall marry her.
Do you intend it?

CASSIO: Ha, ha, ha!

OTHELLO: Do you triumph, Roman?° Do you triumph?

CASSIO: I marry her? What? A customer?° Prithee, bear some   *120*
charity to my wit;° do not think it so unwholesome. Ha,
ha, ha!

OTHELLO: So, so, so, so! They laugh that win.°

IAGO: Faith, the cry° goes that you shall marry her.

CASSIO: Prithee, say true.

---

98 restrain refrain   **101 unbookish** uninstructed.   **conster** construe   **104 addition** title
105 Whose want the lack of which   **109 caitiff** wretch   **115 Go to** (An expression of remonstrance.)   **Well said** well done   **119 Roman** (The Romans were noted for their *triumphs* or tri-
umphal processions.)   **120 customer** i.e., prostitute.   **bear . . . wit** be more charitable to my
judgment   **122 They . . . win** i.e., they that laugh last laugh best   **123 cry** rumor

IAGO: I am a very villain else.° 125

OTHELLO: Have you scored me?° Well.

CASSIO: This is the monkey's own giving out. She is persuaded I will marry her out of her own love and flattery,° not out of my promise.

OTHELLO: Iago beckons me.° Now he begins the story.

CASSIO: She was here even now; she haunts me in every place. 130 I was the other day talking on the seabank° with certain Venetians, and thither comes the bauble,° and, by this hand,° she falls me thus about my neck—

[*He embraces Iago.*]

OTHELLO: Crying, "O dear Cassio!" as it were; his gesture imports it.

CASSIO: So hangs and lolls and weep upon me, so shakes and pulls me. Ha, ha, ha!

OTHELLO: Now he tells how she plucked him to my chamber. 135 O, I see that nose of yours, but not that dog I shall throw it to.°

CASSIO: Well, I must leave her company.

IAGO: Before me,° look where she comes.

Enter Bianca [with Othello's handkerchief].

CASSIO: 'Tis such another fitchew!° Marry, a perfumed one.— What do you mean by this haunting of me? 140

BIANCA: Let the devil and his dam° haunt you! What did you mean by that same handkerchief you gave me even now? I was a fine fool to take it. I must take out the work? A likely piece of work,° that you should find it in your chamber and know not who left it there! This is some minx's token, and I must take out the work? There; give it your hobbyhorse.° 145

---

125 I . . . else call me a complete rogue if I'm not telling the truth   **126 scored me** scored off me, beaten me, made up my reckoning, branded me   **128 flattery** self-flattery, self-deception
129 beckons signals   **131 seabank** seashore   **132 bauble** plaything   **by this hand** I make my vow   **136 not . . . to** (Othello imagines himself cutting off Cassio's nose and throwing it to a dog.)
138 Before me i.e., on my soul   **139 'Tis . . . fitchew** what a polecat she is! Just like all the others. (Polecats were often compared with prostitutes because of their rank smell and presumed lechery.)
141 dam mother   **143 A likely . . . work** a fine story   **145 hobbyhorse** harlot

[*She gives him the handkerchief.*] Wheresoever you had it, I'll take out no work on 't.

CASSIO: How now, my sweet Bianca? How now? How now?

OTHELLO: By heaven, that should be° my handkerchief!

BIANCA: If you'll come to supper tonight, you may; if you will not, come when you are next prepared for.°   *150*

Exit.

IAGO: After her, after her.

CASSIO: Faith, I must. She'll rail in the streets else.

IAGO: Will you sup there?

CASSIO: Faith, I intend so.

IAGO: Well, I may chance to see you, for I would very fain speak with you.   *155*

CASSIO: Prithee, come. Will you?

IAGO: Go to.° Say no more.   [*Exit Cassio.*]

OTHELLO [*advancing*]: How shall I murder him, Iago?

IAGO: Did you perceive how he laughed at his vice?

OTHELLO: O, Iago!   *160*

IAGO: And did you see the handkerchief?

OTHELLO: Was that mine?

IAGO: Yours, by this hand. And to see how he prizes the foolish woman your wife! She gave it him, and he hath given it his whore.

OTHELLO: I would have him nine years a-killing. A fine woman! A fair woman! A sweet woman!   *165*

IAGO: Nay, you must forget that.

OTHELLO: Ay, let her rot and perish, and be damned tonight, for she shall not live. No, my heart is turned to stone; I strike it, and it hurts my hand. O, the world hath not a sweeter creature! She might lie by an emperor's side and command   *170* him tasks.

IAGO: Nay, that's not your way.°

OTHELLO: Hang her! I do but say what she is. So delicate with her needle! An admirable musician! O, she will sing the sav-

---

148 should be must be   **149-150 when . . . for** when I'm ready for you (i.e., never)   **157 Go to** (An expression of remonstrance.)   **172 your way** i.e., the way you should think of her

ageness out of a bear. Of so high and plenteous wit and in-
vention!°   *175*

IAGO: She's the worse for all this.

OTHELLO: O, a thousand, a thousand times! And then, of so
gentle a condition!°

IAGO: Ay, too gentle.°

OTHELLO: Nay, that's certain. But yet the pity of it, Iago! O,
Iago, the pity of it, Iago!   *180*

IAGO: If you are so fond° over her iniquity, give her patent° to
offend, for if it touch not you it comes near nobody.

OTHELLO: I will chop her into messes.° Cuckold me?

IAGO: O, 'tis foul in her.

OTHELLO: With mine officer?   *185*

IAGO: That's fouler.

OTHELLO: Get me some poison, Iago, this night. I'll not ex-
postulate with her, lest her body and beauty unprovide° my
mind again. This night, Iago.

IAGO: Do it not with poison. Strangle her in her bed, even the
bed she hath contaminated.   *190*

OTHELLO: Good, good! The justice of it pleases. Very good.

IAGO: And for Cassio, let me be his undertaker.° You shall hear
more by midnight.

OTHELLO: Excellent good. [*A trumpet within.*] What trumpet
is that same?

IAGO: I warrant, something from Venice.

Enter Lodovico, Desdemona, and attendants.

'Tis Lodovico. This comes from the Duke.   *195*
See, your wife's with him.

LODOVICO: God save you, worthy General!

OTHELLO: With all my heart,° sir.

LODOVICO [*giving him a letter*]:   The Duke and the senators of
Venice greet you.

OTHELLO: I kiss the instrument of their pleasures.

---

175 invention imagination   **177 gentle a condition** well-born and well-bred   **178 gentle** generous, yielding (to other men)   **181 fond** foolish.   **patent** license   **183 messes** portions of meat,
i.e., bits   **188 unprovide** weaken, render unfit   **192 be his undertaker** undertake to dispatch him
197 With all my heart i.e., I thank you most heartily

[*He opens the letter, and reads.*]

DESDEMONA: And what's the news, good cousin Lodovico?   *200*
IAGO: I am very glad to see you, signor.
   Welcome to Cyprus.
LODOVICO: I thank you. How does Lieutenant Cassio?
IAGO: Lives, sir.
DESDEMONA: Cousin, there's fall'n between him and my lord   *205*
   An unkind° breach; but you shall make all well.
OTHELLO: Are you sure of that?
DESDEMONA: My lord?
OTHELLO [*reads*]: "This fail you not to do, as you will—"
LODOVICO: He did not call; he's busy in the paper.   *210*
   Is there division twixt my lord and Cassio?
DESDEMONA: A most unhappy one. I would do much
   T' atone° them, for the love I bear to Cassio.
OTHELLO: Fire and brimstone!
DESDEMONA: My lord?   *215*
OTHELLO: Are you wise?
DESDEMONA: What, is he angry?
LODOVICO: Maybe the letter moved him;
   For, as I think, they do command him home,
   Deputing Cassio in his government.°
DESDEMONA: By my troth, I am glad on 't.°   *220*
OTHELLO: Indeed?
DESDEMONA: My lord?
OTHELLO: I am glad to see you mad.°
DESDEMONA: Why, sweet Othello—
OTHELLO [*striking her*]: Devil!   *225*
DESDEMONA: I have not deserved this.
LODOVICO: My lord, this would not be believed in Venice,
   Though I should swear I saw 't. 'Tis very much.°
   Make her amends; she weeps.
OTHELLO: O devil, devil!

---

206 unkind unnatural, contrary to their natures; hurtful   **213 atone** reconcile   **219 government**
office   **220 on 't** of it   **223 I am . . . mad** i.e., I am glad to see that you are insane enough to rejoice in Cassio's promotion (? Othello bitterly plays on Desdemona's *I am glad.*)   **228 very much**
too much, outrageous

If that the earth could teem° with woman's tears,   230
Each drop she falls would prove a crocodile.°
Out of my sight!

DESDEMONA: I will not stay to offend you. [*Going.*]

LODOVICO: Truly, an obedient lady.
I do beseech your lordship, call her back.

OTHELLO: Mistress!   235

DESDEMONA [*returning*]: My lord?

OTHELLO: What would you with her, sir?°

LODOVICO: Who, I, my lord?

OTHELLO: Ay, you did wish that I would make her turn.
Sir, she can turn, and turn, and yet go on   240
And turn again; and she can weep, sir, weep;
And she's obedient,° as you say, obedient,
Very obedient.—Proceed you in your tears.—
Concerning this, sir—O well-painted passion!°—
I am commanded home.—Get you away;   245
I'll send for you anon.—Sir, I obey the mandate
And will return to Venice.—Hence, avaunt!

                                    [*Exit Desdemona.*]

Cassio shall have my place. And, sir, tonight
I do entreat that we may sup together.
You are welcome, sir, to Cyprus.—Goats and monkeys!° *Exit.*   250

LODOVICO: Is this the noble Moor whom our full Senate
Call all in all sufficient? Is this the nature
Whom passion could not shake? Whose solid virtue
The shot of accident nor dart of chance
Could neither graze nor pierce?

IAGO: He is much changed.   255

LODOVICO: Are his wits safe? Is he not light of brain?

IAGO: He's that he is. I may not breathe my censure
What he might be. If what he might he is not,

---

230 teem breed, be impregnated   **231 falls . . . crocodile** (Crocodiles were supposed to weep hypocritical tears for their victims.)   **237 What . . . sir** (Othello implies that Desdemona is pliant and will do a *turn*, lines 239-241, for any man.)   **242 obedient** (With much the same sexual connotation as *turn* in lines 239-241.)   **244 passion** i.e., grief   **250 Goats and monkeys** (See Act III, Scene iii, line 419.)

I would to heaven he were!°
LODOVICO: What, strike his wife?
IAGO: Faith, that was not so well; yet would I knew   260
  That stroke would prove the worst!
LODOVICO: Is it his use?°
  Or did the letters work upon his blood°
  And new-create his fault?
IAGO: Alas, alas!
  It is not honesty in me to speak
  What I have seen and known. You shall observe him,   265
  And his own courses will denote° him so
  That I may save my speech. Do but go after,
  And mark how he continues.
LODOVICO: I am sorry that I am deceived in him.   *Exeunt.*

Scene II [The Citadel.]

Enter Othello and Emilia.

OTHELLO: You have seen nothing then?
EMILIA: Nor ever heard, nor ever did suspect.
OTHELLO: Yes, you have seen Cassio and she together.
EMILIA: But then I saw no harm, and then I heard
  Each syllable that breath made up between them.   5
OTHELLO: What, did they never whisper?
EMILIA: Never, my lord.
OTHELLO: Nor send you out o' the way?
EMILIA: Never.
OTHELLO: To fetch her fan, her gloves, her mask, nor nothing?   10
EMILIA: Never, my lord.
OTHELLO: That's strange.
EMILIA: I durst, my lord, to wager she is honest,
  Lay down my soul at stake.° If you think other,
  Remove your thought; it doth abuse your bosom.°   15

257-259 I may . . . were i.e., I dare not venture an opinion as to whether he's of unsound mind, as
you suggest, but, if he isn't, then it might be better to wish he were in fact insane, since only that
could excuse his wild behavior   **261 use** custom   **262 blood** passions   **266 courses will denote**
actions will reveal
14 at stake as the wager   **15 abuse your bosom** deceive you

If any wretch have put this in your head,
Let heaven requite it with the serpent's curse!°
For if she be not honest, chaste, and true,
There's no man happy; the purest of their wives
Is foul as slander.

OTHELLO: Bid her come hither. Go.   20

> *Exit Emilia.*

She says enough; yet she's a simple bawd
That cannot say as much.° This° is a subtle whore,
A closet lock and key° of villainous secrets.
And yet she'll kneel and pray; I have seen her do 't.

Enter Desdemona and Emilia.

DESDEMONA: My lord, what is your will?   25
OTHELLO: Pray you, chuck, come hither.
DESDEMONA: What is your pleasure?
OTHELLO: Let me see your eyes.
    Look in my face.
DESDEMONA: What horrible fancy's this?
OTHELLO [*to Emilia*]: Some of your function,° mistress.
    Leave procreants° alone and shut the door;   30
    Cough or cry "hem" if anybody come.
    Your mystery, your mystery!° Nay, dispatch.

> *Exit Emilia.*

DESDEMONA [*kneeling*]: Upon my knees, what doth your
    speech import?
    I understand a fury in your words,
    But not the words.   35
OTHELLO: Why, what art thou?
DESDEMONA: Your wife, my lord, your true
    And loyal wife.

---

17 the serpent's curse the curse pronounced by God on the serpent for deceiving Eve, just as some man has done to Othello and Desdemona. (See Genesis 3:14.)   **21-22 she's . . . much** i.e., any procuress or go-between who couldn't make up as plausible a story as Emilia's would have to be pretty stupid   **22 This** i.e., Desdemona   **23 closet lock and key** i.e., concealer   **29 Some . . . function** i.e., practice your chosen profession, that of bawd (by guarding the door)   **30 procreants** mating couples   **32 mystery** trade, occupation

OTHELLO: Come, swear it, damn thyself,
   Lest, being like one of heaven,° the devils themselves
   Should fear to seize thee. Therefore be double damned:
   Swear thou art honest.

DESDEMONA: Heaven doth truly know it.   *40*

OTHELLO: Heaven truly knows that thou art false as hell.

DESDEMONA: To whom, my lord? With whom? How am I
   false?

OTHELLO [*weeping*]: Ah, Desdemon! Away, away, away!

DESDEMONA: Alas the heavy day! Why do you weep?
   Am I the motive° of these tears, my lord?   *45*
   If haply you my father do suspect
   An instrument of this your calling back,
   Lay not your blame on me. If you have lost him,
   I have lost him too.

OTHELLO: Had it pleased heaven
   To try me with affliction, had they° rained   *50*
   All kinds of sores and shames on my bare head,
   Steeped me in poverty to the very lips,
   Given to captivity me and my utmost hopes,
   I should have found in some place of my soul
   A drop of patience. But, alas, to make me   *55*
   A fixèd figure for the time of scorn°
   To point his° slow and moving finger° at!
   Yet could I bear that too, well, very well.
   But there where I have garnered° up my heart,
   Where either I must live or bear no life,   *60*
   The fountain° from the which my current runs
   Or else dries up—to be discarded thence!
   Or keep it as a cistern° for foul toads
   To knot° and gender° in! Turn thy complexion there,°
   Patience, thou young and rose-lipped cherubin—   *65*

---

38 being . . . heaven looking like an angel   **45 motive** cause   **50 they** i.e., heavenly powers
56 time of scorn i.e., scornful world   **57 his** its.   **slow and moving finger** i.e., hour hand of the
clock, moving so slowly it seems hardly to move at all. (Othello envisages himself as being eternally
pointed at by the scornful world as the numbers on a clock are pointed at by the hour hand.)
59 garnered stored   **61 fountain** spring   **63 cistern** cesspool   **64 knot** couple.   **gender** engender.   **Turn . . . there** change your color, grow pale, at such a sight

Ay, there look grim as hell!°
DESDEMONA: I hope my noble lord esteems me honest.°
OTHELLO: O, ay, as summer flies are in the shambles,°
    That quicken° even with blowing.° O thou weed,
    Who art so lovely fair and smell'st so sweet   70
    That the sense aches at thee, would thou hadst ne'er been
    born!
DESDEMONA: Alas, what ignorant° sin have I committed?
OTHELLO: Was this fair paper, this most goodly book,
    Made to write "whore" upon? What committed?
    Committed? O thou public commoner!°   75
    I should make very forges of my cheeks,
    That would to cinders burn up modesty,
    Did I but speak thy deeds. What committed?
    Heaven stops the nose at it and the moon winks;°
    The bawdy° wind, that kisses all it meets,   80
    Is hushed within the hollow mine° of earth
    And will not hear 't. What committed?
    Impudent strumpet!
DESDEMONA: By heaven, you do me wrong.
OTHELLO: Are not you a strumpet?
DESDEMONA: No, as I am a Christian.   85
    If to preserve this vessel° for my lord
    From any other foul unlawful touch
    Be not to be a strumpet, I am none.
OTHELLO: What, not a whore?
DESDEMONA: No, as I shall be saved.   90
OTHELLO: Is 't possible?
DESDEMONA: O, heaven forgive us!
OTHELLO: I cry you mercy,° then.
    I took you for that cunning whore of Venice
    That married with Othello. [*Calling out.*] You, mistress,
    That have the office opposite to Saint Peter   95

65-66 Patience . . . hell (Even Patience, that rose-lipped cherub, will look grim and pale at this spectacle.) **67 honest** chaste **68 shambles** slaughterhouse **69 quicken** come to life. **with blowing** i.e., with the puffing up of something rotten in which maggots are breeding **72 ignorant sin** sin in ignorance **75 commoner** prostitute **79 winks** closes her eyes. (The moon symbolizes chastity.) **80 bawdy** kissing one and all **81 mine** cave (where the winds were thought to dwell) **86 vessel** body **92 cry you mercy** beg your pardon

And keep the gate of hell!

Enter Emilia.

You, you, ay, you!
We have done our course.° There's money for your
pains.[*He gives money.*]
I pray you, turn the key and keep our counsel.   *Exit.*

EMILIA: Alas, what does this gentleman conceive?°
How do you, madam? How do you, my good lady?   100

DESDEMONA: Faith, half asleep.°

EMILIA: Good madam, what's the matter with my lord?

DESDEMONA: With who?

EMILIA: Why, with my lord, madam.

DESDEMONA: Who is thy lord?

EMILIA: He that is yours, sweet lady.   105

DESDEMONA: I have none. Do not talk to me, Emilia.
I cannot weep, nor answers have I none
But what should go by water.° Prithee, tonight
Lay on my bed my wedding sheets, remember;
And call thy husband hither.   110

EMILIA: Here's a change indeed!   *Exit.*

DESDEMONA: 'Tis meet I should be used so, very meet.°
How have I been behaved, that he might stick°
The small'st opinion° on my least misuse?°

Enter Iago and Emilia.

IAGO: What is your pleasure, madam? How is 't with you?   115

DESDEMONA: I cannot tell. Those that do teach young babes
Do it with gentle means and easy tasks.
He might have chid me so, for, in good faith,
I am a child to chiding.

IAGO: What is the matter, lady?   120

EMILIA: Alas, Iago, my lord hath so bewhored her,
Thrown such despite and heavy terms upon her,
That true hearts cannot bear it.

---

97 course business (with an indecent suggestion of "trick," turn at sex)   **99 conceive** suppose,
think   **101 half asleep** i.e., dazed   **108 go by water** be expressed by tears   **112 meet** fitting
113 stick attach   **114 opinion** censure.   **least misuse** slightest misconduct

DESDEMONA: Am I that name, Iago?

IAGO: What name, fair lady? 125

DESDEMONA: Such as she said my lord did say I was.

EMILIA: He called her whore. A beggar in his drink
Could not have laid such terms upon his callet.°

IAGO: Why did he so?

DESDEMONA [*weeping*]: I do not know. I am sure I am none
such. 130

IAGO: Do not weep, do not weep. Alas the day!

EMILIA: Hath she forsook so many noble matches,
Her father and her country and her friends,
To be called whore? Would it not make one weep?

DESDEMONA: It is my wretched fortune.

IAGO: Beshrew° him for 't! 135
How comes this trick° upon him?

DESDEMONA: Nay, heaven doth know.

EMILIA: I will be hanged if some eternal° villain,
Some busy and insinuating° rogue,
Some cogging,° cozening° slave, to get some office,
Have not devised this slander. I will be hanged else. 140

IAGO: Fie, there is no such man. It is impossible.

DESDEMONA: If any such there be, heaven pardon him!

EMILIA: A halter° pardon him! And hell gnaw his bones!
Why should he call her whore? Who keeps her company?
What place? What time? What form?° What likelihood? 145
The Moor's abused by some most villainous knave,
Some base notorious knave, some scurvy fellow.
O heaven, that° such companions° thou'dst unfold,°
And put in every honest hand a whip
To lash the rascals naked through the world 150
Even from the east to th' west!

IAGO: Speak within door.°

EMILIA: O, fie upon them! Some such squire° he was

---

128 **callet** whore   135 **Beshrew** curse   136 **trick** strange behavior, delusion   137 **eternal** inveterate   138 **insinuating** ingratiating, fawning, wheedling   139 **cogging** cheating.   **cozening** defrauding   143 **halter** hangman's noose   145 **form** appearance, circumstance   148 **that** would that.   **companions** fellows.   **unfold** expose   151 **within door** i.e., not so loud   152 **squire** fellow

That turned your wit the seamy side without°
And made you to suspect me with the Moor.

IAGO: You are a fool. Go to.°

DESDEMONA: Alas, Iago,   155
What shall I do to win my lord again?
Good friend, go to him; for, by this light of heaven,
I know not how I lost him. Here I kneel. [*She kneels.*]
If e'er my will did trespass 'gainst his love,
Either in discourse° of thought or actual deed,   160
Or that° mine eyes, mine ears, or any sense
Delighted them° in any other form;
Or that I do not yet,° and ever did,
And ever will—though he do shake me off
To beggarly divorcement—love him dearly,   165
Comfort forswear° me! Unkindness may do much,
And his unkindness may defeat° my life,
But never taint my love. I cannot say "whore."
It does abhor° me now I speak the word;
To do the act that might the addition° earn   170
Not the world's mass of vanity° could make me.

[*She rises.*]

IAGO: I pray you, be content. 'Tis but his humor.°
The business of the state does him offense,
And he does chide with you.

DESDEMONA: If 'twere no other—   175

IAGO: It is but so, I warrant. [*Trumpets within.*]
Hark, how these instruments summon you to supper!
The messengers of Venice stays the meat.°
Go in, and weep not. All things shall be well.

                    Exeunt Desdemona and Emilia.

Enter Roderigo.

---

153 seamy side without wrong side out   **155 Go to** i.e., that's enough   **160 discourse of thought**
process of thinking   **161 that** if. (Also in line 163.)   **162 Delighted them** took delight   **163 yet**
still   **166 Comfort forswear** may heavenly comfort forsake   **167 defeat** destroy   **169 abhor** (1)
fill me with abhorrence (2) make me whorelike   **170 addition** title   **171 vanity** showy splendor
172 humor mood   **178 stays the meat** are waiting to dine

How now, Roderigo?   180

RODERIGO: I do not find that thou deal'st justly with me.

IAGO: What in the contrary?

RODERIGO: Every day thou daff'st me° with some device,°
Iago, and rather, as it seems to me now, keep'st from me all
conveniency° than suppliest me with the least advantage° of   185
hope. I will indeed no longer endure it, nor am I yet persuaded to put up° in peace what already I have foolishly suffered.

IAGO: Will you hear me, Roderigo?

RODERIGO: Faith, I have heard too much, for your words and
performances are no kin together.

IAGO: You charge me most unjustly.   190

RODERIGO: With naught but truth. I have wasted myself out
of my means. The jewels you have had from me to deliver°
Desdemona would half have corrupted a votarist.° You have
told me she hath received them and returned me expectations and comforts of sudden respect° and acquaintance, but
I find none.   195

IAGO: Well, go to, very well.

RODERIGO: "Very well"! "Go to"! I cannot go to,° man, nor
'tis not very well. By this hand, I think it is scurvy, and begin
to find myself fopped° in it.

IAGO: Very well.

RODERIGO: I tell you 'tis not very well.° I will make myself   200
known to Desdemona. If she will return me my jewels, I will
give over my suit and repent my unlawful solicitation; if not,
assure yourself I will seek satisfaction° of you.

IAGO: You have said now?°

RODERIGO: Ay, and said nothing but what I protest
intendment° of doing.

---

183 thou daff'st me you put me off.   **device** excuse, trick   **184 conveniency** advantage, opportunity   **185 advantage** increase   **186 put up** submit to, tolerate   **192 deliver** deliver to
193 votarist nun   **194 sudden respect** immediate consideration   **197 I cannot go to** (Roderigo
changes Iago's go to, an expression urging patience, to *I cannot go to*, "I have no opportunity for success in wooing.")   **198 fopped** fooled, duped   **200 not very well** (Roderigo changes Iago's *very
well*, "all right, then," to *not very well*, "not at all good.")   **202 satisfaction** repayment. (The term
normally means settling of accounts in a duel.)   **203 You . . . now** have you finished?
204 intendment intention

IAGO: Why, now I see there's mettle in thee, and even from this   *205*
instant do build on thee a better opinion than ever before.
Give me thy hand, Roderigo. Thou hast taken against me a
most just exception; but yet I protest I have dealt most directly in thy affair.

RODERIGO: It hath not appeared.

IAGO: I grant indeed it hath not appeared, and your suspicion   *210*
is not without wit and judgment. But, Roderigo, if thou hast
that in thee indeed which I have greater reason to believe
now than ever—I mean purpose, courage, and valor—this
night show it. If thou the next night following enjoy not
Desdemona, take me from this world with treachery and   *215*
devise engines for° my life.

RODERIGO: Well, what is it? Is it within reason and compass?

IAGO: Sir, there is especial commission come from Venice to de-
pute Cassio in Othello's place.

RODERIGO: Is that true? Why, then Othello and Desdemona
return again to Venice.   *220*

IAGO: O, no; he goes into Mauritania and takes away with him
the fair Desdemona, unless his abode be lingered here by
some accident; wherein none can be so determinate° as the
removing of Cassio.

RODERIGO: How do you mean, removing of him?

IAGO: Why, by making him uncapable of Othello's place—   *225*
knocking out his brains.

RODERIGO: And that you would have me to do?

IAGO: Ay, if you dare do yourself a profit and a right. He sups
tonight with a harlotry,° and thither will I go to him. He
knows not yet of his honorable fortune. If you will watch his
going thence, which I will fashion to fall out° between twelve   *230*
and one, you may take him at your pleasure. I will be near to
second your attempt, and he shall fall between us. Come,
stand not amazed at it, but go along with me. I will show
you such a necessity in his death that you shall think your-

---

214 engines for plots against   **223 determinate** conclusive   **229 harlotry** slut   **230 fall out**
occur

self bound to put it on him. It is now high° suppertime, and
the night grows to waste.° About it.   235
RODERIGO: I will hear further reason for this.
IAGO: And you shall be satisfied.   *Exeunt.*

SCENE III [THE CITADEL.]

*Enter Othello, Lodovico, Desdemona, Emilia, and atten-
dants.*

LODOVICO: I do beseech you, sir, trouble yourself no further.
OTHELLO: O, pardon me; 'twill do me good to walk.
LODOVICO: Madam, good night. I humbly thank your
ladyship.
DESDEMONA: Your honor is most welcome.
OTHELLO: Will you walk, sir?
O, Desdemona!   5
DESDEMONA: My lord?
OTHELLO: Get you to bed on th' instant.
I will be returned forthwith. Dismiss your attendant there.
Look 't be done.
DESDEMONA: I will, my lord.   10

Exit [Othello, with Lodovico and attendants].

EMILIA: How goes it now? He looks gentler than he did.
DESDEMONA: He says he will return incontinent,°
And hath commanded me to go to bed,
And bid me to dismiss you.
EMILIA: Dismiss me?   15
DESDEMONA: It was his bidding. Therefore, good Emilia,
Give me my nightly wearing, and adieu.
We must not now displease him.
EMILIA: I would you had never seen him!
DESDEMONA: So would not I. My love doth so approve him   20
That even his stubbornness,° his checks,° his frowns—
Prithee, unpin me—have grace and favor in them.

234 **high** fully   235 **grows to waste** wastes away
12 **incontinent** immediately   21 **stubbornness** roughness.   **checks** rebukes

[*Emilia prepares Desdemona for bed.*]

EMILIA: I have laid those sheets you bade me on the bed.
DESDEMONA: All's one.° Good faith, how foolish are our
  minds!
  If I do die before thee, prithee shroud me   *25*
  In one of these same sheets.
EMILIA: Come, come, you talk.°
DESDEMONA: My mother had a maid called Barbary.
  She was in love, and he she loved proved mad°
  And did forsake her. She had a song of "Willow."
  An old thing 'twas, but it expressed her fortune,   *30*
  And she died singing it. That song tonight
  Will not go from my mind; I have much to do
  But to go hang° my head all at one side
  And sing it like poor Barbary. Prithee, dispatch.
EMILIA: Shall I go fetch your nightgown?°   *35*
DESDEMONA: No, unpin me here.
  This Lodovico is a proper° man.
EMILIA: A very handsome man.
DESDEMONA: He speaks well.
EMILIA: I know a lady in Venice would have walked barefoot   *40*
  to Palestine for a touch of his nether lip.
DESDEMONA [*singing*]:
    "The poor soul sat sighing by a sycamore tree,
    Sing all a green willow;°
    Her hand on her bosom, her head on her knee,
    Sing willow, willow, willow.   *45*
    The fresh streams ran by her and murmured her moans;
    Sing willow, willow, willow;
    Her salt tears fell from her, and softened the stones—"
    Lay by these.
        [*Singing.*] "Sing willow, willow, willow—"   *50*
  Prithee, hie thee.° He'll come anon.°

---

24 All's one all right. It doesn't really matter   **26 talk** i.e., prattle   **28 mad** wild, i.e., faithless
32-33 I . . . hang I can scarcely keep myself from hanging   **35 nightgown** dressing gown
37 proper handsome   **43 willow** (A conventional emblem of disappointed love.)   **51 hie thee**
hurry.   **anon** right away

[*Singing.*] "Sing all a green willow must be my
garland.
Let nobody blame him; his scorn I approve—"
Nay, that's not next.—Hark! Who is 't that knocks?

EMILIA: It's the wind.

DESDEMONA [*singing*]:
"I called my love false love; but what said he then?   *55*
Sing willow, willow, willow;
If I court more women, you'll couch with more men."
So, get thee gone. Good night. Mine eyes do itch;
Doth that bode weeping?

EMILIA: 'Tis neither here nor there.   *60*

DESDEMONA: I have heard it said so. O, these men, these
men!
Dost thou in conscience think—tell me, Emilia—
That there be women do abuse° their husbands
In such gross kind?

EMILIA: There be some such, no question.

DESDEMONA: Wouldst thou do such a deed for all the world?   *65*

EMILIA: Why, would not you?

DESDEMONA: No, by this heavenly light!

EMILIA: Nor I neither by this heavenly light;
I might do 't as well i' the dark.

DESDEMONA: Wouldst thou do such a deed for all the world?

EMILIA: The world's a huge thing. It is a great price   *70*
For a small vice.

DESDEMONA: Good troth, I think thou wouldst not.

EMILIA: By my troth, I think I should, and undo 't when I had
done. Marry, I would not do such a thing for a joint ring,°
nor for measures of lawn,° nor for gowns, petticoats, nor
caps, nor any petty exhibition.° But for all the whole world!   *75*
Uds° pity, who would not make her husband a cuckold to
make him a monarch? I should venture purgatory for 't.

DESDEMONA: Beshrew me if I would do such a wrong
For the whole world.

---

63 abuse deceive   **74 joint ring** a ring made in separate halves.   **lawn** fine linen   **75 exhibition**
gift   **76 Uds** God's

EMILIA: Why, the wrong is but a wrong i' the world, and hav-   *80*
ing the world for your labor, 'tis a wrong in your own world,
and you might quickly make it right.
DESDEMONA: I do not think there is any such woman.
EMILIA: Yes, a dozen, and as many
To th' vantage° as would store° the world they played° for.   *85*
But I do think it is their husbands' faults
If wives do fall. Say that they slack their duties°
And pour our treasures into foreign laps,°
Or else break out in peevish jealousies,
Throwing restraint upon us? Or say they strike us,°   *90*
Or scant our former having in despite?°
Why, we have galls,° and though we have some grace,
Yet have we some revenge. Let husbands know
Their wives have sense° like them. They see, and smell,
And have their palates both for sweet and sour,   *95*
As husbands have. What is it that they do
When they change us for others? Is it sport?°
I think it is. And doth affection° breed it?
I think it doth. Is 't frailty that thus errs?
It is so, too. And have not we affections,   *100*
Desires for sport, and frailty, as men have?
Then let them use us well; else let them know,
The ills we do, their ills instruct us so.
DESDEMONA: Good night, good night. God me such uses° send
Not to pick bad from bad, but by bad mend!°   *105*

Exeunt.

---

85 **To th' vantage** in addition, to boot.   **store** populate.   **played** (1) gambled (2) sported sexually
87 **duties** marital duties   88 **pour . . . laps** i.e., are unfaithful, give what is rightfully ours (semen)
to other women   90 **Throwing . . . us** i.e., jealously restricting our freedom to see other men
91 **scant . . . despite** reduce our allowance to spite us   92 **have galls** i.e., are capable of resenting
injury and insult   94 **sense** physical sense   97 **sport** sexual pastime   98 **affection** passion
104 **uses** habit, practice   105 **Not . . . mend** i.e., not to learn bad conduct from others' badness (as
Emilia has suggested women learn from men), but to mend my ways by perceiving what badness is,
making spiritual benefit out of evil and adversity

ACT V

SCENE I [A STREET IN CYPRUS.]

Enter Iago and Roderigo.

IAGO: Here stand behind this bulk.° Straight will he come.
Wear thy good rapier bare,° and put it home.
Quick, quick! Fear nothing. I'll be at thy elbow.
It makes us or it mars us. Think on that,
And fix most firm thy resolution.   5
RODERIGO: Be near at hand. I may miscarry in 't.
IAGO: Here, at thy hand. Be bold, and take thy stand.

[*Iago stands aside. Roderigo conceals himself.*]

RODERIGO: I have no great devotion to the deed;
And yet he hath given me satisfying reasons.
'Tis but a man gone. Forth, my sword! He dies.   10

[*He draws.*]

IAGO: I have rubbed this young quat° almost to the sense,°
And he grows angry. Now, whether he kill Cassio
Or Cassio him, or each do kill the other,
Every way makes my gain. Live Roderigo,°
He calls me to a restitution large   15
Of gold and jewels that I bobbed° from him
As gifts to Desdemona.
It must not be. If Cassio do remain,
He hath a daily beauty in his life
That makes me ugly; and besides, the Moor   20
May unfold° me to him; there stand I in much peril.
No, he must die. Be 't so. I hear him coming.

Enter Cassio.

RODERIGO [*coming forth*]: I know his gait, 'tis he.—Villain,
thou diest!

---

1 bulk framework projecting from the front of a shop   **2 bare** unsheathed   **11 quat** pimple, pustule.   **to the sense** to the quick   **14 Live Roderigo** if Roderigo lives   **16 bobbed** swindled
21 unfold expose

[*He attacks Cassio.*]

CASSIO: That thrust had been mine enemy indeed,
But that my coat° is better than thou know'st.   25
I will make proof° of thine.

[*He draws, and wounds Roderigo.*]

RODERIGO: O, I am slain! [*He falls.*]

[*Iago, from behind, wounds Cassio in the leg, and exits.*]

CASSIO: I am maimed forever. Help, ho! Murder! Murder!

Enter Othello.

OTHELLO: The voice of Cassio! Iago keeps his word.
RODERIGO: O, villain that I am!
OTHELLO: It is even so.   30
CASSIO: O, help, ho! Light! A surgeon!
OTHELLO: 'Tis he. O brave Iago, honest and just,
That hast such noble sense of thy friend's wrong!
Thou teachest me. Minion,° your dear lies dead,
And your unblest fate hies.° Strumpet, I come.   35
Forth of° my heart those charms, thine eyes, are blotted;
Thy bed, lust-stained, shall with lust's blood be spotted.

Exit Othello.

Enter Lodovico and Gratiano.

CASSIO: What ho! No watch? No passage?° Murder! Murder!
GRATIANO: 'Tis some mischance. The voice is very direful.
CASSIO: O, help!   40
LODOVICO: Hark!
RODERIGO: O wretched villain!
LODOVICO: Two or three groan. 'Tis heavy° night;
These may be counterfeits. Let's think 't unsafe
To come in to° the cry without more help.   45

___

25 coat (Possibly a garment of mail under the outer clothing, or simply a tougher coat than Roderigo expected.)   **26 proof** a test   **34 Minion** hussy (i.e., Desdemona)   **35 hies** hastens on   **36 Forth of** from out   **38 passage** people passing by   **43 heavy** thick, dark   **45 come in to** approach

[*They remain near the entrance.*]

RODERIGO: Nobody come? Then shall I bleed to death.

Enter Iago [*in his shirtsleeves, with a light*].

LODOVICO: Hark!

GRATIANO: Here's one comes in his shirt, with light and weapons.

IAGO: Who's there? Whose noise is this that cries on° murder?

LODOVICO: We do not know.

IAGO: Did not you hear a cry? 50

CASSIO: Here, here! For heaven's sake, help me!

IAGO: What's the matter?

[*He moves toward Cassio.*]

GRATIANO [*to Lodovico*]: This is Othello's ancient, as I take it.

LODOVICO [*to Gratiano*]: The same indeed, a very valiant fellow.

IAGO [*to Cassio*]: What° are you here that cry so grievously?

CASSIO: Iago? O, I am spoiled,° undone by villains! 55
Give me some help.

IAGO: O me, Lieutenant! What villains have done this?

CASSIO: I think that one of them is hereabout,
And cannot make° away.

IAGO: O treacherous villains!

[*To Lodovico and Gratiano.*]

What are you there? Come in, and give some help. [*They advance.*] 60

RODERIGO: O, help me there!

CASSIO: That's one of them.

IAGO: O murderous slave! O villain!

[*He stabs Roderigo.*]

RODERIGO: O damned Iago! O inhuman dog!

---

49 cries on cries out   **54 What** who (also at lines 60 and 66)   **55 spoiled** ruined, done for
59 make get

IAGO: Kill men i' the dark?—Where be these bloody
thieves?—
How silent is this town!—Ho! Murder, murder!— 65
[*To Lodovico and Gratiano.*] What may you be? Are you of
good or evil?
LODOVICO: As you shall prove us, praise° us.
IAGO: Signor Lodovico?
LODOVICO: He, sir.
IAGO: I cry you mercy.° Here's Cassio hurt by villains. 70
GRATIANO: Cassio?
IAGO: How is 't, brother?
CASSIO: My leg is cut in two.
IAGO: Marry, heaven forbid!
Light, gentlemen! I'll bind it with my shirt. 75

[*He hands them the light, and tends to Cassio's wound.*]

Enter Bianca.

BIANCA: What is the matter, ho? Who is 't that cried?
IAGO: Who is 't that cried?
BIANCA: O my dear Cassio!
My sweet Cassio! O Cassio, Cassio, Cassio!
IAGO: O notable strumpet! Cassio, may you suspect
Who they should be that have thus mangled you? 80
CASSIO: No.
GRATIANO: I am sorry to find you thus. I have been to seek
you.
IAGO: Lend me a garter. [*He applies a tourniquet.*] So.—O,
for a chair,°
To bear him easily hence!
BIANCA: Alas, he faints! O Cassio, Cassio, Cassio! 85
IAGO: Gentlemen all, I do suspect this trash
To be a party in this injury.—
Patience awhile, good Cassio.—Come, come;
Lend me a light. [*He shines the light on Roderigo.*] Know
we this face or no?

---

67 praise appraise   **70 I cry you mercy** I beg your pardon   **83 chair** litter

Alas, my friend and my dear countryman   90
Roderigo! No.—Yes, sure.—O heaven! Roderigo!

GRATIANO: What, of Venice?

IAGO: Even he, sir. Did you know him?

GRATIANO: Know him? Ay.

IAGO: Signor Gratiano? I cry your gentle° pardon.   95
These bloody accidents° must excuse my manners
That so neglected you.

GRATIANO: I am glad to see you.

IAGO: How do you, Cassio? O, a chair, a chair!

GRATIANO: Roderigo!

IAGO: He, he, 'tis he. [*A litter is brought in.*] O, that's well
said;° the chair.   100
Some good man bear him carefully from hence;
I'll fetch the General's surgeon. [*To Bianca.*] For you,
mistress,
Save you your labor.°—He that lies slain here, Cassio,
Was my dear friend. What malice° was between you?

CASSIO: None in the world, nor do I know the man.   105

IAGO [*to Bianca*]:   What, look you pale?—O, bear him out o'
th' air.°

> [*Cassio and Roderigo are borne off.*]

Stay you,° good gentlemen.—Look you pale, mistress?—
Do you perceive the gastness° of her eye?—
Nay, if you stare,° we shall hear more anon.—
Behold her well; I pray you, look upon her.   110
Do you see, gentlemen? Nay, guiltiness
Will speak, though tongues were out of use.

[*Enter Emilia.*]

EMILIA: 'Las, what's the matter? What's the matter, husband?

IAGO: Cassio hath here been set on in the dark

---

95 gentle noble   **96 accidents** sudden events   **100 well said** well done   **103 Save . . . labor**
i.e., never you mind tending Cassio   **104 malice** enmity   **106 bear . . . air** (Fresh air was thought
to be dangerous for a wound.)   **107 Stay you** (Lodovico and Gratiano are evidently about to leave.)
108 gastness terror   **109 stare** (Iago pretends to interpret Bianca's wild looks as an involuntary
confession of guilt.)

By Roderigo and fellows that are scaped.   *115*

He's almost slain, and Roderigo dead.

EMILIA: Alas, good gentleman! Alas, good Cassio!

IAGO: This is the fruits of whoring. Prithee, Emilia,

Go know° of Cassio where he supped tonight.

[*To Bianca.*] What, do you shake at that?   *120*

BIANCA: He supped at my house, but I therefore shake not.

IAGO: O, did he so? I charge you go with me.

EMILIA: O, fie upon thee, strumpet!

BIANCA: I am no strumpet, but of life as honest°

As you that thus abuse me.   *125*

EMILIA: As I? Faugh! Fie upon thee!

IAGO: Kind gentlemen, let's go see poor Cassio dressed.°—

Come, mistress, you must tell's another tale.

Emilia, run you to the citadel

And tell my lord and lady what hath happed.—   *130*

Will you go on afore? [*Aside.*] This is the night

That either makes me or fordoes° me quite.   *Exeunt.*

SCENE II [A BEDCHAMBER IN THE CITADEL.]

Enter Othello [with a light], and Desdemona in her bed.°

OTHELLO: It is the cause,° it is the cause, my soul.

Let me not name it to you, you chaste stars!

It is the cause. Yet I'll not shed her blood,

Nor scar that whiter skin of hers than snow,

And smooth as monumental° alabaster.   *5*

Yet she must die, else she'll betray more men.

Put out the light, and then put out the light.°

If I quench thee, thou flaming minister,°

I can again thy former light restore,

Should I repent me;° but once put out thy light,   *10*

Thou cunning'st pattern° of excelling nature,

---

119 know learn   **124 honest** chaste   **127 Cassio dressed** Cassio's wounds dressed   **132 fordoes** undoes, ruins
[s.d.] in her bed (Either the curtains are drawn back to reveal the bed in a recessed area backstage, or the bed is "thrust out" onstage as the scene begins.)   **1 cause** i.e., cause of justice, the offense itself, which Othello must correct as an agent of justice   **5 monumental** i.e., used in making tombs and funeral monuments   **7 the light . . . light** the torch or lamp . . . Desdemona's life   **8 flaming minister** torch or lamp that serves me   **10 repent me** change my mind

I know not where is that Promethean heat°
That can thy light relume.° When I have plucked thy rose,
I cannot give it vital growth again;
It needs must wither. I'll smell thee on the tree.   15

[*He kisses her.*]

O balmy breath, that dost almost persuade
Justice to break her sword! One more, one more.
Be thus when thou art dead, and I will kill thee,
And love thee after. One more, and that's the last.

[*He kisses her.*]

So sweet was ne'er so fatal. I must weep,   20
But they are cruel° tears. This sorrow's heavenly;
It strikes where it doth love.° She wakes.
DESDEMONA: Who's there? Othello?
OTHELLO: Ay, Desdemona.
DESDEMONA: Will you come to bed, my lord?   25
OTHELLO: Have you prayed tonight, Desdemon?
DESDEMONA: Ay, my lord.
OTHELLO: If you bethink yourself of any crime°
  Unreconciled as yet to heaven and grace,
  Solicit° for it straight.°   30
DESDEMONA: Alack, my lord, what may you mean by that?
OTHELLO: Well, do it, and be brief. I will walk by.
  I would not kill thy unprepared spirit.
  No, heaven forfend!° I would not kill thy soul.
DESDEMONA: Talk you of killing?
OTHELLO: Ay, I do.
DESDEMONA: Then heaven   35
  Have mercy on me!
OTHELLO: Amen, with all my heart!
DESDEMONA: If you say so, I hope you will not kill me.
OTHELLO: Humh!

---

11 Thou . . . pattern you skillfully wrought perfect example   **12 Promethean heat** divine fire.
(Alluding to the theft of fire from heaven by Prometheus.)   **13 relume** rekindle   **21 cruel** unrelenting   **22 It . . . love** (Compare Hebrews 12:6: "For whom the Lord loveth he chasteneth.")
28 crime sin   **30 Solicit** petition, pray.   **straight** immediately   **34 forfend** forbid

DESDEMONA: And yet I fear you; for you're fatal then
   When your eyes roll so. Why I should fear I know not,   *40*
   Since guiltiness I know not; but yet I feel I fear.
OTHELLO: Think on thy sins.
DESDEMONA: They are loves I bear to you.°
OTHELLO: Ay, and for that thou diest.
DESDEMONA: That death's unnatural that kills for loving.
   Alas, why gnaw you so your nether lip?   *45*
   Some bloody passion shakes your very frame.
   These are portents; but yet I hope, I hope,
   They do not point on° me.
OTHELLO: Peace, and be still!
DESDEMONA: I will so. What's the matter?   *50*
OTHELLO: That handkerchief which I so loved and gave thee
   Thou gav'st to Cassio.
DESDEMONA: No, by my life and soul!
   Send for the man and ask him.
OTHELLO: Sweet soul, take heed, take heed of perjury.
   Thou art on thy deathbed.   *55*
DESDEMONA: Ay, but not yet to die.
OTHELLO: Yes, presently.°
   Therefore confess thee freely of thy sin;
   For to deny each article with oath
   Cannot remove nor choke the strong conception°
   That I do groan withal.° Thou art to die.   *60*
DESDEMONA: Then Lord have mercy on me!
OTHELLO: I say, amen.
DESDEMONA: And have you mercy too! I never did
   Offend° you in my life; never loved Cassio
   But with such general warranty° of heaven
   As I might love. I never gave him token.   *65*
OTHELLO: By heaven, I saw my handkerchief in 's hand.
   O perjured woman! Thou dost stone° my heart,
   And makes me call what I intend to do

---

42 They are . . . you i.e., if I sinned, it was in loving you more than my father or more than God
48 point on point at, predict what is to happen to   **56 presently** immediately   **59 conception** (1)
belief in your guilt (2) plan in my mind   **60 groan withal** (1) groan at in sorrow (2) as in giving
birth   **63 Offend** wrong   **64 warranty** sanction   **67 stone** turn to stone, harden

A murder, which I thought a sacrifice.
I saw the handkerchief.

DESDEMONA: He found it, then.   70
I never gave it him. Send for him hither;
Let him confess a truth.

OTHELLO: He hath confessed.

DESDEMONA: What, my lord?

OTHELLO: That he hath used thee.

DESDEMONA: How? Unlawfully?

OTHELLO: Ay.

DESDEMONA: He will not say so.

OTHELLO: No, his mouth is stopped;   75
Honest Iago hath ta'en order° for 't.

DESDEMONA: O, my fear interprets. What, is he dead?

OTHELLO: Had all his hairs been lives, my great revenge
Had stomach for them all.

DESDEMONA: Alas, he is betrayed and I undone! [*She weeps.*]   80

OTHELLO: Out, strumpet! Weep'st thou for him to my face?

DESDEMONA: O, banish me, my lord, but kill me not!

OTHELLO: Down, strumpet!

DESDEMONA: Kill me tomorrow; let me live tonight!

OTHELLO: Nay, if you strive—   85

DESDEMONA: But half an hour!

OTHELLO: Being done,° there is no pause.

DESDEMONA: But while I say one prayer!

OTHELLO: It is too late.

Smothers her.

EMILIA [*at the door*]:   My lord, my lord! What, ho! My lord,
my lord!

OTHELLO: What noise is this? Not dead? Not yet quite dead?
I that am cruel am yet merciful;   90
I would not have thee linger in thy pain.

[*He dispatches her.*]

---

76 ta'en order taken measures   **86 Being done** i.e., since justice has begun its relentless course

So, so.

EMILIA [*within*]:   What, ho! My lord, my lord!

OTHELLO: Who's there?

EMILIA [*within*]:   O, good my lord, I would speak a word with
you!

OTHELLO: Yes, 'tis Emilia.—By and by.—She's dead.
'Tis like° she comes to speak of Cassio's death.—   95
The noise was here.° Ha! No more moving?
Still as the grave. Shall she come in? Were 't good?—
I think she stirs again. No. What's best to do?
If she come in, she'll sure speak to my wife.
My wife! My wife! What wife? I have no wife.   100
O, insupportable! O heavy hour!
Methinks it should be now a huge eclipse
Of sun and moon, and that th' affrighted globe
Should yawn° at alteration.°

EMILIA [*within*]:   I do beseech you
That I may speak with you, O, good my lord!   105

OTHELLO: I had forgot thee. O, come in, Emilia.—
Soft,° by and by. Let me the curtains draw.—

[*He closes the bed-curtains and opens the door.*]

Where art thou?

Enter Emilia.

What's the matter with thee now?

EMILIA: O, my good lord, yonder's foul murders done!

OTHELLO: What, now?   110

EMILIA: But now, my lord.

OTHELLO: It is the very error° of the moon;
She comes more nearer earth than she was wont,
And makes men mad.

EMILIA: Cassio, my lord, hath killed a young Venetian   115

---

95 like likely that   **96 here** (The Folio's *high* is possible, suggesting that the commotion of the attack on Cassio was loud.)   **104 yawn** gape in amazement, i.e., move in an earthquake. (According
to Pliny, earthquakes often happen during eclipses.)   **at alteration** at these cataclysmic events in
nature, well-suited to express the horror of Desdemona's death   **107 Soft** wait a minute   **112 error**
aberration, irregularity

Called Roderigo.

OTHELLO: Roderigo killed?
And Cassio killed?

EMILIA: No, Cassio is not killed.

OTHELLO: Not Cassio killed? Then murder's out of tune,
And sweet revenge grows harsh.

DESDEMONA: O, falsely, falsely murdered! 120

EMILIA: O Lord, what cry is that?

OTHELLO: That? What?

EMILIA: Out° and alas, that was my lady's voice.

[She opens the bed-curtains.]

Help, help, ho, help! O lady, speak again!
Sweet Desdemona! O sweet mistress, speak! 125

DESDEMONA: A guiltless death I die.

EMILIA: O, who hath done this deed?

DESDEMONA: Nobody; I myself. Farewell.
Commend me to my kind lord. O, farewell! *[She dies.]*

OTHELLO: Why, how should she be murdered?

EMILIA: Alas, who knows? 130

OTHELLO: You heard her say herself it was not I.

EMILIA: She said so. I must needs report the truth.

OTHELLO: She's like a liar gone to burning hell!
'Twas I that killed her.

EMILIA: O, the more angel she,
And you the blacker devil! 135

OTHELLO: She turned to folly,° and she was a whore.

EMILIA: Thou dost belie° her, and thou art a devil.

OTHELLO: She was false as water.

EMILIA: Thou art rash as fire to say
That she was false. O, she was heavenly true! 140

OTHELLO: Cassio did top her. Ask thy husband else.°
O, I were damned beneath all depth in hell
But that I did proceed upon just grounds
To this extremity. Thy husband knew it all.

---

123 Out (A cry of dismay, intensifying *alas*.) **136 folly** i.e., wantonness, fleshly sin **137 belie**
slander **141 else** i.e., if you don't believe me

EMILIA: My husband?   *145*

OTHELLO: Thy husband.

EMILIA: That she was false to wedlock?

OTHELLO: Ay, with Cassio. Nay, had she been true,
    If heaven would make me such another world
    Of one entire and perfect chrysolite,°   *150*
    I'd not have sold her for it.

EMILIA: My husband?

OTHELLO: Ay, 'twas he that told me on her first.
    An honest man he is, and hates the slime
    That sticks on filthy deeds.   *155*

EMILIA: My husband?

OTHELLO: What needs this iterance,° woman? I say thy
    husband.

EMILIA: O mistress, villainy hath made mocks with° love!
    My husband say she was false?

OTHELLO: He, woman;
    I say thy husband. Dost understand the word?   *160*
    My friend, thy husband, honest, honest Iago.

EMILIA: If he say so, may his pernicious soul
    Rot half a grain a day! He lies to th' heart.
    She was too fond of her most filthy bargain.

OTHELLO: Ha?   *[He draws.]*   *165*

EMILIA: Do thy worst!
    This deed of thine is no more worthy heaven
    Than thou wast worthy her.

OTHELLO: Peace, you were best.°

EMILIA: Thou hast not half that power to do me harm
    As I have to be hurt.° O gull!° O dolt!   *170*
    As ignorant as dirt! Thou hast done a deed—
    I care not for thy sword; I'll make thee known,
    Though I lost twenty lives.—Help! Help, ho, help!
    The Moor hath killed my mistress! Murder, murder!

Enter Montano, Gratiano, and Iago.

---

150 **chrysolite** precious topaz   157 **iterance** iteration, repetition   158 **made mocks with** derided, made sport of   168 **you were best** it would be best for you   170 **to be hurt** i.e., to endure hurt. **gull** dupe

MONTANO: What is the matter? How now, General?   *175*

EMILIA: O, are you come, Iago? You have done well,

That men must lay their murders on your neck.

GRATIANO: What is the matter?

EMILIA [*to Iago*]:   Disprove this villain, if thou be'st a man.

He says thou toldst him that his wife was false.   *180*

I know thou didst not; thou'rt not such a villain.

Speak, for my heart is full.

IAGO: I told him what I thought, and told no more

Than what he found himself was apt° and true.

EMILIA: But did you ever tell him she was false?   *185*

IAGO: I did.

EMILIA: You told a lie, an odious, damnèd lie!

Upon my soul, a lie, a wicked lie.

She false with Cassio? Did you say with Cassio?

IAGO: With Cassio, mistress. Go to, charm° your tongue.   *190*

EMILIA: I will not charm my tongue; I am bound to speak.

My mistress here lies murdered in her bed—

ALL: O heavens forfend!

EMILIA: And your reports have set the murder on.

OTHELLO: Nay, stare not, masters. It is true indeed.   *195*

GRATIANO: 'Tis a strange truth.

MONTANO: O monstrous act!

EMILIA: Villainy, villainy, villainy!

I think upon 't—I think I smell 't! O villainy!

I thought so then°—I'll kill myself for grief—

O villainy, villainy!   *200*

IAGO: What, are you mad? I charge you, get you home.

EMILIA: Good gentlemen, let me have leave to speak.

'Tis proper I obey him, but not now.

Perchance, Iago, I will ne'er go home.

Othello: O! O! O!   [*Othello falls on the bed.*°]

EMILIA: Nay, lay thee down and roar,   *205*

For thou hast killed the sweetest innocent

---

184 apt plausible   **190 charm** keep silent (as though by a magic spell)   **199 then** (Perhaps at Act III, Scene iii, lines 331-332 and Act IV, Scene ii, lines 137-154.)   **205 [s.d.] Othello . . . bed** (This direction is from the Quarto, as also *He kisses her* at line 19 and *She dies* at line 129.)

That e'er did lift up eye.°
OTHELLO [*rising*]:   O, she was foul!
I scarce did know you, uncle. There lies your niece,
Whose breath indeed these hands have newly stopped.
I know this act shows° horrible and grim.   210
GRATIANO: Poor Desdemon! I am glad thy father's dead.
Thy match was mortal to him, and pure grief
Shore his old thread° in twain. Did he live now,
This sight would make him do a desperate turn,°
Yea, curse his better angel from his side,   215
And fall to reprobance.°
OTHELLO: 'Tis pitiful. But yet Iago knows
That she with Cassio hath the act of shame
A thousand times committed. Cassio confessed it;
And she did gratify° his amorous works   220
With that recognizance° and pledge of love
Which I first gave her. I saw it in his hand;
It was a handkerchief, an antique token
My father gave my mother.
EMILIA: O God! O heavenly God!   225
IAGO: Zounds, hold your peace.
EMILIA: 'Twill out, 'twill out! I peace?
No, I will speak as liberal as the north.°
Let heaven and men and devils, let them all,
All, all, cry shame against me, yet I'll speak.
IAGO: Be wise, and get you home.
EMILIA: I will not.

[*Iago threatens Emilia.*]

GRATIANO: Fie   230
Your sword upon a woman?
EMILIA: O thou dull Moor! That handkerchief thou speak'st of
I found by fortune and did give my husband;
For often, with a solemn earnestness,

---

207 lift up eye i.e., lift her eyes to heaven   **210 shows** looks   **213 Shore . . . thread** sheared the thread of his old age (as Atropos, one of the three Fates, was thought to do)   **214 turn** deed
216 reprobance damnation, i.e., suicide   **220 gratify** reward   **221 recognizance** token
227 liberal as the north freely as the north wind (blows)

More than indeed belonged° to such a trifle,   235
He begged of me to steal 't.

IAGO: Villainous whore!

EMILIA: She give it Cassio? No, alas! I found it,
And I did give 't my husband.

IAGO: Filth, thou liest!

EMILIA: By heaven, I do not, I do not, gentlemen.
O murderous coxcomb!° What should such a fool   240
Do with so good a wife?

OTHELLO: Are there no stones° in heaven
But what serves for the thunder?—Precious° villain!

[*He runs at Iago; Montano disarms Othello. Iago, from behind, stabs Emilia.°*]

GRATIANO: The woman falls! Sure he hath killed his wife.

EMILIA: Ay, ay. O, lay me by my mistress' side.   245

Exit [*Iago.*]

GRATIANO: He's gone, but his wife's killed.

MONTANO: 'Tis a notorious villain. Take you this weapon,
Which I have here recovered from the Moor.
Come, guard the door without. Let him not pass,
But kill him rather. I'll after that same villain,   250
For 'tis a damnèd slave.

Exit [*with all but Othello and Emilia, who has been laid by
Desdemona's side*].

OTHELLO: I am not valiant neither,
But every puny whipster° gets my sword.
But why should honor° outlive honesty?°
Let it go all.

EMILIA: What did thy song bode, lady?   255
Hark, canst thou hear me? I will play the swan,

---

235 belonged was appropriate   **240 coxcomb** fool. (Addressed to Othello.)   **242 stones** bolts, such as those used for thunderbolts   **243 Precious** i.e., arrant, utter.   **[s.d.] He . . . Emilia** (The Quarto text reads, "The Moor runs at Iago. Iago kills his wife." The Quarto also specifies the exit of Iago at line 245 and the death of Emilia at line 260.)   **253 whipster** contemptible fellow (one who is always ready to whip out his sword)   **254 honor** i.e., the bravery for which one enjoys a soldier's reputation.   **honesty** true integrity

And die in music. [*She sings.*] "Willow, willow, willow."
Moor, she was chaste. She loved thee, cruel Moor.
So come my soul to bliss as I speak true.
So speaking as I think, alas, I die.   [*She dies.*]   260
OTHELLO: I have another weapon in this chamber;
It was a sword of Spain, the ice-brook's temper°—
O, here it is. [*He finds a sword.*] Uncle, I must come forth.
GRATIANO [*within*]:   If thou attempt it, it will cost thee dear.
Thou hast no weapon, and perforce must suffer.   265
OTHELLO: Look in upon me then and speak with me,
Or, naked° as I am, I will assault thee.

[*Enter Gratiano.*]

GRATIANO: What is the matter?
OTHELLO: Behold, I have a weapon;
A better never did itself sustain
Upon a soldier's thigh. I have seen the day   270
That, with this little arm and this good sword,
I have made my way through more impediments
Than twenty times your stop.° But O, vain boast!
Who can control his fate? 'Tis not so now.
Be not afraid, though you do see me weaponed;   275
Here is my journey's end, here is my butt°
And very seamark° of my utmost sail.

[*Gratiano steps back.*]

Do you go back dismayed? 'Tis a lost° fear;
Man but a rush° against Othello's breast
And he retires. Where should Othello go?   280

[*He turns to Desdemona.*]

Now, how dost thou look now? O ill-starred wench!
Pale as thy smock! When we shall meet at compt,°
This look of thine will hurl my soul from heaven,

---

262 **the ice-brook's temper** tempered in ice-cold water   267 **naked** unarmed   273 **stop** power (to stop)   276 **butt** goal, limit. (An archery term.)   277 **seamark** beacon (marking his destination or limit)   278 **lost** wasted, unneeded   279 **Man . . . rush** wield no more than a reed   282 **compt** account, judgment day

And fiends will snatch at it. Cold, cold, my girl?
Even like thy chastity. O cursèd, cursèd slave!°   285
Whip me, ye devils,
From the possession of this heavenly sight!
Blow me about in winds! Roast me in sulfur!
Wash me in steep-down gulfs of liquid fire!
O Desdemon! Dead, Desdemon! Dead! O! O!   290

*Enter Lodovico, Cassio [carried in a litter°], Montano, and
Iago [prisoner], with officers.*

LODOVICO: Where is this rash and most unfortunate man?
OTHELLO: That's he that was Othello. Here I am.
LODOVICO: Where is that viper? Bring the villain forth.

[Iago is led forward.]

OTHELLO: I look down towards his feet;° but that's a fable.
If that thou be'st a devil, I cannot kill thee.   295

[He wounds Iago.]

LODOVICO: Wrench his sword from him.

[Othello is disarmed.]

IAGO: I bleed, sir, but not
killed.
OTHELLO: I am not sorry neither. I'd have thee live,
For in my sense° 'tis happiness to die.
LODOVICO: O thou Othello, that was once so good,
Fall'n in the practice° of a cursèd slave,°   300
What shall be said to thee?
OTHELLO: Why, anything.
An honorable murderer, if you will,
For naught I did in hate, but all in honor.
LODOVICO: This wretch hath part confessed his villainy.
Did you and he consent° in Cassio's death?   305

---

285 slave i.e., Othello himself   **290 [s.d.] in a litter** (The Quarto specifies that Cassio is "in a chair.")   **294 towards his feet** i.e., to see if they are cloven, as the devil's are fabled to be   **298 in my sense** to one who feels as I do   **300 in the practice** through the plotting, into the snare.   **slave villain**   **305 consent** agree

OTHELLO: Ay.

CASSIO: Dear General, I never gave you cause.

OTHELLO: I do believe it, and I ask your pardon.
    Will you, I pray, demand that demi-devil
    Why he hath thus ensnared my soul and body?   310

IAGO: Demand me nothing. What you know, you know.
    From this time forth I never will speak word.

LODOVICO: What, not to pray?

GRATIANO: Torments° will ope your lips.

OTHELLO: Well, thou dost best.   315

LODOVICO: Sir, you shall understand what hath befall'n,
    Which, as I think, you know not. Here is a letter
    Found in the pocket of the slain Roderigo;
    And here another. [*He produces letters.*] The one of them
    imports
    The death of Cassio, to be undertook   320
    By Roderigo.

OTHELLO: O villain!

CASSIO: Most heathenish and most gross!°

LODOVICO [*showing another paper*]: Now here's another
    discontented° paper
    Found in his pocket too. And this, it seems,
    Roderigo meant t' have sent this damnèd villain;   325
    But that belike° Iago in the interim
    Came in and satisfied him.°

OTHELLO: O thou pernicious caitiff!—
    How came you, Cassio, by that handkerchief
    That was my wife's?

CASSIO: I found it in my chamber;   330
    And he himself confessed but even now
    That there he dropped it for a special purpose
    Which wrought to his desire.°

OTHELLO: O fool, fool, fool!

CASSIO: There is besides in Roderigo's letter

---

314 **Torments** torture   322 **gross** monstrous   323 **discontented** full of discontent   326 **belike**
most likely   327 **Came . . . him** interposed and gave him satisfactory explanation   333 **wrought**
. . . desire worked out as he wished, fitted in with his plan

How he upbraids Iago, that he made him   *335*
Brave° me upon the watch, whereon it came°
That I was cast;° and even but now he spake,
After long seeming dead, Iago hurt him,
Iago set him on.

LODOVICO [*to Othello*]:   You must forsake this room and go   *340*
with us.
Your power and your command is taken off,°
And Cassio rules in Cyprus. For this slave,
If there be any cunning cruelty
That can torment him much and hold him long,°
It shall be his. You shall close prisoner rest°   *345*
Till that the nature of your fault be known
To the Venetian state.—Come, bring away.

OTHELLO: Soft you;° a word or two before you go.
I have done the state some service, and they know 't.
No more of that. I pray you, in your letters,   *350*
When you shall these unlucky° deeds relate,
Speak of me as I am; nothing extenuate,
Nor set down aught in malice. Then must you speak
Of one that loved not wisely but too well;
Of one not easily jealous but, being wrought,°   *355*
Perplexed° in the extreme; of one whose hand,
Like the base Indian,° threw a pearl away
Richer than all his tribe; of one whose subdued° eyes,
Albeit unusèd to the melting mood,
Drops tears as fast as the Arabian trees   *360*
Their medicinable gum.° Set you down this;
And say besides that in Aleppo once,
Where a malignant and a turbaned Turk
Beat a Venetian and traduced the state,
I took by th' throat the circumcisèd dog   *365*

---

336 Brave defy.   **whereon it came** whereof it came about   **337 cast** dismissed   **341 taken off**
taken away   **344 hold him long** keep him alive a long time (during his torture)   **345 rest** remain
348 Soft you one moment   **351 unlucky** unfortunate   **355 wrought** worked upon, worked into a
frenzy   **356 Perplexed** distraught   **357 Indian** (This reading from the Quarto pictures an ignorant savage who cannot recognize the value of a precious jewel. The Folio reading, *Iudean* or *Judean*,
i.e., infidel or disbeliever, may refer to Herod, who slew Miriamne in a fit of jealousy, or to Judas
Iscariot, the betrayer of Christ.)   **358 subdued** i.e., overcome by grief   **361 gum** i.e., myrrh

And smote him, thus.   [*He stabs himself.*°]

LODOVICO: O bloody period!°

GRATIANO: All that is spoke is marred.

OTHELLO: I kissed thee ere I killed thee. No way but this,
Killing myself, to die upon a kiss.   370

[*He kisses Desdemona and*] *dies.*

CASSIO: This did I fear, but thought he had no weapon;
For he was great of heart.

LODOVICO [*to Iago*]:   O Spartan dog,°
More fell° than anguish, hunger, or the sea!
Look on the tragic loading of this bed.
This is thy work. The object poisons sight;   375
Let it be hid.° Gratiano, keep° the house,

[*The bed curtains are drawn*]

And seize upon° the fortunes of the Moor,
For they succeed on° you. [*To Cassio.*] To you, Lord
Governor,
Remains the censure° of this hellish villain,
The time, the place, the torture. O, enforce it!   380
Myself will straight aboard, and to the state
This heavy act with heavy heart relate.   *Exeunt.*

—1604?

---

366 [s.d.] **He stabs himself** (This direction is in the Quarto text.)   **367 period** termination, conclusion   **372 Spartan dog** (Spartan dogs were noted for their savagery and silence.)   **373 fell** cruel
376 Let it be hid i.e., draw the bed curtains. (No stage direction specifies that the dead are to be carried offstage at the end of the play.)   **keep** remain in   **377 seize upon** take legal possession of
378 succeed on pass as though by inheritance to   **379 censure** sentencing

Henrik Ibsen (1828–1906), universally acknowledged as the first of the great modern playwrights, was born in Skien, a small town in Norway, the son of a merchant who went bankrupt during Ibsen's childhood. Ibsen first trained for a medical career, but drifted into the theatre, gaining, like Shakespeare and Molière, important dramatic training through a decade's service as a stage manager and director. Ibsen was unsuccessful in establishing a theater in Oslo, and he spent almost thirty years living and writing in Germany and Italy. The fame he won through early poetic dramas like Peer Gynt *(1867), which is considered the supreme exploration of the Norwegian national character, was overshadowed by the realistic prose plays he began writing with* Pillars of Society *(1877).* A Doll House *(1879) and* Ghosts *(1881), which deal, respectively, with a woman's struggle for independence and self-respect and with the taboo subject of venereal disease, made Ibsen an internationally famous, if controversial, figure. Although Ibsen's type of realism, displayed in "problem plays" such as these and later psychological dramas like* The Wild Duck *(1885) and* Hedda Gabler *(1890), has become so fully assimilated into our literary heritage that now it is difficult to think of him as an innovator, his marriage of the tightly constructed plots of the conventional "well-made play" to serious discussion of social issues was one of the most significant developments in the history of drama. Interestingly, the conclusion of* A Doll House *proved so unsettling that Ibsen was forced to write an alternate ending in which Nora states her case but does not slam the door on her marriage. His most influential advocate in English-speaking countries was George Bernard Shaw, whose* The Quintessence of Ibsenism *(1891) is one of the earliest and most influential studies of Ibsen's dramatic methods and ideas.*

Henrik Ibsen
A Doll House

CHARACTERS

Torvald Helmer, *a lawyer*
Nora, *his wife*
Dr. Rank
Mrs. Linde
Nils Krogstad, *a bank clerk*
The Helmers' Three Small Children
Anne-Marie, *their nurse*

Translated by Rolfe Fjelde

Helene, *a maid*
A Delivery Boy

The action takes place in Helmer's residence.

Act I

A comfortable room, tastefully but not expensively furnished. A door to the right in the back wall leads to the entryway; another to the left leads to Helmer's study. Between these doors, a piano. Midway in the left-hand wall a door, and farther back a window. Near the window a round table with an armchair and a small sofa. In the right-hand wall, toward the rear, a door, and nearer the foreground a porcelain stove with two armchairs and a rocking chair beside it. Between the stove and the side door, a small table. Engravings on the walls. An étagère with china figures and other small art objects; small bookcase with richly bound books; the floor carpeted; a fire burning in the stove. It is a winter day.

A bell rings in the entryway; shortly after we hear the door being unlocked. Nora comes into the room, humming happily to herself; she is wearing street clothes and carries an armload of packages, which she puts down on the table to the right. She has left the hall door open and through it a Delivery Boy is seen, holding a Christmas tree and a basket, which he gives to the Maid who let them in.

NORA: Hide the tree well, Helene. The children mustn't get a glimpse of it till this evening, after it's trimmed. (*To the Delivery Boy, taking out her purse.*) How much?

DELIVERY BOY: Fifty, ma'am.

NORA: There's a crown. No, keep the change. (*The Boy thanks her and leaves. Nora shuts the door. She laughs softly to herself while taking off her street things. Drawing a bag of macaroons from her pocket, she eats a couple, then steals over and listens at her husband's study door.*) Yes, he's home. (*Hums again as she moves to the table, right.*)

HELMER (*from the study*): Is that my little lark twittering out there?

NORA (*busy opening some packages*): Yes, it is.

HELMER: Is that my squirrel rummaging around?

NORA: Yes!

HELMER: When did my squirrel get in?

NORA: Just now. (*Putting the macaroon bag in her pocket and wiping her mouth.*) Do come in, Torvald, and see what I've bought.

HELMER: Can't be disturbed. (*After a moment he opens the door and peers in, pen in hand.*) Bought, you say? All that there? Has the little spendthrift been out throwing money around again?

NORA: Oh, but Torvald, this year we really should let ourselves go a bit. It's the first Christmas we haven't had to economize.

HELMER: But you know we can't go squandering.

NORA: Oh yes, Torvald, we can squander a little now. Can't we? Just a tiny, wee bit. Now that you've got a big salary and are going to make piles and piles of money.

HELMER: Yes—starting New Year's. But then it's a full three months till the raise comes through.

NORA: Pooh! We can borrow that long.

HELMER: Nora! (*Goes over and playfully takes her by the ear.*) Are your scatter-brains off again? What if today I borrowed a thousand crowns, and you squandered them over Christmas week, and then on New Year's Eve a roof tile fell on my head, and I lay there—

NORA (*putting her hand on his mouth*): Oh! Don't say such things!

HELMER: Yes, but what if it happened—then what?

NORA: If anything so awful happened, then it just wouldn't matter if I had debts or not.

HELMER: Well, but the people I'd borrowed from?

NORA: Them? Who cares about them? They're strangers.

HELMER: Nora, Nora, how like a woman! No, but seriously, Nora, you know what I think about that. No debts! Never borrow! Something of freedom's lost—and something of beauty, too—from a home that's founded on borrowing and debt. We've made a brave stand up to now, the two of us; and we'll go right on like that the little while we have to.

NORA (*going toward the stove*): Yes, whatever you say, Torvald.

HELMER (*following her*): Now, now, the little lark's wings mustn't droop. Come on, don't be a sulky squirrel. (*Taking out his wallet.*) Nora, guess what I have here.

NORA (*turning quickly*): Money!

HELMER: There, see. (*Hands her some notes.*) Good grief, I know how costs go up in a house at Christmastime.

NORA: Ten—twenty—thirty—forty. Oh, thank you, Torvald; I can manage no end on this.

HELMER: You really will have to.

NORA: Oh yes, I promise I will! But come here so I can show you everything I bought. And so cheap! Look, new clothes for Ivar here—and a sword. Here a horse and a trumpet for Bob. And a doll and a doll's bed here for Emmy; they're nothing much, but she'll tear them to bits in no time anyway. And here I have dress material and handkerchiefs for the maids. Old Anne-Marie really deserves something more.

HELMER: And what's in that package there?

NORA (*with a cry*): Torvald, no! You can't see that till tonight!

HELMER: I see. But tell me now, you little prodigal, what have you thought of for yourself?

NORA: For myself? Oh, I don't want anything at all.

HELMER: Of course you do. Tell me just what—within reason—you'd most like to have.

NORA: I honestly don't know. Oh, listen, Torvald—

HELMER: Well?

NORA (*fumbling at his coat buttons, without looking at him*): If you want to give me something, then maybe you could—you could—

HELMER: Come on, out with it.

NORA (*hurriedly*): You could give me money, Torvald. No more than you think you can spare; then one of these days I'll buy something with it.

HELMER: But Nora—

NORA: Oh, please, Torvald darling, do that! I beg you, please. Then I could hang the bills in pretty gilt paper on the Christmas tree. Wouldn't that be fun?

HELMER: What are those little birds called that always fly through their fortunes?

NORA: Oh yes, spendthrifts; I know all that. But let's do as I say, Torvald; then I'll have time to decide what I really need most. That's very sensible, isn't it?

HELMER (*smiling*): Yes, very—that is, if you actually hung onto the money I give you, and you actually used it to buy yourself something. But it goes for the house and for all sorts of foolish things, and then I only have to lay out some more.

NORA: Oh, but Torvald—

HELMER: Don't deny it, my dear little Nora. (*Putting his arm around her waist.*) Spendthrifts are sweet, but they use up a frightful amount of money. It's incredible what it costs a man to feed such birds.

NORA: Oh, how can you say that! Really, I save everything I can.

HELMER (*laughing*): Yes, that's the truth. Everything you can. But that's nothing at all.

NORA (*humming, with a smile of quiet satisfaction*): Hm, if you only knew what expenses we larks and squirrels have, Torvald.

HELMER: You're an odd little one. Exactly the way your father was. You're never at a loss for scaring up money; but the moment you have it, it runs right out through your fingers; you never know what you've done with it. Well, one takes you as you are. It's deep in your blood. Yes, these things are hereditary, Nora.

NORA: Ah, I could wish I'd inherited many of Papa's qualities.

HELMER: And I couldn't wish you anything but just what you are, my sweet little lark. But wait; it seems to me you have a very—what should I call it?—a very suspicious look today—

NORA: I do?

HELMER: You certainly do. Look me straight in the eye.

NORA (*looking at him*): Well?

HELMER (*shaking an admonitory finger*): Surely my sweet tooth hasn't been running riot in town today, has she?

NORA: No. Why do you imagine that?

HELMER: My sweet tooth really didn't make a little detour through the confectioner's?

NORA: No, I assure you, Torvald—

HELMER: Hasn't nibbled some pastry?

NORA: No, not at all.

HELMER: Nor even munched a macaroon or two?

NORA: No, Torvald, I assure you, really—

HELMER: There, there now. Of course I'm only joking.

NORA (*going to the table, right*): You know I could never think of going against you.

HELMER: No, I understand that; and you *have* given me your word. (*Going over to her.*) Well, you keep your little Christmas secrets to yourself, Nora darling I expect they'll come to light this evening, when the tree is lit.

NORA: Did you remember to ask Dr. Rank?

HELMER: No. But there's no need for that; it's assumed he'll be dining with us. All the same, I'll ask him when he stops by here this morning. I've ordered some fine wine. Nora, you can't imagine how I'm looking forward to this evening.

NORA: So am I—And what fun for the children, Torvald!

HELMER: Ah, it's so gratifying to know that one's gotten a safe, secure job, and with a comfortable salary. It's a great satisfaction, isn't it?

NORA: Oh, it's wonderful!

HELMER: Remember last Christmas? Three whole weeks before, you shut yourself in every evening till long after midnight, making flowers for the Christmas tree, and all the other decorations to surprise us. Ugh, that was the dullest time I've ever lived through.

NORA: It wasn't at all dull for me.

HELMER (*smiling*): But the outcome *was* pretty sorry, Nora.

NORA: Oh, don't tease me with that again. How could I help it that the cat came in and tore everything to shreds.

HELMER: No, poor thing, you certainly couldn't. You wanted so much to please us all, and that's what counts. But it's just as well that the hard times are past.

NORA: Yes, it's really wonderful.

HELMER: Now I don't have to sit here alone, boring myself, and you don't have to tire your precious eyes and your fair little delicate hands—

NORA (*clapping her hands*): No, is it really true, Torvald, I don't have to? Oh, how wonderfully lovely to hear! (*Taking his arm.*) Now I'll tell you just how I've thought we should plan things. Right after Christmas—(*The doorbell rings.*) Oh, the bell. (*Straightening the room up a bit.*) Somebody would have to come. What a bore!

HELMER: I'm not at home to visitors, don't forget.

MAID (*from the hall doorway*): Ma'am, a lady to see you—

NORA: All right, let her come in.

MAID (*to Helmer*): And the doctor's just come too.

HELMER: Did he go right to my study?

MAID: Yes, he did.

Helmer goes into his room. The Maid shows in Mrs. Linde,
dressed in traveling clothes, and shuts the door after her.

MRS. LINDE (*in a dispirited and somewhat hesitant voice*): Hello, Nora.

NORA (*uncertain*): Hello—

MRS. LINDE: You don't recognize me.

NORA: No, I don't know—but wait, I think—(*Exclaiming.*) What! Kristine! Is it really you?

MRS. LINDE: Yes, it's me.

NORA: Kristine! To think I didn't recognize you. But then, how could I? (*More quietly.*) How you've changed, Kristine!

MRS. LINDE: Yes, no doubt I have. In nine—ten long years.

NORA: Is it so long since we met! Yes, it's all of that. Oh, these last eight years have been a happy time, believe me. And so now you've come to town, too. Made the long trip in the winter. That took courage.

MRS. LINDE: I just got here by ship this morning.

NORA: To enjoy yourself over Christmas, of course. Oh, how lovely! Yes, enjoy ourselves, we'll do that. But take your coat off. You're not still cold? (*Helping her.*) There now, let's get cozy here by the stove. No, the easy chair there! I'll take the rocker here. (*Seizing her hands.*) Yes, now you have your old look again; it was only in that first moment. You're a bit more pale, Kristine—and maybe a bit thinner.

MRS. LINDE: And much, much older, Nora.

NORA: Yes, perhaps a bit older; a tiny, tiny bit; not much at all. (*Stopping short; suddenly serious.*) Oh, but thoughtless me, to sit here, chattering away. Sweet good Kristine, can you forgive me?

MRS. LINDE: What do you mean, Nora?

NORA (*softly*): Poor Kristine, you've become a widow.

MRS. LINDE: Yes, three years ago.

NORA: Oh, I knew it, of course; I read it in the papers. Oh, Kristine, you must believe me; I often thought of writing you then, but I kept postponing it, and something always interfered.

MRS. LINDE: Nora dear, I understand completely.

NORA: No, it was awful of me, Kristine. You poor thing, how much you must have gone through. And he left you nothing?

MRS. LINDE: No.

NORA: And no children?

MRS. LINDE: No.

NORA: Nothing at all, then?

MRS. LINDE: Not even a sense of loss to feed on.

NORA (*looking incredulously at her*): But Kristine, how could that be?

MRS. LINDE (*smiling wearily and smoothing her hair*): Oh, sometimes it happens, Nora.

NORA: So completely alone. How terribly hard that must be for you. I have three lovely children. You can't see them now; they're out with the maid. But now you must tell me everything—

MRS. LINDE: No, no, no, tell me about yourself.

NORA: No, you begin. Today I don't want to be selfish. I want to think only of you today. But there *is* something I must tell you. Did you hear of the wonderful luck we had recently?

MRS. LINDE: No, what's that?

NORA: My husband's been made manager in the bank, just think!

MRS. LINDE: Your husband? How marvelous!

NORA: Isn't it? Being a lawyer is such an uncertain living, you know, especially if one won't touch any cases that aren't clean and decent. And of course Torvald would never do that, and I'm with him completely there. Oh, we're simply delighted, believe me! He'll join the bank right after New Year's and start getting a huge salary and lots of commissions. From now on we can live quite differently—just as we want. Oh, Kristine, I feel so light and happy! Won't it be lovely to have stacks of money and not a care in the world?

MRS. LINDE: Well, anyway, it would be lovely to have enough for necessities.

NORA: No, not just for necessities, but stacks and stacks of money!

MRS. LINDE (*smiling*): Nora, Nora, aren't you sensible yet? Back in school you were such a free spender.

NORA (*With a quiet laugh*): Yes, that's what Torvald still says. (*Shaking her finger.*) But "Nora, Nora" isn't as silly as you all think. Really, we've been in no position for me to go squandering. We've had to work, both of us.

MRS. LINDE: You too?

NORA: Yes, at odd jobs—needlework, crocheting, embroidery, and such—(*casually*) and other things too. You remember that Torvald left the department when we were married? There was no chance of promotion in his office, and of course he needed to earn more money. But that first year he drove himself terribly. He took on all kinds of extra work that kept him going morning and night. It wore him down, and then he fell deathly ill. The doctors said it was essential for him to travel south.

MRS. LINDE: Yes, didn't you spend a whole year in Italy?

NORA: That's right. It wasn't easy to get away, you know. Ivar had just been born. But of course we had to go. Oh, that was a beautiful trip, and it saved Torvald's life. But it cost a frightful sum, Kristine.

MRS. LINDE: I can well imagine.

NORA: Four thousand, eight hundred crowns it cost. That's really a lot of money.

MRS. LINDE: But it's lucky you had it when you needed it.

NORA: Well, as it was, we got it from Papa.

MRS. LINDE: I see. It was just about the time your father died.

NORA: Yes, just about then. And, you know, I couldn't make that trip out to nurse him. I had to stay here, expecting Ivar any moment, and with my poor sick Torvald to care for. Dearest Papa, I never saw him again, Kristine. Oh, that was the worst time I've known in all my marriage.

MRS. LINDE: I know how you loved him. And then you went off to Italy?

NORA: Yes. We had the means now, and the doctors urged us. So we left a month after.

MRS. LINDE: And your husband came back completely cured?

NORA: Sound as a drum!

MRS. LINDE: But—the doctor?

NORA: Who?

MRS. LINDE: I thought the maid said he was a doctor, the man who came in with me.

NORA: Yes, that was Dr. Rank—but he's not making a sick call. He's our closest friend, and he stops by at least once a day. No, Torvald hasn't had a sick moment since, and the children are healthy and strong, and I am, too. (*Jumping up and clapping her hands.*) Oh, dear God, Kristine, what a lovely thing to live and be happy! But how disgusting of me—I'm talking of nothing but my own affairs. (*Sits on a stool close by Kristine, arms resting across her knees.*) Oh, don't be angry with me! Tell me, is it really true that you weren't in love with your husband? Why did you marry him, then?

MRS. LINDE: My mother was still alive, but bedridden and helpless—and I had my two younger brothers to look after. In all conscience, I didn't think I could turn him down.

NORA: No, you were right there. But was he rich at the time?

MRS. LINDE: He was very well off, I'd say. But the business was shaky, Nora. When he died, it all fell apart, and nothing was left.

NORA: And then—?

MRS. LINDE: Yes, so I had to scrape up a living with a little shop and a little teaching and whatever else I could find. The last three years have been like one endless workday without a rest for me. Now it's over, Nora. My poor mother doesn't need me, for she's passed on. Nor the boys, either; they're working now and can take care of themselves.

NORA: How free you must feel—

MRS. LINDE: No—only unspeakably empty. Nothing to live for now. (*Standing up anxiously.*) That's why I couldn't take it any longer out in that desolate hole. Maybe here it'll be easier to find something to do and keep my mind occupied. If I could only be lucky enough to get a steady job, some office work—

NORA: Oh, but Kristine, that's so dreadfully tiring, and you already look so tired. It would be much better for you if you could go off to a bathing resort.

MRS. LINDE (*going toward the window*): I have no father to give me travel money, Nora.

NORA (*rising*): Oh, don't be angry with me.

MRS. LINDE (*going to her*): Nora dear, don't you be angry with me. The worst of my kind of situation is all the bitterness that's stored away. No one to work for, and yet you're always having to snap up your opportunities. You have to live; and so you grow selfish. When you told me the happy change in your lot, do you know I was delighted less for your sakes than for mine?

NORA: How so? Oh, I see. You think Torvald could do something for you.

MRS. LINDE: Yes, that's what I thought.

NORA: And he will, Kristine! Just leave it to me; I'll bring it up so delicately—find something attractive to humor him with. Oh, I'm so eager to help you.

MRS. LINDE: How very kind of you, Nora, to be so concerned over me—doubly kind, considering you really know so little of life's burdens yourself.

NORA: I—? I know so little—?

MRS. LINDE (*smiling*): Well my heavens—a little needlework and such—Nora, you're just a child.

NORA (*tossing her head and pacing the floor*): You don't have to act so superior.

MRS. LINDE: Oh?

NORA: You're just like the others. You all think I'm incapable of anything serious—

MRS. LINDE: Come now—

NORA: That I've never had to face the raw world.

MRS. LINDE: Nora dear, you've just been telling me all your troubles.

NORA: Hm! Trivia! (*Quietly.*) I haven't told you the big thing.

MRS. LINDE: Big thing? What do you mean?

NORA: You look down on me so, Kristine, but you shouldn't. You're proud that you worked so long and hard for your mother.

MRS. LINDE: I don't look down on a soul. But it *is* true: I'm proud—and happy, too—to think it was given to me to make my mother's last days almost free of care.

NORA: And you're also proud thinking of what you've done for your brothers.

MRS. LINDE: I feel I've a right to be.

NORA: I agree. But listen to this, Kristine—I've also got something to be proud and happy for.

MRS. LINDE: I don't doubt it. But whatever do you mean?

NORA: Not so loud. What if Torvald heard! He mustn't, not for anything in the world. Nobody must know, Kristine. No one but you.

MRS. LINDE: But what is it, then?

NORA: Come here. (*Drawing her down beside her on the sofa.*) It's true—I've also got something to be proud and happy for. I'm the one who saved Torvald's life.

MRS. LINDE: Saved—? Saved how?

NORA: I told you about the trip to Italy. Torvald never would have lived if he hadn't gone south—

MRS. LINDE: Of course; your father gave you the means—

NORA (*smiling*): That's what Torvald and all the rest think, but—

MRS. LINDE: But—?

NORA: Papa didn't give us a pin. I was the one who raised the money.

MRS. LINDE: You? That whole amount?

NORA: Four thousand, eight hundred crowns. What do you say to that?

MRS. LINDE: But Nora, how was it possible? Did you win the lottery?

NORA (*disdainfully*): The lottery? Pooh! No art to that.

MRS. LINDE: But where did you get it from then?

NORA (*humming, with a mysterious smile*): Hmm, tra-la-la-la.

MRS. LINDE: Because you couldn't have borrowed it.

NORA: No? Why not?

MRS. LINDE: A wife can't borrow without her husband's consent.

NORA (*tossing her head*): Oh, but a wife with a little business sense, a wife who knows how to manage—

MRS. LINDE: Nora, I simply don't understand—

NORA: You don't have to. Whoever said I *borrowed* the money? I could have gotten it other ways. (*Throwing herself back on the sofa.*) I could have gotten it from some admirer or other. After all, a girl with my ravishing appeal—

MRS. LINDE: You lunatic.

NORA: I'll bet you're eaten up with curiosity, Kristine.

MRS. LINDE: Now listen here, Nora—you haven't done something indiscreet?

NORA (*sitting up again*): Is it indiscreet to save your husband's life?

MRS. LINDE: I think it's indiscreet that without his knowledge you—

NORA: But that's the point: he mustn't know! My Lord, can't you understand? He mustn't ever know the close call he had. It was to *me* the doctors came to say his life was in danger—that nothing could save him but a stay in the south. Didn't I try strategy then! I began talking about how lovely it would be for me to travel abroad like other young wives; I begged and I cried; I told him please to remember my condition, to be kind and indulge me; and then I dropped a hint that he could easily take out a loan. But at that, Kristine, he nearly exploded. He said I was frivolous, and it was his duty as man of the house not to indulge me in whims and fancies—as I think he called them. Aha, I thought now, you'll just have to be saved—and that's when I saw my chance.

MRS. LINDE: And your father never told Torvald the money wasn't from him?

NORA: No, never. Papa died right about then. I'd considered bringing him into my secret and begging him never to tell. But he was too sick at the time—and then, sadly, it didn't matter.

MRS. LINDE: And you've never confided in your husband since?

NORA: For heaven's sake, no! Are you serious? He's so strict on that subject. Besides—Torvald, with all his masculine pride—how painfully humiliating for him if he ever found out he was in debt to me. That would just ruin our relationship. Our beautiful, happy home would never be the same.

MRS. LINDE: Won't you ever tell him?

NORA (*thoughtfully, half smiling*): Yes—maybe sometime, years from now, when I'm no longer so attractive. Don't laugh! I only mean when Torvald loves me less than now, when he stops enjoying my dancing and dressing up and reciting for him. Then it might be wise to have something in reserve—(*Breaking off.*) How ridiculous! That'll never happen—Well, Kristine, what do you think of my big secret? I'm capable of something too, hm? You can imagine, of course, how this thing hangs over me. It really hasn't been easy meeting the payments on time. In the business world there's what they call quarterly interest and what they call amortization, and these are always so terribly hard to manage. I've had to skimp a little here and there, wherever I could, because Torvald has to live well. I couldn't let the children go poorly dressed; whatever I got for them, I felt I had to use up completely—the darlings!

MRS. LINDE: Poor Nora, so it had to come out of your own budget, then?

NORA: Yes, of course. But I was the one most responsible, too. Every time Torvald gave me money for new clothes and such, I never used more than half; always bought the simplest, cheapest outfits. It was a godsend that everything looks so well on me that Torvald never noticed. But it did weigh me down at times, Kristine. It *is* such a joy to wear fine things. You understand.

MRS. LINDE: Oh, of course.

NORA: And then I found other ways of making money. Last winter I was lucky enough to get a lot of copying to do. I locked myself in and sat writing every evening till late in the night. Ah, I was tired so often, dead tired. But still it was wonderful fun, sitting and working like that, earning money. It was almost like being a man.

MRS. LINDE: But how much have you paid off this way so far?

NORA: That's hard to say, exactly. These accounts, you know, aren't easy to figure. I only know that I've paid out all I could scrape together. Time and again I haven't known where to turn. (*Smiling.*)

Then I'd sit here dreaming of a rich old gentleman who had fallen
in love with me—

MRS. LINDE: What! Who is he?

NORA: Oh, really! And that he'd died, and when his will was opened,
there in big letters it said, "All my fortune shall be paid over in
cash, immediately to that enchanting Mrs. Nora Helmer."

MRS. LINDE: But Nora dear—who *was* this gentleman?

NORA: Good grief, can't you understand? The old man never existed;
that was only something I'd dream up time and again whenever I
was at my wits' end for money. But it makes no difference now; the
old fossil can go where he pleases for all I care; I don't need him or
his will—because now I'm free. (*Jumping up.*) Oh, how lovely to
think of that, Kristine! Carefree! To know you're carefree, utterly
carefree; to be able to romp and play with the children, and to keep
up a beautiful, charming home—everything just the way Torvald
likes it! And think, spring is coming, with big blue skies. Maybe we
can travel a little then. Maybe I'll see the ocean again. Oh yes, it *is*
so marvelous to live and be happy!

The front doorbell rings.

MRS. LINDE (*rising*): There's the bell. It's probably best that I go.

NORA: No, stay. No one's expected. It must be for Torvald.

MAID (*from the hall doorway*): Excuse me, ma'am—there's a gentleman here to see Mr. Helmer, but I didn't know—since the doctor's
with him.

NORA: Who is the gentleman?

KROGSTAD (*from the doorway*): It's me, Mrs. Helmer.

Mrs. Linde starts and turns away toward the window.

NORA (*stepping toward him, tense, her voice a whisper*): You? What is
it? Why do you want to speak to my husband?

KROGSTAD: Bank business—after a fashion. I have a small job in the investment bank and I hear now your husband is going to be our chief—

NORA: In other words, it's—

KROGSTAD: Just dry business, Mrs. Helmer. Nothing but that.

NORA: Yes, then please be good enough to step into the study. (*She
nods indifferently as she sees him out by the hall door, then returns
and begins stirring up the stove.*)

MRS. LINDE: Nora—who was that man?

NORA: That was a Mr. Krogstad—a lawyer.

MRS. LINDE: Then it really was him.

NORA: Do you know that person?

MRS. LINDE: I did once—many years ago. For a time he was a law clerk in our town.

NORA: Yes, he's been that.

MRS. LINDE: How he's changed.

NORA: I understand he had a very unhappy marriage.

MRS. LINDE: He's a widower now.

NORA: With a number of children. There now, it's burning. (*She closes the stove and moves the rocker a bit to one side.*)

MRS. LINDE: They say he has a hand in all kinds of business.

NORA: That may be true; I wouldn't know. But let's not think about business. It's so dull.

> *Dr. Rank enters from Helmer's study.*

RANK (*still in the doorway*): No, no, really—I don't want to intrude, I'd just as soon talk a little while with your wife. (*Shuts the door, then notices Mrs. Linde.*) Oh, beg pardon. I'm intruding here, too.

NORA: No, not at all. (*Introducing him.*) Dr. Rank, Mrs. Linde.

RANK: Well now, that's a name much heard in this house. I believe I passed the lady on the stairs as I came.

MRS. LINDE: Yes, I take the stairs very slowly. They're rather hard on me.

RANK: Uh-hm, some touch of internal weakness?

MRS. LINDE: More overexertion, I'd say.

RANK: Nothing else? Then you're probably here in town to rest up in a round of parties?

MRS. LINDE: I'm here to look for work.

RANK: Is that the best cure for overexertion?

MRS. LINDE: One has to live, Doctor.

RANK: Yes, there's a common prejudice to that effect.

NORA: Oh, come on, Dr. Rank—you really do want to live yourself.

RANK: Yes, I really do. Wretched as I am, I'll gladly prolong my torment indefinitely. All my patients feel like that. And it's quite the same, too, with the morally sick. Right at this moment there's one of those moral invalids in there with Helmer—

MRS. LINDE (*softly*): Ah!

NORA: What do you mean?

RANK: Oh, it's a lawyer, Krogstad, a type you wouldn't know. His character is rotten to the root—but even he began chattering all-importantly about how he had to *live.*

NORA: Oh? What did he want to talk to Torvald about?

RANK: I really don't know. I only heard something about the bank.

NORA: I didn't know that Krog—that this man Krogstad had anything to do with the bank.

RANK: Yes, he's gotten some kind of berth down there. (*To Mrs. Linde.*) I don't know if you also have, in your neck of the woods, a type of person who scuttles about breathlessly, sniffing out hints of moral corruption, and then maneuvers his victim into some sort of key position where he can keep an eye on him. It's the healthy these days that are out in the cold.

MRS. LINDE: All the same, it's the sick who most need to be taken in.

RANK (*with a shrug*): Yes, there we have it. That's the concept that's turning society into a sanatorium.

Nora, lost in her thoughts, breaks out into quiet laughter and claps her hands.

RANK: Why do you laugh at that? Do you have any real idea of what society is?

NORA: What do I care about dreary old society? I was laughing at something different—something terribly funny. Tell me, Doctor—is everyone who in the bank dependent now on Torvald?

RANK: Is that what you find so terribly funny?

NORA (*smiling and humming*): Never mind, never mind! (*Pacing the floor.*) Yes, that's really immensely amusing: that we—that Torvald has so much power now over all those people. (*Taking the bag out of her pocket.*) Dr. Rank, a little macaroon on that?

RANK: See here, macaroons! I thought they were contraband here.

NORA: Yes, but these are some that Kristine gave me.

MRS. LINDE: What? I—?

NORA: Now, now, don't be afraid. You couldn't possibly know that Torvald had forbidden them. You see, he's worried they'll ruin my teeth. But hmp! Just this once! Isn't that so, Dr. Rank? Help yourself! (*Puts a macaroon in his mouth.*) And you too, Kristine. And I'll also have one, only a little one—or two, at the most. (*Walking about again.*) Now I'm really tremendously happy. Now there's just one last thing in the world that I have an enormous desire to do.

RANK: Well! And what's that?

NORA: It's something I have such a consuming desire to say so Torvald could hear.

RANK: And why can't you say it?

NORA: I don't dare. It's quite shocking.

MRS. LINDE: Shocking?

RANK: Well, then it isn't advisable. But in front of us you certainly can. What do you have such a desire to say so Torvald could hear?

NORA: I have such a huge desire to say—to hell and be damned!

RANK: Are you crazy?

MRS. LINDE: My goodness, Nora!

RANK: Go on, say it. Here he is.

NORA (*hiding the macaroon bag*): Shh, shh, shh!

Helmer comes in from his study, hat in hand, overcoat over his arm.

NORA (*going toward him*): Well, Torvald dear, are you through with him?

HELMER: Yes, he just left.

NORA: Let me introduce you—this is Kristine, who's arrived here in town.

HELMER: Kristine—? I'm sorry, but I don't know—

NORA: Mrs. Linde, Torvald dear. Mrs. Kristine Linde.

HELMER: Of course. A childhood friend of my wife's, no doubt?

MRS. LINDE: Yes, we knew each other in those days.

NORA: And just think, she made the long trip down here in order to talk with you.

HELMER: What's this?

MRS. LINDE: Well, not exactly—

NORA: You see, Kristine is remarkably clever in office work, and so she's terribly eager to come under a capable man's supervision and add more to what she already knows—

HELMER: Very wise, Mrs. Linde.

NORA: And then when she heard that you'd become a bank manager—the story was wired out to the papers—then she came in as
fast as she could and—Really, Torvald, for my sake you can do a little something for Kristine, can't you?

HELMER: Yes, it's not at all impossible. Mrs. Linde, I suppose you're a
widow?

MRS. LINDE: Yes.

HELMER: Any experience in office work?

MRS. LINDE: Yes, a good deal.

HELMER: Well, it's quite likely that I can make an opening for you.

NORA (*clapping her hands*): You see, you see!

HELMER: You've come at a lucky moment, Mrs. Linde.

MRS. LINDE: Oh, how can I thank you?

HELMER: Not necessary. (*Putting his overcoat on.*) But today you'll
have to excuse me—

RANK: Wait, I'll go with you. (*He fetches his coat from the hall and
warms it at the stove.*)

NORA: Don't stay out long, dear.

HELMER: An hour; no more.

NORA: Are you going too, Kristine?

MRS. LINDE (*putting on her winter garments*): Yes, I have to see
about a room now.

HELMER: Then perhaps we can all walk together.

NORA (*helping her*): What a shame we're so cramped here, but it's
quite impossible for us to—

MRS. LINDE: Oh, don't even think of it! Good-bye, Nora dear, and
thanks for everything.

NORA: Good-bye for now. Of course you'll be back this evening. And
you too, Dr. Rank. What? If you're well enough? Oh, you've got to
be! Wrap up tight now.

*In a ripple of small talk the company moves out into the hall;
children's voices are heard outside on the steps.*

NORA: There they are! There they are! (*She runs to open the door.
The children come in with their nurse, Anne-Marie.*) Come in, come
in! (*Bends down and kisses them.*) Oh, you darling—! Look at
them, Kristine. Aren't they lovely!

RANK: No loitering in the draft here.

HELMER: Come, Mrs. Linde—this place is unbearable now for anyone but mothers.

Dr. Rank, Helmer, and Mrs. Linde go down the stairs. Anne-Marie goes into the living room with the children. Nora follows, after closing the hall door.

NORA: How fresh and strong you look. Oh, such red cheeks you have! Like apples and roses. (*The children interrupt her throughout the following.*) And it was so much fun? That's wonderful. Really? You pulled both Emmy and Bob on the sled? Imagine, all together! Yes, you're a clever boy, Ivar. Oh, let me hold her a bit, Anne-Marie. My sweet little doll baby! (*Takes the smallest from the nurse and dances with her.*) Yes, yes, Mama will dance with Bob as well. What? Did you throw snowballs? Oh, if I'd only been there! No, don't bother, Anne-Marie: I'll undress them myself. Oh yes, let me. It's such fun. Go in and rest; you look half frozen. There's hot coffee waiting for you on the stove. (*The nurse goes into the room to the left. Nora takes the children's winter things off, throwing them about, while the children talk to her all at once.*) Is that so? A big dog chased you? But it didn't bite? No, dogs never bite little, lovely doll babies. Don't peek in the packages, Ivar! What is it? Yes, wouldn't you like to know. No, no, it's an ugly something. Well? Shall we play? What shall we play? Hide-and-seek? Yes, let's play hide-and-seek. Bob must hide first. I must? Yes, let me hide first. (*Laughing and shouting, she and the children play in and out of the living room and the adjoining room to the right. At last Nora hides under the table. The children come storming in, search, but cannot find her, then hear her muffled laughter, dash over to the table, lift the cloth up and find her. Wild shouting. She creeps forward as if to scare them. More shouts. Meanwhile, a knock at the hall door; no one has noticed it. Now the door half opens, and Krogstad appears. He waits a moment; The game goes on.*)

KROGSTAD: Beg pardon, Mrs. Helmer—

NORA (*with a strangled cry, turning and scrambling to her knees*): Oh! What do you want?

KROGSTAD: Excuse me. The outer door was ajar; it must be someone forgot to shut it—

NORA (*rising*): My husband isn't home, Mr. Krogstad.

KROGSTAD: I know that.

NORA: Yes—then what do you want here?

KROGSTAD: A word with you.

NORA: With—? (*To the children, quietly.*) Go in to Anne-Marie. What? No, the strange man won't hurt Mama. When he's gone, we'll play some more. (*She leads the children into the room to the left and shuts the door after them. Then, tense and nervous*): You want to speak to me?

KROGSTAD: Yes, I want to.

NORA: Today? But it's not yet the first of the month—

KROGSTAD: No, it's Christmas Eve. It's going to be up to you how merry a Christmas you have.

NORA: What is it you want? Today I absolutely can't—

KROGSTAD: We won't talk about that till later. This is something else. You do have a moment to spare, I suppose?

NORA: Oh yes, of course—I do, except—

KROGSTAD: Good. I was sitting over at Olsen's Restaurant when I saw your husband go down the street.

NORA: Yes?

KROGSTAD: With a lady.

NORA: Yes. So?

KROGSTAD: If you'll pardon my asking: wasn't that lady a Mrs. Linde?

NORA: Yes.

KROGSTAD: Just now come into town?

NORA: Yes, today.

KROGSTAD: She's a good friend of yours?

NORA: Yes, she is. But I don't see—

KROGSTAD: I also knew her once.

NORA: I'm aware of that.

KROGSTAD: Oh! You know all about it. I thought so. Well, then let me ask you short and sweet: is Mrs. Linde getting a job in the bank?

NORA: What makes you think you can cross-examine me, Mr. Krogstad—you, one my husband's employees? But since you ask, you might as well know—yes, Mrs. Linde's going to be taken on at the bank. And I'm the one who spoke for her, Mr. Krogstad. Now you know.

KROGSTAD: So I guessed right.

NORA (*pacing up and down*): Oh, one does have a tiny bit of influence, I should hope. Just because I am a woman, don't think it means that—When one has a subordinate position, Mr. Krogstad, one really ought to be careful about pushing somebody who—hm—

KROGSTAD: Who has influence?

NORA: That's right.

KROGSTAD (*in a different tone*): Mrs. Helmer, would you be good enough to use your influence on my behalf?

NORA: What? What do you mean?

KROGSTAD: Would you please make sure that I keep my subordinate position in the bank?

NORA: What does that mean? Who's thinking of taking away your position?

KROGSTAD: Oh, don't play the innocent with me. I'm quite aware that your friend would hardly relish the chance of running into me again; and I'm also aware now whom I can thank for being turned out.

NORA: But I promise you—

KROGSTAD: Yes, yes, yes, to the point: there's still time, and I'm advising you to use your influence to prevent it.

NORA: But Mr. Krogstad, I have absolutely no influence.

KROGSTAD: You haven't? I thought you were just saying—

NORA: You shouldn't take me so literally. I! How can you believe that I have any such influence over my husband?

KROGSTAD: Oh, I've known your husband from our student days. I don't think the great bank manager's more steadfast than any other married man.

NORA: You speak insolently about my husband, and I'll show you the door.

KROGSTAD: The lady has spirit.

NORA: I'm not afraid of you any longer. After New Year's, I'll soon be done with the whole business.

KROGSTAD (*restraining himself*): Now listen to me, Mrs. Helmer. If necessary, I'll fight for my little job in the bank as if it were life itself.

NORA: Yes, so it seems.

KROGSTAD: It's not just a matter of income; that's the least of it. It's something else—All right, out with it! Look, this is the thing. You know, just like all the others, of course, that once, a good many years ago, I did something rather rash.

NORA: I've heard rumors to that effect.

KROGSTAD: The case never got into court; but all the same, every door was closed in my face from them on. So I took up those various activities you know about. I had to grab hold somewhere; and I dare say I haven't been among the worst. But now I want to drop all that. My boys are growing up. For their sakes, I'll have to win back as much respect as possible here in town. That job in the bank was like the first rung in my ladder. And now your husband wants to kick me right back down in the mud again.

NORA: But for heaven's sake, Mr. Krogstad, it's simply not in my power to help you.

KROGSTAD: That's because you haven't the will to—but I have the means to make you.

NORA: You certainly won't tell my husband that I owe you money?

KROGSTAD: Hm—what if I told him that?

NORA: That would be shameful of you. (*Nearly in tears.*) This secret—my joy and my pride—that he should learn it in such a crude and disgusting way—learn it from you. You'd expose me to the most horrible unpleasantness—

KROGSTAD: Only unpleasantness?

NORA (*vehemently*): But go on and try. It'll turn out the worse for you, because then my husband will really see what a crook you are, and then you'll *never* be able to hold your job.

KROGSTAD: I asked if it was just domestic unpleasantness you were afraid of?

NORA: If my husband finds out, then of course he'll pay what I owe at once, and then we'd be through with you for good.

KROGSTAD (*a step closer*): Listen, Mrs. Helmer—you've either got a very bad memory or else no head at all for business. I'd better put you a little more in touch with the facts.

NORA: What do you mean?

KROGSTAD: When your husband was sick, you came to me for a loan of four thousand, eight hundred crowns.

NORA: Where else could I go?

KROGSTAD: I promised to get you that sum—

NORA: And you got it.

KROGSTAD: I promised to get you that sum, on certain conditions. You were so involved in your husband's illness, and so eager to finance your trip, that I guess you didn't think out all the details. It might just be a good idea to remind you. I promised you the money on the strength of a note I drew up.

NORA: Yes, and that I signed.

KROGSTAD: Right. But at the bottom I added some lines for your father to guarantee the loan. He was supposed to sign down there.

NORA: Supposed to? He did sign.

KROGSTAD: I left the date blank. In other words, your father would have dated his signature himself. Do you remember that?

NORA: Yes, I think—

KROGSTAD: Then I gave you the note for you to mail to your father. Isn't that so?

NORA: Yes.

KROGSTAD: And naturally you sent it at once—because only some five, six days later you brought me the note, properly signed. And with that, the money was yours.

NORA: Well, then; I've made my payments regularly, haven't I?

KROGSTAD: More or less. But—getting back to the point—those were hard times for you then, Mrs. Helmer.

NORA: Yes, they were.

KROGSTAD: Your father was very ill, I believe.

NORA: He was near the end.

KROGSTAD: He died soon after?

NORA: Yes.

KROGSTAD: Tell me, Mrs. Helmer, do you happen to recall the date of your father's death? The day of the month, I mean.

NORA: Papa died the twenty-ninth of September.

KROGSTAD: That's quite correct; I've already looked into that. And now we come to a curious thing—(*taking out a paper*) which I simply cannot comprehend.

NORA: Curious thing? I don't know—

KROGSTAD: This is the curious thing: that your father co-signed the note for your loan three days after his death.

NORA: How—? I don't understand.

KROGSTAD: Your father died the twenty-ninth of September. But look. Here your father dated his signature October second. Isn't that curious, Mrs. Helmer? (*Nora is silent*). Can you explain it to me? (*Nora remains silent.*) It's also remarkable that the words

"October second" and the year aren't written in your father's
hand, but rather in one that I think I know. Well, it's easy to understand. Your father forgot perhaps to date his signature, and
then someone or other added it, a bit sloppily, before anyone
knew of his death. There's nothing wrong in that. It all comes
down to the signature. And there's no question about *that*, Mrs.
Helmer. It really *was* your father who signed his own name here,
wasn't it?

NORA (*after a short silence, throwing her head back and looking
squarely at him*):   No it wasn't. *I* signed Papa's name.

KROGSTAD: Wait, now—are you fully aware that this is a dangerous
confession?

NORA: Why? You'll soon get your money.

KROGSTAD: Let me ask you a question—why didn't you send the paper to your father?

NORA: That was impossible. Papa was so sick. If I'd asked him for his
signature, I also would have had to tell him what the money was
for. But I couldn't tell him, sick as he was, that my husband's life
was in danger. That was just impossible.

KROGSTAD: Then it would have been better if you'd given up the trip
abroad.

NORA: I couldn't possibly. The trip was to save my husband's life. I
couldn't give that up.

KROGSTAD: But didn't you ever consider that this was a fraud
against me?

NORA: I couldn't let myself be bothered by that. You weren't any concern of mine. I couldn't stand you, with all those cold complications
you made, even though you knew how badly off my husband was.

KROGSTAD: Mrs. Helmer, obviously you haven't the vaguest idea of
what you've involved yourself in. But I can tell you this: it was
nothing more and nothing worse than I once did—and it wrecked
my whole reputation.

NORA: You? Do you expect me to believe that you ever acted bravely
to save your wife's life?

KROGSTAD: Laws don't inquire into motives.

NORA: Then they must be very poor laws.

KROGSTAD: Poor or not—if I introduce this paper in court, you'll be
judged according to law.

NORA: This I refuse to believe. A daughter hasn't a right to protect her dying father from anxiety and care? A wife hasn't a right to save her husband's life? I don't much about laws, but I'm sure that somewhere in the books these things are allowed. And you don't know anything about it—you who practice law? You must be an awful lawyer, Mr. Krogstad.

KROGSTAD: Could be. But business—the kind of business we two are mixed up in—don't you think I know about that? All right. Do what you want now. But I'm telling you *this:* if I get shoved down a second time, you're going to keep me company. *(He bows and goes out through the hall.)*

NORA *(pensive for a moment, then tossing her head):* Oh, really! Trying to frighten me! I'm not so silly as all that. *(Begins gathering up the children's clothes, but soon stops.)* But—? No, but that's impossible! I did it out of love.

THE CHILDREN *(in the doorway, left):* Mama: that strange man's gone out the door.

NORA: Yes, yes, I know it. But don't tell anyone about the strange man. Do you hear? Not even Papa!

THE CHILDREN: No, Mama. But now will you play again?

NORA: No, not now.

THE CHILDREN: Oh, but Mama, you promised.

NORA: Yes, but I can't now. Go inside; I have too much to do. Go in, go in, my sweet darlings. *(She herds them gently back in the room and shuts the door after them. Settling on the sofa, she takes up a piece of embroidery and makes some stitches, but soon stops abruptly.)* No! *(Throws the work aside, rises, goes to the hall door and calls out.)* Helene! Let me have the tree in here. *(Goes to the table, left, opens the table drawer, and stops again.)* No, but that's utterly impossible!

MAID *(with the Christmas tree):* Where should I put it, ma'am?

NORA: There. The middle of the floor.

MAID: Should I bring anything else?

NORA: No, thanks. I have what I need.

The Maid, who has set the tree down, goes out.

NORA *(absorbed in trimming the tree):* Candles here—and flowers here. That terrible creature! Talk, talk, talk! There's nothing to it at all. The tree's going to be lovely. I'll do anything to please you, Torvald. I'll sing for you, dance for you—

Helmer comes in from the hall, with a sheaf of papers under his arm.

NORA: Oh! You're back so soon?

HELMER: Yes. Has anyone been here?

NORA: Here? No.

HELMER: That's odd. I saw Krogstad leaving the front door.

NORA: So? Oh yes, that's true. Krogstad was here a moment.

HELMER: Nora, I can see by your face that he's been here, begging you to put in a good word for him.

NORA: Yes.

HELMER: And it was supposed to seem like your own idea? You were to hide it from me that he'd been here. He asked you that, too, didn't he?

NORA: Yes, Torvald, but—

HELMER: Nora, Nora, and you could fall for that? Talk with that sort of person and promise him anything? And then in the bargain, tell me an untruth.

NORA: An untruth—?

HELMER: Didn't you say that no one had been here? (*Wagging his finger.*) My little songbird must never do that again. A songbird needs a clean beak to warble with. No false notes. (*Putting his arm about her waist.*) That's the way it should be, isn't it? Yes, I'm sure of it. (*Releasing her.*) And so, enough of that. (*Sitting by the stove.*) Ah, how snug and cozy it is here. (*Leafing among his papers.*)

NORA (*busy with the tree, after a short pause*): Torvald!

HELMER: Yes.

NORA: I'm so much looking forward to the Stenborgs' costume party, day after tomorrow.

HELMER: And I can't wait to see what you'll surprise me with.

NORA: Oh, that stupid business!

HELMER: What?

NORA: I can't find anything that's right. Everything seems so ridiculous, so inane.

HELMER: So my little Nora's come to *that* recognition?

NORA (*going behind his chair, her arms resting on its back*): Are you very busy, Torvald?

HELMER: Oh—

NORA: What papers are those?

HELMER: Bank matters.

NORA: Already?

HELMER: I've gotten full authority from the retiring management to make all necessary changes in personnel and procedure. I'll need Christmas week for that. I want to have everything in order by New Year's.

NORA: So that was the reason this poor Krogstad—

HELMER: Hm.

NORA (*still leaning on the chair and slowly stroking the nape of his neck*): If you weren't so very busy, I would have asked you an enormous favor, Torvald.

HELMER: Let's hear. What is it?

NORA: You know, there isn't anyone who has your good taste—and I want so much to look well at the costume party. Torvald, couldn't you take over and decide what I should be and plan my costume?

HELMER: Ah, is my stubborn little creature calling for a lifeguard?

NORA: Yes, Torvald, I can't get anywhere without your help.

HELMER: All right—I'll think it over. We'll hit on something.

NORA: Oh, how sweet of you. (*Goes to the tree again. Pause.*) Aren't the red flowers pretty—? But tell me, was it really such a crime that this Krogstad committed?

HELMER: Forgery. Do you have any idea what that means?

NORA: Couldn't he have done it out of need?

HELMER: Yes, or thoughtlessness, like so many others. I'm not so heartless that I'd condemn a man categorically for just one mistake.

NORA: No, of course not, Torvald!

HELMER: Plenty of men have redeemed themselves by openly confessing their crime and taking their punishment.

NORA: Punishment—?

HELMER: But now Krogstad didn't go that way. He got himself out by sharp practices, and that's the real cause of his moral breakdown.

NORA: Do you really think that would—?

HELMER: Just imagine how a man with that sort of guilt in him has to lie and cheat and deceive on all sides, has to wear a mask even with the nearest and dearest he has, even with his own wife and children. And with the children, Nora—that's where it's most horrible.

NORA: Why?

HELMER: Because that kind of atmosphere of lies infects the whole life of a home. Every breath the children take in is filled with the germs of something degenerate.

NORA (*coming closer behind him*): Are you sure of that?

HELMER: Oh, I've seen it often enough as a lawyer. Almost everyone who goes bad early in life has a mother who's a chronic liar.

NORA: Why just—the mother?

HELMER: It's usually the mother's influence that's dominant, but the father's works in the same way, of course. Every lawyer is quite familiar with it. And still this Krogstad's been going home year in, year out, poisoning his own children with lies and pretense; that's why I call him morally lost. (*Reaching his hands out toward her.*) So my sweet little Nora must promise me never to plead his cause. Your hand on it. Come, come, what's this? Give me your hand. There, now. All settled. I can tell you it'd be impossible for me to work alongside of him. I literally feel physically revolted when I'm anywhere near such a person.

NORA (*withdraws her hand and goes to the other side of the Christmas tree*): How hot it is here! And I've got so much to do.

HELMER (*getting up and gathering his papers*): Yes, and I have to think about getting some of these read through before dinner. I'll think about your costume, too. And something to hang on the tree in gilt paper, I may even see about that. (*Putting his hand on her head.*) Oh you, my darling little songbird. (*He goes into his study and closes the door after him.*)

NORA (*softly, after a silence*): Oh, really! It isn't so. It's impossible. It must be impossible.

ANNE-MARIE (*in the doorway, left*): The children are begging so hard to come in to Mama.

NORA: No, no, no, don't let them in to me! You stay with them, Anne-Marie.

ANNE-MARIE: Of course, ma'am. (*Closes the door.*)

NORA (*pale with terror*): Hurt my children—! Poison my home? (*A moment's pause; she tosses her head.*) That's not true. Never. Never in all the world.

ACT II

Same room. Beside the piano the Christmas tree now stands stripped of ornaments, burned-down candle stubs on its ragged branches. Nora's street clothes lie on the sofa. Nora, alone in the room, moves restlessly about; at last she stops at the sofa and picks up her coat.

NORA (*dropping the coat again*): Someone's coming! (*Goes toward the door, listens.*) No—there's no one. Of course—nobody's coming today, Christmas Day—or tomorrow, either. But maybe—(*Opens the door and looks out.*) No, nothing in the mailbox. Quite empty. (*Coming forward.*) What nonsense! He won't do anything serious. Nothing terrible could happen. It's impossible. Why, I have three small children.

Anne-Marie, with a large carton, comes in from the room to the left.

ANNE-MARIE: Well, at last I found the box with the masquerade clothes.
NORA: Thanks. Put it on the table.
ANNE-MARIE (*does so*): But they're all pretty much of a mess.
NORA: Ahh! I'd love to rip them in a million pieces!
ANNE-MARIE: Oh, mercy, they can be fixed right up. Just a little patience.
NORA: Yes, I'll go get Mrs. Linde to help me.
ANNE-MARIE: Out again now? In this nasty weather? Miss Nora will catch cold.
NORA: Oh, worse things could happen—How are the children?
ANNE-MARIE: The poor mites are playing with their Christmas presents, but—
NORA: Do they ask for me much?
ANNE-MARIE: They're so used to having Mama around, you know.
NORA: But Anne-Marie, I *can't* be together with them as much as I was.
ANNE-MARIE: Well, small children get used to anything.
NORA: You think so? Do you think they'd forget their mother if she was gone for good?
ANNE-MARIE: Oh, mercy—gone for good!

NORA: Wait, tell me, Anne-Marie—I've wondered so often—how could you ever have the heart to give your child over to strangers?

ANNE-MARIE: But I had to, you know, to become little Nora's nurse.

NORA: Yes, but how could you *do* it?

ANNE-MARIE: When I could get such a good place? A girl who's poor and who's gotten in trouble is glad enough for that. Because that slippery fish, he didn't do a thing for me, you know.

NORA: But your daughter's surely forgotten you.

ANNE-MARIE: Oh, she certainly has not. She's written to me, both when she was confirmed and when she was married.

NORA (*clasping her about the neck*): You old Anne-Marie, you were a good mother for me when I was little.

ANNE-MARIE: Poor little Nora, with no other mother but me.

NORA: And if the babies didn't have one, then I know that you'd— What silly talk! (*Opening the carton.*) Go in to them. Now I'll have to—Tomorrow you can see how lovely I'll look.

ANNE-MARIE: Oh, there won't be anyone at the party as lovely as Miss Nora. (*She goes off into the room, left.*)

NORA (*begins unpacking the box, but soon throws it aside*): Oh, if I dared to go out. If only nobody would come. If only nothing would happen here while I'm out. What craziness—nobody's coming. Just don't think. This muff—needs a brushing. Beautiful gloves, beautiful gloves. Let it go. Let it go! One, two, three, four, five, six—(*With a cry.*) Oh, there they are! (*Poises to move toward the door, but remains irresolutely standing. Mrs. Linde enters from the hall, where she has removed her street clothes.*)

NORA: Oh, it's you, Kristine. There's no one else out there? How good that you've come.

MRS. LINDE: I hear you were up asking for me.

NORA: Yes, I just stopped by. There's something you really can help me with. Let's get settled on the sofa. Look, there's going to be a costume party tomorrow evening at the Stenborgs' right above us, and now Torvald wants me to go as a Neapolitan peasant girl and dance the tarantella that I learned in Capri.

MRS. LINDE: Really, are you giving a whole performance?

NORA: Torvald says yes, I should. See, here's the dress. Torvald had it made for me down there; but now it's all so tattered that I just don't know—

MRS. LINDE: Oh, we'll fix that up in no time. It's nothing more than the trimmings—they're a bit loose here and there. Needle and thread? Good, now we have what we need.

NORA: Oh, how sweet of you!

MRS. LINDE (*sewing*): So you'll be in disguise tomorrow, Nora. You know what? I'll stop by then for a moment and have a look at you all dressed up. But listen, I've absolutely forgotten to thank you for that pleasant evening yesterday.

NORA (*getting up and walking about*): I don't think it was as pleasant as usual yesterday. You should have come to town a bit sooner, Kristine—Yes, Torvald really knows how to give a home elegance and charm.

MRS. LINDE: And you do, too, if you ask me. You're not your father's daughter for nothing. But tell me, is Dr. Rank always so down in the mouth as yesterday?

NORA: No, that was quite an exception. But he goes around critically ill all the time—tuberculosis of the spine, poor man. You know, his father was a disgusting thing who kept mistresses and so on—and that's why the son's been sickly from birth.

MRS. LINDE (*lets her sewing fall to her lap*): But my dearest Nora, how do you know about such things?

NORA (*walking more jauntily*): Hmp! When you've had three children, then you've had a few visits from—from women who know something of medicine, and they tell you this and that.

MRS. LINDE (*resumes sewing; a short pause*): Does Dr. Rank come here every day?

NORA: Every blessed day. He's Torvald's best friend from childhood, and my good friend, too. Dr. Rank almost belongs to this house.

MRS. LINDE: But tell me—is he quite sincere? I mean, doesn't he rather enjoy flattering people?

NORA: Just the opposite. Why do you think that?

MRS. LINDE: When you introduced us yesterday, he was proclaiming that he'd often heard my name in this house; but later I noticed that your husband hadn't the slightest idea who I really was. So how could Dr. Rank—?

NORA: But it's all true, Kristine. You see, Torvald loves me beyond words and, as he puts it, he'd like to keep me all to himself. For a long time he'd almost be jealous if I even mentioned any of my old friends back home. So of course I dropped that. But with Dr. Rank I talk a lot about such things, because he likes hearing about them.

MRS. LINDE: Now listen, Nora; in many ways you're still like a child. I'm a good deal older than you, with a little more experience. I'll tell you something: you ought to put an end to all this with Dr. Rank.

NORA: What should I put an end to?

MRS. LINDE: Both parts of it, I think. Yesterday you said something about a rich admirer who'd provide you with money—

NORA: Yes, one who doesn't exist—worse luck. So?

MRS. LINDE: Is Dr. Rank well off?

NORA: Yes, he is.

MRS. LINDE: With no dependents?

NORA: No, no one. But—

MRS. LINDE: And he's over here every day?

NORA: Yes, I told you that.

MRS. LINDE: How can a man of such refinement be so grasping?

NORA: I don't follow you at all.

MRS. LINDE: Now don't try to hide it, Nora. You think I can't guess who loaned you the forty-eight hundred crowns?

NORA: Are you out of your mind? How could you think such a thing! A friend of ours, who comes here every single day. What an intolerable situation that would have been!

MRS. LINDE: Then it really wasn't him.

NORA: No, absolutely not. It never even crossed my mind for a moment—And he had nothing to lend in those days; his inheritance came later.

MRS. LINDE: Well, I think that was a stroke of luck for you, Nora dear.

NORA: No, it never would have occurred to me to ask Dr. Rank—Still, I'm quite sure that if I had asked him—

MRS. LINDE: Which you won't, of course.

NORA: No, of course not. I can't see that I'd ever need to. But I'm quite positive that if I talked to Dr. Rank—

MRS. LINDE: Behind your husband's back?

NORA: I've got to clear up this other thing; *that's* also behind his back. I've *got to* clear it all up.

MRS. LINDE: Yes, I was saying that yesterday, but—

NORA (*pacing up and down*): A man handles these problems so much better than a woman—

MRS. LINDE: One's husband does, yes.

NORA: Nonsense. (*Stopping.*) When you pay everything you owe, then you get your note back, right?

MRS. LINDE: Yes, naturally.

NORA: And can rip it into a million pieces and burn it up—that filthy scrap of paper!

MRS. LINDE (*looking hard at her, laying her sewing aside, and rising slowly*): Nora, you're hiding something from me.

NORA: You can see it in my face?

MRS. LINDE: Something's happened to you since yesterday morning. Nora, what is it?

NORA (*hurrying toward her*): Kristine! (*Listening.*) Shh! Torvald's home. Look, go in with the children a while. Torvald can't bear all this snipping and stitching. Let Anne-Marie help you.

MRS. LINDE (*gathering up some of the things*): All right, but I'm not leaving here until we've talked this out. (*She disappears into the room, left, as Torvald enters from the hall.*)

NORA: Oh, how I've been waiting for you, Torvald dear.

HELMER: Was that the dressmaker?

NORA: No, that was Kristine. She's helping me fix up my costume. You know, it's going to be quite attractive.

HELMER: Yes, wasn't that a bright idea I had?

NORA: Brilliant! But then wasn't I good as well to give in to you?

HELMER: Good—because you give in to your husband's judgment? All right, you little goose, I know you didn't mean it like that. But I won't disturb you. You'll want to have a fitting, I suppose.

NORA: And you'll be working?

HELMER: Yes. (*Indicating a bundle of papers.*) See. I've been down to the bank. (*Starts toward his study.*)

NORA: Torvald.

HELMER (*stops*): Yes.

NORA: If your little squirrel begged you, with all her heart and soul, for something—?

HELMER: What's that?

NORA: Then would you do it?

HELMER: First, naturally, I'd have to know what it was.

NORA: Your squirrel would scamper about and do tricks, if you'd only be sweet and give in.

HELMER: Out with it.

NORA: Your lark would be singing high and low in every room—

HELMER: Come on, she does that anyway.

NORA: I'd be a wood nymph and dance for you in the moonlight.

HELMER: Nora—don't tell me it's that same business from this morning!

NORA (*coming closer*): Yes, Torvald, I beg you, please!

HELMER: And you actually have the nerve to drag that up again?

NORA: Yes, yes, you've got to give in to me; you *have* to let Krogstad keep his job in the bank.

HELMER: My dear Nora, I've slated his job for Mrs. Linde.

NORA: That's awfully kind of you. But you could just fire another clerk instead of Krogstad.

HELMER: This is the most incredible stubbornness! Because you go and give an impulsive promise to speak up for him, I'm expected to—

NORA: That's not the reason, Torvald. It's for your own sake. That man does writing for the worst papers; you said it yourself. He could do you any amount of harm. I'm scared to death of him—

HELMER: Ah, I understand. It's the old memories haunting you.

NORA: What do you mean by that?

HELMER: Of course, you're thinking about your father.

NORA: Yes, all right. Just remember how those nasty gossips wrote in the papers about Papa and slandered him so cruelly. I think they'd have had him dismissed if the department hadn't sent you up to investigate, and if you hadn't been so kind and open-minded toward him.

HELMER: My dear Nora, there's a notable difference between your father and me. Your father's official career was hardly above reproach. But mine is; and I hope it'll stay that way as long as I hold my position.

NORA: Oh, who can ever tell what vicious minds can invent? We could be so snug and happy now in our quiet, carefree home—you and I and the children, Torvald! That's why I'm pleading with you so—

HELMER: And just by pleading for him you make it impossible for me to keep him on. It's already known at the bank that I'm hiring Krogstad. What if it's rumored around now that the new bank manager was vetoed by his wife—

NORA: Yes, what then—?

HELMER: Oh yes—as long as our little bundle of stubbornness gets her way—! I should go and make myself ridiculous in front of the whole office—give people the idea I can be swayed by all kinds of outside pressure. Oh, you can bet I'd feel the effects of that soon enough! Besides—there's something that rules Krogstad right out at the bank as long as I'm the manager.

NORA: What's that?

HELMER: His moral failings I could maybe overlook if I had to—

NORA: Yes, Torvald, why not?

HELMER: And I hear he's quite efficient on the job. But he was a crony of mine back in my teens—one of those rash friendships that crop up again and again to embarrass you later in life. Well, I might as well say it straight out: we're on a first-name basis. And that tactless fool makes no effort at all to hide it in front of others. Quite the contrary—he thinks that entitles him to take a familiar air around me, and so every other second he comes booming out with his "Yes, Torvald!" and "Sure thing, Torvald!" I tell you, it's been excruciating for me. He's out to make my place in the bank unbearable.

NORA: Torvald, you can't be serious about all this.

HELMER: Oh no? Why not?

NORA: Because these are such petty considerations.

HELMER: What are you saying? Petty? You think I'm petty!

NORA: No, just the opposite, Torvald dear. That's exactly why—

HELMER: Never mind. You call my motives petty; then I might as well be just that. Petty! All right! We'll put a stop to this for good. (*Goes to the hall door and calls.*) Helene!

NORA: What do you want?

HELMER (*searching among his papers*): A decision. (*The Maid comes in.*) Look here; take this letter; go out with it at once. Get hold of a messenger and have him deliver it. Quick now. It's already addressed. Wait, here's some money.

MAID: Yes, sir. (*She leaves with the letter.*)

HELMER (*straightening his papers*): There, now, little Miss Willful.

NORA (*breathlessly*): Torvald, what was that letter?

HELMER: Krogstad's notice.

NORA: Call it back, Torvald! There's still time. Oh, Torvald, call it back! Do it for my sake—for your sake, for the children's sake! Do you hear, Torvald; do it! You don't know how this can harm us.

HELMER: Too late.

NORA: Yes, too late.

HELMER: Nora dear, I can forgive you this panic, even though basically you're insulting me. Yes, you are! Or isn't it an insult to think that *I* should be afraid of a courtroom hack's revenge? But I forgive you anyway, because this shows so beautifully how much you love me. (*Takes her in his arms.*) This is the way it should be, my darling Nora. Whatever comes, you'll see: when it really counts, I have strength and courage enough as a man to take on the whole weight myself.

NORA (*terrified*): What do you mean by that?

HELMER: The whole weight, I said.

NORA (*resolutely*): No, never in all the world.

HELMER: Good. So we'll share it, Nora, as man and wife. That's as it should be. (*Fondling her.*) Are you happy now? There, there, there—not these frightened dove's eyes. It's nothing at all but empty fantasies—Now you should run through your tarantella and practice your tambourine. I'll go to the inner office and shut both doors, so I won't hear a thing; you can make all the noise you like. (*Turning in the doorway.*) And when Rank comes, just tell him where he can find me. (*He nods to her and goes with his papers into the study, closing the door.*)

NORA (*standing as though rooted, dazed with fright, in a whisper*): He really could do it. He will do it. He'll do it in spite of everything. No, not that, never, never! Anything but that! Escape! A way out— (*The doorbell rings.*) Dr. Rank! Anything but that! *Anything*, whatever it is! (*Her hands pass over her face, smoothing it; she pulls herself together, goes over and opens the hall door. Dr. Rank stands outside, hanging his fur coat up. During the following scene, it begins getting dark.*)

NORA: Hello, Dr. Rank. I recognized your ring. But you mustn't go in to Torvald yet; I believe he's working.

RANK: And you?

NORA: For you, I always have an hour to spare—you know that. (*He has entered, and she shuts the door after him.*)

RANK: Many thanks. I'll make use of these hours while I can.

NORA: What do you mean by that? While you can?

RANK: Does that disturb you?

NORA: Well, it's such an odd phrase. Is anything going to happen?

RANK: What's going to happen is what I've been expecting so long—but I honestly didn't think it would come so soon.

NORA (*gripping his arm*): What is it you've found out? Dr. Rank, you have to tell me!

RANK (*sitting by the stove*): It's all over with me. There's nothing to be done about it.

NORA (*breathing easier*): Is it you—then—?

RANK: Who else? There's no point in lying to one's self. I'm the most miserable of all my patients, Mrs. Helmer. These past few days I've been auditing my internal accounts. Bankrupt! Within a month I'll probably be laid out and rotting in the churchyard.

NORA: Oh, what a horrible thing to say.

RANK: The thing itself is horrible. But the worst of it is all the other horror before it's over. There's only one final examination left; when I'm finished with that, I'll know about when my disintegration will begin. There's something I want to say. Helmer with his sensitivity has a sharp distaste for anything ugly. I don't want him near my sickroom.

NORA: Oh, but Dr. Rank—

RANK: I won't have him in there. Under no condition. I'll lock my door to him—As soon as I'm completely sure of the worst, I'll send you my calling card marked with a black cross, and you'll know then the wreck has started to come apart.

NORA: No, today you're completely unreasonable. And I wanted you so much to be in a really good humor.

RANK: With death up my sleeve? And then to suffer this way for somebody else's sins. Is there any justice in that? And in every single family, in some way or another, this inevitable retribution of nature goes on—

NORA (*her hands pressed over her eyes*): Oh, stuff! Cheer up! Please—be gay!

RANK: Yes, I'd just as soon laugh at it all. My poor, innocent spine, serving time for my father's gay army days.

NORA (*by the table, left*): He was so infatuated with asparagus tips and *pâté de foie gras*, wasn't that it?

RANK: Yes—and with truffles.

NORA: Truffles, yes. And then with oysters, I suppose?

RANK: Yes, tons of oysters, naturally.

NORA: And then the port and champagne to go with it. It's so sad that all these delectable things have to strike at our bones.

RANK: Especially when they strike at the unhappy bones that never shared in the fun.

NORA: Oh, that's the saddest of all.

RANK (*looks searchingly at her*):   Hm.

NORA (*after a moment*):   Why did you smile?

RANK: No, it was you who laughed.

NORA: No, it was you who smiled, Dr. Rank!

RANK (*getting up*):   You're even a bigger tease than I'd thought.

NORA: I'm full of wild ideas today.

RANK: That's obvious.

NORA (*putting both hands on his shoulders*):   Dear, dear Dr. Rank, you'll never die for Torvald and me.

RANK: Oh, that loss you'll easily get over. Those who go away are soon forgotten.

NORA (*looks fearfully at him*):   You believe that?

RANK: One makes new connections, and then—

NORA: Who makes new connections?

RANK: Both you and Torvald will when I'm gone. I'd say you're well under way already. What was that Mrs. Linde doing here last evening?

NORA: Oh, come—you can't be jealous of poor Kristine?

RANK: Oh yes, I am. She'll be my successor here in the house. When I'm down under, that woman will probably—

NORA: Shh! Not so loud. She's right in there.

RANK: Today as well. So you see.

NORA: Only to sew on my dress. Good gracious, how unreasonable you are. (*Sitting on the sofa.*) Be nice now, Dr. Rank. Tomorrow you'll see how beautifully I'll dance, and you can imagine then that I'm dancing only for you—yes, and of course for Torvald, too— that's understood. (*Takes various items out of the carton.*) Dr. Rank, sit over here and I'll show you something.

RANK (*sitting*):   What's that?

NORA: Look here. Look.

RANK: Silk stockings.

NORA: Flesh-colored. Aren't they lovely? Now it's so dark here, but to- morrow. No, no, no, just look at the feet. Oh well, you might as well look at the rest.

RANK: Hm—

NORA: Why do you look so critical? Don't you believe they'll fit?

RANK: I've never had any chance to form an opinion on that.

NORA (*glancing at him a moment*): Shame on you. (*Hits him lightly on the ear with the stockings*) That's for you. (*Puts them away again.*)

RANK: And what other splendors am I going to see now?

NORA: Not the least bit more, because you've been naughty. (*She hums a little and rummages among her things.*).

RANK (*after a short silence*): When I sit here together with you like this, completely easy and open, then I don't know—I simply can't imagine—whatever would have become of me if I'd never come into this house.

NORA (*smiling*): Yes, I really think you feel completely at ease with us.

RANK (*more quietly, staring straight ahead*): And then to have to go away from it all—

NORA: Nonsense, you're not going away.

RANK (*his voice unchanged*):—And not even be able to leave some poor show of gratitude behind, scarcely a fleeting regret—no more than a vacant place that anyone can fill.

NORA: And if I asked you now for—? No—

RANK: For what?

NORA: No, I mean—for an exceptionally big favor—

RANK: Would you really, for once, make me so happy?

NORA: Oh, you haven't the vaguest idea what it is.

RANK: All right, then tell me.

NORA: No, but I can't, Dr. Rank—it's all out of reason. It's advice and help, too—and a favor—

RANK: So much the better. I can't fathom what you're hinting at. Just speak out. Don't you trust me?

NORA: Of course. More than anyone else. You're my best and truest friend, I'm sure. That's why I want to talk to you. All right, then, Dr. Rank: there's something you can help me prevent. You know how deeply, how inexpressibly dearly Torvald loves me; he'd never hesitate a second to give up his life for me.

RANK (*leaning close to her*): Nora—do you think he's the only one—

NORA (*with a slight start*): Who—?

RANK: Who'd gladly give up his life for you.

NORA (*heavily*): I see.

RANK: I swore to myself you should know this before I'm gone. I'll never find a better chance. Yes, Nora, now you know. And also you know now that you can trust me beyond anyone else.

NORA (*rising, natural and calm*): Let me by.

RANK (*making room for her, but still sitting*): Nora—

NORA (*in the hall doorway*): Helene, bring the lamp in. (*Goes over to the stove.*) Ah dear Dr. Rank, that was really mean of you.

RANK (*getting up*): That I've loved you just as deeply as somebody else? Was *that* mean?

NORA: No, but that you came out and told me. That was quite unnecessary—

RANK: What do you mean? Have you known—?

The Maid comes in with the lamp, sets it on the table, and goes out again.

RANK: Nora—Mrs. Helmer—I'm asking you: have you known about it?

NORA: Oh, how can I tell what I know or don't know? Really, I don't know what to say—Why did you have to be so clumsy, Dr. Rank! Everything was so good.

RANK: Well, in any case, you now have the knowledge that my body and soul are at your command. So won't you speak out?

NORA (*looking at him*): After that?

RANK: Please, just let me know what it is.

NORA: You can't know anything now.

RANK: I have to. You mustn't punish me like this. Give me the chance to do whatever is humanly possible for you.

NORA: Now there's nothing you can do for me. Besides, actually, I don't need any help. You'll see—it's only my fantasies. That's what it is. Of course! (*Sits in the rocker, looks at him, and smiles.*) What a nice one you are, Dr. Rank. Aren't you a little bit ashamed, now that the lamp is here?

RANK: No, not exactly. But perhaps I'd better go—for good?

NORA: No, you certainly can't do that. You must come here just as you always have. You know Torvald can't do without you.

RANK: Yes, but *you?*

NORA: You know how much I enjoy it when you're here.

RANK: That's precisely what threw me off. You're a mystery to me. So many times I've felt you'd almost rather be with me than with Helmer.

NORA: Yes—you see, there are some people that one loves most and other people that one would almost prefer being with.

RANK: Yes, there's something to that.

NORA: When I was back home, of course I loved Papa most. But I always thought it was so much fun when I could sneak down to the maids' quarters, because they never tried to improve me, and it was always so amusing, the way they talked to each other.

RANK: Aha, so it's *their* place that I've filled.

NORA (*Jumping up and going to him*): Oh, dear, sweet Dr. Rank, that's not what I mean at all. But you can understand that with Torvald it's just the same as with Papa—

The Maid enters from the hall.

MAID: Ma'am—please! (*She whispers to Nora and hands her a calling card.*)

NORA (*glancing at the card*): Ah! (*Slips it into her pocket.*)

RANK: Anything wrong?

NORA: No, no, not at all. It's only some—it's my new dress—

RANK: Really? But—there's your dress.

NORA: Oh, that. But this is another one—I ordered it—Torvald mustn't know—

RANK: Ah, now we have the big secret.

NORA: That's right. Just go in with him—he's back in the inner study. Keep him there as long as—

RANK: Don't worry. He won't get away. (*Goes into the study.*)

NORA (*to the Maid*): And he's standing waiting in the kitchen?

MAID: Yes, he came up by the back stairs.

NORA: But didn't you tell him somebody was here?

MAID: Yes, but that didn't do any good.

NORA: He won't leave?

MAID: No, he won't go till he's talked with you, ma'am.

NORA: Let him come in, then—but quietly. Helene, don't breathe a word about this. It's a surprise for my husband.

MAID: Yes, yes, I understand—(*Goes out.*)

NORA: This horror—it's going to happen. No, no, no, it can't happen, it mustn't. (*She goes and bolts Helmer's door. The Maid opens the hall door for Krogstad and shuts it behind him. He is dressed for travel in a fur coat, boots, and a fur cap.*)

NORA (*going toward him*): Talk softly. My husband's home.

KROGSTAD: Well, good for him.

NORA: What do you want?

KROGSTAD: Some information.

NORA: Hurry up, then. What is it?

KROGSTAD: You know, of course, that I got my notice.

NORA: I couldn't prevent it, Mr. Krogstad. I fought for you to the bitter end, but nothing worked.

KROGSTAD: Does your husband's love for you run so thin? He knows everything I can expose you to, and all the same he dares to—

NORA: How can you imagine he knows anything about this?

KROGSTAD: Ah, no—I can't imagine it either, now. It's not at all like my fine Torvald Helmer to have so much guts.

NORA: Mr. Krogstad, I demand respect for my husband!

KROGSTAD: Why, of course—all due respect. But since the lady's keeping it so carefully hidden, may I presume to ask if you're also a bit better informed than yesterday about what you've actually done?

NORA: More than you ever could teach me.

KROGSTAD: Yes, I *am* such an awful lawyer.

NORA: What is it you want from me?

KROGSTAD: Just a glimpse of how you are, Mrs. Helmer. I've been thinking about you all day long. A cashier, a night-court scribbler, a—well, a type like me also has a little of what they call a heart, you know.

NORA: Then show it. Think of my children.

KROGSTAD: Did you or your husband ever think of mine? But never mind. I wanted to tell you that you don't need to take this thing too seriously. For the present, I'm not proceeding with any action.

NORA: Oh no, really! Well—I knew that.

KROGSTAD: Everything can be settled in a friendly spirit. It doesn't have to get around town at all; it can stay just among us three.

NORA: My husband must never know anything of this.

KROGSTAD: How can you manage that? Perhaps you can pay me the balance?

NORA: No, not right now.

KROGSTAD: Or you know some way of raising the money in a day or two?

NORA: No way that I'm willing to use.

KROGSTAD: Well, it wouldn't have done you any good, anyway. If you stood in front of me with a fistful of bills, you still couldn't buy your signature back.

NORA: Then tell me what you're going to do with it.

KROGSTAD: I'll just hold onto it—keep it on file. There's no outsider who'll even get wind of it. So if you've been thinking of taking some desperate step—

NORA: I have.

KROGSTAD: Been thinking of running away from home—

NORA: I have!

KROGSTAD: Or even of something worse—

NORA: How could you guess that?

KROGSTAD: You can drop those thoughts.

NORA: How could you guess I was thinking of that?

KROGSTAD: Most of us think about *that* at first. I thought about it too, but I discovered I hadn't the courage—

NORA (*lifelessly*): I don't either.

KROGSTAD (*relieved*): That's true, you haven't the courage? You too?

NORA: I don't have it—I don't have it.

KROGSTAD: It would be terribly stupid, anyway. After that first storm at home blows out, why, then—I have here in my pocket a letter for your husband—

NORA: Telling everything?

KROGSTAD: As charitably as possible.

NORA (*quickly*): He mustn't ever get that letter. Tear it up. I'll find some way to get money.

KROGSTAD: Beg pardon, Mrs. Helmer, but I think I just told you—

NORA: Oh, I don't mean the money I owe you. Let me know how much you want from my husband, and I'll manage it.

KROGSTAD: I don't want any money from your husband.

NORA: What do you want, then?

KROGSTAD: I'll tell you what I want to recoup, Mrs. Helmer; I want to get on in the world—and there's where your husband can help me. For a year and a half I've kept myself clean of anything disreputable—all that time struggling with the worst conditions; but I was satisfied, working my way up step by step. Now I've been written right off, and I'm just not in the mood to come crawling back. I tell you, I want to move on. I want to get back in the bank—in a better position. Your husband can set up a job for me—

NORA: He'll never do that!

KROGSTAD: He'll do it. I know him. He won't dare breathe a word of protest. And once I'm in there together with him, you just wait and see! Inside of a year, I'll be the manager's right-hand man. It'll be Nils Krogstad, not Torvald Helmer who runs the bank.

NORA: You'll never see the day!

KROGSTAD: Maybe you think you can—

NORA: I have the courage now—for *that.*

KROGSTAD: Oh, you don't scare me. A smart, spoiled lady like you—

NORA: You'll see; you'll see!

KROGSTAD: Under the ice, maybe? Down in the freezing, coal-black water? There, till you float up in the spring, ugly, unrecognizable, with your hair falling out—

NORA: You don't frighten me!

KROGSTAD: Nor do you frighten me. One doesn't do these things, Mrs. Helmer. Besides, what good would it be? I'd still have him safe in my pocket.

NORA: Afterwards? When I'm no longer—?

KROGSTAD: Are you forgetting that *I'll* be in control then over your final reputation? (*Nora stands speechless, staring at him.*) Good; now I've warned you. Don't do anything stupid. When Helmer's read my letter, I'll be waiting for his reply. And bear in mind that it's your husband himself who's forced me back to my old ways. I'll never forgive him for that. Good-bye, Mrs. Helmer. (*He goes out through the hall.*)

NORA (*goes to the hall door, opens it a crack, and listens*): He's gone. Didn't leave the letter. Oh no, no, that's impossible too! (*Opening the door more and more.*) What's that? He's standing outside—not going downstairs. He's thinking it over? Maybe he'll—? (*A letter falls in the mailbox; then Krogstad's footsteps are heard, dying away down a flight of stairs. Nora gives a muffled cry and runs over toward the sofa table. A short pause.*) In the mailbox. (*Slips warily over to the hall door.*) It's lying there. Torvald, Torvald—now we're lost!

MRS. LINDE (*entering with the costume from the room, left*): There now. I can't see anything else to mend. Perhaps you'd like to try.

NORA (*in a hoarse whisper*): Kristine, come here.

MRS. LINDE (*tossing the dress on the sofa*): What's wrong? You look upset.

NORA: Come here. See that letter? *There!* Look—through the glass in the mailbox.

MRS. LINDE: Yes, yes, I see it.

NORA: That letter's from Krogstad—

MRS. LINDE: Nora—it's Krogstad who loaned you the money!

NORA: Yes, and now Torvald will find out everything.

MRS. LINDE: Believe me, Nora, it's best for both of you.

NORA: There's more you don't know. I forged a name.

MRS. LINDE: But for heaven's sake—?

NORA: I only want to tell you that, Kristine, so that you can be my witness.

MRS. LINDE: Witness? Why should I—?

NORA: If I should go out of my mind—it could easily happen—

MRS. LINDE: Nora!

NORA: Or anything else occurred—so I couldn't be present here—

MRS. LINDE: Nora, Nora, you aren't yourself at all!

NORA: And someone should try to take on the whole weight, all of the guilt, you follow me—

MRS. LINDE: Yes, of course, but why do you think—?

NORA: Then you're the witness that it isn't true, Kristine. I'm very much myself; my mind right now is perfectly clear; and I'm telling you: nobody else has known about this; I alone did everything. Remember that.

MRS. LINDE: I will. But I don't understand all this.

NORA: Oh, how could you ever understand it? It's the miracle now that's going to take place.

MRS. LINDE: The miracle?

NORA: Yes, the miracle. But it's so awful, Kristine. It mustn't take place, not for anything in the world.

MRS. LINDE: I'm going right over and talk with Krogstad.

NORA: Don't go near him; he'll do you some terrible harm!

MRS. LINDE: There was a time once when he'd gladly have done anything for me.

NORA: He?

MRS. LINDE: Where does he live?

NORA: Oh, how do I know? Yes. (*Searches in her pocket.*) Here's his card. But the letter, the letter—!

HELMER (*from the study, knocking on the door*): Nora!

NORA (*with a cry of fear*): Oh! What is it? What do you want?

HELMER: Now, now, don't be so frightened. We're not coming in. You locked the door—are you trying on the dress?

NORA: Yes, I'm trying it. I'll look just beautiful, Torvald.

MRS. LINDE (*who has read the card*): He's living right around the corner.

NORA: Yes, but what's the use? We're lost. The letter's in the box.

MRS. LINDE: And your husband has the key?

NORA: Yes, always.

MRS. LINDE: Krogstad can ask for his letter back unread; he can find some excuse—

NORA: But it's just this time that Torvald usually—

MRS. LINDE: Stall him. Keep him in there. I'll be back as quick as I can. (*She hurries out through the hall entrance.*)

NORA (*goes to Helmer's door, opens it, and peers in*): Torvald!

HELMER (*from the inner study*): Well—does one dare set foot in one's own living room at last? Come on, Rank, now we'll get a look—(*In the doorway.*) But what's this?

NORA: What, Torvald dear?

HELMER: Rank had me expecting some grand masquerade.

RANK (*in the doorway*): That was my impression, but I must have been wrong.

NORA: No one can admire me in my splendor—not till tomorrow.

HELMER: But Nora dear, you look so exhausted. Have you practiced too hard?

NORA: No, I haven't practiced at all yet.

HELMER: You know, it's necessary—

NORA: Oh, it's absolutely necessary, Torvald. But I can't get anywhere without your help. I've forgotten the whole thing completely.

HELMER: Ah, we'll soon take care of that.

NORA: Yes, take care of me, Torvald, please! Promise me that? Oh, I'm so nervous. That big party—You must give up everything this evening for me. No business—don't even touch your pen. Yes? Dear Torvald, promise?

HELMER: It's a promise. Tonight I'm totally at your service—you little helpless thing—but first there's one thing I want to—(*Goes toward the hall door.*)

NORA: What are you looking for?

HELMER: Just to see if there's any mail.

NORA: No, no, don't do that, Torvald!

HELMER: Now what?

NORA: Torvald, please. There isn't any.

HELMER: Let me look, though. (*Starts out. Nora, at the piano, strikes the first notes of the tarantella. Helmer, at the door, stops.*) Aha!

NORA: I can't dance tomorrow if I don't practice with you.

HELMER (*going over to her*): Nora dear, are you really so frightened?

NORA: Yes, so terribly frightened. Let me practice right now; there's still time before dinner. Oh, sit down and play for me, Torvald. Direct me. Teach me, the way you always have.

HELMER: Gladly, if it's what you want. (*Sits at the piano.*)

NORA (*snatches the tambourine up from the box, then a long, vari-colored shawl, which she throws around herself, whereupon she springs forward and cries out*): Play for me now! Now I'll dance!

Helmer plays and Nora dances. Rank stands behind Helmer at the piano and looks on.

HELMER (*as he plays*): Slower. Slow down.

NORA: Can't change it.

HELMER: Not so violent, Nora!

NORA: Has to be just like this.

HELMER (*stopping*): No, no, that won't do at all.

NORA (*laughing and swinging her tambourine*): Isn't that what I told you?

RANK: Let me play for her.

HELMER (*getting up*): Yes, go on. I can teach her more easily then.

Rank sits at the piano and plays; Nora dances more and more wildly. Helmer has stationed himself by the stove and repeatedly gives her directions; she seems not to hear them;

her hair loosens and falls over her shoulders; she does not notice, but goes on dancing. Mrs. Linde enters.

MRS. LINDE (*standing dumbfounded at the door*): Ah—!

NORA (*still dancing*): See what fun, Kristine!

HELMER: But Nora darling, you dance as if your life were at stake.

NORA: And it is.

HELMER: Rank, stop! This is pure madness. Stop it, I say!

Rank breaks off playing, and Nora halts abruptly.

HELMER (*going over to her*): I never would have believed it. You've forgotten everything I taught you.

NORA (*throwing away the tambourine*): You see for yourself.

HELMER: Well, there's certainly room for instruction here.

NORA: Yes, you see how important it is. You've got to teach me to the very last minute. Promise me that, Torvald?

HELMER: You can bet on it.

NORA: You mustn't, either today or tomorrow, think about anything else but you mustn't open any letters—or the mailbox—

HELMER: Ah, it's still the fear of that man—

NORA: Oh yes, yes, that too.

HELMER: Nora, it's written all over you—there's already a letter from him out there.

NORA: I don't know. I guess so. But you mustn't read such things now; there mustn't be anything ugly between us before it's all over.

RANK (*quietly to Helmer*): You shouldn't deny her.

HELMER (*putting his arm around her*): The child can have her way. But tomorrow night, after you've danced—

NORA: Then you'll be free.

MAID (*in the doorway, right*): Ma'am, dinner is served.

NORA: We'll be wanting champagne, Helene.

MAID: Very good, ma'am. (*Goes out.*)

HELMER: So—a regular banquet, hm?

NORA: Yes, a banquet—champagne till daybreak! (*Calling out.*) And some macaroons, Helene. Heaps of them—just this once.

HELMER (*taking her hands*): Now, now, now—no hysterics. Be my own little lark again.

NORA: Oh, I will soon enough. But go on in—and you, Dr. Rank. Kristine, help me put up my hair.

RANK (*whispering, as they go*): There's nothing wrong—really wrong, is there?

HELMER: Oh, of course not. It's nothing more than this childish anxiety I was telling you about. (*They go out, right.*)

NORA: Well?

MRS. LINDE: Left town.

NORA: I could see by your face.

MRS. LINDE: He'll be home tomorrow evening. I wrote him a note.

NORA: You shouldn't have. Don't try to stop anything now. After all, it's a wonderful joy, this waiting here for the miracle.

MRS. LINDE: What is it you're waiting for?

NORA: Oh, you can't understand that. Go in to them; I'll be along in a moment.

Mrs. Linde goes into the dining room. Nora stands a short while as if composing herself; then she looks at her watch.

NORA: Five. Seven hours to midnight. Twenty-four hours to the midnight after, and then the tarantella's done. Seven and twenty-four? Thirty-one hours to live.

HELMER (*in the doorway, right*): What's become of the little lark?

NORA (*going toward him with open arms*): Here's your lark!

Act III

Same scene. The table, with chairs around it, has been moved to the center of the room. A lamp on the table is lit. The hall door stands open. Dance music drifts down from the floor above. Mrs. Linde sits at the table, absently paging through a book trying to read, but apparently unable to focus her thoughts. Once or twice she pauses, tensely listening for a sound at the outer entrance.

MRS. LINDE (*glancing at her watch*): Not yet—and there's hardly any time left. If only he's not—(*Listening again.*) Ah, there he is. (*She goes out in the hall and cautiously opens the outer door. Quiet footsteps are heard on the stairs. She whispers.*) Come in. Nobody's here.

KROGSTAD (*in the doorway*):   I found a note from you at home. What's back of all this?

MRS. LINDE: I just *had* to talk to you.

KROGSTAD: Oh! And it just *had* to be here in this house?

MRS. LINDE: At my place it was impossible; my room hasn't a private entrance. Come in; we're all alone. The maid's asleep, and the Helmers are at the dance upstairs.

KROGSTAD (*entering the room*):   Well, well, the Helmers are dancing tonight? Really?

MRS. LINDE: Yes, why not?

KROGSTAD: How true—why not?

MRS. LINDE: All right, Krogstad, let's talk.

KROGSTAD: Do we two have anything more to talk about?

MRS. LINDE: We have a great deal to talk about.

KROGSTAD: I wouldn't have thought so.

MRS. LINDE: No, because you've never understood me, really.

KROGSTAD: Was there anything more to understand—except what's all too common in life? A calculating woman throws over a man the moment a better catch comes by.

MRS. LINDE: You think I'm so thoroughly calculating? You think I broke it off lightly?

KROGSTAD: Didn't you?

MRS. LINDE: Nils—is that what you really thought?

KROGSTAD: If you cared, then why did you write me the way you did?

MRS. LINDE: What else could I do? If I had to break off with you, then it was my job as well to root out everything you felt for me.

KROGSTAD (*wringing his hands*):   So that was it. And this—all this, simply for money!

MRS. LINDE: Don't forget I had a helpless mother and two small brothers. We couldn't wait for you, Nils; you had such a long road ahead for you then.

KROGSTAD: That may be; but you still hadn't the right to abandon me for somebody else's sake.

MRS. LINDE: Yes—I don't know. So many, many times I've asked myself if I did have that right.

KROGSTAD (*more softly*):   When I lost you, it was as if all the solid ground dissolved from under my feet. Look at me; I'm a half-drowned man now, hanging onto a wreck.

MRS. LINDE: Help may be near.

KROGSTAD: It was near—but then you came and blocked it off.

MRS. LINDE: Without my knowing it, Nils. Today for the first time I learned that it's you I'm replacing at the bank.

KROGSTAD: All right—I believe you. But now that you know, will you step aside?

MRS. LINDE: No, because that wouldn't benefit you in the slightest.

KROGSTAD: Not "benefit" me, hm! I'd step aside anyway.

MRS. LINDE: I've got to be realistic. Life and hard, bitter necessity have taught me that.

KROGSTAD: And life's taught me never to trust fine phrases.

MRS. LINDE: Then life's taught you a very sound thing. But you do have to trust in actions, don't you?

KROGSTAD: What does that mean?

MRS. LINDE: You said you were hanging on like a half-drowned man to a wreck.

KROGSTAD: I've good reason to say that.

MRS. LINDE: I'm also like a half-drowned woman on a wreck. No one to suffer with; no one to care for.

KROGSTAD: You made your choice.

MRS. LINDE: There wasn't any choice then.

KROGSTAD: So—what of it?

MRS. LINDE: Nils, if only we two shipwrecked people could reach across to each other.

KROGSTAD: What are you saying?

MRS. LINDE: Two on one wreck are at least better off than each on his own.

KROGSTAD: Kristine!

MRS. LINDE: Why do you think I came into town?

KROGSTAD: Did you really have some thought of me?

MRS. LINDE: I have to work to go on living. All my born days, as long as I can remember, I've worked, and it's been my best and my only joy. But now I'm completely alone in the world; it frightens me to be so empty and lost. To work for yourself—there's no joy in that. Nils, give me something—someone to work for.

KROGSTAD: I don't believe all this. It's just some hysterical feminine urge to go out and make a noble sacrifice.

MRS. LINDE: Have you ever found me to be hysterical?

KROGSTAD: Can you honestly mean this? Tell me—do you know everything about my past?

MRS. LINDE: Yes.

KROGSTAD: And you know what they think I'm worth around here.

MRS. LINDE: From what you were saying before, it would seem that with me you could have been another person.

KROGSTAD: I'm positive of that.

MRS. LINDE: Couldn't it happen still?

KROGSTAD: Kristine—you're saying this in all seriousness? Yes, you are! I can see it in you. And do you really have the courage, then—?

MRS. LINDE: I need to have someone to care for; and your children need a mother. We both need each other. Nils, I have faith that you're good at heart—I'll risk everything together with you.

KROGSTAD (*gripping her hands*): Kristine, thank you, thank you— Now I know I can win back a place in their eyes. Yes—but I forgot—

MRS. LINDE (*listening*): Shh! The tarantella. Go now! Go on!

KROGSTAD: Why? What is it?

MRS. LINDE: Hear the dance up there? When that's over, they'll be coming down.

KROGSTAD: Oh, then I'll go. But—it's all pointless. Of course, you don't know the move I made against the Helmers.

MRS. LINDE: Yes, Nils, I know.

KROGSTAD: And all the same, you have the courage to—?

MRS. LINDE: I know how far despair can drive a man like you.

KROGSTAD: Oh, if I only could take it all back.

MRS. LINDE: You easily could—your letter's still lying in the mailbox.

KROGSTAD: Are you sure of that?

MRS. LINDE: Positive. But—

KROGSTAD (*looks at her searchingly*): Is that the meaning of it, then? You'll save your friend at any price. Tell me straight out. Is that it?

MRS. LINDE: Nils—anyone who's sold herself for somebody else once isn't going to do it again.

KROGSTAD: I'll demand my letter back.

MRS. LINDE: No, no.

KROGSTAD: Yes, of course. I'll stay here till Helmer comes down; I'll tell him to give me my letter again—that it only involves my dismissal—that he shouldn't read it—

MRS. LINDE: No, Nils, don't call the letter back.

KROGSTAD: But wasn't that exactly why you wrote me to come here?

MRS. LINDE: Yes, in that first panic. But it's been a whole day and night since then, and in that time I've seen such incredible things in this house. Helmer's got to learn everything; this dreadful secret has to be aired; those two have to come to a full understanding; all these lies and evasions can't go on.

KROGSTAD: Well, then, if you want to chance it. But at least there's one thing I can do, and do right away.

MRS. LINDE (*listening*): Go now, go, quick! The dance is over. We're not safe another second.

KROGSTAD: I'll wait for you downstairs.

MRS. LINDE: Yes, please do; take me home.

KROGSTAD: I can't believe it; I've never been so happy. (*He leaves by way of the outer door; the door between the room and hall stays open.*)

MRS. LINDE (*straightening up a bit and getting together her street clothes*): How different now! How different! Someone to work for, to live for—a home to build. Well, it is worth the try! Oh, if they'd only come! (*Listening.*) Ah, there they are. Bundle up. (*She picks up her hat and coat. Nora's and Helmer's voices can be heard outside; a key turns in the lock, and Helmer brings Nora into the hall almost by force. She is wearing the Italian costume with a large black shawl about her; he has on evening dress, with a black domino open over it.*)

NORA (*struggling in the doorway*): No, no, no, not inside! I'm going up again. I don't want to leave so soon.

HELMER: But Nora dear—

NORA: Oh, I beg you, please, Torvald. From the bottom of my heart, *please*—only an hour more!

HELMER: Not a single minute, Nora darling. You know our agreement. Come on, in we go; you'll catch cold out here. (*In spite of her resistance, he gently draws her into the room.*)

MRS. LINDE: Good evening.

NORA: Kristine!

HELMER: Why, Mrs. Linde—are you here so late?

MRS. LINDE: Yes, I'm sorry, but I did want to see Nora in costume.

NORA: Have you been sitting here, waiting for me?

MRS. LINDE: Yes. I didn't come early enough; you were all upstairs; and then I thought I really couldn't leave without seeing you.

HELMER (*removing Nora's shawl*): Yes, take a good look. She's worth looking at, I can tell you that, Mrs. Linde. Isn't she lovely?

MRS. LINDE: Yes, I should say—

HELMER: A dream of loveliness, isn't she? That's what everyone thought at the party, too. But she's horribly stubborn—this sweet little thing. What's to be done with her? Can you imagine, I almost had to use force to pry her away.

NORA: Oh, Torvald, you're going to regret you didn't indulge me, even for just a half hour more.

HELMER: There, you see. She danced the tarantella and got a tumultuous hand—which was well earned, although the performance may have been a bit too naturalistic—I mean it rather overstepped the proprieties of art. But never mind—what's important is, she made a success, an overwhelming success. You think I could let her stay on after that and spoil the effect? Oh no; I took my lovely little Capri girl—my capricious little Capri girl, I should say—took her under my arm; one quick tour of the ballroom, a curtsy to every side, and then—as they say in novels—the beautiful vision disappeared. An exit should always be effective, Mrs. Linde, but that's what I can't get Nora to grasp. Phew, it's hot in here. (*Flings the domino on a chair and opens the door to his room.*) Why's it dark in here? Oh yes, of course. Excuse me. (*He goes in and lights a couple of candles.*)

NORA (*in a sharp, breathless whisper*): So?

MRS. LINDE (*quietly*): I talked with him.

NORA: And—?

MRS. LINDE: Nora—you must tell your husband everything.

NORA (*dully*): I knew it.

MRS. LINDE: You've got nothing to fear from Krogstad, but you have to speak out.

NORA: I won't tell.

MRS. LINDE: Then the letter will.

NORA: Thanks, Kristine. I know now what's to be done. Shh!

HELMER (*reentering*): Well, then, Mrs. Linde—have you admired her?

MRS. LINDE: Yes, and now I'll say good night.

HELMER: Oh, come, so soon? Is this yours, this knitting?

MRS. LINDE: Yes, thanks. I nearly forgot it.

HELMER: Do you knit, then?

MRS. LINDE: Oh yes.

HELMER: You know what? You should embroider instead.

MRS. LINDE: Really? Why?

HELMER: Yes, because it's a lot prettier. See here, one holds the embroidery so, in the left hand, and then one guides the needle with the right—so—in an easy, sweeping curve—right?

MRS. LINDE: Yes, I guess that's—

HELMER: But, on the other hand, knitting—it can never be anything but ugly. Look, see here, the arms tucked in, the knitting needles going up and down—there's something Chinese about it. Ah, that was really a glorious champagne they served.

MRS. LINDE: Yes, good night, Nora, and don't be stubborn any more.

HELMER: Well put, Mrs. Linde!

MRS. LINDE: Good night, Mr. Helmer.

HELMER (*accompanying her to the door*): Good night, good night. I hope you get home all right I'd be very happy to—but you don't have far to go. Good night, good night. (*She leaves. He shuts the door after her and returns.*) There, now, at last we got her out the door. She's a deadly bore, that creature.

NORA: Aren't you pretty tired, Torvald?

HELMER: No, not a bit.

NORA: You're not sleepy?

HELMER: Not at all. On the contrary, I'm feeling quite exhilarated. But you? Yes, you really look tired and sleepy.

NORA: Yes, I'm very tired. Soon now I'll sleep.

HELMER: See! You see! I was right all along that we shouldn't stay longer.

NORA: Whatever you do is always right.

HELMER (*kissing her brow*): Now my little lark talks sense. Say, did you notice what a time Rank was having tonight?

NORA: Oh, was he? I didn't get to speak with him.

HELMER: I scarcely did either, but it's a long time since I've seen him in such high spirits. (*Gazes at her a moment, then comes nearer her.*) Hm—it's marvelous, though, to be back home again—to be completely alone with you. Oh, you bewitchingly lovely young woman!

NORA: Torvald, don't look at me like that!

HELMER: Can't I look at my richest treasure? At all that beauty that's mine, mine alone—completely and utterly.

NORA (*moving around to the other side of the table*): You mustn't talk to me that way tonight.

HELMER (*following her*): The tarantella is still in your blood, I can see—and it makes you even more enticing. Listen. The guests are beginning to go. (*Dropping his voice.*) Nora—it'll soon be quiet through this whole house.

NORA: Yes, I hope so.

HELMER: You do, don't you, my love? Do you realize—when I'm out at a party like this with you—do you know why I talk to you so little, and keep such a distance away; just send you a stolen look now and then—you know why I do it? It's because I'm imagining then that you're my secret darling, my secret young bride-to-be, and that no one suspects there's anything between us.

NORA: Yes, yes; oh, yes, I know you're always thinking of me.

HELMER: And then when we leave and I place the shawl over those fine young rounded shoulders—over that wonderful curving neck—then I pretend that you're my young bride, that we're just coming from the wedding, that for the first time I'm bringing you into my house—that for the first time I'm alone with you—completely alone with you, your trembling young beauty! All this evening I've longed for nothing but you. When I saw you turn and sway in the tarantella—my blood was pounding till I couldn't stand it—that's why I brought you down here so early—

NORA: Go away, Torvald! Leave me alone. I don't want all this.

HELMER: What do you mean? Nora, you're teasing me. You will, won't you? Aren't I your husband—?

A knock at the outside door.

NORA (*startled*): What's that?

HELMER (*going toward the hall*): Who is it?

RANK (*outside*): It's me. May I come in a moment?

HELMER (*with quiet irritation*): Oh, what does he want now? (*Aloud.*) Hold on. (*Goes and opens the door.*) Oh, how nice that you didn't just pass us by!

RANK: I thought I heard your voice, and then I wanted so badly to have a look in. (*Lightly glancing about.*) Ah, me, these old familiar haunts. You have it snug and cozy in here, you two.

HELMER: You seemed to be having it pretty cozy upstairs, too.

RANK: Absolutely. Why shouldn't I? Why not take in everything in life? As much as you can, anyway, and as long as you can. The wine was superb—

HELMER: The champagne especially.

RANK: You noticed that too? It's amazing how much I could guzzle down.

NORA: Torvald also drank a lot of champagne this evening.

RANK: Oh?

NORA: Yes, and that always makes him so entertaining.

RANK: Well, why shouldn't one have a pleasant evening after a well-spent day?

HELMER: Well spent? I'm afraid I can't claim that.

RANK (*slapping him on the back*): But I can, you see!

NORA: Dr. Rank, you must have done some scientific research today.

RANK: Quite so.

HELMER: Come now—little Nora talking about scientific research!

NORA: And can I congratulate you on the results?

RANK: Indeed you may.

NORA: Then they were good?

RANK: The best possible for both doctor and patient—certainty.

NORA (*quickly and searching*): Certainty?

RANK: Complete certainty. So don't I owe myself a gay evening afterwards?

NORA: Yes, you're right, Dr. Rank.

HELMER: I'm with you—just so long as you don't have to suffer for it in the morning.

RANK: Well, one never gets something for nothing in life.

NORA: Dr. Rank—are you very fond of masquerade parties?

RANK: Yes, if there's a good array of odd disguises—

NORA: Tell me, what should we two go as at the next masquerade?

HELMER: You little featherhead—already thinking of the next!

RANK: We two? I'll tell you what: you must go as Charmed Life—

HELMER: Yes, but find a costume for *that*!

RANK: Your wife can appear just as she looks every day.

HELMER: That was nicely put. But don't you know what you're going to be?

RANK: Yes, Helmer, I've made up my mind.

HELMER: Well?

RANK: At the next masquerade I'm going to be invisible.

HELMER: That's a funny idea.

RANK: They say there's a hat—black, huge—have you never heard of the hat that makes you invisible? You put it on, and then no one on earth can see you.

HELMER (*suppressing a smile*): Ah, of course.

RANK: But I'm quite forgetting what I came for. Helmer, give me a cigar, one of the dark Havanas.

HELMER: With the greatest pleasure. (*Holds out his case.*)

RANK: Thanks. (*Takes one and cuts off the tip.*)

NORA (*striking a match*): Let me give you a light.

RANK: Thank you. (*She holds the match for him; he lights the cigar.*) And now good-bye.

HELMER: Good-bye, good-bye, old friend.

NORA: Sleep well, Doctor.

RANK: Thanks for that wish.

NORA: Wish me the same.

RANK: You? All right, if you like—Sleep well. And thanks for the light. (*He nods to them both and leaves.*)

HELMER (*his voice subdued*): He's been drinking heavily.

NORA (*absently*): Could be. (*Helmer takes his keys from his pocket and goes out in the hall.*) Torvald—what are you after?

HELMER: Got to empty the mailbox; it's nearly full. There won't be room for the morning papers.

NORA: Are you working tonight?

HELMER: You know I'm not. Why—what's this? Someone's been at the lock.

NORA: At the lock—?

HELMER: Yes, I'm positive. What do you suppose—? I can't imagine one of the maids—? Here's a broken hairpin. Nora, it's yours—

NORA (*quickly*): Then it must be the children—

HELMER: You'd better break them of that. Hm, hm—well, opened it after all. (*Takes the contents out and calls into the kitchen.*) Helene! Helene, would you put out the lamp in the hall. (*He returns to the room, shutting the hall door, then displays the handful of mail.*) Look how it's piled up. (*Sorting through them.*) Now what's this?

NORA (*at the window*): The letter! Oh, Torvald, no!

HELMER: Two calling cards—from Rank.

NORA: From Dr. Rank?

HELMER (*examining them*): "Dr. Rank, Consulting Physician." They were on top. He must have dropped them in as he left.

NORA: Is there anything on them?

HELMER: There's a black cross over the name. See? That's a gruesome notion. He could almost be announcing his own death.

NORA: That's just what he's doing.

HELMER: What! You've heard something? Something he's told you?

NORA: Yes. That when those cards came, he'd be taking his leave of us. He'll shut himself in now and die.

HELMER: Ah, my poor friend! Of course I knew he wouldn't be here much longer. But so soon—And then to hide himself away like a wounded animal.

NORA: If it has to happen, then it's best it happens in silence—don't you think so, Torvald?

HELMER (*pacing up and down*): He'd grown right into our lives. I simply can't imagine him gone. He with his suffering and loneliness—like a dark cloud setting off our sunlit happiness. Well, maybe it's best this way. For him, at least. (*Standing still.*) And maybe for us too, Nora. Now we're thrown back on each other, completely. (*Embracing her.*) Oh you, my darling wife, how can I hold you close enough? You know what, Nora—time and again I've wished you were in some terrible danger, just so I could stake my life and soul and everything, for your sake.

NORA (*tearing herself away, her voice firm and decisive*): Now you must read your mail, Torvald.

HELMER: No, no, not tonight. I want to stay with you, dearest.

NORA: With a dying friend on your mind?

HELMER: You're right. We've both had a shock. There's ugliness between us—these thoughts of death and corruption. We'll have to get free of them first. Until then—we'll stay apart.

NORA (*clinging about his neck*): Torvald—good night! Good night!

HELMER (*kissing her on the cheek*): Good night, little songbird. Sleep well, Nora. I'll be reading my mail now. (*He takes the letters into his room and shuts the door after him.*)

NORA (*with bewildered glances, groping about, seizing Helmer's domino, throwing it around her, and speaking in short, hoarse, broken whispers*): Never see him again. Never, never. (*Putting her* *shawl over her head.*) Never see the children either—them, too. Never, never. Oh, the freezing black water! The depths—down— Oh, I wish it were over—He has it now; he's reading it—now. Oh no, no, not yet. Torvald, good-bye, you and the children—(*She starts for the hall; as she does, Helmer throws open his door and stands with an open letter in his hand.*)

HELMER: Nora!

NORA (*screams*): Oh—!

HELMER: What is this? You know what's in this letter?

NORA: Yes, I know. Let me go! Let me out!

HELMER (*holding her back*): Where are you going?

NORA (*struggling to break loose*): You can't save me, Torvald!

HELMER (*slumping back*): True! Then it's true what he writes? How horrible! No, no, it's impossible—it can't be true.

NORA: It is true. I've loved you more than all this world.

HELMER: Ah, none of your slippery tricks.

NORA (*taking one step toward him*): Torvald—!

HELMER: What is this you've blundered into?

NORA: Just let me loose. You're not going to suffer for my sake. You're not going to take on my guilt.

HELMER: No more playacting. (*Locks the hall door.*) You stay right here and give me a reckoning. You understand what you've done? Answer! You understand?

NORA (*looking squarely at him, her face hardening*): Yes. I'm beginning to understand everything now.

HELMER (*striding about*): Oh, what an awful awakening! In all these eight years—she who was my pride and joy—a hypocrite, a liar— worse, worse—a criminal! How infinitely disgusting it all is! The shame! (*Nora says nothing and goes looking straight at him. He stops in front of her.*) I should have suspected something of the kind. I should have known. All your father's flimsy values have come out in you. No religion, no morals, no sense of duty—Oh, how I'm punished for letting him off! I did it for your sake, and you repay me like this.

NORA: Yes, like this.

HELMER: Now you've wrecked all my happiness—ruined my whole future. Oh, it's awful to think of. I'm in a cheap little grafter's hands; he can do anything he wants with me, ask for anything, play with me like a puppet—and I can't breathe a word. I'll be swept down miserably into the depths on account of a featherbrained woman.

NORA: When I'm gone from this world, you'll be free.

HELMER: Oh, quit posing. Your father had a mess of those speeches too. What good would that ever do me if you were gone from this world, as you say? Not the slightest. He can still make the whole thing known; and if he does, I could be falsely suspected as your accomplice. They might even think that I was behind it—that I put you up to it. And all that I can thank you for—you that I've coddled the whole of our marriage. Can you see now what you've done to me?

NORA (*icily calm*): Yes.

HELMER: It's so incredible, I just can't grasp it. But we'll have to patch up whatever we can. Take off the shawl. I said, take it off! I've got to appease him somehow or other. The thing has to be hushed up at any cost. And as for you and me, it's got to seem like everything between us is just as it was—to the outside world, that is. You'll go right on living in this house, of course. But you can't be allowed to bring up the children; I don't dare trust you with them— Oh, to have to say this to someone I've loved so much! Well, that's done with. From now on happiness doesn't matter; all that matters is saving the bits and pieces, the appearance—(*The doorbell rings. Helmer starts.*) What's that? And so late. Maybe the worst—? You think he'd—? Hide, Nora! Say you're sick. (*Nora remains standing motionless. Helmer goes and opens the door.*)

MAID (*fully dressed, in the hall*): A letter for Mrs. Helmer.

HELMER: I'll take it. (Snatches the letter and shuts the door.) Yes, it's from him. You don't get it; I'm reading it myself.

NORA: Then read it.

HELMER (*by the lamp*): I hardly dare. We may be ruined, you and I. But—I've got to know. (*Rips open the letter, skims through a few lines, glances at an enclosure, then cries out joyfully.*) Nora! (*Nora looks inquiringly at him.*) Nora! Wait—better check it again—Yes, yes, it's true. I'm saved. Nora, I'm saved!

NORA: And I?

HELMER: You too, of course. We're both saved, both of us. He's sent back your note. He says he's sorry and ashamed—that a happy development in his life—oh, who cares what he says! Nora, we're saved! No one can hurt you. Oh, Nora, Nora—but first, this ugliness all has to go. Let me see—(*Takes a look at the note.*) No, I don't want to see it; I want the whole thing to fade like a dream. (*Tears the note and both the letters to pieces, throws them into the stove and watches them burn.*) There—now there's nothing left— He wrote that since Christmas Eve you—Oh, they must have been three terrible days for you, Nora.

NORA: I fought a hard fight.

HELMER: And suffered pain and saw no escape but—No, we're not going to dwell on anything unpleasant. Well just be grateful and keep on repeating: it's over now, it's over! You hear me, Nora? You don't seem to realize—it's over. What's it mean—that frozen look? Oh, poor little Nora, I understand. You can't believe I've forgiven you. But I have, Nora; I swear I have. I know that what you did, you did out of love for me.

NORA: That's true.

HELMER: You loved me the way a wife ought to love her husband. It's simply the means that you couldn't judge. But you think I love you any the less for not knowing how to handle your affairs? No, no— just lean on me; I'll guide you and teach you. I wouldn't be a man if this feminine helplessness didn't make you twice as attractive to me. You mustn't mind those sharp words I said—that was all in the first confusion of thinking my world had collapsed. I've forgiven you, Nora; I swear I've forgiven you.

NORA: My thanks for your forgiveness. (*She goes out through the door, right.*)

HELMER: No, wait—(*Peers in.*) What are you doing in there?

NORA (*inside*): Getting out of my costume.

HELMER (*by the open door*): Yes, do that. Try to calm yourself and collect your thoughts again, my frightened little songbird. You can rest easy now; I've got wide wings to shelter you with. (*Walking about close by the door.*) How snug and nice our home is, Nora. You're safe here; I'll keep you like a hunted dove I've rescued out of a hawk's claws. I'll bring peace to your poor, shuddering heart. Gradually it'll happen, Nora; you'll see. Tomorrow all this will look different to you; then everything will be as it was. I won't have to go on repeating I forgive you; you'll feel it for yourself. How can you imagine I'd ever conceivably want to disown you—or even blame you in any way? Ah, you don't know a man's heart, Nora. For a man there's something indescribably sweet and satisfying in knowing he's forgiven his wife—and forgiven her out of a full and open heart. It's as if she belongs to him in two ways now: in a sense he's given her fresh into the world again, and she's become his wife and his child as well. From now on that's what you'll be to me—you little, bewildered, helpless thing. Don't be afraid of anything, Nora; just open your heart to me, and I'll be conscience and will to you both—(*Nora enters in her regular clothes.*) What's this? Nor in bed? You've changed your dress?

NORA: Yes, Torvald, I've changed my dress.

HELMER: But why now, so late?

NORA: Tonight I'm not sleeping.

HELMER: But Nora dear—

NORA (*looking at her watch*):   It's still not so very late. Sit down, Torvald; we have a lot to talk over. (*She sits at one side of the table.*)

HELMER: Nora—what is this? That hard expression—

NORA: Sit down. This'll take some time. I have a lot to say.

HELMER (*sitting at the table directly opposite her*):   You worry me, Nora. And I don't understand you.

NORA: No, that's exactly it. You don't understand me. And I've never understood you either—until tonight. No, don't interrupt. You can just listen to what I say. We're closing our accounts, Torvald.

HELMER: How do you mean that?

NORA (*after a short pause*):   Doesn't anything strike you about our sitting here like this?

HELMER: What's that?

NORA: We've been married now eight years. Doesn't it occur to you that this is first time we two, you and I, man and wife, have ever talked seriously together?

HELMER: What do you mean—seriously?

NORA: In eight whole years—longer even—right from our first acquaintance, we've never exchanged a serious word on any serious thing.

HELMER: You mean I should constantly go and involve you in problems you couldn't possibly help me with?

NORA: I'm not talking of problems. I'm saying that we've never sat down seriously together and tried to get to the bottom of anything.

HELMER: But dearest, what good would that ever do you?

NORA: That's the point right there: you've never understood me. I've been wronged greatly, Torvald—first by Papa, and then by you.

HELMER: What! By us—the two people who've loved you more than anyone else?

NORA (*shaking her head*):   You never loved me. You've thought it fun to be in love with me, that's all.

HELMER: Nora, what a thing to say!

NORA: Yes, it's true now, Torvald. When I lived at home with Papa, he told me all his opinions, so I had the same ones too; or if they were different I hid them, since he wouldn't have cared for that. He used to call me his doll-child, and he played with me the way I played with my dolls. Then I came into your house—

HELMER: How can you speak of our marriage like that?

NORA (*unperturbed*):   I mean, then I went from Papa's hands into yours. You arranged everything to your own taste, and so I got the same taste as you—or I pretended to; I can't remember. I guess a little of both, first one, then the other. Now when I look back, it seems as if I'd lived here like a beggar—just from hand to mouth. I've lived by doing tricks for you, Torvald. But that's the way you wanted it. It's a great sin what you and Papa did to me. You're to blame that nothing's become of me.

HELMER: Nora, how unfair and ungrateful you are! Haven't you been happy here?

NORA: No, never. I thought so—but I never have.

HELMER: Not—not happy!

NORA: No, only lighthearted. And you've always been so kind to me. But our home's been nothing but a playpen. I've been your doll-wife here, just as at home I was Papa's doll-child. And in turn the children have been my dolls. I thought it was fun when you played with me, just as they thought it fun when I played with them. That's been our marriage, Torvald.

HELMER: There's some truth in what you're saying—under all the raving exaggeration. But it'll all be different after this. Playtime's over; now for the schooling.

NORA: Whose schooling—mine or the children's?

HELMER: Both yours and the children's, dearest.

NORA: Oh, Torvald, you're not the man to teach me to be a good wife to you.

HELMER: And you can say that?

NORA: And I—how am I equipped to bring up children?

HELMER: Nora!

NORA: Didn't you say a moment ago that that was no job to trust me with?

HELMER: In a flare of temper! Why fasten on that?

NORA: Yes, but you were so very right. I'm not up to the job. There's another job I have to do first. I have to try to educate myself. You can't help me with that. I've got to do it alone. And that's why I'm leaving you now.

HELMER (*jumping up*): What's that?

NORA: I have to stand completely alone, if I'm ever going to discover myself and the world out there. So I can't go on living with you.

HELMER: Nora, Nora!

NORA: I want to leave right away. Kristine should put me up for the night—

HELMER: You're insane! You've no right! I forbid you!

NORA: From here on, there's no use forbidding me anything. I'll take with me whatever is mine. I don't want a thing from you, either now or later.

HELMER: What kind of madness is this!

NORA: Tomorrow I'm going home—I mean, home where I came from. It'll be easier up there to find something to do.

HELMER: Oh, you blind, incompetent child!

NORA: I must learn to be competent, Torvald.

HELMER: Abandon your home, your husband, your children! And you're not even thinking what people will say.

NORA: I can't be concerned about that. I only know how essential this is.

HELMER: Oh, it's outrageous. So you'll run out like this on your most sacred vows.

NORA: What do you think are my most sacred vows?

HELMER: And I have to tell you that! Aren't they your duties to your husband and children?

NORA: I have other duties equally sacred.

HELMER: That isn't true. What duties are they?

NORA: Duties to myself.

HELMER: Before all else, you're a wife and a mother.

NORA: I don't believe in that any more. I believe that, before all else, I'm a human being, no less than you—or anyway, I ought to try to become one. I know the majority thinks you're right, Torvald, and plenty of books agree with you, too. But I can't go on believing what the majority says, or what's written in books. I have to think over these things myself and try to understand them.

HELMER: Why can't you understand your place in your own home? On a point like that, isn't there one everlasting guide you can turn to? Where's your religion?

NORA: Oh, Torvald, I'm really not sure what religion is.

HELMER: What—?

NORA: I only know what the minister said when I was confirmed. He told me religion was this thing and that. When I get clear and away by myself, I'll go into that problem too. I'll see if what the minister said was right, or, in any case, if it's right for me.

HELMER: A young woman your age shouldn't talk like that. If religion can't move you, I can try to rouse your conscience. You do have some moral feeling? Or, tell me—has that gone too?

NORA: It's not easy to answer that, Torvald. I simply don't know. I'm all confused about these things. I just know I see them so differently from you. I find out, for one thing, that the law's not at all what I'd thought—but I can't get it through my head that the law is fair. A woman hasn't a right to protect her dying father or save her husband's life! I can't believe that.

HELMER: You talk like a child. You don't know anything of the world you live in.

NORA: No, I don't. But now I'll begin to learn for myself. I'll try to discover who's right, the world or I.

HELMER: Nora, you're sick; you've got a fever. I almost think you're out of your head.

NORA: I've never felt more clearheaded and sure in my life.

HELMER: And—clearheaded and sure—you're leaving your husband and children?

NORA: Yes.

HELMER: Then there's only one possible reason.

NORA: What?

HELMER: You no longer love me.

NORA: No. That's exactly it.

HELMER: Nora! You can't be serious!

NORA: Oh, this is so hard, Torvald—you've been so kind to me always. But I can't help it. I don't love you any more.

HELMER (*struggling for composure*): Are you also clearheaded and sure about that?

NORA: Yes, completely. That's why I can't go on staying here.

HELMER: Can you tell me what I did to lose your love?

NORA: Yes, I can tell you. It was this evening when the miraculous thing didn't come—then I knew you weren't the man I'd imagined.

HELMER: Be more explicit; I don't follow you.

NORA: I've waited now so patiently eight long years—for, my Lord, I know miracles don't come every day. Then this crisis broke over me, and such a certainty filled me: *now* the miraculous event would occur. While Krogstad's letter was lying out there, I never for an instant dreamed that you could give in to his terms. I was so utterly sure you'd say to him: go on, tell your tale to the whole wide world. And when he'd done that—

HELMER: Yes, what then? When I'd delivered my own wife into shame and disgrace—!

NORA: When he'd done that, I was so utterly sure that you'd step forward, take the blame on yourself and say: I am the guilty one.

HELMER: Nora—!

NORA: You're thinking I'd never accept such a sacrifice from you? No, of course not. But what good would my protests be against you? That was the miracle I was waiting for, in terror and hope. And to stave that off, I would have taken my life.

HELMER: I'd gladly work for you day and night, Nora—and take on pain and deprivation. But there's no one who gives up honor for love.

NORA: Millions of women have done just that.

HELMER: Oh, you think and talk like a silly child.

NORA: Perhaps. But you neither think nor talk like the man I could join myself to. When your big fright was over—and it wasn't from any threat against me, only for what might damage you—when all the danger was past, for you it was just as if nothing had happened. I was exactly the same, your little lark, your doll, that you'd have to handle with double care now that I'd turned out so brittle and frail. (*Gets up.*) Torvald—in that instant it dawned on me that for eight

years I've been living here with a stranger, and that I'd even conceived three children—oh, I can't stand the thought of it! I could
tear myself to bits.

HELMER (*heavily*):   I see. There's a gulf that's opened between us—
that's clear. Oh but Nora, can't we bridge it somehow?

NORA: The way I am now, I'm no wife for you.

HELMER: I have the strength to make myself over.

NORA: Maybe—if your doll gets taken away.

HELMER: But to part! To part from you! No, Nora, no—I can't imagine it.

NORA (*going out, right*):   All the more reason why it has to be. (*She
reenters with her coat and a small overnight bag, which she puts on
a chair by the table.*)

HELMER: Nora, Nora, not now! Wait till tomorrow.

NORA: I can't spend the night in a strange man's room.

HELMER: But couldn't we live here like brother and sister—

NORA: You know very well how long that would last. (*Throws her
shawl about her.*) Good-bye, Torvald. I won't look in on the children. I know they're in better hands than mine. The way I am now,
I'm no use to them.

HELMER: But someday, Nora—someday—?

NORA: How can I tell? I haven't the least idea what'll become of me.

HELMER: But you're my wife, now and wherever you go.

NORA: Listen, Torvald—I've heard that when a wife deserts her husband's house just as I'm doing, then the law frees him from all responsibility. In any case, I'm freeing you from being responsible.
Don't feel yourself bound, any more than I will. There has to be absolute freedom for us both. Here, take your ring back. Give me mine.

HELMER: That too?

NORA: That too.

HELMER: There it is.

NORA: Good. Well, now it's all over. I'm putting the keys here. The
maids knows all about keeping up the house—better than I do.
Tomorrow, after I've left town, Kristine will stop by to pack up everything that's mine from home. I'd like those things shipped up to me.

HELMER: Over! All over! Nora, won't you ever think about me?

NORA: I'm sure I'll think of you often, and about the children and the
house here.

HELMER: May I write you?

NORA: No—never. You're not to do that.

HELMER: Oh, but let me send you—

NORA: Nothing. Nothing.

HELMER: Or help you if you need it.

NORA: No. I accept nothing from strangers.

HELMER: Nora—can I never be more than a stranger to you?

NORA (*picking up the overnight bag*): Ah, Torvald—it would take the greatest miracle of all—

HELMER: Tell me the greatest miracle!

NORA: You and I both would have to transform ourselves to the point that—Oh, Torvald, I've stopped believing in miracles.

HELMER: But I'll believe. Tell me! Transform ourselves to the point that—?

NORA: That our living together could be a true marriage. (*She goes out down the hall.*)

HELMER (*sinks down on a chair by the door, face buried in his hands*): Nora! Nora! (*Looking about and rising.*): Empty. She's gone. (*A sudden hope leaps in him.*) The greatest miracle—?

From below, the sound of a door slamming shut.

—1879

Susan Glaspell (1882–1948) *was born in Iowa and educated at Drake University. Glaspell was one of the founders, with her husband George Cram Cook, of the Provincetown Players. This company, founded in the Cape Cod resort village, was committed to producing experimental drama, an alternative to the standard fare playing in Broadway theaters. Eventually it was relocated to New York. Along with Glaspell, Eugene O'Neill, America's only Nobel Prize–winning dramatist, wrote plays for this group. Trained as a journalist and the author of short stories and novels, Glaspell wrote* Trifles *(1916), her first play, shortly after the founding of the Players, basing her plot on an Iowa murder case she had covered. The one-act play, with both Glaspell and her husband in the cast, premiered during the Players' second season and also exists in a short-story version. Glaspell won the Pulitzer Prize for Drama in 1930 for* Alison's House, *basing the title character on poet Emily Dickinson. A socialist and feminist, Glaspell lived in Provincetown in her last years, writing* The Road to the Temple, *a memoir of her husband's life, and novels.*

Susan Glaspell

Trifles

CHARACTERS

George Henderson, County Attorney
Mrs. Peters
Henry Peters, Sheriff
Lewis Hale, a neighbor
Mrs. Hale

SCENE: *The kitchen in the now abandoned farmhouse of John Wright, a gloomy kitchen, and left without having been put in order—unwashed pans under the sink, a loaf of bread outside the breadbox, a dish towel on the table—other signs of incompleted work. At the rear the outer door opens, and the Sheriff comes in, followed by the County Attorney and Hale. The Sheriff and Hale are men in middle life, the County Attorney is a young man; all are much bundled up and go at once to the stove. They are followed by the two women—the Sheriff's Wife first; she is a slight wiry woman, a thin nervous face. Mrs. Hale is larger and would ordinarily be called more comfortable looking, but she is disturbed now and looks fearfully about as she enters. The women have come in slowly and stand close together near the door.*

COUNTY ATTORNEY (*rubbing his hands*):   This feels good. Come up to the fire, ladies.

MRS. PETERS (*after taking a step forward*):   I'm not—cold.

SHERIFF (*unbuttoning his overcoat and stepping away from the stove as if to the beginning of official business*):   Now, Mr. Hale, before we move things about, you explain to Mr. Henderson just what you saw when you came here yesterday morning.

COUNTY ATTORNEY: By the way, has anything been moved? Are things just as you left them yesterday?

SHERIFF (*looking about*):   It's just the same. When it dropped below zero last night, I thought I'd better send Frank out this morning to make a fire for us—no use getting pneumonia with a big case on; but I told him not to touch anything except the stove—and you know Frank.

COUNTY ATTORNEY: Somebody should have been left here yesterday.

SHERIFF: Oh—yesterday. When I had to send Frank to Morris Center for that man who went crazy—I want you to know I had my hands full yesterday. I knew you could get back from Omaha by today, and as long as I went over everything here myself—

COUNTY ATTORNEY: Well, Mr. Hale, tell just what happened when you came here yesterday morning.

HALE: Harry and I had started to town with a load of potatoes. We came along the road from my place; and as I got here, I said, "I'm going to see if I can't get John Wright to go in with me on a party telephone." I spoke to Wright about it once before, and he put me off, saying folks talked too much anyway, and all he asked was peace and quiet—I guess you know about how much he talked him-self; but I thought maybe if I went to the house and talked about it before his wife, though I said to Harry that I didn't know as what his wife wanted made much difference to John—

COUNTY ATTORNEY: Let's talk about that later, Mr. Hale. I do want to talk about that, but tell now just what happened when you got to the house.

HALE: I didn't hear or see anything; I knocked at the door, and still it was all quiet inside. I knew they must be up, it was past eight o'clock. So I knocked again, and I thought I heard somebody say, "Come in." I wasn't sure, I'm not sure yet, but I opened the door— this door (*indicating the door by which the two women are still* *standing*), and there in that rocker—(*pointing to it*) sat Mrs. Wright. (*They all look at the rocker.*)

COUNTY ATTORNEY: What—was she doing?

HALE: She was rockin' back and forth. She had her apron in her hand and was kind of—pleating it.

COUNTY ATTORNEY: And how did she—look?

HALE: Well, she looked queer.

COUNTY ATTORNEY: How do you mean—queer?

HALE: Well, as if she didn't know what she was going to do next. And kind of done up.

COUNTY ATTORNEY: How did she seem to feel about your coming?

HALE: Why, I don't think she minded—one way or other. She didn't pay much attention. I said, "How do, Mrs. Wright, it's cold, ain't it?" And she said, "Is it?"—and went on kind of pleating at her apron. Well, I was surprised; she didn't ask me to come up to the stove, or to set down, but just sat there, not even looking at me, so I said, "I want to see John." And then she—laughed. I guess you would call it a laugh. I thought of Harry and the team outside, so I said a little sharp: "Can't I see John?" "No," she says, kind o' dull like. "Ain't he home?" says I. "Yes," says she, "he's home." "Then why can't I see him?" I asked her, out of patience. "'Cause he's dead," says she. "*Dead?*" says I. She just nodded her head, not getting a bit excited, but rockin' back and forth. "Why—where is he?" says I, not knowing what to say. She just pointed upstairs—like that (*himself pointing to the room above*). I got up, with the idea of going up there. I walked from there to here—then I says, "Why, what did he die of?" "He died of a rope around his neck," says she, and just went on pleatin' at her apron. Well, I went out and called Harry. I thought I might—need help. We went upstairs, and there he was lyin'—

COUNTY ATTORNEY: I think I'd rather have you go into that upstairs, where you can point it all out. Just go on now with the rest of the story.

HALE: Well, my first thought was to get that rope off. I looked . . . (*Stops, his face twitches.*) . . . but Harry, he went up to him, and he said, "No, he's dead all right, and we'd better not touch anything." So we went back downstairs. She was still sitting that same way. "Has anybody been notified?" I asked. "No," says she, unconcerned. "Who did this, Mrs. Wright?" said Harry. He said it businesslike—and she stopped pleatin' of her apron. "I don't know," she says. "You don't *know?*" says Harry. "No," says she, "Weren't you sleepin' in the bed with him?" says Harry. "Yes," says she, "but I was on the inside." "Somebody slipped a rope round his neck and strangled him, and you didn't wake up?" says Harry. "I didn't wake up," she said after him. We must 'a looked as if we didn't see how that could be, for after a minute she said, "I sleep sound." Harry was going to ask her more questions, but I said maybe we ought to let her tell her story first to the coroner, or the sheriff, so Harry went fast as he could to Rivers' place, where there's a telephone.

COUNTY ATTORNEY: And what did Mrs. Wright do when she knew that you had gone for the coroner?

HALE: She moved from that chair to this over here . . . (*Pointing to a small chair in the corner.*) . . . and just sat there with her hands held together and looking down. I got a feeling that I ought to make some conversation, so I said I had come in to see if John wanted to put in a telephone, and at that she started to laugh, and then she stopped and looked at me—scared. (*The County Attorney, who has had his notebook out, makes a note.*) I dunno, maybe it wasn't scared. I wouldn't like to say it was. Soon Harry got back, and then Dr. Lloyd came, and you, Mr. Peters, and so I guess that's all I know that you don't.

COUNTY ATTORNEY (*looking around*): I guess we'll go upstairs first— and then out to the barn and around there. (*To the Sheriff.*) You're convinced that there was nothing important here—nothing that would point to any motive?

SHERIFF: Nothing here but kitchen things.

(*The County Attorney, after again looking around the kitchen, opens the door of a cupboard closet. He gets up on a chair and looks on a shelf. Pulls his hand away, sticky.*)

COUNTY ATTORNEY: Here's a nice mess.

(*The women draw nearer.*)

MRS. PETERS (*to the other woman*): Oh, her fruit; it did freeze. (*To the Lawyer.*) She worried about that when it turned so cold. She said the fir'd go out and her jars would break.

SHERIFF: Well, can you beat the women! Held for murder and worryin' about her preserves.

COUNTY ATTORNEY: I guess before we're through she may have something more serious than preserves to worry about.

HALE: Well, women are used to worrying over trifles.

(The two women move a little closer together.)

COUNTY ATTORNEY *(with the gallantry of a young politician)*: And yet, for all their worries, what would we do without the ladies? *(The women do not unbend. He goes to the sink, takes a dipperful of water from the pail and, pouring it into a basin, washes his hands. Starts to wipe them on the roller towel, turns it for a cleaner place.)* Dirty towels! *(Kicks his foot against the pans under the sink.)* Not much of a housekeeper, would you say, ladies?

MRS. HALE *(stiffly)*: There's a great deal of work to be done on a farm.

COUNTY ATTORNEY: To be sure. And yet . . . *(With a little bow to her.)* . . . I know there are some Dickson county farmhouses which do not have such roller towels. *(He gives it a pull to expose its full length again.)*

MRS. HALE: Those towels get dirty awful quick. Men's hands aren't always as clean as they might be.

COUNTY ATTORNEY: Ah, loyal to your sex, I see. But you and Mrs. Wright were neighbors. I suppose you were friends, too.

MRS. HALE *(shaking her head)*: I've not seen much of her of late years. I've not been in this house—it's more than a year.

COUNTY ATTORNEY: And why was that? You didn't like her?

MRS. HALE: I liked her all well enough. Farmers' wives have their hands full, Mr. Henderson. And then—

COUNTY ATTORNEY: Yes—?

MRS. HALE *(looking about)*: It never seemed a very cheerful place.

COUNTY ATTORNEY: No—it's not cheerful. I shouldn't say she had the homemaking instinct.

MRS. HALE: Well, I don't know as Wright had, either.

COUNTY ATTORNEY: You mean that they didn't get on very well?

MRS. HALE: No, I don't mean anything. But I don't think a place'd be any cheerfuler for John Wright's being in it.

COUNTY ATTORNEY: I'd like to talk more of that a little later. I want to get the lay of things upstairs now. *(He goes to the left, where three steps lead to a stair door.)*

SHERIFF: I suppose anything Mrs. Peters does'll be all right. She was to take in some clothes for her, you know, and a few little things. We left in such a hurry yesterday.

COUNTY ATTORNEY: Yes, but I would like to see what you take, Mrs. Peters, and keep an eye out for anything that might be of use to us.

MRS. PETERS: Yes, Mr. Henderson.

(The women listen to the men's steps on the stairs, then look about the kitchen.)

MRS. HALE: I'd hate to have men coming into my kitchen, snooping around and criticizing. *(She arranges the pans under sink which the Lawyer had shoved out of place.)*

MRS. PETERS: Of course it's no more than their duty.

MRS. HALE: Duty's all right, but I guess that deputy sheriff that came out to make the fire might have got a little of this on. *(Gives the roller towel a pull.)* Wish I'd thought of that sooner. Seems mean to talk about her for not having things slicked up when she had to come away in such a hurry.

MRS. PETERS *(who has gone to a small table in the left rear corner of the room, and lifted one end of a towel that covers a pan)*: She had bread set. *(Stands still.)*

MRS. HALE *(eyes fixed on a loaf of bread beside the breadbox, which is on a low shelf at the other side of the room. Moves slowly toward it)*: She was going to put this in there. *(Picks up loaf, then abruptly drops it. In a manner of returning to familiar things.)* It's a shame about her fruit. I wonder if it's all gone. *(Gets up on the chair and looks.)* I think there's some here that's all right, Mrs. Peters. Yes—here; *(Holding it toward the window.)* this is cherries, too. *(Looking again.)* I declare I believe that's the only one. *(Gets down, bottle in her hand. Goes to the sink and wipes it off on the outside.)* She'll feel awful bad after all her hard work in the hot weather. I remember the afternoon I put up my cherries last summer. *(She puts the bottle on the big kitchen table, center of the room, front table. With a sigh, is about to sit down in the rocking chair. Before she is seated realizes what chair it is; with a slow look at it, steps back. The chair, which she has touched, rocks back and forth.)*

MRS. PETERS: Well, I must get those things from the front room closet. (*She goes to the door at the right, but after looking into the other room steps back.*) You coming with me, Mrs. Hale? You could help me carry them. (*They go into the other room; reappear, Mrs. Peters carrying a dress and skirt, Mrs. Hale following with a pair of shoes.*)

MRS. PETERS: My, it's cold in there. (*She puts the cloth on the big table, and hurries to the stove.*)

MRS. HALE (*examining the skirt*): Wright was close. I think maybe that's why she kept so much to herself. She didn't even belong to the Ladies' Aid. I suppose she felt she couldn't do her part, and then you don't enjoy things when you feel shabby. She used to wear pretty clothes and be lively, when she was Minnie Foster, one of the town girls singing in the choir. But that—oh, that was thirty years ago. This all you was to take in?

MRS. PETERS: She said she wanted an apron. Funny thing to want, for there isn't much to get you dirty in jail, goodness knows. But I suppose just to make her feel more natural. She said they was in the top drawer in this cupboard. Yes, here. And then her little shawl that always hung behind the door. (*Opens stair door and looks.*) Yes, here it is. (*Quickly shuts door leading upstairs.*)

MRS. HALE (*abruptly moving toward her*): Mrs. Peters?

MRS. PETERS: Yes, Mrs. Hale?

MRS. HALE: Do you think she did it?

MRS. PETERS (*in a frightened voice*): Oh, I don't know.

MRS. HALE: Well, I don't think she did. Asking for an apron and her little shawl. Worrying about her fruit.

MRS. PETERS (*starts to speak, glances up, where footsteps are heard in the room above. In a low voice*): Mr. Peters says it looks bad for her. Mr. Henderson is awful sarcastic in speech, and he'll make fun of her sayin' she didn't wake up.

MRS. HALE: Well, I guess John Wright didn't wake when they was slipping that rope under his neck.

MRS. PETERS: No, it's strange. It must have been done awful crafty and still. They say it was such a—funny way to kill a man, rigging it all up like that.

MRS. HALE: That's just what Mr. Hale said. There was a gun in the house. He says that's what he can't understand.

MRS. PETERS: Mr. Henderson said coming out that what was needed for the case was a motive; something to show anger, or—sudden feeling.

MRS. HALE (*who is standing by the table*): Well, I don't see any signs of anger around here. (*She puts her hand on the dish towel which lies on the table, stands looking down at the table, one half of which is clean, the other half messy.*) It's wiped here. (*Makes a move as if to finish work, then turns and looks at loaf of bread outside the breadbox. Drops towel. In that voice of coming back to familiar things.*) Wonder how they are finding things upstairs? I hope she had it a little more red-up there. You know, it seems kind of *sneaking.* Locking her up in town and then coming out here and trying to get her own house to turn against her!

MRS. PETERS: But, Mrs. Hale, the law is the law.

MRS. HALE: I s'pose 'tis. (*Unbuttoning her coat.*) Better loosen up your things, Mrs. Peters. You won't feel them when you go out.

(*Mrs. Peters takes off her fur tippet, goes to hang it on hook at the back of room, stands looking at the under part of the small corner table.*)

MRS. PETERS: She was piecing a quilt. (*She brings the large sewing basket, and they look at the bright pieces.*)

MRS. HALE: It's log cabin pattern. Pretty, isn't it? I wonder if she was goin' to quilt or just knot it?

(*Footsteps have been heard coming down the stairs. The Sheriff enters, followed by Hale and the County Attorney.*)

SHERIFF: They wonder if she was going to quilt it or just knot it. (*The men laugh, the women look abashed.*)

COUNTY ATTORNEY (*rubbing his hands over the stove*): Frank's fire didn't do much up there, did it? Well, let's go out to the barn and get that cleared up.

(*The men go outside.*)

MRS. HALE (*resentfully*): I don't know as there's anything so strange, our takin' up our time with little things while we're waiting for them to get the evidence. (*She sits down at the big table, smoothing out a block with decision.*) I don't see as it's anything to laugh about.

MRS. PETERS (*apologetically*): Of course they've got awful important things on their minds. (*Pulls up a chair and joins Mrs. Hale at the table.*)

MRS. HALE (*examining another block*): Mrs. Peters, look at this one. Here, this is the one she was working on, and look at the sewing! All the rest of it has been so nice and even. And look at this! It's all over the place! Why, it looks as if she didn't know what she was about! (*After she has said this, they look at each other, then started to glance back at the door. After an instant Mrs. Hale has pulled at a knot and ripped the sewing.*)

MRS. PETERS: Oh, what are you doing, Mrs. Hale?

MRS. HALE (*mildly*): Just pulling out a stitch or two that's not sewed very good. (*Threading a needle.*) Bad sewing always made me fidgety.

MRS. PETERS (*nervously*): I don't think we ought to touch things.

MRS. HALE: I'll just finish up this end. (*Suddenly stopping and leaning forward.*) Mrs. Peters?

MRS. PETERS: Yes, Mrs. Hale?

MRS. HALE: What do you suppose she was so nervous about?

MRS. PETERS: Oh—I don't know. I don't know as she was nervous. I sometimes sew awful queer when I'm just tired. (*Mrs. Hale starts to say something, looks at Mrs. Peters, then goes on sewing.*) Well, I must get these things wrapped up. They may be through sooner than we think. (*Putting apron and other things together.*) I wonder where I can find a piece of paper, and string.

MRS. HALE: In that cupboard, maybe.

MRS. PETERS (*looking in cupboard*): Why, here's a birdcage. (*Holds it up.*) Did she have a bird, Mrs. Hale?

MRS. HALE: Why, I don't know whether she did or not—I've not been here for so long. There was a man around last year selling canaries cheap, but I don't know as she took one; maybe she did. She used to sing real pretty herself.

MRS. PETERS (*glancing around*): Seems funny to think of a bird here. But she must have had one, or why should she have a cage? I wonder what happened to it?

MRS. HALE: I s'pose maybe the cat got it.

MRS. PETERS: No, she didn't have a cat. She's got that feeling some people have about cats—being afraid of them. My cat got in her room, and she was real upset and asked me to take it out.

MRS. HALE: My sister Bessie was like that. Queer, ain't it?

MRS. PETERS (*examining the cage*): Why, look at this door. It's broke. One hinge is pulled apart.

MRS. HALE (*looking, too*): Looks as if someone must have been rough with it.

MRS. PETERS: Why, yes. (*She brings the cage forward and puts it on the table.*)

MRS. HALE: I wish if they're going to find any evidence they'd be about it. I don't like this place.

MRS. PETERS: But I'm awful glad you came with me, Mrs. Hale. It would be lonesome for me sitting here alone.

MRS. HALE: It would, wouldn't it? (*Dropping her sewing.*) But I tell you what I do wish, Mrs. Peters. I wish I had come over sometimes when *she* was here. I—(*Looking around the room.*)—wish I had.

MRS. PETERS: But of course you were awful busy, Mrs. Hale—your house and your children.

MRS. HALE: I could've come. I stayed away because it weren't cheer-ful—and that's why I ought to have come. I—I've never liked this place. Maybe because it's down in a hollow, and you don't see the road. I dunno what it is, but it's a lonesome place and always was. I wish I had come over to see Minnie Foster sometimes. I can see now—(*Shakes her head.*)

MRS. PETERS: Well, you mustn't reproach yourself, Mrs. Hale. Somehow we just don't see how it is with other folks until—something comes up.

MRS. HALE: Not having children makes less work—but it makes a quiet house, and Wright out to work all day, and no company when he did come in. Did you know John Wright, Mrs. Peters?

MRS. PETERS: Not to know him; I've seen him in town. They say he was a good man.

MRS. HALE: Yes—good; he didn't drink, and kept his word as well as most, I guess, and paid his debts. But he was a hard man, Mrs. Peters. Just to pass the time of day with him. (*Shivers.*) Like a raw wind that gets to the bone. (*Pauses, her eye falling on the cage.*) I should think she would 'a wanted a bird. But what do you suppose went with it?

MRS. PETERS: I don't know, unless it got sick and died. (*She reaches over and swings the broken door, swings it again; both women watch it.*)

MRS. HALE: You weren't raised round here, were you? (*Mrs. Peters shakes her head.*) You didn't know—her?

MRS. PETERS: Not till they brought her yesterday.

MRS. HALE: She—come to think of it, she was kind of like a bird herself—real sweet and pretty, but kind of timid and—fluttery. How—she—did—change. (*Silence; then as if struck by a happy thought and relieved to get back to everyday things.*) Tell you what, Mrs. Peters, why don't you take the quilt in with you? It might take up her mind.

MRS. PETERS: Why, I think that's a real nice idea, Mrs. Hale. There couldn't possibly be any objection to it, could there? Now, just what would I take? I wonder if her patches are in here—and her things. (*They look in the sewing basket.*)

MRS. HALE: Here's some red. I expect this has got sewing things in it (*Brings out a fancy box.*) What a pretty box. Looks like something somebody would give you. Maybe her scissors are in here. (*Opens box. Suddenly puts her hand to her nose.*) Why—(*Mrs. Peters bends nearer, then turns her face away.*) There's something wrapped up in this piece of silk.

MRS. PETERS: Why, this isn't her scissors.

MRS. HALE (*lifting the silk*): Oh, Mrs. Peters—it's—(*Mrs. Peters bends closer.*)

MRS. PETERS: It's the bird.

MRS. HALE (*jumping up*): But, Mrs. Peters—look at it. Its neck! Look at its neck! It's all—other side *to.*

MRS. PETERS: Somebody—wrung—its neck.

(*Their eyes meet. A look of growing comprehension of horror. Steps are heard outside. Mrs. Hale slips box under quilt pieces, and sinks into her chair. Enter Sheriff and County Attorney. Mrs. Peters rises.*)

COUNTY ATTORNEY (*as one turning from serious things to little pleasantries*): Well, ladies, have you decided whether she was going to quilt it or knot it?

MRS. PETERS: We think she was going to—knot it.

COUNTY ATTORNEY: Well, that's interesting, I'm sure. (*Seeing the birdcage.*) Has the bird flown?

MRS. HALE (*putting more quilt pieces over the box*): We think the— cat got it.

COUNTY ATTORNEY (*preoccupied*): Is there a cat?

(*Mrs. Hale glances in a quick covert way at Mrs. Peters.*)

MRS. PETERS: Well, not now. They're superstitious, you know. They leave.

COUNTY ATTORNEY (*to Sheriff Peters, continuing an interrupted conversation*): No sign at all of anyone having come from the outside. Their own rope. Now let's go up again and go over it piece by piece. (*They start upstairs.*) It would have to have been someone who knew just the—

(*Mrs. Peters sits down. The two women sit there not looking at one another, but as if peering into something and at the same time holding back. When they talk now, it is the manner of feeling their way over strange ground, as if afraid of what they are saying, but as if they cannot help saying it.*)

MRS. HALE: She liked the bird. She was going to bury it in that pretty box.

MRS. PETERS (*in a whisper*): When I was a girl—my kitten—there was a boy took a hatchet, and before my eyes—and before I could get there—(*Covers her face an instant.*) If they hadn't held me back, I would have—(*Catches herself, looks upstairs where steps are heard, falters weakly.*)—hurt him.

MRS. HALE (*with a slow look around her*): I wonder how it would seem never to have had any children around. (*Pause.*) No, Wright wouldn't like the bird—a thing that sang. She used to sing. He killed that, too.

MRS. PETERS (*moving uneasily*): We don't know who killed the bird.

MRS. HALE: I knew John Wright.

MRS. PETERS: It was an awful thing was done in this house that night, Mrs. Hale. Killing a man while he slept, slipping a rope around his neck that choked the life out of him.

MRS. HALE: His neck. Choked the life out of him.

(Her hand goes out and rests on the birdcage.)

MRS. PETERS (*with a rising voice*):   We don't know who killed him. We don't *know*.

MRS. HALE (*her own feeling not interrupted*):   If there'd been years and years of nothing, then a bird to sing to you, it would be awful—still, after the bird was still.

MRS. PETERS (*something within her speaking*):   I know what stillness is. When we homesteaded in Dakota, and my first baby died—after he was two years old, and me with no other then—

MRS. HALE (*moving*):   How soon do you suppose they'll be through, looking for evidence?

MRS. PETERS: I know what stillness is. (*Pulling herself back.*) The law has got to punish crime, Mrs. Hale.

MRS. HALE (*not as if answering that*):   I wish you'd seen Minnie Foster when she wore a white dress with blue ribbons and stood up there in the choir and sang. (*A look around the room.*) Oh, I *wish* I'd come over here once in a while! That was a crime! That was a crime! Who's going to punish that?

MRS. PETERS (*looking upstairs*):   We mustn't—take on.

MRS. HALE: I might have known she needed help! I know how things can be—for women. I tell you, it's queer, Mrs. Peters. We live close together and we live far apart. We all go through the same things—it's all just a different kind of the same thing. (*Brushes her eyes, noticing the bottle of fruit, reaches out for it.*) If I was you, I wouldn't tell her her fruit was gone. Tell her it *ain't*. Tell her it's all right. Take this in to prove it to her. She—she may never know whether it was broke or not.

MRS. PETERS (*takes the bottle, looks about for something to wrap it in; takes petticoat from the clothes brought from the other room, very nervously begins winding this around the bottle. In a false voice*):   My, it's a good thing the men couldn't hear us. Wouldn't they just laugh! Getting all stirred up over a little thing like a—dead canary. As if that could have anything to do with—with—wouldn't they *laugh!*

(The men are heard coming downstairs.)

MRS. HALE (*under her breath*):   Maybe they would—maybe they wouldn't.

COUNTY ATTORNEY: No, Peters, it's all perfectly clear except a reason for doing it. But you know juries when it comes to women. If there was some definite thing. Something to show—something to make a story about—a thing that would connect up with this strange way of doing it.

(The women's eyes meet for an instant. Enter Hale from outer door.)

HALE: Well, I've got the team around. Pretty cold out there.

COUNTY ATTORNEY: I'm going to stay here awhile by myself. (*To the Sheriff.*) You can send Frank out for me, can't you? I want to go over everything. I'm not satisfied that we can't do better.

SHERIFF: Do you want to see what Mrs. Peters is going to take in?

(The Lawyer goes to the table, picks up the apron, laughs.)

COUNTY ATTORNEY: Oh I guess they're not very dangerous things the ladies have picked up. (*Moves a few things about, disturbing the quilt pieces which cover the box. Steps back.*) No, Mrs. Peters doesn't need supervising. For that matter, a sheriff's wife is married to the law. Ever think of it that way, Mrs. Peters?

MRS. PETERS: Not—just that way.

SHERIFF (*chuckling*): Married to the law. (*Moves toward the other room.*) I just want you to come in here a minute, George. We ought to take a look at these windows.

COUNTY ATTORNEY (*scoffingly*): Oh, windows!

SHERIFF: We'll be right out, Mr. Hale.

(Hale goes outside. The Sheriff follows the County Attorney into the other room. Then Mrs. Hale rises, hands tight together, looking intensely at Mrs. Peters, whose eyes take a slow turn, finally meeting, Mrs. Hale's. A moment Mrs. Hale holds her, then her own eyes point the way to where the box is concealed. Suddenly Mrs. Peters throws back quilt pieces and tries to put the box in the bag she is wearing. It is too big. She opens box, starts to take the bird out, cannot touch it, goes to pieces, stands there helpless. Sound of a knob turning in the other room. Mrs. Hale snatches the box and

puts it in the pocket of her big coat. Enter County Attorney and Sheriff.)

COUNTY ATTORNEY (*facetiously*):   Well, Henry, at least we found out that she was not going to quilt it. She was going to—what is it you call it, ladies?

MRS. HALE (*her hand against her pocket*):   We call it—knot it, Mr. Henderson.

CURTAIN

—1917

Tennessee Williams (1914–1983) *was the first important American playwright to emerge in the post-World War II period. Born Thomas Lanier Williams and raised in St. Louis, he took his professional name from his mother's southern forebears. Williams studied at the University of Missouri and Washington University, ultimately completing a degree in drama at the University of Iowa. After staging some of his early one-act plays with the Group Theater (later known as the Actors Studio), Williams first came to larger public attention with* The Glass Menagerie, *which won a Drama Critics Circle award in 1945.* The Glass Menagerie *is clearly autobiographical, drawing on Williams's memories of life with his faded southern belle mother and his tragically disturbed sister, Rose, who ultimately had to be institutionalized.* The Glass Menagerie *is outwardly a realistic play, but it is suffused with poetic symbolism, passages of intense lyricism, and the soft glow of Laura's candles. In 1947* A Streetcar Named Desire *received the Pulitzer Prize, the first of two Williams would win in a forty-year career.* A Streetcar Named Desire, *which starred the young Marlon Brando on stage and in the film, is, in contrast to* The Glass Menagerie, *a brutally naturalistic tragedy in which no romantic illusions are allowed to survive. Both Jessica Tandy, who orginated the stage role, and Vivien Leigh, who starred in the film, were acclaimed for their portrayals of Blanche DuBois. Williams's plays are constantly revived in little theaters and on Broadway. In the last decade both* Cat on a Hot Tin Roof, *starring Kathleen Turner, and* A Streetcar Named Desire, *with Alec Baldwin, completed New York engagements. An unproduced early play,* Not About Nightingales, *enjoyed successful runs in London and on Broadway in 1999. Some of the film adaptations of Williams's plays, several of which have screenplays written by the author, remain classics, especially Elia Kazan's version of* A Streetcar Named Desire *and John Huston's* The Night of the Iguana, *with Richard Burton, Deborah Kerr, and Ava Gardner. Williams published his autobiography in 1975, and a fascinating collection of his correspondence, which gives insight into both his concerns as a writer and his intensely troubled personal life, appeared in 2000.*

Tennessee Williams

The Glass Menagerie

nobody, not even the rain, has such small hand.

e.e. cummings

LIST OF CHARACTERS

Amanda Wingfield, *the mother.—A little woman of great but confused vitality clinging frantically to another time and place. Her characterization* *must be carefully created, not copied from type. She is not paranoiac, but her life is paranoia. There is much to admire in Amanda, and as much to love and pity as there is to laugh at. Certainly she has endurance and a kind of heroism, and though her foolishness makes her unwittingly cruel at times, there is tenderness in her slight person.*

Laura Wingfield, *her daughter.—Amanda, having failed to establish contact with reality, continues to live vitally in her illusions, but Laura's situation is even graver. A childhood illness has left her crippled, one leg slightly shorter than the other, and held in a brace. This defect need not be more than suggested on the stage. Stemming from this, Laura's separation increases till she is like a piece of her own glass collection, too exquisitely fragile to move from the shelf.*

Tom Wingfield, *her son.—And the narrator of the play. A poet with a job in a warehouse. His nature is not remorseless, but to escape from a trap he has to act without pity.*

Jim O'Connor, *the gentleman caller.—A nice, ordinary young man.*

SCENE: *An alley in St. Louis.*
PART 1. *Preparation for a Gentleman Caller.*
PART 2. *The Gentleman Calls.*
PART 3. *Now and the Past.*

SCENE 1

The Wingfield apartment is in the rear of the building, one of those vast hive-like conglomerations of cellular living-units that flower as warty growths in overcrowded urban centers of lower middle-class population and are symptomatic of the impulse of this largest and fundamentally enslaved section of American society to avoid fluidity and differentiation and to exist and function as one interfused mass of automatism.

The apartment faces an alley and is entered by a fire-escape, a structure whose name is a touch of accidental poetic truth, for all of these huge buildings are always burning with the slow and implacable fires of human desperation. The fire escape is included in the set—that is, the landing of it and steps descending from it.

The scene is memory and is therefore non-realistic. Memory takes a lot of poetic license. It omits some details; others are exaggerated, according to the emotional value of the articles it touches, for memory is seated predominantly in the heart. The interior is therefore rather dim and poetic.

At the rise of the curtain, the audience is faced with the dark, grim rear wall of the Wingfield tenement. This building, which runs parallel to the footlights, is flanked on both sides by dark, narrow alleys which run into murky canyons of tangled clotheslines, garbage cans and the sinister latticework of neighboring fire-escapes. It is up and down these side alleys that exterior entrances and exits are made, during the play. At the end of Tom's opening commentary, the dark tenement wall slowly reveals (by means of a transparency) the interior of the ground floor Wingfield apartment.

Downstage is the living room, which also serves as a sleeping room for Laura, the sofa unfolding to make her bed. Upstage, center, and divided by a wide arch or second proscenium with transparent faded portieres (or second curtain), is the dining room. In an old-fashioned what-not in the living room are seen scores of transparent glass animals. A blown-up photograph of the father hangs on the wall of the living room, facing the audience, to the left of the archway. It is the face of a very handsome young man in a doughboy's First World War cap. He is gallantly smiling, ineluctably smiling, as if to say, "I will be smiling forever."

The audience hears and sees the opening scene in the dining room through both the transparent wall of the building and the transparent gauze portieres of the diningroom arch. It is during this revealing scene that the fourth wall slowly ascends, out of sight.

This transparent exterior wall is not brought down again until the very end of the play, during Tom's final speech.

The narrator is an undisguised convention of the play. He takes whatever license with dramatic convention as is convenient to his purposes.

Tom enters dressed as a merchant sailor from alley, stage left, and strolls across the front of the stage to the fire-escape. There he stops and lights a cigarette. He addresses the audience.

TOM: Yes, I have tricks in my pocket, I have things up my sleeve. But I am the opposite of a stage magician. He gives you the illusion that has the appearance of truth. I give you truth in the pleasant disguise of illusion. To begin with, I turn back time. I reverse it to that quaint period, the thirties, when the huge middle class of America was matriculating in a school for the blind. Their eyes had failed them, or they had failed their eyes, and so they were having their fingers pressed forcibly down on the fiery Braille alphabet of a dissolving economy. In Spain there was revolution. Here there was only shouting and confusion. In Spain there was Guernica. Here there were disturbances of labor, sometimes pretty violent, in otherwise peaceful cities such as Chicago, Cleveland, Saint Louis. . . . This is the social background of the play.

(Music.)

The play is memory. Being a memory play, it is dimly lighted, it is sentimental, it is not realistic. In memory everything seems to happen to music. That explains the fiddle in the wings. I am the narrator of the play, and also a character in it. The other characters are my mother, Amanda, my sister, Laura, and a gentleman caller who appears in the final scenes. He is the most realistic character in the play, being an emissary from a world of reality that we were somehow set apart from. But since I have a poet's weakness for symbols, I am using this character also as a symbol; he is the long delayed but always expected something that we live for. There is a fifth character in the play who doesn't appear except in this larger-than-life photograph over the mantel. This is our father who left us a long time ago. He was a telephone man who fell in love with long distances; he gave up his job with the telephone company and skipped the light fantastic out of town. . . . The last we heard of him was a picture post-card from Mazatlan, on the Pacific coast of Mexico, containing a message of two words—"Hello—Good-bye!" and no address. I think the rest of the play will explain itself. . . .

Amanda's voice becomes audible through the portieres.

(Legend on Screen: "Où Sont Les Neiges?")°

He divides the portieres and enters the upstage area. Amanda and Laura are seated at a drop-leaf table. Eating is indicated by ges-

---

Où Sont Les Neiges refrain from a poem by François Villon (1431–1463?): "Where are the snows of yesteryear?"

tures without food or utensils. Amanda faces the audience. Tom and Laura are seated in profile. The interior has lit up softly and through the scrim we see Amanda and Laura seated at the table in the upstage area.

AMANDA (*calling*): Tom?

TOM: Yes, Mother.

AMANDA: We can't say grace until you come to the table!

TOM: Coming, Mother. (*He bows slightly and withdraws, reappearing a few moments later in his place at the table.*)

AMANDA (*to her son*): Honey, don't *push* with your *fingers.* If you have to push with something, the thing to push with is a crust of bread. And chew—chew! Animals have sections in their stomachs which enable them to digest food without mastication, but human beings are supposed to chew their food before they swallow it down. Eat food leisurely, son, and really enjoy it. A well-cooked meal has lots of delicate flavors that have to be held in the mouth for appreciation. So chew your food and give your salivary glands a chance to function!

(Tom deliberately lays his imaginary fork down and pushes his chair back from the table.)

TOM: I haven't enjoyed one bite of this dinner because of your constant directions on how to eat it. It's you that makes me rush through meals with your hawk-like attention to every bite I take. Sickening—spoils my appetite—all this discussion of animals' secretion—salivary glands—mastication!

AMANDA (*lightly*): Temperament like a Metropolitan star! (*He rises and crosses downstage.*) You're not excused from the table.

TOM: I am getting a cigarette.

AMANDA: You smoke too much. (*Laura rises.*)

LAURA: I'll bring in the blanc mange.

(He remains standing with cigarette by the portieres during the following.)

AMANDA (*rising*): No, sister, no, sister—you be the lady this time and I'll be the darky.

LAURA: I'm already up.

AMANDA: Resume your seat, little sister—I want you to stay fresh and pretty—for gentlemen callers!

LAURA: I'm not expecting any gentlemen callers.

AMANDA (*crossing out to kitchenette. Airily.*): Sometimes they come when they are least expected! Why, I remember one Sunday afternoon in the Blue Mountain—(*Enters kitchenette.*)

TOM: I know what's coming!

LAURA: Yes. But let her tell it.

TOM: Again?

LAURA: She loves to tell it.

(Amanda returns with bowl of dessert.)

AMANDA: One Sunday afternoon in Blue Mountain—your mother received—*seventeen!*—gentlemen callers! Why sometimes there weren't chairs enough to accommodate them all. We had to send the nigger over to bring in folding chairs from the parish house.

TOM (*remaining at portieres*): How did you entertain those gentlemen callers?

AMANDA: I understood the art of conversation!

TOM: I bet you could talk.

AMANDA: Girls in those days *knew* how to talk, I can tell you.

TOM: Yes?

(Image: Amanda as a Girl on a Porch Greeting Callers.)

AMANDA: They knew how to entertain their gentlemen callers. It wasn't enough for a girl to be possessed of a pretty face and a graceful figure—although I wasn't slighted in either respect. She also needed to have a nimble wit and a tongue to meet all occasions.

TOM: What did you talk about?

AMANDA: Things of importance going on in the world! Never anything coarse or common or vulgar. (*She addresses Tom as though he were seated in the vacant chair at the table though he remains by portieres. He plays this scene as though he held the book.*) My callers were gentlemen—all! Among my callers were some of the most prominent young planters of the Mississippi Delta—planters and sons of planters!

(Tom motions for music and a spot of light on Amanda. Her eyes lift, her face glows, her voice becomes rich and elegiac.)

(Screen Legend: "Où Sont Les Neiges?")

There was young Champ Laughlin who later became vice-president of the Delta Planters Bank. Hadley Stevenson who was drowned in Moon Lake and left his widow one hundred and fifty thousand in Government bonds. There were the Cutrere brothers, Wesley and Bates. Bates was one of my bright particular beaux! He got in a quarrel with that wild Wainright boy. They shot it out on the floor of Moon Lake Casino. Bates was shot through the stomach. Died in the ambulance on his way to Memphis. His widow was also well provided for, came into eight or ten thousand acres, that's all. She married him on the rebound—never loved her—carried my picture on him the night he died! And there was that boy that every girl in the Delta had set her cap for! That beautiful, brilliant young Fitzhugh boy from Green County!

TOM: What did he leave his widow?

AMANDA: He never married! Gracious, you talk as though all of my old admirers had turned up their toes to the daisies!

TOM: Isn't this the first you mentioned that still survives?

AMANDA: That Fitzhugh boy went North and made a fortune—came to be known as the Wolf of Wall Street! He had the Midas touch, whatever he touched turned to gold! And I could have been Mrs. Duncan J. Fitzhugh, mind you! But—I picked your *father!*

LAURA (*rising*): Mother, let me clear the table.

AMANDA: No dear, you go in front and study your typewriter chart. Or practice your shorthand a little. Stay fresh and pretty!—It's almost time for our gentlemen callers to start arriving. (*She flounces girlishly toward the kitchenette.*) How many do you suppose we're going to entertain this afternoon?

(Tom throws down the paper and jumps up with a groan.)

LAURA (*alone in the dining room*): I don't believe we're going to receive any, Mother.

AMANDA (*reappearing, airily*): What? No one—not one? You must be joking! (*Laura nervously echoes her laugh. She slips in a fugitive manner through the half-open portieres and draws them gently behind her. A shaft of very clear light is thrown on her face against the faded tapestry of the curtain.*) (*Music: "The Glass Menagerie"*

Under Faintly.) (*Lightly*) Not one gentleman caller? It can't be true! There must be a flood, there must have been a tornado!

LAURA: It isn't a flood, it's not a tornado, Mother. I'm just not popular like you were in Blue Mountain. . . . (*Tom utters another groan. Laura glances at him with a faint, apologetic smile. Her voice catching a little*) Mother's afraid I'm going to be an old maid.

(The Scene Dims Out with "Glass Menagerie" Music.)

SCENE 2

"LAURA, HAVEN'T YOU EVER LIKED SOME BOY?"

On the dark stage the screen is lighted with the image of blue roses. Gradually Laura's figure becomes apparent and the screen goes out. The music subsides. Laura is seated in the delicate ivory chair at the small clawfoot table. She wears a dress of soft violet material for a kimono—her hair tied back from her forehead with a ribbon. She is washing and polishing her collection of glass.

Amanda appears on the fire-escape steps. At the sound of her ascent, Laura catches her breath, thrusts the bowl of ornaments away and seats herself stiffly before the diagram of the typewriter keyboard as though it held her spellbound. Something has happened to Amanda. It is written in her face as she climbs to the landing: a look that is grim and hopeless and a little absurd.

She has one of those cheap or imitation velvety-looking cloth coats with imitation fur collar. Her hat is five or six years old, one of those dreadful cloche hats that were worn in the late twenties, and she is clasping an enormous black patent-leather pocketbook with nickel clasp and initials. This is her full-dress outfit, the one she usually wears to the D.A.R.

Before entering she looks through the door. She purses her lips, opens her eyes wide, rolls them upward and shakes her head. Then she slowly lets herself in the door. Seeing her mother's expression Laura touches her lips with a nervous gesture.

LAURA: Hello, Mother, I was—(*She makes a nervous gesture toward the chart on the wall. Amanda leans against the shut door and stares are Laura with a martyred look.*)

AMANDA: Deception? Deception? (*She slowly removes her hat and gloves, continuing the swift suffering stare. She lets the hat and gloves fall on the floor—a bit of acting.*)

LAURA (*shakily*): How was the D.A.R. meeting? (*Amanda slowly opens her purse and removes a dainty white handkerchief which she shakes out delicately and delicately touches to her lips and nostrils.*) Didn't you go to the D.A.R. meeting, Mother?

AMANDA (*faintly, almost inaudibly*): —No.—No. (*Then more forcibly*) I did not have the strength—to go to the D.A.R. In fact, I did not have the courage. I waited to find a hole in the ground and hide myself in it forever! (*She crosses slowly to the wall and removes the diagram of the typewriter keyboard. She holds it in front of her for a second, starting at it sweetly and sorrowfully—then bites her lips and tears it in two pieces.*)

LAURA (*faintly*): Why did you do that, Mother? (*Amanda repeats the same procedure with the chart of the Gregg Alphabet.*) Why are you—

AMANDA: Why? Why? How old are you, Laura?

LAURA: Mother, you know my age.

AMANDA: I thought that you were an adult; it seems that I was mistaken. (*She crosses slowly to the sofa and sinks down and stares at Laura.*)

LAURA: Please don't stare at me, Mother.

(*Amanda closes her eyes and lowers her head. Count ten.*)

AMANDA: What are we going to do, what is going to become of us, what is the future?

(*Count ten.*)

LAURA: Has something happened, Mother? (*Amanda draws a long breath and takes out the handkerchief again. Dabbing process.*) Mother, has—something happened?

AMANDA: I'll be right in a minute. I'm just bewildered—(*count five*) —by life. . . .

LAURA: Mother, I wish you would tell me what's happened.

AMANDA: As you know, I was supposed to be inducted into my office at the D.A.R. this afternoon. (*Image: A Swarm of Typewriters.*) But I stopped off at Rubicam's Business College to speak to your teachers about your having a cold and ask them what progress they thought you were making down there.

LAURA: Oh. . . .

AMANDA: I went to the typing instructor and introduced myself as your mother. She didn't know who you were. Wingfield, she said. We don't have any such student enrolled at the school! I assured her she did, that you had been going to classes since early in January. "I wonder," she said, "if you could be talking about that terribly shy little girl who dropped out of school after only a few days' attendance?" "No," I said, "Laura, my daughter, has been going to school every day for the past six weeks!" "Excuse me," she said. She took the attendance book out and there was your name, unmistakably printed, and all the dates you were absent until they decided that you had dropped out of school. I still said, "No, there must have been some mistake! There must have been some mix-up in the records!" And she said, "No—I remember her perfectly now. Her hand shook so that she couldn't hit the right keys! The first time we gave a speed-test, she broke down completely—was sick at the stomach and almost had to be carried into the wash-room! After that morning she never showed up any more. We phoned the house but never got any answer"—while I was working at Famous and Barr, I suppose demonstrating those—Oh! I felt so weak I could barely keep on my feet. I had to sit down while they got me a glass of water! Fifty dollars' tuition, all of our plans—my hopes and ambitions for you—just gone up the spout, just gone up the spout like that. (*Laura draws a long breath and gets awkwardly to her feet. She crosses to the victrola and winds it up.*) What are you doing?

LAURA: Oh! (*She releases the handle and returns to her seat.*)

AMANDA: Laura, where have you been going when you've gone out pretending that you were going to business college?

LAURA: I've just been going out walking.

AMANDA: That's not true.

LAURA: It is. I just went walking.

AMANDA: Walking? Walking? In winter? Deliberately courting pneumonia in that light coat? Where did you walk to, Laura?

LAURA: It was the lesser of two evils, Mother. (*Image: Winter Scene in Park.*) I couldn't go back up. I—threw up—on the floor!

AMANDA: From half past seven till after five thirty every day you mean to tell me you walked around in the park, because you wanted to make me think that you were still going to Rubicam's Business College?

LAURA: It wasn't as bad as it sounds. I went inside places to get warmed up.

AMANDA: Inside where?

LAURA: I went in the art museum and the birdhouses at the Zoo. I visited the penguins every day! Sometimes I did without lunch and went to the movies. Lately I've been spending most of my afternoons in the Jewel-box, that big glass house where they raise the tropical flowers.

AMANDA: You did all this to deceive me, just for the deception? (*Laura looks down.*) Why?

LAURA: Mother, when you're disappointed, you get that awful suffering look on your face. Like the picture of Jesus' mother in the museum!

AMANDA: Hush!

LAURA: I couldn't face it.

(Pause: A whisper of strings.)

(Legend: "The Crust of Humility.")

AMANDA (*hopelessly fingering the huge pocketbook*): So what are we going to do the rest of our lives? Stay home and watch the parades go by? Amuse ourselves with the glass menagerie, darling? Eternally play those worn-out phonograph records your father left as a painful reminder of him? We won't have a business career— we've given that up because it gave us nervous indigestion! (*Laughs wearily.*) What is there left but dependency all our lives? I know so well what becomes of unmarried women who aren't prepared to occupy a position. I've seen such pitiful cases in the South—barely tolerated spinsters living upon the grudging patronage of sister's husband or brother's wife!—stuck away in some little mousetrap of a room—encouraged by one inlaw to visit another—little birdlike women without any nest—eating the crust of humility all their life! Is that the future that we've mapped out for ourselves? I swear it's the only alternative I can think of! It isn't a very pleasant alternative, is it? Of course—some girls *do marry*. (*Laura twists her hands nervously.*) Haven't you ever liked some boy?

LAURA: Yes, I liked one once. (*Rises.*) I came across his picture a while ago.

AMANDA (*with some interest*): He gave you his picture?

LAURA: No, it's in the year-book.

AMANDA (*disappointed*): Oh—a high-school boy.

(Screen Image: Jim as a High-School Hero Bearing a Silver Cup.)

LAURA: Yes. His name was Jim. (*Laura lifts the heavy annual from the clawfoot table.*) Here he is in *The Pirates of Penzance.*

AMANDA (*absently*): The what?

LAURA: The operetta the senior class put on. He had a wonderful voice and we sat across the aisle from each other Mondays, Wednesdays, and Fridays in the Aud. Here he is with the silver cup for debating! See his grin?

AMANDA (*absently*): He must have had a jolly disposition.

LAURA: He used to call me—Blue Roses.

(Image: Blue Roses.)

AMANDA: Why did he call you such a name as that?

LAURA: When I had that attack of pleurosis—he asked me what was the matter when I came back. I said pleurosis—he thought I said Blue Roses! So that's what he always called me after that. Whenever he saw me, he'd holler, "Hello, Blue Roses!" I didn't care for the girl that he went out with. Emily Meisenbach. Emily was the best-dressed girl at Soldan. She never struck me, though, as being sincere. . . . It says in the Personal Section—they're engaged. That's—six years ago! They must be married by now.

AMANDA: Girls that aren't cut out for business careers usually wind up married to some nice man. (*Gets up with a spark of revival.*) Sister, that's what you'll do!

(*Laura utters a startled, doubtful laugh. She reaches quickly for a piece of glass.*)

LAURA: But, Mother—

AMANDA: Yes? (*Crossing to photograph.*)

LAURA (*in a tone of frightened apology*): I'm—crippled!

(Image: Screen.)

AMANDA: Nonsense! Laura, I've told you never, never to use that word. Why, you're not crippled, you just have a little defect—hardly noticeable, even! When people have some slight disadvantage like that, they cultivate other things to make up for it—develop charm—and vivacity—and—*charm!* That's all you have to do! (*She turns again to the photograph.*) One thing your father had plenty of—was *charm!*

(Tom motions to the fiddle in the wings.)

(The Scene Fades Out with Music.)

SCENE 3

(LEGEND ON THE SCREEN: "AFTER THE FIASCO — ")

Tom speaks from the fire-escape landing.

TOM: After the fiasco at Rubicam's Business College, the idea of getting a gentleman caller for Laura began to play a more important part in Mother's calculations. It became an obsession. Like some archetype of the universal unconscious, the image of the gentleman caller haunted our small apartment. . . . *(Image: Young Man at Door with Flowers.)* An evening at home rarely passed without some allusion to this image, this specter, this hope. . . . Even when he wasn't mentioned, his presence hung in Mother's preoccupied look and in my sister's frightened, apologetic manner—hung like a sentence passed upon the Wingfields! Mother was a woman of action as well as words. She began to take logical steps in the planned direction. Late that winter and in the early spring—realizing that extra money would be needed to properly feather the nest and plume the bird—she conducted a vigorous campaign on the telephone, roping in subscribers to one of those magazines for matrons called *The Home-maker's Companion*, the type of journal that features the serialized sublimation of ladies of letters who think in terms of delicate cup-like breasts, slim, tapering waists, rich, creamy thighs, eyes like wood-smoke in autumn, fingers that soothe and caress like strains of music, bodies as powerful as Etruscan sculpture.

(Screen Image: Glamour Magazine Cover.)

(Amanda enters with phone on long extension cord. She is spotted in the dim stage.)

AMANDA: Ida Scott? This is Amanda Wingfield! We *missed* you at the D.A.R. last Monday! I said to myself: She's probably suffering with that sinus condition! How is that sinus condition? Horrors! Heaven have mercy!—You're a Christian martyr, yes, that's what you are, a

Christian martyr! Well, I just now happened to notice that your subscription to the *Companion's* about to expire! Yes, it expires with the next issue, honey!—just when that wonderful new serial by Bessie Mae Hopper is getting off to such an exciting start. Oh, honey, it's something that you can't miss! You remember how *Gone With the Wind* took everybody by storm? You simply couldn't go out if you hadn't read it. All everybody *talked* was Scarlett O'Hara. Well, this is a book that critics already compare to *Gone With the Wind*. It's the *Gone With the Wind* of the post-World War generation!— What?—Burning? Oh, honey, don't let them burn, go take a look in the oven and I'll hold the wire! Heavens—I think she's hung up!

(Dim Out.)

(Legend on Screen: "You Think I'm in Love with Continental Shoemakers?")

(Before the stage is lighted, the violent voices of Tom and Amanda are heard. They are quarreling behind the portieres. In front of them stands Laura with clenched hands and panicky expression. A clear pool of light on her figure throughout this scene.)

TOM: What in Christ's name am I—
AMANDA (*shrilly*): Don't you use that—
TOM: Supposed to do!
AMANDA: Expression! Not in my—
TOM: Ohhh!
AMANDA: Presence! Have you gone out of your senses?
TOM: I have, that's true, *driven* out!
AMANDA: What is the mater with you, you—big—big—IDIOT!
TOM: Look—I've got *no thing*, no single thing—
AMANDA: Lower your voice?
TOM: In my life here that I can call my OWN! Everything is—
AMANDA: Stop that shouting!
TOM: Yesterday you confiscated my books! You had the nerve to—
AMANDA: I took that horrible novel back to the library—yes! That hideous book by that insane Mr. Lawrence. (*Tom laughs wildly.*) I cannot control the output of diseased minds or people who cater to them—(*Tom laughs still more wildly.*) BUT I WON'T ALLOW SUCH FILTH BROUGHT INTO MY HOUSE! No, no, no, no, no!

TOM: House, house! Who pays rent on it, who makes a slave of himself to—

AMANDA (*fairly screeching*): Don't you DARE to—

TOM: No, no, *I* musn't say things! *I've* got to just—

AMANDA: Let me tell you—

TOM: I don't want to hear any more! (*He tears the portieres open. The upstage area is lit with a turgid smoky red glow.*)

Amanda's hair is in metal curlers and she wears a very old bathrobe, much too large for her slight figure, a relic of the faithless Mr. Wingfield. An upright typewriter and a mild disarray of manuscripts are on the drop-leaf table. The quarrel was probably precipitated by Amanda's interruption of his creative labor. A chair lying overthrown on the floor. Their gesticulating shadows are cast on the ceiling by the fiery glow.

AMANDA: You *will* hear more, you—

TOM: No, I won't hear more, I'm going out!

AMANDA: You come right back in—

TOM: Out, out out! Because I'm—

AMANDA: Come back here, Tom Wingfield! I'm not through talking to you!

TOM: Oh, go—

LAURA (*desperately*): Tom!

AMANDA: You're going to listen, and no more insolence from you! I'm at the end of my patience! (*He comes back toward her.*)

TOM: What do you think I'm at? Aren't I supposed to have any patience to reach the end of, Mother? I know, I know. It seems unimportant to you, what I'm *doing*—what I *want* to do—having a little *difference* between them! You don't think that—

AMANDA: I think you've been doing things that you're ashamed of. That's why you act like this. I don't believe that you go every night to movies. Nobody goes to the movies night after night. Nobody in their right minds goes to movies as often as you pretend to. People don't go to the movies at nearly midnight, and movies don't let out at two A.M. Come in stumbling. Muttering to yourself like a maniac! You get three hours' sleep and then go to work. Oh, I can picture the way you're doing down there. Moping, doping, because you're in no condition.

TOM (*wildly*): No, I'm in no condition!

AMANDA: What right have you got to jeopardize your job? Jeopardize the security of us all? How do you think we'd manage if you were—

TOM: Listen! You think I'm crazy *about the warehouse?* (*He bends fiercely toward her slight figure.*) You think I'm in love with the Continental Shoemakers? You think I want to spend fifty-five *years* down there in that—*celotex interior!* with—*fluorescent—tubes!* Look! I'd rather somebody picked up a crowbar and battered out my brains than go back mornings! I *go!* Every time you come in yelling that God damn *"Rise and Shine!"* *"Rise and Shine!"* I say to myself "How *lucky dead* people are!" But I get up. I *go!* For sixty-five dollars a month I gave up all that I dream of doing and being *ever!* And you say self—*self's* all I ever think of. Why, listen, if self is what I thought of, Mother, I'd be where he is—GONE! (*Pointing to father's picture.*) As far as the system of transportation reaches! (*He starts past her. She grabs his arm.*) Don't grab at me, Mother!

AMANDA: Where are you going?

TOM: I'm going to the *movies!*

AMANDA: I don't believe that lie!

TOM (*crouching toward her, overtowering her tiny figure. She backs away, gasping*): I'm going to opium dens! Yes, opium dens, dens of vice and criminals' hang-outs, Mother. I've joined the Hogan gang, I'm a hired assassin, I carry a tommy-gun in a violin case! I run a string of cat-houses in the Valley. They call me Killer, Killer Wingfield, I'm leading a double-life, a simple, honest warehouse worker by day, by night a dynamic *czar* of the *underworld, Mother.* I go to gambling casinos, I spin away fortunes on the roulette table! I wear a patch over one eye and a false mustache, sometimes I put on green whiskers. On those occasions they call me—*El Diablo!* Oh, I could tell you things to make you sleepless! My enemies plan to dynamite this place. They're going to blow us all sky-high some night! I'll be glad, very happy, and so will you! You'll go up, up on a broomstick, over Blue Mountain with seventeen gentlemen callers! You ugly—babbling old—*witch.* . . . (*He goes through a series of violent, clumsy movements, seizing his overcoat, lunging to the door, pulling it fiercely open. The women watch him, aghast. His arm catches in the sleeve of the coat as he struggles to pull it*

*on. For a moment he is pinioned by the bulky garment. With an
outraged groan he tears the coat off again, splitting the shoulders
of it, and hurls it across the room. It strikes against the shelf of
Laura's glass collection, there is a tinkle of shattering glass. Laura
cries out as if wounded.*)

(Music Legend: "The Glass Menagerie.")

LAURA (*shrilly*):   My glass! —menagerie. . . . (*She covers her face
and turns away.*)

(*But Amanda is still stunned and stupefied by the "ugly witch" so
that she barely notices this occurrence. Now she recovers her
speech.*)

AMANDA (*in an awful voice*):   I won't speak to you—until you apologize! (*She crosses through the portieres and draws them together
behind her. Tom is left with Laura. Laura clings weakly to the mantel with her face averted. Tom stares at her stupidly for a moment.
Then he crosses to shelf. Drops awkwardly to his knees to collect the
fallen glass, glancing at Laura as if he would speak but couldn't.*)

("The Glass Menagerie" steals in as the Scene Dims Out.)

SCENE 4

*The interior is dark. Faint light in the alley. A deep-voiced bell in a
church is tolling the hour by five as the scene commences.*

*Tom appears at the top of the alley. After each solemn boom of the
bell in the tower, he shakes a little noise-maker or rattle as if to express
the tiny spasm of man in contrast to the sustained power and dignity of
the Almighty. This and the unsteadiness of his advance make it evident
that he has been drinking.*

*As he climbs the few steps to the fire-escape landing light steals up
inside. Laura appears in night-dress, observing Tom's empty bed in the
front room.*

*Tom fishes in his pockets for the door-key, removing a motley as-
sortment of articles in the search, including a perfect shower of movie-
ticket stubs and an empty bottle. At last he finds the key, but just as he
about to insert it, it slips from his fingers. He strikes a match and
crouches below the door.*

TOM (*bitterly*):   One crack—and it falls through!

(*Laura opens the door.*)

LAURA: Tom! Tom, what are you doing?

TOM: Looking for a door-key.

LAURA: Where have you been all this time?

TOM: I have been to the movies.

LAURA: All this time at the movies?

TOM: There was a very long program. There was a Garbo picture and a Mickey Mouse and a travelogue and a newsreel and a preview of coming attractions. And there was an organ solo and a collection for the milk-fund—simultaneously—which ended up in a terrible fight between a fat lady and an usher!

LAURA (*innocently*):   Did you have to stay through everything?

TOM: Of course! And, oh, I forgot! There was a big stage show! The headliner on this stage show was Malvolio the Magician. He performed wonderful tricks, many of them, such as pouring water back and forth between pitchers. First it turned to wine and then it turned to beer and then it turned to whiskey. I know it was whiskey it finally turned into because he needed somebody to come up out of the audience to help him, and I came up—both shows! It was Kentucky Straight Bourbon. A very generous fellow, he gave souvenirs. (*He pulls from his back pocket a shimmering rainbow-colored scarf.*) He gave me this. This is his magic scarf. You can have it, Laura. You wave it over a canary cage and you get a bowl of gold-fish. You wave it over the goldfish bowl and they fly away canaries. . . . But the wonderfulest trick of all was the coffin trick. We nailed him into a coffin and he got out of the coffin without removing one nail. (*He has come inside.*) There is a trick that would come in handy for me—get me out of this 2 by 4 situation! (*Flops onto bed and starts removing shoes.*)

LAURA: Tom—Shhh!

TOM: What you shushing me for?

LAURA: You'll wake up Mother.

TOM: Goody, goody! Pay 'er back for those "Rise an' Shines." (*Lies down, groaning.*) You know it don't take much intelligence to get yourself into a nailed-up coffin, Laura. But who in hell ever got himself out of one without removing one nail?

(As if in answer, the father's grinning photograph lights up.)

(Scene Dims Out.)

Immediately following: The church bell is heard striking six. At the sixth stroke the alarm clock goes off in Amanda's room, and after a few moments we hear her calling: "Rise and Shine! Rise and Shine! Laura, go tell your brother to rise and shine!"

TOM (*sitting up slowly*): I'll rise—but I won't shine.

(The light increases.)

AMANDA: Laura, tell your brother his coffee is ready.

(Laura slips into front room.)

LAURA: Tom! it's nearly seven. Don't make Mother nervous. (*He stares at her stupidly. Beseechingly.*) Tom, speak to Mother this morning. Make up with her, apologize, speak to her!

TOM: She won't to me. It's her that started not speaking.

LAURA: If you just say you're sorry she'll start speaking.

TOM: Her not speaking—is that such a tragedy?

LAURA: Please—please!

AMANDA (*calling from kitchenette*): Laura, are you going to do what I asked you to do, or do I have to get dressed and go out myself?

LAURA: Going, going—soon as I get on my coat! (*She pulls on a shapeless felt hat with nervous, jerky movement, pleadingly glancing at Tom. Rushes awkwardly for coat. The coat is one of Amanda's, inaccurately made-over, the sleeves too short for Laura.*) Butter and what else?

AMANDA (*entering upstage*): Just butter. Tell them to charge it.

LAURA: Mother, they make such faces when I do that.

AMANDA: Sticks and stones may break my bones, but the expression of Mr. Garfinkel's face won't harm me! Tell your brother his coffee is getting cold.

LAURA (*at door*): Do what I asked you, will you, will you, Tom?

(He looks sullenly away.)

AMANDA: Laura, go now or just don't go at all!

LAURA (*rushing out*): Going—going! (*A second later she cries out. Tom springs up and crosses to the door. Amanda rushes anxiously in. Tom opens the door.*)

TOM: Laura?

LAURA: I'm all right. I slipped, but I'm all right.

AMANDA (*peering anxiously after her*): If anyone breaks a leg on those fire-escape steps, the landlord ought to be sued for every cent he possesses! (*She shuts door. Remembers she isn't speaking and returns to the other room.*)

(*As Tom enters listlessly for his coffee, she turns her back to him and stands rigidly facing the widow on the gloomy gray vault of the areaway. Its light on her face with its aged but childish features is cruelly sharp, satirical as a Daumier print.*)

(Music Under: "Ave Maria.")

(*Tom glances sheepishly but sullenly at her averted figure and slumps at the table. The coffee is scalding hot; he sips it and gasps and spits it back in the cup. At his gasp, Amanda catches breath and half turns. Then catches herself and turns back to window.*)

Tom blows on his coffee, glancing sidewise at his mother. She clears her throat. Tom clears his. He starts to rise. Sinks back down again, scratches his head, clears his throat again. Amanda coughs. Tom raises his cup in both hands to blow on it, his eyes staring over the rim of it at his mother for several moments. Then he slowly sets the cup down and awkwardly and hesitantly rises from the chair.)

TOM (*hoarsely*): Mother. I—I apologize. Mother. (*Amanda draws a quick, shuddering breath. Her face works grotesquely. She breaks into childlike tears.*) I'm sorry for that I said, for everything that I said, I didn't mean it.

AMANDA (*sobbingly*): My devotion has made me a witch and so I make myself hateful to my children!

TOM: No, you *don't.*

AMANDA: I worry so much, don't sleep, it makes me nervous!

TOM (*gently*): I understand that.

AMANDA: I've had to put up a solitary battle all these years. But you're my right-hand bower! Don't fall down, don't fail!

TOM (*gently*): I try, Mother.

AMANDA (*with great enthusiasm*): Try and you will SUCCEED! (*The notion makes her breathless.*) Why, you—you're just *full* of natural endowments! Both of my children—they're *unusual* children! Don't you think I know it? I'm so—*proud!* Happy and—feel I've—so much to be thankful for but—Promise me one thing, son!

TOM: What, Mother?

AMANDA: Promise, son, you'll—never be a drunkard!

TOM (*turns to her grinning*): I will never be a drunkard!

AMANDA: That's what frightened me so, that you'd be drinking! Eat a bowl of Purina!

TOM: Just coffee, Mother.

AMANDA: Shredded wheat biscuit?

TOM: No. No, Mother, just coffee.

AMANDA: You can't put in a day's work on an empty stomach. You've got ten minutes—don't gulp! Drinking too-hot liquids makes cancer of the stomach. . . . Put cream in.

TOM: No, thank you.

AMANDA: To cool it.

TOM: No! No, thank you, I want it black.

AMANDA: I know, but it's not good for you. We have to do all that we can to build ourselves up. In these trying times we live in, all that we have to cling to is each other. . . . That's why it's so important to—Tom, I—I sent out your sister so I could discuss something with you. If you hadn't spoken I would have spoken to you. (*Sits down.*)

TOM (*gently*): What is it, Mother, that you want to discuss?

AMANDA: Laura!

(Tom puts his cup down slowly.)

(Legend on Screen: "Laura.")

(Music: "The Glass Menagerie.")

TOM: —Oh.—Laura . . .

AMANDA (*touching his sleeve*): You know how Laura is. So quiet but—still water runs deep! She notices things and I think she—broods about them. (*Tom looks up.*) A few days ago I came in and she was crying.

TOM: What about?

AMANDA: You.

TOM: Me?

AMANDA: She has an idea that you're not happy here.

TOM: What gave her that idea?

AMANDA: What gives her any idea? However, you do act strangely. I—I'm not criticizing, understand *that!* I know your ambitions do not lie in the warehouse, that like everybody in the whole wide world—you've had to—make sacrifices, but—Tom—Tom—life's not easy, it calls for—Spartan endurance! There's so many things in my heart that I cannot describe to you! I've never told you but I—*loved* your father. . . .

TOM (*gently*): I know that, Mother.

AMANDA: And you—when I see you taking after his ways! Staying out late—and—well, you *had* been drinking the night you were in that—terrifying condition! Laura says that you hate the apartment and that you go out nights to get away from it! Is that true, Tom?

TOM: No. You say there's so much in your heart that you can't describe to me. That's true of me, too. There's so much in my heart that I can't describe to *you!* So let's respect each other's—

AMANDA: But, why—*why*, Tom—are you always so *restless?* Where do you go to, nights?

TOM: I—go to the movies.

AMANDA: Why do you go to the movies so much, Tom?

TOM: I go to the movies because—I like adventure. Adventure is something I don't have much of at work, so I go to the movies.

AMANDA: But, Tom, you go to the movies *entirely too much!*

TOM: I like a lot of adventure.

(*Amanda looks baffled, then hurt. As the familiar inquisition resumes he becomes hard and impatient again. Amanda slips back into her querulous attitude toward him.*)

(Image on Screen: Sailing Vessel with Jolly Roger.)

AMANDA: Most young men find adventure in their careers.

TOM: Then most young men are not employed in a warehouse.

AMANDA: The world is full of young men employed in warehouses and offices and factories.

TOM: Do all of them find adventure in their careers?

AMANDA: They do or they do without it! Not everybody has a craze for adventure.

TOM: Man is by instinct a lover, a hunter, a fighter, and none of these instincts are given much play at the warehouse!

ARMANDA: Man is by instinct! Don't quote instinct to me! Instinct is something that people have got away from! It belongs to animals! Christian adults don't want it!

TOM: What do Christian adults want, then, Mother?

AMANDA: Superior things! Things of the mind and the spirit! Only animals have to satisfy instincts! Surely your aims are somewhat higher than theirs! Than monkeys—pigs—

TOM: I reckon they're not.

AMANDA: You're joking. However, that isn't what I wanted to discuss.

TOM (*rising*): I haven't much time.

AMANDA (*pushing his shoulders*): Sit down.

TOM: You want me to punch in red at the warehouse, Mother?

AMANDA: You have five minutes. I want to talk about Laura.

(Legend: "Plans and Provisions.")

TOM: All right! What about Laura?

AMANDA: We have to be making plans and provisions for her. She's older than you, two years, and nothing has happened. She just drifts along doing nothing. It frightens me terribly how she just drifts along.

TOM: I guess she's the type that people call home girls.

AMANDA: There's no such type, and if there is, it's a pity! That is unless the home is hers, with a husband!

TOM: What?

AMANDA: Oh, I can see the handwriting on the wall as plain as I see the nose in front of my face! It's terrifying! More and more you remind me of your father! He was out all hours without explanation—Then *left! Good-bye!* And me with the bag to hold. I saw that letter you got from the Merchant Marine. I know what you're dreaming of. I'm not standing here blindfolded. Very well, then. Then *do* it! But not till there's somebody to take your place.

TOM: What do you mean?

AMANDA: I mean that as soon as Laura has got somebody to take care of her, married, a home of her own, independent—why, then you'll be free to go wherever you please, on land, on sea, whichever way the wind blows! But until that time you've got to look out for your sister. I don't say me because I'm old and don't matter! I say for your sister because she's young and dependent. I put her in business college—a dismal failure! Frightened her so it made her sick to her stomach. I took her over to the Young People's League at the church. Another fiasco. She spoke to nobody, nobody spoke to her. Now all she does is fool with those pieces of glass and play those worn-out records. What kind of life is that for a girl to lead!

TOM: What can I do about it?

AMANDA: Overcome selfishness! Self, self, self is all that you ever think of! (*Tom springs up and crosses to get his coat. It is ugly and bulky. He pulls on a cap with earmuffs.*) Where is your muffler? Put your wool muffler on! (*He snatches it angrily from the closet and tosses it around his neck and pulls both ends tight.*) Tom! I haven't said what I had in mind to ask you.

TOM: I'm too late to—

AMANDA (*catching his arms very importunately. Then shyly.*): Down the warehouse, aren't there some—nice young men?

TOM: No!

AMANDA: There *must* be—*some.*

TOM: Mother—

(Gesture.)

AMANDA: Find out one that's clean-living—doesn't drink and—ask him out for sister?

TOM: What?

AMANDA: For *sister!* To *meet!* Get acquainted!

TOM (*stamping to door*): Oh, my go-osh!

AMANDA: Will you? (*He opens door. Imploringly*) Will you? (*He starts down.*) Will you? *Will* you, dear?

TOM (*calling back*): YES!

(Amanda closes the door hesitantly and with a troubled but faintly hopeful expression.)

(Screen Image: Glamor Magazine Cover.)

(Spot Amanda at phone.)

AMANDA: Ella Cartwright? This is Amanda Wingfield! How are you, honey? How is that kidney condition? (*Count five.*) Horrors!

(*Count five.*) You're a Christian martyr, yes, honey, that's what you are, a Christian martyr! Well, I just happened to notice in my little red book that your subscription to the *Companion* has just run out! I knew that you wouldn't want to miss out on the wonderful serial starting in this new issue. It's by Bessie Mae Hopper, the first thing she's written since *Honeymoon for Three*. Wasn't that a strange and interesting story? Well, this one is even lovelier, I believe. It has a sophisticated society background. It's all about the horsey set on Long Island!

(Fade Out.)

SCENE 5

(LEGEND ON SCREEN: "ANNUNCIATION.") FADE WITH MUSIC.

It is early dusk of a spring evening. Supper has just been finished in the Wingfield apartment. Amanda and Laura in light-colored dresses are removing dishes from the table, in the upstage area, which is shadowy, their movements formalized almost as a dance or ritual, their moving forms as pale and silent as moths. Tom, in white shirt and trousers, rises from the table and crosses toward the fire-escape.

AMANDA (*as he passes her*):   Son, will you do me a favor?

TOM: What?

AMANDA: Comb your hair! You look so pretty when your hair is combed! (*Tom slouches on sofa with evening paper. Enormous caption "Franco Triumphs."*) There is only one respect in which I would like you to emulate your father.

TOM: What respect is that?

AMANDA: The care he always took of his appearance. He never allowed himself to look untidy. (*He throws down the paper and crosses to fire-escape.*) Where are you going?

TOM: I'm going out to smoke.

AMANDA: You smoke too much. A pack a day at fifteen cents a pack. How much would that amount to in month? Thirty times fifteen is how much, Tom? Figure it out and you will be astounded at what you could save. Enough to give you a night-school course in accounting at Washington U! Just think what a wonderful thing that would be for you, son!

(Tom is unmoved by the thought.)

TOM: I'd rather smoke. *(He steps out on landing, letting the screen door slam.)*

AMANDA *(sharply)*: I know! That's the tragedy of it. . . . *(Alone, she turns to look at her husband's picture.)*

(Dance Music: "All the World Is Waiting for the Sunrise!")

TOM *(to the audience)*: Across the alley from us was the Paradise Dance Hall. On evenings in spring the windows and doors were open and the music came outdoors. Sometimes the lights were turned out except for a large glass sphere that hung from the ceiling. It would turn slowly about and filter the dusk with delicate rainbow colors. Then the orchestra played a waltz or a tango, something that had a slow and sensuous rhythm. Couples would come outside, to the relative privacy of the alley. You could see them kissing behind ashpits and telephone poles. This was the compensation for lives that passed like mine, without any change or adventure. Adventure and change were imminent in this year. They were waiting around the corner for all these kinds. Suspended in the mist over Berchtesgaden, caught in the folds of Chamberlain's umbrella—In Spain there was Guernica! But here there was only hot swing music and liquor, dance halls, bars, and movies, and sex that hung in the gloom like a chandelier and flooded the world with brief, deceptive rainbows. . . . All the world was waiting for bombardments!

(Amanda turns from the picture and comes outside.)

AMANDA *(sighing)*: A fire-escape landing's a poor excuse for a porch. *(She spreads a newspaper on a step and sits down, gracefully and demurely as if she were settling into a swing on a Mississippi veranda.)* What are you looking at?

TOM: The moon.

AMANDA: Is there a moon this evening?

TOM: It's rising over Garfinkel's Delicatessen.

AMANDA: So it is! A little silver slipper of a moon. Have you made a wish on it yet?

TOM: Um-hum.

AMANDA: What did you wish for.

TOM: That's a secret.

AMANDA: A secret, huh? Well, I won't tell you mine either. I will be just as mysterious as you.

TOM: I bet I can guess what yours is.

AMANDA: Is my head so transparent?

TOM: You're not a sphinx.

AMANDA: No, I don't have secrets. I'll tell you what I wished for on the moon. Success and happiness for my precious children! I wish for that whenever there's a moon, and when there isn't a moon, I wish for it, too.

TOM: I thought perhaps you wished for a gentleman caller.

AMANDA: Why do you say that?

TOM: Don't you remember asking me to fetch one?

AMANDA: I remember suggesting that it would be nice for your sister if you brought home some nice young man from the warehouse. I think I've made that suggestion more than once.

TOM: Yes, you have made it repeatedly.

AMANDA: Well?

TOM: We are going to have one.

AMANDA: What?

TOM: A gentleman caller!

(The Annunciation Is Celebrated with Music.)

(Amanda rises.)

(Image on Screen: Caller with Bouquet.)

AMANDA: You mean you have asked some nice young man to come over?

TOM: Yep. I've asked him to dinner.

AMANDA: You really did?

TOM: I did!

AMANDA: You did, and did he—*accept?*

TOM: He did!

AMANDA: Well, well—well, well! That's—lovely!

TOM: I thought that you would be pleased.

AMANDA: It's definite, then?

TOM: Very definite.

AMANDA: Soon?

TOM: Very soon.

AMANDA: For heaven's sake, stop putting on and tell me some things, will you?

TOM: What things do you want me to tell you?

AMANDA: Naturally I would like to know when he's *coming!*

TOM: He's coming tomorrow.

AMANDA: Tomorrow?

TOM: Yep. Tomorrow.

AMANDA: But, Tom!

TOM: Yes, Mother?

AMANDA: Tomorrow gives me no time!

TOM: Time for what?

AMANDA: Preparations! Why didn't you phone me at once, as soon as you asked him, the minute that he accepted? Then, don't you see, I could have been getting ready!

TOM: You don't have to make any fuss.

AMANDA: Oh, Tom, Tom, Tom, of course I have to make a fuss! I want things nice, not sloppy! Not thrown together. I'll certainly have to do some fast thinking, won't I?

TOM: I don't see why you have to think at all.

AMANDA: You just don't know. We can't have a gentleman caller in a pig-sty! All my wedding silver has to be polished, the mono-grammed table linen ought to be laundered! The windows have to be washed and fresh curtains put up. And how about clothes? We have to *wear* something, don't we?

TOM: Mother, this boy is no one to make a fuss over!

AMANDA: Do you realize he's the first young man we've had intro-duced to your sister? It's terrible, dreadful, disgraceful that poor lit-tle sister has never received a single gentleman caller! Tom, come inside! (*She opens the screen door.*)

TOM: What for?

AMANDA: I want to ask you some things.

TOM: If you're going to make such a fuss, I'll call it off, I'll tell him not to come.

AMANDA: You certainly won't do anything of the kind. Nothing of-fends people worse than broken engagements. It simply means I'll have to work like a Turk! We won't be brilliant, but we'll pass in-spection. Come on inside. (*Tom follows, groaning.*) Sit down.

TOM: Any particular place you would like me to sit?

AMANDA: Thank heavens I've got that new sofa! I'm also making payments on a floor lamp I'll have sent out! And put the chintz covers on, they'll brighten things up! Of course I'd hoped to have these walls re-papered. . . . What is the young man's name?

TOM: His name is O'Connor.

AMANDA: That, of course, means fish—tomorrow is Friday! I'll have that salmon loaf—with Durkee's dressing! What does he do? He works at the warehouse?

TOM: Of course! How else would I—

AMANDA: Tom, he—doesn't drink?

TOM: Why do you ask me that?

AMANDA: Your father *did!*

TOM: Don't get started on that!

AMANDA: He *does* drink, then?

TOM: Not that I know of!

AMANDA: Make sure, be certain! The last thing I want for my daughter's a boy who drinks?

TOM: Aren't you being a little premature? Mr. O'Connor has not yet appeared on the scene!

AMANDA: But will tomorrow. To meet your sister, and what do I know about his character? Nothing! Old maids are better off than wives of drunkards!

TOM: Oh, my God.

AMANDA: Be still!

TOM (*leaning forward to whisper*): Lots of fellows meet girls whom they don't marry!

AMANDA: Oh, talk sensibly, Tom—and don't be sarcastic! (*She has gotten a hairbrush.*)

TOM: What are you doing?

AMANDA: I'm brushing that cow-lick down! What is this young man's position at the warehouse?

TOM (*submitting grimly to the brush and the interrogation*): This young man's position is that of a shipping clerk, Mother.

AMANDA: Sounds to me like a fairly responsible job, the sort of a job *you* would be in if you just had more *get-up.* What is his salary? Have you got any idea?

TOM: I would judge it to be approximately eighty-five dollars a month.

AMANDA: Well—not princely, but—

TOM: Twenty more than I make.

AMANDA: Yes, how well I know! But for a family man, eighty-five dollars a month is not much more than you can just get by on. . . .

TOM: Yes, but Mr. O'Connor is not a family man.

AMANDA: He might be, mightn't he? Some time in the future?

TOM: I see. Plans and provisions.

AMANDA: You are the only young man that I know of who ignores the fact that the future becomes the present, the present the past, and the past turns into everlasting regret if you don't plan for it!

TOM: I will think that over and see what I can make of it.

AMANDA: Don't be supercilious with your mother! Tell me some more about this—what do you call him?

TOM: James D. O'Connor. The D. is for Delaney.

AMANDA: Irish on *both* sides! *Gracious!* And doesn't drink?

TOM: Shall I call him up and ask him right this minute?

AMANDA: The only way to find out about those things is to make discreet inquiries at the proper moment. When I was a girl in Blue Mountain and it was suspected that a young man drank, the girl whose attentions he had been receiving, if any girl *was*, would sometimes speak to the minister of his church, or rather her father would if her father was living, and sort of feel him out on the young man's character. That is the way such things are discreetly handled to keep a young woman from making a tragic mistake!

TOM: Then how did you happen to make a tragic mistake?

AMANDA: That innocent look of your father's had everyone fooled! He *smiled*—the world was *enchanted!* No girl can do worse than put herself at the mercy of a handsome appearance! I hope that Mr. O'Connor is not too good-looking.

TOM: No, he's not too good-looking. He's covered with freckles and hasn't too much of a nose.

AMANDA: He's not right-down homely, though?

TOM: Not right-down homely. Just medium homely, I'd say.

AMANDA: Character's what to look for in a man.

TOM: That's what I've always said, Mother.

AMANDA: You've never said anything of the kind and I suspect you would never give it a thought.

TOM: Don't be suspicious of me.

AMANDA: At least I hope he's the type that's up and coming.

TOM: I think he really goes in for self-improvement.

AMANDA: What reason have you to think so?

TOM: He goes to night school.

AMANDA (*beaming*): Splendid! What does he do, I mean study?

TOM: Radio engineering and public speaking!

AMANDA: Then he has visions of being advanced in the world! Any young man who studies public speaking is aiming to have an executive job some day! And radio engineering? A thing for the future! Both of these facts are very illuminating. Those are the sort of things that a mother should know concerning any young man who comes to call on her daughter. Seriously or—not.

TOM: One little warning. He doesn't know about Laura. I didn't let on that we had dark ulterior motives. I just said, why don't you come have dinner with us? He said okay and that was the whole conversation.

AMANDA: I bet it was! You're eloquent as an oyster. However, he'll know about Laura when he gets here. When we sees how lovely and sweet and pretty she is, he'll thank his lucky stars he was asked to dinner.

TOM: Mother, you mustn't expect too much of Laura.

AMANDA: What do you mean?

TOM: Laura seems all those things to you and me because she's ours and we love her. We don't even notice she's crippled any more.

AMANDA: Don't say crippled! You know that I never allow that word to be used!

TOM: But face facts, Mother. She is and—that's not all—

AMANDA: What do you mean "not all"?

TOM: Laura is very different from other girls.

AMANDA: I think the difference is all to her advantage.

TOM: Not quite all—in the eyes of others—strangers—she's terribly shy and lives in a world of her own and those things make her seem a little peculiar to people outside the house.

AMANDA: Don't say peculiar.

TOM: Face the facts. She is.

(The Dance-Hall Music Changes to a Tango That Has a Minor and Somewhat Ominous Tone.)

AMANDA: In what way is she peculiar—may I ask?

TOM (*gently*): She lives in a world of her own—a world of—little glass ornaments, Mother. . . . (*Gets up, Amanda remains holding brush, looking at him, troubled.*) She plays old phonograph records and— that's about all—(*He glances at himself in the mirror and crosses to door.*)

AMANDA (*sharply*): Where are you going?

TOM: I'm going to the movies. (*Out screen door.*)

AMANDA: Not to the movies, every night to the movies! (*Follows quickly to screen door.*) I don't believe you always go to the movies! (*He is gone. Amanda looks worriedly after him for a moment. Then vitality and optimism return and she turns from the door. Crossing to portieres.*) Laura! Laura! (*Laura answers from kitchenette.*)

LAURA: Yes, Mother.

AMANDA: Let those dishes go and come in front! (*Laura appears with dish towel. Gaily*) Laura, come here and make a wish on the moon!

LAURA (*entering*): Moon—moon?

AMANDA: A little silver slipper of a moon. Look over your left shoulder, Laura, and make a wish! (*Laura looks faintly puzzled as if called out of sleep. Amanda seizes her shoulders and turns her at angle by the door.*) Now! Now, darling, *wish!*

LAURA: What shall I wish for, Mother?

AMANDA (*her voice trembling and her eyes suddenly filling with tears*): Happiness! Good Fortune!

(*The violin rises and the stage dims out.*)

SCENE 6

(**IMAGE: HIGH SCHOOL HERO.**)

TOM: And so the following evening I brought Jim home to dinner. I had known Jim slightly in high school. In high school Jim was a hero. He had tremendous Irish good nature and vitality with the scrubbed and polished look of white chinaware. He seemed to move in a continual spotlight. He was a star in basketball, captain of the debating club, president of the senior class and the glee club and he sang the male lead in the annual light operas. He was always running or bounding, never just walking. He seemed always at the point of defeating the law of gravity. He was shooting with such velocity through his adolescence that you would logically expect him to arrive at nothing short of the White House by the time he was thirty. But Jim apparently ran into more interference after his graduation from Soldan. His speed had definitely slowed. Six years after he left high school he was holding a job that wasn't much better than mine.

(Image: Clerk.)

He was the only one at the warehouse with whom I was on friendly terms. I was valuable to him as someone who could remember his former glory, who had seen him win basketball games and the silver cup in debating. He knew of my secret practice of retiring to a cabinet of the washroom to work on poems when business was slack in the warehouse. He called me Shakespeare. And while the other boys in the warehouse regarded me with suspicious hostility, Jim took a humorous attitude toward me. Gradually his attitude affected the others, their hostility wore off and they also began to smile at me as people smile at an oddly fashioned dog who trots across their path at some distance.

I knew that Jim and Laura had known each other at Soldan, and I had heard Laura speak admiringly of his voice. I didn't know if Jim remembered her or not. In high school Laura had been as unobtrusive as Jim had been astonishing. If he did remember Laura, it was not as my sister for when I asked him to dinner, he grinned and said, "You know, Shakespeare, I never thought of you as having folks!"

He was about to discover that I did. . . .

(Light upstage.)

(Legend on Screen: "The Accent of a Coming Foot.")

(Friday evening. It is about five o'clock of a late spring evening which comes "scattering poems in the sky." A delicate lemony light is in the Wingfield apartment. Amanda has worked like a Turk in preparation for the gentleman caller. The results are astonishing. The new floor lamp with its rose-silk shade is in place, a colored paper lantern conceals the broken light fixture in the ceiling, new billowing white curtains are at the windows, chintz covers are on chairs, and sofa, a pair of new sofa pillows make their initial appearance.

Open boxes and tissue paper are scattered on the floor.

Laura stands in the middle with lifted arms while Amanda crouches before her, adjusting the hem of the new dress, devout and ritualistic. The dress is colored and designed by memory. The arrangement of Laura's hair is changed; it is softer and more becoming. A fragile, unearthly prettiness has come out in Laura: she is like a piece of translucent glass touched by light, given a momentary radiance, not actual, not lasting.)

AMANDA (*impatiently*): Why are you trembling?

LAURA: Mother, you've made me so nervous!

AMANDA: How have I made you nervous?

LAURA: By all this fuss! You make it seem so important?

AMANDA: I don't understand you, Laura. You couldn't be satisfied with just sitting home, and yet whenever I try to arrange something for you, you seem to resist it. (*She gets up.*) Now take a look at yourself. No, wait! Wait just a moment—I have an idea!

LAURA: What is it now?

(Amanda produces two powder puffs which she wraps in handkerchiefs and stuffs in Laura's bosom.)

LAURA: Mother, what are you doing?

AMANDA: They call them "Gay Deceivers"!

LAURA: I won't wear them!

AMANDA: You will!

LAURA: Why should I?

AMANDA: Because, to be painfully honest, your chest is flat.

LAURA: You make it seem like we were setting a trap.

AMANDA: All pretty girls are a trap, a pretty trap, and men expect them to be.

(Legend: "A Pretty Trap.")

Now look at yourself, young lady. This is the prettiest you will ever be! I've got to fix myself now! You're going to be surprised by your mother's appearance.

(She crosses through portieres, humming gaily.)

(Laura moves slowly to the long mirror and stares solemnly at herself. A wind blows the white curtains inward in a slow, graceful motion and with a faint, sorrowful sighing.)

AMANDA *(offstage)*: It isn't dark enough yet. *(She turns slowly before the mirror with a troubled look.)*

(Legend on Screen: "This Is My Sister: Celebrate Her with Strings!" Music.)

AMANDA *(laughing, off)*: I'm going to show you something. I'm going to make a spectacular appearance!

LAURA: What is it, Mother?

AMANDA: Possess your soul in patience—you will see! Something I've resurrected from that old trunk! Styles haven't changed so terribly much after all. . . . *(She parts the portieres.)* Now just look at your mother! *(She wears a girlish frock of yellowed voile with a blue silk sash. She carries a bunch of jonquils—the legend of her youth is nearly revived. Feverishly)* This is the dress in which I led the cotillion. Won the cakewalk twice at Sunset Hill, wore one spring to the Governor's ball in Jackson! See how I sashayed around the ballroom, Laura? *(She raises her skirt and does a mincing step around the room.)* I wore it on Sundays for my gentleman callers! I had it on the day I met your father—I had malaria fever all that spring. The change of climate from East Tennessee to the Delta— weakened resistance—I had a little temperature all the time—not enough to be serious—just enough to make me restless and giddy! Invitations poured in parties all over the Delta!—"Stay in bed," said Mother, "you have fever!"—but I just wouldn't.—I took quinine but kept on going, going!—Evenings, dances!—Afternoon, long, long rides! Picnics—lovely!—So lovely, that country in May.—All lacy with dogwood, literally flooded with jonquils.—That was the spring I had the craze for jonquils. Jonquils became an absolute obsession. Mother said, "Honey, there's no more room for jonquils." And still I kept bringing in more jonquils. Whenever, wherever I saw them, I'd say, "Stop! Stop! I see jonquils!" I made the young men help me gather the jonquils! It was a joke, Amanda and her jonquils! Finally there were no more vases to hold them, every available space was filled with jonquils. No vases to hold them? All right, I'll hold them myself! And then I—*(She stops in front of the picture.)* *(Music.)* met your father! Malaria fever and jonquils and then—this—boy. . . . (*She switches on the rose-colored lamp.*) I hope they get here before it starts to rain. (*She crosses upstage and places the jonquils in bowl on table.*) I gave your brother a little extra change so he and Mr. O'Connor could take the service car home.

LAURA (*with altered look*):   What did you say his name was?

AMANDA: O'Connor.

LAURA: What is his first name?

AMANDA: I don't remember. Oh, yes, I do. It was—Jim!

(Laura sways slightly and catches hold of a chair.)

(Legend on Screen: "Not Jim!")

LAURA (*faintly*):   Not—Jim!

AMANDA: Yes, that was it, it was Jim! I've never know a Jim that wasn't nice!

(Music: Ominous.)

LAURA: Are you sure his name is Jim O'Connor?

AMANDA: Yes. Why?

LAURA: Is he the one that Tom used to know in high school?

AMANDA: He didn't say so. I think he just got to know him at the warehouse.

LAURA: There was a Jim O'Connor we both knew in high school— (*Then, with effort.*) If that is the one that Tom is bringing to dinner—you'll have to excuse me, I won't come to the table.

AMANDA: What sort of nonsense is this?

LAURA: You asked me once if I'd ever liked a boy. Don't you remember I showed you this boy's picture?

AMANDA: You mean the boy you showed me in the year book?

LAURA: Yes, that boy.

AMANDA: Laura, Laura, were you in love with that boy?

LAURA: I don't know, Mother. All I know is I couldn't sit at the table if it was him!

AMANDA: It won't be him! It isn't the least bit likely. But whether it is or not, you will come to the table. You will not be excused.

LAURA: I'll have to be, Mother.

AMANDA: I don't intend to humor your silliness, Laura. I've had too much from you and your brother, both! So just sit down and compose yourself till they come. Tom has forgotten his key so you'll have to let them in, when they arrive.

LAURA (*panicky*):   Oh, Mother—*you* answer the door!

AMANDA (*lightly*):   I'll be in the kitchen—busy!

LAURA: Oh, Mother, please answer the door, don't make me do it!

AMANDA (*crossing into kitchenette*):   I've got to fix the dressing for the salmon. Fuss, fuss—silliness!—over a gentleman caller!

(*Door swings shut. Laura is left alone.*)

(Legend: "Terror!")

(*She utters a low moan and turns off the lamp—sits stiffly on the edge of the sofa, knotting her fingers together.*)

(Legend on Screen: "The Opening of a Door!")

(*Tom and Jim appear on the fire-escape steps and climb to landing. Hearing their approach, Laura rises with a panicky gesture. She retreats to the portieres.*

The doorbell. Laura catches her breath and touches her throat. Low drums.)

AMANDA (*calling*):   Laura, sweetheart! The door!

(*Laura stares at it without moving.*)

JIM: I think we just beat the rain.

TOM: Uh-huh. (*He rings again, nervously, Jim whistles and fishes for a cigarette.*)

AMANDA (*very, very gaily*):   Laura, that is your brother and Mr. O'Connor! Will you let them in, darling?

(*Laura crosses toward kitchenette door*).

LAURA (*breathlessly*):   Mother—you go to the door!

(*Amanda steps out of the kitchenette and stares furiously at Laura. She points imperiously at the door.*)

LAURA: Please, please!

AMANDA (*in a fierce whisper*):   What is the matter with you, you silly thing?

LAURA (*desperately*):   Please, you answer it, *please!*

AMANDA: I told you I wasn't going to humor you, Laura. Why have you chosen this time to lose your mind?

LAURA: Please, please, please, you go!

AMANDA: You'll have to go to the door because I can't.

LAURA (*despairingly*): I can't either!

AMANDA: Why?

LAURA: I'm *sick?*

AMANDA: I'm sick, too—of your nonsense! Why can't you and your brother be normal people? Fantastic whims and behavior! (*Tom gives a long ring.*) Preposterous goings on! Can you give me one reason—(*Calls out lyrically.*) COMING! JUST ONE SECOND!—why should you be afraid to open a door? Now you answer it, Laura!

LAURA: Oh, oh, oh . . . (*She returns through the portieres. Darts to the victrola and winds it frantically and turns it on.*)

AMANDA: Laura Wingfield, you march right to that door!

LAURA: Yes—yes, Mother.

(A faraway, scratchy rendition of "Dardanella" softens the air and gives her strength to move through it. She slips to the door and draws it cautiously open. Tom enters with the caller, Jim O'Connor.)

TOM: Laura, this is Jim. Jim, this is my sister, Laura.

JIM (*stepping inside*): I didn't know that Shakespeare had a sister!

LAURA (*retreating stiff and trembling from the door*): How—how do you do?

JIM (*heartily extending his hand*): Okay!

(Laura touches it hesitantly with hers.)

JIM: Your hand's *cold*, Laura!

LAURA: Yes, well—I've been playing the victrola. . . .

JIM: Must have been playing classical music on it! You ought to play a little hot swing music to warm you up!

LAURA: Excuse me—I haven't finished playing the victrola. . . .

(She turns awkwardly and hurries onto the front room. She pauses a second by the victrola. Then catches her breath and darts through the portieres like a frightened deer.)

JIM (*grinning*): What was the matter?

TOM: Oh—with Laura? Laura is—terribly shy.

JIM: Shy, huh? It's unusual to meet a shy girl nowadays. I don't believe you ever mentioned you had a sister.

TOM: Well, now you know. I have one. Here is the *Post Dispatch.* You want a piece of it?

JIM: Uh-huh.

TOM: What piece? The comics?

JIM: Sports! (*Glances at it.*) Ole Dizzy Dean is on his bad behavior.

TOM (*disinterest*): Yeah? (*Lights cigarette and crosses back to fire-escape door.*)

JIM: Where are *you* going?

TOM: I'm going out on the terrace.

JIM (*goes after him*): You know, Shakespeare—I'm going to sell you a bill of goods!

TOM: What goods?

JIM: A course I'm taking.

TOM: Huh?

JIM: In public speaking! You and me, we're not the warehouse type.

TOM: Thanks—that's good news. But what has public speaking got to do with it?

JIM: It fits you for—executive positions!

TOM: Awww.

JIM: I tell you it's done a helluva lot for me.

(Image: Executive at Desk.)

TOM: In what respect?

JIM: In every! Ask yourself what is the difference between you an' me in the office down front? Brains?—No!—Ability?—No! Then what? Just one little thing—

TOM: What is that one little thing?

JIM: Primarily it amounts to—social poise! Being able to square up to people and hold your own on any social level!

AMANDA (*off stage*): Tom?

TOM: Yes, Mother?

AMANDA: Is that you and Mr. O'Connor?

TOM: Yes, Mother.

AMANDA: Well, you just make yourselves comfortable in there.

TOM: Yes, Mother.

AMANDA: Ask Mr. O'Connor if he would like to wash his hands.

JIM: Aw—no—no—thank you—I took care of that at the warehouse. Tom—

TOM: Yes?

JIM: Mr. Mendoza was speaking to me about you.

TOM: Favorably?

JIM: What do you think?

TOM: Well—

JIM: You're going to be out of a job if you don't wake up.

TOM: I am waking up—

JIM: You show no signs.

TOM: The signs are interior.

> (Image on Screen: The Sailing Vessel with Jolly Roger Again.)

TOM: I'm planning to change. (*He leans over the rail speaking with quiet exhilaration. The incandescent marquees and signs of the first-run movie houses light his face from across the alley. He looks like a voyager.*) I'm right at the point of committing myself to a future that doesn't include the warehouse and Mr. Mendoza or even a night-school course in public speaking.

JIM: What are you gassing about?

TOM: I'm tired of the movies.

JIM: Movies!

TOM: Yes, movies! Look at them—(*A wave toward the marvels of Grand Avenue.*) All of those glamorous people—having adventures—hogging it all, gobbling the whole thing up! You know what happens? People go to the *movies* instead of *moving!* Hollywood characters are supposed to have all the adventures for everybody in America, while everybody in America sits in a dark room and watches them have them! Yes, until there's a war. That's when adventure becomes available to the masses! *Everyone's* dish, not only Gable's! Then the people in the dark room come out of the dark room to have some adventures themselves—Goody, goody—It's our turn now, to go to the South Sea Island—to make a safari—to be exotic, far-off—But I'm not patient. I don't want to wait till then. I'm tired of the *movies* and I am *about* to move!

JIM (*incredulously*):   Move?

TOM: Yes.

JIM: When?

TOM: Soon!

JIM: Where? Where?

(Theme Three: Music Seems to Answer the Question, While Tom Thinks It Over. He Searches Among His Pockets.)

TOM: I'm starting to boil inside. I know I seem dreamy, but inside— well, I'm boiling! Whenever I pick up a shoe, I shudder a little thinking how short life is and what I am doing!—Whatever that means. I know it doesn't mean shoes—except as something to wear on a traveler's feet! *(Finds paper.)* Look—

JIM: What?

TOM: I'm a member.

JIM *(reading)*: The Union of Merchant Seamen.

TOM: I paid my dues this month, instead of the light bill.

JIM: You will regret it when they turn the lights off.

TOM: I won't be here.

JIM: How about your mother?

TOM: I'm like my father. The bastard son of a bastard! See how he grins? And he's been absent going on sixteen years!

JIM: You're just talking, you drip. How does you mother feel about it?

TOM: Shhh—Here comes Mother! Mother is not acquainted with my plans.

AMANDA *(enters portiere)*: Where are you all?

TOM: On the terrace, Mother.

(They start inside. She advances to them. Tom is distinctly shocked at her appearance. Even Jim blinks a little. He is making his first contact with girlish Southern vivacity and in spite of the night-school course in public speaking is somewhat thrown off the beam by the unexpected outlay of social charm. Certain responses are attempted by Jim but are swept aside by Amanda's gay laughter and chatter. Tom is embarrassed but after the first shock Jim reacts very warmly. Grins and chuckles, is altogether won over.)

(Image: Amanda as a Girl.)

AMANDA *(coyly smiling, shaking her girlish ringlets)*: Well, well, well, so this is Mr. O'Connor. Introductions entirely unnecessary. I've heard so much about you from my boy. I finally said to him, Tom—good gracious!—why don't you bring this paragon to supper? I'd like to meet this nice young man at the warehouse!—Instead of just hearing him sing your praises so much! I don't know why my son is so stand-offish—that's not Southern behavior! Let's sit down and—I think we could stand a little more air in here! Tom, leave the door open. I felt a nice fresh breeze a moment ago. Where has it gone? Mmm, so warm already! And not quite summer, even. We're going to burn up when summer really gets started. However, we're having—we're having a very light supper. I think light things are better fo' this time of year. The same as light clothes are. Light clothes an' light food are what warm weather calls fo'. You know our blood gets so thick during th' winter—it takes a while fo' us to *adjust* ou'selves!—when the season changes . . . It's come so quick this year. I wasn't prepared. All of a sudden—heavens! Already summer!—I ran to the trunk an' pulled out this light dress—Terribly old! Historical almost! But feels so good—so good an' co-ol, y'know. . . .

TOM: Mother—

AMANDA: Yes, honey?

TOM: How about—supper?

AMANDA: Honey, you go ask Sister if supper is ready! You know that Sister is in full charge of supper! Tell her you hungry boys are waiting for it. (*To Jim*) Have you met Laura?

JIM: She—

AMANDA: Let you in? Oh, good, you've met already! It's rare for a girl as sweet an' pretty as Laura to be domestic! But Laura is, thank heavens, not only pretty but also very domestic. I'm not at all. I never was a bit. I never could make a thing but angel-food cake. Well, in the South we had so many servants. Gone, gone, gone. All vestiges of gracious living! Gone completely! I wasn't prepared for what the future brought me. All of my gentleman callers were sons of planters and so of course I assumed that I would be married to one and raise my family on a large piece of land with plenty of servants. But man proposes—and woman accepts the proposal!—To vary that old, old saying a little bit—I married no planter! I married a man who worked for the telephone company!—that gallantly smiling gentleman over there! (*Points to the*

picture.) A telephone man who—fell in love with long distance!—
Now he travels and I don't even know where!—But what am I going on for about my—tribulations! Tell me yours—I hope you don't
have any! Tom?

TOM (*returning*): Yes, Mother?

AMANDA: Is supper nearly ready?

TOM: It looks to me like supper is on the table.

AMANDA: Let me look—(*She rises prettily and looks through
portieres.*) Oh, lovely—but where is Sister?

TOM: Laura is not feeling well and she says that she thinks she'd better not come to the table.

AMANDA: What?—Nonsense!—Laura? Oh, Laura!

LAURA (*off stage, faintly*): Yes, Mother.

AMANDA: You really must come to the table. We won't be seated until
you come to the table! Come in, Mr. O'Connor. You sit over there
and I'll—Laura? Laura Wingfield! You're keeping us waiting,
honey! We can't say grace until you come to the table!

*(The back door is pushed weakly open and Laura comes in. She is
obviously quite faint, her lips trembling, her eyes wide and staring.
She moves unsteadily toward the table.)*

(Legend: "Terror!")

*(Outside a summer storm is coming abruptly. The white curtains
billow inward at the windows and there is a sorrowful murmur and
deep blue dusk. Laura suddenly stumbles—She catches at a chair
with a faint moan.)*

TOM: Laura!

AMANDA: Laura! (*There's a clap of thunder*). (*Legend: "Ah!"*)
(*Despairingly*) Why, Laura, you *are* sick, darling! Tom, help your
sister into the living room, dear! Sit in the living room, Laura—
rest on the sofa. Well! (*To the gentleman caller*) Standing over the
hot stove made her ill! I told her that it was just too warm this
evening, but—(*Tom comes back in. Laura is on the sofa.*) Is Laura
all right now?

TOM: Yes.

AMANDA: What is that? Rain? A nice cool rain has come up? (*She
gives the gentleman caller a frightened look.*) I think we may—have

grace—now . . . (*Tom looks at her stupidly.*) Tom, honey—you say grace!

TOM: Oh . . . "For these and all thy mercies—" (*They bow their heads. Amanda stealing a nervous glance at Jim. In the living room Laura, stretched on the sofa, clenches her hands to her lips, to hold back a shuddering sob.*) God's Holy Name be praised—

(The Scene Dims Out.)

SCENE 7

A SOUVENIR

Half an hour later. Dinner is just being finished in the upstage area which is concealed by the drawn portieres.

As the curtain rises Laura is still huddled upon the sofa, her feet drawn under her, her head resting on a pale blue pillow, her eyes wide and mysteriously watchful. The new floor lamp with its shade of rose-colored silk gives a soft, becoming light to her face, bringing out the fragile, unearthly prettiness which usually escapes attention. There is a steady murmur of rain, but it is slackening and stops soon after the scene begins; the air outside becomes pale and luminous as the moon breaks out.

A moment after the curtain rises, the lights in both rooms flicker and go out.

JIM: Hey, there, Mr. Light Bulb!

(Amanda laughs nervously.)

(Legend: "Suspension of a Public Service.")

AMANDA: Where was Moses when the lights went out? Ha-ha. Do you know the answer to that one, Mr. O'Connor?

JIM: No, Ma'am, what's the answer?

AMANDA: In the dark! (*Jim laughs appreciatively.*) Everybody sit still. I'll light the candles. Isn't it lucky we have them on the table? Where's a match. Which of you gentlemen can provide a match?

JIM: Here.

AMANDA: Thank you, sir.

JIM: Not at all, Ma'am!

AMANDA: I guess the fuse has burnt out. Mr. O'Connor, can you tell a burnt-out fuse? I know I can't and Tom is a total loss when it comes to mechanics. (*Sound: Getting Up: Voices Recede a Little to Kitchenette.*) Oh, be careful, you don't bump into something. We don't want our gentleman caller to break his neck. Now wouldn't that be a fine howdy-do?

JIM: Ha-ha! Where is the fuse-box?

AMANDA: Right there next to the stove. Can you see anything?

JIM: Just a minute.

AMANDA: Isn't electricity a mysterious thing? Wasn't it Benjamin Franklin who tied a key to a kite? We live in such a mysterious universe, don't we? Some people say that science clears up all the mysteries for us. In my opinion it only creates more! Have you found it yet?

JIM: No, Ma'am. All these fuses look okay to me.

AMANDA: Tom!

TOM: Yes, Mother?

AMANDA: That light bill I gave you several days ago. The one I told you we got the notices about?

TOM: Oh.—Yeah.

(Legend: "Ha!")

AMANDA: You didn't neglect to pay it by any chance.

TOM: Why, I—

AMANDA: Didn't! I might have known it!

JIM: Shakespeare probably wrote a poem on the light bill, Mrs. Wingfield.

AMANDA: I might have known better than to trust him with it! There's such a high price for negligence in this world!

JIM: Maybe the poem will win a ten-dollar prize.

AMANDA: We'll just have to spend the remainder of the evening in the nineteenth century, before Mr. Edison made the Mazda lamp!

JIM: Candlelight is my favorite kind of light.

AMANDA: That shows you're romantic! But that's no excuse for Tom. Well, we got through dinner. Very considerate of them to let us get through dinner before they plunged us into everlasting darkness, wasn't it, Mr. O'Connor?

JIM: Ha-ha!

AMANDA: Tom, as a penalty for your carelessness you can help me with the dishes.

JIM: Let me give you a hand.

AMANDA: Indeed you will not!

JIM: I ought to be good for something.

AMANDA: Good for something? (*Her tone is rhapsodic.*) *You?* Why, Mr. O'Connor, nobody, *nobody's* given me this much entertainment in years—as you have!

JIM: Aw, now, Mrs. Wingfield!

AMANDA: I'm not exaggerating, not one bit! But Sister is all by her lonesome. You go keep her company in the parlor! I'll give you this lovely old candelabrum that used to be on the altar at the church of the Heavenly Rest. It was melted a little out of shape when the church burnt down. Lightning struck it one spring. Gypsy Jones was holding a revival at the time and he estimated that the church was destroyed because the Episcopalians gave card parties.

JIM: Ha-ha.

AMANDA: And how about coaxing Sister to drink a little wine? I think it would be good for her! Can you carry both at once?

JIM: Sure, I'm Superman!

AMANDA: Now, Thomas, get into this apron!

(*The door of kitchenette swings closed on Amanda's gay laughter; the flickering light approaches the portieres. Laura sits up nervously as he enters. Her speech at first is low and breathless from the almost intolerable strain of being alone with a stranger.*)

(Legend: "I Don't Suppose You Remember Me at All!")

(*In her first speeches in this scene, before Jim's warmth overcomes her paralyzing shyness, Laura's voice is thin and breathless as though she has run up a steep flight of stairs. Jim's attitude is gently humorous. In playing this scene it should be stressed that while the incident is apparently unimportant, it is to Laura the climax of her secret life.*)

JIM: Hello, there, Laura.

LAURA (*faintly*): Hello. (*She clears her throat.*)

JIM: How are you feeling now? Better?

LAURA: Yes. Yes, thank you.

JIM: This is for you. A little dandelion wine. (*He extends it toward her with extravagant gallantry.*)

LAURA: Thank you.

JIM: Drink it—but don't get drunk! (*He laughs heartily. Laura takes the glass uncertainly; laughs shyly.*) Where shall I set the candles?

LAURA: Oh—oh, anywhere . . .

JIM: How about here on the floor? Any objections?

LAURA: No.

JIM: I'll spread a newspaper under to catch the drippings. I like to sit on the floor. Mind if I do?

LAURA: Oh, no.

JIM: Give me a pillow?

LAURA: What?

JIM: A pillow!

LAURA: Oh . . . (*Hands him one quickly.*)

JIM: How about you? Don't you like to sit on the floor?

LAURA: Oh—yes.

JIM: Why don't you, then?

LAURA: I—will.

JIM: Take a pillow! (*Laura does. Sits on the other side of the candelabrum. Jim crosses his legs and smiles engagingly at her.*) I can't hardly see you sitting way over there.

LAURA: I can—see you.

JIM: I know, but that's not fair, I'm in the limelight. (*Laura moves her pillow closer.*) Good! Now I can see you! Comfortable?

LAURA: Yes.

JIM: So am I. Comfortable as a cow. Will you have some gum?

LAURA: No, thank you.

JIM: I think that I will indulge, with your permission. (*Musingly unwraps it and holds it up.*) Think of the fortune made by the guy that invented the first piece of chewing gum. Amazing, huh? The Wrigley Building is one of the sights of Chicago.—I saw it summer before last when I went up to the Century of Progress. Did you take in the Century of Progress?

LAURA: No, I didn't.

JIM: Well, it was quite a wonderful exposition. What impressed me most was the Hall of Science. Gives you an idea of what the future will be in America, even more wonderful than the present time is! (*Pause. Smiling at her*) Your brother tells me you're shy. Is that right, Laura?

LAURA: I—don't know.

JIM: I judge you to be an old-fashioned type of girl. Well, I think that's a pretty good type to be. Hope you don't think I'm being too personal—do you?

LAURA (*hastily, out of embarrassment*): I believe I *will* take a piece of gum, if you—don't mind. (*Clearing her throat*) Mr. O'Connor, have you—kept up with your singing?

JIM: Singing? Me?

LAURA: Yes. I remember what a beautiful voice you had.

JIM: When did you hear me sing?

(Voice Offstage in the Pause.)

VOICE (*offstage*):
O blow, ye winds, heigh-ho,
A-roving I will go!
I'm off to my love
With a boxing glove—
Ten thousand miles away!

JIM: You say you've heard me sing?

LAURA: Oh, yes! Yes, very often . . . I—don't suppose you remember me—at all?

JIM (*smiling doubtfully*): You know I have an idea I've seen you before. I had that idea soon as you opened the door. It seemed almost like I was about to remember your name. But the name that I started to call you—wasn't a name! And so I stopped myself before I said it.

LAURA: Wasn't it—Blue Roses?

JIM (*springs up, grinning*): Blue Roses! My gosh, yes—Blue Roses! That's what I had on my tongue when you opened the door! Isn't it funny what tricks your memory plays? I didn't connect you with the high school somehow or other. But that's where it was; it was high school. I didn't even know you were Shakespeare's sister! Gosh, I'm sorry.

LAURA: I didn't expect you to. You—barely knew me!

JIM: But we did have a speaking acquaintance, huh?

LAURA: Yes, we—spoke to each other.

JIM: When did you recognize me?

LAURA: Oh, right away!

JIM: Soon as I came in the door?

LAURA: When I heard your name I thought it was probably you. I knew that Tom used to know you a little in high school. So when you came in the door—Well, then I was—sure.

JIM: Why didn't you say something, then?

LAURA (*breathlessly*): I didn't know what to say, I was—too surprised!

JIM: For goodness' sakes! You know, this sure is funny!

LAURA: Yes! Yes, isn't it, though . . .

JIM: Didn't we have a class in something together?

LAURA: Yes, we did.

JIM: What class was that?

LAURA: It was—singing—Chorus!

JIM: Aw!

LAURA: I sat across the aisle from you in the Aud.

JIM: Aw.

LAURA: Mondays, Wednesdays and Fridays.

JIM: Now I remember—you always came in late.

LAURA: Yes, it was so hard for me, getting upstairs. I had that brace on my leg—it clumped so loud!

JIM: I never heard any clumping.

LAURA (*wincing at the recollection*): To me it sounded like—thunder!

JIM: Well, well, well. I never even noticed.

LAURA: And everybody was seated before I came in. I had to walk in front of all those people. My seat was in the back row. I had to go clumping all the way up the aisle with everyone watching!

JIM: You shouldn't have been self-conscious.

LAURA: I know, but I was. It was always such a relief when the singing started.

JIM: Aw, yes. I've placed you now! I used to call you Blue Roses. How was it that I got started calling you that?

LAURA: I was out of school a little while with pleurosis. When I came back you asked me what was the matter. I said I had pleurosis—you thought I said Blue Roses. That's what you always called me after that!

JIM: I hope you didn't mind.

LAURA: Oh, no—I liked it. You see, I wasn't acquainted with many—people. . . .

JIM: As I remember you sort of stuck by yourself.

LAURA: I—I—never had much luck at—making friends.

JIM: I don't see why you wouldn't.

LAURA: Well, I—started out badly.

JIM: You mean being—

LAURA: Yes, it sort of—stood between me—

JIM: You shouldn't have let it!

LAURA: I know but it did, and—

JIM: You were shy with people!

LAURA: I tried not to be but never could—

JIM: Overcome it?

LAURA: No, I—I never could!

JIM: I guess being shy is something you have to work out of kind of gradually.

LAURA (*sorrowfully*): Yes—I guess it—

JIM: Takes time!

LAURA: Yes.

JIM: People are not so dreadful when you know them. That's what you have to remember! And everybody has problems, not just you, but practically everybody has got some problems. You think of yourself as having the only problems, as being the only one who is disappointed. But just look around you and you will see lots of people as disappointed as you are. For instance, I hoped when I was going to high school that I would be further along at this time, six years later, than I am now—You remember that wonderful write-up I had in *The Torch?*

LAURA: Yes! (*She rises and crosses to table.*)

JIM: It said I was bound to succeed in anything I went into! (*Laura returns with the annual.*) Holy Jeez! *The Torch!* (*He accepts it reverently. They smiled across it with mutual wonder. Laura crouches beside him and they begin to turn through it. Laura's shyness is dissolving in his warmth.*)

LAURA: Here you are in *Pirates of Penzance!*

JIM (*wistfully*): I sang the baritone lead in that operatta.

LAURA (*rapidly*): So—*beautifully!*

JIM (*protesting*): Aw—

LAURA: Yes, yes—beautifully—beautifully!

JIM: You heard me?

LAURA: All three times!

JIM: No!

LAURA: Yes!

JIM: All three performances?

LAURA (*looking down*): Yes.

JIM: Why?

LAURA: I—wanted to ask you to—autograph my program.

JIM: Why didn't you ask me to?

LAURA: You were always surrounded by your own friends so much that I never had a chance to.

JIM: You should have just—

LAURA: Well, I—thought you might think I was—

JIM: Thought I might think you was—what?

LAURA: Oh—

JIM (*with reflective relish*): I was beleaguered by females in those days.

LAURA: You were terribly popular!

JIM: Yeah—

LAURA: You had such a—friendly way—

JIM: I was spoiled in high school.

LAURA: Everybody—liked you!

JIM: Including you?

LAURA: I—yes, I—I did, too—(*She gently closes the book in her lap.*)

JIM: Well, well, well!—Give me that program, Laura. (*She hands it to him. He signs it with a flourish.*) There you are—better late then never!

LAURA: Oh, I—what a—surprise!

JIM: My signature isn't worth very much right now. But some day— maybe—it will increase in value! Being disappointed is one thing and being discouraged is something else. I am disappointed but I'm not discouraged. I'm twenty-three years old. How old are you?

LAURA: I'll be twenty-four in June.

JIM: That's not old age!

LAURA: No, but—

JIM: You finished high school?

LAURA (*with difficulty*): I didn't go back.

JIM: You mean you dropped out?

LAURA: I made bad grades in my final examinations. (*She rises and replaces the book and the program. Her voice strained.*) How is— Emily Meisenbach getting along?

JIM: Oh, that kraut-head!

LAURA: Why do you call her that?

JIM: That's what she was.

LAURA: You're not still—going with her?

JIM: I never see her.

LAURA: It said in the Personal Section that you were—engaged!

JIM: I know, but I wasn't impressed by that—propaganda!

LAURA: It wasn't—the truth?

JIM: Only in Emily's optimistic opinion!

LAURA: Oh—

(Legend: "What Have You Done Since High School?")

(*Jim lights a cigarette and leans indolently back on his elbows smiling at Laura with a warmth and charm which light her inwardly with altar candles. She remains by the table and turns in her hands a piece of glass to cover her tumult.*)

JIM (*after several reflective puffs on a cigarette*): What have you done since high school? (*She seems not to hear him.*) Huh? (*Laura looks up.*) I said what have you done since high school, Laura?

LAURA: Nothing much.

JIM: You must have been doing something these six long years.

LAURA: Yes.

JIM: Well, then, such as what?

LAURA: I took a business course at business college—

JIM: How did that work out?

LAURA: Well, not very—well—I had to drop out, it gave me—indigestion—

(*Jim laughs gently.*)

JIM: What are you doing now?

LAURA: I don't do anything—much. Oh, please don't think I sit around doing nothing! My glass collection takes up a good deal of my time. Glass is something you have to take good care of.

JIM: What did you say—about glass?

LAURA: Collection I said—I have one—(*She clears her throat and turns away again, acutely shy.*)

JIM (*abruptly*): You know what I judge to be the trouble with you? Inferiority complex! Know what that is? That's what they call it when someone low-rates himself? I understand it because I had it, too. Although my case was not so aggravated as yours seems to be. I had it until I took up public speaking, developed my voice, and learned that I had an aptitude for science. Before that time I never thought of myself as being outstanding in any way whatsoever! Now I've never made a regular study of it, but I have a friend who says I can analyze people better than doctors that make a profession of it. I don't claim that to be necessarily true, but I can sure guess a person's psychology, Laura. (*Takes out his gum.*) Excuse me, Laura. I always take it out when the flavor is gone. I'll use this scrap of paper to wrap it in. I know how it is to get it stuck on a shoe. Yep—that's what I judge to be your principal trouble. A lack of confidence in yourself as a person. You don't have the proper amount of faith in yourself. I'm basing that fact on a number of your remarks and also on certain observations I've made. For instance that clumping you thought was so awful in high school. You say that you even dreaded to walk into class. You see what you did? You dropped out of school, you gave up an education because of a clump, which as far as I know was practically nonexistent! A little physical defect is what you have? Hardly noticeable even! Magnified thousands of times by imagination! You know what my strong advice to you is? Think of yourself as superior in some way!

LAURA: In what way would I think?

JIM: Why, man alive, Laura! Just look about you a little. What do you see? A world full of common people! All of 'em born and all of 'em going to die! Which of them has one-tenth of your good points! Or mine! Or anyone else's, as far as that goes—Gosh! Everybody excels in some one thing. Some in many! (*Unconsciously glances at himself in the mirror.*) All you've got to do is discover in what! Take me, for instance. (*He adjusts his tie at the mirror.*) My interest happens to lie in electrodynamics. I'm taking a course in radio engineering at night school, Laura, on top of a fairly responsible job at the warehouse. I'm taking that course and studying public speaking.

LAURA: Ohhhh.

JIM: Because I believe in the future of television! (*Turning back to her.*) I wish to be ready to go up right along with it. Therefore I'm planning to get in on the ground floor. In fact, I've already made the right connections and all that remains is for the industry itself to get under way! Full steam—(*His eyes are starry.*) Knowledge—Zzzzp! Money—Zzzzzp! Power! That's the cycle democracy is built on! (*His attitude is convincingly dynamic. Laura stares at him, even her shyness eclipsed in her absolute wonder. He suddenly grins.*) I guess you think I think a lot of myself!

LAURA: No—o-o-o, I—

JIM: Now how about you? Isn't there something you take more interest in than anything else?

LAURA: Well, I do—as I said—have my—glass collection—

(A peal of girlish laughter from the kitchen.)

JIM: I'm not right sure I know what you're talking about. What kind of glass is it?

LAURA: Little articles of it, they're ornaments mostly! Most of them are little animals made out of glass, the tiniest little animals in the world. Mother calls them a glass menagerie! Here's an example of one, if you'd like to see it! This one is one of the oldest. It's nearly thirteen. (*He stretches out his hand.*) (*Music: "The Glass Menagerie."*) Oh, be careful—if you breathe, it breaks!

JIM: I'd better not take it. I'm pretty clumsy with things.

LAURA: Go on. I trust you with him! (*Places it in his palm.*) There now—you're holding him gently! Hold him over the light, he loves the light! You see how the light shines through him?

JIM: It sure does shine!

LAURA: I shouldn't be partial, but he is my favorite one.

JIM: What kind of thing is this one supposed to be?

LAURA: Haven't you noticed the single horn on his forehead?

JIM: A unicorn, huh?

LAURA: Mmm-hmmm!

JIM: Unicorns, aren't they extinct in the modern world?

LAURA: I know!

JIM: Poor little fellow, he must feel sort of lonesome.

LAURA (*smiling*):   Well, if he does he doesn't complain about it. He stays on a shelf with some horses that don't have horns and all of them seem to get along nicely together.

JIM: How do you know?

LAURA (*lightly*):   I haven't heard any arguments among them!

JIM (*grinning*):   No arguments, huh? Well, that's a pretty good sign! Where shall I set him?

LAURA: Put him on the table. They all like a change of scenery once in a while!

JIM (*stretching*):   Well, well, well, well—Look how big my shadow is when I stretch!

LAURA: Oh, oh, yes—it stretches across the ceiling!

JIM (*crossing to door*):   I think it's stopped raining. (*Opens fire-escape door*) Where does the music come from?

LAURA: From the Paradise Dance Hall across the alley.

JIM: How about cutting the rug a little, Miss Wingfield?

LAURA: Oh, I—

JIM: Or is your program filled up? Let me have a look at it. (*Grasps imaginary card.*) Why, every dance is taken! I'll just have to scratch some out. (*Waltz Music: "La Golondrina."*) Ahhh, a waltz! (*He executes some sweeping turns by himself then holds his arms toward Laura.*)

LAURA (*breathlessly*):   I—can't dance!

JIM: There you go, that inferiority stuff!

LAURA: I've never danced in my life!

JIM: Come on, try!

LAURA: Oh, but I'd step on you!

JIM: I'm not made out of glass.

LAURA: How—how—how do we start?

JIM: Just leave it to me. You hold your arms out a little.

LAURA: Like this?

JIM: A little bit higher. Right. Now don't tighten up, that's the main thing about it—relax.

LAURA (*laughing breathlessly*):   It's hard not to.

JIM: Okay.

LAURA: I'm afraid you can't budge me.

JIM: What do you bet I can't? (*He swings her into motion.*)

LAURA: Goodness, yes, you can!

JIM: Let ourself go, now, Laura, just let yourself go.

LAURA: I'm—

JIM: Come on!

LAURA: Trying!

JIM: Not so stiff—Easy does it!

LAURA: I know but I'm—

JIM: Loosen th' backbone! There now, that's a lot better.

LAURA: Am I?

JIM: Lots, lots better! (*He moves her about the room in a clumsy waltz.*)

LAURA: Oh, my!

JIM: Ha-ha!

LAURA: Goodness, yes you can!

JIM: Ha-ha-ha! (*They suddenly bump into the table, Jim stops.*) What did we hit on?

LAURA: Table.

JIM: Did something fall of it? I think—

LAURA: Yes.

JIM: I hope that it wasn't the little glass horse with the horn!

LAURA: Yes.

JIM: Aw, aw, aw. Is it broken?

LAURA: Now it is just like all the other horses.

JIM: It's lost its—

LAURA: Horn! It doesn't matter. Maybe it's a blessing in disguise.

JIM: You'll never forgive me. I bet that was your favorite piece of glass.

LAURA: I don't have favorites much. It's no tragedy, Freckles. Glass breaks so easily. No matter how careful you are. The traffic jars the shelves and things fall off them.

JIM: Still I'm awfully sorry that I was the cause.

LAURA (*smiling*): I'll just imagine he had an operation. The horn was removed to make him feel less—freakish! (*They both laugh.*) Now he will feel more at home with the other horses, the ones that don't have horns . . .

JIM: Ha-ha, that's very funny! (*Suddenly serious.*) I'm glad to see that you have a sense of humor. You know—you're—well—very differ-ent! Surprisingly different from anyone else I know! (*His voice be-comes soft and hesitant with a genuine feeling.*) Do you mind me telling you that? (*Laura is abashed beyond speech.*) You make me feel sort of—I don't know how to put it! I'm usually pretty good at expressing things, but—This is something that I don't know how to say! (*Laura touches her throat, clears it—turns the broken unicorn in her hands.*) (*Even softer.*) Has anyone ever told you that you were pretty? (*Pause: Music.*) (*Laura looks up slowly, with wonder, and shakes her head.*) Well, you are! In a very different way from anyone else. And all the nicer because of the difference, too. (*His voice becomes low and husky. Laura turns away, nearly faint with the novelty of her emotions.*) I wish that you were my sister. I'd teach you to have some confidence in yourself. The different people are not like other people, but being different is nothing to be ashamed of. Because other people are not such wonderful people. They're one hundred times one thousand. You're one times one! They walk all over the earth. You just stay here. They're common as—weeds, but—you—well, you're—Blue Roses!

(Image on Screen: Blue Roses.)

(Music Changes.)

LAURA: But blue is wrong for—roses . . .

JIM: It's right for you—You're—pretty!

LAURA: In what respect am I pretty?

JIM: In all respects—believe me! Your eyes—your hair—are pretty! Your hands are pretty! (*He catches hold of her hand.*) You think I'm making this up because I'm invited to dinner and have to be nice. Oh, I could do that! I could put on an act for you, Laura, and say lots of things without being very sincere. But this time I am. I'm talking to you sincerely. I happened to notice you had this inferiority complex that keeps you from feeling comfortable with people. Somebody needs to build your confidence up and make you proud instead of shy and turning away and—blushing—Somebody ought to—ought to—*kiss* you, Laura!

(*His hand slips slowly up her arm to her shoulder.*) (*Music Swells Tumultuously.*) (*He suddenly turns her about and kisses her on the lips. When he releases her Laura sinks on the sofa with a bright, dazed look. Jim backs away and fishes in his pocket for a cigarette.*) (*Legend on Screen: "Souvenir."*) Stumble-john! (*He lights the cigarette, avoiding her look. There is a peal of girlish laughter from Amanda in the kitchen. Laura slowly raises and opens her hand. It still contains the little broken glass animal. She looks at it with a tender, bewildered expression.) Stumble-john! I shouldn't have done that—That was way off the beam. You don't smoke, do you? (She looks up, smiling, not hearing the question. He sits besides her a little gingerly. She looks at him speechlessly—waiting. He coughs decorously and moves a little farther aside as he considers the situation and senses her feelings, dimly, with perturbation. Gently.) Would you—care for a—mint? (She doesn't seem to hear him but her look grows brighter even.) Peppermint—Life Saver? My pocket's a regular drug store—wherever I go . . . (He pops a mint in his mouth. Then gulps and decides to make a clean breast of it. He speaks slowly and gingerly.) Laura, you know, if I had a sister like you, I'd do the same thing as Tom. I'd bring out fellows—introduce her to them. The right type of boys of a type to—appreciate her. Only—well—he made a mistake about me. Maybe I've got no call to be saying this. This may not have been the idea in having me over. But what if it was? There's nothing wrong about that. The only trouble is that in my case—I'm not in a situation to—do the right thing. I can't take down your number and say I'll phone. I can't call up next week and—ask for a date. I thought I had better explain the situation in case you misunderstood it and—hurt your feelings. . . . (Pause. Slowly, very slowly, Laura's look changes, her eyes returning slowly from his to the ornament in her palm.)*

(Amanda utters another gay laugh in the kitchen.)

LAURA *(faintly)*:   You—won't—call again?

JIM: No, Laura. I can't. *(He rises from the sofa.)* As I was just explaining, I've—got strings on me, Laura, I've—been going steady! I go out all the time with a girl named Betty. She's a home-girl like you, and Catholic, and Irish, and in a great many ways we—get along fine. I met her last summer on a moonlight boat trip up the river to Alton, on the Majestic. Well—right away from the start it was—love! *(Legend: "Love!")* *(Laura sways slightly forward and grips the arm of the sofa. He fails to notice, now enrapt in his own comfortable being.)* Being in love has made a new man of me! *(Leaning stiffly forward, clutching the arm of the sofa, Laura struggles visibly with her storm. But Jim is oblivious, she is a long way off.)* The power of love is really pretty tremendous! Love is something that— changes the whole world, Laura! *(The storm abates a little and*

Laura leans back. He notices her again.) It happened that Betty's aunt took sick, she got a wire and had to go to Centralia. So Tom—when he asked me to dinner—I naturally just accepted the invitation, not knowing that you—that he—that I—(*He stops awkwardly.*) Huh—I'm a stumble-john! (*He flops back on the sofa. The holy candles in the altar of Laura's face have been snuffed out! There is a look of almost infinite desolation. Jim glances at her uneasily.*) I wish that you would—say something. (*She bites her lip which was trembling and then bravely smiles. She opens her hand again on the broken glass ornament. Then she gently takes his hand and raises it level to her own. She carefully places the unicorm in the palm of his hand, then pushes his fingers closed upon it.*) What are you—doing that for? You want me to have him?—Laura? (*She nods.*) What for?

LAURA: A—souvenir . . .

(*She rises unsteadily and crouches beside the victrola to wind it up.*)

(Legend on Screen: "Things Have a Way of Turning Out So Badly.")

(Or Image: "Gentleman Caller Waving Good-Bye—Gaily.")

(*At this moment Amanda rushes brightly back in the front room. She bears a pitcher of fruit punch in an old-fashioned cut-glass pitcher and a plate of macaroons. The plate has a gold border and poppies painted on it.*)

AMANDA: Well, well, well! Isn't the air delightful after the shower? I've made you children a little liquid refreshment. (*Turns gaily to the gentleman caller.*) Jim, do you know that song about lemonade?
   "Lemonade, lemonade
   Made in the shade and stirred with a spade—
   Good enough for any old maid!"

JIM (*uneasily*): Ha-ha! No—I never heard it.

AMANDA: Why, Laura! You look so serious!

JIM: We were having a serious conversation.

AMANDA: Good! Now you're better acquainted!

JIM (*uncertainly*): Ha-ha! Yes.

AMANDA: You modern young people are much more serious-minded than my generation. I was so gay as a girl!

JIM: You haven't changed, Mrs. Wingfield.

AMANDA: Tonight I'm rejuvenated! The gaiety of the occasion, Mr. O'Connor! (*She tosses her head with a peal of laughter. Spills lemonade.*) Oooo! I'm baptizing myself!

JIM: Here—let me—

AMANDA (*setting the pitcher down.*):   There now. I discovered we had some maraschino cherries. I dumped them in, juice and all!

JIM: You shouldn't have gone to that trouble, Mrs. Wingfield.

AMANDA: Trouble, trouble? Why it was loads of fun! Didn't you hear me cutting up in the kitchen? I bet your ears were burning! I told Tom how outdone with him I was for keeping you to himself so long a time! He should have brought you over much, much sooner! Well, now that you've found your way, I want you to be a very frequent caller! Not just occasional but all the time. Oh, we're going to have a lot of gay times together! I see them coming! Mmm, just breathe that air! So fresh, and the moon's so pretty! I'll skip back out—I know where my place is when young folks are having a—serious conversation!

JIM: Oh, don't go out, Mrs. Wingfield. The fact of the matter is I've got to be going.

AMANDA: Going, now? You're joking! Why, it's only the shank of the evening, Mr. O'Connor.

JIM: Well, you now how it is.

AMANDA: You mean you're a young workingman and have to keep workingmen's hours. We'll let you off early tonight. But only on the condition that next time you stay later. What's the best night for you? Isn't Saturday night the best night for you workingmen?

JIM: I have a couple of time-clocks to punch, Mrs. Wingfield. One at morning, another one at night.

AMANDA: My, but you are ambitious! You work at night, too?

JIM: No, Ma'am, not work but—Betty! (*He crosses deliberately to pick up his hat. The band at the Paradise Dance Hall goes into a tender waltz.*)

AMANDA: Betty? Betty? Who's—Betty! (*There is an ominous cracking sound in the sky.*)

JIM: Oh, just a girl. The girl I go steady with! (*He smiles charmingly. The sky falls.*)

(Legend: "The Sky Falls")

AMANDA (*a long-drawn exhalation*):   Ohhhh . . . Is it a serious romance, Mr. O'Connor?

JIM: We're going to be married the second Sunday in June.

AMANDA: Ohhhh—how nice! Tom didn't mention that you were engaged to be married.

JIM: The cat's not out of the bag at the warehouse yet. You know how they are. They call you Romeo and stuff like that. (*He stops at the oval mirror to put on his hat. He carefully shapes the brim and the crown to give a discreetly dashing effect.*) It's been a wonderful evening, Mrs. Wingfield. I guess this is what they mean by Southern hospitality.

AMANDA: It really wasn't anything at all.

JIM: I hope it don't seem like I'm rushing off. But I promised Betty I'd pick her up at the Wabash depot, an' by the time I get my jalopy down there her train'll be in. Some women are pretty upset if you keep 'em waiting.

AMANDA: Yes, I know—The tyranny of women! (*Extends her hand.*) Goodbye, Mr. O'Connor. I wish you luck—and happiness—and success! All three of them, and so does Laura!—Don't you, Laura?

LAURA: Yes!

JIM (*taking her hand*):   Goodbye, Laura. I'm certainly going to treasure that souvenir. And don't you forget the good advice I gave you. (*Raises his voice to a cheery shout.*) So long, Shakespeare! Thanks again, ladies—Good night!

(*He grins and ducks jauntily out. Still bravely grimacing, Amanda closes the door on the gentleman caller. Then she turns back to the room with a puzzled expression. She and Laura don't dare to face each other. Laura crouches beside the victrola to wind it.*)

AMANDA (*faintly*):   Things have a way of turning out so badly. I don't believe that I would play the victrola. Well, well—well—Our gentleman caller was engaged to be married! Tom!

TOM (*from back*):   Yes, Mother?

AMANDA: Come in here a minute. I want to tell you something awfully funny.

TOM (*enters with macaroon and a glass of the lemonade*):   Has the gentleman caller gotten away already?

AMANDA: The gentleman caller has made an early departure. What a wonderful joke you played on us!

TOM: How do you mean?

AMANDA: You didn't mention that he was engaged to be married.

TOM: Jim? Engaged?

AMANDA: That's what he just informed us.

TOM: I'll be jiggered! I didn't know about that.

AMANDA: That seems very peculiar.

TOM: What's peculiar about it?

AMANDA: Didn't you call him your best friend down at the warehouse?

TOM: He is, but how did I know?

AMANDA: It seems extremely peculiar that you wouldn't know your best friend was going to be married!

TOM: The warehouse is where I work, not where I know things about people!

AMANDA: You don't know things anywhere! You live in a dream; you manufacture illusions! (*He crosses to door.*) Where are you going?

TOM: I'm going to the movies.

AMANDA: That's right, now that you've had us make such fools of ourselves. The effort, the preparations, all the expense! The new floor lamp, the rug, the clothes for Laura! All for what? To entertain some other girl's fiancé! Go to the movies, go! Don't think about us, a mother deserted, an unmarried sister who's crippled and has no job! Don't let anything interfere with your selfish pleasure! Just go, go, go—to the movies!

TOM: All right, I will! The more you shout about my selfishness to me the quicker I'll go, and I won't go to the movies!

AMANDA: Go, then! Then go to the moon—you selfish dreamer!

Tom smashes his glass on the floor. He plunges out on the fire-escape, slamming the door. Laura screams—cut by door.

Dance-hall music up. Tom goes to the rail and grips it desperately, lifting his face in the chill white moonlight penetrating the narrow abyss of the alley.

(Legend on Screen: "And So Good-Bye . . .")

(Tom's closing speech is timed with the interior pantomime. The interior scene is played as though viewed through sound-proof glass.

Amanda appears to be making a comforting speech to Laura who is huddled upon the sofa. Now that we cannot hear the mother's speech, her silliness is gone and she has dignity and tragic beauty. Laura's dark hair hides her face until at the end of the speech she lifts it to smile at her mother. Amanda's gestures are slow and graceful, almost dancelike, as she comforts her daughter. At the end of her speech she glances a moment at the father's picture—then withdraws through the portieres. At close of Tom's speech, Laura blows out the candles, ending the play.)

TOM: I didn't go to the moon, I went much further—for time is the longest distance between two places—Not long after that I was fired for writing a poem on the lid of a shoe-box. I left Saint Louis. I descended the steps of this fire-escape for a last time and followed, from then on, in my father's footsteps, attempting to find in motion what was lost in space—I traveled around a great deal. The cities swept about me like dead leaves, leaves that were brightly colored but torn away from the branches. I would have stopped, but I was pursued by something. It always came upon me unawares, taking me altogether by surprise. Perhaps it was a familiar bit of music. Perhaps it was only a piece of transparent glass—Perhaps I am walking along a street at night, in some strange city, before I have found companions. I pass the lighted window of a shop where perfume is sold. The window is filled with pieces of colored glass, tiny transparent bottles in delicate colors, like bits of a shattered rainbow. Then all at once my sister touches my shoulder. I turn around and look into her eyes . . . Oh, Laura, Laura, I tried to leave you behind me, but I am more faithful than I intended to be! I reach for a cigarette, I cross the street, I run into the movies or a bar, I buy a drink, I speak to the nearest stranger—anything that can blow your candles out! (*Laura bends over the candles.*)—for nowadays the world is lit by lightning! Blow out your candles, Laura—and so goodbye . . .

(*She blows the candles out.*)

(The Scene Dissolves.)

—*1944*

Arthur Miller (b. 1915) *gained a reputation as a major American dramatist with his second play, and continues to be productive in his mid 80s. Miller was born in Harlem, the son of prosperous Jewish immigrants who suffered badly during the depression. He studied drama at the University of Michigan and was for a time employed by the Federal Theatre Project, a Roosevelt-era government program dedicated to bringing drama with social themes to audiences in areas outside New York. His first success was* All My Sons *(1947), an Ibsenesque problem play (Miller later adapted Ibsen's* An Enemy of the People *for the New York stage) about a manufacturer who profited during World War II by knowingly supplying defective parts which caused airplanes to crash.* All My Sons, *following closely on the heels of investigations of wartime profiteering, easily found appreciative audiences.* Death of a Salesman *(1949) won Miller a Pulitzer Prize. Originally a short story based to some degree on one of Miller's uncles,* Death of a Salesman *evolved into its final form over many years. When Miller finally sat down at the typewriter to write the play, he said, "All I had was the first two lines and a death." During the height of the play's success, Miller wrote a famous essay titled "Tragedy and the Common Man," in which he dismisses the ancient "rule" that true tragedy can concern only the lives and fates of the famous. "I believe," he said, "that the common man is an apt a subject for tragedy in its highest sense as knigs were. . . . If the exaltation of tragic action were truly a property of the high-bred character alone, it is inconceivable that the mass of mankind should cherish tragedy above all other forms, let alone be capable of understanding it." Miller's fame was further increased by* The Crucible *(1953), a play about the Salem witch trials that had obvious contemporary political overtones, drawing on Miller's own McCarthy-era investigations by the House Un-Amerian Activities Committee into his past political affiliations. Miller risked a jail term for his refusal to cooperate with the committee. His marriage to Marilyn Monroe, which is in part the subject of* After the Fall *(1964), ended unhappily shortly after Miller completed work on the screenplay of* The Misfits, *which proved to be her final film. Other important plays include* A View from the Bridge *(1955), which has been revived several times on Broadway and also exists in an operatic version;* Incident at Vichy *(1964), a play about the Holocaust;* The Price *(1968);* Broken Glass, *another play about anti-Semetism; and* Ride Down Mount Morgan *(1998), which starred Patrick Stewart in its Broadway production. Miller's autobiography,* Timebends, *was published in 1987. In it he proudly recounts his experiences in 1983 directing a Chinese production of* Death of a Salesman *in Beijing, the first contemporary American play produced in China. Like Tennessee Williams's plays, Miller's are frequently revived, the most recent being the award-wining production of* Death of a Salesman *in 1999, the final performance of which was televised on Showtime in 2000.*

Arthur Miller

Death of a Salesman

CHARACTERS

Willy Loman
Linda
Biff
Happy
Bernard
The Woman
Charley
Uncle Ben
Howard Wagner
Jenny
Stanley
Miss Forsythe
Letta

Scene: The action takes place in Willy Loman's house and yard and in various places he visits in the New York and Boston of today.

ACT 1

Scene: A melody is heard, played upon a flute. It is small and fine, telling of grass and trees and the horizon. The curtain rises.

    Before us is the Salesman's house. We are aware of towering, angular shapes behind it, surrounding it on all sides. Only the blue light of the sky falls upon the house and forestage; the surrounding area shows an angry glow of orange. As more light appears, we see a solid vault of apartment houses around the small, fragile-seeming home. An air of the dream clings to the place, a dream rising out of reality. The kitchen at center seems actual enough, for there is a kitchen table with three chairs, and a refrigerator. But no other fixtures are seen. At the back of the kitchen there is a draped entrance, which leads to the living room. To the right of the kitchen, on a level raised two feet, is a bedroom furnished only with a brass bedstead and a straight chair. On a shelf over the bed a silver athletic trophy stands. A window opens onto the apartment house at the side.

Behind the kitchen, on a level raised six and a half feet, is the boys' bedroom, at present barely visible. Two beds are dimly seen, and at the back of the room a dormer window. (This bedroom is above the unseen living room.) At the left a stairway curves up to it from the kitchen.

The entire setting is wholly or, in some places, partially transparent. The roof-line of the house is one-dimensional; under and over it we see the apartment buildings. Before the house lies an apron, curving beyond the forestage into the orchestra. This forward area serves as the back yard as well as the locale of all Willy's imaginings and of his city scenes. Whenever the action is in the present the actors observe the imaginary wall-lines, entering the house only through its door at the left. But in the scenes of the past these boundaries are broken, and characters enter or leave a room by stepping "through" a wall onto the forestage.

From the right, Willy Loman, the Salesman, enters, carrying two large sample cases. The flute plays on. He hears but is not aware of it. He is past sixty years of age, dressed quietly. Even as he crosses the stage to the doorway of the house, his exhaustion is apparent. He unlocks the door, comes into the kitchen, and thankfully lets his burden down, feeling the soreness of his palms. A word-sigh escapes his lips—it might be "Oh, boy, oh, boy." He closes the door, then carries his cases out into the living room, through the draped kitchen doorway.

Linda, his wife, has stirred in her bed at the right. She gets out and puts on a robe, listening. Most often jovial, she has developed an iron repression of her exceptions to Willy's behavior—she more than loves him, she admires him, as though his mercurial nature, his temper, his massive dreams and little cruelties, served her only as sharp reminders of the turbulent longings within him, longings which she shares but lacks the temperament to utter and follow to their end.

LINDA *[hearing Willy outside the bedroom, calls with some trepidation]:* Willy!

WILLY: It's all right. I came back.

LINDA: Why? What happened? (*Slight pause.*) Did something happen, Willy?

WILLY: No, nothing happened.

LINDA: You didn't smash the car, did you?

WILLY (*with casual irritation*): I said nothing happened. Didn't you hear me?

LINDA: Don't you feel well?

WILLY: I'm tired to the death. (*The flute has faded away. He sits on the bed beside her, a little numb.*) I couldn't make it. I just couldn't make it, Linda.

LINDA (*very carefully, delicately*): Where were you all day? You look terrible.

WILLY: I got as far as a little above Yonkers. I stopped for a cup of coffee. Maybe it was the coffee.

LINDA: What?

WILLY (*after a pause*): I suddenly couldn't drive any more. The car kept going off onto the shoulder, y'know?

LINDA (*helpfully*): Oh. Maybe it was the steering again. I don't think Angelo knows the Studebaker.

WILLY: No, it's me, it's me. Suddenly I realize I'm goin' sixty miles an hour and I don't remember the last five minutes. I'm—I can't seem to—keep my mind to it.

LINDA: Maybe it's your glasses. You never went for your new glasses.

WILLY: No, I see everything. I came back ten miles an hour. It took me nearly four hours from Yonkers.

LINDA (*resigned*): Well, you'll just have to take a rest, Willy, you can't continue this way.

WILLY: I just got back from Florida.

LINDA: But you didn't rest your mind. Your mind is overactive, and the mind is what counts, dear.

WILLY: I'll start out in the morning. Maybe I'll feel better in the morning. (*She is taking off his shoes.*) These goddam arch supports are killing me.

LINDA: Take an aspirin. Should I get you an aspirin? It'll soothe you.

WILLY (*with wonder*): I was driving along, you understand? And I was fine. I was even observing the scenery. You can imagine, me looking at scenery, on the road every week of my life. But it's so beautiful up there, Linda, the trees are so thick, and the sun is warm. I opened the windshield and just let the warm air bathe over me. And then all of a sudden I'm goin' off the road! I'm tellin' ya, I absolutely forgot I was driving. If I'd've gone the other way over the white line I might've killed somebody. So I went on again—and five minutes later I'm dreamin' again, and I nearly . . . (*He presses two fingers against his eyes.*) I have such thoughts, I have such strange thoughts.

LINDA: Willy, dear. Talk to them again. There's no reason why you can't work in New York.

WILLY: They don't need me in New York. I'm the New England man. I'm vital in New England.

LINDA: But you're sixty years old. They can't expect you to keep traveling every week.

WILLY: I'll have to send a wire to Portland. I'm supposed to see Brown and Morrison tomorrow morning at ten o'clock to show the line. Goddammit, I could sell them! (*He starts putting on his jacket.*)

LINDA (*taking the jacket from him*): Why don't you go down to the place tomorrow and tell Howard you've simply got to work in New York? You're too accommodating, dear.

WILLY: If old man Wagner was alive I'd a been in charge of New York now! That man was a prince, he was a masterful man. But that boy of his, that Howard, he don't appreciate. When I went north the first time, the Wagner Company didn't know where New England was!

LINDA: Why don't you tell those things to Howard, dear?

WILLY (*encouraged*): I will, I definitely will. Is there any cheese?

LINDA: I'll make you a sandwich.

WILLY: No, go to sleep. I'll take some milk. I'll be up right away. The boys in?

LINDA: They're sleeping. Happy took Biff on a date tonight.

WILLY (*interested*): That so?

LINDA: It was so nice to see them shaving together, one behind the other, in the bathroom. And going out together. You notice? The whole house smells of shaving lotion.

WILLY: Figure it out. Work a lifetime to pay off a house. You finally own it, and there's nobody to live in it.

LINDA: Well, dear, life is a casting off. It's always that way.

WILLY: No, no, some people—some people accomplish something. Did Biff say anything after I went this morning?

LINDA: You shouldn't have criticized him, Willy, especially after he just got off the train. You mustn't lose your temper with him.

WILLY: When the hell did I lose my temper? I simply asked him if he was making any money. Is that a criticism?

LINDA: But, dear, how could he make any money?

WILLY (*worried and angered*): There's such an undercurrent in him. He became a moody man. Did he apologize when I left this morning?

LINDA: He was crestfallen, Willy. You know how he admires you. I think if he finds himself, then you'll both be happier and not fight any more.

WILLY: How can he find himself on a farm? Is that a life? A farm hand? In the beginning, when he was young, I thought, well, a young man, it's good for him to tramp around, take a lot of different jobs. But it's more than ten years now and he has yet to make thirty-five dollars a week!

LINDA: He's finding himself, Willy.

WILLY: Not finding yourself at the age of thirty-four is a disgrace!

LINDA: Shh!

WILLY: The trouble is he's lazy, goddammit!

LINDA: Willy, please!

WILLY: Biff is a lazy bum!

LINDA: They're sleeping. Get something to eat. Go on down.

WILLY: Why did he come home? I would like to know what brought him home.

LINDA: I don't know. I think he's still lost, Willy. I think he's very lost.

WILLY: Biff Loman is lost. In the greatest country in the world a young man with such—personal attractiveness, gets lost. And such a hard worker. There's one thing about Biff—he's not lazy.

LINDA: Never.

WILLY (*with pity and resolve*): I'll see him in the morning; I'll have a nice talk with him. I'll get him a job selling. He could be big in no time. My God! Remember how they used to follow him around in high school? When he smiled at one of them their faces lit up. When he walked down the street . . . (*He loses himself in reminiscences.*)

LINDA (*trying to bring him out of it*): Willy, dear, I got a new kind of American-type cheese today. It's whipped.

WILLY: Why do you get American when I like Swiss?

LINDA: I just thought you'd like a change . . .

WILLY: I don't want a change! I want Swiss cheese. Why am I always being contradicted?

LINDA (*with a covering laugh*): I thought it would be a surprise.

WILLY: Why don't you open a window in here, for God's sake?

LINDA (*with infinite patience*): They're all open, dear.

WILLY: The way they boxed us in here. Bricks and windows, windows and bricks.

LINDA: We should've bought the land next door.

WILLY: The street is lined with cars. There's not a breath of fresh air in the neighborhood. The grass don't grow any more, you can't raise a carrot in the back yard. They should've had a law against apartment houses. Remember those two beautiful elm trees out there? When I and Biff hung the swing between them?

LINDA: Yeah, like being a million miles from the city.

WILLY: They should've arrested the builder for cutting those down. They massacred the neighborhood. (*Lost.*) More and more I think of those days, Linda. This time of year it was lilac and wisteria. And then the peonies would come out, and the daffodils. What fragrance in this room!

LINDA: Well, after all, people had to move somewhere.

WILLY: No, there's more people now.

LINDA: I don't think there's more people. I think . . .

WILLY: There's more people! That's what's ruining this country! Population is getting out of control. The competition is maddening! Smell the stink from that apartment house! And another one on the other side . . . How can they whip cheese?

On Willy's last line, Biff and Happy raise themselves up in their beds, listening.

LINDA: Go down, try it. And be quiet.

WILLY (*turning to Linda, guiltily*): You're not worried about me, are you, sweetheart?

BIFF: What's the matter?

HAPPY: Listen!

LINDA: You've got too much on the ball to worry about.

WILLY: You're my foundation and my support, Linda.

LINDA: Just try to relax, dear. You make mountains out of molehills.

WILLY: I won't fight with him any more. If he wants to go back to Texas, let him go.

LINDA: He'll find his way.

WILLY: Sure. Certain men just don't get started till later in life. Like Thomas Edison, I think. Or B. F. Goodrich. One of them was deaf. (*He starts for the bedroom doorway.*) I'll put my money on Biff.

LINDA: And Willy—if it's warm Sunday we'll drive in the country. And we'll open the windshield, and take lunch.

WILLY: No, the windshields don't open on the new cars.

LINDA: But you opened it today.

WILLY: Me? I didn't. (*He stops.*) Now isn't that peculiar! Isn't that a remarkable . . . (*He breaks off in amazement and fright as the flute is heard distantly.*)

LINDA: What, darling?

WILLY: That is the most remarkable thing.

LINDA: What, dear?

WILLY: I was thinking of the Chevvy. (*Slight pause.*) Nineteen twenty-eight . . . when I had that red Chevvy . . . (*Breaks off:*) That funny? I coulda sworn I was driving that Chevvy today.

LINDA: Well, that's nothing. Something must've reminded you.

WILLY: Remarkable. Ts. Remember those days? The way Biff used to simonize that car? The dealer refused to believe there was eighty thousand miles on it. (*He shakes his head.*) Heh! (*To Linda.*) Close your eyes, I'll be right up. (*He walks out of the bedroom.*)

HAPPY (*to Biff*): Jesus, maybe he smashed up the car again!

LINDA (*calling after Willy*): Be careful on the stairs, dear! The cheese is on the middle shelf. (*She turns, goes over to the bed, takes his jacket, and goes out of the bedroom.*)

Light has risen on the boys' room. Unseen, Willy is heard talking to himself; "Eighty thousand miles," and a little laugh. Biff gets out of bed, comes downstage a bit, and stands attentively. Biff is two years older than his brother Happy, well built, but in these days bears a worn air and seems less self-assured. He has succeeded less, and his dreams are stronger and less acceptable than Happy's. Happy is tall, powerfully made. Sexuality is like a visible color on him, or a scent that many women have discovered. He, like his brother, is lost, but in a different way, for he has never allowed himself to turn his face toward defeat and is thus more confused and hard-skinned, although seemingly more content.

HAPPY (*getting out of bed*): He's going to get his license taken away if he keeps that up. I'm getting nervous about him, y'know, Biff?

BIFF: His eyes are going.

HAPPY: No, I've driven with him. He sees all right. He just doesn't keep his mind on it. I drove into the city with him last week. He stops at a green light and then it turns red and he goes. (*He laughs.*)

BIFF: Maybe he's color-blind.

HAPPY: Pop? Why he's got the finest eye for color in the business. You know that.

BIFF (*sitting down on his bed*): I'm going to sleep.

HAPPY: You're not still sour on Dad, are you, Biff?

BIFF: He's all right, I guess.

WILLY (*underneath them, in the living room*): Yes, sir, eighty thousand miles—eighty-two thousand!

BIFF: You smoking?

HAPPY (*holding out a pack of cigarettes*): Want one?

BIFF (*taking a cigarette*): I can never sleep when I smell it.

WILLY: What a simonizing job, heh!

HAPPY (*with deep sentiment*): Funny, Biff, y'know? Us sleeping in here again? The old beds. (*He pats his bed affectionately.*) All the talk that went across those beds, huh? Our whole lives.

BIFF: Yeah. Lotta dreams and plans.

HAPPY (*with a deep and masculine laugh*): About five hundred women would like to know what was said in this room. (*They share a soft laugh.*)

BIFF: Remember that big Betsy something—what the hell was her name—over on Bushwick Avenue?

HAPPY (*combing his hair*): With the collie dog!

BIFF: That's the one. I got you in there, remember?

HAPPY: Yeah, that was my first time—I think. Boy, there was a pig. (*They laugh, almost crudely.*) You taught me everything I know about women. Don't forget that.

BIFF: I bet you forgot how bashful you used to be. Especially with girls.

HAPPY: Oh, I still am, Biff.

BIFF: Oh, go on.

HAPPY: I just control it, that's all. I think I got less bashful and you got more so. What happened, Biff? Where's the old humor, the old confidence? (*He shakes Biff's knee. Biff gets up and moves restlessly about the room.*) What's the matter?

BIFF: Why does Dad mock me all the time?

HAPPY: He's not mocking you, he . . .

BIFF: Everything I say there's a twist of mockery on his face. I can't get near him.

HAPPY: He just wants you to make good, that's all. I wanted to talk to you about Dad for a long time, Biff. Something's—happening to him. He—talks to himself.

BIFF: I noticed that this morning. But he always mumbled.

HAPPY: But not so noticeable. It got so embarrassing I sent him to Florida. And you know something? Most of the time he's talking to you.

BIFF: What's he say about me?

HAPPY: I can't make it out.

BIFF: What's he say about me?

HAPPY: I think the fact that you're not settled, that you're still kind of up in the air . . .

BIFF: There's one or two other things depressing him, Happy.

HAPPY: What do you mean?

BIFF: Never mind. Just don't lay it all to me.

HAPPY: But I think if you just got started—I mean—is there any future for you out there?

BIFF: I tell ya, Hap, I don't know what the future is. I don't know—what I'm supposed to want.

HAPPY: What do you mean?

BIFF: Well, I spent six or seven years after high school trying to work myself up. Shipping clerk, salesman, business of one kind or another. And it's a measly manner of existence. To get on that subway on the hot mornings in summer. To devote your whole life to keeping stock, or making phone calls, or selling or buying. To suffer fifty weeks of the year for the sake of a two-week vacation, when all you really desire is to be outdoors, with your shirt off. And always to have to get ahead of the next fella. And still—that's how you build a future.

HAPPY: Well, you really enjoy it on a farm? Are you content out there?

BIFF (*with rising agitation*): Hap, I've had twenty or thirty different kinds of jobs since I left home before the war, and it always turns out the same. I just realized it lately. In Nebraska when I herded cattle, and the Dakotas, and Arizona, and now in Texas. It's why I came home now, I guess, because I realized it. This farm I work on, it's spring there now, see? And they've got about fifteen new colts. There's nothing more inspiring or—beautiful than the sight of a mare and a new colt. And it's cool there now, see? Texas is cool now, and it's spring. And whenever spring comes to where I am, I suddenly get the feeling, my God, I'm not gettin' anywhere! What the hell am I doing, playing around with horses, twenty-eight dollars a week! I'm thirty-four years old, I oughta be makin' my future. That's when I come running home. And now, I get here, and I don't know what to do with myself. (*After a pause.*) I've always made a point of not wasting my life, and everytime I come back here I know that all I've done is to waste my life.

HAPPY: You're a poet, you know that, Biff? You're a—you're an idealist!

BIFF: No, I'm mixed up very bad. Maybe I oughta get married. Maybe I oughta get stuck into something. Maybe that's my trouble. I'm like a boy. I'm not married, I'm not in business, I just—I'm like a boy. Are you content, Hap? You're a success, aren't you? Are you content?

HAPPY: Hell, no!

BIFF: Why? You're making money, aren't you?

HAPPY (*moving about with energy, expressiveness*): All I can do now is wait for the merchandise manager to die. And suppose I get to be merchandise manager? He's a good friend of mine, and he just built a terrific estate on Long Island. And he lived there about two months and sold it, and now he's building another one. He can't enjoy it once it's finished. And I know that's just what I would do. I don't know what the hell I'm workin' for. Sometimes I sit in my apartment—all alone. And I think of the rent I'm paying. And it's crazy. But then, it's what I always wanted. My own apartment, a car, and plenty of women. And still, goddammit, I'm lonely.

BIFF (*with enthusiasm*): Listen, why don't you come out West with me?

HAPPY: You and I, heh?

BIFF: Sure, maybe we could buy a ranch. Raise cattle, use our muscles. Men built like we are should be working out in the open.

HAPPY (*avidly*): The Loman Brothers, heh?

BIFF (*with vast affection*): Sure, we'd be known all over the counties!

HAPPY (*enthralled*): That's what I dream about, Biff. Sometimes I want to just rip my clothes off in the middle of the store and outbox that goddam merchandise manager. I mean I can outbox, outrun, and outlift anybody in that store, and I have to take orders from those common, petty sons-of-bitches till I can't stand it any more.

BIFF: I'm tellin' you, kid, if you were with me I'd be happy out there.

HAPPY (*enthused*): See, Biff, everybody around me is so false that I'm constantly lowering my ideals . . .

BIFF: Baby, together we'd stand up for one another, we'd have someone to trust.

HAPPY: If I were around you . . .

BIFF: Hap, the trouble is we weren't brought up to grub for money. I don't know how to do it.

HAPPY: Neither can I!

BIFF: Then let's go!

HAPPY: The only thing is—what can you make out there?

BIFF: But look at your friend. Builds an estate and then hasn't the peace of mind to live in it.

HAPPY: Yeah, but when he walks into the store the waves part in front of him. That's fifty-two thousand dollars a year coming through the revolving door, and I got more in my pinky finger than he's got in his head.

BIFF: Yeah, but you just said . . .

HAPPY: I gotta show some of those pompous, self-important executives over there that Hap Loman can make the grade. I want to walk into the store the way he walks in. Then I'll go with you, Biff. We'll be together yet, I swear. But take those two we had tonight. Now weren't they gorgeous creatures?

BIFF: Yeah, yeah, most gorgeous I've had in years.

HAPPY: I get that any time I want, Biff. Whenever I feel disgusted. The only trouble is, it gets like bowling or something. I just keep knockin' them over and it doesn't mean anything. You still run around a lot?

BIFF: Naa. I'd like to find a girl—steady, somebody with substance.

HAPPY: That's what I long for.

BIFF: Go on! You'd never come home.

HAPPY: I would! Somebody with character, with resistance! Like Mom, y'know? You're gonna call me a bastard when I tell you this. That girl Charlotte I was with tonight is engaged to be married in five weeks. (*He tries on his new hat.*)

BIFF: No kiddin'!

HAPPY: Sure, the guy's in line for the vice-presidency of the store. I don't know what gets into me, maybe I just have an over-developed sense of competition or something, but I went and ruined her, and furthermore I can't get rid of her. And he's the third executive I've done that to. Isn't that a crummy characteristic? And to top it all, I go to their weddings! (*Indignantly, but laughing.*) Like I'm not supposed to take bribes. Manufacturers offer me a hundred-dollar bill now and then to throw an order their way. You know how honest I am, but it's like this girl, see. I hate myself for it. Because I don't want the girl, and, still, I take it and—I love it!

BIFF: Let's go to sleep.

HAPPY: I guess we didn't settle anything, heh?

BIFF: I just got one idea that I think I'm going to try.

HAPPY: What's that?

BIFF: Remember Bill Oliver?

HAPPY: Sure, Oliver is very big now. You want to work for him again?

BIFF: No, but when I quit he said something to me. He put his arm on my shoulder, and he said, "Biff, if you ever need anything, come to me."

HAPPY: I remember that. That sounds good.

BIFF: I think I'll go to see him. If I could get ten thousand or even seven or eight thousand dollars I could buy a beautiful ranch.

HAPPY: I bet he'd back you. 'Cause he thought highly of you, Biff. I mean, they all do. You're well liked, Biff. That's why I say to come back here, and we both have the apartment. And I'm tellin' you, Biff, any babe you want . . .

BIFF: No, with a ranch I could do the work I like and still be something. I just wonder though. I wonder if Oliver still thinks I stole that carton of basketballs.

HAPPY: Oh, he probably forgot that long ago. It's almost ten years. You're too sensitive. Anyway, he didn't really fire you.

BIFF: Well, I think he was going to. I think that's why I quit. I was never sure whether he knew or not. I know he thought the world of me, though. I was the only one he'd let lock up the place.

WILLY (*below*): You gonna wash the engine, Biff?

HAPPY: Shh!

Biff looks at Happy, who is gazing down, listening. Willy is mumbling in the parlor.

HAPPY: You hear that?

They listen. Willy laughs warmly.

BIFF (*growing angry*): Doesn't he know Mom can hear that?

WILLY: Don't get your sweater dirty, Biff!

A look of pain crosses Biff's face.

HAPPY: Isn't that terrible? Don't leave again, will you? You'll find a job here. You gotta stick around. I don't know what to do about him, it's getting embarrassing.

WILLY: What a simonizing job!

BIFF: Mom's hearing that!

WILLY: No kiddin', Biff, you got a date? Wonderful!

HAPPY: Go on to sleep. But talk to him in the morning, will you?

BIFF (*reluctantly getting into bed*): With her in the house. Brother!

HAPPY (*getting into bed*): I wish you'd have a good talk with him.

The light on their room begins to fade.

BIFF (*to himself in bed*): That selfish, stupid . . .

HAPPY: Sh . . . Sleep, Biff.

Their light is out. Well before they have finished speaking, Willy's form is dimly seen below in the darkened kitchen. He opens the refrigerator, searches in there, and takes out a bottle of milk. The apartment houses are fading out, and the entire house and surroundings become covered with leaves. Music insinuates itself as the leaves appear.

WILLY: Just wanna be careful with those girls, Biff, that's all. Don't make any promises. No promises of any kind. Because a girl, y'know, they always believe what you tell 'em, and you're very young, Biff, you're too young to be talking seriously to girls.

Light rises on the kitchen. Willy, talking, shuts the refrigerator door and comes downstage to the kitchen table. He pours milk into a glass. He is totally immersed in himself, smiling faintly.

WILLY: Too young entirely, Biff. You want to watch your schooling first. Then when you're all set, there'll be plenty of girls for a boy like you. (*He smiles broadly at a kitchen chair.*) That so? The girls pay for you? (*He laughs.*) Boy, you must really be makin' a hit.

Willy is gradually addressing—physically—a point offstage, speaking through the wall of the kitchen, and his voice has been rising in volume to that of a normal conversation.

WILLY: I been wondering why you polish the car so careful. Ha! Don't leave the hubcaps, boys. Get the chamois to the hubcaps. Happy, use newspaper on the windows, it's the easiest thing. Show him how to do it, Biff! You see, Happy? Pad it up, use it like a pad. That's it, that's it, good work. You're doin' all right, Hap. (*He pauses, then nods in approbation for a few seconds, then looks upward.*) Biff, first thing we gotta do when we get time is clip that big branch over the house. Afraid it's gonna fall in a storm and hit the roof. Tell you what. We get a rope and sling her around, and then we climb up there with a couple of saws and take her down. Soon as you finish the car, boys, I wanna see ya. I got a surprise for you, boys.

BIFF (*offstage*): Whatta ya got, Dad?

WILLY: No, you finish first. Never leave a job till you're finished—remember that. (*Looking toward the "big trees."*) Biff, up in Albany I saw a beautiful hammock. I think I'll buy it next trip, and we'll hang it right between those two elms. Wouldn't that be something? Just swingin' there under those branches. Boy, that would be . . .

Young Biff and Young Happy appear from the direction Willy was addressing. Happy carries rags and a pail of water. Biff, wearing a sweater with a block "S," carries a football.

BIFF (*pointing in the direction of the car offstage*): How's that, Pop, professional?

WILLY: Terrific. Terrific job, boys. Good work, Biff.

HAPPY: Where's the surprise, Pop?

WILLY: In the back seat of the car.

HAPPY: Boy! (*He runs off.*)

BIFF: What is it, Dad? Tell me, what'd you buy?

WILLY (*laughing, cuffs him*): Never mind, something I want you to have.

BIFF (*turns and starts off*): What is it, Hap?

HAPPY (*offstage*): It's a punching bag!

BIFF: Oh, Pop!

WILLY: It's got Gene Tunney's signature on it!

Happy runs onstage with a punching bag.

BIFF: Gee, how'd you know we wanted a punching bag?

WILLY: Well, it's the finest thing for the timing.

HAPPY (*lies down on his back and pedals with his feet*): I'm losing weight, you notice, Pop?

WILLY (*to Happy*): Jumping rope is good too.

BIFF: Did you see the new football I got?

WILLY (*examining the ball*): Where'd you get a new ball?

BIFF: The coach told me to practice my passing.

WILLY: That so? And he gave you the ball, heh?

BIFF: Well, I borrowed it from the locker room. (*He laughs confidentially.*)

WILLY (*laughing with him at the theft*): I want you to return that.

HAPPY: I told you he wouldn't like it!

BIFF (*angrily*): Well, I'm bringing it back!

WILLY (*stopping the incipient argument, to Happy*): Sure, he's gotta practice with a regulation ball, doesn't he? (*To Biff.*) Coach'll probably congratulate you on your initiative!

BIFF: Oh, he keeps congratulating my initiative all the time, Pop.

WILLY: That's because he likes you. If somebody else took that ball there'd be an uproar. So what's the report, boys, what's the report?

BIFF: Where'd you go this time, Dad? Gee we were lonesome for you.

WILLY (*pleased, puts an arm around each boy and they come down to the apron*): Lonesome, heh?

BIFF: Missed you every minute.

WILLY: Don't say? Tell you a secret, boys. Don't breathe it to a soul. Someday I'll have my own business, and I'll never have to leave home any more.

HAPPY: Like Uncle Charley, heh?

WILLY: Bigger than Uncle Charley! Because Charley is not—liked. He's liked, but he's not—well liked.

BIFF: Where'd you go this time, Dad?

WILLY: Well, I got on the road, and I went north to Providence. Met the Mayor.

BIFF: The Mayor of Providence!

WILLY: He was sitting in the hotel lobby.

BIFF: What'd he say?

WILLY: He said, "Morning!" And I said, "Morning!" And I said, "You got a fine city here, Mayor." And then he had coffee with me. And then I went to Waterbury. Waterbury is a fine city. Big clock city, the famous Waterbury clock. Sold a nice bill there. And then Boston— Boston is the cradle of the Revolution. A fine city. And a couple of other towns in Mass., and on to Portland and Bangor and straight home!

BIFF: Gee, I'd love to go with you sometime, Dad.

WILLY: Soon as summer comes.

HAPPY: Promise?

WILLY: You and Hap and I, and I'll show you all the towns. America is full of beautiful towns and fine, upstanding people. And they know me, boys, they know me up and down New England. The finest people. And when I bring you fellas up, there'll be open sesame for all of us, 'cause one thing, boys: I have friends. I can park my car in any street in New England, and the cops protect it like their own. This summer, heh?

BIFF AND HAPPY (*together*): Yeah! You bet!

WILLY: We'll take our bathing suits.

HAPPY: We'll carry your bags, Pop!

WILLY: Oh, won't that be something! Me comin' into the Boston stores with you boys carryin' my bags. What a sensation!

Biff is prancing around, practicing passing the ball.

WILLY: You nervous, Biff, about the game?

BIFF: Not if you're gonna be there.

WILLY: What do they say about you in school, now that they made you captain?

HAPPY: There's a crowd of girls behind him everytime the classes change.

BIFF (*taking Willy's hand*): This Saturday, Pop, this Saturday—just for you, I'm going to break through for a touchdown.

HAPPY: You're supposed to pass.

BIFF: I'm takin' one play for Pop. You watch me, Pop, and when I take off my helmet, that means I'm breakin' out. Then you watch me crash through that line!

WILLY (*kisses Biff*): Oh, wait'll I tell this in Boston!

Bernard enters in knickers. He is younger than Biff, earnest and loyal, a worried boy.

BERNARD: Biff, where are you? You're supposed to study with me today.

WILLY: Hey, looka Bernard. What're you lookin' so anemic about, Bernard?

BERNARD: He's gotta study, Uncle Willy. He's got Regents next week.

HAPPY (*tauntingly, spinning Bernard around*): Let's box, Bernard!

BERNARD: Biff! (*He gets away from Happy.*) Listen, Biff, I heard Mr. Birnbaum say that if you don't start studyin' math he's gonna flunk you, and you won't graduate. I heard him!

WILLY: You better study with him, Biff. Go ahead now.

BERNARD: I heard him!

BIFF: Oh, Pop, you didn't see my sneakers! (*He holds up a foot for Willy to look at.*)

WILLY: Hey, that's a beautiful job of printing!

BERNARD (*wiping his glasses*): Just because he printed University of Virginia on his sneakers doesn't mean they've got to graduate him, Uncle Willy!

WILLY (*angrily*): What're you talking about? With scholarships to three universities they're gonna flunk him?

BERNARD: But I heard Mr. Birnbaum say . . .

WILLY: Don't be a pest, Bernard! (*To his boys.*) What an anemic!

BERNARD: Okay, I'm waiting for you in my house, Biff.

Bernard goes off. The Lomans laugh.

WILLY: Bernard is not well liked, is he?

BIFF: He's liked, but he's not well liked.

HAPPY: That's right, Pop.

WILLY: That's just what I mean. Bernard can get the best marks in school, y'understand, but when he gets out in the business world, y'understand, you are going to be five times ahead of him. That's why I thank Almighty God you're both built like Adonises. Because the man who makes an appearance in the business world, the man who creates personal interest, is the man who gets ahead. Be liked and you will never want. You take me, for instance. I never have to wait in line to see a buyer. "Willy Loman is here!" That's all they have to know, and I go right through.

BIFF: Did you knock them dead, Pop?

WILLY: Knocked 'em cold in Providence, slaughtered 'em in Boston.

HAPPY (*on his back, pedaling again*): I'm losing weight, you notice, Pop?

Linda enters as of old, a ribbon in her hair, carrying a basket of washing.

LINDA (*with youthful energy*): Hello, dear!

WILLY: Sweetheart!

LINDA: How'd the Chevvy run?

WILLY: Chevrolet, Linda, is the greatest car ever built. (*To the boys.*) Since when do you let your mother carry wash up the stairs?

BIFF: Grab hold there, boy!

HAPPY: Where to, Mom?

LINDA: Hang them up on the line. And you better go down to your friends, Biff. The cellar is full of boys. They don't know what to do with themselves.

BIFF: Ah, when Pop comes home they can wait!

WILLY (*laughs appreciatively*): You better go down and tell them what to do, Biff.

BIFF: I think I'll have them sweep out the furnace room.

WILLY: Good work, Biff.

BIFF (*goes through wall-line of kitchen to doorway at back and calls down*): Fellas! Everybody sweep out the furnace room! I'll be right down!

VOICES: All right! Okay, Biff.

BIFF: George and Sam and Frank, come out back! We're hangin' up the wash! Come on, Hap, on the double! (*He and Happy carry out the basket.*)

LINDA: The way they obey him!

WILLY: Well, that's training, the training. I'm tellin' you, I was sellin' thousands and thousands, but I had to come home.

LINDA: Oh, the whole block'll be at that game. Did you sell anything?

WILLY: I did five hundred gross in Providence and seven hundred gross in Boston.

LINDA: No! Wait a minute. I've got a pencil. (*She pulls pencil and paper out of her apron pocket.*) That makes your commission . . . Two hundred—my God! Two hundred and twelve dollars!

WILLY: Well, I didn't figure it yet, but . . .

LINDA: How much did you do?

WILLY: Well, I—I did—about a hundred and eighty gross in Providence. Well, no—it came to—roughly two hundred gross on the whole trip.

LINDA (*without hesitation*): Two hundred gross. That's . . . (*She figures.*)

WILLY: The trouble was that three of the stores were half-closed for inventory in Boston. Otherwise I woulda broke records.

LINDA: Well, it makes seventy dollars and some pennies. That's very good.

WILLY: What do we owe?

LINDA: Well, on the first there's sixteen dollars on the refrigerator . . .

WILLY: Why sixteen?

LINDA: Well, the fan belt broke, so it was a dollar eighty.

WILLY: But it's brand new.

LINDA: Well, the man said that's the way it is. Till they work themselves in, y'know.

They move through the wall-line into the kitchen.

WILLY: I hope we didn't get stuck on that machine.

LINDA: They got the biggest ads of any of them!

WILLY: I know, it's a fine machine. What else?

LINDA: Well, there's nine-sixty for the washing machine. And for the vacuum cleaner there's three and a half due on the fifteenth. Then the roof, you got twenty-one dollars remaining.

WILLY: It don't leak, does it?

LINDA: No, they did a wonderful job. Then you owe Frank for the carburetor.

WILLY: I'm not going to pay that man! That goddam Chevrolet, they ought to prohibit the manufacture of that car!

LINDA: Well, you owe him three and a half. And odds and ends, comes to around a hundred and twenty dollars by the fifteenth.

WILLY: A hundred and twenty dollars! My God, if business don't pick up I don't know what I'm gonna do!

LINDA: Well, next week you'll do better.

WILLY: Oh, I'll knock 'em dead next week. I'll go to Hartford. I'm very well liked in Hartford. You know, the trouble is, Linda, people don't seem to take to me.

They move onto the forestage.

LINDA: Oh, don't be foolish.

WILLY: I know it when I walk in. They seem to laugh at me.

LINDA: Why? Why would they laugh at you? Don't talk that way, Willy.

Willy moves to the edge of the stage. Linda goes into the kitchen and starts to darn stockings.

WILLY: I don't know the reason for it, but they just pass me by. I'm not noticed.

LINDA: But you're doing wonderful, dear. You're making seventy to a hundred dollars a week.

WILLY: But I gotta be at it ten, twelve hours a day. Other men—I don't know—they do it easier. I don't know why—I can't stop myself—I talk too much. A man oughta come in with a few words. One thing about Charley. He's a man of few words, and they respect him.

LINDA: You don't talk too much, you're just lively.

WILLY (*smiling*): Well, I figure, what the hell, life is short, a couple of jokes. (*To himself:*) I joke too much! (*The smile goes.*)

LINDA: Why? You're . . .

WILLY: I'm fat. I'm very—foolish to look at, Linda. I didn't tell you, but Christmas time I happened to be calling on F. H. Stewarts, and a salesman I know, as I was going in to see the buyer I heard him say something about—walrus. And I—I cracked him right across the face. I won't take that. I simply will not take that. But they do laugh at me. I know that.

LINDA: Darling . . .

WILLY: I gotta overcome it. I know I gotta overcome it. I'm not dressing to advantage, maybe.

LINDA: Willy, darling, you're the handsomest man in the world . . .

WILLY: Oh, no, Linda.

LINDA: To me you are. (*Slight pause.*) The handsomest.

From the darkness is heard the laughter of a woman. Willy doesn't turn to it, but it continues through Linda's lines.

LINDA: And the boys, Willy. Few men are idolized by their children the way you are.

Music is heard as behind a scrim, to the left of the house; The Woman, dimly seen, is dressing.

WILLY (*with great feeling*):   You're the best there is. Linda, you're a pal, you know that? On the road—on the road I want to grab you sometimes and just kiss the life outa you.

The laughter is loud now, and he moves into a brightening area at the left, where The Woman has come from behind the scrim and is standing, putting on her hat, looking into a "mirror" and laughing.

WILLY: 'Cause I get so lonely—especially when business is bad and there's nobody to talk to. I get the feeling that I'll never sell anything again, that I won't make a living for you, or a business, a business for the boys. (*He talks through The Woman's subsiding laughter; The Woman primps at the "mirror."*) There's so much I want to make for . . .

THE WOMAN: Me? You didn't make me, Willy. I picked you.

WILLY (*pleased*):   You picked me?

THE WOMAN (*who is quite proper-looking, Willy's age*):   I did. I've been sitting at that desk watching all the salesmen go by, day in, day out. But you've got such a sense of humor, and we do have such a good time together, don't we?

WILLY: Sure, sure. (*He takes her in his arms.*) Why do you have to go now?

THE WOMAN: It's two o'clock . . .

WILLY: No, come on in! (*He pulls her.*)

THE WOMAN: . . . my sisters'll be scandalized. When'll you be back?

WILLY: Oh, two weeks about. Will you come up again?

THE WOMAN: Sure thing. You do make me laugh. It's good for me. (*She squeezes his arm, kisses him.*) And I think you're a wonderful man.

WILLY: You picked me, heh?

THE WOMAN: Sure. Because you're so sweet. And such a kidder.

WILLY: Well, I'll see you next time I'm in Boston.

THE WOMAN: I'll put you right through to the buyers.

WILLY (*slapping her bottom*):   Right. Well, bottoms up!

THE WOMAN (*slaps him gently and laughs*):   You just kill me, Willy. (*He suddenly grabs her and kisses her roughly.*) You kill me. And thanks for the stockings. I love a lot of stockings. Well, good night.

WILLY: Good night. And keep your pores open!

THE WOMAN: Oh, Willy!

*The Woman bursts out laughing, and Linda's laughter blends in.
The Woman disappears into the dark. Now the area at the kitchen
table brightens. Linda is sitting where she was at the kitchen table,
but now is mending a pair of her silk stockings.*

LINDA: You are, Willy. The handsomest man. You've got no reason to
feel that . . .

WILLY (*coming out of The Woman's dimming area and going over to
Linda*): I'll make it all up to you, Linda, I'll . . .

LINDA: There's nothing to make up, dear. You're doing fine, better
than . . .

WILLY (*noticing her mending*): What's that?

LINDA: Just mending my stockings. They're so expensive . . .

WILLY (*angrily, taking them from her*): I won't have you mending
stockings in this house! Now throw them out!

Linda puts the stockings in her pocket.

BERNARD (*entering on the run*): Where is he? If he doesn't study!

WILLY (*moving to the forestage, with great agitation*): You'll give him
the answers!

BERNARD: I do, but I can't on a Regents! That's a state exam! They're
liable to arrest me!

WILLY: Where is he? I'll whip him, I'll whip him!

LINDA: And he'd better give back that football, Willy, it's not nice.

WILLY: Biff! Where is he? Why is he taking everything?

LINDA: He's too rough with the girls, Willy. All the mothers are afraid
of him!

WILLY: I'll whip him!

BERNARD: He's driving the car without a license!

The Woman's laugh is heard.

WILLY: Shut up!

LINDA: All the mothers . . .

WILLY: Shut up!

BERNARD (*backing quietly away and out*): Mr. Birnbaum says he's
stuck up.

WILLY: Get outa here!

BERNARD: If he doesn't buckle down he'll flunk math! (*He goes off.*)

LINDA: He's right, Willy, you've gotta . . .

WILLY (*exploding at her*): There's nothing the matter with him! You want him to be a worm like Bernard? He's got spirit, personality . . .

As he speaks, Linda, almost in tears, exits into the living room. Willy is alone in the kitchen, wilting and staring. The leaves are gone. It is night again, and the apartment houses look down from behind.

WILLY: Loaded with it. Loaded! What is he stealing? He's giving it back, isn't he? Why is he stealing? What did I tell him? I never in my life told him anything but decent things.

Happy in pajamas has come down the stairs; Willy suddenly becomes aware of Happy's presence.

HAPPY: Let's go now, come on.

WILLY (*sitting down at the kitchen table*): Huh! Why did she have to wax the floors herself? Everytime she waxes the floors she keels over. She knows that!

HAPPY: Shh! Take it easy. What brought you back tonight?

WILLY: I got an awful scare. Nearly hit a kid in Yonkers. God! Why didn't I go to Alaska with my brother Ben that time! Ben! That man was a genius, that man was success incarnate! What a mistake! He begged me to go.

HAPPY: Well, there's no use in . . .

WILLY: You guys! There was a man started with the clothes on his back and ended up with diamond mines!

HAPPY: Boy, someday I'd like to know how he did it.

WILLY: What's the mystery? The man knew what he wanted and went out and got it! Walked into a jungle, and comes out, the age of twenty-one, and he's rich! The world is an oyster, but you don't crack it open on a mattress!

HAPPY: Pop, I told you I'm gonna retire you for life.

WILLY: You'll retire me for life on seventy goddam dollars a week? And your women and your car and your apartment, and you'll retire me for life! Christ's sake, I couldn't get past Yonkers today!

Where are you guys, where are you? The woods are burning! I can't drive a car!

Charley has appeared in the doorway. He is a large man, slow of speech, laconic, immovable. In all he says, despite what he says, there is pity, and, now, trepidation. He has a robe over pajamas, slippers on his feet. He enters the kitchen.

CHARLEY: Everything all right?

HAPPY: Yeah, Charley, everything's . . .

WILLY: What's the matter?

CHARLEY: I heard some noise. I thought something happened. Can't we do something about the walls? You sneeze in here, and in my house hats blow off.

HAPPY: Let's go to bed, Dad. Come on.

Charley signals to Happy to go.

WILLY: You go ahead, I'm not tired at the moment.

HAPPY (*to Willy*): Take it easy, huh? (*He exits.*)

WILLY: What're you doin' up?

CHARLEY (*sitting down at the kitchen table opposite Willy*): Couldn't sleep good. I had a heartburn.

WILLY: Well, you don't know how to eat.

CHARLEY: I eat with my mouth.

WILLY: No, you're ignorant. You gotta know about vitamins and things like that.

CHARLEY: Come on, let's shoot. Tire you out a little.

WILLY (*hesitantly*): All right. You got cards?

CHARLEY (*taking a deck from his pocket*): Yeah, I got them. Someplace. What is it with those vitamins?

WILLY (*dealing*): They build up your bones. Chemistry.

CHARLEY: Yeah, but there's no bones in a heartburn.

WILLY: What are you talkin' about? Do you know the first thing about it?

CHARLEY: Don't get insulted.

WILLY: Don't talk about something you don't know anything about.

They are playing. Pause.

CHARLEY: What're you doin' home?

WILLY: A little trouble with the car.

CHARLEY: Oh. (*Pause.*) I'd like to take a trip to California.

WILLY: Don't say.

CHARLEY: You want a job?

WILLY: I got a job, I told you that. (*After a slight pause.*) What the hell are you offering me a job for?

CHARLEY: Don't get insulted.

WILLY: Don't insult me.

CHARLEY: I don't see no sense in it. You don't have to go on this way.

WILLY: I got a good job. (*Slight pause.*) What do you keep comin' in here for?

CHARLEY: You want me to go?

WILLY (*after a pause, withering*):   I can't understand it. He's going back to Texas again. What the hell is that?

CHARLEY: Let him go.

WILLY: I got nothin' to give him, Charley, I'm clean, I'm clean.

CHARLEY: He won't starve. None a them starve. Forget about him.

WILLY: Then what have I got to remember?

CHARLEY: You take it too hard. To hell with it. When a deposit bottle is broken you don't get your nickel back.

WILLY: That's easy enough for you to say.

CHARLEY: That ain't easy for me to say.

WILLY: Did you see the ceiling I put up in the living room?

CHARLEY: Yeah, that's a piece of work. To put up a ceiling is a mystery to me. How do you do it?

WILLY: What's the difference?

CHARLEY: Well, talk about it.

WILLY: You gonna put up a ceiling?

CHARLEY: How could I put up a ceiling?

WILLY: Then what the hell are you bothering me for?

CHARLEY: You're insulted again.

WILLY: A man who can't handle tools is not a man. You're disgusting.

CHARLEY: Don't call me disgusting, Willy.

Uncle Ben, carrying a valise and an umbrella, enters the forestage from around the right corner of the house. He is a stolid man, in his sixties, with a mustache and an authoritative air. He is utterly certain of his destiny, and there is an aura of far places about him. He enters exactly as Willy speaks.

WILLY: I'm getting awfully tired, Ben.

Ben's music is heard. Ben looks around at everything.

CHARLEY: Good, keep playing; you'll sleep better. Did you call me Ben?

Ben looks at his watch.

WILLY: That's funny. For a second there you reminded me of my brother Ben.

BEN: I only have a few minutes. (*He strolls, inspecting the place. Willy and Charley continue playing.*)

CHARLEY: You never heard from him again, heh? Since that time?

WILLY: Didn't Linda tell you? Couple of weeks ago we got a letter from his wife in Africa. He died.

CHARLEY: That so.

BEN (*chuckling*): So this is Brooklyn, eh?

CHARLEY: Maybe you're in for some of his money.

WILLY: Naa, he had seven sons. There's just one opportunity I had with that man . . .

BEN: I must make a train, William. There are several properties I'm looking at in Alaska.

WILLY: Sure, sure! If I'd gone with him to Alaska that time, everything would've been totally different.

CHARLEY: Go on, you'd froze to death up there.

WILLY: What're you talking about?

BEN: Opportunity is tremendous in Alaska, William. Surprised you're not up there.

WILLY: Sure, tremendous.

CHARLEY: Heh?

WILLY: There was the only man I ever met who knew the answers.

CHARLEY: Who?

BEN: How are you all?

WILLY (*taking a pot, smiling*): Fine, fine.

CHARLEY: Pretty sharp tonight.

BEN: Is Mother living with you?

WILLY: No, she died a long time ago.

CHARLEY: Who?

BEN: That's too bad. Fine specimen of a lady, Mother.

WILLY (*to Charley*): Heh?

BEN: I'd hoped to see the old girl.

CHARLEY: Who died?

BEN: Heard anything from Father, have you?

WILLY (*unnerved*): What do you mean, who died?

CHARLEY (*taking a pot*): What're you talkin' about?

BEN (*looking at his watch*): William, it's half-past eight!

WILLY (*as though to dispel his confusion he angrily stops Charley's hand*): That's my build!

CHARLEY: I put the ace . . .

WILLY: If you don't know how to play the game I'm not gonna throw my money away on you!

CHARLEY (*rising*): It was my ace, for God's sake!

WILLY: I'm through, I'm through!

BEN: When did Mother die?

WILLY: Long ago. Since the beginning you never knew how to play cards.

CHARLEY (*picks up the cards and goes to the door*): All right! Next time I'll bring a deck with five aces.

WILLY: I don't play that kind of game!

CHARLEY (*turning to him*): You ought to be ashamed of yourself!

WILLY: Yeah?

CHARLEY: Yeah! (*He goes out.*)

WILLY (*slamming the door after him*): Ignoramus!

BEN (*as Willy comes toward him through the wall-line of the kitchen*): So you're William.

WILLY (*shaking Ben's hand*): Ben! I've been waiting for you so long! What's the answer? How did you do it?

BEN: Oh, there's a story in that.

Linda enters the forestage, as of old, carrying the wash basket.

LINDA: Is this Ben?

BEN (*gallantly*): How do you do, my dear.

LINDA: Where've you been all these years? Willy's always wondered why you . . .

WILLY (*pulling Ben away from her impatiently*): Where is Dad? Didn't you follow him? How did you get started?

BEN: Well, I don't know how much you remember.

WILLY: Well, I was just a baby, of course, only three or four years old . . .

BEN: Three years and eleven months.

WILLY: What a memory, Ben!

BEN: I have many enterprises, William, and I have never kept books.

WILLY: I remember I was sitting under the wagon in—was it Nebraska?

BEN: It was South Dakota, and I gave you a bunch of wild flowers.

WILLY: I remember you walking away down some open road.

BEN (*laughing*): I was going to find Father in Alaska.

WILLY: Where is he?

BEN: At that age I had a very faulty view of geography, William. I discovered after a few days that I was heading due south, so instead of Alaska, I ended up in Africa.

LINDA: Africa!

WILLY: The Gold Coast!

BEN: Principally diamond mines.

LINDA: Diamond mines!

BEN: Yes, my dear. But I've only a few minutes . . .

WILLY: No! Boys! Boys! (*Young Biff and Happy appear.*) Listen to this. This is your Uncle Ben, a great man! Tell my boys, Ben!

BEN: Why, boys, when I was seventeen I walked into the jungle, and when I was twenty-one I walked out. (*He laughs.*) And by God I was rich.

WILLY (*to the boys*): You see what I been talking about? The greatest things can happen!

BEN (*glancing at his watch*): I have an appointment in Ketchikan Tuesday week.

WILLY: No, Ben! Please tell about Dad. I want my boys to hear. I want them to know the kind of stock they spring from. All I remember is a man with a big beard, and I was in Mamma's lap, sitting around a fire, and some kind of high music.

BEN: His flute. He played the flute.

WILLY: Sure, the flute, that's right!

New music is heard, a high, rollicking tune.

BEN: Father was a very great and a very wild-hearted man. We would start in Boston, and he'd toss the whole family into the wagon, and then he'd drive the team right across the country; through Ohio, and Indiana, Michigan, Illinois, and all the Western states. And we'd stop in the towns and sell the flutes that he'd made on the way. Great inventor, Father. With one gadget he made more in a week than a man like you could make in a lifetime.

WILLY: That's just the way I'm bringing them up, Ben—rugged, well liked, all-around.

BEN: Yeah? (*To Biff.*) Hit that, boy—hard as you can. (*He pounds his stomach.*)

BIFF: Oh, no, sir!

BEN (*taking boxing stance*): Come on, get to me! (*He laughs.*)

WILLY: Go to it, Biff! Go ahead, show him!

BIFF: Okay! (*He cocks his fists and starts in.*)

LINDA (*to Willy*): Why must he fight, dear?

BEN (*sparring with Biff*): Good boy! Good boy!

WILLY: How's that, Ben, heh?

HAPPY: Give him the left, Biff!

LINDA: Why are you fighting?

BEN: Good boy! (*Suddenly comes in, trips Biff, and stands over him, the point of his umbrella poised over Biff's eye.*)

LINDA: Look out, Biff!

BIFF: Gee!

BEN (*patting Biff's knee*): Never fight fair with a stranger, boy. You'll never get out of the jungle that way. (*Taking Linda's hand and bowing.*) It was an honor and a pleasure to meet you, Linda.

LINDA (*withdrawing her hand coldly, frightened*): Have a nice—trip.

BEN (*to Willy*): And good luck with your—what do you do?

WILLY: Selling.

BEN: Yes. Well . . . (*He raises his hand in farewell to all.*)

WILLY: No, Ben, I don't want you to think . . . (*He takes Ben's arm to show him.*) It's Brooklyn, I know, but we hunt too.

BEN: Really, now.

WILLY: Oh, sure, there's snakes and rabbits and—that's why I moved out here. Why, Biff can fell any one of these trees in no time! Boys! Go right over to where they're building the apartment house and get some sand. We're gonna rebuild the entire front stoop right now! Watch this, Ben!

BIFF: Yes, sir! On the double, Hap!

HAPPY (*as he and Biff run off*): I lost weight, Pop, you notice?

Charley enters in knickers, even before the boys are gone.

CHARLEY: Listen, if they steal any more from that building the watchman'll put the cops on them!

LINDA (*to Willy*): Don't let Biff . . .

    Ben laughs lustily.

WILLY: You shoulda seen the lumber they brought home last week. At least a dozen six-by-tens worth all kinds a money.

CHARLEY: Listen, if that watchman . . .

WILLY: I gave them hell, understand. But I got a couple of fearless characters there.

CHARLEY: Willy, the jails are full of fearless characters.

BEN (*clapping Willy on the back, with a laugh at Charley*): And the stock exchange, friend!

WILLY (*joining in Ben's laughter*): Where are the rest of your pants?

CHARLEY: My wife bought them.

WILLY: Now all you need is a golf club and you can go upstairs and go to sleep. (*To Ben.*) Great athlete! Between him and his son Bernard they can't hammer a nail!

BERNARD (*rushing in*): The watchman's chasing Biff!

WILLY (*angrily*): Shut up! He's not stealing anything!

LINDA (*alarmed, hurrying off left*): Where is he? Biff, dear! (*She exits.*)

WILLY (*moving toward the left, away from Ben*): There's nothing wrong. What's the matter with you?

BEN: Nervy boy. Good!

WILLY (*laughing*): Oh, nerves of iron, that Biff!

CHARLEY: Don't know what it is. My New England man comes back and he's bleedin', they murdered him up there.

WILLY: It's contacts, Charley, I got important contacts!

CHARLEY (*sarcastically*): Glad to hear it, Willy. Come in later, we'll shoot a little casino. I'll take some of your Portland money. (*He laughs at Willy and exits.*)

WILLY (*turning to Ben*): Business is bad, it's murderous. But not for me, of course.

BEN: I'll stop by on my way back to Africa.

WILLY (*longingly*): Can't you stay a few days? You're just what I need, Ben, because I—I have a fine position here, but I—well, Dad left when I was such a baby and I never had a chance to talk to him and I still feel—kind of temporary about myself.

BEN: I'll be late for my train.

They are at opposite ends of the stage.

WILLY: Ben, my boys—can't we talk? They'd go into the jaws of hell for me, see, but I . . .

BEN: William, you're being first-rate with your boys. Outstanding, manly chaps!

WILLY (*hanging on to his words*): Oh, Ben, that's good to hear! Because sometimes I'm afraid that I'm not teaching them the right kind of—Ben, how should I teach them?

BEN (*giving great weight to each word, and with a certain vicious audacity*): William, when I walked into the jungle, I was seventeen. When I walked out I was twenty-one. And, by God, I was rich! (*He goes off into darkness around the right corner of the house.*)

WILLY: . . . was rich! That's just the spirit I want to imbue them with! To walk into a jungle! I was right! I was right! I was right!

Ben is gone, but Willy is still speaking to him as Linda, in nightgown and robe, enters the kitchen, glances around for Willy, then goes to the door of the house, looks out and sees him. Comes down to his left. He looks at her.

LINDA: Willy, dear? Willy?

WILLY: I was right!

LINDA: Did you have some cheese? (*He can't answer.*) It's very late, darling. Come to bed, heh?

WILLY (*looking straight up*): Gotta break your neck to see a star in this yard.

LINDA: You coming in?

WILLY: Whatever happened to that diamond watch fob? Remember? When Ben came from Africa that time? Didn't he give me a watch fob with a diamond in it?

LINDA: You pawned it, dear. Twelve, thirteen years ago. For Biff's radio correspondence course.

WILLY: Gee, that was a beautiful thing. I'll take a walk.

LINDA: But you're in your slippers.

WILLY (*starting to go around the house at the left*): I was right! I was! (*Half to Linda, as he goes, shaking his head.*) What a man! There was a man worth talking to. I was right!

LINDA (*calling after Willy*): But in your slippers, Willy!

Willy is almost gone when Biff, in his pajamas, comes down the stairs and enters the kitchen.

BIFF: What is he doing out there?

LINDA: Sh!

BIFF: God Almighty, Mom, how long has he been doing this?

LINDA: Don't, he'll hear you.

BIFF: What the hell is the matter with him?

LINDA: It'll pass by morning.

BIFF: Shouldn't we do anything?

LINDA: Oh, my dear, you should do a lot of things, but there's nothing to do, so go to sleep.

Happy comes down the stair and sits on the steps.

HAPPY: I never heard him so loud, Mom.

LINDA: Well, come around more often; you'll hear him. (*She sits down at the table and mends the lining of Willy's jacket.*)

BIFF: Why didn't you ever write me about this, Mom?

LINDA: How would I write to you? For over three months you had no address.

BIFF: I was on the move. But you know I thought of you all the time. You know that, don't you, pal?

LINDA: I know, dear, I know. But he likes to have a letter. Just to know that there's still a possibility for better things.

BIFF: He's not like this all the time, is he?

LINDA: It's when you come home he's always the worst.

BIFF: When I come home?

LINDA: When you write you're coming, he's all smiles, and talks about the future, and—he's just wonderful. And then the closer you seem to come, the more shaky he gets, and then, by the time you get here, he's arguing, and he seems angry at you. I think it's just that maybe he can't bring himself to—to open up to you. Why are you so hateful to each other? Why is that?

BIFF (*evasively*): I'm not hateful, Mom.

LINDA: But you no sooner come in the door than you're fighting!

BIFF: I don't know why. I mean to change. I'm tryin', Mom, you understand?

LINDA: Are you home to stay now?

BIFF: I don't know. I want to look around, see what's doin'.

LINDA: Biff, you can't look around all your life, can you?

BIFF: I just can't take hold, Mom. I can't take hold of some kind of a life.

LINDA: Biff, a man is not a bird, to come and go with the spring time.

BIFF: Your hair . . . (*He touches her hair.*) Your hair got so gray.

LINDA: Oh, it's been gray since you were in high school. I just stopped dyeing it, that's all.

BIFF: Dye it again, will ya? I don't want my pal looking old.

(He smiles.)

LINDA: You're such a boy! You think you can go away for a year and . . . You've got to get it into your head now that one day you'll knock on this door and there'll be strange people here . . .

BIFF: What are you talking about? You're not even sixty, Mom.

LINDA: But what about your father?

BIFF (*lamely*): Well, I meant him too.

HAPPY: He admires Pop.

LINDA: Biff, dear, if you don't have any feeling for him, then you can't have any feeling for me.

BIFF: Sure I can, Mom.

LINDA: No. You can't just come to see me, because I love him. (*With a threat, but only a threat, of tears.*) He's the dearest man in the world to me, and I won't have anyone making him feel unwanted and low and blue. You've got to make up your mind now, darling, there's no leeway any more. Either he's your father and you pay him that respect, or else you're not to come here. I know he's not easy to get along with—nobody knows that better than me—but . . .

WILLY (*from the left, with a laugh*): Hey, hey, Biffo!

BIFF (*starting to go out after Willy*): What the hell is the matter with him? (*Happy stops him.*)

LINDA: Don't—don't go near him!

BIFF: Stop making excuses for him! He always, always wiped the floor with you. Never had an ounce of respect for you.

HAPPY: He's always had respect for . . .

BIFF: What the hell do you know about it?

HAPPY (*surlily*): Just don't call him crazy!

BIFF: He's got no character—Charley wouldn't do this. Not in his own house—spewing out that vomit from his mind.

HAPPY: Charley never had to cope with what he's got to.

BIFF: People are worse off than Willy Loman. Believe me, I've seen them!

LINDA: Then make Charley your father, Biff. You can't do that, can you? I don't say he's a great man. Willy Loman never made a lot of money. His name was never in the paper. He's not the finest character that ever lived. But he's a human being, and a terrible thing is happening to him. So attention must be paid. He's not to be allowed to fall into his grave like an old dog. Attention, attention must be finally paid to such a person. You called him crazy . . .

BIFF: I didn't mean . . .

LINDA: No, a lot of people think he's lost his—balance. But you don't have to be very smart to know what his trouble is. The man is exhausted.

HAPPY: Sure!

LINDA: A small man can be just as exhausted as a great man. He works for a company thirty-six years this March, opens up unheard-of territories to their trademark, and now in his old age they take his salary away.

HAPPY (*indignantly*): I didn't know that, Mom.

LINDA: You never asked, my dear! Now that you get your spending money someplace else you don't trouble your mind with him.

HAPPY: But I gave you money last . . .

LINDA: Christmas time, fifty dollars! To fix the hot water it cost ninety-seven fifty! For five weeks he's been on straight commission, like a beginner, an unknown!

BIFF: Those ungrateful bastards!

LINDA: Are they any worse than his sons? When he brought them business, when he was young, they were glad to see him. But now his old friends, the old buyers that loved him so and always found some order to hand him in a pinch—they're all dead, retired. He used to be able to make six, seven calls a day in Boston. Now he takes his valises out of the car and puts them back and takes them out again and he's exhausted. Instead of walking he talks now. He drives seven hundred miles, and when he gets there no one knows him any more, no one welcomes him. And what goes through a man's mind, driving seven hundred miles home without having earned a cent? Why shouldn't he talk to himself? Why? When he has to go to Charley and borrow fifty dollars a week and pretend to me that it's his pay? How long can that go on? How long? You see what I'm sitting here and waiting for? And you tell me he has no character? The man who never worked a day but for your benefit? When does he get the medal for that? Is this his reward—to turn around at the age of sixty-three and find his sons, who he loved better than his life, one a philandering bum . . .

HAPPY: Mom!

LINDA: That's all you are, my baby! (*To Biff.*) And you! What happened to the love you had for him? You were such pals! How you used to talk to him on the phone every night! How lonely he was till he could come home to you!

BIFF: All right, Mom. I'll live here in my room, and I'll get a job. I'll keep away from him, that's all.

LINDA: No, Biff. You can't stay here and fight all the time.

BIFF: He threw me out of this house, remember that.

LINDA: Why did he do that? I never knew why.

BIFF: Because I know he's a fake and he doesn't like anybody around who knows!

LINDA: Why a fake? In what way? What do you mean?

BIFF: Just don't lay it all at my feet. It's between me and him—that's all I have to say. I'll chip in from now on. He'll settle for half my paycheck. He'll be all right. I'm going to bed. (*He starts for the stairs.*)

LINDA: He won't be all right.

BIFF (*turning on the stairs, furiously*): I hate this city and I'll stay here. Now what do you want?

LINDA: He's dying, Biff.

Happy turns quickly to her, shocked.

BIFF (*after a pause*): Why is he dying?

LINDA: He's been trying to kill himself.

BIFF (*with great horror*): How?

LINDA: I live from day to day.

BIFF: What're you talking about?

LINDA: Remember I wrote you that he smashed up the car again? In February?

BIFF: Well?

LINDA: The insurance inspector came. He said that they have evidence. That all these accidents in the last year—weren't—weren't—accidents.

HAPPY: How can they tell that? That's a lie.

LINDA: It seems there's a woman . . . (*She takes a breath as:*)

BIFF (*sharply but contained*): What woman?

LINDA (*simultaneously*): . . .and this woman . . .

LINDA: What?

BIFF: Nothing. Go ahead.

LINDA: What did you say?

BIFF: Nothing. I just said what woman?

HAPPY: What about her?

LINDA: Well, it seems she was walking down the road and saw his car. She says that he wasn't driving fast at all, and that he didn't skid. She says he came to that little bridge, and then deliberately smashed into the railing, and it was only the shallowness of the water that saved him.

BIFF: Oh, no, he probably just fell asleep again.

LINDA: I don't think he fell asleep.

BIFF: Why not?

LINDA: Last month . . . (*With great difficulty.*) Oh, boys, it's so hard to say a thing like this! He's just a big stupid man to you, but I tell you there's more good in him than in many other people. (*She chokes, wipes her eyes.*) I was looking for a fuse. The lights blew out, and I went down the cellar. And behind the fuse box—it happened to fall out—was a length of rubber pipe—just short.

HAPPY: No kidding!

LINDA: There's a little attachment on the end of it. I knew right away. And sure enough, on the bottom of the water heater there's a new little nipple on the gas pipe.

HAPPY (*angrily*): That—jerk.

BIFF: Did you have it taken off?

LINDA: I'm—I'm ashamed to. How can I mention it to him? Every day I go down and take away that little rubber pipe. But, when he comes home, I put it back where it was. How can I insult him that way? I don't know what to do. I live from day to day, boys. I tell you, I know every thought in his mind. It sounds so old-fashioned and silly, but I tell you he put his whole life into you and you've turned your backs on him. (*She is bent over in the chair, weeping, her face in her hands.*) Biff, I swear to God! Biff, his life is in your hands!

HAPPY (*to Biff*):   How do you like that damned fool!

BIFF (*kissing her*):   All right, pal, all right. It's all settled now. I've been remiss. I know that, Mom. But now I'll stay, and I swear to you, I'll apply myself. (*Kneeling in front of her, in a fever of self-reproach.*) It's just—you see, Mom, I don't fit in business. Not that I won't try. I'll try, and I'll make good.

HAPPY: Sure you will. The trouble with you in business was you never tried to please people.

BIFF: I know, I . . .

HAPPY: Like when you worked for Harrison's. Bob Harrison said you were tops, and then you go and do some damn fool thing like whistling whole songs in the elevator like a comedian.

BIFF (*against Happy*):   So what? I like to whistle sometimes.

HAPPY: You don't raise a guy to a responsible job who whistles in the elevator!

LINDA: Well, don't argue about it now.

HAPPY: Like when you'd go off and swim in the middle of the day instead of taking the line around.

BIFF (*his resentment rising*):   Well, don't you run off? You take off sometimes, don't you? On a nice summer day?

HAPPY: Yeah, but I cover myself!

LINDA: Boys!

HAPPY: If I'm going to take a fade the boss can call any number where I'm supposed to be and they'll swear to him that I just left. I'll tell you something that I hate to say, Biff, but in the business world some of them think you're crazy.

BIFF (*angered*):   Screw the business world!

HAPPY: All right, screw it! Great, but cover yourself!

LINDA: Hap, Hap!

BIFF: I don't care what they think! They've laughed at Dad for years, and you know why? Because we don't belong in this nuthouse of a city! We should be mixing cement on some open plain or—or carpenters. A carpenter is allowed to whistle!

Willy walks in from the entrance of the house, at left.

WILLY: Even your grandfather was better than a carpenter. (*Pause. They watch him.*) You never grew up. Bernard does not whistle in the elevator, I assure you.

BIFF (*as though to laugh Willy out of it*): Yeah, but you do, Pop.

WILLY: I never in my life whistled in an elevator! And who in the business world thinks I'm crazy?

BIFF: I didn't mean it like that, Pop. Now don't make a whole thing out of it, will ya?

WILLY: Go back to the West! Be a carpenter, a cowboy, enjoy yourself!

LINDA: Willy, he was just saying . . .

WILLY: I heard what he said!

HAPPY (*trying to quiet Willy*): Hey, Pop, come on now . . .

WILLY (*continuing over Happy's line*): They laugh at me, heh? Go to Filene's, go to the Hub, go to Slattery's, Boston. Call out the name Willy Loman and see what happens! Big shot!

BIFF: All right, Pop.

WILLY: Big!

BIFF: All right!

WILLY: Why do you always insult me?

BIFF: I didn't say a word. (*To Linda.*) Did I say a word?

LINDA: He didn't say anything, Willy.

WILLY (*going to the doorway of the living room*): All right, good night, good night.

LINDA: Willy, dear, he just decided . . .

WILLY (*to Biff*): If you get tired hanging around tomorrow, paint the ceiling I put up in the living room.

BIFF: I'm leaving early tomorrow.

HAPPY: He's going to see Bill Oliver, Pop.

WILLY (*interestedly*): Oliver? For what?

BIFF (*with reserve, but trying; trying*): He always said he'd stake me. I'd like to go into business, so maybe I can take him up on it.

LINDA: Isn't that wonderful?

WILLY: Don't interrupt. What's wonderful about it? There's fifty men in the City of New York who'd stake him. (*To Biff.*) Sporting goods?

BIFF: I guess so. I know something about it and . . .

WILLY: He knows something about it! You know sporting goods better than Spalding, for God's sake! How much is he giving you?

BIFF: I don't know, I didn't even see him yet, but . . .

WILLY: Then what're you talkin' about?

BIFF (*getting angry*):   Well, all I said was I'm gonna see him, that's all!

WILLY (*turning away*):   Ah, you're counting your chickens again.

BIFF (*starting left for the stairs*):   Oh, Jesus, I'm going to sleep!

WILLY (*calling after him*):   Don't curse in this house!

BIFF (*turning*):   Since when did you get so clean?

HAPPY (*trying to stop them*):   Wait a . . .

WILLY: Don't use that language to me! I won't have it!

HAPPY (*grabbing Biff, shouts*):   Wait a minute! I got an idea. I got a feasible idea. Come here, Biff, let's talk this over now, let's talk some sense here. When I was down in Florida last time, I thought of a great idea to sell sporting goods. It just came back to me. You and I, Biff—we have a line, the Loman Line. We train a couple of weeks, and put on a couple of exhibitions, see?

WILLY: That's an idea!

HAPPY: Wait! We form two basketball teams, see? Two water-polo teams. We play each other. It's a million dollars' worth of publicity. Two brothers, see? The Loman Brothers. Displays in the Royal Palms—all the hotels. And banners over the ring and the basketball court: "Loman Brothers." Baby, we could sell sporting goods!

WILLY: That is a one-million-dollar idea!

LINDA: Marvelous!

BIFF: I'm in great shape as far as that's concerned.

HAPPY: And the beauty of it is, Biff, it wouldn't be like a business. We'd be out playin' ball again.

BIFF (*enthused*):   Yeah, that's . . .

WILLY: Million-dollar . . .

HAPPY: And you wouldn't get fed up with it, Biff. It'd be the family again. There'd be the old honor, and comradeship, and if you wanted to go off for a swim or somethin'—well, you'd do it! Without some smart cooky gettin' up ahead of you!

WILLY: Lick the world! You guys together could absolutely lick the civilized world.

BIFF: I'll see Oliver tomorrow. Hap, if we could work that out . . .

LINDA: Maybe things are beginning to . . .

WILLY (*widely enthused, to Linda*):   Stop interrupting! (*To Biff.*) But don't wear sport jacket and slacks when you see Oliver.

BIFF: No, I'll . . .

WILLY: A business suit, and talk as little as possible, and don't crack any jokes.

BIFF: He did like me. Always liked me.

LINDA: He loved you!

WILLY (*to Linda*):   Will you stop! (*To Biff.*) Walk in very serious. You are not applying for a boy's job. Money is to pass. Be quiet, fine, and serious. Everybody likes a kidder, but nobody lends him money.

HAPPY: I'll try to get some myself, Biff. I'm sure I can.

WILLY: I see great things for you kids, I think your troubles are over. But remember, start big and you'll end big. Ask for fifteen. How much you gonna ask for?

BIFF: Gee, I don't know . . .

WILLY: And don't say "Gee." "Gee" is a boy's word. A man walking in for fifteen thousand dollars does not say "Gee!"

BIFF: Ten, I think, would be top though.

WILLY: Don't be so modest. You always started too low. Walk in with a big laugh. Don't look worried. Start off with a couple of your good stories to lighten things up. It's not what you say, it's how you say it—because personality always wins the day.

LINDA: Oliver always thought the highest of him . . .

WILLY: Will you let me talk?

BIFF: Don't yell at her, Pop, will ya?

WILLY (*angrily*):   I was talking, wasn't I?

BIFF: I don't like you yelling at her all the time, and I'm tellin' you, that's all.

WILLY: What're you, takin' over this house?

LINDA: Willy . . .

WILLY (*turning to her*):   Don't take his side all the time, goddammit!

BIFF (*furiously*):   Stop yelling at her!

WILLY (*suddenly pulling on his cheek, beaten down, guilt ridden*): Give my best to Bill Oliver—he may remember me. (*He exits through the living room doorway.*)

LINDA (*her voice subdued*):   What'd you have to start that for? (*Biff turns away.*) You see how sweet he was as soon as you talked hopefully? (*She goes over to Biff.*) Come up and say good night to him. Don't let him go to bed that way.

HAPPY: Come on, Biff, let's buck him up.

LINDA: Please, dear. Just say good night. It takes so little to make him happy. Come. (*She goes through the living room doorway, calling upstairs from within the living room.*) Your pajamas are hanging in the bathroom, Willy!

HAPPY (*looking toward where Linda went out*): What a woman! They broke the mold when they made her. You know that, Biff.

BIFF: He's off salary. My God, working on commission!

HAPPY: Well, let's face it: he's no hot-shot selling man. Except that sometimes, you have to admit, he's a sweet personality.

BIFF (*deciding*): Lend me ten bucks, will ya? I want to buy some new ties.

HAPPY: I'll take you to a place I know. Beautiful stuff. Wear one of my striped shirts tomorrow.

BIFF: She got gray. Mom got awful old. Gee, I'm gonna go in to Oliver tomorrow and knock him for a . . .

HAPPY: Come on up. Tell that to Dad. Let's give him a whirl. Come on.

BIFF (*steamed up*): You know, with ten thousand bucks, boy!

HAPPY (*as they go into the living room*): That's the talk, Biff, that's the first time I've heard the old confidence out of you! (*From within the living room, fading off*) You're gonna live with me, kid, and any babe you want just say the word . . . (*The last lines are hardly heard. They are mounting the stairs to their parents' bedroom.*)

LINDA (*entering her bedroom and addressing Willy, who is in the bathroom. She is straightening the bed for him*): Can you do anything about the shower? It drips.

WILLY (*from the bathroom*): All of a sudden everything falls to pieces. Goddam plumbing, oughta be sued, those people. I hardly finished putting it in and the thing . . . (*His words rumble off.*)

LINDA: I'm just wondering if Oliver will remember him. You think he might?

WILLY (*coming out of the bathroom in his pajamas*): Remember him? What's the matter with you, you crazy? If he'd've stayed with Oliver he'd be on top by now! Wait'll Oliver gets a look at him. You don't know the average caliber any more. The average young man today—(*he is getting into bed*)—is got a caliber of zero. Greatest thing in the world for him was to bum around.

Biff and Happy enter the bedroom. Slight pause.

WILLY (*stops short, looking at Biff*): Glad to hear it, boy.

HAPPY: He wanted to say good night to you, sport.

WILLY (*to Biff*): Yeah. Knock him dead, boy. What'd you want to tell me?

BIFF: Just take it easy, Pop. Good night. (*He turns to go.*)

WILLY (*unable to resist*): And if anything falls off the desk while you're talking to him—like a package or something—don't you pick it up. They have office boys for that.

LINDA: I'll make a big breakfast . . .

WILLY: Will you let me finish? (*To Biff.*) Tell him you were in the business in the West. Not farm work.

BIFF: All right, Dad.

LINDA: I think everything . . .

WILLY (*going right through her speech*): And don't undersell yourself. No less than fifteen thousand dollars.

BIFF (*unable to bear him*): Okay. Good night, Mom. (*He starts moving.*)

WILLY: Because you got a greatness in you, Biff, remember that. You got all kinds of greatness . . . (*He lies back, exhausted. Biff walks out.*)

LINDA (*calling after Biff*): Sleep well, darling!

HAPPY: I'm gonna get married, Mom. I wanted to tell you.

LINDA: Go to sleep, dear.

HAPPY (*going*): I just wanted to tell you.

WILLY: Keep up the good work. (*Happy exits.*) God . . . remember that Ebbets Field game? The championship of the city?

LINDA: Just rest. Should I sing to you?

WILLY: Yeah. Sing to me. (*Linda hums a soft lullaby.*) When that team came out—he was the tallest, remember?

LINDA: Oh, yes. And in gold.

Biff enters the darkened kitchen, takes a cigarette, and leaves the house. He comes downstage into a golden pool of light. He smokes, staring at the night.

WILLY: Like a young god. Hercules—something like that. And the sun, the sun all around him. Remember how he waved to me? Right up from the field, with the representatives of three colleges standing by? And the buyers I brought, and the cheers when he came out— Loman, Loman, Loman! God Almighty, he'll be great yet. A star like that, magnificent, can never really fade away!

The light on Willy is fading. The gas heater begins to glow through the kitchen wall, near the stairs, a blue flame beneath red coils.

LINDA (*timidly*): Willy dear, what has he got against you?
WILLY: I'm so tired. Don't talk any more.

Biff slowly returns to the kitchen. He stops, stares toward the heater.

LINDA: Will you ask Howard to let you work in New York?
WILLY: First thing in the morning. Everything'll be all right.

Biff reaches behind the heater and draws out a length of rubber tubing. He is horrified and turns his head toward Willy's room, still dimly lit, from which the strains of Linda's desperate but monotonous humming rise.

WILLY (*staring through the window into the moonlight*): Gee, look at the moon moving between the buildings! (*Biff wraps the tubing around his hand and quickly goes up the stairs.*)

Act 2

Scene: Music is heard, gay and bright. The curtain rises as the music fades away. Willy, in shirt sleeves, is sitting at the kitchen table, sipping coffee, his hat in his lap. Linda is filling his cup when she can.

WILLY: Wonderful coffee. Meal in itself.
LINDA: Can I make you some eggs?
WILLY: No. Take a breath.
LINDA: You look so rested, dear.
WILLY: I slept like a dead one. First time in months. Imagine, sleeping till ten on a Tuesday morning. Boys left nice and early, heh?
LINDA: They were out of here by eight o'clock.
WILLY: Good work!

LINDA: It was so thrilling to see them leaving together. I can't get over the shaving lotion in this house!

WILLY (*smiling*):   Mmm . . .

LINDA: Biff was very changed this morning. His whole attitude seemed to be hopeful. He couldn't wait to get downtown to see Oliver.

WILLY: He's heading for a change. There's no question, there simply are certain men that take longer to get—solidified. How did he dress?

LINDA: His blue suit. He's so handsome in that suit. He could be a— anything in that suit!

Willy gets up from the table. Linda holds his jacket for him.

WILLY: There's no question, no question at all. Gee, on the way home tonight I'd like to buy some seeds.

LINDA (*laughing*):   That'd be wonderful. But not enough sun gets back there. Nothing'll grow any more.

WILLY: You wait, kid, before it's all over we're gonna get a little place out in the country, and I'll raise some vegetables, a couple of chickens . . .

LINDA: You'll do it yet, dear.

Willy walks out of his jacket. Linda follows him.

WILLY: And they'll get married, and come for a weekend. I'd build a little guest house. 'Cause I got so many fine tools, all I'd need would be a little lumber and some peace of mind.

LINDA (*joyfully*):   I sewed the lining . . .

WILLY: I could build two guest houses, so they'd both come. Did he decide how much he's going to ask Oliver for?

LINDA (*getting him into the jacket*):   He didn't mention it, but I imagine ten or fifteen thousand. You going to talk to Howard today?

WILLY: Yeah. I'll put it to him straight and simple. He'll just have to take me off the road.

LINDA: And Willy, don't forget to ask for a little advance, because we've got the insurance premium. It's the grace period now.

WILLY: That's a hundred . . . ?

LINDA: A hundred and eight, sixty-eight. Because we're a little short again.

WILLY: Why are we short?

LINDA: Well, you had the motor job on the car . . .

WILLY: That goddam Studebaker!

LINDA: And you got one more payment on the refrigerator . . .

WILLY: But it just broke again!

LINDA: Well, it's old, dear.

WILLY: I told you we should've bought a well-advertised machine. Charley bought a General Electric and it's twenty years old and it's still good, that son-of-a-bitch.

LINDA: But, Willy . . .

WILLY: Whoever heard of a Hastings refrigerator? Once in my life I would like to own something outright before it's broken! I'm always in a race with the junkyard! I just finished paying for the car and it's on its last legs. The refrigerator consumes belts like a goddam maniac. They time those things. They time them so when you finally paid for them, they're used up.

LINDA (*buttoning up his jacket as he unbuttons it*): All told, about two hundred dollars would carry us, dear. But that includes the last payment on the mortgage. After this payment, Willy, the house belongs to us.

WILLY: It's twenty-five years!

LINDA: Biff was nine years old when we bought it.

WILLY: Well, that's a great thing. To weather a twenty-five year mortgage is . . .

LINDA: It's an accomplishment.

WILLY: All the cement, the lumber, the reconstruction I put in this house! There ain't a crack to be found in it any more.

LINDA: Well, it served its purpose.

WILLY: What purpose? Some stranger'll come along, move in, and that's that. If only Biff would take this house, and raise a family . . . (*He starts to go.*) Good-by, I'm late.

LINDA (*suddenly remembering*): Oh, I forgot! You're supposed to meet them for dinner.

WILLY: Me?

LINDA: At Frank's Chop House on Forty-eighth near Sixth Avenue.

WILLY: Is that so! How about you?

LINDA: No, just the three of you. They're gonna blow you to a big meal!

WILLY: Don't say! Who thought of that?

LINDA: Biff came to me this morning, Willy, and he said, "Tell Dad, we want to blow him to a big meal." Be there six o'clock. You and your two boys are going to have dinner.

WILLY: Gee whiz! That's really somethin'. I'm gonna knock Howard for a loop, kid. I'll get an advance, and I'll come home with a New York job. Goddammit, now I'm gonna do it!

LINDA: Oh, that's the spirit, Willy!

WILLY: I will never get behind a wheel the rest of my life!

LINDA: It's changing, Willy, I can feel it changing!

WILLY: Beyond a question. G'by, I'm late. (*He starts to go again.*)

LINDA (*calling after him as she runs to the kitchen table for a handkerchief*): You got your glasses?

WILLY (*feels for them, then comes back in*): Yeah, yeah, got my glasses.

LINDA (*giving him the handkerchief*): And a handkerchief.

WILLY: Yeah, handkerchief.

LINDA: And your saccharine?

WILLY: Yeah, my saccharine.

LINDA: Be careful on the subway stairs.

She kisses him, and a silk stocking is seen hanging from her hand. Willy notices it.

WILLY: Will you stop mending stockings? At least while I'm in the house. It gets me nervous. I can't tell you. Please.

Linda hides the stocking in her hand as she follows Willy across the forestage in front of the house.

LINDA: Remember, Frank's Chop House.

WILLY (*passing the apron*): Maybe beets would grow out there.

LINDA (*laughing*): But you tried so many times.

WILLY: Yeah. Well, don't work hard today. (*He disappears around the right corner of the house.*)

LINDA: Be careful!

As Willy vanishes, Linda waves to him. Suddenly the phone rings. She runs across the stage and into the kitchen and lifts it.

LINDA: Hello? Oh, Biff! I'm so glad you called, I just . . . Yes, sure, I just told him. Yes, he'll be there for dinner at six o'clock, I didn't forget. Listen, I was just dying to tell you. You know that little rubber pipe I told you about? That he connected to the gas heater? I finally decided to go down the cellar this morning and take it away and destroy it. But it's gone! Imagine? He took it away himself, it isn't there! (*She listens.*) When? Oh, then you took it. Oh—nothing, it's just that I'd hoped he'd taken it away himself. Oh, I'm not worried, darling, because this morning he left in such high spirits, it was like the old days! I'm not afraid any more. Did Mr. Oliver see you?. . . . Well, you wait there then. And make a nice impression on him, darling. Just don't perspire too much before you see him. And have a nice time with Dad. He may have big news too!. . . . That's right, a New York job. And be sweet to him tonight, dear. Be loving to him. Because he's only a little boat looking for a harbor. (*She is trembling with sorrow and joy.*) Oh, that's wonderful, Biff, you'll save his life. Thanks, darling. Just put your arm around him when he comes into the restaurant. Give him a smile. That's the boy . . . Good-by, dear. . . . You got your comb?. . . That's fine. Good-by, Biff dear.

In the middle of her speech, Howard Wagner, thirty-six, wheels in a small typewriter table on which is a wire-recording machine and proceeds to plug it in. This is on the left forestage. Light slowly fades on Linda as it rises on Howard. Howard is intent on threading the machine and only glances over his shoulder as Willy appears.

WILLY: Pst! Pst!

HOWARD: Hello, Willy, come in.

WILLY: Like to have a little talk with you, Howard.

HOWARD: Sorry to keep you waiting. I'll be with you in a minute.

WILLY: What's that, Howard?

HOWARD: Didn't you ever see one of these? Wire recorder.

WILLY: Oh. Can we talk a minute?

HOWARD: Records things. Just got delivery yesterday. Been driving me crazy, the most terrific machine I ever saw in my life. I was up all night with it.

WILLY: What do you do with it?

HOWARD: I bought it for dictation, but you can do anything with it. Listen to this. I had it home last night. Listen to what I picked up. The first one is my daughter. Get this. (*He flicks the switch and "Roll Out the Barrel" is heard being whistled.*) Listen to that kid whistle.

WILLY: That is lifelike, isn't it?

HOWARD: Seven years old. Get that tone.

WILLY: Ts, ts. Like to ask a little favor if you . . .

The whistling breaks off, and the voice of Howard's daughter is heard.

HIS DAUGHTER: "Now you, Daddy."

HOWARD: She's crazy for me! (*Again the same song is whistled.*) That's me! Ha! (*He winks.*)

WILLY: You're very good!

The whistling breaks off again. The machine runs silent for a moment.

HOWARD: Sh! Get this now, this is my son.

HIS SON: "The capital of Alabama is Montgomery; the capital of Arizona is Phoenix; the capital of Arkansas is Little Rock; the capital of California is Sacramento . . ." (*and on, and on.*)

HOWARD (*holding up five fingers*): Five years old, Willy!

WILLY: He'll make an announcer some day!

HIS SON (*continuing*): "The capital . . ."

HOWARD: Get that—alphabetical order! (*The machine breaks off suddenly.*) Wait a minute. The maid kicked the plug out.

WILLY: It certainly is a . . .

HOWARD: Sh, for God's sake!

HIS SON: "It's nine o'clock, Bulova watch time. So I have to go to sleep."

WILLY: That really is . . .

HOWARD: Wait a minute! The next is my wife.

They wait.

HOWARD'S VOICE: "Go on, say something." (*Pause.*) "Well, you gonna talk?"

HIS WIFE: "I can't think of anything."

HOWARD'S VOICE: "Well, talk—it's turning."

HIS WIFE (*shyly, beaten*): "Hello." (*Silence.*) "Oh, Howard, I can't talk into this . . ."

HOWARD (*snapping the machine off*): That was my wife.

WILLY: That is a wonderful machine. Can we . . .

HOWARD: I tell you, Willy, I'm gonna take my camera, and my band-saw, and all my hobbies, and out they go. This is the most fascinating relaxation I ever found.

WILLY: I think I'll get one myself.

HOWARD: Sure, they're only a hundred and a half. You can't do without it. Supposing you wanna hear Jack Benny, see? But you can't be at home at that hour. So you tell the maid to turn the radio on when Jack Benny comes on, and this automatically goes on with the radio . . .

WILLY: And when you come home you . . .

HOWARD: You can come home twelve o'clock, one o'clock, any time you like, and you get yourself a Coke and sit yourself down, throw the switch, and there's Jack Benny's program in the middle of the night!

WILLY: I'm definitely going to get one. Because lots of times I'm on the road, and I think to myself, what I must be missing on the radio!

HOWARD: Don't you have a radio in the car?

WILLY: Well, yeah, but who ever thinks of turning it on?

HOWARD: Say, aren't you supposed to be in Boston?

WILLY: That's what I want to talk to you about, Howard. You got a minute? (*He draws a chair in from the wing.*)

HOWARD: What happened? What're you doing here?

WILLY: Well . . .

HOWARD: You didn't crack up again, did you?

WILLY: Oh, no. No . . .

HOWARD: Geez, you had me worried there for a minute. What's the trouble?

WILLY: Well, tell you the truth, Howard. I've come to the decision that I'd rather not travel any more.

HOWARD: Not travel! Well, what'll you do?

WILLY: Remember, Christmas time, when you had the party here? You said you'd try to think of some spot for me here in town.

HOWARD: With us?

WILLY: Well, sure.

HOWARD: Oh, yeah, yeah. I remember. Well, I couldn't think of anything for you, Willy.

WILLY: I tell ya, Howard. The kids are all grown up, y'know. I don't need much any more. If I could take home—well, sixty-five dollars a week, I could swing it.

HOWARD: Yeah, but Willy, see I . . .

WILLY: I tell ya why, Howard. Speaking frankly and between the two of us, y'know—I'm just a little tired.

HOWARD: Oh, I could understand that, Willy. But you're a road man, Willy, and we do a road business. We've only got a half-dozen salesmen on the floor here.

WILLY: God knows, Howard. I never asked a favor of any man. But I was with the firm when your father used to carry you in here in his arms.

HOWARD: I know that, Willy, but . . .

WILLY: Your father came to me the day you were born and asked me what I thought of the name Howard, may he rest in peace.

HOWARD: I appreciate that, Willy, but there just is no spot here for you. If I had a spot I'd slam you right in, but I just don't have a single solitary spot.

He looks for his lighter. Willy has picked it up and gives it to him. Pause.

WILLY (*with increasing anger*): Howard, all I need to set my table is fifty dollars a week.

HOWARD: But where am I going to put you, kid?

WILLY: Look, it isn't a question of whether I can sell merchandise, is it?

HOWARD: No, but it's business, kid, and everybody's gotta pull his own weight.

WILLY (*desperately*): Just let me tell you a story, Howard . . .

HOWARD: 'Cause you gotta admit, business is business.

WILLY (*angrily*): Business is definitely business, but just listen for a minute. You don't understand this. When I was a boy—eighteen, nineteen—I was already on the road. And there was a question in my mind as to whether selling had a future for me. Because in those days I had a yearning to go to Alaska. See, there were three gold strikes in one month in Alaska, and I felt like going out. Just for the ride, you might say.

HOWARD (*barely interested*): Don't say.

WILLY: Oh, yeah, my father lived many years in Alaska. He was an adventurous man. We've got quite a little streak of self-reliance in our family. I thought I'd go out with my older brother and try to locate him, and maybe settle in the North with the old man. And I was almost decided to go, when I met a salesman in the Parker House. His name was Dave Singleman. And he was eighty-four years old, and he'd drummed merchandise in thirty-one states. And old Dave, he'd go up to his room, y'understand, put on his green velvet slippers—I'll never forget—and pick up his phone and call the buyers, and without ever leaving his room, at the age of eighty-four, he made his living. And when I saw that, I realized that selling was the greatest career a man could want. 'Cause what could be more satisfying than to be able to go, at the age of eight-four, into twenty or thirty different cities, and pick up a phone, and be remembered and loved and helped by so many different people? Do you know? when he died—and by the way he died the death of a salesman, in his green velvet slippers in the smoker of the New York, New Haven and Hartford, going into Boston—when he died, hundreds of salesmen and buyers were at his funeral. Things were sad on a lotta trains for months after that. (*He stands up, Howard has not looked at him.*) In those days there was personality in it, Howard. There was respect, and comradeship, and gratitude in it. Today, it's all cut and dried, and there's no chance for bringing friendship to bear—or personality. You see what I mean? They don't know me any more.

HOWARD (*moving away, to the right*): That's just the thing, Willy.

WILLY: If I had forty dollars a week—that's all I'd need. Forty dollars, Howard.

HOWARD: Kid, I can't take blood from a stone, I . . .

WILLY (*desperation is on him now*): Howard, the year Al Smith was nominated, your father came to me and . . .

HOWARD (*starting to go off*): I've got to see some people, kid.

WILLY (*stopping him*): I'm talking about your father! There were promises made across this desk! You mustn't tell me you've got people to see—I put thirty-four years into this firm, Howard, and now I can't pay my insurance! You can't eat the orange and throw the peel away—a man is not a piece of fruit! (*After a pause.*) Now pay attention. Your father—in 1928 I had a big year. I averaged a hundred and seventy dollars a week in commissions.

HOWARD (*impatiently*): Now, Willy, you never averaged . . .

WILLY (*banging his hand on the desk*): I averaged a hundred and seventy dollars a week in the year of 1928! And your father came to me—or rather, I was in the office here—it was right over this desk—and he put his hand on my shoulder . . .

HOWARD (*getting up*): You'll have to excuse me, Willy, I gotta see some people. Pull yourself together. (*Going out.*) I'll be back in a little while.

On Howard's exit, the light on his chair grows very bright and strange.

WILLY: Pull myself together! What the hell did I say to him? My God, I was yelling at him! How could I? (*Willy breaks off, staring at the light, which occupies the chair, animating it. He approaches this chair, standing across the desk from it.*) Frank, Frank, don't you remember what you told me that time? How you put your hand on my shoulder, and Frank . . . (*He leans on the desk and as he speaks the dead man's name he accidentally switches on the recorder, and instantly*)

HOWARD'S SON: ". . . of New York is Albany. The capital of Ohio is Cincinnati, the capital of Rhode Island is . . ." (*The recitation continues.*)

WILLY (*leaping away with fright, shouting*): Ha! Howard! Howard! Howard!

HOWARD (*rushing in*): What happened?

WILLY (*pointing at the machine, which continues nasally, childishly, with the capital cities*): Shut it off! Shut it off!

HOWARD (*pulling the plug out*): Look, Willy . . .

WILLY (*pressing his hands to his eyes*): I gotta get myself some coffee. I'll get some coffee . . .

Willy starts to walk out. Howard stops him.

HOWARD (*rolling up the cord*): Willy, look . . .

WILLY: I'll go to Boston.

HOWARD: Willy, you can't go to Boston for us.

WILLY: Why can't I go?

HOWARD: I don't want you to represent us. I've been meaning to tell you for a long time now.

WILLY: Howard, are you firing me?

HOWARD: I think you need a good long rest, Willy.

WILLY: Howard . . .

HOWARD: And when you feel better, come back, and we'll see if we can work something out.

WILLY: But I gotta earn money, Howard. I'm in no position to . . .

HOWARD: Where are your sons? Why don't your sons give you a hand?

WILLY: They're working on a very big deal.

HOWARD: This is no time for false pride, Willy. You go to your sons and you tell them that you're tired. You've got two great boys, haven't you?

WILLY: Oh, no question, no question, but in the meantime . . .

HOWARD: Then that's that, heh?

WILLY: All right, I'll go to Boston tomorrow.

HOWARD: No, no.

WILLY: I can't throw myself on my sons. I'm not a cripple!

HOWARD: Look, kid, I'm busy this morning.

WILLY (*grasping Howard's arm*): Howard, you've got to let me go to Boston!

HOWARD (*hard, keeping himself under control*): I've got a line of people to see this morning. Sit down, take five minutes, and pull yourself together, and then go home, will ya? I need the office, Willy. (*He starts to go, turns, remembering the recorder, starts to push off the table holding the recorder.*) Oh, yeah. Whenever you can this week, stop by and drop off the samples. You'll feel better, Willy, and then come back and we'll talk. Pull yourself together, kid, there's people outside.

Howard exits, pushing the table off left. Willy stares into space, exhausted. Now the music is heard—Ben's music—first distantly, then closer, closer. As Willy speaks, Ben enters from the right. He carries valise and umbrella.

WILLY: Oh, Ben, how did you do it? What is the answer? Did you wind up the Alaska deal already?

BEN: Doesn't take much time if you know what you're doing. Just a short business trip. Boarding ship in an hour. Wanted to say good-by.

WILLY: Ben, I've got to talk to you.

BEN (*glancing at his watch*): Haven't the time, William.

WILLY (*crossing the apron to Ben*): Ben, nothing's working out. I don't know what to do.

BEN: Now, look here, William. I've bought timberland in Alaska and I need a man to look after things for me.

WILLY: God, timberland! Me and my boys in those grand outdoors!

BEN: You've a new continent at your doorstep, William. Get out of these cities, they're full of talk and time payments and courts of law. Screw on your fists and you can fight for a fortune up there.

WILLY: Yes, yes! Linda, Linda!

Linda enters as of old, with the wash.

LINDA: Oh, you're back?

BEN: I haven't much time.

WILLY: No, wait! Linda, he's got a proposition for me in Alaska.

LINDA: But you've got . . . (*To Ben.*) He's got a beautiful job here.

WILLY: But in Alaska, kid, I could . . .

LINDA: You're doing well enough, Willy!

BEN (*to Linda*): Enough for what, my dear?

LINDA (*frightened of Ben and angry at him*): Don't say those things to him! Enough to be happy right here, right now. (*To Willy, while Ben laughs.*) Why must everybody conquer the world? You're well liked, and the boys love you, and someday—(*To Ben*)—why, old man Wagner told him just the other day that if he keeps it up he'll be a member of the firm, didn't he, Willy?

WILLY: Sure, sure. I am building something with this firm, Ben, and if a man is building something he must be on the right track, mustn't he?

BEN: What are you building? Lay your hand on it. Where is it?

WILLY (*hesitantly*): That's true, Linda, there's nothing.

LINDA: Why? (*To Ben.*) There's a man eighty-four years old . . .

WILLY: That's right, Ben, that's right. When I look at that man I say, what is there to worry about?

BEN: Bah!

WILLY: It's true, Ben. All he has to do is go into any city, pick up the phone, and he's making his living and you know why?

BEN (*picking up his valise*): I've got to go.

WILLY (*HOLDING BEN BACK*): Look at this boy!

Biff, in his high school sweater, enters carrying suitcase. Happy carries Biff's shoulder guards, gold helmet, and football pants.

WILLY: Without a penny to his name, three great universities are begging for him, and from there the sky's the limit, because it's not what you do, Ben. It's who you know and the smile on your face! It's contacts, Ben, contacts! The whole wealth of Alaska passes over the lunch table at the Commodore Hotel, and that's the wonder, the wonder of this country, that a man can end with diamonds here on the basis of being liked! (*He turns to Biff.*) And that's why when you get out on that field today it's important. Because thousands of people will be rooting for you and loving you. (*To Ben, who has again begun to leave.*) And Ben! when he walks into a business office his name will sound out like a bell and all the doors will open to him! I've seen it, Ben, I've seen it a thousand times! You can't feel it with your hand like timber, but it's there!

BEN: Good-by, William.

WILLY: Ben, am I right? Don't you think I'm right? I value your advice.

BEN: There's a new continent at your doorstep, William. You could walk out rich. Rich! (*He is gone.*)

WILLY: We'll do it here, Ben! You hear me? We're gonna do it here!

Young Bernard rushes in. The gay music of the Boys is heard.

BERNARD: Oh, gee, I was afraid you left already!

WILLY: Why? What time is it?

BERNARD: It's half-past one!

WILLY: Well, come on, everybody! Ebbets Field next stop! Where's the pennants? (*He rushes through the wall-line of the kitchen and out into the living room.*)

LINDA (*to Biff*): Did you pack fresh underwear?

BIFF (*who has been limbering up*): I want to go!

BERNARD: Biff, I'm carrying your helmet, ain't I?

HAPPY: No, I'm carrying the helmet.

BERNARD: Oh, Biff, you promised me.

HAPPY: I'm carrying the helmet.

BERNARD: How am I going to get in the locker room?

LINDA: Let him carry the shoulder guards. (*She puts her coat and hat on in the kitchen.*)

BERNARD: Can I, Biff? 'Cause I told everybody I'm going to be in the locker room.

HAPPY: In Ebbets Field it's the clubhouse.

BERNARD: I meant the clubhouse. Biff!

HAPPY: Biff!

BIFF (*grandly, after a slight pause*): Let him carry the shoulder guards.

HAPPY (*as he gives Bernard the shoulder guards*): Stay close to us now.

Willy rushes in with the pennants.

WILLY (*handing them out*): Everybody wave when Biff comes out on the field. (*Happy and Bernard run off.*) You set now, boy?

The music has died away.

BIFF: Ready to go, Pop. Every muscle is ready.

WILLY (*at the edge of the apron*): You realize what this means?

BIFF: That's right, Pop.

WILLY (*feeling Biff's muscles*): You're comin' home this afternoon captain of the All-Scholastic Championship Team of the City of New York.

BIFF: I got it, Pop. And remember, pal, when I take off my helmet, that touchdown is for you.

WILLY: Let's go! (*He is starting out, with his arm around Biff, when Charley enters, as of old, in knickers.*) I got no room for you, Charley.

CHARLEY: Room? For what?

WILLY: In the car.

CHARLEY: You goin' for a ride? I wanted to shoot some casino.

WILLY (*furiously*): Casino! (*Incredulously.*) Don't you realize what to-day is?

LINDA: Oh, he knows, Willy. He's just kidding you.

WILLY: That's nothing to kid about!

CHARLEY: No, Linda, what's goin' on?

LINDA: He's playing in Ebbets Field.

CHARLEY: Baseball in this weather?

WILLY: Don't talk to him. Come on, come on! (*He is pushing them out.*)

CHARLEY: Wait a minute, didn't you hear the news?

WILLY: What?

CHARLEY: Don't you listen to the radio? Ebbets Field just blew up.

WILLY: You go to hell! (*Charley laughs. Pushing them out.*) Come on, come on! We're late.

CHARLEY (*as they go*): Knock a homer, Biff, knock a homer!

WILLY (*the last to leave, turning to Charley*): I don't think that was funny, Charley. This is the greatest day of his life.

CHARLEY: Willy, when are you going to grow up?

WILLY: Yeah, heh? When this game is over, Charley, you'll be laughing out of the other side of your face. They'll be calling him another Red Grange. Twenty-five thousand a year.

CHARLEY (*kidding*): Is that so?

WILLY: Yeah, that's so.

CHARLEY: Well, then, I'm sorry, Willy. But tell me something.

WILLY: What?

CHARLEY: Who is Red Grange?

WILLY: Put up your hands. Goddam you, put up your hands!

Charley, chuckling, shakes his head and walks away, around the left corner of the stage. Willy follows him. The music rises to a mocking frenzy.

WILLY: Who the hell do you think you are, better than everybody else? You don't know everything, you big, ignorant, stupid . . . Put up your hands!

Light rises, on the right side of the forestage, on a small table in the reception room of Charley's office. Traffic sounds are heard. Bernard, now mature, sits whistling to himself. A pair of tennis rackets and an old overnight bag are on the floor beside him.

WILLY (*offstage*): What are you walking away for? Don't walk away! If you're going to say something say it to my face! I know you laugh at me behind my back. You'll laugh out of the other side of your goddam face after this game. Touchdown! Touchdown! Eighty thousand people! Touchdown! Right between the goal posts.

Bernard is a quiet, earnest, but self-assured young man. Willy's voice is coming from right upstage now. Bernard lowers his feet off the table and listens. Jenny, his father's secretary, enters.

JENNY (*distressed*): Say, Bernard, will you go out in the hall?

BERNARD: What is that noise? Who is it?

JENNY: Mr. Loman. He just got off the elevator.

BERNARD (*getting up*): Who's he arguing with?

JENNY: Nobody. There's nobody with him. I can't deal with him any more, and your father gets all upset every time he comes. I've got a lot of typing to do, and your father's waiting to sign it. Will you see him?

WILLY (*entering*): Touchdown! Touch—(*He sees Jenny.*) Jenny, Jenny, good to see you. How're ya? Workin'? Or still honest?

JENNY: Fine. How've you been feeling?

WILLY: Not much any more, Jenny. Ha, ha! (*He is surprised to see the rackets.*)

BERNARD: Hello, Uncle Willy.

WILLY (*almost shocked*): Bernard! Well, look who's here! (*He comes quickly, guiltily, to Bernard and warmly shakes his hand.*)

BERNARD: How are you? Good to see you.

WILLY: What are you doing here?

BERNARD: Oh, just stopped by to see Pop. Get off my feet till my train leaves. I'm going to Washington in a few minutes.

WILLY: Is he in?

BERNARD: Yes, he's in his office with the accountant. Sit down.

WILLY (*sitting down*): What're you going to do in Washington?

BERNARD: Oh, just a case I've got there, Willy.

WILLY: That so? (*Indicating the rackets.*) You going to play tennis there?

BERNARD: I'm staying with a friend who's got a court.

WILLY: Don't say. His own tennis court. Must be fine people, I bet.

BERNARD: They are, very nice. Dad tells me Biff's in town.

WILLY (*with a big smile*): Yeah, Biff's in. Working on a very big deal, Bernard.

BERNARD: What's Biff doing?

WILLY: Well, he's been doing very big things in the West. But he decided to establish himself here. Very big. We're having dinner. Did I hear your wife had a boy?

BERNARD: That's right. Our second.

WILLY: Two boys! What do you know!

BERNARD: What kind of a deal has Biff got?

WILLY: Well, Bill Oliver—very big sporting-goods man—he wants Biff very badly. Called him in from the West. Long distance, carte blanche, special deliveries. Your friends have their own private tennis court?

BERNARD: You still with the old firm, Willy?

WILLY (*after a pause*): I'm—I'm overjoyed to see how you made the grade, Bernard, overjoyed. It's an encouraging thing to see a young man really—really . . . Looks very good for Biff—very . . . (*He breaks off, then.*) Bernard . . . (*He is so full of emotion, he breaks off again.*)

BERNARD: What is it, Willy?

WILLY (*small and alone*): What—what's the secret?

BERNARD: What secret?

WILLY: How—how did you? Why didn't he ever catch on?

BERNARD: I wouldn't know that, Willy.

WILLY (*confidentially, desperately*): You were his friend, his boyhood friend. There's something I don't understand about it. His life ended after that Ebbets Field game. From the age of seventeen nothing good ever happened to him.

BERNARD: He never trained himself for anything.

WILLY: But he did, he did. After high school he took so many correspondence courses. Radio mechanics; television; God knows what, and never made the slightest mark.

BERNARD (*taking off his glasses*): Willy, do you want to talk candidly?

WILLY (*rising, faces Bernard*): I regard you as a very brilliant man, Bernard. I value your advice.

BERNARD: Oh, the hell with the advice, Willy. I couldn't advise you. There's just one thing I've always wanted to ask you. When he was supposed to graduate, and the math teacher flunked him . . .

WILLY: Oh, that son-of-a-bitch ruined his life.

BERNARD: Yeah, but, Willy, all he had to do was go to summer school and make up that subject.

WILLY: That's right, that's right.

BERNARD: Did you tell him not to go to summer school?

WILLY: Me? I begged him to go. I ordered him to go!

BERNARD: Then why wouldn't he go?

WILLY: Why? Why! Bernard, that question has been trailing me like a ghost for the last fifteen years. He flunked the subject, and laid down and died like a hammer hit him!

BERNARD: Take it easy, kid.

WILLY: Let me talk to you—I got nobody to talk to. Bernard, Bernard, was it my fault? Y'see? It keeps going around in my mind, maybe I did something to him. I got nothing to give him.

BERNARD: Don't take it so hard.

WILLY: Why did he lay down? What is the story there? You were his friend!

BERNARD: Willy, I remember, it was June, and our grades came out. And he'd flunked math.

WILLY: That son-of-a-bitch!

BERNARD: No, it wasn't right then. Biff just got very angry, I remember, and he was ready to enroll in summer school.

WILLY (*surprised*): He was?

BERNARD: He wasn't beaten by it at all. But then, Willy, he disappeared from the block for almost a month. And I got the idea that he'd gone up to New England to see you. Did he have a talk with you then?

Willy stares in silence.

BERNARD: Willy?

WILLY (*with a strong edge of resentment in his voice*): Yeah, he came to Boston. What about it?

BERNARD: Well, just that when he came back—I'll never forget this, it always mystifies me. Because I'd thought so well of Biff, even though he'd always taken advantage of me. I loved him, Willy, y'know? And he came back after that month and took his sneakers—remember those sneakers with "University of Virginia" printed on them? He was so proud of those, wore them every day. And he took them down in the cellar, and burned them up in the furnace. We had a fist fight. It lasted at least half an hour. Just the two of us, punching each other down the cellar, and crying right through it. I've often thought of how strange it was that I knew he'd given up his life. What happened in Boston, Willy?

Willy looks at him as at an intruder.

BERNARD: I just bring it up because you asked me.

WILLY (*angrily*): Nothing. What do you mean, "What happened?" What's that got to do with anything?

BERNARD: Well, don't get sore.

WILLY: What are you trying to do, blame it on me? If a boy lays down is that my fault?

BERNARD: Now, Willy, don't get . . .

WILLY: Well, don't—don't talk to me that way! What does that mean, "What happened?"

Charley enters. He is in his vest, and he carries a bottle of bourbon.

CHARLEY: Hey, you're going to miss that train. (*He waves the bottle.*)

BERNARD: Yeah, I'm going. (*He takes the bottle.*) Thanks, Pop. (*He picks up his rackets and bag.*) Good-by, Willy, and don't worry about it. You know, "If at first you don't succeed . . ."

WILLY: Yes, I believe in that.

BERNARD: But sometimes, Willy, it's better for a man just to walk away.

WILLY: Walk away?

BERNARD: That's right.

WILLY: But if you can't walk away?

BERNARD (*after a slight pause*): I guess that's when it's tough. (*Extending his hand.*) Good-by, Willy.

WILLY (*shaking Bernard's hand*): Good-by, boy.

CHARLEY (*an arm on Bernard's shoulder*): How do you like this kid? Gonna argue a case in front of the Supreme Court.

BERNARD (*protesting*): Pop!

WILLY (*genuinely shocked, pained, and happy*): No! The Supreme Court!

BERNARD: I gotta run. 'By, Dad!

CHARLEY: Knock 'em dead, Bernard!

Bernard goes off.

WILLY (*as Charley takes out his wallet*): The Supreme Court! And he didn't even mention it!

CHARLEY (*counting out money on the desk*): He don't have to—he's gonna do it.

WILLY: And you never told him what to do, did you? You never took any interest in him.

CHARLEY: My salvation is that I never took any interest in anything. There's some money—fifty dollars. I got an accountant inside.

WILLY: Charley, look . . . (*with difficulty.*) I got my insurance to pay. If you can manage it—I need a hundred and ten dollars.

Charley doesn't reply for a moment; merely stops moving.

WILLY: I'd draw it from my bank but Linda would know, and I . . .

CHARLEY: Sit down, Willy.

WILLY (*moving toward the chair*): I'm keeping an account of everything, remember. I'll pay every penny back. (*He sits.*)

CHARLEY: Now listen to me, Willy.

WILLY: I want you to know I appreciate . . .

CHARLEY (*sitting down on the table*): Willy, what're you doin'? What the hell is going on in your head?

WILLY: Why? I'm simply . . .

CHARLEY: I offered you a job. You make fifty dollars a week. And I won't send you on the road.

WILLY: I've got a job.

CHARLEY: Without pay? What kind of a job is a job without pay? (*He rises.*) Now, look, kid, enough is enough. I'm no genius but I know when I'm being insulted.

WILLY: Insulted!

CHARLEY: Why don't you want to work for me?

WILLY: What's the matter with you? I've got a job.

CHARLEY: Then what're you walkin' in here every week for?

WILLY (*getting up*): Well, if you don't want me to walk in here . . .

CHARLEY: I'm offering you a job.

WILLY: I don't want your goddam job!

CHARLEY: When the hell are you going to grow up?

WILLY (*furiously*): You big ignoramus, if you say that to me again I'll rap you one! I don't care how big you are! (*He's ready to fight.*)

Pause.

CHARLEY (*kindly, going to him*): How much do you need, Willy?

WILLY: Charley, I'm strapped. I'm strapped. I don't know what to do. I was just fired.

CHARLEY: Howard fired you?

WILLY: That snotnose. Imagine that? I named him. I named him Howard.

CHARLEY: Willy, when're you gonna realize that them things don't mean anything? You named him Howard, but you can't sell that.

The only thing you got in this world is what you can sell. And the funny thing is that you're a salesman, and you don't know that.

WILLY: I've always tried to think otherwise, I guess. I always felt that if a man was impressive, and well liked, that nothing . . .

CHARLEY: Why must everybody like you? Who liked J. P. Morgan? Was he impressive? In a Turkish bath he'd look like a butcher. But with his pockets on he was very well liked. Now listen, Willy, I know you don't like me, and nobody can say I'm in love with you, but I'll give you a job because—just for the hell of it, put it that way. Now what do you say?

WILLY: I—I just can't work for you, Charley.

CHARLEY: What're you, jealous of me?

WILLY: I can't work for you, that's all, don't ask me why.

CHARLEY (*angered, takes out more bills*): You been jealous of me all your life, you damned fool! Here, pay your insurance. (*He puts the money in Willy's hand.*)

WILLY: I'm keeping strict accounts.

CHARLEY: I've got some work to do. Take care of yourself. And pay your insurance.

WILLY (*moving to the right*): Funny, y'know? After all the highways, and the trains, and the appointments, and the years, you end up worth more dead than alive.

CHARLEY: Willy, nobody's worth nothin' dead. (*After a slight pause.*) Did you hear what I said?

Willy stands still, dreaming.

CHARLEY: Willy!

WILLY: Apologize to Bernard for me when you see him. I didn't mean to argue with him. He's a fine boy. They're all fine boys, and they'll end up big—all of them. Someday they'll all play tennis together. Wish me luck, Charley. He saw Bill Oliver today.

CHARLEY: Good luck.

WILLY (*on the verge of tears*): Charley, you're the only friend I got. Isn't that a remarkable thing? (*He goes out.*)

CHARLEY: Jesus!

Charley stares after him a moment and follows. All light blacks out. Suddenly raucous music is heard, and a red glow rises behind the screen at right. Stanley, a young waiter, appears, carrying a table, followed by Happy, who is carrying two chairs.

STANLEY (*putting the table down*): That's all right, Mr. Loman, I can handle it myself. (*He turns and takes the chairs from Happy and places them at the table.*)

HAPPY (*glancing around*): Oh, this is better.

STANLEY: Sure, in the front there you're in the middle of all kinds of noise. Whenever you got a party, Mr. Loman, you just tell me and I'll put you back here. Y'know, there's a lotta people they don't like it private, because when they go out they like to see a lotta action around them because they're sick and tired to stay in the house by theirself. But I know you, you ain't from Hackensack. You know what I mean?

HAPPY (*sitting down*): So how's it coming, Stanley?

STANLEY: Ah, it's a dog life. I only wish during the war they'd a took me in the Army. I coulda been dead by now.

HAPPY: My brother's back, Stanley.

STANLEY: Oh, he come back, heh? From the Far West.

HAPPY: Yeah, big cattle man, my brother, so treat him right. And my father's coming too.

STANLEY: Oh, your father too!

HAPPY: You got a couple of nice lobsters?

STANLEY: Hundred per cent, big.

HAPPY: I want them with the claws.

STANLEY: Don't worry, I don't give you no mice. (*Happy laughs.*) How about some wine? It'll put a head on the meal.

HAPPY: No. You remember, Stanley, that recipe I brought you from overseas? With the champagne in it?

STANLEY: Oh, yeah, sure. I still got it tacked up yet in the kitchen. But that'll have to cost a buck apiece anyways.

HAPPY: That's all right.

STANLEY: What'd you, hit a number or somethin'?

HAPPY: No, it's a little celebration. My brother is—I think he pulled off a big deal today. I think we're going into business together.

STANLEY: Great! That's the best for you. Because a family business, you know what I mean?—that's the best.

HAPPY: That's what I think.

STANLEY: 'Cause what's the difference? Somebody steals? It's in the family. Know what I mean? (*Sotto voce.*) Like this bartender here. The boss is goin' crazy what kinda leak he's got in the cash register. You put it in but it don't come out.

HAPPY (*raising his head*):   Sh!

STANLEY: What?

HAPPY: You notice I wasn't lookin' right or left, was I?

STANLEY: No.

HAPPY: And my eyes are closed.

STANLEY: So what's the . . . ?

HAPPY: Strudel's comin'.

STANLEY (*catching on, looks around*):   Ah, no, there's no . . .

> *He breaks off as a furred, lavishly dressed Girl enters and sits at the next table. Both follow her with their eyes.*

STANLEY: Geez, how'd ya know?

HAPPY: I got radar or something. (*Staring directly at her profile.*) Ooooooo . . . Stanley.

STANLEY: I think that's for you, Mr. Loman.

HAPPY: Look at that mouth. Oh, God. And the binoculars.

STANLEY: Geez, you got a life, Mr. Loman.

HAPPY: Wait on her.

STANLEY (*going to the Girl's table*):   Would you like a menu, ma'am?

GIRL: I'm expecting someone, but I'd like a . . .

HAPPY: Why don't you bring her—excuse me, miss, do you mind? I sell champagne, and I'd like you to try my brand. Bring her a champagne, Stanley.

GIRL: That's awfully nice of you.

HAPPY: Don't mention it. It's all company money. (*He laughs.*)

GIRL: That's a charming product to be selling, isn't it?

HAPPY: Oh, gets to be like everything else. Selling is selling, y'know.

GIRL: I suppose.

HAPPY: You don't happen to sell, do you?

GIRL: No, I don't sell.

HAPPY: Would you object to a compliment from a stranger? You ought to be on a magazine cover.

GIRL (*looking at him a little archly*):   I have been.

> *Stanley comes in with a glass of champagne.*

HAPPY: What'd I say before, Stanley? You see? She's a cover girl.

STANLEY: Oh, I could see, I could see.

HAPPY (*to the Girl*):   What magazine?

GIRL: Oh, a lot of them. (*She takes the drink.*) Thank you.

HAPPY: You know what they say in France, don't you? "Champagne is the drink of the complexion"—Hya, Biff!

Biff has entered and sits with Happy.

BIFF: Hello, kid. Sorry I'm late.

HAPPY: I just got here. Uh, Miss . . . ?

GIRL: Forsythe.

HAPPY: Miss Forsythe, this is my brother.

BIFF: Is Dad here?

HAPPY: His name is Biff. You might've heard of him. Great football player.

GIRL: Really? What team?

HAPPY: Are you familiar with football?

GIRL: No, I'm afraid I'm not.

HAPPY: Biff is quarterback with the New York Giants.

GIRL: Well, that is nice, isn't it? (*She drinks.*)

HAPPY: Good health.

GIRL: I'm happy to meet you.

HAPPY: That's my name. Hap. It's really Harold, but at West Point they called me Happy.

GIRL (*now really impressed*): Oh, I see. How do you do? (*She turns her profile.*)

BIFF: Isn't Dad coming?

HAPPY: You want her?

BIFF: Oh, I could never make that.

HAPPY: I remember the time that idea would never come into your head. Where's the old confidence, Biff?

BIFF: I just saw Oliver . . .

HAPPY: Wait a minute. I've got to see that old confidence again. Do you want her? She's on call.

BIFF: Oh, no. (*He turns to look at the Girl.*)

HAPPY: I'm telling you. Watch this. (*Turning to the Girl.*) Honey? (*She turns to him.*) Are you busy?

GIRL: Well, I am . . . but I could make a phone call.

HAPPY: Do that, will you, honey? And see if you can get a friend. We'll be here for a while. Biff is one of the greatest football players in the country.

GIRL (*standing up*):   Well, I'm certainly happy to meet you.

HAPPY: Come back soon.

GIRL: I'll try.

HAPPY: Don't try, honey, try hard.

The Girl exits. Stanley follows, shaking his head in bewildered admiration.

HAPPY: Isn't that a shame now? A beautiful girl like that? That's why I can't get married. There's not a good woman in a thousand. New York is loaded with them, kid!

BIFF: Hap, look . . .

HAPPY: I told you she was on call!

BIFF (*strangely unnerved*):   Cut it out, will ya? I want to say something to you.

HAPPY: Did you see Oliver?

BIFF: I saw him all right. Now look, I want to tell Dad a couple of things and I want you to help me.

HAPPY: What? Is he going to back you?

BIFF: Are you crazy? You're out of your goddam head, you know that?

HAPPY: Why? What happened?

BIFF (*breathlessly*):   I did a terrible thing today, Hap. It's been the strangest day I ever went through. I'm all numb, I swear.

HAPPY: You mean he wouldn't see you?

BIFF: Well, I waited six hours for him, see? All day. Kept sending my name in. Even tried to date his secretary so she'd get me to him, but no soap.

HAPPY: Because you're not showin' the old confidence, Biff. He remembered you, didn't he?

BIFF (*stopping Happy with a gesture*):   Finally, about five o'clock, he comes out. Didn't remember who I was or anything. I felt like such an idiot, Hap.

HAPPY: Did you tell him my Florida idea?

BIFF: He walked away. I saw him for one minute. I got so mad I could've torn the walls down! How the hell did I ever get the idea I was a salesman there? I even believed myself that I'd been a salesman for him! And then he gave me one look and—I realized what a ridiculous lie my whole life has been! We've been talking in a dream for fifteen years. I was a shipping clerk.

HAPPY: What'd you do?

BIFF (*with great tension and wonder*): Well, he left, see. And the secretary went out. I was all alone in the waiting room. I don't know what came over me, Hap. The next thing I know I'm in his office—paneled walls, everything. I can't explain it. I—Hap. I took his fountain pen.

HAPPY: Geez, did he catch you?

BIFF: I ran out. I ran down all eleven flights. I ran and ran and ran.

HAPPY: That was an awful dumb—what'd you do that for?

BIFF (*agonized*): I don't know, I just—wanted to take something, I don't know. You gotta help me, Hap. I'm gonna tell Pop.

HAPPY: You crazy? What for?

BIFF: Hap, he's got to understand that I'm not the man somebody lends that kind of money to. He thinks I've been spiting him all these years and it's eating him up.

HAPPY: That's just it. You tell him something nice.

BIFF: I can't.

HAPPY: Say you got a lunch date with Oliver tomorrow.

BIFF: So what do I do tomorrow?

HAPPY: You leave the house tomorrow and come back at night and say Oliver is thinking it over. And he thinks it over for a couple of weeks, and gradually it fades away and nobody's the worse.

BIFF: But it'll go on forever!

HAPPY: Dad is never so happy as when he's looking forward to something!

Willy enters.

HAPPY: Hello, scout!

WILLY: Gee, I haven't been here in years!

Stanley has followed Willy in and sets a chair for him. Stanley starts off but Happy stops him.

HAPPY: Stanley!

Stanley stands by, waiting for an order.

BIFF (*going to Willy with guilt, as to an invalid*): Sit down, Pop. You want a drink?

WILLY: Sure, I don't mind.

BIFF: Let's get a load on.

WILLY: You look worried.

BIFF: N-no. (*To Stanley.*) Scotch all around. Make it doubles.

STANLEY: Doubles, right. (*He goes.*)

WILLY: You had a couple already, didn't you?

BIFF: Just a couple, yeah.

WILLY: Well, what happened, boy? (*Nodding affirmatively, with a smile.*) Everything go all right?

BIFF (*takes a breath, then reaches out and grasps Willy's hand*): Pal . . . (*He is smiling bravely, and Willy is smiling too.*) I had an experience today.

HAPPY: Terrific, Pop.

WILLY: That so? What happened?

BIFF (*high, slightly alcoholic, above the earth*): I'm going to tell you everything from first to last. It's been a strange day. (*Silence. He looks around, composes himself as best he can, but his breath keeps breaking the rhythm of his voice.*) I had to wait quite a while for him, and . . .

WILLY: Oliver?

BIFF: Yeah, Oliver. All day, as a matter of cold fact. And a lot of—instances—facts, Pop, facts about my life came back to me. Who was it, Pop? Who ever said I was a salesman with Oliver?

WILLY: Well, you were.

BIFF: No, Dad, I was a shipping clerk.

WILLY: But you were practically . . .

BIFF (*with determination*): Dad, I don't know who said it first, but I was never a salesman for Bill Oliver.

WILLY: What're you talking about?

BIFF: Let's hold on to the facts tonight, Pop. We're not going to get anywhere bullin' around. I was a shipping clerk.

WILLY (*angrily*): All right, now listen to me . . .

BIFF: Why don't you let me finish?

WILLY: I'm not interested in stories about the past or any crap of that kind because the woods are burning, boys, you understand? There's a big blaze going on all around. I was fired today.

BIFF (*shocked*): How could you be?

WILLY: I was fired, and I'm looking for a little good news to tell your mother, because the woman has waited and the woman has suffered. The gist of it is that I haven't got a story left in my head, Biff.

So don't give me a lecture about facts and aspects. I am not interested. Now what've you got to say to me?

Stanley enters with three drinks. They wait until he leaves.

WILLY: Did you see Oliver?

BIFF: Jesus, Dad!

WILLY: You mean you didn't go up there?

HAPPY: Sure he went up there.

BIFF: I did. I—saw him. How could they fire you?

WILLY (*on the edge of his chair*): What kind of a welcome did he give you?

BIFF: He won't even let you work on commission?

WILLY: I'm out! (*Driving.*) So tell me, he gave you a warm welcome?

HAPPY: Sure, Pop, sure!

BIFF (*driven*): Well, it was kind of . . .

WILLY: I was wondering if he'd remember you. (*To Happy.*) Imagine, man doesn't see him for ten, twelve years and gives him that kind of a welcome!

HAPPY: Damn right!

BIFF (*trying to return to the offensive*): Pop, look . . .

WILLY: You know why he remembered you, don't you? Because you impressed him in those days.

BIFF: Let's talk quietly and get this down to the facts, huh?

WILLY (*as though Biff had been interrupting*): Well, what happened? It's great news, Biff. Did he take you into his office or'd you talk in the waiting room?

BIFF: Well, he came in, see, and . . .

WILLY (*with a big smile*): What'd he say? Betcha he threw his arm around you.

BIFF: Well, he kinda . . .

WILLY: He's a fine man. (*To Happy.*) Very hard man to see, y'know.

HAPPY (*agreeing*): Oh, I know.

WILLY (*to Biff*): Is that where you had the drinks?

BIFF: Yeah, he gave me a couple of—no, no!

HAPPY (*cutting in*): He told him my Florida idea.

WILLY: Don't interrupt. (*To Biff.*) How'd he react to the Florida idea?

BIFF: Dad, will you give me a minute to explain?

WILLY: I've been waiting for you to explain since I sat down here! What happened? He took you into his office and what?

BIFF: Well—I talked. And—and he listened, see.

WILLY: Famous for the way he listens, y'know. What was his answer?

BIFF: His answer was—(*He breaks off, suddenly angry.*) Dad, you're not letting me tell you what I want to tell you!

WILLY (*accusing, angered*): You didn't see him, did you?

BIFF: I did see him!

WILLY: What'd you insult him or something? You insulted him, didn't you?

BIFF: Listen, will you let me out of it, will you just let me out of it!

HAPPY: What the hell!

WILLY: Tell me what happened!

BIFF (*to Happy*): I can't talk to him!

A single trumpet note jars the ear. The light of green leaves stains the house, which holds the air of night and a dream. Young Bernard enters and knocks on the door of the house.

YOUNG BERNARD (*frantically*): Mrs. Loman, Mrs. Loman!

HAPPY: Tell him what happened!

BIFF (*to Happy.*): Shut up and leave me alone!

WILLY: No, no! You had to go and flunk math!

BIFF: What math? What're you talking about?

YOUNG BERNARD: Mrs. Loman, Mrs. Loman!

Linda appears in the house, as of old.

WILLY (*wildly*): Math, math, math!

BIFF: Take it easy, Pop!

YOUNG BERNARD: Mrs. Loman!

WILLY (*furiously*): If you hadn't flunked you'd've been set by now!

BIFF: Now, look, I'm gonna tell you what happened, and you're going to listen to me.

YOUNG BERNARD: Mrs. Loman!

BIFF: I waited six hours . . .

HAPPY: What the hell are you saying?

BIFF: I kept sending in my name but he wouldn't see me. So finally he . . . (*He continues unheard as light fades low on the restaurant.*)

YOUNG BERNARD: Biff flunked math!

LINDA: No!

YOUNG BERNARD: Birnbaum flunked him! They won't graduate him!

LINDA: But they have to. He's gotta go to the university. Where is he? Biff! Biff!

YOUNG BERNARD: No, he left. He went to Grand Central.

LINDA: Grand—You mean he went to Boston!

YOUNG BERNARD: Is Uncle Willy in Boston?

LINDA: Oh, maybe Willy can talk to the teacher. Oh, the poor, poor boy!

Light on house area snaps out.

BIFF (*at the table, now audible, holding up a gold fountain pen*): . . . so I'm washed up with Oliver, you understand? Are you listening to me?

WILLY (*at a loss*): Yeah, sure. If you hadn't flunked . . .

BIFF: Flunked what? What're you talking about?

WILLY: Don't blame everything on me! I didn't flunk math—you did! What pen?

HAPPY: That was awful dumb, Biff, a pen like that is worth—

WILLY (*seeing the pen for the first time*): You took Oliver's pen?

BIFF (*weakening*): Dad, I just explained it to you.

WILLY: You stole Bill Oliver's fountain pen!

BIFF: I didn't exactly steal it! That's just what I've been explaining to you!

HAPPY: He had it in his hand and just then Oliver walked in, so he got nervous and stuck it in his pocket!

WILLY: My God, Biff!

BIFF: I never intended to do it, Dad!

OPERATOR'S VOICE: Standish Arms, good evening!

WILLY (*shouting*): I'm not in my room!

BIFF (*frightened*): Dad, what's the matter? (*He and Happy stand up.*)

OPERATOR: Ringing Mr. Loman for you!

WILLY: I'm not there, stop it!

BIFF (*horrified, gets down on one knee before Willy*): Dad, I'll make good, I'll make good. (*Willy tries to get to his feet. Biff holds him down.*) Sit down now.

WILLY: No, you're no good, you're no good for anything.

BIFF: I am, Dad, I'll find something else, you understand? Now don't worry about anything. (*He holds up Willy's face.*) Talk to me, Dad.

OPERATOR: Mr. Loman does not answer. Shall I page him?

WILLY (*attempting to stand, as though to rush and silence the Operator*): No, no, no!

HAPPY: He'll strike something, Pop.

WILLY: No, no . . .

BIFF (*desperately, standing over Willy*): Pop, listen! Listen to me! I'm telling you something good. Oliver talked to his partner about the Florida idea. You listening? He—he talked to his partner, and he came to me . . . I'm going to be all right, you hear? Dad, listen to me, he said it was just a question of the amount!

WILLY: Then you . . . got it?

HAPPY: He's gonna be terrific, Pop!

WILLY (*trying to stand*): Then you got it, haven't you? You got it! You got it!

BIFF (*agonized, holds Willy down*): No, no. Look, Pop. I'm supposed to have lunch with them tomorrow. I'm just telling you this so you'll know that I can still make an impression, Pop. And I'll make good somewhere, but I can't go tomorrow, see.

WILLY: Why not? You simply . . .

BIFF: But the pen, Pop!

WILLY: You give it to him and tell him it was an oversight!

HAPPY: Sure, have lunch tomorrow!

BIFF: I can't say that . . .

WILLY: You were doing a crossword puzzle and accidentally used his pen!

BIFF: Listen, kid, I took those balls years ago, now I walk in with his fountain pen? That clinches it, don't you see? I can't face him like that! I'll try elsewhere.

PAGE'S VOICE: Paging Mr. Loman!

WILLY: Don't you want to be anything?

BIFF: Pop, how can I go back?

WILLY: You don't want to be anything, is that what's behind it?

BIFF (*now angry at Willy for not crediting his sympathy*): Don't take it that way! You think it was easy walking into that office after what I'd done to him? A team of horses couldn't have dragged me back to Bill Oliver!

WILLY: Then why'd you go?

BIFF: Why did I go? Why did I go! Look at you! Look at what's become of you!

Off left, The Woman laughs.

WILLY: Biff, you're going to go to that lunch tomorrow, or . . .

BIFF: I can't go. I've got no appointment!

HAPPY: Biff, for . . . !

WILLY: Are you spiting me?

BIFF: Don't take it that way! Goddammit!

WILLY (*strikes Biff and falters away from the table*): You rotten little louse! Are you spiting me?

THE WOMAN: Someone's at the door, Willy!

BIFF: I'm no good, can't you see what I am?

HAPPY (*separating them*): Hey, you're in a restaurant! Now cut it out, both of you! (*The girls enter.*) Hello, girls, sit down.

The Woman laughs, off left.

MISS FORSYTHE: I guess we might as well. This is Letta.

THE WOMAN: Willy, are you going to wake up?

BIFF (*ignoring Willy*): How're ya, miss, sit down. What do you drink?

MISS FORSYTHE: Letta might not be able to stay long.

LETTA: I gotta get up very early tomorrow. I got jury duty. I'm so excited! Were you fellows ever on a jury?

BIFF: No, but I been in front of them! (*The girls laugh.*) This is my father.

LETTA: Isn't he cute? Sit down with us, Pop.

HAPPY: Sit him down, Biff!

BIFF (*going to him*): Come on, slugger, drink us under the table. To hell with it! Come on, sit down, pal.

On Biff's last insistence, Willy is about to sit.

THE WOMAN (*now urgently*): Willy, are you going to answer the door!

The Woman's call pulls Willy back. He starts right, befuddled.

BIFF: Hey, where are you going?

WILLY: Open the door.

BIFF: The door?

WILLY: The washroom . . . the door . . . where's the door?

BIFF (*leading Willy to the left*): Just go straight down.

Willy moves left.

THE WOMAN: Willy, Willy, are you going to get up, get up, get up, get up?

Willy exits left.

LETTA: I think it's sweet you bring your daddy along.

MISS FORSYTHE: Oh, he isn't really your father!

BIFF (*at left, turning to her resentfully*): Miss Forsythe, you've just seen a prince walk by. A fine, troubled prince. A hardworking, unappreciated prince. A pal, you understand? A good companion. Always for his boys.

LETTA: That's so sweet.

HAPPY: Well, girls, what's the program? We're wasting time. Come on, Biff. Gather round. Where would you like to go?

BIFF: Why don't you do something for him?

HAPPY: Me!

BIFF: Don't you give a damn for him, Hap?

HAPPY: What're you talking about? I'm the one who . . .

BIFF: I sense it, you don't give a good goddam about him. (*He takes the rolled-up hose from his pocket and puts it on the table in front of Happy.*) Look what I found in the cellar, for Christ's sake. How can you bear to let it go on?

HAPPY: Me? Who goes away? Who runs off and . . .

BIFF: Yeah, but he doesn't mean anything to you. You could help him—I can't! Don't you understand what I'm talking about? He's going to kill himself, don't you know that?

HAPPY: Don't know it! Me!

BIFF: Hap, help him! Jesus . . . help him . . . Help me, help me, I can't bear to look at his face! (*Ready to weep, he hurries out, up right.*)

HAPPY (*starting after him*): Where are you going?

MISS FORSYTHE: What's he so mad about?

HAPPY: Come on, girls, we'll catch up with him.

MISS FORSYTHE (*as Happy pushes her out*): Say, I don't like that temper of his!

HAPPY: He's just a little overstrung, he'll be all right!

WILLY (*off left, as The Woman laughs*): Don't answer! Don't answer!

LETTA: Don't you want to tell your father . . .

HAPPY: No, that's not my father. He's just a guy. Come on, we'll catch Biff, and, honey, we're going to paint this town! Stanley, where's the check! Hey, Stanley!

They exit. Stanley looks toward left.

STANLEY (*calling to Happy indignantly*): Mr. Loman! Mr. Loman!

Stanley picks up a chair and follows them off. Knocking is heard off left. The Woman enters, laughing. Willy follows her. She is in a black slip; he is buttoning his shirt. Raw, sensuous music accompanies their speech:

WILLY: Will you stop laughing? Will you stop?

THE WOMAN: Aren't you going to answer the door? He'll wake the whole hotel.

WILLY: I'm not expecting anybody.

THE WOMAN: Whyn't you have another drink, honey, and stop being so damn self-centered?

WILLY: I'm so lonely.

THE WOMAN: You know you ruined me, Willy? From now on, whenever you come to the office, I'll see that you go right through to the buyers. No waiting at my desk anymore, Willy. You ruined me.

WILLY: That's nice of you to say that.

THE WOMAN: Gee, you are self-centered! Why so sad? You are the saddest, self-centeredest soul I ever did see-saw. (*She laughs. He kisses her.*) Come on inside, drummer boy. It's silly to be dressing in the middle of the night. (*As knocking is heard.*) Aren't you going to answer the door?

WILLY: They're knocking on the wrong door.

THE WOMAN: But I felt the knocking. And he heard us talking in here. Maybe the hotel's on fire!

WILLY (*his terror rising*): It's a mistake.

THE WOMAN: Then tell him to go away!

WILLY: There's nobody there.

THE WOMAN: It's getting on my nerves, Willy. There's somebody standing out there and it's getting on my nerves!

WILLY (*pushing her away from him*): All right, stay in the bathroom here, and don't come out. I think there's a law in Massachusetts about it, so don't come out. It may be that new room clerk. He looked very mean. So don't come out. It's a mistake, there's no fire.

The knocking is heard again. He takes a few steps away from her, and she vanishes into the wing. The light follows him, and now he is facing Young Biff, who carries a suitcase. Biff steps toward him. The music is gone.

BIFF: Why didn't you answer?

WILLY: Biff! What are you doing in Boston?

BIFF: Why didn't you answer? I've been knocking for five minutes, I called you on the phone . . .

WILLY: I just heard you. I was in the bathroom and had the door shut. Did anything happen home?

BIFF: Dad—I let you down.

WILLY: What do you mean?

BIFF: Dad . . .

WILLY: Biffo, what's this about? (*Putting his arm around Biff.*) Come on, let's go downstairs and get you a malted.

BIFF: Dad, I flunked math.

WILLY: Not for the term?

BIFF: The term. I haven't got enough credits to graduate.

WILLY: You mean to say Bernard wouldn't give you the answers?

BIFF: He did, he tried, but I only got a sixty-one.

WILLY: And they wouldn't give you four points?

BIFF: Birnbaum refused absolutely. I begged him, Pop, but he won't give me those points. You gotta talk to him before they close the school. Because if he saw the kind of man you are, and you just talked to him in your way, I'm sure he'd come through for me. The class came right before practice, see, and I didn't go enough. Would you talk to him? He'd like you, Pop. You know the way you could talk.

WILLY: You're on. We'll drive right back.

BIFF: Oh, Dad, good work! I'm sure he'll change it for you!

WILLY: Go downstairs and tell the clerk I'm checkin' out. Go right down.

BIFF: Yes, sir! See, the reason he hates me, Pop—one day he was late for class so I got up at the blackboard and imitated him. I crossed my eyes and talked with a lithp.

WILLY (*laughing*): You did? The kids like it?

BIFF: They nearly died laughing!

WILLY: Yeah? What'd you do?

BIFF: The thquare root of thixthy twee is . . . (*Willy bursts out laughing; Biff joins.*) And in the middle of it he walked in!

Willy laughs and The Woman joins in offstage.

WILLY (*without hesitation*): Hurry downstairs and . . .

BIFF: Somebody in there?

WILLY: No, that was next door.

The Woman laughs offstage.

BIFF: Somebody got in your bathroom!

WILLY: No, it's the next room, there's a party . . .

THE WOMAN (*enters, laughing; she lisps this*): Can I come in? There's something in the bathtub, Willy, and it's moving!

Willy looks at Biff; who is staring open-mouthed and horrified at The Woman.

WILLY: Ah—you better go back to your room. They must be finished painting by now. They're painting her room so I let her take a shower here. Go back, go back . . . (*He pushes her.*)

THE WOMAN (*resisting*): But I've got to get dressed, Willy, I can't . . .

WILLY: Get out of here! Go back, go back . . . (*Suddenly striving for the ordinary.*) This is Miss Francis, Biff, she's a buyer. They're painting her room. Go back, Miss Francis, go back . . .

THE WOMAN: But my clothes, I can't go out naked in the hall!

WILLY (*pushing her offstage*): Get outa here! Go back, go back!

Biff slowly sits down on his suitcase as the argument continues offstage.

THE WOMAN: Where's my stockings? You promised me stockings, Willy!

WILLY: I have no stockings here!

THE WOMAN: You had two boxes of size nine sheers for me, and I want them!

WILLY: Here, for God's sake, will you get outa here!

THE WOMAN (*enters holding a box of stockings*): I just hope there's nobody in the hall. That's all I hope. (*To Biff.*) Are you football or baseball?

BIFF: Football.

THE WOMAN (*angry, humiliated*): That's me too. G'night. (*She snatches her clothes from Willy, and walks out.*)

WILLY (*after a pause*): Well, better get going. I want to get to the school first thing in the morning. Get my suits out of the closet. I'll get my valise. (*Biff doesn't move.*) What's the matter! (*Biff remains motionless, tears falling.*) She's a buyer. Buys for J. H. Simmons. She lives down the hall—they're painting. You don't imagine—(*He breaks off. After a pause.*) Now listen, pal, she's just a buyer. She sells merchandise in her room and they have to keep it looking just so . . . (*Pause. Assuming command.*) All right, get my suits. (*Biff doesn't move.*) Now stop crying and do as I say. I gave you an order. Biff, I gave you an order! Is that what you do when I give you an order? How dare you cry! (*Putting his arm around Biff.*) Now look, Biff, when you grow up you'll understand about these things. You mustn't—you mustn't overemphasize a thing like this. I'll see Birnbaum first thing in the morning.

BIFF: Never mind.

WILLY (*getting down beside Biff*): Never mind! He's going to give you those points. I'll see to it.

BIFF: He wouldn't listen to you.

WILLY: He certainly will listen to me. You need those points for the U. of Virginia.

BIFF: I'm not going there.

WILLY: Heh? If I can't get him to change that mark you'll make it up in summer school. You've got all summer to . . .

BIFF (*his weeping breaking from him*): Dad . . .

WILLY (*infected by it*): Oh, my boy . . .

BIFF: Dad . . .

WILLY: She's nothing to me, Biff. I was lonely, I was terribly lonely.

BIFF: You—you gave her Mama's stockings! (*His tears break through and he rises to go.*)

WILLY (*grabbing for Biff*): I gave you an order!

BIFF: Don't touch me, you—liar!

WILLY: Apologize for that!

BIFF: You fake! You phony little fake! You fake! (*Overcome, he turns quickly and weeping fully goes out with his suitcase. Willy is left on the floor on his knees.*)

WILLY: I gave you an order! Biff, come back here or I'll beat you! Come back here! I'll whip you!

Stanley comes quickly in from the right and stands in front of Willy.

WILLY (*shouts at Stanley*): I gave you an order . . .

STANLEY: Hey, let's pick it up, pick it up, Mr. Loman. (*He helps Willy to his feet.*) Your boys left with the chippies. They said they'll see you home.

A second waiter watches some distance away.

WILLY: But we were supposed to have dinner together.

Music is heard, Willy's theme.

STANLEY: Can you make it?

WILLY: I'll—sure, I can make it. (*Suddenly concerned about his clothes.*) Do I—I look all right?

STANLEY: Sure, you look all right. (*He flicks a speck off Willy's lapel.*)

WILLY: Here—here's a dollar.

STANLEY: Oh, your son paid me. It's all right.

WILLY (*putting it in Stanley's hand*): No, take it. You're a good boy.

STANLEY: Oh, no, you don't have to . . .

WILLY: Here—here's some more, I don't need it any more. (*After a slight pause.*) Tell me—is there a seed store in the neighborhood?

STANLEY: Seeds? You mean like to plant?

As Willy turns, Stanley slips the money back into his jacket pocket.

WILLY: Yes. Carrots, peas . . .

STANLEY: Well, there's hardware stores on Sixth Avenue, but it may be too late now.

WILLY (*anxiously*): Oh, I'd better hurry. I've got to get some seeds. (*He starts off to the right.*) I've got to get some seeds, right away. Nothing's planted. I don't have a thing in the ground.

Willy hurries out as the light goes down. Stanley moves over to the right after him, watches him off. The other waiter has been staring at Willy.

STANLEY (*to the waiter*):   Well, whatta you looking at?

The waiter picks up the chairs and moves off right. Stanley takes the table and follows him. The light fades on this area. There is a long pause, the sound of the flute coming over. The light gradually rises on the kitchen, which is empty. Happy appears at the door of the house, followed by Biff. Happy is carrying a large bunch of long-stemmed roses. He enters the kitchen, looks around for Linda. Not seeing her, he turns to Biff, who is just outside the house door, and makes a gesture with his hands, indicating "Not here, I guess." He looks into the living room and freezes. Inside, Linda, unseen, is seated, Willy's coat on her lap. She rises ominously and quietly and moves toward Happy, who backs up into the kitchen, afraid.

HAPPY: Hey, what're you doing up? (*Linda says nothing but moves toward him implacably.*) Where's Pop? (*He keeps backing to the right, and now Linda is in full view in the doorway to the living room.*) Is he sleeping?

LINDA: Where were you?

HAPPY (*trying to laugh it off*):   We met two girls, Mom, very fine types. Here, we brought you some flowers. (*Offering them to her.*) Put them in your room, Ma.

She knocks them to the floor at Biff's feet. He has now come inside and closed the door behind him. She stares at Biff, silent.

HAPPY: Now what'd you do that for? Mom, I want you to have some flowers . . .

LINDA (*cutting Happy off, violently to Biff*):   Don't you care whether he lives or dies?

HAPPY (*going to the stairs*):   Come upstairs, Biff.

BIFF (*with a flare of disgust, to Happy*):   Go away from me! (*To Linda.*) What do you mean, lives or dies? Nobody's dying around here, pal.

LINDA: Get out of my sight! Get out of here!

BIFF: I wanna see the boss.

LINDA: You're not going near him!

BIFF: Where is he? (*He moves into the living room and Linda follows.*)

LINDA (*shouting after Biff.*):   You invite him for dinner. He looks forward to it all day—(*Biff appears in his parents' bedroom, looks around, and exits*)—and then you desert him there. There's no stranger you'd do that to!

HAPPY: Why? He had a swell time with us. Listen, when I—(*Linda comes back into the kitchen*)—desert him I hope I don't outlive the day!

LINDA: Get out of here!

HAPPY: Now look, Mom . . .

LINDA: Did you have to go to women tonight? You and your lousy rotten whores!

Biff re-enters the kitchen.

HAPPY: Mom, all we did was follow Biff around trying to cheer him up! (*To Biff.*) Boy, what a night you gave me!

LINDA: Get out of here, both of you, and don't come back! I don't want you tormenting him any more. Go on now, get your things together! (*To Biff.*) You can sleep in his apartment. (*She starts to pick up the flowers and stops herself.*) Pick up this stuff, I'm not your maid any more. Pick it up, you bum, you!

Happy turns his back to her in refusal. Biff slowly moves over and gets down on his knees, picking up the flowers.

LINDA: You're a pair of animals! Not one, not another living soul would have had the cruelty to walk out on that man in a restaurant!

BIFF (*not looking at her*):   Is that what he said?

LINDA: He didn't have to say anything. He was so humiliated he nearly limped when he came in.

HAPPY: But, Mom, he had a great time with us . . .

BIFF (*cutting him off violently*):   Shut up!

Without another word, Happy goes upstairs.

LINDA: You! You didn't even go in to see if he was all right!

BIFF (*still on the floor in front of Linda, the flowers in his hand; with self-loathing*):   No. Didn't. Didn't do a damned thing. How do you like that, heh? Left him babbling in a toilet.

LINDA: You louse. You . . .

BIFF: Now you hit it on the nose! (*He gets up, throws the flowers in the wastebasket.*) The scum of the earth, and you're looking at him!

LINDA: Get out of here!

BIFF: I gotta talk to the boss, Mom. Where is he?

LINDA: You're not going near him. Get out of this house!

BIFF (*with absolute assurance, determination*): No. We're gonna have an abrupt conversation, him and me.

LINDA: You're not talking to him.

Hammering is heard from outside the house, off right. Biff turns toward the noise.

LINDA (*suddenly pleading*): Will you please leave him alone?

BIFF: What's he doing out there?

LINDA: He's planting the garden!

BIFF (*quietly*): Now? Oh, my God!

Biff moves outside, Linda following. The light dies down on them and comes up on the center of the apron as Willy walks into it. He is carrying a flashlight, a hoe, and a handful of seed packets. He raps the top of the hoe sharply to fix it firmly, and then moves to the left, measuring off the distance with his foot. He holds the flashlight to look at the seed packets, reading off the instructions. He is in the blue of night.

WILLY: Carrots . . . quarter-inch apart. Rows . . . one-foot rows. (*He measures it off.*) One foot. (*He puts down a package and measures off.*) Beets. (*He puts down another package and measures again.*) Lettuce. (*He reads the package, puts it down.*) One foot—(*He breaks off as Ben appears at the right and moves slowly down to him.*) What a proposition, ts, ts. Terrific, terrific. 'Cause she's suffered, Ben, the woman has suffered. You understand me? A man can't go out the way he came in, Ben, a man has got to add up to something. You can't, you can't—(*Ben moves toward him as though to interrupt.*) You gotta consider now. Don't answer so quick. Remember, it's a guaranteed twenty-thousand-dollar proposition. Now look, Ben, I want you to go through the ins and outs of this thing with me. I've got nobody to talk to, Ben, and the woman has suffered, you hear me?

BEN (*standing still, considering*): What's the proposition?

WILLY: It's twenty thousand dollars on the barrelhead. Guaranteed, gilt-edged, you understand?

BEN: You don't want to make a fool of yourself. They might not honor the policy.

WILLY: How can they dare refuse? Didn't I work like a coolie to meet every premium on the nose? And now they don't pay off? Impossible!

BEN: It's called a cowardly thing, William.

WILLY: Why? Does it take more guts to stand here the rest of my life ringing up a zero?

BEN (*yielding*): That's a point, William. (*He moves, thinking, turns.*) And twenty thousand—that is something one can feel with the hand, it is there.

WILLY (*now assured, with rising power*): Oh, Ben, that's the whole beauty of it! I see it like a diamond, shining in the dark, hard and rough, that I can pick up and touch in my hand. Not like—like an appointment! This would not be another damned-fool appointment, Ben, and it changes all the aspects. Because he thinks I'm nothing, see, and so he spites me. But the funeral . . . (*Straightening up.*) Ben, that funeral will be massive! They'll come from Maine, Massachusetts, Vermont, New Hampshire! All the old-timers with the strange license plates—that boy will be thunder-struck, Ben, because he never realized—I am known! Rhode Island, New York, New Jersey—I am known, Ben, and he'll see it with his eyes once and for all. He'll see what I am, Ben! He's in for a shock, that boy!

BEN (*coming down to the edge of the garden*): He'll call you a coward.

WILLY (*suddenly fearful*): No, that would be terrible.

BEN: Yes. And a damned fool.

WILLY: No, no, he mustn't, I won't have that! (*He is broken and desperate.*)

BEN: He'll hate you, William.

The gay music of the Boys is heard.

WILLY: Oh, Ben, how do we get back to all the great times? Used to be so full of light, and comradeship, the sleigh-riding in winter, and the ruddiness on his cheeks. And always some kind of good news coming up, always something nice coming up ahead. And never even let me carry the valises in the house, and simonizing, simonizing that little red car! Why, why can't I give him something and not have him hate me?

BEN: Let me think about it. (*He glances at his watch.*) I still have a little time. Remarkable proposition, but you've got to be sure you're not making a fool of yourself.

Ben drifts off upstage and goes out of sight. Biff comes down from the left.

WILLY (*suddenly conscious of Biff, turns and looks up at him, then begins picking up the packages of seeds in confusion*): Where the hell is that seed? (*Indignantly.*) You can't see nothing out here! They boxed in the whole goddam neighborhood!

BIFF: There are people all around here. Don't you realize that?

WILLY: I'm busy. Don't bother me.

BIFF (*taking the hoe from Willy*): I'm saying good-by to you, Pop. (*Willy looks at him, silent, unable to move.*) I'm not coming back any more.

WILLY: You're not going to see Oliver tomorrow?

BIFF: I've got no appointment, Dad.

WILLY: He put his arm around you, and you've got no appointment?

BIFF: Pop, get this now, will you? Everytime I've left it's been a—fight that sent me out of here. Today I realized something about myself and I tried to explain it to you and I—I think I'm just not smart enough to make any sense out of it for you. To hell with whose fault it is or anything like that. (*He takes Willy's arm.*) Let's just wrap it up, heh? Come on in, we'll tell Mom. (*He gently tries to pull Willy to left.*)

WILLY (*frozen, immobile, with guilt in his voice*): No, I don't want to see her.

BIFF: Come on! (*He pulls again, and Willy tries to pull away.*)

WILLY (*highly nervous*): No, no, I don't want to see her.

BIFF (*tries to look into Willy's face, as if to find the answer there*): Why don't you want to see her?

WILLY (*more harshly now*): Don't bother me, will you?

BIFF: What do you mean, you don't want to see her? You don't want them calling you yellow, do you? This isn't your fault; it's me, I'm a bum. Now come inside! (*Willy strains to get away.*) Did you hear what I said to you?

Willy pulls away and quickly goes by himself into the house. Biff follows.

LINDA (*to Willy*): Did you plant, dear?

BIFF (*at the door, to Linda*): All right, we had it out. I'm going and I'm not writing any more.

LINDA (*going to Willy in the kitchen*): I think that's the best way, dear. 'Cause there's no use drawing it out, you'll just never get along.

Willy doesn't respond.

BIFF: People ask where I am and what I'm doing, you don't know, and you don't care. That way it'll be off your mind and you can start brightening up again. All right? That clears it, doesn't it? (*Willy is silent, and Biff goes to him.*) You gonna wish me luck, scout? (*He extends his hand.*) What do you say?

LINDA: Shake his hand, Willy.

WILLY (*turning to her, seething with hurt*): There's no necessity—to mention the pen at all, y'know.

BIFF (*gently*): I've got no appointment, Dad.

WILLY (*erupting fiercely*): He put his arm around . . . ?

BIFF: Dad, you're never going to see what I am, so what's the use of arguing? If I strike oil I'll send you a check. Meantime forget I'm alive.

WILLY (*to Linda*): Spite, see?

BIFF: Shake hands, Dad.

WILLY: Not my hand.

BIFF: I was hoping not to go this way.

WILLY: Well, this is the way you're going. Good-by.

Biff looks at him a moment, then turns sharply and goes to the stairs.

WILLY (*stops him with*): May you rot in hell if you leave this house!

BIFF (*turning*): Exactly what is it that you want from me?

WILLY: I want you to know, on the train, in the mountains, in the valleys, wherever you go, that you cut down your life for spite!

BIFF: No, no.

WILLY: Spite, spite, is the word of your undoing! And when you're down and out, remember what did it. When you're rotting some-

where beside the railroad tracks, remember, and don't you dare
blame it on me!

BIFF: I'm not blaming it on you!

WILLY: I won't take the rap for this, you hear?

*Happy comes down the stairs and stands on the bottom step,
watching.*

BIFF: That's just what I'm telling you!

WILLY (*sinking into a chair at a table, with full accusation*): You're
trying to put a knife in me—don't think I don't know what you're
doing!

BIFF: All right, phony! Then let's lay it on the line. (*He whips the rubber tube out of his pocket and puts it on the table.*)

HAPPY: You crazy . . .

LINDA: Biff! (*She moves to grab the hose, but Biff holds it down with
his hand.*)

BIFF: Leave it there! Don't move it!

WILLY (*not looking at it*): What is that?

BIFF: You know goddam well what that is.

WILLY (*caged, wanting to escape*): I never saw that.

BIFF: You saw it. The mice didn't bring it into the cellar! What is this
supposed to do, make a hero out of you? This supposed to make me
sorry for you?

WILLY: Never heard of it.

BIFF: There'll be no pity for you, you hear it? No pity!

WILLY (*to Linda*): You hear the spite!

BIFF: No, you're going to hear the truth—what you are and what I
am!

LINDA: Stop it!

WILLY: Spite!

HAPPY (*coming down toward Biff*): You cut it now!

BIFF (*to Happy*): The man don't know who we are! The man is gonna
know! (*To Willy.*) We never told the truth for ten minutes in this
house!

HAPPY: We always told the truth!

BIFF (*turning on him*): You big blow, are you the assistant buyer?
You're one of the two assistants to the assistant, aren't you?

HAPPY: Well, I'm practically . . .

BIFF: You're practically full of it! We all are! and I'm through with it. (*To Willy.*) Now hear this, Willy, this is me.

WILLY: I know you!

BIFF: You know why I had no address for three months? I stole a suit in Kansas City and I was in jail. (*To Linda, who is sobbing.*) Stop crying. I'm through with it.

Linda turns away from them, her hands covering her face.

WILLY: I suppose that's my fault!

BIFF: I stole myself out of every good job since high school!

WILLY: And whose fault is that?

BIFF: And I never got anywhere because you blew me so full of hot air I could never stand taking orders from anybody! That's whose fault it is!

WILLY: I hear that!

LINDA: Don't, Biff!

BIFF: It's goddam time you heard that! I had to be boss big shot in two weeks, and I'm through with it!

WILLY: Then hang yourself! For spite, hang yourself!

BIFF: No! Nobody's hanging himself, Willy! I ran down eleven flights with a pen in my hand today. And suddenly I stopped, you hear me? And in the middle of that office building, do you hear this? I stopped in the middle of that building and I saw—the sky. I saw the things that I love in this world. The work and the food and time to sit and smoke. And I looked at the pen and said to myself, what the hell am I grabbing this for? Why am I trying to become what I don't want to be? What am I doing in an office, making a contemptuous, begging fool of myself, when all I want is out there, waiting for me the minute I say I know who I am! Why can't I say that, Willy? (*He tries to make Willy face him, but Willy pulls away and moves to the left.*)

WILLY (*with hatred, threateningly*): The door of your life is wide open!

BIFF: Pop! I'm a dime a dozen, and so are you!

WILLY (*turning on him now in an uncontrolled outburst*): I am not a dime a dozen! I am Willy Loman, and you are Biff Loman!

Biff starts for Willy, but is blocked by Happy. In his fury, Biff seems on the verge of attacking his father.

BIFF: I am not a leader of men, Willy, and neither are you. You were never anything but a hard-working drummer who landed in the ash can like all the rest of them! I'm one dollar an hour, Willy! I tried seven states and couldn't raise it. A buck an hour! Do you gather my meaning? I'm not bringing home any prizes any more, and you're going to stop waiting for me to bring them home!

WILLY (*directly to Biff*): You vengeful, spiteful mutt!

Biff breaks from Happy. Willy, in fright, starts up the stairs. Biff grabs him.

BIFF (*at the peak of his fury*): Pop! I'm nothing! I'm nothing, Pop. Can't you understand that? There's no spite in it any more. I'm just what I am, that's all.

Biff's fury has spent itself and he breaks down, sobbing, holding on to Willy, who dumbly fumbles for Biff's face.

WILLY (*astonished*): What're you doing? What're you doing? (*To Linda.*) Why is he crying?

BIFF (*crying, broken*): Will you let me go, for Christ's sake? Will you take that phony dream and burn it before something happens? (*Struggling to contain himself, he pulls away and moves to the stairs.*) I'll go in the morning. Put him—put him to bed. (*Exhausted, Biff moves up the stairs to his room.*)

WILLY (*after a long pause, astonished, elevated*): Isn't that—isn't that remarkable? Biff—he likes me!

LINDA: He loves you, Willy!

HAPPY (*deeply moved*): Always did, Pop.

WILLY: Oh, Biff! (*Staring wildly.*) He cried! Cried to me. (*He is choking with his love, and now cries out his promise.*) That boy—that boy is going to be magnificent!

Ben appears in the light just outside the kitchen.

BEN: Yes, outstanding, with twenty thousand behind him.

LINDA (*sensing the racing of his mind, fearfully, carefully*): Now come to bed, Willy. It's all settled now.

WILLY (*finding it difficult not to rush out of the house*): Yes, we'll sleep. Come on. Go to sleep, Hap.

BEN: And it does take a great kind of a man to crack the jungle.

In accents of dread, Ben's idyllic music starts up.

HAPPY (*his arm around Linda*): I'm getting married, Pop, don't forget it. I'm changing everything. I'm gonna run that department before the year is up. You'll see, Mom. (*He kisses her.*)

BEN: The jungle is dark but full of diamonds, Willy.

Willy turns, moves, listening to Ben.

LINDA: Be good. You're both good boys, just act that way, that's all.

HAPPY: 'Night, Pop. (*He goes upstairs.*)

LINDA (*to Willy*): Come, dear.

BEN (*with greater force*): One must go in to fetch a diamond out.

WILLY (*to Linda, as he moves slowly along the edge of the kitchen, toward the door*): I just want to get settled down, Linda. Let me sit alone for a little.

LINDA (*almost uttering her fear*): I want you upstairs.

WILLY (*taking her in his arms*): In a few minutes, Linda. I couldn't sleep right now. Go on, you look awful tired. (*He kisses her.*)

BEN: Not like an appointment at all. A diamond is rough and hard to the touch.

WILLY: Go on now. I'll be right up.

LINDA: I think this is the only way, Willy.

WILLY: Sure, it's the best thing.

BEN: Best thing!

WILLY: The only way. Everything is gonna be—go on, kid, get to bed. You look so tired.

LINDA: Come right up.

WILLY: Two minutes.

Linda goes into the living room, then reappears in her bedroom. Willy moves just outside the kitchen door.

WILLY: Loves me. (*Wonderingly.*) Always loved me. Isn't that a remarkable thing? Ben, he'll worship me for it!

BEN (*with promise*): It's dark there, but full of diamonds.

WILLY: Can you imagine that magnificence with twenty thousand dollars in his pocket?

LINDA (*calling from her room*): Willy! Come up!

WILLY (*calling into the kitchen*): Yes! Yes. Coming! It's very smart, you realize that, don't you, sweetheart? Even Ben sees it. I gotta go, baby. 'By! 'By! (*Going over to Ben, almost dancing.*) Imagine? When the mail comes he'll be ahead of Bernard again!

BEN: A perfect proposition all around.

WILLY: Did you see how he cried to me? Oh, if I could kiss him, Ben!

BEN: Time, William, time!

WILLY: Oh, Ben, I always knew one way or another we were gonna make it, Biff and I.

BEN (*looking at his watch*): The boat. We'll be late. (*He moves slowly off into the darkness.*)

WILLY (*elegiacally, turning to the house*): Now when you kick off, boy, I want a seventy-yard boot, and get right down the field under the ball, and when you hit, hit low and hit hard, because it's important, boy. (*He swings around and faces the audience.*) There's all kinds of important people in the stands, and the first thing you know . . . (*Suddenly realizing he is alone.*) Ben! Ben, where do I . . .? (*He makes a sudden movement of search.*) Ben, how do I . . .?

LINDA (*calling*): Willy, you coming up?

WILLY (*uttering a gasp of fear, whirling about as if to quiet her*): Sh! (*He turns around as if to find his way; sounds, faces, voices, seem to be swarming in upon him and he flicks at them, crying.*) Sh! Sh! (*Suddenly music, faint and high, stops him. It rises in intensity, almost to an unbearable scream. He goes up and down on his toes, and rushes off around the house.*) Shhh!

LINDA: Willy?

There is no answer. Linda waits. Biff gets up off his bed. He is still in his clothes. Happy sits up. Biff stands listening.

LINDA (*with real fear*): Willy, answer me! Willy!

There is the sound of a car starting and moving away at full speed.

LINDA: No!

BIFF (*rushing down the stairs*): Pop!

As the car speeds off the music crashes down in a frenzy of sound, which becomes the soft pulsation of a single cello string. Biff slowly returns to his bedroom. He and Happy gravely don their jackets. Linda slowly walks out of her room. The music has developed into a dead march. The leaves of day are appearing over everything. Charley and Bernard, somberly dressed, appear and knock on the kitchen door. Biff and Happy slowly descend the stairs to the kitchen as Charley and Bernard enter. All stop a moment when Linda, in clothes of mourning, bearing a little bunch of roses, comes through the draped doorway into the kitchen. She goes to Charley and takes his arm. Now all move toward the audience, through the wall-line of the kitchen. At the limit of the apron, Linda lays down the flowers, kneels, and sits back on her heels. All stare down at the grave.

REQUIEM

CHARLEY: It's getting dark, Linda.

Linda doesn't react. She stares at the grave.

BIFF: How about it, Mom? Better get some rest, heh? They'll be closing the gate soon.

Linda makes no move. Pause.

HAPPY (*deeply angered*):   He had no right to do that. There was no necessity for it. We would've helped him.

CHARLEY (*grunting*):   Hmmm.

BIFF: Come along, Mom.

LINDA: Why didn't anybody come?

CHARLEY: It was a very nice funeral.

LINDA: But where are all the people he knew? Maybe they blame him.

CHARLEY: Naa. It's a rough world, Linda. They wouldn't blame him.

LINDA: I can't understand it. At this time especially. First time in thirty-five years we were just about free and clear. He only needed a little salary. He was even finished with the dentist.

CHARLEY: No man only needs a little salary.

LINDA: I can't understand it.

BIFF: There were a lot of nice days. When he'd come home from a trip; or on Sundays, making the stoop; finishing the cellar; putting on the new porch; when he built the extra bathroom; and put up the garage. You know something, Charley, there's more of him in that front stoop than in all the sales he ever made.

CHARLEY: Yeah. He was a happy man with a batch of cement.

LINDA: He was so wonderful with his hands.

BIFF: He had the wrong dreams. All, all, wrong.

HAPPY (*almost ready to fight Biff*): Don't say that!

BIFF: He never knew who he was.

CHARLEY (*stopping Happy's movement and reply; to Biff*): Nobody dast blame this man. You don't understand: Willy was a salesman. And for a salesman, there is no rock bottom to the life. He don't put a bolt to a nut, he don't tell you the law or give you medicine. He's a man way out there in the blue, riding on a smile and a shoeshine. And when they start not smiling back—that's an earthquake. And then you get yourself a couple of spots on your hat, and you're finished. Nobody dast blame this man. A salesman is got to dream, boy. It comes with the territory.

BIFF: Charley, the man didn't know who he was.

HAPPY (*infuriated*): Don't say that!

BIFF: Why don't you come with me, Happy?

HAPPY: I'm not licked that easily. I'm staying right in this city, and I'm gonna beat this racket! (*He looks at Biff, his chin set.*) The Loman Brothers!

BIFF: I know who I am, kid.

HAPPY: All right, boy. I'm gonna show you and everybody else that Willy Loman did not die in vain. He had a good dream. It's the only dream you can have—to come out number-one man. He fought it out here, and this is where I'm gonna win it for him.

BIFF (*with a hopeless glance at Happy, bends toward his mother*): Let's go, Mom.

LINDA: I'll be with you in a minute. Go on, Charley. (*He hesitates.*) I want to, just for a minute. I never had a chance to say good-by.

Charley moves away, followed by Happy. Biff remains a slight distance up and left of Linda. She sits there, summoning herself. The flute begins, not far away, playing behind her speech.

LINDA: Forgive me, dear. I can't cry. I don't know what it is, but I can't cry. I don't understand it. Why did you ever do that? Help me, Willy, I can't cry. It seems to me that you're just on another trip. I keep expecting you. Willy, dear, I can't cry. Why did you do it? I search and search and I search, and I can't understand it, Willy. I made the last payment on the house today. Today, dear. And there'll be nobody home. (*A sob rises in her throat.*) We're free and clear. (*Sobbing mournfully, released.*) We're free. (*Biff comes slowly toward her.*) We're free . . . We're free . . .

Biff lifts her to her feet and moves out up right with her in his arms. Linda sobs quietly. Bernard and Charley come together and follow them, followed by Happy. Only the music of the flute is left on the darkening stage as over the house the hard towers of the apartment buildings rise into sharp focus and the curtain falls.

—1949

August Wilson *(b. 1945), whose birth name was Federick August Kittel, was born in Pittsburgh's predominantly African-American Hill District, the setting of many of his plays. The child of a mixed-race marriage, he grew up fatherless and credits his real education in life and, incidentally, in language to the older men in his neighborhood, whose distinctive voices echo memorably in his plays. A school dropout at fifteen after a teacher unjustly accused him of plagiarism, he joined in the Black Power movement of the 1960s, eventually founding the Black Horizon on the Hill, an African-American theater company. Wilson admits to having had little confidence in his own ability to write dialogue during his early career, and his first publications were poems. A move to St. Paul, Minnesota, led to work with the Minneapolis Playwrights' Center. After his return to Pittsburgh he wrote* Jitney *and* Fullerton Street, *which were staged by regional theaters. His career hit full stride with the successful debut of* Ma Rainey's Black Bottom *(1984), which was first produced at the Yale Repertory Theater and later moved to Broadway.* Joe Turner's Come and Gone *(1986) was his next success, and* Fences *(1987) and* The Piano Lesson *(1990) both won Pulitzer Prizes and other major awards, establishing Wilson as the most prominent African-American dramatist. In most of Wilson's plays a historical theme is prominent, as Wilson attempts to piece together the circumstances that led African Americans to northern cities, depicting how they remain united and sometimes divided by a common cultural heritage that transcends even the ties of friendship and family. But to these social concerns Wilson brings a long training in the theatre and a poet's love of language. As he said to an interviewer in 1991, "[Poetry] is the bedrock of my playwriting. . . . The idea of metaphor is a very large idea in my plays and something that I find lacking in most contemporary plays. I think I write the kinds of plays that I do because I have twenty-six years of writing poetry underneath all of that."* Two Trains Running *(1992),* Seven Guitars *(1995), and* King Hedley II *(2001) are his more recent plays.*

August Wilson
Fences

for Lloyd Richards,
who adds to whatever he touches.

When the sins of our fathers visit us
We do not have to play host.
We can banish them with forgiveness
As God, in His Largeness and Laws.

—August Wilson

LIST OF CHARACTERS

Troy Maxson
Jim Bono, *Troy's friend*
Rose, *Troy's wife*
Lyons, *Troy's oldest son by previous marriage*
Gabriel, *Troy's brother*
Cory, *Troy and Rose's son*
Raynell, *Troy's daughter*

Setting: *The setting is the yard which fronts the only entrance to the Maxson household, an ancient two-story brick house set back off a small alley in a big-city neighborhood. The entrance to the house is gained by two or three steps leading to a wooden porch badly in need of paint.*

A relatively recent addition to the house and running its full width, the porch lacks congruence. It is a sturdy porch with a flat roof. One or two chairs of dubious value sit at one end where the kitchen window opens onto the porch. An old-fashioned icebox stands silent guard at the opposite end.

The yard is a small dirt yard, partially fenced, except for the last scene, with a wooden saw horse, a pile of lumber, and other fence-building equipment set off to the side. Opposite is a tree from which hangs a ball made of rags. A baseball bat leans against the tree. Two oil drums serve as garbage receptacles and sit near the house at right to complete the setting.

The Play: *Near the turn of the century, the destitute of Europe sprang on the city with tenacious claws and an honest and solid dream. The city devoured them. They swelled its belly until it burst into a thousand furnaces and sewing machines, a thousand butcher shops and bakers' ovens, a thousand churches and hospitals and funeral parlors and money-lenders. The city grew. It nourished itself and offered each man a partnership limited only by his talent, his guile, and his willingness and capacity for hard work. For the immigrants of Europe, a dream dared and won true.*

The descendants of African slaves were offered no such welcome or participation. They came from places called the Carolinas and the Virginias, Georgia, Alabama, Mississippi, and Tennessee. They came strong, eager, searching. The city rejected them and they fled and settled along the riverbanks and under bridges in shallow, ramshackle houses made of sticks and tarpaper. They collected rags and wood. They sold the use of their muscles and their bodies. They cleaned houses and washed clothes, they shined shoes, and in quiet desperation and vengeful pride, they stole, and lived in pursuit of their own dream. That they could breathe free, finally, and stand to meet life with the force of dignity and whatever eloquence the heart could call upon.

By 1957, the hard-won victories of the European immigrants had solidified the industrial might of America. War had been confronted and won with new energies that used loyalty and patriotism as its fuel. Life was rich, full, and flourishing. The Milwaukee Braves won the World Series, and the hot winds of change that would make the sixties a turbulent, racing, dangerous, and provocative decade had not yet begun to blow full.

ACT 1

SCENE 1

It is 1957. Troy and Bono enter the yard, engaged in conversation. Troy is fifty-three years old, a large man with thick, heavy hands; it is this largeness that he strives to fill out and make an accommodation with. Together with his blackness, his largeness informs his sensibilities and the choices he has made in his life.

Of the two men, Bono is obviously the follower. His commitment to their friendship of thirty-odd years is rooted in his admiration of Troy's honesty, capacity for hard work, and his strength, which Bono seeks to emulate.

It is Friday night, payday, and the one night of the week the two men engage in a ritual of talk and drink. Troy is usually the most talkative and at times he can be crude and almost vulgar, though he is capable of rising to profound heights of expression. The men carry lunch buckets and wear or carry burlap aprons and are dressed in clothes suitable to their jobs as garbage collectors.

BONO: Troy, you ought to stop that lying!

TROY: I ain't lying! The nigger had a watermelon this big. (*He indicates with his hands.*) Talking about . . . "What watermelon, Mr. Rand?" I liked to fell out! "What watermelon, Mr. Rand?" . . . And it sitting there big as life.

BONO: What did Mr. Rand say?

TROY: Ain't said nothing. Figure if the nigger too dumb to know he carrying a watermelon, he wasn't gonna get much sense out of him. Trying to hide that great big old watermelon under his coat. Afraid to let the white man see him carry it home.

BONO: I'm like you . . . I ain't got no time for them kind of people.

TROY: Now what he look like getting mad cause he see the man from the union talking to Mr. Rand?

BONO: He come to me talking about . . . "Maxson gonna get us fired." I told him to get away from me with that. He walked away from me calling you a troublemaker. What Mr. Rand say?

TROY: Ain't said nothing. He told me to go down the Commissioner's office next Friday. They called me down there to see them.

BONO: Well, as long as you got your complaint filed, they can't fire you. That's what one of them white fellows tell me.

TROY: I ain't worried about them firing me. They gonna fire me cause I asked a question? That's all I did. I went to Mr. Rand and asked him, "Why? Why you got the white mens driving and the colored lifting?" Told him, "what's the matter, don't I count? You think only white fellows got sense enough to drive a truck. That ain't no paper job! Hell, anybody can drive a truck. How come you got all whites driving and the colored lifting?" He told me "take it to the union." Well, hell, that's what I done! Now they wanna come up with this pack of lies.

BONO: I told Brownie if the man come and ask him any questions . . . just tell the truth! It ain't nothing but something they done trumped up on you cause you filed a complaint on them.

TROY: Brownie don't understand nothing. All I want them to do is change the job description. Give everybody a chance to drive the truck. Brownie can't see that. He ain't got that much sense.

BONO: How you figure he be making out with that gal be up at Taylor's all the time . . . that Alberta gal?

TROY: Same as you and me. Getting just as much as we is. Which is to say nothing.

BONO: It is, huh? I figure you doing a little better than me . . . and I ain't saying what I'm doing.

TROY: Aw, nigger, look here . . . I know you. If you had got anywhere near that gal, twenty minutes later you be looking to tell somebody. And the first one you gonna tell . . . that you gonna want to brag to . . . is me.

BONO: I ain't saying that. I see where you be eyeing her.

TROY: I eye all the women. I don't miss nothing. Don't never let nobody tell you Troy Maxson don't eye the women.

BONO: You been doing more than eyeing her. You done bought her a drink or two.

TROY: Hell yeah, I bought her a drink! What that mean? I bought you one, too. What that mean cause I buy her a drink? I'm just being polite.

BONO: It's all right to buy her one drink. That's what you call being polite. But when you wanna be buying two or three . . . that's what you call eyeing her.

TROY: Look here, as long as you known me . . . you ever known me to chase after women?

BONO: Hell yeah! Long as I done known you. You forgetting I knew you when.

TROY: Naw, I'm talking about since I been married to Rose?

BONO: Oh, not since you been married to Rose. Now, that's the truth, there. I can say that.

TROY: All right then! Case closed.

BONO: I see you be walking up around Alberta's house. You supposed to be at Taylors' and you be walking up around there.

TROY: What you watching where I'm walking for? I ain't watching after you.

BONO: I seen you walking around there more than once.

TROY: Hell, you liable to see me walking anywhere! That don't mean nothing cause you see me walking around there.

BONO: Where she come from anyway? She just kinda showed up one day.

TROY: Tallahassee. You can look at her and tell she one of them Florida gals. They got some big healthy women down there. Grow them right up out the ground. Got a little bit of Indian in her. Most of them niggers down in Florida got some Indian in them.

BONO: I don't know about that Indian part. But she damn sure big and healthy. Woman wear some big stockings. Got them great big old legs and hips as wide as the Mississippi River.

TROY: Legs don't mean nothing. You don't do nothing but push them out of the way. But them hips cushion the ride!

BONO: Troy, you ain't got no sense.

TROY: It's the truth! Like you riding on Goodyears!

Rose enters from the house. She is ten years younger than Troy, her devotion to him stems from her recognition of the possibilities of her life without him: a succession of abusive men and their babies, a life of partying and running the streets, the Church, or aloneness with its attendant pain and frustration. She recognizes Troy's spirit as a fine and illuminating one and she either ignores or forgives his faults, only some of which she recognizes. Though she doesn't drink, her presence is an integral part of the Friday night rituals. She alternates between the porch and the kitchen, where supper preparations are under way.

ROSE: What you all out here getting into?

TROY: What you worried about what we getting into for? This is men talk, woman.

ROSE: What I care what you all talking about? Bono, you gonna stay for supper?

BONO: No, I thank you, Rose. But Lucille say she cooking up a pot of pigfeet.

TROY: Pigfeet! Hell, I'm going home with you! Might even stay the night if you got some pigfeet. You got something in there to top them pigfeet, Rose?

ROSE: I'm cooking up some chicken. I got some chicken and collard greens.

TROY: Well, go on back in the house and let me and Bono finish what we was talking about. This is men talk. I got some talk for you later. You know what kind of talk I mean. You go on and powder it up.

ROSE: Troy Maxson, don't you start that now!

TROY (*puts his arm around her*): Aw, woman . . . come here. Look here, Bono . . . when I met this woman . . . I got out that place, say, "Hitch up my pony, saddle up my mare . . . there's a woman out there for me somewhere. I looked here. Looked there. Saw Rose and latched on to her." I latched on to her and told her—I'm gonna tell you the truth—I told her, "Baby, I don't wanna marry, I just wanna be your man." Rose told me . . . tell him what you told me, Rose.

ROSE: I told him if he wasn't the marrying kind, then move out the way so the marrying kind could find me.

TROY: That's what she told me. "Nigger, you in my way. You blocking the view! Move out the way so I can find me a husband." I thought it over two or three days. Come back—

ROSE: Ain't no two or three days nothing. You was back the same night.

TROY: Come back, told her . . . "Okay, baby . . . but I'm gonna buy me a banty rooster and put him out there in the backyard . . . and when he see a stranger come, he'll flap his wings and crow. . . ." Look here, Bono, I could watch the front door by myself . . . it was that back door I was worried about.

ROSE: Troy, you ought not talk like that. Troy ain't doing nothing but telling a lie.

TROY: Only thing is . . . when we first got married . . . forget the rooster . . . we ain't had no yard!

BONO: I hear you tell it. Me and Lucille was staying down there on Logan Street. Had two rooms with the outhouse in the back. I ain't mind the outhouse none. But when that goddamn wind blow through there in the winter . . . that's what I'm talking about! To this day I wonder why in the hell I ever stayed down there for six long years. But see, I didn't know I could do no better. I thought only white folks had inside toilets and things.

ROSE: There's a lot of people don't know they can do no better than they doing now. That's just something you got to learn. A lot of folks still shop at Bella's.

TROY: Ain't nothing wrong with shopping at Bella's. She got fresh food.

ROSE: I ain't said nothing about if she got fresh food. I'm talking about what she charge. She charge ten cents more than the A&P.

TROY: The A&P ain't never done nothing for me. I spends my money where I'm treated right. I go down to Bella, say, "I need a loaf of bread, I'll pay you Friday." She give it to me. What sense that make when I got money to go and spend it somewhere else and ignore the person who done right by me? That ain't in the Bible.

ROSE: We ain't talking about what's in the Bible. What sense it make to shop there when she overcharge?

TROY: You shop where you want to. I'll do my shopping where the people been good to me.

ROSE: Well, I don't think it's right for her to overcharge. That's all I was saying.

BONO: Look here . . . I got to get on. Lucille going be raising all kind of hell.

TROY: Where you going, nigger? We ain't finished this pint. Come here, finish this pint.

BONO: Well, hell, I am . . . if you ever turn the bottle loose.

TROY (*hands him the bottle*): The only thing I say about the A&P is I'm glad Cory got that job down there. Help him take care of his school clothes and things. Gabe done moved out and things getting tight around here. He got that job. . . . He can start to look out for himself.

ROSE: Cory done went and got recruited by a college football team.

TROY: I told that boy about that football stuff. The white man ain't gonna let him get nowhere with that football. I told him when he first come to me with it. Now you come telling me he done went and got more tied up in it. He ought to go and get recruited in how to fix cars or something where he can make a living.

ROSE: He ain't talking about making no living playing football. It's just something the boys in school do. They gonna send a recruiter by to talk to you. He'll tell you he ain't talking about making no living playing football. It's a honor to be recruited.

TROY: It ain't gonna get him nowhere. Bono'll tell you that.

BONO: If he be like you in the sports . . . he's gonna be all right. Ain't but two men ever played baseball as good as you. That's Babe Ruth and Josh Gibson.[1] Them's the only two men ever hit more home runs than you.

TROY: What it ever get me? Ain't got a pot to piss in or a window to throw it out of.

ROSE: Times have changed since you was playing baseball, Troy. That was before the war. Times have changed a lot since then.

TROY: How in hell they done changed?

ROSE: They got lots of colored boys playing ball now. Baseball and football.

---

[1]African-American ballplayer (1911–1947).

BONO: You right about that, Rose. Times have changed, Troy. You just come along too early.

TROY: There ought not never have been no time called too early! Now you take that fellow . . . what's that fellow they had playing right field for the Yankees back then? You know who I'm talking about, Bono. Used to play right field for the Yankees.

ROSE: Selkirk?

TROY: Selkirk! That's it! Man batting .269, understand? .269. What kind of sense that make? I was hitting .432 with thirty-seven home runs! Man batting .269 and playing right field for the Yankees! I saw Josh Gibson's daughter yesterday. She walking around with raggedy shoes on her feet. Now I bet you Selkirk's daughter ain't walking around with raggedy shoes on the feet! I bet you that!

ROSE: They got a lot of colored baseball players now. Jackie Robinson[2] was the first. Folks had to wait for Jackie Robinson.

TROY: I done seen a hundred niggers play baseball better than Jackie Robinson. Hell, I know some teams Jackie Robinson couldn't even make! What you talking about Jackie Robinson. Jackie Robinson wasn't nobody. I'm talking about if you could play ball then they ought to have let you play. Don't care what color you were. Come telling me I come along too early. If you could play . . . then they ought to have let you play.

Troy takes a long drink from the bottle.

ROSE: You gonna drink yourself to death. You don't need to be drinking like that.

TROY: Death ain't nothing. I done seen him. Done wrassled with him. You can't tell me nothing about death. Death ain't nothing but a fastball on the outside corner. And you know what I'll do to that! Lookee here, Bono . . . am I lying? You get one of them fastballs, about waist high, over the outside corner of the plate where you can get the meat of the bat on it . . . and good god! You can kiss it goodbye. Now, am I lying?

BONO: Naw, you telling the truth there. I seen you do it.

TROY: If I'm lying . . . that 450 feet worth of lying! (*Pause.*) That's all death is to me. A fastball on the outside corner.

[2]Robinson (1919–1972) became the first African-American to play baseball in the major leagues, starring for the Brooklyn Dodgers.

ROSE: I don't know why you want to get on talking about death.

TROY: Ain't nothing wrong with talking about death. That's part of life. Everybody gonna die. You gonna die, I'm gonna die. Bono's gonna die. Hell, we all gonna die.

ROSE: But you ain't got to talk about it. I don't like to talk about it.

TROY: You the one brought it up. Me and Bono was talking about baseball . . . you tell me I'm gonna drink myself to death. Ain't that right, Bono? You know I don't drink this but one night out of the week. That's Friday night. I'm gonna drink just enough to where I can handle it. Then I cuts it loose. I leave it alone. So don't you worry about me drinking myself to death. 'Cause I ain't worried about Death. I done seen him. I done wrestled with him.

Look here, Bono . . . I looked up one day and Death was marching straight at me. Like Soldiers on Parade! The Army of Death was marching straight at me. The middle of July, 1941. It got real cold just like it be winter. It seem like Death himself reached out and touched me on the shoulder. He touch me just like I touch you. I got cold as ice and Death standing there grinning at me.

ROSE: Troy, why don't you hush that talk.

TROY: I say . . . what you want, Mr. Death? You be wanting me? You done brought your army to be getting me? I looked him dead in the eye. I wasn't fearing nothing. I was ready to tangle. Just like I'm ready to tangle now. The Bible say be ever vigilant. That's why I don't get but so drunk. I got to keep watch.

ROSE: Troy was right down there in Mercy Hospital. You remember he had pneumonia? Laying there with a fever talking plumb out of his head.

TROY: Death standing there staring at me . . . carrying that sickle in his hand. Finally he say, "You want bound over for another year?" See, just like that . . . "You want bound over for another year?" I told him, "Bound over hell! Let's settle this now!"

It seem like he kinda fell back when I said that, and all the cold went out of me. I reached down and grabbed that sickle and threw it just as far as I could throw it . . . and me and him commenced to wrestling.

We wrestled for three days and three nights. I can't say where I found the strength from. Everytime it seemed like he was gonna get the best of me, I'd reach way down deep inside myself and find the strength to do him one better.

ROSE: Everytime Troy tell that story he find different ways to tell it. Different things to make up about it.

TROY: I ain't making up nothing. I'm telling you the facts of what happened. I wrestled with Death for three days and three nights and I'm standing here to tell you about it. (*Pause.*) All right. At the end of the third night we done weakened each other to where we can't hardly move. Death stood up, throwed on his robe . . . had him a white robe with a hood on it. He throwed on that robe and went off to look for his sickle. Say, "I'll be back." Just like that. "I'll be back." I told him, say, "Yeah, but . . . you gonna have to find me!" I wasn't no fool. I wasn't going looking for him. Death ain't nothing to play with. And I know he's gonna get me. I know I got to join his army . . . his camp followers. But as long as I keep my strength and see him coming . . . as long as I keep up my vigilance . . . he's gonna have to fight to get me. I ain't going easy.

BONO: Well, look here, since you got to keep up your vigilance . . . let me have the bottle.

TROY: Aw hell, I shouldn't have told you that part. I should have left out that part.

ROSE: Troy be talking that stuff and half the time don't even know what he be talking about.

TROY: Bono know me better than that.

BONO: That's right. I know you. I know you got some Uncle Remus[3] in your blood. You got more stories than the devil got sinners.

TROY: Aw hell, I done seen him too! Done talked with the devil.

ROSE: Troy, don't nobody wanna be hearing all that stuff.

Lyons enters the yard from the street. Thirty-four years old, Troy's son by a previous marriage, he sports a neatly trimmed goatee, sport coat, white shirt, tieless and buttoned at the collar. Though he fancies himself a musician, he is more caught up in the rituals and "idea" of being a musician than in the actual practice of the music. He has come to borrow money from Troy, and while he knows he will be successful, he is uncertain as to what extent his lifestyle will be held up to scrutiny and ridicule.

LYONS: Hey, Pop.

---

[3]Narrator of dialect/written tales in a book by Joel Chandler Harris.

TROY: What you come "Hey, Popping" me for?

LYONS: How you doing, Rose? (*He kisses her.*) Mr. Bono. How you doing?

BONO: Hey, Lyons . . . how you been?

TROY: He must have been doing all right. I ain't seen him around here last week.

ROSE: Troy, leave your boy alone. He come by to see you and you wanna start all that nonsense.

TROY: I ain't bothering Lyons. (*Offers him the bottle.*) Here . . . get you a drink. We got an understanding. I know why he come by to see me and he know I know.

LYONS: Come on, Pop . . . I just stopped by to say hi . . . see how you was doing.

TROY: You ain't stopped by yesterday.

ROSE: You gonna stay for supper, Lyons? I got some chicken cooking in the oven.

LYONS: No, Rose . . . thanks. I was just in the neighborhood and thought I'd stop by for a minute.

TROY: You was in the neighborhood all right, nigger. You telling the truth there. You was in the neighborhood cause it's my payday.

LYONS: Well, hell, since you mentioned it . . . let me have ten dollars.

TROY: I'll be damned! I'll die and go to hell and play blackjack with the devil before I give you ten dollars.

BONO: That's what I wanna know about . . . that devil you done seen.

LYONS: What . . . Pop done seen the devil? You too much, Pops.

TROY: Yeah, I done seen him. Talked to him too!

ROSE: You ain't seen no devil. I done told you that man ain't had nothing to do with the devil. Anything you can't understand, you want to call it the devil.

TROY: Look here, Bono . . . I went down to see Hertzberger about some furniture. Got three rooms for two-ninety-eight. That what it say on the radio. "Three rooms . . . two-ninety-eight." Even made up a little song about it. Go down there . . . man tell me I can't get no credit. I'm working every day and can't get no credit. What to do? I got an empty house with some raggedy furniture in it. Cory ain't got no bed. He's sleeping on a pile of rags on the floor. Working every day and can't get no credit. Come back here—Rose'll tell you—madder than hell. Sit down . . . try to figure what I'm gonna do. Come a knock on the door. Ain't been living here but three days. Who know I'm here? Open the door . . . devil standing there bigger than life. White fellow . . . white fellow . . . got on good clothes and everything. Standing there with a clipboard in his hand. I ain't had to say nothing. First words come out of his mouth was . . . "I understand you need some furniture and can't get no credit." I liked to fell over. He say, "I'll give you all the credit you want, but you got to pay the interest on it." I told him, "Give me three rooms worth and charge whatever you want." Next day a truck pulled up here and two men unloaded them three rooms. Man what drove the truck give me a book. Say send ten dollars, first of every month to the address in the book and every thing will be all right. Say if I miss a payment the devil was coming back and it'll be hell to pay. That was fifteen years ago. To this day . . . the first of the month I send my ten dollars, Rose'll tell you.

ROSE: Troy lying.

TROY: I ain't never seen that man since. Now you tell me who else that could have been but the devil? I ain't sold my soul or nothing like that, you understand. Naw, I wouldn't have truck with the devil about nothing like that. I got my furniture and pays my ten dollars the first of the month just like clockwork.

BONO: How long you say you been paying this ten dollars a month?

TROY: Fifteen years!

BONO: Hell, ain't you finished paying for it yet? How much the man done charged you?

TROY: Ah hell, I done paid for it. I done paid for it ten times over! The fact is I'm scared to stop paying it.

ROSE: Troy lying. We got that furniture from Mr. Glickman. He ain't paying no ten dollars a month to nobody.

TROY: Aw hell, woman. Bono know I ain't that big a fool.

LYONS: I was just getting ready to say . . . I know where there's a bridge for sale.

TROY: Look here, I'll tell you this . . . it don't matter to me if he was the devil. It don't matter if the devil give credit. Somebody has got to give it.

ROSE: It ought to matter. You going around talking about having truck with the devil . . . God's the one you gonna have to answer to. He's the one gonna be at the Judgment.

LYONS: Yeah, well, look here, Pop . . . Let me have that ten dollars. I'll give it back to you. Bonnie got a job working at the hospital.

TROY: What I tell you, Bono? The only time I see this nigger is when he wants something. That's the only time I see him.

LYONS: Come on, Pop, Mr. Bono don't want to hear all that. Let me have the ten dollars. I told you Bonnie working.

TROY: What that mean to me? "Bonnie working." I don't care if she working. Go ask her for the ten dollars if she working. Talking about "Bonnie working." Why ain't you working?

LYONS: Aw, Pop, you know I can't find no decent job. Where am I gonna get a job at? You know I can't get no job.

TROY: I told you I know some people down there. I can get you on the rubbish if you want to work. I told you that the last time you came by here asking me for something.

LYONS: Naw, Pop . . . thanks. That ain't for me. I don't wanna be carrying nobody's rubbish. I don't wanna be punching nobody's time clock.

TROY: What's the matter, you too good to carry people's rubbish? Where you think that ten dollars you talking about come from? I'm just supposed to haul people's rubbish and give my money to you cause you too lazy to work. You too lazy to work and wanna know why you ain't got what I got.

ROSE: What hospital Bonnie working at? Mercy?

LYONS: She's down at Passavant working in the laundry.

TROY: I ain't got nothing as it is. I give you that ten dollars and I got to eat beans the rest of the week. Naw . . . you ain't getting no ten dollars here.

LYONS: You ain't got to be eating no beans. I don't know why you wanna say that.

TROY: I ain't got no extra money. Gabe done moved over to Miss Pearl's paying her the rent and things done got tight around here. I can't afford to be giving you every payday.

LYONS: I ain't asked you to give me nothing. I asked you to loan me ten dollars. I know you got ten dollars.

TROY: Yeah, I got it. You know why I got it? Cause I don't throw my money away out there in the streets. You living the fast life . . . wanna be a musician . . . running around in them clubs and things . . . then, you learn to take care of yourself. You ain't gonna find me going and asking nobody for nothing. I done spent too many years without.

LYONS: You and me is two different people, Pop.

TROY: I done learned my mistake and learned to do what's right by it. You still trying to get something for nothing. Life don't owe you nothing. You owe it to yourself. Ask Bono. He'll tell you I'm right.

LYONS: You got your way of dealing with the world . . . I got mine. The only thing that matters to me is the music.

TROY: Yeah, I can see that! It don't matter how you gonna eat . . . where your next dollar is coming from. You telling the truth there.

LYONS: I know I got to eat. But I got to live too. I need something that gonna help me to get out of the bed in the morning. Make me feel like I belong in the world. I don't bother nobody. I just stay with the music cause that's the only way I can find to live in the world. Otherwise there ain't no telling what I might do. Now I don't come criticizing you and how you live. I just come by to ask you for ten dollars. I don't wanna hear all that about how I live.

TROY: Boy, your mamma did a hell of a job raising you.

LYONS: You can't change me, Pop. I'm thirty-four years old. If you wanted to change me, you should have been there when I was growing up. I come by to see you . . . ask for ten dollars and you want to talk about how I was raised. You don't know nothing about how I was raised.

ROSE: Let the boy have ten dollars, Troy.

TROY (*to Lyons*): What the hell you looking at me for? I ain't got no ten dollars. You know what I do with my money. (*To Rose.*) Give him ten dollars if you want him to have it.

ROSE: I will. Just as soon as you turn it loose.

TROY (*handing Rose the money*): There it is. Seventy-six dollars and forty-two cents. You see this, Bono? Now, I ain't gonna get but six of that back.

ROSE: You ought to stop telling that lie. Here, Lyons. (*She hands him the money.*)

LYONS: Thanks, Rose. Look . . . I got to run . . . I'll see you later.

TROY: Wait a minute. You gonna say, "thanks, Rose" and ain't gonna look to see where she got that ten dollars from? See how they do me, Bono?

LYONS: I know she got it from you, Pop. Thanks. I'll give it back to you.

TROY: There he go telling another lie. Time I see that ten dollars . . . he'll be owing me thirty more.

LYONS: See you, Mr. Bono.

BONO: Take care, Lyons!

LYONS: Thanks, Pop. I'll see you again.

Lyons exits the yard.

TROY: I don't know why he don't go and get him a decent job and take care of that woman he got.

BONO: He'll be all right, Troy. The boy is still young.

TROY: The *boy* is thirty-four years old.

ROSE: Let's not get off into all that.

BONO: Look here . . . I got to be going. I got to be getting on. Lucille gonna be waiting.

TROY (*puts his arm around Rose*): See this woman, Bono? I love this woman. I love this woman so much it hurts. I love her so much . . . I done run out of ways of loving her. So I got to go back to basics. Don't you come by my house Monday morning talking about time to go to work . . .'cause I'm still gonna be stroking!

ROSE: Troy! Stop it now!

BONO: I ain't paying him no mind, Rose. That ain't nothing but gin-talk. Go on, Troy. I'll see you Monday.

TROY: Don't you come by my house, nigger! I done told you what I'm gonna be doing.

The lights go down to black.

SCENE 2

The lights come up on Rose hanging up clothes. She hums and sings softly to herself. It is the following morning.

ROSE (*sings*):

Jesus, be a fence all around me every day
Jesus, I want you to protect me as I travel on my way.
Jesus, be a fence all around me every day.

Troy enters from the house.

Jesus, I want you to protect me
As I travel on my way.

(*To Troy.*) 'Morning. You ready for breakfast? I can fix it soon as I finish hanging up these clothes?

TROY: I got the coffee on. That'll be all right. I'll just drink some of that this morning.

ROSE: That 651 hit yesterday. That's the second time this month. Miss Pearl hit for a dollar . . . seem like those that need the least always get lucky. Poor folks can't get nothing.

TROY: Them numbers don't know nobody. I don't know why you fool with them. You and Lyons both.

ROSE: It's something to do.

TROY: You ain't doing nothing but throwing your money away.

ROSE: Troy, you know I don't play foolishly. I just play a nickel here and a nickel there.

TROY: That's two nickels you done thrown away.

ROSE: Now I hit sometimes . . . that makes up for it. It always comes in handy when I do hit. I don't hear you complaining then.

TROY: I ain't complaining now. I just say it's foolish. Trying to guess out of six hundred ways which way the number gonna come. If I had all the money niggers, these Negroes, throw away on numbers for one week—just one week—I'd be a rich man.

ROSE: Well, you wishing and calling it foolish ain't gonna stop folks from playing numbers. That's one thing for sure. Besides . . . some good things come from playing numbers. Look where Pope done bought him that restaurant off of numbers.

TROY: I can't stand niggers like that. Man ain't had two dimes to rub together. He walking around with his shoes all run over bumming money for cigarettes. All right. Got lucky there and hit the numbers . . .

ROSE: Troy, I know all about it.

TROY: Had good sense, I'll say that for him. He ain't throwed his money away. I seen niggers hit the numbers and go through two thousand dollars in four days. Man bought him that restaurant down there . . . fixed it up real nice . . . and then didn't want nobody to come in it! A Negro go in there and can't get no kind of service. I seen a white fellow come in there and order a bowl of stew. Pope picked all the meat out of the pot for him. Man ain't had nothing but a bowl of meat! Negro come behind him and ain't got nothing but the potatoes and carrots. Talking about what numbers do for people, you picked a wrong example. Ain't done nothing but make a worser fool out of him than he was before.

ROSE: Troy, you ought to stop worrying about what happened at work yesterday.

TROY: I ain't worried. Just told me to be down there at the Commissioner's office on Friday. Everybody think they gonna fire me. I ain't worried about them firing me. You ain't got to worry about that. (*Pause.*) Where's Cory? Cory in the house? (*Calls.*) Cory?

ROSE: He gone out.

TROY: Out, huh? He gone out 'cause he know I want him to help me with this fence. I know how he is. That boy scared of work.

Gabriel enters. He comes halfway down the alley and, hearing Troy's voice, stops.

TROY (*continues*): He ain't done a lick of work in his life.

ROSE: He had to go to football practice. Coach wanted them to get in a little extra practice before the season start.

TROY: I got his practice . . . running out of here before he get his chores done.

ROSE: Troy, what is wrong with you this morning? Don't nothing set right with you. Go on back in there and go to bed . . . get up on the other side.

TROY: Why something got to be wrong with me? I ain't said nothing wrong with me.

ROSE: You got something to say about everything. First it's the numbers . . . then it's the way the man runs his restaurant . . . then you done got on Cory. What's it gonna be next? Take a look up there and see if the weather suits you . . . or is it gonna be how you gonna put up the fence with the clothes hanging in the yard.

TROY: You hit the nail on the head then.

ROSE: I know you like I know the back of my hand. Go on in there and get you some coffee . . . see if that straighten you up. 'Cause you ain't right this morning.

Troy starts into the house and sees Gabriel. Gabriel starts singing. Troy's brother, he is seven years younger than Troy. Injured in World War II, he has a metal plate in his head. He carries an old trumpet tied around his waist and believes with every fiber of his being that he is the Archangel Gabriel. He carries a chipped basket with an assortment of discarded fruits and vegetables he has picked up in the strip district and which he attempts to sell.

GABRIEL (*singing*):
> Yes, ma'am I got plums
> You ask me how I sell them
> Oh ten cents apiece
> Three for a quarter
> Come and buy now
> 'Cause I'm here today
> And tomorrow I'll be gone

Gabriel enters.

Hey, Rose!
ROSE: How you doing Gabe?
GABRIEL: There's Troy . . . Hey, Troy!
TROY: Hey, Gabe.

Exit into kitchen.

ROSE (*to Gabriel*): What you got there?
GABRIEL: You know what I got, Rose. I got fruits and vegetables.
ROSE (*looking in basket*): Where's all these plums you talking about?
GABRIEL: I ain't got no plums today, Rose. I was just singing that. Have some tomorrow. Put me in a big order for plums. Have enough plums tomorrow for St. Peter and everybody.

Troy reenters from kitchen, crosses to steps.

(*To Rose.*) Troy's mad at me.
TROY: I ain't mad at you. What I got to be mad at you about? You ain't done nothing to me.
GABRIEL: I just moved over to Miss Pearl's to keep out from in your way. I ain't mean no harm by it.
TROY: Who said anything about that? I ain't said anything about that.
GABRIEL: You ain't mad at me, is you?
TROY: Naw . . . I ain't mad at you, Gabe. If I was mad at you I'd tell you about it.

GABRIEL: Got me two rooms. In the basement. Got my own door too. Wanna see my key? (*He holds up a key.*) That's my own key! My two rooms!

TROY: Well, that's good, Gabe. You got your own key . . . that's good.

ROSE: You hungry, Gabe? I was just fixing to cook Troy his breakfast.

GABRIEL: I'll take some biscuits. You got some biscuits? Did you know when I was in heaven . . . every morning me and St. Peter would sit down by the gate and eat some big fat biscuits? Oh, yeah! We had us a good time. We'd sit there and eat us them biscuits and then St. Peter would go off to sleep and tell me to wake him up when it's time to open the gates for the judgment.

ROSE: Well, come on . . . I'll make up a batch of biscuits.

Rose exits into the house.

GABRIEL: Troy . . . St. Peter got your name in the book. I seen it. It say . . . Troy Maxson. I say . . . I know him! He got the same name like what I got. That's my brother!

TROY: How many times you gonna tell me that, Gabe?

GABRIEL: Ain't got my name in the book. Don't have to have my name. I done died and went to heaven. He got your name though. One morning St. Peter was looking at his book . . . marking it up for the judgment . . . and he let me see your name. Got it in there under M. Got Rose's name . . . I ain't seen it like I seen yours . . . but I know it's in there. He got a great big book. Got everybody's name what was ever been born. That's what he told me. But I seen your name. Seen it with my own eyes.

TROY: Go on in the house there. Rose going to fix you something to eat.

GABRIEL: Oh, I ain't hungry. I done had breakfast with Aunt Jemimah. She come by and cooked me up a whole mess of flapjacks. Remember how we used to eat them flapjacks?

TROY: Go on in the house and get you something to eat now.

GABRIEL: I got to sell my plums. I done sold some tomatoes. Got me two quarters. Wanna see? (*He shows Troy his quarters.*) I'm gonna save them and buy me a new horn so St. Peter can hear me when it's time to open the gates. (*Gabriel stops suddenly. Listens.*) Hear that? That's the hellhounds. I got to chase them out of here. Go on get out of here! Get out!

Gabriel exits singing.

Better get ready for the judgment
Better get ready for the judgment
My Lord is coming down

Rose enters from the house.

TROY: He's gone off somewhere.

GABRIEL (*offstage*):
Better get ready for the judgment
Better get ready for the judgment morning
Better get ready for the judgment
My God is coming down

ROSE: He ain't eating right. Miss Pearl say she can't get him to eat nothing.

TROY: What you want me to do about it, Rose? I done did everything I can for the man. I can't make him get well. Man got half his head blown away . . . what you expect?

ROSE: Seem like something ought to be done to help him.

TROY: Man don't bother nobody. He just mixed up from that metal plate he got in his head. Ain't no sense for him to go back into the hospital.

ROSE: Least he be eating right. They can help him take care of himself.

TROY: Don't nobody wanna be locked up, Rose. What you wanna lock him up for? Man go over there and fight the war . . . messin' around with them Japs, get half his head blow off . . . and they give him a lousy three thousand dollars. And I had to swoop down on that.

ROSE: Is you fixing to go into that again?

TROY: That's the only way I got a roof over my head . . . cause of that metal plate.

ROSE: Ain't no sense you blaming yourself for nothing. Gabe wasn't in no condition to manage that money. You done what was right by him. Can't nobody say you ain't done what was right by him. Look how long you took care of him . . . till he wanted to have his own place and moved over there with Miss Pearl.

TROY: That ain't what I'm saying, woman! I'm just stating the facts. If my brother didn't have that metal plate in his head . . . I wouldn't have a pot to piss in or a window to throw it out of. And I'm fifty-three years old. Now see if you can understand that!

Troy gets up from the porch and starts to exit the yard.

ROSE: Where you going off to? You been running out of here every Saturday for weeks. I thought you was gonna work on this fence?

TROY: I'm gonna walk down to Taylor's. Listen to the ball game. I'll be back in a bit. I'll work on it when I get back.

He exits the yard. The lights go to black.

SCENE 3

The lights come up on the yard. It is four hours later. Rose is taking down the clothes from the line. Cory enters carrying his football equipment.

ROSE: Your daddy like to had a fit with you running out of here this morning without doing your chores.

CORY: I told you I had to go to practice.

ROSE: He say you were supposed to help him with this fence.

CORY: He been saying that the last four or five Saturdays, and then he don't never do nothing, but go down to Taylors'. Did you tell him about the recruiter?

ROSE: Yeah, I told him.

CORY: What he say?

ROSE: He ain't said nothing too much. You get in there and get started on your chores before he gets back. Go on and scrub down them steps before he gets back here hollering and carrying on.

CORY: I'm hungry. What you got to eat, Mama?

ROSE: Go on and get started on your chores. I got some meat loaf in there. Go on and make you a sandwich . . . and don't leave no mess in there.

Cory exits into the house. Rose continues to take down the clothes. Troy enters the yard and sneaks up and grabs her from behind.

Troy! Go on, now. You liked to scared me to death. What was the score of the game? Lucille had me on the phone and I couldn't keep up with it.

TROY: What I care about the game? Come here, woman. (*He tries to kiss her.*)

ROSE: I thought you went down Taylors' to listen to the game. Go on, Troy! You supposed to be putting up this fence.

TROY (*attempting to kiss her again*): I'll put it up when I finish with what is at hand.

ROSE: Go on, Troy. I ain't studying you.

TROY (*chasing after her*): I'm studying you . . . fixing to do my homework!

ROSE: Troy, you better leave me alone.

TROY: Where's Cory? That boy brought his butt home yet?

ROSE: He's in the house doing his chores.

TROY (*calling*): Cory! Get your butt out here, boy!

> *Rose exits into the house with the laundry. Troy goes over to the pile of wood, picks up a board, and starts sawing. Cory enters from the house.*

TROY: You just now coming in here from leaving this morning?

CORY: Yeah, I had to go to football practice.

TROY: Yeah, what?

CORY: Yessir.

TROY: I ain't but two seconds off you noway. The garbage sitting in there overflowing . . . you ain't done none of your chores . . . and you come in here talking about "Yeah."

CORY: I was just getting ready to do my chores now, Pop . . .

TROY: Your first chore is to help me with this fence on Saturday. Everything else come after that. Now get that saw and cut them boards.

> *Cory takes the saw and begins cutting the boards. Troy continues working. There is a long pause.*

CORY: Hey, Pop . . . why don't you buy a TV?

TROY: What I want with a TV? What I want one of them for?

CORY: Everybody got one. Earl, Ba Bra . . . Jesse!

TROY: I ain't asked you who had one. I say what I want with one?

CORY: So you can watch it. They got lots of things on TV. Baseball games and everything. We could watch the World Series.

TROY: Yeah . . . and how much this TV cost?

CORY: I don't know. They got them on sale for around two hundred dollars.

TROY: Two hundred dollars, huh?

CORY: That ain't that much, Pop.

TROY: Naw, it's just two hundred dollars. See that roof you got over your head at night? Let me tell you something about that roof. It's been over ten years since that roof was last tarred. See now . . . the snow come this winter and sit up there on that roof like it is . . . and it's gonna seep inside. It's just gonna be a little bit . . . ain't gonna hardly notice it. Then the next thing you know, it's gonna be leaking all over the house. Then the wood rot from all that water and you gonna need a whole new roof. Now, how much you think it cost to get that roof tarred?

CORY: I don't know.

TROY: Two hundred and sixty-four dollars . . . cash money. While you thinking about a TV, I got to be thinking about the roof . . . and whatever else go wrong here. Now if you had two hundred dollars, what would you do . . . fix the roof or buy a TV?

CORY: I'd buy a TV. Then when the roof started to leak . . . when it needed fixing . . . I'd fix it.

TROY: Where you gonna get the money from? You done spent it for a TV. You gonna sit up and watch the water run all over your brand new TV.

CORY: Aw, Pop. You got money. I know you do.

TROY: Where I got it at, huh?

CORY: You got it in the bank.

TROY: You wanna see my bankbook? You wanna see that seventy-three dollars and twenty-two cents I got sitting up in there?

CORY: You ain't got to pay for it all at one time. You can put a down payment on it and carry it on home with you.

TROY: Not me. I ain't gonna owe nobody nothing if I can help it. Miss a payment and they come and snatch it right out of your house. Then what you got? Now, soon as I get two hundred dollars clear, then I'll buy a TV. Right now, as soon as I get two hundred and sixty-four dollars, I'm gonna have this roof tarred.

CORY: Aw . . . Pop!

TROY: You go on and get you two hundred dollars and buy one if ya want it. I got better things to do with my money.

CORY: I can't get no two hundred dollars. I ain't never seen two hundred dollars.

TROY: I'll tell you what . . . you get you a hundred dollars and I'll put the other hundred with it.

CORY: All right, I'm gonna show you.

TROY: You gonna show me how you can cut them boards right now.

Cory begins to cut the boards. There is a long pause.

CORY: The Pirates won today. That makes five in a row.

TROY: I ain't thinking about the Pirates. Got an all-white team. Got that boy . . . that Puerto Rican boy . . . Clemente. Don't even half-play him. That boy could be something if they give him a chance. Play him one day and sit him on the bench the next.

CORY: He gets a lot of chances to play.

TROY: I'm talking about playing regular. Playing every day so you can get your timing. That's what I'm talking about.

CORY: They got some white guys on the team that don't play every day. You can't play everybody at the same time.

TROY: If they got a white fellow sitting on the bench . . . you can bet your last dollar he can't play! The colored guy got to be twice as good before he get on the team. That's why I don't want you to get all tied up in them sports. Man on the team and what it get him? They got colored on the team and don't use them. Same as not having them. All them teams the same.

CORY: The Braves got Hank Aaron and Wes Covington. Hank Aaron hit two home runs today. That makes forty-three.

TROY: Hank Aaron ain't nobody. That what you supposed to do. That's how you supposed to play the game. Ain't nothing to it. It's just a matter of timing . . . getting the right follow-through. Hell, I can hit forty-three home runs right now!

CORY: Not off no major-league pitching, you couldn't.

TROY: We had better pitching in the Negro leagues. I hit seven home runs off of Satchel Paige.[4] You can't get no better than that!

CORY: Sandy Koufax. He's leading the league in strikeouts.

TROY: I ain't thinking of no Sandy Koufax.

CORY: You got Warren Spahn and Lew Burdette. I bet you couldn't hit no home runs off of Warren Spahn.

---

[4]Paige (1906–1982) was a pitcher in the Negro leagues and later played briefly in the majors.

TROY: I'm through with it now. You go on and cut them boards. (*Pause.*) Your mama tell me you done got recruited by a college football team? Is that right?

CORY: Yeah. Coach Zellman say the recruiter gonna be coming by to talk to you. Get you to sign the permission papers.

TROY: I thought you supposed to be working down there at the A&P. Ain't you suppose to be working down there after school?

CORY: Mr. Stawicki say he gonna hold my job for me until after the football season. Say starting next week I can work weekends.

TROY: I thought we had an understanding about this football stuff? You suppose to keep up with your chores and hold that job down at the A&P. Ain't been around here all day on a Saturday. Ain't none of your chores done . . . and now you telling me you done quit your job.

CORY: I'm going to be working weekends.

TROY: You damn right you are! And ain't no need for nobody coming around here to talk to me about signing nothing.

CORY: Hey, Pop . . . you can't do that. He's coming all the way from North Carolina.

TROY: I don't care where he coming from. The white man ain't gonna let you get nowhere with that football noway. You go on and get your book-learning so you can work yourself up in that A&P or learn how to fix cars or build houses or something, get you a trade. That way you have something can't nobody take away from you. You go on and learn how to put your hands to some good use. Besides hauling people's garbage.

CORY: I get good grades, Pop. That's why the recruiter wants to talk with you. You got to keep up your grades to get recruited. This way I'll be going to college. I'll get a chance . . .

TROY: First you gonna get your butt down there to the A&P and get your job back.

CORY: Mr. Stawicki done already hired somebody else 'cause I told him I was playing football.

TROY: You a bigger fool than I thought . . . to let somebody take away your job so you can play some football. Where you gonna get your money to take out your girlfriend and whatnot? What kind of foolishness is that to let somebody take away your job?

CORY: I'm still gonna be working weekends.

TROY: Naw . . . naw. You getting your butt out of here and finding you another job.

CORY: Come on, Pop! I got to practice. I can't work after school and play football too. The team needs me. That's what Coach Zellman say . . .

TROY: I don't care what nobody else say. I'm the boss . . . you understand? I'm the boss around here. I do the only saying what counts.

CORY: Come on, Pop!

TROY: I asked you . . . did you understand?

CORY: Yeah . . .

TROY: What?!

CORY: Yessir.

TROY: You go on down there to that A&P and see if you can get your job back. If you can't do both . . . then you quit the football team. You've got to take the crookeds with the straights.

CORY: Yessir. (*Pause.*) Can I ask you a question?

TROY: What the hell you wanna ask me? Mr. Stawicki the one you got the questions for.

CORY: How come you ain't never liked me?

TROY: Liked you? Who the hell say I got to like you? What law is there say I got to like you? Wanna stand up in my face and ask a damn foolass question like that. Talking about liking somebody. Come here, boy, when I talk to you.

Cory comes over to where Troy is working. He stands slouched over and Troy shoves him on his shoulder.

Straighten up, goddammit! I asked you a question . . . what law is there say I got to like you?

CORY: None.

TROY: Well, all right then! Don't you eat every day? (*Pause.*) Answer me when I talk to you! Don't you eat every day?

CORY: Yeah.

TROY: Nigger, as long as you in my house, you put that sir on the end of it when you talk to me.

CORY: Yes . . . sir.

TROY: You eat every day.

CORY: Yessir!

TROY: Got a roof over your head.

CORY: Yessir!

TROY: Got clothes on your back.

CORY: Yessir.

TROY: Why you think that is?

CORY: Cause of you.

TROY: Ah, hell I know it's cause of me . . . but why do you think that is?

CORY (*hesitant*): Cause you like me.

TROY: Like you? I go out of here every morning . . . bust my butt . . . putting up with them crackers every day . . . cause I like you? You are the biggest fool I ever saw. (*Pause.*) It's my job. It's my responsibility! You understand that? A man got to take care of his family. You live in my house . . . sleep you behind on my bedclothes . . . fill you belly up with my food . . . cause you my son. You my flesh and blood. Not cause I like you! Cause it's my duty to take care of you. I owe a responsibility to you! Let's get this straight right here . . . before it go along any further . . . I ain't got to like you. Mr. Rand don't give me my money come payday cause he likes me. He gives me cause he owe me. I done give you everything I had to give you. I gave you your life! Me and your mama worked that out between us. And liking your black ass wasn't part of the bargain. Don't you try and go through life worrying about if somebody like you or not. You best be making sure they doing right by you. You understand what I'm saying boy?

CORY: Yessir.

TROY: Then get the hell out of my face, and get on down to that A&P.

Rose has been standing behind the screen door for much of the scene. She enters as Cory exits.

ROSE: Why don't you let the boy go ahead and play football, Troy? Ain't no harm in that. He's just trying to be like you with the sports.

TROY: I don't want him to be like me! I want him to move as far away from my life as he can get. You the only decent thing that ever happened to me. I wish him that. But I don't wish him a thing else from my life. I decided seventeen years ago that boy wasn't getting involved in no sports. Not after what they did to me in the sports.

ROSE: Troy, why don't you admit you was too old to play in the major leagues? For once . . . why don't you admit that?

TROY: What do you mean too old? Don't come telling me I was too old. I just wasn't the right color. Hell, I'm fifty-three years old and can do better than Selkirk's .269 right now!

ROSE: How's was you gonna play ball when you were over forty? Sometimes I can't get no sense out of you.

TROY: I got good sense, woman. I got sense enough not to let my boy get hurt over playing no sports. You been mothering that boy too much. Worried about if people like him.

ROSE: Everything that boy do . . . he do for you. He wants you to say "Good job, son." That's all.

TROY: Rose, I ain't got time for that. He's alive. He's healthy. He's got to make his own way. I made mine. Ain't nobody gonna hold his hand when he get out there in that world.

ROSE: Times have changed from when you was young, Troy. People change. The world's changing around you and you can't even see it.

TROY (*slow, methodical*): Woman . . . I do the best I can do. I come in here every Friday. I carry a sack of potatoes and a bucket of lard. You all line up at the door with your hands out. I give you the lint from my pockets. I give you my sweat and my blood. I ain't got no tears. I done spent them. We go upstairs in that room at night . . . and I fall down on you and try to blast a hole into forever. I get up Monday morning . . . find my lunch on the table. I go out. Make my way. Find my strength to carry me through to the next Friday. (*Pause.*) That's all I got, Rose. That's all I got to give. I can't give nothing else.

Troy exits into the house. The lights go down to black.

Scene 4

It is Friday. Two weeks later. Cory starts out of the house with his football equipment. The phone rings.

CORY (*calling*): I got it! (*He answers the phone and stands in the screen door talking.*) Hello? Hey, Jesse. Naw . . . I was just getting ready to leave now.

ROSE (*calling*): Cory!

CORY: I told you, man, them spikes is all tore up. You can use them if you want, but they ain't no good. Earl got some spikes.

ROSE (*calling*):   Cory!

CORY (*calling to Rose*):   Mam? I'm talking to Jesse. (*Into phone.*) When she say that? (*Pause.*) Aw, you lying, man. I'm gonna tell her you said that.

ROSE (*calling*):   Cory, don't you go nowhere!

CORY: I got to go to the game, Ma! (*Into the phone.*) Yeah, hey, look, I'll talk to you later. Yeah, I'll meet you over Earl's house. Later. Bye, Ma.

Cory exits the house and starts out the yard.

ROSE: Cory, where you going off to? You got that stuff all pulled out and thrown all over your room.

CORY (*in the yard*):   I was looking for my spikes. Jesse wanted to borrow my spikes.

ROSE: Get up there and get that cleaned up before your daddy get back in here.

CORY: I got to go to the game! I'll clean it up *when I get back.*

Cory exits.

ROSE: That's all he need to do is see that room all messed up.

Rose exits into the house. Troy and Bono enter the yard. Troy is dressed in clothes other than his work clothes.

BONO: He told him the same thing he told you. Take it to the union.

TROY: Brownie ain't got that much sense. Man wasn't thinking about nothing. He wait until I confront them on it . . . then he wanna come crying seniority. (*Calls.*) Hey, Rose!

BONO: I wish I could have seen Mr. Rand's face when he told you.

TROY: He couldn't get it out of his mouth! Liked to bit his tongue! When they called me down there to the Commissioner's office . . . he thought they was gonna fire me. Like everybody else.

BONO: I didn't think they was gonna fire you. I thought they was gonna put you on the warning paper.

TROY: Hey, Rose! (*To Bono.*) Yeah, Mr. Rand like to bit his tongue.

Troy breaks the seal on the bottle, takes a drink, and hands it to Bono.

BONO: I see you run right down to Taylors' and told that Alberta gal.

TROY (*calling*):   Hey Rose! (*To Bono.*) I told everybody. Hey, Rose! I went down there to cash my check.

ROSE (*entering from the house*):   Hush all that hollering, man! I know you out here. What they say down there at the Commissioner's office?

TROY: You supposed to come when I call you, woman. Bono'll tell you that. (*To Bono.*) Don't Lucille come when you call her?

ROSE: Man, hush your mouth. I ain't no dog . . . talk about "come when you call me."

TROY (*puts his arm around Rose*):   You hear this, Bono? I had me an old dog used to get uppity like that. You say, "C'mere, Blue!" . . . and he just lay there and look at you. End up getting a stick and chasing him away trying to make him come.

ROSE: I ain't studying you and your dog. I remember you used to sing that old song.

TROY (*he sings*):
Hear it ring! Hear it ring! I had a dog his name was Blue.

ROSE: Don't nobody wanna hear you sing that old song.

TROY (*sings*):
You know Blue was mighty true.

ROSE: Used to have Cory running around here singing that song.

BONO: Hell, I remember that song myself.

TROY (*sings*):
You know Blue was a good old dog.
Blue treed a possum in a hollow log.
That was my daddy's song. My daddy made up that song.

ROSE: I don't care who made it up. Don't nobody wanna hear you sing it.

TROY (*makes a song like calling a dog*):   Come here, woman.

ROSE: You come in here carrying on, I reckon they ain't fired you. What they say down there at the Commissioner's office?

TROY: Look here, Rose . . . Mr. Rand called me into his office today when I got back from talking to them people down there . . . it come from up top . . . he called me in and told me they was making me a driver.

ROSE: Troy, you kidding!

TROY: No I ain't. Ask Bono.

ROSE: Well, that's great, Troy. Now you don't have to hassle them people no more.

Lyons enters from the street.

TROY: Aw hell, I wasn't looking to see you today. I thought you was in jail. Got it all over the front page of the *Courier* about them raiding Sefus's place . . . where you be hanging out with all them thugs.

LYONS: Hey, Pop . . . that ain't got nothing to do with me. I don't go down there gambling. I go down there to sit in with the band. I ain't got nothing to do with the gambling part. They got some good music down there.

TROY: They got some rogues . . . is what they got.

LYONS: How you been, Mr. Bono? Hi, Rose.

BONO: I see where you playing down at the Crawford Grill tonight.

ROSE: How come you ain't brought Bonnie like I told you? You should have brought Bonnie with you, she ain't been over in a month of Sundays.

LYONS: I was just in the neighborhood . . . thought I'd stop by.

TROY: Here he come . . .

BONO: Your daddy got a promotion on the rubbish. He's gonna be the first colored driver. Ain't got to do nothing but sit up there and read the paper like them white fellows.

LYONS: Hey, Pop . . . if you knew how to read you'd be all right.

BONO: Naw . . . naw . . . you mean if the nigger knew how to drive he'd be all right. Been fighting with them people about driving and ain't even got a license. Mr. Rand know you ain't got no driver's license?

TROY: Driving ain't nothing. All you do is point the truck where you want it to go. Driving ain't nothing.

BONO: Do Mr. Rand know you ain't got no driver's license? That's what I'm talking about. I ain't asked if driving was easy. I asked if Mr. Rand know you ain't got no driver's license.

TROY: He ain't got to know. The man ain't got to know my business. Time he find out, I have two or three driver's licenses.

LYONS (*going into his pocket*): Say, look here, Pop . . .

TROY: I knew it was coming. Didn't I tell you, Bono? I know what kind of "Look here, Pop" that was. The nigger fixing to ask me for some money. It's Friday night. It's my payday. All them rogues down there on the avenue . . . the ones that ain't in jail . . . and Lyons is hopping in his shoes to get down there with them.

LYONS: See, Pop . . . if you give somebody else a chance to talk sometimes, you'd see that I was fixing to pay you back your ten dollars like I told you. Here . . . I told you I'd pay you when Bonnie got paid.

TROY: Naw . . . you go ahead and keep that ten dollars. Put it in the bank. The next time you feel like you wanna come by here and ask me for something . . . you go on down there and get that.

LYONS: Here's your ten dollars, Pop. I told you I don't want you to give me nothing. I just wanted to borrow ten dollars.

TROY: Naw . . . you go on and keep that for the next time you want to ask me.

LYONS: Come on, Pop . . . here go your ten dollars.

ROSE: Why don't you go on and let the boy pay you back, Troy?

LYONS: Here you go, Rose. If you don't take it I'm gonna have to hear about it for the next six months. (*He hands her the money.*)

ROSE: You can hand yours over here too, Troy.

TROY: You see this, Bono. You see how they do me.

BONO: Yeah, Lucille do me the same way.

Gabriel is heard singing off stage. He enters.

GABRIEL: Better get ready for the Judgment! Better get ready for . . . Hey!. . . Hey!. . . There's Troy's boy!

LYONS: How are you doing, Uncle Gabe?

GABRIEL: Lyons . . . The King of the Jungle! Rose . . . hey, Rose. Got a flower for you. (*He takes a rose from his pocket.*) Picked it myself. That's the same rose like you is!

ROSE: That's right nice of you, Gabe.

LYONS: What you been doing, Uncle Gabe?

GABRIEL: Oh, I been chasing hellhounds and waiting on the time to tell St. Peter to open the gates.

LYONS: You been chasing hellhounds, huh? Well . . . you doing the right thing, Uncle Gabe. Somebody got to chase them.

GABRIEL: Oh, yeah . . . I know it. The devil's strong. The devil ain't no pushover. Hellhounds snipping at everybody's heels. But I got my trumpet waiting on the judgment time.

LYONS: Waiting on the Battle of Armageddon, huh?

GABRIEL: Ain't gonna be too much of a battle when God get to waving that Judgment sword. But the people's gonna have a hell of a time trying to get into heaven if them gates ain't open.

LYONS (*putting his arm around Gabriel*): You hear this, Pop. Uncle Gabe, you all right!

GABRIEL (*laughing with Lyons*):   Lyons! King of the Jungle.

ROSE: You gonna stay for supper, Gabe? Want me to fix you a plate?

GABRIEL: I'll take a sandwich, Rose. Don't want no plate. Just wanna eat with my hands. I'll take a sandwich.

ROSE: How about you, Lyons? You staying? Got some short ribs cooking.

LYONS: Naw, I won't eat nothing till after we finished playing. (*Pause.*) You ought to come down and listen to me play, Pop.

TROY: I don't like that Chinese music. All that noise.

ROSE: Go on in the house and wash up, Gabe . . . I'll fix you a sandwich.

GABRIEL (*to Lyons, as he exits*):   Troy's mad at me.

LYONS: What you mad at Uncle Gabe for, Pop?

ROSE: He thinks Troy's mad at him cause he moved over to Miss Pearl's.

TROY: I ain't mad at the man. He can live where he want to live at.

LYONS: What he move over there for? Miss Pearl don't like nobody.

ROSE: She don't mind him none. She treats him real nice. She just don't allow all that singing.

TROY: She don't mind that rent he be paying . . . that's what she don't mind.

ROSE: Troy, I ain't going through that with you no more. He's over there cause he want to have his own place. He can come and go as he please.

TROY: Hell, he could come and go as he please here. I wasn't stopping him. I ain't put no rules on him.

ROSE: It ain't the same thing, Troy. And you know it.

Gabriel comes to the door.

Now, that's the last I wanna hear about that. I don't wanna hear nothing else about Gabe and Miss Pearl. And next week . . .

GABRIEL: I'm ready for my sandwich, Rose.

ROSE: And next week . . . when that recruiter come from that school . . . I want you to sign that paper and go on and let Cory play football. Then that'll be the last I have to hear about that.

TROY (*to Rose as she exits into the house*):   I ain't thinking about Cory nothing.

LYONS: What . . . Cory got recruited? What school he going to?

TROY: That boy walking around here smelling his piss . . . thinking he's grown. Thinking he's gonna do what he want, irrespective of what I say. Look here, Bono . . . I left the Commissioner's office and went down to the A&P . . . that boy ain't working down there. He lying to me. Telling me he got his job back . . . telling me he working weekends . . . telling me he working after school . . . Mr. Stawicki tell me he ain't working down there at all!

LYONS: Cory just growing up. He's just busting at the seams trying to fill out your shoes.

TROY: I don't care what he's doing. When he get to the point where he wanna disobey me . . . then it's time for him to move on. Bono'll tell you that. I bet he ain't never disobeyed his daddy without paying the consequences.

BONO: I ain't never had a chance. My daddy came on through . . . but I ain't never knew him to see him . . . or what he had on his mind or where he went. Just moving on through. Searching out the New Land. That's what the old folks used to call it. See a fellow moving around from place to place . . . woman to woman . . . called it searching out the New Land. I can't say if he ever found it. I come along, didn't want no kids. Didn't know if I was gonna be in one place long enough to fix on them right as their daddy. I figured I was going searching too. As it turned out I been hooked up with Lucille near about as long as your daddy been with Rose. Going on sixteen years.

TROY: Sometimes I wish I hadn't known my daddy. He ain't cared nothing about no kids. A kid to him wasn't nothing. All he wanted was for you to learn how to walk so he could start you to working. When it come time for eating . . . he ate first. If there was anything left over, that's what you got. Man would sit down and eat two chickens and give you the wing.

LYONS: You ought to stop that, Pop. Everybody feed their kids. No matter how hard times is . . . everybody care about their kids. Make sure they have something to eat.

TROY: The only thing my daddy cared about was getting them bales of cotton in to Mr. Lubin. That's the only thing that mattered to him. Sometimes I used to wonder why he was living. Wonder why the devil hadn't come and got him. "Get them bales of cotton in to Mr. Lubin" and find out he owe him money . . .

LYONS: He should have just went on and left when he saw he couldn't get nowhere. That's what I would have done.

TROY: How he gonna leave with eleven kids? And where he gonna go? He ain't knew how to do nothing but farm. No, he was trapped and I think he knew it. But I'll say this for him . . . he felt a responsibility toward us. Maybe he ain't treated us the way I felt he should have . . . but without that responsibility he could have walked off and left us . . . made his own way.

BONO: A lot of them did. Back in those days what you talking about . . . they walk out their front door and just take on down one road or another and keep on walking.

LYONS: There you go! That's what I'm talking about.

BONO: Just keep on walking till you come to something else. Ain't you never heard of nobody having the walking blues? Well, that's what you call it when you just take off like that.

TROY: My daddy ain't had them walking blues! What you talking about? He stayed right there with his family. But he was just as evil as he could be. My mama couldn't stand him. Couldn't stand that evilness. She run off when I was about eight. She sneaked off one night after he had gone to sleep. Told me she was coming back for me. I ain't never seen her no more. All his women run off and left him. He wasn't good for nobody.

When my turn come to head out, I was fourteen and got to sniffing around Joe Canewell's daughter. Had us an old mule we called Greyboy. My daddy sent me out to do some plowing and I tied up Greyboy and went to fooling around with Joe Canewell's daughter. We done found us a nice little spot, got real cozy with each other. She about thirteen and we done figured we was grown anyway . . . so we down there enjoying ourselves . . . ain't thinking about nothing. We didn't know Greyboy had got loose and wandered back to the house and my daddy was looking for me. We down there by the creek enjoying ourselves when my daddy come up on us. Surprised us. He had them leather straps off the mule and commenced to whupping me like there was no tomorrow. I jumped up, mad and embarrassed. I was scared of my daddy. When he commenced to whupping on me . . . quite naturally I run to get out of the way. (*Pause.*) Now I thought he was mad cause I ain't done my work. But I see where he was chasing me off so he could have the gal for himself. When I see what the matter of it was, I lost all fear of my daddy. Right there is where I become a man . . . at fourteen years of age. (*Pause.*) Now it was my turn to run him off. I picked up them same reins that he had used on me. I picked up them reins and commenced to whupping on him. The gal jumped up and run off . . . and when my daddy turned to face me, I could see why the devil had never come to get him . . . cause he was the devil himself. I don't know what happened. When I woke up, I was laying right there by the creek, and Blue . . . this old dog we had . . . was licking my face. I thought I was blind. I couldn't see nothing. Both my eyes were swollen shut. I laid there and cried. I didn't know what I was gonna do. The only thing I knew was the time had come for me to leave my daddy's house. And right there the world suddenly got big. And it was a long time before I could cut it down to where I could handle it.

Part of that cutting down was when I got to the place where I could feel him kicking in my blood and knew that the only thing that separated us was the matter of a few years.

Gabriel enters from the house with a sandwich.

LYONS: What you got there, Uncle Gabe?

GABRIEL: Got me a ham sandwich. Rose gave me a ham sandwich.

TROY: I don't know what happened to him. I done lost touch with everybody except Gabriel. But I hope he's dead. I hope he found some peace.

LYONS: That's a heavy story, Pop. I didn't know you left home when you was fourteen.

TROY: And didn't know nothing. The only part of the world I knew was the forty-two acres of Mr. Lubin's land. That's all I knew about life.

LYONS: Fourteen's kinda young to be out on your own. (*Phone rings.*) I don't even think I was ready to be out on my own at fourteen. I don't know what I would have done.

TROY: I got up from the creek and walked on down to Mobile. I was through with farming. Figured I could do better in the city. So I walked the two hundred miles to Mobile.

LYONS: Wait a minute . . . you ain't walked no two hundred miles, Pop. Ain't nobody gonna walk no two hundred miles. You talking about some walking there.

BONO: That's the only way you got anywhere back in them days.

LYONS: Shhh. Damn if I wouldn't have hitched a ride with somebody!

TROY: Who you gonna hitch it with? They ain't had no cars and things like they got now. We talking about 1918.

ROSE (*entering*): What you all out here getting into?

TROY (*to Rose*): I'm telling Lyons how good he got it. He don't know nothing about this I'm talking.

ROSE: Lyons, that was Bonnie on the phone. She say you supposed to pick her up.

LYONS: Yeah, okay, Rose.

TROY: I walked on down to Mobile and hitched up with some of them fellows that was heading this way. Got up here and found out . . . not only couldn't you get a job . . . you couldn't find no place to live. I thought I was in freedom. Shhh. Colored folks living down there on the riverbanks in whatever kind of shelter they could find for themselves. Right down there under the Brady Street Bridge. Living in shacks made of sticks and tarpaper. Messed around there and went from bad to worse. Started stealing. First it was food. Then I figured, hell, if I steal money I can buy me some food. Buy me some shoes too! One thing led to another. Met your mama. I was young and anxious to be a man. Met your mama and had you. What I do that for? Now I got to worry about feeding you and her. Got to steal three times as much. Went out one day looking for somebody to rob . . . that's what I was, a robber. I'll tell you the truth. I'm ashamed of it today. But it's the truth. Went to rob this fellow . . . pulled out my knife . . . and he pulled out a gun. Shot me in the chest. I felt just like somebody had taken a hot branding iron and laid it on me. When he shot me I jumped at him with my knife. They told me I killed him and they put me in the penitentiary and locked me up for fifteen years. That's where I met Bono. That's where I learned how to play baseball. Got out that place and your mama had taken you and went on to make life without me. Fifteen years was a long time for her to wait. But that fifteen years cured me of that robbing stuff. Rose'll tell you. She asked me when I met her if I had gotten all that foolishness out of my system. And I told her, "Baby, it's you and baseball all what count with me." You hear me, Bono? I meant it too. She say, "Which one comes first?" I told her, "Baby, ain't no doubt it's baseball . . . but you stick and get old with me and we'll both outlive this baseball." Am I right, Rose? And it's true.

ROSE: Man, hush your mouth. You ain't said no such thing. Talking about, "Baby you know you'll always be number one with me." That's what you was talking.

TROY: You hear that, Bono. That's why I love her.

BONO: Rose'll keep you straight. You get off the track, she'll straighten you up.

ROSE: Lyons, you better get on up and get Bonnie. She waiting on you.

LYONS (*gets up to go*): Hey, Pop, why don't you come on down to the Grill and hear me play?

TROY: I ain't going down there. I'm too old to be sitting around in them clubs.

BONO: You got to be good to play down at the Grill.

LYONS: Come on, Pop . . .

TROY: I got to get up in the morning.

LYONS: You ain't got to stay long.

TROY: Naw, I'm gonna get my supper and go on to bed.

LYONS: Well, I got to go. I'll see you again.

TROY: Don't you come around my house on my payday.

ROSE: Pick up the phone and let somebody know you coming. And bring Bonnie with you. You know I'm always glad to see her.

LYONS: Yeah, I'll do that, Rose. You take care now. See you, Pop. See you, Mr. Bono. See you, Uncle Gabe.

GABRIEL: Lyons! King of the Jungle!

Lyons exits.

TROY: Is supper ready, woman? Me and you got some business to take care of. I'm gonna tear it up too.

ROSE: Troy, I done told you now!

TROY (*puts his arm around Bono*): Aw hell, woman . . . this is Bono. Bono like family. I done known this nigger since . . . how long I done know you?

BONO: It's been a long time.

TROY: I done know this nigger since Skippy was a pup. Me and him done been through some times.

BONO: You sure right about that.

TROY: Hell, I done know him longer than I known you. And we still standing shoulder to shoulder. Hey, look here, Bono . . . a man can't ask for no more than that. (*Drinks to him.*) I love you, nigger.

BONO: Hell, I love you too . . . I got to get home see my woman. You got yours in hand. I got to get mine.

Bono starts to exit as Cory enters the yard, dressed in his football uniform. He gives Troy a hard, uncompromising look.

CORY: What you do that for, Pop?

He throws his helmet down in the direction of Troy.

ROSE: What's the matter? Cory . . . what's the matter?

CORY: Papa done went up to the school and told Coach Zellman I can't play football no more. Wouldn't even let me play the game. Told him to tell the recruiter not to come.

ROSE: Troy . . .

TROY: What you Troying me for. Yeah, I did it. And the boy know why I did it.

CORY: Why you wanna do that to me? That was the one chance I had.

ROSE: Ain't nothing wrong with Cory playing football, Troy.

TROY: The boy lied to me. I told the nigger if he wanna play football . . . to keep up his chores and hold down that job at the A&P. That was the conditions. Stopped down there to see Mr. Stawicki . . .

CORY: I can't work after school during the football season, Pop! I tried to tell you that Mr. Stawicki's holding my job for me. You don't never want to listen to nobody. And then you wanna go and do this to me!

TROY: I ain't done nothing to you. You done it to yourself.

CORY: Just cause you didn't have a chance! You just scared I'm gonna be better than you, that's all.

TROY: Come here.

ROSE: Troy . . .

Cory reluctantly crosses over to Troy.

TROY: All right! See. You done made a mistake.

CORY: I didn't even do nothing!

TROY: I'm gonna tell you what your mistake was. See . . . you swung at the ball and didn't hit it. That's strike one. See, you in the batter's box now. You swung and you missed. That's strike one. Don't you strike out!

Lights fade to black.

ACT 2

SCENE 1

The following morning. Cory is at the tree hitting the ball with the bat. He tries to mimic Troy, but his swing is awkward, less sure. Rose enters from the house.

ROSE: Cory, I want you to help me with this cupboard.

CORY: I ain't quitting the team. I don't care what Poppa say.

ROSE: I'll talk to him when he gets back. He had to go see about your Uncle Gabe. The police done arrested him. Say he was disturbing the peace. He'll be back directly. Come on in here and help me clean out the top of this cupboard.

Cory exits into the house. Rose sees Troy and Bono coming down the alley.

Troy, . . . what they say down there?

TROY: Ain't said nothing. I give them fifty dollars and they let him go. I'll talk to you about it. Where's Cory?

ROSE: He's in there helping me clean out these cupboards.

TROY: Tell him to get his butt out here.

Troy and Bono go over to the pile of wood. Bono picks up the saw and begins sawing.

TROY (*to Bono*): All they want is the money. That makes six or seven times I done went down there and got him. See me coming they stick out their hands.

BONO: Yeah. I know what you mean. That's all they care about . . . that money. They don't care about what's right. (*Pause.*) Nigger, why you got to go and get some hard wood? You ain't doing nothing but building a little old fence. Get you some soft pine wood. That's all you need.

TROY: I know what I'm doing. This is outside wood. You put pine wood inside the house. Pine wood is inside wood. This here is outside wood. Now you tell me where the fence is gonna be?

BONO: You don't need this wood. You can put it up with pine wood and it'll stand as long as you gonna be here looking at it.

TROY: How you know how long I'm gonna be here, nigger? Hell, I might just live forever. Live longer than old man Horsely.

BONO: That's what Magee used to say.

TROY: Magee's damn fool. Now you tell me who you ever heard of gonna pull their own teeth with a pair of rusty pliers.

BONO: The old folks . . . my granddaddy used to pull his teeth with pliers. They ain't had no dentists for the colored folks back then.

TROY: Get clean pliers! You understand? Clean pliers! Sterilize them! Besides we ain't living back then. All Magee had to do was walk over to Doc Goldblum's.

BONO: I see where you and that Tallahassee gal . . . that Alberta . . . I see where you all done got tight.

TROY: What you mean "got tight"?

BONO: I see where you be laughing and joking with her all the time.

TROY: I laughs and jokes with all of them, Bono. You know me.

BONO: That ain't the kind of laughing and joking I'm talking about.

Cory enters from the house.

CORY: How you doing. Mr. Bono?

TROY: Cory? Get that saw from Bono and cut some wood. He talking about the wood's too hard to cut. Stand back there, Jim, and let that young boy show you how it's done.

BONO: He's sure welcome to it.

Cory takes the saw and begins to cut the wood.

Whew-e-e! Look at that. Big old strong boy. Look like Joe Louis. Hell, must be getting old the way I'm watching that boy whip through that wood.

CORY: I don't see why Mama want a fence around the yard noways.

TROY: Damn if I know either. What the hell she keeping out with it? She ain't got nothing nobody want.

BONO: Some people build fences to keep people out . . . and other people build fences to keep people in. Rose wants to hold on to you all. She loves you.

TROY: Hell, nigger, I don't need nobody to tell me my wife loves me. Cory . . . go on in the house and see if you can find that other saw.

CORY: Where's it at?

TROY: I said find it! Look for it till you find it!

Cory exits into the house.

What's that supposed to mean? Wanna keep us in?

BONO: Troy . . . I done known you seem like damn near my whole life. You and Rose both. I done know both of you all for a long time. I remember when you met Rose. When you was hitting them baseball out the park. A lot of them old gals was after you then. You had the pick of the litter. When you picked Rose, I was happy for you. That was the first time I knew you had any sense. I said . . . My man Troy knows what he's doing . . . I'm gonna follow this nigger . . . he might take me somewhere. I been following you too. I done learned a whole heap of things about life watching you. I done learned how to tell where the shit lies. How to tell it from the alfalfa. You done learned me a lot of things. You showed me how to not make the same mistakes . . . to take life as it comes along and keep putting one foot in front of the other. (*Pause.*) Rose a good woman, Troy.

TROY: Hell, nigger, I know she a good woman. I been married to her for eighteen years. What you got on your mind, Bono?

BONO: I just say she a good woman. Just like I say anything. I ain't got to have nothing on my mind.

TROY: You just gonna say she a good woman and leave it hanging out there like that? Why you telling me she a good woman?

BONO: She loves you, Troy. Rose loves you.

TROY: You saying I don't measure up. That's what you trying to say. I don't measure up cause I'm seeing this other gal. I know what you trying to say.

BONO: I know what Rose means to you, Troy. I'm just trying to say I don't want to see you mess up.

TROY: Yeah, I appreciate that, Bono. If you was messing around on Lucille I'd be telling you the same thing.

BONO: Well, that's all I got to say. I just say that because I love you both.

TROY: Hell, you know me . . . I wasn't out there looking for nothing. You can't find a better woman than Rose. I know that. But seems like this woman just stuck onto me where I can't shake her loose. I done wrestled with it, tried to throw her off me . . . but she just stuck on tighter. Now she's stuck on for good.

BONO: You's in control . . . that's what you tell me all the time. You responsible for what you do.

TROY: I ain't ducking the responsibility of it. As long as it sets right in my heart . . . then I'm okay. Cause that's all I listen to. It'll tell me right from wrong every time. And I ain't talking about doing Rose no bad turn. I love Rose. She done carried me a long ways and I love and respect her for that.

BONO: I know you do. That's why I don't want to see you hurt her. But what you gonna do when she find out? What you got then? If you try and juggle both of them . . . sooner or later you gonna drop one of them. That's common sense.

TROY: Yeah, I hear what you saying, Bono. I been trying to figure a way to work it out.

BONO: Work it out right, Troy. I don't want to be getting all up between you and Rose's business . . . but work it so it come out right.

TROY: Ah hell, I get all up between you and Lucille's business. When you gonna get that woman that refrigerator she been wanting? Don't tell me you ain't got no money now. I know who your banker is. Mellon don't need that money bad as Lucille want that refrigerator. I'll tell you that.

BONO: Tell you what I'll do . . . when you finish building this fence for Rose . . . I'll buy Lucille that refrigerator.

TROY: You done stuck your foot in your mouth now!

Troy grabs up a board and begins to saw. Bono starts to walk out the yard.

Hey, nigger . . . where you going?

BONO: I'm going home. I know you don't expect me to help you now. I'm protecting my money. I wanna see you put that fence up by yourself. That's what I want to see. You'll be here another six months without me.

TROY: Nigger, you ain't right.

BONO: When it comes to my money . . . I'm right as fireworks on the Fourth of July.

TROY: All right, we gonna see now. You better get out your bankbook.

Bono exits, and Troy continues to work. Rose enters from the house.

ROSE: What they say down there? What's happening with Gabe?

TROY: I went down there and got him out. Cost me fifty dollars. Say he was disturbing the peace. Judge set up a hearing for him in three weeks. Say to show cause why he shouldn't be recommitted.

ROSE: What was he doing that cause them to arrest him?

TROY: Some kids was teasing him and he run them off home. Say he was howling and carrying on. Some folks seen him and called the police. That's all it was.

ROSE: Well, what's you say? What'd you tell the judge?

TROY: Told him I'd look after him. It didn't make no sense to recommit the man. He stuck out his big greasy palm and told me to give him fifty dollars and take him on home.

ROSE: Where's he at now? Where'd he go off to?

TROY: He's gone about his business. He don't need nobody to hold his hand.

ROSE: Well, I don't know. Seem like that would be the best place for him if they did put him into the hospital. I know what you're gonna say. But that's what I think would be best.

TROY: The man done had his life ruined fighting for what? And they wanna take and lock him up. Let him be free. He don't bother nobody.

ROSE: Well, everybody got their own way of looking at it I guess. Come on and get your lunch. I got a bowl of lima beans and some cornbread in the oven. Come and get something to eat. Ain't no sense you fretting over Gabe.

Rose turns to go into the house.

TROY: Rose . . . got something to tell you.

ROSE: Well, come on . . . wait till I get this food on the table.

TROY: Rose!

She stops and turns around.

I don't know how to say this. (*Pause.*) I can't explain it none. It just sort of grows on you till it gets out of hand. It starts out like a little bush . . . and the next thing you know it's a whole forest.

ROSE: Troy . . . what is you talking about?

TROY: I'm talking, woman, let me talk. I'm trying to find a way to tell you . . . I'm gonna be a daddy. I'm gonna be somebody's daddy.

ROSE: Troy . . . you're not telling me this? You're gonna be . . . what?

TROY: Rose . . . now . . . see . . .

ROSE: You telling me you gonna be somebody's daddy? You telling your *wife* this?

Gabriel enters from the street. He carries a rose in his hand.

GABRIEL: Hey, Troy! Hey, Rose!

ROSE: I have to wait eighteen years to hear something like this.

GABRIEL: Hey, Rose . . . I got a flower for you. (*He hands it to her.*) That's a rose. Same rose like you is.

ROSE: Thanks, Gabe.

GABRIEL: Troy, you ain't mad at me is you? Them bad mens come and put me away. You ain't mad at me is you?

TROY: Naw, Gabe, I ain't mad at you.

ROSE: Eighteen years and you wanna come with this.

GABRIEL (*takes a quarter out of his pocket*): See what I got? Got a brand new quarter.

TROY: Rose . . . it's just . . .

ROSE: Ain't nothing you can say, Troy. Ain't no way of explaining that.

GABRIEL: Fellow that give me this quarter had a whole mess of them. I'm gonna keep this quarter till it stop shining.

ROSE: Gabe, go on in the house there. I got some watermelon in the Frigidaire. Go on and get you a piece.

GABRIEL: Say, Rose . . . you know I was chasing hellhounds and them bad mens come and get me and take me away. Troy helped me. He come down there and told them they better let me go before he beat them up. Yeah, he did!

ROSE: You go on and get you a piece of watermelon, Gabe. Them bad mens is gone now.

GABRIEL: Okay, Rose . . . gonna get me some watermelon. The kind with the stripes on it.

Gabriel exits into the house.

ROSE: Why, Troy? Why? After all these years to come dragging this in to me now. It don't make no sense at your age. I could have expected this ten or fifteen years ago, but not now.

TROY: Age ain't got nothing to do with it, Rose.

ROSE: I done tried to be everything a wife should be. Everything a wife could be. Been married eighteen years and I got to live to see the day you tell me you been seeing another woman and done fathered a child by her. And you know I ain't never wanted no half nothing in my family. My whole family is half. Everybody got different fathers and mothers . . . my two sisters and my brother. Can't hardly tell who's who. Can't never sit down and talk about Papa and Mama. It's your papa and your mama and my papa and my mama . . .

TROY: Rose . . . stop it now.

ROSE: I ain't never wanted that for none of my children. And now you wanna drag your behind in here and tell me something like this.

TROY: You ought to know. It's time for you to know.

ROSE: Well, I don't want to know, goddamn it!

TROY: I can't just make it go away. It's done now. I can't wish the circumstance of the thing away.

ROSE: And you don't want to either. Maybe you want to wish me and my boy away. Maybe that's what you want? Well, you can't wish us away. I've got eighteen years of my life invested in you. You ought to have stayed upstairs in my bed where you belong.

TROY: Rose . . . now listen to me . . . we can get a handle on this thing. We can talk this out . . . come to an understanding.

ROSE: All of a sudden it's "we." Where was "we" at when you was down there rolling around with some godforsaken woman? "We" should have come to an understanding before you started making a damn fool of yourself. You're a day late and a dollar short when it comes to an understanding with me.

TROY: It's just . . . She gives me a different idea . . . a different understanding about myself. I can step out of this house and get away

from the pressures and problems . . . be a different man. I ain't got
to wonder how I'm gonna pay the bills or get the roof fixed. I can
just be a part of myself that I ain't never been.

ROSE: What I want to know . . . is do you plan to continue seeing her.
That's all you can say to me.

TROY: I can sit up in her house and laugh. Do you understand what
I'm saying. I can laugh out loud . . . and it feels good. It reaches all
the way down to the bottom of my shoes. (*Pause.*) Rose, I can't give
that up.

ROSE: Maybe you ought to go on and stay down there with her . . . if
she's a better woman than me.

TROY: It ain't about nobody being a better woman or nothing. Rose,
you ain't the blame. A man couldn't ask for no woman to be a better wife than you've been. I'm responsible for it. I done locked myself into a pattern trying to take care of you all that I forgot about
myself.

ROSE: What the hell was I there for? That was my job, not somebody
else's.

TROY: Rose, I done tried all my life to live decent . . . to live a clean
. . . hard . . . useful life. I tried to be a good husband to you. In
every way I knew how. Maybe I come into the world backwards, I
don't know. But . . . you born with two strikes on you before you
come to the plate. You got to guard it closely . . . always looking
for the curve ball on the inside corner. You can't afford to let none
get past you. You can't afford a call strike. If you going down . . .
you going down swinging. Everything lined up against you. What
you gonna do. I fooled them, Rose. I bunted. When I found you and
Cory and a halfway decent job . . . I was safe. Couldn't nothing
touch me. I wasn't gonna strike out no more. I wasn't going back to
the penitentiary. I wasn't gonna lay in the streets with a bottle of
wine. I was safe. I had me a family. A job. I wasn't gonna get that
last strike. I was on first looking for one of them boys to knock me
in. To get me home.

ROSE: You should have stayed in my bed, Troy.

TROY: Then when I saw that gal . . . she firmed up my backbone.
And I got to thinking that if I tried . . . I just might be able to steal
second. Do you understand after eighteen years I wanted to steal
second.

ROSE: You should have held me tight. You should have grabbed me and held on.

TROY: I stood on first base for eighteen years and I thought . . . well, goddamn it . . . go on for it!

ROSE: We're not talking about baseball! We're talking about you going off to lay in bed with another woman . . . and then bring it home to me. That's what we're talking about. We ain't talking about no baseball.

TROY: Rose, you're not listening to me. I'm trying the best I can to explain it to you. It's not easy for me to admit that I been standing in the same place for eighteen years.

ROSE: I been standing with you! I been right here with you, Troy. I got a life too. I gave eighteen years of my life to stand in the same spot with you. Don't you think I ever wanted other things? Don't you think I had dreams and hopes? What about my life? What about me. Don't you think it ever crossed my mind to want to know other men? That I wanted to lay up somewhere and forget about my responsibilities? That I wanted someone to make me laugh so I could feel good? You not the only one who's got wants and needs. But I held on to you, Troy. I took all my feelings, my wants and needs, my dreams . . . and I buried them inside you. I planted a seed and watched and prayed over it. I planted myself inside you and waited to bloom. And it didn't take me no eighteen years to find out the soil was hard and rocky and it wasn't never gonna bloom.

But I held on to you, Troy. I held you tighter. You was my husband. I owed you everything I had. Every part of me I could find to give you. And upstairs in that room . . . with the darkness falling in on me . . . I gave everything I had to try and erase the doubt that you wasn't the finest man in the world. And wherever you was going . . . I wanted to be there with you. Cause you was my husband. Cause that's the only way I was gonna survive as your wife. You always talking about what you give . . . and what you don't have to give. But you take too. You take . . . and don't even know nobody's giving!

Rose turns to exit into the house; Troy grabs her arm.

TROY: You say I take and don't give!

ROSE: Troy! You're hurting me!

TROY: You say I take and don't give!

ROSE: Troy . . . you're hurting my arm! Let go!

TROY: I done give you everything I got. Don't you tell that lie on me.

ROSE: Troy!

TROY: Don't you tell that lie on me!

Cory enters from the house.

CORY: Mama!

ROSE: Troy. You're hurting me.

TROY: Don't you tell me about no taking and giving.

Cory comes up behind Troy and grabs him. Troy, surprised, is thrown off balance just as Cory throws a glancing blow that catches him on the chest and knocks him down. Troy is stunned, as is Cory.

ROSE: Troy. Troy. No!

Troy gets to his feet and starts at Cory.

Troy . . . no. Please! Troy!

Rose pulls on Troy to hold him back. Troy stops himself.

TROY (*to Cory*): All right. That's strike two. You stay away from around me, boy. Don't you strike out. You living with a full count. Don't you strike out.

Troy exits out the yard as the lights go down.

Scene 2

It is six months later, early afternoon. Troy enters from the house and starts to exit the yard. Rose enters from the house.

ROSE: Troy, I want to talk to you.

TROY: All of a sudden, after all this time, you want to talk to me, huh? You ain't wanted to talk to me for months. You ain't wanted to talk to me last night. You ain't wanted no part of me then. What you wanna talk to me about now?

ROSE: Tomorrow's Friday.

TROY: I know what day tomorrow is. You think I don't know tomorrow's Friday? My whole life I ain't done nothing but look to see Friday coming and you got to tell me it's Friday.

ROSE: I want to know if you're coming home.

TROY: I always come home, Rose. You know that. There ain't never been a night I ain't come home.

ROSE: That ain't what I mean . . . and you know it. I want to know if you're coming straight home after work.

TROY: I figure I'd cash my check . . . hang out at Taylors' with the boys . . . maybe play a game of checkers . . .

ROSE: Troy, I can't live like this. I won't live like this. You livin' on borrowed time with me. It's been going on six months now you ain't been coming home.

TROY: I be here every night. Every night of the year. That's 365 days.

ROSE: I want you to come home tomorrow after work.

TROY: Rose . . . I don't mess up my pay. You know that now. I take my pay and I give it to you. I don't have no money but what you give me back. I just want to have a little time to myself . . . a little time to enjoy life.

ROSE: What about me? When's my time to enjoy life?

TROY: I don't know what to tell you, Rose. I'm doing the best I can.

ROSE: You ain't been home from work but time enough to change your clothes and run out . . . and you wanna call that the best you can do?

TROY: I'm going over to the hospital to see Alberta. She went into the hospital this afternoon. Look like she might have the baby early. I won't be gone long.

ROSE: Well, you ought to know. They went over to Miss Pearl's and got Gabe today. She said you told them to go ahead and lock him up.

TROY: I ain't said no such thing. Whoever told you that is telling a lie. Pearl ain't doing nothing but telling a big fat lie.

ROSE: She ain't had to tell me. I read it on the papers.

TROY: I ain't told them nothing of the kind.

ROSE: I saw it right there on the papers.

TROY: What it say, huh?

ROSE: It said you told them to take him.

TROY: Then they screwed that up, just the way they screw up everything. I ain't worried about what they got on the paper.

ROSE: Say the government send part of his check to the hospital and the other part to you.

TROY: I ain't got nothing to do with that if that's the way it works. I ain't made up the rules about how it work.

ROSE: You did Gabe just like you did Cory. You wouldn't sign the paper for Cory . . . but you signed for Gabe. You signed that paper.

The telephone is heard ringing inside the house.

TROY: I told you I ain't signed nothing, woman! The only thing I signed was the release form. Hell, I can't read, I don't know what they had on that paper! I ain't signed nothing about sending Gabe away.

ROSE: I said send him to the hospital . . . you said let him be free . . . now you done went down there and signed him to the hospital for half his money. You went back on yourself, Troy. You gonna have to answer for that.

TROY: See now . . . you been over there talking to Miss Pearl. She done got mad cause she ain't getting Gabe's rent money. That's all it is. She's liable to say anything.

ROSE: Troy, I seen where you signed the paper.

TROY: You ain't seen nothing I signed. What she doing got papers on my brother anyway? Miss Pearl telling a big fat lie. And I'm gonna tell her about it too! You ain't seen nothing I signed. Say . . . you ain't seen nothing I signed.

Rose exits into the house to answer the telephone. Presently she returns.

ROSE: Troy . . . that was the hospital. Alberta had the baby.

TROY: What she have? What is it?

ROSE: It's a girl.

TROY: I better get on down to the hospital to see her.

ROSE: Troy . . .

TROY: Rose . . . I got to go see her now. That's only right . . . what's the matter . . . the baby's all right, ain't it?

ROSE: Alberta died having the baby.

TROY: Died . . . you say she's dead? Alberta's dead?

ROSE: They said they done all they could. They couldn't do nothing for her.

TROY: The baby? How's the baby?

ROSE: They say it's healthy. I wonder who's gonna bury her.

TROY: She had family, Rose. She wasn't living in the world by herself.

ROSE: I know she wasn't living in the world by herself.

TROY: Next thing you gonna want to know if she had any insurance.

ROSE: Troy, you ain't got to talk like that.

TROY: That's the first thing that jumped out your mouth. "Who's gonna bury her?" Like I'm fixing to take on that task for myself.

ROSE: I am your wife. Don't push me away.

TROY: I ain't pushing nobody away. Just give me some space. That's all. Just give me some room to breathe.

Rose exits into the house. Troy walks about the yard.

TROY (*with a quiet rage that threatens to consume him*): All right . . . Mr. Death. See now . . . I'm gonna tell you what I'm gonna do. I'm gonna take and build me a fence around this yard. See? I'm gonna build me a fence around what belongs to me. And then I want you to stay on the other side. See? You stay over there until you're ready for me. Then you come on. Bring your army. Bring your sickle. Bring your wrestling clothes. I ain't gonna fall down on my vigilance this time. You ain't gonna sneak up on me no more. When you ready for me . . . when the top of your list say Troy Maxson . . . that's when you come around here. You come up and knock on the front door. Ain't nobody else got nothing to do with this. This is between you and me. Man to man. You stay on the other side of that fence until you ready for me. Then you come up and knock on the front door. Anytime you want. I'll be ready for you.

The lights go down to black.

Scene 3

The lights come up on the porch. It is late evening three days later. Rose sits listening to the ball game waiting for Troy. The final out of the game is made and Rose switches off the radio. Troy enters the yard carrying an infant wrapped in blankets. He stands back from the house and calls.

Rose enters and stands on the porch. There is a long, awkward silence, the weight of which grows heavier with each passing second.

TROY: Rose . . . I'm standing here with my daughter in my arms. She ain't but a wee bittie little old thing. She don't know nothing about grownups' business. She innocent . . . and she ain't got no mama.

ROSE: What you telling me for, Troy?

She turns and exits into the house.

TROY: Well . . . I guess we'll just sit out here on the porch.

He sits down on the porch. There is an awkward indelicateness about the way he handles the baby. His largeness engulfs and seems to swallow it. He speaks loud enough for Rose to hear.

A man's got to do what's right for him. I ain't sorry for nothing I done. It felt right in my heart. (*To the baby.*) What you smiling at? Your daddy's a big man. Got these great big old hands. But sometimes he's scared. And right now your daddy's scared cause we sitting out here and ain't got no home. Oh, I been homeless before. I ain't had no little baby with me. But I been homeless. You just be out on the road by your lonesome and you see one of them trains coming and you just kinda go like this . . .

He sings as a lullaby.

Please, Mr. Engineer let a man ride the line
Please, Mr. Engineer let a man ride the line
I ain't got no ticket please let me ride the blinds.

Rose enters from the house. Troy, hearing her steps behind him, stands and faces her.

She's my daughter, Rose. My own flesh and blood. I can't deny her no more than I can deny them boys. (*Pause.*) You and them boys is my family. You and them and this child is all I got in the world. So I guess what I'm saying is . . . I'd appreciate it if you'd help me take care of her.

ROSE: Okay, Troy . . . you're right. I'll take care of your baby for you . . . cause . . . like you say . . . she's innocent . . . and you can't visit the sins of the father upon the child. A motherless child has got a hard time. (*She takes the baby from him.*) From right now . . . this child got a mother. But you a womanless man.

Rose turns and exits into the house with the baby. Lights go down to black.

SCENE 4

It is two months later. Lyons enters the street. He knocks on the door and calls.

LYONS: Hey, Rose! (*Pause.*) Rose!

ROSE (*from inside the house*): Stop that yelling. You gonna wake up Raynell. I just got her to sleep.

LYONS: I just stopped by to pay Papa this twenty dollars I owe him. Where's Papa at?

ROSE: He should be here in a minute. I'm getting ready to go down to the church. Sit down and wait on him.

LYONS: I got to go pick up Bonnie over her mother's house.

ROSE: Well, sit it down there on the table. He'll get it.

LYONS (*enters the house and sets the money on the table*): Tell Papa I said thanks. I'll see you again.

ROSE: All right, Lyons. We'll see you.

Lyons starts to exit as Cory enters.

CORY: Hey, Lyons.

LYONS: What's happening, Cory? Say man, I'm sorry I missed your graduation. You know I had a gig and couldn't get away. Otherwise, I would have been there, man. So what you doing?

CORY: I'm trying to find a job.

LYONS: Yeah I know how that go, man. It's rough out here. Jobs are scarce.

CORY: Yeah, I know.

LYONS: Look here, I got to run. Talk to Papa . . . he know some people. He'll be able to help get you a job. Talk to him . . . see what he say.

CORY: Yeah . . . all right, Lyons.

LYONS: You take care. I'll talk to you soon. We'll find some time to talk.

Lyons exits the yard. Cory wanders over to the tree, picks up the bat, and assumes a batting stance. He studies an imaginary pitcher and swings. Dissatisfied with the result, he tries again. Troy enters. They eye each other for a beat. Cory puts the bat down and exits the yard. Troy starts into the house as Rose exits with Raynell. She is carrying a cake.

TROY: I'm coming in and everybody's going out.

ROSE: I'm taking this cake down to the church for the bake sale. Lyons was by to see you. He stopped by to pay you your twenty dollars. It's laying in there on the table.

TROY (*going into his pocket*): Well . . . here go this money.

ROSE: Put it in there on the table, Troy. I'll get it.

TROY: What time you coming back?

ROSE: Ain't no use in you studying me. It don't matter what time I come back.

TROY: I just asked you a question, woman. What's the matter . . . can't I ask you a question?

ROSE: Troy, I don't want to go into it. Your dinner's in there on the stove. All you got to do is heat it up. And don't you be eating the rest of them cakes in there. I'm coming back for them. We having a bake sale at the church tomorrow.

Rose exits the yard. Troy sits down on the steps, takes a pint bottle from his pocket, opens it, and drinks. He begins to sing.

TROY:

Hear it ring! Hear it ring!
Had an old dog his name was Blue
You know Blue was mighty true
You know Blue as a good old dog
Blue trees a possum in a hollow log
You know from that he was a good old dog.

Bono enters the yard.

BONO: Hey, Troy.

TROY: Hey, what's happening, Bono?

BONO: I just thought I'd stop by to see you.

TROY: What you stop by and see me for? You ain't stopped by in a month of Sundays. Hell, I must owe you money or something.

BONO: Since you got your promotion I can't keep up with you. Used to see you every day. Now I don't even know what route you working.

TROY: They keep switching me around. Got me out in Greentree now . . . hauling white folks' garbage.

BONO: Greentree, huh? You lucky, at least you ain't got to be lifting them barrels. Damn if they ain't getting heavier. I'm gonna put in my two years and call it quits.

TROY: I'm thinking about retiring myself.

BONO: You got it easy. You can drive for another five years.

TROY: It ain't the same, Bono. It ain't like working the back of the truck. Ain't got nobody to talk to . . . feel like you working by yourself. Naw, I'm thinking about retiring. How's Lucille?

BONO: She all right. Her arthritis get to acting up on her sometime. Saw Rose on my way in. She going down to the church, huh?

TROY: Yeah, she took up going down there. All them preachers looking for somebody to fatten their pockets. (*Pause.*) Got some gin here.

BONO: Naw, thanks. I just stopped by to say hello.

TROY: Hell, nigger . . . you can take a drink. I ain't never known you to say no to a drink. You ain't got to work tomorrow.

BONO: I just stopped by. I'm fixing to go over to Skinner's. We got us a domino game going over his house every Friday.

TROY: Nigger, you can't play no dominoes. I used to whup you four games out of five.

BONO: Well, that learned me. I'm getting better.

TROY: Yeah? Well, that's all right.

BONO: Look here . . . I got to be getting on. Stop by sometime, huh?

TROY: Yeah, I'll do that, Bono. Lucille told Rose you bought her a new refrigerator.

BONO: Yeah, Rose told Lucille you had finally built your fence . . . so I figured we'd call it even.

TROY: I knew you would.

BONO: Yeah . . . okay. I'll be talking to you.

TROY: Yeah, take care, Bono. Good to see you. I'm gonna stop over.

BONO: Yeah. Okay, Troy.

Bono exits. Troy drinks from the bottle.

TROY:
Old Blue died and I dig his grave
Let him down with a golden chain
Every night when I hear old Blue bark
I know Blue treed a possum in Noah's Ark.
Hear it ring! Hear it ring!

Cory enters the yard. They eye each other for a beat. Troy is sitting in the middle of the steps. Cory walks over.

CORY: I got to get by.

TROY: Say what? What's you say?

CORY: You in my way. I got to get by.

TROY: You got to get by where? This is my house. Bought and paid for. In full. Took me fifteen years. And if you wanna go in my house and I'm sitting on the steps . . . you say excuse me. Like your mama taught you.

CORY: Come on, Pop . . . I got to get by.

Cory starts to maneuver his way past Troy. Troy grabs his leg and shoves him back.

TROY: You just gonna walk over top of me?

CORY: I live here too!

TROY (*advancing toward him*): You just gonna walk over top of me in my own house?

CORY: I ain't scared of you.

TROY: I ain't asked if you was scared of me. I asked you if you was fixing to walk over top of me in my own house? That's the question. You ain't gonna say excuse me? You just gonna walk over top of me?

CORY: If you wanna put it like that.

TROY: How else am I gonna put it?

CORY: I was walking by you to go into the house cause you sitting on the steps drunk, singing to yourself. You can put it like that.

TROY: Without saying excuse me???

Cory doesn't respond.

I asked you a question. Without saying excuse me???

CORY: I ain't got to say excuse me to you. You don't count around here no more.

TROY: Oh, I see . . . I don't count around here no more. You ain't got to say excuse me to your daddy. All of a sudden you done got so grown that your daddy don't count around here no more . . . Around here in his own house and yard that he done paid for with the sweat of his brow. You done got so grown to where you gonna take over. You gonna take over my house. Is that right? You gonna wear my pants. You gonna go in there and stretch out on my bed. You ain't got to say excuse me cause I don't count around here no more. Is that right?

CORY: That's right. You always talking this dumb stuff. Now, why don't you just get out my way?

TROY: I guess you got someplace to sleep and something to put in your belly. You got that, huh? You got that? That's what you need. You got that, huh?

CORY: You don't know what I got. You ain't got to worry about what I got.

TROY: You right! You one hundred percent right! I done spent the last seventeen years worrying about what you got. Now it's your turn, see? I'll tell you what to do. You grown . . . we done established that. You a man. Now, let's see you act like one. Turn your behind around and walk out this yard. And when you get out there in the alley . . . you can forget about this house. See? Cause this is my house. You go on and be a man and get your own house. You can forget about this. Cause this is mine. You go on and get yours cause I'm through with doing for you.

CORY: You talking about what you did for me . . . what'd you ever give me?

TROY: Them feet and bones! That pumping heart, nigger! I give you more than anybody else is ever gonna give you.

CORY: You ain't never gave me nothing! You ain't never done nothing but hold me back. Afraid I was gonna be better than you. All you ever did was try and make me scared of you. I used to tremble every time you called my name. Every time I heard your footsteps in the house. Wondering all the time . . . what's Papa gonna say if I do this?. . . What's he gonna say if I do that?. . . What's Papa gonna say if I turn on the radio? And Mama, too . . . she tries . . . but she's scared of you.

TROY: You leave your mama out of this. She ain't got nothing to do with this.

CORY: I don't know how she stand you . . . after what you did to her.

TROY: I told you to leave your mama out of this!

He advances toward Cory.

CORY: What you gonna do . . . give me a whupping? You can't whup me no more. You're too old. You just an old man.

TROY (*shoves him on his shoulder*): Nigger! That's what you are. You just another nigger on the street to me!

CORY: You crazy! You know that?

TROY: Go on now! You got the devil in you. Get on away from me!

CORY: You just a crazy old man . . . talking about I got the devil in me.

TROY: Yeah, I'm crazy! If you don't get on the other side of that yard . . . I'm gonna show you how crazy I am! Go on . . . get the hell out of my yard.

CORY: It ain't your yard. You took Uncle Gabe's money he got from the army to buy this house and then you put him out.

TROY (*advances on Cory*): Get your black ass out of my yard!

Troy's advance backs Cory up against the tree. Cory grabs up the bat.

CORY: I ain't going nowhere! Come on . . . put me out! I ain't scared of you.

TROY: That's my bat!

CORY: Come on!

TROY: Put my bat down!

CORY: Come on, put me out.

Cory swings at Troy, who backs across the yard.

What's the matter? You so bad . . . put me out!

Troy advances toward Cory.

CORY (*backing up*): Come on! Come on!

TROY: You're gonna have to use it! You wanna draw that bat back on me . . . you're gonna have to use it.

CORY: Come on!. . . Come on!

Cory swings the bat at Troy a second time. He misses. Troy continues to advance toward him.

TROY: You're gonna have to kill me! You wanna draw that bat back on me. You're gonna have to kill me.

Cory, backed up against the tree, can go no farther. Troy taunts him. He sticks out his head and offers him a target.

Come on! Come on!

Cory is unable to swing the bat. Troy grabs it.

TROY: Then I'll show you.

Cory and Troy struggle over the bat. The struggle is fierce and fully engaged. Troy ultimately is the stronger and takes the bat from Cory and stands over him ready to swing. He stops himself.

Go on and get away from around my house.

Cory, stung by his defeat, picks himself up, walks slowly out of the yard and up the alley.

CORY: Tell Mama I'll be back for my things.

TROY: They'll be on the other side of that fence.

Cory exits.

TROY: I can't taste nothing. Helluljah! I can't taste nothing no more. (*Troy assumes a batting posture and begins to taunt Death, the fastball on the outside corner.*) Come on! It's between you and me now! Come on! Anytime you want! Come on! I be ready for you . . . but I ain't gonna be easy.

The lights go down on the scene.

Scene 5

The time is 1965. The lights come up in the yard. It is the morning of Troy's funeral. A funeral plaque with a light hangs beside the door. There is a small garden plot off to the side. There is noise and activity in the house as Rose, Lyons, and Bono have gathered. The door opens and Raynell, seven years old, enters dressed in a flannel nightgown. She crosses to the garden and pokes around with a stick. Rose calls from the house.

ROSE: Raynell!

RAYNELL: Mam?

ROSE: What you doing out there?

RAYNELL: Nothing.

Rose comes to the door.

ROSE: Girl, get in here and get dressed. What you doing?

RAYNELL: Seeing if my garden growed.

ROSE: I told you it ain't gonna grow overnight. You got to wait.

RAYNELL: It don't look like it never gonna grow. Dag!

ROSE: I told you a watched pot never boils. Get in here and get dressed.

RAYNELL: This ain't even no pot, Mama.

ROSE: You just have to give it a chance. It'll grow. Now you come on and do what I told you. We got to be getting ready. This ain't no morning to be playing around. You hear me?

RAYNELL: Yes, mam.

Rose exits into the house. Raynell continues to poke at her garden with a stick. Cory enters. He is dressed in a Marine corporal's uniform, and carries a duffelbag. His posture is that of a military man, and his speech has a clipped sternness.

CORY (*to Raynell*): Hi. (*Pause.*) I bet your name is Raynell.

RAYNELL: Uh huh.

CORY: Is your mama home?

Raynell runs up on the porch and calls through the screen door.

RAYNELL: Mama . . . there's some man out here. Mama?

Rose comes to the door.

ROSE: Cory? Lord have mercy! Look here, you all!

Rose and Cory embrace in a tearful reunion as Bono and Lyons enter from the house dressed in funeral clothes.

BONO: Aw, looka here . . .

ROSE: Done got all grown up!

CORY: Don't cry, Mama. What you crying about?

ROSE: I'm just so glad you made it.

CORY: Hey Lyons. How you doing, Mr. Bono.

Lyons goes to embrace Cory.

LYONS: Look at you, man. Look at you. Don't he look good, Rose. Got them Corporal stripes.

ROSE: What took you so long?

CORY: You know how the Marines are, Mama. They got to get all their paperwork straight before they let you do anything.

ROSE: Well, I'm sure glad you made it. They let Lyons come. Your Uncle Gabe's still in the hospital. They don't know if they gonna let him out or not. I just talked to them a little while ago.

LYONS: A Corporal in the United States Marines.

BONO: Your daddy knew you had it in you. He used to tell me all the time.

LYONS: Don't he look good, Mr. Bono?

BONO: Yeah, he remind me of Troy when I first met him. (*Pause.*) Say, Rose, Lucille's down at the church with the choir. I'm gonna go down and get the pallbearers lined up. I'll be back to get you all.

ROSE: Thanks, Jim.

CORY: See you, Mr. Bono.

LYONS (*with his arm around Raynell*): Cory . . . look at Raynell. Ain't she precious? She gonna break a whole lot of hearts.

ROSE: Raynell, come and say hello to your brother. This is your brother, Cory. You remember Cory.

RAYNELL: No, Mam.

CORY: She don't remember me, Mama.

ROSE: Well, we talk about you. She heard us talk about you. (*To Raynell.*) This is your brother, Cory. Come on and say hello.

RAYNELL: Hi.

CORY: Hi. So you're Raynell. Mama told me a lot about you.

ROSE: You all come on into the house and let me fix you some breakfast. Keep up your strength.

CORY: I ain't hungry, Mama.

LYONS: You can fix me something, Rose. I'll be in there in a minute.

ROSE: Cory, you sure you don't want nothing? I know they ain't feeding you right.

CORY: No, Mama . . . thanks. I don't feel like eating. I'll get something later.

ROSE: Raynell . . . get on upstairs and get that dress on like I told you.

Rose and Raynell exit into the house.

LYONS: So . . . I hear you thinking about getting married.

CORY: Yeah, I done found the right one, Lyons. It's about time.

LYONS: Me and Bonnie been split up about four years now. About the time Papa retired. I guess she just got tired of all them changes I was putting her through. (*Pause.*) I always knew you was gonna make something out yourself. Your head was always in the right direction. So . . . you gonna stay in . . . make it a career . . . put in your twenty years?

CORY: I don't know. I got six already, I think that's enough.

LYONS: Stick with Uncle Sam and retire early. Ain't nothing out here. I guess Rose told you what happened with me. They got me down the workhouse. I thought I was being slick cashing other people's checks.

CORY: How much time you doing?

LYONS: They give me three years. I got that beat now. I ain't got but nine more months. It ain't so bad. You learn to deal with it like anything else. You got to take the crookeds with the straights. That's what Papa used to say. He used to say that when he struck out. I seen him strike out three times in a row . . . and the next time up he hit the ball over the grandstand. Right out there in Homestead Field. He wasn't satisfied hitting in the seats . . . he want to hit it over everything! After the game he had two hundred people standing around waiting to shake his hand. You got to take the crookeds with the straights. Yeah, Papa was something else.

CORY: You still playing?

LYONS: Cory . . . you know I'm gonna do that. There's some fellows down there we got us a band . . . we gonna try and stay together when we get out . . . but yeah, I'm still playing. It still helps me to get out of bed in the morning. As long as it do that I'm gonna be right there playing and trying to make some sense out of it.

ROSE (*calling*): Lyons, I got these eggs in the pan.

LYONS: Let me go on and get these eggs, man. Get ready to go bury Papa. (*Pause.*) How you doing? You doing all right?

Cory nods. Lyons touches him on the shoulder and they share a moment of silent grief. Lyons exits into the house. Cory wanders about the yard. Raynell enters.

RAYNELL: Hi.

CORY: Hi.

RAYNELL: Did you used to sleep in my room?

CORY: Yeah . . . that used to be my room.

RAYNELL: That's what Papa call it. "Cory's room." It got your football in the closet.

Rose comes to the door.

ROSE: Raynell, get in there and get them good shoes on.

RAYNELL: Mama, can't I wear these? Them other one hurt my feet.

ROSE: Well, they just gonna have to hurt your feet for a while. You ain't said they hurt your feet when you went down to the store and got them.

RAYNELL: They didn't hurt then. My feet done got bigger.

ROSE: Don't you give me no backtalk now. You get in there and get them shoes on.

Raynell exits into the house.

Ain't too much changed. He still got that piece of rag tied to that tree. He was out here swinging that bat. I was just ready to go back in the house. He swung that bat and then he just fell over. Seem like he swung it and stood there with this grin on his face . . . and then he just fell over. They carried him on down to the hospital, but I knew there wasn't no need . . . why don't you come on in the house?

CORY: Mama . . . I got something to tell you. I don't know how to tell you this . . . but I've got to tell you . . . I'm not going to Papa's funeral.

ROSE: Boy, hush your mouth. That's your daddy you talking about. I don't want hear that kind of talk this morning. I done raised you to come to this? You standing there all healthy and grown talking about you ain't going to your daddy's funeral?

CORY: Mama . . . listen . . .

ROSE: I don't want to hear it, Cory. You just get that thought out of your head.

CORY: I can't drag Papa with me everywhere I go. I've got to say no to him. One time in my life I've got to say no.

ROSE: Don't nobody have to listen to nothing like that. I know you and your daddy ain't seen eye to eye, but I ain't got to listen to that kind of talk this morning. Whatever was between you and your daddy . . . the time has come to put it aside. Just take it and set it over there on the shelf and forget about it. Disrespecting your daddy ain't gonna make you a man, Cory. You got to find a way to come to that on your own. Not going to your daddy's funeral ain't gonna make you a man.

CORY: The whole time I was growing up . . . living in his house . . . Papa was like a shadow that followed you everywhere. It weighed on you and sunk into your flesh. It would wrap around you and lay there until you couldn't tell which one was you anymore. That shadow digging in your flesh. Trying to crawl in. Trying to live through you. Everywhere I looked, Troy Maxson was staring back at me . . . hiding under the bed . . . in the closet. I'm just saying I've got to find a way to get rid of that shadow, Mama.

ROSE: You just like him. You got him in you good.

CORY: Don't tell me that, Mama.

ROSE: You Troy Maxson all over again.

CORY: I don't want to be Troy Maxson. I want to be me.

ROSE: You can't be nobody but who you are, Cory. That shadow wasn't nothing but you growing into yourself. You either got to grow into it or cut it down to fit you. But that's all you got to make life with. That's all you got to measure yourself against that world out there. Your daddy wanted you to be everything he wasn't . . . and at the same time he tried to make you into everything he was. I don't know if he was right or wrong . . . but I do know he meant to do more good than he meant to do harm. He wasn't always right. Sometimes when he touched he bruised. And sometimes when he took me in his arms he cut.

When I first met your daddy I thought . . . Here is a man I can lay down with and make a baby. That's the first thing I thought when I seen him. I was thirty years old and had done seen my share of men. But when he walked up to me and said, "I can dance a waltz that'll make you dizzy," I thought, Rose Lee, here is a man that you can open yourself up to and be filled to bursting. Here is a man that can fill all them empty spaces you been tipping around the edges of. One of them empty spaces was being somebody's mother.

I married your daddy and settled down to cooking his supper and keeping clean sheets on the bed. When your daddy walked through the house he was so big he filled it up. That was my first mistake. Not to make him leave some room for me. For my part in the matter. But at that time I wanted that. I wanted a house that I could sing in. And that's what your daddy gave me. I didn't know to keep up his strength I had to give up little pieces of mine. I did that. I took on his life as mine and mixed up the pieces so that you couldn't hardly tell which was which anymore. It was my choice. It was my life and I didn't have to live it like that. But that's what life offered me in the way of being a woman and I took it. I grabbed hold of it with both hands.

By the time Raynell came into the house, me and your daddy had done lost touch with one another. I didn't want to make my blessing off of nobody's misfortune . . . but I took on to Raynell like she was all them babies I had wanted and never had.

The phone rings.

Like I'd been blessed to relive a part of my life. And if the Lord see fit to keep up my strength . . . I'm gonna do her just like your daddy did you . . . I'm gonna give her the best of what's in me.

RAYNELL (*entering, still with her old shoes*): Mama . . . Reverend Tollivier on the phone.

Rose exits into the house.

RAYNELL: Hi.

CORY: Hi.

RAYNELL: You in the Army or the Marines?

CORY: Marines.

RAYNELL: Papa said it was the Army. Did you know Blue?

CORY: Blue? Who's Blue?

RAYNELL: Papa's dog what he sing about all the time.

CORY (*singing*):

Hear it ring! Hear it ring!
I had a dog his name was Blue
You know Blue was mighty true
You know Blue was a good old dog
Blue treed a possum in a hollow log
You know from that he was a good old dog.
Hear it ring! Hear it ring!

Raynell joins in singing.

CORY AND RAYNELL:

Blue treed a possum out on a limb
Blue looked at me and I looked at him
Grabbed that possum and put him in a sack
Blue stayed there till I came back
Old Blue's feets was big and round
Never allowed a possum to touch the ground.

Old Blue died and I dug his grave
I dug his grave with a silver spade
Let him down with a golden chain
And every night I call his name
Go on Blue, you good dog you
Go on Blue, you good dog you.

RAYNELL:

Blue laid down and died like a man
Blue laid down and died . . .

BOTH:

Blue laid down and died like a man
Now he's treeing possums in the Promised Land
I'm gonna tell you this to let you know
Blue's gone where the good dogs go

When I hear old Blue bark
When I hear old Blue bark
Blue treed a possum in Noah's Ark
Blue treed a possum in Noah's Ark.

Rose comes to the screen door.

ROSE: Cory, we gonna be ready to go in a minute.

CORY (*to Raynell*): You go on in the house and change them shoes like Mama told you so we can go to Papa's funeral.

RAYNELL: Okay, I'll be back.

Raynell exits into the house. Cory gets up and crosses over to the tree. Rose stands in the screen door watching him. Gabriel enters from the alley.

GABRIEL (*calling*): Hey, Rose!

ROSE: Gabe?

GABRIEL: I'm here, Rose. Hey Rose, I'm here!

Rose enters from the house.

ROSE: Lord . . . Look here, Lyons!

LYONS: See, I told you, Rose . . . I told you they'd let him come.

CORY: How you doing, Uncle Gabe?

LYONS: How you doing, Uncle Gabe?

GABRIEL: Hey, Rose. It's time. It's time to tell St. Peter to open the gates. Troy, you ready? You ready, Troy. I'm gonna tell St. Peter to open the gates. You get ready now.

Gabriel, with great fanfare, braces himself to blow. The trumpet is without a mouthpiece. He puts the end of it into his mouth and blows with great force, like a man who has been waiting some twenty-odd years for this single moment. No sound comes out of the trumpet. He braces himself and blows again with the same result. A third time he blows. There is a weight of impossible description that falls away and leaves him bare and exposed to a frightful realization. It is a trauma that a sane and normal mind would be unable to withstand. He begins to dance. A slow, strange dance, eerie and life-giving. A dance of atavistic signature and ritual. Lyons attempts to embrace him. Gabriel pushes Lyons away. He begins to howl in what is an attempt at song, or perhaps a song turning back into itself in an attempt at speech. He finishes his dance and the gates of heaven stand open as wide as God's closet.

That's the way that go!

BLACKOUT

—1987

David Ives (b. 1950) grew up on Chicago's South Side, the son of working-class parents, writing his first play at the age of nine: "But then I realized you had to have a copy of the script for each person in the play, so that was the end of it." Impressed by theatrical productions he saw in his teens, Ives entered Northwestern University and after graduation attended Yale School of Drama. After several attempts to become a "serious writer" he decided to "aspire to silliness on a daily basis" and began creating the short comic plays on which his reputation rests. An evening of six one-act comedies, All in the Timing, *had a successful off-Broadway production in 1994, running over two years. In 1996, it was the most performed contemporary play in the nation, and* Sure Thing *(1988), its signature piece, remains popular, especially with student drama groups. A second collection of one acts,* Mere Mortals, *had a successful run at Primary Stages in 1997, and a third collection,* Lives of Saints, *was produced in 1999. Two of his collections,* All in the Timing *(1995) and* Time Flies *(2001), have been published. Ives's comedic skills range from a hilarious parody of David Mamet's plays (presented at an event honoring Mamet) to his witty revision of a legendary character in the full-length* Don Juan in Chicago. *His short plays, in many cases, hinge on brilliant theatrical conceits; in* Time Flies, *a boy mayfly and girl mayfly must meet, court, and consummate their relationship before dying as their one day of life ends.* Sure Thing, *a piece that plays witty tricks with time, resembles a scene in the Bill Murray film* Groundhog Day, *the script of which was written some years after Ives's play. In an article titled "Why I Shouldn't Write Plays," Ives notes, among other reasons, "All reviews should carry a Surgeon General's warning. The good ones turn your head, the bad ones break your heart."*

David Ives

Sure Thing

CHARACTERS

Betty
Bill

Scene: *A café.*

Betty, a woman in her late twenties, is reading at a café table. An empty chair is opposite her. Bill, same age, enters.

BILL: Excuse me. Is this chair taken?
BETTY: Excuse me?

BILL: Is this taken?

BETTY: Yes it is.

BILL: Oh. Sorry.

BETTY: Sure thing.

(*A bell rings softly.*)

BILL: Excuse me. Is this chair taken?

BETTY: Excuse me?

BILL: Is this taken?

BETTY: No, but I'm expecting somebody in a minute.

BILL: Oh. Thanks anyway.

BETTY: Sure thing.

(*A bell rings softly.*)

BILL: Excuse me. Is this chair taken?

BETTY: No, but I'm expecting somebody very shortly.

BILL: Would you mind if I sit here till he or she or it comes?

BETTY (*glances at her watch*): They do seem to be pretty late. . . .

BILL: You never know who you might be turning down.

BETTY: Sorry. Nice try, though.

BILL: Sure thing.

(*Bell.*)

Is this seat taken?

BETTY: No it's not.

BILL: Would you mind if I sit here?

BETTY: Yes I would.

BILL: Oh.

(*Bell.*)

Is this chair taken?

BETTY: No it's not.

BILL: Would you mind if I sit here?

BETTY: No. Go ahead.

BILL: Thanks. (*He sits. She continues reading.*) Everyplace else seems to be taken.

BETTY: Mm-hm.

BILL: Great place.

BETTY: Mm-hm.

BILL: What's the book?

BETTY: I just wanted to read in quiet, if you don't mind.

BILL: No. Sure thing.

(*Bell.*)

BILL: Everyplace else seems to be taken.

BETTY: Mm-hm.

BILL: Great place for reading.

BETTY: Yes, I like it.

BILL: What's the book?

BETTY: *The Sound and the Fury.*

BILL: Oh. Hemingway.

(*Bell.*)

What's the book?

BETTY: *The Sound and the Fury.*

BILL: Oh. Faulkner.

BETTY: Have you read it?

BILL: Not . . . actually. I've sure read *about* it, though. It's supposed to be great.

BETTY: It is great.

BILL: I hear it's great. (*Small pause.*) Waiter?

(*Bell.*)

What's the book?

BETTY: *The Sound and the Fury.*

BILL: Oh. Faulkner.

BETTY: Have you read it?

BILL: I'm a Mets fan, myself.

(*Bell.*)

BETTY: Have you read it?

BILL: Yeah, I read it in college.

BETTY: Where was college?

BILL: I went to Oral Roberts University.

(*Bell.*)

BETTY: Where was college?
BILL: I was lying. I never really went to college. I just like to party.

(*Bell.*)

BETTY: Where was college?
BILL: Harvard.
BETTY: Do you like Faulkner?
BILL: I love Faulkner. I spent a whole winter reading him once.
BETTY: I've just started.
BILL: I was so excited after ten pages that I went out and bought everything else he wrote. One of the greatest reading experiences of my life. I mean, all that incredible psychological understanding. Page after page of gorgeous prose. His profound grasp of the mystery of time and human existence. The smells of the earth . . . What do you think?
BETTY: I think it's pretty boring.

(*Bell.*)

BILL: What's the book?
BETTY: *The Sound and the Fury.*
BILL: Oh! Faulkner!
BETTY: Do you like Faulkner?
BILL: I love Faulkner.
BETTY: He's incredible.
BILL: I spent a whole winter reading him once.
BETTY: I was so excited after ten pages that I went out and bought everything else he wrote.
BILL: All that incredible psychological understanding.
BETTY: And the prose is so gorgeous.
BILL: And the way he's grasped the mystery of time—
BETTY: —and human existence. I can't believe I've waited this long to read him.
BILL: You never know. You might not have liked him before.
BETTY: That's true.
BILL: You might not have been ready for him. You have to hit these things at the right moment or it's no good.
BETTY: That's happened to me.
BILL: It's all in the timing. (*Small pause.*) My name's Bill, by the way.

BETTY: I'm Betty.

BILL: Hi.

BETTY: Hi. (*Small pause.*)

BILL: Yes I thought reading Faulkner was . . . a great experience.

BETTY: Yes. (*Small pause.*)

BILL: *The Sound and the Fury* . . . (*Another small pause.*)

BETTY: Well. Onwards and upwards. (*She goes back to her book.*)

BILL: Waiter—?

(*Bell.*)

You have to hit these things at the right moment or it's no good.

BETTY: That's happened to me.

BILL: It's all in the timing. My name's Bill, by the way.

BETTY: I'm Betty.

BILL: Hi.

BETTY: Hi.

BILL: Do you come in here a lot?

BETTY: Actually I'm just in town for two days from Pakistan.

BILL: Oh. Pakistan.

(*Bell.*)

My name's Bill, by the way.

BETTY: I'm Betty.

BILL: Hi.

BETTY: Hi.

BILL: Do you come in here a lot?

BETTY: Every once in a while. Do you?

BILL: Not so much anymore. Not as much as I used to. Before my nervous breakdown.

(*Bell.*)

Do you come in here a lot?

BETTY: Why are you asking?

BILL: Just interested.

BETTY: Are you really interested, or do you just want to pick me up?

BILL: No, I'm really interested.

BETTY: Why would you be interested in whether I come in here a lot?

BILL: I'm just . . . getting acquainted.

BETTY: Maybe you're only interested for the sake of making small talk long enough to ask me back to your place to listen to some music, or because you've just rented this great tape for your VCR, or because you've got some terrific unknown Django Reinhardt record, only all you really want to do is fuck—which you won't do very well—after which you'll go into the bathroom and pee very loudly, then pad into the kitchen and get yourself a beer from the refrigerator without asking me whether I'd like anything, and then you'll proceed to lie back down beside me and confess that you've got a girlfriend named Stephanie who's away at medical school in Belgium for a year, and that you've been involved with her—*off and on*—in what you'll call a very "intricate" relationship, for the past *seven YEARS*. None of which *interests* me, mister!

BILL: Okay.

(*Bell.*)

Do you come in here a lot?

BETTY: Every other day, I think.

BILL: I come in here quite a lot and I don't remember seeing you.

BETTY: I guess we must be on different schedules.

BILL: Missed connections.

BETTY: Yes. Different time zones.

BILL: Amazing how you can live right next door to somebody in this town and never even know it.

BETTY: I know.

BILL: City life.

BETTY: It's crazy.

BILL: We probably pass each other in the street every day. Right in front of this place, probably.

BETTY: Yep.

BILL (*looks around*): Well the waiters here sure seem to be in some different time zone. I can't seem to locate one anywhere. . . . Waiter! (*He looks back.*) So what do you—(*He sees that she's gone back to her book.*)

BETTY: I beg pardon?

BILL: Nothing. Sorry.

(*Bell.*)

BETTY: I guess we must be on different schedules.

BILL: Missed connections.

BETTY: Yes. Different time zones.

BILL: Amazing how you can live right next door to somebody in this town and never even know it.

BETTY: I know.

BILL: City life.

BETTY: It's crazy.

BILL: You weren't waiting for somebody when I came in, were you?

BETTY: Actually I was.

BILL: Oh. Boyfriend?

BETTY: Sort of.

BILL: What's a sort-of boyfriend?

BETTY: My husband.

BILL: Ah-ha.

(*Bell.*)

You weren't waiting for somebody when I came in, were you?

BETTY: Actually I was.

BILL: Oh. Boyfriend?

BETTY: Sort of.

BILL: What's a sort-of boyfriend?

BETTY: We were meeting here to break up.

BILL: Mm-hm . . .

(*Bell.*)

What's a sort-of boyfriend?

BETTY: My lover. Here she comes right now!

(*Bell.*)

BILL: You weren't waiting for somebody when I came in, were you?

BETTY: No, just reading.

BILL: Sort of a sad occupation for a Friday night, isn't it? Reading here, all by yourself?

BETTY: Do you think so?

BILL: Well sure. I mean, what's a good-looking woman like you doing out alone on a Friday night?

BETTY: Trying to keep away from lines like that.

BILL: No, listen—

(*Bell.*)

You weren't waiting for somebody when I came in, were you?

BETTY: No, just reading.

BILL: Sort of a sad occupation for a Friday night, isn't it? Reading here all by yourself?

BETTY: I guess it is, in a way.

BILL: What's a good-looking woman like you doing out alone on a Friday night anyway? No offense, but . . .

BETTY: I'm out alone on a Friday night for the first time in a very long time.

BILL: Oh.

BETTY: You see, I just recently ended a relationship.

BILL: Oh.

BETTY: Of rather long standing.

BILL: I'm sorry. (*Small pause.*) Well listen, since reading by yourself *is* such a sad occupation for a Friday night, would you like to go elsewhere?

BETTY: No . . .

BILL: Do something else?

BETTY: No thanks.

BILL: I was headed out to the movies in a while anyway.

BETTY: I don't think so.

BILL: Big chance to let Faulkner catch his breath. All those long sentences get him pretty tired.

BETTY: Thanks anyway.

BILL: Okay.

BETTY: I appreciate the invitation.

BILL: Sure thing.

(*Bell.*)

You weren't waiting for somebody when I came in, were you?

BETTY: No, just reading.

BILL: Sort of a sad occupation for a Friday night, isn't it? Reading here all by yourself?

BETTY: I guess I was trying to think of it as existentially romantic. You know—cappuccino, great literature, rainy night . . .

BILL: That only works in Paris. We *could* hop the late plane to Paris. Get on a Concorde. Find a café . . .

BETTY: I'm a little short on plane fare tonight.

BILL: Darn it, so am I.

BETTY: To tell you the truth, I was headed to the movies after I finished this section. Would you like to come along? Since you can't locate a waiter?

BILL: That's a very nice offer, but . . .

BETTY: Uh-huh. Girlfriend?

BILL: Two, actually. One of them's pregnant, and Stephanie—

(*Bell.*)

BETTY: Girlfriend?

BILL: No, I don't have a girlfriend. Not if you mean the castrating bitch I dumped last night.

(*Bell.*)

BETTY: Girlfriend?

BILL: Sort of. Sort of.

BETTY: What's a sort-of girlfriend?

BILL: My mother.

(*Bell.*)

I just ended a relationship, actually.

BETTY: Oh.

BILL: Of rather long standing.

BETTY: I'm sorry to hear it.

BILL: This is my first night out alone in a long time. I feel a little bit at sea, to tell you the truth.

BETTY: So you didn't stop to talk because you're a Moonie, or you have some weird political affiliation—?

BILL: Nope. Straight-down-the-ticket Republican.

(*Bell.*)

Straight-down-the-ticket Democrat.

(*Bell.*)

Can I tell you something about politics?

(*Bell.*)

I like to think of myself as a citizen of the universe.

(*Bell.*)

I'm unaffiliated.

BETTY: That's a relief. So am I.

BILL: I vote my beliefs.

BETTY: Labels are not important.

BILL: Labels are not important, exactly. Take me, for example. I mean, what does it matter if I had a two-point at—

(*Bell.*)

three-point at—

(*Bell.*)

four-point at college? Or if I did come from Pittsburgh—

(*Bell.*)

Cleveland—

(*Bell.*)

Westchester County?

BETTY: Sure.

BILL: I believe that a man is what he is.

(*Bell.*)

A person is what he is.

(*Bell.*)

A person is . . . what they are.

BETTY: I think so too.

BILL: So what if I admire Trotsky?

(*Bell.*)

So what if I once had a total-body liposuction?

(*Bell.*)

So what if I don't have a penis?

(*Bell.*)

So what if I spent a year in the Peace Corps? I was acting on my convictions.

BETTY: Sure.

BILL: You just can't hang a sign on a person.

BETTY: Absolutely. I'll bet you're a Scorpio.

(*Many bells ring.*)

Listen, I was headed to the movies after I finished this section. Would you like to come along?

BILL: That sounds like fun. What's playing?

BETTY: A couple of the really early Woody Allen movies.

BILL: Oh.

BETTY: You don't like Woody Allen?

BILL: Sure. I like Woody Allen.

BETTY: But you're not crazy about Woody Allen.

BILL: Those early ones kind of get on my nerves.

BETTY: Uh-huh.

(*Bell.*)

BILL: Y'know I was headed to the—

BETTY (*simultaneously*): I was thinking about—

BILL: I'm sorry.

BETTY: No, go ahead.

BILL: I was going to say that I was headed to the movies in a little while, and . . .

BETTY: So was I.

BILL: The Woody Allen festival?

BETTY: Just up the street.

BILL: Do you like the early ones?

BETTY: I think anybody who doesn't ought to be run off the planet.

BILL: How many times have you seen *Bananas?*

BETTY: Eight times.

BILL: Twelve. So are you still interested? (*Long pause.*)

BETTY: Do you like Entenmann's crumb cake . . . ?

BILL: Last night I went out at two in the morning to get one. Did you have an Etch-a-Sketch as a child?

BETTY: Yes! And do you like Brussels sprouts? (*Pause.*)

BILL: No, I think they're disgusting.

BETTY: They *are* disgusting!

BILL: Do you still believe in marriage in spite of current sentiments against it?

BETTY: Yes.

BILL: And children?

BETTY: Three of them.

BILL: Two girls and a boy.

BETTY: Harvard, Vassar, and Brown.

BILL: And will you love me?

BETTY: Yes.

BILL: And cherish me forever?

BETTY: Yes.

BILL: Do you still want to go to the movies?

BETTY: Sure thing.

BILL AND BETTY (*together*):   *Waiter!*

BLACKOUT

—1988

Wendy Wasserstein (b. 1950), born in Brooklyn, has led the way among a gener-ation of important new women playwrights, among them prize-winners Beth Henley and Marsha Norman. Wasserstein was educated at Mount Holyoke, City University of New York, and the Yale School of Drama, where her contemporaries included included fellow playwrights Christopher Durang and Albert Innaurato and actress Meryl Streep. Having come of age during the first years of the feminist era, Wasserstein takes the changing roles of women in American society as her chief theme. One of her earliest short plays was a satire of beauty contests, and her first full-length play, Uncommon Women *(1977), examines how a group of college students in the late 1960s react to both the opportunities and uncertainties created by the women's movement, a subject which is further explored in* The Heidi Chronicles. The Heidi Chronicles *opened in New York in 1988 and won the Pulitzer Prize, the Antoinette Perry Award, and the New York Drama Critics Circle Award. Subsequent plays include,* The Sisters Rosenweig, *a Broadway hit in 1993, and* An American Daughter *(1997), which was televised on the Lifetime Channel in 2000.* Old Money, *her most recent play, opened late in 2000. Wasserstein has also written a collection of essays,* Bachelor Girls, *which includes advice on ranking "the world's worst boyfriends." In 1998 she sponsored a program in which eight New York high school students accompanied her to plays and kept journals of their impressions. Wasserstein notes that the students overcame their ini-tial fears that the plays would be boring and aimed toward elite audiences, eventually finding that "the art from was gloriously compelling. Now the trick is to eliminate 'only the rich and elegant.' If the price was right — which is not only a high school student's dream — and the theater became the undisputed birthright of every New Yorker, it would be way cool, indeed."*

Wendy Wasserstein
The Man in a Case

CHARACTERS

Byelinkov
Varinka

SCENE: A small garden in the village of Mironitski, 1898

[*Byelinkov is pacing. Enter Varinka out of breath.*]

BYELINKOV: You are ten minutes late.
VARINKA: The most amazing thing happened on my way over here. You know the woman who runs the grocery store down the road.

She wears a black wig during the week, and a blond wig on Saturday nights. And she has the daughter who married an engineer in Moscow who is doing very well thank you and is living, God bless them, in a three-room apartment. But he really is the most boring man in the world. All he talks about is his future and his station in life. Well, she heard we were to be married and she gave me this basket of apricots to give to you.

BYELINKOV: That is a most amazing thing!

VARINKA: She said to me, "Varinka, you are marrying the most honorable man in the entire village. In this village he is the only man fit to speak with my son-in-law."

BYELINKOV: I don't care for apricots. They give me hives.

VARINKA: I can return them. I'm sure if I told her they give you hives she would give me a basket of raisins or a cake.

BYELINKOV: I don't know this woman or her pompous son-in-law. Why would she give me her cakes?

VARINKA: She adores you!

BYELINKOV: She is emotionally loose.

VARINKA: She adores you by reputation. Everyone adores you by reputation. I tell everyone I am to marry Byelinkov, the finest teacher in the country.

BYELINKOV: You tell them this?

VARINKA: If they don't tell me first.

BYELINKOV: Pride can be an imperfect value.

VARINKA: It isn't pride. It is the truth. You are a great man!

BYELINKOV: I am the master of Greek and Latin at a local school at the end of the village of Mironitski.

[*Varinka kisses him.*]

VARINKA: And I am to be the master of Greek and Latin's wife!

BYELINKOV: Being married requires a great deal of responsibility. I hope I am able to provide you with all that a married man must properly provide a wife.

VARINKA: We will be very happy.

BYELINKOV: Happiness is for children. We are entering into a social contract, an amicable agreement to provide us with a secure and satisfying future.

VARINKA: You are so sweet! You are the sweetest man in the world!

BYELINKOV: I'm a man set in his ways who saw a chance to provide himself with a small challenge.

VARINKA: Look at you! Look at you! Your sweet round spectacles, your dear collar always starched, always raised, your perfectly pressed pants always creasing at right angles perpendicular to the floor, and my most favorite part, the sweet little galoshes, rain or shine, just in case. My Byelinkov, never taken by surprise. Except by me.

BYELINKOV: You speak about me as if I were your pet.

VARINKA: You are my pet! My little school mouse.

BYELINKOV: A mouse?

VARINKA: My sweetest dancing bear with galoshes, my little stale babka.

BYELINKOV: A stale babka?

VARINKA: I am not Pushkin.[1]

BYELINKOV [*laughs*]: That depends what you think of Pushkin.

VARINKA: You're smiling. I knew I could make you smile today.

BYELINKOV: I am a responsible man. Every day I have for breakfast black bread, fruit, hot tea, and every day I smile three times. I am halfway into my translation of the *Aeneid*[2] from classical Greek hexameter[3] into Russian alexandrines.[4] In twenty years I have never been late to school. I am a responsible man, but no dancing bear.

VARINKA: Dance with me.

BYELINKOV: Now? It is nearly four weeks before the wedding!

VARINKA: It's a beautiful afternoon. We are in your garden. The roses are in full bloom.

BYELINKOV: The roses have beetles.

VARINKA: Dance with me!

BYELINKOV: You are a demanding woman.

VARINKA: You chose me. And right. And left. And turn. And right. And left.

BYELINKOV: And turn. Give me your hand. You dance like a school mouse. It's a beautiful afternoon! We are in my garden. The roses are in full bloom! And turn. And turn. [*twirls* Varinka *around*]

[*Byelinkov stops dancing.*]

---

[1]**Alexander Pushkin** a famous Russian poet and dramatist (1799–1837)   [2]**Aeneid** epic poem written by Vergil (70–19 B.C.)   [3]**hexameter** a line of verse having six metric units   [4]**alexandrine** a line of verse having six metric units

BYELINKOV: To place a lilac in your hair. Every year on this day I will place a lilac in your hair.

VARINKA: Will you remember?

BYELINKOV: I will write it down. [*takes a notebook from his pocket*] Dear Byelinkov, don't forget the day a young lady, your bride, entered your garden, your peace, and danced on the roses. On that day every year you are to place a lilac in her hair.

VARINKA: I love you.

BYELINKOV: It is convenient we met.

VARINKA: I love you.

BYELINKOV: You are a girl.

VARINKA: I am thirty.

BYELINKOV: But you think like a girl. That is an attractive attribute.

VARINKA: Do you love me?

BYELINKOV: We've never spoken about housekeeping.

VARINKA: I am an excellent housekeeper. I kept house for my family on the farm in Gadyatchsky. I can make a beetroot soup with tomatoes and aubergines which is so nice. Awfully, awfully nice.

BYELINKOV: You are fond of expletives.

VARINKA: My beet soup, sir, is excellent!

BYELINKOV: Please don't be cross. I too am an excellent housekeeper. I have a place for everything in the house. A shelf for each pot, a cubby for every spoon, a folder for favorite recipes. I have cooked for myself for twenty years. Though my beet soup is not outstanding, it is sufficient.

VARINKA: I'm sure it's very good.

BYELINKOV: No. It is awfully, awfully not. What I am outstanding in, however, what gives me greatest pleasure, is preserving those things which are left over. I wrap each tomato slice I haven't used in a wet cloth and place it in the coolest corner of the house. I have had my shoes for seven years because I wrap them in the galoshes you are so fond of and every night before I go to sleep I wrap my bed in quilts and curtains so I never catch a draft.

VARINKA: You sleep with curtains on your bed?

BYELINKOV: I like to keep warm.

VARINKA: I will make you a new quilt.

BYELINKOV: No. No new quilt. That would be hazardous.

VARINKA: It is hazardous to sleep under curtains.

BYELINKOV: Varinka, I don't like change very much. If one works out the arithmetic, the final fraction of improvement is at best less than an eighth of value over the total damage caused by disruption. I never thought of marrying till I saw your eyes dancing among the familiar faces at the headmaster's tea. I assumed I would grow old preserved like those which are left over, wrapped suitably in my case of curtains and quilts.

VARINKA: Byelinkov, I want us to have dinners with friends and summer country visits. I want people to say, "Have you spent time with Varinka and Byelinkov? He is so happy now that they are married. She is just what he needed."

BYELINKOV: You have already brought me some happiness. But I never was a sad man. Don't ever think I thought I was a sad man.

VARINKA: My sweetest darling, you can be whatever you want! If you are sad, they'll say she talks all the time, and he is soft-spoken and kind.

BYELINKOV: And if I am difficult?

VARINKA: Oh, they'll say he is difficult because he is highly intelligent. All great men are difficult. Look at Lermontov, Tchaikovsky, Peter the Great.

BYELINKOV: Ivan the Terrible.

VARINKA: Yes, him too.

BYELINKOV: Why are you marrying me? I am none of these things.

VARINKA: To me you are.

BYELINKOV: You have imagined this. You have constructed an elaborate romance for yourself. Perhaps you are the great one. You are the one with the great imagination.

VARINKA: Byelinkov, I am a pretty girl of thirty. You're right, I am not a woman. I have not made myself into a woman because I do not deserve that honor. Until I came to this town to visit my brother I lived on my family's farm. As the years passed I became younger and younger in fear that I would never marry. And it wasn't that I wasn't pretty enough or sweet enough, it was just that no man ever looked at me and saw a wife. I was not the woman who would be there when he came home. Until I met you I thought I would lie all my life and say I never married because I never met a man I loved. I will love you, Byelinkov. And I will help you to love me. We deserve the life everyone else has. We deserve not to be different.

BYELINKOV: Yes. We are the same as everyone else.

VARINKA: Tell me you love me.

BYELINKOV: I love you.

VARINKA [*takes his hands*]:   We will be very happy. I am very strong. [*pauses*] It is time for tea.

BYELINKOV: It is too early for tea. Tea is at half past the hour.

VARINKA: Do you have heavy cream? It will be awfully nice with apricots.

BYELINKOV: Heavy cream is too rich for teatime.

VARINKA: But today is special. Today you placed a lilac in my hair. Write in your note pad. Every year we will celebrate with apricots and heavy cream. I will go to my brother's house and get some.

BYELINKOV: But your brother's house is a mile from here.

VARINKA: Today it is much shorter. Today my brother gave me his bicycle to ride. I will be back very soon.

BYELINKOV: You rode to my house by bicycle! Did anyone see you?

VARINKA: Of course. I had such fun. I told you I saw the grocery store lady with the son-in-law who is doing very well thank you in Moscow, and the headmaster's wife.

BYELINKOV: You say the headmaster's wife!

VARINKA: She smile at me.

BYELINKOV: Did she laugh or smile?

VARINKA: She laughed a little. She said, "My dear, you are very progressive to ride a bicycle." She said, "You and your fiancé Byelinkov must ride together sometime. I wonder if he'll take off his galoshes when he rides a bicycle."

BYELINKOV: She said that?

VARINKA: She adores you. We had a good giggle.

BYELINKOV: A woman can be arrested for riding a bicycle. That is not progressive, it is a premeditated revolutionary act. Your brother must be awfully, awfully careful on behalf of your behavior. He has been careless—oh so careless—in giving you the bicycle.

BYELINKOV: Dearest Byelinkov, you are wrapping yourself under curtains and quilts! I made friends on the bicycle.

BYELINKOV: You saw more than the headmaster's wife and the idiot grocery woman.

VARINKA: She is not an idiot.

BYELINKOV: She is a potato-vending, sausage-armed fool!

VARINKA: Shhh! My school mouse. Shhh!

BYELINKOV: What other friends did you make on this bicycle.

VARINKA: I saw students from my brother's classes. They waved and shouted, "Anthropos in love! Anthropos in love!!"

BYELINKOV: Where is that bicycle?

VARINKA: I left it outside the gate. What are you doing?

BYELINKOV [*muttering as he exits*]: Anthropos in love, anthropos in love.

VARINKA: They were cheering me on. Careful, you'll trample the roses.

BYELINKOV [*returning with the bicycle*]: Anthopos is the Greek singular for man. Anthropos in love translates as the Greek and Latin master in love. Of course they cheered you. Their instructor, who teaches them the discipline and contained beauty of the classics, is in love with a sprite on a bicycle. It is a good giggle, isn't it? A very good giggle! I am returning this bicycle to your brother.

VARINKA: But it is teatime.

BYELINKOV: Today we will not have tea.

VARINKA: But you will have to walk back a mile.

BYELINKOV: I have my galoshes on. [*gets on the bicycle*] Varinka, we deserve not to be different. [*Begins to pedal. The bicycle doesn't move.*]

VARINKA: Put the kickstand up.

BYELINKOV: I beg your pardon.

VARINKA [*giggling*]: Byelinkov, to make the bicycle move, you must put the kickstand up.

[*Byelinkov puts it up and awkwardly falls off the bicycle as it moves.*]

[*laughing*] Ha ha ha. My little school mouse. You look so funny! You are the sweetest dearest man in the world. Ha ha ha!

[*pause*]

BYELINKOV: Please help me up. I'm afraid my galosh is caught.

VARINKA [*trying not to laugh*]: Your galosh is caught! [*explodes in laughter again*] Oh, you are so funny! I do love you so. [*helps Byelinkov up*] You were right, my pet, as always. We don't need heavy cream for tea. The fraction of improvement isn't worth the damage caused by the disruption.

BYELINKOV: Varinka, it is still too early for tea. I must complete two stanzas of my translation before late afternoon. That is my regular schedule.

VARINKA: Then I will watch while you work.

BYELINKOV: No. You had a good giggle. That is enough.

VARINKA: Then while you work I will work too. I will make lists of guests for our wedding.

BYELINKOV: I can concentrate only when I am alone in my house. Please take your bicycle home to your brother.

VARINKA: But I don't want to leave you. You look so sad.

BYELINKOV: I never was a sad man. Don't ever think I was a sad man.

VARINKA: Byelinkov, it's a beautiful day, we are in your garden. The roses are in bloom.

BYELINKOV: Allow me to help you on to your bicycle. [*takes Varinka's hand as she gets on the bike*]

VARINKA: You are such a gentleman. We will be very happy.

BYELINKOV: You are very strong. Good day, Varinka.

[*Varinka pedals off. Byelinkov, alone in the garden, takes out his pad and rips up the note about the lilac, strews it over the garden, then carefully picks up each piece of paper and places them all in a small envelope as lights fade to black.*]

Appendix

Literature: Thematic and Critical Approaches

Because it is possible to classify the stories, poems, and plays in the anthology in many different ways, the following appendix is not exhaustive. It should, however, provide suggestions for reading and writing about works from the same genre or works from different genres that share thematic similarities. Following the thematic listing is a brief discussion of several key critical approaches and their applications to the thematic groups.

Works are listed by genre, and works in each genre are listed in chronological order. Consult the *Index to Authors; Titles of Stories, Poems, and Plays; and First Lines of Poems* for their page numbers in the text.

Thematic Approaches

Aging (See also Carpe Diem)

Stories

Porter, "The Jilting of Granny Weatherall"
Faulkner, "A Rose for Emily"
Steinbeck, "The Chrysanthemums"
Welty, "Livvie"
García Márquez, "A Very Old Man with Enormous Wings"

Poems

Queen Elizabeth, "When I Was Fair and Young"

Shakespeare, "Sonnet 73"
Milton, "How Soon Hath Time"
Tennyson, "Ulysses"
Eliot, "The Love Song of J. Alfred Prufrock"
Kennedy, "In a Prominent Bar in Secaucus One Day"
Phillips, "Compartments"

Plays

Williams, *The Glass Menagerie*
Miller, *Death of a Salesman*

Allegorical and Symbolic Works

Stories

Hawthorne, "Young Goodman Brown"
Poe, "The Fall of the House of Usher"
Lawrence, "The Rocking-Horse Winner"
Borges, "The Gospel According to Mark"
Welty, "Livvie"
Jackson, "The Lottery"
García Márquez, "A Very Old Man with Enormous Wings"
Oates, "Where Are You Going, Where Have You Been?"

Poems

Southwell, "The Burning Babe"
Herbert, "Redemption"
Burns, "John Barleycorn"
Poe, "The Haunted Palace"
Dickinson, "Because I Could Not Stop for Death"
Rossetti, "Up-hill"
Stevens, "Anecdote of the Jar"
Stevens, "The Snow Man"
Eliot, "Journey of the Magi"
Larkin, "Next, Please"
Kizer, "The Ungrateful Garden"
Creeley, "Oh No"
Merwin, "The Last One"
Rich, "Diving into the Wreck"

Plays

Williams, The Glass Menagerie
Miller, Death of a Salesman

Animals

Stories

Lawrence, "The Rocking-Horse Winner"

Poems

Smart, "Jubilate Agno" (selection)
Blake, "The Tyger"
Tennyson, "The Eagle"
Dickinson, "A Narrow Fellow in the Grass"
Moore, "The Fish"
cummings, "r-p-o-p-h-e-s-s-a-g-r"
Bishop, "The Fish"
Stafford, "Traveling Through the Dark"
Dickey, "The Heaven of Animals"
Wright, "A Blessing"
Hughes, "Pike"
Harjo, "Song for the Deer and Myself to Return On"

Plays

Glaspell, Trifles

Art

Stories

Cather, "Paul's Case"

Poems

Spenser, "Amoretti: Sonnet 75"
Shakespeare, "Sonnet 18"
Shelley, "Ozymandias"
Keats, "Ode on a Grecian Urn"
Browning, "My Last Duchess"
Yeats, "Sailing to Byzantium"
Stevens, "Anecdote of the Jar"
Auden, "Musée des Beaux Arts"

Plays

Wasserstein, The Man in a Case

Ballads and Narrative Poetry

Anonymous, "Bonny Barbara Allen"
Anonymous, "Sir Patrick Spens"
Burns, "John Barleycorn"

Hurston, "Sweat"
Welty, "Livvie"
Ellison, "A Party Down at the Square"
Jackson, "The Lottery"
O'Connor, "A Good Man Is Hard to Find"
Achebe, "Dead Men's Path"
Carver, "A Small, Good Thing"
Erdrich, "The Red Convertible"

Poems

Donne, "Holy Sonnet 10"
Keats, "When I Have Fears"
Browning, "My Last Duchess"
Browning, "Porphyria's Lover"
Dickinson, "Because I Could Not Stop for Death"
Dickinson, "I Died for Beauty—But Was Scarce"
Dickinson, "I Heard a Fly Buzz— When I Died"
Hardy, "Ah, Are You Digging on My Grave?"
Housman, "Eight O'Clock"
Frost, "Home Burial"
Williams, "Last Words of My English Grandmother"
Thomas, "Do Not Go Gentle into That Good Night"
Jarrell, "The Death of the Ball Turret Gunner"
Brooks, "We Real Cool"
Larkin, "Next, Please"
Merwin, "For the Anniversary of My Death"
Gunn, "Terminal"
Phillips, "Compartments"

Plays

Sophocles, *Oedipus the King*
Shakespeare, *The Tragedy of Othello, the Moor of Venice*

Glaspell, *Trifles*
Miller, *Death of a Salesman*

Dramatic Dialogues (Poetry)

Hardy, "Ah, Are You Digging on My Grave"
Hardy, "The Ruined Maid"
Frost, "Home Burial"
Ransom, "Piazza Piece"
Randall, "Ballad of Birmingham"
Chappell, "Narcissus and Echo"

Dramatic Monologues and Related Poetry

Blake, "The Chimney Sweeper"
Blake, "The Little Black Boy"
Blake, "A Poison Tree"
Tennyson, "Ulysses"
Browning, "My Last Duchess"
Browning, "Porphyria's Lover"
Pound, "The River-Merchant's Wife: A Letter"
Eliot, "Journey of the Magi"
Eliot, "The Love Song of J. Alfred Prufrock"
Jarrell, "The Death of the Ball Turret Gunner"
Brooks, "We Real Cool"
Wright, "Saint Judas"
Kennedy, "In a Prominent Bar in Secaucus One Day"
Atwood, "Siren Song"
Hall, "Maybe Dats Your Pwoblem Too"
Cortez, *"Tu Negrito"*

Duty

Stories

Maupassant, "Mother Savage"
Camus, "The Guest"

Poems

Anonymous, "Sir Patrick Spens"
Lovelace, "To Lucasta, Going to the
    Wars"
Tennyson, "Ulysses"
Lowell, "For the Union Dead"

Plays

Sophocles, *Oedipus the King*
Shakespeare, *The Tragedy of
    Othello, the Moor of Venice*

Elegy (Poetry)

Jonson, "On My First Son"
Dryden, "To the Memory of Mr.
    Oldham"
Gray, "Elegy Written in a Country
    Churchyard"
Longfellow, "The Cross of Snow"
Tennyson, "In Memoriam A.H.H., 54"
Ransom, "Bells for John Whiteside's
    Daughter"
Millay, "Sonnet 5"
O'Hara, "The Day Lady Died"
Sexton, "The Truth the Dead Know"
Gunn, "Terminal"
Gioia, "Planting a Sequoia"

Fate

Stories

Hawthorne, "Young Goodman
    Brown"
Lawrence, "The Rocking-Horse
    Winner"
Borges, "The Gospel According to
    Mark"
Camus, "The Guest"
Jackson, "The Lottery"
O'Connor, "A Good Man Is Hard to
    Find"

Poems

Randall, "Ballad of Birmingham"
Frost, "Design"
Yeats, "Leda and the Swan"
Auden, "The Unknown Citizen"

Plays

Sophocles, *Oedipus the King*
Shakespeare, *The Tragedy of
    Othello, the Moor of Venice*
Williams, *The Glass Menagerie*
Miller, *Death of a Salesman*
Ives, *Sure Thing*

History

Stories

Hawthorne, "Young Goodman
    Brown"
Maupassant, "Mother Savage"
Faulkner, "A Rose for Emily"
Camus, "The Guest"
Ellison, "A Party Down at the
    Square"
Jackson, "The Lottery"
Achebe, "Dead Men's Path"
Walker, "Everyday Use"

Poems

Milton, "On the Late Massacre in
    Piedmont"
Gray, "Elegy Written in a Country
    Churchyard"
Shelley, "Ozymandias"
Yeats, "The Second Coming"
Jeffers, "The Purse-Seine"
Lowell, "For the Union Dead"
Wilbur, "Year's End"
Merrill, "Casual Wear"
Walcott, "Central America"
Heaney, "Punishment"

Adcock, "Digression on the Nuclear
  Age"
Forché, "The Colonel"

Plays

Sophocles, *Oedipus the King*
Shakespeare, *The Tragedy of
  Othello, the Moor of Venice*
Wasserstein, *The Man in a Case*

Holocaust

Poems

Hecht, "More Light! More Light!"
Williams, "The Book"
Shomer, "Women Bathing at Bergen-
  Belsen"
Plath, "Daddy"
Hudgins, "Air View of an Industrial
  Scene"

Humanity

Stories

Gautreaux, "Died and Gone to
  Vegas"
Gilb, "Look on the Bright Side"

Poems

Arnold, "Dover Beach"
Whitman, "Crossing Brooklyn Ferry"
cummings, "nobody loses all the time"
Crane, "Chaplinesque"
Auden, "As I Walked Out One
  Evening"
Stafford, "Traveling Through the
  Dark"
Nemerov, "A Primer of the Daily
  Round"
Justice, "Counting the Mad"
Ginsberg, "A Supermarket in
  California"
Wright, "Saint Judas"

Levine, "Genius"
Phillips, "Compartments"
Mayers, "All-American Sestina"
Steele, "Sapphics Against Anger"
Nye, "The Traveling Onion"
Song, "Stamp Collecting"

Language

Stories

Hurston, "Sweat"
Atwood, "Happy Endings"

Poems

cummings, "r-p-o-p-h-e-s-s-a-g-r"
Hollander, "Adam's Task"
Hass, "Picking Blackberries with a
  Friend Who Has Been Reading
  Jacques Lacan"
Martin, "E.S.L."
Raine, "A Martian Sends a Postcard
  Home"
Alvarez, "Bilingual Sestina"

Plays

Ives, *Sure Thing*

Love

Stories

Wharton, "Roman Fever"
Joyce, "Eveline"
Hemingway, "Hills like White
  Elephants"
Steinbeck, "The Chrysanthemums"
Welty, "Livvie"
Atwood, "Happy Endings"

Poems

Shakespeare, "Sonnet 29"
Shakespeare, "Sonnet 30"
Shakespeare, "Sonnet 116"

Donne, "The Canonization"
Wroth, "In This Strange Labyrinth
    How Shall I Turn"
Burns, "A Red, Red Rose"
Browning, "Sonnets from the
    Portuguese, 43"
Browning, "Porphyria's Lover"
Eliot, "The Love Song of J. Alfred
    Prufrock"
Dugan, "Love Song: I and Thou"
Walker, "Even As I Hold You"

Plays

Shakespeare, *The Tragedy of
    Othello, the Moor of Venice*
Williams, *The Glass Menagerie*
Ives, *Sure Thing*

Love, Loss of

Stories

Joyce, "Eveline"
Faulkner, "A Rose for Emily"

Poems

Anonymous, "Western Wind"
Wyatt, "They Flee from Me"
Keats, "La Belle Dame sans Merci"
Poe, "The Raven"
Hardy, "Neutral Tones"
Millay, "What Lips My Lips Have
    Kissed"
Bishop, "One Art"
Snodgrass, "Mementos, I"
Stokesbury, "Evening's End"

Love: Marital Relationships

Stories

Hawthorne, "Young Goodman
    Brown"
Chopin, "The Story of an Hour"
Hurston, "Sweat"

Welty, "Livvie"
Atwood, "Happy Endings"
Mason, "Shiloh"

Poems

Shakespeare, "Sonnet 116"
Donne, "A Valediction: Forbidding
    Mourning"
Browning, "My Last Duchess"
Arnold, "Dover Beach"
Robinson, "Firelight"
Frost, "Home Burial"
Pound, "The River-Merchant's Wife:
    A Letter"
Eliot, "Love Song: I and Thou"
Levertov, "The Ache of Marriage"
Dugan, "Love Song: I and Thou"
Rich, "Aunt Jennifer's Tigers"
Morgan, "Mountain Bride"

Plays

Shakespeare, *The Tragedy of
    Othello, the Moor of Venice*
Ibsen, *A Doll House*
Miller, *Death of a Salesman*

Myth

Stories

Borges, "The Gospel According to
    Mark"
Welty, "Livvie"
Jackson, "The Lottery"
García Márquez, "A Very Old Man
    with Enormous Wings"

Poems

Poe, "To Helen"
Yeats, "Leda and the Swan"
Eliot, "The Love Song of J. Alfred
    Prufrock"
Hope, "Imperial Adam"

Auden, "Musée des Beaux Arts"
Merwin, "The Last One"
Hollander, "Adam's Task"
Plath, "Edge"
Chappell, "Narcissus and Echo"
Atwood, "Siren Song"

Plays

Sophocles, *Oedipus the King*

Nature and God

Stories

Welty, "Livvie"

Poems

Wordsworth, "It Is a Beauteous Evening"
Wordsworth, "Ode: Intimations of Immortality"
Whitman, "A Noiseless Patient Spider"
Whitman, "Song of Myself, 6"
Whitman, "When I Heard the Learn'd Astronomer"
Hopkins, "God's Grandeur"
Frost, "Design"
Stevens, "The Snow Man"
Stevens, "Sunday Morning"
Willard, "A Hardware Store As Proof of the Existence of God"

Nature: Descriptive Poetry

Swift, "Description of a City Shower"
Freneau, "The Wild Honey Suckle"
Wordsworth, "I Wandered Lonely As a Cloud"
Wordsworth, "Lines (Composed a Few Miles Above Tintern Abbey . . .)"
Bryant, "To the Fringed Gentian"
Hopkins, "Pied Beauty"

Frost, "The Need of Being Versed in Country Things"
Frost, "Stopping by Woods on a Snowy Evening"
H. D., "Pear Tree"
H. D., "Sea Rose"
Kunitz, "Halley's Comet"
Roethke, "Root Cellar"
Thomas, "Fern Hill"
Swenson, "How Everything Happens"
Snyder, "A Walk"
Heaney, "Bogland"
Sáenz, "To the Desert"
Murphy, "The Track of a Storm"
Hongo, "Crossing Ka'u Desert"

Nature: The Environment

Poems

Hopkins, "God's Grandeur"
Jeffers, "The Purse-Seine"
cummings, "pity this busy monster"
Bishop, "The Fish"
Stafford, "Traveling Through the Dark"
Kizer, "The Ungrateful Garden"
Kumin, "Noted in the *New York Times*"
Merwin, "The Last One"
Oliver, "The Black Walnut Tree"
Harjo, "Song for the Deer and Myself to Return On"

Nature: Seasons of the Year

Stories

Welty, "Livvie"

Poems

Shakespeare, "When Daisies Pied (Spring and Winter)"
Shelley, "Ode to the West Wind"
Bryant, "To the Fringed Gentian"

Williams, "Spring and All"
Toomer, "Reapers"
Wilbur, "Year's End"
Pastan, "Crocuses"

Parents and Children

Stories

Maupassant, "Mother Savage"
Wharton, "Roman Fever"
Lawrence, "The Rocking-Horse
    Winner"
Faulkner, "A Rose for Emily"
Lawrence, "Hills like White
    Elephants"
Cheever, "Reunion"
O'Connor, "A Good Man Is Hard to
    Find"
Munro, "Vandals"
Oates, "Where Are You Going,
    Where Have You Been?"
Carver, "A Small, Good Thing"
Walker, "Everyday Use"
Tan, "Two Kinds"
Moore, "How to Talk to Your Mother
    (Notes)"

Poems

Coleridge, "Frost at Midnight"
Moore, "Silence"
Roethke, "My Papa's Waltz"
Hayden, "Those Winter Sundays"
Thomas, "Do Not Go Gentle into
    That Good Night"
Kees, "For My Daughter"
Brooks, "The Mother"
Wilbur, "The Writer"
Larkin, "This Be the Verse"
Simpson, "My Father in the Night
    Commanding No"
Sexton, "The Truth the Dead Know"
Plath, "Daddy"
Heaney, "Digging"
Voight, "Daughter"

Cortez, "*Tu Negrito*"
Tufariello, "Useful Advice"

Plays

Sophocles, *Oedipus the King*
Shakespeare, *Othello*
Ibsen, *A Doll House*
Williams, *The Glass Menagerie*
Miller, *Death of a Salesman*
Wilson, *Fences*
Wasserstein, *The Man in a Case*

Physical Handicaps

Poems

Milton, "When I Consider How My
    Light Is Spent"
Miller, "Subterfuge"
Ruark, "The Visitor"

Plays

Sophocles, *Oedipus the King*
Shakespeare, *Tragedy of Othello, the
    Moor of Venice*
Williams, *The Glass Menagerie*

Poetry

Bradstreet, "The Author to Her Book"
Pope, "Essay on Criticism" (selection)
Wordsworth, "Nuns Fret Not at
    Their Convent's Narrow Room"
Keats, "On First Looking into
    Chapman's Homer"
Housman, "Terence, This Is Stupid
    Stuff"
Ashbery, "Paradoxes and Oxy-
    morons"
Heaney, "Digging"
Tate, "Teaching the Ape to Write
    Poems"

Gwynn, "Approaching a Significant
Birthday, He Peruses *The Norton
Anthology of Poetry*"

Poetry: Inspiration

Sidney, "Astrophel and Stella:
Sonnet I"
Coleridge, "Kubla Khan"
Keats, "Ode to a Nightingale"
Whitman, "Out of the Cradle
Endlessly Rocking"
Wilbur, "The Writer"

Political and Social Themes

Stories

Maupassant, "Mother Savage"
Joyce, "An Upheaval"
Hemingway, "Hills like White
Elephants"
Camus, "The Guest"
Achebe, "Dead Men's Path"
Gautreaux, "Died and Gone to Vegas"
Gilb, "Look on the Bright Side"
Tan, "Two Kinds"
Erdrich, "The Red Convertible"

Poems

Milton, "On the Late Massacre in
Piedmont"
Blake, "The Chimney Sweeper"
Housman, "Eight O'Clock"
Robinson, "The Mill"
Auden, "The Unknown Citizen"
Roethke, "Dolor"
Brooks, "The Mother"
Simpson, "American Classic"
Merrill, "Casual Wear"
Walcott, "Central America"
Ai, "Child Beater"
Cortez, "*Tu Negrito*"

Forché, "The General"
Song, "Stamp Collecting"

Plays

Sophocles, *Oedipus the King*
Shakespeare, *The Tragedy of
Othello, the Moor of Venice*
Ibsen, *A Doll House*
Wasserstein, *The Man in a Case*

Racial Identity and Racism

Stories

Wright, "The Man Who Was Almost
a Man"
Camus, "The Guest"
Ellison, "A Party Down at the Square"
O'Connor, "A Good Man Is Hard to
Find"
Walker, "Everyday Use"
Tan, "Two Kinds"
Cisneros, "Barbie-Q"
Erdrich, "The Red Convertible"

Poems

Blake, "The Little Black Boy"
Dunbar, "We Wear the Mask"
Hughes, "Dream Boogie"
Hughes, "Theme for English B"
Cullen, "Incident"
Cullen, "Yet Do I Marvel"
Randall, "Ballad of Birmingham"
Walker, "For Malcolm X"
Lowell, "For the Union Dead"
Nelson, "Ballad of Aunt Geneva"
Jones, "Winter Retreat: Homage to
Martin Luther King, Jr."

Plays

Shakespeare, *The Tragedy of
Othello, the Moor of Venice*
Wilson, *Fences*

Satire and Humor

Stories

O'Connor, "A Good Man Is Hard to Find"
Walker, "Everyday Use"
Gautreaux, "Died and Gone to Vegas"

Poems

Swift, "Description of a City Shower"
Byron, "Stanzas"
Hardy, "The Ruined Maid"
Stevens, "Disillusionment of Ten O'Clock"
Auden, "The Unknown Citizen"
Wilbur, "Playboy"
Martin, "E.S.L."
Tate, "Teaching the Ape to Write Poems"
Fenton, "God, a Poem"
Disch, "Ballade of the New God"
Hall, "Maybe Dat's Your Pwoblem Too"

Plays

Wasserstein, *The Man in a Case*
Ives, *Sure Thing*

Sexual Themes (See also Carpe Diem)

Stories

Poe, "The Fall of the House of Usher"
Wharton, "Roman Fever"
Lawrence, "The Rocking-Horse Winner"
Faulkner, "A Rose for Emily"
Hemingway, "Hills like White Elephants"
Steinbeck, "The Chrysanthemums"
Munro, "Vandals"
Updike, "A & P"

Oates, "Where Are You Going, Where Have You Been?"

Poems

Shakespeare, "Sonnet 20"
Donne, "The Flea"
Marvell, "To His Coy Mistress"
Hardy, "The Ruined Maid"
Eliot, "The Love Song of J. Alfred Prufrock"
Wilbur, "Playboy"
Rich, "Rape"
Rogers, "Foreplay"
Ríos, "The Purpose of Altar Boys"

Plays

Sophocles, *Oedipus the King*
Wasserstein, *The Man in a Case*

Solitude

Stories

Poe, "The Fall of the House of Usher"
Cather, "Paul's Case"
Faulkner, "A Rose for Emily"
Welty, "Livvie"
Camus, "The Guest"

Poems

Pope, "Ode on Solitude"
Dickinson, "The Soul Selects Her Own Society"
Yeats, "The Lake Isle of Innisfree"
Thomas, "Acquainted With the Night"
Frost, "Stopping by Woods on a Snowy Evening"

Plays

Glaspell, *Trifles*

Sports and Games

Stories

Lawrence, "The Rocking-Horse Winner"
Gautreaux, "Died and Gone to Vegas"

Poems

Housman, "To an Athlete Dying Young"
Gunn, "From the Wave"
Gildner, "First Practice"
Fairchild, "Body and Soul"
Bottoms, "Sign for My Father, Who Stressed the Bunt"

Plays

Miller, *Death of a Salesman*
Wilson, *Fences*

Suicide

Stories

Poe, "The Fall of the House of Usher"
Cather, "Paul's Case"
Erdrich, "The Red Convertible"

Poems

Anonymous, "Bonny Barbara Allen"
Robinson, "The Mill"
Robinson, "Richard Cory"
Parker, "Résumé"
Wright, "Saint Judas"
Plath, "Edge"

Plays

Sophocles, *Oedipus the King*
Othello, *The Tragedy of Othello, the Moor of Venice*
Miller, *Death of a Salesman*

War

Stories

Maupassant, "Mother Savage"
Camus, "The Guest"

Poems

Longfellow, "The Arsenal at Springfield"
Whitman, "A Sight in Camp in the Daybreak Gray and Dim"
Crane, "War Is Kind"
Sassoon, "Dreamers"
Owen, "Dulce et Decorum Est"
Jarrell, "Death of the Ball Turret Gunner"
Snodgrass, "Mementos, I"
Adcock, "Digression on the Nuclear Age"
Komunyakaa, "Facing It"
Salter, "Welcome to Hiroshima"

Plays

Shakespeare, *The Tragedy of Othello, the Moor of Venice*

Women's Issues

Stories

Chopin, "The Story of an Hour"
Wharton, "Roman Fever"
Joyce, "Eveline"
Porter, "The Jilting of Granny Weatherall"
Hemingway, "Hills like White Elephants"
Hurston, "Sweat"
Oates, "Where Are You Going, Where Have You Been?"
Atwood, "Happy Endings"
Mason, "Shiloh"

Walker, "Everyday Use"
Moore, "How to Talk to Your Mother
(Notes)"

Poems

Pound, "Portrait d'une Femme"
Millay, "Oh, Oh, You Will Be Sorry
for That Word"
Parker, "One Perfect Rose"
Bogan, "Women"
Wilbur, "Playboy"
Sexton, "Cinderella"
Rich, "Aunt Jennifer's Tigers"
Rich, "Rape"
Plath, "Daddy"

Plath, "Metaphors"
Stevenson, "Sous-entendu"
Clifton, "to my last period"
Piercy, "Barbie Doll"
Atwood, "Siren Song"
Cardiff, "Combing"
Olds, "The One Girl at the Boys
Party"
Cope, "Rondeau Redoublé"
Tufariello, "Useful Advice"

Plays

Ibsen, *A Doll House*
Glaspell, *Trifles*
Wasserstein, *The Man in a Case*

Critical Approaches to Literature

An extensive overview of strategies for reading and analyzing fiction, poetry, and drama lies outside the scope of this book, but it may safely be said that each era in the history of literature has given rise to critics and theorists who redefine the very nature of what literature is. Neoclassical critics of the eighteenth century, with their insistence on balance, reason, and order, yielded in the next century to their Romantic successors, who stressed qualities that were diametrically opposed. The so-called New Critics of the mid-twentieth century focused on literary works as autonomous verbal texts that should be read with little or no reference to the writers' biographies or to the social conditions under which they lived. More recent theories of poetic interpretation focus precisely on those things the New Critics avoided, stressing matters of race, class, and gender as essential to understanding texts. As we enter a new century, new strategies for reading and understanding literature will doubtless emerge to challenge the preconceptions of the past and offer readers further ways to "make it new."

You may be asked to analyze works from two or three genres at once; the themes that one encounters in short stories will also be found in poems and plays. Similarly, a single critical approach—deconstruction, feminist criticism, new historicist techniques—may be employed to look at literary works by employing a specific methodology. For example, suppose you are asked to explore a general topic like "The Isolated Woman in Literature." You might pick Faulkner's Emily Grierson, Williams's Laura Wingfield, and the poet Emily Dickinson as three examples. Here you would be looking at characters and, in one case, a creator from three different genres. A thematic approach to such a topic might find some common thread that links the three. A feminist approach

might examine how all three characters choose their isolation as a means of sub-
verting a dominant patriarchy, whereas a psychological approach might explore
the backgrounds and experiences of these women to locate the causes of their
withdrawal from the world. The possibilities are numerous, and these groupings
of stories, poems, and plays that would lend themselves to shared thematic or
critical approaches are offered as suggestions. The brief discussion of several
leading theoretical strategies that follows will further assist you in using the thematic index.

Formalism

Formalist Criticism

Formalism, in its American incarnation as the New Criticism, devoted much of
its early attention to the works of metaphysical poets like Donne, Marvell, and
Herbert. In the hands of such New Critics as Cleanth Brooks, William K.
Wimsatt, Jr., and Monroe Beardsley, the formalist approach stressed the internal
qualities of literary works by close reading and explication, attempting to
demonstrate unity of form and content in successful poems. Such matters as authors' biographies, historical situations, or intentions, and the effect that works
produced on readers were considered less important than analysis that would
demonstrate and justify the "tensions" in a given work as contributing to a unified whole. In essence, the New Criticism stressed that in literature the whole is
always more than the sum of the individual parts. Formalist approaches may be
used to examine any kind of literary work, but they are perhaps most useful in
explications of short poems (especially those, like sonnets, which have a clear
formal structure), or in explications of selected passages from stories and plays.
Because this book contains a number of contemporary poems written in traditional forms, a formalist approach to them might focus on the relationship of
poetic form to content and use of language. As far as short stories and plays are
concerned, works translated from other languages would not be good candi-
dates for explication because many of the nuances of the original language may
have been lost in translation.

Biographical Criticism

Writers whose life stories continue to intrigue us are always likely choices for biographical criticism, which tries to locate literary works and their genesis within
the known facts about the lives and working habits of authors. Although you
should be wary of making connections between life and art that are too direct,
biographical criticism can be useful in examining the sources of stories, poems,
and plays and, in the case where an author's preliminary drafts have been pre-

served, in articulating the process of literary creation. Among fiction writers, Poe, Chopin, Cather, Hemingway, Cheever, and Carver, to mention only a few, have undergone quite a bit of scrutiny by biographers and memoirists. In poetry, one obvious source of much biographical speculation has been Shakespeare's sonnets, which have been read, in the absence of any substantial biographical information about Shakespeare, as revelatory of the poet's friendships, sexual preferences, and jealousies. It is only with the rise of romanticism that the poet becomes the true subject of the poem, and it is easy to see why Wordsworth made such an impact on literary history and, in his long autobiographical poem *The Prelude*, made his own life his primary subject. In this respect, Wordsworth parallels Coleridge; indeed, John Livingston Lowes's *The Road to Xanadu* remains a classic critical biography that traces the sources of Coleridge's "Kubla Khan" through rigorous examination of the poet's education and reading. In more recent times, the confessional poetry of the 1960s, as practiced by Lowell, Plath, and Sexton, still attracts interest, especially because multiple biographies and memoirs of all three writers are now available. In drama, only one play here, Tennessee Williams's *The Glass Menagerie*, could be called an autobiographical work, but Arthur Miller's own autobiography, *Timebends*, gives quite a bit of information about how *Death of a Salesman* grew into its present form over a number of years.

Historical and Sociological Criticism

Old-style historical and sociological criticism focused on the contexts of the authors' historical eras, demonstrating how events and cultural forces influenced their works. With the rise of naturalism in the late nineteenth century, critics began to apply the theories and practices of "social Darwinism" to literary works, often finding that the emphasis on heredity and environment in them was directly influenced by many of the new ideas of what we now term the social sciences; in this respect we think of the naturalist novelist Frank Norris's heavy debt to the Italian criminologist Lombroso in the characterization in his novel *McTeague*, or of the socialist political agenda that informs Upton Sinclair's novel *The Jungle*. In recent times, the new historicism, which reevaluates such matters as race, class, and gender as essential forces shaping literary creation, and various types of Marxist criticism (we note especially critics Fredric Jameson and Terry Eagleton in this regard) have been prominent. Works that deal with such likely topics for historical and sociological analysis as war and political ideology are listed above thematically and would lend themselves to historical/sociological approaches. The use of historical and sociological contexts to analyze fiction requires an understanding of the culture out of which the story arose, so you may need to investigate this background possibly as part of a research assignment. Obvious choices among short stories would be "Mother Savage," an account of an act of political terrorism and revenge during the Franco-Prussian War, and "The Guest," which is set during the early days of the Algerian War for Independence. Virtually all of the selections listed thematically under *Racial Identity and Racism* would be good choices for sociological/historical analysis. An investigation of the journalistic accounts of lynchings in the South might reveal Ellison's sources for "A Party Down at the Square," and research into the 1970s African American lifestyle would reveal the point of Alice Walker's satire in "Everyday Use." Faulkner, whose novels chronicle the history of his fictional Yoknapatapha County, includes in "A Rose for Emily" a short history lesson on the changes in the South in the half-century following the Civil War. Even a comic story like Tim Gautreaux's "Died and Gone to Vegas" is best read with some understanding of Louisiana Cajun culture. A number of poems directly deal with such historical topics as the Holocaust and are good subjects for historical analysis, and an examination of such plays as *Death of a Salesman* and *Fences* might focus on how they reveal the changes in American society following World War II.

Feminist and Gender Criticism

Feminist critical approaches focus on both the woman as reader of (male) literature and the woman-as-writer. To look at the latter first, the thematic listing under *Women's Issues* or under *Love: Marital* would be a starting point for feminist analysis of how women writers have viewed these subjects. The recent rediscovery of writers like Chopin and Hurston has been a chief concern of feminist criticism, and there are many writers here who are outspoken feminists and critics as well (Atwood and Rich are the two most prominent). As far as the perspective of woman-as-reader is concerned, one potentially useful topic for analysis from the feminist perspective would be to examine the role of the silent auditors in such classic love poems as "To His Coy Mistress," "The Flea," and "Dover Beach." Students might be asked to examine the stereotypes of female behavior that male authors perpetuate in these works. Some women fiction writers, interestingly, have not yet attracted a great deal of response from feminist critics; among them we would list Welty, O'Connor, and Moore. Among poets, Dickinson has perhaps been the subject of the most feminist scrutiny, with Plath a close second; some others, like Wylie and Bogan, have not received much attention at all. The relatively late but prominent arrival of women playwrights as a major force in drama can only be hinted at with the limited selection of plays this book contains, but both Glaspell and Wasserstein clearly use feminist themes in their work. Obviously, many of the stories, poems, and plays listed under *Sexual Themes* would also benefit from feminist or other types of gender-based analysis, such as gay studies (also known as queer theory), the study of how a writer's sexual orientation shapes his or her work. Shakespeare's sonnets have long provided fuel for this kind of speculation, as have Whitman's and Dickinson's poems in recent years. Obvious subjects are writers who were either openly gay or whose sexual orientation has been the subject of controversy:

Tennessee Williams, Hart Crane, Willa Cather, and Langston Hughes are a few who are commonly mentioned in this regard.

Structuralism: Mythological and Psychological Approaches

Under the structuralist banner are included mythological (archetypal or Jungian) and Freudian approaches, as well as a number of other structuralist methods of critical analysis that began to appear in the 1970s in the works of Roland Barthes, Tzvetan Todorov, Jacques Lacan, and others. The thematic category of *Myth* lists works that draw heavily on traditional mythology and folklore and would be ideal for Jungian analysis; you may find the Bill Moyers/Joseph Campbell video series *The Power of Myth* helpful in recognizing some of these archetypes. Some of the choices from earlier eras of works that derive from myth are obvious here (*Oedipus the King*, "Leda and the Swan"), but more intriguing might be contemporary works by such writers as Welty, Plath, and Atwood which adapt ancient myths to new cultural settings. Welty's use of vegetation symbolism in "Livvie" reveals her debt to Fraser's *The Golden Bough*, and Atwood and Plath provide new contexts from which to inspect stories from Homer and Euripides. One area of fiction that has been deeply concerned with mythic subtexts has been magic realism, as practiced by García Márquez. Among contemporary poets W. S. Merwin stands out as one example of a writer who uses myth prominently. Freudian psychological approaches can be used on virtually any selection from the fiction section of the anthology, although the obvious choices are those which present characters like Poe's, Maupassant's, or Oates's who are in extreme situations. Poets who are of interest for their psychological histories—Blake, Lowell, Plath, Sexton—will readily lend themselves to psychological approaches. Two plays here, *The Glass Menagerie* and *Death of a Salesman*, deal directly with mental illness, incipient in one, terminal in the other. Purely structuralist approaches such as those employed by Todorov in *The Fantastic* might be employed to distinguish between the different uses of fantastic material in such fiction writers as Hawthorne, Poe, Jackson, and Oates.

Post-Structuralism: Reader-Response Theory and Deconstruction

These most recent critical methods, both of which attempt to demonstrate that language itself cannot impose a definite meaning upon a reader's interpretation of a given work, involve in-depth study, and the critical theories of Stanley Fish, Jacques Derrida, and Paul de Man may be too abstruse for serious application in lower-division courses. Still, in theory (so to speak), reader-response criticism and deconstruction can be applied to any literary text, and a brief demonstration of their main points might lead to some lively classroom discussion about how language and meaning operate. A demonstration of how reader-response theory proceeds might be performed by having you, without any prior preparation, write about such short, cryptic modernist poems as Stevens's "Anecdote of the Jar" or Williams's "The Red Wheelbarrow." Because it stresses the indeterminacy of language itself, deconstruction seems a likely choice for works that clearly use experimental techniques; cummings's or Ashbery's poems might provide good examples for post-structuralist analysis, as would stories and plays that employ unconventional techniques: Atwood's "Happy Endings" and Ives's *Sure Thing*.

Acknowledgments

Fiction

Chinua Achebe, "Dead Men's Path" from *Girls at War and Other Stories*. Reprinted by permission of Doubleday, a division of Random House, Inc., and Harold Ober Associates.

Margaret Atwood, "Happy Endings" from *Good Bones and Simple Murders* by Margaret Atwood, copyright © 1983, 1992, 1994 by O.W. Toad, Ltd. A Nan A. Talese Book. Used by permission of Doubleday, a division of Random House.

Jorge Luis Borges, "The Gospel According to Mark" from *Collected Fictions* by Jorge Luis Borges, translated by Andrews Hurley, copyright © 1998 by Maria Kodama; translation copyright © 1998 by Penguin Putnam, Inc. Used by permission of Viking Penguin, a division of Penguin Putnam, Inc.

Albert Camus, "The Guest" from *Exile and the Kingdom* by Albert Camus, translated by Justin O'Brien, copyright © 1957, 1958 by Alfred A. Knopf, a division of Random House, Inc. Used by permission of Alfred A. Knopf, a division of Random House, Inc.

Raymond Carver, "A Small Good Thing" from *Cathedral* by Raymond Carver, copyright © 1983 by Raymond Carver. Used by permission of Alfred A. Knopf, a division of Random House, Inc.

John Cheever, "Reunion" from *The Stories of John Cheever* by John Cheever, copyright © 1978 by John Cheever. Used by permission of Alfred A. Knopf, a division of Random House, Inc.

Sandra Cisneros, "Barbie-Q" from *Woman Hollering Creek*. Copyright © 1991 by Sandra Cisneros. Published by Vintage Books, a division of Random House, Inc., New York and originally in hardcover by Random House, Inc. Reprinted by permission of Susan Bergholz Literary Services, New York. All rights reserved.

Ralph Ellison, "A Party Down at the Square" from *Flying Home and Other Stories* by Ralph Ellison, copyright © 1996 by Fanny Ellison; Introduction copyright © 1996 by John F. Callahan. Used by permission of Random House, Inc.

Louise Erdrich, "The Red Convertible" from *Love Medicine, New and Expanded Version* by Louise Erdrich. © 1984, 1993 by Louise Erdrich. Reprinted by permission of Henry Holt & Company LLC.

William Faulkner, "A Rose for Emily" by William Faulkner, copyright 1930 & renewed by William Faulkner, from *Collected Stories of William Faulkner* by William Faulkner. Used by permission of Random House, Inc.

Tim Gautreaux, "Died and Gone to Vegas". Copyright © 1996 by Tim Gautreaux. From *Same Place, Same Things* by Tim Gautreaux. Originally published in *The Atlantic Monthly*. Reprinted by permission of St. Martin's Press, LLC.

Dagoberto Gilb, "Look on the Bright Side" from *The Magic of Blood*. Copyright © 1993. Reprinted by permission of the University of New Mexico Press.

Ernest Hemingway, "Hills Like White Elephants" reprinted with permission of Scribner's, a Division of Simon & Schuster, Inc. from *The Short Stories of Ernest Hemingway*. Copyright 1927 by Charles Scribner's Sons. Copyright renewed 1955 by Ernest Hemingway.

Zora Neale Hurston, "Sweat" from *The Complete Stories* by Zora Neale Hurston. Introduction copyright © 1995 by Henry Louis Gates, Jr. and Sieglinde Lemke. Compilation copyright © 1995 by Vivian Bowden, Lois J. Hurston Gaston, Clifford Hurston, Lucy Ann Hurston, Winifred Hurston Clark, Zora Mack Goins, Edgar Hurston, Sr., and Barbara Hurston Lewis. Afterword and Bibliography copyright © 1995 by Henry Louis Gates. Reprinted by permission of HarperCollins Publishers, Inc.

Shirley Jackson, "The Lottery" from *The Lottery* by Shirley Jackson. Copyright © 1948, 1949 by Shirley Jackson. Copyright renewed 1976, 1977 by Laurence Hyman, Barry Hyman, Mrs. Sarah Webster and Mrs. Joanne Schnurer. Reprinted by permission of Farrar, Straus & Giroux, Inc.

James Joyce, "Eveline" from *Dubliners* by James Joyce, copyright 1916 by B.W. Heubsch. Definitive text copyright © 1967 by the Estate of James Joyce. Used by permission of Viking Penguin, a division of Penguin Putnam, Inc.

D. H. Lawrence, "The Rocking Horse Winner". Copyright 1933 by the Estate of D. H. Lawrence, renewed © 1961 by Angelo Ravagli and C. M. Weekley, Executors of the Estate of Freida Lawrence, from *Complete Short Stories of D. H.*

1423

Lawrence by D. H. Lawrence. Used by permission of Viking Penguin, a division of Penguin Putnam, Inc.

Gabriel García Márquez, "A Very Old Man with Enormous Wings" from Leaf Storm and Other Stories by Gabriel García Márquez and translated by Gregory Rabassa. Copyright © 1971 by Gabriel García Márquez. Reprinted by permission of HarperCollins Publishers, Inc.

Guy de Maupassant, Mother Savage, translated by Lafcadio Hearn; revised by R. S. Gwynn. Used by permission of R. S. Gwynn.

Lorrie Moore, "How to Talk to Your Mother" from *Self-Help* by Lorrie Moore, copyright © 1985 by ML Moore. Used by permission of Alfred A. Knopf, a division of Random House Inc.

Alice Munro, "Vandals" from *Open Secrets* by Alice Munro. Copyright 1994. Reprinted with permission of Alfred A. Knopf.

Flannery O'Connor, "A Good Man is Hard to Find" from *A Good Man is Hard to Find and Other Stories*, copyright 1953 by Flannery O'Connor and renewed in 1981 by Regina O'Connor, reprinted by permission of Harcourt, Inc.

Joyce Carol Oates, "Where are You Going? Where Have You Been?" by Joyce Carol Oates from *The Wheel of Love and Other Stories*. Copyright © 1970 by Joyce Carol Oates. Reprinted by permission of John Hawkins & Associates, Inc.

Katherine Anne Porter, "The Jilting of Granny Weatherall" from *Flowering Judas and Other Stories*, copyright 1930 and renewed in 1958 by Katherine Anne Porter, reprinted by permission of Harcourt, Inc.

John Steinbeck, "The Chrysanthemums". Copyright 1937, renewed © 1965 by John Steinbeck, from *The Long Valley* by John Steinbeck. Used by permission of Viking Penguin, a division of Penguin Putnam, Inc.

Amy Tan, "Two Kinds" reprinted by permission of The Putnam Publishing Group, Inc., from *The Joy Luck Club* by Amy Tan. Copyright © 1989 by Amy Tan.

John Updike, "A&P" from *Pigeon Feathers and Other Stories* by John Updike, copyright © 1962 by John Updike. Used by permission of Alfred A. Knopf, a division of Random House, Inc.

Alice Walker, "Everyday Use" from *Love & Trouble: Stories of Black Women*, copyright © 1973 by Alice Walker, reprinted by permission of Harcourt, Inc.

Eudora Welty, "Livvie" from *The Wide Net and Other Stories*. Copyright © 1942 and renewed © 1970 by Eudora Welty. Reprinted by permission of Harcourt Brace Jovanovich, Inc.

Edith Wharton, "Roman Fever", reprinted with the permission of Scribner's, a Division of Simon & Schuster, Inc. from *Roman Fever and Other Stories* by Edith Wharton. Copyright © 1934 by Liberty Magazine, copyright renewed © 1962 by William R. Tyler.

Richard Wright, "The Man Who Was Almost a Man" from *Eight Men* by Richard Wright. Copyright 1940 © 1961 by Richard Wright. Copyright renewed 1989 by Ellen Wright. Reprinted by permission of HarperCollins Publishers.

Poetry

Betty Adcock, "Digression on the Nuclear Age" reprinted by permission of Louisiana State University Press from *Beholdings* by Betty Adcock. Copyright © 1988 by Betty Adcock.

Ai, "Child Beater" from *Cruelty* published by Houghton Mifflin Company. Reprinted by permission of the author.

Julia Alvarez, "Bilingual Sestina" from *The Other Side/El Otro Lado*. Copyright © 1995 by Julia Alvarez. Published by Dutton, a division of Penguin Putnam Inc. Reprinted by permission of Susan Bergholz Literary Services, New York. All rights reserved.

John Ashberry, "Farm Implements and Rutabagas in a Landscape" from *Shadow Train* (New York: Viking, 1981). Reprinted by permission of Georges Borchardt, Inc., for the author. Copyright © 1980, 1981 John Ashberry.

Margaret Atwood, "Siren Song" from *You are Happy. Selected Poems 1965–1975*. Copyright © 1976 by Margaret Atwood. Reprinted by permission of Houghton Mifflin Co. All rights reserved.

W. H. Auden, "As I Walked Out One Evening" "Musee des Beaux Arts" and "The Unknown Citizen" from *W. H. Auden: Collected Poems* by W. H. Auden. Reprinted by permission of Random House, Inc.

Gerald Barrax, "Strangers Like Us: Pittsburgh, Raleigh, 1945–1985" reprinted by permission of Louisiana State University Press from *A Person Sitting in Darkness* by Gerald Barrax. Copyright © 1998 by Gerald Barrax.

Elizabeth Bishop, "One Art" and "The Fish" from *The Complete Poems 1927–1979* by Elizabeth Bishop. Copyright © 1979, 1983 by Alice Helen Methfessel. Reprinted by permission of Farrar, Straus & Giroux, Inc.

Louise Bogan, "Women" from *The Blue Estuaries*. Copyright © 1968 by Louise Bogan. Copyright renewed © 1996 by Ruth Limmer. Reprinted by permission of Farrar, Straus & Giroux, Inc.

David Bottoms, "Sign for My Father, Who Stressed the Bunt" from *Armored Hearts: Selected and New Poems*. Copyright © 1995 by David Bottoms. Reprinted with the permission of Copper Canyon Press, P.O. Box 271, Port Townsend, WA 98368-0271, USA.

Gwendolyn Brooks, "the mother" and "We Real Cool" from *Blacks* by Gwendolyn Brooks. Copyright © 1991 by Gwendolyn Brooks. Reprinted by permission of the author.

Gladys Cardiff, "Combing." Copyright © 1971 by Gladys Cardiff. Reprinted from *To Frighten a Storm* (Copper Canyon Press, 1976) by permission of the author.

Fred Chappell, "Narcissus and Echo" reprinted by permission of Louisiana State University Press from *Source* by Fred Chappell. Copyright © 1985 by Fred Chappell.

Wendy Cope, "Rondeau Redoublé" from *Making Cocoa for Kingsley Amis* by Wendy Cope. Copyright © Wendy Cope 1986. Reproduced by permission of the publishers Faber and Faber Limited.

Hart Crane, "Chaplinesque" from *Complete Poems of Hart Crane* by Marc Simon, editor. Copyright © 1933, © 1958, 1966 by Liveright Publishing Corporation. Copyright © 1986 by Marc Simon. Reprinted by permission of Liveright Publishing Corporation.

Robert Creeley, "I Know a Man" from *Collected Poems of Robert Creeley, 1945–1975*. Copyright © 1983 The Regents of the University of California. Reprinted by permission.

Countee Cullen, "Incident" and "Yet I DO Marvel" published in *On These I Stand* © 1947 Harper & Bros. Renewed 1975 Ida M. Cullen. Copyrights held by The Amistad Research Center Administered by Thompson and Thompson, New York, NY.

E. E. Cummings, "nobody loses all the time" copyright 1926, 1954, © 1991 by the Trustees for the E. E. Cummings Trust. Copyright © 1976 by George James Firmage, "pity this busy monster,manunkind" copyright 1944, © 1972, 1991 by the Trustees of the E. E. Cummings Trust,

"r-p-o-p-h-e-s-s-a-g-r" copyright 1935, © 1963, 1991 by the Trustees for the E. E. Cummings Trust. Copyright © 1978 by George James Firmage, from *Complete Poems: 1904–1962* by E. E. Cummings, edited by George J. Firmage. Reprinted by permission of Liveright Corporation.

James Dickey, "The Heaven of Animals" from *Poems: 1957–1967*. Copyright © 1968 by James Dickey. Reprinted by permission of Wesleyan University Press.

Emily Dickinson, "A Narrow Fellow in the Grass," "Because I Could Not Stop for Death," "I Died for Beauty But Was Scarce," "I Heard a Fly Buzz When I Died," "My Life Closed Twice Before Its Close," and "The Soul Selects Her Own Society" reprinted by permission of the publishers and the Trustees of Amherst College from *The Poems of Emily Dickinson*, Thomas H. Johnson, ed., Cambridge, Mass: The Belknap Press of Harvard University Press, Copyright © 1951, 1955, 1979 by the President and Fellows of Harvard College.

Tom Disch, "Ballade of the New God" from *The Dark Horse*. Copyright © 1966 Tom Disch. Reprinted by permission of the author.

H. D. Doolittle, "Pear Tree" and "Sea Rose" from *Collected Poems 1912–1944*, copyright © 1982 by The Estate of Hilda Doolittle. Reprinted by permission of New Directions Publishing Corp.

Rita Dove, "Adolescence. . . III" from *The Yellow House on the Corner*, Carnegie-Mellon University Press, copyright © 1980 by Rita Dove. Used by permission of the author.

Alan Dugan, "Love Song: I and Thou" from *New and Collected Poems*. Reprinted by permission of The Ecco Press.

Stephen Dunn, "The Sacred" from *Between Angels* by Stephen Dunn. Copyright © 1989 by Stephen Dunn. Used by permission if W. W. Norton & Company, Inc.

T. S. Eliot, "Journey of the Magi" and "The Love Song of J. Alfred Profrock" from *Collected Poems*, copyright © 1936 by Harcourt Brace & Company, copyright © 1964, 1963 by T. S. Eliot, reprinted by permission of Harcourt Brace & Company, Inc. and Faber and Faber Ltd.

James Fenton, "God: a Poem." From *Children in Exile* by James Fenton. Copyright © 1972, 1978, 1980, 1982, 1983 by James Fenton. Reprinted by permission of Random House, Inc.

Lawrence Ferlinghetti, " A Coney Island of the Mind # 15" from *Constantly Risking Absurdity*, copyright © 1958 by Lawrence Ferlinghetti. Reprinted by permission of New Directions Publishing Corp.

Carolyn Forché, "The Colonel" from *The Country Between Us* by Carolyn Forché. Copyright © 1980 by Carolyn Forché. Reprinted by permission of HarperCollins Publishers.

Robert Frost, "Acquainted with the Night," "Design," "Stopping Woods on a Snowy Evening" and "The Need of Being Versed in Country Things" from *The Poetry of Robert Frost* edited by Edward Connery Lathem. Copyright © 1923, 1928, © 1969 by Henry Holt & Co., © 1936, 1951, 1956 by Robert Frost, © 1964 by Lesley Frost Ballantine. Reprinted by permission of Henry Holt and Company, LLC.

Gary Gildner, "First Practice" from *First Practice* by Gary Gildner, © 1969 by University of Pittsburgh Press. Reprinted by permission of the University of Pittsburgh Press.

Allen Ginsberg, "A Supermarket in California." Copyright © 1955 by Allen Ginsberg. From *Collected Poems 1947–1980*. Reprinted by permission of HarperCollins Publishers.

Dana Gioia, "Planting a Sequoia" copyright 1991 by Dana Gioia. Reprinted from *The Gods of Winter* with the permission of Graywolf Press, Saint Paul, Minnesota.

Thom Gunn, "From the Wave" and "Terminal" from *Collected Poems*, copyright © 1994 by Thom Gunn. Reprinted by permission of Farrar, Straus & Giroux, Inc., and Faber & Faber Ltd.

R. S. Gwynn, "Approaching a Significant Birthday, He Peruses the *Norton Anthology of Poetry*" from *No Word of Farewell: Selected Poems 1970–2000* by R. S. Gwynn. Copyright © 2001 by R. S. Gwynn. Reprinted by permission of Story Line Press, Inc., www.storylinepress.com.

Jim Hall, "Maybe Dats Your Pwoblem Too" from *The Mating Reflex*. By permission of Carnegie Mellon University Press, © 1980 by Jim Hall.

Joy Harjo, "Song for the Deer and Myself to Return On" from *In Mad Love and War*, copyright 1990 by Joy Harjo and reprinted by permission of Wesleyan University Press.

Robert Hass, "Picking Blackberries with a Friend Who Has Been Reading Jacques Lacan" from *Praise*. Reprinted by permission of The Ecco Press.

Robert Hayden, "Those Winter Sundays." Copyright © 1966 by Robert Hayden, from *Collected Poems of Robert Hayden* by Robert Hayden, edited by Frederick Glaysher. Used by permission of Liveright Publishing Corporation.

Seamus Heaney, "Bogland," "Digging" and "Punishment" from *Selected Poems 1966–1987* by Seamus Heaney. Copyright © 1990 by Seamus Heaney. Reprinted by permission of Farrar, Straus & Giroux, Inc., and Faber & Faber Ltd.

Anthony Hecht, "More Light! More Light!" from *Collected Earlier Poems* by Anthony Hecht, copyright © 1990 by Anthony Hecht. Used by permission of Alfred A. Knopf, a division of Random House, Inc.

John Hollander, "Adam's Task" from *Selected Poetry* by John Hollander, copyright © 1993 by John Hollander. Used by permission of Alfred A. Knopf, a division of Random House, Inc.

Janet Holmes, "Cinquains for Rocky" from *The Physicist at the Mall*. Tallahassee, FL. 1994. Reprinted with permission of Anhinga Press.

Garrett Hongo, "Crossing Ka'u Desert" from *The River of Heaven* by Garrett Hongo, copyright © 1988 by Garrett Hongo. Used by permission of Alfred A. Knopf, a division of Random House, Inc.

A. D. Hope, "Imperial Adam" from *Collected Poems* by A. D. Hope. Copyright © 1968 A. D. Hope. Reprinted by permission of Collins/Angus & Robertson Publishers.

A. E. Housman, "Eight O'Clock" and "Stars, I Have Seen them Fall" by A. E. Housman from *The Collected Poems of A. E. Housman* copyright 1936, © 1950 by Barclays Bank, Ltd. © 1964, 1967, 1968 by Robert E. Symons, © 1922, 1939, 1940, 1965 by Henry Holt and Co. Reprinted by permission of Henry Holt and Company, LLC.

Andrew Hudgins, "Air View of an Industrial Scene" from *Saints and Strangers*. Copyright © 1985 by Andrew Hudgins. Reprinted by permission of Houghton Mifflin Co. All rights reserved.

Langston Hughes, "Dream Boogie" and "Theme for English B" from *The Collected Poems of Langston Hughes* by Langston Hughes, copyright © 1994 by The Estate of Langston Hughes. Used by permission of Alfred A. Knopf, Inc., a division of Random House, Inc.

Ted Hughes, "Pike" and "The Thought-Fox" from *Selected Poems 1957–1981*. Reprinted by permission of HarperCollins and Faber & Faber Ltd.

Mark Jarman, "Questions for Ecclesiates" by Mark Jarman. Copyright © 1997 by Mark Jarman. Reprinted by permission of Story Line Press, Inc., www.storylinepress.com.

Randall Jarrell, "The Death of the Ball Turret Gunner" from *The Complete Poems*. Copyright © 1969 by Mrs. Randall Jarrell. Reprinted by permission of Farrar, Straus & Giroux, Inc.

Robinson Jeffers, "The Purse-Seine" copyright 1938 & renewed 1966 by Donnan & Garth Jeffers, from *The Selected Poems of Robinson Jeffers* by Robinson Jeffers. Used by permission of Random House, Inc.

Rodney Jones, "Winter Retreat: Homage to Martin Luther King, Jr." from *Transparent Gestures*. Copyright © 1989 by Rodney Jones. Reprinted by permission of Houghton Mifflin Co. All rights reserved.

Donald Justice, "Counting the Mad" from *New and Selected Poems* by Donald Justice, copyright © 1995 by Donald Justice. Used by permission of Alfred A. Knopf, a division of Random House, Inc.

Weldon Kees, "For My Daughter" reprinted from *The Collected Poems of Weldon Kees*, edited by Donald Justice, by permission of the University of Nebraska Press. Copyright 1975, by the University of Nebraska Press.

X. J. Kennedy, "In a Prominent Bar in Secaucus One Day." Copyright © 1961 by X. J. Kennedy. Reprinted by permission of Curtis Brown, Ltd.

Caroline Kizer, "The Ungrateful Garden" from *Midnight Was My Cry: New and Selected Poems*. Copyright © 1961. Reprinted by the permission of the author.

Yusef Komunyakaa, "Facing It" from *Dai Cai Dau* by Yusef Komunyakaa. © 1988 by Yusef Komunyakaa. Reprinted by permission of Wesleyan University Press

Maxine Kumin, "Noted in the *New York Times*" from *Nurture* by Maxine Kumin. Copyright © 1989 by Maxine Kumin. Used by permission of Viking Penguin, a division of Penguin Books USA Inc.

Philip Larkin, "Next, Please" from *The Less Deceived*. Reprinted by permission of The Marvell Press, England and Australia. "Aubade" from *Collected Poems* by Philip Larkin. Copyright © 1988, 1989 by the Estate of Philip Larkin. Reprinted by permission of Farrar, Straus & Giroux, Inc. "This Be the Verse" from *High Windows*. Reprinted by permission of Farrar, Straus and Giroux, Inc., and Faber & Faber, Ltd.

Denise Levertov, "The Ache of Marriage" from *Denis Levertov: Poems 1960–1967*. Copyright © 1964 by Denise Levertov Goodman. Reprinted by permission of New Directions Publishing Corporation.

Robert Lowell, "For the Union Dead" from *For the Union Dead* by Robert Lowell. Copyright © 1959 by Robert Lowell. Copyright renewed © 1987 by Harriet Lowell, Caroline Lowell, and Sheridan Lowell. Reprinted by permission of Farrar, Straus & Giroux, Inc.

David Mason, "Song of the Powers" from *The Country I Remember*, 1996. Story Line Press. No portion of this text may be reprinted without permission.

Florence Cassen Mayers, "All American Sestina." First published in *The Atlantic Monthly*. Reprinted by permission of the author.

James Merrill, "Casual Wear" and "Charles on Fire" from *Selected Poems 1946–1985* by James Merrill, copyright © 1992 by James Merrill. Used by permission of Alfred A. Knopf, Inc., a division of Random House, Inc.

W. S. Merwin, "For the Anniversary of My Death" and "The Last One" from *The Lice*, © 1963, 1964, 1965, 1966, 1967 by W. S. Merwin. No portion of this text may be reprinted without permission of Georges Borchardt, Inc.

Edna St. Vincent Millay, "If I Should Learn in Some Quiet Casual Way," "Not in a Silver Casket," "Oh, Oh, You Will Be Sorry for That Word," and "What Lips My Lips Have Kissed" by Edna St. Vincent Millay. From *Collected Poems*, HarperCollins. Copyright © 1917, 1923, 1931, 1945, 1951, 1958 by Edna St. Vincent Millay and Norma Millay Ellis. All rights reserved. Reprinted by permission of Elizabeth Barnett, Literary Executor.

Vassar Miller, "Subterfuge" from *If I Had Wheels of Love: Collected Poems*. Reprinted by permission of Martha Failing & Co. (Houston, TX).

Marianne Moore, "Silence" and "The Fish" reprinted with the permission of Scribner, a Division of Simon & Schuster, Inc., from *The Collected Poems of Marianne Moore* by Marianne Moore. Copyright © 1935 by Marianne Moore, copyright renewed © 1963 by Marianne Moore and T. S. Eliot.

Robert Morgan, "Mountain Bride" from *Groundwork*, Gnomon Press. Copyright © 1979. Reprinted by permission of the author.

Timothy Murphy, "The Track of a Storm" from *The Dead of Gift* by Timothy Murphy.

Copyright © 2001 by Timothy Murphy. Reprinted by permission of Story Line Press, Inc., www.storylinepress.com.

Howard Nemerov, "A Primer of the Daily Round" from *New and Selected Poems* by Howard Nemerov, copyright © 1960 by Howard Nemerov (University of Chicago Press). Reprinted by permission of Margaret Nemerov.

Naomi Shihab Nye, "The Traveling Onion." Reprinted by permission of Naomi Shihab Nye from *Yellow Glove*, Breitenbush Books, Portland, OR. Copyright © 1986 by Naomi Shihab Nye.

Frank O'Hara, "The Day the Lady Died" from *Lunch Poems*. Copyright © 1964 by Frank O'Hara. Reprinted by permission of City Lights Books.

Sharon Olds, "The One Girl at the Boy's Party" from *The Dead and the Living* by Sharon Olds, copyright © 1987 by Sharon Olds. Used by permission of Alfred A. Knopf, a division of Random House, Inc.

Mary Oliver, "The Black Walnut Trees" from *Twelve Moons* by Mary Oliver. Copyright © 1972, 1973, 1974, 1975, 1976, 1977, 1978, 1979 by Mary Oliver; first appeared in *The Ohio Review*. By permission of Little, Brown & Company.

Simon J. Ortiz, "The Serenity in Stones." Permission to reprint given by author Simon J. Ortiz, Copyright 1975.

Wilfred Owen, "Dulce et Decorum Est" from *Wilfred Owen: Collected Poems of Wilfred Owen*. Copyright © 1963 by Chatto & Witndus Ltd. Reprinted by permission of New Directions Publishing Corporation.

Dorothy Parker, "One Perfect Rose" and "Résumé" copyright 1926, renewed © 1954 by Dorothy Parker from *The Portable Dorothy Parker* by Dorothy Parker. Used by permission of Viking Penguin, a division of Penguin Putnam, Inc.

Linda Pastan, "Crocuses." Copyright © 1989 by Linda Pastan, from *Heroes in Disguise* by Linda Pastan. Used by permission of W. W. Norton & Company, Inc.

Robert Phillips, "Compartments" from *Spinach Days*. Copyright © 2000. Reprinted by permission of The Johns Hopkins University Press.

Marge Piercy, "Barbie Doll" from *Circles on the Water* by Marge Piercy, © 1982 by Marge Piercy. Used by permission of Alfred A. Knopf, a division of Random House, Inc.

Sylvia Plath, "Daddy," "Edge" and "Metaphors" from *The Collected Poems of Sylvia Plath*. Reprinted by permission of HarperCollins Publishers and Faber and Faber Ltd.

Ezra Pound, "In the Station at the Metro," "Portrait d'une Femme" and "The River Merchant's Wife: A Letter" by Ezra Pound, from *Personae*, copyright © 1926 by Ezra Pound. Reprinted by permission of New Directions Publishing Corporation.

Craig Raine, "A Martian Sends a Postcard Home" by Craig Raine from *A Martian Sends a Postcard Home*. Reprinted by permission of David Goodwin Associates.

Dudley Randall, "Ballad of Birmingham" from *Cities Burning* by Dudley Randall. Copyright © 1979. Reprinted by permission of Broadside Press.

John Crowe Ransom, "Piazza Piece." Copyright 1927 by Alfred A. Knopf, Inc. and renewed 1955 by John Crowe Ransom. From *Selected Poems* by John Crowe Ransom. Reprinted by permission of the publisher.

Adrienne Rich, "Aunt Jennifer's Tigers," "Diving into a Wreck" and "Rape" from *The Fact of a Doorframe: Poems Selected and New 1950–1984* by Adrienne Rich. Copyright © 1975, 1978 by W. W. Norton & Company, Inc. Copyright © 1981 by Adrienne Rich. Reprinted by permission of the author and W. W. Norton & Company, Inc.

Alberto Ríos, "The Purpose of Altar Boys" from *Whispering to Fool the Wind* (Sheep Meadow Press). Copyright © 1982 by Alberto Ríos. Reprinted by permission of the author.

Theodore Roethke, "My Papa's Waltz" copyright 1942 by Hearst Magazines, Inc. "Root Cellar" copyright 1943 by Modern Poetry Association from *The Collected Poems of Theodore Roethke* by Theodore Roethke. Used by permission of Doubleday, a division of Random House, Inc.

Pattiann Rogers, "Foreplay" from *Firekeeper: New and Selected Poems* by Pattiann Rogers (Milkweed Editions, 1994). Copyright © 1994 by Pattian Rogers. Reprinted by permission of Milkweed Editions and Pattiann Rogers.

Gibbons Ruark, "The Visitor" is reprinted by permission of Louisiana State University Press from *Passing Through Customs: New and Selected Poems*, by Gibbons Ruark.

Benjamin Alire Sáenz, "To the Desert" from *Dark and Perfect Angels*, Cinco Punto Press. Copyright © 1995 by Benjamin Alire Sáenz. Used by permission of the author and Cinco Punto Press.

Index of Authors, Titles, and First Lines of Poems

Mary Jo Salter, "Welcome to Hiroshima" from *Henry Purcell in Japan* by Mary Jo Salter, copyright © 1984 by Mary Jo Salter. Used by permission of Alfred A. Knopf, a division of Random House, Inc.

May Sarton, "A Guest." Copyright © 1967 by May Sarton, from *Collected Poems 1930–1993* by May Sarton. Used by permission of W. W. Norton & Company, Inc.

Siegfried Sassoon, "Dreamers" from *Collected Poems*. Copyright by Siegfried Sassoon. Reprinted by permission of George T. Sassoon, c/o Barbara Levy Literary Agency, London.

Enid Shomer, "Women Bathing at Bergen-Belson," winner of Negative Capability's Eve of St. Agnes Award. Reprinted from *Stalking the Florida Panther*, published by The Word Works. Copyright © 1987 by Enid Shomer. Reprinted by permission of the author.

Charles Simic, "Stone" from *Selected Poems 1963–1983*. Copyright © 1971 by Charles Simic. Reprinted by permission of George Braziller, Inc.

Louis Simpson, "American Classic" from *Caviare at the Funeral* by Louis Simpson. Copyright © 1980 by Louis Simpson. Used with permission of the publisher Franklin Watts, Inc., New York. "My Father in the Night Commanding No" from *At the End of the Open road* by Louis Simpson, copyright 1963 by Louis Simpson, Wesleyan University Press. Reprinted by permission of University Press of New England.

W. D. Snodgrass, "Mementos, I" reprinted by permission of Soho Press Inc. from W. D. Snodgrass, *Selected Poems 1957–1987*, © 1968, 1978 by W. D. Snodgrass.

Gary Snyder, "A Walk" from *Gary Snyder: The Back Country*. Copyright © 1968 by Gary Snyder. Reprinted by permission of New Directions Publishing Corporation.

Cathy Song, "Stamp Collecting" from *Frameless Windows, Squares of Light: Poems by Cathy Song*. Copyright © 1988 by Cathy Song. Used by permission of W. W. Norton & Company, Inc.

Gary Soto, "The Skeptics" from *Junior College* by Gary Soto, © 1996, published by Chronicle Books, San Francisco. Reprinted by permission of Chronicle Books.

William Stafford, "Traveling Through the Dark." Copyright © 1960 by William Stafford. Reprinted from *Stories That Could Be True* by permission of the author.

Timothy Steele, "Sapphics Against Anger," by Timothy Steele from *Sapphics and Uncertainties: Poems 1970–1986*. Reprinted by permission of the University of Arkansas Press.

Wallace Stevens, "Anecdote of the Jar," "Disillusionment of Ten O'Clock," "Sunday Morning" and "The Snow Man" from *The Collected Poems of Wallace Stevens* by Wallace Stevens, Copyright 1954 by Wallace Stevens. Used by permission of Alfred A. Knopf, Inc., a division of Random House, Inc.

Anne Stevenson, "Sous-Entendu" (1970). Reprinted from *The Collected Poems of Anne Stevenson 1955–1996* by Anne Stevenson (1996) by permission of Oxford University Press.

Leon Stokesbury, "Evening's End" from *Autumn Rhythm: New & Selected Poems by Leon Stokesbury*. Copyright © 1996. Reprinted by permission of the University of Arkansas Press, Inc.

Mark Strand, "The Tunnel" from *Selected Poems* by Mark Strand, copyright © 1979, 1980 by Mark Strand. Used by permission of Alfred A. Knopf, Inc., a division of Random House.

Dabney Stuart, "Discovering My Daughter" from *Light Years: New and Selected Poems*, 1994. Copyright © 1990, 1991, 1992, 1993, 1994 by Dabney Stuart. Reprinted by permission of Louisiana State University Press.

May Swenson, "How Everything Happens (Based on a Study of the Wave)." Reprinted with permission of Simon & Schuster Books for Young Readers, an imprint of Simon & Schuster Children's Publishing Division for *The Complete Poems to Solve* by May Swenson. Copyright © 1993 by The Literary Estate of May Swenson.

James Tate, "Teaching the Ape to Write Poems." Reprinted by permission of James Tate.

Dylan Thomas, "Do Not Go Gentle into That Good Night" from *Poems of Dylan Thomas*. Copyright © 1952 by Dylan Thomas. Reprinted by permission of David Hgham Associates, and New Directions Publishing Corporation.

Jean Toomer, "Reapers" from *Cane* by Jean Toomer. Copyright © 1923 by Boni & Liveright, renewed 1951 by Jean Toomer. Used by permission of Liveright Publishing Corporation.

Catherine Tufariello, "Useful Advice" from *Tar River Poetry*. Reprinted by permission.

Ellen Bryant Voigt, "Daughter" from *The Forces of Plenty* by Ellen Voigt. Copyright © 1983 by Ellen Bryant Voigt. Used by permission of W. W. Norton & Company, Inc.

Derek Walcott, "Central America" from *The Arkansas Testament.* Copyright © 1987 by Derek Walcott. Reprinted by permission of Farrar, Straus & Giroux, Inc.

Alice Walker, "Even as I Hold You" from *Good Night Willie Lee, I'll See you in the Morning* by Alice Walker, copyright © 1975, 1976, 1979 by Alice Walker. Used by permission of Doubleday, a Division of Random House, Inc.

Margaret Walker, "For Malcom X" from *This is My Century: New and Selected Poems.* Reprinted by permission of the University of Georgia Press.

Richard Wilbur, "Junk" from *Advice to a Prophet and Other Poems.* Copyright © 1961 and renewed 1989. Reprinted by permission of Harcourt Inc. "Playboy" from *Walking to Sleep: New Poems and Translations,* copyright © 1968 by Richard Wilbur. Reprinted by permission of Harcourt Brace & Company, Inc. "The Writer" from *The Mind Reader,* copyright © 1971 by Richard Wilbur. Reprinted by permission of Harcourt Brace & Company, Inc. "Year's End" from *Ceremony and Other Poems,* copyright © 1949 and renewed 1977 by Richard Wilbur. Reprinted by permission of Harcourt Brace & Company, Inc.

Nancy Willard, "A Hardware Store as Proof of the Existence of God" from *Water Walker* by Nancy Willard, copyright © 1989 by Nancy Willard. Used by permission of Alfred A. Knopf, a division of Random House, Inc.

Miller Williams, "The Book" from *Living on the Surface: New and Selected Poems.* Copyright © 1989 by Miller Williams. Reprinted by permission of Louisiana State University Press.

William Carlos Williams, "The Last Words of My English Grandmother," "The Red Wheelbarrow" and "Spring and All" from *Collected Poems: 1909–1939, Volume 1,* copyright © 1938 by New Directions Publishing Corp. Reprinted by permission of New Directions Publishing Corp.

James Wright, "A Blessing" from *The Branch Will Not Break?* by James Wright. © 1959 by James Wright. "Saint Judas" from *Saint Judas* by James Wright. © 1959 by James

Wright. Reprinted by permission of Wesleyan University Press.

William Butler Yeats, "Leda and the Swan," "Sailing to Byzantium," "The Lake Isle of Innesfree," "The Second Coming" and "the Song of Wandering Aengus" reprinted with the permission of Scribner's, a Division of Simon & Schuster, Inc., from *The Collected Poems of W. B. Yeats: Revised Second Edition,* edited by Richard J. Finneran. (New York: Scribner, 1996).

Drama

David Ives, "Sure Thing" from *All in the Timing* by David Ives. Copyright © 1944 by David Ives. Reprinted by permission of Vintage Books, a division of Random House, Inc. CAUTION: Professionals and amateurs are hereby warned that this play, being fully protected under the copyright laws of the United States of America, the British Empire including the Dominion of Canada, and all other countries of the Copyright Union, is subject to royalty. All rights, including professional, amateur, motion picture, recitation, lecturing, public reading, radio and television broadcasting, and the rights of translation are strictly reserved. All inquiries concerning performance rights for this play should be addressed to William Craver, Writers and Artists Agency, 19 West 44th Street, Suite 1000, New York, NY 10036.

Arthur Miller, "Death of a Salesman" from *Death of a Salesman* by Arthur Miller, copyright 1949, renewed © 1977 by Arthur Miller. Used by permission of Viking Penguin, a division of Penguin Putnam, Inc.

Wendy Wasserstein, "The Man in the Case" from *Orchards: Seven Stories by Anton Chekhov and Seven Plays They Have Inspired,* published by Knopf. Copyright © 1986 by Wendy Wasserstein. Reprinted by permission of Rosenstone/Wender.

Tennessee Williams, "The Glass Menagerie" by Tennessee Williams, copyright 1945 by Tennessee Williams and Edwina D. Williams. Copyright renewed 1973 by Tennessee Williams. Used by permission of Random House, Inc.

August Wilson, "Fences" by August Wilson. Copyright © 1986 by August Wilson. Used by permission of Dutton Signet, a division of Penguin Putnam, Inc.

Index of Critical Terms